W9-BHS-704

LEGAL PERSPECTIVES
OF
AMERICAN BUSINESS ASSOCIATIONS

GRID SERIES IN LAW

Consulting Editor
THOMAS W. DUNFEE, The Wharton School, University of Pennsylvania

Atteberry, Pearson, & Litka, *Real Estate Law*
Dunfee & Gibson, *Modern Business Law: An Introduction to Government and Business,* Second Edition
Dunfee, Gibson, Lamber & McCarty, *Modern Business Law: An Introduction to the Legal Environment of Business*
Erickson, Dunfee, & Gibson, *Antitrust and Trade Regulations: Cases and Materials*
Francois, *Mass Media Law and Regulation*
Litka, *Business Law,* Second Edition
Litka & Inman, *The Legal Environment of Business: Text, Cases, and Readings*
Miller, *Government Policy Toward Labor: An Introduction to Labor Law*
Stern and Yaney, *Cases In Labor Law*
Warren, *Antitrust in Theory and Practice*
Wolfe & Naffziger, *Legal Perspectives of American Business Associations*

OTHER BOOKS IN THE GRID SERIES IN LAW

Naffziger & Knauss, *Basic Guide to Federal Labor Law*
Zwarensteyn, *Introduction to the Legal System,* Third Edition

LEGAL PERSPECTIVES OF AMERICAN BUSINESS ASSOCIATIONS

ARTHUR D. WOLFE

Member of the Ohio, Indiana, Virgin Islands
and Federal Bars

Associate Professor of Business Law
Michigan State University

FREDERICK J. NAFFZIGER

Member of the Illinois, District of Columbia
and Federal Bars

Associate Professor of Business Administration
Indiana University at South Bend

Grid Inc., Columbus, Ohio

1 2 3 4 5 6 ▨ 2 1 0 9 8 7

This book is dedicated to
Susie Wolfe and Carol Naffziger,
and to the miraculous incentive:
"Publica aut peri."

TABLE OF CONTENTS

PART I:
INTRODUCTION TO THE STUDY OF LAW
AND AMERICAN BUSINESS ASSOCIATIONS

1 **Introduction To The Study Of Law** 3

Definition of the Law
Rule Creation
Rule Application
Structure and Method of This Book
The Study of Appellate Cases
Briefing Appellate Cases
Review Problems

2 **An Overview Of American Business Associations** 29

State-Level Restraints in Forming Business Associations
Federal-Level Restraints on Business Associations
Types of American Business Associations
Review Problems, Part I

PART II: AGENCY LAW

3 **The Mutual Legal Duties Of Principal And Agent** 59

Creation of the Agency Relationship
Duties of the Agent to the Principal
Remedies
Duties of the Principal to the Agent
Capacity
Husband and Wife as Principal and Agent
Review Problems

4 **Contractual Liability Of Principals And Agents To Third Parties** 83

Contractual Liability of Principals to Third Parties
Contractual Liability of the Agent to Third Parties
Review Problems

5 **Tort Liability Of Principal And Agent To Third Parties** 113

Tort Liability
Tort Liability of a Principal to a Third Party
Vicarious Liability of the Principal
Speculations as to "Respondeat Superior"
The Master as a Cause
The Justice of Liability Without Moral Fault
Liability without Legal Fault
Justification for "Respondeat Superior"
Review Problems

6 Agency Operation And Termination **165**

Agency Operation
Agency Termination
Review Problems, Part II

PART III: PARTNERSHIPS

7 The Partnership Form Of Association:
Creation And Partnership Property **195**

Definition
Creation
Partnership Property and a Partner's Interest
Joint Ventures
Limited Partnership
Review Problems

8 Partnership Operation And Dissolution **221**

Partnership Operation: Contract Liability
Partnership Operation: Tort Liability
Incoming Partners
Partnership Dissolution
Dissolution Notice to Third Parties
Review Problems

PART IV: CORPORATIONS

9 Corporations: Introduction, Formation And Corporate Personality **259**

Introduction
Corporate Nature
Whether to Incorporate
Where to Incorporate
How to Incorporate
Promoters
Incorporation Process
Defectively Formed Corporations
Disregarding the Corporate Entity
Lifting the Corporate Veil: Corporate Entity in the Modern Day Court
Foreign Corporations
Powers of a Corporation
Review Problems

10 Shareholders And The Corporate Capital Structure **293**

The Shareholder
Corporate Capital Structure
Corporate Control Devices
Close Corporations
Shareholders' Remedial Rights
Review Problems

11 Managing The Corporation: The Role Of The Directors And Officers . .**323**

    Illinois Business Corporation Act
    Board Authority and Meetings
    Qualifications and Removal
    The Duty of Care and the Business Judgment Defense
    Officers
    Crimes and Torts
    Indemnification of Directors and Officers
    Executive Compensation
    Review Problems

12 Dividends **373**

    Sources for Dividends
    Declaration of Dividends
    Directors, Liability for Impermissible Dividends
    Types of Dividends
    Directors' Discretion in Dividend Matters
    Review Problems

13 Fiduciary Obligation **391**

    Corporate Opportunities
    Sale of Control
    Interested Directors and Interlocking Directorates
    Employee — Competitor
    Review Problems

14 Altering The Corporate Structure And Dissolution **435**

    Amending the Articles
    Merger, Consolidation and Sale of Assets
    Dissolution
    Review Problems

PART V: SECURITIES REGULATION

15 Securities Regulation **461**

    Blue Sky Laws
    Federal Securities Regulation
    The Securities and Exchange Commission
    Going Public
    What is a Security?
    Registration Requirements
    Review Problems

16 Insider Trading **485**

    Short Swing Profits — Section 16 (b) of the '34 Act
    Section 10 (b) of the '34 Act and Rule 10b-5
    Tipper and Tippee Liability
    Who May Recover for Section 10 (b) and Rule 10b-5 Violations?
    Other Fradulent Activities
    Review Problems

17 Liability Of Directors, Accountants, And Attorneys
    Under The Securities Law 529

    Director's Liability
    Accountant's Liability
    Attorney's Liability
    Statutory Liability for Securities Law Violations
    Review Problems

18 Regulation Of The Proxy Process And Tender Offers 573

    Proxy Regulation
    Tender Offers
    Corporate Reporting
    Securities and the Uniform Commercial Code
    Review Problems

PART VI: RECENT FEDERAL LEGISLATION
AND THE AMERICAN BUSINESS ASSOCIATION

19 Corporate Duties To Employees And The Public 595

    Recent Federal Legislation on Employers' Duties to Employees
    Recently Developed Legal Duties of Business Associations to
      the Public
    Social Responsibilities of American Business Associations
    Review Problems

PART VII: EPILOGUE

20 The New Form Of Property 663

APPENDICES

    Review Problems
    Uniform Partnership Act
    Glossary

    Index 719

CASES

Abresch v. Northwestern Bell Tel. Co. 60
ADT v. Grinnell 378
Albemarle Paper Co. v. Moody 602
Allen Mfg. Co. v. Loika 66
Allenberg Cotton v. Pittman 283
Aluma Kraft Mfg. Co. & Solmica, Inc., v. Elmer Fox & Co. 10
Aluminum Co. of America v. Ward 176
American Smelting and Refining Co. v. OSAHRC 613
App'l of Delaware Racing Assoc. 443
Baltimore & Ohio R. Co. v. Foar 351
Bancroft Whitney v. Glen 428
Barber Agency W.H. v. Co-operative Barrel Co. 174
Barnes v. Andrews 331
Bates v. Dresser 328
Blau v. Lehman 487
Brooks v. St. Bd. of Funeral Dir. & Embalmers 31
Blue Chip Stamps v. Manor Drug 517
B-OK Inc. v. Storey 245
Brantman, In re 378
Browe, v. Fenner & Beane 75
Burch v. Americus Grocery Co. 187
Cady, Roberts & Co., In re 494
Calvert Cliffs' v. A.E.C. 641
Central Trust & Safe Deposit Co. v. Respass 51
Channon v. Channon 378
Chicago Flexotile Floor Co. v. Lane 391
Clement v. Clement 209
Coblentz v. Riskin 88
Consolidated Sun Ray, Inc., v. Oppenstein 278
Cooper v. Cooper 79
Cote Bros. Inc., v. Granite Lake Realty 345
Cox v. Bowling 185
Davidsville First National Bank v. St. John's Church 85

Dempsey v. Chambers 151

Dodge v. Ford Motor Co. 378

Donahue v. Permacel Tape Corp. 70

Ellingson v. Walsh, O'Connor & Barneson 239

Ernst & Ernst v. Hochfelder 556

Escott v. Barchris Construction Corp. 529

Essex Universal Corp. v. Yates 419

Farris v. Glen Alden Corp. 438

Flick, Melba Jean v. Elmer Crouch 130

Foremost-McKesson, Inc. v. Provident Securities Co. 487

Galler v. Galler 308

Gizzi v. Texaco, Inc. 146

Globe Woolen Co. v. Utica Gas & Elec. Co. 426

Goldenberg v. Bartell Broadcasting 347

Gottfried v. Gottfried 383

Gratz v. Claughton 486

Greenman v. Yuba Power Prod. Inc. 637

Guth v. Loft 393

Heckel v. Cranford Country Club 92

Henningsen v. Bloomfield Motors, Inc. and Chrysler Corp. 625

Hobbs v. U.S. 430

Holzman v. De Escamilla 215

Huff v. United Van Lines Inc. 166

Humphrey v. Virginian Ry. Co. 158

Irving Trust Co. v. Deutsch 404

Johnson v. Greene 399

Jones v. Mutual Creamery Co. 153

Kelley v. Comm'r I.R.S. 300

Lamb v. Leroy 437

Larsen v. General Motors 634

Lawer v. Kline 222

Ledbetter-Johnson Co. v. Hawkins 156

Lind v. Schenley Industries Inc. 98

Litwin v. Allen 335

Lyons v. American Legion Post No. 650 48

Malloy v. Fong 169

Manufacturing Trust Co. v. Becker 407

Mayer v. Adams 317

McClennen v. Comm'r of I.R.S. 242

Mitchell v. Vulture Min. & Mill. Co. 182
Murray v. Modoc State Bank 114
Myzel v. Fields 480
Northway v. TSC Industries 580
Nye v. Lovelace 63
Patton v. Nicholas 378
Perlman v. Feldman 412
Philipsborn & Co. v. Suson 264
Phillips v. Cook 228
Pierce v. Commonwealth 306
Poretta v. Superior Dowel Company 107
Radom & Neidorff, In re 452
Reliance Elec. Co. v. Emerson Elec. Co. 487
Rockwell v. Stone 179
Rogers v. Hill 366
Rosenfeld v. Fairchild Engine 575
Rouse v. Pollard 224
Sandman v. Hagan & Striegel 138
Schein v. Chasen 513
School Dist. of Phila. v. Frankford Grocery Co. 45
Sec. of Labor v. Pecosteel 617
S.E.C. v. Capital Grains Research Bureau 524
S.E.C. v. Howey 467
S.E.C. v. National Student Marketing 563
S.E.C. v. Ralston Purina Co. 476
S.E.C. v. Texas Gulf Sulphur 496
S.E.C. v. Transamerica Corp. 576
Shapiro v. Merrill Lynch 512
Sheldon v. Little 200
Sinclair Oil v. Levien 378
Smith Mfg. Co. v. Barlow 288
Smolowe v. Delendo Corp. 486
Solomon v. Kirkwood 352
Southwestern Portland Cement v. Beavers 94
State v. Elsbury 212
Stockwell v. Morris 133
Thomas v. McBride Exp. Co. 136
United Brokers Co. v. Dose 237
United Housing Foundation v. Formaan 470

U.S. v. Park 359
U.S. v. Reserve Mining Co. 652
U.S. v. Simon 549
U.S. Liability Ins. Co. v. Haidinger-Hayes Inc. 356
Von Au v. Magenhemer 378
Vrabel v. Acri 234
Wellington Print Works v. Magid 430
Wilkins v. Waldo Lumber Co. 102
Winkleman v. General Motors Corp. 368
Zajac v. Harris 198

EDITOR'S PREFACE

Legal Perspectives of American Business Associations is a significant newcomer to the Grid Series in Law. The concept of the Series is to develop a group of innovative teaching materials designed especially for non-law school legal instruction. *Perspectives* is an apt addition to the Series for a number of reasons. First and foremost, it is student oriented. Professor Wolfe is well known for his ideas regarding educational theory[1] and he and his co-author Fred Naffziger have put these ideas in practice with the writing of this text. Second, a variety of teaching materials is presented including carefully selected cases, documents, and excerpts from classic writings in the fields of law covered. Third, the text is written and organized in a very straightforward, comprehendible manner.

Perspectives is designed for upper-level and graduate courses in the law of business associations. In the past many business law instructors teaching business association courses have had to make use of selected chapters from one of the various multi-topic basic business law texts. In so doing, the instructor often ended up requiring students to purchase a text of which a third or less would actually be used. Further, the business associations coverage in such texts tended to be excessively rule oriented with very little analysis of policy issues. In contrast, *Perspectives* covers many of the current policy issues in the law of business associations and provides cohesive, integrated coverage of the topics of agency, employment, partnerships and corporations.

The law of business organizations is a very important part of business law. Business people continually face important decisions regarding the operational implications of particular forms of business association. This fact is reflected in the growing interest in business association law in management oriented continuing education programs.

In addition, many important policy issues are posed by the nature of business associations recognized by the state. General Motors will probably survive all humans alive today. Enormous implications flow from this fact. Similarly, many proposals for dealing with the thorny question of corporate social responsibility relate to changing the law of corporations in some specific manner. Issues regarding securities regulation and the functioning of our financial markets intertwine in the law of this field.

The need for a separate business school course in business associations where the student is exposed to a wide-ranging treatment of these important topics and issues is great. The old approach of Business Law I, II and III must give way to a more selective curriculum that is relevant to student needs and to the times. In fact, many schools have already added policy-oriented business association courses. Others will soon follow. *Perspectives* will serve as an excellent foundation for such a course.

Thomas W. Dunfee, The Wharton School, University of Pennsylvania

[1] Wolfe, *Expressing the Educational Objectives of Business Law: A proposed Method and Framework,* 12 **Am. B.L.J.** *1* (1974).

PREFACE

Most new textbooks are motivated by a perceived gap between the real world and the knowledge of that world provided by conventional instructional materials. The gap we perceive has at least two dimensions. First, a major source of wealth and property exchange is provided by corporate securities, yet the law applicable to this phenomenon has been neglected by established textbooks on the law of business associations. These textbooks focus primarily upon corporate formation and control under *state law*. Only recently have fragmented presentations of federal securities law appeared. We could find no source outside of law school texts which presented a comprehensive treatment of the federal law governing the trading of corporate securities. Almost one fifth of this text is devoted to the law of federal securities.

Second, we perceive that the usual treatment of the law of business associations is too rule oriented. The traditional attention of the quantity of rules rather than quality has lead to an over emphasis on student behavior in the simplest of all cognitive acts, recall. The nature of the material in this text will enable the instructor to emphasize the more complex cognitive acts of comprehension, analysis, application and synthesis. To strengthen a student's comprehension of significant rules of law, we have included law review articles and other material explaining the historical development of the rules and how they are applied, and how they may change in the future. The cases are longer than in most other comparable texts so that the student is required to analyze the factual pattern (break it apart into relevant and irrelevant portions) as he or she would have to do when confronting the problem outside the classroom. Most cases are followed by review questions which will focus the reader's attention on our purpose for including the case in the text. Following each chapter, and in the appendix, we present a series of review questions, some of which are from past CPA exams. Some of these problems are quite lengthy and will require that the student carefully analyze the facts, correctly recall and then apply one or more legal principles and, finally, synthesize an answer by, in some cases, considering both legal and policy issues. Thus, this textbook on the law of American business associations differs from those currently available both in the substance presented and in the manner in which it is presented.

We intend this book for use in advanced undergraduate courses and graduate courses outside the law school. It is divided into seven parts followed by an appendix which includes, first, review problems, and, second, the Uniform Partnership Act. The appendix is followed by a glossary of important terms used in the text.

Part I of the book is written with the assumption that the student has never taken a law course. In Chapter 1, we present the process of rule creation by legislatures, individuals, and judges in addition to rule application through the court system. The studying and briefing of appellate cases is given special emphasis. In Chapter 2, we present an overview of the most prominent forms of

American business associations including the Subchapter "S" corporation and the cooperative.

Part II has four chapters on the law of agency. The instructor will note that the text in these chapters, as in the ones that follow, is not burdened with the terse statements of all the possible rules on agency law. Rather, the textual material emphasizes the fundamental rules of agency: the nature of the fiduciary relationship, the concepts of contractual authority and vicarious liability. Also included are major articles by Professor Warran A. Seavey on the reasons for the doctrine of respondeat superior and William H. Dickey, Jr. on the growing uses of apparent authority.

Part III again combines text and appellate cases together with sections of the Uniform Partnership Act in order to explain partnership law. The presentation uses a typical partnership agreement as an organizational guide. Partnership formation, the duties of partners to one another and to the partnership, and partnership property are emphasized in Chapter 7. Chapter 8 presents the contractual and tort liabilities of the partnership and partners, and concludes with an emphasis on the liability of incoming partners and partnership dissolution.

Part IV has six chapters: corporate formation and personality; the shareholders and the corporate capital structure; the role of directors and officers; dividends; fiduciary obligations of management, and, altering the corporate structure and dissolution. Statutes from various states are used together with text, appellate cases, and corporate documents to illustrate the circumstances in which courts apply corporate law. A semi-scholarly article provides background on one of the basic issues discussed: piercing the corporate veil.

Part V presents four chapters on federal securities law. The increasing importance of this area of law for business persons is manifested not only by the increasing number of major CPA examination questions but also by increased litigation involving corporations, their owners and managers. Chapter 15 begins the analysis with an overview of blue sky laws, the Federal Securities Act of 1933 and 1934, and explanations of "going public," the definition of a "security," and elaboration of registration requirements including SEC Rules 146 and 144. Chapters 16 and 17 are closely related. Chapter 16 covers insider trading liability based upon Section 16 of the '34 Act and SEC Rule 10 (b) 5. The famous case of *SEC* v. *Texas Gulf Sulphur* is reproduced for analysis. Chapter 17 continues to explore the liability of directors, accountants, and attorneys based upon the federal securities law. Chapter 18 concludes this part by presenting text, cases, and review problems on proxy and tender-offer regulation, corporate reporting to the SEC and corporate securities and the Uniform Commercial Code.

Part VI offers an overview of very recent federal legislation and how it affects the business association's duties to employees and the public. Chapter 19 begins by presenting some of the leading cases on and major points of the following federal laws and their amendments which create new duties running from *employers* to *employees:* Title VII, 1964 Civil Rights Act; Equal Pay Act of 1963; Age Discrimination in Employment Act, 1967; Occupational Safety and Health Act of 1970; and, the Employment Retirement Income Security Act of 1974. This chapter also includes cases and text on recently developed legal duties of the business association to the public in the areas of product liability and the environment. The chapter concludes with a section on the Reserve Mining litigation and the "social responsibility" of American business associations.

Since about one-half of this book is devoted to the corporate form of business association, its ownership and control, the book concludes with a major piece written by Professor Adolph Berle, noted legal and social commentator. In Part VII, Professor Berle explores the social ramifications of the relatively recent ascendency of the corporate form of business association. His thesis, which first appeared in 1932 in *The Modern Corporation and Private Property,* co-authored with Dr. Gardiner C. Means, argues that the separation of corporate ownership — vested in shareholder — and corporate control - vested in management — has bread a new form of property. He suggests that while the outlines and consequences of this new form of property are dimly perceived, continued inquiry into the new property will reveal some of the directions of the continued evolution of American society.

Acknowledgments

The text writing and case selection responsibility were divided between the co-authors as follows: Professor Wolfe was primarily responsible for the material in Chapter 1-8, 19 and 20; Professor Naffziger was primarily responsible for the material in Chapters 9 through 18 and the first section of Chapter 19 on the Civil Rights Laws. This book, however, is the product of the efforts of many. We thank the administration, staff, students, and Professor Tom Vander Ven of the English Department, all of Indiana University at South Bend for their important contributions. Also, we gratefully acknowledge the kind contributions of the Columbia Law Review; Harvard University Law School; Harvard University Press; University of Pittsburgh Law Review; the American Bar Association and its Section of Corporation, Banking, and Business Law; American Institute of Certified Public Accountants; the Commercial Law League of America; Matthew Bender and Company, Inc.; and the National Conference of Commissioners on Uniform State Laws. We also thank Winnebago Industries, Inc., for permission to reprint their stock certificate.

Also, we acknowledge the extensive contributions of the numerous judges who authored the opinions reproduced herein. Without their careful analysis and lucid prose this work would suffer significantly. Finally, we note the special contributions of Professor Thomas Dunfee of the Wharton School of Finance, University of Pennsylvania, whose criticism and encouragement helped us immensely.

In conclusion, we offer a caveat. Significant time passes between submission of a final manuscript and its appearance in print. In the rapidly changing areas of law such as those covered in Chapters 15 through 19 it is possible that substantial changes have occurred since manuscript submission. With this caveat we accept full responsibility for the accuracy of the information, and the opinions presented.

Arthur D. Wolfe
Frederick J. Naffziger

PART I

INTRODUCTION TO THE STUDY OF LAW AND AMERICAN BUSINESS ASSOCIATIONS

INTRODUCTION TO THE STUDY OF LAW 1

If laws were unchanging and if human behavior were simple, then the study of law would be a matter of memorization — of fixed rules and of the situations they govern. The student of law would merely master the constitutions and statute books of federal, state, and local legislation, the rulings of administrative agencies, and the opinions of the courts. But the body of society has the complex vitality of a living organism, and its legal system has the energy of process rather than the inert mass of fixed rules.

DEFINITION OF THE LAW

To perceive law as a process, as activity, we must observe its rules at work in a complex and changing social, economic, political, and moral environment. The focus of law study must not only include the written rules; but it must also include the activity of law application. A working definition of law must include these minimum descriptions: 1) the rules, written and unwritten, generated by the sovereign or other rule source; 2) how these rules are applied: 3) how persons and institutions respond to rule applications; and 4) how the rule-making bodies change old rules and generate new ones.

Our discussion of law begins with the creation of rules and then expands to the judicial process of the application of rules by the court system. Through such a course of study, we can begin to learn to predict with some certainty when and how the rules will be enforced and how those affected will react. This development of the ability to predict when and how laws will be applied is the primary objective of law study; memorization of some rules is simply a convenient starting point.

RULE CREATION

The ultimate source of rules in American law is the U.S. Constitution. This document proclaims that it is the supreme law of the land and that any other law or "legal" activity which conflicts with it is unconstitutional or illegal.

LEGISLATIVE

The federal constitution creates our three, co-equal branches of government: the legislature whose prime responsibility is to pass the laws; the executive whose prime responsibility is to implement and enforce the laws, and the judiciary whose responsibility is to adjudicate; that is, to provide a framework for deciding if there has been a violation of law.

Since the U.S. Constitution delegates to the Congress the duty to pass laws, any law passed by the Congress which is consistent with the powers delegated to Congress by the U.S. Constitution is the supreme law of the land and forms the second level in our scheme of legislative rule creation.

Congress, like state legislatures, may delegate some of its rule making powers to other governmental units called administrative agencies. For example, the Sixteenth Amendment to the U.S. Constitution gives Congress the authority to levy a tax on incomes. After the Congress passed income tax legislation (the most recent comprehensive law is the Internal Revenue Code of 1954), it delegated the authority to enforce the code to the Secretary of the Treasury. Congress further provided that the president, with the advice and consent of the Senate, should appoint a Commissioner of Internal Revenue who ". . . shall be in the Department of the Treasury,"[1] and that the Secretary or his delegate (usually the Commissioner) shall prescribe all necessary rules and regulations for the enforcement of the Internal Revenue Code.[2] So both the Secretary of the Treasury and the Commissioner of Internal Revenue have substantial rule making authority. There are numerous federal administrative agencies, some may be "independent" such as the Federal Trade Commission, and some more directly controlled by Congress such as the Internal Revenue Service, or are controlled by the president, such as the Department of Health, Education and Welfare. All of these administrative agencies make rules, formally called "regulations," which are applied by the agency itself.

The Tenth Amendment to the U.S. Constitution provides that those powers not expressly given (or necessarily implied in) the grant of authority given to the federal government are reserved to the states. The rule creating power within each state follows the same general pattern as that of the federal government. Each state has a constitution which creates the basic rights, duties and privileges of the residents of the state as well as organizes the state system of government. The legislature, one of three branches of state government, is the primary rule making body, and any rules made by it which are consistent with the state constitution's fundamental guidelines are the supreme law of the state. State rules which are consistent with state constitutional provisions are valid unless they conflict with a federal rule which has been made by Congress and this latter rule is consistent with the U.S. Constitution. If a state-made rule or the official acts of a state agency conflicts with a federal statute or the U.S. Constitution, this state rule or activity is unconstitutional or illegal.

State legislatures may also create administrative agencies; state departments of welfare, taxation and education which have rule making authority are just a few examples. Moreover, the state may also delegate some of its rule making authority to local governments such as county and city governments which enact ordinances.

INDIVIDUAL RULE CREATION

Another major source of our rules comes from individuals who voluntarily make rules to govern a transaction between themselves. These rules form the body of our contract law. Contract law is rule creation in every sense of the term because the rules are recognized by the courts as enforceable obligations. This means that upon a violation of them, one party may be compelled through our court system to pay damages to the injured party.

Other examples of individual or institutional rule creation such as the rules adopted by a particular religion or fraternal group or the rules adopted and followed in sporting or competitive events are generally not considered "legal" rules because the breach of them is not punishable by a *court imposed* fine or loss of freedom. This is not to say that the infraction of these rules might not be severely punished; indeed, they may be and those arguing for a very broad definition of law would probably include these rules. We believe, however, that convenient and useful classification of individual rule creation is limited to those rules for which the judiciary provides a remedy.

JUDICIAL RULE CREATION

The role of the judiciary (court system) in rule creation may be divided into two broad categories. First, the judiciary in applying (and in this process interpreting) legislative rules inevitably creates rules of its own. However, these rules, whether in the form of an exception to the rule or otherwise, become part of the meaning of the legislative rules.

Second, and more applicable to this section, is the fact that the judiciary may create substantive duties and rights where none existed in the statutory law. Generally, the rules of the law of negligence are made by the judiciary, as well as the rules regarding agency law, the subject of the first portion of this book. The entire body of the law of contracts was created by the judiciary, but recently the rules regarding contracts for the sale of goods were enacted by almost all of the state legislatures in the Uniform Commercial Code, Article 2, thus becoming part of the legislative rule scheme.

This second class of rules which is separate from legislative enactments and which derives its authority from custom as adopted and recognized by the courts is often referred to as the common law. The common law of this country is determined only after reading decision after decision in which judges have attempted to describe the substantive rules in areas in which the legislatures have not acted and in which rules are needed to govern activity. To bring some uniformity into our system of common law, legal scholars have collected and codified what they believe to be the best judicially created rules on a subject. These scholars publish and, from time to time, revise these rules which are found in volumes entitled *Restatements of the Law.* In the chapters following we will discuss the *Restatement of the Law of Agency* which, although stated in the form of a comprehensive code, remains non-legislative.

Another important source of judicially created rules which is not thought of as part of the common law, but as a distinct body of judicially generated rules is called equity law. Since equity law or equitable principles will be discussed throughout this book we must provide a brief overview of how this body of law developed.

The word "equity" is derived from the Latin word "aequitas" which means equality or justice. Like much of our law this body of rules comes from England. As the English sovereigns began to gather legislative power to themselves in the thirteenth and fourteenth centuries, the "law" became more and more the very word of the sovereign. The law became rigid and inflexible and often a very literal application of the law had such severe repercussions that the effect of its application served to defeat the intent of the rule. To create flexibility in the application of law the English sovereign (beginning about 1350) allowed his immediate subordinate, the Chancellor, to hear grievances arising because of the harsh application of the law or where no remedy existed in the sovereign's law. The Chancellor would hear only those cases he believed to be worthy and would decide each case according to his conscience and sense of justice. In short, he was to provide equity when the literal application of the law failed in some respect.

Thus, equity law became a supplementary legal system which operated only when the established legal system of the sovereign would not provide that which in good conscience should be done. The Tudor and Stuart sovereigns and the Puritan Revolution somewhat confined the powers of the Chancellor, but, by the colonial period, there were still two discernible legal systems: that based upon the word of the sovereign (by then the Parliament) enforced in "courts of law" and that based upon principles of what was fair given the circumstances, enforced in "courts of equity."

During and after colonization the American legal system continued to provide separate "law" and "equity" courts, but by the middle of the nineteenth century the two separate courts were made one and a single judge administered both bodies of rules. Today the federal system and all of the states have but one system of courts, but the judges presiding may, from time to time, invoke certain "equitable" principles in those situations in which the remedies provided by the law (or, today the legislative and individual rules) are either inadequate to do "justice" or work an "injustice" by their direct application. These equitable rules are still applied in the discretion of the judge and remain supplementary in nature. Two examples of present day "equitable" principles are the remedies of the issuance of an injunction (a court order prohibiting activity) or the decree of specific performance (a court order directing that certain activity take place). Both of these remedies are given to a party in a law suit where the traditional remedy at law of awarding money damages would be insufficient to compensate the injured party.

RULE APPLICATION

Learning the circumstances in which rules are applied is at the heart of the legal instructional process. However, before we examine the process of rule application we must distinguish between the types of rules which are applied.

TYPES OF RULES

The types of rules generated by the three primary sources discussed above, the legislature, private persons and the judiciary, are divided into two broad categories, criminal and civil. Neither the judiciary nor private persons can create criminal rules. These are created only by the federal and state legislatures. The criminal law is distinguished fom the civil law primarily by: 1) who initiates the prosecution process after a violation; 2) the standard of proof; and, 3) the potential punishment or remedy.

A crime is an illegal act the prosecution of which is initiated by a federal, state or county prosecutor, and the person being tried for the crime (the defendant) is tried on behalf of and in the name of the federal or state government. The civil law is usually "enforced" by private persons or by a governmental unit suing for the breach of a civil rule. The "wrong" involved in a criminal prosecution is one which usually manifests an "evil" intent. It is the purpose of the criminal law to punish this evil intent. If the defendant does not plead guilty, punishment may be imposed only after a trial by a jury (unless trial by jury is waived by the defendant in which case the judge acts as a jury). In some less significant crimes (traffic violations, etc.) there is no right to a trial by jury.

In a criminal case, the government has the burden of proving guilt beyond a reasonable doubt. This differs substantially from the standard of proof in a civil case. In the latter instance, the plaintiff must prove that it is more probable than not that the defendant committed the act complained of. Obviously, this standard of proof is less than that required in criminal cases.

Finally, in the prosecution of a criminal case the action sought (from the court and jury) is the imposition of a fine or imprisonment. In a civil case, the law seeks to compensate the injured party, not punish the defendant. Thus, the plaintiff seeks money damages for compensation or an equitable decree.

The criminal law is usually subdivided into two more categories: felonies and misdemeanors. A felony is a crime of a serious nature and is defined by the federal and state legislatures as an offense, the punishment for which may be a penitentiary sentence of over one year, or in some states, over six months. A misdemeanor, a less serious crime, is usually punishable by fine or imprisonment for less than one year or six months in some states. Since the state legislatures have the duty of creating rules for the health and welfare of the residents of the state, most of the commonly known criminal rules are created by state legislatures.

In summary, these differences discussed above between the two broad rule classifications are only generalizations, and are subject to exception. In some instances, a governmental unit may initiate a proceeding which is civil in nature. The remedy sought may be the payment of damages for some harm done, or a request for an injunction to prohibit some threatened harm to the federal or state government.

Most of the rules in this book about business associations are "civil" in nature and not criminal. Therefore, you will find that a person such as an individual, a partnership or a corporation and not a governmental unit initiates the prosecution, suing for damages. If it is found by the jury (or the judge sitting as a jury) that it is more probable than not that the one being sued did the act complained of, and that the act of the defendant breached a duty owed to the plaintiff, and that the damages requested will compensate for the injury done, then the court will award a judgment to the one bring the suit.

JUDICIAL SYSTEMS

Since the U.S. Constitution and all the state constitutions create judicial systems for the redress of the breach of a rule, there are fifty-one different systems, one federal system and fifty state systems. The federal system is nationwide and is composed of three levels of courts. The courts on the initial level, the trial courts, are called the federal district courts. Each state is divided into districts and there may be as many federal district courts in each district as congress deems adequate.

If a litigant in the federal system believes an error was committed at the trial stage, an appeal may be taken to the second level of the system, the federal circuit court of appeals. Currently there are eleven appellate circuits in the federal system. An appeal from the circuit court level goes to the third level, the U.S. Supreme Court, composed of nine justices sitting in Washington, D.C. Usually, appeals will be heard by the Supreme Court if four justices vote to hear the case. That is, almost all appeals to the Supreme Court are heard in the discretion of the court and very few appeals will be heard as a matter of right.

Generally, the various state systems are also of a three-level nature. There is an initial trial court, an appellate court level and a final appellate court, usually called the supreme court of the state. This basic scheme may be varied by adding township, city or small claims courts in which the amount in dispute may not exceed a given amount (usually $500) or by adding courts of special jurisdiction such as those limited to probate, juvenile or domestic relations. Nevertheless, the general scheme is similar to the federal scheme: one trial court level followed by two appellate levels.

The state and federal judicial systems are administered separately. The application of the criminal law provides the best example of the division of duties between the two systems. Prosecutions for the breach of the criminal rules generated by Congress must take place in the federal system. This is necessary to secure a uniform application of the federal criminal laws. The action must begin at the federal district court level and is prosecuted by a federal official, the U.S. Attorney, for the district or his assistant. These U.S. Attorneys are agents of the U.S. Department of Justice under the U.S. Attorney General.

Most crimes such as murder, assault and battery, larceny, etc., are defined by state legislatures. The prosecution of these crimes must begin at the trial court level in the state. These prosecutions are initiated by a state, or, usually, a county prosecutor who may be elected or may, in some cases, be appointed.

The judicial system selected by a *civil* litigant is determined by which legislative source, federal or state, created the rule which is the subject of the complaint. For example, if a violation of the Clayton Act is alleged (adopted by Congress in 1914) and damages are sought, the suit must begin in the federal judiciary. If the failure to meet some rule standard created by the state legislature is the subject of the case, it usually begins in the state judicial system. The reason for this is, again, the necessity to preserve the uniformity of the rule application.

The two judicial systems overlap in at least two important respects. First, to alleviate the local prejudice which might be present when a resident of one state is suing a resident of another in the state court system (usually in the state of the defendant's residence), Congress has created federal power (jurisdiction) to hear the case if the amount in controversy exceeds $10,000. In most of the cases based upon this type of federal jurisdiction, called "diversity jurisdiction" because of the necessity of needing residents from different states as parties of the case, the rule source sued upon is usually created by state-level sources. It is assumed that local prejudice will be minimized in the federal district courts because the judges are appointed by the president, and not a local political body, and they serve until they voluntarily retire or are impeached. They need not stand for election as do some state or county judges. Moreover, the federal district is usually geographically larger than that of the state trial court, hence the jury members in the federal court are picked from a wider area, again minimizing the chance for local prejudice to influence the matter.

In summary, a private civil litigant may use the federal system if the subject matter of the case primarily involves the breach of a federally created rule or if the case involves a rule created by state-level sources and the parties to the case are:

1. from different states *and*
2. the amount in controversy exceeds $10,000.

A second major area of overlap between the federal and state judicial systems involves appeals from the state system to the federal. In a state-level trial, if either party raises issues of the state substantive or procedural law conflicting with the U.S. Constitution, then, after appeals raising these same issues are taken through the highest state court which could hear the case, then the party may appeal from that court to the U.S. Supreme Court.

The U.S. Supreme Court has the final word on all interpretations of the U.S. Constitution whether or not the case originated on the state or federal level. This does not mean, however, that the U.S. Supreme Court must hear a case appealed to it from the federal or state system; in matters of this sort, the Supreme Court has discretion whether or not to hear the case.

THE CIVIL TRIAL PROCESS

Rule application takes place at many levels. Administrative agencies and individuals apply rules made by them everyday, but the judiciary has the formal task of adjudicating or declaring whether the activity complained of violates the rules. Knowledge of this formal process of rule application or adjudication is absolutely necessary to understanding most rules because it illustrates how those in charge of enforcing the rules do, in fact, enforce them. Remember that the real value in studying the law is to be able to predict when and how rules will be applied. The process of rule application, then, as manifested by the judicial process of adjudication is at the heart of the study of the law.

Below is presented the broad outlines of the trial of a civil case. The processes used may vary slightly from state to state, but, in general, the definition of the terms below are widely accepted.

A civil suit is initiated by the plaintiff who files several documents in a trial court of general jurisdiction (usually a county court located in the county government building). The document of greatest importance is called the complaint, which is filed by the plaintiff. The complaint must contain the following information:

1. The names of the parties to the case, the plaintiff(s) and defendant(s);
2. A statement sufficient to show that the court has jurisdiction to hear the matter;
3. A short and plain statement of the facts which indicate:
   a. the existence of a legal duty, and
   b. the breach of this duty; and
   c. a claim for relief in the form of a request for a given amount of money damages and/or a claim for equitable relief such as a request for an injunction or an order for specific performance.

Following is a copy of the complaint filed by the plaintiffs, Aluma Kraft Manufacturing Company Inc., and Solmica, Inc. for the first appellate case you will read later in this chapter. It is here reproduced almost entirely so that the reader can see that it is the complaint which sets the outlines of the case. Search the complaint (called "Petition" in Missouri) for the assertion of the existence of a legal duty and allegations which indicate a breach of this duty. The assertion of the legal duty and its breach are often referred to as the cause of action.

STATE OF MISSOURI
COUNTY OF ST. LOUIS

IN THE CIRCUIT COURT OF THE COUNTY OF ST. LOUIS
STATE OF MISSOURI

ALUMA KRAFT MANUFACTURING COMPANY
a corporation, and SOLMICA, INC,
a corporation,

Plaintiffs,
vs.

ELMER FOX & COMPANY,
Certified Public Accountants,
a partnership, 7750 Clayton Road,
Clayton, Missouri, comprising,
H. LEE SCHNURE, JR., RICHARD F. ASH,
M. GUY HARDIN and VICTOR JACQUEMIN, III.

Defendants

Filed
May 20, 1971

Cause No. 321920
Division _____

PETITION

Plaintiffs, for their claim for relief, state as follows:

1. That at the times herein mentioned, plaintiff, ALUMA KRAFT MANUFACTURING COMPANY, ("ALUMA KRAFT") was and is a corporation duly organized and existing according to law with its principal office in the City of Manchester, St. Louis County, Missouri, and the plaintiff, SOLMICA, INC., ("SOLMICA") was and is a corporation duly organized and existing according to law with its principal office in the City of St. Louis, Missouri; that the said corporations join herewith as co-plaintiffs for the complete adjudication of the rights of the said plaintiffs with respect to the claim as herein set forth.

2. That defendant, ELMER FOX & COMPANY, is a partnership of certified public accountants engaged in the general practice of accountancy, consisting of partners registered and licensed in accordance with the laws of Missouri; that the said partnership maintains an office at 7750 Clayton Road, St. Louis County, Missouri; that the said partners had, at the time herein mentioned, the following named defendants as partners: H. LEE SCHNURE, JR., RICHARD F. ASH, M. GUY HARDIN and VICTOR JACQUEMIN, III: that in addition to the said named defendants, the said partnership had other partners, the identity of which persons is not presently known to the plaintiffs.

3. That the defendant auditors, at the times herein mentioned and for many years prior thereto, had been regularly and routinely engaged by the plaintiff, ALUMA KRAFT, to perform general accounting and auditing services for it, and that in connection therewith, prepared plaintiff ALUMA KRAFT's financial statements, balance sheets and tax returns.

4. That on and prior to the 1st day of August, 1969, only T.J. BOTTOM ("BOTTOM") was the President, chief executive officer, principal director and

the owner of substantially all of the issued and outstanding shares of ALUMA KRAFT: that on or about the 29th day of Apri. 1969, negotiations were entered into between BOTTOM and SOLMICA whereby SOLMICA would acquire from BOTTOM eighty percent (80%) of the issued and outstanding capital stock of ALUMA KRAFT, the remaining twenty percent (20%) to be retained by BOTTOM, and BOTTOM would then continue to manage the affairs of ALUMA KRAFT as chief executive officer; that the negotiations culminated in a contract on August 1, 1969, which provided, *inter alia,* as follows:

"1(b) The purchase price of said shares of stock shall be the book value of such shares as of June 30th, 1969, which book value shall be determined as follows:

(i) Seller shall cause to be prepared by Aluma Kraft's auditors an interim financial statement reflecting the operations of the business from January 1, 1969, through June 30th, 1969, consisting of a profit and loss statement and balance sheet (subject to the auditors' notes and qualifications as set forth herein) showing the financial condition of said business at that date.

5. That pursuant to the said contract of August 1, 1969, SOLMICA acquired eighty percent (80%) of the issued and outstanding shares of stock of ALUMA KRAFT in conformity to the formula as hereinabove specified, for which plaintiff SOLMICA paid the sum of Two Hundred and Twenty-Nine Thousand Ninety and 40/100 Dollars ($229,090.40). Thereafter, on the 31st day of December, 1969, SOLMICA and BOTTOM mutually agreed to terminate BOTTOM's services as chief executive officer of ALUMA KRAFT, and SOLMICA purchased the balance of the shares of stock of ALUMA KRAFT.

6. That in contemplation of the Agreement for Purchase and in accordance with the provisions thereof, the plaintiff, ALUMA KRAFT, engaged its regular auditors, ELMER FOX & COMPANY, the defendant auditors herein, to perform the services required in preparing the financial statements.

7. Thereafter, on August 5, 1969, the defendant auditors furnished to the plaintiff, ALUMA KRAFT, its formal report setting forth the scope and opinion of the audit as follows:

The Board of Directors
Aluma Kraft Manufacturing Company
Manchester, Missouri

We have examined the balance sheet of Aluma Kraft Manufacturing Company as of June 30, 1969. Our examination was made in accordance with generally accepted auditing standards and accordingly included such tests of the accounting records and such other auditing procedures as we considered necessary in the circumstances.

In our opinion, the accompanying balance sheet presents fairly the financial position of Aluma Kraft Manufacturing Company at June 30, 1969 in conformity with generally accepted accounting principles.

/s/ Elmer Fox & Company

8. In reliance upon the said report, the plaintiff SOLMICA closed on the transaction at the sale price computed in accordance with the balance sheet as determined by the defendant auditors in its formal audit statement.

9. The plaintiffs state that the defendant auditors, in truth and in fact, failed to conduct their examination in accordance with "generally accepted auditing standards" and failed to furnish an opinion in conformity to "generally accepted accounting principles" and that both the scope and opinion of the said audit were false, erroneous, inaccurate and misleading and were made in disregard of the professional standards required of certified public accounts. Plaintiffs further state that the audit report was so sloppy that the defendant auditors failed to include as a liability on their audit the amounts due and unpaid to themselves by the plaintiff, ALUMA KRAFT, as of the dåte of the audit.

10. The failures of the defendant auditors, ELMER FOX & COMPANY, as hereinabove alleged, to conform to generally accepted auditing standards and to furnish an opinion in accordance with generally accepted accounting principles in the said audit were, amongst others, the following:*

Item 4.

Prepaid advertising was carried at $4,000.00. There was no substantiation of this item and no inventory record, and it covered obsolete literature. There was no proper evaluation of the item and it was an unverified estimate. The entire sum amounted to an overstatement of valuation in the amount of $4,000.00

Item 6.

Reynolds Metals was one of the principal suppliers and creditors of Aluma Kraft. No attempt was made to properly verify the amounts due either as payables or by shrinkage of consignment inventory:

(a) Invoices submitted by this supplier prior to June 30, 1969, were not recorded on the books as a liability in the amount of . . $3,934.79

(b) Reynolds Metals inventory shortage as of
June 30, 1969 . . . . $26,496.69
Reynolds Metals — Total $30,431.48

Item 7.

Accrued vacation pay not disclosed on the books. No attempt was made to determine this liability and the obligations of Aluma Kraft to its Union staff. The liability was understated in the amount of
$ 2,070.10

Item 10.

Skillform equipment was carried on the books at a cost of $59,292.58, less depreciation of $32,116.25. This was useless and obsolete junk and not used by Aluma Kraft for many years. Fifty-nine machines were originally built; thirteen of the machines are still at the Aluma Kraft

---

*Author's note: Many of the "Items" set out under paragraph 10 were deleted. Only a selection of those stated were reproduced to show the reader the type of items included.

factory; five machines are believed to be in the field; and forty-one machines are unaccounted for. No attempt was made to verify the physical assets or economic value of these assets, and the assets were overstated in the amount of $27,176.33

Item 13.

In addition to the Skillform equipment, a parts inventory for the Skillform equipment in the amount of $12,594.49 was likewise carried as an asset, which was obsolete and useless junk. The overstatement of the assets $12,594.49

The total of these specific items aggregates the sum of $106,584.91

In addition to the foregoing specific items, the plaintiffs state that the defendant auditors, in disregard of their professional obligations, condoned numerous instances which constituted a departure from generally accepted accounting principles and generally accepted auditing standards in reevaluations of inventory by inclusion of hundreds of minor items which had not been previously carried as inventory items in prior examinations conducted by the defendant auditors. This included a detailing of all of the minuscule individual items of supplies, resulting in an overstatement of valuation of the assets by many thousands of dollars, the exact amount of which has not been presently determined by the plaintiffs. In addition thereto, the defendant auditors made no attempt whatsoever to determine the ownership of assets appearing on the premises which appeared to be the property of the corporation, such as the chairs and desks which were subsequently claimed to be the property of others and not that of the plaintiff corporation, ALUMA KRAFT. The value of this furniture has not been presently determined by the plaintiffs.

11. The plaintiffs state that the defendant auditors knew that the said audit was being prepared for the purpose of determining the amounts which plaintiff SOLMICA would pay for the ALUMA KRAFT shares, and that the plaintiff SOLMICA would rely upon the said audit. Plaintiff SOLMICA states that it was entitled to rely and did in fact rely on the said audit, all to its damage in the sum of $150,000.00.

12. The plaintiff, ALUMA KRAFT, states that the audit furnished by the defendant auditors was useless, valueless and misleading; that plaintiff, ALUMA KRAFT, paid the defendant auditors the sum of $4,100.00 and is entitled to a refund of said fees.

13. Plaintiffs state that the conduct of the audit by the defendant auditors was handled in a willfully careless and wantonly negligent manner in disregard of the professional standards required to be exercised by the defendant auditors, and that by reason thereof, the plaintiffs are entitled to exemplary damages in addition to their actual damages.

WHEREFORE, the premises considered, the plaintiff, SOLMICA, INC., prays for judgment against the defendants for actual damages in the sum of $150,000.00 and exemplary damages in the sum of $150,000.00; and the plaintiff, ALUMA KRAFT MANUFACTURING COMPANY, prays for judgment against the defendants in the amount of $4,100.00, together with the costs of the plaintiffs herein expended.

ACKERMAN, SCHILLER & SCHWARTZ
By: Gideon H. Schiller
Attorneys for Plaintiffs
7701 Forsyth Boulevard
Clayton, Missouri 63105
863-4654

The complaint is filed together with a summons which directs the server of the papers (usually a county sheriff if the case is filed in state court or a federal marshall if the case is filed in the federal court) to the last known address of the defendant. A copy of the complaint is included for the purpose of this "service." When the server of the papers locates the defendants or, in some states, when the server locates the permanent residence of the defending parties, the papers are left with someone of suitable age and discretion residing therein. The server then files a sworn statement with the court, often called a "return," in which the server swears that the defendants were served.

The defendants may file a document with the court responding to the complaint, called an "Answer" within a given time period, usually twenty to thirty days. A copy of the answer is given to the plaintiff. The answer may admit all or part of the facts as alleged in the complaint and may admit or deny any or all of the legal consequences. In addition, the answer may include a claim for relief against the plaintiff, called a counterclaim, if the grounds exist.

If it appears that a party not originally a plaintiff or defendant may be liable to either of these parties as a result of the pleadings (the collective designation given to the complaint, answer, counter claims and motions) or that this party has a claim against either the plaintiffs or defendants arising from the subject of the law suit then this party may be "joined" as a party to the suit and must be served with all of the pleadings and must respond.

The general rule defining those persons who may be plaintiffs or defendants, is that they must have a direct interest in the subject matter of the suit; that is, these persons must be directly affected by the outcome. This rule has been expanded somewhat recently by permitting "class action" suits.

Class action suits were first widely used on the federal level, but gradually states have been adopting procedures which provide for this type of litigation. The class action procedural rules provide that one or more members of a class may sue or be sued *as representatives of a class of persons if:* 1) the class is so numerous that joinder of all members of the class is not practicable; 2) there are questions of law or fact that are common to all members of the class; 3) the claims or defenses of the parties representing the class are typical of the claims or defenses of the class; 4) the representatives of the class will fairly protect the interests of the class, and judicial interpretation has now added a fifth prerequisite which is that all the members of the class must be identifiable (within reason). In addition to these prerequisites the court must find that the class action is superior to other available methods for the fair and efficient adjudication of the controversy. While the matter of class action remains the subject of controversy, the student should be aware that this procedure exists and, in some cases, represents the most effective remedy available.

If a party is properly served with the complaint and fails to file an answer within the time period provided by law, then the plaintiff may ask the court to enter a "default" judgment. If such is entered, the court is making a judgment that the plaintiff is entitled to the relief claimed in the complaint.

As stated earlier, a defendant may "answer" or the defendant may challenge the plaintiff's case by "motion" before the issue is formally tried. There are several motions the parties may use to challenge the legal arguments of the other party asserted through the pleadings filed with the court. The first such opportunity to present such a motion is presented to the defendant who may make a motion to the court — in this case the motion is made by filing a document labeled "Motion" with the court — to dismiss the complaint for failure to state a claim upon which relief may be granted. This motion achieves the same result that used to be accomplished by the filing of a "demurrer." Today, however, the word demurrer is no longer used by the federal courts or many state courts to designate formal pleadings.

The filing of the "Motion to Dismiss for Failure to State a Claim" by the defendant requires the judge to rule on whether or not the plaintiff has stated the existence and breach of a legal duty. The judge must consider the complaint and the facts stated therein and resolve every inference created by the facts in favor of the plaintiff. When this is done, and the judge determines that the complaint presents no legal claim, then the court will grant the motion to dismiss.

If the defendants file an answer, then the litigation moves into a phase of the process generally called the discovery stage. Generally, the objectives of this pre-trial procedure are to: 1) simplify the issues; 2) obtain admissions of fact to avoid unnecessary arguments and avoid surprise; 3) limit the number of expert witnesses; and other matters which would expedite the trial. In order to accomplish these objectives, several procedures are allowed which should be familiar to a student of the law of business associations.

The following legal devices permit an adverse party to "discover" almost all business records, communications, documents and other relevant material. The best known discovery device is the deposition. A deposition is a sworn statement of any person, including a party to the action (the plaintiffs or defendants) or any witness, which is made in response to questions from the attorneys for the opposing side. The deposition is used to discover physical evidence, to discover what a witness will say at trial or to discover any other relevant matter to the subject of the case. A deposition is usually taken in front of attorneys for both parties and is transcribed by a court reporter. The final copy is signed as a true statement by the one being deposed and is filed with the court. This signed statement may be used at the trial to challenge the testimony of the witness if this testimony varies from that in the deposition.

If the party or witness cannot be interviewed in person, then a series of written questions may be sent and must be answered under oath. These written questions are called interrogatories.

In addition to depositions and interrogatories, a party may ask the court to order another party, if good cause is shown, to produce documents and other items of evidence for inspection, copying or photographing. The subject of this order may be books, papers, accounts, letters, photographs, objects or tangible things, or other items which constitute evidence relating to the subject of the suit. The court may also order any party to permit entry upon designated land or other property in the control of the party for the purpose of measuring, inspecting, surveying or photographing the property. If the mental or physical condition of the party is in controversy, the court may order the party to submit to a physical or mental examination by a physician if good cause is shown. This latter method of "discovery" is used in many cases where personal injury is the subject of the case.

Courts in the various states adopted many of these discovery procedures in the 1960's so they are viewed as relatively new. This adoption has resulted in many more cases being settled out of court because the procedures allow a party to discover almost all of the relevant evidence of the opposing party. The only evidence which is not obtainable by an opposing party are those materials which are "privileged." Generally, such materials are an attorney's work product (thoughts and research on a case). Because of these procedures the attorneys for the parties can more accurately assess the chances for success if the matter should proceed to trial.

If the parties decide to "settle" the case out of court, the attorneys ask the permission of the judge to dismiss the case. If this dismissal is done "with prejudice" it means that a party will be barred from filing the suit again. If the pre-trial procedures do not result in settlement, then the parties usually ask the judge to rule on another series of motions challenging the legal assertions of the adverse parties. After the pleadings are all filed either party may make a motion to dismiss the claims of an adverse party and enter judgment for the moving party by moving for a "Judgment on the Pleadings" or "Summary Judgment." Some procedural systems make a distinction between these two motions but, in essence, they are the same. Like the initial motion to dismiss or the demurrer, described above, these motions require the judge to consider the arguments made in all of the pleadings, resolve every reasonable inference against the moving party, and make a finding as to whether or not the arguments made and facts asserted warrant submission of the case to the jury. Generally, if the judge finds that the legal arguments and facts presented could lead but to one reasonable conclusion, and that is in favor of the moving party, then the motion must be granted. If there are issues of fact present which would lead reasonable minds to differ, then the motion should be overruled.

If a court grants or sustains a motion to dismiss, or a motion for judgment on the pleadings or for summary judgment, then the aggrieved party may appeal this decision. The first appellate decision in the book, for example, the *Aluma Kraft* case, concerns whether or not a trial court properly entered a judgment dismissing the complaint of the plaintiff. If the judge does not grant the motion, then the trial process proceeds.

A matter may be tried before a jury or a judge alone. If a party in a civil suit desires a jury trial it must be demanded, usually during the initial pleading phase. In Federal Courts, the Constitution guarantees a trial by jury in all civil actions at common law where the value of the controversy exceeds twenty dollars. The U.S. Constitution does not guarantee the right of a trial by jury in civil cases in state courts. However, the constitutions of the states usually provide that there is such a right in cases similar to those where the common law gave such a right at the time the constitution was adopted. Practically speaking, this means that almost all matters involving judgments of fact and requests for money damages may be tried before a jury. Usually negligence cases, and other personal injury cases are thus tried. On the other hand, cases involving the equity powers of the court or those involving very complex issues such as antitrust suits or breaches of industrial contracts and other cases where evaluation of the evidence requires rigorous analysis and expertise are usually tried before the judge alone. In very exceptional cases, the judge may appoint a master or referee to hear some of the evidence and make findings of fact.

The process of questioning prospective jurors to determine which of them will be permitted to sit by the court and adverse parties is called voire dire. This phrase is French in origin and means "to speak the truth". The voire dire procedure allows the court and parties to reject a prospective juror if, after questioning, it is revealed that juror might be prejudiced or unable to render an impartial judgment. Usually, each party is given three challenges to use for any reason they so determine and additional challenges can be made for sufficient cause.

At the trial, the plaintiff, through the attorney representing the plaintiff's interests, presents its side of the evidence. After each witness is sworn and directly examined by the plaintiff's attorney, the defendant's attorney may cross-examine the witness on matters brought out on direct examination. It must be emphasized at this point that since most of the cases which proceed to trial do involve disputes of fact, the process by which the facts are "found" is the process of direct examination of a witness by one side followed by cross examination from the attorneys for the other side. The jury or the judge, by watching the witnesses respond to the questions asked must determine if they are telling the truth or accurately recalling an event. Not only the answers which are given by the witness are considered by the fact finder, but the witness's demeanor (facial expressions, and hand movements) all go into the final determination of whether or not they are credible.

Following the plaintiff's version of the facts in the case, the defendant presents the evidence relevant to its side.

During the trial itself, a party may challenge the entire case of an adverse party by moving for a Directed Verdict. Either party may move this and it requires the judge to rule on whether or not there are still issues of fact present which warrant the continuation of the trial. If reasonable minds could differ about the interpretation or existence of certain crucial facts, or the inferences to be drawn from the facts, then the court will overrule the motion and the trial will proceed.

At the close of the defendant's case, both sides make summary arguments emphasizing the aspects of the testimony and other evidence they believe most pertinent to their arguments. Before the jury retires to make its finding of fact, the judge instructs the jury as to the appropriate rules of law to apply. Below is an example of the type of "instruction" the judge may give to the jury in a negligence case:

Negligence is lack of ordinary care. It is a failure to exercise that degree of care which a reasonably prudent person would have exercised under the same circumstances. It may arise from doing an act which a reasonable prudent person would not have done under the same circumstances, or, on the other hand, from failing to do an act which a reasonably prudent person would have done under the circumstances.[3]

In applying this statement of the law, each juror must decide by using his or her own life experience as a guide whether or not the defendant acted as a "reasonably prudent person" would have, given the circumstances.

The judge gives the jury instructions on each matter of law argued in the case. After the instructions, the jury retires to the jury room where it applies all the rules stated by the judge to the facts as presented to them at the trial by the parties, witnesses, attorneys, and other evidence and reaches a verdict both as to liabilty — was the defendant legally at fault for a breach of a rule — and damages — if the defendant was liable, what is the appropriate amount of damages that will compensate the plaintiff for the breach of the rule.

A motion for "Judgment notwithstanding the Verdict" — formally called a Judgment Non Obstante Veredicto or Judgment N. O. V. — may be made by an aggrieved party against whom the verdict has been announced after the trial of the issues. This motion requires the judge to rule on whether or not the jury could reasonably have reached the verdict it did given the evidence and the court's instructions. This motion is granted only when the judge believes that the jury reached a verdict by ignoring his instructions, or where, after hearing and seeing all of the evidence, the jury could not logically have reached the verdict it did. This motion, like the one for summary judgment or the one for a directed verdict, essentially challenges the legal sufficiency of a party's case. It must not be confused with a motion for a new trial, which may be made after a verdict is reached but is granted only where substantial errors in the trial process occurred.

THE APPELLATE PROCESS

If either of the parties believe that there was an error during the trial and this error caused an unfavorable verdict, they may appeal. The error must be one in the process of introducing evidence, or in the statement of the law or in the application of the rule to the facts. Parties usually cannot appeal the finding of a fact. For example, if the jury finds that as a matter of fact the defendant did sign the agreement in question on a given date, then this may not be appealed. However, a party may appeal the issue of whether or not signing the agreement did legally bind the party. This latter conclusion is one which is a mixture of fact finding and law application and is appropriate for appeal. The reasons for this are that a party should get only one chance to introduce the evidence the party deems appropriate. Therefore, the trial courts are set up to take evidence; all the procedures at this level are adopted to insure the fairness of the evidence producing process. The right to cross examination, the right to demand and examine other evidence and the right to object to the introduction of irrelevant or excessively prejudicial evidence all exist at the trial level.

Appellate courts are not equipped to hear testimony or inspect evidence. Appellate courts are composed of three or more judges who hear the arguments of the appealing parties as to why the statements of the rules in the trial court were erroneous or why the process of rule application was erroneous.

An appeal may be initiated by either party. The one appealing is called the appellant or, in some courts, the petitioner. The one answering the appeal is the appellee or the respondent. At the trial stage, the case is given a name or "style" (in legal language) and almost always this is done by putting the name of the plaintiff first followed by the name of the defendant. However, on appeal some courts, but not all, put the name of the appellant first when reporting the case. So, if the defendant appeals, this name goes first in the official report. The student should be cautioned, therefore, that the appellate case's style does not reveal who is the plaintiff or defendant in the original trial of the matter. This may only be determined by reading the appellate opinion.

The appellant must file with the appellate court at least two documents. One is the transcribed version of the trial court. During the trial a court reporter took down all of the testimony, all objections and motions, and other relevant happenings in a special form of short hand. This short hand version of the trial is not transcribed into prose unless it is requested and paid for by one of the parties. Together with this transcript, the appellant files a legal brief which contains the legal arguments of the party. The appellate court considers the trial transcript, the written legal arguments (briefs) of both parties, and in many cases allows attorneys for the parties to appear before it to orally answer questions asked by the appellate court and, in general, to argue the merits of the issues advanced. For the reasons stated above the appellate court does not consider additional evidence, cannot call new or recall the old witnesses or, generally, view the evidence again. The facts as found by the trial court must be taken as given.

The appellate court then takes the matter into consideration, does considerable legal research on the matter, votes and writes its opinion. If some of the judges do not agree with the majority of the court, they may write dissenting opinions stating their reasons. This appellate opinion is usually published and is available to all. The numbers after the name of the cases reprinted in this text indicate the volume which contains the opinion.

If either party is still of the belief that a substantial error in the statement of the rule or in the application of the rule to the facts was made by either the trial or intermediate appellate court, the party may appeal the case to the next higher level, the supreme court of the state or federal system, which is usually the highest level. Again, the party appealing this is called the appellant or petitioner and the answering party is the appellee or respondent. The name of the appellant usually is placed first again. The same general practice is followed in filing the appeals papers and hearing the arguments except that additional arguments are made either supporting or attacking the decision of the first appellate court.

An appellate court (either intermediate or supreme court) may do one of three things with the case before it. It may affirm the holding of the trial court (or intermediate appellate court) and state its reasons for affirming the holding. If it affirms the decision, the same party who won the case in the trial court wins again.

The appellate court may reverse the decision being appealed and enter its own judgment, giving the reasons. The third option is to order all or part of the case tried again using the interpretation of the law as stated by the appellate court. In this case, if the parties so desire, the case will be tried again.

This concludes our presentation of material on the trial and appeal of a civil case. The terms defined above and the processes outlined are crucial to our understanding of how to study law because the published opinions of appellate judges are the best source available to indicate how the law is applied. For this reason much of the information about the law in this text will come from reading the appellate opinions reproduced herein. We have made an attempt to edit the irrelevant portions out of these opinions, and have attempted to leave in enough information so that the student may discern the complete outlines of how the dispute developed and how the legal rules were applied to solve the dispute.

STRUCTURE AND METHOD OF THIS BOOK

At the beginning of this chapter we stated that the definition of law is a statement of: 1) the rules written or unwritten generated by one of the rule sources; 2) how those rules are applied by those persons in charge of rule application; 3) how persons and institutions respond to the application; and 4) how the old rules are changed or new ones generated.

KINDS OF MATERIAL IN THIS BOOK

Within the chapters that follow we have presented four different kinds of material which represent the four aspects of law study stated above. First, there is textual material which presents a statement of the general rules of law applicable to business associations. These rules are both legislative and judicial in origin. Where the law varies from state to state, this will be noted by pointing out that most states take one approach (the "majority" rule) while fewer take a different approach (the "minority" rule).

However, presenting the written rules is only a starting point. A second type of information illustrates how some of the important rules are applied by those in charge of rule application, either the state or federal governments or private individuals. This rule application is illustrated by presenting long excerpts from appellate case opinions. These case opinions demonstrate how the abstract statements presented by the written rules are applied to reality. The cases literally breathe life into the rules and are absolutely necessary to an understanding of how the law "works." Much, if not most, of the information in the text is contained in these appellate opinions; therefore, the student is encouraged to read them carefully and make notes on them as described later.

A third kind of material is presented which assesses how the persons and institutions respond to a given rule and how the rule should be changed. This information is usually in the form of an excerpt from an article written by a recognized expert in the field or from an article written by a law professor or law student who has done research in the area.

Fourth, we have presented at the end of some appellate cases and at the end of most chapters review questions and review problems which are another source of material requiring the student ot integrate several of the rules discussed and to assess whether or not a rule should be the way that it is. Some of these review problems were created by us, so they should be reviewed as not portraying an actual factual pattern.

A final word about footnoting. The footnotes within the appellate cases and articles have been renumbered to conform to our editing of the material. These footnotes have been numbered in italic and placed at the bottom of the page because they add to an understanding of the case or article. Footnotes substantiating assertions we make in the text appear at the end of the chapter as endnotes.

ANALYSIS, RECALL, EVALUATION AND SYNTHESIS AS EDUCATION OBJECTIVES

As we stated at the beginning of this chapter, the study of law has little permanent value if rule memorization is the sole objective. The intellectual activity of memorizing and then recalling numerous rules is the easiest of the cognitive activities and should be thought of as necessary for the study of law, but not the ultimate objective. The prediction of when and with what results a rule will be enforced by those in charge of rule enforcement should be a central objective. Essentially this involves a detailed assessment of rule application. Rule application involves the process of analyzing, recalling, evaluating and synthesizing. These intellectual or cognitive skills therefore should be the central focus of the instructional process in the study of law.

More specifically, law application involves, first, the precise comprehension of a factual pattern. This means the student should be able to segregate the essential elements of a communication into parts which are recognized as familiar and parts which are, at first, unfamiliar or cannot be grouped together. Once this is done, the familiar parts of the factual pattern should call forth some abstraction, principle, or, in the case of law study, a rule, which will be used if a solution to the factual problem is needed or if relationships between the facts are to be discerned. This recall of principles or rules is the second cognitive element in law application. When recalling the principles and rules used in the past to solve similar factual problems the student may find that several alternative rules are presented. When this is true, the student must evaluate which rule is the best one to apply in the circumstances. Finally, the student must be able to synthesize (create) an answer to the question of when and with what result rules will be applied.

Law application demonstrates that the law is not a static phenomenon, but a relation; it cannot exist in a vacuum as a mere statement of a rule rather, it is relative to time, place, and persons. Assessing the legal rules relative to time, place and persons develops, we believe, an intellectual pattern which may have educational significance for the student beyond the objectives of this course and this text. The process of analyzing, recalling, evaluating, and synthesizing is one which we all engage in when we are asked to render a judgment. It should be pointed out that this process is not completely described by a series of steps, it is more accurately portrayed, we believe, as being circular in nature. For example, when one is presented with a factual pattern some facts may immediately stand out as relevant to an ultimate decision. However, when the principles or rules are recalled and evaluated, they may suggest facts necessary to the proper application of the principle which were initially discarded as irrelevant. One may actually alternate from analyzing (mentally dissecting and arranging) to recalling and synthesizing and then back to analyzing (rearranging) before an acceptable solution is synthesized.

THE STUDY OF APPELLATE CASES

The process of rule application is best illustrated in the published reports of appellate cases. You will note that in these appellate cases a judge has analyzed a factual pattern, has isolated similar or "pertinent" facts, has recalled several possible rules which could be applied, has evaluated their application, selected one or more to apply, has integrated the pertinent facts with the proper principle and has thereby resolved the dispute. You are encouraged to take note of this analytical process in each case presented by making a brief outline. At first this process of "briefing" a case will appear clumsy, time consuming and of no apparent value. However, over the course of a semester notice how the ability to brief a case develops; how the ability to spot the "pertinent" facts becomes almost instinctive and how the ability to critically assess the opinion develops. There is no reason to doubt that if analysis of an appellate opinion improves, analysis of other forms of written communication also improves.

Following we have printed portions of an appellate decision and followed it with an explanation of how we suggest the student take notes or brief the case. We suggest the student first read the opinion and the briefing instructions which follow, then reread the case briefing it as it is read.

ALUMA KRAFT MANUFACTURING COMPANY & SOLMICA, INC.
v.
ELMER FOX AND COMPANY
493 SW3d 378 (1973)

◆ ◆ ◆

SIMEONE, Judge

Plaintiff Solmica, Incorporated (hereinafter Solmica), appeals from the judgment of the Circuit Court of St. Louis County entered April 18, 1972, dismissing with prejudice Solmica's amended petition against defendants Elmer Fox & Company, certified public accountants, a partnership, (hereinafter Fox). Solmica's amended petition, containing two counts, sought damages against Fox and its individual partners for negligently performing an audit and expressing an unqualified opinion regarding a balance sheet of its client which was allegedly relied on by Solmica in the purchase of the stock of Aluma Kraft Manufacturing Company to its damage.

The issue presented, one of first impression in this state, is whether the defendants, certified public accountants, are under a duty to exercise due care to protect a third party from economic injury and are liable for damages caused by their alleged negligence, even though there is a lack of privity of contract.

Solmica's amended petition, filed on October 27, 1971, was in two counts. The first count was based on the ground that the auditors failed to comply with professional standards in making an audit; the second count was based on the alleged negligence of the auditors. The petition alleged that for many years Fox had been the regular auditors for Aluma Kraft, and one T. J. Bottom was the president, chief executive officer, principal director and owner of substantially all of the shares of Aluma Kraft. The petition alleged that in April of 1969 negotiations were entered into between Bottom and Solmica concerning the acquisition of eighty percent of the shares of Aluma Kraft which resulted in a contract specifying that the purchase price of the shares of stock would be the book value of the shares as of June 30, 1969. The contract further privided that Bottom ". . . shall cause to be prepared by Aluma Kraft's auditors an interim financial statement reflecting the operations of the business from January 1, 1969, through June 30th, 1969, consisting of a profit and loss statement and balance sheet . . . showing the financial condition of said business at that date," and that the statement would be prepared in accordance with generally accepted accounting standards. Fox was engaged and Solmica alleges that ". . . in contemplation that the (financial statement) would be utilized by plaintiff, SOLMICA, INC., the defendant auditors furnished to ALUMA KRAFT its formal report setting forth the scope and opinion. . . ." The opinion directed to the Board of Directors of Aluma Kraft stated that the balance sheet of Aluma Kraft had been examined and the examination was made in accordance with generally accepted auditing standards. The report stated that, "In our opinion, the accompanying balance sheet presents fairly the financial position of Aluma Kraft Manufacturing Company at June 30, 1969. . . ." Thereafter, and in reliance on the report, the petition states that Solmica closed the transaction for the purchase of the stock at the sale price ". . . computed in accordance with the balance sheet as determined by the defendant auditors in its formal audit statement", and paid the sum of $229,090.40. Later, the other twenty percent of the shares was also purchased.

Solmica then alleged that the auditors failed to conduct their examination in accordance with generally accepted auditing standards and failed to furnish an opinion in conformity with generally accepted accounting principles. Solmica listed some thirteen separate items which were allegedly inaccurate or misleading and which resulted in the book value of Aluma Kraft's stock being erroneously stated in the amount of $150,000.00 in excess of its true value.

Solmica contends that the defendants, certified public accounts, having negligently performed an audit and having rendered an unqualified opinion, are liable to it without regard to contractual privity. Solmica urges that such liability may be grounded upon (1) a duty imposed by the Missouri Statutes and the rules and regulations governing the professional conduct of the accountant, and (2) common law negligence.

On the other hand, the defendants urge that the long-standing rule of privity should be retained and that " . . . an accounting firm is liable only to the person or firm with which it is in contractual privity when the claimed liability is based on ordinary negligence" when such alleged negligence causes harm to intangible economic interests.

In determining whether the petition filed states a claim, we assume as true all facts well pleaded and give the appellant the benefit of every favorable inference to be drawn from the facts pleaded.

Plaintiff contends that Count I of the petition states a claim based upon the Missouri Statutes regulating the conduct and establishing the standards for accountants, . . . and inferentially upon the various codes of professional conduct. In effect, Solmica contends that the statutes and roles create a cause of action based on negligence without regard to privity.

We believe that the statutes and rules of professional practice establish certain legislative and professional standards of care to be observed by accountants in the performance of their duties and may assist in the determination of the standard of reasonable care required of the accountant. However, §§ 326.111 and 326.120 (12), which impose criminal penalties for the violation of Chapter 326, do not demonstrate that a civil action is created independently from an action for common law negligence. Criminal sanctions against doing or not doing some act do not automatically include authority for civil actions. Therefore, we hold that Count I of the petition fails to state a claim. We now turn to Count II, which alleges common law negligence.

The precise issue to be determined under these facts is whether an accounting firm may be liable to a third party not a privity when it is alleged that the public accountant knows the audit would be utilized and relied upon by the plaintiff, and knows the audit was being performed for the purpose of determining the price the plaintiff would pay for the shares of stock.

The accountant's liability to a third person not in privity with him for ordinary negligence, as distinguished from fraud, begins with the well-known decision by Mr. Justice Cardozo in *Ultramares Corp.* v. *Touche,* 174 N. E. 441. The New York Court of Appeals held that the firm of accountants could be held responsible for fraud but rejected the accountants' liability for ordinary negligence. Discussing the question as to whether the accountants were under a duty to third persons, Justice Cardozo stated:

" . . . If liability for negligence exists (to third parties), a thoughtless slip or blunder . . . may expose accountants to liability in an indeterminate amount for an indeterminate time to an indetermine class. . . . Liability for negligence is one that is bounded by the contract, and is to be enforced between the parties by whom the contract has been made." The court held (in Ultramares) that since " . . . public accountants are public only in the sense that their services are offered to any one who chooses to employ them," privity or a bond so close so as to approach privity is essential to impose liability upon the public accountant.

The necessity of privity of contract when a petition is based on ordinary negligence was decided recently by our Supreme Court in *Westerhold* v. *Carroll,* Mo., 419 S. W. 2d 73. An action was brought by an indemnitor of a surety on a performance bond against an architect for incorrectly certifying the amount of material furnished and work performed in the construction of a church. There was no privity between the defendant architect and the indemnitor or surety. The Supreme Court rejected the rule requiring privity and held that the petition stated a claim against the architect.

While not abandoning the doctrine of privity under all circumstances, Westerhold held that the extension of limits of liability should be done on a "case-to-case basis" and where the third party is known, the requirement of privity is not applicable.

The liability of the accountant has been discussed in recent years. The view that the rule of privity is to be rejected as to those third persons for whose benefit and guidance the accountant intends to supply such information to a limited class of persons, has been upheld in recent decisions and has been adopted by the *Restatement of the Law, Second, Torts,* §552, *Tentative Draft No. 12.*[1]

We also reject the privity requirement when, as alleged in the petition, the accountant knows the audit is to be used by the plaintiff for its benefit and guidance, or knows the recipient intends to supply the information to prospective users such as the plaintiff here. Therefore, we hold that a third party in such situations, although not in privity, has a claim for the alleged negligence of an accountant who renders an unqualified opinion upon which the third person relies to its detriment.

The allegations of the amended petition filed by Solmica brings this case within our holding and the decisions of Westerhold . . . , supra. The allegations are that the defendants knew the financial statement and opinion would be utilized by the plaintiff Solmica. The petition stated that " . . . in contemplation

---

[1]*Restatement of the Law, Second, Torts, Tentative Draft, No. 12* §552, p. 14 "(1) One who, in the course of his business, profession or employment, or in a transaction in which he has a pecuniary interest, supplies false information for the guidance of others in their business transactions, is subject to liability for pecuniary loss caused to them by their justifiable reliance upon the information, if he fails to exercise reasonable care or competence in obtaining or communicating the information. (2) Except as stated in subsection (3) the liability stated in subsection (1) is limited to loss suffered (a) by the person for whose benefit and guidance he intends to supply the information, or knows that the recipient intends to supply it; and (b) through reliance upon it in a transaction which he intends the information to influence, or knows that the recipient so intends, or in a substantially similar transaction. (3) The liability of one who is under a public duty to give the information extends to loss suffered by any of the class of persons for whose benefit the duty is created in any of the transactions in which it is intended to protect them."

that (the report) would be utilized by plaintiff . . . the defendant auditors furnished . . . its formal report setting forth the scope and opinion of the audit. . . ." The petition further stated that the " . . . auditors knew that the said audit was being prepared for the purpose of determining the amounts which plaintiff . . . would pay for the ALUMA KRAFT shares, and that the plaintiff . . . would rely upon the said audit." These allegations are sufficient to show that Fox knew its opinion would be utilized by the plaintiff, knew a purchase of the stock was contemplated, knew the purchase price was to be computed based upon the audit, and knew the audit would be furnished to the purchasers, Solmica. Therefore, these allegations are sufficient to state a claim for relief.

We have examined the cases cited by the respondents and do not believe they control this case.

In conclusion, we hold the amended petition filed by Solmica states a claim for relief against respondents Fox & Company although there is no privity of contract between Solmica and the respondents.

Therefore, the judgment of the Circuit Court is reversed and remanded for further proceedings.

◆◆◆

BRIEFING APPELLATE CASES

The traditional starting point for briefing an appellate case is to start with a statement of the legal position of the parties before the court. That is, in the trial court, who was the plaintiff, and who was the defendant and what, at the appellate court level, is the status of the litigation.

PARTIES

Plaintiff: Aluma Kraft Manufacturing Co., and Solmica, Inc. (The "Inc." is important and should be noted because it indicates the nature of the legal entity suing, a corporation).

Defendant: Elmer Fox & Co., a CPA accounting firm (partnership), and individual partners.

Trial Court: The plaintiff Solmica, alleged that the defendant was negligent in preparing an audit of Aluma Kraft. The trial court dismissed the petition of Solmica without a hearing on the evidence. Solmica appeals.

After the parties to the suit are identified and the current posture of the litigation identified, a brief explanation of the "facts" of the case is presented:

FACTS

Solmica negotiated with T. J. Bottom, president and principal owner of Aluma Kraft concerning the purchase of 80 percent of the stock of Aluma Kraft. They negotiated a contract in which Solmica was to purchase 80 percent of Aluma paying a purchase price based on the book value of the shares of Aluma as of June 30, 1969. Aluma was to prepare a financial statement from Jan. 1, 1969, to June 30, 1969, showing the financial condition of the business. Aluma engaged (contracted with) Fox to prepare the audit and Fox knew the reasons for the audit. Relying on the audit, Solmica purchased 80 percent of Aluma for $229,090.40 and later purchased the remaining 20 percent of the firm. Solmica alleges that Fox, the defendant, made errors which resulted in an overstatement of the book value of Aluma's stock.

CAUSE OF ACTION

The Cause of Action and Legal Question (or, the statement of the legal duty and the breach thereof), and the Defense.

The plaintiff alleges that a state statute imposes a duty on the defendant to act as a reasonably prudent accountant and, secondly, alleges that the defendant has committed a negligent act, as defined by the common law of the state, and that the defendant is therefore liable to the plaintiff for damages.

The defendant alleges that it is not liable to any legal person with whom it has not contracted, that this bond between contracting parties (called "privity") is a necessary element of the plaintiff's case.

The legal question or issue presented is stated succinctly by the court: " . . . is . . . an accounting firm . . . liable to a third party not in privity (with it) when it is alleged that the public accountant knows the audit would be utilized and relied upon by the (third party) plaintiff . . . "

COURT'S DECISION AND REASONING

The court relies on *Westerhold* and the *Restatement* and holds that where it is alleged that a CPA knows that a third party will rely on an audit, and it is alleged that the audit was negligently prepared, then the third party may bring a cause of action against the CPA where it relied on the audit to its detriment even though the third party and the CPA never directly contracted for the audit. The court reversed the decision of the trial court and remanded the case to the trial court. Presumably a trial on the merits will follow.

1. The established law directly pertinent to this case is stated in the *Ultramares Corp.* case (a New York case) in which it was held that liability for negligence is bounded by contract; that is, one not a party to the contract with the alleged wrongdoer (tortfeasor) cannot recover for negligence.
2. But, the court apparently rejects the reasoning of *Ultramares* and relies instead on the *Westerhold* case (a Missouri case) in which it was held that a party not in contract with an architect could sue the architect for negligence when the architect knew the third party might rely on his assertions.
3. The court also relies on the *Restatement of the Law,* which provides that if one in the course of business supplies false information for the guidance of others in their business, he is subject to liability for loss caused by the justifiable reliance on the information.

Studying appellate cases to sharpen one's analytical skills and, just as important, to learn the circumstances under which some of the major rules governing business associations are applied is not without some drawbacks. Appellate cases are not a perfect instructional tool.

Sometimes an appellate court will not clearly define exactly what the trial court held. One might think that an appellate court would clearly outline the posture of the case before it, but some courts seem to assume the reader already knows or can pick out by inference or deduction what the trial court did. Another somewhat confusing aspect of reading appellate cases is that in a case involving many parties the style or title of the case may not reveal all of the names. Some reporters may arrange several plaintiffs or defendants alphabetically and then select only the first name in each list as the title to the case. Thus, a particular named plaintiff or defendant referred to in the appellate decision may not be mentioned in the style of the case.

One will find that some questions presented by the factual pattern will often remain unanswered. Generally, they remain unanswered because the appellate court has not deemed them relevant to the issue before it. For example, in the *Solmica* case one may be left wondering how a CPA firm can make what is alleged to be such a gross error. The book value of eighty percent of the shares according to Fox was supposed to be about $229,090, when, according to the "true" market value of the assets, it was substantially less.

Be careful not to read more into the case than is presented in the opinion. Judge Simeone said nothing about what constitutes negligence in the preparation of an audit, nor did he indicate whether or not the plaintiffs would ultimately prevail. The "rule" of this case is that in Missouri a CPA firm now owes a legal duty to persons with whom it has not contracted when it furnishes an opinion and knows that a specific third person might reasonably rely on it to its detriment. The plaintiffs may now pursue the case in the trial court and proceed to obtain a judgment on the merits of the case if they can prove negligence.

If you believe several or, perhaps, numerous issues are presented in an appellate case you may narrow these by considering the chapter heading and subheading in the text which immediately precede the case. These will provide some guide as to what our objectives are in presenting a case. For example, the *Solmica* case may have been used to accomplish many possible objectives: the case illustrates the phenomenon of judicial rule creation; it illustrates the use of case precedent (the court followed the holding in *Westerhold* and rejected the holding in *Ultramares* even though the facts of *Ultramares* were more like the ones in *Solmica*); it also illustrates one use of the *Restatement of Law* and, finally, it provides a concise statement of one of the rules of law which may at some time be of value to the student. While all of these potential uses of the case exist, our objective here is rather narrow: it is important that you carefully read the case and clearly understand the process of briefing the decision.

Most of the cases reproduced in this text were chosen for their instructional value. That is, they probably illustrate the "classic" factual outlines of the conflict under discussion or explain thoroughly the rationale for the application for a given principle. Since this was our criteria for case selection, the age of the case is not important. For purposes of illustrating the circumstances under which a rule will be applied by officials or illustrating the reasons why a rule is so applied, an 1890s opinion by Oliver Wendall Holmes may be just as instructive as a 1970s case.

REVIEW PROBLEMS

1. In the *Aluma Kraft* case, why wasn't T.J. Bottom, President of Aluma Kraft, made a defendant? According to the information presented in the complaint and the appellate decision, did T.J. Bottom have any legal duties which ran to Solmica and which were breached?

2. Summarize the holding of the appellate court in the *Solmica* case in a few concise sentences. Should this holding include the statement that the CPA firm has a duty of care only to those it knew would rely on the audit? Can an argument be made that the holding should not be so limited? Read the *Restatement*, Section 552, quoted in the case. Didn't the court rely on this in forming its' judgment?

3. Below are some terms which will be used repeatedly throughout the text. They appear in the approximate order in which they were discussed in this chapter. You should be able to recall and write down the definition of each term and explain its use in the context where the term was discussed. If you can not, then reread this chapter or refer to the glossary of terms at the end of the text. Another alternative is to refer to *Black's Law Dictionary*, 4th ed., which should be available in your library.

law, study of
statute, statutory law
administrative agency
ordinance
breach of duty
Restatement of the Law
common law
equity law, equitable principles
injunction
specific performance
appellate court
criminal law/civil law
defendant
plaintiff
felony/misdemeanor
diversity jurisdiction
complaint
cause of action
summons
service of process
answer
pleadings

counterclaim
class action cases
default judgement
motion to dismiss for failure to state a claim
discovery procedures/devices
deposition
interrogatories
dismissal with prejudice
judgment on the pleadings
summary judgment
verdict
voire dire
direct verdict
judge's instructions
judgment notwithstanding the verdict
judgment N.O.V.
intermediate appellate court
appellant/petitioner
appellee/respondent
trial transcript
appellate brief

ENDNOTES

1. 26 USCA §7802
2. 26 USCA §7805
3. 1 *New York Pattern Jury Instruction — Civil 126* (2nd ed. 1974).

AN OVERVIEW OF AMERICAN BUSINESS ASSOCIATIONS

Gathered in this chapter are the definitions of the most prominent forms of business associations used in this country today. More comprehensive definitions of agency, partnership, and corporations will be found in the appropriate following chapters. In addition to the definitions in this chapter, the reader should focus on the relative advantages and disadvantages of using each form of association, and the government's power to regulate the form of association. A table contrasting the various business associations presented may be found at the end of this chapter.

STATE-LEVEL RESTRAINTS IN FORMING BUSINESS ASSOCIATIONS

State governments have the power to enact legislation to promote and preserve the health and welfare of the citizens of the state. This power is called the "police power" of the state. Pursuant to this power, most states have adopted comprehensive regulatory schemes which affect almost all business associations. Generally, partnerships and corporations are regulated by state statute. Also, this police power gives most states the right to promulgate licensing schemes for various professions and businesses. These licensing schemes require those rendering certain types of personal service deemed potentially dangerous to the public to comply with certain conditions in order to receive a state license. The purpose of this requirement is *to control* those individuals affecting public health and welfare. This type of licensing must be distinguished from licensing for tax purposes. The latter is imposed pursuant to a state's taxing power and has as its prime objective the raising of revenue. Almost all business and professional persons are subject to this latter form of taxation and are required, therefore, to buy a business license each year.

Those who are regulated under the police power of the state such as doctors, attorneys, real estate brokers, electricians, plumbers, barbers and others engaged in a "profession" or business requiring special training and skill, usually need to receive only the initial license to operate: this license is good for as long as the professional remains qualified.

Practicing without a license when one is required may result in a permanent denial of the privilege to practice the profession or the assessment of a fine. The only way to determine if a license is needed is to consult the state statutes or a professional advisor in the state of proposed activity. States vary greatly in their licensing requirements. California, Illinois and Pennsylvania, for example, list over 160 licensed occupations, others list less than 70.[1]

A second general restraint applicable to all business organizations is the requirement that if an organization is going to use a name other than the surname of the proprietor or the partners, then the name must be registered with the secretary of state in the state where business is conducted. This name is usually called a "trade-name." Many authorities do not distinguish between trade-names and trade-marks because the same principles and procedures are applicable to both. Most agree, however, that a trade-name is a broader concept referring to the designation of the entire business; a trade-mark is usually thought of as a distinguishable mark placed on goods for sale, but for purposes of registration and protection by the state they are treated similarly, and in many states the same statute requires registration.

States require registration of trade-names to protect established businesses from those who would confuse or mislead the public by adopting the same name as the established business. If confusion between a previously registered name and proposed new business would result, then states refuse to register the trade-name of the new business and the owners must adopt another name. For example, most states would not permit one to use the name, General Motors, for a business producing automobiles.

The following is an example of a statute requiring trademark registration. Note here that the definition of a "trade mark" includes the name adopted by persons to refer to services rendered or goods sold.

Ind. Ann. Stat. § 24-2-1-2 (Burns, 1974)

Definitions
    (a) The term "trade-mark" means any work, name, symbol or device or any combination thereof, adopted and used by a person to identify goods or services made, sold or rendered by him . . . .
    (b) The term "person," means any individual, firm, partnership, corporation, association . . . or other organization.

Ind. Ann. Stat. § 24-2-1-3 (Burns, 1974)

Marks not subject to registration:

A trade-mark by which the goods or services of any applicant for registration may be distinguished from the goods or services of others shall not be registered if it:

    (a) consists of . . . immoral, deceptive or scandalous matter; or
    (b) consists of . . . matter which may disparge or falsely suggest a connection with persons, living or dead, institutions, beliefs or national symbols . . . or,
    (c) consists of . . . the . . . insignia of the United States, or of any state or municipality, or of the United States, or of any foreign nation . . . or,
    (d) consists of the name, signature or portrait of any living individual, except with his written consent; or
    (e) consists of a mark which . . . (3) is primarily merely a surname . . .
    (f) consists of . . . a trade mark which so resembles a trade-mark registered in this state . . . as to be likely, when applied to the goods or services of the applicant, to cause confusion or mistake or to deceive unless there shall be filed with the state the written consent of the registrant of such trade-mark. . . .

Ind. Ann. Stat. § 24-2-1-4 (Burns, 1974)

Improper use of registered mark or imitation-damages . . . (A)ny person who shall

(a) use, without the consent of the registrant, any reproduction; counterfeit, copy or colorable imitation of a trade-mark registered under this act . . . which . . . is likely to cause confusion or mistake or to deceive as to the source or origin of such goods or services; . . . shall be liable to a civil action by the owner of such registered trade-mark. . . .

A subsequent section, 24-2-1-14, provides that the registrant may sue for an injunction to prohibit the use of the unregistered trade-mark as well as profits derived from its use if the illegal user did so with the intent to confuse the public.

In addition to requiring associations or individuals to procure licenses and register trade names, states may, again pursuant to the police power they possess, enact comprehensive regulatory schemes for types of business invested with a vital public interest. For example, most states have enacted very complex regulatory schemes for banks or those planning to offer some banking activity to the public. Also, insurance companies, trust companies, mortgage companies and others are regulated by special statutes and professional advice should be sought in complying with registration under these laws.

Also partnerships and corporations must meet numerous filing requirements which are propounded by the state legislatures and regulative agencies. All such organizations should request of the secretary of state in the state(s) in which they do business a list of all such filing requirements (such as an annual report of a corporation) as well as tax filing requirements which are necessary to operate in good standing within the state.

The following case discusses two central issues. The first is the power of the state legislature to pass laws which regulate the form or capacity in which one does business, and a related sub-issue of the power of state legislatures to discriminate between existing corporations and those to be formed in the future; secondly, the court addresses itself to the power of a legislature to regulate the practice of a given profession or business through licensing.

This case is long and, at first reading, it appears complex. We suggest you read it twice; first read it rapidly looking for the discussion of the facts and rules which apply to the two central issues. Next, read it again, briefing it as you read.

BROOKS

v.

STATE BOARD OF FUNERAL DIRECTORS AND EMBALMERS
233 Md. 98, 195 A2d 728, 1963

BRUNE, Chief Judge

The State Board of Funeral Directors and Emblamers (the Board) on April 12, 1962, ordered the suspension of the license of the appellant, L. Scott Brooks as a funeral director, and the next day notified him that it was for one year. Brooks appealed to the Circuit Court for Baltimore County. That Court, in accordance with an oral opinion delivered after a hearing on January 31, 1963, entered an order on February 21, 1963, affirming the Board's order. . . .

The questions here presented arise out of the provisions of Section 360 of Article 43 of the 1957 Code which permit corporations previously licensed as funeral directors (in 1937 as to some, in 1945 as to others) to continue to engage in the "business or profession of funeral directing," sometimes referred to below as the "undertaking business," but which prohibit other corporations from doing so.

The appellant makes three contentions: first, that these provisions are invalid and unconstitutional because they bear no substantial relationship to the public, health, safety or welfare; second, that they are invalid because they discriminate between corporations engaged in the business before a certain date and corporations thereafter seeking to enter it; . . .

The pertinent facts disclosed by the record may be briefly summarized. Mr. Brooks, the appellant, was duly licensed as an individual as a funeral director and also as an embalmer, holding a separate license for each of these occupations. In August 1960 (not through his present counsel) he caused to be organized under the general corporation laws of Maryland, a corporation known as Brooks Funeral Service, Inc. and on August 10th of that year he wrote the Board a letter requesting the issuance of a license to the corporation as a funeral director. He stated that he was aware of the statute against granting such a license but contended that the statute was unconstitutional. The Board refused to license the corporation. About January 1, 1962, the corporation, nevertheless, started to carry on the business of a funeral director. Mr. Brooks is the sole stockholder and an officer and director of the corporation.

All of the employees of the corporation who are active in the conduct of its business (except a woman who does only cleaning or domestic work) are licensed as funeral directors or embalmers, or both. The Board found after a hearing on April 12, 1962, at which Mr. Brooks appeared as a witness and renewed his attack on the statute, that Mr. Brooks had operated the corporation, that it had engaged in the business of a funeral director without a license, and that Mr. Brooks had "purposely, knowingly, and deliberately operated" the corporation "for the purpose, among others of testing the validity of * * * Section 360 * * *" It concluded that, as a matter of law, Mr. Brooks had violated Section 360 and suspended his license pursuant to Section 352(2)(i). . . .

On the question of due process the appellant contends, among other things, that undertaking is essentially a business, rather than a profession, and he challenges the validity of any regulation of the business which prevents its being conducted in corporate form. We are inclined to agree with the appellant's contention that the occupation is a business, rather than a profession. It was referred to in our statutes, without exception so far as we are advised, as a business from 1902 to 1937, and in Sections 345, 346, and 357 (1957 numbering) down to and including the 1957 code. The amendment of Section 360 made by Ch. 503 of the Acts of 1937 introduced the phrase "business or profession" as applied to the occupation of a funeral director, but the same Chapter spoke consistently of the "profession" of embalmer.

Nothing appears in the record in this case to show what, if any, changes had occurred in the nature of the occupation of a funeral director between 1902 and 1937 to bring about even the equivocal change then made in its characterization in Section 360. . . .

We shall, for the purpose of this case, but without undertaking to foreclose the question for the future when a more adequate record might be presented, regard the occupation of a funeral director as a business and not a profession. Accordingly, in our view, cases upholding the right of a legislature to bar corporations from the practice of a profession are not here applicable. . . .

That undertaking be regarded as a business and not a profession does not of itself solve the problems presented by this case. The occupation is one which bears such a relation to public health as to make it appropriate for regulation through licensing. . . .

Requirements stated in Section 346 as to the subjects upon which applicants for licenses are to be examined show that the business is concerned with matters affecting the public health. This section, after providing that applicants must meet certain requirements, including two years of practical experience as an apprentice, further provides that they shall be examined as to the proper sanitation and disinfection of the clothing and bedding of persons dying from infectious or contagious diseases and the premises in which they shall have died; . . . (and) as to the laws of this State and the local laws . . . relative to burials and burial permits and the proper care, preparation for burial or shipment of dead human bodies . . . .

It is evident, of course, that corporations as such could not be examined on the above matters and that corporations can act only through agents. Just why the statute does not of itself contain a requirement . . . that corporations licensed under the statute may act only through or under the director of licensed individuals, is not clear. . . .

The present case arises upon the suspension of the appellant's license as a funeral director, and his corporation is not itself a party to the case. The right or rights which the appellant claims here are seemingly partly individual and partly corporate. He claims as an individual the right to engage in the undertaking business through a corporation, and he also seems to seek to assert the right of his corporation to engage in it. The rights of an individual to engage in a lawful business are entitled to protection under the due process and equal protection clauses of the Fourteenth Amendment and by the due process clause, Art. 23, of the State Declaration of Rights. . . .

It is also well established and is not disputed that corporations are entitled to protection Clauses of the Fourteenth Amendment and under Article 23 of the Declaration of Rights. . . .

There may be, however, some important differences between corporations and individuals as to whether rights which an individual may have, actually have been or may be acquired by corporations. A non-existent corporate right could scarcely receive constitutional protection. The right of individuals to form a corporation to carry on a business is not so extensive as to authorize the formation of corporations for purposes contrary to a statute. . . .

Our General Corporation Law (Code 1957, Art. 23, Sec. 3) provides that corporations (with exceptions not here relevant) may be formed under Art. 23 for any one or more lawful purposes. The charter of Brooks Funeral Service, Inc. is not in the record, but it does appear from the record that it was conducting the business of a funeral director, notwithstanding the prohibition contained in Sec. 360 of Art. 43 against corporations formed after 1937 doing so. If, as we think it reasonable to suppose, a purpose stated in the charter of the Brooks corporation was to conduct the business of funeral director, it is difficult to see how, in the face of Sec. 360 of Art. 43, this could qualify as a "lawful purpose," if Sec. 360 is valid.

It follows, we think, that any right of the appellant as an individual to form or cause to be formed a corporation to conduct the business of a funeral director can be established only if that prohibition is for some reason invalid.

The appellant relies heavily upon *Liggett Co.* v. *Baldridge, Dasch* v. *Jackson,* and *Schneider* v. *Duer* to support his contention that the statutory prohibition against new corporations conducting the business of a funeral director and against granting them licenses so to do involve a denial of due process of law. None of these cases seems to us to be controlling here.

Dasch v. *Jackson* . . . a licensing case, held invalid unreasonable statutory restrictions upon the right of an individual to engage in a lawful, common calling, that of a paperhanger. *Schneider* v. *Duer* . . . was a similar case involving the trade of barbering. There was no controversy over the right of a corporation to engage in either the business of paperhanging or that of barbering in spite of a statute prohibiting a corporation from doing so, since no corporation was involved, nor, for that matter, was there any such statute, so far as appears. The right of individuals to work themselves at their respective callings was at issue; not their right to carry on their trades through corporations organized by them.

Liggett Co. v. *Baldridge* . . . held invalid, as a denial of due process of law, a Pennsylvania statute requiring that all stockholders in corporations owning drugstores be registered pharmacists. This statute contained an exception in favor of existing corporations authorized to do business in the state, which permitted them to continue to own and conduct drug stores or pharmacies owned and conducted by them when the statute took effect, but they could not own and conduct new stores.

The Liggett Co. had acquired and wished to operate new drug stores in the state and sought an injunction to prevent enforcement of the statute to keep it from doing so. The Supreme Court, with Justices Holmes and Brandeis dissenting, held the statute void as an undue restriction upon the Liggett Company's business, since the requirement as to ownership of stock bore no reasonable relation to the public health. . . .

According to the majority in *Liggett*, a state cannot "under the guise of protecting the public, arbitrarily interfere with private business or prohibit lawful occupations or impose unreasonable and unnecessary restrictions upon them." . . .

Very recently, in *Ferguson* v. *Skrupa,* 372 U.S. 726, 83 S. Ct. 1028, 10 L. Ed. 2d 93, the Supreme Court unanimously sustained a Kansas statute which flatly prohibited the business of debt adjustment, except as an incident to the lawful practice of law. The opinion of the Court referred to its "abandonment of the use of the 'vague contours' of the Due Process clause to nullify laws which a majority of the Court believed to be economically unwise * * *," and went on to say: "We refuse to sit as a 'superlegislature to weigh the wisdom of legislation,' and we emphatically refuse to go back to the time when courts used the Due Process Claim 'to strike down state laws, regulatory of business and industrial conditions, because they may be unwise, improvident, or out of harmony with a particular school of thought.' " . . .

The appellant . . . relies heavily upon the case of *Trinka Services* v. *State Board of Mortuary Science.* A decision by a single Judge of the New Jersey Superior Court. That case is directly in point and it supports the appellant's position. The court struck down a statute excluding corporations from the undertaking business as going beyond the proper exercise of the police power. The court found that what it regarded as the technical side of the business (as indicated below) was only a small part of the business of an undertaker, and concluded that "once the State and its Board of Mortuary Science have secured the health and welfare of the public in the usual sense, by its (the Board's, we infer) education, licensing and like provisions pertaining to the technical treatment of the human remains, ... that ... is as far as the State can go in regulating what is otherwise a private property right, i.e., the doing of business in the corporate frame."

The opinion makes no reference to the general principle of corporation law that corporations may have and exercise only such powers as the legislature confers upon them.

This is the only case which has come to our attention which seems to hold that individuals have the absolute right to organize a corporation to conduct any business which they might conduct as individuals without interference or limitation by the legislature except in the exercise of the police power of the state. In this respect we believe that the court's holding is not supported by authority generally, and we do not believe that either the Federal or the State Constitution so restricts the power of the General Assembly of this State. Sec. 48 of Art. 3 of our Constitution provides that corporations may be formed under general laws and prohibits incorporation by special acts when general laws are available. This certainly does not say that the General Assembly must permit corporations to be formed to carry on any and every kind of business open to individuals, unless their formation for any of such purposes may be prevented by an exercise of the police power.

We are accordingly unable to accept for this State the sweeping premise upon which the decision of the New Jersey Superior Court seems to rest. Nor are we aware of any rule of law which would bar the legislature from amending the law as to the purposes for which corporations may be formed.

We think that the legislature can, for the protection of the public health, require that the business of undertaking be conducted only by individuals possessing the qualifications, skills and knowledge specified by Sec. 346. It could accomplish this result in either of these two ways; one by limiting the conducting of the business to such individuals, and the other by permitting not only individuals but also corporations to engage in the business, provided that the actual operations of corporations are carried on by or under the direction of duly licensed individuals.

We do not think that the legislature was bound to adopt the second method or, if it had once been adopted, to adhere to it for corporations formed after the legislature determined to abandon it. It may be that the legislature thought that individual responsibility in this field would be promoted by restricting the conduct of the business to individuals or partnerships of which they are members.

The above views relate to the power of the legislature to exclude corporations entirely from conducting the business of funeral directors. This brings us to the question of unreasonableness of the statutory regulation and of discrimination arising from the fact that pre-1937 and World War II servicemen's corporations are permitted to conduct the business.

Not every difference amounts to an arbitrary or invidious discrimination. In

Williamson v. *Lee Optical Co.*, the U.S. Supreme Court upheld as against an attack under the Equal Protection Clause of the Fourteenth Amendment a state statute which subjected opticians to a regulatory system, but exempted all sellers of ready-to-wear glasses. "The problem of legislative classification is a perennial one, admitting of no doctrinaire definition. Evils in the same field may be of different dimensions and proportions requiring different remedies. Or so the legislature may think.

Or the reform may take one step at a time, addressing itself to the phase of the problem which seems most acute to the legislative mind. The legislature may select one phase of one field and apply a remedy there, neglecting the others. The prohibition of the Equal Protection Clause goes no further than the invidious discrimination." . . .

As was held by the Supreme Court of the United States in *Sperry & Hutchinson Co.* v. *Rhodes,* 220 U.S. 502, 505, 31 S. Ct. 490, the Fourteenth Amendment does not prevent a statute or a statutory change from having a beginning and thus to discriminate between the right of those of an earlier and those of a later time. . . .

We think that the appellant has failed to demonstrate that the provisions in favor of existing corporations as of a past date and of corporations formed to carry on the business of persons serving in the armed forced during World War II constitute invidious discriminations. On the contrary, we deem the preservation of existing investments or values a sufficient basis to warrant separate classification and treatment.

In accordance with our views that Sec. 360 is not unconstitutional as a denial of due process of law under either the Federal or the State Constitution or as a denial of the equal protection of the laws, the order of the Circuit Court will be affirmed.

◆◆◆

Case Questions

1. Why does the state in this case have the authority to require examinations and licenses of those who enter the embalming occupation?
2. Is there a principle or rule you discern which could be used to reconcile the holding of the *Liggett* case discussed in the above decision and the holding of *Brooks?* In the former, the court held the legislative restriction on the association illegal; in the latter *(Brooks)* the court held the legislative restriction legal. Why?
3. Does the *Brooks* case imply that as long as there si some "reasonable" connection between the commercial activity to be carried out and the public health and welfare, state legislatures may enact rules governing both the qualifications of those who engage in the activity and form of business association used?

FEDERAL-LEVEL RESTRAINTS ON BUSINESS ASSOCIATIONS

The technical aspects of forming a business association such as a partnership or corporation are governed by state law. However, there are numerous federal laws which apply to individuals, business associations, or other organizations which intend to engage in commerce. Every corporation, for example, must request from the Internal Revenue Service an identification number for tax purposes.

If an individual's or association's activity affects interstate commerce, then that activity may be subject to regulation by the federal government. The federal government derives the power from Article I, Section Eight of the United States Constitution which provides, "the Congress shall have Power . . . to regulate Commerce with foreign Nations, and among the several states . . ." Except for the Federal Securities Laws, and a brief consideration of employment discrimination, job safety, and the new pension reform law, environmental legislation and the new federal regulation of product warranties, federal regulation of American business associations is beyond the scope of this book. However, the student should be aware that the following kinds of activities may be subject to federal law if the interstate-commerce requirement is met:

1. Anticompetitve Behavior — regulated by application of the Antitrust Laws: Sherman Act; Clayton Act, as amended; Federal Trade Commission Act, as amended;
2. Employment Practices — regulated by application of the Civil Rights Acts, Wagner Act, Hours of Work and Minimum Wage legislation, and Pension Reform legislation;
3. Safety Conditions — regulated by application of the William-Steiger Act, (referred to as the Occupational, Safety and Health Act or OSHA).
4. Environmental Activities — regulated by the application of several federal Environmental Protection acts — as well as rules created by the National Environmental Protection Agency.
5. The Sale or Purchase of Securities of the Corporation — regulated by the application of the Securities Acts of 1933 and 1934.
6. Transportation, Banking, Insurance, Broadcasting and other industries invested with a special public trust are regulated by the application of numerous rules and regulations as generated by the various federal regulatory agencies such as the I. C. C., F. P. C. , F. C. C. , A. E. C. , etc.

TYPES OF AMERICAN BUSINESS ASSOCIATIONS

Next we define and discuss several forms of American business associations. The list of associations discussed is far from being a complete one. Variations in the standard forms of associations are being created constantly. We offer just a brief overview of the more conventional business associations.

AGENCY

Agency is not a form of association in the same sense that partnerships and corporations are. Agency is much more pervasive than any other form of business association and exists usually when one voluntarily consents to act on behalf of or under the control of another person. It exists within the framework of corporations; the officers, for example, are agents of the corporation when they deal with outsiders on corporate business. Partnership law provides that all partners are agents of the partnership for conducting the business of the partnership. Comparing partnerships and corporations to agency is like comparing an organization to one of its inner parts. Agency law together with state common law and state statutes forms the building material of business associations. In fact, corporations could not exist as we know them without agents. This point will be more greatly appreciated after reading the chapters on Agency.

PROPRIETORSHIP

A proprietorship is a business association conducted by one individual who owns all or most of the business property and who may hire employees to act as agents. The chief advantage of this form is that it is the simplest, and for this reason the most numerous. It is estimated there are about ten times as many proprietorships as partnerships with a volume of business twice that of partnerships. However, proprietorships account for only one-fifth of the volume of business of all corporations.[2]

The business assets and liabilities of the proprietorship are one and the same as the proprietor's individual assets and liabilities. There is no separate legal entity, thus those who extend credit to the proprietorship rely upon the individual's assets and credit standing. The proprietor makes all decisions in the operation of the business including what employees are to be hired, if any, and the nature of their work; and, he owns all of the profit of the organization, splitting it with no one. The business suffers the same fate as the proprietor and stops or is incapacitated (legally) whenever the proprietor dies or suffers incapacity.

PARTNERSHIP

A partnership is an association of two or more persons to carry on as co-owners a business for profit. Individuals form partnerships when they wish to share the management, profits, or ownership of an enterprise for profit. In some instances where these aspects of co-ownership are intended but the partnership form was not intended, courts will nevertheless impose the partnership form on individuals. This is discussed in greater detail in the chapters on partnerships.

Partnerships are created by the contractual understanding, expressed or implied, of the partners. The usual process involves the drafting of written "Articles of Partnership" agreed to by all partners. Although this is the usual method of creation, a partnership can be created without a written contract.

While there is some disagreement on whether or not partnerships are a separate legal entity apart from the owners, we believe the best view is that it is separate for some purposes. A partnership contracts in its own name, holds the title to assets in its own name, can be sued in its own name and files income tax returns in its name, and is treated as a separate entity by the bankruptcy statutes. The Uniform Partnership Act, the act adopted by all of the states which governs the rights and duties of partners, does not expressly state that a partnership is a separate legal entity, but would have done so had the original chief draftsman, Dean James Barr Ames, lived to complete the drafting.[3]

For the purposes mentioned above, the partnership is a separate legal entity. For the purposes of paying off those who obtain a court judgment against the partnership, the owner/partner can not separate his own individual assets from those of the partnership. The partner can not "limit" his liability for partnership obligations.

This is a chief distinction between corporations and partnerships; owners of the former being able to limit their liability. This means that judgment creditors of the corporation must be paid from the corporation's assets, not the owner's assets.

Other disadvantages of the partnership form as contrasted with corporation include the limited life of a partnership; any time a partner dies, is incapacitated or voluntarily leaves the partnership, the old partnership is dissolved. Any time a new partner joins, the old partnership is dissolved and a new partnership is created. Also, the ability and opportunities to raise capital are not as diverse as the corporation because in a partnership this ability rests solely on the financial resources of the partners.

Advantages of this form of organization are its simplicity in creation and the democratic methods it offers in operation which allow, for example, one partner to contribute cash, one to contribute technical know-how and another to contribute manual work and all three then share equally their profits and management of the partnership.

LIMITED PARTNERSHIP

There are several variations of the partnership form in use today. A limited partnership is a partnership formed by two or more persons, one of whom is a general partner and one of whom is a limited partner, and who have filed with the state as a limited partnership. The Uniform Limited Partnership Act, in force in most states, requires that such partnerships file a certificate with the state which reveals all essential obligations of the partners. The limited partnership is formed once the filing is complete or there is substantial compliance in good faith with the filing requirement.

The essential characteristic of a limited partnership is that the limited partner is not liable as a general partner unless he takes part in the control of the business. Thus, a limited partner may contribute cash to the partnership and his liability will be limited to this amount; he is an investor rather than an active partner. Presently, the limited partnership is popular as a form of organization for real estate investment groups and theatrical promotion.[4]

JOINT VENTURE

A joint venture is another variation of the partnership form which is more narrow in function and duration than a partnership, usually contemplating a single business operation. The law of partnership applies to joint ventures. The primary purpose for this form of organization is to share the risks and profits of a specific business undertaking.

A few state courts have found difficulty with a corporation becoming a general partner. The reason for this is that statutes require corporations to be managed by a board of directors; if they joined a partnership, the corporate partner would be subject to additional management authority since every partner is controlled by a vote of a majority of the partners. However, the Uniform Partnership Act defines a corporation as a person allowing it thus to be a partner; and, many states allow corporations to be partners as a matter of corporate law. Almost all states allow corporations to be a joint venturer. Indeed, today many of the large corporations combine in joint ventures to explore for oil and to develop experimental products and manufacturing facilities.

CORPORATION

The corporate form of business association has three fundamental characteristics which distinguish it from proprietorships and partnerships. Perhaps the most important characteristic is that it is considered to be a separate legal entity from the shareholders or owners. The corporation can own property, sue and be sued, contract to buy and sell, and be fined, all in its own name. Most importantly, however, the owners under most circumstances, cannot be made to pay debts of the corporation. That is, the liability of the owners is limited to the amount of money they have paid or promised to pay into the corporation. A few states such as New York make the shareholders liable for certain obligations to the employees; but, the general rule is that the corporate form offers limited liability. Exceptions to this rule will be disclosed in the chapters on corporations.

A second characteristic of the corporate form is that it may have perpetual life. It is not dissolved upon the death of the owner as are the proprietorship and partnership. This result follows from the notion that a corporation is a separate legal entity with a life of its own established by the articles of incorporation filed with the secretary of state pursuant to a general incorporation statute. Also, the owners may choose to sell or transfer their ownership and this may be freely done without altering the corporate form if there is a market for the ownership shares. So, besides perpetual life, there is a measure of flexibility in the transfer of ownership not available in other forms of business associations.

A third characteristic of the corporate form is the way in which it is owned and managed. Corporations issue ownership shares in the form of, usually, common stock. The owners of this stock may vote individually or combine in numerous ways to elect a board of directors who manage the corporation for the shareholders. Thus, at least in the case of large corporations, practical control of the corporation is removed from the owners by a board of directors. Issues raised by the method of ownership and control of corporations will be more fully explored in later chapters.

One characteristic which most believe to be a disadvantage is the "double taxation" of the owners of the corporation. The corporation must pay federal income tax on its income. After income taxes are paid, some of the earnings may be distributed to the shareholders in the form of dividends which is again taxed by the federal government as income to the shareholders. Thus, a shareholder suffers taxation twice on accretions to his initial, single investment. This is not true for proprietorships and partnerships. A partnership is required to file a separate federal income tax return but it is for informational purposes only. The income tax is levied upon the partner's distributive share of the partnership's income whether the partner receives it as income, or whether it stays in the partnership account. A sole proprietor includes all business income and deductions on his individual tax return.

The disadvantage of double taxation is, in the case of large publicly held corporations, far outweighed by the advantages of limited liability, perpetual life, ease of transferability of ownership and the ability to raise new capital by selling more stock. In the case of small corporations, those owned by one family or a very few people, this disadvantage is minimized since the owners of these corporations are usually officers or employees of the corporation and may gain an indirect return for their investment by drawing salaries from the corporation.

These amounts which must be "reasonable" are deducted from corporate income as an expense and are paid out before determining taxable income to the corporation. The shareholder-employee, however, must pay income tax on this salary.

A final disadvantage of the corporate form is the expense of creation. Proprietorships cost very little to form, partnerships cost more because usually an attorney is paid to draw up the contractual understanding of the parties. Corporations cost the most because fees must be paid to the state (the amount varies according to the number of shares authorized) and fees must also be paid to an attorney to help form the corporation. The attorney usually buys a corporate minute book, arranges for the printing of stock certificates and the purchase of a seal. At a minimum, it costs 300 to 500 dollars to form a corporation.

There are numerous variations of the corporate form all offering the same advantages of a completely separate entity, thus, limited liability for the owners, perpetual life, and the advantages that flow from the share ownership. Some of the more widely used variations are explained in the following.

Subchapter S Corporations

Another method of minimizing the disadvantages of double taxation of the corporate form as well as securing other tax advantages is provided by the *Internal Revenue Code* (Sections 1371-1379). The code allows corporations with ten or fewer shareholders who are individuals or estates (not partnerships or corporations) with one class of stock plus other requirements to qualify under "Subchapter S" for special tax treatment. This special status allows the *shareholders* to treat the income or loss of such a corporation as their personal income or loss. Owners of a Subchapter S Corporation may, for example, offset their share of corporate losses against their personal income resulting in less individual tax liability. If a corporation elects to file under Subchapter S, the tax treatment of the corporation income and loss is very similar to that of a partnership.

Section 1244 of the *Internal Revenue Code* offers further tax advantages to *small* corporations which qualify. Generally, it provides that a qualifying corporation may issue stock pursuant to a plan which meets the requirements of Section 1244 and any loss sustained by an individual shareholder on the sale of this stock will be treated as an ordinary loss of the individual and can be deducted from the shareholders ordinary income up to a maximum amount of $25,000.

Thus, Subchapter S and Section 1244 could permit, for instance, a doctor with an individual income of $75,000 per year to buy a small cattle ranch and incorporate it. The ranch would be the chief asset of the Subchapter S Corporation. By paying ranch hands salaries which just equalled the ranch income and by taking depreciation on buildings at the ranch, it could be run at a paper loss of say, $5,000 per year, which could be transferred through the corporation to the doctor (presumably the sole or chief shareholder) and deducted by him from his income resulting in a $5,000 deduction from his salary before he arrived at his taxable income. This would result in a reduction of his cost basis on the buildings but would still result in a substantial present tax savings. Also, if he should sell his corporate ownership shares at a loss, he may offset as much as $25,000 from his individual income.

Do not confuse the privilege of offsetting Subchapter S corporate losses against one's individual income with limited liability. Subchapter S Corporations still offer limited liability in that the shareholders cannot be made to pay out-of-pocket for corporate debts. What they are offered is the privilege of offsetting losses against their income to reduce their tax liability. They pay nothing; they receive, in essence, a credit which is a substantial benefit to them.

Public Versus Private Corporations

The corporate form may be used to conduct any activity, unless prohibited from doing so by law. We are accustomed to the fact that private corporations may pursue many objectives but often overlooked are public corporations. These corporations are created primarily for purposes connected with the administration of government. Municipalities, school districts and townships are a few examples of "municipal corporations," the name given to these public corporations. The ownership of these corporations is vested by state statute in the sovereign (the state) and the management of the corporation is subject to a charter issued by the state. These public corporations are beyond the scope of this book.

Private corporations may be divided into those which are operated for a profit and those not for a profit. The former are probably the most familiar to you and are the subject of the last one-half of this book. Corporations not for profit are created by state statutes which are separate from the corporation for profit statutes and provide, generally, that organizations for religious, charitable, or educational purposes shall be issued a corporate charter upon complying with several filing requirements. Thus, churches, private hospitals, private schools and universities and philanthropic organizations may all enjoy corporate status.

Classifying private corporations for profit is beyond the scope of this book, but two types of such corporations should be mentioned. Holding companies are corporations, chartered primarily for the purpose of owning the shares of other companies. Today these companies own and control a substantial number of our large manufacturing companies.

Another type of private corporation which is somewhat similar in objective is the conglomerate corporation. Although frequently the conglomerate takes the name of an established manufacturing corporation the object is to diversify the original company into both related and unrelated markets. The conglomerate owns numerous other corporations.

Restrictions on the Use of the Corporate Form

As discussed before a chief advantage of the corporate form is the concept of the limited liability of the owners of the corporation. Limited liability is a legal privilege for the owners bestowed by the state; this privilege may be withheld in the exercise of the state's police powers. Until recently those offering a professional service such as doctors, lawyers, dentists and optometrists were forbidden by many states from incorporating. The reason for this was that it was believed inappropriate for one offering a professional service to be able to separate his personal assets from his business assets when he was sued for the negligent performance of the service offered. Patients or clients relied on the personal skill and judgment of the professional in the rendering of the service and thus the professional should not be able to shield his personal assets from the risks of his profession. Another reason for denying such a professional the use of the corporate form was that it would not be appropriate for this individual to subject his actions and judgment to the discretion of a board of directors who, by state law, manage the business of corporations.

However, within the last decade many states have passed special statutes allowing the formation of professional corporations. This special legislation was in response to the pressure of these professionals to allow members of the profession to share in some of the special tax benefits which are offered by the corporate form. Although the owners of the professional corporation are subject to double taxation if they pay themselves dividends, the tax advantages for their retirement plans and insurance programs are considerable, and more than offset the double taxation disadvantage. For example, if the professional were a partner and the partnership decided to use some of its income to pay into a retirement plan or pay for insurance premiums on the life of a partner, then these payments (premiums) would be taxed as income to the partner in the year in which they were made. However, if the professional were an employee of a corporation, the corporation could make contributions to the retirement plan or insurance program of the employee which would, first, be deducted by the corporation as a business expense, and, second, would not be taxed to the owner as income when the payments to the plan were made. The owner would, of course, pay income tax on the benefits of the plan when they were distributed to him. These retirement plans and insurance programs, generally, allow the professional to simply postpone taxation on a portion of his income. At the peak income years it would be advantageous to be able to postpone some of the income to the wanning years and thereby suffer less of a current tax liability. This is the central advantage of the professional corporation.

The Internal Revenue Service has argued that for the professional corporation to be taxed as a regular for-profit corporation the professional's potential liability to third parties can be no greater than that of a shareholder in a regular for-profit corporation. This view has not prevailed, however, since most state laws on professional corporations do not allow professionals to limit their personal liability for their own tortious acts or the acts of associates.[5] Thus, a professional's potential liability to third parties is much greater than that of a shareholder in a regular, for-profit corporation, yet the courts are still allowing the professionals to enjoy the tax benefits just described. In short, many states have allowed the creation of a hybrid form of corporation which permits professionals to incorporate for tax purposes but not for the purpose of limiting personal liability.

COOPERATIVES

A form of organization which combines the democratic management aspects of a partnership with some of the advantages of a corporation is the cooperative. Cooperatives are being popularized today at both ends of the economic spectrum. Large land developers are concentrating much of their resources into the construction of cooperative apartment buildings (and the related legal form, the condominium) and smaller associations are forming food and consumer cooperatives. These enterprises have at least two things in common which cause them to be classified as cooperatives. First, they are organized primarily to provide the members (not the public) an economic benefit or service and, second, each member, usually an individual, has one vote in the management of the enterprise thus resulting in substantial equality of ownership.

In addition to these two general characteristics, it should be emphasized that while a cooperative may make a profit, this is not the primary purpose of the organization. The members usually expect no monetary return for putting their money into a cooperative. What they expect is to enjoy whatever non-monetary, but economically useful benefits the association provides. The emphasis on *economically useful* benefits for members distinguishes the cooperative from charitable, religious, educational or political associations.

Generalizations about this form of association which is used for so many different tasks should be attempted with caution, but it has been suggested that the following are some characteristics of a cooperative:[6]

1. Control and ownership is substantially equal;
2. Members are limited to those who avail themselves of the services furnished by the cooperative;
3. Transfer of a membership is prohibited or limited;
4. Capital investment receives either no return or a limited return;
5. Economic benefits pass to members on a substantially equal basis;
6. Members are not personally liable for obligations of the association unless they agree to such liability;
7. Death, bankruptcy or withdrawal of one or more of the members does not terminate the association; and
8. Services of the association are furnished primarily for the use of the members.

Cooperatives are not a new form of association. Rural communities have been served by cooperatives since the early 1900s with, first, the formation of marketing cooperatives to sell farmers' produce, and then the development of rural electrification cooperatives to furnish electricity to rural areas.

Cooperatives may be either incorporated or unincorporated associations. With the exception of labor unions (which have generally remained unincorporated because they prefer no regulation from the state) most cooperatives do incorporate. Since the management of the cooperative is conducted by a vote of the members and not by a board of directors, the enterprise is not managed as is the typical corporation. This difference in management is allowed in almost all states by the existence of special cooperative statutes which provide for the incorporation and operation of cooperatives.

In concluding this rather brief overview of American business associations, we must again mention that any such presentation is far from complete. Attorneys, accountants, entrepreneurs and other creative business people are always creating new business association forms or hybrids of the established ones to take advantage of new tax incentives or to share in the ever changing character of business risks.

Comprehensive discussions of the law of agency, partnerships and corporations are presented in the following chapters. In concluding this chapter we first present three cases which exemplify some of the legal principles one should understand when operating a business association.

The first case, *School District of Philadelphia* v. *Frankford Grocery Co.*, illustrates one set of circumstances in which individuals adopted the cooperative form of business association to achieve their goals.

The next case, *Lyons* v. *American Legion Post No. 650 Realty Co.*, is intended to reveal the circumstances in which the law will impose liability on members of an unincorporated association which was created primarily for social as opposed to profit-making purposes. As noted in this case, if the purpose of the unincorporated association is to make a profit by co-owning assets of the association, then the law of partnership (discussed in later chapters) will apply. However, the rights and duties of the members of non-profit, unincorporated associations are treated differently depending on whether or not state statute controls.

The final case, *Central Trust & Safe Deposit Co.,* v. *Respass,* reveals the typical attitude of courts when presented with the legal obligations of members of an association founded for illegal purposes.

**SCHOOL DISTRICT OF PHILADELPHIA v.
FRANKFORD GROCERY CO.
376 Pa. 542; 103 A. 2d 738 (1954)**

◆◆◆

CHIDSEY, Justice

In this action . . . the School District of Philadelphia sought to recover the sum of $29,056.03 as additional tax due under a levy made in 1950 upon the gross receipts of the defendant for the calendar year 1949. . . . The defendant's gross receipts in 1949 amounted to $29,358,488.33 and it paid tax on $302,464.06 thereof, claiming that the balance of its gross receipts represented receipts from the distribution of commodities and services rendered as a purely cooperative association to its constituent members, and therefore not within the purview of the statute authorizing the tax. The case was heard by Judge Levinthal of the Common Pleas Court of Philadelphia sitting without a jury, and after a submission of briefs and oral argument to the court . . . , judgment was entered for the defendant. The School District appeals therefrom.

The history, structure and operation of the defendant are well summarized from the evidence adduced in the following portion of the opinion of the learned trial judge:"* * * The company originated in 1905 as the Frankford Retail Grocer Association, which name was changed to the present one in 1909. It was formed by a small group of fourteen or fifteen retailers to purchase goods in large quantities and eliminate wholesalers' profits because of chain store competition. The articles of incorporation stated that the purpose of the organization was to act as a purely cooperative enterprise of retail grocers. Every member stockholder in the corporation is obligated to buy sufficient capital stock to cover his average weekly purchases, and to deposit the stock with the company in escrow, and then to pay his bills weekly. This system eliminates credit losses. A member is not obligated to obtain all his supplies from the company. But ordinarily merchandise is distributed only to retail grocer members. Occasionally it is sold at cost to charities. In some instances a surplus of a commodity is sold on the open market in order to dispose of it. Each member receives only one weekly delivery. The company employs no salesmen and all orders are received by mail or in person on written order blanks. Delivery of merchandise is controlled so that a truck covers a territory without duplication. In making deliveries the drivers deposit the goods on the pavements and do not carry them into the members' stores. . . . The goods which the company purchases for distribution are insured by it and title taken in its name. The company provides advertising, accounting and promotion assistance to members. It operates schools to give instruction in the best methods of meat cutting and meat and produce merchandising. A construction department rebuilds stores for members, installs fixtures and display stands and equipment, and services refrigeration equipment. The company also purchases store equipment for members. It has established and promoted a 'Unity' brand name which it owns and which represents a valuable good will. . . .

Officers and employees own about 321 shares of the total number of 12,393 shares of stock outstanding. As already pointed out, the retail grocer members who own the rest of the shares were required to invest in sufficient capital stock to cover average weekly withdrawals. Upon retirement from the organization the member must surrender his stock for its par value. The same applies to stock held by officers and employees. The withdrawal 'price' of merchandise to retail grocer members is determined as near to cost as possible. Usually at the end of a fiscal year there is an excess of receipts over total costs. This fund is distributed to members in proportion to the withdrawals they have made, as a patronage dividend. A permissive dividend on shares of $5.00 each has also been customarily declared; this dividend also goes to employees who hold shares. The company has some surplus, part of which is in the form of securities of a market value of $304,006.25. . . .

The Act of 1949 imposing the tax provides: "Every person engaging in any business in any school district of the first class shall pay an annual tax at the rate of one (1) mill on each dollar of the annual receipts thereof." 24 P.S. § 584.3. Section 1 (2) defines "business" as follows: "Carrying on or exercising *for gain or profit* within a school district of the first class, any trade, business, including financial business as hereinafter defined, profession, vocation, or commercial activity, or making sales to persons within such school district of the first class." (Emphasis supplied.) . . .

The plaintiff contended in the lower court, as it does here, that the word "business" as defined in the Act should be given a broad meaning so as to include any commercial activity and not be limited to a business carried on for gain or profit; that the defendant is organized as a business corporation and not as a nonprofit or cooperative association; that its by-laws and contracts with its retail grocer members refer to its activities as "business"; that its receipts exceed cost and hence result in a profit. The defendant admits that it is engaged in business but not in business for profit in so far as its cooperative functioning is concerned. As to the latter, it asserts that the business it conducts is really the business of its constituent retail grocer members who pay the general business tax; that it must be considered the alter ego of its members or their agent. The defendant's corporate purpose, as stated in its by-laws, is: "The purpose for which this Company is organized and incorporated is to act as a purely cooperative enterprise of retail grocers in the purchasing and warehousing of food and merchandise for its retail-grocer shareholders and to distribute said food and merchandise to them on their respective orders." . . .

We think it clear that business as contemplated by the Act means business for "gain or profit," that is, for (the) profit motive. . . .

The matter therefore reduces itself to the question whether the defendant in its cooperative functioning is carrying on a business for gain or profit, and therefore within the purview of the tax. We deem it important that it is incorporated under the Business Corporation Law. We are not concerned with the form but with the substance of its structure and operation in its cooperative activites. That it pays the tax on some of its activites does not prevent immunity from tax on its nonprofit activities, . . . to the same extent that a nonprofit corporation may be liable for the tax on some of its activities. . . .

We think there is a persuasive indication that the Legislature did not contemplate the inclusion of cooperatives in that double taxation would result. Each individual retail grocer member would not only pay, as he does, the tax on his gross receipts, but also on his intermediate purchasing methods. In the case of a chain store, the tax is paid only on receipts from retail sales and not on the purchase, storage and distribution of the merchandise to its retail outlets.

While it is true that the defendant conducts its operation as a corporation, which is the tendency of most cooperative associations today, it possesses all of the attributes of a purchasing cooperative. In their present form and mode of operation, purchasing cooperatives are of comparatively recent origin and, like all cooperatives, they are somewhat of a hybrid, partaking both of the nature of a corporation and of a partnership. But basically a purchasing cooperative acts as the joint agent of all its member principals in purchasing in bulk and distributing at cost the products sold by its members. That it also acts as such agent in supplying at cost equipment and services incidental to and in furtherance of the economic objectives of its principals, does not change its character. By means of this principle of unified action the merchants secure the advantages of quantity buying, eliminate wholesalers' profits and attain a position where they can compete on even terms with the giant grocery chains. Viewing the defendant as an enterprise separate and distinct from its members, it has what superficially resembles a profit, that is, an excess of receipts over cost of operation. Realistically, however, the apparent profit is due entirely to the fact that each cooperator has paid in more than enough to cover the cost of the products he obtains for himself. By reason of the contract between the organization and each cooperator, this money belongs to the latter. When a group of individuals enter into an agreement to pool their resources for a common purpose and state therein that their contributions to the extent not required for that purpose shall be repaid to them, it is hard to conceive how the contributions returned to them should be regarded as a gain or profit to the entity acting as their mutual agent. The activities of the agent are the activities of its principals with the result that it is the retail grocer members who are purchasing the merchandise, storing it, distributing and selling it at retail, and they are the parties who realize the profit from the sale to the ultimate consumer. They owe and pay the tax on their gross receipts. Surely reimbursements or advancements made by them as principals to their agent for merchandise purchased by the agent for them is not subject to the tax. Indeed this is recognized by the School District in the regulations covering taxability under the Act. . . .

Conflicting views are expressed in the appellate courts of other States as to the tax status of cooperatives under the particular state statutes involved.

Confining ourselves to the Pennsylvania statute here in question, we are of the opinion that the defendant in its cooperative functioning is not conducting an independent business separate and apart from its constituent members, and its receipts from them in payment for their withdrawal of merchandise purchased for their account, are not taxable. . . .

Judgment affirmed.

◆◆◆

Case Questions

1. Why did the groceries choose the cooperative form of association?
2. Why do you suppose the Frankford Grocery was compelled to pay some taxes?

Case Comment

When competing businesses combine to form purchasing cooperatives there is a chance that the federal government through the Federal Trade Commission or the Justice Department might become interested. Can you guess why? Could Ford Motor Co. and General Motors form a purchasing cooperative? The federal antitrust laws and especially Section 1 of the *Sherman Act* prohibit conspiracies and combinations in restraint of trade. Generally, competitors are not permitted to "cooperate". However, the court mentions that the formation of the cooperative was to counter the competitive impact of large chain stores. So, one may conclude that the extent of cooperation allowed between competing enterprises depends upon the reasons for the cooperation; that is, the competitiveness of the market, the size of the firms in the market and the outcome or results of the cooperation are all weighed by the federal government before it takes action.

LYONS v. AMERICAN LEGION POST NO. 650
172 Ohio St. 331; 175 N.E. 2nd 733,
(S.Ct., Ohio, 1961)

(Author's note: William A. Lyons attended a fish fry conducted by the defendant and was injured and later died as a result of the alleged negligence of the defendant and its agents in maintaining a defective gas heater owned or leased by the defendant. Also sued as defendants were 81 members of the defendant association. The plaintiff is the administratrix of the estate of the deceased, Martha A. Lyons.)

ZIMMERMAN, Judge

In the cases of *Koogler et al., Trustees* v. *Koogler,* 1933, 127 Ohio St. 57, 186 N.E. 725; . . . it was either indicated or held that, since a voluntary unincorporated association had no status as a legal entity, an action against it as such would not lie, and that ordinarily any action had to be brought against the individual members of such an association collectively and conjointly.

Or stating it in another way, "In the absence of an enabling statute, a voluntary association cannot be sued by its association name. It has no legal existence, and the persons composing it must be joined individually." *Kimball* v. *Lower Columbia Fire Ass'n.*, 67 Or. 249, 252, 135 P. 877, 878. . . .

Then effective on September 30, 1955, the General Assembly enacted legislation which is now Sections 1745.01 through 1745.04, Revised Code. Section 1745.01 provides:

> Any unincorporated association may contract or sue in behalf of those who are members and, in its own behalf, be sued as an entity under the name by which it is commonly known and called.

Section 1745.02 reads:

> All assets, property, funds and any right or interest, at law or in equity, of such unincorporated association shall be subject to judgment, execution and other process. A money judgment against such unincorporated association shall be enforced only against the association as an entity and shall not be enforceable against the property of an individual member of such association. . . .

. . . Ordinarily, it is for the Legislature to determine who may sue or be sued so long as it does not interfere with vested rights, deny any remedy or transgress constitutional inhibitions. As a general rule, every state has control over the remedies it offers litigants in its courts. It may give a new and additional remedy as to a right or equity already in existence and it may abolish old remedies and substitute new. . . .

In the early case of *Darling* v. *Peck*, 15 Ohio 65, 72, the following statement appears:

> Where a statute gives a new remedy without impairing or denying one already known to the law, the rule is, to consider it as cumulative, allowing either the new or the old remedy to be pursued at the option of the party seeking redress. . . .

Is it the purpose and intent of the statutes quoted and referred to above to limit actions solely against unincorporated associations as entities in the names they commonly use, as determined by the two lower courts herein, or may the individual members of such associations still be sued as under the former practice? We think the new statutes are no more than cumulative and do not abrogate the right to sue the members of the associations if the suitor chooses to proceed in that way. It is to be noted that Section 1745.01, Revised Code, uses the permissive word, "may," and that, under Section 1745.02, Revised Code, when a suitor does take advantage of the enabling statutes by suing an unincorporated association by the name it uses, the collection of any judgment obtained against such association must be satisfied out of its property alone and the property of its members is immune from seizure. Surely, had the General Assembly intended to eliminate actions against the individuals composing an unincorporated association, it would have so expressed itself.

That statutes like Section 1745.01 et seq., Revised Code, represent an alternative mode of procedure appears to be the established rule. Thus, in 7 C.J.S. Associations § 36, p. 91, the following statement is made:

It has been said that it is only by virtue of statute that an unincorporated association may be sued as an entity. In some states statutes have been enacted which expressly or impliedly authorize the bringing of actions against unincorporated associations in their common name * * *.

And at page 92, ibid., it is stated that such statutes do "not take away the right previously existing at common law. The individuals composing such an association do not, by force of such statutes, acquire any immunity from individual liability, and it is optional with a creditor to sue either the association as such or the individuals composing it." . . .

However, a recognized difference exists between an unincorporated association organized for the transaction of business and one organized for fraternal or social purposes. This is illustrated in *Azziolina* v. *Order of Sons of Italy, Conte Luigi Cadorna,* No. 440, 119 Conn. 681, 691, 179 A. 201, 204, where it is stated in the opinion:

In the case of a voluntary association formed for the purpose of engaging in business and making profits, its members are liable, as partners, to third persons upon contracts which are within its scope and are entered into with actual or apparent authority, and a joint judgment against them is justified. * * * But when, as here, the purpose of the association is not business or profit, the liability, if any, of its members is not in its nature that of partners but that arising out of the relation of principal and agent, and only those members who authorize or subsequently ratify an obligation are liable on account of it.

The same principle is recognized in relation to torts. In *Thomas, Potentate* v. *Dunne,* 131 Colo. 20, 30, 279 P.2d 427, 432, the following language is found in the course of the opinion:

We cannot subscribe to the proposition that one who becomes a member of an unincorporated association such as a fraternal organization, a veterans organization or any one of numerous other societies which might be mentioned, subjects himself to liability for injuries sustained in ceremonies held under the auspices of that organization, in the absence of any allegation in the complaint against him that he took an active part in the act resulting in the injury or in some manner had knowledge of the proposed initiation rites or 'stunts' to be employed and gave assent or encouragement to the use thereof.

. . . In the instant case the petition alleges that the defendants, American Legion Post No. 650 . . . and the individual members of American Legion Post No. 650 . . . conducted or caused to be conducted within said building a social affair known as a fish fry for which they charged each person attending the sum of one dollar ($1.00)," and that "defendants, and each of them, were negligent in failing to provide a safe heating system in the building; in equipping and maintaining the building with a defective heating system; in failing to provide proper ventilation in the building; and in failing to warn invitees in the building, including decedent, of the presence of carbon monoxide fumes therein."

Such petition . . . states causes of action good as against demurrer . . . but on the trial of the action to establish liability on the part of individual defendants evidence would have to be produced linking them as active participants in the affair resulting in plaintiff's decedent's alleged injuries, and, furthermore, that they knew or in the exercise of ordinary care should have known of the defective condition of the instrumentality claimed to have caused the injury. And, of course, the other elements necessary to support recovery would have to be proved.

The judgment of the Court of Appeals is reversed, and the cause is remanded to the trial court for further proceedings.

Judgment reversed.   ◆ ◆ ◆

Case Questions

1. If a judgment were recovered against the American Legion Post No. 650 as the sole defendant, could the property of the president of the post be taken to satisfy the judgment?
2. Under what circumstances could the property of the president of the Post be taken to satisfy the judgment?
3. Why would an injured plaintiff want to sue an unincorporated association as a separate entity?
4. What is the difference between the liability of a member of an unincorporated association organized for business and the liability of a member of an unincorporated association organized for social purposes?

Case Comment

In this case one may say that the opinion is not clearly written. We are not told the holding of the trial court nor the holding of the Ohio Court of Appeals. Further, the facts of the case appear at the end of the opinion, not the beginning. There is no required pattern that an appellate opinion must follow. Even though judge Zimmerman does present an opinion which varies from the usual pattern, we can nevertheless learn from it.

CENTRAL TRUST & SAFE DEPOSIT CO. v. RESPASS
112 Ky. 606, 66 S.W. 421 (Ct. of App. Ky., 1902)

◆ ◆ ◆

DU RELLE, J.

Jerome B. Respass and Solomon L. Sharp appear to have formed a copartnership, extending over several years, in the business of managing a racing stable, and, in connection with that business, were engaged in "book-making, or making wagers upon race horses. They seem, also, to have had an interest in a pool room at Newport. For the book business a separate account was kept by a cashier employed for the purpose. They had no regular time for making settlements with each other, but at various times, when requested, the cashier made out statements of the booking business of the firm. It appears from the testimony of Bernard, the cashier, that Sharp in November, 1897, handed him $4,724, and told him to deposit it to his (Sharp's) credit in the Merchants'

National Bank of Cincinnati, Ohio, which was done. Sharp appears to have stated at the time that one-half of this fund belonged to Respass. It appears further that this was the "bank roll" of the bookmaking concern, in which each partner had an equal interest. At the same time he remarked that Respass had paid out $1,500 for the firm, and that he would see him in a few days and settle with him. Sharp died suddenly, before any such settlement was made. The money in the bank roll was on deposit to Sharp's credit. The racing business of the firm seems to have been almost entirely in the hands of Respass, who attended to the horses, trained them, entered them in races, and at times wagered on them for the benefit of the firm, which divided the profits or shared the losses, as the case might be. Respass brought suit against Sharp's executors for a settlement of the partnership accounts. . . . The business of breeding, training, and racing horses for purses is legal. The partnership for that purpose can undoubtedly be settled by the chancellor. The only question presented as to this matter is upon the correctness of the settlement made. . . .

An . . . item to which exception is taken consists of $700; being the amount of two bets made, lost, and paid by Respass on the horses "Fair Deceiver" and "Shannon." In view of the statutory law of Kentucky . . . we think it is well settled that a man who lends money to another, to be bet on a horse race, cannot recover it back. And so it would seem that if A. agrees with B. that B. shall advance the money, and himself bet upon a horse race for their joint account, no action will lie by B. to compel A. to respond for his share of a bet which is lost. . . . It is a contract for an illegal venture. The whole contract is illegal. No right of action can arise out of that contract. This is exactly the position of Respass as to the two bets. He advanced the money to make them for himself and Sharp, relying upon Sharp's express or implied agreement to pay half the losses if loss should be incurred. Such a contract cannot be enforced in this state.

A closer question is presented by the claim for a division of the "bank roll." This $4,724 was, as found by the chancellor, earned by the firm composed of Respass and Sharp in carrying on an illegal business — that of "bookmaking" — in the state of Illinois. But though this amount had been won upon horse races in Chicago, it is claimed that, though secured illegally, "the transaction has been closed, and the appellee is only seeking his share from the realized profits from the illegal contracts, if they are illegal." On the other hand, it is claimed for appellants that, as to the bank roll, this proceeding is a bill for an accounting of profits from the business of gambling.

It does not seem to be seriously contended that the business of "bookmaking," whether carried on in Chicago or in this commonwealth, was legal, for by the common law of this country all wagers are illegal. . . . In *McMullen* v. *Hoffman* (174 U.S. 639) it appeared that a partnership was formed for the purpose of obtaining a public contract by unlawful means, upon the terms of sharing the profits equally, and that the profits came into the hands of one partner. The other filed a bill for an accounting, and was denied relief. Said the court: "We must therefore come back to the proposition that to permit a recovery in this case is, in substance, to enforce an illegal contract, and one which is illegal because it is against public policy to permit it to stand. The court refuses to enforce such a contract, and it permits defendant to set up its illegality, not out of any regard for defendant who sets it up, but only on account of the public interest. * * * To refuse to grant either party to an illegal contract judicial aid for the enforcement of his alleged rights under it tends strongly towards reducing the number of such transactions to a minimum. The more plainly parties understand that when they enter into contracts of this nature they place themselves outside the protection of the law, so far as that protection consists in aiding them to enforce such contracts, the less inclined they will be to enter into them. . . .

We conclude that in this country, in the case of a partnership in a business confessedly illegal, whatever may be the doctrine where there has been a new contract in relation to, or a new investment of, the profits of such illegal business, and whatever may be the doctrine as to the rights or liabilities of a third person who assumes obligations with respect to such profits, or by law becomes responsible therefor, the decided weight of authority is that a court of equity will not entertain a bill for an accounting.

The judgment of the chancellor is therefore reversed, and the cause remanded, with directions to enter a judgment in accordance with this opinion.

Case Question

1. Do you believe the court is correct when it states that if courts refuse to enforce illegal contracts it tends to reduce the number of such transactions? Did the court have any choice but not to enforce the agreement?

REVIEW PROBLEMS
PART I

1. We have listed more terms below which will be used repeatedly throughout the text. You should be able to recall and write down the definition of each term. Remember that if you believe the text discussion of the term is inadequate, you should refer to the glossary and *Black's Law Dictionary*, 4th ed.

state police power	corporation
trade mark/trade name	limited liability
differentiate: federal law v. state law	double taxation
agency	Subchapter S Corporations
proprietorship	Section 1244 stock
partnership	public v. private corporations
judgment creditor	municipal corporations
limited partnership	cooperative association
joint venture	unincorporated association

2. Assume that you and a friend wish to start a business selling discount merchandise at the retail level which would be ordered through catalogues available in your store. You would carry some inventory, but the main intent of the business would be to provide the customer with catalogue information and guidance in ordering, reasonable prices and delivery service. Besides a small store, you plan to lease warehouse space and either buy or lease a delivery truck. For the present time you do not plan to hire any employees because you and your friend could do all of the required work. You and your friend plan to furnish $2,500 each to the enterprize and you are hoping to borrow another $2,500 from a bank. Assume you have decided to call your business the "Quality Discount Service."

List the procedures for starting such a business. Which type of business association would you choose and why?

ENDNOTES

1. U.S. Dept. of Labor Manpower Administration, *Manpower Research Monograph No. 11,* 1969, as quoted in A. Conrad, R. Knauss and S. Siegel, *Enterprize Organization,* 9-10 (1972).
2. J. Crane and A. Bromberg, *Law of Partnership,* 9-10 (1968).
3. *Id.,* at 26.
4. A. Conrad, *Supra,* note 1 at 336.
5. *Id.,* at 122.
6. I. Packel, *The Organization and Operation of Cooperatives,* 4-5 (1970).
7. *Id.,* at 11-12.
8. *Id.,* at 32.

Table 2-1

COMPARATIVE LEGAL ASPECTS OF MOST OFTEN USED BUSINESS ASSOCIATIONS

	PROPRIETORSHIP	PARTNERSHIP	CORPORATION
LEGAL BASIS	common law	express contract of owners consistent with UPA or contract implied in law by courts	state statute
LEGAL ENTITY	not separate from owner	separate from owner for some purposes	separate legal person
OWNER'S LIABILITY	owner liable for all debts.	general partner liable for all debts; limited partner liable for amounts contributed	owners liable only to the extent of paid in capital
LENGTH OF LIFE	same as owner	agreed to by partners usually life of any partner	perpetual
MANAGEMENT CONTROL	by owner directly	by majority vote of partners owners manage	by vote of board of directors elected by owners — owners do not manage.
CAPITAL	limited to what the single owner can raise	limited to what partners can raise — may necessitate a new partner, thus a new partnership.	sale of more ownership shares
FEDERAL INCOME TAXES	profits taxed to owner as individual	profits taxed proportionately to each owner as agreed in contract or all share equally.	profits of corp taxed to corp — owners pay income tax on dividends.
COMPLEXITY OF CREATION/OPERATION	simplest, no agreement with other individuals or filings with state required unless doing business under a name other than owner's name.	should have partnership agreement and must file partnership name if name is other than those of partners.	numerous filings required and formalities of organization imposed by state statute must be followed.

PART II
AGENCY LAW

THE MUTUAL LEGAL DUTIES OF PRINCIPAL AND AGENT

3

Commercial activity is almost always conducted by agents of various kinds. These agents are usually individuals who are acting on behalf of other individuals, partnerships, corporations, governments or other legal entities. The legal relationship created by an agent on behalf of his principal with a third party is defined by that body of rules referred to as agency law. Agency law is a large part of the total legal framework which governs the employer-employee relationship. This law has been created primarily by state judicial decisions and today it remains one of the most important bodies of law still based almost entirely on the common law. Since the common law varies from state to state, studying agency law could be very confusing. We have attempted to simplify the presentation of the most important agency rules by focusing on one widely recognized reference work, *The Restatement of Agency, 2nd,*[1] referred to hereafter as the Restatement. The Restatement was written by legal practitioners, jurists and scholars who comprise the American Law Institute (an organization founded in 1923 to promote the clarification and simplification of the law). Also, from time to time, we will cite material from a respected treatise on Agency Law by Harvard Professor Warren A. Seavey entitled, *Law of Agency.*[2] The reader should remember that these rules do not have the force of legislative law or even a court decision but represent a synthesis of what some legal scholars believe the law is or should be.

As we pointed out in the last chapter, agency law does not present a body of principles which define a business association in the same sense that proprietorships, partnerships and corporations are so defined. Neither the federal nor state statutes, nor administrative agencies such as the Internal Revenue Service recognize agency law as creating a distinct form of business association. In essence, agency law is just one component, although a major one, of all business associations. For example, Section 9 of the *Uniform Partnership Act* provides that partners are agents of the partnership for performing partnership business. Similarly, the common law provides that all employees of a corporation who are authorized to contract with persons outside of the corporation are its agents. A knowledge of agency law then is a logical necessity for understanding some aspects of American business associations and most properly precedes the direct study of such associations.

The advantages in using others (agents) to do one's work are numerous. They enable an individual or corporation or other legal person to extend his physical reach. One may safely negotiate a binding contract in Europe or Africa by sending an agent, properly authorized, to conduct the negotiating and contracting. Also, one's intellectual reach may be likewise extended by hiring experts or others specially trained to act for and at the direction of the employer.

Although many of the agency law issues involve a third party there is an essential portion of agency law which involves only the principal and agent. For the sake of convenience we start by defining the agency relationship and then proceed to analyze the mutual legal duties of the principal and agent. The final portion of the chapter presents material on the legal capacity of one to be an agent.

CREATION OF THE AGENCY RELATIONSHIP

The *Restatement* (Section 1) defines an agency as follows:

1. Agency is: The fiduciary relation which results from the manifestation of consent by one person to another that the other shall act on his behalf and subject to his control, and consent by the other so to act.
2. The one for whom action is to be taken is the principal.
3. The one who is to act is the agent.

In this instance perhaps Professor Seavey provides a clearer definition. He states: Agency is a consensual, fiduciary relation between two persons, created by law by which one, the principal, has a right to control the conduct of the agent, and the agent has the power to affect the legal relations of the principal.[3]

Most agency relationships are created by contract, but, as the definition indicates, consent, and not a formal "enforceable" contract, is all that is needed. One who *voluntarily acts at the direction of another* is an agent, although nothing is received by the actor. However, for a court to impose the full range of duties discussed below on the principal more than mere consent is required. In addition to consent, there must be an act by the agent, and finally, *reliance* on the agent's act by the principal or a third party. The following case illustrates the existence of the bare elements needed for the formation of an agency relationship. In this case it was necessary for the plaintiff to establish the existence of an agency relationship in order to recover from the telephone company. Note carefully how the court reasons that an agency existed for the purpose of transmitting the message even though the principal had expressly forbidden it.

ABRESCH v. NORTHWESTERN BELL TELEPHONE COMPANY
246 Minn. 408; 75 N.W. 2d 206 (1956)

◆ ◆ ◆

KNUTSON, Justice

Appeal from a judgment . . . granting defendant's motion for summary judgment.

This action was commenced to recover damages suffered by plaintiff in a fire in which his building was destroyed. A pretrial deposition of plaintiff was taken, and the following facts appear from the pleadings and such deposition.

Plaintiff owned and operated a business, specializing in cleaning and reconditioning barrels and drums, in a large one-story frame building located in Washington County in this state. Defendant furnished plaintiff with telephone service, one telephone being located in his home, which was about 300 feet from his place of business, with an extension installed in his business building. Both were dial telephones.

On July 27, 1954, at about 3:45 p.m., a fire started inside plaintiff's business building. His attention was called to the fire, and he immediately went to the telephone and dialed "0" and heard someone say "Number, please." He thereupon requested the operator to call the North St. Paul and East County Line Fire Departments, giving the operator the location of his place of business. He then left the telephone to assist in fighting the fire. A short time later, when he became aware of the fact that the fire departments were not coming, he requested his wife to contact the fire departments by telephone from his home. He contends that the telephone then was out of order and that he could not contact the fire departments for about 20 minutes. In the meantime one of the fire departments had been contacted by a neighbor. By the time the fire departments arrived the fire was out of control, and the entire building was destroyed.

Plaintiff alleges in his complaint: "That defendant through its agents and servants negligently and carelessly failed to transmit said message . . . and negligently and carelessly caused plaintiff's telephone connections to be out of service and delayed for more than thirty minutes, and that defendant was otherwise negligent in failing and neglecting to furnish plaintiff with proper telephone service; and that as the result thereof, said fire department was delayed more than thirty minutes in getting to plaintiff's place of business.

"That solely and proximately by reason of the delay of thirty minutes, plaintiff's building and contents thereof were completely destroyed by fire and plaintiff's business ceased to operate as a business."

Defendant denied liability and as affirmative defense: . . .

"Alleges that among the regulations which have been on file with said Commission and available for public inspection at defendant's offices is the following regulation, which has been in force and effect for many years, to-wit:

" 'Transmission of Messages — The function of the Telephone Company is to furnish means of communication between telephone stations. Acceptance, by employees of written or verbal communications from the public, for transmission or delivery, is forbidden.' " . . .

After the pretrial deposition of plaintiff was taken by defendant, a motion was made for summary judgment, which was granted by the trial court. The court was of the opinion that the rights of plaintiff are based on contract and that no tort action could be maintained. This appeal is from the judgment. The question presented for our determination is whether plaintiff, under the circumstances, can maintain a tort action to recover his damages.

Plaintiff contends that, . . . defendant has held itself out to the public as willing to convey messages in case of certain emergencies such as a fire. The question then arises, assuming such fact can be proved, is defendant liable in a tort action for a negligent failure to perform such promise: We think that this question must be answered in the affirmative. . . .

Restatement, Agency, § 378,:

"One who, by a gratuitous promise or other conduct which he should realize will cause another reasonably to rely upon the performance of definite acts of service by him as the other's agent, causes the other to refrain from having such acts done by other available means is subject to a duty to use care to perform such service or, while other means are available, to give notice that he will not perform." . . .

" * * * Telephone companies cannot be required to furnish a service which they do not hold themselves out as undertaking to furnish. * * * The record does not disclose any obligation imposed by public authority requiring a telephone operator to transmit or relay emergency messages in the circumstances here disclosed."

In this limited area of accepting emergency messages, . . . while the telephone company is under no duty to assume the responsibility of delivering messages in cases of emergency, if it does voluntarily assume such responsibility and thereby leads others to rely on such assumption of duty and to refrain from taking other and more direct action to protect themselves, the company is required to exercise reasonable care in performing the duty so assumed for a failure of which it may become liable in a tort action. Whether there was such assumption of responsibility and whether defendant failed to exercise reasonable care in the performance thereof involve questions of fact which cannot be determined on a motion for summary judgment.

Reversed.

Case Questions

1. Why would the plaintiff be more interested in suing Northwestern Bell Telephone Co. than the telephone operator?
2. Does the opinion of the court state that the telephone company or its agent was negligent? Clearly state in your own words the precise holding of this court.

DUTIES OF THE AGENT TO THE PRINCIPAL

Most of the duties of the agent to the principal are implied by describing the relationship between principal and agent as a fiduciary one. A fiduciary relationship is one that is vested with a special form of trust; it is derived from the Roman Law, and defines (as a noun) a person who acts as a trustee and who is required to display scrupulous good faith and candor toward the body of the trust.[4] In agency law, the agent is a fiduciary and this imposes on the agent the following duties:

1. To act with the utmost loyalty for and on behalf of the principal;
2. To act with due care and diligence;
3. To render complete and accurate information to the principal;
4. To account for all receipts and profits;
5. To follow directions of the principal.

The fiduciary duties outlined apply to the agent only for acts conducted pursuant to the purpose of the agency. To determine if there has been a breach of the fiduciary duties the first step must usually be to determine the exact nature or scope of the agency relationship. This determination is made by inquiring about the authority of the agent which is defined by a contract, if there is one; if there is no contract, then it is defined by the usual and normal authority of other agents in similar circumstances. The process of defining the authority or scope or agency is explained in greater detail in the following chapters. It suffices to say here that for an agent to be liable for a breach of a fiduciary duty, it must be found that the breach was within the ambit of employment. For example, an agent employed to buy personal property such as goods for his principal may compete with his principal for the purchase of real property (land) and not be liable.[5]

However, if an agent is instructed to buy designated property on a map provided by the principal he may not even buy for himself property outside of that designated if it could reasonably be thought of as related to the purpose of the agency. The closer the competing opportunity taken by the agent is to the purpose of the agency, the greater the chance is that a court will hold that the agent must tender the opportunity to the principal before it is taken by the agent.

The following case illustrates a circumstance in which the agent obviously violated the special trust placed upon him and therefore created liability for himself. Note carefully the arguments of the defendant and how the court reasons that what the agent took for himself really belonged to the principal.

NYE v. LOVELACE
228 F. 2d 599 (5th Cir., 1956)

(Author's note: The express objective of the agency in this case was the procurement of mineral rights under land designated by the principal on a map of the area. One parcel of land, the Johnson tract, was entirely within the designated area. The Crosby parcel of 1,260 acres had 400 acres within the designated tract. One of the owners of the Crosby parcel, Hart, also owned the Gray parcel, no part of which was within the designated tract.)

BROWN, Circuit Judge

Appellant Nye, an Oklahoma oil investor, in the spring of 1951 made arrangements through his agent, Tom Gorton, with the appellee, Lovelace, to procure mineral interests in an area later on known as the Pollard Field in Alabama. The last transaction was concluded August 16, 1951. Later on, perhaps inadvertently, Nye learned that Lovelace had purchased in his own name and held for his own account one-half of the minerals under 40 acres known as the Gray tract. In pre-trial discovery deposition in Nye's suite to recover the Gray tract, Nye learned, for the first time, that in procuring the mineral acreage Lovelace, instead of drawing on Nye's account for actual cost, had treated each of the transactions as though it were a purchase by him (Lovelace) from the landowner and a resale to Nye at substantial profits totaling over $2,500.00.

After a full trial, the court made a finding having, to us, extraordinary and dominant significance. The court rejected Lovelace's contention that his engagement was to get together such acreage within the outlined area on the best terms obtainable to himself and then submit them to Nye's agent, Gorton, at a mutually acceptable price, the difference to be his compensation. In so doing, the court adopted altogether Nye's contention that Lovelace's compensation was to be his out-of-pocket expenses and an interest, later to be determined, in specific minerals. Additionally, without ever informing Nye or Gorton, Lovelace purchased the Johnson tract, admittedly within the designated buying area, for his own account. This means that from the very outset Lovelace was, and continued to be, an unfaithful servant who sought private gain to the detriment of his principal. The district court required Lovelace to repay the withheld profits and convey the Johnson tract. Lovelace has acquiesced in both.

But not so as to the Gray tract. The trial court held that this was properly purchased by Lovelace for his own account since it lay outside the designated buying area, and its purchase was not necessary to the acquisition of interests within the area. And this, even though Gray was purchased from the same person (Hart) and simultaneously with the Crosby tract, one concededly within the agency. We cannot agree.

In the beginning Nye furnished to Gorton, and through him, to Lovelace a plat on which lines, following strictly the perpendiculars of sections, were traced outlining the area in which minerals were desired. Nye had confidential information as to the location of a test well (later dry) and the area, roughly 7 miles in width east and west and 1-1/2 miles in depth north and south, ran generally northwest to southeast in stairstep fashion roughly paralleling the supposed location of a fault. Offsetting the well-site, in part, in the adjacent section was the Crosby tract, owned in equal one-third shares by James Hart and two other partners. . . .

The trial court placed great reliance on the fact that, since the Gray tract happened to be just outside of the lines on the plat, Nye had himself excluded it from the buying area even though he knew it was a physical, diagonal, offset to the well-site. The court recognized, however, that it could not automatically exclude from the agency all land outside of the designated buying area, since so much had been, and had to be, procured beyond it to acquire interests within it. In the trial court's view, the outside acreage was within the agency only when necessarily procured in a single transaction as a condition to acquiring acreage within the area. On this approach the court then held that these were two separate transactions, separately negotiated so that procurement of Gray was wholly unrelated to acquisition of the desired interest in Crosby. . . .

Disregarding Lovelace's subjective attitude whether this was one or two transactions and the factual conflict between Hart and Lovelace on whether the original trade was for 100 acres or something more or less, it is uncontradicted that so far as Hart was concerned, it was a common transaction, whether in one or two parts, or more, and under no circumstance would he have sold the Gray tract had not he been selling Crosby. While the trial court rejected, as Hart's conclusion, his insistence that it was one transaction, the court did not, could not, find that had Lovelace approached him solely to procure Gray, he would have made the trade for the equivalent of $180.00. Everything about the course of dealing between Lovelace and the owners of Crosby bespeaks the recognition by Lovelace that these people were not going to permit a purchaser to pick and choose the good and reject the bad. Requiring Lovelace to take 560 acres of Crosby outside the designated area to procure the interest in 400 within makes practically absolute Hart's assertion that Gray would not have been sold alone.

The trial court, we think, became so preoccupied with the notion that Hart did not require purchase of Gray as a condition precedent to delivery of Crosby, that the vital importance of Hart's unwillingness to sell Gray unless they bought Crosby completely escaped him. This meant that the opportunity to procure a valuable interest in Gray was due entirely to Lovelace's position as agent for Nye. It was not simply the case of an agent acquiring knowledge of an attractive opportunity through performance of the master's work. When the door was opened solely because of Lovelace's dealings for his principal — when the only way to exploit the collateral opportunity was to consummate concurrently the principal's transaction — he was under an obligation to tender the co-incidental benefits to his principal or at least advise him of his personal tentative interest in it. It is not for the agent to determine for the principal whether the fruits are, or are not, attractive or desired, nor is it open to the servant under his heavy obligation of high fidelity to analyze, in reverse, what must have been in his principal's mind at the time the general outline of the area was made, or to determine that, because the particular tract was separately owned under a title unrelated to the larger purchase, the principal would adhere to the strict artificial lines of the area instead of acquiring, as was otherwise frequently done, interests in the seller's outside acreage.

Here, an unfaithful servant, whose activities from the inception were in breach of his heavy duties, undertook, with circumstances strongly suggesting a studied furtiveness, to capitalize upon the information which had come to him under an obligation of trust, and in doing so, he sought to make decisions and resolve questions for his principal in which he stood to gain or lose as self-interest prevailed or was submerged. That which he was obtained by these means, he must restore.

As we think the total record is an overpowering portrayal of an agent unfaithful to his trust, the denial by the trial court of equitable relief to recapture the diverted fruits of his actions leaves us with the conviction that an injustice has been done and a mistake has been committed. ... and the judgment, insofar as it concerns the Gray tract, must be reversed and rendered in favor of appellant, Clark C. Nye.

Reversed and rendered.   ◆ ◆ ◆

Case Questions

1. At issue in the *Nye* case was whether or not the scope of the agency should be limited to the property described in the map provided by the principal or whether it should be broader than the property so described. What did the court hold?
2. Would Lovelace be liable to the principal if he had purchased land 1/4 mile away from that designated on the map and was unconnected from any parcel within the designated area?
3. Defining the ambit or scope of the agency may not always be easily accomplished. Often principals give general instructions to agents such as, "Sell my product in the Chicago area" or, "Manage my business." When this is how the relationship is defined how would you go about discovering the intended scope of the agency?

Agency relationships cover such a wide variety of circumstances (ranging from the confidential relation of attorney and client to the relatively slight fiduciary relationship which exists between a land owner and a real estate salesman), that the duties finally imposed by a court may vary greatly.

The fiduciary nature of the agency relationship may continue even after termination of the agency. The very essence of the relationship is one based on trust and, in some circumstances such as the attorney-client relationship, trust implies confidentiality. Thus, even after the completion of such a relationship, the attorney may not reveal or use confidential information. In the typical employer-employee context, the employer who exposes his employee to confidential information usually attempts to guard his interest in such information by asking the employee to agree by contract not to use the information in a manner detrimental to the interests of the employer after the employment is terminated. Such a contractual agreement is called a "restrictive convenant." Generally, *in the absence of a restrictive covenant* limiting the right of an employee to use information gained from the work experience, or to compete with the employer after employment termination, courts will permit employees to compete with the previous employer. The one exception to this is when an employee takes with him and uses information which was regarded as secret by the employer. In the typical employer-employee relationship, such information may be referred to as a trade secret.

In the two following cases the employees may not be technically defined as agents, but, nevertheless, the rules discussed are applicable to the agency relationship. On one hand, we see that the common law protects the employer by giving it a remedy against an agent who takes and converts a trade secret. On the other hand, the common law also protects the employee from the unreasonable use of restrictive covenants.

ALLEN MANUFACTURING COMPANY v. LOIKA
145 Ct. 509; 144 A. 2d 306 (1958)

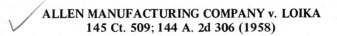

MELLITZ, Associate Justice

This is an appeal taken by the defendants from a decree enjoining them from disclosing a trade secret, knowledge of which they acquired while in the employ of the plaintiff. The secret involved the use of a process, known as warm heading, in the manufacture of screws.

The plaintiff has been manufacturing screws and similar products for many years. The defendant Edward Loika was hired by it in 1936 as a drill press operator and worked in various capacities in the plant until 1954, when he became chief of the production engineering department. The defendant James Fiorino entered the plaintiff's employ in 1953 as an electronics engineer. In 1949 or 1950 Loika had suggested to his superiors the installation of the warm heading process for shaping wire into blanks for screws. It is not a new process, having been patented by others in 1920. Its advantages are faster production, longer tool and die life, lesser cost and reduction of plant equipment and space. Except for the purchase of a small induction heating unit, the plaintiff did nothing concerning the introduction of warm heading until late in 1954, when Loika and others participated in further discussions about it. Early in 1955, preliminary to installing warm heading, the plaintiff ordered a single die, two blow, heading machine for the process. Loika was in charge of the tooling, setting up and operation of this new header, and Fiorino worked on the induction heating phase under Loika's direction. . . .

The heading unit proved unsatisfactory, and in early 1956 the plaintiff consulted with the New Rochelle Tool Corporation and ordered from it a generator type of induction heating unit, which the New Rochelle representatives installed on the plaintiff's heading machine. The New Rochelle representatives worked in close proximity to the heading machine and were considered by the plaintiff to be free to reveal the idea of this tie-up to others. The New Rochelle Company advertises its equipment for use in warm heading and that it will give advice on installing a warm heading process. The plaintiff encountered difficulties with its warm heading process, and the defendants assisted in overcoming them. The plaintiff expended a sum estimated to be $180,000 in developing the process. The process was installed in the plaintiff's plant in an ordinary production department, visible from the street, without being specially segregated or guarded in any way. The diagrams and tool and die drawings in connection with the process were not marked secret or confidential. Plant tours for customers, suppliers and salesmen often included the warm heading department. Observation of the process in operation would not, however, enable anyone to learn sufficient details to duplicate it, and, furthermore, no competitor of the plaintiff was permitted to view the process in operation.

In late August, 1957, while on their vacation, the defendants called at the Chicago Screw Company, a competitor of the plaintiff, inquiring if it would be interested in hiring them as engineering consultants on warm heading production of screws. Loika gave the assistant chief engineer of the Chicago Screw Company a sample of the plaintiff's production from warm heading, explained the advantages of two blow screw machines, and indicated that he could solve the lubrication problem involved in the warm heading process. Although asked, the defendants did not tell what lubricant, wire coating and temperature was used by the plaintiff in the process. On September 4, 1957, the defendants resigned their employment with the plaintiff. At no time prior to that date did the plaintiff request any of its employees to keep secret or confidential the details of its warm heading process. Of the plaintiff's many competitors, only one has developed a warm heading process, and that varies from the plaintiff's process. The plaintiff's warm heading process gives it a competitive advantage. It would take a competitor about two years to develop a process like that of the plaintiff, and if the defendants revealed their knowledge, the plaintiff would lose its competitive advantage in a matter of weeks. The court concluded that the warm heading process as used by the plaintiff was a trade secret which the defendants learned while employed by the plaintiff in a position of confidence and that the plaintiff was entitled to protection by injunction against its disclosure by the defendants. An injunction for one year was granted. . . .

The facts essential to a disposition of the ultimate issue are not in dispute. The defendants, as employees of the plaintiff, participated over a period of years in the development of a warm heading process for the manufacture of screws in the plaintiff's plant. The process is not generally known in the trade and gives the plaintiff a substantial advantage over its competitors. The position of the defendants is that they may take the knowledge they acquired while participating in the perfection of the process as employees of the plaintiff and freely use it for their own advantage by imparting that knowledge to the plaintiff's competitors, to the harm of the plaintiff. They assert that the plaintiff has no property interest in the process which a court will protect since warm heading is not a secret process and the materials and methods by which the plaintiff developed it are well known and generally available, and further that the plaintiff did not take steps indicating that it regarded warm heading at its plant as a trade secret.

The law is well settled that knowledge acquired by an employee during his employment cannot be used for his own advantage to the injury of the employer during the employment; and after the employment has ceased the employee remains subject to a duty not to use trade secrets, or other confidential information which he had acquired in the course of his employment, for his own benefit or that of a competitor to the detriment of his former employer. ... It matters not that there is no specific agreement on the part of the employee not to disclose the knowledge he has so acquired. "(T)he law will import into the contract (or employment) a prohibition against a betrayal of (the employer's) trust and confidence and against imparting confidential information to others. In fact, such a stipulation probably is a part of every employment, whether actually expressed or not. Employees are bound by such an implied obligation even though they be not under contract at all." 1 Nims, *Unfair Competition & Trade-Marks* (4th Ed.) § 150; ... "The principle upon which courts proceed in the protection of trade secrets is stated in *Du Pont (de Nemours) Powder Co.* v. *Masland*, 244 U.S. 100, 102, 37 S.Ct. 575, 576, 61 L.Ed. 1016, where the court, by Justice Holmes, said: 'The word "property," as applied to trademarks and trade secrets, is an unanalyzed expression of certain secondary consequences of the primary fact that the law makes some rudimentary requirements of good faith. Whether the plaintiffs have any valuable secret or not the defendant knows the facts, whatever they are, through a special confidence that he accepted. The property may be denied but the confidence cannot be. Therefore the starting point for the present matter is not property or due process of law, but that the defendant stood in confidential relations with the plaintiffs, or one of them. These have given place to hostility, and the first thing to be made sure of is that the defendant shall not fraudulently abuse the trust reposed in him. It is the usual incident of confidential relations.' "

The defendants base their position first on the contention that since the materials by which the warm heading process was developed in the plaintiff's plant are all common, commercially available components, and the warm heading process is itself a recognized form of heading, no trade secret could have resulted. This claim is effectively answered in the conclusion reached by the trial court: "Although the header, heating unit, lubricant or coolant, and wire used might be available to competitors, plaintiff's ability to combine these elements into a successful warm heading process, like the creation of a recipe from common cooking ingredients, is a trade secret entitled to protection." ... Definitions of "trade secret" abouund in the reported cases. ... In *Restatement*, 4 Torts § 757, comment b, the following definition is given: A trade secret may consist of any formula, pattern, device or compilation of information which is used in one's business, and which gives him an opportunity to obtain an advantage over competitors who do not know or use it. It may be a formula for a chemical compound, a process of manufacturing, treating or preserving materials, a pattern for a machine or other device, or a list of customers. * * * A trade secret is a process or device for continuous use in the operation of the business." There can be no question that the plaintiff's warm heading process fits clearly into this definition. The defendants argue that an essential element of a trade secret is secrecy and that this factor was lacking in the manner in which use of the process was carried on in the plaintiff's plant. The trial court concluded on the evidence before it that the plaintiff reasonably protected the secrecy of its process so that no competitor or member of the public had discovered it. Reasonable precautionary measures for maintaining the secrecy of the process were all that were required. The question was one of fact for the trial court, and the finding fully supports its conclusion.

The defendants point to *Samuel Stores, Inc.,* v. *Abrams,* 94 Conn. 248, 252, 108 A. 541, 9 A.L.R. 1450, and urge that the result of the judgment restraining them from pursuing their activities is an unreasonable restriction upon the rights of employees and the freedom to exercise their talents to earn a livelihood. ... The basis for the protection of trade secrets is that the recipient obtains through a confidential relationship something he did not know previously. ... The comment in *Sun Dial Corporation* v. *Rideout,* 16 N.J. 252, 260, 108 A. 2d ´442, 447, is apt: "There is undoubtedly * * * an important policy which 'encourages employees to seek better jobs from other employers or to go into business for themselves.' * * * But there is also a policy which is designed to protect employers against improper disclosures of information which their employees have received in confidence and this policy may perhaps be receiving increased recognition in the light of the marked changes in the attitude of the law towards the need for commercial morality. * * * Our judicial decisions have faithfully sought to vindicate both policies by preserving to employees their unfettered right to leave their employment and use elsewhere their acquired skill and knowledge of the trade generally as distinguished, however, from any trade secrets imparted to them in confidence and which they must continue to honor as such." The opportunities for the defendants to pursue their economic interests continue open to them despite the injunction, provided they refrain from appropriating to themselves the plaintiff's property right in the warm heading process developed and employed by it in the conduct of its business.

There is no error.

In this opinion the other Judges concurred.

◆◆◆

Case Questions

1. List the factors which you believe the court relied upon in reaching its conclusion that the plaintiff had a property interest in the information taken.
2. Derive your own definition of a trade secret.
3. If the plaintiff had developed a pattern or process which might be labeled a trade secret yet did not use the pattern or process but merely kept it secret, would the law, in your opinion, protect the plaintiff if an employee tried to use the pattern or process elsewhere?

DONAHUE v. PERMACEL TAPE CORPORATION
234 Ind. 398; 127 N.E. 2d. 235 (S. Ct.Ind., 1955)

◆◆◆

ANCHOR, Judge

Appellee is engaged in the manufacture and sale of adhesives and adhesive tapes. Appellant was formerly a sales representative for appellee. During such employment the parties entered into a written contract, the pertinent sections of which are as follows:

1. Employee shall not divulge to others or use for his own benefit any confidential information obtained during the course of his employment with Company relating to sales, sales volume or strategy, customers, number or location of salesmen, formulae, processes, methods, machines, manufacturers, compositions, idea, improvements or invention belonging to or relating to the affairs of the company, Johnson & Johnson or its subsidiary or affiliated companies, without first obtaining Company's written permission.

2. Employee for a period of three (3) years after leaving Company's employment for any reason whatsoever, shall not, in the United States or Canada without first obtaining Company's written permission, engage in or enter the employment of or act as a sales agent or broker for the products of or as an advisor or consultant to any person, firm or corporation engaged in or about to become engaged in the manufacture of adhesive or adhesive tapes.

Thereafter appellant terminated his employment with appellee and, without the consent of appellee, became a sales representative for a competitor. An action for temporary and permanent injunctive relief followed. A temporary restraining order was issued and it is from that decree that this appeal is prosecuted.

In support of his appeal, appellant contends among other things that whereas, the scope of his employment with appellee was limited to northern Indiana, the restrictive covenant contained in the contract was unreasonably restrictive in that the restricted territory (United States and Canada) encompassed too large an area, and that therefore the contract in its entirety was contrary to public policy and void. ... It is upon these facts that the validity of the restrictive covenant in issue must be determined.

Appellee asserts that precedent is uniformly and firmly established that negative covenants in restraint of trade are valid if limited to the area of the business "sought to be protected" and cites numerous cases in support of that position. Appellee then relies on the fact that appellee's business which it sought to protect covered the entire area of the United States and Canada. However, it is to be observed that the "business involved" in each of the cases related to either (1) employer-employee contracts where the use of divulgence of "trade secrets" is involved or (2) the sale of a business or profession, in which cases the "business sought to be protected" is that of the business or profession sold by the covenantor.

Do the cases involved in either of the two above classifications provide either precedent or reason by which to support the validity of the covenant before us? It is admitted that an employee who is entrusted with "trade secrets" may make a valid covenant against the competitive use or disclosure of such trade secrets to the full extent of the affected area of the business of the employer. ...

It is appellee's contention that the facts in this case bring it within the precedent of the above cited cases for the reason that the contract in the case before us, by its express terms, contemplates that processes would be disclosed to appellant, and in addition confidential selling information, including ideas, customer lists and the like would be made available to appellant as a result of his employment; that appellant did, in fact, acquire "confidential information" by virtue of his employment and that such information is classified by law as of the kind appellee is entitled to protect to the extent of the area of its business operations, which include United States and Canada.

However, the rule is firmly established, ... that in determining the validity of a negative covenant in restraint of competition that such contracts are to be strictly construed against the covenantee, and the test of their validity is dependent not merely upon the covenant itself but upon the entire contract and the situation to which it is related. ...

We therefore give our consideration to the covenant, the contract and the situation to which it related. While it is true that section one of the contract refers to "confidential information obtained during the course of employment" the pleadings, ... do not allege, nor can it reasonably be inferred therefrom, that appellant obtained any "confidential information" which was of such a nature that it was related to the business of the covenantee in more than a general way outside the limited territory assigned to the covenantor as a sales representative. In fact, the express allegation of the complaint upon the subject of the breach of covenant indicates that appellee's only cause of complaint is that appellant is working for a competitor and is "soliciting trade" for it in competition with appellee. There is no allegation of fact as to the use or abuse of either "trade secrets" or "confidential information." ...

As far as we are able to ascertain or could reasonably infer from the facts before us, no "trade secrets" were divulged to appellant as a result of his employment and the only "confidential information" which he acquired, used and/or disclosed was the ordinary general information which a sales representative would acquire, such as related to sales methods, lists of customers, customer requirements, etc., in the area worked. ...

We proceed to analyze the second class of cases which state that covenants in restraint of trade will be enforced if limited to the "area of the business involved" — those related to ... the sale of a business or profession. The rule is well established that a vendor may enter into a valid covenant not to compete within the area of the business or profession sold. ...

It must be noted that these cases relate to the good will, which is "the interest to be protected" in the business or profession sold, and they do not relate to the scope of the business of the buyer. For example, if the seller operated stores in cities A, B, and C, and he sells the store in city A, the cases do not hold that a negative covenant may be enforced prohibiting seller from continuing business in cities B and C, neither do they hold that the mere fact that the buyer operates a business throughout the state of Indiana that he may preclude a seller whose business was limited to a single county, from operating elsewhere within the State of Indiana. . . .

By clear analogy the precedent of these cases, when applied to employer-employee covenants, clearly supports the conclusion that such covenants will be upheld, if limited to the area in which operation of the employee's activity was related to the good will of the employer's business. Also, they provide strong precedent in support of the position that covenants which would restrict the competitive employment of an employee beyond the area of his former employment are void, unless such subsequent employment involves that use or divulgence of "trade secrets" of the former employer which are related to the scope of the latter's business throughout the "restricted area."

As far as we are informed, our courts of review have not heretofore been called upon to consider the validity of a covenant not to subsequently engage in competitive activity (not involving "trade secrets") which covenant restricted the activity of the employee outside the area of his former employment. . . .

When we look to the reported cases from other states and the authors of texts on the subject, we find that they provide strong precedent and pursuasive reasoning in support of the position that (where "trade secrets" effecting the entire business are not involved), a covenant which would restrict an employee beyond the area of his prior operation are void, notwithstanding the fact that the employer's business covers a much greater area. . . .

As heretofore stated, the facts before us present a case of first impression in this state. It is therefore our opportunity and responsibility to decide the case upon those principles which most fully do justice to both the parties themselves and to the public.

The general principles governing the legality of a contract in restraint of trade have been stated by *Williston on Contracts,* § 1636, pp. 4580-4581:

> It is everywhere agreed that in order to be valid a promise imposing a restraint in trade or occupation must be reasonable. The question of reasonableness is for the court, not the jury; and in considering what is reasonable, regard must be paid to (a) the question whether the promise is wider than is necessary for the protection of the covenantee in some legitimate interest, (b) the effect of the promise upon the covenantor, and (c) the effect upon the public. * * *

To what conclusion do we arrive when we apply the first above stated test to the facts in this case? Was (a) the covenant wider than was necessary for the protection of the covenantee (appellee) in some legitimate interest? There was no evidence from which the court could assume that the "confidential sales information, including ideas, customer lists and the like * * * made available" to appellant, were related (except in a general way) to appellee's business outside the limited area of his employment with appellee in northern Indiana. Therefore, the case clearly fails to meet the first test of "necessity for the protection of the covenantee" in the area prescribed, — "the United States and Canada."

Furthermore, when we consider the second test above stated, namely (b) the effect upon the covenantor, we find that the covenant also fails to meet the test of validity in this respect. We are here concerned with one of the most basic rights of man as recognized by our Judean-Anglican civilization, "that man is endowed by his Creator with the rights of life, liberty and the pursuit of happiness." We perceive that these rights are inherent and therefore inalienable — whether on the part of governments or by man individually through his own act. By way of illustration only, because we perceive that man is inherently free, our courts will not interfere even with the folly of a man who voluntarily (without mistake, fraud or duress) bargains away his property accumulated through all his past years for a consideration of grossly disproportionate value. Courts will purposely close their eyes to such transactions, as Isaac was unwittingly blinded to the folly of Esau who sold his birthright to Jacob. Our society recognizes and is committed to guard the sacredness of every human personality and to make possible its fullest possible development. Therefore, in order to guarantee that every man shall, as of now and in the future, enjoy the freedom of "life, liberty and the pursuit of happiness" our courts will zealously guard every individual against even his own commitments which would limit or thwart the greatest constructive employment and enjoyment of his faculties from this moment forward, unless the manner of his living would contravene public policy or the personal property rights of another.

This brings us to a consideration of the property rights of both the parties to this action. As an incident to his business the appellee (employer) was entitled to contract with regard to and thus to protect the good will of his business. Elements of this good will include "secret or confidential information," such as the names and addresses and requirements of customers and the advantage acquired through representative contact with the trade in the area of their application. These are property rights which the employer is entitled to protect. However, is not the same true regarding the skill . . . the employee has acquired, or the general knowledge or information he has obtained which is not directly related to the good will or value of his employer's business. Knowledge, skill and information (except trade secrets and confidential information) become a part of the employee's personal equipment. They belong to him as an individual for the transaction of any business in which he may engage, just the same as any part of the skill, knowledge, information or education that was received by him before entering the employment. Therefore, on terminating his employment he has a right to take them with him. These things cannot be taken from him, although he may forget them or abandon them. . . . An employee may contract to conditionally forego these personal attainments as a consideration for his employment only where their use adverse to his employer would result in irreparable injury to the employer. This would occur only in the area of his employment. Therefore, a covenant which would limit his employment with a competitor beyond the scope of his present employment is void. . . .

Appellant's employment with appellee was limited to northern Indiana. There is no evidence that he acquired "trade secrets" or "confidential information" from appellee, the competitive use of which was related to or could result in irreparable injury to the business of the appellee throughout the breadth of "the United States and Canada," where the covenant attempted to restrict appellant's employment. We conclude, therefore, . . . that the covenant of the contract before us was unreasonable to the extent that it attempted to restrict the gainful employment of appellant beyond the area of his former employment with appellee.

The above conclusion gives rise to the final issue in the case. It is asserted that even though the covenant of the contract may not be enforceable as to all the area interdicted, that the equities of the case require enforcement in the area of appellant's former actual employment. ... However, we are not permitted to consider that question or the equities which might support such a decision in this case. ... Whereas the contract before us does not describe the area of appellee's former employment but, on the contrary, the restricted territory is described in one indivisible whole — "The United States and Canada." We cannot rewrite the contract made by the parties and add to it matters which it does contain and then use the contract as rewritten as a basis for litigation, however justifiable equitable interference under the circumstances might seem to be. We conclude, therefore, the covenant of contract upon which this action is predicated, is unenforceable in its entirety. ...

Therefore, the temporary restraining order heretofore issued is ordered dissolved.

◆◆◆

Case Questions

1. Develop a clear statement of the circumstances in which courts will enforce restrictive covenants.
2. Assume that you work for a company which has valuable information which it wishes to protect. Write your own restrictive covenant for employees to sign.
3. Companies have a habit of writing restrictive covenants much broader than necessary. In spite of the law of the *Donahue* case and numerous others like it employers continue to use language almost identical to that used in *Donahue*. Why is this so?
4. The court in *Donahue* even refused to enforce the restrictive covenant in Northern Indiana. This attitude of the court indicates the same general attitude of the court expressed in the *Central Trust* case presented earlier in which a court refused to enforce an illegal agreement. When a court believes an agreement is unfair, it usually will refuse to reform or rewrite the agreement to make it fair.

REMEDIES

The most obvious remedy available to the principal for a breach of duty by the agent is to discharge the agent. In the absence of a contractual provision stating that an agent shall be employed for a given length of time, there is no duty on the part of the principal to keep the agent employed. An agency relationship is created by consent and can, therefore, be terminated by either party by withdrawing the consent.

Another common remedy was sought by the principal in the case of *Nye* v. *Lovelace*. In that case the plaintff-principal asked the court for and was awarded the ownership of the Gray parcel of land. Of course, the principal would have to pay the agent what the agent had to pay for the land. The general rule is that when an agent breaches the fiduciary duty of loyalty owed to the principal by converting to his own use a business opportunity which belonged to the principal then the principal may recover the ownership of that which is converted, just as if it had belonged to the principal in the first place. Moreover, if the agent sells that which was wrongfully purchased by him and realizes a profit, then the principal may recover the profit.

If that which is converted by the agent cannot be traced (a legal term for "specifically identified"), or it is impossible to assess in money terms the measure of damages suffered by the principal, then the principal, as in the case of *Allen Manufacturing Company* v. *Loika,* may ask the court for an equitable remedy such as an injunction. Remember that equitable remedies are awarded only if the court finds that the remedies at law (primarily money damages) are inadequate to fully compensate the injured plaintiff.

In the *Allen* case, had the employees started a firm of their own using the warm head technique for screw production, then the employer might be able to recover any profits derived by the employees if it could trace the profits to the use of the technique.

Obviously, if the agent takes property of value from the principal and either destroys it or disposes of it so that tracing is impossible, then the agent is liable to the principal for the value of that taken.

DUTIES OF THE PRINCIPAL TO THE AGENT

Primarily, the duties of the principal to the agent are based upon the contractual understanding of the parties. Where there is no formal contract between the agent and the principal, or if there is a contract and it does not mention these duties, then the duties are based upon the prior relation of the parties, the customs of the particular type of business involved and common law.

The common law provides that in exchange for the fiduciary duties owed by the agent to the principal, the principal owes the following duties to the agent:

1. not to interfere with the work of the agent;
2. to keep reasonably accurate records indicating the amount due to the agent;
3. to indemnify the agent for liabilities properly incurred by the agent in the scope of the agency;
4. to pay the agent a reasonable amount for the performance of the work contemplated by the subject of the agency.

The following case illustrates the application of the common law principal of indemnification.

BROWER v. FENNER & BEANE
237 Ala. 632, 188 So. 240 (S. Ct. Ala., 1939)

KNIGHT, Justice

Winnowed of all immaterial and irrelevant matter, the evidence shows: That the defendant in February, 1929, owned 355 shares of the capital stock of the Insurance Securities Company, Inc., represented by a single certificate numbered 6205—; that he desired to sell 300 shares of this stock, and to that end, on February 15, 1929, he delivered said certificate to the Birmingham office of the plaintiffs, with directions that 300 shares thereof be sold; that pursuant to defendant's said instructions, 300 shares of said stock were, in fact, sold on the

New York Curb Exchange on February 15, 1929, at the price of $32 per share, or a total of $9,600, and that, after deducting, their commissions and taxes, the plaintiffs, on February 19, 1929, paid to the defendant the residue of the sale price of said 300 shares, amounting to $9,553.80.

Subsequent to the sale of said 300 shares of stock, that is to say, on March 8, 1929, a dividend of 35 cents per share was declared on said stock to the stockholders of record as of March 8, 1929. This dividend was actually paid on April 1, 1929.

The evidence further shows, without conflict, that although Brower had sold and delivered, through the plaintiffs, the 300 shares of stock prior to March 8, 1929, the said shares had not been on that date actually transferred on the books of the company to the purchasers of the same. So that, on said date, the 300 shares of stock, along with the other 55 shares, appeared on the books of the company as still belonging to the defendant, although, as a matter of fact, 200 shares of said stock had been sold to Arthur Lipper and 100 shares had been sold to R. B. Logan, and said purchasers were on the day the dividends were declared the legal and equitable owners of the 300 shares of stock, and the defendant had no real interest in the same. . . .

On the books of the company, the said Brower appeared as the sole owner of the said stock. In distributing the dividend, the Insurance Securities Company, Inc., paid to said Brower the entire dividend declared on said 355 shares. . . .

The brokers, plaintiffs, paid to the said purchasers of the 300 shares the amount of the dividend declared on their stock, to-wit, $124.25, and also remitted to Brower $19.25, representing the dividend on 55 shares of said stock still owned by the defendant:

Demand was made on defendant by the plaintiffs for the payment to them of the dividend on the 300 shares of stock paid by the Insurance Securities Company, Inc., and retained by him, . . .

Brower refused to pay the plaintiffs the said dividend of $124.25 so paid to him by the Insurance Securities Company, Inc., . . .

This suit is to enforce the payment of the said $124.25, and the interest thereon.

The only question of merit presented by this appeal is: Under the undisputed evidence, are plaintiffs, as a matter of law, entitled to recover of the defendant the amount of the dividend, $124.25, which the Insurance Securities Company, Inc., has paid to the defendant under the assumption that he was still the owner of said stock, and which these plaintiffs had made good to the said Lipper and Logan, the purchasers?

We excerpt the following statement from brief of counsel for appellant: " . . . we submit that the facts in this case show beyond peradventure . . . that the appellees were, at best, merely volunteers, who may have (or may not have) paid the claim of the transferees of appellant's stock, without any legal compulsion so to do, and as a result thereof are not only not entitled to recover of the appellant as for money had and received, but, by such payment, have extinguished any obligation which may have been due by the appellant to the transferees of such stock."

We cannot agree with counsel for appellant that in paying to the purchasers of the defendant's 300 shares of stock the dividend declared thereon by the company on March 8, 1929, the plaintiffs were, "at best, merely volunteers, and as such have no right to reimbursement of the amount so paid out by them."

These purchasers, as a matter of law, were entitled to the dividends as against the defendant.

These plaintiffs were the brokers, and, therefore, the agents of defendant to whom the latter had intrusted the sale of certain of its stock upon the New York Curb Exchange, and this appointment, of course, carried with it the authority, and imposed the duty, of doing all acts necessary, or customary, to complete the transaction intrusted to them as such brokers and agents.

"As a general rule, where an agent is employed or directed by another to do an act in his behalf, the law implies a promise of indemnity of the principal for damages resulting to an agent proximately from the execution of the agency, and of reimbursement for necessary expenses advanced or incurred by the agent in order to consummate that which he is directed to do."

"It is another general proposition, in respect to the relation between principal and agent, that a request to undertake an agency or employment, the proper execution of which does or may involve the loss or expenditure of money on the part of the agent, operates as an implied request on the part of the principal, but also as a promise to repay it or reimburse the agent. So that the employment of a broker to sell property for future delivery implies not only an undertaking to indemnify the broker in respect to the execution of his agency, but likewise implies a promise on the part of the principal to repay or reimburse him for such losses or expenditures as may become necessary or may result from the performance of his agency." *Bibb* v. *Allen,* 149 U.S. 481, 13 S.Ct. 950, 956. ...

Under the facts in this case, and the law applicable thereto, the plaintiffs, in paying the dividends in question, were not mere volunteers and are not precluded from recovery in this action upon that theory. The defendant has shown no legal right whatsoever to retain the dividends paid to him by the Insurance Securities Company, Inc., while on the contrary, upon all legal and equitable principles, applicable to the undisputed evidence in this case, the plaintiffs were entitled to recover of the defendant the amount paid by them, as dividends, to the purchasers of said stock, the amount being $124.25, and upon this amount plaintiffs were entitled to interest. ...

Under the undisputed evidence in this case, the plaintiffs were entitled to recover, ...

It follows that the judgment of the court below is due to be affirmed. It is so ordered.

Affirmed.

◆◆◆

Case Question

1. Draw a diagram in which you illustrate who was the principal, the agent and the third party in the above case.

CAPACITY

Legal capacity as we use the term here refers to the legal qualification of one to contract. Most states have statutes defining this legal capacity. Generally, they state that minors, persons declared insane or those deprived of their civil rights (those in prison for a felony or aliens) lack this capacity. The common law of some states may further provide that if one is so under the influence of drugs or alcohol that he could not understand or appreciate the legal effect of his acts then such a person lacks the legal capacity to accomplish the act.

In an agency relationship, it is most important that the principal have the legal capacity to act. If the principal has the capacity to give a legally operative consent, then an agent may be appointed by the principal to conduct all of those transactions which the principal could conduct if he were present.[6] This is so even if the agent lacks capacity to act for himself unless the agent is so drunk or similarly incapacitated that a third party would see that the agent did not know what he was doing. For example, if a state declares that those under eighteen years of age lack capacity to contract, a principal of legal age may appoint a seventeen year old agent to act on his behalf and will be bound by contracts made for the principal by the agent. Similarly, when the principal lacks capacity he cannot appoint one who, by himself, would have the capacity. When the capacity of the principal is removed, an agent who acts for the principal also lacks capacity.

HUSBAND AND WIFE AS PRINCIPAL AND AGENT

Closely related to the discussion on capacity are the issues of when a husband and wife may act as agents for one another. At common law, a wife was denied the capacity to contract. Today this is not so but the law nevertheless does treat the contracts between husband and wife as well as those by a husband and wife for the benefit of the marriage with a third person as special. Neither the husband nor the wife has the power to contractually bind the other by virtue of the marriage relation alone.[7] However, the relation is such that circumstances which would not create an agency relationship between strangers might create an agency relationship between husband and wife. For example, consider this illustration from the *Restatement:*[8]

> P tells A, his wife, that she can open accounts for household supplies with certain designated local stores but with no others. A opens accounts in P's name with such stores and also with others; the latter accounts not being revealed to P. Modest bills for such supplies are incurred. Each month P gives A the money to pay the household bills, making no inquiries as to the creditors. At the end of six months P discovers the facts and refuses to pay the current bills of the undesignated stores. It may be found that A had apparent authority to incur such indebtedness on P's account.

In this case, the marriage relationship does create apparent authority (this concept of apparent authority is discussed in the next chapter) which would contractually bind the husband. Without additional facts, if P and A were strangers P would not be liable.

Except in the case of "necessaries" (needed food, clothing and shelter), a contract signed by one spouse does not bind the other unless there are additional circumstances indicating that one is acting on behalf of the other. Where one spouse contracts with regard to jointly owned property, then this is usually sufficient to bind the other party. Also, where one receives a benefit from jointly owned property, the recipient owns one half of that received and holds the other half in trust as an agent for the other. The following case highlights this principle.

COOPER v. COOPER
284 S.W. 2d 617 (S.Ct. of Arkansas, 1955)

(Author's note: An "estate by the entirety" is a legal form of joint ownership in which a husband and wife each have an equal right to possess all of the property owned and, upon the death of either spouse, the remaining partner becomes owner of the entire property).

◆◆◆

ROBINSON, Justice

The principal issues here are the validity of a divorce granted by a court in the State of Nevada, and the wife's interest in funds received on a fire insurance policy for the loss of a house owned as an estate by the entirety. Appellant and appellee were married on August 29, 1950, in Columbia County, Arkansas, where they had lived all their lives. A son was born in January, 1952. On May 24, 1951, they purchased two acres of land as an estate by the entirety and built a house on the property. The house was insured for $2,500 against fire; later it burned and the loss was settled for $2,250 which was paid to appellant J. W. Cooper.

A short time later, he departed for the State of Nevada where it appears that he ... filed suit for divorce. Dorothy was not notified, and he obtained a decree of divorce on March 26, 1953. Two days after this divorce was granted he returned to Arkansas and immediately married another person.

Appellee, Dorothy Cooper, then filed this suit in which she ... asks for maintenance for herself and support for the child. She further asks that appellant be required to account to her for one-half of the proceeds from the insurance policy, ... Cooper answered, alleging that he had been granted a valid divorce in the State of Nevada. Dorothy replied, denying the validity of the Nevada divorce and stating that it was invalid because proper service was not obtained and further alleging that the Nevada court did not have jurisdiction to grant a divorce because the plaintiff, Cooper, was not domiciled there.

The Chancellor made a finding that the Nevada court was without jurisdiction to grant a divorce to Cooper, and ordered appellant to pay $12.50 a week for support of his child. The court also rendered a judgment against appellant for one-half of the proceeds of the insurance policy. ...

Next is the question of the ownership of the proceeds of a policy of fire insurance. The house owned by the parties was destroyed by fire and Cooper collected and kept the insurance money. He had taken out the policy of insurance in his own name, but in doing so he was acting as agent for his wife as well as for himself.

The husband is not an agent for the wife solely by reason of the marital relationship. "But slight evidence of actual authority is sufficient proof of the agency of the husband for the wife in matters of domestic nature." ...

And, it is said in *Restatement of Agency,* § 22: "Neither husband nor wife by virtue of the relationship has power to act as agent for the other. The relationship is of such a nature, however, that circumstances which in the case of strangers would not indicate the creation of authority or apparent authority may indicate it in the case of husband or wife." In the case at bar, the husband secured a policy of fire insurance in his name only on property which is an estate by the entirety. In these circumstances, the fact that the husband was acting as agent for his wife in addition to acting for himself is established if any reasonable inference to be deduced from the evidence leads to that conclusion.

In the case at bar, the circumstantial evidence proves that at the time Cooper obtained the policy of insurance not only was he acting for himself but he was also acting as an agent for his wife. . . .

As evidence of the fact that Cooper was acting as agent for his wife, she testified that she knew he had taken out the fire insurance policy, but she did not know that he had taken it out in his name only. She was present in the insurance company office, along with Cooper, when the settlement was agreed on, but she was not present when the check was delivered to him. In fact, she did not know that he had received the check. . . .

Cooper testified that the insurance company paid him $2,750. (This figure included $500 for personal property.) He further said: "I told her, I says, "Well, I have the money now; I might as well get started paying on bills; we won't have any money, as I want to pay the bills." "And that's what I did." On direct examination he was asked this question: "How much did you pay out of that on indebtedness you and Dorothy already owed?" Cooper then testified as to a long list of items which he claims that both owed and which he paid from the insurance money. He also said that he paid an old account of Dorothy's on which he personally was not liable at all. From the above testimony, it can be inferred that Cooper was acting as agent for his wife when he secured the policy of fire insurance. . . .

In the case at bar the evidence is convincing that Mrs. Cooper did not know that her husband had collected the insurance money, although there is some evidence to the contrary. Cooper held his wife's interest in the funds as trustee, and the court correctly found that he was indebted to Mrs. Cooper for one-half of the amount of the insurance he had collected on the house, . . .

The decree is affirmed.

Case Questions

1. What single fact caused the court to say that the husband was the agent of the wife?
2. The cause of action by the wife against the husband was based upon the breach of what type of duty?

REVIEW PROBLEMS

1. M started a small manufacturing firm in Ohio to produce and market a new form of skin protection which was formed by mixing suntan lotion with a bug repellant and perfume. The advantages of using such a solution seemed so

obvious to M that he was sure the firm would make a profit. He made his own suntan lotion from a combination of coconut oils and iodine and combined this with spruce wood sap and alcohol with a pinch of rose bud fragrance thrown in. M hired P to be chief production engineer and as part of the employment contract P agreed in writing that he would not:

> ... for a period of five years after leaving M's employment for any reason whatsoever in an area east of the Mississippi River engage in or consult with any person or firm in or about to be engaged in the manufacture of suntan lotions or bug repellants or other skin protection lotions.

M also hired S, a salesperson, to develop the market for the product in Illinois, Ohio, and surrounding states. S was to drive his own car, pay for his own gas and determine his own route. Additionally, M hired an office staff which consisted of a secretary, G, a receptionist, R, and an office manager, O.

The firm was an overnight success and sales and profits shot skyward. The firm even began selling throughout the midwest. The idea seemed so simple M never did apply for a patent. All of the employees wondered why no one had ever tried it before. Unknown to M, the secretary he hired was a brilliant mathematician whose hobby was theoretical chemistry. She immediately discerned that it would take no great effort to make her own combination suntan-bug repellant-perfume lotion so she quit the firm taking with her the production manager, P. They set up their firm in Kentucky, but had a disagreement and P went to Florida to set up a firm of his own while G continued to develop her firm.

Neither G nor P used the same identical ingredients as M but used chemicals which could be substituted for M's substances. They did use the same proportions of materials which P and M had calculated as being a uniquely stable combination of ingredients. P had informed G of this combination.

Assume that you are M and you wish to do everything possible to protect your business. Write a short essay in which you explain how the legal arguments would be developed. First list the legal principles or rules you learned from this chapter which you believe might help your case. Next write down a complete and precise definition of these rules. Following the definition of the rules, apply the definition to the factual pattern above by integrating the facts of the case with the statement of the rule. Be sure to list the "relevant facts"; that is, list those facts which lead you to believe that the principle should be applied. If there is a question in your mind about whether or not the principle would be applied, then state the facts of the case which cause you to question the rule's applicability. Perhaps there are some facts missing which would cause you to definitely conclude that the principle is applicable. State these facts and how they would influence your decision.

Finally, based upon your conclusions as to the applicability of the rules discussed in this chapter, you should conclude whether or not M can legally restrain P and G from operating their respective businesses.

2. In addition to the above facts in problem 1, assume that one day M could not get away from work to pick up an important package at the post office so he asked a neighbor, N, to do so and N agreed. Was an agency formed between M and N?

3. The office manager in the above factual pattern, O, was a very generous type and was always looking out for and protecting the interests of the office staff.

O paid for a new typewriter for M's business out of his own pocket when the firm was short of cash. Also, O used his own money to pay for a color TV for employees to watch on their coffee and lunch breaks. Could M be required to reimburse O for these expenditures?

In answering this question, construct your answer in the same way you answered question 1. First state and then define the legal principle which you believe will control this case. Then integrate the facts with the principle and finally state your conclusion.

ENDNOTES

1. Vol.'s 1 & 2, Am. L. Inst., *The Restatement of Agency*, 2d (1958).
2. W.A. Seavey, *Law of Agency*, 1964.
3. *Id.*, at 3.
4. *Black's Law Dictionary*, Rev. *4th ed.*, 753 (1957).
5. Seavey, *Supra*, note 2 at 243.
6. *Restatement, supra*, note 1 at 91.
7. *Id.*, at 94.
8. *Id.*, at 95.

CONTRACTUAL LIABILITY OF PRINCIPALS AND AGENTS TO THIRD PARTIES

In Chapter 3 the first two elements of the agency definition were presented. They were 1) the relationship is a fiduciary one and 2) it is based upon consent. The remainder of the agency definition presented in Chapter 3 stated that the relationship is one in which one person, the agent, shall act on behalf of the principal and subject to his control.

All corporations, partnerships, governmental units and some individuals employ others to act on their behalf and subject to their control. The last part of the definition of agency implies that agents are utilized primarily to act for the principal in dealings with persons who are strangers to the agency relationship. These strangers are called "third parties". Indeed, the real heart of agency law is that body of legal principles which create legal duties that run from the principal to third parties because of the promises, representations or acts of the agent. The circumstances in which the agent can create legal duties, that is, legally bind the principal to third parties, are the subjects of this and the following chapter.

Before proceeding with an analysis of these circumstances it would be helpful for the reader to keep in mind a basic distinction between the two central branches of the civil law. Civil duties (as opposed to criminal duties) are imposed primarily by the common law of *torts* and *contracts.*

Tort liability arises because of injury to one's person, property, reputation or some other legally protected interest. The common torts such as negligence, battery, defamation, etc., are defined in the next chapter and the methods the law uses to impute the tort liability of the agent to the principal when the agent tortiously injures a third party are also explained there. Generally speaking, these methods vary depending upon the degree of control exercised by the principal over the agent.

Contract duties or liabilities arise because one breaches a promise or set of promises made to another party. These promises may be stated, either in writing or orally; that is, *expressed.* Or they may be imposed on the agent or principal because of the acts of the principal or agent. These promises are *implied* by the law. Most of the circumstances in which principals will be liable to third parties based upon a breach of either expressed or implied promises made by the agent are presented in this chapter.

The reader should be cautioned, however, that "compartmentalizing" the law into tort liability and contract liability for purposes of presenting this agency material is not without drawbacks. Simply stated, some factual patterns just do not neatly fit into either category. Hence, if an agent (A) is given money by a third party (T/P) for delivery to the principal (P) and A absconds with it, the act of absconding may be both a breach of contract to the T/P (if the P fails to deliver the goods the money was intended to pay for) as well as a tort (a conversion of T/P's money). Nevertheless, we believe the reader will be helped in understanding the agency material if a factual pattern is first read for an understanding of the basic violation of duty (either contract or tort) and then read for an understanding of the court's reasoning.

If this method of analysis is used the reader will find that cases involving a breach of promise are usually resolved by employing legal principles which define *authority*; and that cases involving torts are resolved by employing legal principles which define the right of the principal to *control* the physical acts of the agent.

CONTRACTUAL LIABILITY OF PRINCIPALS TO THIRD PARTIES

Courts will impose liability upon a principal for the promises or representations made by an agent to a third party when the court finds that the principal authorized the agent to make the promise or representation.

Courts have defined two broad types of authority: actual authority — either express or implied; and, circumstantial authority — either apparent or inherent. The doctrines of estoppel and ratification, discussed below, achieve the same result as the application of principles of authority but are not usually considered to be types of authority.

ACTUAL AUTHORITY — EXPRESS OR IMPLIED

Expressed authority is defined as that authority which the principal gives either in writing or by spoken word to the agent when instructing the agent when and how to act on his behalf. Expressed authority may take the form of a formal document such as a Power of Attorney which is a sworn statement in writing that another is to act for and in the place of the principal, or it may be manifested in less formal ways such as a board of directors resolution or a mere statement in an employment contract that the employee (agent) is to "sell the goods of the employer."

In a commercial transaction of any complexity at all, however, it is impossible for the principal to express all of the kinds of authority that may be needed by the agent to complete the transaction. Therefore, the law recognizes "implied" authority which is that authority which is reasonably necessary to accomplish the act for which the express authority was given. Implied authority is found by examining the facts of the particular case, defining the expressed authority and then asking whether or not a reasonable person familiar with the customs and ways of dealings of agents in the particular line of business could believe that the agent had the authority to act. The key difference between implied authority and the kinds of circumstantial authority described below is that the implied authority flows from the grant of expressed authority and must be reasonably necessary to accomplish the purpose of the expressed authority. If there is not expressed authority, there can be no implied authority; yet, there may be circumstantial authority.

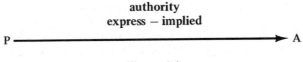

authority
express — implied

P ⟶ A

Figure 4-1

Since implied authority is primarily authority by necessity it also includes the authority to act in an emergency to protect the interests of the principal when no express authority was given. Of course if there is time to communicate with the principal, the agent must do so. But if the agent can not communicate by any reasonable means and the circumstances appear to call for action in order to prevent loss for the principal then the agent has the authority to act as necessary. For example, a chauffeur employed only "to drive" may be authorized to have repairs made to the limousine when it breaks down on the road and the principal can not be contracted. He may have this authority even though it was contrary to the expressed authority so long as there is a reasonable probability of further loss to the principal.[1]

Most of the cases in the remaining material on agency will involve three parties; the principal, agent and the third party. It is essential to understand at the outset who is the plaintiff and who is the defendant and who committed the breach of duty alleged. So, when analyzing the remainder of the textual material on agency and the appellate cases, the reader may find it helpful to draw a diagram to clarify the identity of the parties and the rules being discussed. For example, the first case presented could be diagrammed as shown in Figure 4-2.

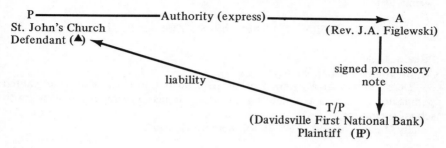

Figure 4-2

The two cases that follow present factual patterns involving, first, express authority and then implied authority. The first case illustrates that even though the agent is expressly authorized to contract, the third party is held to a certain standard of reasonableness. There is no absolute right to rely on the express authority of the principle.

DAVIDSVILLE FIRST NATIONAL BANK v.
ST. JOHN'S CHURCH
296 Pa. 467 (1929)

(Author's note: The trial court found for the plaintiff and defendant appeals.)

♦♦♦

Opinion By Mr. Justice Walling.

The defendant, St. John's Church, Windber, Pa., is an unincorporated Roman Catholic Church organization, located in Somerset County, of which Rev. J. A.

Figlewski was pastor or priest, and as such gave the plaintiff bank a note as follows:

"2500.00/100 Davidsville, Pa., Nov. 30, 1925.

"On demand after date, we or either of us promise to pay to the order of THE FIRST NATIONAL BANK, DAVIDSVILLE, Pa., at the FIRST NATIONAL BANK, DAVIDSVILLE, Pa., Two thousand five hundred and no/100 — dollars without defalcation, value received. . . .
"WITNESS OUR HANDS AND SEALS
   "St. John's Church, Windber, Pa. (Seal)."
   "Rev. J. A. Figlewski, Pastor (Seal)." . . .

In the summer of 1923, the church membership, at a properly convened meeting, decided to repair their school building and erect a convent and to secure a loan of $15,000 for that purpose. Under the rule of the church a parish like the defendant could not incur an indebtedness exceeding $500 without the consent of the bishop of the diocese. Hence, the pastor sought and obtained a permit, as follows:

"CHANCERY 1211 Thirteenth St., Altoona, Pa., July 7-23

"Rev. J. Figlewski:
   "St. John's Church, Windber.
   "Dear Father: At a meeting of the Diocesian Consultors you were granted permission to contract a debt of $15,000 for masonry repairs & changes to school & convent.
   "By Order of the Rt. Rev. Bishop Bernard Conlay

"Sec'y Consultors."

Some two years and four months after the permit was issued the pastor presented it to the plaintiff and obtained thereon a loan of $2,500, for which he gave the note in suit. There was oral testimony that he told the bank the permit was not nearly exhausted. So far as appears, he made no representations to the bank as to the action taken by the congregation. The evidence for the defendant was that the church had obtained loans to the amount of the $15,000 from two local banks shortly after the date of the permit; with which, and some $10,000 additional raised by the congregation, the specific improvements were made during 1923 and 1924. The loan in suit was the only one made by the pastor from plaintiff for defendant, although he was known to the bank and had previously done business with it. The proof tends to show that soon after making the loan in suit the pastor absconded with the $2,500. From the church funds the succeeding pastor paid the interest on this note for two years, but testified that he did so in ignorance of the true situation and without the knowledge or approval of the lay members. . . .

By law the bishop cannot create an indebtedness without the consent of the congregation nor under the canons of the church can it incur an indebtedness exceeding $500 without his permit. Each is a check upon the other.

The trial court erred in treating the mere permit and assurance of the pastor that it was not exhausted as warranting the loan. The age of the permit, nearly two and a half years, was such as to require inquiry of the congregation. The plaintiff bank and the church were close neighbors and slight inquiry by the former would doubtless have disclosed the fact that the improvements stated in the permit had been completed and paid for, inter alia, by funds secured from other banks, to the full amount of the permit and that the congregation had refused to request a further permit. . . .

One who gives credit to a pastor on the faith of an old permit without inquiry from the congregation does so at his peril. Otherwise a pastor might bankrupt the church for his own purposes despite the limit in the permit. Happily, it is rare that a priest or pastor betrays his church. That the pastor had possession of the old permit proved nothing as to its vitality. The money having been secured from different banks, there was nothing strange in his retention of the permit, especially as it was his warrant for executing the notes. That it had been fully exhausted shortly after its date, quite clearly appeared by the evidence for the defense, yet the proof as to that, being oral, was probably for the jury.

Here the agency of the pastor was to borrow $15,000 for the church; when that was done and obligations given therefore, the permit was exhausted and the agency terminated. . . . "A person dealing with an agent must not act negligently, but must use reasonable diligence to ascertain whether the agent acts within the scope of his power. He is not authorized under any circumstances blindly to trust the agent's statements as to the extent of his powers:" 21 R.C.L., page 853. If this loan was valid, one for the entire $15,000 would have been. So the bishop's express limit and the like limit of the congregation would go for nought.

Had the church received the $2,500 the case would present a different aspect . . . , but there is no evidence or even averment that it received the money or any part of it, and the burden as to that was upon the plaintiff.

True, the new pastor receiving bills for interest on the note paid them for two years, supposing, as he testified, that it was a bona fide note of the church; but if done in ignorance, that would not constitute a ratification on the part of the church. In any event the burden of showing ratification was upon the plaintiff and the priest could not ratify the note without authority from the lay members. A principal can ratify the unauthorized act of an agent only when he has knowledge thereof. This may be a hard case for the bank; if so, it results from its overconfidence in the pastor, for which neither the bishop nor the congregation was blamable. . . .

The judgment is reversed. . . .

◆◆◆

Case Questions

1. St. John's Church was an unincorporated association. Under what circumstances could it be sued in its own name?
2. In this case there was a contract signed between the old pastor, Figlewski, and the bank for the purported benefit of the church. The legal issue may be stated in broad terms thusly: Did the signing of the contract by the pastor legally bind the church? In a few concise sentences state why or why not?

3. A third party who does business with an agent has a duty to ascertain the authority of the agent. How do you define this duty?

COBLENTZ v. RISKIN
74 Nev. 53, 322 P. 2d 905 (S. Ct. Nev., 1958)

MERRILL, Justice

The sole question upon this appeal is whether the record supports the determination of the trial court (sitting without jury) that the acts of the employee in receiving the merchandise and in executing the consignment agreement were on behalf of the defendants and were authorized by them. We have concluded that the record provides such support and that judgment should be affirmed.

Appellants are owners of the Thunderbird Jewel Shop in Clark County, Nevada. Respondent Riskin is a diamond broker and wholesale jeweler of Los Angeles, California. In August, 1955 appellants employed Hyman Davidson for services in connection with their store. In January, 1956 Davidson entered into a consignment agreement with Riskin pursuant to which he received, for purposes of retail sale, two expensive items of jewelry. In his dealings with Riskin, Davidson represented himself as manager of the jewel shop with full authority to receive merchandise on consignment. Riskin did not check these representations with appellants but did check with others in the jewelry trade and satisfied himself as to Davidson's authority. The jewelry pieces were reconsigned by Davidson without Riskin's approval or consent. The person to whom they were reconsigned has disappeared. Riskin demanded of appellants the return of the jewelry or its agreed value pursuant to the terms of the agreement. Upon failure of appellants to comply with his demand this action was brought. Judgment in favor of Riskin was given in the sum of $16,300.

Appellants contend that there is no evidence from which the trial court could have found the essentials of either actual or apparent authority to exist. . . .

In support of its conclusion of authority the court found, "That during the month of August, 1955 the defendants * * * engaged and employed one Hyman Davidson * * * as manager of the Thunderbird Jewel Shop * * * . That the said Hyman Davidson was and acted as manager of the said Thunderbird Jewel Shop at all times between August, 1955 and the beginning of March, 1956 on behalf of, for the account of and for the benefit of the said defendants and each of them. That the said Hyman Davidson, during the period aforesaid, with the knowledge, consent and approval of the defendants, and each of them, held himself out to the jewelry trade and to persons dealing with the said Thunderbird Jewel Shop as the manager of the said Thunderbird Jewel Shop, with full authority to receive merchandise on behalf of the said Thunderbird Jewel Shop on memorandum and/or consignment."

Although in many respects the evidence is in dispute the record unquestionably provides support for this finding.

Riskin testified that it was the custom in the jewelry trade to take expensive pieces of jewelry on consignment rather than by purchase at wholesale. This testimony is compellingly supported by reason when the nature of consignment transactions and the benefit to retail merchants of this commercial practice are considered. By consignment retail merchants are not financially committed to the purchase of expensive items until they have themselves resold the items. Until resale their only financial commitment is that of safekeeping. Thus there is substantial benefit to be realized at the minimum of financial commitment. It can hardly be questioned that the engaging in consignment transactions would be regarded by those in the jewelry trade as a customary, proper and necessary function of store management.

Davidson testified positively that he had been employed as manager of the store with instructions to run the store as he saw fit; ...

Actual authority includes ... implied authority ... Implied authority is that which the agent reasonably believes himself to possess as a result of representations by the principal or of acts of the agent permitted by the principal over a course of time in which the principal has acquiesced. ... (or) that which is reasonably necessary, proper and usual to carry into effect the main authority granted. ...

The trial court has found that Davidson was employed to serve as manager and that he did so serve. The evidence we have recited presents a clear case of ... implied authority. ... We conclude that the trial court's determination of actual authority is supported by the record and that appellants are bound by Davidson's actions in their behalf in committing them to the consignment agreement with Riskin.

Affirmed.

◆◆◆

Case Questions

1. In your own words define "implied authority."
2. If you hire an agent and instruct him or her to "manage" your business, what other limitations, if any, are placed upon his or her authority to act for you? To help answer this question some legal scholars and courts recognize a distinction between general and special agents. A general agent is one who is employed as a permanent employee to conduct a series of transactions. A general manager is such an agent and if a person has such a title, third parties can reasonably rely upon the fact that such person has the authority to act which most general managers in that business possess. In the above case, note that an important element of proof for the plaintiff was the fact that much of the business between jewel owners and jewel sellers or retailers was done on a consignment basis.

   A special agent is one employed to conduct a specific task. Usually there is authority to conduct only one transaction. If the circumstances reveal to a third party that an employee is a special agent, the third party should inquire about the precise nature of the authority possessed. With regard to the *Davidsville* case, the pastor might well be labeled a special agent. Why?

CIRCUMSTANTIAL AUTHORITY — APPARENT AUTHORITY, ESTOPPEL AND INHERENT AUTHORITY

Circumstantial authority is authority which courts recognize and impose on an agency relationship even though there is no express or implied authority. Courts do this because the circumstances of the third party's dealing with the agent could reasonably lead a third party to believe that the agent was authorized. A key difference between actual and circumstantial authority is that the actual authority is defined by asking what measure of authority was really given to the agent by the principal, while circumstantial authority is defined by asking what measure of authority could a third party reasonably believe the agent to have under the circumstances.

Circumstantial authority is often divided into several categories or types. The most comprehensive type of circumstantial authority is called apparent authority. The *Restatement* defines apparent authority as follows:

> Apparent authority is the power to affect the legal relations of another person by transactions with third parties, professedly as agent for the other, arising from and in accordance with the others manifestations to such third party.[2]

Generally, there are two factual elements which a court must find in order to conclude that the agent was apparently authorized. Firstly, it must find that the *principal*, referred to in the definition above as the "other" person, not the agent, created some of the circumstances leading the third party to believe the agent was authorized, and secondly that the third party reasonably relied upon these circumstances. It makes no difference if the principal has expressly forbidden the agent to act, or has otherwise secretly placed restrictions upon the agent's authority. So long as the court or jury can find the two basic factual elements mentioned above, they most probably will find that the agent's promise or conduct was apparently authorized.

The concept of apparent authority was created to protect the reasonable expectations of those in commerce who do business with agents. It is one of the more dynamic principles in the law of agency and today occupies a central, almost dominating position in the agency field.[3] The concept is growing and changing not only a principal's liability for an agent's contracts but, just as important, it is imposing new types of liability on the principal for the agent's tortious conduct. This will be more fully explained in the next chapter.

The circumstances in which the courts will impose apparent authority on the agent when none existed in fact are very similar to those circumstances in which some courts will invoke the doctrine of estoppel. Estoppel is a well established legal principle created from the law of equity. In general terms it means that one's own act or failure to act when a reasonable person would have, will stop or close his mouth to plead the truth.[4]

The *Restatement* provides a more elaborate definition:

1. A person who is not otherwise liable as a party to a transaction purported to be done on his account, is nevertheless subject to liability to persons who have changed their positions because of their belief that the transaction was entered into by or for him, if

a) he intentionally or carelessly caused such belief, or

b) knowing of such belief and that others might change their positions because of it, he did not take reasonable steps to notify them of the facts. . . .

3. Change of position, as the phrase is used in the restatement, indicates the payment of money, expenditure of labor, suffering a loss or subjection to legal liability.[5]

There is some disagreement as to whether or not "estoppel" is a distinctly separate legal doctrine in the law of agency. Some courts believe that estoppel forms the real basis for apparent authority and therefore seem to use apparent authority in circumstances which would support the use of an estoppel argument (see the *Southwestern Portland Cement* case). Other authorities such as the *Restatement* and Professor Warren Seavey assert that estoppel is more narrowly defined than apparent authority.[6] The *Restatement*, for example, admits that in most circumstances in which apparent authority exists, estoppel may also exist.[7] However, estoppel is appropriately argued when there have been: 1) circumstances created by the principal which 2) cause a third party to reasonably believe the agent has authority (these two elements are identical to the elements for apparent authority) and 3) the third party has changed his position. Thus estoppel is more narrow than apparent authority because it requires an additional element of proof — change in position.

Another difference that some perceive between apparent authority and estoppel is that estoppel may not be pleaded by the principal as the basis for a cause of action against a third party but apparent authority may be. That is, if an agent does not have the express authority to contract with a third party, but does so anyway, and the third party could reasonably believe the agent was authorized to contract by relying on circumstances created by the principal, then most courts would allow the principal to sue the third party upon a theory of apparent authority. Most courts would not apply the doctrine of estoppel to either the principal or the third party in this case.

Perhaps an example of the different circumstances in which courts would usually apply the doctrines of apparent authority and estoppel will help in understanding the need for and use of the two principles.

Assume that P, by letter, authorizes A to sell his real property. The letter is given to A who shows it to T/P who then contracts with A for the purchase of P's real property. Assume that P telephones A and revokes the authority in the letter just before A signs the contract with T/P. Nevertheless, A signs the contract. The contract was not expressly authorized because P did revoke A's authority by telephone; therefore, there could be no implied authority to contract either. However, P would be liable to T/P based upon apparent authority. Without changing his position, T/P could sue P if P refused to abide by the contractual provisions. Even though P revoked the actual authority, P could also hold T/P liable if T/P breached the contract.[8] Estoppel would not be properly applied in this case because T/P suffered no change of position or out of pocket loss.

Now consider the following example: assume A, in the presence of P, states to T/P that he, A, is authorized by P to sell P's painting. P heard this statement of A and said nothing. A contracts with T/P for the sale of P's painting and T/P thereby refrains from buying another painting he had an opportunity to buy. In this example, if T/P sued P for breach of contract, a court most probably would estopp (not allow) P to defend on the basis of the lack of authority. In essence, the court would be reasoning that because P had a duty to speak up if A lacked authority, but did not do so, the court will not permit him to speak now. In this example, A was not actually authorized to sell the painting. Further, the use of apparent authority here would be a weak argument because of the lack of positive acts of P clothing A with authority to act. Yet, it appears that T/P has changed his position by refraining from buying another printing, which is presumably not available now, so that it would be unfair to allow P to deny he authorized the sale.

We have selected two appellate cases to illustrate the application of the principles of apparent authority and estoppel. The first case presents the classic outlines of the use of apparent authority. In this case make a note especially of the facts which make it appear to the third party that the principal has authorized the agent to buy the food for it when, in reality, the agent was not to buy food for the principal but for itself.

In the second case, the facts are more similar to our estoppel example. The circumstances creating the authority of the agent are vague and there was a substantial change of position by the third party. Note that in this case, the court states that apparent authority is really based upon estoppel. While the authors of the *Restatement* would probably dispute this assertion, it is nevertheless the view of many courts.

In summary, in any given factual pattern involving acts by the principal which reasonably lead a third party to believe the agent is authorized, it is sometimes difficult to predict whether or not a court will apply the principles of apparent authority or estoppel. So, we believe the best approach is to argue both existed.

HECKEL et al. v. CRANFORD COUNTRY CLUB
97 N.J. Law 538; 117 A. 607 (1922)

◆◆◆

KATZENBACH, J.

This action was instituted to recover the value of articles of food alleged to have been sold by the plaintiffs-respondents to the defendant-appellant. The plaintiffs were engaged in the meat and produce business in Bloomfield. The defendant was the Union County Country Club, subsequently known as the Cranford Golf Club, and later as the Echo Lake Country Club. The articles were purchased between August 1, 1918, and December 10, of the same year. They were ordered by one Roachman, who had been engaged about March 29, 1918, as manager of the club, and was known and is referred to in the testimony as the club manager or steward. Roachman was paid a salary of $200 a month, and also had the restaurant privilege of the club; that is, Roachman was to furnish the members with meals and refreshments to be supplied by him and for which they were to pay him, and the profit, if any, was to supplement his salary. Roachman was the steward during the entire period of the purchases from the plaintiffs. At the time of the first purchase, he introduced himself as the steward of the club, and as the person of whom the steward of the Baltursrol Club, which was located near the defendant's grounds, had spoken to the plaintiffs. The goods ordered by Roachman were charged by the plaintiffs to the club, delivered to the clubhouse, accompanied by charge slips addressed to the club, with each order delivered. Bills were sent by mail monthly by the plaintiffs, addressed to the club. There was also evidence given by the plaintiffs' bookkeeper that one or more checks of the club had been received and applied in part payment of the account. This was denied. One of the plaintiffs also testified that on one occasion he met the president of the club, and the president spoke to him of the money which the club owed his firm, and assured him that it would be paid. This was denied by the president, who said he merely told Mr. Heckel, the plaintiff who spoke to him, that the club would pay Roachman what it owed him. From these facts the plaintiffs contended that the club was responsible to them for the goods ordered by Roachman, and the defendant contended that Roachman was the plaintiffs' debtor, and no liability to pay the account attached to the club. There was no dispute as to the delivery of the goods or the correctness of the charges made therefor. The one question at issue was that of liability. The trial judge permitted the case to go to the jury, which rendered a verdict for the plaintiffs for the full amount of their claim. From the judgment entered upon the verdict the club has appealed.

The appellant contends that there was no evidence of Roachman's power to bind the club for the payment of the goods ordered by him, and in the absence of such evidence it was the duty of the trial court to grant either the defendant's motion for a nonsuit or for the direction of a verdict in its favor.

Mr. Justice Trenehard, in the case of *J. Wiss & Sons Co.* v. *H. G. Vogel Co.,* 86 N. J. Law, 618, 92 Atl. 360, stated the law with . . . clearness when he said:

"As between the principal and third persons the true limit of the agent's power to bind the principal is the apparent authority with which the agent is invested. The principal is bound by the acts of the agent within the apparent authority which he knowingly permits the agent to assume, or which he holds the agent out to the public as possessing. And the reason is that to permit the principal to dispute the authority of the agent in such cases would be to enable him to commit a fraud upon innocent persons. * * *

"The question in every such case is whether the principal has by his voluntary act placed the agent in such a situation that a person of ordinary prudence, conversant with business usages, and the nature of the particular business, is justified in presuming that such agent has authority to perform the particular act in question, and when the party relying upon such apparent authority presents evidence which would justify a finding in his favor, he is entitled to have the question submitted to the jury."

The difficulty always arises in the application of the law to the facts of the given case. In the present case, did the club place Roachman in such a situation that a person of ordinary prudence, conversant with business usages and the nature of the particular business, would be justified in presuming that Roachman had authority to order provisions for the club? Did the plaintiffs present such evidence of Roachman's apparent authority as to justify the trial court in submitting to the jury the question of his authority to bind the club? We think these two questions should be answered in the affirmative.

It was admitted that the club employed Roachman as manager or steward, and paid him a salary. It is a matter of common knowledge that one of the duties of a steward of a country club is to obtain the supplies necessary to serve the members of the club with meals and refreshments. While it is true that as between Roachman and the club, Roachman was to be responsible for the payment of the supplies ordered by him, yet by his employment as steward the club had apparently clothed Roachman with the powers usually appertaining to the position of steward, of which one was the purchase of supplies for a club. When, therefore, Roachman approached the plaintiffs, informed them of the position he held with the club, ordered provisions, which were charged to the club, delivered to the clubhouse, and bills therefore were mailed to the club monthly, and this course of dealing continued for approximately five months, without either repudiation of Roachman's authority or any intimation from the club that he was without authority to bind it, we feel that such evidence presented a question for the determination of the jury.

In addition to the evidence referred to, which was not disputed, there was also testimony, which was disputed, as to the receipt of the check or checks of the club which were applied to the account, and the president's statement to one of the plaintiffs that the club owed him money, but not to worry; that he would get it. If the check or checks received by the plaintiffs were the club's checks, the sending of them to the plaintiffs was a recognition or ratification of the agency of Roachman, as was also the statement of the president. The plaintiffs were also entitled to have this testimony submitted to a jury. . . .

The judgment was affirmed, with costs.

◆◆◆

Case Questions

1. Can you explain why the court in *Heckel* applied the principle of apparent authority to hold the principal liable when the court in the *Coblentz* case, earlier in the chapter, on facts very similar to those in *Heckel*, applied the principle of implied authority? This question indicates how the law can sometimes split hairs. Could the answer be that the agent in *Coblentz* was not forbidden to accept consignments but was given the authority to "manage." It seems Roachman was specifically forbidden to contract for his principal.
2. What could the principal have done in this case to protect itself from the type of liability which was the subject of this case?

SOUTHWESTERN PORTLAND CEMENT v. BEAVERS
82 N.M. 218, 478 P.2d 546 (S. Ct., New Mex., 1970)

McKENNA, Justice

Appellee Southwestern Portland Cement brought this suit to collect payment on an account in the amount of $1,647.00, plus costs and attorney fees, against appellants Beavers and Glasgow, doing business as Plains Sand and Gravel, and defendant Adams. Judgment was entered against all three . . . for the sum sued for, plus costs and attorney fees of $549.31. Only Beavers and Glasgow appealed.

In February of 1968, the appellants formed a partnership known as Plains Sand and Gravel to provide concrete for a construction project at Cannon Air Force Base. The general contractor for the project was Wilkerson-Webb. Defendant Adams had no proprietary interest in the partnership. In March, 1968, the partnership entered into an oral agreement with Adams to use his ready-mix concrete batching plant and delivery trucks to mix and deliver concrete to the project. The partnership made arrangements with appellee Southwestern to furnish bulk cement to Adams at his plant. The method of payment for the delivered concrete was for Wilkerson-Webb to issue their check payable jointly to Plains Sand and Gravel and to Southwestern.

On March 20, 1968, and again on April 30, 1968, Southwestern delivered cement to Adams' plant for the partnership account. Adams received these deliveries at his plant and signed truck tickets for the cement on behalf of Plains Sand and Gravel for the Cannon Air Force job. These two deliveries of cement were paid for by Wilkerson-Webb's joint check in the amount of $1,052.70.

On July 10, 13 and 16, Adams ordered cement from Southwestern telling it that the order was for Plains Sand and Gravel. Similarly, Adams received the three deliveries at his plant, signed truck tickets for receipt of the cement on behalf of Plains Sand and Gravel for the Cannon Air Force job.

It was established during trial that prior to the last three deliveries by Southwestern, Adams' equipment broke down and he was unable to deliver the concrete to the job site and Plains Sand and Gravel made other arrangements with another firm to deliver the concrete. However, the appellants did not inform Southwestern of this prior to the last three deliveries. After the last of the three deliveries, Southwestern contacted Wilkerson-Webb to "confirm" the amount of concrete usage on the job and to "reconfirm" the guarantee of payments. It was then informed that only a negligible amount of concrete was supplied by Plains Sand and Gravel for the job, and Wilkerson-Webb refused to issue a joint check for the delivered cement. Thereupon, Southwestern called one of the appellant partners who denied that Adams had authority to order the cement.

Southwestern then sued Beavers, Glasgow and Adams for the last three loads delivered. . . .

The findings of fact pertinent to this appeal are: . . .

"9. Plains Sand & Gravel authorized Adams to order cement from plaintiff for use on said project, and Adams ordered the cement which was delivered to him by plaintiff on March and April, 1968. Adams' authority to so order cement was not cancelled until after July, 1968. This course of dealing gave Adams apparent authority to place other orders for cement from plaintiff on behalf of Plains Sand & Gravel. * * * "

"11. On July 10 and 13, 1968, Adams ordered additional loads of bulk cement from plaintiff on the Plains Sands & Gravel account, without specific authority from Plains Sand & Gravel. * * * "

The court concluded:

"2. Plains Sand & Gravel as principal is estopped to deny the authority of Adams as its agent to order the cement involved in this action, having clothed Adams with apparent authority to order same, and plaintiff having acted on said apparent authority in good faith and to its detriment."

For reversal, the appellants argue that there was no substantial evidence to support the finding that Adams had apparent authority from the course of dealing to order the last three loads of cement and Southwestern was negligent by not inquiring into the scope of Adams' authority and this negligence precluded appellee from any recovery. ...

Obviously, the course of dealing was not lengthy, and was limited, in terms of time span and deliveries, but this must be viewed in light of the limited business relationship which was involved — it was for only one project at Cannon Air Force Base. It is equally obvious that the component acts in the course of dealing were identical and reflected a common pattern. ... Each of the deliveries made to Adams was for the account of Plains Sand & Gravel for use on the particular project in accordance with the pre-arranged procedure. Each delivery was made to the same location; each was receipted for by Adams for the partnership. If Southwestern had not been paid for the first two loads, it would have been warned or alerted — at least the law would so view it ... but having been paid for the first two loads by the very procedure agreed upon, Southwestern could reasonably construe this as ratification of the previous course of business. We cannot say that under these circumstances Southwestern acted in bad faith or without reasonable prudence in delivering the last three shipments. As between Southwestern and the partners, it is the latter's conduct which fails to meet the test of reasonable prudence, for not only did they have the responsibility for the relationship, they neglected to notify Southwestern that they had made different arrangements for delivery of the concrete when Adams' equipment broke down. If they had done this, Southwestern's delivery of the last three shipments would have been at its peril.

An agent's scope of authority embraces not only his actual authority but also that apparently delegated. A settled course of conduct does serve to create apparent authority in the agent binding upon the principal where the acts are not timely disavowed and a third party is thereby induced to rely on the ostensible authority of the agent and does so in good faith and with reasonable prudence. The doctrine is based upon an estoppel: the principal will not be permitted to establish that the agent's authority was less than what was apparent from the course of dealing for when one of two innocent parties must suffer, the loss must fall upon the party who created the enabling circumstances. ...

The appellants argue that Southwestern did not act with reasonable diligence and was negligent in failing to inquire into Adams' authority as evidence by Southwestern's statement that after the delivery of the last three shipments, it did contact Wilkerson-Webb to check into the cement usage at the Air Force Base and to reconfirm the guarantee of payment. ...

Standing by itself, under the circumstances presented, we do not believe that the inquiry made *after* the cement was delivered constitutes as a matter of law negligence or failure to exercise reasonable diligence. It is the appellants who should bear the loss since they are responsible for a course of business with the necessary apparent authority and are now estopped to deny that authority, the appellant having reasonably relied upon it. Furthermore, balancing the positions of both sides, the appellants fall short for they could have easily averted their loss by advising Southwestern that they had made other arrangements for the concrete because of Adams' equipment failure. . . .

The judgment is affirmed. . . .

Case Questions

1. Define the three factual elements of an estoppel and then locate them in the opinion.
2. Did the court apply the principle of apparent authority or estoppel?
3. Were there not two principals in this case: the partnership, Plains Sand and Gravel, and Beavers and Glasgow? Who was the agent?

Case Comment

One of the more subtle costs to society of doing business through agents is that principals may be required to pay for damages to an injured third party caused by an agent's promises or representations when the third party and the principal are both innocent of any intentional wrongdoing; yet, because the principal benefits from the use of agents and because he can best guard against these misrepresentations by properly training his agents, he is required to compensate the third party. We attempt to put labels on the circumstances when the principal is required to pay for injury to third parties. The existence of express and implied authority as legal doctrines is well recognized and understood. It should be obvious that circumstantial authority is less precisely defined. Nevertheless the law quests for certainty and in this quest it has developed the related doctrines of apparent authority and estoppel. Upon close analysis it may be very difficult to explain the difference between the two. Do you agree?

Another type of circumstantial authority which is similar to apparent authority is inherent authority. The *Restatement* provides:

Inherent agency power is a term used in the *Restatement* to indicate the power of an agent which is derived not from authority, apparent authority or estoppel, but solely from the agency relation and exists for the protection of persons harmed by or dealing with . . . an agent.[9]

In some circumstances the existence of a binding, enforceable contract between the third party and agent for the benefit of the principal are questionable; or the breach of duty being sued upon is quasi-contractual (this term is usually used to designate a circumstance in which someone has unfairly benefited at the expense of someone else); or the breach of duty may look like the breach of one of the generally recognized torts but it is not; thus the other principles of circumstantial authority do not fit the factual pattern. The common law has developed the principle of inherent agency power to be applied in such situations. This power is derived from the view that the primary function of agency law in recent times is to make possible commercial undertakings which might not otherwise be possible. As stated earlier, corporations which conduct most of the large and complex commercial transactions in this country today depend upon agency rules for conducting their business with third parties. It is obvious that corporate agents will harm third parties in ways which are unauthorized. So, believing it unfair for the commercial enterprize to have the benefit of the agency law without making it responsible for the agent's actions, courts developed the doctrine of inherent agency power.[10]

Inherent authority differs from implied authority in that the former is created by the circumstance of position and not the express delegation of authority. Inherent authority may exist when the principal has expressly forbidden the agent to act in certain matters, yet failed to take measures to inform third parties of this limitation causing them to reasonably believe the position of the agent carried with it the authority asserted.

The doctrine of inherent authority is another example of courts' recognition that it is vital to protect the reasonable expectations of businessmen. To this end, the principles of apparent authority, estoppel and inherent authority are all directed and all achieve the same practical result: In a commercial transaction where the principal stands to benefit by the utilization of agents, this principal should bear the loss as between itself, who is innocent of any intentional wrong, and a third party who is likewise innocent when it can be reasonably found that the principal created the impression that the agent was authorized.

In any given factual situation any third party plaintiff may argue all of the types of authority. There is no inconsistency in this. If the facts reasonably lend themselves to the creation of circumstantial authority it is best to argue apparent authority, estoppel, and inherent authority. The following case illustrates the application of the doctrine of inherent authority as well as the difficulty some courts experience in attempting to delineate between the various types of circumstantial authority.

LIND v. SCHENLEY INDUSTRIES INC.
278 F. 2d 79 (C.C.A. 3rd, 1960)

◆◆◆

BIGGS, Chief Judge

This is a diversity case: Lind, the plaintiff-appellant, sued Park & Tilford Distiller's Corp.,[1] the defendant-appellee, for compensation that he asserts is due him by virtue of a contract expressed by a written memorandum supplemented by oral conversations as set out hereinafter. Lind also sued for certain expenses he incurred when moving from New Jersey to New York when his position as New Jersey State Manager of Park & Tilford terminated on January 31, 1957. The evidence, including Lind's own testimony, taking the inferences most favorable to Lind, shows the following. Lind had been employed for some years by Park & Tilford. In July 1950, Lind was informed by Herrfeldt, then Park & Tilford's vice-president and general salesmanager, that he would be appointed assistant to Kaufman, Park & Tilford's sales-manager for metropolitan

---

[1]Park & Tilford Distiller's Corp. was merged into Schenley Industries, Inc., a Delaware corporation, before the commencement of this action, with Schenley assuming all of Park & Tilford's obligations.

New York. Herrfeldt told Lind to see Kaufman to ascertain what his new duties and his salary would be. Lind embarked on his new duties with Kaufman and was informed in October 1950, that some "raises" had come through and that Lind should get official word from his "boss", Kaufman. Subsequently, Lind received a communication, dated April 19, 1951, signed by Kaufman, informing Lind that he would assume the title of "District Manager." The letter went on to state: "I wish to inform you of the fact that you have as much responsibility as a State Manager and that you should consider yourself to be of the same status." The letter concluded with the statement: "An incentive plan is being worked out so that you will not only be responsible for increased sales in your district, but will benefit substantially in a monetary way." The other two district managers under Kaufman received similar memoranda. Lind assumed his duties as district sales manager for metropolitan New York. During the weeks following Lind's new appointment, Lind inquired of Kaufman frequently what his remuneration would be under the incentive plan referred to in the letter of April 19, 1951, and was informed that details were being worked out. In July 1951, Kaufman informed Lind that he was to receive one percent commission on the gross sales of the men under him. This was an oral communication and was completely corroborated by Mrs. Kennan, Kaufman's former secretary, who was present. On subsequent occasions Lind was assured by Kaufman that he would get his money. Lind was also informed by Herrfeldt in the autumn of 1952 that he would get a one percent commission on the sales of the men under him. Early in 1955, Lind negotiated with Brown, then president of Park & Tilford, for the sale of Park & Tilford's New Jersey Wholesale House, and Brown agreed to apply the money owed to Lind by reason of the one percent commission against the value of the goodwill of the Wholesale House. The proposed sale of the New Jersey Wholesale House was not consummated. . . .

The court . . . requested the jury to answer the following five questions: "1. Did Kaufman offer plaintiff one percent of gross sales effected by the salesmen under plaintiff?" "2. If the answer to question 1 is yes, when was plaintiff to commence such commissions?" "3. If the answer to question 1 is yes, when was the commission arrangement to terminate?" "4. Did defendant cause the plaintiff to believe that Kaufman had authority to make the offer to plaintiff referred to in question 1?" "5. Was plaintiff justified in presuming that Kaufman had the authority to make the offer?"

The answers provided by the jury amounted to a determination that Kaufman did offer Lind a one percent commission on the gross sales of the men under him; that the agreement commenced April 19, 1951; that the agreement terminated February 15, 1952, the date of Lind's transfer to New Jersey; that Park & Tilford did cause Lind to believe that Kaufman had authority to offer him the one percent commission; and that Lind was justified in assuming that Kaufman had the authority to make the offer. In addition, the jury awarded Lind $353 as reimbursement for moving expenses incurred by him at the termination of his position as New Jersey State Manager. . . .

(J)udgement was rendered by the jury in favor of Lind against Schenley for $36,953.10 plus interest for the commission and $353.00 for the moving expenses. However, the judgment was nullified by the court's decision to enter a verdict for the defendant. . . .

The decision to reverse the verdict for Lind with respect to the one percent commission was based on two alternative grounds. First, the court found that

Lind had failed to prove a case of apparent authority in that the evidence did not disclose that Park & Tilford acted in such a manner as to induce Lind to believe that Kaufman had been authorized to offer him the one percent commission. Also the court concluded that the issues of "actual" and "implied" authority had somehow been eliminated from the case. Second, the court reasoned, that even if the jury could find apparent authority, the alleged contract was not sufficiently definite nor specific to be enforceable against Park & Tilford. . . .

The problems of "authority" are probably the most difficult in that segment of law loosely termed, "Agency." Two main classifications of authority are generally recognized, "actual authority," and "apparent authority." The term "implied authority" is often seen but most authorities consider "implied authority" to be merely a sub-group of "actual" authority. Mechem, *Agency,* §§51-60 (4th ed. 1952). An additional kind of authority has been designated by the *Restatement*, Agency 2d, §§8A and 161(b) as "inherent agency." Actually this new term is employed to designate a meaning frequently ascribed to "implied authority."

"Actual authority" means, as the words connote, authority that the principal, expressly or implicitly, gave the agent. "Apparent authority" arises when a principal acts in such a manner as to convey the impression to a third party that an agent has certain powers which he may or may not actually possess. "Implied authority" has been variously defined. It has been held to be actual authority given implicitly by a principal to his agent. Another definition of "implied authority" is that it is a kind of authority arising solely from the designation by the principal of a kind of agent who ordinarily possesses certain powers. It is this concept that is called "inherent authority" by the *Restatement*. . . . Usually it is not necessary for a third party attempting to hold a principal to specify which type of authority he relies upon, general proof of agency being sufficient. . . .

In the case at bar Lind attempted to prove all three kinds of agency; actual, apparent, and inherent, although most of his evidence was directed to proof of "inherent" or "apparent" authority. From the evidence it is clear that Park & Tilford can be held accountable for Kaufman's action on the principle of "inherent authority." Kaufman was Lind's direct superior, and was the man to transfer communications from the upper executives to the lower. Moreover, there was testimony tending to prove that Herrfeldt, the vice-president in charge of sales, had told Lind to see Kaufman for information about his salary and that Herrfeldt himself had confirmed that one percent commission arrangement. Thus Kaufman, so far as Lind was concerned, was the spokesman for the company. . . .

The *Restatement, Agency 2d* § 8, defines "apparent agency" as "the power to affect the legal relations of another person by transactions with third persons, professedly as agent for the other, arising from and in accordance with the other's manifestations to such third persons." There is some uncertainty as to whether or not the third person must change his position in reliance upon these manifestations of authority, but this is of no consequence in the case at bar since Lind clearly changed his position when he accepted the job of district manager with its admittedly increased responsibilities. . . .

Testimony was adduced by Schenley tending to prove that Kaufman had no authority to set salaries, that power being exercisable solely by the president of the corporation, and that the president had not authorized Kaufman to offer

Lind a commission of the kind under consideration here. However, this testimony, even if fully accepted, would only prove lack of actual or implied authority in Kaufman but is irrelevant to the issue of apparent authority. . . .

On the basis of the foregoing it appears that there was sufficient evidence to authorize a jury finding that Park & Tilford had given Kaufman apparent authority to offer Lind one percent commission of gross sales of the salesmen under him and that Lind reasonably had relied upon Kaufman's offer. . . .

The judgment of the court below will be reversed and the case will be remanded . . . to reinstate the verdict and judgment in favor of Lind.

♦♦♦

Case Questions

1. Can you pinpoint in time when the "contract" between Lind and the corporation was made?
2. Is there sufficient evidence in this case for you to feel comfortable in applying the principle of apparent authority or estoppel? What facts are there which indicate that Lind's superiors were authorized by the corporation to promise him a commission upon all sales made by those under his direction?

RATIFICATION

Ratification is another legal principle applied by courts to hold the principal liable to third parties for a promise or act which was not initially authorized by the principal. The *Restatement* defines it in this way:

Ratification is the affirmance by a person of a prior act which did not bind him but which was done professedly on his account, whereby the act, as to some or all persons, is given effect as if originally authorized by him.[11]

Stated in the above definition are several important notions. The first is that the promise or act was not authorized either actually or circumstantially and that the promise or act was done for the benefit of the principal. This means that the promise or act must be of the kind that could have been authorized initially but was not. If the promise or act could not have been authorized initially, it can not be ratified.

Just as important is the notion that the principal must *affirm* by some word, action, or perhaps a failure to act, the transaction in question. The principal must have *knowledge* either actual or implied — which means the principal *should have known* if he did not actually know — of the transaction being affirmed.

A common instance involving ratification is exemplified by the agent's contracting to sell something he is not authorized to sell. If the principal knows of this contract, but says nothing and accepts the proceeds of the sale, then courts will most probably hold he has ratified the contract to sell.

Ratification relates back to the time of the initial transaction and results in the creation of authority as of that time.

In concluding this section on the rules the law has developed to hold the principal liable to third parties for an agents' promises or representations we wish to emphasize two points. First, it must be remembered that the agents' promises or representations to a third party can not, *by themselves,* confer authority on the agent. No agent can create liability for a principal by a forged instrument, or other false assertion. Usually, there must be circumstances present in which it seems fair and reasonable to hold the principal liable. This means one must find that the principal is in some way responsible for creating the circumstances which lead the third party to believe the agent was authorized or otherwise accepts the benefits of the transaction.

Second, in analyzing a factual pattern involving contractual liability the reader should be prepared to argue more than one, perhaps all, of the types of authority discussed herein if it is appropriate. It is seldom that a factual pattern of any complexity will yield to a direct, obvious application of just one of the authority rules. Note for example that in the first case in this chapter, the bank must have argued at the trial level not only the existence of express authority but ratification as well. In fact almost all of the cases in this chapter contain discussions of more than one of the authority rules.

In closing this section we present a case illustrating the application of the doctrine of ratification.

WILKINS v. WALDO LUMBER CO., 130 ME. 5; 153 A. 191 (S. Ct. Maine, 1931)

(Author's note: The plaintiff, Wilkins, was the administrator of the estate of George W. Staples.)

STURGIS, J.

In the late summer or early fall of 1928 Daniel F. Adams, a salesman for the Waldo Lumber company of Bangor, Me., began negotiations for the purchase by the company of a lot of sawed hardwood lumber then on the sticks at Temple, Me., and for sale by the plaintiff as administrator of the estate of George W. Staples.

Mr. Adams examined the lumber, and, upon an interview with the administrator, obtained a price of $15 per M on the sticks. He also arranged with one F. C. Metcalf of West Farmington to haul and mill the lumber if it was purchased, and incidentally learned that the Gem Crib & Cradle Company of Gardner, Mass., was in the market for finished hardwood lumber.

Reporting these facts to Irving G. Stetson, the general manager of the Waldo Lumber Company, Mr. Adams was directed to obtain an order from the Gem Crib & Cradle Company, if possible, and to arrange with Mr. Metcalf for hauling and tallying the lumber at a price of $5.50 per M and for milling it at $12 per M.

Mr. Adams obtained an order from the Gem Crib & Cradle Co. for 180 M feet of hardwood squares, with the stipulation that "above order may be increased to take care of lot at Temple, Maine," went to Wilton, directed Mr. Metcalf to begin hauling and milling the lumber, and, on November 24, 1928, signing for the Waldo Lumber Company as agent, joined the plaintiff in the execution of a written contract, under seal, for the sale to and purchase by the Waldo Lumber

Company of all sawed lumber belonging to the Staples estate then on the sticks in Temple. The price fixed for the lumber was $15 per M on the sticks, and the contract was signed by Mr. Adams subject to confirmation by the Waldo Lumber Company.

Within a few days, the order of the cradle company and the contract made by Mr. Adams and Mr. Wilkins was submitted to Mr. Stetson, the general manager, for confirmation. On November 27, 1928, Mr. Metcalf, pursuant to the orders given him by Mr. Adams, began hauling the Staples lumber from the sticks to his mill, tallying it as it came in, and milling it to the specifications of the Crib & Cradle Company order.

It appears, however, that Mr. Stetson did not formally confirm the lumber contract. Although he had directed Mr. Adams to get the order from the cradle company, and undoubtedly knew that the lumber was being moved to the Metcalf mill on Mr. Adams' orders, he withheld confirmation while he attempted to work out a more advantageous and profitable arrangement. He wrote the Crib & Cradle Company asking for a modification of its orders. On December 6, 1928, he wrote the plaintiff asking for more detailed information than appeared in the contract, noting lack of confirmation, but not repudiating the instrument executed by Mr. Adams. On the same day he wrote Mr. Adams expressing a doubt as to the profits to be made on filling the cradle company order, closing his letter with this paragraph:

"We wish that you would figure this over in view of the requirements stated in this letter, check up on the thickness of the plank and talk it over with Mr. Metcalf. It would surely be better to back out now, which we can do, but naturally do not want to do if there is a reasonable chance of going through with a whole skin."

Replying upon and reiterating the fact that the contract signed by Mr. Adams had not been confirmed, he attempted to get the plaintiff to sign a new contract of a modified tenor and more advantageous to the lumber company. He sought and obtained an agreement from Mr. Metcalf to mill the lumber at a reduced cost. He endeavored to get Mr. Metcalf to take over the purchase from the plaintiff and the order of the crib company, and finally, on January 2, 1929, wrote the plaintiff repudiating the contract signed by Mr. Adams with the statement that the plaintiff must look to Mr. Metcalf, the mill man for his pay for the lumber belonging to the Staples estate. The plaintiff did not reply. . . .

All this time, upon the authority of the orders originally given by Mr. Adams and with the knowledge of the general manager of the lumber company, Mr. Metcalf had been hauling the lumber from the lot where it lay, was milling it upon the specifications of the cradle company order, and had begun shipments.

In December, the exact date not appearing, the lumber company arranged to finance the transaction through the People's National Bank of Farmington, Me., and, although Mr. Stetson called his remittances advances, checks therefor payable to Mr. Metcalf's order were turned over to him from time to time to cover his hauling and milling charges. Through January, February, and March, 1929, Mr. Metcalf, with Mr. Stetson's knowledge, kept on hauling and milling or piling up the lumber, and during the same period four more cars were shipped to the Crib & Cradle Company on orders sent to Metcalf from the Waldo Lumber Company, which billed the cars direct from its Bangor office and made collections in due course. April 9, 1929, Mr. Stetson ordered Metcalf to stop milling on this order. . . .

The plaintiff's contention is that he at all times insisted that his rights were measured by the contract which he had signed on November 24, 1928.

The defendant's claim is that, because of the failure of its manager to confirm the contract in controversy, including his notifications to the plaintiff to that effect, it is not bound to pay the plaintiff for the lumber taken from his intestate's property. Its position is that the plaintiff must look for his pay to Metcalf, who milled the lumber. It even asserts through the testimony of its manager and its bookkeeping that it only sold the lumber on commission for Metcalf.

From the evidence, including the somewhat disconnected and confusing correspondence introduced as exhibits, the jury found for the plaintiff for the full amount of lumber covered by the contract with interest from the date of demand by the plaintiff's attorney. We cannot find in the record evidence which justifies a conviction that the verdict was manifestly wrong.

The evidence warranted a finding, we think, that, with full knowledge of all material facts, the defendant company through its general manager took and retained a part . . . of the benefits of the unauthorized contract which its salesman, Mr. Adams, made. It directed and acquiesced in the hauling of the lumber from the Staples lot to the Metcalf mill and the finishing of enough of it to fill the order of the Gem Crib & Cradle Company until five cars had been shipped. It must be held in law to have impliedly ratified the transaction in part at least, and that binds it for the entirety. . . .

Even though the manager of this defendant lumber company did not actually intend to bind his corporation, his acts and statements, rather than his professions, must determine the questions of ratification. . . .

In *Mechem on Agency* §§ 146 and 148, we read:

> Ratification, like authorization of which it is the equivalent, is generally the creature of intent, but that intent may often be presumed by the law in cases where the principal, as a matter of fact, either had no express intent at all, or had an express intent not to ratify.
>
> If the principal has knowingly appropriated and enjoyed the fruits and benefits of an agent's act, he will not afterwards be heard to say that the act was unauthorized. One who voluntarily accepts the proceeds of an act done by one assuming, though without authority, to be his agent's act, he will not afterwards be heard to say that the act was unauthorized. One who voluntarily accepts the proceeds of an act done by one assuming, though without authority, to be his agent, ratifies his act and takes it as his own, with all its burdens as well as all its benefits. He may not take the benefits and reject the burdens, but he must either accept them or reject them as a whole.

And in *St. Louis Gunning Advertising Co.* v. *Wanamaker & Brown*, 115 Mo. App. 270, 280, 90 S.W. 737, 739, that court says: . . .

In its genuine sense ratification depends on intention. It is the voluntary assumption, on full information, of an unauthorized act or agreement by the party in whose behalf it was done or made. The intention to ratify may be manifested by express words or by conduct. Either may establish that the principal elected to adopt the act or agreement as his own; and the election once made with knowledge of the facts becomes irrevocable. Besides a true ratification intentionally made, the law recognizes a constructive one where none was intended. The latter sort of ratification is a legal presumption, raised against the principal because he has behaved in such a way that the party dealt with by the agent would be injured if the transaction was repudiated. . . .

One more branch of the rule of ratification needs mention. Where the principal receives the benefits of an unauthorized act of his agent, when he is apprised of the facts, if he has suffered no prejudice and can make restitution, he must elect whether to ratify or disaffirm, and, if he decides not to ratify, he must return the fruits of the unauthorized act within a reasonable time. If thereafter he retains, uses, or disposes of what he has received, he will be held to have ratified the act of his agent, unless restoration would be of no practical value to the other party. . . .

Under the rules stated, the verdict must stand. . . .

◆◆◆

Case Question

1. The salesman in this case, Adams, appears to have been authorized to only negotiate and not to contract for Waldo Lumber Co. The contract which he took to Wilkins as the administrator of the Staples estate was subject to confirmation by Waldo. Many businesses write their contracts in this manner. It pays to read the fine print. Many persons upon signing a "contract" believe they are binding both themselves and the other party when, legally, if the contract is subject to "confirmation" at the home office or the like, all they are doing is making an offer. In this case, the contract was finally "confirmed." How?

CONTRACTUAL LIABILITY OF THE AGENT TO THIRD PARTIES

Implicit in the factual patterns discussed in the first portion of this chapter is the fact that the third party knew of the existence of the principal-agent relationship at the time the transaction occured or shortly thereafter. When an agent is contracting for a principal the contract or the circumstances usually indicate that the agent is acting in a representative capacity. One of the most common ways to indicate this representative capacity is for the agent to sign the contract as follows:

> Artie Agent for Peter Principal; or
> Peter Principal by Artie Agent; or
> The P Corporation, by A, President.

In the above examples the agent may sign both the names of the principal and agent. Of course other circumstances such as the use of a letterhead or the use of an office in the same building area as the principal or even the use of a company car with a name on it may indicate that the agent is indeed acting for and on behalf of someone else.

When the contract is signed in a representative capacity, the agent is not liable to the third party unless:

1. he signed a negotiable instrument (a promisory note, check, or the like) without the principal's authority and a third party took it in good faith and paid value for it; or
2. the agent made a personal promise to perform; or
3. the agent misrepresented his authority or the existence or the capacity of the principal.

Only the circumstances of each case will reveal if the contract signed was a negotiable instrument or if a personal promise to perform was made, or there was some misrepresentation. A very important circumstance revealing whether or not an agent personally promised to perform is whether or not the principal was disclosed to the third party, partially disclosed or undisclosed *at the time the contract was made.*

The *Restatement* defines these classifications of principals as follows:[12]

1) If, at the time of a transaction conducted by an agent, the other party thereto has notice that the agent is acting for a principal and of the principal's identity, the principal is a disclosed principal.
2) If the other party has notice that the agent is or may be acting for a principal but has no notice of the principal's identity, the principal for whom the agent is acting is a partially disclosed principal.
3) If the other party has no notice that the agent is acting for a principal, the one for whom he acts is an undisclosed principal.

The difference between (1) and (2) above is slight. In the case of a disclosed principal, the third party can identify the principal by name; this is not so of the partially disclosed principal, yet the existence of a principal is indicated. If a principal is disclosed, the law assumes the contract signed by the agent and the promises therein are made for the benefit of the principal unless otherwise specifically indicated. Therefore, the third party may enforce the contract against the principal *but not the agent.* If the principal is partially disclosed, the law assumes that both the principal and agent may have personally promised to perform and one should carefully search the contractual language for the agent's personal promise. If such a promise is found then both principal and agent may be liable to the third party.

If a principal is undisclosed, the law assumes that the agent has personally promised to perform the contract.[13] *Therefore, the agent is liable* for the breach of the promise(s) made. But, just as important, is the rule that the *principal is also liable* even though its existence is not known to the third party. This result may be contrary to your natural instincts. The reason for imposing liability on the undisclosed principal is that it is the one that initiated the activities of the agent and has a right to control the agent. Since the third party may sue an undisclosed principal the law also recognizes the right of the undisclosed principal to enforce the contract against the third party so long as the agent intended that the contract benefit the principal and the agent acted within the authority possessed. This latter result is perhaps more surprising than the rule which allows a third party to sue an undisclosed principal. However, if the agent induces the third party to enter the contract by positively representing that no principal is involved or if the contract "excludes all principals," then the third party may be granted the remedy of recision of the contract.

It should be clear at this point that even though the agent may not be liable to a third party when the principal is disclosed or partially disclosed, either the principal or third party may compel the agent to plead in the case for purposes of determining the respective liabilities between these parties and the agent. For example, assume a principal gives his horse to an agent to sell for him, and while conducting the sale the agent promises that the horse is, "a fine working horse that can plow all day." The third party buys the horse and it dies of heart failure after plowing 100 feet. If the third party sues the principal for a breach of warranty, the principal may join the agent in the case so that the liability between the three parties is worked out in one forum.

If a third party finds out about the existence of the principal after the contract is made the best course of action for the third party who wishes to sue for the breach of the contract is to join both the principal and agent in the case. However, if either the principal or agent objects the third-party plaintiff *must elect* to continue against either one or the other and may secure a judgment only against the one whom he elects to hold.[14] If the third party knows the identity of the initially undisclosed principal and does not join the principal and recovers a judgment against the agent, the principal is discharged from liability.[15] If the third party does not know the identity of the undisclosed principal at the time of trial and recovers a judgment against the agent, the principal is not discharged from liability by such a recovery.[16]

The following case illustrates one court's reasoning on the liability of an undisclosed principal who has paid the agent for the goods the agent was directed to order. The agent did not pay the third party seller. In this case both the undisclosed principal and the third party are innocent of any wrongdoing causing the court to go to great lengths to explain precisely why the former should be liable and, in effect, be required to pay twice for the same goods.

PORETTA v. SUPERIOR DOWEL COMPANY
153 Me. 308, 137 A2d 361 (S. Ct., Me., 1957)

(Author's note: In this case the plaintiff, Poretta, delivered wood worth $2,574.44 to R. H. Young & Son, Inc. The plaintiff was not paid by R. H. Young & Son, Inc., referred to by the court as "Company," and the plaintiff brought this suit against the Superior Dowel Company, referred to by the court as "Superior," alleging that Superior was the undisclosed principal for Company. The appellate court affirmed the finding of the referee which was in favor of the plaintiff and which established that the wood was purchased by the Company in the capacity as agent for Superior and that the Company was within its scope of authority when it purchased the wood. On the final issue before the court, Superior argued that it had paid the agent, Company (presumably insolvent), and this discharged its liability.)

♦♦♦

The issue thus raised presents a problem of novel impression in this State. The issue is:

Is an undisclosed principal absolved from liability to his agent's vendor who has sold goods to the agent upon the credit of the agent who has received payment or advances, or a settlement of accounts from his undisclosed principal, before discovery of the undisclosed principal by the agent's vendor?

There are two different rules bearing upon the issue. The first one, which appears to be supported by the weight of authority is that an undisclosed principal is generally relieved of his liability for his agent's contracts to the extent that he has settled with his agent prior to the discovery of the agency. The other rule is, that an undisclosed principal is discharged only where he has been induced to settle with the agent by conduct on the part of the third person leading him to believe that such person has settled with the agent.

The decisions appear to be in a state of hopeless confusion. . . .

> "It is often said that persons dealing in their own names are presumed to deal for themselves as principals, yet if one authorized by another to act as his agent, in acting on behalf of the principal, fails to disclose the principal to the third person, or to disclose that he is acting as agent, the principal, when discovered, may become liable for the acts done in his behalf, and may be sued thereon just as if, at the time the transaction was entered into, the agent had disclosed the fact of his agency and the identity of the principal, unless the principal and the agent have so adjusted their accounts that to hold the principal liable would work an injustice to him." 2 *Am. Jur., Agency*, § 393.

The expression "unless the principal and the agent have so adjusted their accounts that to hold the principal liable would work an injustice to him," is qualified by 2 *Am. Jur.* § 399, which reads as follows:

> The general rule which allows a third person to have recourse against an undisclosed principal is subject to the qualification that the principal shall not be prejudiced by being made personally liable because he has in good faith relied upon the conduct of the third person and has paid or settled with the agent; conversely, the rule is that a third person who deals with the agent of an undisclosed principal can, upon discovering the principal, resort to the latter for payment, unless by his conduct he has led the principal in the meanwhile to pay or settle with the agent. . . .

The American Law Institute, as of May 4, 1933, adopted and promulgated the following rule:

> "An undisclosed principal is discharged from liability to the other party to the contract if he has paid or settled accounts with an agent reasonably relying upon conduct of the other party, not induced by the agent's misrepresentations, which indicates that the agent has paid or otherwise settled the account. 1 *Am. Law. Inst. Restatement of Agency*, §208. . . .

We are, therefore, called upon to determine which rule shall become the law in this State.

Manifestly, if we adopt the rule which we have designated as the first rule, as distinguished from the rule laid down in the *Restatement of the Law of Agency*, then, . . . the exceptions of Superior would have to be sustained. On the other hand, if we adopt the rule laid down in the *Restatement*, then the decision of the referee was correct and Superior's exceptions should be overruled. . . .

Mr. Mechem in his Treatise on the *Law of Agency*, 2nd Ed., Vol. 2, points out that the subject of discussion has not very frequently arisen in the United States and has not been thoroughly considered in any recent case by a court of last resort. . . .

In arriving at his conclusion that the law as now set forth in the *Restatement* was the correct law, Mr. Mechem had this to say in his Treatise on the *Law of Agency*, 2nd Ed. § 1749, Vol. II,

> Nevertheless, the rule of Parke, B., seems on the whole to be reasonable and just. If a principal sends an agent to buy goods for him and on his account, it is not unreasonable that he should see that they are paid for. Although the seller may consider the agent to be the principal, the actual principal knows better. He can easily protect himself by insisting upon evidence that the goods have been paid for or that the seller with full knowledge of the facts has elected to rely upon the responsibility of the agent, and if he does not, but, except where misled by some action of the seller, voluntarily pays the agent without knowing that he has paid the seller, there is no hardship in requiring him to pay again. If the other party has the right, within a reasonable time, to charge the undisclosed principal upon his discovery, — and this right seems to be abundantly settled in the law of agency — it is difficult to see how this right of the other party can be defeated, while he is not himself in fault, by dealings between the principal and the agent, of which he had no knowledge, and to which he was not a party.

It is interesting to note that this work on Agency by Mechem was published in 1914.

We think it is pertinent at this point to record something of the establishment, organization and object of the American Law Institute. The Institute was organized on February 23, 1923. The organization meeting was attended by the Chief Justice of the United States, and other representatives of the Supreme Court, representatives of the United States Circuit Courts of Appeals, the highest courts of a majority of the States, the Association of American Law Schools, and the American and State Bar Associations. The Institute was composed of Justices of the Supreme Court of the United States, senior judges of the United States Circuit Court of Appeals, the chief justices of the highest courts of the several States, and president and members of the Executive Committee of the American Bar Association, the presidents of certain legal societies, and the deans of member schools of the Association of American Law Schools. Its object as expressed in its charter was "to promote the clarification and simplification of the law and its better adaptation to social needs, to secure the better administration of justice and to carry on scholarly and scientific legal work."

The Restatement may be regarded both as the product of expert opinion and as the expression of the law by the legal profession.

The Committee on Agency which prepared the *Restatement of the Law of Agency* was composed of outstanding representatives of the leading law schools of the country. It was headed by Mr. Floyd R. Mechem, who at the time was regarded as the foremost living authority on the subject of agency. Its rule as set forth in § 208 promulgated on May 4, 1933 expounds the thinking of some of the best legal minds in the country.

The purpose of the Institute in the promotion of clarification of the law can be applied to no more needy situation than that of the question before us for determination. It is our opinion that the reasoning of Mr. Mechem in support of the doctrine promulgated in the *Restatement* is sound. The adoption of this doctrine by this court will establish a clear cut and explicit rule of law free from the confusion, complications and perplexities which have existed throughout the years.

We, therefore, adopt the rule as laid down in the *Restatement of the Law of Agency*.

Having already ruled that the Company was the duly authorized agent of Superior and that when it purchased the wood from the plaintiff, it was acting within the scope of its authority, we now rule that the referee applied the proper law and that his decision was correct and should be affirmed.

Exceptions overruled.

◆◆◆

Case Questions

1. In this case it appears that the principal was required to pay twice for the same goods. How could the principal have protected itself against such an event?
2. On the facts of this case, could R. H. Young and Son, Inc., be liable to Poretta? Why?

SUMMARY

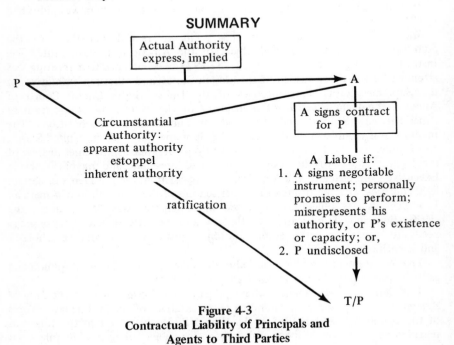

Figure 4-3
Contractual Liability of Principals and Agents to Third Parties

REVIEW PROBLEMS

1. In this chapter we have stated that a principal will be liable to third parties for the contracts made by an agent if there are circumstances present which indicate that the principal authorized or ratified the contract. List and define five types of authority discussed in this chapter and using factual patterns not similar to any of the cases in the chapter, give an example of each.

2. P made store fronts and other additions to commercial buildings and employed A to call on contractors and older commercial enterprizes to promote the sales of P. A was specifically forbidden to collect payment for the erection of the store fronts and other improvements. T went to P's place of business and inquired about a new front for his store and was directed to A's office. A negotiated a contract and signed on behalf of P and P's men began work. P did not keep very good account of his workmen or accounts receivable. A pocketed the payments made by T to A and absconded. P discovers this and since A is unavailable he sues T to recover the payments owed to him for the work done. Can he collect?

3. Henry Wilson & Sons, Inc., manufactured and sold custom-made shoes. Henry Wilson, Sr., the president of the company, hired his grandson, James Wilson, age 17, as a salesman during his summer vacation. James was instructed not to make any contracts in excess of $500 without first obtaining approval from his father, Frank Wilson, the vice president of marketing. All other salesmen could make contracts up to $1,500 without approval. James Wilson made numerous contracts on the corporation's behalf; two of these were for $750. Discuss whether or not James had capacity to contract on behalf of Henry Wilson & Sons, Inc., and whether or not the latter would be liable to those who contracted for orders in excess of $750. (Material from the Uniform CPA Examination, copyright © 1973 by the American Institute of Certified Public Accountants, Inc. is here reprinted with permission. This is adapted from Question Number 3, E of the May 11, 1973 Exam.)

4. Explain how your arguments in the above case would change if it appeared that Frank Wilson accepted payment for the two orders which were in excess of $750.

5. P employs A as the general manager of his manufacturing plant instructing A to purchase certain materials from specifically named suppliers and no others. A, realizing that some of the materials supplied by the designated suppliers are inferior and without consultation with P, contracts with other suppliers for better materials at a more reasonable price. The contracts with the new suppliers are written on plain paper (no letterhead) and A signs the contracts at P's headquarters in the presence of the new suppliers as follows: "A, general manager for P." Will P be bound by these contracts? Why?

6. A uses his own name in conducting a business but is in reality a general agent for P in the management of the business. He, A, contracts with T/P to buy goods which are customarily used in the business not disclosing in any way that he is P's agent. In fact, A has been directed by P to sign contracts for the business only after P has okayed the contract. In this instance P did not OK the contract.
   a. Assume that A fails to pay for the goods and T/P finds out about P's existence. May T/P sue P? May T/P sue A?
   b. Assume T/P fails to deliver the goods. May A sue T/P? May P sue T/P?

ENDNOTES

1. W. A. Seavey, *Law of Agency,* 40 (1964).
2. Am. L. Inst., The Restatement of Agency, 2d § 8 (1958).
3. A. Conrad, R. Knauss, and S. Siegel, *Enterprize Organization,* 418 (1972).
4. *Black's Law Dictionary* Rev. 4th Ed., 648 (1957).
5. *Restatement, supra* note 2, § 8B.
6. See Seavey, *supra* note 1 at 14-15.
7. *Restatement,* supra note 2, at 33 and 40.
8. *Id.,* Illustration 7, at 33.
9. *Id.,* § 8A.
10. *Id.,* at 36-37.
11. *Id.,* § 82.
12. *Id.,* § 4.
13. See Seaney, *supra* note 1 at 120-121.
14. *Restatement,* § 210 A.
15. *Id.,* § 210(1).
16. *Id.,* § 210(2).

TORT LIABILITY OF PRINCIPAL AND AGENT TO THIRD PARTIES

We suggested in Chapter 4 that it would be useful to divide the discussion of the principal's liability to third persons into two broad categories depending upon the nature of the breach of duty sued upon. We stated in Chapter 4 that when the breach of a *contract duty* is alleged the courts usually search for a principle of *authority* to apply. The second category of cases involves a principal's liability to third parties based upon a breach of a *tort duty*. When the breach of a *tort duty* is alleged courts focus upon the degree of *control* exercised by the principal over the agent's physical conduct. Precisely how and when courts use rules of *control* by the principal will be the primary subject of this chapter.

TORT LIABILITY

Before proceeding with the subject of the principal's control over the physical conduct of the agent, an understanding of the nature of tort liability is essential. A tort may be variously defined as a private or civil wrong (breach of duty) independent of contract.[1] Or, a more comprehensive definition is, "Any intentional invasion of, or interference with property, property rights, personal rights or personal liberties causing injury without just cause or excuse".[2]

Torts are divided broadly into unintentional torts and intentional ones. The most pervasive unintentional tort is negligence. Negligence is defined broadly as any conduct which falls below the standard established by law for the protection of others against unreasonable risk of harm.[3] The standard referred to is that of a reasonable person under like circumstances.[4]

Two other torts which may exist either with or without the intent of the wrongdoer (sometimes called a tortfeasor) are conversion and trespass. Conversion is the act of wrongfully exercising ownership over another's personal property. For example, if a third party (T/P) orders from a principal (P) and pays for a set of furniture and P directs an agent (A) to deliver the furniture to T/P and A wrongfully delivers it to X who absconds with it, A and P may both be liable for converting T/P's furniture.

Trespass is the unintentional or intentional interference with another's real or personal property.

Some common torts usually requiring an element of intent on the part of the tortfeasor are defined as follows:

1. Assault — an act other than the speaking of words which puts another person in apprehension of an immediate and harmful contact (e.g., threatening to strike another by raising a fist).
2. Battery — unpermitted, unprivileged, physical contact with another person (e.g., striking another with a fist).
3. False imprisonment — an unprivileged confinement of another for any time where the other is aware of the confinement. (e.g., a manger closes

his store thirty minutes early and locks in several customers for the night).

4. Defamation — the unprivileged publication of false matter which damages another's reputation. Defamation is subdivided into libel (written or printed defamation) and slander (spoken dafamation).

5. Deceit or Misrepresentation — Knowingly making a misrepresentation of fact or opinion for the purpose of inducing another to act or refrain from acting.

Other less common torts are malicious prosecution, abuse of process, interference with one's right of privacy and the intentional infliction of mental distress.

The precise definition of these common torts is beyond the scope of this book. However, pertinent to this chapter is the notion that, generally speaking, a third party injured by the intentional tortious conduct of an agent cannot hold the principal liable for the resulting harm unless the principal authorized the tort or the tort was committed to directly further or protect the interests of the principal. If the tortious conduct was unintentional, the injured party may hold the principal liable even though the conduct was not authorized; this result is more fully explained below.

TORT LIABILITY OF A PRINCIPAL TO A THIRD PARTY

A fundamental principle of law is that an individual is always liable for his own torts. If one is acting as an agent and negligently operates the principal's car injuring a third party, the agent is liable to the third party. However, the agent is usually seldom as wealthy as the principal. Therefore, the injured third party is more concerned with finding a legal way to impute the agent's tortious conduct to the principal than he is in recovering a judgment against the agent. It is fair to assume then that in most of the cases presented, the agent would be liable to the third party for his tortious conduct. The important inquiry is, under what circumstances will the principal be liable for the torts of the agent? A corollary to this first important issue is that if the third party does succeed in recovering a judgment against the principal, the principal can then usually hold the agent liable. That is, the agent is usually required to indemnify the principal for loss suffered as a result of the agent's negligence.

PRINCIPAL NEGLIGENT WITH RESPECT TO HIRING AN AGENT OR ENTRUSTING PROPERTY TO THE AGENT

Since one is almost always liable for his or her own negligence, a principal may be liable to a third party because of his or her own negligence in hiring the agent or entrusting potentially harmful tools to an agent. This is an act of negligence independent of the agent's act. Such liability is well demonstrated in the following case.

MURRAY v. MODOC STATE BANK
181 Kan. 642, 313 P.2d 304 (S. Ct. Kan., 1957)

SCHROEDER, Justice

The petition in substance alleges that one Donald Breithaupt was employed as the cashier and managing officer of the defendant, The Modoc State Bank, a banking corporation at Modoc, Kansas, on January 1, 1952, and was employed continuously in that capacity until on and after March 9, 1954; that plaintiff and Breithaupt had business transactions involving plaintiff and defendant and also involving plaintiff and Breithaupt; that the relationship between plaintiff and Breithaupt was strained and angry; that Breithaupt had threatened bodily harm to the plaintiff; that once when plaintiff had gone to the defendant bank to transact business with defendant, Breithaupt had assaulted him; that the violence and antagonism of Breithaupt grew so great that plaintiff could not in safety go to the defendant bank to transact business but was compelled to do so by mail, all of which facts were known and understood by the defendant; that plaintiff was indebted to the defendant; that on or about the 9th day of March, 1954, plaintiff attempted to transact business with the defendant by mail, particularly the depositing of checks to his personal account, that Breithaupt telephonically requested plaintiff to come to the defendant bank to discuss the transaction with him, but that plaintiff declined to do so; that thereafter and on the 9th day of March, 1954, Breithaupt went to the plaintiff's home and demanded to see the plaintiff; that plaintiff went onto the porch of his home to see Breithaupt; that Breithaupt demanded that plaintiff deposit said checks as he, Breithaupt, directed and further demanded that plaintiff execute and deliver to the defendant a property statement for the benefit of defendant; that plaintiff declined to forthwith comply with said demand, whereupon Breithaupt jerked plaintiff from the porch, struck him with his fists, threw him to the ground, and fell upon him, inflicting upon the plaintiff the injuries complained of.

The petition then specifically alleges:

That said injuries complained of were caused by and as a direct result of the negligence of the defendant in the following particulars, without which negligence the injuries would not have occurred, to wit:

1. In permitting the aforementioned Donald Breithaupt to manage and conduct the affirs of said defendant with this plaintiff. . . .
3. In continuing the aforenamed Donald Breithaupt in its employ after having notice or when it should have had notice, of his violent, aggressive, and antagonistic disposition toward this plaintiff.
4. In directing and permitting said Donald Breithaupt to transact business with this plaintiff when it knew, or by the exercise of reasonable care, should have known, that such would reasonably result in an assault on and injury to this plaintiff. . . .

X

That as a result of the acts committed by this defendant, this plaintiff suffered a broken left leg, a comminuted fracture involving the upper tibia, and a comminuted fracture of the proximal end of the left tibia, one of the fracture lines entering the mid portion of the articular surface of the tibia at the left knee. That such break caused a puncture wound below the tibial tuberosity; that this plaintiff suffered a fracture of the left fibula, all of which necessitated an open reduction of said fractures and breaks, the removal of both menisci, the placement of a tibial bolt across the upper tibia with plates along both sides of the upper tibia, and the alignment and fixation of the fracture fragments by means of wire, metal bolts and two metal plates.

The petition further sets up the various items for which the plaintiff seeks damages and prays judgment for $65,822 and costs. Breithaupt was not joined in the action. The petition was filed on March 8, 1956.

The defendant filed a demurrer to the petition of the plaintiff on the ground that the petition failed to state a cause of action in favor of the plaintiff and against this defendant. After hearing argument the district court overruled the demurrer. The defendant appeals and specifies as error the overruling of defendant's demurrer to the plaintiff's petition.

It will be observed that the cause of action arose on the 9th day of March, 1954, and the petition was filed March 8, 1956, which was one day less than two years.

The first question considered is whether or not the plaintiff's cause of action is outlawed by the statute of limitations.

The defendant argues that this is simply a case of assault and battery and that if an action had been brought against the servant, Breithaupt, or if the servant had been joined as a party defendant in this action, the case could have been nothing more than assault and battery. . . .

Admittedly, if this petition is construed as one charging the defendant with the assault and battery committed by Breithaupt, the managing officer of the bank, the one-year limitation under G.S. 1949, 60-306, Fourth, bars recovery by the plaintiff in that the face of the petition discloses the action was filed more than one year after the cause of action arose. However, if the petition is construed as one alleging actionable negligence against the bank, then a two-year limitation under G.S. 1949, 60-306, Third, applies and the plaintiff's right to maintain the action is not barred under the statute of limitations.

The defendant argues that the injury of which the plaintiff complains was occasioned and caused by the assault and battery, and his attempt to change the cause of action into a negligence action by alleging the negligence of the defendant in hiring and retaining a cashier and general manager with known violent, quarrelsome and antagonistic tendencies, is an effort to circumvent the statute of limitation. . . .

This subject has been thoroughly discussed in earlier decisions of this court and the law is now clear that the fundamental distinction between assault and battery, on the one hand, and negligence, on the other, is that the former is *intentional* and the later is *unintentional.* . . .

In *McMillen* v. *Summunduwot* Lodge, 143 Kan. 502, 54 P.2d 985, this court quoted with approval from 45 C.J. 631, defining actionable negligence as follows:

> To constitute actionable negligence there must be not only a lack of care, but such lack of care must involve a breach of some duty owed to a person who is injured in consequence of such breach. * * * In every case involving negligence there are necessarily three elements essential to its existence: (1) The existence of a duty on the part of defendant to protect plaintiff from the injury; (2) failure of defendant to perform that duty; and (3) injury to plaintiff from such failure of defendant. When these elements are brought together, they unitedly constitute actionable

negligence, and the absence of any one of these elements renders the complaint bad or the evidence insufficient. A judicial definition bringing out with admirable conciseness the elements of actionable negligence is as follows: 'Negligence is an unintentional breach of a legal duty causing damage reasonably foreseeable without which breach the damage would not have occurred.' 143 Kan. at page 509, 54 P.2d at page 989.

It is not a necessary element of negligence that the defendant anticipate the precise injury sustained. . . .

The Restatement of Law, Torts,§ 284, pp. 744, 745, defines "negligent conduct" thus:

> Negligent conduct may be either:
> (a) an act which the actor as a reasonable man should realize as involving an unreasonable risk of causing an invasion of an interest of another, or
> (b) a failure to do an act which is necessary for the protection or assistance of another and which the actor is under a duty to do.

The precise point before this court for decision is a matter of first impression. Simply stated, the question is whether a master may be held liable for injuries to a third person proximately resulting from the incompetence or unfitness of his servant, where the master was negligent in selecting or retaining an incompetent or unfit servant. . . .

The petition filed in the instant case was not attacked by motion. It is thus entitled to a liberal construction most favorable to the pleader. Allegations to the plaintiff's detriment are excluded. The petition does not allege a cause of action under the doctrine of *respondeat superior*. Fairly construed, the petition alleges a cause of action in negligence against the bank and not a tort by its servant or agent. The allegations of the petition meet all the requirements for actionable negligence. . . .

We hold that the doctrine of *respondeat superior* is not involved in the instant case. Construing the pleading most favorably to the petitioner as we must, the issue presented is whether the employer, The Modoc State Bank, was negligent in retaining its managing officer, Breithaupt, who had propensities toward violence. What the evidence will disclose upon trial of the case we are not at liberty to speculate. . . .

Some of the cases in which it was held there was sufficient showing that a master was negligent in keeping his servant in employment are: *Duckworth v. Apostalis*, D.C., 208 F. 936, where a guest sued to recover for injuries inflicted by an employee known by the master to have made previous assaults on guests; *Crawford* v. *Exposition Cotton Mills*, 63 Ga. App. 458, 11 S.E.2d 234, where a customer of a store sued to recover for injuries by a servant known by the master to have an unusual and abnormally high temper; *Priest* v. *F.W. Woolworth Five & Ten Cent Store*, 228 Mo. App. 23, 62 S.W.2d 926, where a customer sought recovery for injuries inflicted by a servant while he was engaged in an act of horseplay and who was known by the manager to have been guilty of previous acts; and *Hall* v. *Smathers*, 240 N.Y. 486, 148 N.E. 654, where a tenant of an apartment house sought to recover as against the master for injuries by a servant known by the master to be a drunkard and incompetent and dangerous.

The following jurisdictions have expressly or impliedly indicated that an employer may be primarily liable for a personal assault by an employee upon a customer, patron, or other invitee, if he has failed to exercise due care to avoid the selection or retention of employees who will assault such invitees: California, Dakota, Georgia, Kentucky, Massachusetts, Michigan, Missouri, Mississippi, Nebraska, New York, Ohio, Pennsylvania, Washington, and several federal districts. . . .

In conclusion, we hold that the plaintiff has alleged a cause of action against The Modoc State Bank on the theory of negligence.

The ruling of the trial court in overruling the demurrer to plaintiff's petition should be and hereby is affirmed.

PRICE, Justice (dissenting).

In my opinion the decision of the court confuses form and substance. What plaintiff actually is attempting to do is to recover, under the guise of a negligence action, for an assault and battery. Despite the language in which the petition is couched, the real wrong complained of, and the real basis of his action — is the assault and battery. An action to recover for an assault and battery must be brought within one year (G.S. 1949), 60-306, Fourth). This action was brought too late. Defendant's demurrer should have been sustained. For this reason I respectfully dissent.

PARKER, C. J., joins in the foregoing dissent.

◆◆◆

Case Questions

1. Why did not the injured plaintiff also sue Donald Breithaupt?
2. Carefully define the negligent act for which the defendant was liable.

VICARIOUS LIABILITY OF THE PRINCIPAL

Vicarious liability is a type of liability imposed upon the principal for the tortious acts of the agent when the principal was not directly liable for the tort and the tortious conduct had not been authorized. Vicarious liability of the principal is based upon the doctrine of Respondeat Superior ("let the master answer"). There is no legal doctrine or principle more vital to the law of agency and more necessary to the understanding of the law of business associations than respondeat superior. This doctrine and the reasons therefor are fully explained in the following edited article. The reader is asked to read the article carefully and to make a list of the reasons supporting the need for the doctrine of respondeat superior.

SPECULATIONS AS TO "RESPONDEAT SUPERIOR"
Warren Abner Seavey

(Reprinted by permission of the publisher and Harvard Law School from *Harvard Legal Essays,* Written in Honor of and Presented to Joseph Henry Beale and Samuel Williston, Cambridge, Mass.: Harvard University Press, 1934; edited by the authors with some footnotes deleted. Copyright © 1934, Harvard Law School.)

Respondeat superior, as the phrase is commonly used, summarizes the doctrine that a master or other principal is responsible, under certain conditions, for the conduct of a servant or other agent although he did not intend or direct it. In practice, it is used chiefly with reference to the liability of a master for the torts of a servant, but its principle includes, as well, the liability of one who is not a master for the undirected contracts made for him by his agent in cases in which there is not the obvious contract basis, such as exists where the agent has apparent authority. Similar reasons lie back of the rules established for both types of situation.

The entire field of vicarious liability is far broader than that of respondeat superior, but in most other cases there is at present liability for the conduct of others only where it is said that there is some fault on the part of the person made responsible, as in the case of the parent who has not used care to restrain the activities of a dangerous child. That the principal is made responsible for certain injurious conduct of the agent, although the principal did not intend it and was not negligent in failing to foresee it or to control the agent, is said to make the doctrine unjust, and a number of unkind remarks have been made about its ancestry. . . .

It is . . . interesting to me to speculate upon whether the principles upon which the rules of respondeat superior are based are in accordance with current legal conceptions and are reasonably just to the individuals involved and to society. If we agree with Mr. Justice Holmes that "common sense is opposed to making one man pay for another man's wrong unless he actually brought the wrong to pass," and if we agree with Holmes that a master has not brought to pass the wrong done by a servant when the master neither commanded nor intended the result, we must view with suspicion the extra-ordinary vitality of the doctrine. It is difficult to believe, however, that a principle opposed to common sense should have existed so long and still be so vigorous. . . . The fact that the supposed victims of the rule, the employing class, usually powerful and vocal in the protection of their interests, have not been militant in demanding a change, and that the rule is constantly expanding without meeting substantial opposition during a time of searching analysis and self-revelation, is some evidence that it does not greatly depart from the common feeling of justice which it is the primary function of the law to satisfy.

It is quite true that we have no sure tests of the ethical basis or economic expediency of respondeat superior. We have no authoritative code of ethics, nor are the economists or psychologists likely soon to be successful in so uniting upon principles that those whom they would make the beneficiaries of their views will accept them as the basis of conduct. In the absence of such definitive information, it appears feasible only to set down some a priori reasons for my belief that respondeat superior is not out of line with our 1934 conceptions of liability or of justice to the employer; that the field of liability without either personal or "constructive" fault is rapidly widening both as to those who are within the classic categories of principal and master and as to others whom we term independent contractors and bailees.

THE MASTER AS A CAUSE

... In a very large proportion of the master and servant cases, the servant either causes the harm by the use of some instrumentality given to him by the employer, or the harm arises in the course of or because of a transaction entrusted to him by the master. ... Where a servant uses excessive force in ejecting a trespasser or in recapturing a chattel for the master, the wrongful act is usually performed in an excess of zeal to protect the interests which the master has entrusted to him. Even in the very modern cases, which sometimes permit recovery against the master for blows given by a servant in a personal quarrel resulting from a business dispute, the employment has a very close physical connection with the result, although we may think it is unfair that the master should be subjected to liability. If there is not this reasonably intimate connnection between the employment and the injury to the third person, the master is not liable, a result which, using the language of causation, may be explained on the theory that the employment has so little connection with the final result that it may be disregarded. This point of view is brought out in the "detour" cases where, if the servant has departed widely from the territorial limits within which he has been commanded to remain, the employer is not liable, even though the harm would not have been occasioned had the instrumentality not been entrusted to the servant for the master's business. ...

THE JUSTICE OF LIABILITY WITHOUT MORAL FAULT

This leads to a consideration of the second objection, that it is unjust to subject to liability a person who has caused a result but has been guilty of no fault in producing it. ...

Mr. Justice Holmes once said that;

> unless my act is of a nature to threaten others, unless under the circumstances a prudent man would have foreseen the possibility of harm, it is no more justifiable to make me indemnify my neighbor against the consequences, than to make me do the same thing if I had fallen upon him in a fit, or to compel me to insure him against lightning.

... It has been suggested that what we now consider a primitive idea of "liability without fault" is merely liability for falling below a standard which includes taking sufficient precautions to prevent harm to others. ...

It must be admitted, however, that little argument is possible as to justice between individuals, since the factors determining this are too indefinite for computation, and the feeling of each person is almost entirely moulded by his upbringing. This applies perhaps even more strongly to Holmes's second distinction. Here, however, something more may be said, since it is generally agreed that a person whose physical being comes into injurious contact with another is more closely associated with the catastrophe than one who merely observes it. It may be that this feeling comes from the days when the act was not disassociated from the result, from the time of the taboo, when the tree that crushed was burned, and the ox which gored was destroyed. . . . Our feelings with reference to things and events are dependent upon our psychological inheritance and training. Whether or not in such cases it is expedient for the community as a whole to have the loss shifted from one to another is a matter disassociated from the matter of justice between the parties. . . .

* * *

In fact, legal fault upon which liability is based has little connection with personal morality or with justice to the individual; it is always tinctured with a supposed expediency in shifting the loss from one harmed to one who has caused the harm by acting below the standard imposed by the courts or legislators. But even this emasculated form of fault, while very important in the hierarchy of legal ideas, plays no part in many situations. It may be worth while briefly to indicate some of those in which it is recognized that fault is not essential to liability.

LIABILITY WITHOUT LEGAL FAULT

The cases which at once leap to mind are those of trespass to land, to chattels, or to persons, where there has been an intentional entry, asportation, or touching under a mistake as to ownership or consent. An innocent converter is subject to liability for the full value of the goods, and this although he obtains no benefit from them, as where an agent innocently sells goods which have been given to him by his principal but which in fact belong to another. For defamation, it would appear that one is liable to a person defamed although there is no intent to make a defamatory statement about the plaintiff or about anyone. . . .

Possession of land or chattels may also lead to liability without fault. One acquiring buildings improperly constructed apparently becomes responsible at once for their condition if it causes harm to third persons, irrespective of his opportunity to remedy the defect. Likewise, the owner of land may be responsible for the escape of injurious substance from his land into that of another, provided the situation may be described as a nuisance. The commonlaw rule as to the liability for the straying of domestic animals or for harm done by wild or vicious animals, after having been abrogated in some jurisdictions, is now substantially where it was four hundred years ago. . . . The use or keeping of explosives, and the use of airplanes, are other prominent illustrations of activities in which liability is divorced from fault. . . .

Without considering the field of vicarious liability, . . . it would appear that after nearly a century and a half devoted to the philosophic conception that there should be liability only if there is fault, the net result has been only to make a modified form of it an inlay in the common-law idea that the price of action is liability for harm caused by it. . . . (I)n any event there are enough situations where fault, even in its artificial legal sense of failing to live up to a specified standard of conduct, plays no part, to indicate that the imposition of liability upon a master for the commanded acts of his servant or upon a principal for the misrepresentations and unauthorized contracts of an agent is not out of line with current ideas of justice.

JUSTIFICATION FOR "RESPONDEAT SUPERIOR"

Considering the reasons which have been given for the existence of liability of an individual who has been guilty of no legal fault, it would appear that most of these reasons apply with somewhat the same force to the liability of a master or other principal. The predominant reason for the objective standard in contracts is the advancement of trade through the comparative certainty created by a fixed standard. In many situations, the same reason applies to the imposition of liability upon a principal for the unauthorized contracts of an agent. If the business of the world is to be done by agents, third persons in dealing with them must be relieved, so far as is possible, from uncertainty as to the extent of their authority, and it is for the general advantage of the entire class of persons acting as principals that occasionally an individual principal should be held liable for contracts which he did not authorize. . . .

Similar reasons apply to cases where an agent employed to manage a business deals in an unauthorized manner with a third person who does not know the position which the agent occupies. In many of these cases there is no basis for finding apparent authority, and hence, if the principal is liable upon the authorized contract it is not because of a "holding out," since the agent was not held out to the plaintiff, but because of a business policy which requires that third persons be reasonably protected in their dealings with those who in fact have been placed in a position of authority by the principal, although the authority has been abused. . . .

Perhaps the strongest reason which can be given for the imposition of "absolute" liability applies even more strongly in the case of vicarious liability, that is, the fact that one who is responsible for all consequences is more apt to take precautions to prevent injurious consequences from arising. If the law requires a perfect score in result, the actor is more likely to strive for that than if the law requires only the ordinary precautions to be taken; the cases where, . . . an actor is made absolutely liable for consequences indicated that this reason plays a very large part. The extent to which the law of torts has a preventative function is of course debatable, and it is doubtful if reliable statistics can be obtained as to its effect upon the ordinary individual. To me, however, it seems fairly obvious that the likelihood of personal liability plays a very important part in our affairs. . . .

But whether or not the law of torts has an appreciable deterrent effect upon individuals, it has important consequences where servants are employed. Without further investigation, our self-questioning inevitably leads us to believe that respondeat superior results in greater care in the selection and instruction of servants than would be used otherwise. . . .

Another reason for liability without fault in many cases is the difficulty of proving negligence. This reason is particularly cogent in imposing liability upon a master. Whether an employee was unfit at the time of the accident or whether there was improper supervision would ordinarily have to be proved by the testimony of fellow workers. Truthful testimony in such cases is difficult to obtain from the members of a well-disciplined organization. Aside from self-interest, which is obvious, only disgruntled fellow-workers are likely to subject themselves to the name commonly applied to a "tattle tale" within the organization. If the instructions of the master are such as to require acts likely to be tortious, if obeyed, ordinarily the instructions will be brought to light by the servant only in the comparatively rare case where he does so in self-protection.

Another reason not frequently acknowledged specifically by the courts is the "long purse" cynicism of Baty. The bald statement that the master should pay because he can pay may have little more than class appeal, although it is in conformity with the spirit of our times to believe that if one is successful enough either to operate a business or to employ servants, in addition to the income taxes taking off the upper layers of soft living, he should pay for the misfortunes caused others by his business or household. This, of itself, may not be a sufficiently strong reason; the liability of a master for the negligence of his domestic servants is less obvious than that of one employing his servants in business. Today, however, we realize that the loss from accident usually falls upon the community as a whole, and that a cause of action is not money in pocket. . . . The business enterprise, until it becomes insolvent, can shift losses imposed upon it because of harm to third persons to the consumers who ultimately pay, and it is not unjust to have the burden of misfortune shared by those who benefit from the work in the course of which liability occurs. It is this which is leading to the extension of absolute liability. . . .

Finally, in the situations most frequently occurring, that is, those in which a corporation or other business organization is a defendant, it is reasonably obvious that the doctrine of respondeat superior is practically a necessity. Without this, the members of the organization, normally free in any event from personal liability, would be released as to the funds contributed, not only for the harms caused by the physical negligence of servants, but also for the wrongs done by the deceit and other similar torts of the directors and other corporate executives. To permit a group of persons so to organize that without personal liability they can secure the profits resulting both from the lawful and the unlawful conduct of those in charge of the organization without having the assets subject to liability for the harm caused by the unlawful conduct, is so shocking that it would seem to be unnecessary to do more than to state the alternatives. Whether or not the rule of respondeat superior was sustainable as a matter of justice when it originated, it is reasonably clear that in the modern world we cannot get along without it.

SPREAD OF "RESPONDEAT SUPERIOR"

Irrespective of its justice or injustice, its expediency or inexpediency, the doctrine of respondeat superior is spreading rapidly, both within and without the field of agency.

In the cases involving unauthorized contracts made by an agent, the liability of a principal has been widely extended, very largely through an expansion in the original meaning of "apparent authority." It is reasonably clear that where a person represents to another that his agent is authorized to do a specified class of acts, such person should be liable for what the agent does within the field as thus defined. It is becoming increasingly recognized, however, that in many cases the person who is given a cause of action against the principal has not relied upon any statement or representation for which the principal is in any way responsible. In a wide variety of situations the courts find a contract where an agent, usually a manager, has disobeyed orders in dealing with a person who had no notice of the extent of his authority. That there is no apparent authority in such cases is obvious where the agent of an undisclosed principal acts. Yet the principle of *Watteau* v. *Fenwick,* in which the undisclosed principal was held liable for the unauthorized acts of his manager, although causing much comment at the time, has now become a commonplace, frequently under the pseudonym of apparent authority.

Again, there has been a wide expansion of the principal's liability for the fraud of his agent. . . . The present nearly universal liability-invoking formula is that "the principal is liable if he has placed the agent in a position which enables him to make the fraud possible". . . . The same tendency to expand the unauthorized power of the agent is seen in those cases where the principal has entrusted an agent with goods for a particular purpose and the agent has disposed of them in violation of the principal's orders. The older cases tended to limit the agent's power of conveyance to the precise authority given; the modern cases tend to deprive the principal of the subject matter if it comes to the hands of a person who buys, reasonably believing the agent to be the owner or to have authority to sell.

The liability of a master to a third person for the torts of a servant has been widely extended by aid of the elastic phrase "scope of the employment" which may be used to include all which the court wishes to put into it. At the beginning of the nineteenth century, the courts were cautiously expanding the master's liability beyond the field of commanded acts, liability for the main part being confined to negligent acts resulting in physical harm and to cases involving mistake by a servant as to the subject matter. Where the servant performed what was described as a "wilful act," the master was not responsible. . . . Likewise the master was not held liable for the conduct of a servant while he was going on "a frolic of his own" and the extent of the frolic was interpreted liberally in favor of the master. The expansion in this field has been rapid. In the detour case, the tendency is more and more to find that even a very extended detour is within the scope of the employment, and in many jurisdictions, at least, the servant reenters his employment, although far from his sphere of action, as soon as he decides so to do. . . .

On the fringes of the master and servant relationship are groups of cases where liability has been created through the wide use of fictions. Thus, the liability of a carrier to a passenger for an injury caused by a servant and that of a bailee to a bailor for the theft by a servant in charge of goods is imposed on the theory that the carrier or the bailee contracted to be responsible for unlawful conduct by the servant. The older cases imposed such liability only upon public utilities; the modern trend is to impose liability upon all employers. Another large group of cases includes those where the head of the household is made responsible for the negligent operation of an automobile in the hands of a dependent member of it. It is perhaps in these cases, in which a spurious relationship of master and servant has been created, that the reasons for respondeat superior most clearly indicate liability, since there is a delivery to a person financially irresponsible and frequently of an age to be reckless, of a machine very dangerous to others which, but for the entrusting, he would not have operated. It is only to be regretted that, in reaching a result which is consistent with modern tendencies, the courts should have felt constrained to use fictions which would have been praiseworthy two hundred years ago but which now seem unnecessary. . . .

The year 1934 is not a time for prophecies. The changes in the world are so great and so recent that to attempt a forecast concerning either the trend of legislation or of judicial opinion is an extra hazardous occupation. There would seem, however, to be an adequate basis for a guess that . . . the absence of negligence or fault . . . will play a continually smaller part, and that we are likely to revert to the primitive rule by which liability for harm, at least of certain types, is not dependent upon either legal or moral fault. Whether or not, however, this guess proves to be correct, it seems clear that until we have an entirely changed form of political organization, the principles of respondeat superior will not disappear.

Article Review Questions

1. Professor Seavey dicusses at least five reasons for the doctrine of respondeat superior. What are they?
2. Professor Seavey suggests at one point that the doctrine of respondeat superior is based more upon expediency than justice. Why is it not "just" that a principal/master who is in business to make a profit should be required to pay the cost incurred in conducting the business. Certainly this cost includes injury by servants to innocent third persons. Obviously, our perceptions of what is "just" change over the decades. Note that many businesses still behave as though it is "unjust" for them to bear the cost of eliminating the pollution caused by the business; or, that it is "unjust" that they should be required to provide a safe working environment for the employees.

BASIC DISTINCTIONS: MASTER, SERVANT, INDEPENDENT CONTRACTOR

Mentioned throughout the article by Seavey are the terms master and servant. Some authorities believe that the law of master and servant exists independently from the law of principal and agent. However, we believe that the *Restatement* is correct when it defines master and servant as a subclassification of principal and agent. The *Restatement* provides:[5]

1. A master is a principal who employs an agent to perform service in his affairs and who controls or has the right to control the physical conduct of the other in the performance of the service.
2. A servant is an agent employed by a master to perform service in his affairs whose physical conduct in the performance of the service is controlled or is subject to the right to control by the master.
3. An independent contractor is a person who contracts with another to do something for him but who is not controlled by the other nor subject to the other's right to control with respect to his physical conduct in the performance of the undertaking. He may or may not be an agent.

Examining the circumstances in which courts apply the definitions above is very important because of the legal consequences which flow from the designation of a master-servant relationship, rather than a principal-independent contractor relationship. Simply stated, these legal consequences are that a *master is liable for the unintentional torts of his servant committed while acting in the scope of employment.*[6] One who employs an independent contractor suffers *no liability based upon respondeat superior for this agent's torts!* However, liability of a principal in the latter case may be imposed if the activity of the independent contractor is ultrahazardous or a state or federal statute or public policy holds that principal shall be liable (discussed later in this chapter).

The key to understanding the above definitions is to focus on who has the *right to control the physical conduct* of the supposed servant. The control need not be exercised, it is the *right* to control that is important. What are some typical circumstances which indicate this right to control? The *Restatement* suggests the following:[7]

1. The extent of control the principal may exercise over the details of the agent's work;
2. Whether or not the agent is engaged in a generally recognized occupation of his own in which he exercises his own independent skill and judgment;
3. Whether the principal or the agent supplies the instrumentalities, tools and place of work; and
4. The method of payment, whether by time or by the job.

Generally, if the main objective of the agency is to accomplish a *physical result* such as building, destroying or altering something in the physical environment and the principal is to direct this work then chances are good that a master-servant relationship exists. If the main objective of the agency is to accomplish a more abstract, non-physical or legal result such as negotiating, contracting, auditing, etc., then chances are that a principal-independent contractor relationship exists.

The *Restatement* distinguishes between two types of independent contractors.[8] An independent contractor may be an agent of the principal (sometimes called a non-servant agent) if he has the authority to contract for the principal (eg., a salesman); or an independent contractor may not be an agent. For example, if an independent contractor (I/C) contracts with an owner (O) to construct a home for O, and O reserves no right of direction over I/C and I/C is not authorized to contract for O, then I/C is not an agent of O, but is properly called an independent contractor.[9] However, the I/C may become an agent of O if O begins to interfere and direct the work of I/C.

The above classifications are only generalizations and sometimes the application of these abstract general principles to reality can be very difficult. Perhaps the most difficult circumstances involve traveling salesmen. These agents are hired to contract for the principal and must do so in circumstances where a physical act (traveling by auto) is usually necessary. Should the principal be liable when the agent negligently operates an auto on a business-related trip? The answer depends upon whether or not this agent can be classified as a servant at the moment the negligent act occurred. Such facts as the ownership of the auto, the principal's right to control the route traveled and the right to designate who should be called upon by the agent become very important. Usually if the agent owns his own car and selects his own route and customers, the principal will not be liable. Conversely, if the auto is owned by the principal and the principal selects the route and customers, the agent may be termed a servant, thus creating liability for the principal/master for his unintentional torts.

In a few instances a non-servant agent or independent contractor may create tort liability of the principal based upon respondent superior or a doctrine very similar to it. These instances are the commission of a tort within the *inherent scope* of the agency; that is, those torts committed during the very act for which the agent was employed. Since most non-servant agents are hired to achieve a legal or other rather abstract, non-physical result, the torts creating the principal's liability are those of a non-physical nature. These torts are, typically, misrepresentation, fraud, deceit, conversion and interference with contractual relations. Thus, while a principal who employs a traveling salesman who owns his own auto, selects his own route and customers may not be liable to a third party for the agent's tortious operations of the auto, he may be liable for the agent's misrepresentations or fraud in the negotiations for an authorized contract. Similarly, if a young accountant working for a Certified Public Accounting firm is negligent while driving his own car to see a client, most courts would not hold the firm liable for this act. However, if he negligently prepared an audit or misrepresented a firm's financial picture then the principal (the firm) most probably would be liable.

If it is found that a master-servant relationship exists, then a second inquiry must be made: was the tortious act committed within the scope of employment. The scope of employment is defined by the authority which the principal/master gives to the agent/servant. Generally, for an act to be within the scope of employment, it must be so related in substance and time to the reasons for the employment that courts can conclude that it is of the same general nature as that conduct which is authorized, and was accomplished while benefiting the principal/master. Of crucial importance here is that the liability of the master is expanded to cover not only those torts inherently connected with the employment situation but those *incidental* to it. That is, a master is liable for the incidental torts of his servants as well as those inherently connected with the employment.

For example, if a principal hires an agent to cut weeds in his field, and carefully explains how the weeds are to be cut and provides the tools for cutting, then the agent may be classified as a servant. If the servant is negligent in lighting a fire in the field to cook his lunch and burns up a third party's crops on adjacent land, the principal/master will be liable.[10]

The negligent act was not within the inherent scope of employment (cutting weeds) but was incidental to the employment.

If the servant commits a tort during activity which is intended to benefit only the servant, but may be on the master's time, courts might well hold that the servant was on a "detour" or "frolic" of his own and was beyond the scope of employment. This results in no liability for the principal. The beginning of the detour or frolic is relatively easy to establish. This occurs when the servant substantially departs from the established route with the intent to benefit himself. While some courts have said that deviating one block or a relatively short distance is not a detour, most courts would hold that a deviation of several miles or a deviation of considerable proportion was a detour.

What if the tort occurred after the servant had accomplished his objective and was returning to the established route? In this instance the courts are divided on the definition of the "scope of employment": some have held that the servant reenters the scope of employment at the moment of turning back; others have said that he reenters when he is reasonably close to the point of departure; others allow recovery from the principal only when the servant is back on the authorized road.[11]

In concluding this textual section on vicarious liability we wish to point out that utilizing the concepts of master-servant, principal-non-servant agent and independent contractor is not as simple or easy as one might at first think. Do not think of the term servant as denoting an agent who does only menial or manual work. Many servants perform work requiring brains rather than brawn. Corporate officers, highly skilled engineers, interns in hospitals and most of those other employees who are employed to achieve a physical result and to give their time rather than their product to their employers may be servants.[12] Moreover, it may be possible for one person to be an independent contractor for some tasks and a servant for others. For resolving complex issues in this area we suggest the reader look first for a precise definition of the conduct or work being performed for the principal at the time of the tortious conduct. Secondly, the reader should confine his or her focus to this circumstance and ask what was the purpose of the agency and what degree of control was exercised or was exercisable by the principal over the physical conduct of the agent? If the purpose of the agency was to achieve a physical result and there was a high degree of control over the physical conduct of the agent then a master-servant relationship might exist. Thirdly, if a master-servant relationship exists, the reader must then determine if, with regard to this specific act, it was within the scope of the agency or was incidental to the agency or beyond the scope of the agency.

Adopting an iron clad rule in this matter is impossible. Definitions of the scope of the agency relationship and matters of control are presented in terms of degrees. An agency relationship and a principal's control are dynamic, always changing. It might be best to think of control on a scale where the legal result varies as you vary the control. (see Fig. 5-1)

The following cases exemplify the application of some of the legal terms already discussed.

In the first case, *Flick* v. *Crouch*, the distinction between a master-servant relationship and principal-independent contractor is most important. If the persons employed to do the work were "employees" or servants of the employer, then the plaintiff would be denied use of the court system to seek damages for the death of her husband because cases by or on behalf of servants are to be brought under the workmen's compensation laws. These laws usually provide for compensation to an injured employee according to established tables which list the amounts to be paid in cases of injury. Workmen's Compensation Acts, prevalent in most of the states, are nothing more than a form of insurance. States (and in a few instances, private companies) undertake to insure employees against job related injury. Employers are required to pay a certain premium in exchange for this insurance coverage. If employees are covered by the Workmen's Compensation Laws, they are forbidden from using the state court system to seek damages for job related injuries.

The *Stockwell* case presents the classic outlines of a dispute between an injured third party and an alleged principal/master. As in the *Flick* case, the classification of the agent as a servant is crucial to the outcome.

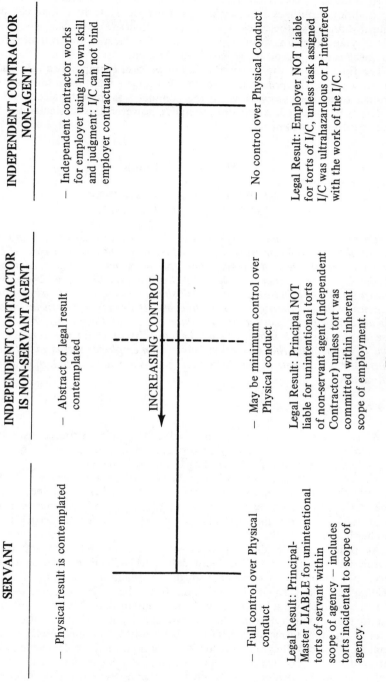

SERVANT

— Physical result is contemplated

— Full control over Physical conduct

Legal Result: Principal-Master LIABLE for unintentional torts of servant within scope of agency — includes torts incidental to scope of agency.

INDEPENDENT CONTRACTOR IS NON-SERVANT AGENT

— Abstract or legal result contemplated

INCREASING CONTROL

— May be minimum control over Physical conduct

Legal Result: Principal NOT liable for unintentional torts of non-servant agent (Independent Contractor) unless tort was committed within inherent scope of employment.

INDEPENDENT CONTRACTOR NON-AGENT

— Independent contractor works for employer using his own skill and judgment: I/C can not bind employer contractually

— No control over Physical Conduct

Legal Result: Employer NOT Liable for torts of I/C, unless task assigned I/C was ultrahazardous or P interfered with the work of the I/C.

Figure 5-1

The *McBride Express Co.* case is also a 'classic" in the sense that it portrays the traditional outlines of a servant on a detour. Note here that because the company furnished the truck it was assumed that the driver was a servant. Had the Maytag company furnished the auto for Morris, the outcome of the *Stockwell* case would probably have been different.

The final case in the group, the *Sandman* case, exemplifies a rule discussed earlier. That is, the principal or master will not be held liable for the tortious conduct of an agent/servant when the conduct was intentional or willful and could not be expected. As the dissent argues, however, this particular principle is applied differently in many states.

MELBA JEAN FLICK

v.

ELMER CROUCH, AND OTHERS
434 P.2d. 256 (S.Ct. Okl., 1967)

(Author's note: At issue in this case was the legal status of Crouch and others. This legal status determined which legal forum should hear this case. If Crouch were an "employee" of Parker, then the Workmen's Compensation Act of Oklahoma provided that the wrongful death action by the widow should be heard by the State Industrial Court, and state courts of general jurisdiction were specifically denied the right to hear the case. If Crouch were not an employee, but an independent contractor, the state court was the proper forum for the case. In this case it is proper to read the word "servant" for the word employee. That is, in this case the distinction between an employee versus an independent contractor is the same as the distinction between a servant and an independent contractor.)

◆ ◆ ◆

While working as a roughneck at a well site, decedent suffered instantaneous death when the derrick suddenly collapsed. At that time he was doing the duties of his employment with Parker Drilling Company (Parker).

This action by the widow attributes the collapse to faulty welds at the base of the derrick which failed to adhere and hold it together. She joined as parties-defendant eight persons engaged in welding business under various trade names. Their defective workmanship, she alleges, is responsible for the derrick's collapse and her husband's death.

At issue in the evidentiary proceedings on the defendant's plea to the jurisdiction was the status of these defending welders in relation to Parker, decedent's employer. The welders sought to establish that at the time of the welding operations, to which the defects are ascribed, they occupied the relation of Parker's employees; hence the welders maintain that they are entitled in this suit to that immunity from common-law liability in tort for negligence which extends by the terms of 85 O.S. 1961,§ 44(b) to "the employer and his employees." According to the widow's contention, these welders were independent contractors. The widow complains that under the evidence adduced below the status of the welders in relation to Parker presented a jury question. She asserts error in treating that issue as one of law.

The record adduced in support of the pleas to the jurisdiction discloses the following facts:

About a month before its collapse the derrick in question underwent certain modifications designed to reinforce it so that it could be used for drilling to a greater depth. The decision to do this work was made by Parker's superintendent who went to Odessa, Texas, to procure specifications for this job. The derrick in question was then brought to Parker's Oklahoma City yard for what is referred to as "relegging." This work consists of welding steel reinforcements onto the "legs" (base) of the rig.

The first person engaged for this operation was Elmer Crouch. It was he who procured other welders. He knew all of the welders in the area. There is nothing to indicate that he was told how many men, with how much equipment were to be engaged.

Crouch, who owns a truck and welding equipment, supplies his own welding rods and arc. He does business with Parker under the trade name of Crouch Welding Company. He "is not on the payroll of Parker." Although he "has the right" to take other jobs if he wants them, he stopped doing "outside" work because "there is no use looking for any place else if you are busy." He has been "in the welding business right at fifteen years." According to Parker's assistant secretary, Crouch is treated as a contractor. Parker's relation with him is the same as with "other contracted work." Under the terms of an arrangement of long standing Crouch maintains his own insurance coverage. He submits monthly an invoice to Parker's Tulsa office. His statements are computed on a time basis at the rate of $7.00 per hour. So far as the record discloses, Crouch keeps his time records and is not required to work regular hours.

When questioned why on the relegging job Crouch was also signing invoices submitted by other welders, Parker's assistant secretary stated that Crouch was "overseeing these other welding contractors" but denied that he was acting as a foreman for Parker. Parker's drilling superintendent, as well as his assistant, both unequivocally testified that Crouch and the other welders engaged for the jobs were instructed only as to that which was "ultimately" sought to be accomplished. According to them, Parker was interested neither in the details of the welding activities nor in the number of welders to be engaged; what they wanted was the "ultimate complete job of that rig being relegged." They had a sketch from which the dimensions of the steel to be attached to the rig could be determined. The steel was procured by Parker and "stacked * * * up there (in the yard) to be welded onto the rig." Crouch, who was procured to do the welding and who in turn engaged the other welders, was told neither how to use his equipment or what kind of equipment to use.

There is other evidence in the record from which it may be inferred that Crouch's status in relation to Parker was that of an employee.

As a general rule the line of demarcation between an independent contractor and a servant is not clearly drawn. The question of such relationship must be determined from the facts peculiar to each case. The various elements to be considered, as set forth in *Page* v. *Hardy*, Okl., 334 P.2d 782, 784, are:

"(a) the nature of the contract between the parties, whether written or oral; (b) the degree of control which, by the agreement, the employer may exercise on the details of the work or the independence enjoyed by the contractor or agent; (c) whether or not the one employed is engaged in a distinct occupation or business for others; (d) the kind of occupation with reference to whether, in the locality, the work is usually done under the direction of the employer or by a specialist without supervision; (e) the skill required in the particular occupation; (f) whether the employer or the workman supplies the instrumentalities, tools and the place or work for the person doing the work; (g) the length of time for which the person is employed; (h) the method of payment, whether by the time or by the job; (i) whether or not the work is a part of the regular business of the employer; (j) whether or not the parties believe they are creating the relationship of master and servant; and (k) the right of either to terminate the relationship without liability."

An independent contractor is one who engages to perform a certain service for another, according to his own method and manner, free from control and direction of his employer in all matters connected with the performance of the service, except as to the result thereof. Those who render service but retain control over the manner of doing it are not servants. Where the defendant's status forms a material issue in the case and the facts bearing on that issue are disputed, or where there is room for reasonable difference of opinion as to the proper inference to be drawn from the known facts, the issue is for the jury under proper instructions by the court. . . .

When a defendant's status forms a material issue in an evidentiary proceeding, such as in this case, which has for its object to determine whether the action sought to be prosecuted is one abrogated or taken away by the Workmen's Compensation Law, . . . or "reserved" to the workman (or his widow) . . . the rule to be applied by the trial court should be the same as that which governs at the trial: if the evidence concerning the status of a party defendant is reasonably susceptible of but a single inference, the question is one purely of law to be decided by the court. . . . but where the facts bearing on such issue are either disputed, or conflicting inferences may be reasonably drawn from the known facts, it is error to withhold the issue from the determination of the jury. . . .

Conflicting inferences may be drawn from the evidence as to the crucial issue of Crouch's relationship to Parker. This issue may not be decided by the court but must be submitted to the. . . .

When the case is tried on its merits, should the evidence then submitted on the issue of defendants' status be reasonably susceptible of but a single inference, the question of the court's jurisdiction is to be treated as one purely of law and be decided by the court; but if such evidence is either disputed or conflicting inferences may be reasonably drawn therefrom, the question of the defendants' status should be submitted to the jury along with other issues in the case.

Judgment dismissing cause for want of jurisdiction of the subject matter is accordingly reversed.

◆◆◆

Case Questions

1. State in three sentences or less what the holding of the court was in the above case.
2. If you were sitting on the jury when this case was tried in the state court what would you decide based upon the facts presented above? Was Crouch a servant or an independent contractor? List the circumstances or facts which lead you to this conclusion.

STOCKWELL v. MORRIS
46 Wyo. 1, 22 P.2d 189 (S. Ct. Wyo., 1933)

◆◆◆

BLUME, Justice

In this case Morris, salesman for the Maytag Intermountain Company, was driving his automobile from Hudson to Lander and collided with the automobile of plaintiff. The latter sued the salesman, as well as his principal, for damages caused by the collision. The court directed a verdict for the company, and the sole question herein is — assuming the agent to have been negligent — as to whether or not the court's action was right. The testimony herein is uncontradicted.

Morris was a salesman for the company in selling washing machines, and had been working for it for some years. That was his only occupation. He received a commission on all sales made, and no further compensation. He made no collections, but occasionally seems to have delivered washing machines sold. He drove his own automobile in the performance of his work, and paid his own expenses. He appointed and discharged subsalesmen under him, receiving a commission on their sales, and he took them out from time to time to show them how to sell washing machines. . . . The company furnished him with no rules or regulations as to his work, except as to the terms of the contracts to be made for the sale of washing machines. The details of the work were left to him. . . . On May 27, 1930 the date of his collision above mentioned, Morris, in company with his wife, drove his automobile to Lander to see a Mr. Tyler, a salesman under him, to see if he could help him in his work. After reaching Lander, he, at the suggestion of Tyler, and in company with him, drove to Hudson, to see Mrs. Radovitch, who had a Maytag washing machine which was out of repair, though repairs of machines were ordinarily made by a special representative of the company. Tyler discovered the trouble, fixed the machine, gratuitously, and he and Morris then drove back to Lander, and the collision occurred while doing so. Morris wrote the Maytag Company as to that fact.

Counsel for appellant argue that the Maytag Intermountain Company was the principal and Morris was its agent, and that the former is, accordingly, liable herein, and they say that the cases which hold contrary to their contention deal with the relationship of master and servant, and that such cases have no application here. But an attorney is an agent. If, then, in attempting to manage his client's case, he, without specific directions, travels in an automobile to see a man who, in his opinion, might become an important witness in his case, is his client responsible? So we have "Ford agencies," "Buick agencies," and other similar "agencies," handling products of automobile manufacturers. While today the managers of these agencies, ordinarily, perhaps, buy such products, they might handle them tomorrow on commission. They are agents, in the broad sense of that term, but should the manufacturer be held responsible for all the torts that the former might commit in disposing of these products? The Curtis

Publishing Company, located at Philadelphia, every week sends its *Saturday Evening Posts* throughout the country. If a boy in Cheyenne, while on the errand of soliciting subscriptions for the magazine, or delivering it, negligently runs into another with his bicycle, should the company be held responsible? The citation to these examples, which might be multiplied many times, shows that the solution of the problem before us is not as easy as counsel for appellant seem to think, and in view of the fact that the case before us is one of the first impression here, we have deemed it expedient to give it more attention than counsel for appellant apparently have thought it necessary.

Prior to the latter part of the seventeenth century, a master was not responsible for the torts of his servants, unless committed by his express command or subsequent assent. But in the case of *Jones* v. *Hart*, . . . decided in 1699, it was held that if a servant driving a cart negligently runs into another cart, the master is liable. And from about that time commenced to be developed the modern doctrine that a master is responsible for the torts of his servant committed within the scope of his employment. . . . Voices against this doctrine were heard from time to time. As late as 1876 Lord Bramwell told a Parliamentary committee that he could not "see why the law should be so * * * why a man should be liable for the negligence of his servant, there being no relation constituted between him and the party complaining." . . . But dissenting voices have been swept aside. Shaw, C. J. said in *Farwell* v. *Railroad Corporation* . . . that the "rule is obviously founded on the great principle of social duty, that every man, in the management of his own affairs, whether by himself or by his agents or servants, shall so conduct them as not to injure another." The doctrine was carried to its logical conclusion. Independent agents or contractors were treated as servants. It was not until the second quarter of the nineteenth century that it was doubted that the doctrine of respondeat superior should be applied in all cases in which one man was employed to perform an act for another. . . . (B)y the middle of that century it came to be recognized that there are many cases in which a man should not be held responsible for the acts of a representative, if the latter is not under his immediate control, direction, or supervision. Such representative has generally been called an independent contractor, a phrase that has acquired almost a technical meaning, originally, of course, applied to one who actually performed services under an independent contract.

Courts in cases of the character now before us have ordinarily ignored the difference between an agent and a servant, and have ordinarily merely attempted to determine in a particular case whether the person through whose instrumentality a negligent act was committed was a servant or ordinary agent on the one hand, or an independent contractor, or independent agent, pursuing a separate occupation, on the other. The controlling or principal test is generally stated to be as to whether or not the employer, using that term in a broad sense, has the right to control the details of the work to be done by the servant or agent, or whether the latter represents the former only as to the result to be accomplished. . . . The rules governing principal and agent are a later development in our law than those governing master and servant, and have branched off from the latter. A servant is defined as a person employed to perform personal service for another in his affairs, and who, in respect to his physical movements in the performance of the service is subject to the other's control or right to control, while an agent is defined as a person who represents another in contractual negotiations or transactions akin thereto. The reason assigned for the importance of making the distinction is that an agent who is not at the same time acting as servant cannot ordinarily make his principal liable for incidental negligence in connection with the means incidentally employed to accomplish the work intrusted to his care. . . . Of course, an agent may, as to some work performed for his principal, be a servant. But no personal service, not even the delivery of washing machines, is involved in this case, unless the driving of the automobile may be called such. And the gist of the controversy herein is as to whether the principal is liable for its agent's negligence while engaged in a more or less necessary physical act which is incidental to the performance of his general duties. . . .

One of the best statements which we have seen, particularly applicable in a case of the character now before us, is that of Professor Seavy in Tentative Draft No. 5 of the Restatement of the Law of Agency, page 100, where it is said: "A principal employing another to achieve a result but not controlling the details of his physical movements is not responsible for incidental negligence while such person is conducting the authorized transaction. Thus the principal is not responsible for the negligent physical conduct of an attorney, a broker, a factor or a rental agent, as such. In their movements and their control of physical forces, they are in the relation of independent contractors to the principal. It is only when to the relationship of principal and agent there is added that right to control physical details as to the manner of performance, which is characteristic of the relation of master and servant, that the person in whose service the act is done, becomes subject to liability for the physical conduct of the actor."

In this view, then, that the right of control of the physical movements – the automobile – is the decisive inquiry, it becomes important what the record discloses in that regard. The evidence shows that the Maytag Company furnished Morris no rules or regulations to govern him in the performance of the work but that the means and manner thereof was left to him. That, perhaps, does not definitely show that the right of control was not in the company. The fact that the company did not exercise control does not show that it did not have the right of control, though it may be some evidence thereof. It has been held that in the absence of a stipulation the existence or nonexistence of the right must be determined by reasonable inferences shown by the evidence. . . .

In the case at bar there was no express reservation of control, and none can be implied. In fact it would seem that in view of the fact that actual control of an automobile driven hundreds of miles away from the place of the employer can at best be theoretical only, even though actual control has been reserved, the right of such control should, in the case of this character, be able to be implied only from reasonably clear evidence showing it.

We think, accordingly, that the employer in this case ought not to be held liable. . . . Some criticism has been leveled at courts for their disagreement on this subject and for not finding a more decisive and clear-cut test. But it must be remembered that the rule that a master is liable for the negligence of his servant committed in the course of his employment – which is at the basis of the cases holding the employer in cases of this character liable – is founded not upon a rule of logic, but upon a rule of public policy, and hence the digression, not constituting an abrogation of the rule, must necessarily also involve the question as to how far public policy requires the digression to be made, and it is not to be wondered at that one court answers the question one way, another another way. . . .

Every rule should, of course, have a reason. Why should we depart from the ordinary rule applicable in the case of master and servant? Is that departure, in the case at bar, based on reason? We think it is. We have, it may be noted, laid some emphasis on the fact of the ownership of the automobile in question. . . .

Practically, in a case of the character before us, the agent has the sole power of control of his automobile. He, as owner, can distribute the risk of driving it by taking out insurance better than, or at least as well as, his principal. If he alone is held responsible for his negligence, that has a tendency to cause him to exercise care to prevent accidents. To put a man upon his own responsibility generally has that effect. And that prevention of automobile accidents is a matter of considerable, nay vital, importance today is, of course, attested by daily experience. And while this reason cannot be held to be controlling, or perhaps should not be even considered, in some cases, it furnishes at least some basis in the application of public policy.

The judgment of the trial court is, accordingly,

Affirmed.

◆◆◆

Case Questions

1. List the circumstances in which a traveling salesperson may cause liability for a principal through the negligent operation of an auto.
2. In your opinion would Maytag be liable to an injured third party if Morris were negligent in the process of repairing a washing machine?

THOMAS v. MCBRIDE EXP. CO.
266 S.W. 2d 11 (Ct. of App., Mo., 1954)

◆◆◆

ANDERSON, Presiding Judge

This is an action by Flody E. Thomas, Jr., as plaintiff, against defendant, McBride Express Company, a corporation, to recover damages for personal injuries alleged to have been sustained on September 14, 1952, as the result of a collission at the intersection of California and Caroline Avenues in the City of St. Louis between a motorbicycle being operated by plaintiff and a tractor type truck owned by defendant and operated by Michael Smyser, defendant's employee. The trial below resulted in a verdict and judgment in favor of plaintiff in the sum of $4,000. Defendant has appealed.

It was admitted by the defendant that it owned the tractor-trailer involved in the accident, and that Michael Smyser was in the company's general employ. Defendant was engaged in the business of long distance hauling from Mattoon,

Illinois, to St. Louis, Missouri. . . . He made trips during the week, and every other Sunday made what was known as the "long bread run." Such a trip was made on Sunday, September 14, 1952. Smyser's sixteen year old son Edward, with defendant's permission, accompanied Smyser on this trip. They arrived at defendant's St. Louis terminal at 1141 South Sixth Street about 12:30 p.m. Smyser left his equipment there and he and his son went by bus to visit friends named Scanlon who lived at 2709 Caroline Street. Smyser then left his son at this address and went to a ball game at Sportsman's Park. After the ball game had been in progress for about an hour it started to rain, whereupon Smyser left the park and returned to the Scanlon home about 3:00 or 3:30 p.m. He ate supper with his friends about 4:00 p.m. After supper he left and went to defendant's terminal to get the tractor-trailer. At the terminal miscellaneous freight was loaded onto the trailer. . . .

Smyser had been on this run for approximately six weeks. He testified that in leaving St. Louis "we always used Chouteau Avenue. That is the direct route to McArthur Bridge;" and his route back to Mattoon was through Litchfield, Taylorville, Springfield, and Decatur. Deliveries were made in each of these towns. To reach Chouteau Avenue . . . Smyser would drive south on Taylor Avenue to Chouteau, then east to the bridge. On cross-examination Smyser testified that he was not told by his employer what streets to travel, or told to follow any certain route. . . .

The witness . . . testified that on none of the nineteen or twenty runs that he had made had he never gone any other way . . . to McArthur Bridge except by way of Chouteau Avenue.

Smyser further testified that on the occasion in question he did not continue east on Chouteau Avenue, as he customarily did, but made a right turn onto California Avenue, intending to go south on California to Caroline Street to pick up his son Edward. Caroline Street runs east and west and is four or five blocks south of Chouteau Avenue. The Scanlon home on Caroline Street is located about one block east of California Avenue. Smyser further testified:

"Q. * * * Now, I will ask you, Mr. Smyser, did you have any load on your truck that had to be delivered or was destined to be delivered or picked up at any place south of Chouteau Avenue? A. No, sir.

"Q. Did you have any instructions or business to perform for the McBride Express Company that would require you to get off Chouteau Avenue and turn south on California? A. No, sir.

"Q. Did you have any other purpose in mind in doing that except to pick up your son? A. No, sir."

The collision with plaintiff occurred while Smyser was making a left turn into Caroline Street.

Liability in this case can only be imposed in the event it can be said that Smyser was, at the time of the accident, acting within the scope of his employment. An act of a servant is not within the scope of employment if it is done with no intention to perform it as a part of or incident to a service on account of which the servant is employed.

The solution of the problem presented is not merely a matter of measuring the distance, the time, or the direction of the departure from what may be called the path of authorized conduct. Such circumstances may guide the judgment, but will not be suffered to control it aside from other circumstances which may characterize the intent of the transaction.

A servant may in certain instances deviate from the most direct or authorized route and still be in the master's service. Thus it may be that one turns aside to avoid heavy traffic, or to seek a smoother route. There may be parallel routes leading in the direction of his ultimate destination, either of which could be said to be within his sphere of service, on the theory that it might be reasonably expected that he would, in the exercise of his best judgment, choose either while in the pursuit of his master's business; or he might turn aside to attend to necessary personal wants which are considered incidental to his employment. But any turning aside from the designated or customary route, where the sole motive is self interest, unmixed with any intent to serve the master, separates the servant from the master's service, regardless of the extent of the deviation. Any other rule would lead to inconsistencies and ultimate confusion in the law.

Smyser, defendant's servant, while making the journey to the Caroline Street address to pick up his son, was performing no service for his master. He was not within his contemplated sphere of service at the time, nor performing an act which could be said to be incidental to his employment. His deviation was not made to facilitate the movement of the freight he was employed to haul. His intent was to serve a private purpose. As a matter of law, Smyser was not within the scope of his employment when the collision occured.

Judgment Reversed.

◆◆◆

Case Questions

1. Was Smyser a servant or a non-servant agent?
2. Even if it were determined that Smyser were a non-servant agent, would not it be reasonable to argue that McBride might still be held liable for a tort within the scope of employment because driving was not merely incidental to the scope of employment, but was the very act for which he was hired?

SANDMAN v. HAGAN & STRIEGEL, d/b/a
Bean Plumbing and Heating Co., and Andrew Montagne
154 N.W. 2d 113 (S.Ct., Iowa, 1967)

It appears from the record that on November 7, 1963, the plaintiff Jerry Sandman, employed by the Sioux City Sewer Department, was directed to inspect a job at 2213 Pierce Street in Sioux City, Iowa, and arrived on the job between 8 and 9 A.M. His duty that particular morning was to inspect the installation, the hookup, and the backfill of the connection to the city water system being done by Beane Plumbing and Heating Co., hereafter referred to as the employer. The defendant Montagne and two other employees of Beane Plumbing and Heating Co., Lloyd Brunssen and Martin Wilde, were doing the actual work. A hole had been dug in the street approximately three to four feet wide, five feet long, and six feet deep. The installation and hookup had been completed and the backfill operation involving the refilling of the hole was awaiting the arrival of Sandman. In this operation a small quantity of dirt is first dumped into the excavation and then this dirt must be firmly tamped beneath the water pipe and main. . . . Inspector Sandman was there to see that the dirt was properly compacted under the main by the installing workmen. At the time of this incident defendant Montagne was on the street helping scoop dirt into the hole with a hand shovel. Lloyd Brunssen was in the hole spreading the dirt and tamping it under the pipes, and Martin Wilde was on the street near the hole attending his frontend loader tractor. An air compressor nearby that powered a pneumatic tamper was running during this time, which made it difficult to hear conversations in the area.

Sandman testified he was observing the backfill operation from above when he noticed that dirt had not been properly compacted under the main, and he brought this to the attention of Brunssen. Not being satisfied with the results of his directions, he jumped down in the hole to show Brunssen that there was a void under the main.

Brunssen testified that Sandman had said nothing to him about improper backfilling, but rather jumped into the hole with him and began shoving dirt into a gap under the main. Both testified that no altercation or abusive language occurred until Sandman had demonstrated to Brunssen that there was indeed a gap between the main and the ground. At this point Sandman testified that Brunssen called him an s. o. b. and other derogatory names, told him to get out of the hole, and said he had no business down there. . . .

Immediately following this name-calling, a fight took place between Sandman and Brunssen. Sandman testified that to the best of his recollection he struck Brunssen only once and that the fight lasted about two minutes. Brunssen testified that he did not strike Sandman, but doubled up to protect himself and that Sandman struck him several times on the face and body, and that the fight lasted about 15 to 30 seconds.

Montagne testified that he did not hear the conversation between Sandman and Brunssen prior to the fight because the noisy air compressor was running at the time, that the first thing he knew Sandman was pounding on Brunssen and he yelled at Sandman to stop but that he did not stop, and that he (Montagne) became scared that Brunssen might be hurt. Montagne then struck Sandman on the back of the head with a shovel. Although Sandman testified he saw Montagne swing the shovel at him, he did not hear Montagne say anything to him before he got hit with the shovel.

Martin Wilde testified that he saw Sandman striking Brunssen about the head and neck, that this lasted about 10 or 15 seconds, and that while Sandman was striking Brunssen he heard Montagne yell at Sandman to stop. He also said Sandman then looked up at Montagne and called him an s. o. b. and asked him if he wanted some too. . . .

After he was struck with the shovel, Sandman climbed out of the hole and said he asked for help and that the employees told him there was a phone booth on 20th and Pierce. . . .

It further appears there was a dispute between Sandman and Montagne over another backfill job two weeks before, in the presence of the employer's foreman. . . .

The jury returned a verdict for Sandman against all defendants. On motion by the employer, the trial court granted judgment notwithstanding the verdict for it, concluding there was insufficient evidence to sustain a finding that Montagne was acting within the scope of his employment. The trial court denied Montagne's motion for a new trial based upon his claim of insufficient evidence to sustain a verdict in the sun (sic) allowed and prejudicial errors in trial procedure. Plaintiff appeals from the granting of the employer's motion, and the employee cross-appeals.

The sole issue presented on appeal by appellant Sandman is whether at the time in question employee Montague was acting within the scope of his apparent authority so as to make the defendant employer liable and sustain the jury determination on that issue.

The trial court concluded there was no evidence to sustain a finding that Montagne's authority extended beyond that of putting in water lines and refilling excavations, or that his duties contemplated conflict with others, or that the assault was done in the furtherance of the employer's business or interests within the scope of his employment. We must agree.

I. It is well established in Iowa that under the common law the master and servant may each and both be liable for a servant's torts committed within the course of employment. ...

The difficulty encountered by various courts in cases of willful torts committed by servants has resulted in irreconcilable decisions, and unless carefully scrutinized, the authorities seem to be in hopeless confusion. ... The difficulty is in defining and applying the concept of acts within the course of employment or the scope of the servant's authority. These terms are often used loosely and not carefully analyzed. Even the text writers seem to have trouble relating the servant's duty and authority to scope of employment and, due to various decisions, use the words, "implied," "apparent," and "actual authority," to expand or diminish the duty of the servant upon which liability rests when courts seek evidence as to whether the tort was committed in the furtherance of the employer's business or interests.

It has been said an act is "within the scope of the servant's employment" where such act is necessary to accomplish the purpose of the employment and is intended for such purpose, although in excess of the powers actually conferred on the servant by the master. ...

It is safe to say that "within the scope of the employment" requires that the conduct complained of must be of the same general nature as that authorized or incidental to the conduct authorized. ... The facts in the Kentucky Wood case and the Minnesota Plotkin case are not greatly different. Both result in no employer liability. In each case, after an altercation with another vehicle on the highway, the bus company driver stopped his bus and assaulted the operator of the other vehicle. Both courts recognize the rule that to determine whether an agent's act is within the scope of employment so as to make the master liable therefore, the question is whether the agent's conduct is so unlike that authorized that it is "substantially different." Both state that, to render a master liable for a servant's battery, it is not sufficient that the battery is due to anger arising from the performance of the servant's duties. Consideration was also given therein to the claim that such driver action was employment-related because the employer's business was to keep the bus on schedule, but this was not deemed sufficient. ...

II. As we have pointed out, a deviation from the employer's business, or interest to pursue the employee's own business or interest must be substantial in nature to relieve the employer from liability. . . . Here, the employer contends the assault was clearly a deviation substantial in nature, for under no theory advanced would the duty of installing water lines and digging ditches include the exercise of force upon others. It is difficult to see how his employer's business or interest would ever be furthered by such an employee attack, especially on an inspector. The trial court found nothing was shown to sustain a finding that the act of defendant Montagne was anything his employment contemplated or was something which, if he would do lawfully, he might do in his employer's name. We agree. Of course, a deviation need not be of long duration in order to relieve the employer of liability if the deviation is substantial in nature. . . .

Although the question of whether an act is within the scope of employment is ordinarily a jury question, depending on the surrounding facts and circumstances, the question as to whether the act which departs markedly from the employer's business is still within the scope of employment may well be for the court. . . .

III. We are aware of the so-called modern trend to find liability in this class of cases on the basis that such wrongs are committed by the employee only because of the employment situation, and that since the employer has the benefit of the enterprise as between two innocent third parties, he is better able to bear the risk of loss. If he cannot altogether avoid such wrongs, he can at least minimize them. In those cases it is argued that a general sense of fairness requires that the employer, as the person interested and benefited by the business, rather than the persons who have no concern in or control over it, should bear the burden of such wrongs as incidental to such business. . . .

If employer liability is to be extended this far, we believe it should come from the legislature, and do not find that this concept has substantial support in judicial decisions.

We are satisfied here that the employee Montagne's assault on Inspector Sandman was a substantial deviation from his duties, that his act was substantially different in nature from that authorized by the employer, and that at the time thereof he was acting outside the scope of his employment. The trial court was correct in granting the employer's motion for judgment notwithstanding the verdict and must be affirmed on appellant Sandman's appeal. . . .

V. On cross-appeal defendant Montagne contends the trial court erred in denying his motion for directed verdict and his motion for a new trial. He relies on the following propositions for reversal: (1) that he was privileged to use reasonable force to come to the defense of Brunssen as a matter of law; . . .

It is well established in Iowa that a person is privileged to come to the defense of another about to be injured. Section 691.3 of the code states: "Any other person, in aid or defense of the person about to be injured, may make resistance sufficient to prevent the same." However, this section must be read in connection with section 691.1, which states: "Lawful resistance to the commission of a public offense may be made by the party about to be injured, or by others." The import of these two sections is to give a third party the right to come to the aid of another, but in doing so he must use lawful resistance. Lawful resistance, or self-defense, is tested by whether the force used to repel the attack was reasonable. Once the force used becomes unreasonable, the privilege ceases. . . .

Whether the force used was reasonable is generally a jury question, and the jury's conclusion will be sustained if there is any substantial evidence to support it. It does not appear the shovel was the only reasonable method to stop the fight. The jury so found, and there was no objection to the court's instruction on this issue.

In any event, we conclude that the reasonableness of the force used here was a jury question and the evidence is sufficient to sustain its finding that the force used was unreasonable under the circumstances. . . .

Having found no basis for reversal, the judgment of the trial court must be affirmed.

Affirmed.

BECKER, Justice

I dissent as to plaintiff's appeal from judgment in favor of defendant employer.

Thompson-Starrett Co. v. *Heinold* . . . involves a situation where an employee hit the employee of a subcontractor with a lead pipe when the plaintiff didn't move his equipment as ordered. "It is undisputed that in the early cases a master was held not liable for the tortious act of his servant, when the act was wanton and malicious. In later cases, the master is held liable for the wrongful act of the servant, notwithstanding its wanton and malicious character, if the act was done in the course and within the scope of his employment, and the determination of the question whether the tort was committed while the servant was acting in the course and within the scope of his employment is for the jury."

The foregoing statement is a short summation of the law as it has developed in the past thirty years. Standing alone the case would not necessarily persuade. But a careful reading of the very authorities cited by the majority; i.e., *Restatement, Second Agency* §245, Comment a (as amended by the Appendix, Restatement, *Second, Agency* § 245) . . . indicates the rule stated in *Thompson-Starrett Co.* v. *Heinold, supra,* is the majority view. It should be followed by this court. . . .

The change in *Restatement, Second, Agency,* § 245 as indicated in the Appendix written 23 years later should be especially noted because the change is substantial and weakens the authority upon which the majority relies. At page 389 the author of the Appendix states: "It is believed that it is now desirable to state a rule invoking a somewhat greater liability because of the cases in the intervening years. The courts of some states are more conservative in subjecting the master to liability than those of other states, but the tendency of the courts is to broaden the area within which the principal is found liable." The author then carefully reviews the history of the developments of the doctrine and cites numerous cases supporting his conclusion.

There are so many cases reaching divergent results that this matter should be determined by the broad general principles as they have developed in this field. In *Carr* v. *William C. Crowell Co.,* . . . Traynor, J., analyzes the problem in a closely analogous case and sets forth several principles that should govern our consideration here.

"The employer's responsibility for the tortious conduct of his employee 'extends far beyond his actual or possible control over the conduct of the servant. It rests on the broader ground that every man who prefers to manage his affairs through others remains bound to so manage them that third persons are not injured by any breach of legal duty on the part of such others' while acting in the scope of their employment. In the present case, defendant's enterprise required an association of employees with third parties, attended by the risk that someone might be injured. 'The risks of such associations and conditions were risks of the employment. . . .Such associations 'include the faults and derelictions of human beings as well as their virtues and obediences. Men do not discard their personal qualities when they go to work. Into the job they carry their intelligence, skill, habits of care and rectitude. Just as inevitably they take along also their tendencies to carelessness and camaraderie, as well as emotional makeup. In bringing men together, work brings these qualities together, causes frictions between them, creates occasions for lapses into carelessness, and for fun-making and emotional flareup. Work could not go on if men became automatons repressed in every natural expression * * * These expressions of human nature are incidents inseparable from working together. They involve risks of injury and these risks are inherent in the working environment.' * * *

"If an employee inflicts an injury out of personal malice, not engendered by the employment, the employer is not liable."

Such views are also in harmony with what is said in Prosser, *Law of Torts,* 3rd Ed., section 69, p. 476. "It may be said, in general that the master is held liable for any intentional tort committed by the servant where its purpose, however misguided, is wholly or in part to further the master's business."

Here the employees' duties regularly brought them in contact with the inspector. The inspector and Montagne had had previous altercations. This fight developed over the method of performing the employer's business of laying the pipe. Montagne entered the fray on the side of the fellow employee, if not on his behalf. It is for the jury to decide whether this employee was acting within the scope of his employment or on a venture of his own. I would affirm as to defendant Montagne but would reverse and reinstate the verdict as to employer-defendants.

◆◆◆

Case Questions

1. In your own words state:
   a. how and why the law uses the phrase, " . . . within the scope of employment."
   b. define when an act is, ". . . within the scope of employment."
2. List and define the torts which are, according to some courts, not within the scope of employment. List and define those torts which are within the scope of employment. For the purposes of this chapter you may consider willful and intentional torts as the same thing.
3. Does the dissent suggest that as a general rule intentional torts are within the scope of employment? Or, is the dissenting view more narrow in its statement of the rule?

Case Comment

The *Sandman* majority opinion indicates that in Iowa the general rule is that intentional torts of the servant are not within the scope of employment even if they are engendered by the employment; therefore, the master will not be liable for injury caused by a servant's intentional torts. Note that the dissent states that this rule is a minority view. The authors of the *Restatement* and the noted California authority, Judge Traynor, both would reach a decision for the plaintiff here. Note especially the *reasoning* of Judge Traynor cited in the dissent. Although he does not state it explicitly, it appears his reasons for the principal's liability in cases such as *Sandman* bear a distinct similarity to the reasons why some courts invoke the doctrine of inherent authority in quasi-contract cases.

AUTHORIZATION AND RATIFICATION OF THE AGENT'S TORTIOUS CONDUCT

In the previous section we presented material on one of the most significant areas of agency law — vicarious liability, or a statement of those circumstances in which the law will hold the principal liable to a third party for the tortious conduct of the agent when the principal neither intended, knew of, or otherwise assented to the conduct.

It should be obvious that if the law will impose liability on the principal for unauthorized conduct, it most certainly will impose liability on the principal for authorized conduct. Thus, where a principal either expressly or impliedly authorizes tortious conduct, usually in cases of misrepresentation or deceit, the principal will be liable.

The doctrine of apparent authority has been expanded by some courts in recent years to hold principals liable for their agent's torts when the doctrines of respondeat superior could not be appropriately utilized. We have reproduced an edited version of a law review article which explains this recent development. Following this article we present two cases illustrating that when a principal accepts the benefit of an agents' act and the agent committed a tort in accomplishing the act, the principal will be held to have ratified the tort so long as the principal was aware of the tort when the benefit was accepted.

"YOU CAN TRUST YOUR CAR TO THE MAN WHO WEARS THE STAR" — OR CAN YOU? THE USE OF APPARENT AUTHORITY TO ESTABLISH A PRINCIPAL'S TORT LIABILITY

by
William H. Dickey, Jr.

Reprinted with permission of the publisher; copyright©, 1971, University of Pittsburgh Law Review 257. From: Univ. of Pitt. L. Rev. 257 (Winter, 1971).

(Author's note: This article has been edited, footnotes renumbered and citations simplified.)

INTRODUCTION

Charlie Customer regularly patronized "Frankie's Fill-Up" service station. Frankie leased his station from a third party and sold exclusively the petroleum products of the Adverto Oil Company, one of the largest oil companies in the country. The Adverto sign was displayed prominently on the front of the premises, and the attendants all wore shirts bearing the word "Adverto." In nonpetroleum products, however, such as tires, tools, and other various mechanic's instruments, Frankie had stocked an inventory purchased from companies other than Adverto Oil. He also made all decisions concerning who and how many he should employ.

Recently, Adverto had embarked upon a large-scale nationwide advertising campaign in order to increase the sales of its products. Television commercials appeared during prime-time viewing hours extolling the quality and competence of Adverto service station attendants and products. Each commercial ended with the phrase, "Adverto — People Who Care For Your Car." Billboards carried pictures of an Adverto serviceman gently smiling upon the highway with the Adverto motto directly beneath his beaming face.

Customer had frequented "Frankie's" for several years and had even acquired an Adverto credit card. Since it was the only credit card he owned, he stopped only at gas stations which accepted the Adverto card. One day, while filling up at "Frankie's," Customer told Frankie that he had been having some problems with his brakes; they squeaked quite a bit and did not seem to "catch" soon enough. Frankie told Customer, "Don't sweat it, old buddy. Frankie will fix them up like new." When Customer returned for the car several days later, he was informed that Frankie had installed new brake shoes and wheel drums in order to correct the problem. Since Customer knew nothing about the mechanical aspects of his car, he merely gave Frankie the Adverto credit card, accepted a receipt and drove off.

While proceeding down a steep downgrade on his way home, Customer noticed a large truck in front of him. When he depressed the brake pedal to slow down, nothing happened. Customer was frantically pumping the brakes and sounding the horn as his car crashed into the rear of the truck. The injuries sustained by Customer were extremely severe; and hospital and medical expenses were substantial. Although there is evidence that the accident was solely the result of Frankie's negligent repair work, customer decides to sue Adverto Oil Company.

The facts contained in the preceding hypothetical are not far removed from a situation which could occur in everyday life. When viewed in the modern context of mass media advertising, however, these same facts threaten to greatly increase the scope of tort liability in such cases. The primary vehicle utilized to enter this potentially expanding realm is the agency theory of apparent authority.[1]

---

[1] Apparent authority is the power to affect the legal relations of another person by transactions with third persons, professedly as agent for the other, arising from and in accordance with the other's manifestations to such third persons. *Restatemment (Second) of Agency* § 8 (1957). In cases of this nature, although not expressly speaking in terms of respondeat superior, we are generally considering that doctrine; but this does not decide the question of the scope of authority within which the servant-agent must operate. It is in defining the scope of that authority that the use of the apparent authority theory has recently assumed an important role.

THE TRADITIONAL VIEW OF THE RELATIONSHIP

In the given hypothetical, the only contact Frankie maintained with Adverto Oil was in the purchase of its petroleum products. Hiring and firing policies were within the complete discretion of Frankie, and he also paid his assistants and kept the daily records of his business. The property on which the gas station stood was leased to Frankie by a third party. Thus, Frankie, the proprietor, surely thought of himself as an independent businessman using the Adverto Oil Company as a means to an end, who owed allegiance to no one but himself. He could even negotiate with other oil companies if he wished to terminate his relationship with Adverto.

The concept of the independent dealer in such situations has also been furthered by the courts. The major element under consideration when courts faced the problem of determining the proper relationship between the parties has been "control."

> Though 'control' is an important factor, and in some cases still a decisive factor, it is wrong to overestimate its value. Furthermore, in applying the control test, the question is not whether in practice the work was done subject to a direction and control exercised by an actual supervision or whether an actual supervision was possible, but whether ultimate authority over the man in the performance of his work resided in the employer so that he was subject to the employer's orders and directions.[2]

Using this criterion, tort actions brought against major oil companies have met with little success; the companies simply have not been involved in the operation of the station other than supplying the proprietor with gasoline, oil, and signs advertising the brand name. . . . (C)ourts have repeatedly recognized the relationship between the service station and the supplying oil company as they themselves view it: an independent entrepreneur obtaining the products of a company as an independent contractor.

GIZZI v. TEXACO, INC.

The recent Third Circuit case of *Gizzi* v. *Texaco, Inc.* 437 F. 2d 308 (3d Cir., 1971), shattered the traditional interpretation given the service station-oil company relationship. Briefly, the facts involved are as follows: A Texaco station operator in New Jersey offered for sale to one of his regular patrons a 1958 Volkswagen van. The price of $400 included the installation and complete inspection of a new master braking system. When completed, the patron paid the $400, received a Texaco receipt and departed with a friend to Philadelphia. Needless to say, the brakes failed to work, and the van crashed on the Schuylkill Expressway. Plaintiff brought an action against Texaco in the United States District Court for the Eastern District of Pennsylvania. . . . When that court granted defendant Texaco's motion for a direct verdict, plaintiff appealed to the Third Circuit Court of Appeals. . . .

Plaintiff's theory of liability embraced the agency concepts of apparent authority and estoppel. It was argued that Texaco had clothed the station

---

2 Carby-Hall, *Contract of Services, Contract for Services: The Modern Theories,* 113 Sol. J. 356 (1969).

operator with the apparent authority to make all necessary repairs and even sell the vehicle on its behalf. Moreover, since plaintiff had entered into the transaction relying on this apparent authority, Texaco was estopped from denying the existence of the agency.

> The concepts of apparent authority, and agency by estoppel are closely related. Both depend on manifestations by the alleged principal to a third person, and reasonable belief by the third person that the alleged agent is authorized to bind the principal. (Gizzi, cit. 309)

The court, with one judge dissenting, accepted plaintiff's argument. Vital to this acceptance was the fact that Texaco's advertising campaign which used the famous slogan, "Trust Your Car to the Man Who Wears the Star," had instilled a great degree of confidence in plaintiff concerning Texaco. Also important in the determination were the presence of the Texaco sign and certain equipment on the premises which belonged to the company.

> In order for the third person to recover against the principal, he must have relied on the indicia of authority originated by the principal, and such reliance must have been reasonable under the circumstances. (Gizzi, cit. 309)

From the record, the court determined that Texaco exercised a sufficient amount of control over the station so that the agency relationship could be reasonably established. . . .

THE GIZZI RATIONALE

The majority in Gizzi placed much reliance on certain applicable sections of the *Restatement (Second) of Agency.* Aside from the definition of apparent authority, the court's discussion revolved around the principal's manifestation to third parties.

> The manifestation of the principal may be made directly to a third person, or may be made to the community, by signs, by advertising, by authorizing the agent to state that he is authorized, or by continuously employing the agent.[3]

When viewed in the light of the above statement, the presence of the Texaco signs and use of the slogan become crucial factors in the court's determination of liability. But another requirement for liability is reasonable reliance by the third party on the representations made by the alleged principal to the third party:

> A purported master or other principal is subject to liability for physical harm caused to others or to their belongings by their reasonable reliance upon the tortious representations of one acting within his apparent authority or apparent scope of employment.[4]

---

[3] *Restatement (Second) of Agency,* § 8, Comment b (1957). . . .

[4] *Id.,* § 266.

Thus, the question becomes: Is it reasonable to assume that Texaco will indemnify a third person who, relying on signs, slogans, and ads, is injured as a result of the tort of the gas station attendant?

Case support for the majority, in answering the above question affirmatively, involved a variety of circumstances. ... However, it is interesting to note the scarcity of cases relied upon by the majority which involved similar gas station situations. Admittedly, the task would be difficult, because courts which have treated instances relating to the torts of service stations attendants have invariably found it unreasonable to believe that an oil company could be held responsible through the application of an agency theory. Simply stated, it appears that the majority in Gizzi put the "wagon before the horse." It had determined — almost assumed — that an agency relationship existed between the gas station operator and Texaco, and the resulting rationale was drawn from diverse factual situations in order to support the existence of apparent authority. Thus, it is not the rationale of Gizzi which deserves closer attention; it is the development and establishment of the apparent authority relationship in a situation which had previously been viewed in an independent context.

WHY THE SUDDEN SHIFT?

The facts presented in Gizzi offered the majority a change "to break new ground" in the Third Circuit. The plaintiff convinced them that he actually placed a great deal of faith in the motto, "You Can Trust Your Car to the Man Who Wears the Star." But the decision can also be viewed as an attempt to bolster the standing of America's beleaguered consumer. As stated earlier, courts traditionally viewed the gas station-oil company relationship in its proper context (at least to those parties): since no effective control was exercised by the oil company over the gas station, the two were considered independent of each other in terms of day-to-day business routine. Such paraphernalia as signs, pumps, and ads were merely a part of the business. The Gizzi court, however, took the same facts and placed a different emphasis on them. Actual control was not a prime factor in determining Texaco's liability. Mass media advertising had bludgeoned the average consumer into believing that Texaco exercised control over every Texaco service station in the country, even though this was not necessarily a fact. Taking into account the power of advertising and the relative business ignorance of the average consumer, it became reasonable to rely on manifestations perceived through countless television commercials that the "man who wears the star" was in fact clothed with the apparent authority to act for Texaco. Since mass media advertising appears to be one of the principal reasons for the shift, if not the principal reason, a close examination of oil company advertising is in order.

THE POWER OF THE TELEVISION COMMERCIAL

Like any major business or industry, all of the major oil companies expend great sums of money on advertising in order to improve their image and increase their profits. Texaco may have succeeded more than it wished when "You Can Trust Your Car to the Man Who Wears the Star" was coupled with an earpleasing musical jingle. In one commercial, potential customers were greeted with the sight of clean-cut, efficient Texaco attendants marching around their station, descending upon a customer, performing typical service station tasks, and singing the Texaco jingle throughout. From this television fantasy, is a consumer actually to believe that Texaco is the indemnifying principal for every one of its service stations?

Gulf Oil recently advertised that its attendants would be servicing a customer's car within ten seconds of its arrival at the station. Gulf publicized this claim by picturing Gulf attendants taking part in rigorous training sessions reminescent of football workouts. Calisthenics and running through a tire obstacle course, with the out-of-shape falling by the wayside, were the activities to which Gulf men subjected themselves in order to reach the potential customer within the ten second time period. Competitively, however, Gulf did not produce as "catchy" a jingle as Texaco. Because Gulf created the impression that its men actually trained to improve their efficiency, is it liable for the negligent act of its attendants through the utilization of the apparent authority concept?

Atlantic-Richfield, now known as ARCO, advertised under the sign of the "Redball." The "Redball" was intended to signify that the particular Atlantic station displaying it provided Atlantic "Redball" service; in other words, a customer could expect fast, efficient, and complete service at his local "independent" Atlantic dealer. This oil company was also blessed with a good jingle — "Atlantic Keeps Your Car on the Go" — but its words specifically referred to the gasoline, not the servicemen. Has Atlantic, by stressing dealer independence and gasoline efficiency, protected itself from possible tort actions by injured consumers?

RELATING *GIZZI* TO THE HYPOTHETICAL

The facts of the hypothetical closely resemble Gizzi. Adverto, like Texaco has coined a motto — "Adverto — People Who Care For Your Car" — which could imply that it is guaranteeing all aspects of Frankie's service. Customer can point to the fact that the motto gave him security whenever he dealt with an Adverto serviceman. And this can be buttressed by the fact that the Adverto credit card was the only such card he carried. Actually the hypothetical is more susceptible to a decision similar to Gizzi than the facts of the principal case itself. Frankie was performing a service which every service station offers: mechanical repairwork. The question of a "sideline" enterprise is not even present. Thus, should the hypothetical result in a *Gizzi* like decision?

At the trial level, other factors could be introduced which should cast doubt upon the reasonable reliance of Customer. To what extent would Customer's being a regular patron of "Frankie's" affect the decision? Also, when Frankie said, "Don't sweat it, old buddy. Frankie will fix them up like new," could he possibly have meant that Adverto's training would assist him in the repairwork? The presence of the credit card is also not an insurmountable obstacle in defense of Adverto. It is a widely practiced custom for service stations to honor more than one credit card. In many instances, the various gas stations may be affiliated with each other, but there are many small independent stations which honor any gasoline credit card. If Customer had stopped at one of these stations, could he still present the same argument utilizing apparent authority? Obviously he could not. Thus, it appears that Gizzi could be used only in specific cases where the oil company, to its great disadvantage, has "over-advertised." And the hypothetical falls into that category. . . .

CONCLUSION

Applying the *Gizzi* rationale to the hypothetical, Customer stands an excellent chance to recover against the Adverto Oil Company. Applying pre-*Gizzi* rationale to the same hypothetical, Customer could not sustain his argument against Adverto but could recover against Frankie's Fill-Up. It appears that mass media advertising and its interpretation are the sole reasons for the shift in the theory of liability.

Assuming *Gizzi* correct as a proper index for measuring the impact of extensive nationwide advertising campaigns, what are the alternatives. Does *Gizzi* imply that oil companies should personally supervise every gas station displaying their respective brand names — or certify the competence of each individual attendant? Clearly, this would be an unreasonable demand on both the oil companies and the proprietors. Perhaps *Gizzi* serves as a warning to oil companies to tread lightly in the mass media advertising field, or that if it is gasoline and petroleum products that are to be extolled, make certain that the advertisements do not contain any hints of service.

As emphasized earlier, because of its unique factual situation, Gizzi does not appear to embrace all oil companies. But it is not difficult to foresee the eventual expansion of the situations to which *Gizzi* could apply, including the hypothetical set forth in this comment. Perhaps in some instances, this expansion could be warranted. For example, Texaco has recently buttressed its advertising campaign with a commercial showing a company employee making a surprise inspection of one of its gas stations. The employee, with clipboard in hand, inspects all aspects of the service station, from its rest room cleanliness to the appearance of the station itself. The ad invited potential customers to write to the company if any Texaco station does not appear to be offering the kind of service depicted in the commercial. In this context, an injured party would have a much stronger argument for sustaining an apparent authority theory of tort liability. The element of apparent control is seemingly much more obvious. When this type of advertising is coupled with the hypothetical, it would not seem so unjust to allow recovery against the supplying oil company. Thus, *Gizzi* can be viewed in two different extremes; at best, as a warning to oil companies that the courts will protect the average consumer when advertising techniques border on guaranteeing all aspects of service station routines; and at worst, as an unwarranted distortion of the actual relationship which exists between an oil company and a service station. The latter interpretation would open the "floodgates" for any number of possible suits under the concept of apparent authority.

Article Review Questions

1. In the *Sandman* case, dissenting Justice Becker quotes Judge Traynor as follows:

    The employer's responsibility for the tortious conduct of his employee extends far beyond his actual or possible control over the conduct of the servant. It rests on the broader ground that every man who prefers to manage his affairs through others remains bound to so manage them that third persons are not injured by any breach of legal duty on the part of such others' while acting in the scope of their employment. In the present case, defendant's enterprise required an association of employees with third parties, attended by the risk that someone might be injured. The risks of such associations and conditions were risks of the employment.

Do you believe that Traynor's conception of vicarious liability is so broad as to justify the holding in the *Gizzi* case? That is, can Traynor's reasoning in the *Sandman* case be used to justify the *Gizzi* result?

2. Is the author of the above article correct when he states, "Thus the question becomes: Is it reasonable (for third parties) to assume that Texaco will indemnify a third person who, relying on signs, slogans, and ads, is injured as a result of the tort of the gas station attendant?" That is, what is the precise nature of the "reasonable reliance" required of third parties for apparent authority to be applied? Must third parties rely on facts indicating the principal intends to indemnify injured third parties, or must they rely on circumstances which simply indicate that the purported agent is indeed acting as an agent and is authorized to do the act in question? Reread the definition of apparent authority in Chapter 4.

DEMPSEY v. CHAMBERS
154 Mass. 330, 28 N.E. 279, (Sup. Ct., Mass., 1891)

(Plaintiff ordered coal of defendant, which a third person, without defendant's knowledge or authority, undertook to deliver, and in so doing negligently damaged plaintiff's building. Afterwards, and *with knowledge* of the accident, defendant demanded payment for the coal.)

◆◆◆

HOLMES, J.

This is an action of tort to recover damages for the breaking of a plate-glass window. The glass was broken by the negligence of one McCullock while delivering some coal which had been ordered of the defendant by the plaintiff. It is found as a fact that McCullock was not the defendant's servant when he broke the window, but that the "delivery of the coal by (him) was ratified by the defendant, and that such ratification made McCullock in law the agent and servant of the defendant in the delivery of the coal." On this finding the court ruled "that the defendant, by his ratification of the delivery of the coal by McCullock, became responsible for his negligence in the delivery of the coal." The defendant excepted to this ruling, and to nothing else. . . .

If we were contriving a new code today we might hesitate to say that a man could make himself a party to a bare tort in any case merely by assenting to it after it had been committed. But we are not at liberty to refuse to carry out to its consequences any principle which we believe to have been part of the common law simply because the grounds of policy on which it might be justified seem to us to be hard to find, and probably to have belonged to a different state of society. . . .

The earliest instances of liability by way of ratification in the English law, so far as we have noticed, were where a man retained property acquired through the wrongful act of another. . . . But in these cases the defendant's assent was treated as relating back to the original act, and at an early date the doctrine of relation was carried so far as to hold that, where a trespass would have been justified if it had been done by the authority by which it purported to have been done, a subsequent ratification might also justify it. . . .

If we assume that an alleged principal, by adopting an act which was unlawful when done can make it lawful, it follows that he adopts it at his peril, and is liable if it should turn out that his previous command would not have justified the act. . . .

The question remains whether the ratification is established. As we understand the bill of exceptions, McCullock took on himself to deliver the defendant's coal for his benefit, and as his servant, and the defendant afterwards assented to McCullock's assumption. The ratification was not directed specifically to McCullock's trespass, and that act was not for the defendant's benefit, if taken by itself, but it was so connected with McCullock's employment that the defendant would have been liable as master if McCullock really had been his servant when delivering the coal. We have found hardly anything in the books dealing with the precise case, but we are of opinion that consistency with the whole course of authority requires us to hold that the defendant's ratification of the employment established the relation of master and servant from the beginning, with all its incidents, including the anomalous liability for his negligent acts. . . . The ratification goes to the relation, and established it ab initio. The relation existing, the master is answerable for torts which he has not ratified specifically, just as he is for those which he has not commanded, and as he may be for those which he has expressly forbidden. . . . Exceptions overruled.

◆ ◆ ◆

Case Question

1. Refer to your brief of the first case in Chapter 4, *Davidsville First National Bank* v. *St. John's Church*, and note that the new pastor of the church made payments on the unauthorized note signed by Figlewski. Why was this not a ratification?

Case Comment

Justice Holmes states that if he were "contriving" a new set of rules in agency law he would hesitate to apply the doctrine of ratification to an agent's torts. Certainly this indicates an uncomfortable feeling in applying ratification to the facts of this case. Do you feel this same uneasiness? Do you believe that the principal would have demanded payment for the coal had he known he would also be liable for the broken window? The answer probably depends upon weighing the relative values of the coal delivered and the value of the new window. Is it "fair" to allow the principal to do this when, essentially, the intent of the initial act, although not consented to by the principal, was to benefit the principal? Yet, it appears unfair to make the principal liable for an act arising out of a relationship he did not initially consent to. If the principle of ratification appears clumsy to you when applying it to tort cases, try to derive a principle which is more equitable.

JONES v. MUTUAL CREAMERY CO.
81 Ut. 223, 17 P.2d 256 (S. Ct., Utah, 1932)

◆◆◆

STRAUP, J.

This action was brought by the plaintiff to recover damages against the Mutual Creamery Company for the death of his minor son alleged to have been caused through the negligence of the company. It was alleged and claimed by the plaintiff that L.D. Mecham was in the employ of the company, and that in the course of his employment, and through his negligence in driving a truck on a public highway, he collided with and ran over plaintiff's son and killed him. The company denied the alleged negligence, and denied that Mecham at the time was, or that he prior thereto had been, in its employ, or that the truck was driven for or on its behalf or in pursuit of its business. That issue was the controlling point in the case. At the conclusion of plaintiff's evidence, the court granted a nonsuit on the ground that it was not sufficiently shown that Mecham was an employee of the company or that it was responsible for any act of negligence that might have been committed by him in driving the truck. On dismissal of the action, the plaintiff appeals.

The creamery company, among other things, at American Fork City, was engaged in the business of buying eggs from nearby poultry raisers. Its general manager at its place of business was Morris Hanson. It also had in its employ one Sager, who two days of the week acted as salesman in selling butter, eggs, cheese, and ice cream. The other five days of the week he was employed to gather eggs from those who had eggs to sell, using his own truck for such purpose, and was paid 25 cents a case for gathering eggs for the company. He gathered the eggs nearby wherever eggs were procurable. In such particular he was employed by the company to solicit and gather eggs for the company on a commission of 25 cents a case, and in doing so he was at liberty to go when and where and to work as early and late as he pleased. He furnished and used his own car for the purpose, and was paid a commission on the amount of eggs procured by him. Mecham in no sense was or had been in the employ of the company or in any manner connected with its business. On the late afternoon of the day in question Mecham accompanied Sager on his truck to the company's plant. It is not claimed that Mecham went there to do anything for the company. When they arrived at the plant, Sager was informed that a customer, a Mrs. Robinson, had telephoned the company that she had some eggs ready to be delivered and to come and get them. It was Sager's duty to get the eggs. He and Mecham had contemplated going "to a show" that evening. Sager, learning he was to go for the eggs, stated to Mecham (not in the presence of anyone) that because of other work he could not get the eggs and go to the show, whereupon Mecham volunteered to Sager that he would go for the eggs to help him out. Sager assented to that, went inside, got a case, put it on the truck, and Mecham drove off. Hanson, the manager of the company, seeing Mecham drive away, asked Sager where Mecham was going and was told to get Mrs. Robinson's eggs. Hanson made no reply thereto. It is not made to appear that Mecham then was yet in hailing distance or that sufficient opportunity was afforded Hanson to counterdemand what Sager in such particular had done or permitted. On the way, plaintiff's minor child was killed through the alleged negligence of Mecham driving the truck with defective and insufficient brakes, etc., driving at an excessive speed of thirty miles an hour and partly off the paved portion of the highway, and not with due care and circumspection. After the incident, Mecham procured the eggs and delivered them to the company, which thereafter were paid for by the company to Mrs. Robinson. It is not shown that when the eggs were received or paid for by the company it had knowledge of the accident or of the particulars thereof.

In view of such facts, we think no liability is shown against the company. . . .

It is not claimed that he either expressly or impliedly was employed by the company. The record without dispute shows that he was not. It, however, is urged that he ostensibly held himself out as the agent of the company, or with the acquiescence of the company (of its manager) assumed to act for it. In our opinion, neither statement is supported by the record. Mecham was not driving the company's truck. He drove Sager's truck. In doing so and going after the eggs he did not assume to act for any one except for Sager and for his convenience, and in fact did so act for him, and for no one else. Against such direct and indisputable testimony, no inference is permissible that he was acting for, or assumed to act for, the company or for any one except for Sager. The question asked by the manager of the company as to where Mecham was going as he was driving away with Sager's truck, and was told by Sager that he was going to get Robinson's eggs and the manager making no reply thereto, does not show any admission or acknowledgement that Mecham for such purpose was the employee of the company, nor as constituting an assent for and on behalf of the company.

It, however, is further urged that the company became liable for the negligent acts of Mecham on the theory of ratification. The law is well settled and not seriously disputed that, where it is sought to hold a person or company civilly liable for torts committed by another, it must be made to appear that the relation of principal and agent or master and servant existed between the two at the time the tort was committed, and that the tortious act was committed in the course of employment or within the scope of the agency. Here indisputably no such relation was shown to exist. By invoking the doctrine of ratification, it necessarily is implied that no such relation existed between the company and Mecham at the time the tort was committed, but that something thereafter was done by the company which gave sanction and validity to an unauthorized act or acts of Mecham whereby such act or acts became the act or acts of the company. And since, as it is contended, the company sanctioned or gave validity to a particular act of Mecham, therefore it became responsible and liable for all he did or failed to do, including his alleged negligence resulting in the death of plaintiff's child.

As we understand it, the claimed ratification is based on the fact that the company, after the commission of the tort, received the eggs from Mrs. Robinson brought to the company's plant by Mecham and thereafter paid her for them, without any showing that the company when it received or paid for the eggs had any knowledge of the commission of the tort or of any of the particulars thereof, which, as is claimed, constituted a ratification, not only of the authorized act of Mecham procuring the eggs from Mrs. Robinson and delivering them to the company and as to the negotiations had between him and

Mrs. Robinson, but also an acknowledgment or ratification by the company of a relation of master and servant or of an agency between it and Mecham, rendering it liable for the tort committed by him.

The case of *Dempsey* v. *Chambers,* 154 Mass. 330, 28 N.E. 279, is cited as an authority rendering the company here liable on the theory of ratification. In that case the plaintiff ordered coal from the defendant, a coal dealer, which a third person, without the defendant's knowledge or authority, undertook to deliver, and in so delivering the coal injured the plaintiff's buidling by breaking a plate glass window. Afterwards, and with knowledge of the accident, the defendant demanded payment for the coal. It was held that the defendant was liable for the injury because his demand for payment was a ratification of the acts of the person delivering the coal. There the unauthorized person assumed to act for the defendant. . . .

While we think the doctrine of ratification was there carried about to the breaking point, yet the case in hand is even distinguishable from that case, in the particulars that here no showing was made that the company, when it received or paid for the eggs, had knowledge of the commission of the tort or of the circumstances thereof. . . .

Though it be assumed that the company by receiving the eggs and paying Mrs. Robinson therefor, as between the company and Mrs. Robinson, adopted and ratified the unauthorized act of Mecham in procuring the eggs and delivering them to the company, yet, because thereof, to carry the doctrine further and as an acknowledgment or confirmation or ratification of master and servant or of an agency between the company and Mecham rendering it liable to all the world for his torts, is to carry the doctrine even beyond anything decided in the Massachusetts case.

We therefore are of the opinion that the judgment of the court below should be affirmed. Such is the order. Costs to the respondent.

◆◆◆

Case Questions

1. Although the Mutual Creamery was not liable in this case, does this mean the plaintiff was without a remedy against anyone?
2. If you believe the holding in this case is unduly harsh for the plaintiff then attempt to derive a principle of agency law which would result in the principal's being liable.

LIABILITY OF PRINCIPAL TO THIRD PARTIES BASED UPON PUBLIC POLICY OR STATUTORY LAW.

In a limited number of circumstances the law will impose liability upon a principal for the tortious acts of an agent/employee where the act was not authorized and the doctrine of respondeat superior does not apply.

The first set of such circumstances involves an independent contractor who is hired to perform ultrahazardous activities. Ultrahazardous activities are those which pose a substantial threat of harm to the public but are not specifically illegal because they are of benefit to society. Such activities are blasting with dynamite or other explosives, the spraying of noxious solutions on crops or indoors for fumigation, transporting highly toxic chemicals or drilling for oil in a populated area. Simply stated, the law as a matter of public policy recognizes the danger in these and similar activities and therefore holds that the employer cannot avoid liability for injury caused by hiring an independent contractor.

Closely related to the circumstances just discussed are other duties of an employer which cannot be delegated to an agent either because of statute or public policy. For example, The Occupational Safety and Health Act (O.S.H.A.) imposes a duty on certain employers to provide a place of work free from recognized danger. If an employer subject to the act hires an independent contractor to perform work on his factory and an employee of the independent contractor is injured in the factory the initial employer might well be liable if there are circumstances present revealing the employer (the principal) did not provide a work place free from recognized hazards.

Finally, if a principal promises to personally perform and then hires an independent contractor to help, the principal may be liable. This result is based upon the assumption that the injured third party relied primarily upon the principal for performance and, as a matter of public policy, he should not be allowed to avoid liability by hiring an independent contractor to perform. That is, if the principal personally promised to perform certain duties, then these duties can not be delegated to others, unless, of course, the third party consents. An exact list of all of those duties which are non-delegable is beyond the scope of this book. Many of these duties are peculiar to individual states and the answer may be found only by reference to state law.

We present the following two cases to illustrate the first two principles stated in this section.

LEDBETTER-JOHNSON COMPANY v. HAWKINS
103 So. 2d 748 (S. Ct. Alabama, 1958)

MERRILL, Justice

Plaintiff Hawkins, appellee here, recovered a judgment against appellant for damages to his dwelling resulting from blasting operations in a chert pit near his home, which were conducted by appellant or its subcontractor in connection with its contract with the City of Fort Payne to grade, chart and pave certain streets. After a motion for a new trial was overruled, this appeal was taken.

The trial court submitted the case to the jury on two negligence counts. Count E charged that "an agent, servant or employee of the defendant, while acting in the line and scope of his authority, negligently set off or exploded a large charge of dynamite or other explosive near the dwelling house of the plaintiff" etc. Count F charged that "defendant, its agents, servants or employees, while acting within the scope of their employment," failed to handle the explosives as was their duty and negligently set off the explosion. Demurrer to these counts being overruled, appellant pleaded . . . that the acts complained of were done by an independent contractor for whose acts appellant would not be liable.

Appellee . . . in replication to the independent contractor plea said that appellant ought not to prevail under said plea because the contract between appellant and the alleged independent contractor required the use of inherently dangerous explosives and such fact was known to appellant. . . .

A few rules in blasting cases are stated as applicable to the questions here.

It is settled in this state that one who has work done which is intrinsically dangerous cannot avoid responsibility in its execution by letting or subletting the work to an independent contractor; and whether the blasting, which caused the damage, is intrinsically dangerous has been held to be a question for the jury. . . .

A principal is liable for the acts of an independent contractor employed by him where the work to be done is intrinsically dangerous, however skillfully performed. . . .

We think that, according to the best-considered decisions, the rule is that if one, in blasting upon his own lands, invades the premises of his neighbor, by throwing stones and debris thereon, he is liable for the resulting injury, but for any other injury, such as may result from the mere concussion of the atmosphere, sound, or otherwise, there is no liability, unless it is shown that the work was done negligently and that the injury was the result of negligence, and not the result of blasting according to the usual methods and with reasonable care. . . .

The appellee's evidence was that he had previously complained to appellant's vice president about the effects of the blasting in the chert pit which was a short distance from his home. Later, the heavy blast complained of here, shook appellee's house causing the rock veneer, the foundation and the chimney to crack, the doors to warp, the floors to buck and stones and debris to be thrown upon his property. Other homes in the vicinity were damaged by the blast.

There was evidence that appellant selected the chert pit to be used, leased it from the owner, directed its subcontractor to use that pit, paid for all the chert removed and directed where the chert should be placed on the streets. . . .

Applying the rules stated to this evidence, we conclude that a jury question was presented and the affirmative charge for appellant was correctly refused. . . .

Lastly, it is argued that the motion for a new trial was improperly overruled because the verdict was contrary to the law and the evidence. In view of what has already been said, it is obvious that the motion was properly overruled.

The judgment is affirmed.

◆◆◆

Case Questions

1. What is the reason for the law requiring debris to be thrown upon a plaintiff's land before he could sue in a case such as this? Is it not possible that the concussion could cause just as much if not more damage than the debris?
2. The court states, "A principal is liable for the acts of an independent contractor employed by him where the work to be done is intrinsically dangerous, however skillfully performed." This means negligence is not

a part of the cause of action. The plaintiff proves the act of blasting and that this caused his injury. Where liability for personal or property damage is imposed in the absence of negligence the law is creating a form of absolute or unlimited liability.

HUMPHREY v. VIRGINIAN RY. CO.
54 S.E. 2d 204
(S. Ct. of App., West Virginia, 1948)

♦ ♦ ♦

Plaintiff, Alfred Humphrey, instituted this action in the Circuit Court of Fayette County against The Virginian Railway Company, C. T. Wade, B. L. Murphee, Ray Thompson and Cecil Terry to recover damages for personal injuries, which included the loss of both legs above the knees, a fractured scapula and numerous bruises and lacerations. The jury rendered a verdict against the railway company in the sum of forty thousand dollars and acquitted the individual defendants. To the judgment against it, based upon the jury verdict, the railway company prosecutes this writ of error.

The declaration, consisting of two counts, charged, and the evidence established, that plaintiff was injured by a train of the defendant railway company on or adjacent to the west end of a public crossing at Willis Branch, Fayette County. The first count of the declaration, directed against the railway company, C. T. Wade, its engineer, and its fireman, B. L. Murphee, and other agents, servants and employees unnamed in the declaration, charges plaintiff's injuries to the negligent operation of the train by defendant's said engineer and fireman and "other agents, servants and employees" of defendant corporation; and the second count of the declaration charges that the railway company and the defendants, Thompson and Terry, its section foreman and road master in charge of the construction and maintenance of the crossing and defendant's railway tracks, respectively, and other agents, servants and employees, carelessly and negligently failed to perform the alleged duty of inspecting, keeping, repairing and maintaining the crossing in a safe and usable condition, as a result of which plaintiff caught his left foot between the plank of the crossing and the rail so that he was struck by defendant's train before he could extricate himself. ...

On Saturday evening, July 14, 1945, plaintiff, after attended a picture show at Pax, a town a short distance east of the crossing, went to Long Branch to a pool room, immediately west of the crossing, where beer was served. He remained there until the proprietor closed the place at midnight. While there he said he drank four or five bottles of beer, but one witness, W. E. Sweeny, testified that plaintiff and one Jack Penn, ... were drinking what witness thought was moonshine whiskey, and that plaintiff was intoxicated. Plaintiff denies this, and asserts he was not intoxicated. Other witnesses testified variously as to whether plaintiff was, in fact, intoxicated. After the closing of the pool room, plaintiff and Jack Penn went to the latter's home, where they played cards until nearly two o'clock Sunday morning, when plaintiff started toward his home at Willis Branch. ... After catching his foot, plaintiff testified that he injured his ankle, became excited and tried vainly for three or four minutes to free himself, when he saw the headlight of defendant corporation's approaching train, and remembered nothing thereafter until he regained consciousness in the hospital. In his excitement and terror he testified he did not think of removing his foot from the caught shoe. . . .

The first ground for reversal is to the effect that the individual defendants having been acquitted of negligence, there can be no recovery against their employer, the railway company. In the appraisal of this ground, it is necessary that we consider the two counts of the declaration separately.

The gravamen of the first count of the declaration is that plaintiff was injured as the result of the joint negligence of the railway company, C. T. Wade, its engineer, and B. L. Murphee, its fireman, and "the other agents, servants and employees" of said defendant railway corporation in the operation of the railway company's locomotive. It is to be noted that this count of the declaration alleges acts of negligence which are grouped under a single charge that the locomotive was being operated negligently. It contains no allegation that defendant railway company had or took any active charge of the operation of the locomotive, or that the defendant employees were incompetent, so that the railway company's liability under the first count of the declaration is necessarily predicted solely upon the alleged negligent acts of the employees, Wade and Murphee, and the jury verdict having affirmatively exonerated these defendants, the railway company has violated no duty under the allegations of this count of the declaration. The railway's liability resting solely upon the servants' acts, the verdict finding for the latter and against the railway company is inconsistent and will not support the judgment against the railway company on the first count of the declaration. . . . As, under the first count of the declaration, plaintiff seeks to recover against the railway company, as well as the employees, for injuries caused solely by the alleged negligence of the employees, no recovery can be had under this count, and, as the record stands, it is as though the count had not been proved.

But the question whether recovery may be had against the railway company under the second count of the declaration, though the jury found that defendants, Ray Thompson, section foreman, and Cecil Terry, road master, were not guilty, presents an entirely different situation. Section 8, Chapter 40, Acts of the Legislature . . . Code, 17-4-8-, reads as follows: "Whenever any railroad or electric or other railway, heretofore or hereafter constructed, shall cross any state road, it shall be required to keep its own roadbed, and the bed of the road or highway at such crossings, in proper repair, or else to construct and maintain an overhead or undergrade crossing, subject to the approval of the state road commissioner; and the tracks of such railroad or railway at grade crossings shall be so constructed as to give a safe and easy approach to and across the same * * * ". . . .

The second count alleges that plaintiff's injuries were the result of the carelessness and negligence of the defendant railway company, Ray Thompson, its section foreman, Cecil Terry, its road master, "and the other agents, servants and employees of the defendant corporation" in failing to "inspect, keep, repair and maintain [the crossing in question] and otherwise use due and reasonable care to keep the same in safe and useable condition for people, and this plaintiff lawfully using the public crossing in question upon and over the defendant's railroad tracks." Reading Code, 17-4-8, into the second count, . . . this count unlike the first count, alleges two separate derelictions of duty, one, the failure of the railway company to perform its statutory duty to keep and maintain the crossing in safe condition, and, two, the alleged failure of Thompson and Terry, and "the other agents, servants and employees" to perform their alleged duties as such employees. . . . The statute here involved . . . is, in our opinion, absolute and nondelegable, and though the railroad company like a municipality or county, is not an insurer, the statute casts upon the railway company the non-assignable duty in any event to keep and maintain the crossing in a reasonably safe condition.

The railway company's duty being non-delegable, this case, in our opinion, is controlled by *Willis* v. *Fontfair Gas Coal Co.,* 104 W. Va. 12 . . . . The declaration in that case charged the defendant coal company and one Jarrett, its superintendent, with alleged negligence in employing as a snapper, against the express wishes of the father, plaintiff's decedent, a minor, in the company's coal mine, in violation of the then statute, Barnes' Code, 1923, Chapter 15H, Section 72, which provided that "no child under the age of sixteen years shall be employed, permitted, or suffered to work in any mine, quarry, tunnel or excavation." The jury rendered a verdict in favor of plaintiff and against the coal company, which verdict was silent as to the superintendent Jarrett, and judgment was entered on such verdict. On writ of error to this Court the coal company contended that the verdict being silent as to Jarrett, constituted an acquittal by jury verdict of that defendant, and that under the doctrine of respondeat superior the verdict should fail as to the coal company. This Court held, in effect, that the statutory duty imposed upon the coal company was absolute, and therefore the doctrine of respondeat superior should not apply to defeat recovery against the coal company. . . . Also . . . see *Devine* v. *Kroger Grocery & Baking Co.* 349 Mo. 621, 162 S.W. 2d 813, 817. In that case the action was brought by plaintiff against the employer, Kroger Grocery & Baking Company, Henry Boemler, the manager of the defendant store, and John Fromm, the owner of the building to recover damages for injury alleged to have been sustained by plaintiff, a customer, by reason of the alleged dangerous and unsafe condition of the floor of the grocery store. The building owner Fromm was dismissed, a demurrer to plaintiff's petition having been sustained as to him, and upon a trial on the merits of the case, the jury found for the plaintiff and against the defendant grocery company and against the plaintiff in favor of the store manager. The Court held that two distinct torts were in issue, one on the part of the manager, and the other by the grocery company, and that the jury's verdict exonerating the manager and fixing the liability of the grocery company, was not inconsistent, so as to render a judgment based on that verdict reversible. . . . In that case it was held that the duty of the grocery company to keep the premises in a reasonably safe condition cannot be delegated so as to avoid personal responsibility. . . . The Court discussing the distinction between the duties of the defendant manager and defendant grocery company, and the absolute duty on the grocery company, said: "In short the appellant, Kroger Grocery & Baking Company, irrespective of whether its manager was found to be negligent, owed a duty to the respondent to maintain the store in such a manner as not to injure her by reason of a hole in the entrance of which it knew or should have known and which was unknown to her. It is not the type of tort which may be sustained solely upon a finding of negligence on the part of its manager or some other agent. *Others may or may not* have been negligent with respect to the condition complained of and yet liability fastens on the appellant for its wrong which does not depend on *respondeat superior.* Consequently, there is no inconsistency in the jury's verdict and the motion in arrest of judgment was properly overruled." (italics supplied.). . . . The duty of the railroad company here being nondelegable, absolute and nonassignable, is a duty which rests upon the railway company by virtue of statute, and is distinct so far as the second count of the declaration is concerned from the duties charged to the employees, Thompson and Terry. That the declaration charges the named defendants with joint negligence is of no moment, in our opinion, under the holding in the Wills and Devine cases. If the duty is nondelegable, as we think it is, it is nondelegable for all purposes, and it matters not whether the railway company has delegated it either to an independent contractor or to employees. . . . Perceiving no reversible error in this record, we affirm the judgment of the trial court.

Affirmed.

FOX, Judge (dissenting)

I concur in the majority opinion in this case on all points except that relating to the inconsistency of the verdict returned by the jury. . . . It is assumed here, as it is in the majority opinion, that the jury verdict against the railway company was based on the allegations of the second count of the declaration, relating solely to alleged defect in its road crossing at the point where plaintiff was injured.

This being true, but one act of negligence is charged. . . . The declaration then proceeds to explain how plaintiff's injuries occurred and charges that the injury resulted: "because of the carelessness and negligence of the defendant corporation, and Ray Thompson and Cecil Terry, and the other agents, servants and employees of the defendant corporation as aforesaid." Thus it will be seen that the single act of negligence charged against all of the defendants, named in the second count of the declaration, was the failure to inspect, keep in repair and maintain a particular road crossing.

The railway company, Thompson and Terry were jointly charged with the negligence alleged in the second count of the declaration. The road crossing was, as a physical fact, either in a proper state of repair, or it was not. The duty to keep it in proper repair, whether under the statutory requirement, or under the common law against negligence, was present; and, on the theory of plaintiff's declaration, equally binding on the railway company and Thompson and Terry. If the crossing was not in proper repair, then Thompson and Terry were guilty of common law negligence; if the crossing was not in proper repair, then the railway company was guilty of negligence, under its common law obligation, and guilty of a violation of a statute on which a recovery might be had if such violation was the proximate cause of an injury resulting therefrom. On the assumption of a failure to keep the crossing in proper repair, each of the defendants was guilty of one and the same act of negligence; whereas if the crossing was in proper state of repair, there was no common law negligence on the part of all or either of the said defendants, and the statutory provision had not been violated. The matter is reduced to the simple proposition that there could not have been a justifiable verdict of guilty against any one or all of the defendants unless the crossing was in a bad state of repair.

If all this be true, how can a jury verdict be upheld which releases two of the defendants, equally guilty with the third, if any are guilty, and convict the third defendant of the single act of negligence charged against all of them in the declaration? It is but common sense to say that, in such circumstances, if one is guilty all are guilty; and in a court of justice the verdict of a jury which punishes one and releases the other two, should be set aside in its entirety. . . .

◆◆◆

Case Questions

1. The case of *Devine* v. *Kroger Grocery & Baking Co.,* mentioned in the above case, is, perhaps, a more typical case than the one presented. Describe what happened in that case.
2. Write a short essay in which you explain whether you agree with the majority or dissenting opinion. Could it be that one of the reasons state legislatures pass statutes declaring certain duties nondelegable is to avoid the logical decision rendered by the dissenting judge? It seems that the existence of the statute created a form of absolute liability in which the existence or non-existence of negligence is unimportant.

SUMMARY

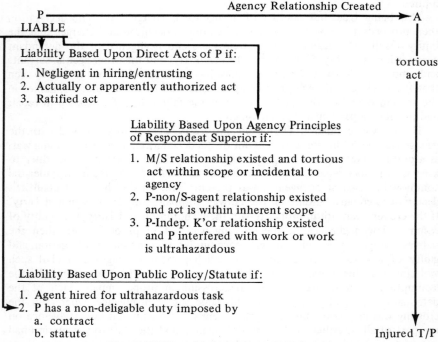

Tort Liability of Principal to Third Parties

Figure 5-2

REVIEW PROBLEMS

1. In this chapter we have presented material illustrating the concept of vicarious liability as applied to the agency relationship. In some circumstances the principal will be held liable for the torts of its agents when it neither authorized, ratified or otherwise intended that the tortious act occur. List and define these circumstances and give an example of each by using factual patterns not similar to those of the cases in this chapter.

2. On October 1, Great Puppet Shows, Inc., (The "Company") hired Mandrake as its new purchasing agent. The Company knew that Puppetland Corp. was interested in selling certain stage scenery and props but it believed that it could purchase the property for less money if it did not disclose its identity. Therefore, it instructed Mandrake to drive over to Puppetland's office the next day and negotiate for the purchase of the property in his own name without disclosing the Company's identity. Mandrake was authorized to spend up to $5,000.

   On October 2, Mandrake negotiated and signed a contract with Puppetland for the purchase of the property for $4,500 and for delivery and payment on October 15. After signing the contract Mandrake began to drive back to the Company office. On the way he stopped at a bar for a few drinks which he knew was in violation of a Company policy which prohibited drinking of alcoholic beverages during working hours. After becoming intoxicated he left the bar and began driving to the office. Enroute he negligently struck and killed a pedestrian. Upon learning these facts the Company immediately discharged Mandrake who then advised Puppetland that when he signed the contract in his own name he was really doing so for his former employer's benefit and that he wanted nothing to do with the contract.

   a. Discuss fully the liability which might arise between Great Puppet Shows, Inc., and Mandrake on the one hand and Puppetland Corp. on the other. That is, may Puppetland Corp. enforce the contract against Mandrake? Against Great Puppet Shows, Inc.? May Great Puppet Shows, Inc., enforce the contract against Puppetland Corp.?

   b. Does the pedestrian's estate have a right to recover against Mandrake and Great Puppet Shows? State what facts you would need in order to reach an affirmative answer with regard to Great Puppet Shows, Inc.

   c. Does Great Puppet Shows Inc. have a right to recover from Mandrake if it incurs liability to the estate? (Material from the Uniform CPA Examination, copyright © 1971 by the American Institute of Certified Public Accountants, Inc., is here reprinted with permission. This is adapted from Question Number 8 of the November 5, 1971, exam.)

3. "Texas Family-Style Restaurants" was the name of a nationwide chain of restaurants. These restaurants were operated on a franchise system in which the parent organization, "Texas Family-Style Restaurants, International, Inc.," agreed to let a local owner of a restaurant use both its name and style of cooking and serving food. The local owner agreed to maintain certain standards of service and cooking in exchange for using the name, etc., and also agreed to give the parent organization a percentage of the profits earned. The parent organization also engaged in a national advertising campaign in which it made a pitch for family business and specifically emphasized that this chain of restaurants stood for unrivaled service to the public and dependable food quality.

   O was the owner of a local "Texas Family-Style Restaurant" and hired primarily younger people to serve the public because he found them eager and courteous. He even sent some of them, including W, to a national school operated by the parent organization to learn the latest in the preparation and serving of food. W was captain of his high school wrestling team and had a reputation for being a very tough, almost beligerent, person.

One evening T and his family attended the restaurant for dinner and ordered the special for the evening which was stuffed chicken. The chicken was held together with toothpicks and some of these were buried in the chicken so that a reasonable person could not have detected them. T swallowed a toothpick and became very ill and was hospitalized for surgery.

During the commotion caused in the restaurant when T swallowed the toothpick people became scared and rushed for the door. W, thinking that many of the persons would leave without paying attempted to restrain them and in the process negligently struck an elderly lady, L, in the head. She also was hospitalized.

(Fully) Discuss the entities which would be liable to both T and L. Against whom may they recover and why?

4. P formed a charter bus company which provided transportation for groups of 30 or more persons. P owned 5 busses and employed 6 professional drivers. P did all of the negotiating for the bus rental but left the route selection to the drivers. D was one of the drivers who had driven for P for a long time. On a trip from Chicago to Las Vegas, D became extremely agitated when a van load of teenagers first followed him too closely and then passed him and slowed down. At a stop light in the next town D stopped in back of the van, got out and in rather unfriendly language began a discussion with the van's driver. The van driver used vile language whereupon D hit him in the head with his fist knocking the van driver out and causing the loss of 5 teeth.

   a. Describe whether or not P will be liable for the damage caused. Discuss the possible causes of action.
   b. Would the result differ if D intentionally ran *the bus* into the rear of the van at the stop light?
   c. On the facts above, could the members of the charter party be held liable?
   d. How and why would your answer change if you knew that P knew that D had a very bad temper and had been arrested and convicted several times of assault and battery?
   e. What if, after striking the van driver, D resumed his travels and negligently ran into T. Explain the liability of D and P to T.

ENDNOTES

1. *Black's Law Dictionary,* Rev. 4th Ed., p. 1660 (1957).
2. *Green* v. *Victor Talleying Mach. Co.,* C.C.A.N.Y., 24 Fed. 378, cited as headnote definition in 86 *Corpus Juris Secundum,* 954.
3. *Vol. II, Restatement of the Law of Torts, Negligence,* 738 (1934).
4. *Id.,* at 742.
5. *Restatement of the Law, Agency 2nd,* § 2, (1958).
6. *Id.,* §219 (1).
7. *Id.,* §220.
8. *Id.,* at 14.
9. *Id.*
10. See, *Bugge* v. *Brown,* High Ct. Anst., 1919, 2 Comm. L.R. 110.
11. See W. A. Seavey, *Law of Agency* 151 (1964).
12. *Id.,* pp. 145-146.

AGENCY OPERATION AND TERMINATION

There are some important legal aspects of the agency relationship which do not conveniently fit into the discussions in the first three chapters on agency. These legal aspects we present in this chapter.

AGENCY OPERATION

Agency operation includes first of all those matters, primarily contractual or quasi-contractural in nature, in which the agent and principal are considered one and the same person. These are matters of notice, knowledge, and payment. Following this we will discuss the legal consequences of appointing sub-agents and delegating part or all of the duties of the agent imposed by the agency relationship. The last category of agency operations provides a discussion of the loaned or borrowed servant doctrine.

NOTICE, KNOWLEDGE AND PAYMENT

Notice and knowledge both concern the same thing: notification of a fact. In many kinds of contractural understandings notification by a third party to a principal through an agent or vice versa is crucial to triggering certain events provided for in the contract. What happens, for example, when a large corporation (T/P) is to respond to another corporation (P) by a given date as to whether or not it will accept an alteration in their contractual understanding? A day before the given date the T/P calls the vice president (A) of P to notify P of its acceptance of the alteration. The vice president leaves that evening on a two-week vacation without telling anyone else. Was "notice" given? The *Restatement* provides:[1] . . .

> (2) A person is given notification of a fact by another if the latter
>   (a) informs him of the fact by adequate or specified means or of other facts from which he has reason to know or should know the facts. . . .
> (3) A person has notice of a fact if his agent has knowledge of the fact, reason to know it or should know it. . . .

This rule from the *Restatement* makes it clear that notice was indeed legally given to the P, if the vice president was *authorized* to receive such notice. In determining issues of authority one must refer to those types of authority set out in Chapter 4. If an agent is actually, apparently or inherently authorized to receive notice of the kind given, and if it is given to the agent but is not in fact communicated to the principal, the law assumes that it was given.

The same assumption usually exists with regard to payment. For example, if T/P orders goods from P through A and T/P receives the goods and pays A who absconds with the payment, P will not be allowed to recover the payment from

T/P. If the agent is authorized to receive payment, payment to the agent is payment to the principal. Of course, in this particular example P may sue A for a breach of A's duties as agent if A can be found.

Generally, there will be no imputation of notice or knowledge where the agent is acting adversely to the principal or beyond the scope of the agency. As we have already pointed out the majority rule is that knowledge of an agent's intentionally dishonest acts will not be imputed to the principal (and thereby render it liable) because it is assumed such acts are beyond the scope of the agency. However, the *Restatement* would impute such knowledge to the principal if the principal benefited from the intentionally dishonest act.[2]

Likewise, payment to an agent who is not authorized either actually or circumstantially to receive it, will not be payment to the principal. In summary, where the agent is authorized to either give or accept notice or payment then the concept of oneness is applied if the agent does so act. If the agent is not authorized to give or accept notice or payment then courts will not hold the principal liable; however, the agent will be liable based upon the fact that the agent misrepresented his or her authority.

In the following case was the notice or knowledge referred to by the court given by the agent to the third party or received by the agent? Note how this knowledge does bind the principal.

HUFF v. UNITED VAN LINES, INC.
28 N.W. 2d 793 (S. Ct. Iowa, 1947)

◆◆◆

BLISS, Justice

Plaintiff's petition set out the written order for services or contract under which defendant agreed to transport the household goods of plaintiff from his old home in Sioux City to his new home in Palo Alto, California, with "reasonable dispatch." . . . The petition alleged that in reliance on defendant's agreement to deliver the goods in a reasonable time plaintiff's wife and child came to Palo Alto, but because of the defendant's breach of the contract in its unreasonable and avoidable delay in delivering the goods, plaintiff and his wife and children were compelled to procure lodging and board at a hotel from November 10, 1944 to January 3, 1945, to his expense and damage in the sum of $442.50 for lodging and $140.89 for meals.

Defendant's answer admitted the execution of the written order and the time consumed in the trip as alleged in the petition. Defendant denied any breach of contract or unreasonable delay, any oral agreement, or agreement other than the written contract, and any liability for the hotel expense, and averred that such expense was not a proper measure of damages. It answered that under the written contract it was not liable for any delay or damage caused by authority of law, or by any breakdown or mechanical defects of the vehicle or equipment. It further answered that it was operating under the rules and regulations of the Office of Defense Transportation, and particularly General Order No. 3, Section 501.6, which provided: "(a) No common carrier shall operate any motor truck in over-the-road service unless it is loaded to capacity." It averred that it used all reasonable and necessary diligence in procuring cargo additional to the plaintiff's goods to load to full capacity a van by December 14, 1944. ...

The trial court found that the goods were not being transported with reasonable dispatch during the period of thirty-seven days of storage at St. Louis, and held that defendant was properly chargeable with notice of the pressing needs of plaintiff and his family, and the necessity of reasonable dispatch in delivering the goods and that it was therefore liable for the expense to which plaintiff was put for hotel lodging for himself and family for thirty-seven days. ... The court held that this was the proper measure of damages. Nothing was allowed for money expended for meals.

Plaintiff, with his wife and minor child, had been a resident of Sioux City, Iowa. After his return from military service, he entered the school of medicine at Palo Alto, California, in September, 1944. Desiring to live there, he purchased a home on October 5th of that year, which was ready for occupancy on the fifth of the following November. ... On October 30, 1944, Wilson brought to the Huff home the paper, designated as an "order for service" — four copies of it — which she signed. ... Mrs. Huff, and the father and brother of plaintiff were at the latter's home when the truck was loaded. Each of them testified to talks with the driver; of his inquiry as to the best route between Sioux City and Palo Alto; of his examination and acceptance of roadmaps showing the route across Wyoming and westward; of his intention to go the next morning directly west from Sioux City over this "northern" route — U. S. Highway No. 20 — in order to save mileage. Mrs. Huff testified: "I asked the driver how long he thought the trip to California would take him. He replied that he would arrive in Palo Alto by Friday, November 13, 1944. I told him I was planning to fly out with my year-old child on November 10th in time to meet the van. I left Sioux City with my year-old child November 8, 1944. My furniture and household goods did not arrive in Palo Alto until January 3, 1945. ... The Huffs were not informed that the truck, instead of proceeding directly to Palo Alto from Sioux City, had been routed circuitously through St. Louis. Wilson had not told them, for he testified: "I don't believe the fact that this shipment would be consolidated with another load was discussed with the Huffs." The Huffs at Sioux City had no knowledge of the rerouting, until word was received from the plaintiff about a week after the goods were due to arrive, that they had not been delivered. ... It was disclosed at the trial by the deposition testimony of defendant's witnesses that when the Huff shipment reached St. Louis it weighed 6,730 pounds which was less than 80 percent of the capacity of defendant's cross-country van, and therefore further progress had to wait the arrival of sufficient goods to make up the 20 percent deficiency and complete a full load, as required by the above-mentioned ODT regulation. The Huff goods, which, according to the driver of the cross-country van, occupied about 75 percent of the cubage of the van was then placed in storage until a cargo weighing 3,160 pounds from Cleveland consigned to Palo Alto arrived and was consolidated with the Huff shipment. After remaining in storage 37 days the coast-bound van left St. Louis on December 15, 1944, with a load of 9,890 pounds, and after a trip of 19 days arrived and was unloaded at Palo Alto January 2, 1945. ...

Defendant in this court assigns errors for reversal as follows: ... The court erred in presuming that the driver of its truck at Sioux City informed defendant of the alleged conversations at the time of loading. ...

Defendant stressed the contract provision that it was required to use only reasonable dispatch. This term is merely a statement of the common-law rule. For many years the statutes of this state have required transportation by railroads to be made with "reasonable dispatch." Under the decisions of this court the burden is upon the shipper to establish the unusual and apparently unreasonable delay, and the burden is then on the common carrier to explain, account for, and justify the delay, consistently with the exercise of ordinary diligence and reasonable dispatch. . . .

Plaintiff fully met its burden, and defendant failed to exculpate itself. We cannot disturb the judgment on the ground of lack of evidence to sustain it.

Defendant complains that nothing supports the court's presumption that the truck driver at Sioux City advised defendant of the alleged conversations he had with the Huffs at the time the truck was loaded. It is contended that these acts of the driver were outside the scope of his authority. Whether he could vary the terms of the writing which Wilson had procured from Mrs. Huff is a matter we need not pass on. But he was an authorized representative of the defendant sent by it to Sioux City to load the goods and apparently to take them to California. The defendant gave him the appearance of having such authority. He certainly was not barred from expressing his opinion as to what "reasonable dispatch" under the contract meant and was respecting this trip. Mrs. Huff was justified in placing some reliance on what he said and in informing him of why she wished to know. The notice and knowledge which he and Wilson received from the Huffs were notice and knowledge to the defendant, and it was bound thereby. It was the duty of each of these agents and representatives to impart this information to the defendant. It is presumed that they did so. And the fact that they may not have does not defeat or rebut the presumption. Plaintiff was not required to establish by direct testimony that the knowledge was in fact communicated to defendant. The court was justified in indulging in the presumption complained of. It is a general rule that the knowledge of an agent gained in the performance of his authorized work or duty and within its scope . . . is the knowledge of the one for whom he is acting. . . .

Even without considering any alleged oral contract, and limiting defendant's liability strictly to the written "order for services," it is our conclusion that the judgment should be, and it is,

Affirmed.

Case Questions

1. In this case the notice or knowledge concerned the clarification of a provision in the contract between the parties. Describe the notice or knowledge received by the agent (or was it given the third party)?
2. In this case was the agent authorized to give or accept notice or knowledge? How was he so authorized?

SUB-AGENTS

The *Restatement* defines a sub-agent as follows:[3]

A sub-agent is a person appointed by an agent empowered to do so, to perform functions undertaken by the agent for the principal, but for whose conduct the agent agrees with the principal to be primarily responsible.

It is very important to note that a sub-agent is appointed by the agent to work directly for the agent in accomplishing tasks for the principal. Thus, a sub-agent is the agent of the agent who has appointed him and the sub-agent of the principal. A sub-agent owes duties of loyalty to both the appointing agent and the principal; and, of utmost importance is that a sub-agent can create contract and tort liability for both the appointing agent and the principal. The *Restatement* provides:[4]

The liability of an agent to third persons for the conduct of his servants, subservants, and other sub-agents is the same as that of a master or other principal for the conduct of his servants and other agents.

A third party damaged by a properly appointed sub-agent may sue both the appointing agent and the principal. As between the initial agent and the principal, the former should bear the loss in the absence of a contractual provision to the contrary.[5] Of course, in the case of a breach of tort duty, the sub-agent is the one who should ultimately bear the loss.

In order to impose liability on the agent for the tortious conduct of a sub-agent, the same type of analysis we used when presenting the respondeat superior doctrine must be utilized. The relationship between agent and sub-agent must be properly classified as a master-servant one if a tort within the scope of (or incidental to the purpose of) the agency has been committed.

An agent who hires a sub-agent must be distinguished from an agent whose job it is to hire employees for the employer. For example, a personnel officer for a corporation may hire employees for the corporation, but they become the agents of the corporation and not the sub-agents of the personnel officer. One way to determine if an agent is a sub-agent is to focus upon the activity for which the person was hired. If the activity primarily involves functions already undertaken by the appointing agent for the principal, then this person may be a sub-agent.

As you read and then brief the following case, concentrate upon the reasons why the court states Antisdale is liable to the plaintiff. There are at least two reasons. Be sure to not why the court holds that the Presbytery of San Francisco is liable to the plaintiff.

MALLOY v. FONG
232 P.2d 241 (Sup. Ct., Calif., 1951)

TRAYNOR, Justice.

Plaintiff brought this action for damages for personal injuries allegedly caused by the concurrent negligence of defendants Holmes, Fong, and Antisdale.

Plaintiff alleged that Fong and Antisdale were acting as agents of defendant Presbytery of San Francisco. The jury exonerated defendant Holmes, but returned a verdict in favor of plaintiff in the amount of $41,500 against defendants Fong, Antisdale, and the Presbytery of San Francisco. On motion of defendant Presbytery, the trial court entered a judgment notwithstanding the verdict as to it. . . .

During the summer vacation of 1943, plaintiff, then a boy of thirteen, attended a vacation Bible school conducted at the San Mateo Presbyterian Church for the children of members of the Church, then a "mission" under the jurisdiction of defendant Presbytery of San Francisco. Defendant Antisdale, pastor of the Church, was in charge of the school and gave the Bible instruction. The Bible classes were supplemented by classes in arts and crafts and by supervised recreation at a nearby playground to which the children were taken in automobiles and from which they were returned to the Church at the conclusion of the recreation period.

Antisdale became ill several days before July 1, 1943, the day plaintiff was injured, and was unable to conduct the school. It was therefore left without an instructor qualified to conduct the Bible classes. Defendant Fong, a 19-year-old divinity student, was at that time vacationing at the home of his guardian, Dr. Jones, a retired Presbyterian minister, in San Mateo. Fong agreed to conduct the Bible instruction in Antisdale's absence so that Antisdale might stay home and rest. In addition to conducting the Bible classes, Fong drove the children to the playground for their recreation period in his guardian's automobile, a Ford station wagon lent to him for that purpose.

Antisdale returned to the Church on the day of the accident, but he was occupied in his office the greater part of the morning, and Fong remained in charge of the class. At the conclusion of the Bible instruction, Fong released the children to wait outside the Church for transportation to the playground for the recreation period. Antisdale emerged from his office to see the children climbing into Fong's station wagon and several boys, including plaintiff, standing on the running boards. Antisdale then informed the children that he would take some of them in his car to relieve the congestion in the station wagon, and several of them entered the back seat of his car. Two of the boys left Fong's station wagon and stood on the running boards of Antisdale's car. The other children remained in Fong's station wagon, plaintiff standing on the left running board and another boy standing on the right running board. Antisdale testified that he ordered the children off the running boards. It is undisputed, however, that Antisdale did not insist on compliance with his order and that the children continued to stand on the running boards of his car and Fong's. . . .

During the trip the children in each vehicle were shouting and challenging the children in the other vehicle to race to the playground. Although the evidence is conflicting on this point, there is testimony that Fong and Antisdale entered into the spirit of the competition and increased the speed of their vehicles. After the vehicles turned west on Twenty-eighth Avenue, Fong pulled out to the left and endeavored to pass Antisdale, who increased the speed of his car to prevent Fong from passing. Fong pulled up parallel to Antisdale but was unable to pass him because Antisdale had increased his speed. Twenty-eighth Avenue has only one lane for vehicular traffic proceeding in each direction, so that Fong's station wagon during the time he was attempting to pass Antisdale was being driven well over in the left-hand lane, almost to the opposite curb. The two vehicles approached the intersection of Twenty-eighth and Isabelle Avenues in that position, Fong still unsuccessfully attempting to pass Antisdale. Antisdale stopped his car at the intersection, but Fong proceeded out into the intersection at an excessive rate of speed, still on the left-hand side of the road. Defendant Holmes was driving her car north on Isabelle Avenue and had just pulled out into the intersection when Fong drove by her. The vehicles were too close for her to stop in time and, according to her testimony, Fong made no effort to stop. Her right front fender and Fong's station wagon collided, striking plaintiff standing on the left running board. As a result of the collision, plaintiff lost his left leg below the knee and sustained injuries of a permanently disabling nature to his right leg, necessitating prolonged hospitalization and medical treatment.

Plaintiff's complaint was in three counts. In the first count he alleged that Fong was the agent of Antisdale and the Presbytery, that he was a passenger in Fong's car at the time of the accident, and that the accident was caused by the concurrent negligence of defendants Fong and Holmes. In the second count he alleged that Antisdale was the agent of the Presbytery, and that his negligence was a cause of the injuries to plaintiff in that he "negligently and carelessly increased the speed of his said Chevrolet sedan automobile, so as to render it impossible for said Ford Station Wagon (driven by Fong), in which plaintiff was riding, to pass and return to the right side of the roadway, so that the two (2) vehicles ran abreast into the intersection of said 28th Avenue with Isabelle Avenue, proximately causing and precipitating a collision between said Ford Station Wagon in which plaintiff was riding and that said Chevrolet sedan automobile being driven by defendant Eleanor Holmes." In the third count, plaintiff alleged that Antisdale and Fong were negligent in failing to exercise proper care for the safety of the children for whom they were responsible in that they negligently permitted several of them, including plaintiff, to ride on the running boards of the two vehicles, and that such negligence was a proximate cause of plaintiff's injuries. . . .

The Presbytery contends that public policy requires the preservation of its immunity from liability for torts committed by its agents or nonpaying beneficiaries of its charity. The declared public policy of this state, however, is contrary to that view: "Everyone is responsible, not only for the result of his willful acts, but also for an injury occasioned to another by his want of ordinary care or skill in the management of his property or person * * *". Civil Code, § 1714. That policy admits of no exception based upon the objectives, however laudable, of the tortfeasor. . . . Professor Harper, in his book *The Law of Torts,* points out that 'the immunity of charitable corporations in tort is based upon very dubious grounds'. Continuing, he concludes: 'It would seem that a sound social policy ought, in fact, to require such organizations to make just compensation for harm legally caused by their activities under the same circumstances as individuals before they carry on their charitable activities. The policy of the law requiring individuals to be just before generous seems equally applicable to charitable corporations. To require an injured individual to forego compensation for harm when he is otherwise entitled thereto, because the injury was committed by the servants of a charity, is to require him to make an unreasonable contribution to the charity, against his will, and a rule of law imposing such burdens can not be regarded as socially desirable nor consistent with sound policy.' Sec. 294. . . .

The Presbytery next contends that Antisdale and Fong were not agents of the Presbytery.

As the judicatory in charge of all Presbyterian churches in the San Francisco Bay area, the Presbytery of San Francisco had primary responsibility for the extension of the Presbyterian movement into new localities in that region. It was the Presbytery that organized the San Mateo group in 1942 and undertook the task of transforming it into a full-fledged church. During this early period, the Presbytery not only held the Church property but was in charge of Church activities. Speaking of churches in the mission stage, an officer of the defendant Presbytery testified: "that really is the place where the presbytery does exercise control." The establishment and maintenance of religious education for children was an important part of the Presbytery's project in San Mateo. The jury could properly conclude, therefore, that the agents who conducted the Daily Vacation Bible School were the agents of the Presbytery. . . .

The Presbytery has cited a number of decisions in other states to the effect that bishops and similar ecclesiastical bodies are not liable for the torts of local ministers. None of these cases involved supervision of a mission church. Furthermore, some were contract actions and turned upon specific findings that the act of the subordinate was beyond his contractual authority. . . .

The Presbytery contends that even if Antisdale was engaged in work for the Presbytery, he was an independent contractor for whose negligence the Presbytery was not responsible.

Whether a person performing work for another is an agent or an independent contractor depends primarily upon whether the one for whom the work is done has the legal right to control the activities of the alleged agent. . . . The power of the principal to terminate the services of the agent gives him the means of controlling the agent's activities. . . . It is not essential that the right of control be exercised or that there be actual supervision of the work of the agent. The existence of the right of control and supervision establishes the existence of an agency relationship. . . . The evidence clearly supports the conclusion of the jury that such control existed in the present case. The right of the Presbytery to install and remove its ministers, to approve or disapprove their transfer to other jurisdictions, and to supervise and control the activities of the local churches, particularly those in the mission stage, is inconsistent with a contrary conclusion.

Although the evidence as to Antisdale's negligence is conflicting, there is substantial evidence to support the finding that he was negligent and that his negligence was a cause of the injury to plaintiff. Such a finding is supported on either of two grounds: (1) that Antisdale negligently permitted and participated in a race between his automobile and the station wagon driven by Fong, causing both vehicles to travel at an excessive speed, and forcing Fong to enter the intersection of Twenty-eighth and Isabelle Avenues on the wrong side of the roadway, thus causing the accident; and (2) that Antisdale was negligent in permitting plaintiff among others to ride on the running boards of the vehicles, and that such negligence caused the injuries of which plaintiff complains. It is clear that Antisdale was acting in the scope of his agency at the time the tort was committed. As his principal, the Presbytery is liable for injuries to plaintiff resulting therefrom.

The verdict against the Presbytery may be supported not only on Antisdale's negligence but on that of Fong as well. Civil Code section 2351 provides: "A subagent, lawfully appointed, represents the principal in like manner with the original agent * * * ." Antisdale was an agent of the Presbytery, i.e., the "original" agent, and he lawfully appointed Fong a subagent.

An agency relationship may be informally created. No particular words are necessary, nor need there be consideration. All that is required is conduct by each party manifesting acceptance of a relationship whereby one of them is to perform work for the other under the latter's direction. . . .

There is ample evidence to support a finding that Antisdale and Fong entered into just such a relationship. Antisdale, as pastor of the Church was in charge of the Vacation Bible School. It was his responsibility to supervise and control the instruction and all activities connected with the School. He was in charge of the transportation of the children from the Church to the playground and of their return to the Church. He had authority to direct the activities of the children attending the school and to direct them into vehicles for transportation to the playground. He determined how long the children should remain at the playground and when they should be returned to the Church. . . .

The evidence that Fong, with Antisdale's knowledge and consent, performed duties for which the latter was responsible, that his performance of those duties was subject to Antisdale's supervision and control, and that his services could be terminated by Antisdale at any time, supports the conclusion that Fong was a subagent acting within the scope of his agency at the time of the accident. This conclusion is not negatived by the fact that Fong was not paid. *Restatement, Agency*, § 225. . . .

The evidence shows that Daily Vacation Bible Schools were conducted by virtually all churches of the Presbyterian denomination, including those within the area governed by the Presbytery of San Francisco, and in fact the Daily Vacation Bible School of the San Mateo Church antedated Antisdale's arrival there. In many respects the organization of such schools is similar to that of Sunday Schools and necessarily involves the work of volunteer teachers who assist the minister. Antisdale testified that the children were divided into age groups and that he gave the Bible instruction to those of plaintiff's age and above. There were classes in handwork and classes in worship and the supervised recreation periods. Extensive volunteer assistance was customarily rendered by the friends and members of the Church. Authority to organize the school and its staff was inherent in the nature and scope of Antisdale's duties. Fong was appointed in the exercise of this authority, and therefore . . . the Presbytery may be held liable for Fong's negligence. Civil Code, § 2349. . . .

The judgment in favor of Presbytery of San Francisco is reversed, and the trial court is directed to enter judgment against Presbytery in accordance with the verdict of the jury.

◆◆◆

Case Questions

1. It appears from the opinion that Fong was not paid for his work for the Presbytery. Was he an agent? Why?
2. Was Fong a sub-agent?
3. Who were the defendants in this case and against whom did the plaintiff recover?

4. Note the various possible causes of action against Antisdale and the Presbytery. Could Antisdale be vicariously liable to the plaintiff?
5. A state statute may displace or add to the common law in a state. Does the California statute cited in the opinion change the common law of sub-agents as we have presented it? In the absence of the state statute could the Presbytery have been liable to the plaintiff?
6. Was Antisdale a servant of Presbytery; or was he a non-servant agent?

DELEGATION OF AGENCY DUTIES

Closely related to the sub-agent discussion is the delegation of the entire agency task to someone else. If the principal is aware of the delegation and consents to it, then a new agency relationship is formed. In the absence of this consent, however, an agent's power to delegate is extremely limited. It is generally recognized that an agent cannot delegate to another any task involving the exercise of judgment or discretion in the use of authority held for the principal's benefit.[6] Remember that agents are fiduciaries; thus the relationship between the parties is invested with special qualities of confidentiality. However, in some agency relationships the fiduciary quality is not nearly as strong as others. Thus, the rule that fiduciaries cannot delegate matters requiring discretion has been labeled an overstatement by some authorities.[7] Just what "discretion" means must be defined by the trade customs and usages. Clearly, there can be no delegation where a principal forbids it. Where the exercise of discretion is minimal and many principals do allow delegation, the power to delegate may be inferred. This may be true when a principal employs a corporation for a task which is not generally thought of as involving personal service. However, when a principal deals with a partnership and, in particular, where a principal selects one of the partners to deal with, the agency may not be delegated.

The following case presents the general view that an agency relationship involving one's individual skill and judgment cannot be delegated.

W.H. BARBER AGENCY CO. v. CO-OPERATIVE BARREL CO.
133 Minn. 207, 158 N.W. 38 (S. Ct. Minn., 1916)

TAYLOR, C.

Plaintiff appealed from an order sustaining a demurrer to its complaint.

The complaint sets forth that W.H. Barber was a broker and maintained an organization for the sale of commercial products; that he made a contract with defendant to have the exclusive sale, at a stated commission, for a term of years, of all the butter tubs manufactured by defendant; that after performing such contract for more than four years and establishing a large and lucrative business in the sale of such tubs, he organized the plaintiff corporation which took over all his business and his organization, and has ever since continued the same without any change in the personnel or management thereof; that defendant refused to permit the plaintiff corporation to perform the remainder of Barber's contract for the sale of its tubs; and that plaintiff has been damaged thereby in the amount of the commissions which it could have earned during the remainder of the term.

The sole question presented and argued is whether Barber could transfer his contract to the plaintiff corporation without the consent of the defendant.

Barber was defendant's sales agent, and the case is controlled by the rules governing agency, ... The powers conferred upon an agent are based upon the confidence which the principal has in the agent's ability and integrity; and it is the universal rule that an agent cannot transfer to another powers calling for the exercise of discretion, skill or judgment. ... It is held that, where a principal has authorized a partnership to act as his agent, the subsequent dissolution of the partnership terminates the agency, and that a partner who takes over the business cannot continue to act as such agent unless the principal authorizes him to do so. ...

In *Meysenburg* v. *Littlefield* (C.C.) 135 Fed. 184, Meysenburg and Littlefield were selling agents for the Lorain Steel Company. We quote the opinion:

> It was the skill and diligence of Littlefield and Meysenburg, as partners, with all that term implies, which the Lorain Steel Company contracted for, and when Littlefield and Meysenburg dissolved that relation the consideration so far failed that the contract ceased to be enforceable; and the firm's action in dissolving the copartnership would be such a breach of the contract in question as to justify the steel company in subsequently ignoring it.

In *Wheaton* v. *Cadillac Automobile Co.*, 143 Mich. 21, 106 N.W. 399, the New Jersey Automobile Company, a partnership composed of two members, was defendant's selling agent in the state of New Jersey. One of the partners withdrew from the firm and assigned all his interest in the business to the other. The court held that this gave defendant the right to abrogate the contract.

In the present case, defendant made Barber its agent. He assumed to transfer to a corporation the powers conferred upon him personally. The corporation is a separate entity controlled by a board of at least three directors, and its stockholders and officers are subject to change at any time. If it acquired Barber's rights under his contract with defendant, it would retain such rights even if Barber should entirely sever his connection with it. To permit a person, employed as an agent, to transfer his duties and powers to a corporation without the consent of his principal would involve a more radical violation of the rules governing the relation of principal and agent than to permit a partnership, employed as an agent, to devolve its powers and duties upon one of its members. Barber could no more substitute plaintiff for himself as defendant's agent, without defendant's consent, than he could so substitute any other corporation or individual.

Order affirmed.

◆◆◆

Case Questions

1. What is there about the structure of a corporation which caused the principal to object to the delegation of the agency in this case?

2. What could W.H. Barber have done to secure a valid delegation of authority?

LOANED OR BORROWED SERVANTS

Sometimes a principal/master will permit his agent/servant to work for or help someone else. A common example of this is where a building contractor leases or gratuitously provides (to another person) heavy equipment with an operator. If the operator commits a tort while working for the other person, which employer is liable? The question is answered by determining which employer had control of the servant. The *Restatement* concludes that the master exercising control over the servant at the time of the tortious act is liable;[8] it also suggests that where the issue of control is not clear a person may be a servant of two masters thus creating liability for both to a tortiously injured third party.[9]

The following cases present circumstances where courts have attempted to resolve factual disputes centering on the issues of control over a servant by a second master. The second case is of special interest for at least two reasons. First, it illustrates that even a highly trained professional such as an anesthesiologist may be a servant. Second, it illustrates that sometimes courts may apply a well-established principle of law incorrectly. Do you agree?

ALUMINUM COMPANY OF AMERICA v. WARD
231 F.2d 376 (C.C.A. 6th, 1956)

◆◆◆

SIMONS, Chief Judge.

For the death of her husband, William A. Ward, the appellee sought and obtained a judgment against the appellant based upon negligence. . . .

Ward was a truck driver for the Dixie-Ohio Express Company, (D.O.X.) a common carrier by motor vehicle. His equipment was a tractor and trailer. With it on the day of the accident he was transporting a load of aluminum from the appellant's plant at Alcoa, Tennessee, to points in Ohio and New York. While making a left turn from one street to another, in Knoxville, both tractor and trailer overturned, resulting in Ward's death. There is substantial and cumulative evidence that the accident was caused by the shifting of the load on the trailer and this the appellant appears to concede, for it suggests no negligence of Ward in respect to speed or carelessness in making the turn. The theory upon which the appellant was sought to be held was that the Aluminum Company undertook to load the trailer, as it did with the many trailers employed by it for delivery of its product, that it had negligently loaded and braced its cargo and that, as a result, the tractor and trailer overturned and killed the decedent.

The principle upon which the Aluminum Company seeks to defeat liability is that it did not load and brace the cargo; that such work was being performed solely by the carrier; that although the loading and bracing was done by the Aluminum Company's general employees they were loaned to the carrier for that purpose and, so, came within the loaned servant doctrine. . . .

The proofs show that Davis, a fellow employee of Ward, had towed the trailer from the Aluminum Company plant where it had been partially loaded to a cafe where he had stopped for coffee; that the decedent there joined him, having arrived towing an empty trailer; that they there exchanged trailers; that Davis advised the decedent of the approximate weight of the cargo in the front of the trailer and also that there were two boxes at the back that were to go off at the carrier's loading dock in Knoxville where the loading of the trailer was to be completed by taking on a cargo from another trailer which the decedent had towed from Alcoa to Knoxville and that the decedent then proceeded to drive the tractor-trailer toward Knoxville, to the place where the accident occurred.

Davis said he was not only a truck driver but for a year prior to the accident had been a supervisor *for the carrier*, (emphasis added) supervising the loading of all its trailers at the Aluminum Company's Alcoa plant, and had supervised the loading of the trailer here involved. Although the Aluminum Company paid the loading crew, furnished the wood, timbers, nails and steel bands in bracing the cargo and performed this work with its own equipment, it was under his direction and supervision, the loaders doing only the actual mechanical work. . . .

Davis further testified that the procedure followed in the loading and bracing of the aluminum in the trailer was in accordance with the method pursued in the loading of all D.O.X. trailers at Alcoa. He always backed his trailer into the dock, told the company checker what and how he wanted it done, and the trailers were loaded according to his instructions; that on occasions, when the loading or bracing was not done as instructed, he refused to move the trailer until it was loaded and braced as he had directed; that sometimes he would not require boxes of aluminum to be braced, where in his judgment it was unnecessary; that no one but he at any time gave any directions for loading D.O.X. trailers and that on the occasions when he thought a load was not braced safely he went to the loading or bracing crew and told them what to do. Occasionally, however, he went to the Aluminum Company foreman, if this was more convenient, and told him what changes were to be made and had no trouble in getting the crew to follow his instructions. Davis' evidence, in this respect, was in part corroborated by other supervisors, by the Assistant Business Agent in Knoxville for the Teamsters' Union and some of the members of the loading crew.

On the basis of this evidence, the Aluminum Company insists a legal conclusion follows that the responsibility for the loading and bracing was upon the trucker because the employees who performed the loading and bracing became servants of the trucker, and if such employees were negligent the Aluminum Company was not responsible. This leads us to a consideration of the loaned servant doctrine as it may be spelled out from relevant decisions. In *Charles* v. *Barrett,* 233 N.Y. 127, 135 N.E. 199, 200, Chief Judge Cardozo stated the general principle in these words: "The rule now is that, as long as the employee is furthering the business of his general employer by the service rendered to another, there will be no inference of a new relation unless command has been surrendered, and no inference of its surrender from the mere fact of its division." In an illuminating opinion of Mr. Justice Christianson of the Minnesota Supreme Court in *Nepstad* v. *Lambert*, 235 Minn. 1, 50 N.W. 2d 614, 620, it was pointed out that the courts have relied principally on two tests, in determining when a worker becomes a loaned servant. The first of these is the " 'whose business' test" but this test is practically valueless where the general employer's business consists of furnishing men to perform work for the special employer because by doing his job the worker is necessarily furthering and doing the business of both employers. A second test is the so-called "control" test but one danger in using this test is failing to define sufficiently the scope and meaning of the term. In a general sense, both employers frequently have powers over the employee which may be considered elements of control. He comes to the conclusion, however, that "the orders of the borrowing employer must be commands and not requests if the worker is to be found. to be a loaned servant. * * * The right to discharge is one element in measuring the authoritativeness of the order, but it should not be made decisive. * * * Authority to designate only the result to be reached is not sufficient under the control test. There must be the authority to exercise detailed authoritative control over the manner in which the work is to be done." ...

With these observations, we turn to the record to determine whether complete control over the loading force was placed in the trucking company, having in mind that upon a contested issue of fact we are bound by the verdict, if substantial evidence supports it. Hubert Payne was a driver for another carrier and also Assistant Business Agent of the local Teamsters' Union. He testified as to the general practices of the Aluminum Company, in respect to loading, and was asked this question: "Did you ever attempt to tell the workmen what to do or did the foreman pass the work to them?" to which his reply was: "I would tell the foreman and he normally would ask me what I thought was wrong with it and he in turn would instruct the people." To the question: "Did you ever attempt to boss or supervise workmen in their work or did their own foreman do that?" his reply was: "I did not supervise, no sir." The supervisor Davis, hereinbefore referred to, was asked this question: "But you didn't feel like you had direct control over the employees yourself?" and his answer was: "I didn't have any control over the employees." Burnett, a checker for D.O.X. testifying for the appellee, was asked whether the Aluminum Company had a head man there, said that it had both a checker and a foreman; that the checker checks the net weight and gross weight and the number of boxes; then was asked this question: "And who else do you say the Aluminum Company has there?" His reply was: "They have, I would imagine, a superintendent." And when asked what he did the answer was: "He is the boss over the whole thing, the shipping department." Asked whether the Dixie-Ohio employees do anything at all in actually loading the aluminum in the trailer and in bracing it, he testified: "No, that's one thing you can't do it. You strike the Aluminum Company if you do their work. They would strike. They do their own work."

In view of this evidence, even though controverted, the jury was warranted in drawing the inference that the Aluminum Company had not surrendered complete control of its employees to the trucking company. It had its own foreman or superintendent on the job. This was fully recognized by the trucking company supervisors who, on occasion, transmitted their instructions to the loading crew through the foreman or superintendent. The most that can be said on the subject of control is that there was divided authority and this falls short of that power to command which is the necessary element in the determination of a surrender of complete control by the general employer to the temporary employer under the loaned servant doctrine. . . .

Affirmed.

◆◆◆

Case Questions

1. Concisely state the defense of Aluminum Company of America and whether or not it was successful.
2. Was Davis a loaned servant?

ROCKWELL v. STONE
404 Pa. 574, 173 A. 2d 54 (S. Ct., Pa., 1961)

◆◆◆

BOK, Justice.

* * * Suffice it to say that plaintiff recovered a verdict against both doctors, who have separately appealed. Dr. Kaplan, the subject of this opinion, asks judgment n. o. v. or, if he may not have it, a new trial. Both requests were refused below and this appeal is from the ensuing judgment. . . .

Dr. Kaplan's liability rests on two piers, either one of which will support it: his own negligence and his responsibility as principal for Dr. Stone's negligence, . . .

The following facts appear in the record: Dr. Kaplan said that he was "the boss of the surgical end of it and that the plaintiff was his patient; he chose the hospital and arranged the patient's admission; he chose to use a minor elective surgical procedure to remove the bursa from plaintiff's right arm, which procedure could be postponed or done at the patient's convenience; he overruled his patient, who wanted local anesthesia, and ordered a general one; if he did not choose Dr. Stone, who was the chief of the hospital's anesthesiology department, he chose Dr. Stone's hospital and was satisfied with him and with his choice of sodium pentothal as the induction agent and a gas for the general anesthesia; . . . plaintiff was presented to Dr. Kaplan for surgery fifteen minutes after the injection; . . . the injection in plaintiff's left arm missed the vein and went in or around an artery; . . . although Dr. Stone chose not to tell Dr. Kaplan of the "catastrophe" that had occurred at induction with the sodium pentothal, which is a very dangerous drug, Dr. Kaplan could and did see that the plaintiff's left arm was extended on the intravenous board when the patient entered the operating room; . . . he assumed that when the patient was presented to him in the operating room he was ready for surgery; . . . he made no inquiry about the plaintiff's reaction to the anesthesia, . . . the arm visibly deteriorated during the operation and the pulse vanished while in the recovery room afterwards; and . . . he left the operating room and the hospital without seeing the plaintiff in the recovery room. . . .

Hence the basic question of fact was whether Dr. Kaplan should have seen the condition of the arm or should have asked about it and having found out should have refused to operate until it had been taken care of. In leaving such matters generally to the jury on the ground of negligence, the trial judge gave Dr. Kaplan more than he deserved when he said:

> There is no testimony in the record that I can recall whereby such a standard of care is required under those circumstances of a surgeon in attendance. Therefore, if you find that there has been no violation of his duty in that regard there would be no basis for a finding of responsibility on the part of Dr. Kaplan on the first ground alone, namely, negligence.

There is no dispute that the misuse of sodium pentothal caused the condition of plaintiff's arm, which in turn caused its amputation. The jury needed no expert testimony of what Dr. Kaplan's duty was: it was, so far as they were concerned, to do something quickly for a dangerous condition which the evidence shows was visible and urgent. Something specific was done, though too late, ...

Plaintiff's personal negligence was therefore properly left to the jury under the full range of the circumstances. . . .

As for Dr. Kaplan's responsibility for Dr. Stone's negligence, Dr. Stone testified that a surgeon could use the hospital's anesthesiologist or bring in his own. Dr. Kaplan testified that he was "the boss of the surgical end of it," and that "as long as Dr. Stone had anything to do with the anesthesia I was perfectly satisfied." He chose the hospital in which Dr. Stone worked and chose a general rather than a local anesthetic. Dr. Stone testified that Dr. Kaplan had the authority to ask or tell him what sort of anesthesia he wanted, although it was not the practice at the Graduate Hospital to do so. Dr. Kaplan said that if it was best for his patient's safety he could discontinue the operation and tell the anesthesiologist to stop giving anesthetic, particularly in minor elective surgical procedure. His words were, on the latter point:

Q. Suppose you felt that anesthesia should stop and the anesthetist felt that it sould continue, and you felt that continuation would create a critical condition for your patient?

A. I would stop immediately, regardless of what he had to say, if I felt strongly that this should stop, I would stop it.

Q. And you would tell the anesthetist to stop it, wouldn't you?

A. I would.

Q. And he would stop, wouldn't he?

A. I think he would have to.

The foregoing is very different from the independent contractor-like language of Dr. Kaplan's brief. We think it points clearly to the language concerning borrowed employees in *Mature* v. *Angelo*, 1953, 373 Pa. 593, 97 A. 2d 59, 60: "A servant is the employee of the person who has the *right* of controlling the manner of his performance of the work, irrespective of whether he actually *exercises* that control or not." . . .

Nor was there a conflict of evidence on the question of right of control. Dr. Kaplan and Dr. Stone did not disagree in their testimony as it has been condensed above, nor can there be doubt based on common sense that Dr. Stone acted on Dr. Kaplan's business: he had to or the surgeon could not operate. The undisputed evidence clearly shores up the instruction of the trial judge. "And in the eyes of the law, in this case, Dr. Stone was the agent for a step in the operative procedure, the anesthesia step. He was the agent of Dr. Kaplan."

It is clear, . . . that doctors are subject to the law of agency and may at the same time be agent both of another physician and of a hospital, even though the employment is not joint.

This establishes the theory of respondeat superior and also answers the heart of defendant's motion for a new trial. We have carefully read the charge and see no error in it when looked at it in the round. . . .

Judgment affirmed.

* * *

BENJAMIN R. JONES, Justice (dissenting).

Although alleged, the case at bar in my opinion presents no evidence of any *direct* negligence on the part of Dr. Kaplan and Dr. Kaplan's liability, if any, must be premised on the theory of vicarious liability. Stated otherwise, is Dr. Kaplan liable for malpractice under the doctrine of respondeat superior for an act of negligence which occurred, outside his presence and without his knowledge, during preoperative procedure involved in the administration of an anesthesia?

Certain factual circumstances must be noted. Dr. Kaplan neither requested nor exercised any choice in the selection of any particular anesthesiologist to administer the anesthesia. Although Dr. Kaplan, as any other surgeon, was at liberty to select any anesthesiologist he so desired, he simply indicated to Dr. Stone, the Chief of the Department of Anesthesiology, that he wanted a general anesthesia administered and relied upon Dr. Stone's professional competency for selection of the type of anesthesia and the person or persons to administer it. Such service was provided by the hospital and the compensation for such service would be billed by the hospital to the patient and would be paid by the latter directly to the hospital. The personnel of the Department were employed by, paid by and under the general control and direction of the hospital which had the sole power to dismiss such personnel.

When the incident occurred, as previously stated, Dr. Kaplan was not present nor was his presence required at that time and, while the injection and ensuing incident took place at approximately 9:45 a.m., Dr. Kaplan was unaware of it until approximately noon. . . .

In the case at bar, Dr. Kaplan neither prescribed nor was he advised of the use of sodium pentothal; he did not administer it, was not present when it was administered and, in fact, did not know of it until hours later. Moreover, he exercised no direction, control or authority over Drs. Stone and Jiminez, or Molnar, while in the induction room and he did not request any of them to administer this drug. Dr. Kaplan was simply using the hospital facilities and its personnel, a service for which Rockwell would be billed directly.

The sodium pentothal was administered outside of Dr. Kaplan's presence, in the induction room over which, to employ the language of McConnell, he was not the "captain of the ship:" . . . at that time *only* Dr. Stone was in command. . . .

Under such circumstances, in my opinion, Dr. Kaplan could not be held liable upon any theory of respondeat superior and the judgment as to Dr. Kaplan should be reversed and judgment . . . entered in his favor.

◆◆◆

Case Questions

1. Dr. Kaplan was liable on two separate grounds. What were they?
2. Did Dr. Kaplan have the right to control at the time of the negligent act? At the time of the negligent act (before the operation) was not Dr. Stone an independent contractor?
3. Could the injured third party in this case sue the hospital and allege that Dr. Kaplan was the hospital's agent and Dr. Stone a sub-agent? From the facts given, would this case be successful? What additional facts, if any, would you need to know?

AGENCY TERMINATION

The agency relationship may be terminated by consent or renunciation by either party, or termination may be inferred from events. Such events as the loss of capacity (death, insanity, illegality) or impossibility, the destruction of the subject matter, lapse of time, or declarations of bankruptcy will terminate the agency relationship. When we use the term "termination", we are speaking of an end to the agency relationship which usually involves two phases. The first phase is the end of the legal relationship between the principal and agent. The second is the end of the agent's authority as perceived by others — third parties and potential third parties.

TERMINATION BY CONSENT

As between the principal and agent, their mutual legal duties may be terminated by mutual consent at any time, or in accordance with the terms of their agreement. This includes the completion of the authorized task. If no specific task is identified or if no time limit is set, then the relationship ends when the agent should know that the principal no longer desires him to act.

An agency relationship may end before the date set in a contract by the expression of either party; however, this might not relieve the parties of contractual liability. For example, a board of directors may contract with A for service as president of the corporation for a period of three years. State statutes usually provide that corporate officers may be removed at will by the board. The board then may discharge A as president at any time, but may be required to pay damages for the breach of the three-year contract. The next case illustrates the application of the principle.

MITCHELL v. VULTURE MINING & MILLING CO.
47 Az. 249; 55 P. 2d 636 (S. Ct., Ariz., 1936)

McALISTER, Judge.

This is an appeal by F. H. Mitchell from a judgment in favor of the Vulture Mining & Milling Company, a corporation, . . .

The substance of the second amended complaint on which the case was tried is that in the summer of 1930 the Vulture Mining & Milling Company, a corporation, hereinafter called defendant, owned thirty-one mining claims, patented and unpatented, near Wickenburg, Arizona. It had an authorized capital of one million shares of the par value of one dollar each, six hundred thousand of which were treasury stock it desired to sell for the purpose of raising funds to develop its mining property. F. H. Mitchell, hereinafter called plaintiff, was an experienced mining engineer and salesman who had friends in the eastern section of the United States through whom he felt he could contact prospective purchasers. So, on or about August 10, 1930, he and the defendant entered into an agreement by which he was granted for a reasonable time "the exclusive right to sell in the eastern states of the United States the treasury stock of the defendant," and pursuant to this agreement the defendant's board of directors appointed him its agent and gave him power to hire assistants, to select a bank as depository for funds from the sale of stock, and to issue certificates thereof on behalf of the defendant. It was agreed that the plaintiff would go to the Eastern States at his own expense and for a reasonable time devote his efforts exclusively to presenting the stock to prospective purchasers and making sales thereof at eighty cents a share and that he should receive as compensation therefor twenty-five per cent of the proceeds of the sales made by or through him. For the purpose of fulfilling this agreement the plaintiff went east on August 21, 1930, and expended large sums of money in an effort to sell the stock, the defendant being kept advised at all times of his activities and prospects. On October 7, 1930, the oral agreement was modified by the parties in writing in such a way that the plaintiff's exclusive right to sell the treasury stock of the defendant was limited to three hundred thousand shares, the other three hundred thousand being reserved for these two purposes: One hundred thousand for sale in the west by the defendant and two hundred thousand to remain unsold for the time being. Some of those he contacted desired to purchase all the treasury stock and upon the defendant's being advised of this it informed plaintiff that it did not care to sell a controlling interest, but would be glad to dispose of the three hundred thousand shares or any part thereof through him and encouraged him to continue his efforts to that end.

On the 29th day of October, 1930, while the plaintiff was actively endeavoring to sell the three hundred thousand shares and had reasonable prospects of completing a sale, the defendant, without advising him, granted a ten day option on the six hundred thousand shares of treasury stock to the United Verde Extension Mining Company, a corporation, organized under the laws of Delaware and having its legal office in that state and its financial office in the state of New York. It is then averred that the option was granted to a purchaser in the Eastern States, territory in which plaintiff had been given the right to sell, that the option was thereafter exercised by the United Verde Extension Mining Company, and that the result of this was to disable the defendant from performing its agreement and to deprive the plaintiff of the opportunity to fulfill his and to receive compensation for his services and to reimburse himself for the monies expended by him, in the sum of $60,000, amended later, however, to read $10,000. It alleged also that in going East and maintaining himself there in an endeavor to sell the stock, in sending telegrams in connection therewith and in obtaining permits to sell, he expended approximately $2,000 and devoted seventy-five days of time, the reasonable value of each day's service being $100.

The defendant answered, admitting the execution of the option and its exercise by the company. It denied, however, that either act was performed in the East and alleged that the option and the sale of the stock covered thereby was made, exercised and fulfilled within the state of Arizona where the company had been authorized to and had actually carried on business for more than ten years. Every other allegation, not specifically admitted, was denied. . . . According to the evidence the plaintiff and the defendant entered into an agreement by which the plaintiff was authorized to sell in the Eastern States within a reasonable time three hundred thousand shares of the defendant's treasury stock at eighty cents a share for a commission of twenty-five percent, the plaintiff agreeing to go from his home in Arizona to that section and devote his entire time and energy to making a sale of this stock, all at his own expense. Pursuant to this agreement he went East and actively endeavored to sell the stock until October 29, 1930, when the defendant terminated his authority in respect thereto by optioning the stock to the Verde Extension Mining Company, and the plaintiff contends that the agreement and his actual partial performance of it was sufficient to make a binding contract not revocable without rendering defendant liable for breaching it, either in damages sustained as a result thereof or for the recovery of the reasonable value of his time and efforts and the expenditures incurred by him in attempting to carry out his part of the undertaking. It occurs to us that this contention is correct, because the agreement, even if merely unilateral prior to plaintiff's going East and entering upon its performance, became, when this took place, bilateral and mutual, the plaintiff's acceptance and actual part performance of it being sufficient consideration for the contract of employment. . . . In *2d Mechem on Agency*, p. 2052, § 2454, the author says: "The negotiations may also take another form. The principal may say to the broker in substance and effect, if not expressly, 'I will promise to pay you a commission if you will promise to list it, advertise it, or otherwise endeavor to find a purchaser.' This is the offer of a bilateral contract. The broker's promise may be made in words or it may be inferred as a fact from his conduct, as, for example, in accepting the employment and entering upon the performance. In this case both parties are bound, and the principal will be liable to the broker for any breach of the terms of the contract."

The contract being mutual, the giving of an option and thus placing it beyond the power of the defendant to live up to its terms was just as effectively a breach as a sale by the defendant of the stock in the East, the territory the plaintiff alleged to be exclusively his, would have been. The defendant, it is true, had the power to terminate it any time it saw fit but no right to do so without subjecting itself to liability for whatever damages its act may have caused the plaintiff. *Mechem on Agency,*, page 405, § 568. It is utterly unthinkable that after he had entered into the agreement, gone east and, at an expense to himself of $2,000, devoted his entire time and effort for two months to selling the stock, the plaintiff's contractual status should have been such that the defendant could, before he had had a reasonable time in which to complete the undertaking, deprive him of the right to do so without rendering itself liable, at least, for the reasonable value of his services and reimbursement for expenditures made or incurred by him. The agreement specified no particular time in which he could make the sale but under all the authorities a reasonable time was implied. ...

The evidence, as we view it, is such that it cannot reasonably be inferred from it that it was intended by the parties that the defendant was retaining the right to sell in the West the stock it was giving the plaintiff the right to dispose of in the East, or, in other words, that the general rule, that one who gives another the exclusive right to sell property in certain territory does not deprive himself of the right to sell in other territory, ...

The judgment is reversed and the cause remanded for a new trial.

◆ ◆ ◆

Case Questions

1. Does this decision hold that the principal could not have revoked the agent's authority when it wished to do so?
2. Upon retrial, how do you think the court would instruct the jury as to how it should calculate the measure of damages?

TERMINATION BY EVENTS

Generally any event which would cause the agent to reasonably believe that the principal would no longer wish him to act will cause a termination of the agency.[10] Some of the common events are the loss of capacity of the principal, impossibility, death of either party, destruction of the subject matter or declarations of bankruptcy or illegality.

Capacity as it is used here refers to the legal capacity to conduct business transactions or contracts. Capacity is defined by state statute and usually all persons who are of sound mind and who are over eighteen years of age have the capacity to contract. Obviously, both a formal declaration of insanity or death terminate the principal's capacity to contract thus terminating the agent's capacity to act for the principal.

COX v. BOWLING
54 Mo. App. 289 (Kan. City Ct. of App., 1893)

GILL, J.

This is a suit for commissions for sale of real estate. Plaintiff had judgment below, and defendant appealed. The material facts are about as follows: Bowling owned a house and lot in Lamar, Missouri, which he desired to sell. He agreed with Cox, an agent, that if he, Cox, would find a purchaser for the house and lot at the price of $2,500 he would allow him $100 as commissions. Cox entered into negotiations with one Snyder, a resident of Lamar, and made an effort to sell the property to Snyder at the fixed price of $2,500. Snyder refused to give that sum and offered to purchase at a less amount, which Bowling then declined. Cox made repeated efforts to get the parties together, but to no purpose, and the negotiations then ceased. A short time thereafter the building on the lot was destroyed by fire. A few days after the fire Bowling and Snyder met on the street, and after a brief interview Bowling sold the lot (then vacant) to Snyder for $2,000.

Plaintiff originally brought his action before the justice of the peace on the special contract which, as already stated, was that defendant was to pay plaintiff the agreed price of $100 if he sold the property for $2,500; . . .

Even if there had been no change in the nature and condition of the property subsequent to plaintiff's employment, the right to commissions in this case may well be questioned, since according to the testimony of both parties the nature of plaintiff's engagement was, it seems, that he was to be paid $100 *if he found a purchaser able and willing to give $2,500 for the house and lot,* and otherwise no compensation was to be paid. Nor is there any evidence to show that this original contract was ever changed or modified.

But, however, this may be, plaintiff did not secure a purchaser for the house and lot he engaged to sell. Snyder and Bowling were never able to agree on a price for the property as it stood when Cox conducted the negotiations. Bowling's price — and that, too, at which Cox undertook to sell — was $2,500, but Snyder was not willing to pay that for the property. Subsequently, however, when the building was destroyed and the property became materially changed (so that indeed it was not the same as when Cox was employed to sell it), Bowling and Snyder came together and a sale of the vacant lot was effected. But his was not the property that Cox was empowered to sell. There was nothing said between Bowling and Cox after the destruction of the building. So material a change in the subject-matter of the agency amounted to a revocation of Cox's authority as agent. It is well settled that the authority of the agent is terminated by the destruction of the subject-matter of the agency. . . .

◆◆◆

Case Questions

1. Define a "material alteration" of the subject matter of the agency which will most likely result in a court's order terminating the agency relationship.
2. What if Cox made a contract to sell the property to Snyder for $2,500 after the house was materially altered but neither Cox nor the purchaser, Snyder, knew, or through the exercise of reasonable care, could have known about the alteration. Could Cox collect his commission? This is a very close question, and the outcome could go either way depending upon which one of the parties, Cox or Bowling or Snyder assumed the risk of the destruction of the subject matter. This may be established either by contract or the "usual methods and conduct of doing business." In the absence of one of the parties assuming the risk of destruction, Cox most probably could collect his commission because he has done all that was required of him: he secured a purchaser.

3. What if Cox discovered a small uranium deposit on the land making it worth five times the $2,500 he was authorized to sell it for? Could he, without incurring liability to Bowling, sell it for $2,500 assuming that Bowling had no knowledge of the deposit?

TERMINATION OF THE AGENT'S AUTHORITY AS PERCEIVED BY THIRD PARTIES

Circumstantial authority, primarily apparent and inherent authority, was created by the common law to protect the reasonable expectations of those dealing with agents. This authority is generally not terminated when the formal actual authority between principal and agent is terminated. The general rule is that the agent's circumstantial authority continues until the third party knows or has reason to know of the termination. The *Restatement* takes the position that death or incapacity of the principal or declared illegality of the agency relationship are events of such notoriety that it will be inferred that all third parties have notice of the event.[11] Thus where the death or incapacity of a principal terminates the agency relationship and the agent subsequently contracts with a third party for the benefit of the principal and neither the agent nor the third party have actual knowledge of the death or incapacity, the contract cannot be enforced against the principal. Although this approach is theoretically sound it does work a hardship on the third party and seems to contradict (or at least be an exception to) the reasons for the creation of circumstantial authority.[12]

If the agency is not terminated by death, incapacity, or illegality, the principal is required to notify third parties of the termination of the agent's authority. In this case, the principal must proceed to give notice in one of two ways.

A third party who has contracted with or begun to contract with an agent based upon the agent's apparent authority must be given actual notice of termination of the agent's authority. This is notice which is given to the third party personally or mailed to his business or posted in a place where, in view of the business customs between the parties, the third party could reasonably be expected to look for such a notice.[13]

With respect to those persons with whom the agent has not dealt prior to the termination of authority, notice of the agent's termination of apparent authority may be given by advertising the fact in a newspaper of general circulation in the place where the agency operates or by some other manner reasonably calculated to give notice to such third parties.[14]

If a third party who has dealt with an agent on the basis of apparent authority does not receive actual notice of the agency termination and enters into a contract with the agent for the benefit of the principal after the actual authority is terminated, the principal is bound.

BURCH v. AMERICUS GROCERY CO.
125 Ga. 153, 53 S.E. 1008 (S. Ct., Ga., 1906)

EVANS, J.

The Americus Grocery Company sued J. B. Burch for a balance alleged to be due on open account. The only item in dispute was one of May 8, 1903, for a certain quantity of tobacco. The defendant contended that this item was purchased by his clerk, Mike Burch, after he had left his employment, and that he neither authorized nor ratified the purchase nor received the tobacco. On the other hand, the plaintiff insisted that Mike Burch was the general agent of the defendant in the management of his store, and as such, on previous occasions, had ordered goods of plaintiff on defendant's account, and that the plaintiff, without notice that Mike Burch was no longer employed by the defendant, took the order in the defendant's name and shipped the goods to the defendant, as was usual in the past transactions. On the trial it appeared that the defendant operated a sawmill and in connection therewith conducted a store or commissary. The commissary was in the charge of Mike Burch, who purchased all the merchandise therein sold and managed the business. On former occasions, the plaintiff had sold merchandise to the defendant upon the order of his agent, Mike Burch. When the merchandise, to recover the price of which the present action was brought, was ordered of the plaintiff by Mike Burch, he was not in the employment of the defendant, and had not been for two months past. Niether the plaintiff company nor its "drummer" was aware at the time of receiving the order that Mike Burch was no longer in the service of the defendant. The plaintiff's salesman called at the commissary of the defendant and asked for Mike Burch, as he had always done, and was informed that Mike Burch was about three miles away, superintending the putting down of a sawmill. There he found him and took the order for the merchandise. It was shipped to the defendant and the bill of lading was mailed to him. The defendant testified that the goods were never received by him, but were taken possession of by Mike Burch without his knowledge, and that he never received the bill of lading for the goods. Upon these facts the jury returned a verdict in favor of the plaintiff for the value of the goods, which verdict the trial judge refused to set aside on motion for a new trial.

1. In the management of the business of the commissary, the agent, Mike Burch, had general powers. Relatively to this business, he was the general agent of the defendant in the purchase of merchandise. "Whenever a general agency has been established for any purpose, all persons who have dealt with such agent, or who have known of the agency and are apt to deal with him, have a right to presume that such authority will continue until it is shown to have been terminated in one way or another; and they also have a right to anticipate that if the principal revokes such authority, they will be given due notice thereof. It is a general rule of law, therefore, upon which there seems to be no conflict of authorities, that all acts of a general agent within the scope of his authority, as respects third persons, will be binding on the principal, even though done after revocation, unless notice of such revocation has been given to those persons who have had dealings with and who are apt to have other dealings with the agent upon the strength of his former authority." 1 *Clark & Skyles on Agency,* § 173 (b). . . .

In the present case no express notice was shown, and the controlling issue was whether or not the plaintiff had "implied notice" that there had been a revocation of the agency, . . . The only circumstance upon which the defendant could rely as suggesting the necessity of making inquiry whether the agency had been terminated was that the order for the goods was given to the plaintiff's salesman three miles from the defendant's store, where the agent had been employed. The defendant was engaged in the sawmill business, and his "commissary" was run in connection with that business, as an adjunct to it, and not as a wholly independent enterprise. When the order for the goods was taken, Mike Burch, who still assumed to act as the defendant's agent, was superintending the erection of a sawmill. That it did not belong to the defendant or was not to be used in connection with his business was not self-apparent, nor was the fact that Mike Burch was not at the time engaged in his customary duties at the commissary calculated to put the plaintiff's salesman on notice that he had left the service of the defendant. Moreover, the salesman had first driven by the store of the defendant and inquired for Mike Burch, who had theretofore been in charge of it. Instead of being notified that Mike Burch was no longer in the defendant's employ, the salesman was told where Mike Burch could be found. Under these circumstances it is not strange that the salesman should assume that the employees at the store of the defendant understood that he had called on business, as theretofore, and wished to see the defendant's representative, nor is it remarkable that, after being informed as to his whereabouts but given no intimation that he was no longer the defendant's agent, the drummer should entertain no doubt as to the continuance of the general agency. The jury, after considering all facts and circumstances brought to light at the trial, found against the contention of the defendant that due caution and prudence on the part of the plaintiff's drummer ought to have suggested to him the propriety of making inquiry, if he did not divine the truth. ... The defendant was admittedly at fault, having failed to take any steps to give notice to the plaintiff, whereas the plaintiff had not omitted to perform any legal duty owing to the defendant, and the plaintiff's drummer admittedly acted in entire good faith. The jury took the view that the plaintiff should not be called on to suffer the loss. "In this there is no hardship upon the defendant," as was pointed out by Rapallo, J., In *Clafin* v. *Lenheim*, ... who added that it was the defendant's duty, "after he had accredited his brother for a series of years as authorized to deal in his name and on his responsibility, when he terminated that authority, to notify all parties who had been in the habit of dealing with his agent, as the plaintiffs had been to his knowledge. This was an act easily performed, and would have been a perfect protection to him and prevented the plaintiffs from being deceived. Justice to parties dealing with agents requires that the rule requiring notice in such cases should not be departed from on slight grounds, or dubious or equivocal circumstances substituted in place of notice. If notice was not in fact given, and loss happens to the defendant, it is attributable to his neglect of a most usual and necessary precaution." The verdict of the jury appears to be in accord both with the strict law and the common justice of the case, ...

Judgment affirmed.

Case Questions

1. Since the third party recovered from the principal in this case, could the principal recover from the agent? What must be alleged and proved for this to happen?

2. When a principal discharges an agent who has had the authority to contract with third persons, what course of conduct should the principal adopt to be sure it will be free from liability for acts of the agent after discharge?

REVIEW PROBLEMS
PART II

1. The following was taken from a local newspaper:

A local insurance man, who has provided health insurance coverage for city employees for the past six years, admitted today that he misused premiums paid to him by the city.

Michael Daher of M. Daher and Associates, Lakeshore Bank Building, made the admission to a newsman after Mayor Randall Miller said in a news release this morning that the city had been informed by the Golden Rule Insurance Co. that claims filed by city employees during June, July and August of this year would not be honored by the company. The mayor said that the city was informed of the company's decision last week. He said at that time the company informed city officials that insurance premiums for those three months had not been remitted to the company by Daher.

The mayor said that the city had paid the premiums in good faith to Daher and Daher agreed that the city was not at fault. He said, "The mayor is correct, the premiums were remitted to me. The city did act in good faith." Daher went on, "I admit I have misused the funds."

The mayor said today that during conversations with company officials the city had been informed that the company would be willing to honor the claims if the premiums ($17,000 per month) are paid. He said that the city has contacted the office of the State Insurance Commissioner in Indianapolis and that the office is sending an investigator to examine the situation. The mayor said that since the premiums have been paid to Daher, the company has a duty to honor the claims.

He said if they continue to refuse to pay the claims we will vigorously pursue any and every course of action to insure the payment of claims to our employees including legal action against Golden Rule Insurance Co., and Mr. Daher as their agent.

Assume that you are the investigator sent by the state to examine the situation:

a. Clearly state the legal rules under which the Golden Rule Co. could be held liable.

b. What kinds of evidence will you look for to substantiate your proper use of the above listed legal rules?

c. Clearly state whether or not Mr. Daher could be liable to either the Golden Rule Insurance Co., or the city for the premiums taken.

2. A hired C, a contractor to build an addition to his home. Although A provided the plans for the addition and relied on C's practical skills in

construction, he nevertheless went home early every day to make comments about how the job was going and to give C his impressions of the work done. C hired S to work for him. S had basic carpentry skills, but mostly did the driving, clean up work, painting and whatever else C told him to do.

A's house was in the city and the addition was very close to a busy sidewalk and street. When a mild rainstorm passed through the city, the frame of the new structure collapsed on the sidewalk severely injuring P. S was sent by C to get a trailer to haul away the mess and negligently ran into Q.

Discuss the causes of action that P and Q have. Whom may they sue and will they succeed?

3. O owned a small plastics manufacturing business which served the mobile home and recreational vehicle industry in north central Indiana. He employed a traveling salesman, S, who made calls on customers in the area served. S sold O's products for a period of 2 years and was authorized not only to sign the contracts on behalf of O but also accept payment by check from those placing orders. O became increasingly concerned with the decline in sales as a result of his customers selling fewer of their products because of the energy crisis. He decided to change his method of selling. On September 1, 1975 he discharged S and on that date ran an advertisement in a local newspaper informing the public that:

S, general sales agent, for O, was discharged from employment as of this date, due to a new and innovative sales organization being implemented by O.

S was angry with O and had no hopes of employment. He was desperate for money so after his discharge he wen o C, a good customer of O's in the past who had not read the newspaper notice, and secured an order for $10,000 worth of plastics; S was paid by check and then cashed the check.

Also, S contracted with N, a new customer who knew of O's business but had never done business with O, and similarly took payment and absconded with it.

Of course, the plastics are never shipped to C and N and both bring suit against O for breach of contract. Should they recover? Why?

Would there be a difference in the outcome if O's business had filed for bankruptcy on Sept. 1, 1975 and notice of this was carried in the local newspaper?

ENDNOTES

1. *The Restatement of the Law,* 2nd, §9 (1958).
2. *Id.,* § 282.
3. *Id.,* § 5(1).
4. *Id.,* § 362.
5. W. A. Seavey, *Law of Agency,* 10-11 (1964).
6. *Restatement, supra,* note 1, § 18.
7. Seavey, *supra,* note 5, p. 25.
8. *Restatement, supra,* note 1, § 226.
9. *Id.*
10. *Id.,* § 108.
11. *Id.,* § 134.
12. Seavey, *supra,* note 5, p. 89.
13. *Restatement, supra,* note 1, § 136.
14. *Id.*

PART III
PARTNERSHIPS

THE PARTNERSHIP FORM OF ASSOCIATION: CREATION AND PARTNERSHIP PROPERTY 7

In this chapter and the next we will present material illustrating the circumstances in which the courts will recognize the partnership form, and as a consequence will establish legal duties among partners, and among the partnership, the partners, and third parties. A statement of these circumstances is called Partnership Law. Partnership Law differs from Agency Law in that the former has been codified in most states in the form of partnership statutes while the latter is not in statutory form, but is based upon the common law.

The National Conference of Commissioners on Uniform State Laws is a body of well-known lawyers, judges, and law professors who meet yearly to draft and make available for adoption by the various state legislatures uniform laws covering a wide variety of topics. It is believed that in some areas of the law, Partnership Law being one, uniformity in law application among the states is desirable. Many partnerships do business in more than one state and if such an association was subject to a different set of laws governing the association form in each state then an unnecessary element of complexity would be confronted. Today at least forty-four states have adopted the Uniform Partnership Act with very little change in the language from that originally proposed in 1916.[1] Throughout the next two chapters, we will use the Uniform Partnership Act as a key to our presentation of material and will refer to it only as the U.P.A. This act is reproduced in its entirety in the Appendix.

The reader should note that even though Partnership Law is mostly statutory, case law is by no means insignificant in understanding the statutory language. Appellate cases still provide, better than any other source, a statement of the circumstances in which the legal system will act to enforce either statutory, contractual or common law duties.

At this point the reader might wish to refer to Chapter 2 and table 2-1 provided there for a list of advantages and disadvantages of using this form of business association.

DEFINITION

A partnership is defined by Section 6 of the U.P.A. as follows:

A partnership is an association of two or more persons to carry on as co-owners a business for profit.

One of the unresolved issues of Partnership Law is presented by the use of the word "association" in the definition. The issue is whether or not this association is a legal entity separate from the partners. Is it like a corporation which is a distinct legal entity or like a proprietorship in which the business and personal assets of the owner are not separate? The U.P.A. does not answer this question, but, as we pointed out in Chapter 2, it is stated that the original chief draftsman of the U.P.A., Dean James Barr Ames of the Harvard Law School, would have defined a partnership as a legal entity had he lived to complete the drafting.[2] Today, as a general rule, the partnership is recognized by most courts as a separate legal entity for limited purposes. More specifically, a partnership can contract, own both personal and real property and sue and be sued in its own name. Also, the Internal Revenue Laws require that partnerships file income tax returns and the bankruptcy statutes also specifically provide for partnerships.

The glaring exception to the above statements is that a partner may not shield his personal assets (savings accounts, home, auto, etc.) from the business creditors of the partnership. This means that if the partnership is unable to pay its debts, the judgment creditors of the partnership may ask the court to order the sheriff to seize the partner's personal assets and sell them to satisfy the judgment. Practically speaking, most suits against partnerships also join partners as individuals so that any judgment is recovered against both. For an example of this type of joinder refer back to the complaint in the *Solmica* case (Chapter 1) and note that both the partnership, Elmer Fox & Co., and its partners were defendants.

The definition further states that a partnership, " . . . is an association of . . . persons . . ." The U.P.A., Section 2 states that the word person includes, " . . . individuals, partnerships, corporations and other associations." Thus the U.P.A. permits humans to be partners with other humans or with any other legal form of business association. As we noted in Chapter 2, some state legislatures in the nineteenth century did not permit a corporation to become a partner on the theory that the statutory mandate that a corporation be managed by a board of directors was incompatible with the corporation's being subject to control by a vote of the other partners. Today many legislatures and courts will allow a corporation to be a partner especially where the power to control the partner is limited by the narrow purpose of the partnership (such as being a joint venturer) or by having its authority to act eliminated (such as being a limited partner).[3] The point to be remembered is that state Partnership Law does not limit those who may become partners; State Corporation Law, however, may.

Implied in the use of the term "persons" in the definition above is the principle that to be a partner one must have the legal capacity to contract. As previously noted in Chapter 3 in the section on capacity, the term is defined by state statute. Generally, minors, persons declared insane or those deprived of their civil rights such as those in prison for a felony or aliens may lack the legal capacity to contract. In the last century many legislatures forbade married women and trustees from becoming partners but today these restrictions have been removed almost everywhere. However, in some jurisdictions, cases in the early twentieth century held that husband-wife partnerships are not permitted because the potential for disagreement and consequent litigation is considered incompatible with the family relationship.[4] It is doubtful today if these courts would reach the same result. Similarly, older cases held it improper for a trustee to invest in a partnership because it was too risky. Today, as long as the investment is prudent, it will be allowed.

In many jurisdictions the contracts of a minor are treated differently than those of insane persons or others lacking capacity to contract. Minors contracts are usually voidable at the option of the minor; in the case of insane persons their contracts are usually void and unenforceable by either party. Therefore, although a minor may be a partner if he or she wishes, obligations to the partnership and its creditors may be repudiated at the minors option in most jurisdictions.

The definition of a partnership further states that persons must "carry on as co-owners." This element of co-ownership is one of the chief features which distinguishes the partnership form of business from the proprietorship (employer-employee relationship). Often one partner may act for another or at the control of another partner, but if there is an intent to co-own, a partnership exists. One of the surest signs of co-ownership is the sharing of profits. The U.P.A. Section 7(4) recognizes this when it states:

> The receipt by a person of the profits of a business is prima facie evidence that he is a partner in the business, but no such inference shall be drawn if such profits were received in payment:
> a. As a debt by installment or otherwise;
> b. As wages . . . or rent. . . .
> c. As an annuity. . . .
> d. As interest on a loan, though the amount of payment may vary with the profits of the business.
> e. As the consideration for the sale of good will of a business . . .

In addition to sharing profits other evidence of an intent to co-own may be found in the joint ownership of property, and in the joint obligation to contribute capital to the enterprise.

Finally, the U.P.A. requires that the association be one carried on for *profit*. This means that those associations created *primarily* for charitable, religious, fraternal or social purposes are not partnerships even though they may share in the revenue of a fund-raising project or devote such revenue to further their purpose.

CREATION

Partnerships may be implied in law by courts where the circumstances meet the requirements of the definition or they may be created by contract between the partners. In *some* instances a contract or a writing of some kind is required. Most states for example have a statute which requires agreements for the sale of an interest in real property or agreements which require performance lasting over one year to be in writing. So, if a partnership confers authority on a partner to contract in real property, such authority should be in writing. If it is not and the partner contracts with a third person to buy or sell the real property, the contract may not be enforced against or by the partnership. Also, if the partners intend the partnership to exist for longer than one year, they should place their understanding in writing.

With the exceptions noted, the general rule is that to form a partnership, a written agreement is not necessary — although it is advisable. There are many instances in which an informal business relationship may be formed for the purpose of co-owning an enterprise. Little thought may be given to the formal, legal implications of the association until the circumstances of ownership conflict occur. Before a resolution of the conflict can be achieved courts must determine if a partnership did exist. If the facts of the case reveal the elements of a partnership as stated in the definition above, then courts will hold a partnership existed. As indicated before if the parties are partners, rather than employer-employee a different set of legal consequences will follow.

Following are two cases in which the issue is whether or not a partnerhsip was intended. See if you can determine why the court in the first case, where there was no written agreement, concluded that there was a partnership; whereas, in the next case, where there was an agreement, the court concluded the opposite.

ZAJAC v. HARRIS
241 Ark. 737, 410 S.W. 2d 593 (S. Ct., Ark., 1967)

♦♦♦

GEORGE ROSE SMITH, Justice.

The appellee, George Harris, brought this suit to compel the appellant, Carl A. Zajac, to account for the profits and assets of a partnership that assertedly existed between the parties for some two years. Zajac denied that a partnership existed, insisting that Harris was merely an employee in a business owned by Zajac. The chancellor concluded that Harris had met the burden of proving the partnership relationship. The court accordingly referred the case to a master for a statement of the partnership accounts. The essential question here is whether the chancellor's recognition of the partnership is against the weight of the evidence.

At first blush the testimony appears to be in such hopeless conflict that the controlling issue at the trial must have been one of credibility. Upon reflection, however, we arrive at a somewhat different view of the case. The business association that is known in the law as a partnership is not one that can be defined with precision. To the contrary, a partnership is a contractual relationship that may vary, in form and substance, in an almost infinite variety of ways. The draftsmen of the controlling statute, the Uniform Partnership Act, tacitly acknowledged that fact by stating only in the most general language an assortment of rules that are to be considered in determining whether a partnership exists. . . .

In the case at bar there is the . . . consideration that these two laymen went into business together without consulting a lawyer or attempting to put their agreement into writing. It is apparent from the testimony that neither man had any conscious or deliberate intention of entering into a particular legal relationship. When the testimony is viewed in this light the conflicts are not so sharp as they might otherwise appear to be. Our problem is that of determining from the record as a whole whether the association they agreed upon was a partnership or an employer-employee relationship.

Before the two men became business associates Zajac had conducted a combination garage-and-salvage company, filling station, and grocery store in the Marche community in Pulaski County. This dispute relates only to the salvage branch of the enterprise.

In the salvage operation now in controversy the parties bought wrecked automobiles from insurance companies and either rebuilt them for resale or cannibalized them by reusing or reselling the parts. Harris, the plaintiff, testified that he and Zajac agreed to go into business together, splitting the profits equally—except that Harris was to receive one fourth of the proceeds from any parts sold by him. Harris borrowed $9,000 from a bank, upon the security of property that he owned, and placed the money in a bank account that he used in buying cars for the firm. The profits were divided from time to time as the cars were resold, so that Harris's capital was used and reused. He identified checks totaling more than $73,000 that he signed in making purchases for the business.

Zajac, by contrast, took the position that Harris was merely an employee working for a commission of one half the profits realized from cars that Harris himself had bought. Zajac denied that he had ever agreed that Harris would spend his own money in buying cars. "I told him, when you go out there, when you bid on a car, make a note that I will pay for it." We have no doubt, however, that Harris *did* use his own money in the venture and that Zajac knew that such expenditures were being made.

Counsel for Zajac put much stress upon their client's controlling voice in the management of the business. Zajac and his wife and their accountant had charge of the books and records. No partnership income tax return was ever filed. Harris was ostensibly treated as an employee, in that federal withholding and Social Security taxes were paid upon his share of the profits. The firm also carried workmen's compensation insurance for Harris's protection. In our opinion, however, any inferences that might ordinarily be drawn from these bookkeeping entries are effectively rebutted by the undisputed fact that Harris, apart from being able to sign his name, was unable to read or write. There is no reason to believe that he appreciated the significance of the accounting practices now relied upon by Zajac. They were unilateral.

We attach much weight to Zajac's candid admissions, elicited by the chancellor's questions, that Zajac paid Harris one half of the profits derived from cars that Zajac bought with his own money and sold by his own efforts. Zajac had insisted from the outset that Harris was working upon a commission basis, but that view cannot be reconciled with Harris's admitted right to receive his share of the profits derived from business conducted by Zajac alone.

There is no real dispute between the parties about the governing principles of law. The ultimate question is whether the two men intended to become partners, as that term is used in the law. . . . Harris's receipt of a share of the net profits is prima facie evidence that he was a partner, unless the money was paid to him as wages. . . . He invested, as we have seen, substantial sums of his own money in the acquisition of cars for the firm. Zajac concedes that Harris was entitled to a share of the profits from transactions that Harris certainly did not handle on a commission basis. When the testimony is reconciled, as we have attempted to do, it does not appear that the chancellor was wrong in deciding that a partnership existed.

Affirmed.

◆◆◆

Case Questions

1. What facts did the court rely upon in reaching its conclusion that a partnership existed?

2. Why do you think it was advantageous for Harris to establish that a partnerhsip existed?

SHELDON v. LITTLE
111 Vt. 301, 15 A.2d 574 (S. Ct., Vt., 1940)

(Authors' note: In this case the plaintiff, Adelaide W. Sheldon, sued C. Russell Little for amounts allegedly due her. Russell's motion to dismiss the case was overruled. Russell argued that he and the defendant were partners and that no formal settlement of the partnership accounts had taken place and that the cause of action should not be one for money owed, but for an "accounting" – a legal term meaning a complete settlement of accounts. The defendant admitted that the cause of action for the money due was proper if no partnership had been formed. In the first part of the opinion, the court addressed itself to the issue of whether or not a partnership had been formed. This part of the opinion which affirms the dismissal of the defendant's motion is below.)

BUTTLES, Justice

From the facts found it appears that prior to March, 1925, the plaintiff and defendant each conducted an insurance business in Fair Haven, Vermont, that of the defendant being such that he gave only a part of his time thereto. On March 5, 1925, the parties executed a written agreement providing for the consolidation of their two insurance agencies. Thereafter the consolidated business was conducted in accordance with such agreement until October 1, 1932, when the parties ceased to do business together under such agreement or in any other way. During all of the time that the business was so conducted it was actively managed by the defendant who took general charge of the same, kept the books and handled the finances. Meanwhile the plaintiff was away from Fair Haven much of the time and took no active part in the business except that during the year 1932 she gave it some attention and participated in its management. At the end of each year except 1932 the defendant submitted to the plaintiff a written report or statement purporting to give certain data regarding the business for that year. Each of these reports states the amount of money or value that each of the parties had received from the business during the year and the difference between those amounts. . . . Each of them contains a tabulation of expenses and a tabulation by months of what appears to be, in each instance, the commission income of the business. None of the reports are balanced and on each report the difference between the sums of the two tabulations referred to exceeds by a substantial amount the sum of the amounts received by the plaintiff and the defendant.

Said written agreement provided that the said agencies, after being consolidated, should be run as the property of the plaintiff and under the name as theretofore of the Sheldon Agency; that the defendant should have the supervision and management of said agency, bringing to the Sheldon office the books, files, papers, and other personal property previously used by him in his own agency and continue there the general business of the consolidated agencies, devoting his entire working time to the management and development thereof; that the plaintiff might give such time to the management of the business as she cared to give from time to time, but should be under no obligation at any time to give the same her personal attention and care; that from the gross income of the business there should be paid the running expenses including rent, heat, light, office supplies, stenographer and other incidental expenses usual in the conduct of such a business, and that the net profits after the payment of such expenses should be equally divided between the parties to the agreement. Other provisions of the agreement will be considered later.

The question for determination is whether the plaintiff and defendant were partners or sustained some other relation to each other. Where the rights of the parties . . . are concerned, and no question as to third parties is involved, the criterion to determine whether the contract is one of partnership or not must be: What did the parties intend by the contract which they made as between themselves? . . . This intention may be shown by their express agreement or inferred from their conduct and dealings with one another. But we have here no indication of the intention of the parties other than their written agreement, so that their intention is to be ascertained by a construction of that writing.

Many definitions of partnership have been given, no one of which would, perhaps, fit all cases, and various tests for determining the existence of the partnership relation have been applied by the courts. The test most generally applied, subject to various conditions and limitations, is that of profit sharing. This Court has recently said that the indispensable constituent of a partnership is that the parties shall be jointly interested in the profits and affected by the losses of the business. . . . Such joint interest may result even though one party furnishes the capital or stock and the other contributes his labor and skill. . . . But there is a clear distinction between agreements whereby the parties have a specific interest in the profits themselves as profits, and agreements which give to the person sought to be charged not a specific interest in the business or profits but a stipulated proportion of the proceeds as compensation for his labor and services. The former constitute a partnership but the latter do not. . . .

This distinction between profits received as profits and profits received in payment of an obligation is generally recognized. . . .

In *Gibson* v. *Smith*, 31 Neb. 354, 47 N.W. 1052, it is concisely stated that to have the effect of making a participant in the profits of a business a partner, his participation must be in the profits as such under circumstances which give him a proprietary interest in them as principal before they are divided. . . .

But such proprietary interest, as principal, in the profits before they are divided involves ownership of an interest in the business that produces the profits. . . .

In the case we are considering by the terms of the agreement the business was to be run as the property of the plaintiff; no substantial increase in expenses of management could be incurred by the defendant as manager except with the approval of the plaintiff; the plaintiff could terminate the agreement at any time, resume control of the business and discharge the defendant as manager by paying him a sum equal to one half of the earnings for another year; the plaintiff could see the business at any time, but before selling to another she was required to offer it to the defendant at a price to be based on the business done by the agency during the year 1924; in case of plaintiff's death the defendant was to have a similar option to purchase the business from plaintiff's personal representatives. Clearly it was the intent of the parties that the plaintiff should have the sole proprietary interest in the business and in the profits resulting therefrom before they were divided. The defendant received a portion of the profits not as profits, but as compensation for his services as manager of the plaintiff's business. We hold that the parties were not partners and there was no error in the denial of the defendant's motion as made.

◆◆◆

Case Questions

1. The general rule is that if the evidence reveals the parties intended to form a partnership but they never expressly agreed to this, the courts will create one or imply one for them to protect the interests of one or more of the partners. Also, if the evidence reveals no intent to form such an association, the courts will not imply one. What evidence caused the court in this case to conclude that no partnership existed?
2. Can you reconcile the holdings of *Zajac* and *Sheldon*?

In both of the cases presented, one of the remedies sought was for the court to order an "accounting." This term as used in Partnership Law designates an equitable remedy in which the court orders a comprehensive investigation of the transactions of the partnership, and a complete statement of accounts. Section 22 of the U.P.A. provides that any partner shall have the rights to a formal account as to partnership affairs:

a. if he is wrongfully excluded from the partnership business or possession of its property by his co-partners,
b. if the right exists under the terms of any agreement,
c. as provided in Section 21 (Section 21 deals with a partner receiving a partnership benefit without the consent of other partners),
d. whenever other circumstances render it just and reasonable.

Before this remedy is available, the court must find that the party requesting the remedy is a partner. This was the issue that was before the courts in the *Zajac* and *Sheldon* cases, and is often the first issue presented in partnership litigation. Moreover, most courts hold that an action *between partners* for money owed is inappropriate. The appropriate remedy is to seek an accounting. Once a complete statement of partnership accounts has been made, then the partners and the court may more clearly decide who is owed which amounts.

In addition to the circumstances discussed above where the court created a partnership, courts will also impose the duties of a partner upon one under circumstances in which there may be no partnership in fact, but *third parties* are lead to believe there is one and have dealt either with the supposed partnership or one representing himself to be a partner. The circumstances under which this will occur create a partnership by estoppel. The word, "estoppel," is used here in the same manner as it was used in the agency material. It is an equitable doctrine imposed upon a relationship to protect the reasonable expectations of the third parties.

Section 16 of the U.P.A. recognizes a partner by estoppel in two circumstances:

1. When a person ... represents himself ... as a partner in an existing partnership ... he is liable to any ... person to whom such representation has been made (and) who has ... given credit to the actual or apparent partnership. ...
2. When a person has been ... represented to be a partner in an existing partnership, or with one or more persons not actual partners, he is an agent of the persons consenting to such representation ... to the same extent and in the same manner as though he were a partner in fact, with respect to persons who rely upon the representation. ...

In the first circumstance, the law recognizes a partnership when, for example, A expressly or implicitly represents he is a partner in "P Associates & Co." although in reality he is not; and a T/P extends credit to P Associates & Co., and does not directly contract with A. By recognizing a partnership in this instance, A would become liable to T/P since a court would estopp A from denying he was a partner in P Associates & Co.

In the second circumstance, the law recognizes a partnership when some member or members or a partnership, P Associates & Co., allow or have knowledge that one who is not a partner, "A", is holding himself out as a partner and a third party T/P extends credit to or otherwise contracts with A believing him to be a partner. If all partners consent to or know about the representation, then the partnership is liable. If fewer than all partners consent or know, only they are liable.

The results reached in these two instances illustrate that Partnership Law, like Agency Law, will protect the reasonable expectations of third persons who deal with an apparent partner or apparent partnership to his detriment. Note that though there is liability running from the "partnership" to the third party in both cases, it is a very restricted form of partnership. Partnership by estoppel establishes an actual partnership relation between the partnership and third parties only for the purpose of providing a remedy to the injured third party. This equitable remedy does not create an actual partnership between the parties so that they can enforce other duties of partners on one another.

The most conventional way to establish a partnership is for the parties to sign a contractual agreement declaring their intent to form a partnership. This agreement, customarily referred to as "Articles of Partnership," may be as complex as the parties desire. We have reproduced a rather simple partnership agreement. We suggest you read it carefully and take notes on the provisions which make the partnership form of association distinct from other associations. These provisions are the ones concerning capital, profit and loss, salaries, management, and termination.

PARTNERSHIP AGREEMENT*

AGREEMENT made June 4, 1973, between John O'Connell and Harry Jones, both of New York, New York.

1. Name and business. The parties hereby form a partnership under the name of Ace Advertising Co. to conduct a general advertising business. The principal office of the business shall be in New York, New York.

2. Term. The partnership shall begin on June 4, 1973, and shall continue until terminated as herein provided.

3. Capital. The capital of the partnership shall be contributed in cash by the partners as follows:

John O'Connell	$20,000
Harry Jones	$20,000

A separate capital account shall be maintained for each partner. Neither partner shall withdraw any part of his capital account. . . .

Upon the demand of either partner, the capital accounts of the partners shall be maintained at all times in the proportions in which the partners share in the profits and losses of the partnership.

4. Profit and loss. The net profits of the partnership shall be divided equally between the partners and the net losses shall be borne equally by them. A separate income account shall be maintained for each partner. Partnership profits and losses shall be charged or credited to the separate income account of each partner. If a partner has no credit balance in his income account, losses shall be charged to his capital account.

5. Salaries and drawings. Neither partner shall receive any salary for services rendered to the partnership. Each partner may, from time to time, withdraw the credit balance in his income account. No additional share of profits shall inure to either partner by reason of his capital or income account being in excess of the capital or income account of the other.

6. Interest. No interest shall be paid on the initial contributions to the capital of the partnership or on any subsequent contributions of capital.

7. Management, duties, and restrictions. The partners shall have equal rights in the management of the partnership business, and each partner shall devote his entire time to the conduct of the business. . . . Without the consent of the other partner neither partner shall on behalf of the partnership borrow or lend money, or make, deliver or accept any commercial paper, or execute any mortgage, security agreement, bond, or lease, or purchase or contract to purchase, or sell or contract to sell any property for or of the partnership other than the type of property bought and sold in the regular course of its business. Neither partner shall, except with the consent of the other partner, assign, mortgage, grant a security interest in, or sell his share in the partnership or in its capital assets or property, or enter into any agreement as a result of which any person shall become interested with him in the partnership, or do any act detrimental to the best interests of the partnership or which

Source: *Current Legal Forms with Tax Analyses,* Vol. 1, Matthew Bender, 1975, p. 1-1004 Form 1.01. Copyright © 1975 by Matthew Bender & Co., Inc., and reprinted from Rabkin & Johnson *Current Legal Forms* with permission from the publisher.

would make it impossible to carry on the ordinary business of the partnership.

8. Banking. All funds of the partnership shall be deposited in its name in such checking account or accounts as shall be designated by the partners. All withdrawals therefrom are to be made upon checks signed by either partner.

9. Books. The partnership books shall be maintained at the principal office of the partnership, and each partner shall at all times have access thereto. The books shall be kept on a fiscal year basis, commencing July 1 and ending June 30, and shall be closed and balanced at the end of each fiscal year. An audit shall be made as of the closing date.

10. Voluntary termination. The partnership may be dissolved at any time by agreement of the partners, in which event the partners shall proceed with reasonable promptness to liquidate the business of the partnership. The partnership name shall be sold with the other assets of the business. The assets of the partnership business shall be used and distributed in the following order: (a) to pay or provide for the payment of all partnership liabilities and liquidating expenses and obligations; (b) to equalize the income accounts of the partners; (c) to discharge the balance of the income accounts of the partners; (d) to equalize the capital accounts of the partners; and (e) to discharge the balance of the capital accounts of the partners.

11. Retirement. Either partner shall have the right to retire from the partnership at the end of any fiscal year. Written notice of intention to retire shall be served upon the other partner at the office of the partner at the office of the partnership at least three months before the end of the fiscal year. The retirement of either partner shall have no effect upon the continuance of the partnership business. The remaining partner shall have the right either to purchase the retiring partner's interest in the partnership or to terminate and liquidate the partnership business. If the remaining partner elects to purchase the interest of the retiring partner, he shall serve notice in writing of such election upon the retiring partner at the office of the partnership within two months after receipt of his notice of intention to retire.

(a) If the remaining partner elects to purchase the interest of the retiring partner in the partnership, the purchase price and method of payment shall be the same as stated in paragraph 12 with reference to the purchase of a decedent's interest in the partnership.

(b) If the remaining partner does not elect to purchase the interest of the retiring partner in the partnership, the partners shall proceed with reasonable promptness to liquidate the business of the partnership. The procedure as to liquidation and distribution of the assets of the partnership business shall be the same as stated in paragraph 10 with reference to voluntary termination.

12. Death. Upon the death of either partner, the surviving partner shall have the right either to purchase the interest of the decedent in the partnership or to terminate and liquidate the partnership business. If the surviving partner elects to purchase the decedent's interest, he shall service notice in writing of such election, within three months after the

death of the decedent, upon the executor or administrator of the decedent, or, if at the time of such election no legal representative has been appointed upon any one of the known legal heirs of the decedent at the last known address of such heir.

(a) If the surviving partner elects to purchase the interest of the decedent in the partnership, the purchase price shall be equal to the decedent's capital account as at the date of his death plus the decedent's income account as at the end of the prior fiscal year, increased by his share of partnership profits or decreased by his share of partnership losses for the period from the beginning of the fiscal year in which his death occurred until the end of the calendar month in which his death occurred, and decreased by withdrawals charged to his income account during such period. No allowance shall be made for goodwill, trade name, patents, or other intangible assets, except as those assets have been reflected on the partnership books immediately prior to the decedent's death; but the survivor shall nevertheless be entitled to use the trade name of the partnership. The purchase price shall be paid without interest in four semi-annual installments beginning six months after the end of the calendar month in which the decedent's death occurred.

(b) If the surviving partner does not elect to purchase the interest of the decedent in the partnership, he shall proceed with reasonable promptness to liquidate the business of the partnership. The surviving partner and the estate of the deceased partner shall share equally in the profits and losses of the business during the period of liquidation, except that the decedent's estate shall not be liable for losses in excess of the decedent's interest in the partnership at the time of his death. No compensation shall be paid to the surviving partner for his services in liquidation. Except as herein otherwise stated, the procedure as to liquidation and distribution of the assets of the partnership business shall be the same as stated in paragraph 10 with reference to voluntary termination. . . .

In witness whereof the parties have signed this agreement.

s/. . . . .

John O'Connell

s/. . . . .

Harry Jones

The remaining material on partnerships will be presented by using the agreement above as an organizing guide. The first two paragraphs of the partnership agreement are self-explanatory. Remember that if a partnership adopts a name which is *not* composed of the surnames of the partners, it must register such name with the state as a tradename or trade mark, whichever is appropriate; additionally it must procure licenses for engaging in regulated professions and businesses.

PARTNERSHIP PROPERTY AND A PARTNER'S INTEREST

Paragraphs 3 to 9 of the partnership agreement concern the right of a partner vis-a-vis the property he brings to the partnership and the property subsequently owned by the partnership. The nature of partnership property will be more fully explained in the remaining portions of this chapter. Partnership operations and partnership termination (paragraphs 10 through 12) will be the focus of Chapter 8.

The initial capital of the enterprise is whatever the partners contribute to the partnership. It may be cash or other personal or real property. This capital is used by the partnership to buy assets for operation of the partnership. Seldom does it stay in the original form of cash or other property.

All of the property originally brought into the partnership and all of that subsequently acquired by purchase or otherwise on account of the partnership become partnership property [U.P.A. § 8(1)]. If there is a dispute over whether a partner or the partnership owns the property the intent of the parties controls. The problem usually is in ascertaining this intent. The best evidence of intent is the articles of partnership and the property described as partnership property therein. In the absence of an agreement, other evidence of intent must be found. If partnership funds are used to acquire property, then the law assumes, unless a contrary intention appears, that it is partnership property [U.P.A. § 8(2)]. This is true even though the title to the property is in the name of one of the partners, not the partnership.

Once the partnership has been formed, a partner has certain rights in the partnership and its property which are unique features of a partnership. Section 24 of the U.P.A. provides:

> The property rights of a partner are 1) his rights in specific partnership property, 2) his interest in the partnership and 3) his right to participate in the management.

The manner in which the U.P.A. § 24(1) characterizes a partner's rights in specific partnership property may be somewhat misleading. Generally, a partner has *no* "individual" right to specific partnership property. He only has an equal right shared with other partners to possess such property for the purpose of carrying out the partnership business. That is, once the partner's capital has been committed to the enterprise, he loses his right to repossess or control it to the exclusion of others (unless he wishes to dissolve the partnership) and must share it with the other partners. This form of ownership is not unique but exists whenever persons jointly own property. Perhaps the ownership of your home is jointly owned by you and your spouse, or perhaps your parents jointly own a home. This means the owners have an equal right to possess all of it; they have a right to enter any portion they wish, but so do all the owners. No specific portion may be appropriated by any one of the owners. The same is true of partnership property.

This duty to share partnership property and the right to possess partnership property for partnership purposes cannot be sold or given to someone else without the consent of all other partners, nor may an individual creditor of a partner seize this "right." That is, to a limited degree, a partner may shield his personal assets from individual creditors by conveying some of them to a partnership and becoming a partner. To this extent a partnership does look like a distinct legal entity apart from the individuals that compose it.[5] This partnership property is subject, of course, to seizure by *partnership* creditors, and may be seized by individual creditors if the partnership is dissolved and specific partnership property is conveyed back to a partner. The right to possess partnership property for partnership purposes is accompanied by the right to repayment for the intial capital contribution upon dissolution of the partnership. We will discuss this more fully in the next chapter.

The second kind or classification of partnership rights provided for in U.P.A. § 24(2) is his "interest" in the partnership. "A partner's interest in the partnership is his share of the profits . . ." (U.P.A. § 26). This right of interest in profits is a property right which can be assigned by the partner, (sold or given to someone else) and which is subject to a court order directing the partner to pay it to an individual judgment creditor. Such an order is called a "charging order."

A third property right of a partner provided for in U.P.A. § 24(3) is the right to participate in the management. Some items of management may be specifically delegated in the partnership agreement to specific partners. If it is not or if differences arise as to the ordinary matters connected with the partnership business, they are settled by a majority vote of the partners. Any act which would be in violation of the partnership agreement, however, must have the consent of all partners [(U.P.A. § 18(h)]. This right to vote is given to a partner regardless of the type or amount of his capital contribution to the partnership.

In addition to the three classifications of a partner's property right in the partnership the U.P.A. and most partnership agreements provide for the following rights:

1. the right to be repaid for contributions or loans (advancements) to the partnership, if there are funds available, at dissolution [§ 18(a)]
2. the right to indemnification for payments made in the ordinary course of business [§18(b)]
3. the right to have access and to copy the firm books (§ 19), and
4. the right to an accounting (§ 22)

Generally, a partner is under a duty imposed by the U.P.A. to the partnership to act as a fiduciary. The designation of the relationship between the partners and the partnerships as a fiduciary one imposes on the partners all of those duties of a fiduciary discussed in Chapter 3. The partner must act in the best interest of the partnership, can not compete with it, and must render true and full information to the partnership of all things affecting the partnership business (U.P.A. § 20). Issues of the breach of a fiduciary relationship or other matters in which it is alleged a partner owes money to the partnership are litigated by means of a cause of action for an accounting. Economy of litigation and convenience require this. For these reasons it is usually held as we noted earlier, that a direct lawsuit by one partner against another or the partnership against an individual partner will not lie until an accounting has been conducted.

In addition to the duties of a partner noted no partner is to receive interest on the capital contributed to the partnership unless it is held by the partnership after the date when it was supposed to be repaid (U.P.A. § 18d) nor is he entitled to a salary or other fixed compensation except when the partnership is dissolved and he is winding up partnership affairs (U.P.A. § 18f). However, remember that the contractual understanding of the parties revealed in the articles of partnership create duties between parties and if it provides for salaries or guaranteed minimum income to some partner or unequal sharing of profits or unequal voting power such provisions will be enforced. The reason for the statutory provision against interest and compensation is that one type of compensation (salary) will not be inferred where another type (profit sharing) has been expressly provided for.

We have reproduced two cases to illustrate some of the principles already discussed. An important point to remember is that in addition to the duties imposed upon the partners by the articles of partnership and the U.P.A., partners are under a duty to act as a fiduciary. The *Clement* case illustrates that a court will presume that a partner acted to the detriment of the partnership when he grew relatively wealthy and could not explain the source of the wealth.

The *Elsbury* case is a very unique but excellent one for describing the nature of partnership property.

CLEMENT v. CLEMENT
436 Pa. 466, 260 A.2d 728 (S. Ct., Pa., 1970)

◆◆◆

ROBERTS, Justice.

Charles and L. W. Clement are brothers whose forty-year partnership has ended in acrimonious litigation. The essence of the conflict lies in Charles' contention that L. W. has over the years wrongfully taken for himself more than his share of the partnership's profits. Charles discovered these misdeeds during negotiations with L. W. over the sale of Charles' interest in the partnership in 1964. He then filed an action in equity, asking for dissolution of the partnership, appointment of a receiver, and an accounting. Dissolution was ordered and a receiver appointed. After lengthy hearings on the issue of the accounting the chancellor decided that L. W., who was the brighter of the two and who kept the partnership books, had diverted partnership funds. The chancellor awarded Charles a one-half interest in several pieces of property owned by L. W. and in several insurance policies on L. W.'s life on the ground that these had been purchased with partnership assets.

The court . . . then heard the case and reversed the chancellor's decree in several material respects. The reversal was grounded on two propositions: that Charles' recovery could only be premised on a showing of fraud and that this burden was not met, and that the doctrine of laches foreclosed Charles' right to complain about the bulk of the alleged misdeeds.

We disagree with the court's . . . statement of the applicable law and therefore reverse. Our theory is simple. There is a fiduciary relationship between partners. Where such a relationship exists actual fraud need not be shown. There was ample evidence of self-dealing and diversion of partnership assets on the part of L. W. — more than enough to sustain the chancellor's conclusion that several substantial investments made by L. W. over the years were bankrolled with funds improperly withdrawn from the partnership. Further, we are of the opinion that the doctrine of laches is inapplicable because Charles' delay in asserting his rights was as much a product of L. W.'s concealment and misbehavior as of any negligence on his part. In all this we are strongly motivated by the fact that the chancellor saw and heard the various witnesses for exhausting periods of time and was in a much better position than we could ever hope to be to taste the flavor of the testimony.

The Act of 1915, March 26, P.L. 18, part IV, § 21, 59 P.S. § 54, very simply and unambiguously provides that partners owe a fiduciary duty one to another. One should not have to deal with his partner as though he were the opposite party in an arms-length transaction. One should be allowed to trust his partner, to expect that he is pursuing a common goal and not working at cross-purposes. This concept of the partnership entity was expressed most ably by Mr. Justice, then Judge, Cardozo in *Meinhard* v. *Salmon*, 249 N.Y. 458, 164 N.E. 545, 62 A.L.R. 1 (1928):

> Joint adventurers, like copartners, owe to one another, while the enterprise continues, the duty of the finest loyalty. Many forms of conduct permissible in a workaday world for those acting at arm's length are forbidden to those bound by fiduciary ties. A trustee is held to something stricter than the morals of the marketplace. Not honesty alone, but the punctilio of an honor the most sensitive, is then the standard of behavior. As to this there has developed a tradition that is unbending and inveterate. Uncompromising rigidity has been the attitude of courts of equity when petitioned to undermine the rule of undivided loyalty by the 'disintegrating erosion' of particular exceptions. * * * Only thus has the level of conduct for fiduciaries been kept at a level higher than that trodden by the crowd. It will not consciously be lowered by any judgment of this court.

It would be unduly harsh to require that one must prove actual fraud before he can recover for a partner's derelictions. Where one partner has so dealt with the partnership as to raise the probability of wrongdoing it ought to be his responsibility to negate that inference. It has been held that "where a partner fails to keep a record of partnership transactions, and is unable to account for them, every presumption will be made against him." *Bracht* v. *Connell*, 313 Pa. 397, 405, 170 A. 297, 301 (1933). Likewise, where a partner commingles partnership funds with his own and generally deals loosely with partnership assets he ought to have to shoulder the task of demonstrating the probity of his conduct.

In the instant case L. W. dealt loosely with partnership funds. At various times he made substantial investments in his own name. He was totally unable to explain where he got the funds to make these investments. The court . . . held that Charles had no claim on the fruits of these investments because he could not trace the money that was invested therein dollar for dollar from the partnership. Charles should not have had this burden. He did show that his brother had diverted substantial sums from the partnership funds under his control. The inference that these funds provided L. W. with the wherewithall to make his investments was a perfectly reasonable one for the chancellor to make and his decision should have been allowed to stand.

The doctrine of laches has no role to play in the decision of this case. It is true that the transactions complained of cover a period of many years. However, we do not think that it can be said that Charles negligently slept on his rights to the detriment of his brother. L. W. actively concealed much of his wrongdoing. He cannot now rely upon the doctrine of laches — that defense was not intended to reward the successful wrongdoer.

The decree is vacated and the case remanded for further proceedings consistent with this opinion.

EAGEN, Justice (dissenting).

In 1923, L. W. Clement and his younger brother, Charles, formed a partnership for the purpose of engaging in the plumbing business under the name of Clement Brothers. They agreed to share the profits of the business equally after payment of the debts. L. W. was the more alert and aggressive of the two. He attended special training schools to upgrade his plumbing skills, and became a master plumber. He alone conducted the business here involved, and had complete control of its finances. He frequently worked nights, Sundays and holidays. Charles, on the other hand, refused to be "bothered" with the administration of the business or its finances. He insisted also on limiting his work to a regular eight-hour shift and confining his contribution to the business to the performance of various plumbing jobs assigned to him.

Over the years, L. W. accumulated assets which eventually became quite valuable. For instance, in 1945 he purchased two lots of land for $5500, and subsequently constructed a commercial building thereon. This construction was financed in most part by money secured through placing a mortgage on the property. In 1951 he purchased another piece of real estate for $3500, and in 1927, 1936, 1938, 1945, 1947, 1955, and 1965 purchased policies of life insurance on his own life. There are presently existing substantial loans against some of these policies.

In 1964, Charles for the first time accused his brother, L. W., of misusing partnership funds to gain the assets he had accumulated. Charles did not have any evidence to substantiate the accusation, but surmised something must be wrong since L. W. had so much while he had so little.

At trial, not a scintilla of evidence was introduced to establish that L. W. diverted any partnership funds to purchase any of his personal assets. In view of this, a majority of the court . . . below ruled that Charles failed to establish that he had any interest or property rights therein. With this I agree. The majority of this Court now rule, in effect, that, because of the fiduciary relationship existing, it is L. W.'s burden to prove that he did not misuse partnership funds. This I cannot accept. . . .

I dissent and would affirm the decree of the court below.

◆◆◆

Case Questions

1. Under what circumstances will a court hold that there is sufficient evidence of a breach of a partner's fiduciary duty so that the issue of liability is one for the jury?
2. The doctrine of laches precludes a party from recovering when he has not pursued his remedies in a timely manner. Why was not this doctrine properly asserted by the defendant in this case?

STATE v. ELSBURY
63 Nev. 463; 175 P2d 430 (S. Ct. Nev., 1946)

◆◆◆

Appellant was convicted of the crime of grand larceny. He has appealed from both the judgment and the order denying his motion for a new trial, and has assigned twelve alleged errors.

The information charged appellant with having stolen the sum of $1,000 from one S. L. Corsino.

The evidence shows that at the time of the alleged theft appellant and S. L. Corsino were general partners, engaged as such in operating a cafe, under written articles of partnership; that the sum of $1,000, admittedly taken and retained by appellant, constituted part of the proceeds from the business on deposit in the bank in a checking account in the firm name; and that the partnership was heavily in debt. It also shows that S. L. Corsino originally furnished the largest amount of the firm's capital.

The statute defining grand larceny reads as follows:

> Every person who shall feloniously steal, take, and carry away, lead or drive away, the personal goods or property of another, of the value of fifty dollars or more shall be deemed guilty of grand larceny, * * * . . .

Under this statute, it is essential that money which has been unlawfully taken and retained must be the "property of another." . . .

But the State relies upon section 10339, N.C.L. which provides that:

> It shall be no defense to a prosecution for larceny * * * that the money or property appropriated was partly the property of another and partly the property of the accused.

The important question to be decided, therefore, is whether this statute is applicable to a general partner who takes and retains partnership property during the existence of the partnership.

The title to partnership property is of a different class and with characteristics quite distinct from that of the title to property owned and held by individuals.

Section 24 of the Uniform Partnership Act reads:

> The property rights of a partner are (1) his rights in specific partnership property, (2) his interest in the partnership, and (3) his right to participate in the management.

By the statement that one of the property rights of a partner is his right in specific partnership property is meant simply that a partner, subject to any contrary agreement, has an equal right with his copartners to use or possess any partnership property for any proper partnership purpose. . . .

Under section 25 of the Uniform Partnership Act, a partner is co-owner with his partners of specific partnership property holding as a tenant in partnership. The incidents of this tenancy are such that: A partner, subject to the provisions of the act and to any agreement between the partners, has an equal right with his partners to possess specific partnership property for partnership purposes, but cannot otherwise possess same without the consent of his partners. His rights in specific partnership property are not assignable except in connection with the assignment of rights of all the partners in the same property, nor are they subject to attachment or execution upon a personal claim against him. . . . On the death of a partner his right in specific partnership property vests not in the partner's personal representative but in the surviving partner. A partner's right in specific partnership property is not subject to dower, curtesy, or allowances to widows, heirs or next of kin. . . .

Section 26 of the same statute specifically provides:

A partner's interest in the partnership is his share of the profits and surplus, and the same is personal property.

A partner has no individual property in any specific assets of the firm. . . .

Instead, the interest of each partner in the partnership property is his share in the surplus, after the partnership debts are paid and the partnership accounts have been settled. . . .

Until that time arrives, it cannot be known what property will have to be used to satisfy the debts and, therefore, what property will remain after the debts are paid. . . .

The amounts of money invested by the partners respectively in the firm would be no criterion in determining their ownership of the partnership property, for the partner who furnished in the first instance the largest amount of capital, on final settlement might be found to have no interest whatever in the assets then on hand. . . .

When a partnership is admittedly insolvent, as was the partnership in the case at bar at the time of the alleged larceny, neither of the partners can possibly have any separate interest in the firm property. . . .

A partner's right in partnership property is a mere choose in action, and carries with it a right to an accounting. . . .

As each partner is the ultimate owner of an undivided interest in all the partnership property, none of such property "Can be said, with reference to any partner, 'to be the property of another.' "

Therefore, it seems plain that the statute relied upon by the State does not apply where, as in this case, partnership property is appropriated by one of the partners during the existence of the partnership.

This conclusion disposes of the case in appellant's favor, and makes it unnecessary to pass upon the other alleged errors.

The judgment of conviction and the order . . . are reversed, and the money heretofore deposited instead of bail will be refunded to the appellant.

◆◆◆

Case Comment

If the $1,000 did not belong to the partner who withdrew it and it was not the property of another for purposes of the application of the grand larceny statute, then to whom did it belong? This question highlights the logical bind which results when courts refuse—by implication—to recognize the partnership as a distinct, separate legal entity.

JOINT VENTURES

A joint venture, or joint adventure as it is sometimes called, is a business association similar to a partnership except that it is more narrow in purpose. Usually a joint venture is formed for a single undertaking or a series of related undertakings of fairly short duration which might not involve the complete attention of the members.[6] It is a form of partnership and the members and the association are subject to the U.P.A., and the court interpretations thereof.

One of the most significant reasons for distinguishing between a partnership and a joint venture is that in the few states which prohibit corporations from being general partners counts are likely to allow them to be participants in a joint venture. This exception is based upon the premise that becoming a participant in a joint venture requires less delegation of managerial authority from the board of directors to the joint ventures than participating in a general partnership requires.[7] This premise arises because of the limited nature of joint ventures.

LIMITED PARTNERSHIP

A limited partnership, in contrast to a joint venture and partnership, is a distinctly different form of association. The chief distinguishing features are in the formation and the nature of the liability of the limited partner. Limited partnerships, like corporations, can only exist where state legislatures have passed statutes providing for their formation. For this purpose, the National Conference of Commissioners on Uniform State Laws drafted the Uniform Limited Partnership Act (U.L.P.A.) which has been passed by almost all of the states. The U.L.P.A. § 1 defines a limited partnership as:

> ... a partnership formed by two or more persons under the provisions of § 2, having as members one or more general partners and one or more limited partners.

A limited partnership is a partnership and unless the U.L.P.A. in a specific section says differently, Partnership Law applies. The U.L.P.A. does depart from partnership law in at least two important respects. Firstly, Section 2 of the U.L.P.A. requires that the persons desiring to form a limited partnership sign an agreement which states, among other things:

1. The name, character and location of the business; and the name and residence of each member including the limited partner;
2. The term of the partnership and contributions of the limited partner; and
3. The right of a limited partner to withdraw or the right to add additional limited partners.

This agreement must be filed with the appropriate registration office where the limited partnership does business. This is usually the county recorder's office. The reason for the filing is to make public, especially to potential creditors, the limited nature of the liability of the limited partners.

The second, and perhaps most drastic departure from Partnership Law, is that provided by the U.L.P.A., § 7:

A limited partner shall not become liable as a general partner unless, in addition to the exercise of his rights and powers as a limited partner, he takes part in the control of the business.

Thus, the U.L.P.A. limits the liability of the limited partner. It is limited to the property which he has contributed or promised to contribute to the firm. For this benefit, he gives up the right to manage. This privilege of management resides with the general partner or partners. In all other respects the limited partner is treated as a general partner. Specifically, § 10 of the U.L.P.A. provides that he have the right of access to the partnership books, to have dissolution and winding up by a court decree and have a right to receive a share of the profits.

The interest of a limited partner in the partnership is his right to profit which is like the general partner's interest and may be assigned or attached by a creditor.

Limited partnerships offer the advantage of limited liability to those who are desirious of investing in the ownership of a business. Why not form a corporation? Generally, the corporate form is more highly regulated by the states and is subject to additional tax burdens. As mentioned in Chapter 2, owners of corporations are taxed twice on their investment (the earnings of the corporation are taxed to the corporation and the dividends are taxable to the shareholders) whereas a partner's return on his investment is taxed only once. Also, recently corporations have been subject to an "excess profits" tax, not partnerships.

The following case reveals the typical response of a court when faced with the liability of limited partners who have engaged in management. In short, you can't have your cake and eat it too!

HOLZMAN v. DE ESCAMILLA
86 Cal. App. 2d 858; 195 P.2d 833
(Cal. D. Ct. of App., 1948)

◆◆◆

MARKS, Justice.

This is an appeal by James L. Russell and H. W. Andrews from a judgment decreeing they were general partners in Hacienda Farms, Limited, a limited partnership, from February 27, to December 1, 1943, and as such were liable as general partners to the creditors of the partnership.

Early in 1943, Hacienda Farms, Limited, was organized as a limited partnership . . . with Ricardo de Escamilla as the general partner and James L. Russell and H. W. Andrews as limited partners.

The partnership went into bankruptcy in December, 1943, and Lawrence Holzman was appointed and qualified as trustee of the estate of the bankrupt. On November 13, 1944, he brought this action for the purpose of determining that Russell and Andrews, by taking part in the control of the partnership business, had become liable as general partners to the creditors of the partnership. The trial court found in favor of the plaintiff on this issue and rendered judgment to the effect that the three defendants were liable as general partners.

The findings supporting the judgment are so fully supported by the testimony of certain witnesses, although contradicted by Russell and Andrews, that we need mention but a small part of it. We will not mention conflicting evidence as conflicts in the evidence are settled in the trial court and not here.

De Escamilla was raising beans on farm lands near Escondido at the time the partnership was formed. The partnership continued raising vegetable and truck crops which were marketed principally through a produce concern controlled by Andrews.

The record shows the following testimony of de Escamilla:

Q. Did you have a conversation or conversations with Mr. Andrews or Mr. Russell before planting the tomatoes?

A. We always conferred and agreed as to what crops we would put in. * * *

Q. Who determined that it was advisable to plant watermelons?

A. Mr. Andrews. * * *

Q. Who determined that string beans should be planted?

A. All of us. There was never any planting done — except the first crop that was put into the partnership as an asset by myself, there was never any crop that was planted or contemplated in planting that wasn't thoroughly discussed and agreed upon by the three of us; particularly Andrews and myself.

De Escarmilla further testified that Russell and Andrews came to the farms about twice a week and consulted about the crops to be planted. He did not want to plant peppers or egg plant because, as he said "I don't like that country for peppers or egg plant; no sir," but he was overruled and those crops were planted. The same is true of the watermelons.

Shortly before October 15, 1943, Andrews and Russell requested de Escamilla to resign as manager, which he did, and Harry Miller was appointed in his place.

Hacienda Farms, Limited, maintained two bank accounts, one in a San Diego bank and another in an Escondido bank. It was provided that checks could be drawn on the signatures of any two of the three partners. It is stated in plaintiff's brief, without any contradiction (the checks are not before us) that money was withdrawn on twenty checks signed by Russell and Andrews and that all other checks except three bore the signature of de Escamilla, the general partner, and one of the other defendants. The general partner had no power to withdraw money without the signature of one of the limited partners.

Section 2483 of the Civil Code provides as follows:

A limited partner shall not become liable as a general partner, unless, in addition to the exercise of his rights and powers as a limited partner, he takes part in the control of the business.

The foregoing illustrations sufficiently show that Russell and Andrews both took "part in the control of the business." The manner of withdrawing money from the bank accounts is particularly illuminating. The two men had absolute power to withdraw all the partnership funds in the banks without the knowledge or consent of the general partner. Either Russell or Andrews could take control of the business from de Escamilla by refusing to sign checks for bills contracted by him and thus limit his activities in the management of the business. They required him to resign as manager and selected his successor. They were active in dictating the crops to be planted, some of them against the wishes of de Escamilla. This clearly shows they took part in the control of the business of the partnership and thus became liable as general partners. ...

Judgment affirmed.

Case Question

1. List the facts which caused the appellate court to conclude that the status of a limited partner was lost for Russell and Andrews.

REVIEW PROBLEMS

1. P went to C and told him that he had contracted for about two car loads of hogs to be delivered the next day, and he did not have the money to pay for them. P asked C to advance the money to him and take an ownership interest in the hogs in return. C refused this. P then proposed that if C would let him have the money to pay for the hogs he had bought and others he might have to buy to make two car loads, he (C) could have a security interest in the hogs which would enable C to take the hogs and sell them to repay the money advanced and in addition C would receive 1/2 of the profits of the sale of the hogs to repay him for the risk he was taking; and that in no event should C sustain any loss. C accepted this proposition and advanced $2,500 to P. Shortly thereafter P bought the hogs from H on his own credit. The hogs could not be sold at a profit. C took possession of the hogs and had them sold. P still owed money to C since the sale price of the hogs did not cover the amount of the advance and P paid to C this deficiency. Meanwhile H was not paid by P for the hogs. H sues C as a partner. Should he recover? (*Harvey* v. *Childs*, 28 Ohio St. 319).

2. B leased land from F upon which he conducted the business of a fruit farm and nursery for a period of six years. P sold fruit trees to B and received documents from time to time signed "F & B", indicating joint ownership. P also proved that advertisements for "F & B" were published in newspapers in F's area over a three month period. B prepared and paid for these advertisements without F's consent but F did have knowledge of them. P was not paid for the trees and B dies. P sues F as a partner of B's. F defends alleging that he merely leased some land to B and that he had no knowledge that the documents showing a "B & F" enterprise existed and that he did not know of the advertisements until he read them in the newspaper and at that time instructed B never to do it again. Should P's cause of action be sustained? (*Flectheer* v. *Pullen,* 70 Md. 205, 16A. 887, 1889).

3. S was a young college grad who returned to his home town to start his own business. He had never been exceptionally bright and was relatively unknown compared with his father (F) who was the recently-retired football coach of the local high school. S founded a small insurance business, and, with his father's permission, called it, "F & Son Insurance." As between F and S it was agreed S was the owner and would make all decisions in the business. F was employed from time to time to greet potential business clients and to seek out business in the community. He was paid a straight hourly wage for

this and only worked a few days each week. When S was purchasing office furniture from P, P came to S's place of business, recognized F who happened to be there, and, primarily on the strength of F's reputation in the community as a leader and a man of his word, sold on credit $5,000 worth of furniture to "F and Son Insurance" with S signing the purchase agreement. Later S defaults. Does P have a remedy against F? Explain fully.

4. A, B and C agree to form a business association in which the net profits are to be split evenly. A is exceptionally bright but financially without a cent so he agrees to contribute his technical knowledge and labor which will be used in the production phase of the business. The purpose of the business will be to develop new applications of plastic (PVC) to metal surfaces to reduce friction in fast moving, heavy, industrial machines.

B is very wealthy and agrees to contribute $15,000 but will not take part in the day-to-day operation of the business but will be available to consult and vote in important managerial decisions.

C agrees to contribute $5,000 and to work in the marketing phase of the business and will be primarily responsible for keeping the books, placing orders for suppliers and developing new markets for their product.

The association becomes mildly successful. They acquire, in the firm name, "A,B,C and Associates," a small plant, several expensive materials handling machines, and about fifteen employees. One of the employees, D, is very responsible and gradually becomes a favored employee directly responsible to C. Although C was never given the actual authority to contract for the firm, C allowed him to negotiate, on a preliminary basis only, some matters for the firm. In one instance, C and D were negotiating with E, with D doing most of the talking. C was called out of the meeting and shortly thereafter D initiated an agreement with E for the benefit of the firm. C was later told of this and did not object. A and B were never aware of D's representations.

Although A was a smart technician he was a very poor businessman especially regarding his own personal affairs. He overextended himself in purchasing new home furnishings, rugs and drapes, and was unable to pay for them when the balances became due. The seller of the furnishings, J, obtained a judgment against A which has remained uncollected.

B also suffered a severe shortage of cash. He figures since he contributed more money than the other partners he was entitled to a return on the investment in lieu of interest. He wrote a check on partnership funds for a motorcycle he needed and took title in his own name.

In a carefully worded essay describe the rights, if any, of E, J, and the partnership.

5. P and D were partners, who operated a tavern in a good location of town. The partnership leased the building in which the business was conducted and this lease expired on the same day that the partners had agreed to terminate their partnership. The partnership had spent a relatively large sum on improving the property during the life of the lease. Over one year before the expiration of the lease, D went to the owner of the property and obtained a lease in his own name to begin when the present lease and partnership were terminated. P learns of this and sues D in an attempt to have the lease declared partnership property. What breach of duty, if any, is the basis for the cause of action? Will P succeed?

ENDNOTES

1. 6 *Uniform Laws Annot., Master Edition,* p. iii.
2. J. Crane and A. Bromberg, *Law of Partnership,* 26, (1968).
3. *Id.,* at 52-54.
4. *Id.,* at 48.
5. *Id.,* at 244-245.
6. *Id.,* at 189.
7. *Id.,* at 195.

PARTNERSHIP OPERATION AND DISSOLUTION   8

This chapter is divided into two sections; the first, partnership operation, emphasizes the portion of the Partnership Law which creates contract and tort liability for the partners and partnership. The second section, partnership dissolution, emphasizes the manner in which partnerships may be dissolved and the resultant duties between partners.

PARTNERSHIP OPERATION: CONTRACT LIABILITY

In presenting the material on the liability of the partnership and partners to third parties we again believe it is convenient to divide this liability into two kinds: contract and tort. The law of agency is applicable to partnerships and the resolution of conflicts between the partners themselves, and the partnership, on the one hand and third parties on the other, are resolved by a direct application of the same principles discussed in the chapters on Agency Law.

When a partner contracts on partnership business the partnership is the principal and the partner or partners acting for it are the agents. An agent will bind his principal contractually when he has the actual or circumstantial authority to act. This is expressed by § 9 of the U.P.A. as follows:

> Every partner is an agent of the partnership for the purpose of its business, and the act of every partner, . . . for apparently carrying on in the usual way the business of the partnership . . . binds the partnership. . . .

The articles of partnership usually state the actual authority the partners are granted. This may include the right to do any business act which may be the subject of lawful delegation of authority. In addition agents have the circumstantial authority to act in carrying on the business in the usual way. This circumstantial authority is defined by considering the business purpose or nature of the partnership, the ordinary usages and methods in which similar businesses are conducted and the reasonable expectations of third parties. According to Section 9(3) of the U.P.A., this authority *does not* include extraordinary acts such as assigning partnership property in trust for creditors, disposing of the firm's good will, confessing a judgment or submitting a partnership claim to arbitration, or doing any other act which would make it impossible to carry on the ordinary business of the partnership.

Case law has developed a useful analytical device for establishing liability of the partnership when the evidence shows no expressed authority existed. In cases involving the borrowing of money and the executing of negotiable instruments some courts recognize a distinction between trading and non-trading partnerships. A trading partnership is one which is organized primarily to buy and sell property for profit. Those partnerships which are organized primarily to offer a service and in which the passage of title to property *is not* the central means of making a profit are non-trading partnerships. The latter include professional partnerships (such as doctors, lawyers, and accountants) and partnerships formed to provide a service such as to operate theatres, or sell insurance. If the partnership is a trading partnership some courts will presume that implied or circumstantial authority to obligate the partnership on a loan or other negotiable instrument exists. If the partnership is a non-trading one, some courts may require actual authority for a partner to bind the partnership on loan obligations or other negotiable instruments.

Whether or not this distinction would be used by most courts today is questionable.[1] With the growing diversity of activities of a single association and the increasing variety of financing methods, this rather simplistic approach to establishing implied or circumstantial authority may not be useful. Furthermore one may question the logical connection between buying and selling, and borrowing. The best approach is to treat the partnership as the principal, the contracting partner as the agent, the other contracting party as the "third party" and then search the facts for evidence of actual or circumstantial authority, estoppel or ratification as those terms were defined and used in Chapter 4.

In addition to the types of authority mentioned above, a partnership may also be bound by any knowledge or notice communicated to a partner relating to partnership affairs. (U.P.A. § 12)

The next two cases present a good illustration of the circumstances in which a partner's acts will or will not bind the partnership to third parties in contractual or quasi-contractual cases.

LAWER v. KLINE
39 Wyo. 285, 270 P. 1077
(S. Ct. Wyo., 1928)

◆◆◆

BLUME, C. J.

This was an action for rent, brought by H. C. Lawer against E. A. Kline, David Kline, and Morris Kline, copartners doing business under the firm name of Kline's. . . . The plaintiff recovered judgment for the sum of $1,699.94, less a deduction of $416.06, and the costs of the action. From the judgment so rendered, the defendants appeal. The parties will be hereinafter named as in the court below. The partnership conducted a clothing business in the town of Riverton. The term during which it was to last does not appear, but it seems to have been unlimited as to time.

The actions were brought to recover rent, though for different periods, under a written lease made and executed on January 8, 1923, and signed by H. C. Lawer as lessor, and the partnership above named by David Kline, one of the partners, as lessee. The lease was for the period of five years, and reserved a monthly rental of $177.50 for the first two years and a monthly rental of $190.00 during the remainder of the term. The dispute herein arises by reason of the increased rental during the last three years. It was contended by the defendants that, according to the verbal arrangements made previous to the execution of the written lease, it had been agreed that the lease of January 8, 1923, should be upon the same terms and conditions as a previous lease for these premises, which, too, was for five years, and which reserved a rental of $177.50 per month throughout the term, and that David Kline, one of the partners, had no authority to execute the lease in question, and that the only partner who had such right was E. A. Kline. . . .

The main question herein is as to whether or not the lease of January 8, 1923, was binding on the partnership. Counsel for defendant contend that it was void, for the reason that the person signing had no authority to bind the partnership or the other members of the partnership to a lease for a term of years, . . .

The assignment of error involves, . . . whether a partner has implied authority to execute a lease on behalf of the partnership for a term of years, in this case for five years; . . .

The case of *Stillman* v. *Harvey*, 47 Conn. 26, decided in 1879, involved a lease for seven years, which was taken over by one of the partners for the partnership, but where the agreement of the other partner was not obtained. The court said:

"The purchase of the right to use a brewery for the period of about seven years by a member of a partnership formed for the purpose of brewing, and which was without limitation as to time, is so directly in the line and so necessary to the prosecution of its business, that if it be effected by one partner his act and signature will bind the partnership to the contract. Haviland (the party not agreeing) stands precisely where he would if he had himself negotiated and signed the assumption."

The case of *Seaman* v. *Ascherman*, 57 Wis. 547, 15 N. W. 788, involved an agreement made by one partner on behalf of a commerical partnership to enter into a lease for five years. The court held the agreement binding, saying in part as follows:

"The rule of law is that a firm, is liable prima facie for the act of one partner in its behalf, necessarily done for carrying on the partnership business in the ordinary way, although such act was not authorized by the other partners. 1 *Lindley on Part.* 236. In such matters each partner is the general agent of the firm, and the above rule has its foundation in the law of agency. It was certainly necessary to the carrying on of the business of the defendants in the ordinary way that they should have a proper building in which to transact it." . . .

The review of these cases, . . . show, we think, that the decided weight of authority is to the effect that a partner has implied authority to execute leases of the character here under discussion, when they are necessary and appropriate to carry on the business of the partnership, and that such leases are binding upon it, unless of course, the partner who signs has no actual authority, and the want thereof is known to the lessor. Such holding seems to simply carry to its logical conclusion the general rule that each partner has implied authority to bind the firm and each member thereof by contracts in the firm name which are within the scope of the firm business as that is ordinarily conducted. Aside from these authorities, however, we must further bear in mind section 9 of the Uniform Partnership Act, which was adopted in this state in 1917, and which appears as section 4180, Wyo. Comp. Stat. 1920, and which reads in part as follows:

"Every partner is an agent of the partnership for the purpose of its business, and the act of every partner, including the execution in the partnership name of any instrument, for apparently carrying on in the usual way the business of the partnership of which he is a member binds the partnership, unless the partner so acting has in fact no authority to act for the partnership, in the particular matter, and the person with whom he is dealing has knowledge of the fact that he has no such authority." ... The controlling point in this case, accordingly, seems to be as to whether or not the lease in question is within the limitation expressed in the section; namely, that it was executed to carry on the business of the partnership in the usual way. We think it is. The partnership needed some lease to carry on its business. We do not think that leases lasting for five years are at all out of the ordinary. ... Past transactions may be taken into consideration in determining this point. ... And, as we have seen, the partnership had a lease lasting for five years previous to the time that the lease in question was taken. In fact, leases lasting only a short time could, in the nature of things, not be satisfactory unless perchance in those cases in which a partnership is formed for only a short and definite period of time. We conclude that David Kline had implied authority to execute the lease in question, which was binding upon the partnership in the absence of knowledge by plaintiff of his actually limited power.

If, however, we are wrong in the foregoing conclusion, still the defendants in error, must be held to have ratified the lease in question through E. A. Kline, who at least had authority to sign it. The partnership had the benefit of the lease for the period of two years without in any way questioning it. The claim that E. A. Kline supposed that the new lease was upon the same terms as the old one is without merit. It is altogether unreasonable to think that he, who claimed to be executive head of the partnership, should not, during all that time, have made some inquiry into the actual terms embodied therein. Further than that, it stands undisputed that in October, 1924, plaintiff sent him a copy of the lease, and he admits that he read it, but he made no objection to it whatever. ...

Affirmed.

◆◆◆

Case Questions

1. What type of authority did the court say the signing partner possessed?
2. What circumstances lead the court to conclude this?
3. If the rent would have been increased to $290.00 for the remaining three years of the lease term would the result have been the same?
4. Would the result have been the same if the non-signing partners objected to the increase in rent within a reasonable time?

ROUSE v. POLLARD
130 N.J. Eq. 204; 21 A.2d 801 (Ct. of Er. & App., N.J., 1941)

◆◆◆

CASE, Justice.

This is an appeal by the complainant from a final decree in Chancery dismissing the bill as to all of the partners formerly of the law firm of Riker and

Riker except Thomas E. Fitzsimmons against whom the decree ran as a judgment in the amount of $20,500 with interest and costs. The suit was to charge all of the members of the firm with liability for what was, in effect, an embezzlement of complainant's funds by the defendant Fitzsimmons in the above named amount.

The appeal presents two main questions, one of fact and the other a mixed question of fact and law. Did complainant intend to entrust her funds to the firm of Riker and Riker, or did she intend to entrust them to Thomas E. Fitzsimmons personally? If she purposed to place them with Riker and Riker through the agency of Fitzsimmons, is she entitled, under the law as applied to the facts, to hold the members of the firm, other than Fitzsimmons, liable?

Complainant sought a separation from her husband, In or about the month of June, 1927, she went to the firm of Riker and Riker, stated her case and was referred to Fitzsimmons, a member of the firm. The separation agreement was signed, and there were a few other legal services rendered. In the course of the incidental conferences Fitzsimmons asked Mrs. Rouse what money she possessed and was informed by her of the amount thereof and the manner in which it was invested. According to Mrs. Rouse:

"He said the securities was a bad thing for a woman in my position to have and he suggested that I turn over my securities and sell them and turn the money over to the firm, that they dealt in gilt edge mortgage bonds, as he said. He said that they did that for their clients and it was perfectly secure. I asked if it was all right for me and he said that is the only way they would take care of it and I would get my check every six months. He said if I handed it at once they would place it the first of July and I did place it . . . and the 15th of January was the first check."

Mrs. Rouse wrote to her brokers directing them to sell her securities and to "forward a check for the same payable to me to my attorney, Mr. Thomas E. Fitzsimmons. . . . A check for $28,252.67 was sent as directed, was endorsed by Mrs. Rouse "Pay to the order of Thos. E. Fitzsimmons" and was deposited by Fitzsimmons in his personal bank account. No part ever came to the firm except $350, or thereabouts, which was paid by Fitzsimmons to the firm for the legal services rendered, and no member of the firm, other than Fitzsimmons, knew of the transaction. The bill of complaint specifically exonerates the remaining members from any fraud, deceit or misappropriation. On January 16, 1928, Fitzsimmons wrote Mrs. Rouse: "Enclosed herewith find my check for $825, being six months' interest at 6 percent on the $27,500., which I have invested for you. . . . For more than ten years interest payments went to Mrs. Rouse by Fitzsimmons' personal check. . . .

(T)he documentary and circumstantial evidence leans heavily towards the conclusion that Mrs. Rouse did not, . . . intend to place her money with the firm of Riker and Riker; that, on the contrary, she confided in, and rested upon the integrity of, Fitzsimmons and placed her money with him individually for investment; and that she constantly knew of that status although she probably did not appraise the legal significance of it until Fitzsimmons' financial integrity had been shattered. Perhaps the initial respect which Mrs. Rouse entertained for Fitzsimmons' business sagacity and investment acumen was seeded in the fact that he was a member of the Riker firm; but he was a member of that firm for the practice of law, and that membership did not per se create liability by his partners for his acts outside the general scope of the practice of law. There is a quality intimately personal to Fitzsimmons in all of the communications that passed between him and Mrs. Rouse about her money affairs. It was to him, personally, that Mrs. Rouse endorsed the check for the original funds. It was he who, according to his letters to complainant, had "invested" the money for her. It was he who, by his personal checks, paid the interest. . . . We conclude that Mrs. Rouse knowingly placed her funds with Fitzsimmons, personally, for investment by him, likewise personally, and that Riker and Riker were neither the depositaries nor the proposed investors. . . .

Appellant contends that the investment of the funds in mortgages was within the scope of the defendant firm's practice or within the scope of Fitzsimmons' apparent authority. The proofs do not sustain the implication that the practice of this particular firm embraced the acceptance of clients' money to be placed at the firm's discretion in investments thereafter to be ascertained and selected, whether in first mortgages or otherwise. The firm did engage extensively in what is known as a "real estate practice;" it represented bank, building and loan associations and estates; it examined titles, closed mortgages and drew necessary documents relating to mortgage investments by clients; it had clients' funds and trust funds on deposit awaiting the closing or other requirements of transactions for which such funds were held; it did not do a general investment business and it did not accept funds for future, unspecified investment, at the firm's discretion, in mortages or otherwise.

It has long been a recognized incident to the general practice of law, more extensively developed in some offices than in others, to make note of such clients as have moneys to invest on bond and mortgage, to bring the attention of those clients to the applications of proposed borrowers and, after the principals come to an agreement, to search the title, draw the necessary documents, even hold the money against the event, place the recordable papers on record and in general superintend the closing of the transaction. But we do not understand that it is a characteristic function of the practice of law to accept clients' money for deposit and future investment in unspecified securities at the discretion of the attorney, and we find to the contrary. . . .

We have found that the incident sued upon, that is, the placing of money for the purposes named, is not a function of the practice of law and that it was not a part of any practice indulged in by the respondents; but beyond this appellant contends that it was within Fitzsimmons' apparent authority and so seeks to fasten liability upon respondents under that well known rule in the law of agency. The facts for the application of the principle do not exist. The respondents did nothing to indicate that Fitzsimmons had any authority to act in their behalf outside the practice of law.

Another point is that respondents should be made to answer for the loss upon the theory that inasmuch as they and the complainant were both innocent the burden should rest upon them because they put Fitzsimmons in the position where he was able to perpetrate the fraud upon complainant; and, yet another, that the respondents received a part of the funds and so are estopped from denying the authority of Fitzsimmons. These contentions also rest upon a warped view of the facts. The paying over of the money to Fitzsimmons not only was not an act in the practice of law, it was not a part of or connected with any transaction which Fitzsimmons was conducting or was authorized to conduct for the firm. The amount of $350 did not go to respondents as a participation in a tortious transaction but from money that belonged to Mrs. Rouse and in payment of legal services that were performed by the firm for her. The existence of the debt and the propriety of the charge were not in dispute. The money was paid to them in ignorance on their part, then and for many years thereafter, of any wrongdoing by Fitzsimmons, and without facts in their knowledge, or chargeable to their knowledge, which served to put them on notice. We find no element of estoppel.

The decree in the court below will be affirmed.

◆◆◆

Case Question

1. In this case how was the plaintiff to know what the ordinary course of business of the partnership was? It appears that this case is a very close one. One of the elements emphasized by courts in applying apparent authority is the reasonable expectations of the third party. This case, if it were heard today, might well be decided for the plaintiff because, from the facts given, it may have appeared to the plaintiff that the firm did handle other people's money for investment in real estate.

PARTNERSHIP OPERATION: TORT LIABILITY

The liability of a partnership to damaged third parties for the tortious acts of a partner is based upon the same reasoning which supports the doctrine of Respondeat Superior in Agency Law. The principle of a partnership's vicarious liability is clearly stated by the U.P.A. §13:

> Where, by any wrongful act or omission of any partner acting in the ordinary course of the business of the partnership or with the authority of his co-partners, loss or injury is caused to any person, not being a partner in the partnership, or any penalty is incurred the partnership is liable therefor to the same extent as the partner so acting or omitting to act.

In the above provision, the key words are " . . . acting in the ordinary course of business of the partnership or with the authority of his co-partners. . . ." The basic issue then is whether or not the tort was within the ordinary course of business or authorized. In defining the ordinary course of business, some courts have hesitated to use the control test provided by the master-servant-type of analysis of Agency Law because they believe that a partner who has, usually, as much management authority as every other partner, cannot be a servant. This point is made in the *Phillips* v. *Cook* case. Of course, an *employee* of a partnership may be a servant if the control test is met. Generally the tort liability of a partnership is established by using the same kind of analysis as used by courts in establishing the tort liability of a principal for the torts of a non-servant agent. In the agency material we stated that the principal is liable for the torts of a non-servant agent when the tort was committed within the inherent scope of the agency. As applied to Partnership Law this means that the tort must have occured while furthering the *very purpose* of the partnership. Torts committed by a partner *incidental* to the partnership purpose do not usually create liability for the partnership.

An area of frequent litigation involves the liability of the partnership for the negligence of a partner when traveling by auto on partnership business. In this case two facts are very important. The first is the ownership of the auto. If it is owned by the partnership and the partner is traveling on partnership business, liability for the partnership usually results. However, if the partner owns the auto and it is under his control, and he is traveling on partnership business, liability is usually determined by the second important fact, *the nature of the partnership.* While there is some conflict in the decisions in this area, we believe the best view is that unless the partnership inherently involves the delivery of goods and or services (for example, the delivery of coal[2] or the providing of pinball repair service during the day or evening[3]), the partnership should not be held liable for the partner's negligence in the operation of his own auto. This result is consistent with that of the often cited agency case of *Stockwell* v. *Morris* reproduced in Chapter 5.

In the case of professional partnership such as attorneys, physicians, accountants, etc., it has been suggested that no partnership liability results when a partner negligently drives his own car when traveling from one business site to another.[4]

One of the best cases illustrating the circumstances when a court will hold a partnership liable for a partner's negligent operation is the *Phillips* v. *Cook* case. When reading this case try to discern the facts that the court thinks are important in deciding to impose liability on the partnership.

PHILLIPS v. COOK
239 Md. 215; 210 A. 2d 743 (Ct. of App., Md., 1965)

MARBURY, Judge.

This is an appeal by Daniel Phillips individually, and trading as "Dan's Used Cars," one of the defendants below, from a judgment in favor of Delores Cook and Marshall Cook, her husband, plaintiffs below, entered upon the verdict of a jury in favor of the plaintiffs against the defendants. Isadore Harris and Daniel Phillips, individually and as co-partners trading as Dan's Used Cars, in the Superior Court of Baltimore City. The verdict was rendered in an action by the Cooks to recover damages for injuries sustained by them as a result of a collision involving a partnership automobile operated by Harris and bearing dealer plates issued to Dan's Used Cars by the Department of Motor Vehicles.

The Cooks sued Harris and Phillips, individually, and as co-partners trading as Dan's Used Cars. The accident in question occurred on January 7, 1960, at about 6:50 p.m., when a partnership automobile operated by Harris struck the rear of a vehicle driven by one Smith, which in turn hit an automobile operated by Delores Cook. ... Harris was on his way home from the used car lot when the accident occurred. He was using the most direct route from the partnership lot and was only five blocks from his home at the time of the incident.

In October 1959, Harris and Phillips entered into a partnership on an equal basis under the name of "Dan's Used Cars" for the purpose of buying and selling used automobiles. Phillips owned the lot and a gas station adjacent to it. He went into the partnership with Harris because the latter had the experience and money which he did not have to put into the business. This partnership agreement was oral and it was agreed between the partners that each would have an equal voice in the conduct and management of the business.

Neither of the partners owned a personal automobile or had one titled in his individual name. It was agreed as a part of the partnership arrangement that Harris would use a partnership vehicle for transportation to and from his home. Under this agreement, he was authorized to demonstrate and sell such automobiles, call on dealers for the purpose of seeing and purchasing used cars, or go to the Department of Motor Vehicles on partnership business after leaving the lot in the evening and before returning the next day. Both Harris and Phillips could use a partnership automobile as desired. Such vehicles were for sale at any time during the day or night and at various times and places they had "for sale" signs on the windshields. Harris had no regular hours to report to the used car lot but could come and go as he saw fit. Phillips testified that it was essential that Harris have a partnership automobile for his transportation to and from his home, and that it was the most practical way to operate. It is also significant to note that both Harris and Phillips testified at the trial that each paid for the gasoline used in the partnership automobiles they drove. However, Phillips said at the time of the taking of his deposition, which was admitted in evidence, that the gasoline used came out of the used car business and was for cars that were for sale on the lot. He admitted that the Mercury sedan involved in the collision was for sale and had been sitting on the lot. This car was titled in the name of the partnership and Phillips could have used it if he wanted to. ...

I

If there was any evidence, no matter how slight, viewed in the light most favorable to appellees, that Harris, is using the partnership vehicle, was acting within the scope of the partnership agreement and business, i.e., the use was of some benefit or incidental to the partnership arrangement, then the question was for the jury's determination. Appellant contends that because Harris was on his way home from the used car lot at the time of the accident, the evidence was insufficient to support a finding by the jury that he was acting within the scope of the partnership arrangement or that such use of the vehicle was of benefit to the partnership.

In a case involving a partnership, the contract of partnership constitutes all of its members as agents of each other and each partner acts both as a principal and as the agent of the others in regard to acts done within the apparent scope of the business, purpose and agreement of the partnership or for its benefit. It is clear that the partnership is bound by the partner's wrongful act if done within the scope of the partnership's business. Code (1957), Article 73A, Section 13 provides:

Where, by any wrongful act or omission of any partner acting in the ordinary course of the business of the partnership, or with the authority of his copartners, loss or injury is caused to any person, not being a partner in the partnership, or any penalty is incurred, the partnership is liable therefor to the same extent as the partner so acting or omitting to act.

The test of the liability of the partnership and of its members for the torts of any one partner is whether the wrongful act was done within what may reasonably be found to be the scope of the business of the partnership and for its benefit. The extent of the authority of a partner is determined essentially by the same principles as those which measure the scope of an agent's authority. . . . Partnership cases may differ from principal and agent and master and servant relationships because in the non-partnership cases, the element of control or authorization is important. This is not so in the case of a partnership for a partner is also a principal, and control and authorization are generally within his power to exercise.

In the past, we have held both in workmen's compensation cases and others that where an employer authorizes or furnishes the employee transportation to and from his work as an incident to his employment, or as a benefit to the employer, the employee is considered in the course of his employment when so traveling. This is so whether it be to his place to eat, sleep or to the employee's home. . . .

Here, the fact that the defendant partners were in the used car business; that the very vehicle involved in the accident was one of the partnership assets for sale at all times, day or night, at any location; that Harris was on call by Phillips or customers at his home — he went back to the lot two or three times after going home; that he had no set time and worked irregular hours, coupled with the fact that he frequently stopped to conduct partnership business on the way to and from the lot; drove partnership vehicles to the Department of Motor Vehicles, and to dealers in Baltimore to view and buy used cars while on his way to or from his home; that one of the elements of the partnership arrangement was that each partner could have full use of the vehicles; that the use of the automobile by Harris for transportation to and from his home was admittedly "essential" to the partnership arrangement and the most practical and convenient way to operate; and that Harris conducted partnership business both at the used car lot and from his home requires that the question of whether the use of the automobile at the time of the accident was in the partnership interest and for its benefit be submitted to the jury. We find that the lower court did not err in refusing to grant appellant's motions for a directed verdict as to him in the capacity of a co-partner trading as Dan's Used Cars.

II

The appellant next complains that the lower court committed reversible error in charging the jury that the burden of proof was upon the defendants to show that the vehicle was not at the time being operated on partnership business. The trial court in its charge instructed the jury that the ownership of the automobile by the partnership raised the presumption that it was being operated by Harris on partnership business at the time of the collision and instructed that the jury would have to determine from the evidence whether or not Harris was, in fact, operating the automobile on partnership business at the time of the accident. Judge Carter went on to say:

> When I say it is a rebuttable presumption, what do I mean? You have the presumption in the first instance, and then it is rebuttable, and then it becomes the duty of the defendant — that would be Harris and Phillips, operating the partnership — to go forward with the evidence to establish to your satisfaction by a fair preponderance of the evidence that the car was not at that time being operated on partnership business. So again you will have to determine from the facts of the case whether or not at the time of this accident this car was in fact then and there being operated by Mr. Harris on partnership business.

Appellant contends that the above quoted part of the court's charge cast the burden of proof upon the defendants to show that the automobile was not being operated on partnership business. It is the established law in Maryland that the legal presumption arising from the ownership of a motor vehicle places the burden of overcoming the presumption on the owner. We see no difference between a master and servant situation and one involving a partnership. We have held that in a collision caused by an automobile operated by the servant of the owner, there is a reasonable presumption that the servant was acting in the scope of his employment and upon the business of his master, and the burden of overcoming this presumption is upon the master by showing that the servant was employed in business other than his employer's. . . .

III

At the conclusion of the plaintiff's evidence and again at the conclusion of all the evidence, Phillips, the appellant, moved for a directed verdict in his favor as an individual. These motions were apart from and in addition to the motions with regard to directing a verdict in Phillip's favor as a copartner. Phillips contends that, in any event, he could not be held liable as an individual because partnership assets must first be used in the payment of partnership liabilities and the individual assets in the payment of individual liabilities, although, concededly, a partner's individual assets may be held liable for the payment of partnership debts where partnership assets are insufficient.

The principle prevails both at common law and under the Uniform Partnership Act when suit is brought on an alleged contractual obligation of the partnership. . . . The rule is otherwise, however, both at common law and under the Uniform Partnership Act, where the claim is based upon an alleged tortious act committed in the course of the partnership business. . . .

It has been held that the language of the Uniform Partnership Act, in making all partners jointly and severally liable for tortious acts chargeable to the partnership . . . reaffirms the common law doctrine. . . . We agree with the reasoning of these cases that in tort actions, as contrasted with contractual claims, each member of the partnership may be held personally liable. . . . If the tortious act may reasonably be found to be done within the scope of the business of the partnership, the individual partner against whom judgment is obtained may have a right of contribution from the partnership and from the other partners, but that right does not limit the remedy of the plaintiff to proceed against the members of the partnership as individuals as well as co-partners.

The motions of the appellant for directed verdicts in his favor as an individual were properly denied.

Judgment affirmed: Costs to be paid by appellant.

HAMMOND, Judge (dissenting).

I dissent because I think the evidence conclusively rebutted the presumption that the operator of a motor vehicle owned by another is the agent or servant of the owner, acting within the scope of the owner's business, and left no room for the jury to find the partnership liable. The holding of the majority extends the liability of a partnership for the tortious acts of a partner to new and, to me, unjustified lengths.

There was no contradiction or impeachment of, or reason to doubt, the testimony that Harris had left the used car lot on the evening of the accident for the day and was driving home to eat supper and spend the evening. He planned to remain at home and to drive back to the used car lot the next morning. It is undisputed that both Harris and Phillips were free to treat vehicles owned by the partnership as their own for personal trips and uses. In the months that the partnership had existed, Harris had returned to the used car lot, after he had gone home, only two or three times. He never kept a car at home for sale, always on the partnership lot. The car he drove he had paid for although it was titled in the name of the partnership. He did not solicit business away from the lot and apparently had not sold a car away from there, but if some one had asked him to sell the car he was driving he would have done so at the right price.

Restatement, Second, Agency Sec. 14A (a) says that the rights and liabilities of partners with respect to each other and to third persons are largely determined by agency principles so that the members of a partnership are liable in tort for the acts of a partner when the act is within the agency power of a partner. . . .

Restatement, Second, Agency, Sec. 238, Comment b of that section says:

> The mere fact that the master habitually allows the servant to use the instrumentality, or even that the master maintains the instrumentality entirely for the use of the servant, does not of itself subject the master to liability. The master is liable only when the instrumentality is being used by the servant for the purpose of advancing the employer's business or interests, as distinguished from the private affairs of the servant. Thus, a master who purchases an automobile for the convenience of his servants is not subject to liability when a servant is using it for his own purposes; * * *.

The test is not whether the servant on another occasion or at another time might use the instrumentality in furtherance of the master's business or interests or within the scope of the business of the partnership, it is whether at the time the servant causes harm he then reasonably could be found to be so acting. If the servant's activities at the time of the infliction of the harm were for his own purposes, or in his own behalf, the master is not liable. It matters not that earlier he had acted for his master or that later he would again act for him; at the time of the harm the immediately predominating purpose of the servant must have some significant relation to the business of the master, if the master is to be held liable. . . .

The majority finds evidence that the driving of the car home to supper and for the night was within the scope of the partnership business because "for sale" signs were on the partnership cars "at various times and places," the car was always for sale, Harris had on two or three occasions over a number of months gone back to the used car lot at night, and at times in the morning had driven from his home, before going to the lot, to the Department of Motor Vehicles or to an automobile dealer on partnership business. I find no support in the record for a finding that "for sale" signs were ever on the cars except when they were standing on the lot, certainly none that such a sign was on the car Harris was driving on the night of the accident. The fact that Harris would have sold the car for a price if some purchaser had flagged him down while he was en route home or telephoned him at home, does not make his purpose in driving home to supper and an evening of television and sleep less predominantly personal and unmixed with business than that of a lawyer driving home from his office with a briefcase full of files (which he may or may not open). If the lawyer negligently injures someone while driving home, his partners certainly would not be liable because of the briefcase or because a client involved in a street accident might flag him down en route or another client call him at home for advice. . . .

The defendant's prayer for an instructed verdict should have been granted.

◆◆◆

Case Questions

1. Does this case stand for the legal principle that whenever a partner commits a tort while on partnership business, the partnership will be liable? Isn't this statement too broad?
2. List the facts which caused the court to conclude that the plaintiffs had stated a good cause of action against the partnership. That is, what circumstances establish the negligent partner was operating the vehicle in the ordinary course of the business?
3. Do you agree with the majority or the dissent? Should not the majority have focused upon the intent and purpose of the very trip which was taken? Was not the partner going home for the evening?
4. Note that the court does not discuss the elements of control needed to establish liability in a master-servant case. The analysis here is very similar to that used by courts in an agency case where it is alleged that the relationship of principal-non-servant agent existed.
5. Must liability for a partner's tort be satisfied first out of partnership property; or, may the negligent partner be required to directly pay the injured party? Who ultimately bears the loss?

In the *Phillips* v. *Cook* case the majority thought the ordinary course of business, selling autos, could be conducted anywhere and, therefore, even though one partner was on his way home for the evening, there was still a potential to conduct business. Usually the "ordinary course of business" is easier to define. It should be obvious that the negligent preparation of an audit by a partner will subject a C. P. A. partnership to liability,[5] even though the other partners did not participate; the same is true of a partnership of physicians when one of them breaches a duty owed to a patient.[6]

Generally, a partnership is not liable on the basis of respondeat superior for the willful or malicious torts or crimes of a partner. In these cases the intent to commit the act is necessary and intent will not be imputed to those who did not engage in or authorize the act. However, some state and federal regulatory laws describe acts which are criminal and intent may not be an element. When this is the case, the partnership may be liable.[7]

Tort liability of a partnership is treated differently procedurally from contract liability. Section 15 of the U.P.A. provides that partners are jointly and severally liable for all wrongful acts and omissions and breaches of trust, but only jointly liable for all contractual debts. Joint and several liability means that as a procedural matter, any partner may be sued alone for the tortious acts of another partner and the other partners need not be joined. A judgment against any one partner, if it remains uncollected, is not a bar to a subsequent law suit against another partner for the same negligent act. The law in this instance seeks to protect the injured third party by providing a remedy against any one of the partners once it has been determined that the tort was within the scope of the partnership. If a tort judgment is recovered against the partnership or one of the partners who *did not in fact cause* the tort then, as between the partners, the one who *did in fact cause* the tort must indemnify the partnership or other partners for their loss.

Joint liability for contractual obligations means that all partners must be joined (named) in the suit. If they are not, then a judgment recovered against fewer than all the partners cannot be enforced against those not joined. Practically this means that all the partners must be made individual defendants and the court must have jurisdiction over all of them. This is needed only for securing a judgment against the individual partners. If the partnership is named a defendant and there is proper service of process on a partner as agent of the partnership, then a judgment creditor may attach partnership assets.

The following cases serve to illustrate some of the principles discussed above. Note that in the *United Brokers* case the principle that one is almost always ultimately liable for his own negligent acts is applicable to partnerships.

VRABEL v. ACRI

156 Ohio St. 467; 103 N.E.2d 564 (S. Ct., Ohio, 1952)

Zimmerman, J.

It will be noted that the amended petition seeks to fix the liability of defendant to plaintiff for his injuries on the theory of negligence. Plaintiff contends that defendant and Michael Acri were joint proprietors of the Acri Cafe and that defendant, as a joint proprietor, was negligent in failing to exercise ordinary measures and precautions to protect patrons of the cafe from unprovoked attacks by Michael Acri, a person known to the defendant to be vicious and irresponsible.

The evidence presented on the trial supports the claims in the amended petition as to the manner in which plaintiff was injured. It shows that, while plaintiff and his companion were sitting quietly at the bar of the Acri Cafe on the night of February 17, 1947, partaking of alcoholic beverages, Michael Acri, for no apparent cause, shot and killed plaintiff's companion and afterwards viciously attacked plaintiff. Evidence was also introduced which might justify the conclusion that at the time of plaintiff's injuries Michael Acri and the defendant, then husband and wife, were joint proprietors of the Acri Cafe which had been started in 1933, although defendant herself denied any such relationship.

Other undisputed evidence discloses that on a number of occasions from 1931, when defendant and Michael Acri were married, until sometime in 1946, the latter was a patient in different hospitals, clinics and sanitariums and under treatment by physicians, and that one of the sanitariums he entered "was a hospital for mental disorders and nervousness." However, no evidence was presented as to the nature of Michael Acri's mental or nervous trouble, if any existed, or as to its manifestations, and there was no evidence that he ever attacked, abused or mistreated anyone except defendant during occasions when they were experiencing marital difficulties.

Additional undisputed evidence shows that . . . that defendant's operation and management of the Acri Cafe were confined principally to those times when Michael Acri was away on account of illness; that Michael Acri and his wife, the defendant, separated permanently in September of 1946; that shortly thereafter she sued him for divorce; and that, from sometime in September 1946 until plaintiff's injuries, defendant had no direct connection with the Acri Cafe, the sole management and control thereof being exercised by Michael Acri to the exclusion of defendant.

It also appears from the evidence that plaintiff secured a judgment for $10,000 against Michael Acri for the injuries received at Acri's hands, and that Acri is now serving a life sentence in the Ohio Penitentiary for killing plaintiff's companion.

For the purpose of the discussion which follows, we shall accept plaintiff's claim, supported by some evidence, that defendant and Michael Acri were joint proprietors of the Acri Cafe at the time plaintiff was assaulted by Acri.

The authorities are in agreement that whether a tort is committed by a partner or a joint adventurer, the principles of law governing the situation are the same. So, where a partnership or a joint enterprise is shown to exist, each member of such project acts both as principal and agent of the others as to those things done within the apparent scope of the business of the project and for its benefit. . . .

Section 8105-13, General Code, a part of the Uniform Partnership Act, provides:

> Where, by any wrongful act or omission of any partner acting in the ordinary course of the business of the partnership or with the authority of his co-partners, loss or injury is caused to any person, not being a partner

in the partnership, or any penalty is incurred, the partnership is liable therefor to the same extent as the partner so acting or omitting to act.

Such section, although enacted after the cause of action in the instant case arose, corresponds with the general law on the subject.

However, it is equally true that where one member of a partnership or joint enterprise commits a wrongful and malicious tort not within the actual or apparent scope of the agency or the common business of the particular venture, to which the other members have not assented, and which has not been concurred in or ratified by them, they are not liable for the harm thereby caused. . . .

The proposition is stated as follows in *Tarlecka* v. *Morgan*, 125 Ohio St. 319, 322, 181 NE 450, 451:

> A tortious act committed by one partner, which is outside the general partnership agency, renders that partner alone responsible, because he acts only for himself.

Because at the time of plaintiff's injuries and for a long period prior thereto defendant had been excluded from the Acri Cafe and had no voice or control in its management as to the hiring of employees or anything else, and because there is no showing that defendant knew or had good reason to believe that Michael Acri was a dangerous individual prone to assault cafe patrons, it seems to us that the theory of negligence adopted and urged by plaintiff is hardly tenable.

We cannot escape the conclusion, therefore, that the above rules, relating to the nonliability of a partner or joint adventurer for wrongful and malicious torts committed by an associate outside the purpose and scope of the business, must be applied in the instant case. The wilful and malicious attack by Michael Acri upon the plaintiff in the Acri Cafe cannot reasonably be said to have come within the scope of the business of operating the cafe, so as to have rendered the absent defendant, assuming her joint proprietorship of the cafe, accountable.

Since the liability of one partner or of one engaged in a joint enterprise for the acts of his associates is founded upon the principles of agency, the statement is in point that an intentional and willful attack committed by an agent or employee, to vent his own spleen or malevolence against the injured person, is a clear departure from his employment and his principal or employer is not responsible therefor. . . .

Therefore, under the evidence in this case, we entertain the view that the trial court should have directed a verdict for the defendant at the close of the evidence, in response to her motion. The judgments of the Court of Common Pleas and of the Court of Appeals are reversed and final judgment is rendered for the defendant.

Judgment reversed.

Case Questions

1. If the plaintiff in this case could prove that the other member of the

partnership knew or should have known about the violent tendencies of Michael Acri would the result have been the same?

2. If a partnership did exist in this case and if Michael Acri were negligent in merely throwing a patron out of the cafe who was causing a disturbance should the partnership be liable? (see the dissent in the *Sandman* case in Chapter 5)

UNITED BROKERS' CO. v. DOSE
143 Or. 283, 22 P. 2d 204 (S. Ct. Or., 1933)

◆◆◆

BELT, Justice.

In April, 1929, plaintiff and defendant entered into a joint adventure whereby they agreed to finance and assist one Luther Harrel in producing a crop of potatoes on 200 acres of land owned by Harrel. It was agreed that one-half of the profits derived from sale of potatoes should go to Harrel, the other half to be divided equally between the plaintiff and the defendant. Pursuant to this contract, a crop of potatoes was produced which netted a profit of $36,772.16. Of this amount plaintiff and defendant were each entitled to $9,193.04. Plaintiff charges in his complaint that defendant, who collected the partnership share, has paid to him only the sum of $8,227.13, and there is still due $965.91 which defendant has failed and refused to pay.

The second cause of action is based upon advances made by plaintiff to defendant, amounting to $1,009.06, one-half of which amount the defendant agreed to repay. There is no dispute relative to this cause of action.

Defendant admits the contract as alleged in the complaint and the amount of money received as profit from sale of the potatoes. . . .

Defendant as a further defense and counterclaim alleges that there is due him, as compensation for services rendered as general manager and in the sale of the potatoes, the sum of $1,155.

Defendant also, as a part of his counterclaim, demands contribution from plaintiff by reason of money which defendant expended in settlement of an automobile accident which occurred while acting within the scope of the partnership business.

Plaintiff in its reply denied the new matter alleged by way of counterclaim.

The trial court denied the counterclaims, and, on the first cause of action, entered a decree in favor of plaintiff for $929.91, together with interest thereon at rate of 6 percent per annum until paid, and, on the second cause of action, entered a decree in favor of plaintiff for $504.33, together with the interest thereon at rate of 6 percent per annum from April 25, 1930, until paid. Defendant appeals.

Relative to the claim of compensation for services rendered by defendant, it is clear that the court was right in denying the same. There is no evidence of any express agreement that defendant was to receive compensation for his services. The rule applicable is thus stated in 20 R. C. L. 877: "The general rule is that a partner is not entitled to compensation for services in conducting the partnership business beyond his share of the profits unless there is a stipulation to that effect, and that he has no right by implication to claim anything extra by reason of any inequality of services rendered by him, as compared with those rendered by his copartners."

The second counterclaim arose out of an automobile accident which occurred while defendant, Dose, was driving to Washington to inspect some potatoes. The trip was made with the knowledge and consent of the plaintiff. Dan Schuler, who accompanied Dose, was injured as a result of the latter's negligence. Schuler threatened to bring an action. Dose thereupon, without the knowledge or consent of the plaintiff, paid to Schuler, in settlement of his claim, the sum of $2,000. The further sum of $1,214.60 was paid by Dose to cover hospital bills for Schuler and himself. The liability of the partnership to a third person for the negligence of one of the partners while acting within the scope of the partnership business is not involved. Neither is this a case where the injury was caused by the negligence of an employee of the partnership.

The law of partnership is the law of agency. Each partner is the agent of the other, and impliedly agrees that he will exercise reasonable care and diligence in the operation of the partnership business. When a loss is paid by a partnership, there is a right of indemnity against the partner whose negligence caused the loss. . . . It is the same rule where the principal is held liable for the negligent act of his agent to be indemnified for the loss sustained: . . . In "The Law of Partnership" by Shumaker (2d Ed.) 160, it is said: "A partner has no right to charge the firm with losses or expenses caused by his own negligence or want of skill. * * * " . . .

In *Kiffer* v. *Bienstock*, 128 Misc. 451, 218 N.Y.S. 526, it was held that, where a judgment was recovered against a partner individually by a person injured by a partner's sole negligence in operating partnership automobile in firm business, partner was not entitled to contribution by copartner on dissolution of partnership. . . .

The decree of the lower court is affirmed.

◆◆◆

Case Question

1. A partner or joint venturer is entitled to indemnity from the association. Why was this denied in this case? Generally, under what circumstances will a court order a partnership to indemnify a partner?

INCOMING PARTNERS

The addition of new partners is an essential part of partnership operation. Unless the articles of partnership provide otherwise, the consent of all partners is needed to expand the partnership. A new partner is given a form of limited liability in that his *personal assets* cannot be attached by a partnership judgment creditor for a partnership obligation which arose before his admission (U.P.A. § 17). Only his property brought to the partnership and his interest therein is subject to attachment for such obligations. The next case illustrates this principle plus provides an explanation for the rather unique obligation created by leasing property.

ELLINGSON v. WALSH, O'CONNOR & BARNESON
15 Cal. 2d 673, 104 P. 2d 507
(S. Ct. Cal, 1940)

◆◆◆

GIBSON, Chief Justice

This is an action against a partnership and its members for rent due under a written lease. The case was submitted upon an agreed statement of facts. Judgment was rendered against the partnership and all general partners, and from this judgment Lionel T. Barneson, one of the general partners, appeals. Appellant admits his liability for rent, but contends that the obligation therefor arose before his admission to the partnership, and that . . . liability must be satisfied only out of partnership property.

On October 4, 1929, the First National Corporation, as lessor, let the premises in question to Walsh, O'Connor & Company, a special partnership, as lessee, for a period of ten years, at a total rental of $66,000, payable in monthly installments of various amounts. In September, 1930, the original lessor assigned the lease to the First National Bank of Beverly Hills, of which plaintiff is receiver. In December, 1930, the limited partnership of Walsh, O'Connor & Barneson was formed, and all of the rights of the original lessee were assigned to the new partnership, which thereafter occupied the premises and paid rent to the bank as lessor.

On April 21, 1931, H. J. Barneson withdrew as a general partner. On April 28, 1931, appellant Lionel T. Barneson was taken in as a general partner, and ever since has enjoyed all of the rights and privileges and assumed the obligations as a general partner of said partnership. . . . During the period between April, 1931, and March, 1932, the partnership paid the full rent due under the lease to the lessor. The judgment herein is for rent claimed to be due for the period commencing March 1, 1932, and ending January 25, 1933, in the sum of $2,374.13, after deducting certain credits and payments. The judgment was a general one against all defendants, with no proviso restricting its enforcement or satisfaction against appellant.

The issue in this case is not the liability of the partnership as such, nor the liability of its assets. There is no doubt whatever that the plaintiff may satisfy his claim against the partnership out of any of its properties. The sole question is whether the appellant's liability as an incoming partner may be satisfied by resort to his personal assets.

Section 2411 of the Civil Code (sec. 17 of the Uniform Partnership Act) provides: "A person admitted as a partner into an existing partnership is liable for all the obligations of the partnership arising before his admission as though he had been a partner when such obligations were incurred, except that this liability shall be satisfied only out of partnership property." It is this section upon which appellant relies, and the interpretation urged by appellant is the sole basis of his case. Appellant contends that since the lease was executed before he became a partner, the obligation of the lease arose before his admission, and therefore his liability can only be satisfied out of partnership property.

This contention would be sound if the only obligation of the partnership in this transaction was one which arose prior to appellant's admission to the firm. For example, if a promissory note had been executed by the partnership for a consideration then passing to it, the obligation would have arisen at the time of execution of the note and the case would plainly be within the statute. But appellant's contention overlooks the fact that a tenant of real property is not liable for rent solely by reason of the contract of lease. Tenancies in property need not necessarily be created . . . by leases. One may become a tenant at will or a periodic tenant under an invalid lease, or without any lease at all, by occupancy with consent. Such tenancies carry with them the incidental obligation of rent, and the liability therefore arises not from contract but from the relationship of landlord and tenant. The tenant is liable by operation of law. Where there is a lease the liability of the tenant arising by operation of law is not superseded by the contractual obligation.

Both liabilities exist simultaneously. . . .

Under the above principles, the first partnership, which did not include appellant as a member, was bound by these dual obligations; that is, having expressly assumed the obligations of the lease, it was bound in contract and also by reason of its tenancy. When appellant became a member, the first partnership was, in legal theory, dissolved and a new partnership came into being composed of the old members and appellant. This second partnership did not expressly assume the obligations of the lease, but it occupied the premises. Whether it was liable contractually on the lease is immaterial; it became liable for rent as a tenant. . . .

The only remaining question is whether the section of the Uniform Partnership Act, quoted above, has changed the rule. Appellant's theory is that he, as a member of the second partnership, may receive the benefits of years of occupancy under the lease, but that his personal assets cannot be reached in satisfaction of liability therefor if the lease was executed before he became a member of the partnership. The statute, however, neither contemplates nor accomplished any such result. . . . Under the general law the obligation of a tenant arising from occupation of the premises is a continuing one; that is, it arises and binds him continually throughout the period of his occupation. This obligation on the part of appellant first arose when the new partnership, of which he was a member, occupied the premises as a tenant. It follows that his obligation as a tenant arose after his admission to the partnership and the immunity given by section 2411 does not apply.

The judgment is affirmed.

◆◆◆

Case Questions

1. If the liability in this case had arisen from the signing of a promissory note before Barneson was admitted as a partner would the result have been the same?

2. Develop your own definition of partnership property. What facts or circumstances will you look for in developing this definition?

PARTNERSHIP DISSOLUTION

Ending the partnership association is achieved by a two-part process. First is the dissolution of the partnership. This is defined as " . . . a change in the relation of the partners caused by any partner ceasing to be associated in the carrying on . . . of the business (U.P.A. §29). In essence, dissolution dissolves the authority of the partners to act for the partnership in the ordinary course of business. The partnership and a partner's authority continues for purposes of liquidating the partnership assets and paying partnership obligations. This process of liquidation is called winding up and is the second step in ending the association. When the winding up is completed, the partnership has been terminated. The reader should be careful to distinguish between these three legal terms: dissolution, winding up, and termination, the first two of which represent a two phase process of ending the partnership association.

Before proceeding to a full discussion of dissolution and winding up, we wish to point out what happens when one of the partners dies, retires or withdraws and the surviving or continuing partners wish to continue to do business as before. Perhaps this is the most often occuring form of dissolution, although it is only a technical dissolution.

In many of the large law and accounting partnerships for example, partners are withdrawing and new ones are added yearly. Technically, this is a dissolution of the partnership because there is a " . . . change in the relation of the partners." Indeed, a new association, either plus or minus one or more partners, results. However, the partnership does not end its business activity. If the partners are prudent, this type of dissolution will be one of the most important items covered in the articles of partnership. Generally, under the provisions of these articles, upon the retirement or death of a partner, the partner's *interest in the partnership* is valued. At this point it would be beneficial to refer to paragraphs 11-12 of the partnership agreement provided in the last chapter. This partnership interest is composed of both a right to the return of some property in exchange for that which he brought to the partnership and a right to profits, if any, plus, if the agreement so provides, a right to a payment for his contribution to the good will of the firm. The entire interest is valued, perhaps somewhat arbitrarily by a pre-set formula, and the partner is paid this value, usually out of the revenues of the firm. We assume here that the partnership was a solvent, going enterprize at dissolution. In those cases where the partnership is insolvent and does not have the funds to pay the partners or the creditors, the partners upon dissolution may have to contribute more to the partnership to pay the creditors.

If there is *no partnership agreement* and one of the partners retires or dies and if the members of the partnership wish to continue then Section 42 of the U.P.A. provides in part that the retiring partner or the estate of the deceased partner:

> . . . may have the value of his interest at the date of dissolution ascertained, and shall receive as an ordinary creditor an amount equal to the

value of his interest in the dissolved partnership with interest, or, at his option, . . . in lieu of interest, the profits attributable to the use of his right in the property of the dissolved partnership; provided that the creditors of the dissolved partnership as against separate creditors . . . of the retired or deceased partner, shall have priority on any claim arising under this Section, as provided by Section 41 (8) of this act.

Section 41 (8) provides for the prior right of partnership creditors over individual creditors upon dissolution of the old partnership and the continuation of business as a new partnership. They also have a prior right over the claim of the retiring partner or his estate for sums advanced to the partnership as loans.

Even though, technically, the old association has been dissolved, the creditors of the old association become creditors of the partnership continuing the business. (U.P.A. § 41). The retiring partner or, in the case of death, a partner's estate, remains liable to creditors of the partnership for obligations incurred before dissolution and even in some cases after dissolution where the creditor has no notice of the dissolution. A partner is discharged from partnership liability existing at time of dissolution by an agreement to that effect between the retired or deceased partner, the surviving partners and the creditors [U.P.A. § 36 (2)]. An agreement between only the retiring or deceased partner and the surviving partners will not discharge the former from partnership obligations to third party creditors existing at dissolution.

We have provided two cases which demonstrate the application of some of the legal rules just discussed. In the *McClemen* v. *Commissioner of Internal Revenue* decision the issue, broadly stated, was the nature of a partner's interest in the partnership when he died. The representatives of the estate treated this interest as income and not a return of capital and thus did not include the partnership interest as part of the deceased's estate when filing the federal estate tax return. The I.R.S. took a different view arguing that although the interest in the partnership was to be paid out of partnership revenues, it was a return of property brought to the partnership and was therefore includable in the gross estate at death as part of the property owned by the deceased.

McCLENNEN v. COMMISSIONER OF INTERNAL REVENUE
131 F2d 165 (C.C.A. 1st, 1942)

♦♦♦

MAGRUDER, Circuit Judge

George R. Nutter had been a partner in the firm of Nutter, McClennen & Fish, practicing law in Boston, Massachusetts. The firm kept its accounts on the cash receipts and disbursements basis. Its receipts were derived solely from personal services. Under the partnership agreement Mr. Nutter's share of the firm's net profits was 8 percent. The agreement also contained the following provision:

On the retirement of a partner or on his death — the other continuing the business — the retiring partner or his estate in the case of his death shall, in addition to his percentage of net profits of the Firm received by it in cash up to the date of such death or retirement, also receive the same percentage of net profits of the Firm received by it in cash until the expiration of the eighteen (18) calendar months next after such retirement, or death, and this shall be in full of the retiring or deceasing member's interest in the capital, the assets, the receivables, the possibilities of the Firm. The continuing members shall have the right to the good will and the use of the Firm name except that the deceasing or retiring member's name shall not be used without his written consent or that of his estate. . . .

After the death of George R. Nutter the other partners continued the business. Eight percent of the net profits of the firm for the 18 calendar months next after the death, computed on the basis of cash receipts and disbursements, amounted to $34,069.99, which amount was paid over to the petitioners as executors. Of this amount $28,069.46 represented 8 percent of the net profits for the period of the year next after the death, and the remainder represented 8 percent of the net profits for the last six months of the agreed 18 month's period.

Petitioners filed an estate tax return with the Collector of Internal Revenue at Boston, and paid the tax thereon shown to be due. On the said return they duly elected to have the property includable in the gross estate valued as of one year after decedent's death, in accordance with the method authorized by § 202 of the Revenue Act of 1935, . . . The sum of $6,136.21, which had been received by the executors as representing the decedent's share of the undistributed profits as of the date of the death, was included in the estate tax return as part of the decedent's gross estate. But beyond this nothing was included on account of the value of the decedent's interest in the partnership.

In his notice of deficiency the Commissioner determined that $34,069.99 should have been included in the gross estate as the value of decedent's "interest in partnership Nutter, McClennen & Fish." The Board has upheld the Commissioner in this determination. We think the Board was right.

In the absence of a controlling agreement in the partnership articles the death of a partner dissolves the partnership. The survivors have the right and duty, with reasonable dispatch, to wind up the partnership affairs, to complete transactions begun but not then finished, to collect the accounts receivable, to pay the firm debts, to convert the remaining firm assets into cash, and to pay in cash to the partners and the legal representative of the deceased partner the net amounts shown by the accounts to be owing to each of them in respect of capital contributions and in respect of their shares of profits and surplus. The representative of a deceased partner does not succeed to any right to specific partnership property. In substance the deceased partner's interest, to which his representative succeeds, is a chose in action, a right to receive in cash the sum of money shown to be due him upon a liquidation and accounting. . . . The same substantive results are reached under the Uniform Partnership Act which, in form at least, proceeds on the aggregate theory. . . . That act, which is law in Massachusetts, conceives of the partner as a "co-owner with his partners of specific partnership property holding as a tenant in partnership;" but provides that on the death of a partner "his right in specific partnership property vests in the surviving partner or partners." Another enumerated property rights of a partner, "his interest in the partnership," is described as "his share of the profits and surplus, and the same is personal property," regardless of whether the firm holds real estate or personalty or both. . . .

This chose in action to which the representative of the deceased partner succeeds, the right to receive payment of a sum of money shown to be due upon a liquidation and accounting, is of course a part of the deceased partner's wealth, and includable in the decedent's gross estate, for purposes of computing the estate tax. . . . This is none the less true even though the net amount thus shown to be due to the estate is derived in whole or in part from past earnings or profits of the partnership resulting from personal services — profits which the decedent, if he had lived, would have had to report as income. The valuation of this chose in action might be a matter of difficulty, especially in the case of a partnership which cannot be speedily liquidated and whose accounts are complicated. Nevertheless, for estate tax purposes, the valuation must be made by the legal representatives of the deceased partner, on the basis of the best evidence available at the applicable valuation date.

In the case at bar, if there had not been the controlling provision in the partnership articles, above quoted, or if the survivors had not come to some agreement otherwise with the executors of Mr. Nutter, the survivors would have had to proceed to wind up the affairs of the partnership, to conclude all unfinished legal business on hand at the date of the death, to realize upon all of the assets of the firm, tangible or intangible, to pay the debts, to return to Mr. Nutter's estate his contribution of capital, if any, and to pay to his estate in cash the amount shown to be due in respect of his "interest in the partnership," that is, his "share of the profits and surplus," as determined upon an accounting. Among other things to be taken into account, "the earned proportion of the unfinished business" would have had "to be valued to determine the decedent's interest in the partnership assets." . . .

To obviate the necessity of a liquidation, or to eliminate accounting difficulties in determining the value of the deceased partner's interest, partners often make specific provision in the partnership articles.

Sometimes the partnership agreement merely provides for the postponement of liquidation, say, to the end of the term for which the partnership was created. Thus, a partnership agreement between A, B and C might provide that "should any partner die during the term of said co-partnership the firm shall not be dissolved thereupon, but the business shall be continued by the survivors until the expiration of said partnership term, the estate of the deceased partner to bear the same share in profits and losses as would have been received and borne by the deceased partner had he lived." Under such an agreement, if A dies, B and C do not buy out A's interest in the partnership. Unless more appears, A's executor does not become personally liable as a general partner, . . . Nor is A's general estate in the executor's hands liable as a partner for new debts created by B and C in continuing the business. . . . For the remainder of the term, A's share already embarked in the business remains in, subject to the risks of the business. It would seem not improper to describe the continuing business as now being owned by B and C as general partners, with A's estate (or A's executor as trustee under the will of A) as a limited partner therein, sharing in the profits, but not liable beyond the amount or interest already embarked in the business. . . .

In the case at bar the partnership agreement contains another familiar arrangement, whereby no liquidation and final accounting will ever be necessary in order to satisfy the claim of the deceased partner. In place of the chose in action to which Mr. Nutter's executor would have succeeded in the absence of specific provision in the partnership articles, that is, a right to receive payment in cash of the amount shown to be due the deceased partner upon a complete liquidation and accounting, a different right is substituted, a right of the estate to receive a share of the net profits of the firm for 18 calendar months after the partner's death.

The language of the partnership agreement in the present case is couched in terms of a purchase of the deceased partner's interest. What the estate is to receive "shall be in full of the retiring or deceasing member's interest in the capital, the assets, the receivables, the possibilities and the good will of the Firm." There is to be an extinguishment of the decedent's interest in the totality of the firm assets, tangible and intangible, as they stood at the moment of death, and the interests therein of the surviving partners are to be correspondingly augmented. . . .

In the present case the Commissioner valued Mr. Nutter's interest in the partnership at the sum of $34,069.99, which happened to be the exact amount received by the executors from the survivors as representing 8 percent of the net profits of the partnership for the 18 calendar months after the death. There is no contention that this was an overvaluation. . . .

The decision of the Board of Tax Appeals is affirmed.

◆◆◆

Case Question

1. Valuing a partner's contribution to the goodwill of a partnership and the present value of his initial capital contribution are considerable problems and should be discussed when the partnership is formed. No formula is perfect. Reread the provisions for valuing the interest of a retiring or deceased partner in the partnership agreement (paragraph 12 a) reproduced in Chapter 7. How does it differ from the provisions of the agreement which were the subject of the case above?

B-OK, INC., v. STOREY
3 Wash. App. 226; 473 P. 2d 426
(Ct. of App., Wash., 1970)

◆◆◆

EVANS, Chief Judge

This is an appeal from an order of dismissal entered at the conclusion of plaintiff's case. Plaintiff's only assignment of error is that "the trial court erred in entering judgment of dismissal against William E. Storey." Plaintiff does not assign error to the findings of fact entered by the trial court. They are, therefore, verities. Since they accurately state the factual background of this case they are set forth below:

I

For several years prior to April 30, 1962, defendants were partners in the petroleum products business at CleElum, doing business as Storey Distributing Company. On April 30, 1962, the defendants dissolved their partnership. At the time of dissolution of the partnership, defendants' account with plaintiff had a balance of $3,515.80.

II

On December 27, 1963, plaintiff obtained a judgment against defendant Earl Storey, in Cause No. 15849, in the above entitled Court for $3,735.47. Defendant William E. Storey was not a named defendant in Cause No. 15849. The judgment in Cause No. 15849 was based upon the identical account involved in this account.

III

Plaintiff and defendants had a debtor-creditor relationship regarding this account which was based upon the sale of petroleum products by plaintiff to defendants. Defendants incurred this debt while they were partners. Defendants liability toward plaintiff in no way involved a breach of trust or a tortious situation.

IV

The dissolution of the partnership by the defendants on April 30, 1962, in no way involved any fraudulent transactions between them effecting their creditors. It was a bona fide dissolution and division of assets, without any evidence of fraud on their creditors.

V

There was no prayer for relief against defendant Earl Storey and his wife in the Amended Complaint herein.

VI

After April 30, 1962, defendant Earl Storey continued doing business selling petroleum products in CleElum, at the same location as before, without any visible alteration of the premises, under the assumed name of Storey Distributing Company, for approximately three years.

Plaintiff concedes that he is charged with notice of the partnership dissolution and that Earl M. Storey was continuing to do business as the Storey Distributing Company, as the "only person conducting or intending to conduct said business or having interest therein." The court entered the following conclusions of law:

I

Defendants, as partners, were jointly indebted to plaintiff on the account sued upon in this action, and not jointly and severally liable.

II

The judgment obtained by plaintiff against Earl Storey in Cause No. 15849, in the above entitled Court, merged the plaintiff's claim against William E. Storey. Said judgment is a bar to this action.

III

This action should be dismissed with prejudice against William E. Storey and his wife, and without prejudice against Earl Storey and his wife.

The conclusion by the trial court that defendant William E. Storey should be dismissed is based on RCW 25.04.150, providing:

Nature of partner's liability. All partners are liable:

1. Jointly and severally for everything chargeable to the partnership under RCW 25.04.130 and 25.04.140.
2. Jointly for all other debts and obligations of the partnership; but any partner may enter into a separate obligation to perform a partnership contract.

and *Warren* v. *Rickles,* 129 Wash. 443, 225 P. 422 (1924), holding that:

It is a very generally accepted rule of law that, where an obligation is joint and not joint and several, a judgment rendered on such obligation against one or more, but less than the whole number of obligors, is a bar to any action of the same claim against the obligors not parties to the judgment, because the claim is merged in the judgment and is extinguished thereby. . . .

There is no claim that the alleged liability did not arise out of a partnership obligation. Plaintiff, however, contends that the provisions of RCW 25.04.150 and the holding in *Warren* v. *Rickles,* supra, do not apply after a partnership is dissolved. We disagree. RCW 25.04.360 provides:

Effect of dissolution on partner's existing liability.

1. The dissolution of the partnership does not of itself discharge the existing liability of any partner.
2. A partner is discharged from any existing liability upon dissolution of the partnership by an agreement to that effect between himself, the partnership creditor and the person or partnership continuing the business; and such agreement may be inferred from the course of dealing between the creditor having knowledge of the dissolution and the person or partnership continuing the business.
3. Where a person agrees to assume the existing obligations of a dissolved partnership, the partners, whose obligations have been assumed shall be discharged from any liability to any creditor of the partnership who, knowing of the agreement, consents to a material alteration in the nature or time of payment of such obligations.
4. The individual property of a deceased partner shall be liable for all obligations of the partnership incurred while he was a partner but subject to the prior payment of his separate debts.

This statute, taken from the Uniform Partnership Act § 36, is consistent with prior Washington cases holding that the retiring partner remains liable to creditors of the partnership for all existing debts of the partnership to the same extent as if he had not retired. In other words, while creditors of a partnership existing at the time of the withdrawal of the retiring partner may, by their own voluntary agreement, look to the remaining active partner for payment of their debts, they are not required to do so. . . .

We hold the trial court correctly concluded that after dissolution the liability of the retiring partner William Storey to plaintiff remained a joint liability, and that plaintiff's claim against him was merged in the prior judgment taken against the continuing partner, Earl Storey. The trial court, therefore, did not err in dismissing William Storey.

The judgment is affirmed.

◆◆◆

Case Question

1. Under what circumstances is a retiring partner discharged from liability for partnership obligations?

Case Comment

Many states have differing procedural requirements as to joinder of parties. Because some states may cling to the old notion that a partnership is not a distinct legal entity apart from the partners, the best course of action when suing a partnership on a partnership obligation is to name not only the partnership as a defendant, but also join as defendants and serve the proper papers on all partners. As the case above illustrates, if only a partner is named defendant and is served with the proper papers then a judgment arising from the breach of contractual duty against this partner distinguishes the obligation of other partners. Moreover, if only the partnership is named as a defendant and a judgment is recovered, this judgment, in most states, may be satisfied only out of partnership assets. The case presented was subsequently reversed (485 P 2d 987) based on an issue and facts not discussed above.

The Articles of Partnership usually cover most circumstances resulting in a dissolution. In addition to retirement and death, many agreements provide that dissolution may be caused by the termination of the partnership term, by the express will of all the partners before the end of the term, or the expulsion of any partner from the business in accordance with such a power conferred by the articles. [U.P.A. § 31 (1)].

If the articles do not provide for dissolution or if there is no agreement then the U.P.A. provides that a partnership is dissolved by:

1. illegality of the partnership business [U.P.A. § 31 (3)],
2. death of any partner [(U.P.A. § 31 (4)],
3. bankruptcy of any partner or bankruptcy of the partnership [U.P.A. § 31 (5)] or,

4. by decree of court under § 32 [U.P.A. § 31 (6)] .

Any of the circumstances set out above is sufficient to cause a dissolution of the partnership without further acts of the partners. Section 32 of the U.P.A. adds to this list but requires a judicial declaration of the existence of the circumstances. It provides that a court shall declare dissolution upon the application by or for a partner when it is proved that:

1. a partner is incapacitated by insanity or is in any other way incapable of performing his part of the agreement;
2. a partner has been guilty of conduct which affects prejudicially the partnership business so that it is not reasonably practicable to carry on the business;
3. the business can only be carried on at a loss; or
4. other circumstances which render a dissolution equitable.

If the surviving partner or partners do not wish to continue the business then, at dissolution, the authority of all partners to act for the others in the ordinary course of business ends (U.P.A. § 33) and the partners wind up the business. Winding up involves selling the firms' assets, the payment of the firms obligations to third parties and then distributing the remaining amounts to the partners. More specifically, section 40 of the U.P.A. provides for distribution of the remaining assets in the following order:

1. those owing to creditors other than partners
2. those owing to partners other than for capital and profits (advancements or loans)
3. those owing to partners in respect of capital
4. those owing to partners in respect of profits

The sections of the U.P.A. providing for the distribution of property after dissolution make no special distinction between personal and real property thus greatly simplifying a matter of considerable historical complexity. Some courts still refuse to free their analysis of partnership property from the historical analysis so we present here just a brief recounting of how the law treated partnership ownership of real property.

English law recognized a distinction between real and personal property upon the owner's death by providing that the ownership to the real property vested in the eldest son. Ownership of personal property vested in a living representative of the "estate" who was to pay the deceased's debts and then distribute the remainder to the "next of kin"[8] This fundamental distinction between real and personal property (the former being regarded as "the" standard of wealth) manifests itself in many areas of our law. For a long time, courts refused to recognize a partnership as a distinct legal person and held, therefore, that real property could not be owned by a partnership, but only the partners. A conveyance of real property at common law was held to either vest title in the partners as individuals or to be a nullity. This result was changed by § 8(3) of the U.P.A. which allows:

Any estate in real property may be acquired in the partnership name.
Title so acquired can be conveyed only in the partnership name.

This section clearly indicates a partnership, as a separate entity, may own real property, but the custom of treating real property as unique continued in other respects. Upon dissolution of the partnership caused by death some courts distinguished between real and personal property by holding that the personal property must be sold first to liquidate partnership debts. The ownership of real estate used in the partnership business passed not to the partners but to the heirs of the deceased. The parties did have an equitable right to sell the real property, but only to pay partnership debts if the personal property was inadequate. Thus, courts asserting this view held there was an equitable conversion of the real property for the payment of partnership debts. This view introduced many problems as to the point at which this "conversion" begins and ends.[9] The U.P.A. appears to clarify this by providing, as we noted in chapter 7, that a partner's right to occupy specific partnership property is not assignable and, upon death, this right vests in the surviving partner or partners [(U.P.A. § 25(2) (d)]. Again, note this section makes no distinction between real and personal property. Despite the clear intent and wording of the U.P.A. some courts may still give deference to this historical distinction between real and personal property causing a lingering view that personal property is to be sold first to liquidate a partnership's assets.

Section 40 (d) of the U.P.A. is one of the most important since it is the section that states the nature of the unlimited liability of a partner. It states:

> The partners shall contribute . . . the amount necessary to satisfy the liabilities. but if any, but not all, of the partners are insolvent, or, not being subject to process, refuse to contribute, the other partners shall contribute their share of the liability, . . .

This provision provides that creditors of the firm will be paid if some of the partners are insolvent but others are able to pay. If a firm suffers a loss at dissolution, then, as between the partners, this loss should be adjusted so that they bear the loss according to their share in profits. When partners contribute equal amounts to the partnership and share profits equally the loss distribution is easily determined. However, the matter is complicated where different amounts were contributed. Using Figure 8-1 as an example, assume that the

CASH CONTRIBUTED	DISSOLUTION	INDIVIDUAL LOSS
A. $ 5,000	$10,000 owed to partners	$3,300 divided
B. $ 4,000	6,700 available to pay	by 3, equals
C. $ 1,000	partners	$1,100
$10,000	loss $ 3,300	

PAYMENT OF DISSOLUTION

Payment to A. $5,000 minus $1,100 is $3,900
Payment to B. $4,000 minus $1,100 is $2,900
C. paid only $1,000 and must pay $100 more to suffer loss of $1,100

Figure 8-1

partners contributed cash as indicated and agreed that they would share profits (and therefore, losses) equally. At dissolution, the assets are sold and only $6,700 remains. This means that the partnership suffered a loss of $3,300. This amount must be shared equally by the three partners requiring partner C to contribute more cash to the partnership.

Further, as noted in the *United Broker's Co.* case each partner must suffer the loss caused by his own wrongful conduct; and, the partnership must indemnify each partner for amounts reasonably expended by him in the ordinary course of business. Moreover, if one or more of the partners caused the dissolution of the partnership in violation of the partnership agreement, they may be liable [U.P.A. Section 38 (2) (a) (II)] for the damages caused by such a breach to the other partners. This amount of damages must be calculated or figured into the respective distributions.

DISSOLUTION NOTICE TO THIRD PARTIES

Dissolution ends the actual authority of a partner to act for the partnership unless he is winding up. However, third parties who knew of the partnership in the past who contracted with or otherwise dealt with a partner within the scope of past partnership authority after dissolution and who have no notice of the dissolution may hold the partnership liable on the basis of the partner's apparent authority or estoppel.

Such apparent authority may be terminated only by notice to the third parties. More specifically, Section 35 (1) (b) (I) of the U.P.A. requires that a third party who has *given credit* to the partnership *prior to dissolution* is entitled to be given actual notice of the dissolution. This type of notice must be communicated directly to the third party or its agent. If such notice is not given and the third party does not have knowledge of the dissolution, then a partner acting in the ordinary course of business (as established before dissolution) binds the partnership.

If the third party had not extended credit to the partnership but only knew of the partnership, then constructive notice is sufficient to terminate a partner's apparent authority. Such notice may be given by publishing the fact of dissolution in a newspaper of general circulation in the place where the partnership business was regularly carried on.

Section 35(3) of the U.P.A. provides that no notice is needed where dissolution is caused by the partnership business being declared illegal, or the bankruptcy of a *partner*. Note that when dissolution is caused by the death of a partner, the U.P.A. does not declare this event so notorious as to negate the necessity of notice. Thus the U.P.A. provides a change from the *Restatement of Agency* for the requirements of notice in the case of death. Remember that the *Restatement* said that in the case of the death of the principal, no notice to third parties who had dealt with the agent was required.

We present an old case which illustrates the kind of notice requirement which must be met by a partnership upon dissolution.

FREDERICK M. SOLOMON v. CHARLES H. KIRKWOOD AND THEODORE HOLLANDER
55 Mich. 256 (1844)

(Authors' note: The trial court found for the defendants. This appellate court affirmed this judgment with respect to the two issues discussed below, but reversed with regard to an issue not here important.)

◆◆◆

COOLEY, C. J.

The plaintiffs, who are, in the city of Chicago, dealers in jewelry, seek to charge the defendants, as partners, upon a promissory note for seven hundred and ninety-one, 92/100 dollars, bearing date Nov. 9, 1882, and signed "Hollander & Kirkwood." The note was given by the defendant Hollander, but Kirkwood denies that any partnership existed between the defendants at the date of the note.

The evidence on the trial tends to show that on July 6, 1882, Hollander & Kirkwood entered into a written agreement for a partnership for one year from the first day of the next ensuing month, in the business of buying and selling jewelry, clocks, watches, etc., and in repairing clocks, watches and jewelry, at Ishpeming, Michigan. Business was begun under this agreement, and continued until the latter part of October, 1882, when Kirkwood, becoming dissatisfied, locked up the goods and excluded Hollander altogether from the business. He also caused notice to be given to all persons with whom the firm had had dealings that the partnership was dissolved, and had the following inserted in the local column of the paper published at Ishpeming: "The copartnership heretofore existing between Mr. C. H. Kirkwood and one Hollander, as jewelers, has ceased to exist, Mr. Kirkwood having purchased the interest of the latter." This was not signed by any one.

A few days later Hollander went to Chicago, and there, on November 9, 1882, he bought, in the name of Hollander & Kirkwood, of the plaintiffs goods in their line amounting to $791.92, and gave to the plaintiffs therefor the promissory note now in suit. The note was made payable December 15, 1882, at a bank in Ishpeming. When the purchase was completed Hollander took away the goods in his satchel. The plaintiffs had before had no dealings with Hollander & Kirkwood, but they had heard there was such a firm, and were not aware of its dissolution. They claim to have made the sale in good faith, and in the belief that the firm was still in existence. . . .

The questions principally contested on the trial were — First, whether the acts of Kirkwood amounted to a dissolution of the partnership; and second, whether sufficient notice of dissolution was given; . . . The trial judge, in submitting the case to the jury, instructed them that Kirkwood, notwithstanding the written agreement, had a right to withdraw from the partnership at any time, leaving matters between him and Hollander to be adjusted between them amicably or in the courts; and for the purpose of this case it made no difference whether Kirkwood was right or wrong in bringing the partnership to an end: if wrong, he might be liable to Hollander in damages for the breach of his contract.

Also, that when partners are dissatisfied, or they cannot get along together, and one partner withdraws, the partnership is then at an end as to the public and parties with whom the partnership deals, and neither partner can make contracts in the future to bind the partnership, provided the retiring partner gives the proper notice. Also, that if they should find from the evidence that there was trouble between Hollander and Kirkwood prior to the sale of the goods and the giving of the note; that Kirkwood informed Hollander, in substance, that he would have no more dealings with him as partner; that he took possession of all the goods and locked them up, and from that time they ceased to do business, — then the partnership was dissolved. Further, that whether sufficient notice had been given of the dissolution was a question for the jury. Kirkwood was not bound to publish notice in any of the Chicago papers; he was only bound to give actual notice to such parties there as had dealt with the partnership. But Kirkwood was bound to use all fair means to publish as widely as possible the fact of a dissolution. Publication in a newspaper is one of the proper means of giving notice, but it is not absolutely essential; and on this branch of the case the question for the jury was whether Kirkwood gave such notice of the dissolution as under the circumstances was fair and reasonable. If he did, then he is not liable on the note: if he did not, he would still continue liable. . . .

I. We think the judge committed no error in his instructions respecting the dissolution of the partnership. The rule on this subject is thus stated in an early New York case. The right of a partner to dissolve, it is said, "is a right inseparably incident to every partnership. There can be no such thing as an indissoluble partnership. Every partner has an indefeasible right to dissolve the partnership as to all future contracts by publishing his own volition to that effect; and after such publication the other members of the firm have no capacity to bind him by any contract. Even where partners covenant with each other that the partnership shall continue seven years, either partner may dissolve it the next day by proclaiming his determination for that purpose; the only consequence being, that he thereby subjects himself to a claim for damages for a breach of his covenant. The power given by one partner to another to make joint contracts for them both, is not only a revocable power, but a man can do no act to divest himself of the capacity to revoke it." . . . When one partner becomes dissatisfied there is commonly no legal policy to be subserved by compelling a continuance of the relation, and the fact that a contract will be broken by the dissolution is no argument against the right to dissolve. Most contracts may be broken at pleasure, subject however to responsibility in damages. And that responsibility would exist in breaking a contract of partnership as in other cases.

II. The instruction respecting notice was also correct. No court can determine for all cases what shall be sufficient notice and what shall not be: the question must necessarily be one of fact. Publication of notice of dissolution in a local newspaper is common, but it is not the only method in which notice can be given. The purpose of the notice is to make notorious in the local community the fact that a dissolution has taken place; and publication of a notice may or may not be the most effectual means for that purpose. Very few persons in any community probably read all the advertisements published in the local papers; and matters of local importance which are advertised are quite as likely to come to them from other sources as from the published notices. . . .

One who derives knowledge of the fact from public notoriety is sufficiently notified; ... and probably in many small communities a fact would sooner be made notorious by a notice in the local column of the county or village paper than in any other way. In a large city it might be otherwise. But all that can be required in any case is that such notice be given as is likely to make the fact generally known locally. ... When that is done the party giving the notice has performed his duty, and any one contemplating for the first time to open dealings with the partnership must at his peril ascertain the facts. This, in effect, was the instruction given. ...

Case Question

1. Distinguish between actual and constructive notice. In many of the large law and accounting partnerships, partnerships are technically dissolved every year upon the addition of new partners or the death or retirement of a partner. Are these partnerships required to send notice of dissolution every year to those who extend credit to them?

REVIEW PROBLEMS

1. P owned a small farm, a part of which he leased to E and F who jointly operated a small pig raising business. E and F split profits and jointly managed the business. Later, the city prevented use of the land for such a purpose. E went to the premises to remove some lumber, some fencing and the pigs. An altercation with P developed over his right to remove the lumber and fencing and E intentionally struck and injured P. Immediately before the fight E negligently allowed most the pigs to escape confinement into P's corn field. They trampled and ate some of P's crop. A few days after the altercation, while P was still in the hospital, E returned for the lumber, the fencing and the wandering pigs. E leaves town. P sues F for the bodily injury caused by E, the damage to his crop and conversion of his lumber and fencing. Will F be liable? Explain.

2. Your client, Williams, Watkins, and Glenn, is a general partnership engaged primarily in the real estate brokerage business; however, in addition, it buys and sells real property for its own account. Williams and Watkins are almost exclusively responsible for the brokerage part of the business, and Glenn devotes almost all of his time to partnership acquisitions and sales of real estate. The firm letterhead makes no distinction along these functional lines and all members are listed as licensed real-estate brokers. Normally acquisitions are made in the firm name; although for convenience or other reason, Glenn occasionally takes title in his own name for and on behalf of the firm.

   The partnership agreement contains, among other provisions, the following:

   • No partner shall reduce the standard real estate commission charged (6%) without the consent of at least one other partner.

   • No partner shall purchase or sell real property for or on behalf of the partnership without the consent of all other partners. Title to real property so acquired shall be taken exclusively in the partnership name, unless otherwise agreed to by all the partners.

• All checks received which are payable to the partnership and all checks and cash received for or on behalf of the partnership shall be deposited intact in one of the partnership's bank accounts.

Part A. Watkins showed a magnificent $350,000 ranch estate, listed for over a year with the firm by John Foster, to numerous prospective purchasers. The firm's exclusive listing had recently expired and Watkins was afraid the firm would lose the sale. Foster's price was firm, and he had repeatedly refused to negotiate with interested parties or accept an offer below $350,000. The most recent prospective buyer offered $340,000 but would not budge from that price. Watkins, fearing that a rival broker might obtain a buyer and cause him to lose the commission, agreed to lower the commission to $11,000 which was acceptable to Foster. Watkins did this without the consent of either of the other partners.

Required

1. Can Williams, Watkins, and Glenn or Williams and Glenn recover from Foster the $10,000 reduction in the commission granted by Watkins to Foster? Explain.
2. What recourse does the partnership or the other partners have against Watkins? Explain.

Part B. During your firm's annual examination of the financial statements of Williams, Watkins, and Glenn, the staff auditor discovered that Glenn had recently engaged in a series of questionable transactions affecting the firm's financial position. Following is a description of these transactions.

First, Glenn sold a tract of land to Bill Sparks for $18,500. Title to the land was held in the name of the partnership. Spark's check was payable to the partnership and was cashed by Glenn at the First City Bank which handled the firm's checking account. Glenn indorsed the firm name "Per Donald Glenn, Partner" and took the cash. Obtaining this amount of cash at the First City Bank was not an uncommon practice for the partnership because the firm paid its substantial weekly payroll and commissions in cash.

Glenn's second series of transactions involved the sale of the firm's former office building for $38,000 to Charles Whitmore. Whitmore was formerly associated with the firm but had left to establish his own real-estate business and was currently a tenant in the firm's old offices. Whitmore was cognizant of the express limitations on the partners' authority contained in the Williams, Watkins, and Glenn partnership agreement. However, Whitmore was assured by Glenn that the requisite consent for his individual actions had been obtained from the other partners regarding the sale in question. Glenn also persuaded Whitmore, "for convenience sake," to make the check payable to his individual order. Glenn cashed the check at one of the savings banks in which the firm had a balance in excess of $50,000.

Glenn's third series of transactions began when he acquired a tract of land for $55,000 from Arthur Douglas. Glenn paid for the land with a partnership check but took record title in his own name. A few days later, two days before leaving for vacation, Glenn closed the sale of this property to Frank Carlson and received a certified check for $58,500 payable to his own order. The proceeds of this sale were not deposited in any of the firm's bank accounts. Glenn has not returned from his vacation. In fact, he is five days overdue and has not communicated with the firm. It was subsequently learned that he cashed the check and retained the funds for his personal use.

Required

1. What rights does the partnership or Williams and Watkins have against Bill Sparks or First City Bank? Explain.
2. What rights does the partnership or Williams and Watkins have against Charles Whitmore? Explain.
3. What rights does the partnership or Williams and Watkins have against Frank Carlson? Explain.
4. What rights does the partnership or Williams and Watkins have against Glenn?

Material from the Uniform CPA Examination, copyright ©, 1975, by the American Institute of Certified Public Accountants, Inc., is here reprinted with permission. This is adapted from Question Number 7 of the November 7, 1975 exam.

3. X, Y, and Z each contributed $75,000 in capital to their partnership in which each partner was to share equally in all profits and losses. X elected to withdraw from the partnership because his personal assets were depleted. An accounting was ordered. It was found that X had advanced to the firm an additional $10,000 several years before the dissolution and this remained unpaid. Y had drawn out $25,000 of his capital before dissolution and Z had drawn out the whole of his, and owed the firm $2,000 which remains unpaid. After selling all of the assets, the partnership had $141,000 but owed $18,000 to firm creditors, and $2,000 to Y for services rendered in winding up the business. Shortly before dissolution P recovered a $12,000 judgment against X as an individual. What amounts should be distributed, if any, at the time of the final distribution. Will P recover anything? If so when and how much?

ENDNOTES

1. J. Crane and A. Bromberg, *Law of Partnership* 280 (1968).
2. See *Dixon* v. *Haynes*, 146 Wash. 163; 262 P. 119 (1927).
3. See Melosevich v. *Cichy,* 30 Wash. 2d. 702, 193 P. 2d 342 (1948).
4. Crane, *supra* note 1 at 309.
5. See, annot. at 54 ALR 2d 330.
6. See, *Hyrne* v. *Erwin,* 23 S.C. 226, 55 Am. Rep. 15 (1885).
7. Crane, *supra* note 1, at 319.
8. A. Conrad, R. Knauss & S. Siegel, *Enterprize Organization,* 645 (1972).
9. *Id.,* at 646.

PART IV
CORPORATIONS

CORPORATIONS: 9
INTRODUCTION, FORMATION
AND CORPORATE PERSONALITY

A corporation has a distinct existence separate from its shareholders. It is an entity in and of itself. This is the noteworthy feature of the corporate form of doing business that provides shareholders with limited liability. The shareholders only put to risk the amount of their investment. If the corporation should go bankrupt the shareholders will lose their investment but they will not be personally liable to the unsatisfied creditors of the corporation. The corporation sues, and is sued, in its own name. It owns property and makes contracts in its own name. The shareholders own the corporation but, they are not the corporation.

The shareholders possess ultimate legal control over corporate affairs. This control is exercised through voting their shares of stock. The shareholders elect the members of the board of directors. The directors have the exclusive authority to manage the corporation. The directors elect the officers, who carry out board policy on a day-to-day basis. It is not infrequent for an individual to be a shareholder, director and officer. In upcoming chapters we will examine in depth the role that each occupies within the corporate sphere.

INTRODUCTION

Corporations come in a variety of forms. There are the "for profit" corporations. This is what most individuals visualize when they hear the term "corporation." It is the ordinary enterprise that has been incorporated and is operated to make a profit which will be distributed to its owners as dividends. In fact, the corporation may suffer a loss or even go bankrupt. Nonetheless, it is still called a "for profit" corporation. "Close" or "closed" corporations are for profit corporations that have very few shareholders, possibly no more than thirty. Typically it is a family enterprise or a former partnership that has been incorporated solely to enjoy the benefits of corporate organization. There are "not-for-profit" corporations. They are incorporated under special corporation statutes. They are reserved for charitable, religious, educational, fraternal and social enterprises. They can be money making operations. However, these profits cannot be distributed to the owners or members. The profits must be devoted to the enterprise's philanthropic causes. There are government corporations created by Congress for specific purposes, the Federal Deposit Insurance Corporation for example. Under the provision of the Internal Revenue Code there can be so-called Sub-Chapter S corporations. There are also joint stock companies, joint ventures, the Massachusetts business trust, and non profit associations. Each serves a limited purpose and is not important for our consideration.

Corporation law is state law. That is not to say that one can ignore the presence of the federal government in corporate matters. We will later observe the significant impact the federal securities laws have on corporate affairs. There are also the federal tax, wage and hour, labor, and civil rights laws to contend with. The regulatory agencies such as the C.A.B. and F.T.C., to just mention two of many, must be dealt with at the federal level. However, the federal government does not grant corporate charters, the individual states possess that power.

At first the privilege of a particular firm doing business as a corporation was granted by special legislative action. Passage of such a bill involved all the normal lobbying, exertions of political pressure, campaign contributions and, some would say, corruption. When the legislature did grant a charter, it placed severe restrictions upon the purpose for which that corporation could operate. The entire process was cumbersome and not pragmatic in a country experiencing tremendous industrial growth. Legislative grants of special business privileges to only a favored few citizens also had an undemocratic flavor. Gradually the states began to enact general incorporation laws. New York was first in 1811. New Jersey did not enact one until 1875 but it was the first "modern" law granting a wide spectrum of powers to its corporations. Such general incorporation statutes changed the granting of a corporate charter from a legislative act to a ministerial task. The corporate form became available to any individual that complied with the law's formalities. The incorporation process became a routine one administered by a state official, typically the Secretary of State.

Each corporation is governed by the business corporation statute of its respective state of incorporation. Because of the important role that these statutes play in corporation law, we have frequently included statutory excerpts. They should be read carefully because they provide a realistic context within which to examine a variety of legal questions. The most frequently quoted statute is that of Illinois. It was selected because it served as the pattern in drafting the Model Business Corporation Act (we have not relied upon the Model Act because it is not actually the "law"). The Delaware statute is oftentimes quoted because of Delaware's popularity as a state of incorporation. Elsewhere, excerpts from the New York and Pennsylvania statutes are included where appropriate.

CORPORATE NATURE

Because a corporation is a legal entity apart from the shareholders does not mean that it automatically enjoys the same rights as an individual. The Constitution speaks in terms of "citizens" or "persons." Do such references include corporations? It depends. The Fourteenth Amandment says that no "person" shall be deprived of due process nor denied equal protection of the laws. Within this context "person" does include corporations. The Fourteenth Amendment also prohibits states from enforcing laws that abridge the privileges or immunities of "citizens" of the United States. Within this context, corporations are not considered "citizens." A corporation incorporated in one state is not free to go into a neighboring state and do business. It must first qualify as a foreign corporation. Yet, a corporation is a citizen of its state of incorporation for diversity of citizenship purposes. The Fifth Amendment protects a "person" from being compelled to be a witness against himself. This self incrimination provision is not available to a corporation. It can be forced to produce documents and records that are incriminating to it and its employees. As one can see, it is impossible to provide generalizations as to when a corporation qualifies as a person or citizen. An interesting discussion of this issues is contained in *Wheeling Steel* v. *Glander,* 337 U.S. 562 (1949).

Until recently corporations were prevented from engaging in a learned profession, such as law or medicine. Licenses to practice such professions are granted to individual human beings. A corporation cannot qualify for such a license. The corporation was also barred from practicing such a profession through its shareholders or employees who were properly licensed. To permit such activity was viewed as being inappropriate, unethical, and against public policy, primarily because the professionals would be able to avail themselves of limited liability. Thus, members of the medical and legal profession were forced to be solo practitioners or to form a partnership. This put them at a disadvantage for some income tax purposes. After a great deal of lobbying by the various professions, many states enacted special incorporation statutes. These statutes permit members of a profession to incorporate and to engage in their profession through that corporation. This allows them to enjoy the tax benefits of corporations. At the same time the statutes are designed to protect the interests of the public that deal with these professions. Protection of the public is accomplished by not allowing the professionals, who incorporate under these statutes, to limit their liability for their acts or for the tortious acts of fellow associates.

WHETHER TO INCORPORATE

The entrepreneur can operate his enterprise as a sole proprietorship, partnership or corporation. The biggest advantage inherent in the corporate form is the limited liability that is extended to the owners. The shareholder limits his risk to the amount of his investment; he bears no unlimited personal liability as does the sole proprietor or general partner. Other advantages are the continuity of existence of the enterprise regardless of additions, withdrawals or death of the owners; the freedom with which ownership interests can be transferred and; the ability to raise capital through the sale of stock. The greatest potential disadvantage is the double taxation-the fact that the corporation pays tax on its profits and, in turn, when these profits are distributed in the form of dividends it constitutes taxable income to the shareholders. However, taxes constitute a two sided coin as the corporate form does offer certain tax advantages. For instance, reasonable salaries paid to employee-shareholders are deductable from gross income and a corporation may reasonably accumulate earnings. A partnership does not deduct partners' salaries as a business expense and a partner is taxed on his share of partnership profits whether they are distributed or not. Another disadvantage of the corporate form is that the necessary corporate formalities of board meetings, shareholder meetings, etc. are more cumbersome and restrictive than the operating procedures in a partnership. See table 2-1 in Chapter 2, *supra,* for a complete outline of the pros and cons of the alternate forms of business associations.

WHERE TO INCORPORATE

An individual is free to incorporate his enterprise in the geographical location of his choice. It is not necessary to have the corporate headquarters, manufacturing facilities or warehouse in the state of incorporation. It may not even be necessary to do business in the state of incorporation; although it may be necessary to have a registered agent and office located in the state. It is usually wise for small and medium size corporations to incorporate in the state where they do their primary business. Different considerations are present for the large corporation which often has a complex capital structure and which engages in business in many states. The corporation statutes can vary in important respects from state to state. Certain features of a given law might be unattractive, such as the Illinois prohibition (contained in § 28) against non voting stock. Another state may permit a type of management flexibility that is inviting.

Delaware has traditionally enjoyed popularity as a state of incorporation. Many of our country's corporate giants are incorporated there. Why is that? Because Delaware has a modern statute that permits corporations to operate with wide flexibility. A large number of technical requirements do not exist as obstacles to management action. One can say, without being derogatory, that the Delaware statute is "pro business." It supplies a favorable corporate atmosphere. To maintain this position in times of changing social and economic conditions, the legislature is not hesitant to amend the statute.

The decision as to where to incorporate is based upon self-interest. One selects the location that is most favorable to him. A state's tax advantages, its degree of management flexibility and the powers granted to shareholders, the obstacles it places in front of those attempting a corporate take over, etc. are some of the factors to be weighed. What constitutes an important factor to one group considering incorporation can be relatively unimportant to another group with different needs and interests.

HOW TO INCORPORATE

A corporation doesn't simply blossom into existence. Someone must perform the work necessary to breath corporate life into an enterprise. Planning and work must be done before the required incorporation documents are filed. The design of the corporation must be formulated. Subscriptions for its shares of stock must be solicited, property and employees acquired, and all the other necessary items leading up to incorporation performed. The individuals that occupy this role are called "promoters."

PROMOTERS

Naturally the promotion process involves certain expenses. The promoter will desire reimbursement of these expenses and possibly compensation for his services as a promoter. The promoter will be paid if: the state's business corporation statute makes the corporation responsible for the reasonable expenses of its promotion; the articles of incorporation specify payment; or the corporation, once formed, agrees to pay. Whether or not promotion expenses will be paid is not a problem. The promoter typically will also be an influential shareholder and director of the resulting corporation. He will be in a position to see that he is paid. Legal issues can arise over the amount or form taken by such compensation. The fiduciary duties created by an agency-principal relationship occupy a significant position in corporation law. The promoter stands in a fiduciary relationship to the corporation and the initial group of shareholders. Thus, while he is permitted to make a profit, he cannot make a secret profit. A promoter can legitimatize his profit pursuing one of four courses: (a) He may provide an independent board of officers in no respect directly or indirectly under his control, and make full disclosure to the corporation through them. (b) He may make a full disclosure of all material facts to each original subscriber of shares in the corporation. (c) He may procure a ratification of the contract after disclosing its circumstances by vote of the stockholders of the completely established corporation. (d) He may be himself the real subscriber of all the shares of the capital stock. [*Old Dominion Copper Mining & Smelting Co.* v. *Bigelow,* 89 N.E. 193 (1909)]. The promoter does not owe a fiduciary duty towards persons who subsequently acquire the stock from the original shareholders. However, these subsequent shareholders can rely upon the state and federal securities laws to provide them with some degree of protection against fraud.

In the booming speculative investment days of the late 1800s and early 1900s, a common method of fleecing the public was through "watered stock." A promoter might have shares issued to him as fully paid when, in fact, he had not paid full value. He might greatly inflate the value of his services as promoter and then take his payment in stock. Or, he might sell property, of slight or dubious value, to the corporation at an inflated price taking payment either in cash or stock. Suppose the promoter received $1,000 worth of stock in return for property whose value did not exceed $100. That corporation has $900 of watered stock; it has issued $900 worth of stock for which it has received no assets or services. A subsequent investor would become an owner of a company whose true assets were below those reflected on its books. His stock would be worth less than the value he paid. The individual receiving watered stock is liable to the corporation for the unpaid value of his stock. Today, stock watering is a rare occurence.

Oftentimes, it will be necessary for the promoter to make contracts during the promotion process. The corporation is not liable on the pre-incorporation contract unless, after it was incorporated, it incurred liability through its action or inaction. For example, the board might pass a resolution accepting the contract; it might start making installment payments under the contract; or it may refrain from taking action but accept the benefits of the contract. In such instances, the corporation is said to have "adopted" the contract. Adoption is the functional equivalent of ratification in agency law. The corporation is not liable on the contract in the first instance because it was not in existence when the contract was made. Although the promoter made the contract for the future benefit of the corporation, legally he was acting for himself. One cannot be an agent for a non-existent principal.

What of the promoter's personal contract liability? The promoter is not automatically relieved of liability simply because the corporation has adopted the contract. The general rule is that the promoter is liable on such pre-incorporation contracts unless: 1) the contract provides that he is relieved of personal liability; or 2) a novation occurs (the promoter, corporation and the contracting third party all agree to release the promoter from liability). The *Philipsborn* v. *Suson* case that follows breaks new ground on the question of promoter's contract liability. The Illinois Supreme Court holds that the intentions of the parties, at the time the contract was made, determines the promoter's liability. Whether this legal position gains widespread acceptance remains to be seen.

H.F. PHILIPSBORN & CO. v. SUSON
322 N.E. 2d 45 (1974) (S. Ct. Ill.)

◆◆◆

The testimony shows that plaintiff was an Illinois corporation engaged in the business of mortgage banking and that it had previously financed two apartment projects for Suson, a real estate developer. Following several discussions between Suson and officials of plaintiff concerning financing for a proposed real estate development, an application in the name of Estates, for a construction and mortgage loan, was prepared by plaintiff. The application, prepared on a printed form, was signed "North Shore Estates, Inc., by Morris Suson Pres." It stated that Estates applied for a "construction and permanent first mortgage loan" in the amount of $5,488,000. The following words were printed on one line of the loan application form: "Title to be in the name of." In a space following those words there was typed "Trust to be formed." Immediately following, printed in ink, appeared the words "or corporation to be formed." The parties agree that this last addition was printed by Suson. The application also provided that acceptance by plaintiff within 60 days "shall constitute a binding contract to make said loan" and that "In such event we agree to pay you a commission equal to 2 percent of the loan."

The testimony shows that while the parties were discussing a performance bond and other matters relating to the loan Suson applied to another mortgage banker for a construction and mortgage loan on the same project. This application was for a larger principal amount at a lower interest rate. This second application was accepted, and sometime thereafter, when plaintiff sent Estates the mortgage documents and the note to be executed, they were returned unsigned.

The loan application, which consisted of two printed pages and a one-page typewritten "Rider," contained provisions concerning, *inter alia,* interest rates, amortization schedules and prepayment privileges and premiums. It provided for the erection of the improvements in three sections, designated A, B, and C, and set forth the stages of the completion of those sections when the mortgage funds would be disbursed. The printed portion of the loan application contained a provision for the deposit of a standby fee, and in the space provided for the insertion of the amount of the fee there appeared the typed words "See attached rider." The rider provided that "In lieu of a standby fee, Morris Suson will execute and deliver 3 demand judgment notes, each in the amount of $10,000.00, payable to you without interest. Upon the opening of the loan in each section, one of said notes is to be cancelled and returned to us."

The record reflects that Suson executed three notes payable to the order of plaintiff, each being in the principal amount of $10,000, payable on demand and providing for no interest. Each note bears the legend "This note is subject to application dated September 17, 1963, under all the terms and conditions under such application."

The judgment in the amount of $109,760 was entered on the count in plaintiff's complaint which sought to recover the 2 percent commission due upon acceptance of the loan. The judgment in the amount of $30,000 was entered on plaintiff's count based on the three promissory notes executed by Suson. The issues concerning a third count of plaintiff's complaint, on which the verdicts were directed, will be discussed later.

Plaintiff concedes that it intended Estates to be the obligor on the loan application and that the application, of itself, imposed no individual liability on Suson for the payment of its commission. It contends, however, that Estates, which purportedly applied for the loan, did not, at the time of the application, exist as a corporate entity, and that plaintiff, at that time, was not aware of that fact. The record shows that on September 17, 1963, when the application was signed, there was no corporate entity named North Shore Estates, Inc. It was incorporated on November 12, 1963, with a paid-in capital of $1,000 and with Suson as the sole shareholder and director. The corporate minutes reflect that the Board of Directors "approved and adopted all acts of Morris Suson to date and assumed liability therefor."

It is plaintiff's theory "that in the absence of a knowing agreement to the contrary" Suson, as the promoter of Estates, "is personally liable on a pre-incorporation contract and is not released by subsequent incorporation and ratification of the contract." It argues that "The general rule concerning promoters' contracts is that the promoter will be personally liable on contracts signed on behalf of a non-existent corporation unless the contract provides to the contrary." The record shows that the circuit court admitted testimony on the question whether plaintiff knew that Estates was not in existance when the application was executed. This testimony was admitted on the theory that the language "or corporation to be formed" which appeared on the line on which were printed the words "Title to be in the name of" was ambiguous as to whether the corporation to be formed was North Shore Estates, Inc., the applicant for the loan, or a corporate titleholder mortgagor. Plaintiff contends that the question whether it was unaware of the nonexistence of Estates was properly submitted to the jury and that the appellate court erred in holding that the verdict was against the manifest weight of the evidence.

The parties to this appeal appear to be in agreement that, unless the parties to the transaction agree otherwise, an individual who conducts the ordinary affairs of a business in the name of a nonexistent corporation is personally liable, both at common law (*Bigelow* v. *Gregory*, 73 Ill. 197), and by statute (Ill. Rev. Stat. 1973, ch. 32, par. 157.150), on contracts made in connection with the business. However, the authorities dealing with a promoter's personal liability on contracts made for the benefit of a proposed corporation present a wide array of factual situations and many so-called general rules. ... A number of the decisions of this court and the appellate court are relevant to the liability of persons who exercise corporate powers without authority ... but none deal with the precise issue here presented. A number of the decisions of the courts of review of other jurisdictions state that where a promoter had become liable on a pre-incorporation contract, he was not, in the absence of an agreement to that effect, discharged from liability merely because the corporation was later organized and ratified the contract. . . . We have examined these cases and find that, in many, either the statement was *dicta* [see, *e.g.,* King features *Syndicate* v. *Courrier* (1950), 241 Iowa 870, 43 N.W. 2d 718, 41 A.L.R. 2d 467, the corporation was never formed], the contract was in the name of the promoter [see, *e.g., Mansfield* v. *Lang* (1936), 293 Mass. 386, 200 N.E. 110], or the rule was not applied [see *e.g., Strause* v. *Richmond* Woodworking Co. (1909), 109 Va. 724, 65 S.E. 659].

We find the facts of *Whitney* v. *Wyman,* 101 U.S. 392 (1879) . . . similar to those of this case and the reasoning more persuasive. In that case a letter was sent to Baxter Whitney stating, "Our company being so far organized, by direction of the officers, we now order from you * * *" certain machinery and was signed "Charles Wyman, Edward P. Ferry, Carlton L. Storrs, Prudential Committee Grand Haven Fruit Basket Co." Baxter, in a letter addressed to the Grand Haven Fruit Basket Co., accepted the order for the machinery. The machinery was delivered but Baxter's sight draft on Wyman, Ferry and Storrs was protested because it was addressed to them individually. The letters of order and acceptance were dated February 1, 1869, and February 10, 1869, respectively, which was before the articles of incorporation were filed with the Secretary of State and the county clerk and, therefore, before the corporation was authorized to do business. Whitney filed an action against Wyman, Ferry and Storrs, individually, to recover the value of the machinery.

The rule applied by the court was that whether liability will be imposed upon the promoter depends upon the intent of the parties. It found from the exchange of letters "that both parties understood and meant that the contract was to be and, in fact, was with the corporation and not with the defendants individually." (101 U.S. at 396) . . . In response to the argument that his intent could not be given effect because the corporation was forbidden to do any business when the letters were written, the court said: "The corporation subsequently ratified the contract by recognizing and treating it as valid. This made it in all respects what it would have been if the requisite corporate power had existed when it was entered into." . . .

In our opinion, insofar as the loan commission and the notes executed by Suson and delivered in lieu of the standby fee were concerned, the question whether there was acceptance of the loan application, and one other issue discussed later in this opinion, were the only issues of fact for determination by the jury. A contract is to be construed to give effect to the intent of the parties, . . . and effect must be given to the contract as written and any documents executed contemporaneously therewith. . . . In this transaction, so far as this record reflects, plaintiff required no showing of Estates' assets nor did it make any inquiry concerning its solvency. Estates was organized within 60 days of the execution of the loan application, and upon its approval and adoption of Suson's acts to date, and its assumption of liability for those acts, plaintiff had received everything for which it had bargained. The record shows that when the loan application was signed Suson had an option to acquire, but did not own, the land on which the proposed project was to be built, and that upon acquisition title was to be taken in either a trust or corporation, in either event, not in existence, but "to be formed." Clearly, under these circumstances, plaintiff looked only to Estates for its commission, and the fact that Estates had not at that time been formed furnished no basis for the imposition of personal liability on Suson for the payment of the loan commission. In contrast, plaintiff required, and Suson executed and delivered in lieu of the standby fee, notes on which he was personally liable. On this record we hold that whether or not Estates existed as a corporate entity at the time the application was executed, or whether plaintiff knew that it was not, was not controlling, and that although we do not agree with its rationale, the appellate court correctly reversed the judgment entered against Suson in the amount of $109,760.

We do not agree with the appellate court that the circuit court erred in entering the judgment against Suson based on the promissory notes. Here, too, the intent of the parties is clear. The purpose of depositing the notes in lieu of the standby fee was to obtain the commitment from the lender that the mortgage funds would be made available in accordance with the terms of the loan agreement. The record shows that such commitment was obtained, and when Estates breached its agreement to borrow the money thus committed, plaintiff was entitled to demand payment of the notes. We have considered Suson's contentions that there was no consideration for the standby fee and that it cannot be recovered by plaintiff for the reason that it was a penalty, and not liquidated damages, and find them to be without merit. Except for the provision contained in the notes that they are subject to the terms and conditions of the application, they are in the usual form of promissory notes and contain the usual cognovit clause, and there is nothing in the record which serves to relieve Suson of personal liability to pay them. . . . We hold that in reversing the judgment against Suson in the amount of $30,000 the appellate court erred.

We turn now to plaintiff's contention that the circuit court erred in directing a verdict in favor of Suson on the third count of its complaint and that the appellate court erred in affirming the judgment entered on the directed verdict. This count was predicated on the theory that Suson, as sole shareholder and director of Estates, had tortiously induced Estates to breach its loan agreement with plaintiff. In affirming the judgment the appellate court held that plaintiff failed to show that Suson had induced Estates to breach the contract. . . .

Since *Doremus* v. *Hennessy,* 176 Ill. 608, 52 N.E. 924, decided in 1898, there has been no question in this jurisdiction that the tortious inducement of breach of contract will give rise to an action for damages. It is equally clear however that a corporate officer may, for a proper business purpose and in good faith, influence the actions of the corporation. . . . In order to recover from Suson on the theory here advanced, plaintiff was required to show that Suson acted either without justification or maliciously, and this it failed to do. The evidence shows that he obtained a loan for more money at a lower interest rate and fails to show that he acted by reason of malice or for any unlawful purpose. The circuit court did not err in directing a verdict in favor of Suson. . . .

Affirmed in part and reversed in part.

◆ ◆ ◆

Case Questions

1. Based upon the limited factual pattern sketched in this decision, what does the intention of the parties appear to have been?
2. Is it more pragmatic to impose liability by retroactive speculation as to the parties intent or by applying a mechanical rule that the promoter is liable unless the contract provides to the contrary? Which is the more equitable rule?
3. In light of the fact that Suson was the sole shareholder, and a director, was the court too quick in saying that he did not maliciously obtain the second loan?

INCORPORATION PROCESS

To actually incorporate a business, one must comply with the statutory formalities of the particular state. A document referred to variously as the "articles of incorporation," "certificate of incorporation" or corporate "charter" is filed with the secretary of state. It is signed by the "incorporators." Many times the promoters will also be the incorporators. The information required in the articles is fairly standardized. The Illinois articles of incorporation that follow provide a good illustration. The amount of the required filing fees is indicated at the end of the form.

ARTICLES OF INCORPORATION

The undersigned.

Name	Number	Street	Address City	State
. . . .				
. . . .				
. . . .				
. . . .				

being one or more natural persons of the age of twenty-one years or more or a corporation, and having subscribed to shares of the corporation to be organized pursuant hereto, for the purpose of forming a corporation under "The Business Corporation Act" of the State of Illinois, do hereby adopt the following Articles of Incorporation:

ARTICLE ONE

The name of the corporation hereby incorporated is: . . . .

. . . .

ARTICLE TWO

The *address* of its initial registered office in the State of Illinois is: . . . . . .

. . . . Street, in the . . . . of . . . . . .

. . . . (. . . . .) County of . . . .
(Zip Code)

and the *name* of its initial Registered Agent at *said address* is: . . . .

. . . .

ARTICLE THREE

The duration of the corporation is: . . . .

ARTICLE FOUR

The purpose or purposes for which the corporation is organized are:

ARTICLE FIVE

Paragraph 1: The aggregate number of shares which the corporation is authorized to issue is . . . ., divided into . . . . classes. The designation of each class, the number of shares of each class, and the par value, if any, of the shares of each class, or a statement that the shares of any class are without par value, are as follows:

Class	Series (If any)	Number of Shares	Par value per share or statement that shares are without par value

Paragraph 2: The preferences, qualifications, limitations, restrictions and the special or relative rights in respect of the shares of each class are:

ARTICLE SIX

The class and number of shares which the corporation proposes to issue without further report to the Secretary of State, and the consideration (expressed in dollars) to be received by the corporation therefor, are:

Class of shares	Number of shares	Total consideration to be received therefor:
		$ _____
		$ _____

ARTICLE SEVEN

The corporation will not commence business until at least one thousand dollars has been received as consideration for the issuance of shares.

ARTICLE EIGHT

The number of directors to be elected at the first meeting of the shareholders is: . . . .

ARTICLE NINE

Paragraph 1: It is estimated that the value of all property to be owned by the corporation for the following year wherever located will be $ . . . .
Paragraph 2: It is estimated that the value of the property to be located within the State of Illinois during the following year will be $ . . . .
Paragraph 3: It is estimated that the gross amount of business which will be transacted by the corporation during the following year will be $ . . . .
Paragraph 4: It is estimated that the gross amount of business which will be transacted at or from places of business in the State of Illinois during the following year will be $ . . . .

NOTE: If all the property of the corporation is to be located in this State and all of its business is to be transacted at or from places of business in this State, or if the incorporators elect to pay the initial franchise tax on the basis of its entire stated capital and paid-in surplus, then the information called for in Article Nine need not be stated.

. . . .

. . . .
                                                    Incorporators
. . . .

. . . .

NOTE: There may be one or more incorporators. Each incorporator shall be either a corporation, domestic or foreign, or a natural person of the age of twenty-one years or more. If a corporation acts as incorporator, the name of the corporation and state of incorporation shall be shown and the execution must be by its President or Vice-President and verified by him, and the corporate seal shall be affixed and attested by its Secretary or an Assistant Secretary.

OATH AND ACKNOWLEDGEMENT

The following fees are required to be paid at the time of issuing certificate of corporation: Filing fee, $75.00; Initial license fee of 50¢ per $1,000.00 or 1/20th of 1% of the amount of stated capital and paid-in surplus the corporation proposes to issue without further report (Article Six); Initial franchise tax of 1/10th of 1% of the issued, as above noted. However, the minimum initial franchise tax is $100.00.

Once the articles are filed the Secretary of State checks them to ascertain if they comply with all the formal statutory requirements. If they do, and if all the required fees have been paid, the Secretary will file one copy in his office and return the other copy to the incorporators accompanied by a certificate of incorporation. Many states also require the incorporators to then file a copy of the articles and certificate of incorporation in the county of the corporation's principal place of business. Although the enterprise now has a corporate existence, it must be organized before beginning business.

Organization of a corporation is a two step process. The first step is a meeting of the subscribers to the corporation's shares and the incorporators. They elect the directors and adopt a set of by-laws. The articles are very general in nature. The by-laws are rather detailed and contain the specifics for regulating the internal affairs of the corporation. For example, the articles will specify the number of directors but will be silent as to their qualifications, term of office, compensation, etc. These latter matters are covered in the by-laws. The by-laws also cover such items as: the time and place of shareholders and directors meetings; the percentage of affirmative votes for approval of a measure; quorum requirements and notice provisions for meetings; the selection and removal process for directors and officers; and the officers and their respective duties. The power to alter, amend or repeal the by-laws rests with either the directors or shareholders depending upon the particular state's law. Occasionally a conflict may exist between the provisions of the by-laws, articles or state statute. Which document is supreme and will control? The by-laws are subordinate to the articles, which in turn, are subordinate to the business corporation statute.

Suppose a corporation complies with all the statutory requirements and then the state amends the statute. Can the state force the corporation to alter its articles to conform with the amendment? In 1819 the Supreme Court in *Dartmouth College* v. *Woodward,* 4 Wheat 518, held that when a state grants a charter to a corporation it is entering a contract with that corporation. The U.S. Constitution prohibits the enactment of legislation which would impair the obligations of a contract. Therefore, a state cannot amend its statute and force corresponding alterations in a corporate charter unless it reserves this right to itself in the business corporation statute. For practical reasons most states do reserve this power in their legislative branch (See § 162 Illinois statute).

The second step in the organization process is the first formal meeting of the board of directors. It usually follows immediately after the meeting of the subscribers. The directors proceed to elect the officers, accept stock subscription agreements, adopt the form of the share certificate, accept contracts, and perform any other actions necessary to get the corporation underway.

DEFECTIVELY FORMED CORPORATIONS

A "de jure" corporation is a legal, validly formed corporation. If a corporation has not been perfectly formed, yet is in substantial compliance with the business corporation statute, it is said to be a "de facto" corporation. This simply means that the state of incorporation can challenge its existence as a corporation in a quo warranto proceeding. (A quo warranto proceeding is a legal action compelling a corporation to show by what authority it is transacting business). The state can force the corporation to comply with the law or, if it refuses, force it to cease doing business as a corporation. Once a corporation has been perfectly formed, it must continue to comply with the statutory requirements. In some states if a corporation does not file the required reports and pay its franchise tax the state attorney general can force its involuntary dissolution. There is a third category of corporation that is no corporation at all. For lack of a better name it is called a "defectively formed" corporation. It is carrying on business as a corporation without substantial compliance with the state's corporation-statute. The owners of this business are personally liable for the debts of the alleged corporation. Where does one draw the line between a de facto and a defectively formed corporation? What constitutes substantial compliance with the business corporation statute? At one time such questions provoked litigation. Today, the problem is almost non existent because of statutes like the following one in Illinois:

§ 49. EFFECT OF ISSUANCE OF CERTIFICATE OF INCORPORATION.

Upon the issuance of the certificate of incorporation by the Secretary of State, the corporate existence shall begin, and such certificate of incorporation shall be conclusive evidence, except as against the State, that all conditions precedent required to be performed by the incorporators have been complied with and that the corporation has been incorporated under this Act.

Such a statute operates to make all corporations receiving a certificate of incorporation at the very least, a de facto corporation.

DISREGARDING THE CORPORATE ENTITY

After annunciating the general proposition that a corporation is an entity separate and distinct from its shareholders, let us now examine an exception. Under certain circumstances a court will "disregard the corporate entity" or "pierce the corporate veil" and hold the owner liable for the actions of his corporation. The power to pierce the corporate veil is an equitable one designed to prevent the evasion of statutes, perpetration of frauds or any other activity that is against public policy. For example, if an individual is ordered by a court to cease and desist from an activity, he cannot avoid the prohibition by forming a corporation to continue that activity. In such an instance, a court would disregard the corporate entity and would attribute the corporation's actions to the individual. He would be in contempt of court for violating the cease and desist order. Sometimes a court will speak of disregarding the corporate entity when the owner is the "alter ego" of the corporation. The following are other examples of the abuse of the corporate privilege leading to the disregard of the corporate entity: 1) Where the owners of the corporation add or withdraw capital from the corporation at will, thereby treating the corporate assets as their own. 2) Where the owner almost predestines the corporation to financial failure by inadequately capitalizing the venture. 3) Where the owner has previously held himself out to be personally liable for the corporate debts.

It is not infrequent for questions of piercing the corporate veil to arise within the context of parent-subsidiary corporate relationships. A subsidiary corporation is one that has a majority of its stock owned by another corporation, called the parent corporation. If the parent owns 100 percent of the stock it is called a "wholly owned" subsidiary. Subsidiaries are very common and are formed for a large number of legitimate reasons. Perhaps a new venture is highly risky and success is speculative. A corporation may want to engage in the venture and simultaneously limit its liability. It can achieve this by forming a subsidiary to conduct the venture. Or, maybe a corporation exports raw materials from other countries and one of those countries enacts a higher tax on exports by foreign corporations. The corporation then incorporates a subsidiary in that country to export the material and qualify for the lower tax rate.

Usually the directors and officers of the parent will serve in the same capacity for the subsidiary. The respective corporate headquarters may be in the same building. These factors, in and of themselves, do not automatically make the parent liable for the contracts or torts of its subsidiary. The courts examine the degree to which the corporate formalities are honored and the manner in which the parent controls the subsidiary. The separateness of the two entities will usually be recognized if: 1) the subsidiary is adequately capitalized considering the nature of the undertaken enterprise; 2) the corporate formalities are observed, i.e. separate board meetings, etc.; 3) the corporate records and accounts are not commingled; and 4) care is taken to maintain the corporation's separate identities in the eyes of the public.

The article by George Ashe that follows examines in greater detail the issue of disregarding the corporate entity. The article is then followed by the *Consolidated Sun Ray* v. *Oppenstein* case. It illustrates a situation where the parent corporation completely dominates its subsidiary so as to lose its limited liability and incur financial responsibility to a creditor of the subsidiary.

LIFTING THE CORPORATE VEIL: CORPORATE ENTITY IN THE MODERN DAY COURT*

I. INTRODUCTION

One of the most difficult and frustrating problems that constantly arises to plague the commercial lawyer is the Siamese twin of corporate entity, and individual liability in the contractual obligations created by creditor-debtor relationships. What is the extent of responsibility of a single or small group of stockholders vis-a-vis the corporation in which they own all the stock? Or to what extent is liability applicable as between a parent corporation and its wholly owned subsidiary? What affect does complete and dominant control have on the concept of separate identity and limited liability, and is domination alone sufficient to sustain an attack on corporate entity? The test, as will be noted, whenever the claim of separateness is advanced to ward off attacks on corporate entity, usually revolves around the question of substantial identity. In a word, is the corporation being attacked the alter ego of its' owners, that is, simply a shell intended to insulate the owners from personal liability? ...

The logical question invariably posed is why one who contracted with a corporation, and performed his obligation only to learn that fulfillment by the corporation was impossible, should be allowed to seek recovery from the

*By George Ashe Reprinted with permission from Vol. 78 No. 4 of the *Commercial Law Journal* (April 1973) pp 121-129 Copyright©1973 Commercial Law League of America.

individual stockowners, or from a parent corporation. On the basis of the contract alone, the claim must be denied, the exception being when there are compelling facts that require otherwise.

What are these other factors that would sustain an attack designed to destroy the fiction of corporate entity and deny to its' owners the limited liability they sought? What are the circumstances that would warrant disregarding separate entity? It is well to remember that the primary purpose underlying the creation of corporate entities is the limited liability it affords stockholders, and that when the state granted the status of a corporation to engage in a business enterprise, the stockowners had every right to believe the entity was inviolable. But while the acceptance of this fiction was intended to protect stockholders from individual liability for any corporate obligations, and limited liability was and still is the primary function, it was never intended that the corporate body was to be used as a vehicle to perpetrate fraud, injustice or wrongdoing. . . .

The rapid growth of the closely held corporate entity with stock ownership found in one or a few dominant stockowners, or where there are a group of small corporations owned and controlled by the same persons engaged in what should be viewed as a single enterprise, compels the application of equitable remedies with greater frequency whenever separate identity is under attack. Examples of these conditions are generally found in the multi-corporate aggregations resorted to in the development and construction of large housing or apartment projects, modern shopping centers, industrial parks, or similar enterprises, where one corporation is used to acquire and own land, another corporation to undertake actual construction, and possibly a third to function as a purchaser of materials and services required for construction.

Investigation of these separate entities almost invariably discloses that all are closely held, with the same limited group of stockholders invariably constituting all the officers and directors. And although it may appear that all the corporate trappings exist, i.e., charter, organization meeting, and the election of officers and directors, thereafter all semblance of separateness ceases, and corporate activities are conducted as though they were a single enterprise, having the same headquarters, the same employees, and sometimes even one set of books. When these conditions exist courts no longer mechanically regard the corporation as a rigid legal device having definite, settled and invariable consequences. Emphasis is more and more directed to examination of underlying factors as they affect the entity when sole and dominant stockholders seek to insulate themselves from liability by using the corporate concept to conceal what actually is their dealing as individuals.

The concept of immunity from individual liability applies only as long as the stockholders do not use the corporation for their own purposes, for then the corporation is simply the alter ego or instrumentality of the individuals. . . .

Significant factors in considering separate entity cases are whether there has been a lack of observance of corporate formalities, or evidence of fraud or deception, of unfair dealings benefiting insiders, or injustice or imposition to the detriment of corporate creditors, and not merely ownership control or even domination. . . .

II. SINGLE OR SEPARATE IDENTITY

The modern approach to a resolution of the thorny problem of separateness, with some isolated exceptions where strict adherence to proof of substantive deviation is the rule, is to avoid obeisance to the rigid concept of the sanctity of corporate entity. Where the equities demand such a solution, the fiction will be disregarded, especially when facts are alleged and proved that substantiate an assertion of oneness. Hence it is important to ascertain, as far as possible, what factors are present that will support a claim directed against corporate entity, allege these facts precisely, and support them with proof at trial.

Unquestionably in these entity cases it is reasonable to assume that when the laws of a state are utilized in order to do business in the corporate form, the stockowners have every right to rely on such laws as a shield against personal liability. But where there is evidence of bad faith or other imposition, or where it is obvious that its formation or subsequent use were intended to subserve some fraudulent, unlawful or unjust purpose, or where there is strong evidence of mismanagement coupled with overreaching or self serving transactions favoring insiders, then the corporate entity should be disregarded and the veil lifted, otherwise it would encourage such dealings and certainly would be an invitation to their continuance. . . .

But this disregard of the corporate entity is not lightly undertaken, purely on a basis of sole ownership of stock, or even domination, either by an individual or a small group of stockowners, or of a parent corporation. The issue is a factual one and each case must be decided on its own merits; the facts must be alleged in the pleadings, and they must be proved by a sufficient preponderance of evidence to convince a tryer of the facts that the entity under attack is nothing more than an instrumentality, or alter ego, of its controlling stockowners, that it serves no real business purpose, and to all intents and purposes simply is an agency created to insulate the principals from personal liability, while they pursue their personal advancement in complete disregard of corporate responsibility.

The broad scope of the equitable powers of the courts in going behind the corporate screen is quite evident in those cases in which dominant or controlling stockowners have been charged with the liabilities of the dominated corporation merely on evidence of a violation of the tenets of fair dealing, of fraud whether active or constructive, or any breach of good faith due the corporation. The very nature of such relationships makes this treatment essential so that the interests of creditors in less favored positions will be protected, and, hopefully, that it will act as a deterrent to others bent on the same practices. But the evidence of such misconduct must be convincing since the veil will not be lifted merely to give a litigant an advantage at law to which the facts and circumstances do not entitle him.

The thrust of court rulings in such cases is to disregard separate entity only when it is clearly shown that such separate existence is a mere sham, that the dominated corporation serves no real purpose, and actually is being used as a shield to conceal the depredations of its controllers. . . .

The importance of presenting convincing evidence is evident in numerous cases where attacks were made on corporate entity, but failed to accomplish their object, because as stated in *Maley* v. *Carroll,"*[1] . . . the occurrences here do

[1] 381 F.2d 147, 155 (1967).

not add up to malevolent manipulations, "warranting disregard of corporate identity. . . . It is quite obvious from a comparison of the cases in which claims of oneness were denied with those involving the "malevolent manipulations' . . . that disregard of corporate entity can only follow where it is clear that the corporation itself was not treated as a separate and distinct entity by their directors or managers. . . .

In *Maule Industries*[2] an attempt was made to "pierce the corporate veil" asserting identity of names of stockholders and officers, and close stockownership, as sufficient ground for disregard. The Court did not consider this sufficient to justify a disregard of separate entity absent affirmative proof that the corporation existed in form only, and not in substance.

A reverse application of the single identity concept is evident in *American Indemnity Co.* v. *Southern Missionary College*[3] where separate entities were ignored. Here a college mercantile enterprise was created, wholly owned and controlled by the college. The store was burglarized and the college sought to recover under its' insurance policy. Although the Court recognized there were separate entities, nevertheless in the application of equitable principles it chose to disregard the separate entity in holding the dual existence to be a mere fiction of law, since the college dominated the activities of the store down to the last detail and therefore considered them to be identical to all intents and purposes.

III. CRITERIA TO SUPPORT DISREGARD

Just what factors must be present to support efforts to "pierce the corporate veil?" Essentially, each case must be judged on its own merits, and does not necessarily require the presence of every factor. Some of the factors that would be persuasive in arriving at a single identity determination are that the corporation was formed (1) to conceal the perpetration of fraud or other illegality; (2) to aid in the working of an injustice; (3) to provide a business conduit or instrumentality, or alter ego, of the individuals, dominant stockowners, or related corporations; (4) that there are indicia of insider deals between controlling or dominant stockholders and the corporation; (5) that there is a lack of corporate voice in directing its activities; (6) that there is an indiscriminate commingling of assets; (7) the dominated corporation was under-capitalized.

The extent and variety of criteria that will sustain a disregard of corporate entity may be seen in the decision of *Auto Del Golfo* v. *Resnick*[4] . . . [T]he issue was whether the trial court was correct in "piercing the corporate veil" and holding stockholder defendants liable as individuals for the price of autos. On appeal the verdict was sustained on findings that (1) the alleged corporation never issued any stock; (2) its capital was grossly inadequate for the amount of business it did; (3) it did not maintain a bank account; (4) that there had been no contributions to capital, and so ruled notwithstanding a complete absence of any evidence of fraud or other misconduct usually present in such cases. . . .

---

[2] 232 F.2d 294, (1956)
[3] 260 S.W. 2d 269 (1953)
[4] 306 P2d 1 (1957)

IV. DOMINATION-MISMANAGEMENT-INSTRUMENTALITY

Dealings between dominant stockowners or persons closely related to them, between managing officers or directors, or other insiders, and the dominated corporation quite obviously must be suspect. When there is evidence of dealings to advance self-interest, or when there is a conflict of interest, mismanagement or consistent spoliation, these would be indicative of a domination that casts the dominated corporation in the role of agent or instrumentality, in short the alter ego of the principals. If these conditions prevail then disregard of the corporate fiction of separate entity would be warranted. . . .

In the *Deep Rock Case*[5] the evidence indicated not only mismanagement by the parent but other abuses, such as loans made during financial stringency to enable payment of dividends to preferred stockholders in order to deny them exercising a voice or vote in management, a dubious lease arrangement, questionable payments for alleged management, engineering and financial advice, as well as wholly inadequate capitalization. These and a variety of other questionable devices used to siphon off assets were deemed sufficient to warrant "piercing the corporate veil." . . .

But reliance on any one facet alone indicative of domination of the satellite, absent fraud, will not suffice to induce a disregard of corporate entity. It is only when under-capitalization, domination or identical ownership, by themselves or together is evident in conjunction with other criteria such as fraud, misconduct, over-reaching, insider deals and manipulation that the veil should be lifted so as to expose as invalid the claims of limited liability which are the absolute concomitant of corporate entity. It is only when a combination of these criteria appear simultaneously that the different segments begin to lose their identity. . . .

Additionally, the concept has sometimes been applied in a reverse manner, where separate entity was disregarded not to charge stockowners with liability but to achieve equity in enabling them to recoup losses, as witness *Kendall* v. *Klapperthal.*[6] In this case a number of persons had associated themselves together in four different corporations to promote the development of land near Reading, Pa. Each of the corporations engaged in a separate function of the whole enterprise. Some of the directors endorsed notes of one of the four, the money being used for proper corporate purposes of that particular entity. The operations of this corporation were unsuccessful, and its assets suffered considerable shrinkage. By fortuitous circumstances, one of the other corporations realized a substantial profit and the directors then voted to repay from its funds the directors who had assumed the note. The plaintiff sued to set aside this action, asserting the separate identity. The court gave scant consideration to this claim and had this to say of such assertions: ". . . not to be reimbursed as far as possible out of such assets simply because of the absence of strict legal identity between the two organizations is one which is wholly barren of real merit in a court of equity. . . ."

V. CONCLUSION

From the foregoing analysis it is abundantly clear that the doctrine of corporate entity invariably will be sustained when it is evident that the purpose

---

[5] 306 U.S. 309 (1939)
[6] 202 Pa. 596 (1902)

of incorporation was to carry on a legitimate business, that in fact, such activities actually were carried on by the organization for corporate purposes, and that all requisite formalities of corporate functions were observed. But where the contrary is shown, and there is a lack of substantial evidence to support assertions of separate identity, then the most ardent protestations against imposing personal liability will be of no avail. When the facts demonstrate that the corporate entity was no more than the alter ego, a marionette, and that all its activities disclosed a complete avoidance of corporate responsibility, such claims are unworthy of consideration.

Additionally, it is quite evident that whenever a contractual creditor-debtor relationship is the subject of litigation, and efforts are made to "pierce the corporate veil", there are no fixed rules or formulae that will make a judicial determination predictable. Rather we find there must be a combination of circumstances among which insufficient capitalization would be a persuasive factor. Lack of adequate financial or business records, common officers and directors with the same personnel using the same facilities are important factors in sustaining attacks on corporate entity. But the most persuasive criteria would be fraud, manipulation, insider deals, or other conduct denoting a complete disregard of fiduciary responsibility. . . .

The whole concept of disregard can be summed up thusly: where control by dominant or sole stockowners, or by a parent corporation is carried out in a normal manner, with due regard for all the necessary formalities and for the rights of creditors, separate entity should be sustained. However, where the dominated corporation is totally without a voice, where there is manipulation of the assets of the dominated corporation, and where corporate and personal activities are so intertwined that no separation is discernible, then the courts must look behind the facade and consider the identities as one.

CONSOLIDATED SUN RAY, INC., v. OPPENSTEIN, et al.
335 F 2d. 801 (8th Cir., 1964)

◆◆◆

VOGEL, Circuit Judge.

This suit, originally commenced in the Circuit Court of Jackson County, Missouri, at Kansas City, sought a declaratory judgment by Michael Oppenstein against appellant Consolidated Sun Ray, Inc., (Consolidated) and Berkson Brothers, Inc., (Berkson), with respect to a lease entered into on December 4, 1939, by Oppenstein and his since deceased brothers as Lessors and Berkson as Lessee. Oppenstein asked judgment declaring Consolidated liable under the lease on the theory that Berkson was the wholly owned subsidiary of Consolidated, under its complete domination and control beginning in June 1955 and continuing thereafter, and was accordingly the alter ego of Consolidated and as a result thereof Consolidated was liable on the lease as though it were in fact a named lessee. Diversity of citizenship and the amount involved justified removal to federal court. . . .

On March 27, 1963, judgment was entered against Berkson on the jury's verdict with the provision that it would become final upon entry of judgment on the claim against Consolidated. On April 5, 1963, the court made its Findings of Fact and Conclusions of Law and, based thereon, entered a declaratory judgment holding Consolidated also liable on the lease. Such judgment was entered on that date against both Berkson and Consolidated. On July 12, 1963, Oppenstein filed a "Motion for Further Relief Based on a Declaratory Judgment" by which he sought a determination of the amount of damages which had accrued to July 1, 1963. On October 22, 1963, before submitting the case to a jury, the District Court entered an ... order holding, as a matter of law, that Oppenstein was under no duty to mitigate damages. On October 24, 1963, the case ... (as to damages) went to trial before a jury and on October 25, 1963, the jury returned a verdict in favor of Oppenstein and against Consolidated and Berkson in the sum of $102,674.73 as appellee's damages to July 1, 1963, plus attorneys' fees in the sum of $10,000. Judgment of $112,674.73 was entered thereon, from which judgment Consolidated and Berkson noticed appeals to this court. ...

Appellant Consolidated bases this appeal upon the following grounds:

1. The District Court erred in holding that the separate corporate entity of Berkson should be disregarded and that Berkson was the alter ego of Consolidated. ...

The District Court, in its Findings of Fact, which, after examination, we conclude were based upon substantial evidence in the record, found that all of the stock of Berkson was owned by Consolidated; that on December 4, 1939, Oppenstein leased certain property to Berkson for a term of 26 years and 11 months ending June 30, 1967; that prior to June or July 1955 Berkson was the sole obligor as lessee under the lease; that after June or July 1955 Consolidated made certain changes in its dealings with its wholly-owned subsidiary Berkson, such as (a) eliminated Berkson's control of money received from its retail store which was operated at the leased premises and reserved to Consolidated alone the right to issue checks on the bank account deposited in the Commerce Trust Company in Kansas City; (b) in 1959 closed the bank account, opening a new one in Consolidated's name so that thereafter Berkson operated without an account in its own name; (c) pledged Berkson's accounts receivable as security for a loan Consolidated negotiated for itself from Walter Heller and Company; (d) took from Berkson its former independent buying discretion and merchandising policies, buying merchandise for Berkson in New York and warehousing it in its own building in New York and directed complete retail price details; (e) changed fire and liability insurance on the leased premises from the name of Berkson to Consolidate; (f) prepared in New York and completely controlled all advertising; (g) arranged so that the directors and officers of Berkson were persons employed by Consolidated and were the same persons who were directors or officers of Consolidated, and no director or officer of Berkson lived in the Kansas City, Missouri trade area, and the local store manager was not a director or officer of Berkson; (h) charged against Berkson a share of the cost of Consolidated's accounting and warehousing operations; (i) in 1956, just after the change-over, Consolidated entered into a Chapter XI Reorganization Plan under the Bankruptcy Laws. At the same time Berkson's operating costs increased despite reductions in personnel; (j) in 1956 Berkson's sales dropped $224,000 and its merchandise cost for inventory was reduced by

Consolidated in the amount of $220,000; (k) many of the corporate minutes of Berkson were printed forms apparently used by Consolidated for all of its subsidiaries, with the name "Berkson's" typed in; (1) all correspondence pertaining to the business of the lessee under the lease, whether written to the lessor, to third parties or to agent of Consolidated, was on Consolidated's letterhead and was for the most part signed "Consolidated Retail Stores by;" in such correspondence Consolidated referred to the lease, the leasehold estate and the demised premises as "its lease," "its property" and "its rent;" (m) Consolidated employed a realty firm and in letters exchanged between the two companies and third parties, efforts were made for Consolidated to sell the leasehold estate for a consideration to be paid to Consolidated; (n) in October 1961 the retail store on the leased premises was closed and the inventory was sold to Macy's; the consideration therefor was paid to and kept by Consolidated, no part being made available to apply on the rent due Oppenstein for November 1961 or thereafter; (o) Consolidated operated Berkson the same as if it were one of the division stores of Consolidated rather than a wholly-owned subsidiary; (p) Consolidated did maintain substantially all the legal formalities required of Berkson as a separate corporation, such as filling necessary papers, reports and corporate tax returns.

The court also found there was a default in the payment of rent beginning November 1961 with notices, etc. From these findings the District Court made its Conclusions of Law:

1. That Consolidated had complete and absolute control over the actions and rights of Berkson from and after July 1955; that Consolidated used its power and control for the benefit of Consolidated and not for the benefit of Berkson;

2. That from June or July 1955 Consolidated did not respect the separateness of the corporate entity of Berkson, treating Berkson as a division, department, or adjunct of Consolidated; caused Berkson's assets to be intermingled with its own, making Berkson the alter ego of Consolidated;

3. That the use by Consolidated of Berkson as a division, conduit or instrumentality of Consolidated and Berkson's loss of control of its own destiny and inability to protect its own assets and the imposition of excessive financial burdens on Berkson was an injustice to Oppenstein, who sustained damage thereby;

4. That Consolidated should be held liable for the actions and obligations of Berkson, the same as though they were the acts and obligations of Consolidated.

Obviously, Consolidated's testimony and evidence and the deductions which could be drawn therefrom indicated contrary conclusions. Consolidated asserts that there was nothing improper in its domination of Berkson and that the new arrangement beginning in 1955 was for the benefit of Berkson and Oppenstein as well; that by its beneficial control of Berkson it enabled that company to stay in business years longer than would otherwise have been possible. . . .

From the evidence in this case there can be no reasonable doubt but that Consolidated did completely control and use Berkson as a mere conduit, instrumentality or adjunct of Consolidated itself. The ultimate fact question for determination, then, was Consolidated's purpose in so doing. If that purpose was unlawful or improper or for some illegitimate purpose which might result in damage to Oppenstein, then the court has the power to look behind Berkson, the alter ego, and hold Consolidated liable for Berkson's obligations. This necessitates a determination by the trier of the facts. Here the court, with the aid of an advisory jury, found against Consolidated on that issue. The law of Missouri is that, where the subsidiary is a mere conduit, instrumentality, or adjunct through which the parent corporation achieves some improper end, its own corporate entity will be disregarded. . . .

Both parties cite, quote from and rely on *May Department Stores Co.* v. *Union Electric Light & Power Co.,* (341 Mo. 299, 107 S.N. 2d 41, 1937) *supra,* as being the leading case in Missouri on the question of piercing the corporate veil. In May, the parent owned the subsidiary, as in the instant case; both companies had the same offices and the same manager, as herein; the parent corporation paid the payroll of the subsidiary and all other expenses, as in the present case; the parent paid the subsidiary's plant rent, as in the instant case; all receipts by the subsidiary were turned over to the parent, as was the fact herein; intercompany accounts recorded credits and debits from the moneys taken in and expended as between the two, as in the instant case; the subsidiary maintained its apparent separate identity for customer relation purposes, as in the instant case; and, as is true herein, all corporate reports were made in the name of the subsidiary in order to preserve its paper identity. In finding an improper purpose had been established in that case, the Supreme Court of Missouri said at page 55 of 107 S.W. 2d:

"* * * It does seem, however, that the determination of whether there is a case for equitable relief could and should be decided by the test of whether or not the arrangement involved is being used for a proper purpose. Should not all these other suggested tests be used only as aids for determining the true purpose of the arrangement? *Making a corporation a supplemental part of an economic unit and operating it without sufficient funds to meet obligations to those who must deal with it would be circumstantial evidence tending to show either an improper purpose or reckless disregard of the rights of others.* . . .

We hold here that Consolidated's complete and absolute control over Berkson, making Berkson a supplemental part of Consolidated's economic unit, and operating Berkson without sufficient funds to meet its obligations to its creditors, constituted circumstantial evidence from which the advisory jury and the court, as the finders of the facts, could reasonably draw the inference that Consolidated's purpose was improper and was detrimental to Oppenstein. Such inference is sustained by substantial evidence. It may not be disturbed here on appeal. . . .

As to the first issue wherein the court and jury held Consolidated liable, this case is affirmed. . . .

◆◆◆

Case Questions

1. In view of the high degree of control that Consolidated exerted over Berkson, why did it bother to form Berkson as a subsidiary?
2. Did the amount involved, $112,674.73, justify an appeal by Consolidated? Is it possible that a factor in deciding to appeal was that other creditors of Berkson, and possibly of other subsidiaries as well, were watching the ultimate outcome of this litigation? *yes*

FOREIGN CORPORATIONS

A corporation operating within the state of its incorporation is called a domestic corporation. In all other states and countries it is called a foreign corporation. Each state has the power to regulate foreign corporations that are doing business within its borders. Before legally commencing business, the corporation must first qualify to do business as a foreign corporation. Qualification usually involves filing certain routine information with the Secretary of State and payment of a fee. The primary purpose behind the qualification requirement is to facilitate the assessment and collection of state ad valorem and franchise taxes. Failure to qualify can result in the imposition of monetary penalties and/or criminal misdemeanor charges. Also, some states deny access to their courts to any corporation that has failed to properly qualify.

The difficult issue is determining whether or not a foreign corporation is doing business within a given state. Article 1, Section 8, of the U.S. Constitution (commonly referred to as the "Commerce Clause") provides that "Congress shall have power . . . to regulate commerce . . . among the several states . . ." Thus, if a foreign corporation is engaged in purely interstate commerce, the states lack the authority to subject it to their qualification statutes. However, if a foreign corporation is engaged in intrastate commerce, it is doing business within that state and is subject to state regulation. In deciding whether a corporation is engaged in interstate or intrastate commerce, the courts examine a variety of factors. The presence or absence of any one of these factors is generally not conclusive. Many times, the test is a balancing one as some factors indicate an interstate nature while others are of an intrastate character. Among the examined factors are: 1) Presence of an office. Is the office maintained for the benefit of the corporate employees, such as furnishing salesmen with a place to use the telephone and complete paperwork? If so, this is not the type of activity that constitutes doing business. Or, is the office utilized for holding corporate meetings or for the storage of a stock of goods to fill the small emergency orders of customers? The latter will require the corporation to qualify as a foreign corporation. 2) Property ownership. For what purpose is the property held, mere investment or the fulfillment of corporate objectives within that state? 3) Solicitation of business. The solicitation of orders from within a state that are then accepted outside the state and filled from an inventory located outside the state is interstate in nature. Likewise, it is interstate commerce to sell or purchase goods within a state if these goods are to be delivered outside that state. However, the solicitation, acceptance and delivery of goods all within one state is clearly doing business within that state. 4) Frequency of business. The consumation of a single or isolated business transaction is not doing business within that state.

The *Allenberg Cotton Co.* v. *Pittman* case that follows demonstrates the complexities involved in judging the interstate or intrastate nature of a business venture. Also note that the issue arises in a state that denys the use of its courts to foreign corporations that fail to qualify.

ALLENBERG COTTON CO., INC. v. PITTMAN
419 U.S. 20 (1974)

◆◆◆

Mr. Justice Douglas delivered the opinion of the Court.

This is an appeal from a judgment of the Supreme Court of Mississippi, 276 So. 2d 678 (1973), which held that under the applicable Mississippi statute appellant might not recover damages for breach of a contract to deliver cotton because of its failure to qualify to do business in the State. Appellant claims that that Mississippi statute as applied to the facts of this case is repugnant to the Commerce Clause of the Constitution. . . .

Appellant is a cotton merchant with its principal office in Memphis, Tenn. It had arranged with one Covington, a local cotton buyer in Marks, Miss., "to contract cotton" to be produced the following season by farmers in Quitman County, Miss. The farmer, Pittman, in the present case, made the initial approach to Covington, seeking a contract for his cotton; in other instances Covington might contact the local farmers. In either event, Covington would obtain all the information necessary for a purchase contract and telephone the information to appellant in Memphis, where a contract would be prepared, signed by an officer of appellant, and forwarded to Covington. The latter would then have the farmer sign the contract. For these services Covington received a commission on each bale of cotton delivered to appellant's account at the local warehouse. When the farmers delivered the cotton, Covington would draw on appellant and pay them the agreed price.

The Supreme Court of Mississippi held that appellant's transactions with Mississippi farmers were wholly intrastate in nature, being completed upon delivery of the cotton at the warehouse, and that the fact that appellant might subsequently sell the cotton in interstate commerce was irrelevant to the federal question "as the Mississippi transaction had been completed and the cotton then belonged exclusively to Allenberg, to be disposed of as it saw fit, at its sole election and discretion," . . . Under the contract which Covington negotiated with appellee, Pittman, the latter was to plant, cultivate, and harvest a crop of cotton on his land, deliver it to a named company in Marks, Miss., for ginning, and then turn over the ginned cotton to appellant at a local warehouse. The suit brought by appellant alleged a refusal of Pittman to deliver the cotton and asked for injunctive relief and damages. One defense tendered by Pittman was that appellant could not use the courts of Mississippi to enforce its contracts, as it was doing business in the State without the requisite certificate. The Supreme Court of Mississippi sustained that plea, reversing a judgment in favor of appellant, and dismissed the complaint.

Appellant's arrangements with Pittman and the broker, Covington, are representative of a course of dealing with many farmers whose cotton, once sold to appellant, enters a long interstate pipeline. That pipeline ultimately terminates at mills across the country or indeed around the world, after a complex sorting and matching process designed to provide each mill with the particular grade of cotton which the mill is equipped to process.

Due to differences in soil, time of planting, harvesting, weather, and the like, each bale of cotton, even though produced on the same farm, may have a different quality. Traders or merchants like appellant, with the assistance of the Department of Agriculture, must sample each bale and classify it according to grade, staple length, and color. Similar bales, whether from different farms even from different collection points, are then grouped in multiples of 100 into "even-running lots" which are uniform as to all measurable characteristics. This grouping process typically takes place in card files in the merchant's office; when enough bales have been pooled to make an even-running lot, the entire lot can be targeted for a mill equipped to handle cotton of that particular quality, and the individual bales in the lot will then be shipped to the mill from their respective collection points. It is true that title often formally passes to the merchant upon delivery of the cotton at the warehouse, and that the cotton may rest at the warehouse pending completion of the classification and grouping processes; but, as the description above indicates, these fleeting events are an integral first step in a vast system of distribution of cotton in interstate commerce. . . .

We deal here with a species of control over an intricate interstate marketing mechanism. The cotton exchange . . . has federal protection under the Commerce Clause. In *Dahnke-Walker Milling Co.* v. *Bondurant,* 257 U.S. 282 (1921), wheat raised in Kentucky was purchased by a miller in Tennessee, payment and delivery to a common carrier being made in Kentucky. There, as here, a suit against the farmer in a Kentucky court was defended on the grounds that the buyer had not qualified to do business in Kentucky and that, therefore, the contract was unenforceable. The Court held that the Kentucky statute could not be applied to defeat this transaction which, though having intrastate aspects, was in fact "a part of interstate commerce," . . . The same observation is pertinent here. Delivery of the cotton to a warehouse, taken in isolation, is an intrastate transaction. But that delivery is also essential for the completion of the interstate transaction, for sorting and classification in the warehouse are essential before the precise interstate destination of the cotton, whether in this country or abroad, is determined. The determination of the precise market cannot indeed be made until the classification is made. The cotton is this Mississippi sale, . . . though temporarily in a warehouse, was still in the stream of interstate commerce. . . .

Much reliance is placed on *Eli Lilly & Co.* v. *Sav-On-Drugs, Inc.*, 366 U.S. 276 (1961), for sustaining Mississippi's action. The case is not in point. There the Court found that the foreign corporation had an office and salesmen in New Jersey selling drugs intrastate. Since it was engaged in an intrastate business it could be required to obtain a license even though it also did an interstate business.

Reliance is also placed on *Union Brokerage Co.* v. *Jensen,* 322 U.S. 202 (1944), which is likewise not in point, It is true that the customhouse broker in that case was in the business of dealing with goods in interstate transit. Nevertheless, we expressly noted that "[Union's] activities are not confined to its services at the port of entry. It has localized its business, and to function effectively it must have a wide variety of dealings with the people in the community." . . . As in Eli Lilly, this element of localization was held to be distinguishable from cases such as Dahnke-Walker in which a foreign corporation enters the State "to contribute to or to conclude a unitary interstate transaction." . . . In this respect we have found appellant's transactions, when viewed against the background of customary trade practices in the cotton market, to be indistinguishable from the activities in Dahnke-Walker in any significant regard.

The Mississippi Supreme Court, as noted, ruled that appellant was doing business in Mississippi. Appellant, however, has no office in Mississippi, nor does it own or operate a warehouse there. It has no employees soliciting business in Mississippi or otherwise operating there on a regular basis; its contracts are arranged through an independent broker, whose commission is paid either by appellant or by the farmer himself and who has no authority to enter into contracts on behalf of appellant. These facts are in sharp contrast to the situation in Eli Lilly, where Lilly operated a New Jersey office with 18 salaried employees whose job was to promote use of Lilly's products. . . . There is no indication that the cotton which makes up appellant's "perpetual inventory" in Mississippi is anything other than what appellant has claimed it to be, namely, cotton which is awaiting necessary sorting and classification as a prerequisite to its shipment in interstate commerce.

In short, appellant's contacts with Mississippi do not exhibit the sort of localization or intrastate character which we have required in situations where a State seeks to require a foreign corporation to qualify to do business. Whether there were local tax incidents of those contacts which could be reached is a different question on which we express no opinion. Whether the course of dealing would subject appellant to suits in Mississippi is likewise a different question on which we express no view. We hold only that Mississippi's refusal to honor and enforce contracts made for interstate or foreign commerce is repugnant to the Commerce Clause.

The judgment is reversed and the cause remanded for proceedings not inconsistent with this opinion. . . .

Mr. Justice Rehnquist, dissenting.

The question in this case is whether Mississippi may require appellant, a Tennessee corporation, to qualify as a foreign corporation under Mississippi law before it may sue in the courts of Mississippi to enforce a contract. The Supreme Court of Mississippi summarized the facts of the transaction, which it stated were "without substantial dispute," as follows:

> It is apparent that these transactions of Allenberg in each case, including that with Pittman, took place wholly in Mississippi. The contract was negotiated in Mississippi, executed in Mississippi, the cotton was produced in Mississippi, delivered to Allenberg at the warehouse in Mississippi, and payment was made to the producer in Mississippi. All interest of the producer in the cotton terminated finally upon delivery to Allenberg at the warehouse in Marks. The fact that afterward Allenberg might or might not sell the cotton in interstate commerce is irrelevant to the issue here, as the Mississippi transaction had been completed and the cotton then belonged exclusively to Allenberg . . . .

The Supreme Court of Mississippi might have added that through an exclusive agent, who was a Mississippi resident, Allenberg entered into over 20 similar contracts in 1971 with farmers in Quitman County alone, contracts covering cotton production from over 9,000 acres in this one county. Allenberg's total 1971 purchases of cotton grown in Mississippi under substantially identical contracts exceeded 25,000 bales. . . .

For reasons which are not entirely clear to me, the Court holds that Mississippi may not require Allenberg to qualify as a foreign corporation as a condition of using Mississippi courts to enforce its contract with appellee Pittman.

The Court says that "[d]elivery of the cotton to a warehouse, taken in isolation, is an intrastate transaction. But that delivery is also essential for the completion of the interstate transaction, for sorting and classification in the warehouse are essential before the precise interstate destination of the cotton, whether in this country or abroad, is determined." . . . Yet in *Parker* v. *Brown*, 317 U.S. 341, 361 (1943), this Court stated that "no case has gone so far as to hold that a state could not license or otherwise regulate the sale of articles within the state because the buyer, after processing and packing them, will, in the normal course of business, sell and ship them in interstate commerce." . . .

It has been settled since Mr. Chief Justice Taney's opinion for the Court in *Bank of Augusta* v. *Earle*, 13 Pet. 519 (1839), that a corporation organized in one State which seeks to do business in another State may be required by the latter to qualify under its law before doing such business. An exception to this general rule was established in cases such as *Crutcher* v. *Kentucky*, 141 U.S. 47 (1891), in which the Court held that such a license might not be required of an express company engaged only in interstate commerce. . . . That exception was subsequently applied in *International Textbook Co.* v. *Pigg*, 217 U.S. 91 (1910), and expanded in *Dahnke-Walker Milling Co.* v. *Bondurant*, 257 U.S. 282 (1921), and *Shafer* v. *Farmers Grain Co.*, 268 U.S. 189 (1925). . . .

In *Union Brokerage Co.* v. *Jensen*, 322 U.S. 202 (1944), this Court upheld Minnesota's denial of access to its courts to a North Dakota customhouse broker, whose sole business in Minnesota was interstate commerce, where the broker had failed to qualify as required of such foreign corporations:

> [T]he Commerce Clause does not cut the States off from all legislative relation to foreign and interstate commerce. *South Carolina Highway Dept.* v. *Barnwell Bros.*, 303 U.S. 177. . . . The incidence of the particular state enactment must determine whether it has transgressed the power left to the States to protect their special state interests although it is related to a phase of a more extensive commercial process. . . .

Mississippi's qualification statute is concededly not discriminatory. Domestic corporations organized under her laws must submit themselves to her taxing jurisdiction, to service of process within the State, and to a number of other incidents of corporate existence which state law may impose. Union Brokerage recognized that qualification statutes were important in the collection of state taxes by identifying foreign corporations operating within the State and in the protection of citizens within the State through insuring ready susceptibility of the corporation to the service of process. The qualification statute also serves an important informational function making available to citizens of the State who may deal with the foreign corporation details of its financing and control. Although the result of Allenberg's failure to comply with the qualification statute is a drastic one, our decisions hold that the burden imposed on interstate commerce by such statutes is to be judged with reference to the measures required to comply with such legislation, and not to the sanctions imposed for violation of it. . . . The steps necessary in order to comply with this statute are not unreasonably burdensome. . . .

I would affirm the judgment of the Supreme Court of Mississippi.

◆◆◆

Case Questions

1. Did Mr. Justice Douglas or Rhenquist author the more persuasive opinion?
2. The court stated that delivery of cotton to a warehouse, taken in isolation, is an intrastate transaction. Should not that conclusion have been determinative of the issue?
3. Since the disputed events took place in Mississippi, why did the court shift its focus to the interstate aspects of cotton distribution?
4. Does the legal reasoning in this case usurp states rights and give the federal government undue control over intrastate transactions?

NOTE:

Qualifying to do business in Mississippi as a foreign corporation does not present a difficult obstacle. Certain information must be filed with the Mississippi Secretary of State accompanied by a fee of between $20 and $500. The amount of the fee is determined by the amount of the corporation's capital. Miss. Code. Ann. 79-3-219 and 79-3-255(q) (1972).

POWERS OF A CORPORATION

The business corporation statute of each state enumerates the general powers held by every corporation. These powers include: the ability to have a name and seal; make contracts; sue and be sued; purchase, lease and convey property and; all powers necessary to effect any or all of the purposes for which the corporation is formed. The latter are called implied powers. They permit the corporation to perform actions that, while necessary to achieve a proper corporate purpose, are not specifically listed in the state statute or corporate charter. This does not mean that a corporation can do anything it so desires. For example, a corporation that has as its stated corporate purpose the operation of airline passenger service cannot enter the business of selling new and used aircraft. Yet, it would have the implied power to sell its used planes as they are replaced with new aircraft.

Some areas pose more difficult questions than others. For example, it will later be observed that the directors of a corporation possess the exclusive authority to manage the corporation. Does a corporation possess the power to enter a partnership, where the partners share management responsibility? A corporation will only have the power to enter a partnership where the statute or charter specifically grants that power. Or consider the question of making loans. Banks are in the business of, among other things, making loans. To enter the banking business requires a special process. Does this then bar a corporation from making loans? A corporation that lacks a bank charter cannot enter the loan business. However, it could lend funds to a corporate subsidiary. A corporation cannot give away or permit the waste of its assets. These assets belong to the corporation and indirectly to the shareholders. They are only to be used to advance the proper corporate purposes. Are donations to charitable, scientific, religious or educational institutions allowable or, do they constitute an impermissible gift of corporate assets? Some state business corporation statutes allow such contributions, i.e. Ill § 5 (m); whereas other statutes are silent on the matter. The *Smith Mfg. Co.* v. *Barlow* case that follows examines the question in a state with a silent statute. The case illustrates the prevalent liberal judicial attitude in approving such corporate expenditures.

A. P. SMITH MFG. CO. v. BARLOW
13 N.J. 145, 98 A.2d 581 (S. Ct. N.J., 1953)

◆◆◆

JACOBS, J.

The Chancery Division, in a well-reasoned opinion by Judge Stein, determined that a donation by the plaintiff The A.P. Smith Manufacturing Company to Princeton University was intra vires. Because of the public importance of the issues presented, the appeal duly taken to the Appellate Division has been certified directly to this court. . . .

The company was incorporated in 1896 and is engaged in the manufacture and sale of valves, fire hydrants and special equipment, mainly for water and gas industries. Its plant is located in East Orange and Bloomfield and it has approximately 300 employees. Over the years the company has contributed regularly to the local community chest and on occasions to Upsala College in East Orange and Newark University, now part of Rutgers, the State University. On July 24, 1951 the board of directors adopted a resolution which set forth that it was in the corporation's best interests to join with others in the 1951 Annual Giving to Princeton University, and appropriated the sum of $1,500 to be transferred by the corporation's treasurer to the university as a contribution towards its maintenance. When this action was questioned by stockholders the corporation instituted a declaratory judgment action in the Chancery Division and trial was had in due course.

Mr. Hubert O'Brien, the president of the company, testified that he considered the contribution to be a sound investment, that the public expects corporations to aid philanthropic and benevolent institutions, that they obtain good will in the community by so doing, and that their charitable donations create favorable environment for their business operations. In addition, he expressed the thought that in contributing to liberal arts institutions, corporations were furthering their self-interest in assuring the free flow of properly trained personnel for administrative and other corporate employment. Mr. Frank W. Abrams, chairman of the board of the Standard Oil Company of New Jersey, testified that corporations are expected to acknowledge their public responsibilities in support of the essential elements of our free enterprise system. He indicated that it was not "good business" to disappoint "this reasonable and justified public expectation," nor was it good business for corporations "to take substantial benefits from their membership in the economic community while avoiding the normally accepted obligations of citizenship in the social community." Mr. Irving S. Olds, former chairman of the board of the United States Steel Corporation, pointed out that corporations have a self-interest in the maintenance of liberal education as the bulwark of good government. He stated that "Capitalism and free enterprise owe their survival in no small degree to the existence of our private, independent universities" and that if American business does not aid in their maintenance it is not "properly protecting the long-range interest of its stockholders, its employees and its customers." . . .

The objecting stockholders have not disputed any of the foregoing testimony nor the showing of great need by Princeton and other private institutions of higher learning and the important public service being rendered by them for democratic government and industry alike. . . . Nevertheless, they have taken the position that . . . the plaintiff's certificate of incorporation does not expressly authorize the contribution and under common-law principles the company does not possess any implied or incidental power to make it. . . .

In his discussion of the early history of business corporations Professor Williston refers to a 1702 publication where the author stated flatly that "The general intent and end of all civil incorporations is for better government." And he points out that the early corporate charters, particularly their recitals, furnish additional support for the notion that the corporate object was the public one of managing and ordering the trade as well as the private one of profit for the members. . . . However, with later economic and social developments and the free availability of the corporate device for all trades, the end of private profit became generally accepted as the controlling one in all businesses other than those classed broadly as public utilities. . . . 45 HLR 1145. . . . As a concomitant the common-law rule developed that those who managed the corporation could not disburse any corporate funds for philanthropic or other worthy public cause *unless* the expenditure would benefit the corporation. . . . During the 19th Century when corporations were relatively few and small and did not dominate the country's wealth, the common-law rule did not significantly interfere with the public interest. But the 20th Century has presented a different climate. . . . Control of economic wealth has passed largely from individual entrepreneurs to dominating corporations, and calls upon the corporations for reasonable philanthropic donations have come to be made with increased public support. In many instances such contributions have been sustained by the courts within the common-law doctrine upon liberal findings that the donations tended reasonably to promote the corporate objectives. . . .

Over 20 years ago Professor Dodd, supra, 45 Harv. L. Rev., at 1159, 1160, cited the views of Justice Letton in State ex rel. *Sorensen* v. *Chicago B. & Q. R. Co., supra,* with seeming approval and suggested the doctrine that corporations may properly support charities which are important to the welfare of the communities where they do business as soundly representative of the public attitude and actual corporate practice. Developments since he wrote leave no doubts on this score.

When the wealth of the nation was primarily in the hands of individuals they discharged their responsibilities as citizens by donating freely for charitable purposes. With the transfer of most of the wealth to corporate hands and the imposition of heavy burdens of individual taxation, they have been unable to keep pace with increased philanthropic needs. They have therefore, with justification, turned to corporations to assume the modern obligations of good citizenship in the same manner as humans do. ... In actual practice corporate giving has correspondingly increased. Thus, it is estimated that annual corporate contributions throughout the nation aggregate over 300 million dollars, with over 60 million dollars thereof going to universities and other educational institutions. Similarly, it is estimated that local community chests receive well over 40 percent of their contributions from corporations. ...

More and more they have come to recognize that their salvation rests upon sound economic and social environment which in turn rests in no insignificant part upon free and vigorous nongovernmental institutions of learning. It seems to us that just as the conditions prevailing when corporations were originally created required that they serve public as well as private interests, modern conditions require that corporations acknowledge and discharge social as well as private responsibilities as members of the communities within which they operate. Within this broad concept there is no difficulty in sustaining, as incidental to their proper objects and in aid of the public welfare, the power of corporations to contribute corporate funds within reasonable limits in support of academic institutions. But even if we confine ourselves to the terms of the common-law rule in its application to current conditions, such expenditures may likewise readily be justified as being for the benefit of the corporation; indeed, if need be the matter may be viewed strictly in terms of actual survival of the corporation in a free enterprise system. The genius of our common law has been its capacity for growth and its adaptability to the needs of the times. Generally courts have accomplished the desired result indirectly through the molding of old forms. Occasionally they have done it directly through frank rejection of the old and recognition of the new. But whichever path the common law has taken it has not been found wanting as the proper tool for the advancement of the general good. ...

We find that it was a lawful exercise of the corporation's implied and incidental powers under common-law principles and that it came within the express authority of the pertinent state legislation. As has been indicated, there is now widespread belief throughout the nation that free and vigorous non-governmental institutions of learning are vital to our democracy and the system of free enterprise and that withdrawal of corporate authority to make such contributions within reasonable limits would seriously threaten their continuance. Corporations have come to recognize this and with their enlightenment have sought in varying measures, as has the plaintiff by its contributions, to insure and strengthen the society which gives them existence and the means of aiding themselves and their fellow citizens. Clearly then, the appellants, as individual stockholders whose private interests rest entirely upon the well-being of the plaintiff corporation, ought not be permitted to close their eyes to present day realities and thwart the long-visioned corporate action in recognizing and voluntarily discharging its high obligations as a constituent of our modern social structure.

The judgment entered in the Chancery Division is in all respects

Affirmed.

◆◆◆

Case Questions

1. When their resolution created questions with the shareholders, the directors held their decision in abeyance pending a judicial resolution of the issue. Is such a course of action appropriate or practical in every instance where stockholders object to board actions?
2. Is the purpose of a corporation to earn maximum profits or to be a social "do-gooder?" If the purpose is a blend of these two elements, in what proportion are they to be mixed?
3. Federal law prohibits a corporation from contributing to a candidate for federal office. Approximately one-half the states bar corporation contributions to state candidates. If the survival of the corporation rests upon a sound economic and social environment and the preservation of the free enterprise system, is it logical to outlaw political contributions? If the individual, and not the corporation, is to select the candidate he wishes to support, should not the selection of philanthropic causes likewise be an individual decision?

REVIEW PROBLEMS

1. Bigelow and Lewisohn formed the Old Dominion Corporation in July 1895. Its authorized stock was 150,000 shares of $25 par value for a total capitalization of $3,750,000. During May and June of 1895 Lewisohn and Bigelow acquired certain mining property at a cost of $1,000,000. The market value of the property did not exceed $2,000,000. They sold this property to Old Dominion in return for 130,000 shares of stock valued at $3,250,000. They completely dominated the Old Dominion board of directors. Thereafter the remaining 20,000 shares were sold to the public to raise working capital. The shares were sold at par, raising $500,000, but the subscribers did not know of the Lewisohn and Bigelow secret profit. Several years later, when the profit comes to light, the corporation sues to recover the secret profit alleging a breach of trust by the two promoters. What results? [*Old Dominion Copper Mining & Smeling Co.* v. *Lewishohn*, 210 U.S. 206 (1908); contra, *Old Dominion Copper Mining & Smelting Co.* v. *Bigelow*, 89 N.E. 193 (Mass S. Ct. 1908), aff'd 225 U.S. 111 (1912)].
2. Seminole, a California corporation, operated a public swimming pool that it leased from its owner. The plaintiffs' daughter drowned in the pool and they won a $10,000 wrongful death action. The judgment remained unsatisfied. The plaintiffs now attempt to hold Cavaney personally liable for the judgment against Seminole. Cavaney was a director and secretary-treasurer of Seminole. He was not a shareholder. At one point in time Seminole sought to issue three shares of stock; one of them to go to Cavaney. This effort was abandoned and no shares were ever issued. Seminole had no assets by Cavaney's own admission. He also stated that "The corporation was duly organized but never functioned as a corporation." Seminole used Cavaney's office for a time to keep records and receive mail. Cavaney contends that this evidence does not support a determination that he is an alter ego of the corporation and therefore personally liable for Seminole's debts. Should the court disregard the corporate entity and hold the defendant liable? [*Minton* v. *Cavaney,* 364 P. 2d 473 (Cal. S. Ct. 1961)]
3. The plaintiff has been run down and injured by a negligently operated taxicab. The cab is owned by Seon Cab Corp. Seon has only two cabs and carries only the legally required minimum automobile liability insurance

($10,000) on each cab. The defendant Carlton is a stockholder in ten corporations, including Seon. Each corporation has only two cabs and carries the minimum amount of insurance. The plaintiff alleges that the stockholders are personally liable for his damages because the multiple corporate structure constitutes an unlawful attempt to defraud members of the general public who might be injured by the cabs. The defendant argues that the law permits taxi owner - operators to form such corporations and corporations are designed to permit the owners to escape personal liability. Furthermore, he points out that he has complied with the legislative branch's insurance mandates. What decision? [*Walkovszky* v. *Carlton,* 223 N.E. 2d 6 (N.Y. Ct. App. 1966)]. *They don't disregard the corp. entity*

4. The plaintiff is injured by the negligent operation of a taxicab. It was owned and operated by one of four corporations affiliated with Terminal. Terminal is not a stockholder in any of the four operating corporations. For the most part, the individuals that own Terminal also own the four corporations. Terminal actually serviced, inspected, repaired and dispatched all the taxis of the four corporations. The Terminal name was conspicuously displayed on the sides of all the taxis used in the enterprise. Should the veil of the operating company, whose cab injured the plaintiff, be pierced to hold Terminal liable? [*Mangan* v. *Terminal Transp. System,* 286 N.Y.S. 666].

5. Should the results in the above two cases differ because in one an attempt is made to hold an individual liable whereas, in the other, the plaintiff seeks to hold liable another corporation? *No — the facts were different*

SHAREHOLDERS AND THE CORPORATE CAPITAL STRUCTURE

10

Legally it is the shareholders that exercise ultimate control of the corporation. We will later observe that the board of directors possess the exclusive authority to manage the corporation but, it is the shareholders that select the directors. It is also the shareholders that approve any basic changes in the corporation's structure. The shareholders are the owners of the corporation. True, the corporation, as a separate entity distinct from the shareholders, holds title to the corporate assets. Yet the shareholders own the corporation and indirectly its assets. This, at least, is the orthodox theory of corporation law. There is another perspective to the issue — a perspective that regards the theory of shareholder control and shareholder democracy as fiction. (As used here, the term shareholder democracy refers to the idea that shareholders control corporate affairs through the exercise of their voting rights.)

THE SHAREHOLDER

In 1932, A. Berle and G. Means published their classic book, *The Modern Corporation and Private Property*. In their book they noted that within the realm of corporations ownership was being separated from control. Control was shifting out of the hands of the shareholder into the hands of the professional manager. Today, some individuals would regard the shift as having been completely consumated with management able to perpetuate itself in office and dominate corporate affairs.

Where in does the truth lie? Somewhere in between, depending upon the type of corporation involved. If one is discussing the closely held corporations, shareholder democracy is alive and working. The corporation will be of a family or partnership nature. The shareholders will either be the managers or will carefully follow the details of the corporate operation. Numerically, these corporations compose a large percentage of the total number of corporations. In the middle of the spectrum are the corporations that, while not close corporations, are not corporate giants. Those corporations are also substantial in number. It is difficult to generalize about these. A corporation may have 500 shareholders who have an active interest in corporate affairs. Under such circumstances management is probably directly responsible to the shareholders. Yet, that same corporation could have a substantial number of nonchalant shareholders that merely rubber stamp all management proposals. Finally, we come to the corporate giants that dominate industries and whose shares are widely distributed. Some have assets that dwarf the combined gross national product of many countries. Although they are an important force in the corporate scheme, they are relatively few in number. Let's pause briefly and take a closer look at these immense corporations.

American Telephone & Telegraph Company (AT&T) is the largest corporation in terms of both outstanding shares and number of shareholders. At the end

of 1975 AT&T had approximately 668.6 million outstanding shares held by about
2.9 million shareholders. On October 1, 1975, it sold 12 million common shares
at $46 each. AT&T realized $531 million from the sale (an additional $21
million went to the underwriters). Figures from other representatives publicly
traded corporations follow.

Corporation	Outstanding Shares*	Shareholders*
Pan Am**	41.3 million	158,123
Polaroid	32.9 million	50,730
Sears Roebuck	2-1 split 157.8 million	270,000 †
Winnebago	25.2 million	18,976

*These are approximate figures for 1975 except for Winnebago whose figures represent
1973.
**Pan Am has 80 million authorized shares.
† no one holds more than 5%

Now let us examine who owns stock and in what amount. In 1972 a peak of
32.5 million shareholders was recorded. This represents about 15 percent of the
1972 U.S. population. According to New York Stock Exchange figures, the
number of individual shareholders had declined to 25.2 million in 1975. As of
mid 1971 individual Americans owned an estimated 780 billion dollars in stock.
Although the value of the stock and the number of shareholders are large,
ownership is concentrated in the wealthiest segment of the population. In 1971
the wealthiest 1 percent of the population owned 51 percent of the market value
of all stock held by families and received 47 percent of all dividend income. The
wealthiest 10 percent owned 74 percent of the market value and received 71
percent of the dividend income. In 1973, financial institutions held 24 percent
of the market value of all noninvestment company outstanding stock. Bank
administered personal trusts account for 10 percent.[1]

After an examination of the tremendous number of shares issued by the large
corporation, their wide distribution and, at the same time, concentrated
ownership within a wealthy but small population, it strains one's credulity to
suggest that the average shareholder exerts control over corporate affairs.
Shortly we will discuss the proxy process, which is designed to allow the
shareholder to vote on various matters. Theoretically, it is shareholder
democracy in action. Yet, in the large corporation the process favors
management. Management selects its nominees for the board of directors and
proposes various shareholder resolutions, both of which will be voted on by
proxy. The corporation, and indirectly the shareholders, bear the proxy
solicitation expense (printing, postage, etc.) If a shareholder wishes to mount a
challenge to management, he must bear the financial burden himself while
corporate lawyers and funds oppose his efforts. If the shareholder surmounts
these barriers and elects a board majority then the corporation will pay his
expenses. However, it is an extremely rare event when an insurgent group
succeeds in winning a proxy fight against an entrenched management.

Generally if a shareholder dislikes corporate policy, his protest takes the form
of selling his stock. The large institutional investors usually vote their stock in
support of management or refrain entirely from voting. There are some slight

indications that institutional investors are beginning to reappraise this traditional passive role. Keep these various ideas in mind when reading the material in this chapter on shareholder control devices.

SHAREHOLDER LIABILITY

Generally the shareholder enjoys limited liability. He puts to risk only his investment and has no personal liability. But, as we have learned, there can be exceptions to the general rule of limited shareholder liability. If the shareholder has failed to pay the subscription price of his shares, his liability for the unpaid balance is quite clear. The shareholder made a contract with the corporation for those shares and he must pay the corporation. Suppose a shareholder has not paid in full for his shares when the corporation topples into bankruptcy. Can the shareholder escape payment? No. The creditors look to the shareholders' investment as support for their extension of credit to the corporation. If the corporation does not pay, the creditor can look to the corporate assets for payment. If there are insufficient assets, but, there are unpaid shareholder subscriptions, an unsatisfied judgment creditor of the corporation can pursue and collect the unpaid balance.

CORPORATE CAPITAL STRUCTURE

Many states permit an enterprise to be incorporated with only $1,000 of capital. Naturally, the corporation will require continued infusions of funds as it continues to grow. Where are the sources for such funds and in what forms can capital be raised?

FINANCING THE CORPORATION

There are two basic sources for financing the new corporation: 1) the issuance and sale of bonds, called debt financing and, 2) the issuance and sale of stock, called equity financing.

A bond is simply a written promise by the corporation to pay a stated sum of money at a specific date accompanied by a stated interest rate. The bondholder is a creditor of the corporation. The corporation has borrowed money from him with the promise to pay him interest in the interim with repayment of the principal to occur at a future maturity date. Generally the corporation will reserve the right to redeem the bonds prior to the maturity date.

Bonds can assume a variety of forms. Usually bonds will be issued in series and secured by a lien or a mortgage making the bondholder a secured creditor. A debenture is a debt instrument that is unsecured. A bond can be convertible into shares of stock of the corporation. The issuance and sale of bonds is a source of long term borrowing that is usually only available to the large corporation.

Normally the only method of raising capital available to the new corporation is through the sale of stock. The stockholder or shareholder is an owner of the corporation and not a creditor. His ownership of the corporation is represented by a stock certificate. As an example, Winnebago Industries, Inc. has graciously granted permission to reprint their stock certificate which is shown in Figures 10-1 and 10-2.

Figure 10-1.

The following abbreviations, when used in the inscription on the face of this certificate, shall be construed as though they were written out in full according to applicable laws or regulations:

TEN COM —as tenants in common

TEN ENT —as tenants by the entireties

JT TEN —as joint tenants with right of survivorship and not as tenants in common

UNIF GIFT MIN ACT—_____Custodian_____
(Cust)   (Minor)
under Uniform Gifts to Minors
Act_____
(State)

Additional abbreviations may also be used though not in the above list.

For value received,_____ hereby sell, assign and transfer unto

PLEASE INSERT SOCIAL SECURITY OR OTHER
IDENTIFYING NUMBER OF ASSIGNEE

(PLEASE PRINT OR TYPEWRITE NAME AND ADDRESS, INCLUDING ZIP CODE, OF ASSIGNEE)

_____ shares of the capital stock represented by the within Certificate, and do hereby irrevocably constitute and appoint _____ Attorney to transfer the said stock on the books of the within named Corporation with full power of substitution in the premises.

Dated _____

Notice: The signature to this assignment must correspond with the name as written upon the face of the certificate in every particular, without alteration or enlargement or any change whatever.

THIS SPACE MUST NOT BE COVERED IN ANY WAY

Figure 10-2.

If an individual wishes to purchase stock in an existing corporation it can be done in two ways. Usually the individual will purchase the stock from a shareholder that desires to sell all or some of his stock. The other method is to enter into a postincorporation stock subscription agreement. This is simply a contract whereby the individual agrees to buy a particular number and type of shares at a specified price when issued by the corporation.

Preincorporation stock subscriptions are used by the promoters to finance the soon to be created corporation. When the corporation is formed, the board of directors accepts the subscription, issues the stock and collects the money. Problems can arise over the question whether a subscriber can revoke his subscription and what constitutes acceptance by the corporation. To settle the first question, a number of states have provided by statute that a preincorporation stock subscription shall be irrevocable for a stated period. The Illinois Business Corporation Act § 16 sets this period at six months. In regard to what constitutes acceptance, the courts require either an express acceptance or some act that implies acceptance.

TYPES OF SHARES

Authorized shares are the number of shares that the Articles permit the corporation to issue. The number of authorized shares can be increased or decreased by amending the Articles. Issued shares are the shares that the corporation has actually distributed to shareholders. They are the shares outstanding. Treasury shares are shares of the corporation which have been issued and then have been subsequently acquired by the corporation. Although they belong to the corporation, they cannot be voted by management at a shareholders' meeting and they are not paid dividends.

Prior to 1912 all stock had a stated par value and consequently was called par stock. The board of directors would fix the par value of the shares and they could not be issued for less than the stated par value. If they were issued for less than par this was considered to work a fraud on the corporate creditors. The creditors had the legal right to assume that the corporation received money, property or services equal to the total par value of the issued shares. These assets would then be available to the creditor if he were not paid. Par value created a number of problems. For instance, what is a corporation to do when the market price of its stock dropped below its par value? If the corporation cannot issue shares, it cannot secure financing and; it cannot sell shares at less than par. To avoid problems like this, the various states began to allow no par stock starting in 1912. No par stock lacks a stated value. However, it does have an inherent monetary value since it does represent the shareholder's proportionate interest in the corporation. This value will be measured by the stock's market value. Although lacking a stated value, the corporation must receive consideration when it issues them.

Voting and nonvoting stock is aptly described by those designations. The shareholder will either have the right to vote his shares or he will not depending upon the type of stock. Nonvoting stock is a device to keep control of the corporation within a certain group and, at the same time, secure financing. Two classes of stock are created, one voting and the other nonvoting. The nonvoting and voting stock is sold to the public while the control group retains all, or a majority of, the voting stock. Some states will not permit nonvoting stock. The idea is that as an owner, the shareholder deserves a say in corporate affairs. Illinois Business Corporation Act § 28 states that each outstanding share, regardless of class, shall be entitled to one vote on each matter submitted to a vote at a shareholders' meeting.

Now that we have defined some terms applied to stock let us examine the two basic types of stock: common and preferred. Common stock is the most frequently issued type of stock. The common shareholders usually control the corporation since common stock traditionally is voting stock. They receive their portion of the corporate profits in the form of dividends. Upon dissolution they share in any assets that remain after payment of the creditors. The common shareholder assumes the biggest risk and can enjoy the largest benefits. Preferred stockholders are entitled to certain preferences over the common shareholders. Generally they enjoy the right to receive dividends at a specified rate before any dividends can be distributed to the common shareholders. In practice this will sometimes mean that the preferred shareholders will receive dividends and the common shareholders will not. The preferred shareholders are also given a preference over the holders of common stock to assets of the corporation upon dissolution. Usually preferred shareholders will be denied voting privileges. Sometimes there will be an exception allowing the preferred shareholders to vote if no dividends have been paid for a certain number of years.

Some preferred stock can enjoy a preference over other preferred stock. For example, two classes of preferred stock may be issued with one class having a preference over the other in certain matters, such as sharing in the assets upon dissolution. If the difference is in the amount of dividends, the preferred is said to be issued in "series" not "classes." Series A might be entitled to eight percent dividends whereas Series B receives dividends in the amount of six percent. It is possible to have convertible preferred. This allows the preferred shareholder to convert his preferred stock into common stock. The rate at which it can be converted into other shares and under what conditions it may be converted will be specified when issued.

Preferred stock will either be cumulative or non-cumulative. If dividends are not paid on cumulative preferred stock in a given year, those dividends will cumulate. In other words, the shareholders will be entitled to the payment of all dividend arrearages before any dividends can be paid to the common shareholders. With noncumulative stock, if the dividends are not paid in a given year, the dividends will be forever lost. The next year all the corporation need do is pay the current dividend to the preferred shareholder and then it may pay dividends to the common shareholders. Preferred stock is cumulative unless specifically indicated otherwise.

Preferred stock will also be either non-participating or participating. If it is non-participating, once it has been paid its dividends the remaining surplus may be distributed among the common shareholders in any amount. With participating preferred, once it has received its dividends and, an equal amount has been distributed to the common, it and the common can both share in the remaining funds. Of course, it is the unusual corporation that enjoys such a surplus of profits so as to face this issue. For preferred to be participating, it must be explicitly so indicated.

In their pure form it is easy to distinguish a stock from a bond or a share of common stock from a preferred share. But all securities do not have definite attributes exclusive of a debt security or an equity security. Oftentimes an element of a bond will be combined with an element of a stock as a lawyer tailors a hybrid security to fit the requirements of a specific corporation. Sometimes these hybrid securities will amost defy classification. The *John Kelley Co.* v. *Commissionor of IRS* case that follows involves such hybrid securities. Notice how in each situation, the attributes of a stock are blended with the attributes of a debt so as to blur the dividing line.

JOHN KELLY CO. v. COMM'R OF I.R.S.
326 U.S. 521 (1946)

◆◆◆

Opinion of the Court by Mr. Justice Reed, announced by Mr. Justice Frankfurter.

These writs of certiorari were granted to examine the deductibility as interest of certain payments which the taxpayer corporations made to holders of their corporate obligations. Although the obligations of the two taxpayers had only one striking difference, the noncumulative in one and the cumulative quality in the other of the payments reserved under the characterization of interest, the Tax Court ... held that the payments under the former, the Kelley Company case, were interest and under the Talbot Mills were dividends. The Circuit Court of Appeals reversed the Tax Court in the Kelley case and another circuit affirmed the Talbot Mills decision. On account of the diversity of approach in the Tax Court and the reviewing courts, we granted certiorari.

In the Kelley case, a corporation, all of whose common and preferred stock was owned directly or as trustee by members of a family group, was reorganized by authorizing the issue of $250,000 income debenture bearer bonds, issued under a trust indenture, calling for 8 percent interest, noncumulative. They were offered only to shareholders of the taxpayer but were assignable. The debentures were payable in twenty years, December 31, 1956, with payment of general interest conditioned upon the sufficiency of the net income to meet the obligation. The debenture holders had priority of payment over stockholders but were subordinated to all other creditors. The debentures were redeemable at the taxpayer's option and carried the usual acceleration provisions for specific defaults. The debenture holders had no right to participate in management. Other changes not material here were made in the corporate structure. Debentures were issued to the amount of $150,000 face value. The greater part, $114,648, was issued in exchange for the original preferred, with six percent cumulative guaranteed dividends, at its retirement price and the balance sold to stockholders at par, which was eventually paid with sums obtained by the purchasers from common stock dividends. Common stock was owned in the same proportions by the same stockholders before and after the reorganization.

In the Talbot Mills case the taxpayer was a corporation which, prior to its recapitalization, had a capital stock of five thousand shares of the par value of $100 or $500,000. All of the stock with the exception of some qualifying shares was held by members, through blood or marriage, of the Talbot family. In an effort to adjust the capital structure to the advantage of the taxpayer, the company was recapitalized just prior to the beginning of the fiscal year in question, by each stockholder surrendering four-fifths of his stock and taking in lieu thereof registered notes in aggregate face value equal to the aggregate par value of the stock retired. This amounted to an issue of $400,000 in notes to the then stockholders. These notes were dated October 2, 1939, and were payable to a specific payee or his assignees on December 1, 1964. They bore annual interest at a rate not to exceed 10 percent nor less than 2 percent, subject to a computation that took into consideration the net earnings of the corporation for the fiscal year ended last previous to the annual interest paying date. There was, therefore, a minimum amount of 2 percent and a maximum of 10 percent due annually and between these limits the interest payable varied in accordance with company earnings. The notes were transferable only by the owner's endorsement and the notation of the transfer by the company. The interest was cumulative and payment might be deferred until the note's maturity when "necessary by reason of the condition of the corporation." Dividends could not be paid until all then due interest on the notes was satisfied. The notes limited the corporation's right to mortgage its real assets. The notes could be subordinated by action of the Board of Directors to any obligation maturing not later than the maturity of the notes. For the fiscal year in question the maximum payment of 10 percent was made on the notes. . . .

Both corporations deducted the payments as interest from their reports of gross income. . . . The Commissioner asserted deficiencies because the payments were considered dividends and not interest. . . .

From the foregoing statements of facts, it appears that the characteristics of all the obligations in question and the surrounding circumstances were of such a nature that it is reasonably possible for determiners to reach the conclusion that the secured annual payments were interest to creditors in one case and dividends to stockholders in the other case. In the Kelley case there were sales of the debentures as well as exchanges of preferred stock for debentures, a promise to pay a certain annual amount, if earned, a priority for the debentures over common stock, the debentures were assignable without regard to any transfer of stock, and a definite maturity date in the reasonable future. These indicia of indebtedness support the Tax Court conclusion that the annual payments were interest on indebtedness. On the other hand, in the Talbot Mills case, the Tax Court found the factors there present of fluctuating annual payments with a two percent minimum, the limitation of the issue of notes to stockholders in exchange only for stock, to be characteristics which distinguish the Talbot Mills notes from the Kelley Company debentures. Upon an appraisal of all the facts, the Tax Court reached the conclusion that the annual payments by Talbot Mills were in reality dividends and not interest.

We think these conclusions should be accepted by the Circuit Courts of Appeals and by ourselves. . . .

These cases now under consideration deal with well understood words as used in the tax statutes — "interest" and "dividends." They need no further definition. . . . The Tax Court is fitted to decide whether the annual payments under these corporate obligations are to be classified as interest or dividends. The Tax Court decisions merely declare that the undisputed facts do or do not bring the payments under the definition of interest or dividends. The documents under consideration embody elements of obligations and elements of stock. There is no one characteristic, not even exclusion from management, which can be said to be decisive in the determination of whether the obligations are risk investments in the corporations or debts. So-called stock certificates may be authorized by corporations which are really debts, and promises to pay may be executed which have incidents of stock. . . .

This leads us to affirm the Talbot Mills decree and to reverse the Kelley judgment.

It is so ordered.

Mr. Justice Rutledge (concurring in part, dissenting in part).

I think the judgments in both cases should be affirmed. On the records presented, I can see no satisfactory basis for deciding one case one way and the other differently. And I agree with the Courts of Appeals that, on the substantially identical facts, the payments were dividends and not interest. . . .

There were some highly technical differences in the two types of "security" which were devised to replace the pre-existing preferred stock issues. But in both instances the original stock and the replacing security were closely held. There was no substantial change in the distribution after the "reorganization." The difference between the stock and the substituted security was so small, in its effect upon the holders' substantial rights, that for all practical purposes it was negligible. . . .

The Court indeed does not attempt to find a substantial differentiating factor other than in the Tax Court's "appraisal of all the facts," in other words its ultimate conclusion. That is true as between the two cases and also as effects the positions of the respective shareholders before and after the wash. Rather the opinion concedes that in each case the circumstances were such that determiners reasonably could conclude that the so-called annual payments were either interest or dividends. Hence, it seems to follow, the conclusion may be drawn in squarely conflicting ways, if the Tax Court sees fit so to draw it; and it is immaterial that no factor of substantial difference is or can be pointed out. . . .

Tax liability should depend upon the subtle refinements of corporate finance no more than it does upon the niceties of conveyancing. Sheer technicalities should have no more weight to control federal tax consequences in one instance than in the other. The taxing statute draws the line broadly between "interest" and "dividend." This requires one who would claim the interest deduction to bring himself clearly within the class for which it was intended. That is not done when the usual signposts between bonds and stock are so obliterated that they become invisible or point equally in both directions at the same time.

"Dividend" and "interest," "stock" and "bond," "debenture" or "note," are correlative and clearly identifiable conceptions in their simpler and more traditional exemplifications. But their distinguishing features vanish when astute manipulation of the broad permissions of modern incorporation acts results in a "security device" which is in truth neither stock nor bond, but the halfbreed offspring of both. At times only the label enables one to ascertain what the manipulator intended to bring forth. But intention clarified by label alone is not always legally effective for the purpose in mind. And there is scarcely any limit to the extent or variety to which this kind of intermingling of the traditional features of stock and bonds or other forms of debt may go, as the books abundantly testify. The taxpayer should show more than a label or a hybrid security to escape his liability. He should show at the least a substantial preponderance of fact pointing to "interest" rather than "dividends." . . .

♦♦♦

Case Questions

1. If there is no one characteristic which can be said to be decisive in the determination of whether securities are equity or debt, what exactly did the Supreme Court base its decision upon?
2. Whose reasoning do you find more persuasive, that of the Court or of Mr. Justice Rutledge? The case certainly drew diverse reactions from the various Justices: five agreed on all issues, three agreed on some issues while disagreeing on others, and one did not take part in the decision.
3. Is the result in the Kelley case an example of an ingenious draftsman slipping a corporation through a tax loophole? Tas evasion is illegal; tax avoidance is legal.

CORPORATE CONTROL DEVICES

Under the law it is the shareholders that possess ultimate corporate power. A major method of exerting this power is through voting their shares. We will now turn to an examination of several devices created to aid the shareholder in exercising his or her control.

PROXY

In a large publicly held corporation one would not expect a large number of shareholders to personally attend shareholder meetings. The time and expense necessary to attend the meeting can be substantial. Yet, this lack of attendance raises two potential problems. First, if shareholders desire to attend but, are unable, they will be denied their suffrage. Secondly, a quorum is necessary at the meeting for shareholder action to be valid. In 1973, Bank of America had 268 shareholders attend its annual meeting, Chrysler 450 and Westinghouse 200 (in 1956 shareholder attendance was 1,600).[2] How were these corporations able to legally conduct these meetings? The proxy system provides the solution. A proxy is the shareholder's equivalent of the absentee ballot. The shareholder casts his vote without attending the meeting and, at the same time, his shares are counted towards the requirements of a quorum.

The shareholder appoints an agent, called a proxy, (which is not to be confused with the written instrument creating the agency relationship also called a proxy), to vote the shares at the meeting. Each share has one vote (except for nonvoting stock). The shareholder can limit the authority of the proxy to voting the shares in a specified manner. Or, the shareholder can delegate general authority to the proxy permitting him to vote the shares according to his own judgment. Figure 10-2 shows a sample of a proxy. The proxy cannot vote for fundamental corporate changes, i.e., mergers, dissolution, basic amendments to the articles, etc., unless the shareholder specifically delegates such authority. The law of agency governs proxies. Thus, a proxy is revocable by the shareholder — principal. The shareholder may revoke his proxy by personally attending the meeting and voting his shares. Subsequently granting a proxy to another individual will revoke the first proxy. However, a proxy coupled with an interest is irrevocable. For example, if A sells his shares to B after the record date for the shareholders' meeting and gives his proxy to B, that proxy is irrevocable. A has coupled his proxy with B's interest in those shares.

The Securities Exchange Act of 1934 subjects the process of proxy solicitation to vigorous regulation. It is unlawful to solicit proxies without complying with the requirements of the '34 Act. These requirements are discussed in detail in Chapter 18.

PROXY FOR ANNUAL MEETING ON MAY 22, 1973

WINNEBAGO INDUSTRIES, INC.

Forest City, Iowa

The undersigned hereby appoints JOHN K. HANSON, ELLIOTT E. COOPER and GERALD E. BOMAN, or any one of them, the undersigned's attorneys and proxies, with full power of substitution, to vote all shares of Common Stock of Winnebago Industries, Inc., which the undersigned is entitled to vote, as fully as the undersigned could do if personally present, at the Annual Meeting of Shareholders of said Corporation to be held in the Forest City Municipal Auditorium, situated at 146 West L Street in Forest City, Iowa, on the 22nd day of May, 1973, at 7:30 P.M., Central Daylight Time, and at any and all adjournments thereof:

(1) For the election of eleven directors; and

(2) In their discretion on such other matters as may properly come before the meeting.

(Continued, and to be signed, on other side)

(Continued from other side)

This proxy is solicited by the management of the corporation.

Dated_____, 1973 _____

I plan to attend the meeting. ☐

Share Owner's Signature—please sign name exactly as imprinted below. (do not print)

PLEASE INDICATE IS ANY CHANGE IN ADDRESS

NOTE: Executors, administrators, trustees and others signing in a representative capacity should indicate the capacity in which they sign. If shares are held jointly EACH holder should sign.

PLEASE DATE, SIGN AND RETURN THIS PROXY

Source: Winnebago Industries, Inc.

Figure 10-2

VOTING TRUSTS

A voting trust is created when any number of shareholders transfer their shares to a trustee for voting purposes. Legal title accompanied by the voting rights to the shares is vested in the trustee. The trustee issues "voting trust certificates" to the shareholders to indicate their respective proportionate share the voting trust. The shareholders retain beneficial ownership of the stock and the trustee forwards any dividends to them. A voting trust agreement sets out the terms and conditions of the voting trust. A voting trust is not to be confused with a proxy, which is revocable. Once established, a voting trust is irrevocable. Typically, the agreement will be limited by statute to a duration of ten years. See Ill. § 30a.

The most famous example of a voting trust is probably the one involving Howard Hughes and TWA, of which he was the majority shareholder. During 1960, Hughes attempted to borrow funds to finance the purchase of jet aircraft for TWA's fleet. The banks and insurance companies disliked his method of managing TWA and refused to lend the funds unless he placed his shares in a voting trust. The trust was to have three trustees, two of which were to be named by the financial institutions. Hughes resisted until, finally, on December 30, 1960, he agreed to the voting trust arrangement. The financial institution's two trustees installed a new management team in TWA. Management then instituted an unsuccessful antitrust suit against Hughes concerning his previous management of the corporation. Shortly after the expiration of the voting trust agreement Hughes sold his 75.18 percent interest at approximately $86 per share. After the deduction of brokerage fees and expenses he received $546,549,711.

PRE-EMPTIVE RIGHTS

A shareholder has the right to purchase his pro rata share of any newly authorized and issued shares of the corporation. This right, called the pre-emptive right, was developed by the common law to enable a shareholder to maintain his proportionate interest in the corporation. The shares must be offered to the shareholder before they can be offered to other prospective purchasers. It is the shareholders' choice whether or not he elects to exercise this right. The right does not exist in shares issued for property,[3] or in connection with a merger,[4] or for payment of debts.[5]

The pre-emptive right doctrine is easily applied in the closely held corporation that has only one class of common stock. Shareholders in such a corporation will likewise be concerned that their voting and financial interest not be diluted by the issuance of shares to other individuals. The situation is quite different in a publicly held corporation. The typical shareholder will have only a small fractional ownership interest in the corporation. Thus, he will be unconcerned with the small dilution to his proportionate voting and dividend rights brought about by a new issue of stock. The administrative burden and expense (paper, postage, secretarial time, etc.) involved in offering pre-emptive rights to a large number of shareholders can be heavy. Pre-emptive rights also pose a delay in securing financing. The shareholders are entitled to a reasonable period of time to consider and accept the offer. In the interim, the public market for such securities may decline. Finally, the widely held corporation may have both common and preferred shares and several different classes within each that have different legal rights. Such a situation can present a legal morass in determining which shareholders are entitled to pre-emptive rights and in what amounts.

Since pre-emptive rights can prove to be troublesome, may a corporation dispense with them? Yes. The states take two approaches. At one end of the spectrum is the elimination of pre-emptive rights unless the articles specifically call for them, i.e., Ind. Corp. Act § 25-205 (i). The opposite position is to permit pre-emptive rights unless they are limited or denied in the articles. See Ill. § 24. In actual operation pre-emptive rights tend to be confined to close corporations.

CUMULATIVE VOTING

Cumulative voting is designed to enable a minority group of shareholders to gain representation on the board of directors. The representatives of the majority shareholders will dominate board affairs, but the minority board members will have an input and gain first hand knowledge of corporate affairs. Typically, management will oppose cumulative voting. The stated reason for such opposition will usually be that the board is to represent the best interests of the corporation and that representatives of special interests have no place in the corporate scheme. The "real" reason for opposition is probably management's desire to avoid having its policies vigorously questioned by segments of the board. Since cumulative voting does preserve majority rule and, since even minority shareholders are owners of the corporation, valid objections to cumulative voting are absent.

Cumulative voting allows a shareholder to mutiply the number of votes given him by his shares times the number of directors to be elected. The shareholder can cast all his votes for a single director candidate or allocate them among several candidates. From a tactical standpoint, the minority shareholder, or shareholders, will desire to cumulate their votes so as to elect the greatest possible number of directors. How is this to be achieved? A formula is available to determine the most advantageous distribution of the cumulated votes.[6] Under the formula: Let X = number of shares needed to elect a given number of directors; Y = total number of shares at the meeting; N^1 = number of directors desired to elect and; N = total number of directors to be elected. The formula assumes that each share is entitled to one vote.

$$X = \frac{Y \times N^1}{N + 1} + 1$$

Let us now examine the formula in operation. Suppose a corporation has a five person board and 3,000 shares outstanding. It is expected that 2,400 shares will be represented at the meeting. If a dissident group of shareholders desires to get one individual elected to the board, how many shares, if cumulated, will be necessary?

$$X = \frac{2,400 \times 1}{5 + 1} + 1$$

$$X = 401 \text{ shares}$$

Thus, for the minority shareholders to place one person on the board of directors, they will need 401 shares if cumulated. To place two individuals on the board will require 801 shares, etc. The five individuals receiving the highest number of votes will be elected.

It is mathematically possible for a minority to use cumulative voting and seize control of the board if the majority errors. Such an error can result from sloppy majority cumulation or a failure to cumulate. In *Pierce v. Commonwealth*, 104

Pa. 150 (1883), the minority cumulated its votes, distributing them among four candidates, while the majority failed to cumulate its votes while distributing them evenly among six candidates. The result was that the four minority candidates were elected to a six person board. The court upheld the result.

Staggering the terms of the directors is a method of circumventing the effect of cumulative voting. For example, if a corporation's board is composed of three members serving staggered three year terms, only one will be elected annually. The majority shareholders will always be victorious in such an election, thereby frustrating the intent of cumulative voting. Such a result will not be permitted in a state that mandates, either constitutionally or by statute, cumulative voting.[7] In slightly less than one half the states cumulative voting is mandatory; slightly less than the remaining one half have permissive cumulative voting, and the remaining handful of states have statutes that are silent on the issue.[8]

SHAREHOLDER MEETINGS

The corporation must hold an annual meeting. The bylaws provide the time and place of the meeting as well as the manner of calling the meeting. The state statute will indicate what percentage of shares, represented in person or by proxy, will constitute a quorum. Oftentimes the statute will prescribe a minimum quorum requirement but allow the corporation to establish a higher requirement if it so desires. If the corporation is granted flexibility in this regard, it should not establish a quorum requirement so high as to make it difficult to hold a meeting nor so low as to allow a small minority to dominate shareholder affairs. The statute will also provide for the closing of the stock transfer books for a stated period (usually mandating a maximum and minimum number of days) to determine the shareholders entitled to notice of or to vote at a meeting. The notice of a regular meeting does not have to contain an agenda for the meeting.

Whenever a special meeting is called, the notice to the shareholder must specify the time, place and the purpose of the meeting. Who has the power to call a special shareholders' meeting? Typically the statute will permit the president, board of directors or such other officers or persons as provided in the articles or bylaws to call a special meeting. Some states allow the holders of a specified number of shares to call a special meeting. See Illinois Business Corporation Act § 26 permitting the holders of not less than one-fifth of all the outstanding shares to call a meeting.

Delaware's corporation law contains a unique feature in § 228. It allows the shareholders to take action without holding an annual or special meeting. It also dispenses with the requirement of prior notice and a vote. If the shareholders holding the minimum number of votes necessary to authorize the action at a meeting, consent in writing to that action, a meeting is not necessary. The shareholders that did not consent must be furnished prompt notice of the action. This provision will permit, in effect, a stockholders meeting to be held by mail. Publicly held corporations incorporated in Delaware have not used this device to avoid hostile questioning by various shareholder groups at the annual meeting. Why? The New York Stock Exchange requires that all companies with stock listed on the Big Board hold annual meetings. Thus, even though management may wish to avoid the annual meeting, and legally may do so, practical obstacles can prevent it.

CLOSE CORPORATIONS

In reality there are two distinctly different types of corporations — 1) the corporation whose shares are widely distributed and, 2) the close corporation with a small number of shareholders. In the latter instance, the shareholders may consist of family members or partners that incorporated for the benefit of limited liability. Are the courts to regard the rights of a shareholder in a publicly traded corporation as being different than those of a shareholder in a closely held enterprise? If so, upon what grounds should a distinction be made when the business corporation statute fails to make such a distinction. The following case, *Galler* v. *Galler*, is indicative of the judicial attitude towards the close corporation.

GALLER v. GALLER
32 Ill. 2d 16, 203 N.E. 2d 577 (S. Ct., Ill., 1964)

♦♦♦

UNDERWOOD, Justice.

Plaintiff, Emma Galler, sued in equity for an accounting and for specific performance of an agreement made in July, 1955, between plaintiff and her husband, of one part, and defendants, Isadore A. Galler and his wife, Rose, of the other. Defendants appealed from a decree of the superior court of Cook County granting the relief prayed. The First District Appellate Court reversed the decree and denied specific performance, affirming in part the order for an accounting, and modifying the order awarding master's fees. . . . That decision is appealed here. . . .

There is no substantial dispute as to the facts in this case. From 1919 to 1924, Benjamin and Isadore Galler, brothers, were equal partners in the Galler Drug Company, a wholesale drug concern. In 1924 the business was incorporated under the Illinois Business Corporation Act, each owning one half of the outstanding 220 shares of stock. In 1945 each contracted to sell 6 shares to an employee, Rosenberg, at a price of $10,500 for each block of 6 shares, payable within 10 years. . . .

In March, 1954, Benjamin and Isadore, on the advice of their accountant, decided to enter into an agreement for the financial protection of their immediate families and to assure their families, after the death of either brother, equal control of the corporation. In June, 1954, while the agreement was in the process of preparation by an attorney-associate of the accountant, Benjamin suffered a heart attack. Although he resumed his business duties some months later, he was again stricken in February, 1955, and thereafter was unable to return to work. During his brother's illness, Isadore asked the accountant to have the shareholders' agreement put in final form in order to protect Benjamin's wife, and this was done by another attorney employed in the accountant's office. On a Saturday night in July, 1955, the accountant brought the agreement to Benjamin's home, and 6 copies of it were executed there by the two brothers and their wives. . . . It appears from the evidence that some months after the agreement was signed, the defendants Isadore and Rose Galler and their son, the defendant, Aaron Galler sought to have the agreements destroyed. The evidence is undisputed that defendants had decided prior to Benjamin's death they would not honor the agreement, but never disclosed their intention to plaintiff or her husband.

On July 21, 1956, Benjamin executed an instrument creating a trust naming his wife as trustee. The trust covered, among other things, the 104 shares of Galler Drug Company stock and the stock certificates were endorsed by Benjamin and delivered to Emma. When Emma presented the certificates to defendants for transfer into her name as trustee, they sought to have Emma abandon the 1955 agreement or enter into some kind of a noninterference agreement as a price for the transfer of the shares. Finally, in September, 1956, after Emma had refused to abandon the shareholders' agreement, she did agree to permit defendant Aaron to become president for one year and agreed that she would not interfere with the business during that year. The stock was then reissued in her name as trustee. During the year 1957 while Benjamin was still alive, Emma tried many times to arrange a meeting with Isadore to discuss business matters but he refused to see her.

Shortly after Benjamin's death, Emma went to the office and demanded the terms of the 1955 agreement be carried out. Isadore told her that anything she had to say could be said to Aaron, who then told her that his father would not abide by the agreement. He offered a modification of the agreement by proposing the salary continuation payment but without her becoming a director. When Emma refused to modify the agreement and sought enforcement of its terms, defendants refused and this suit followed.

During the last few years of Benjamin's life both brothers drew an annual salary of $42,000. Aaron, whose salary was $15,000 as manager of the warehouse prior to September, 1956, has since the time that Emma agreed to his acting as president drawn an annual salary of $20,000. In 1957, 1958, and 1959 a $40,000 annual dividend was paid. Plaintiff has received her proportionate share of the dividend.

The July, 1955, agreement in question here, entered into between Benjamin, Emma, Isadore and Rose, recites that Benjamin and Isadore each own 47½% of the issued and outstanding shares of the Galler Drug Company, an Illinois corporation, and that Benjamin and Isadore desired to provide income for the support and maintenance of their immediate families. . . . The essential features of the contested portions of the agreement are substantially as set forth in the opinion of the Appellate. Court: (2) that the bylaws of the corporation will be amended to provide for a board of four directors; that the necessary quorum shall be three directors; and that no directors' meeting shall be held without giving ten days notice to all directors. (3) The shareholders will cast their votes for the above named persons (Isadore, Rose, Benjamin and Emma) as directors at said special meeting and at any other meeting held for the purpose of electing directors. (4,5) In the event of the death of either brother his wife shall have the right to nominate a director in place of the decedent. (6) Certain annual dividends will be declared by the corporation. The dividend shall be $50,000 payable out of the accumulated earned surplus in excess of $500,000. If 50% of the annual net profits after taxes exceeds the minimum $50,000, then the directors shall have discretion to declare a dividend up to 50% of the annual net profits. If the net profits are less than $50,000, nevertheless the minimum $50,000 annual dividend shall be declared, providing the $500,000 surplus is maintained. Earned surplus is defined. (9) The certificates evidencing the said shares of Benjamin Galler and Isadore Galler shall bear a legend that the shares are subject to the terms of this agreement. (10) A salary continuation agreement shall be entered into by the corporation which shall authorize the corporation upon the death of Benjamin Galler or Isadore Galler, or both, to pay a sum equal to twice the salary of such officer, payable monthly over a five-year period. Said sum shall be paid to the widow during her widowhood, but should be paid to such widow's children if the widow remarries within the five-year period. (11,12) . . . In the event either Benjamin or Isadore decides to sell his shares he is required to offer them first to the remaining shareholders and then to the corporation at book value, according each six months to accept the offer.

The Appellate Court found the 1955 agreement void because "the undue duration, stated purpose and substantial disregard of the provisions of the Corporation Act outweigh any considerations which might call for divisibility" and held that "the public policy of this state demands voiding this entire agreement."

While the conduct of defendants towards plaintiff was clearly inequitable, the basically controlling factor is the absence of an objecting minority interest, together with the absence of public detriment. . . .

The power to invalidate the agreements on the grounds of public policy is so far reaching and so easily abused that it should be called into action to set aside or annul the solemn engagement of parties dealing on equal terms only in cases where the corrupt or dangerous tendency clearly and unequivocally appears upon the face of the agreement itself or is the necessary inference from the matters which are expressed, and the only apparent exception to this general rule is to be found in those cases where the agreement, though fair and unobjectionable on its face, is a part of a corrupt scheme and is made to disguise the real nature of the transaction. . . .

At this juncture it should be emphasized that we deal here with a so-called close corporation. Various attempts at definition of the close corporation have been made. . . . For our purposes, a close corporation is one in which the stock is held in a few hands, or in a few families, and wherein it is not at all, or only rarely, dealt in by buying or selling. . . . Moreover, it should be recognized that shareholder agreements similar to that in question here are often, as a practical consideration, quite necessary for the protection of those financially interested in the close corporation. While the shareholder of a public-issue corporation may readily sell his shares on the open market should management fail to use, in his opinion, sound business judgment, his counterpart of the close corporation often has a large total of his entire capital invested in the business and has no ready market for his shares should he desire to sell. He feels, understandably, that he is more than a mere investor and that his voice should be heard concerning all corporate activity. Without a shareholder agreement, specifically enforceable by the courts, insuring him a modicum of control, a large minority shareholder might find himself at the mercy of an oppressive or unknowledgeable majority. Moreover, as in the case at bar, the shareholders of a close corporation are often also the directors and officers thereof. With substantial shareholding interests abiding in each member of the board of directors, it is often quite impossible to secure, as in the large public-issue corporation, independent board judgment free from personal motivations concerning corporate policy. For these and other reasons too voluminous to enumerate here, often the only sound basis for protection is afforded by a lengthy, detailed shareholder agreement securing the rights and obligations of all concerned. . . .

As the preceding review of the applicable decisions of this court points out, there has been a definite, albeit inarticulate, trend toward eventual judicial treatment of the close corporation as sui generis. Several shareholder-director agreements that have technically "violated" the letter of the Business Corporation Act have nevertheless been upheld in the light of the existing practical circumstances, i.e., no apparent public injury, the absence of a complaining minority interest, and no apparent prejudice to creditors. However, we have thus far not attempted to limit these decisions as applicable only to close corporations and have seemingly implied that general considerations regarding judicial supervision of all corporate behavior apply. . . .

Courts have long ago quite realistically, we feel, relaxed their attitudes concerning statutory compliance when dealings with close corporate behavior, permitting "slight deviations" from corporate "norms" in order to give legal efficacy to common business practice. . . . This attitude is illustrated by the following language in *Clark* v. *Dodge*: "Public policy, the intention of the Legislature, detriment to the corporation, are phrases which in this connection (the court was discussing a shareholder-director agreement whereby the directors pledged themselves to vote for certain people as officers of the corporation) mean little. Possible harm to bona fide purchasers of stock or to creditors or to stockholding minorities have more substance; but such harms are absent in many instances. If the enforcement of a particular contract damages nobody — not even, in any perceptible degree, the public — one sees no reason for holding it illegal, even though it impinges slightly upon the broad provisions of (the relevant statute providing that the business of a corporation shall be managed by its board of directors.). Damage suffered or threatened is a logical and practical test, and has come to be the one generally adopted by the courts. . . .

Numerous helpful textual statements and law review articles dealing with the judicial treatment of the close corporation have been pointed out by counsel. One article concludes with the following: "New needs compel fresh formulation of corporate 'norms'. There is no reason why mature men should not be able to adapt the statutory form to the structure they want, so long as they do not endanger other stockholders, creditors, or the public, or violate a clearly mandatory provision of the corporation laws. In a typical close corporation the stockholders' agreement is usually the result of careful deliberation among all initial investors. In the large public-issue corporation, on the other hand, the 'agreement' represented by the corporate charter is not consciously agreed to by the investors; they have no voice in its formulation, and very few ever read the certificate of incorporation. Preservation of the corporate norms may there be necessary for the protection of the public investors." Hornstein, "Stockholders' Agreements in the Closely Held Corporation," 59 Yale L. Journal, 1040, 1056. . . .

At any rate, however, the courts can no longer fail to expressly distinguish between the close and public-issue corporation when confronted with problems relating to either. What we do here is to illuminate this problem — before the bench, corporate bar, and the legislature, in the context of a particular fact situation. To do less would be to shirk our responsibility, to do more would, perhaps be to invade the province of the legislative branch.

We now, in the light of the foregoing, turn to specific provisions of the 1955 agreement.

The Appellate Court correctly found many of the contractual provisions free from serious objection, and we need not prolong this opinion with a discussion of them here. That court did, however, find difficulties in the stated purpose of the agreement as it relates to its duration, the election of certain persons to specific offices for a number of years, the requirement for the mandatory declaration of stated dividends (which the Appellate Court held invalid), and the salary continuation agreement.

Since the question as to the duration of the agreement is a principal source of controversy, we shall consider it first. The parties provided no specific termination date, and while the agreement concludes with a paragraph that its terms "shall be binding upon and shall inure to the benefits of" the legal representatives, heirs and assigns of the parties, this clause is, we believe, intended to be operative only as long as one of the parties is living. It further provides that it shall be so construed as to carry out its purposes, and we believe these must be determined from a consideration of the agreement as a whole. Thus viewed, a fair construction is that its purposes were accomplished at the death of the survivor of the parties. . . . While defendants argue that the public policy evinced by the legislative restrictions upon the duration of voting trust agreements . . . should be applied here, this agreement is not a voting trust, but as pointed out by the dissenting justice in the Appellate Court, is a straight contractual voting control agreement which does not divorce voting rights from stock ownership. . . . While limiting voting trusts in 1947 to a maximum duration of 10 years, the legislature has indicated no similar policy regarding straight voting agreements although these have been common since prior to 1870. In view of the history of decisions of this court generally upholding, in the absence of fraud or prejudice to minority interests or public policy, the right of stockholders to agree among themselves as to the manner in which their stock will be voted, we do not regard the period of time within which this agreement may remain effective as rendering the agreement unenforceable.

The clause that provides for the election of certain persons to specified offices for a period of years likewise does not require invalidation. . . .

We turn next to a consideration of the effect of the stated purpose of the agreement upon its validity. The pertinent provision is: "The said Benjamin A. Galler and Isadore A. Galler desire to provide income for the support and maintenance of their immediate families." Obviously, there is no evil inherent in a contract entered into for the reason that the persons originating the terms desired to so arrange their property as to provide post-death support for those dependent upon them. . . .

The terms of the dividend agreement require a minimum annual dividend of $50,000, but this duty is limited by the subsequent provision that it shall be operative only so long as an earned surplus of $500,000 is maintained. It may be noted that in 1958, the year prior to commencement of this litigation, the corporation's net earnings after taxes amounted to $202,759 while its earned surplus was $1,543,270, and this was increased in 1958 to $1,680,079 while earnings were $172,964. The minimum earned surplus requirement is designed for the protection of the corporation and its creditors, and we take no exception to the contractual dividend requirements as thus restricted. . . .

The salary continuation agreement is a common feature, in one form or another, of corporate executive employment. It requires that the widow should receive a total benefit, payable monthly over a five-year period, aggregating twice the amount paid her deceased husband in one year. . . .

We hold defendants must account for all monies received by them from the corporation since September 25, 1956, in excess of that theretofore authorized.

Accordingly, the judgment of the Appellate Court is reversed. . . . The cause is remanded to the circuit court of Cook County with directions to proceed in accordance herewith.

Affirmed in part and reversed in part, and remanded with directions.

Case Questions

1. What exactly is "public policy" and who ascertains its dictates? Doesn't the legislature establish the public policy toward corporations when it enacts the business corporation act?
2. Is different judicial treatment of the close corporation vis-a-vis the public corporation justifiable?
3. Does the decision reflect sympathy for Emma Galler, sound judicial reasoning, or both?

Only a mere handful of states have included special provisions for close corporations in their business corporation statutes. Instead, most state legislatures have permitted the judicial branch to carve out exceptions for them as was done in *Galler* v. *Galler.* Delaware provides the most complete statutory treatment of closely held corporations. In 1967, it added a number of special provisions to govern the close corporation, which is defined as one having thirty or fewer shareholders. Among the more significant provisions of the Delaware General Corporation Law on close corporations are the following:

§ 350. AGREEMENTS RESTRICTING DISCRETION OF DIRECTORS.

A written agreement among the stockholders of a close corporation holding a majority of the outstanding stock entitled to vote, whether solely among themselves or with a party not a stockholder, is not invalid, as between the parties to the agreement, on the ground that it so relates to the conduct of the business and affairs of the corporation as to restrict or interfere with the discretion or powers of the board of directors. The effect of any such agreement shall be to relieve the directors and impose upon the stockholders who are parties to the agreement the liability for managerial acts or omissions which is imposed on directors to the extent and so long as the discretion or powers of the board in its management of corporate affairs is controlled by such agreement.

§ 351. MANAGEMENT BY STOCKHOLDERS.

The certificate of incorporation of a close corporation may provide that the business of the corporation shall be managed by the stockholders of the corporation rather than by a board of directors. So long as this provision continues in effect:

1. No meeting of stockholders need be called to elect directors;
2. Unless the context clearly requires otherwise, the stockholders of the corporation shall be deemed to be directors for purposes of applying provisions of this chapter; and
3. The stockholders of the corporation shall be subject to all liabilities of directors.

Such a provision may be inserted in the certificate of incorporation by amendment if all incorporators and subscribers or all holders of record of all of the outstanding stock, whether or not having voting power, authorize such a provision. An amendment to the certificate of incorporation to delete such a provision shall be adopted by a vote of the holders of a majority of all outstanding stock of the corporation, whether or not otherwise entitled to vote. If the certificate of incorporation contains a provision authorized by this section, the existence of such provision shall be noted conspicuously on the face or back of every stock certificate issued by such corporation.

§ 354. OPERATING CORPORATION AS PARTNERSHIP.

No written agreement among stockholders of a close corporation, nor any provision of the certificate of incorporation or of the bylaws of the corporation, which agreement or provision relates to any phase of the affairs of such corporation, including but not limited to the management of its business or declaration and payment of dividends or other division of profits or the election of directors or officers or the employment of stockholders by the corporation or the arbitration of disputes, shall be invalid on the ground that it is an attempt by the parties to the agreement or by the stockholders of the corporation to treat the corporation as if it were a partnership or to arrange relations among the stockholders or between the stockholders and the corporation in a manner that would be appropriate only among partners.

§ 355. STOCKHOLDERS' OPTION TO DISSOLVE CORPORATION.

a. The certificate of incorporation of any close corporation may include a provision granting to any stockholder, or to the holders of any specified number or percentage of shares of any class of stock, an option to have the corporation dissolved at will or upon the occurrence of any specified event or contingency. Whenever any such option to dissolve is exercised, the stockholders exercising such option shall give written notice thereof to all other stockholders. After the expiration of thirty days following the sending of such notice, the dissolution of the corporation shall proceed as if the required number of stockholders having voting power had consented in writing to dissolution of the corporation as provided by § 228 of this title.

b. If the certificate of incorporation as originally filed does not contain a provision authorized by subsection (a), the certificate may be amended to include such provision if adopted by the affirmative vote of the holders of all the outstanding stock, whether or not entitled to vote, unless the certificate of incorporation specifically authorizes such an amendment by a vote which shall be not less than two thirds of all the outstanding stock whether or not entitled to vote.

SHAREHOLDERS' REMEDIAL RIGHTS

As the owners of the corporation, the shareholders legally can control the corporation through election of the board of directors. Yet, at times the right to vote for directors may be insufficient to protect the shareholders' interests. The shareholders' power may be thwarted if information regarding director and officer impropriety does not come to their attention or, if they have no weapon to halt such abuses. We will explore two shareholder remedies for combating improper activities: the right to inspect the corporate books and shareholder derivative suits.

RIGHT TO INSPECT CORPORATE BOOKS AND RECORDS.

Common law grants to a shareholder the right to inspect the corporate books and records for a legitimate purpose. The shareholder can select another, such as an attorney or accountant, to perform the inspection on his behalf.

The requirement of a legitimate purpose is designed to protect the corporation, and its other shareholders, from harrassment or other abuses. For example, an officer of a chemical manufacturer, who is also a shareholder of a competing enterprise, could not see the competitor's books to learn trade secrets or obtain customer lists. A dissident shareholder can obtain a list of shareholders in order to solicit their proxies for his attempt to remove current management. Such an effort constitutes a proper purpose, as does an inspection of the records to discover relevant evidence for a lawsuit against the directors and officers. Other legitimate purposes include a determination of the corporation's financial position and/or its ability to pay dividends and the investigation of possible mismanagement. This is not an all inclusive listing of proper reasons for access to the books. A shareholder can inspect the books and records for any reason so long as he convinces a court that it is necessary to protect the interests of the corporation and himself. It should go without saying that the shareholder must conduct the inspection in a reasonable manner and at a reasonable time.

What books and records are available for inspection? At common law any and all the records relevant to the shareholder's inquiry. Some statutes specifically list the books and records available to the shareholder. His right to inspect records not named on that list is generally protected by his common law rights. Some statutes will require that the shareholder either have owned the stock for a specified period of time or own a certain minimum percentage of the outstanding stock before he can examine the books. The Illinois law, § 45, specifies a either six month period of ownership or ownership of at least five percent of the stock.

A wrongful refusal to produce the records for inspection will subject the wrongdoer to liability for damages caused the shareholder. A computation of actual damages will usually be difficult, if not impossible. This shortcoming is provided for in some statutes by establishing arbitrary penalities. For instance, § 45, of the Illinois Act sets as a penalty ten percent of the value of the shares owned by the shareholder in addition to any other damages.

SHAREHOLDERS' DERIVATIVE SUITS

What is a shareholder to do if a director or officer is violating his fiduciary duties thereby damaging the corporation, and the directors refuse to halt the activity and seek reimbursement? Institute a *shareholders' derivative suit* to call the corporate managers to account.

A shareholders' derivative or representative suit is brought by the plaintiff shareholder against the wrongdoing directors and/or officers and the corporation. Actually, the lawsuit is brought on behalf of the corporation. Despite its legal status as a defendant, the corporation is the real party at interest while the shareholder only serves as the nominal plaintiff. If the lawsuit is successful and results in a monetary award, those funds (minus the plaintiff's attorney's fees and costs) will go into the corporate treasury. A derivative action will be proper: 1) where a valid claim exists on which the corporation could sue and, 2) the corporation has refused to proceed after suitable demand, unless excused by extraordinary circumstances.

It is important to distinguish a derivative suit from a direct private action from a class action. In a derivative suit, the shareholder derives the right to sue from the corporation itself and seeks to remedy a wrong done to the corporation. In a direct private action the shareholder is suing because of a wrong done to him personally. In a class action the plaintiff is suing for himself and all others similarly situated. Suppose a shareholder sues the directors and the corporation to halt a proposed ultra vires act or to recover funds embezzled by a director. Such a lawsuit is derivative in nature. The corporation will, or has, suffered the wrongful act and the shareholder is suing on behalf of the corporation. If the shareholder has instituted legal action against an officer and the corporation because the officer, while in the course of his employment, collided with the shareholder's automobile, that is a direct action. The shareholder is suing because of a wrong done to him personally. If, however, the shareholder was accompanied by guests, who were also injured in the collision, and he now sues the corporation for damages done to all the car's occupants, it is a class action. The shareholder is suing for a personal injury to himself and for all others who themselves suffered injuries. Derivative suits and class actions can be easily confused since, in each, the plaintiff represents the legal interests of, and brings the suit on behalf of, many other persons.

Oftentimes management will regard derivative suits as a legalized form of extortion. Since defending against a derivative is both expensive and time consuming, an out-of-court settlement is not uncommon. Management sometimes feels that the shareholder's claim is frivolous and is brought only for its nuisance value. Nuisance value meaning that the corporation will find it cheaper to pay the shareholder a sum to settle the lawsuit than to conduct a full blown successful defense. A derivative suit that lacks merit is frequently called a "strike suit." In an effort to eliminate strike suits some states have enacted security for costs statutes. Such legislation will require certain categories of shareholders to post security for costs as a condition to maintaining their derivative action. If the plaintiff shareholders are unsuccessful in their suit, the defendants may be able to gain reimbursement for expenses incurred in their defense.

The first and most famous of the security for costs (or expenses) statutes is § 627 of the New York Business Corporation Law. It provides that plaintiffs who hold less than five percent of the outstanding shares of any class of stock, unless the market value of their stock exceeds $50,000, must furnish security upon request by the corporation. The request can be made at any time during the legal proceedings prior to final judgment. When computing the reasonable expenses for which security must be posted, attorneys' fees are included. California has taken a different approach in § 834 (b) of its corporation code. The defendant must move for the posting of security within thirty days after service of process. Then, if his motion is to prevail, he must show that there is no reasonable possibility that the derivative action will benefit the corporation and shareholders.

How do the shareholder plaintiffs finance their portion of the derivative suit? Generally the attorney will accept the suit based upon the expectation of victory. If victorious, the courts award the attorney his fees from the corporation. The courts are not tightfisted in awarding such fees. The judiciary recognizes worthwhile legal and social purposes in a suit that protects a corporation and its shareholders. The generous award of attorneys' fees in such cases guarantees that they will continue to be instituted whenever appropriate. If the derivative suit fails to benefit the corporation, the attorney will typically receive no fee. This serves as an economic incentive to accept only legitimate cases and reject cases of a strike suit nature.

Let us turn to an actual derivative action. The *Mayer* v. *Adams* case that follows deals with the issue of what constitutes extraordinary circumstances excusing the shareholder's demand prior to instituting a derivative suit. We have already observed that a derivative suit can only be brought: 1) where the corporation has a valid legal claim and, 2) the corporation declined to proceed after suitable demand, unless excused by the presence of exceptional conditions.

MAYER v. ADAMS
141 A. 2d 458, (S. Ct., Del. 1958)

◆◆◆

SOUTHERLAND, Chief Justice.

The case concerns Rule 23 (b) of the Rules of the Court of Chancery, Del. C. Ann. relating to stockholders' derivative suits. The second sentence of paragraph (b) provides:

> The complaint shall also set forth with particularity the efforts of the plaintiff to secure from the managing directors or trustees and, if necessary, from the shareholders such action as he desires, and the reasons for his failure to obtain such action or the reasons for not making such effort.

The question is:

Under what circumstances is a preliminary demand on shareholders necessary?

Plaintiff is a stockholder of the defendant Phillips Petroleum Company. She brought an action to redress alleged frauds and wrongs committed by the defendant directors upon the corporation. They concern dealings between Phillips and defendant Ada Oil Company, in which one of the defendant directors is alleged to have a majority stock interest.

The amended complaint set forth reasons why demand on the directors for action would be futile and the sufficiency of these reasons was not challenged. It also set forth reasons seeking to excuse failure to demand stockholder action. The principal reasons were 1) that fraud was charged, which no majority of stockholders could ratify; and 2) that to require a minority stockholder to circularize more than 100,000 stockholders — in effect, to engage a proxy fight with the management — would be an intolerably oppressive and unreasonable rule, and in any event would be a futile proceeding. All defendants moved to dismiss on the ground that the reasons set forth were insufficient in law to excuse such failure.

The Vice Chancellor was of opinion that, notwithstanding these allegations, demand on stockholders would not necessarily have been futile. He accordingly dismissed the complaint. Plaintiff appeals.

In the view we take of the case, the issue between the ligitants narrows itself to this:

If the ground of the derivative suit is fraud, is demand for stockholder action necessary under the rule?

When it is said that a demand on stockholders is necessary in a case involving fraud, the inquiry naturally arises: demand to do what?

Let us suppose that the objecting stockholder submits to a stockholders' meeting a proposal that a suit be brought to redress alleged wrongs. He may do so either by attending the meeting, or, if the regulations of the Securities and Exchange Commission are applicable, by requiring the management to mail copies of the proposal to the other stockholders. (He is limited to 100 words of explanation. Rule X-14A-Sb.) Let us further suppose — a result quite unlikely — that the stockholders approve the resolution. What is accomplished by such approval? The stockholder is about to file his suit. What additional force is given to the suit by the approval?

Let us suppose again that the proposal is disapproved by the majority stockholders — as common knowledge tells us it will ordinarily be. What of it? They cannot ratify the alleged fraud. ...

If the foregoing is a correct analysis of the matter, it follows that the whole process of stockholder demand in a case of alleged fraud is futile and avails nothing.

The defendants vigorously assail this view of the matter. They say that the rule requires demand for action to be made upon the stockholders in all cases in which the board of directors is disqualified (as here) to pass upon the matter of bringing suit, because in such a case the power to determine the question of policy passes to the body of the stockholders. The stockholders may determine, when the matter is presented to them, upon any one of a number of courses. Thus, defendants say, they may authorize plaintiff's suit' they may determine to file the suit collectively — "take it over," so to speak' they may take other remedial action; they may remove the directors; and, finally, they may decide that the suit has no merit, or, as a matter of corporate policy, that it should not in any event be brought.

These answers do not impress us. As we have said, why is it "necessary" to have stockholders' approval of plaintiff's suit? Defendants say: to comply with the rule. This is arguing in a circle. The question is, does the rule make it necessary?

Finally it is suggested that the stockholders may 1) determine that the suit has no merit, or 2) that it is not good policy to press it.

As to the first suggestion, we think it clear that in the ordinary case the stockholders in meeting could not satisfactorily determine the probable merits of a minority stockholder's suit without a reasonably complete presentation and consideration of evidentiary facts. Perhaps some very simple cases might be handled in another manner, but they must be few. A stockholders' meeting is not an appropriate forum for such a proceeding.

The second suggestion, that the stockholders may, as a matter of policy, determine that the claim shall not be enforced and bind the minority not to sue, is really the cruz of this case. If the majority stockholders have this power, there would be much to be said for defendants' argument that in case of a disqualified or non-functioning board, the stockholders should decide the matter. . . .

But a decision not to press a claim for alleged fraud committed by the directors means, in effect, that the wrong cannot be remedied. It is conceded that the wrong cannot be ratified by the majority stockholders . . . To construe Rule 23 (b) as making necessary a submission of the matter to stockholders, because the stockholders have the power to prevent the enforcement of the claim, is to import into our law a procedure that would inevitably have the effect of seriously impairing the minority stockholder's now existing right to seek redress for frauds committed by directors of the corporation. This right he has always had under the Delaware law and practice. The policy of the General Corporation law for many years has been to grant to the directors, and to the majority stockholders in certain matters, very broad powers to determine corporate management and policy. But, correlatively, the policy of our courts has always been to hold the directors and the majority stockholders to strict accountability for any breach of good faith in the exercise of these powers, and to permit any minority stockholder to seek redress in equity on behalf of the corporation for wrongs committed by the directors or by the majority stockholders. We cannot believe that Rule 23 (b) was intended to import into our law and procedural a radical change of this judicial policy.

We hold that if a minority stockholders' complaint is based upon an alleged wrong committed by the directors against the corporation, of such a nature as to be beyond ratification by a majority of the stockholders, it is not necessary to allege or prove an effort to obtain action by the stockholders to redress the wrong.

The question may be asked: In what circumstances is such demand necessary? Obviously the rule contemplates that in some cases a demand is necessary; otherwise, it would have not been adopted.

We are not called upon in this case to attempt to enumerate the various circumstances in which demand on stockholders is excused; and likewise we do not undertake to enumerate all the cases in which demand is necessary. It seems clear that one instance of necessary demand is a case involving only an irregularity or lack of authority in directorate action. . . .

The phrase "if necessary" is thus, we think susceptible of a reasonable construction that comports with Delaware law and practice.

We are accordingly compelled to disagree with the holding of the Vice Chancellor that the bill should be dismissed as to all the defendants for failure to comply with Rule 23 (b).

For the reasons above stated, the judgement below must be reversed, without prejudice to the four defendants Emery, Oberfell, Dimit and Rice, to renew below at an appropriate time the motion to dismiss above referred to.

The cause is remanded to the Court of Chancery for New Castle County, with instructions to vacate the judgment of October 8, 1957, and to take such further proceedings as may not be inconsistent with this opinion.

◆◆◆

Case Questions

1. Is the court here "interpreting" the law or is it "making" law?
2. Why didn't the court enumerate the various circumstances in which a demand on stockholders is necessary or is excused? If the court had done so, it would probably avoid the necessity of future litigation over such questions.
3. Is the demand on stockholders requirement superfluous?

REVIEW PROBLEMS

1. An officer of a corporation makes an illegal $100,000 contribution of corporate funds to a candidate for federal office. Upon discovery of this fact, the corporation hires legal counsel and expends $50,000 in an unsuccessful defense of the resulting criminal charge. The corporation is fined $5,000 for the violation. If the directors refuse to seek recovery of the funds from the officer, would a derivative suit be available? If so, should it seek to have the corporation reimbursed for the $100,000 plus interest from the date of contribution, the $50,000 in legal fees plus the $5,000 fine?
2. The bylaws of a corporation provide that it shall be the duty of the president to call a special meeting whenever requested in writing to do by stockholders owning a majority of the stock. The holders of slightly more than 55 percent of the stock request such a meeting in writing. The president refuses to call the meeting and so the shareholders institute court proceedings to force him to make the call. The purpose of the meeting is to: a) endorse the administration of the prior president, whom the board removed; b) to amend the articles and bylaws to permit the shareholders to fill board vacancies; c) to hear preferred charges against four directors, determine whether their conduct was inimical to the corporation and, if so, to vote upon their removal and for the election of their successors. Will the court order the calling of a special meeting? [*Auer* v. *Dressel*, 118 N.E. 2d 590 (1954)].
3. A corporation issues two classes of stock. The articles provide that "none of the shares of Class B stock shall be entitled to dividends either upon voluntary or involuntary dissolution or otherwise." The shares had voting rights but, the plaintiffs' claim that the Class B shares do not in fact constitute stock because they are deprived of the economic incidents of stock, or of the proportionate interest in the corporate assets. The defense contends that ownership of stock may consist of one or more of the rights to participate in the control of the corporation, in its surplus or profits, or in the distribution of its assets. Do the Class B shares represent valid stock? [*Stroh* v. *Blackhawk Holding Corporation* 272 N.E. 2d 1 (1971)].
4. Why would an individual be willing to purchase non-voting securities?
5. A corporation has a thirteen member board split into two equal factions plus a neutral director. Subsequently four directors resign leaving one faction, led by the president (the Vogel faction), with four directors and the other faction (the Tomlinson faction) with five directors. Seven directors are needed for a

quorum. The president then calls a special stockholders' meeting to a) fill the director vacancies; b) increase the board size to nineteen and a quorum to ten and elect these directors; c) to remove two of the directors of the Tomlinson faction and to fill these vacancies. Naturally, the president proposes a slate of nominees for the vacancies. The bylaws provide that the president shall have power to call special meetings of the stockholders for any purpose or purposes.

The Tomlinson faction seeks to prohibit the meeting. They alleged that the president lacks the power to call a special meeting for such a purpose and, alternatively, that the shareholders have no power to remove directors from office even for cause. If directors can be removed for cause, they argue that the directors must be afforded a reasonable opportunity to be heard by the stockholders on the charges made. They seek an injunction to prevent the Vogel faction from using corporate funds, employees and facilities for the solicitation of proxies. They also seek to have it made clear in the solicitation process that the Vogel group, although representing current corporate policy and administration, is not representing a majority of the board. How should this legal can of worms be solved? [*Campbell* v. *Loew's Inc.*, 134 A. 2d 852 (1957)].

ENDNOTES

1. These figures on stock ownership are taken from Blume, Crockett and Friend, *Stockownership in the U.S.*; *Characteristics and Trends, Survey of Current Business*, Nov. 1974, Vol. 54, No. 11.
2. *Wall Street Journal,* April 19, 1973, at 1, col. 5.
3. *Thom* v. *Baltimore Trust Co.,* 148 A 234 (1930).
4. *Musson* v. *N.Y. & Queens Elect.,* 247 N.Y.S. 406 (1931).
5. *Dunlay* v. *Ave. M Garage & Repair,* 170 N.E. 917 (1930).
6. Williams, *Cumulative Voting for Directors,* pp. 40-46, (1951) (Harvard).
7. *Erie Technological Products Inc.* v. *Erie Technological Products,* 248 F. Supp. 380 (1965).
8. Lattin, *Lattin On Corporations* (2nd Ed. 1971) § 91 p. 374.

MANAGING THE CORPORATION: THE ROLE OF THE DIRECTORS AND OFFICERS

11

After our scrutiny of the shareholders' role in the corporate scheme let us shift our focus to the directors and officers. It is not the shareholders who formulate corporate policy nor, do they execute this policy on a day-to-day basis. The directors fulfill the former function while the officers accomplish the latter task. Frequently an individual will wear three hats, that of a shareholder, director and officer. The law judges the authority and obligations of such an individual according to the specific capacity within which he or she is operating. Let us now examine, in turn, the role occupied by directors and officers.

DIRECTORS

Before discussing the directors' position within the corporate hierarchy we will first sketch the legal backdrop against which they operate. Carefully read the following statutory excerpt keeping in mind that the powers of a board of directors are determined by the relevant state's business corporation statute.

ILLINOIS BUSINESS CORPORATION ACT:

§ 33. BOARD OF DIRECTORS.

The business and affairs of a corporation shall be managed by a board of directors. Directors need not be residents of this State or shareholders of the corporation unless the articles of incorporation or by-laws so require. The articles of incorporation or by-laws may prescribe other qualifications for directors. Unless otherwise provided in the articles of incorporation or by-laws, the board of directors, by the affirmative vote of a majority of the directors then in office, and irrespective of any personal interest of any of its members, shall have authority to establish reasonable compensation of all directors for services to the corporation as directors, officers or otherwise.

§ 34. NUMBER AND ELECTION OF DIRECTORS.

The number of directors of a corporation shall be not less than three, except that in cases where all the shares of a corporation are owned of record by either one or two shareholders, the number of directors may be less than three but not less than the number of shareholders. Subject to such limitation, the number of directors shall be fixed by the by-laws, except as to the number of directors to be elected at the first meeting of shareholders, which number shall be fixed by the articles of incorporation. The number of directors so fixed by the articles of incorporation shall be elected by the shareholders at the first meeting of shareholders after the filing of the articles of incorporation, to hold office until the first annual meeting of shareholders. The number of directors may be increased or decreased from time to time by amendment to the by-laws. In the absence of a by-law fixing the number of directors, the number shall be the same as that stated in the articles of incorporation. At the first annual meeting of shareholders and at each annual meeting thereafter the shareholders shall elect directors to hold office until the next succeeding annual meeting, except as hereinafter provided. Each director shall hold office for the term for which he is elected or until his successor shall have been elected and qualified.

§ 36. VACANCIES.

Any vacancy occurring in the board of directors and any directorship to be filled by reason of an increase in the number of directors may be filled by election at an annual meeting or at a special meeting of shareholders called for that purpose. A director elected to fill a vacancy shall be elected for the unexpired term of his predecessor in office.

§ 37. QUORUM OF DIRECTORS.

A majority of the number of directors fixed by the by-laws, or in the absence of a by-law fixing the number of directors, then of the number stated in the articles of incorporation, shall constitute a quorum for the transaction of business unless a greater number is required by the articles of incorporation or the by-laws. The act of the majority of the directors present at a meeting at which a quorum is present shall be the act of the board of directors, unless the act of a greater number is required by the articles of incorporation or the by-laws.

§ 38. EXECUTIVE COMMITTEE.

If the articles of incorporation or the by-laws so provide, the board of directors, by resolution adopted by a majority of the number of directors fixed by the by-laws, or in the absence of a by-law fixing the number of directors, then of the number stated in the articles of incorporation, may designate two or more directors to constitute an executive committee, which committee, to the extent provided in such resolution or in the articles of incorporation or the by-laws of the corporation, shall have and may exercise all of the authority of the board of directors in the management of the corporation, provided such committee shall not have the authority of the board of directors in reference to amending the articles of incorporation, adopting a plan of merger or adopting a plan of consolidation with another corporation or corporations, . . . amending, altering or repealing the by-laws of the corporation, electing or removing officers of the corporation . . . declaring dividends or amending, altering or repealing any resolution of the board of directors which by its terms provides that it shall not be amended, altered or repealed by the executive committee. The designation of such committee and the delegation thereto of authority shall not operate to relieve the board of directors, or any member thereof, of any responsibility imposed upon it or him by law.

§ 39. PLACE OF DIRECTORS' MEETINGS.

Meetings of the board of directors, regular or special, may be held either within or without this State.

§ 40. NOTICE OF DIRECTORS' MEETINGS.

Meetings of the board of directors shall be held upon such notice as the by-laws may prescribe. Attendance of a director at any meeting shall constitute a waiver of notice of such meeting except where a director attends a meeting for the express purpose of objecting to the transaction of any business because the meeting is not lawfully called or convened. Neither the business to be transacted at, nor the purpose of, any regular or special meeting of the board of directors need be specified in the notice or waiver of notice of such meeting.

§ 42.9. DISSENT — HOW MADE.

A director of a corporation who is present at a meeting of its board of directors at which action on any corporate matter is taken shall be conclusively presumed to have assented to the action taken unless his dissent shall be entered in the minutes of the meeting or unless he shall file his written dissent to such action with the person acting as the secretary of the meeting before the adjournment thereof or shall forward such dissent by registered mail to the secretary of the corporation immediately after the adjournment of the meeting. Such right to dissent shall not apply to a director who voted in favor of such action.

§ 147.1. INFORMAL ACTION BY DIRECTORS.

Unless specifically prohibited by the articles of incorporation or by-laws, any action required by this Act to be taken at a meeting of the board of directors of a corporation, or any other action which may be taken at a meeting of the board of directors or the executive committee thereof, may be taken without a meeting if a consent in writing, setting forth the action so taken, shall be signed by all of the directors entitled to vote with respect to the subject matter thereof, or by all the members of such committee, as the case may be.

Any such consent signed by all the directors or all the members of the executive committee shall have the same effect as a unanimous vote, and may be stated as such in any document filed with the Secretary of State under this Act.

BOARD AUTHORITY AND MEETINGS

Each state gives the board of directors exclusive authority to manage the corporation. They establish the overall operating policy which is then carried out by the officers and their subordinates. The shareholders completely lack any right to establish management policy by direct action. The shareholders are left to influence management of the company indirectly through their election of the directors. However, since the company does belong to the shareholders, there are certain matters that the directors lack authority to undertake. Any transaction that would alter the corporation in a fundamental manner requires shareholder approval. Examples of such fundamental changes include, among others: mergers, consolidation, sale or lease of all the assets, dissolution, charter amendments, and alteration of the stock structure.

The directors exercise authority as a group. They are a body that acts collectively; acting separately as individuals has no legal effect. The concept embodies the old adage that two heads are better than one. Theoretically the best decision will result from the give and take of a meeting where several individuals can supply different perspectives. In this same vein is the rule that a director cannot vote by proxy. To preserve the collegial nature of board deliberations there are quorum requirements. (See § 37 of the Illinois statute). To prevent secret meetings all states have notice requirement similar to § 40. The directors need to know the time and place of the meeting. If the requisite notice is not provided, the action taken at that meeting will have no legal effect. In such an instance it would be necessary for the board to ratify the action at a properly called subsequent meeting. However, if the director attends the meeting, that constitutes a waiver of notice unless his attendance is to protest the legality of the meeting. (See § 40). Although not legally compelled, if a matter of a unique or important nature is on the agenda, it is wise to supply the directors with that knowledge in advance of the meeting.

Notice that 147.1 contains an exception to the general requirement of formal board action by allowing informal action under certain circumstances. Also, section 25a of the Illinois statute permits the adoption of emergency by-laws. These can establish special procedures relative to quorum, and notice requirements and the number of votes necessary for action by the board or the shareholders. These emergency by-laws will be effective if the president, Congress or the governor proclaim a civil defense emergency. It could be expected that a court would give effect to informal action by all the board members where the directors were the only shareholders.

Because of the practical obstacles confronting frequent meetings of the entire board, many statutes provide for the existence of executive committees. (See § 38). Such a committee, like the board itself, can act only as a body. Likewise notice and quorum requirements must be met. The authority of such committees must be determined by examining the relevant state statute and court decisions. The Illinois statute reserves certain important items to the entire board of directors. The use of executive committees is common among large corporations. Frequently, other director committees will also exist. While their actions will require board approval, there is always the tendency of a board to defer to the "expertise" of its committees. During 1975 Sears, Roebuck & Company had the following board committees: executive, finance, salary and supplemental compensation, audits, nominating and proxy, and public issues.

There is usually a minimum board size prescribed by statute but, otherwise, it is a matter of discretion for the shareholders or the board. The board may be composed of inside directors (corporate employees, usually officers), outside directors (non-employees), or both. During 1975 Pan Am had eighteen directors of which fourteen were outside directors, while Sears, Roebuck & Company had twenty-three directors only ten of whom were outside directors (two of which are former corporate officials). Directors are not entitled to compensation for their duties unless authorized by statute, articles or by-laws. Common practice is to pay the outside board members a set fee for each meeting attended plus expenses or an annual fee. The 1975 outside director fees of Sears, Roebuck & Company consisted of an annual fee of $7,500; $500 for each meeting attended; and $500 for each committee meeting attended ($200 on days when the board also met).

QUALIFICATIONS AND REMOVAL

A director need not be a shareholder or a resident of the state unless the statute, charter or by-laws so require. He does have to be of legal age. The qualifications for directors are established by the by-laws. The usual term of office is one year or until a successor takes office. Sometimes the directors will be divided into classes and serve staggered terms. The directors are elected by the shareholders. Vacancies created by death, resignation, or removal may be filled by either shareholder or board action, depending upon the particular statute or by-law. The Illinois statute quoted at the opening of this chapter is silent on the matter of removing a director from office. However, it has been long accepted in every state that the shareholders may remove a director for "cause" i.e. some wrongdoing in his position. Examples of cause would be: gross neglect of his duties as a director; diverting a corporate opportunity to his own benefit; or divulging confidential information to a competitor. The sticky question arises over whether directors may be removed without cause, i.e. at will. Views on this matter conflict. On the one hand, it is the shareholders company and they should be free to control it as they see fit. But, if the directors can be removed at whim, this undermines the directors' management authority and disrupts the orderly conduct of business. Some states now explicitly permit the removal of directors at will. (See Cal. Corp. Code § 810) If a statute or court decision will not permit removal of directors at will, there is another device that will allow the shareholders to work their desire. The shareholders need only expand the size of the board. Then they proceed to elect a sufficient number of directors, who share the stockholders' views, to constitute a majority of the new board.

THE DUTY OF CARE AND THE BUSINESS JUDGMENT DEFENSE

The directors must act in accordance with federal and state law, the corporate charter and by-laws, and board resolutions. They occupy a fiduciary relationship towards the corporation and its shareholders and must meet those resulting standards. Yet, acting in a lawful manner and fulfilling their fiduciary obligations does not terminate their responsibilities. They owe a duty of care to their corporation. The standard of care required is that which would be exercised by a prudent man in the conduct of his own affairs under similar circumstances. Some would apply a prudent director standard. The difference between the two is probably only a semantic one. When a judge or jury decides such a case it is probably more from gut feelings than a clear intellectual grasp of the distinction between a prudent man and a prudent director.

When an individual assumes his post as a director, he is obligated to exercise his best business judgment on behalf of the corporation. When sued over the degree of care exercised in his decisions as director, he can assert as a defense the business judgment rule. If he can show that his decision was based on the reasonable exercise of his judgment and was undertaken in good faith the courts will support his decision. The fact that his decision turned out to be a poor one, or that someone else would have undertaken a different course of action, is irrelevant. The court will not substitute its judgment for that of the director or second guess the director with the benefit of 20-20 hindsight. The courts defer to the directors' expertise so long as they exercise it reasonably. It is negligence in the fulfillment of their duties that is actionable.

The duty of care extends to all directors, whether they be inside or outside directors, and whether they assume an active or passive role in corporate affairs. The duty can be breached by commission as well as omission. If a director opposed a board resolution as improvident and immoderate, he must record his objection if he wishes to avoid legal liability. His dissent to the action must be either recorded in the minutes of the meeting or filed in writing with the secretary of the corporation. (See § 42.9).

The *Bates* v. *Dresser* case examines the dramatic and swift demise of a bank and the respective responsibility of the directors and the president. *Barnes* v. *Andrews* raises the question of who bears the burden of proof in a duty of care lawsuit. Once it is shown that a director failed in his duty, must the plaintiff also prove the amount of the resulting loss; or does the burden of proof shift to the director to prove that the amount of loss is not attributable to his neglect? The answer is controversial. *Litwin* v. *Allen* scrutinizes the exercise of the directors' judgment within the context of a complex business transaction. The case is an excellent illustration of the failure to exhibit reasonable judgment. However, be careful to note that towards the end of the opinion one segment of the board's action is upheld — the retention of the bonds after April 16, 1931.

BATES v. DRESSER
251 U.S. 524 (1920)

◆◆◆

MR. JUSTICE HOLMES delivered the opinion of the court.

This is a bill in equity brought by the receiver of a national bank to charge its former president and directors with the loss of a great part of its assets through the thefts of an employee of the bank while they were in power. The case was sent to a master who found for the defendants; but the District Court entered a decree against all of them. ... The Circuit Court of Appeals reversed this decree, dismissed the bill as against all except the administrator of the estate of Edwin Dresser, the president, cut down the amount with which he was charged and refused to add interest from the date of the decree of the District Court. ... Dresser's administrator and the receiver both appeal, the latter contending that the decree of the District Court should be affirmed with interest and costs.

The bank was a little bank at Cambridge with a capital of $100,000 and average deposits of somewhat about $300,000. It had a cashier, a bookkeeper, a teller and a messenger. Before and during the time of the losses Dresser was its president and executive officer, a large stockholder, with an inactive deposit of from $35,000 to $50,000. From July, 1903, to the end, Frank L. Earl was cashier. Coleman, who made the trouble, entered the service of the bank as messenger in September, 1903. In January, 1904, he was promoted to be bookkeeper, being then not quite eighteen but having studied bookkeeping ... Coleman kept the deposit ledger and that was the work that fell into his hands. There was no cage in the bank, and in 1904 and 1905 there were some small shortages in the accounts of three successive tellers that were not accounted for, and the last of them, Cutting, was asked by Dresser to resign on that ground. Before doing so he told Dresser that someone had taken the money and that if he might be allowed to stay he would set a trap and catch the man, but Dresser did not care to do that and thought that there was nothing wrong. From Cutting's resignation on October 7, 1905, Coleman acted as paying and receiving teller, in addition to his other duty, until November, 1907. During this time there were no shortages disclosed in the teller's accounts. In May, 1906, Coleman took $2,000 cash from the vaults of the bank, but restored it the next morning. In November of the same year he began the thefts that come into question here. Perhaps in the beginning he took the money directly. But as he ceased to have charge of the cash in November, 1907, he invented another way. Having a small account at the bank, he would draw checks for the amount he wanted, exchange checks with a Boston broker, get cash for the broker's check and when his own check came to the bank through the clearing house, would abstract it from the envelope, enter the others on his book and conceal the difference by a charge to some other account or a false addition in the column of drafts or deposits in the depositor's ledger. He handed to the cashier only the slip from the clearing house that showed the totals. The cashier paid whatever appeared to be due and thus Coleman's checks were honored. So far as Coleman thought it necessary, in view of the absolute trust in him on the part of all concerned, he took care that his balances should agree with those in the cashier's book.

By May 1, 1907, Coleman had abstracted $17,000 concealing the fact by false additions in the column of total checks, and false balances in the deposit ledger. Then for the moment a safer concealment was effected by charging the whole to Dresser's account. Coleman adopted this method when a bank examiner was expected. Of course when the fraud was disguised by overcharging a depositor it could not be discovered except by calling in the pass-books, or taking all the deposit slips and comparing them with the depositors' ledger in detail. By November, 1907, the amount taken by Coleman was $30,100 and the charge on Dresser's account was $20,000. In 1908 the sum was raised from $33,000 to $49,671. In 1909 Coleman's activity began to increase. In January he took $6,829.26; in March, $10,833.73; in June, his previous stealings amounting to $83,390.94, he took $5,152.06; in July, 18,050; in August, $6,250; in September, $17,350; in October, $47,277.08; in November $51,847; in December, $46,956.44; in January, 1910, $27,395.53; in February, $6,473.97; making a total of $310,143.02, when the bank closed on February 21, 1910. As a result of this the amount of the monthly deposits seemed to decline noticeably and the directors considered the matter in September, 1909, but concluded that the falling off was due in part to the springing up of rivals, whose deposits were increasing, but was parallel to a similar decrease in New York. An examination by a bank examiner in December, 1909, disclosed nothing wrong to him.

In this connection it should be mentioned that in the previous semi-annual examinations by national bank examiners nothing was discovered pointing to malfeasance. The cashier was honest and everybody believed that they could rely upon him, although in fact he relied too much upon Coleman, who also was unsuspected by all. If Earl had opened the envelopes from the clearing house, and had seen the checks or had examined the deposit ledger with any care he would have found out what was going on. The scrutiny of anyone accustomed to such details would have discovered the false additions and other indicia of fraud that were on the face of the book. But it may be doubted whether anything less than a continuous pursuit of the figures through pages would have done so except by a lucky chance.

The question of the liability of the directors in this case is the question whether they neglected their duty by accepting the cashier's statement of liabilities and failing to inspect the depositors' ledger. The statements of assets always were correct. A by-law that had been allowed to become obsolete or nearly so is invoked as establishing their own standard of conduct. By that a committee was to be appointed every six months "to examine into the affairs of the bank, to count its cash, and compare its assets and liabilities with the balances on the general ledger for the purpose of ascertaining whether or not the books are correctly kept, and the condition of the bank is in a sound and solvent condition." Of course liabilities as well as assets must be known to know the condition and, as this case shows, peculations may be concealed as well by a false understatement of liabilities as by a false show of assets. But the former is not the direction in which fraud would have been looked for, especially on the part of one who at the time of his principal abstractions was not in contact with the funds. A debtor hardly expects to have his liability understated. Some animals must have given at least one exhibition of dangerous propensities before the owner can be held. This fraud was a novelty in the way of swindling a bank so far as the knowledge of any experience had reached Cambridge before 1910. We are not prepared to reverse the finding of the master and the Circuit Court of Appeals that the directors should not be held answerable for taking the cashier's statement of liabilities to be as correct as the statement of assets always was. . . . Their confidence seem warranted by the semi-annual examinations by the government examiner and they were encouraged in their belief that all was well by the president, whose responsibility, as executive officer; interest, as large stockholder and depositor; and knowledge, from long daily presence in the bank, were greater than theirs. They were not bound by virture of the office gratuitously assumed by them to call in the pass-books and compare them with the ledger, and until the event showed the possibility they hardly could have seen that their failure to look at the ledger opened a way to fraud. . . . We are not laying down general principles, however, but confine our decision to the circumstances of the particular case.

The position of the president is different. Practically he was the master of the situation. He was daily at the bank for hours, he had the deposit ledger in his hands at times and might have had it at any time. He had had hints and warnings in addition to those that we have mentioned, warnings that should not be magnified unduly, but still that taken with the auditor's report of 1903, the unexplained shortages, the suggestion of the teller, Cutting, in 1905, and the final seeming rapid decline in deposits, would have induced scrutiny but for an invincible repose upon the status quo. In 1908 one Fillmore learned that a package contained $150 left with the bank for safe keeping was not to be found, told Dresser of the loss, wrote to him that he could but conclude that the package had been destroyed or removed by someone connected with the bank, and in later conversation said that it was evident that there was a thief in the bank. He added that he would advise the president to look after Coleman, that he believed he was living at a pretty fast pace, and that he had pretty good authority for thinking that he was supporting a woman. In the same year or the year before, Coleman, whose pay was never more than twelve dollars a week, set up an automobile, as was known to Dresser and commented on unfavorably, to him. There was also some evidence of notice to Dresser that Coleman was dealing in copper stocks. In 1909 came the great and inadequately explained seeming shrinkage in the deposits. No doubt plausible explanations of his conduct came from Coleman and the notice as to speculations may have been slight, but taking the whole story of the relations of the parties, we are not ready to say that the two courts below erred in finding that Dresser had been put upon his guard. However little the warnings may have pointed to the specific facts, had they been accepted they would have led to an examination of the depositors' ledger, a discovery of past and a prevention of future thefts. . . .

In accepting the presidency Dresser must be taken to have comtemplated responsibility for losses to the bank, whatever they were, if chargeable to his fault. Those that happened were chargeable to his fault, after he had warnings that should have led to steps that would have made fraud impossible, even though the precise form that the fraud would take hardly could have been foreseen. We accept with hesitation the date of December 1, 1908, as the beginning of Dresser's liability, but think it reasonable that interest should be charged against his estate upon the sum found by the Circuit Court of Appeals to be due. It is a question of discretion, not of right . . . it seems to us just upon all the circumstances that it should run until the receiver interposed a delay by his appeal to this Court. . . .

Decree modified by charging the estate of Dresser with interest from February 1, 1916, to June 1, 1918, upon the sum found to be due, and affirmed.

◆◆◆

Case Questions

1. If the fraud was not of a novel variety, should the directors have been held liable?
2. Is a reduced standard of care imposed upon directors when, as here, a governmental agency has authority and responsibility to examine the corporation's financial accounts?
3. Why would Dresser ignore the various warning signals and not conduct even a slight investigation?

BARNES v. ANDREWS
298 F. 614 (1924)

Don't lean on this too heavily

◆◆◆

In Equity. Suit by Earl B. Barnes, as receiver of the Liberty Starters Corporation, against Charles Lee Andrews. Decree for Defendant.

Final hearing on a bill in equity, . . . to hold liable the defendant as director for misprision of office. The corporation was organized under the laws of that state to manufacture starters for Ford motors and aeroplanes. On October 9, 1919, about a year after its organization, the defendant took office as a director, and served until he resigned on June 21, 1920. During that period over $500,000 was raised by the sales of stock of the company, made through an agent working on commission. A force of officers and employees was hired at substantial salaries, and the factory, already erected when the defendant took office, was equipped with machinery. Starter parts were made in quantity, but delays were experienced in the production of starters as a whole, and the funds of the company were steadily depleted by the running charges.

After the defendant resigned, the company continued business until the spring of 1921, when the plaintiff was appointed receiver, found the company without funds, and realized only a small amount on the sale of its assets. During the incumbency of the defendant there had been only two meetings of directors, one of which (i.e., that of October 9, 1919) he attended; the other happening at a day when he was forced to be absent because of his mother's death. He was a friend of the president, who had induced him as the largest stockholder to become a director, and his only attention to the affairs of the company consisted of talks with the president as they met from time to time.

The theory of the bill was that the defendant had failed to give adequate attention to the affairs of the company, which had been conducted incompetently and without regard to the waste in salaries during the period before production was possible. This period was unduly prolonged by the incompetence of the factory manager, and disagreements between him and the engineer, upon whose patents the company depended. The officers were unable to induce these men to compose their differences, and the work languished from incompetence and extravagance. More money was paid the engineer than his royalty contracts justified, and the money was spent upon fraudulent circulars to induce the purchase of stock. . . .

LEARNED HAND, District Judge (after stating the facts as above). This may be divided into three parts: First, the defendant's general liability for the collapse of the enterprise; second, his specific liability for overpayments made to Delano; third, his specific liability for the expenses of printing pamphlets and circulars used in selling the corporate shares. (Discussion of the latter two items is omitted.)

The first liability must rest upon the defendant's general inattention to his duties as a director. He cannot be charged with neglect in attending directors' meetings, because there were only two during his incumbency, and of these he was present at one and had an adequate excuse for his absence from the other. His liability must therefore depend upon his failure in general to keep advised of the conduct of the corporate affairs. The measure of a director's duties in this regard is uncertain; the courts contenting themselves with vague declarations, such as that a director must give reasonable attention to the corporate business. While directors are collectively the managers of the company, they are not expected to interfere individually in the actual conduct of its affairs. To do so would disturb the authority of the officers and destroy their individual responsibility, without which no proper discipline is possible. To them must be left the initiative and the immediate direction of the business; the directors can act individually only by counsel and advice to them. Yet they have an individual duty to keep themselves informed in some detail, and it is this duty which the defendant in my judgment failed adequately to perform.

All he did was to talk with Maynard as they met, while commuting from Flushing, or at their homes. That, indeed, might be enough, because Andrews had no reason to suspect Maynard's candor, nor has any reason to question it been yet disclosed. But it is plain that he did not press him for details, as he should. It is not enough to content oneself with general answers that the business looks promising and that all seems prosperous. Andrews was bound, certainly as the months wore on, to inform himself of what was going on with some particularity, and, if he had done so, he would have learned that there were delays in getting into production which were putting the enterprise in most serious peril. It is entirely clear from his letters of April 14, 1920, and June 12, 1920, that he had made no effort to keep advised of the actual conduct of the corporate affairs, but had allowed himself to be carried along as a figurehead, in complete reliance upon Maynard. In spite of his own substantial investment in the company, which I must assume was as dear to him as it would be to other men, his position required of him more than this. Having accepted a post of confidence, he was charged with an active duty to learn whether the company was moving to production, and why it was not, and to consider, as best he might, what could be done to avoid the conflicts among the personnel, or their incompetence, which was slowly bleeding it to death.

Therefore I cannot acquit Andrews of misprision of his office, though his integrity is unquestioned. The plaintiff must, however, go further than to show that he should have been more active in his duties. This cause of action rests upon a tort, as much though it be a tort of omission as though it had rested upon a positive act. The plaintiff must accept the burden of showing that the performance of the defendant's duties would have avoided loss, and what loss it would have avoided. I pressed Mr. Alger to show me a case in which the courts have held that a director could be charged generally with the collapse of a business in respect of which he had been inattentive, and I am not aware that he has found one. . . .

When the corporate funds have been illegally lent, it is a fair inference that a protest would have stopped the loan, and the director's neglect caused the loss. But when a business fails from general mismanagement, business incapacity, or bad judgment, how is it possible to say that a single director could have made the company successful, or how much in dollars he could have saved? Before this cause can go to a master, the plaintiff must show that, had Andrews done his full duty, he could have made the company prosper, or at least could have broken its fall. He must show what sum he could have saved the company. Neither of these has he made any effort to do.

The defendant is not subject to the burden of proving that the loss would have happened, whether he had done his duty or not. If he were, it would come to this: that, if a director were once shown slack in his duties, he would stand charged prima facie with the difference between the corporate treasury as it was, and as it would be, judged by a hypothetical standard of success. How could such a standard be determined? How could any one guess how far a director's skill and judgment would have prevailed upon his fellows, and what would have been the ultimate fate of the business, if they had? How is it possible to set any measure of liability, or to tell what he could have contributed to the event? Men's fortunes may not be subjected to such uncertain and speculative conjectures. It is hard to see how there can be any remedy, except one can put one's finger on a definite loss and say with reasonable assurance that protest would have deterred, or counsel persuaded, the managers who caused it. No men of sense would take the office, if the law imposed upon them a guaranty of the general success of their companies as a penalty for any negligence.

It is, indeed, hard to determine just what went wrong in the management of this company. Any conclusion is little better than a guess. Still some discussion of the facts is necessary, and I shall discuss them. The claim that there were too many general employees turned out to be true, but, so far as I can see, only because of the delay in turning out the finished product. Had the factory gone into production in the spring of 1920, I cannot say, and the plaintiff cannot prove, that the selling department would have been prematurely or extravagantly organized. The expense of the stock sales was apparently not undue, and in any event Andrews was helpless to prevent it, because he found the contract an existing obligation of the company. So far as I can judge, the company had a fair chance of life, if the factory could have begun to turn out starters at the time expected. Whether this was the fault of Delano, as I suspect, is now too uncertain to say. It seems to me to make no difference in the result whether Delano, through inattention, or through sickness, or through contempt for Taylor, or for all these reasons, did not send along "Van Dycks," or whether Taylor should have got along without them, or should have shown more initiative and competence than he did. Between them the production lagged, until it was too late to resuscitate the dying company; its funds had oozed out in fixed payments, till there was nothing left with which to continue the business.

Suppose I charge Andrews with a complete knowledge of all that we have now learned. What action should he have taken, and how can I say that it would have stopped the losses? The plaintiff gives no definite answer to that question. Certainly he had no right to interject himself personally into the tangle; that was for Maynard to unravel. He would scarcely have helped to a solution by adding another cook to the broth. What suggestion could he have made to Maynard, or to his colleagues? The trouble arose either from an indifferent engineer, on whom the company was entirely dependent, or from an incompetent factory manager, who should have been discharged, or because the executives were themselves inefficient. Is Andrews to be charged for not insisting upon Taylor's discharge, or for not suggesting it? Suppose he did suggest it; have I the slightest reason for saying that the directors would have discharged him? Or, had they discharged him, is it certain that a substitute employed in medias res would have speeded up production? Was there not as a fair chance that Delano and Taylor might be brought to an accomodation as there was in putting in a green man at that juncture? How can I, sitting here, lay it down that Andrews' intervention would have brought order out of this chaos, or how can I measure in dollars the losses he would have saved? Or am I to hold Andrews because he did not move to discharge Maynard? How can I know that a better man was available? It is easy to say that he should have done something, but that will not serve to harness upon him the whole loss, nor is it the equivalent of saying that, had he acted, the company would now flourish.

True, he was not very well-suited by experience for the job he had undertaken, but I cannot hold him on that account. After all, it is the same corporation that chose him which now seeks to charge him. I cannot agree with the language of *Hun* v. *Cary*, *supra*. that in effect he gave an implied warranty of any special fitness. Directors are not specialists, like lawyers or doctors. They must have good sense, perhaps they must have acquaintance with affairs; but they need not — indeed, perhaps they should not — have any technical talent. They are the general advisers of the business, and if they faithfully give such ability as they have to their charge, it would not be lawful to hold them liable. Must a director guarantee that his judgment is good? Can shareholders call him to account for deficiencies which their votes assured him did not disqualify him for his office? While he may not have been the Cromwell for that Civil War, Andrews did not engage to play any such role.

I conclude, therefore, as to this first claim that there is no evidence that the defendant's neglect caused any losses to the company, and that, if there were, that loss cannot be ascertained. . . .

Case Questions

♦♦♦

1. Is it correct to say that directors are not specialists? Since the law gives the directors exclusive authority to manage the corporation, would it be appropriate to measure their performance against a specialist standard?
2. Does this decision confer complete immunity upon a director whose company has failed?
3. Is it not inconsistent to hold Andrews guilty of misprison of office and then relieve him of liability because the plaintiff did not show what loss would have been avoided if Andrews has diligently performed? Would it be more equitable that a director, who has been found guilty of misprison of office, bear the burden of showing that amount of the loss which was not caused by his negligence?
4. Does a director possess the legal right to personally interject himself into a corporate tangle like this one? What form could a director's interjection take?

LITWIN v. ALLEN
25 N.Y.S. 2d667 (1940)

♦♦♦

These actions are derivative stockholders' actions brought on behalf of persons owning 36 shares of the stock of Guaranty Trust Company of New York out of 900,000 shares outstanding. The defendants are directors and the estates of deceased directors of Guaranty Trust Company of New York (hereinafter referred to as the Bank or Trust Company) and its wholly owned subsidiary, now in liquidation, Guaranty Company of New York (hereinafter referred to as the Company or Guaranty Company), together with members of the banking firm of J.P. Morgan & Co.

[Although four transactions were at issue in this case, only one will be examined as relevant for our purposes.]

I shall now proceed to consider generally the rules to be applied in determining the liability of directors. It has sometimes been said that directors are trustees. If this means that directors in the performance of their duties stand in a fiduciary relationship to the company, that statement is essentially correct. . . . "The directors are bound by all those rules of conscientious fairness, morality, and honesty in purpose which the law imposes as the guides for those who are under the fiduciary obligations and responsibilities. They are held, in official action, to the extreme measure of candor, unselfishness, and good faith. Those principles are rigid, essential, and salutary." . . .

It is clear that a director owes loyalty and allegiance to the company — a loyalty that is undivided and an allegiance that is influenced in action by no consideration other than the welfare of the corporation. Any adverse interest of a director will be subjected to a scrutiny rigid and uncompromising. He may not profit at the expense of his corporation and in conflict with its rights; he may not for personal gain divert unto himself the opportunities which in equity and fairness belong to his corporation. He is required to use his independent judgment. In the discharge of his duties a director must, of course, act honestly and in good faith, but that is not enough. He must also exercise some degree of skill and prudence and diligence.

In a leading case the Court of Appeals, in referring to the duties of directors, said: "They should know of and give direction to the general affairs of the institution and its business policy, and have a general knowledge of the manner in which the business is conducted, the character of the investments, and the employment of the resources. No custom or practice can make a directorship a mere position of honor void of responsibility, or cause a name to become a substitute for care and attention. The personnel of a directorate may give confidence and attract custom; it must also afford protection." *Kavanaugh* v. *Commonwealth Trust Co.,* 223 N.Y. 103, 106, 119 N.E. 237, 238.

In other words, directors are liable for negligence in the performance of their duties. Not being insurers, directors are not liable for errors of judgment or for mistakes while acting with reasonable skill and prudence. It has been said that a director is required to conduct the business of the corporation with the same degree of fidelity and care as an ordinarily prudent man would exercise in the management of his own affairs of like magnitude and importance. General rules, however, are not altogether helpful. In the last analysis, whether or not a director has discharged his duty, whether or not he has been negligent, depends upon the facts and circumstances of a particular case, the kind of corporation involved, its size and financial resources, the magnitude of the transaction, and the immediacy of the problem presented. A director is called upon "to bestow the care and skill" which the situation demands. . . . Undoubtedly, a director of a bank is held to stricter accountability than the director of an ordinary business corporation. A director of a bank is entrusted with the funds of depositors, and the stockholders look to him for protection from the imposition of personal liability. . . . But clairvoyance is not required even of a bank director. The law recognizes that the most conservative director is not infallible, and that he will make mistakes, but if he uses that degree of care ordinarily exercised by prudent bankers he will be absolved from liability although his opinion may turn out to have been mistaken and his judgment faulty.

Finally, in order to determine whether transactions approved by a director subject him to liability for negligence, we must "look at the facts as they exist at the time of their occurrence, not aided or enlightened by those which subsequently take place." *Purdy* v. *Lynch,* 145 N.Y. 462, 475, . . . "A wisdom developed after an event, and having it and its consequences as a source, is a standard no man should be judged by." *Costello* v. *Costello* 209 N.Y. 252, 262, . . .

THE MISSOURI PACIFIC BOND TRANSACTION

This transaction involves the participation by the Trust Company or Guaranty Company or both, to the extent of $3,000,000, in a purchase of Missouri Pacific Convertible debentures on October 16, 1930, through the firm of J.P. Morgan & Co. at par, with an option to the seller, Alleghany Corporation to repurchase them at the same price at any time within six months.

In the fall of 1930, the question of putting Alleghany Corporation in funds to the extent of $10,500,000 was first broached. Alleghany had purchased certain terminal properties in Kansas City and St. Joseph, Missouri, and the balance of the purchase price, amounting to slightly in excess of $10,000,000 and interest, had to be paid by October 16. Alleghany needed money to make this payment. Because of the borrowing limitation in Alleghany's charter (which limitation had been reached or exceeded in October 1930) Alleghany was unable to borrow the money. To overcome this borrowing limitation and solely to enable Alleghany to consummate the purchase of the terminal properties, discussions were commenced concerning the means whereby the necessary money could be raised. It is important that this circumstance be constantly kept in mind, in order that the purpose and pattern of the transaction as it did take place be fully understood.

Not being able to make a loan, the way that Alleghany could raise the necessary funds was by sale of some of the securities that it held. Among them was a large block of about $23,500,000 of Missouri Pacific convertible 5½ percent debentures. These were unsecured and subordinate to other Missouri Pacific bond issues. They were convertible into common stock at the rate of ten shares for each $1,000 bond. In 1929, Guaranty Company had participated to the extent of $1,500,000 in the underwriting of these bonds at 97½. At one time in 1929 the bonds had sold as high as 124 and had never gone below par except in November 1929 when they sold at 97. Between October 1 and October 10, 1930 Missouri Pacific common stock had dropped from 53 to 44. There was a decline in the bonds from 113 in April 1930 to 107 on October 1, 1930, and thereafter a decline of about two more points to 105½ by the date of the consummation of the transaction we are considering on October 16, 1930.

The Van Sweringens suggested that $10,000,000 of these bonds be sold to J.P. Morgan & Co. for cash at par, the latter to give an option to Alleghany to buy them back within six months for the price paid. If the transaction were carried through on that basis, namely, a sale by Alleghany with an option to them to repurchase at the same price, the same purpose would be accomplished, for Alleghany at any rate, as if a loan had been made.

The defendants testified that they were informed that the Van Sweringens insisted upon the option to repurchase within six months in order that there might be no possibility of their loss of control of Missouri Pacific through Alleghany, since these bonds were convertible and the privilege to do so might be exercised by third parties in the event of a distribution of these bonds in the market; this, despite the fact that the common stock of Missouri Pacific was then quoted in the neighborhood of 44, while the conversion price was 100.

The fact is that the only purpose served by the option was to make the transaction conform as closely as possible to a loan without the usual incidents of a loan transaction.

As between J.P. Morgan & Co. and Alleghany Corporation, the transaction is represented by two letters, both dated October 15, 1930, from J.P. Morgan & Co. to Alleghany Corporation. These letters separately confirm the purchase and grant an option to repurchase. . . .

As between J.P. Morgan & Co. and the Trust Company, the participation of $3,000,000 in the purchase was plainly a participation by the Trust Company on terms fixed by the exchange of letters dated October 15 and 16, 1930. J.P. Morgan & Co.'s letter of October 15, enclosing the letters to Alleghany Corporation . . . was addressed in care of Mr. Swan as vice president of the Trust Company and said:

"In accordance with our telephone conversation, we beg to advise you that we have purchased from Alleghany Corporation at 100 percent and accrued interest for delivery and payment on October 16, 1930, $10,500,000 Missouri Pacific Railroad Company Twenty Year Convertible Debentures, Series A, 5½ percent Bonds, due May 1, 1949, and have given Alleghany Corporation an option to repurchase such bonds up to the close of business on April 16, 1931, at 100 percent and accrued interest.

"We enclose herewith copies of letters exchanged with Alleghany Corporation with regard to this transaction.

"We beg to offer you an interest of $3,000,000 principal amount of the bonds covered by our purchase as indicated, subject to the conditions set forth in our letter extending to Alleghany Corporation an option to repurchase such bonds.

"Kindly advise us whether you care to accept this offer on the terms indicated."

The Trust Company's acceptance was signed by Mr. Garner as vice-president and treasurer on October 16, . . .

The Trust Company took delivery of the bonds on October 16, and paid for them by its check for $3,075,625, which included accrued interest. As regards J.P. Morgan & Co., the exchange of letters under date of October 15 and 16 obviously represented the participation contract for the $3,000,000 interest in the bonds, and such contract was made only by the Trust Company. Together with J.P. Morgan & Co.'s letters of October 15 to Alleghany Corporation, they fixed the terms of the purchase and of the option and the Guaranty Company was not a party to those terms.

At or shortly before the time that the Trust Company made its written commitment to J.P. Morgan & Co. to participate in the bond purchase, the Guaranty Company committed itself to the Trust Company to take up the bonds from the Trust Company at the end of the six months' period, on April 16, 1931, for the same price that the Trust Company paid, that is, par and interest, if Alleghany failed to exercise its option to repurchase.

There is no evidence in this case of any improper influence or domination of the directors or officers of the Trust Company or of the Guaranty Company by J.P. Morgan & Co. . . . Moreover, there is no evidence to indicate that any of the defendants' officers or directors acted in bad faith or profited or attempted to profit or gain personally by reason of any phase of this transaction. . . .

Regardless of who initiated the transaction, and what form it was originally thought the transaction would take, I do not see why the court should give it a construction other than that placed upon it by all of the interested parties at the time and after it was consummated. Every contemporaneous memorandum and record establishes, and I am bound to find, that this was a Trust Company purchase with a commitment by the Guarantee Company to repurchase the bonds from the Trust Company if, at the end of six months, Alleghany failed to exercise its option so to do.

The decline in the market continued. On October 23, 1930, when the Executive Committee of the Trust Company approved the transaction the Missouri Pacific bonds were at 103 7/8. On November 5, 1930, when the Board of Directors of the Trust Company gave its approval, the bonds sold for 102 7/8, and on November 18, 1930, when the board of the Guaranty Company approved its commitment, the bonds had dropped to 98 5/8. At the end of the six months' period, on April 16, 1931, the bonds sold at 86 high and 81 low (the quotations being for the week ending April 18), and Guaranty Company took them over from the Trust Company at par and accrued interest and carried them on its books as an investment.

Under the circumstances of this case, I do not attach the same significance as do counsel on both sides to the question as to whether this was a purchase by the Trust Company, with an agreement by the Guaranty Company to repurchase if Alleghany failed to exercise its option, or whether it was in effect a purchase by Guaranty Company, with an option to Alleghany to repurchase, financed for six months by the Trust Company, and which was approved in its entirety by the directors of both companies. So far as this case is concerned, there is, as will hereinafter be indicated, no fundamental difference in legal consequences, whichever view of the transaction may be adopted.

Of course, if the transaction was a subterfuge for a loan, as the plaintiffs claim, then it clearly was improper because the essential and most elementary requirement of a loan was lacking; no one obligated himself to repay it. I reject this contention. The transaction was not a subterfuge for a loan; it was a substitute for a loan, and should be viewed on that basis. The fact that a transaction, from the point of view of the party receiving the funds, answers substantially all the requirements of a loan, does not make it a loan in law. . . .

Considering it a purchase by the Trust Company at par, with an option to the seller to repurchase for the same price within a period of six months, at which time if the option was not exercised the wholly owned subsidiary of the Trust Company would take over the securities at the price paid, the question is whether such option agreement was ultra vires. Enough has been alleged in the complaint to raise that question.

There is no case directly in point. Courts have passed upon the legality or enforceability of contracts under which a bank sold securities or property and gave the purchaser an option to resell such securities or property to the bank upon stated terms. . . .

In all of the foregoing cases . . . an option of resale given by a bank to a purchaser was condemned as illegal and unenforceable. . . .

The defendants contend that there is a fundamental difference between an option to compel the bank to buy back securities which the cases cited condemned as ultra vires and unenforceable against the bank and the option in this case to compel the bank to re-sell securities which it has bought and holds. They point out that the cases emphasize the impairment of the liquidity of the bank; that while the liquidity of the bank may be impaired because it is obligated to pay cash and take back securities it has previously sold, the liquidity of the bank is not impaired, in fact it is strengthened when the bank is obligated to take cash and give back the securities it has previously purchased.

However, the cases rest on a broader and more substantial basis. Thus, in *Rothschild* v. *Manufacturers Trust Company,* the plaintiff sued the bank to recover damages for the failure of the bank to repurchase from him, pursuant to an oral agreement by one of its officers, at the full purchase price, various securities bought by the plaintiff from the bank during certain years. The court held that the agreement sought to be enforced was ultra vires and in violation of public policy. It pointed out that "a banking corporation occupies a different relation to the public than do ordinary corporations, and its transactions frequently are subjected to a closer scrutiny and tested by a higher standard than that applied to ordinary commercial affairs." [279 N.Y. 355,] . . . The court reiterated the holding of the United States Supreme Court that banking is a business affected with a public interest (*Noble State Bank* v. *Haskell,* 219 U.S. 104) and continued: "An agreement, valid and enforceable if made by an ordinary corporation or business, may, by reason of public policy, be void and unenforceable against a banking institution." It further pointed out that the "stability of banks is a matter of such public conern that the State should not sanction any device intended to give a false appearance to a transaction or increase the apparent stability as contrasted with the true condition of a bank" and that "this rule of public policy in no wise depends upon the solvency or insolvency of the bank." Such agreements to repurchase, it was emphasized, may constitute serious contingent liabilities on the part of the bank, not reflected on its books, and that the power to make such repurchase agreements will not be regarded as a necessary or proper banking power but will be prescribed as being positively dangerous.

Although, as I have said, there is no case precisely in point, it would seem that if it is against public policy for a bank, anxious to dispose of some of its securities, to agree to buy them back at the same price, it is even more so where a bank purchases securities and gives the seller the option to buy them back at the same price, thereby incurring the entire risk of loss with no possibility of gain other than the interest derived from the securities during the period that the bank holds them. Here, if the market price of the securities should rise, the holder of the repurchase option would exercise it in order to recover his securities from the bank at the lower price at which he sold them to the bank. If the market price should fall, the seller holding the option will not exercise it and the bank will sustain the loss. Thus, any benefit of a sharp rise in the price of the securities is assured the seller and any risk of heavy loss is inevitably assumed by the bank. If such an option agreement as is here involved were sustained, it would force the bank to set aside for six months whatever securities it had purchased. A bank certainly could not free itself from this obligation by engaging in a "short sale". In other words, while a resale option would force a bank to freeze an amount of cash equal to the selling price of the securities sold by it, a repurchase option would force a bank to freeze the securities themselves for the period of the option. In both situations the true financial condition of the bank could not be determined wholly from its books. It would depend upon the fluctuations of the market. In both cases there is a contingent liability which the balance sheet does not show.

I am strengthened in this conclusion by a dictum of Mr. Justice Stone in *Awotin* v. *Atlas Exchange Bank,* 295 U.S. 209, . . . in which he makes no distinction between the two kinds of options, where "the bank assumes the risk of loss which would otherwise fall on the buyer of securities, or undertakes to insure the seller the benefit of an increase in value of securities which would otherwise accrue to the bank." . . . Such contracts are "forms of contingent liability inimical to sound banking and perilous to the interest of depositors and the public." . . .

But, it is said, the Trust Company as such, from the very outset, relieved itself from any risk of loss because it received a commitment from its wholly owned subsidiary whereby the latter undertook to take up the bonds from the Trust Company at the price paid for them in the event that Alleghany Corporation failed to exercise its option by the end of six months. Merely to state that proposition indicates how untenable it is. To say that the option arrangement would be ultra vires the Bank, but that the taint of illegality would be removed if the Bank took an agreement from its wholly owned subsidiary to act as the receptacle for any possible loss, is contrary to law, to reason and to every sense of justice. Assuming that for some purposes the two corporations were separate entities, "in considering the practical effect of such intercorporate dealings, especially as bearing upon the duties of the common directors * * * we need not and ought not to overlook the identity of stock ownership." . . .

It seems clear on principle as well as analogous authority that, although they differ in certain respects, either kind of option would be held ultra vires and unenforceable against a bank.

Plaintiffs urge that if the purchase subject to the option is found to be ultra vires, that finding, in and of itself, imposes absolute liability upon the defendants. It is doubtful whether any such strict rule would apply where directors as here, act honestly and particularly where no violation of a statute is involved. . . .

Directors are not in the position of trustees of an express trust who, regardless of good faith, are personally liable for losses arising from an infraction of their trust deed. . . . If liability is to be imposed on these directors it should rest on a more solid foundation. I find liability in this transaction because the entire arrangement was so improvident, so risky, so unusual and unnecessary as to be contrary to fundamental conceptions of prudent banking practices. A bank director when appointed or elected takes oath that he will, so far as the duty devolves on him "diligently and honestly administer the affairs on the bank or trust company." Banking Law, § 117. The oath merely adds solemnity to the obligation which the law itself imposes. Honesty alone does not suffice; the honesty of the directors in this case is unquestioned. But there must be more than honesty — there must be diligence, and that means care and prudence, as well. This transaction, it has been said, was unusual; it was unique, yet there is nothing in the record to indicate that the advice of counsel was sought. It is not surprising that a precedent cannot be found dealing with such a situation.

What sound reason is there for a bank, desiring to make an investment, short term or otherwise, to buy securities under an arrangement whereby any appreciation will inure to the benefit of the seller and any loss will be borne by the bank? The five and one-half point differential is no answer. It does not meet the fundamental objection that whatever loss there is would have to be borne by the Bank and whatever gain would go to the customer. There is more here than a question of business judgment as to which men might well differ. The directors plainly failed in this instance to bestow the care which the situation demanded. Unless we are to do away entirely with the doctrine that directors of a bank are liable for negligence in administering its affairs liability should be imposed in connection with this transaction.

The same result would be reached if we adopted the defendants' version of this transaction, namely, that it was initially a purchase by the Guaranty Company, with an option to the Alleghany Corporation to rebuy at the same price, and that the transaction was financed by the Bank, so that the immediate interest that the Bank had in it was a short term 5½ percent investment. I should reach that conclusion for the following reasons:

1. The Guaranty Company is an investment company organized under the provisions of the Banking Law, subject to the supervision of the Superintendent of Banks.
2. It is a wholly owned subsidiary of the Trust Company; what loss it sustains is a loss to the Trust Company, to its depositors and to its stockholders.
3. The Trust Company and the Guaranty Company were treated by their officers and directors as one and the same. . . .
4. On January 17, 1934, Mr. Potter, as president of the Bank, sent a letter to its stockholders in which is contained the following: "In 1920 the Trust Company, which had been doing a security business since 1907, organized the Guaranty Company of New York and to it transferred its security operations. Although it is an entirely separate company and not subject to certain restrictions which apply to the Trust Company, the policy of the Guaranty Company from the start has been to do only such business as the Trust Company itself could do."
5. The transaction was just as wasteful and improvident from the standpoint of the Guaranty Company as it was from the standpoint of the Bank, and even more so, because there was not even the 5½ percent interest return to the Guaranty Company during the period not exceeding six months, for which the option was to be outstanding.
6. The transaction in its entirety was approved by the board of directors of both companies. . . .

Whichever way we look at this transaction, therefore, it was so improvident, so dangerous, so unusual and so contrary to ordinary prudent banking practice as to subject the directors who approved it to liability in a derivative stockholders' action.

Having determined that the transaction in litigation is such as to impose liability upon the participating defendants, the next question is what part of the loss can be attributed to the improper transaction? . . .

The real issue as to damages is whether the directors should be liable for the total loss suffered when the bonds were ultimately sold, approximately an 81 percent loss, or only for that portion of the loss which accrued within the six months option period, making allowance for a period thereafter during which defendants could make reasonable and diligent efforts to sell the bonds. The record discloses that none of the bonds were sold until October 8, 1931, about six months after the Alleghany option had expired, and that they were not completely disposed of until December 28, 1937. The Missouri Pacific Railroad went into receivership in April, 1933, and between August 2 and September 25,

1933, $126,000 more of the bonds were purchased by the Company in an attempt to reduce the loss. A total loss was sustained on the bonds of approximately $2,250,000.

I believe that as to the decline of the bonds after April 16, 1931, there is no causal connection with the option which had expired on that date. A director is not liable for loss or damage other than what was proximately caused by his own acts or omissions in breach of his duty. ... The portion of the present transaction which is tainted with improvidence and negligence is the repurchase option. ... Once the option had expired, there was nothing to prevent the directors of the Company, which had taken over the bonds in accordance with its agreement, from selling them. Any loss on the bonds which was incurred after the option had expired on April 16, 1931, was occasioned as a result of the directors' independent business judgment in holding them thereafter. The further loss should not be laid at the door of the improper but already expired repurchase option. ...

Therefore, defendants are only liable for the loss attributable to the improper repurchase option itself, and this option ceased to be the motivating cause of the loss within a reasonable time after April 16, 1931. The price of the bonds for the week ending April 18, 1931, was 86 high and 81 low and closing. The matter will be referred to a Referee for assessment of damages to determine what price could have been obtained for these bonds if defendants had proceeded to sell them after April 16, 1931. ...

◆◆◆

Case Questions

1. Does this decision impose a more stringent standard upon directors than does the *Barnes* v. *Andrews* case?
2. A director of a bank is held to a higher standard than a director of an ordinary business corporation. If the transaction in the instant case had involved, not a bank but, an ordinary corporation, would the directors' business judgment defense have been successful?
3. What reasons could a bank, conservative by its very nature, have for entering a transaction where it bore all the risk and the other party enjoyed all the advantages?

OFFICERS

Corporate officers frequently draw handsome salaries and enjoy plush surroundings. Since the directors have the exclusive legal authority to manage the corporation, what is it that officers do to justify such a privileged existence? A great deal. The board establishes the direction in which the corporation is to go by setting overall basic policy. The officers carry on the day to day operations of the enterprise within that framework. There is one school of thought that views the officers as actually running the corporation while the directors merely serve as their rubber stamps. The Illinois Business Corporation Act provides:

§ 43. OFFICERS The officers of a corporation shall consist of a president, one or more vice-presidents as may be prescribed by the by-laws, a secretary, and a treasurer, each of whom shall be elected by the board of directors at such time and in such manner as may be prescribed by the by-laws. Such other officers and assistant officers and agents as may be deemed necessary may be elected or appointed by the board of directors or chosen in such other manner as may be prescribed by the by-laws. If the by-laws so provide, any two or more offices may be held by the same person, except the offices of president and secretary.

All officers and agents of the corporation, as between themselves and the corporation, shall have such authority and perform such duties in the management of the property and affairs of the corporation as may be provided in the by-laws, or as may be determined by resolution of the board of directors not inconsistent with the by-laws.

§ 44. REMOVAL OF OFFICERS. Any officer or agent may be removed by the board of directors whenever in its judgment the best interests of the corporation will be served thereby, but such removal shall be without prejudice to the contract rights, if any, of the person so removed. Election or appointment of an officer or agent shall not of itself create contract rights.

The officers can have actual (either express or implied) authority. This authority will be found in the charter, by-laws or board resolutions. Like any agent he may also have apparent authority. Authority may be absent but the directors will ratify the officer's actions. His action may be beneficial to the corporation and so the board will willingly accede to it. On the other hand, the board may be displeased yet coerced into ratification by the public relations or other costs inherent in rejection. A good deal of litigation crops up over the degree of authority posessed by an officer by virtue of his office. At one end of the legal spectrum is the view that the office bestows no authority upon an officer. The more realistic and developing position is that the president has the residual authority to enter contracts binding upon the corporation that are within the ordinary course of its business. Determining what constitutes "ordinary" must be done on a case by case basis. It will depend upon, among other factors: the industry concerned, the custom and practice within the trade, past practice, the dollar amount of the transaction relative to the corporation's financial status, the presence or absence of an emergency, etc. An officer lacks the inherent power to execute a contract of an unusual or extraordinary nature. It should be mentioned that the fact that an officer is also a director adds nothing to his authority.

A third party enters contractual transactions with a corporate officer at his own peril. It is the third party's obligation to inquire as to the officer's authority. If the by-laws do not grant the authority, the third party should request a copy of the pertinent board resolution that has been attested to by the secretary of the corporation.

As already mentioned, the courts are recognizing the grant of a certain degree of authority to the president, by virtue of his office, acting within the scope of ordinary matters. This unwritten authority is confined to the president; it does not extend to other corporate officers. A certain amount of confusion is engendered by different companies utilizing different labels for equivalent positions. The term "president" as used here, indicates the officer of highest authority within the respective organization. Some companies will call that individual the: chief executive officer; chairman of the board; chief operating officer; or general manager. The title is irrelevant. It is the individual's duties and function within the organization that determine his authority.

The authority of the remaining corporate officers is established by agency law, the by-laws, or by a specific delegation by board resolution. The vice-president's duties extend to presiding in the place of the president, upon his absence. The secretary keeps the corporate books and records. He also keeps the minutes of shareholder and directors meetings. The treasurer has the power to accept funds and give receipts, on behalf of the corporation. The business corporation statutes typically provide that an individual may hold more than one office if the by-laws so provide. However, they do prohibit one from occupying both the post of the president and secretary. Sometimes corporate documents will require the signature of the president and secretary or, the president's signature accompanied by the corporate seal (kept by the secretary). If two individuals occupy these offices the chances of error or fraud are minimized.

The next three cases examine an officer's authority to enter contracts binding upon the corporation in the absence of express authority. The first one is a straightforward example of an officer consummating an ordinary commercial transaction with a third party. The remaining two examine the authority of an officer to hire employees. The *Goldenberg* v. *Bartell Broadcasting* case illustrates a contract that contains such extraordinary terms that the officer is rendered powerless to execute it. In *Baltimore* v. *Foar* the unusual circumstances that exist, serious labor strife, lead the court to uphold the contract's validity.

COTE BROTHERS, INC. v. GRANITE LAKE REALTY CORP.
105 N.H. 111, 193 A.2d 884 (S. Ct., N.H., 1963)
(The trial court entered judgment for the plaintiff)

◆◆◆

KENISON, Chief Justice

The defendant corporation and its allied corporation Granite Lake Camp Associates, Inc. were both small close corporations which were organized, operated and managed by the same three individuals as stockholders, officers and directors. The issue in this case is whether the defendant is liable on a mercantile claim for merchandise delivered which, it is argued, no officer of the corporation was authorized to purchase. The guide lines for deciding this issue were set forth in *Holman-Baker Company* v. *Pre-Design Company,* 104 N.H. 116, 117-118, 179, A2d 454, 455 as follows: "In the world of credit there is emerging a rule, consistent with modern business practices, under which a principal is bound by the promise to his general agent, whether or not authorized, when such promise is made within the scope of the agent's power." ... The rule has been developed and nurtured over some period of time by an eminent authority. Seavey, "The Rationale of Agency," 29 *Yale L.J.* 859 (1920). ... The rationale of the rule is not based on express authority, implied authority, apparent authority or estoppel 'but (is derived) solely from the agency relation and exists for the protection of persons harmed or dealing with a servant or other agent' and is described as 'inherent agency power.' *Restatement, Second, Agency,* § 8A."

The defendant owned the premises known as Granite Lake Camp which was leased to and operated by another corporation, Granite Lake Camp Associates, Inc. The corporations were organized by three individuals for the purpose of acquiring and operating Granite Lake Camp as "a summer camp." The same three individuals (Chester Gusick, Charles Gusick and Milton Lubow) were the sole stockholders, officers and directors of both corporations. One of the three stockholders, directors, and officers, "Milton Lubow, was the man who handled the finances." At the beginning of their operation a letter was circularized to prospective merchants and suppliers signed by Milton Lubow as secretary-treasurer of Granite Lake Camp Associates, Inc. The letter, which was admitted as an exhibit over the defendants' objection, stated that the three individuals named above were the only persons authorized to order merchandise for Granite Lake Camp and that "we operate our business through Granite Lake Camp Associates, Inc., and Granite Lake Realty Corporation." During the period of time when the plaintiff's bill was due and owing rental payments were made by Granite Lake Camp Associates, Inc. to the defendant. From 1959 to 1962 the mortgage on the real estate in the original amount of $127,500 was reduced to "approximately seventy thousand dollars."

While both Chester Gusick and Charles Gusick testified that they had no knowledge of the letter sent to prospective merchants and that it was not authorized by them, it is evident that the letter was written in furtherance of the everyday business of the corporations and that it was done by Milton Lubow who was selected by the Gusick brothers as "the man who handled the finances." ... *The Restatement (Second), Agency,* § 161 comment (a) states in part: "Commercial convenience requires that the principal should not escape liability where there have been deviations from the usually granted authority by persons who are such essential parts of his business enterprise. In the long run it is of advantage to business, and hence to employers as a class, that third persons should not be required to scrutinize too carefully the mandates of permanent or semi-permanent agents who do no more than what is usually done by agents in similar positions." It is reasonably clear that Lubow as a stockholder, officer and financial manager of two allied close corporations had inherent agency power to purchase ordinary supplies for the business conducted through the two corporations. ...

The Trial Court's rulings, procedural and substantive, were correct.

Judgment on the verdict.

All concurred.

◆◆◆

Case Question

1. Did the court hold Granite liable for the debt because Lubow was one of three stockholders, directors and officers, or because Lubow was the man who handled the finances and the purchased supplies were of an ordinary nature?

GOLDENBERG v. BARTELL BROADCASTING CORPORATION
262 N.Y.S. 2d 274 (1965)

WILFRED A. WALTEMADE, Justice

This court's research has failed to find a case decided by either the State courts in New York or Delaware, in which the precise issue of the case at bar has been passed upon. Nor has counsel for either the plaintiff or defendants directed this court's attention to any such case.

In the case on trial, the plaintiff sets forth two causes of action, both of which seek recovery of damages for an alleged breach of a written contract of employment. The first cause of action is against the defendant Bartell Broadcasting Corporation, an entity incorporated under the laws of the State of Delaware. It is alleged in substance that on or about March 16, 1961, the plaintiff and the defendant Bartell Broadcasting Corporation entered into a written contract wherein the plaintiff was engaged as an Assistant to Gerald A. Bartell, the president of the defendant Bartell Broadcasting Corporation. The plaintiff's primary duties were to engage in corporate development in the field of pay television. The contract which was for a period of three years, provided for (1) the payment to the plaintiff of $1,933.00 per month; and (2) for the delivery to plaintiff of 12,000 shares of "Free Registered" stock of defendant Bartell Broadcasting Corporation, which stock was payable in three installments of 4,000 shares each in the months of January 1962, 1963 and 1964; and (3) the payment of plaintiff's traveling and living expenses in connection with his services to the employer; and (4) that defendant Bartell Broadcasting Corporation would provide the plaintiff with a private office and proper office facilities; and (5) that the agreement would be binding on any successor corporation or any corporation with which defendant Bartell Broadcasting Corporation would merge.

This written contract was signed by the plaintiff and by Gerald A. Bartell, in his capacity as the president of Bartell Broadcasting Corporation. It is further claimed that on or about May 1961, this contract was amended to increase plaintiff's monthly compensation from $1,933.00 to $2,400.00. It is further contended that the plaintiff was not paid his monthly compensation commencing with the month of November 1961; that the defendant Bartell Broadcasting Corporation failed to deliver the 4,000 shares of stock allegedly due in January 1962; and that in July 1962, the defendant Bartell Broadcasting Corporation denied the validity of plaintiff's employment contract. . . .

Granting to the plaintiff a most favorable view of the testimony and giving to him the benefit of every favorable inference to be drawn from such evidence, the court has assumed the making and execution of the contract in litigation, although it should be observed that the defendants have vigorously contended that the contract was fraudulently secured by the plaintiff. . . .

The court will now turn its consideration to the first cause of action set forth in the complaint.

A corporation can only act through its directors, officers and employees. They are the conduit by and through which the corporation is given being and from which its power to act and reason springs. Therefore in every action in which a person sues a corporation on a contract executed on behalf of the corporation by one of its officers, one of the issues to be determined is whether the officer had the express, implied or apparent authority to execute the contract in question. . . .

The authority of an officer to act on behalf of a corporation may be express, implied or apparent. There has been no proof offered in this case indicating that Gerald A. Bartell, as president of the defendant Bartell Broadcasting Corporation, had express authority to enter into the agreement, dated March 16, 1961, which is the subject of the first cause of action.

Did Gerald A. Bartell then have either *implied* or *apparent authority* to execute the contract?

Implied authority is a species of actual authority, which gives an officer the power to do the necessary acts within the scope of his usual duties. Generally, the president of a corporation has the implied authority to hire and fire corporate employees and to fix their compensation. However the president of a corporation does *not* have the implied power to execute "unusual or extraordinary" contracts of employment. . . .

The agreement of March 16, 1961 not only provides for the payment of a substantial monthly compensation, but also requires the delivery of 12,000 shares of "free registered" stock of the defendant Bartell Broadcasting Corporation. While the payment of the monthly compensation would not make the contract of March 16, 1961, *"unusual or extraordinary,"* the Court is of the opinion that the inclusion in the contract of the provision requiring the delivery to plaintiff of 12,000 shares of "free registered stock," does bring the agreement within the category of being an *"unusual and extraordinary"* contract.

A consideration of the cases of *Gumpert* v. *Bon Ami Company,* 2 Cir., 251 F.2d 735, *Noyes* v. *Irving Trust Company,* 250 App.Div. 274, 294 N.Y.S. 2, aff'd 275 N.Y. 520, 11 N.E.2d 323; . . . convinces this court to conclude that the contract of March 16, 1961 was *unusual and extraordinary* and therefore beyond the scope of the implied authority of the president of the defendant Bartell Broadcasting Corporation.

In the *Gumpert* v. *Bon Ami Company* case, the plaintiff there sued on a one year employment contract under which he was to be paid $25,000 in cash and $25,000 in defendant's corporate stock. The contract was signed on behalf of the corporation's executive committee. At page 739, of 251 F.2d, the Federal court there wrote:

> *Even if Rosenberg was chief executive officer * * * it is doubtful that he would possess power to make such an arrangement as a normal incident of his position.* . . . (Emphasis supplied)

In the case of *Noyes* v. *Irving Trust Company,* the plaintiff there sued on an employment contract under which he was to be paid $400 per month together with a bonus based upon the net profits. The contract was signed on behalf of the defendant corporation by its sales manager. At pages 276, and 277 of 250 App. Div., 294 N.Y.S. page 5, the court there wrote:

> It is well settled that a contract of this character is not the usual and ordinary contract which one authorized to employ agents and servants may make. *It would require express authority.* . . .

The reason for the rule enunciated in the cases just cited, is easily discernible. Corporate stock is the sinew, muscle and bone upon which the financial structure of a corporation is constructed. Corporate stock is sold, traded or disposed of in exchange for money, labor, services or other property. Thus in this manner a corporation acquires the necessary assets needed for the fulfillment of the corporate purposes. . . .

The case of *Field* v. *Carlisle Corp.*, 31 Del.Ch.227, 68 A.2d 817, although not involving an employment contract, contains language appropriate here. At page 232, 68 A.2d page 819, the Delaware court there wrote:

> The quoted statutes impose the duty on the directors to fix the value of property received for the corporation's stock. Section 14 (now section 152) explicitly states that the corporation's stock may be issued 'for such consideration as may be fixed from time to time by the board of Directors. * * * Furthermore, Section 14 says that in the absence of actual fraud the judgment of the directors as to the value of the property received for the stock shall be conclusive. * * * Leaving aside other contentions, I do not believe the power to delegate this vitally important duty can be fairly implied from the language of the statute. This is particularly true where the statute imposes the duty on the directors to deal with the particular subject matter. *The importance to the corporation of the subject matter—ownership of the corporation—tends also to negative implication that the directors might delegate it in a manner not explicitly authorized by statute.* (Emphasis supplied.)

To permit the president of a corporation, without the express authority and approval of the corporation's Board of Directors, to barter or contract away the corporation's unissued (free) stock, would not only be an express violation of the statutes, but would also make possible the denudation of a corporation's assets, and the dilution of the value of the stock already issued to the detriment and disadvantage of the corporate stockholders. It should be noted here that in the case at bar, the stock of both defendant corporations is publicly owned and traded.

Apparent authority is the authority which the principal permits the agent to represent that he possesses. Generally, persons dealing with officers of a corporation are bound to take notice that the powers of an officer are derived from statutes, by-laws and usages which more or less define the extent of the officer's authority. In a doubtful case one must at his peril acquaint himself with the exact extent of the officer's authority. . . . The right of a third party to rely on the apparent authority of a corporate officer is subject to the condition that such third person has no notice or knowledge of a limitation in such authority. . . . Although it is true that secret instructions or limitations upon the apparent general authority of an officer of a corporation will not affect one who deals with the officer in the general line of his authority, and knows nothing of such limitations; however, this rule is not applicable to any limitations which are provided for in statutes. Those who contract with a corporation do so with knowledge of the statutory conditions pertaining to a corporation. . . .

The plaintiff is not a naive person, uninitiated in the business world, nor is he without knowledge of corporate financing or business practices. By his own testimony he is and was a stockholder, officer and director of several corporations. There is testimony that the plaintiff has engaged in the sale of securities to the general public. . . .

With the varied and broad business experience acquired by the plaintiff in his wide business associations as evidenced by his career resume furnished to the defendants . . . and by plaintiff's own testimony, it can be truly said that he not only was presumed to have knowledge of the statutory provisions of the law pertaining to corporations, but that he apparently also had actual knowledge of such laws. It is reasonable to infer that the plaintiff was aware, or at the least, had reason to be aware, that the authority for the issuance of corporate stock rests solely within the powers of the Board of Directors of the corporation, and that in the absence of express authority, the president of a corporation does not have the implied or apparent authority to enter into an employment contract which provides for the issuance of corporate stock as compensation. . . .

Some comment is necessary relative to the legal effect of the affixing of the seal of the defendant Bartell Broadcasting Corporation to the contract of March 16, 1961.

The plaintiff's testimony establishes that the seal was not affixed on the date of the execution of the contract, but on some date thereafter. The plaintiff testified that some time after the execution of the contract, he had a conversation with Gerald A. Bartell in which he, the plaintiff, suggested that the corporate seal should be affixed to the contract; that Mr. Bartell agreed with the plaintiff's suggestion, whereupon the plaintiff procured the seal from one of the file cabinets in the corporation's offices, and he then affixed the seal. The plaintiff contends that the placement of the seal on the contract creates the rebuttable presumption that the defendant Bartell Broadcasting Corporation authorized its president to execute the contract dated March 16, 1961. There is no merit to plaintiff's contention in law or fact.

The question of the legal effect of a corporate seal upon a contract is discussed in Hornstein, *Corporate Law and Practice,* Vol. 1, section 264, where he said:

> To-day, the one significant consequence of a seal — if coupled with an acknowledgement by an officer that it was attached by proper authority — is that it gives rise to a presumption (not conclusive) that the instrument to which it is attached was duly authorized by the board of directors.

Absent from the case on trial is any evidence of an acknowledgement by any officer that the seal was attached by proper authority. To the contrary, the plaintiff's own testimony is that he placed the seal on the contract, albeit, allegedly with the consent of Gerald A. Bartell.

The Court concludes, after a careful analysis of the evidence and the application of the law reviewed herein, that the plaintiff has not made out a prima facie case of express, implied or apparent authority of the president of the defendant Bartell Broadcasting Corporation to execute the contract of employment. On the basis of the findings herein stated, the cause of action against Macfadden-Bartell Corporation must also fall.

Accordingly, the motion by the defendants to dismiss the complaint against both defendants is granted.

◆◆◆

Case Questions

1. Should the court have enforced the salary portion of the contract since it was not unusual or extraordinary?
2. The plaintiff signed the contract in March of 1961; during May the monthly compensation was increased. Salary payments did not cease until November, 1961. Under such circumstances could it be said that the directors had ratified the contract?
3. If Bartell Broadcasting is a closely held corporation, do you believe the court's decision is correct?

BALTIMORE & O.R. CO. v. FOAR
84 F.2d 67 (C.C.A. 7th 1936)

◆◆◆

SPARKS, Circuit Judge.

This was an action by appellee to recover damages for breach of an oral contract. The jury returned a verdict for $4500, upon which a judgement was rendered, and from that judgment this appeal is prosecuted.

The errors assigned and relied upon are (1) overruling appellant's demurrer to the complaint, (2) refusing to direct a verdict for appellant at the close of the evidence, and (3) failure to give to the jury appellant's requested instruction to find for the appellant.

The material allegations of the complaint are in substance as follows: appellant, a railroad corporation organized under the laws of Maryland, had for many years operated its road through Indiana, where it owned and operated repair, machine, and construction shops at Garrett, in which a large number of men were employed. In 1911 appellee was employed by appellant as a machinist's helper in the repair shop, and continued in such employment until 1919, when he was transferred to the car department as a carman's helper, where he continued to work as such until July, 1922. In that month a general strike was called by the machinists and other crafts in the shops at Garrett and at all other points on appellant's line from Baltimore to Chicago, and appellee and all other members of his craft, and of the union organization, walked out.

Thereafter, appellant, by Howard W. Mountz and the company's shop superintendent, Robinson, and by its officers and representatives in charge, requested and urged appellee to return to his work, and promised him that if he would do so during the pendency of the strike, appellant would provide permanent and continuous employment for him during his lifetime at the same wages received by him previous to the strike. Appellee accepted the promise and in reliance thereon returned to his work in August, at a daily wage of $4.72. He was retained in said employment by appellant, which acknowledged the same to be in consideration of its promise and agreement, until May 15, 1931, when he was discharged without cause or fault on his part. Appellee had performed his part of the contract and was at all times ready, willing and able to continue to do so, but was prevented by appellant from so doing. . . .

At the time of the strike, Howard W. Mountz was a member of the firm of Mountz and Brinkerhoff, local counsel for appellant. After the strike was called, Mountz called at appellee's home and in the presence of appellee's wife and children said that appellant wanted appellee to return to work; that they needed someone to break the ice so that the others would follow, and that if appellee would return to work the company would give him a lifetime job at the same wages that he had been getting. The wife refused to assent, and Mountz urged her to do so because her husband would then have a lifetime job, which he would need in order to educate his children. He further assured them that the company would protect him and his family. The next day appellee called at Mountz' office where Mountz repeated the promise to him of a lifetime job at his previous wage, and protection to him and his family, whereupon appellee agreed to return to work under those conditions. The next morning before daylight appellee went to the shops by a by-path so that the union pickets around the shops would not see him. The shops were surrounded by a high fence and guarded by over one hundred armed special police officers. There appellee was taken charge of by Robinson, hereinbefore referred to, who had formerly been a superintendent on the road, but at and for some time previous to the strike was an executive officer of the railroad, being the superintendent of fuels over the entire system of eleven thousand miles. At that time, there were no other persons at work except officials and strangers who were brought in and housed in coach cars and fed from a commissary in the shop yards.

On the night following appellee's return to work, his house was surrounded by union pickets who threatened to blow it up. They remained there all night, some staying on the porch, and the family was kept up all night by their threats. They returned to appellee's home the next night and conducted themselves in the same manner as before, threatening to blow up the house, to break the windows, and to kill appellee's cow. The next morning appellee's wife, with her five-month-old baby, went over the gate surrounding the shop yards. She sent for her husband and told him of the actions and threats of the pickets, and he told her he would go home. When he started to do so he was met by Robinson and one Sapp, who was chief of the railroad police at Garrett. Robinson urged him not to go home; that the damage had already been done; that the union men would have it in for him anyhow, and that he had a life job with the company if he would stay. Appellee insisted on going home and Robinson accompanied him, and conferred with appellee's wife. At that time, two dozen strikers were on a nearby overhead bridge watching the house. Robinson urged upon appellee and his wife the duty of appellee to return to work; that he had a life job and that it was necessary for him to rear and educate his children, and give them an opportunity, and if he would return, the company would protect him and his family from harm. Thereupon, appellee returned to his work.

The strike was settled in September, and the returning strikers immediately began to harass appellee. They put grease in his lunch, hid his tools, called him names and interfered with his work in order to make trouble between him and the company. As a result of this conduct, appellee went to consult Mr. Mountz at his office and Mountz gave him a letter to Robinson at Baltimore. He went to Baltimore but Robinson was not in and he delivered the letter to Robinson's clerk. He undertook to see vice-president Galloway, and waited all day for that purpose, but without avail. Upon his return he was reproached by the master mechanic, the general foreman and the division superintendent for going to Baltimore over their heads. The division superintendent told him they did not want him to do this any more and they would give him satisfaction, as he had orders from Baltimore to protect him and take care of him.

In 1926 appellee was furloughed. He consulted with the master mechanic, Short, and reminded him of his life contract with the company, and asked him if he should take the matter up with Baltimore. Short instructed him to return the next day. This he did and he was asked if he would take a job cleaning coaches at the depot, to which he replied that he would do anything to make a living so long as he was not discharged, and Short then told him he would not be discharged. The regular scale for cleaning coaches was thirty-nine cents an hour, but the company paid him fifty-four cents per hour for that work. In about three months the superintendent notified him that he was being paid fifty-four cents for work which should be paid for at the rate of thirty-nine cents per hour, whereupon, he wrote to the superintendent, and his wages were not cut.

He was furloughed again on May 15, 1931. At that time he reminded the division superintendent of the promise that had been made to him during the strike. Thereafter he made repeated applications to appellant for employment; he talked to Mountz, and again went to Baltimore and saw President Willard, but without avail. He was never afterwards given any work by appellant, although he was at all times ready, able and willing to return to work. He made repeated efforts to secure employment elsewhere, but he was black-listed by the unions at other plants. He was on furlough from May 15, 1931 to December, 1932, when he was discharged by appellant.

The verdict of the jury establishes the fact that the contract was made with appellee by Mountz and Robinson who for that purpose essayed to act as representatives of appellant. It must be conceded that in so doing, neither Mountz as local counsel, nor Robinson as superintendent of fuel for the entire system of appellant's railroad, acted within the scope of the duties of those respective employments. Even so, their duties may have been enlarged by appellant, under the exigencies of the situation then present, to such an extent as to authorize the contract; or appellant may have subsequently ratified the unauthorized contract, in which event it would be valid ab initio. The record discloses no direct evidence that the authority of either Mountz or Robinson was expressly enlarged beyond their usual duties, but we think it does disclose facts and circumstances which tended to prove that appellant had ratified the contract.

The consensus of judicial opinion throughout the United States is that a corporation by its proper officers may lawfully enter into a life contract with an employee. It is equally well settled that a corporation by its proper officers may ratify such a contract entered into by certain of its officers without authority, but the unauthorized contract may not be ratified by those who have no authority to make it, and there can be not ratification unless those so acting with authority have full knowledge of all the material facts at the time of the ratification. These propositions are not controverted by counsel.

Primarily, the board of directors is the true agent of a corporation, and the actions of the directors as a board, if within the scope of the corporate charter, are binding upon it. Theoretically, no act of any employee or officer is binding on the corporation unless it is authorized or subsequently approved by the board of directors. The duties of officers and heads of departments are usually defined in the by-laws, and what is actually done in the operation of the business comes to the knowledge of the board of directors, as a rule, through reports of the officers and the heads of departments. The court judicially knows that the ordinary contract of employment in a highly organized corporation, such as appellant, is not entered into by the board of directors, and yet it theoretically approves such contract subsequently by approving the report from that department. It is said, however, that the contract at bar is an unusual one in that it purported to run during the life of appellee, and that it should not be upheld unless express authorization or approval by the board is shown. Such contracts were properly characterized in the earlier decisions as unusual. However, from the number disclosed in the more recent cases, we are impressed with the fact that they are not now as unusual as they were. Be that as it may, it is worthy of note that the defense is usually the same, that is to say, that the contract was entered into without authority from the board, and without their knowledge or ratification.

A board of directors is not only bound by what it actually knows, but it may be bound by what it ought to have known, or by proper attention to its business would have known. In *Knights of Pythias* v. *Kalinski*, 163 U.S. 289, . . . the Court said, "If the company ought to have known of the facts, or, with proper attention to its own business, would have been apprised of them, it has no right to set up its ignorance as an excuse."

It is fair to presume that the board of directors and the higher officers at Baltimore were fully aware of the serious situation occasioned by the strike. It not only involved appellant's entire properties, but it was nation-wide in its scope. Appellant's huge repair, machine and construction shops were at Garrett, where practically all the population of that city were employed. So far as the record discloses, none of the directors or high officers of appellant resided nearer than Baltimore. All of the men at Garrett, save the heads of departments, walked out, and the appellant moved in strike-breakers, and maintained and sustained them night and day at the plant. Windows were broken in large numbers, bombs were thrown on the premises, and property was being destroyed. Summary and substantial direction and assistance were imperative, in order to protect property and to keep the trains running. Robinson was sent there by appellant's authorities at Baltimore. It is true that he was appellant's superintendent of fuel, but it is not disclosed that he performed any of the duties of that office on that trip. It is obvious from the record that he came there to lend whatever assistance he could in protecting appellant's property and in breaking the strike. The heads of the departments likewise were doing the same and all engaged in manual labor which ordinarily was not within the scope of their respective employment. . . .

There was contradictory evidence as to whether Robinson's authority while at Garrett exceeded that of the regular superintendent or superintendents of the plant. That, however, is not material. They were all there with a large group of strike-breakers and special guards, and from the record we are warranted in believing that they were armed with power, by authority from headquarters at Baltimore, to handle the situation at Garrett during the strike as seemed best to them for the interests of the company. The record discloses that one of their great desires was to induce the striking men to return to their work, and appellee was the first striker to return. For years he had been their faithful and trusted workman, and they were sure if he returned others would follow. The record also discloses that when he returned to work he was paid not less than union wages measured by the character of work he did immediately before the strike.

With respect the appellant's knowledge of and acquiescence in the contract sued upon, we think it fair to assume that those in authority at Garrett performed their duties with reference to reporting to their superiors both at Garrett and at Baltimore. We further think it fair to assume that those in authority at Baltimore, including the board of directors, gave proper attention to the reports made to them, and to the company's business and operations during and after this very serious labor controversy. . . .

Judgment affirmed.

♦♦♦

Case Questions

1. Does a lifetime contract of employment seem to be unusual or extraordinary? Would a lifetime contract appear irregular for a carman's helper, while not being out of the ordinary for a high corporate official?
2. The court characterizes Foar as a faithful and trusted workman of the corporation. It presumes that the directors were fully aware of the strike situation. It assumes that the employees properly reported to their superiors and assumes that those in authority, including the board, gave proper attention to these reports. Does this leave the impression that the court was sympathetic to Foar's plight and was determined to find a legal rationale to support his position?
3. Does the decision in this case conflict with the legal reasoning expressed in the *Goldenberg* v. *Bartell Broadcasting* case?

CRIMES AND TORTS

Officers can incur civil tort liability for their corporations and themselves. The corporation will be liable for any torts committed by its officers within the course and scope of their employment. The corporation cannot avoid liability by showing that the officers' action was outside the corporate charter and hence *ultra vires*. The normal master-servant rules are applicable. Therefore, it must be shown that the officer's actions were done within the scope of his employment and were not merely the actions of a private individual. Suppose that a corporate official, upon learning of the candidacy of a personal enemy for the presidency of a university, sends a defamatory letter to that university. The purpose of the letter is to defeat his candidacy and, to add to the letter's credibility, it is written on corporate stationery. In such an instance the corporation would not be liable. However, suppose that two corporations are competing for a consulting contract to be awarded by a municipality. In an effort to defeat its rival, the president of the corporation writes a defamatory letter to a newspaper. Written on corporate stationery, the letter accuses the rival corporation of giving illegal bribes and kickbacks. Is the corporation liable for the tort of its president? Yes. The president's action was within the course and scope of his employment. The action was taken to benefit the corporation. If the corporation will have its interests advanced or property protected by the officers' actions, the corporation will incur liability. The corporation cannot raise as a defense the officer's questionable judgment or exorbitant zeal.

The upcoming *Liability Ins. Co.* v. *Haidinger-Hayes* case examines a slight twist on the question of a corporation's tort liability. It deals with the issue of the extent of an officer's personal liability for his active participation in the corporation's tortious act.

UNITED STATES LIABIL. INS. CO. v. HAIDINGER-HAYES, INC. ·
83 Cal Rptr. 418, 463 P.2d 770 (S. Ct. Cal., 1970)

◆◆◆

McCOMB, Justice.

Plaintiff insurance company, an out of state corporation, entered into a general agency contract with defendant Haidinger-Hayes, Inc., a licensed California insurance agent, effective March 31, 1959. Under the terms of their agreement defendant corporation had authority to solicit and underwrite proposals for insurance, to determine the premium rate, and to issue contracts of insurance in the eleven western states in plaintiff's behalf. The consideration to it was 20 percent of the premiums paid. Numerous policies were solicited, underwritten and issued pursuant to this agreement. It was cancelled on December 12, 1963, at the request of plaintiff because of excessive loss history under a policy of liability insurance issued to Crescent Wharf and Warehouse Company and its wholly-owned subsidiaries (hereinafter all referred to as "Crescent").

The negotiations for the Crescent policy were the responsibility of defendant V. M. Haidinger, president and principal executive officer of defendant corporation. Acting for and on behalf of the corporation he issued the policy on October 10, 1061, for a period of three years, at the premium rate of $1.05 per $100 reportable payroll. The policy covered Crescent's legal liability for claims arising out of the work, operations and other business activities of Crescent up to a limit of liability of $25,000 per claim or casualty, plus expenses of adjusting and defending such claims. The risk under this policy was "self-rated" and was not measurable by any published standard or comparable rate. The policy by its nature anticipated the occurrence of monetary claims for injuries sustained by employees of Crescent and that a premium rate was required which would produce a reasonable profit for the insurer after the settlement, defense and payment of such claims. This policy was cancelled at the request of plaintiff on February 28, 1963. ... This action was filed November 1, 1965, for damages resulting from the Crescent risk. ...

The complaint therein stated several causes of action. During the trial plaintiff dismissed the breach of contract cause of action. Findings were made against both defendants on the issue of negligence in issuing the policy at the premium rate of $1.05 per $100 payroll, and judgment was based solely thereon. In their favor, however, the court found that neither was guilty of failure to disclose any material fact to plaintiff with respect to this coverage; that neither willfully or intentionally placed their own interests or that of others ahead of plaintiff's; and ·

that neither was guilty of any dishonest, fraudulent or malicious acts in connection therewith. Damages were found to have been proximately caused by defendants' negligence in the sum of $137,606.20 as of the date of the conclusion of the trial, plus an undetermined amount on open unsettled claims. . . .

The issues on appeal are: the sufficiency of the evidence to support the findings of negligence; liability to plaintiff of the individual defendant; . . .

The trail was long and the evidence was conflicting. There were discrepancies in the testimony of defendant V.M. Haidinger. Under well-settled rules on appeal the evidence and the inferences arising therefrom must be viewed in the light most favorable to respondent plaintiff.

Question: *Does the evidence support the findings of negligence?*

Yes, as to negligence of both defendants in the computation of the premium rate. *No,* as to the finding of personal responsibility to plaintiff on the part of the individual defendant.

The court found that during the time the agency relationship existed defendants owed a duty to plaintiff to exercise reasonable care in handling plaintiff's business and, in the investigation and underwriting of each insurance risk, to also make a reasonable effort to produce a profit for plaintiff. During the late spring and early summer of 1961, the individual defendant had carried on negotiations with Crescent's insurance broker, Bayly, Martin & Fay, Inc., and had been supplied with current, accurate and detailed underwriting information concerning the Crescent risk going back to October 1, 1954. This information was reviewed and analyzed personally by defendant V.M. Haidinger. . . .

The court found that at the time this policy was issued a "loss ratio" of a maximum of 60 percent was required in order to produce a reasonable allowance for profit to plaintiff on this coverage, and that defendant V.M. Haidinger, acting on behalf of defendant Haidinger-Hayes, Inc. should in the exercise of reasonable care have known this. The court further found that, based on information in the possession of, or readily available to, these defendants at that time it was reasonable to anticipate that Crescent's losses under the policy would be at least $85,000 per year, that its reportable payroll would not exceed $7,000,000 per year, and that it was not reasonable to anticipate that the losses of payroll would be otherwise. In the exercise of reasonable care defendants should have known, the court found, that at the premium rate of $1.05 per $100 of payroll the loss ratio was "in excess of One Hundred Ten Percent (110%) and that the policy would probably result in substantial financial loss to plaintiff. . . .

Among the information furnished or available to defendants and which, in the exercise of reasonable care, they should have considered in determining the premium rate for this policy, was that none of the coverages issued to Crescent by other companies since October 1, 1954, had gone to expiration, each having been cancelled by prior insurers because of loss experience thereunder; that losses under prior Crescent policies had been substantial; that there had been a sharp upward trend in these losses; and that there were payroll-reducing occurrences which might affect the anticipated payroll. These included the loss by Crescent of a major customer, — and with it one-third of its anticipated payroll, and the effects of automation which had begun prior to the issuance of the policy. There was evidence that defendant V.M. Haidinger knew that the anticipated payroll would not exceed $7,000,000, that if the loss ratio was over 60 percent that plaintiff would suffer a financial loss, and that Crescent would not accept the coverage at a substantially higher premium. . . . He anticipated a reduction in the loss picutre through his better efficiency in handling claims, but he did not inquire as to the facts of prior claims or the costs of defending them. . . .

The trial court found that each defendant owed a duty to plaintiff to exercise reasonable care and to make a reasonable effort to produce a profit for plaintiff; that each acted negligently toward plaintiff in this regard; and, as a conclusion of law, found that defendant V.M. Haidinger was liable to plaintiff "by reason of his personal participation as an officer and agent of defendant Haidinger-Hayes, Inc. in the tortious conduct of defendant Haidinger-Hayes, Inc."

What is negligence under a particular set of circumstances is a question for the trier of fact. Actionable negligence involves a legal duty to use due care, a breach of such legal duty, and the breach as the proximate or legal cause of the resulting injury. . . . Defendant corporation was a fiduciary to plaintiff during the existence of the agency agreement. A professional agent is required to have the particular knowledge and to exercise the particular skill and diligence expected of it. . . . If an insurance agent negligently induces an insurer to assume coverage on which it suffers a loss the agent is liable. . . . Liability is not incurred by a mere error of judgment in the exercise of discretion unless the error is based on want of care or diligence. . . . Here there was an express finding of negligence and the "business judgment" rule does not exonerate defendant corporation. . . .

The relationship of defendant V.M. Haidinger to plaintiff is somewhat different. Liability was imposed upon him for his active participation in the tortious (negligent) act of his principal which caused pecuniary harm to a third person. . . . Liability imposed upon agents for active participation in tortious acts of the principal have been mostly restricted to cases involving physical injury, not pecuniary harm, to third person. . . . More must be shown than breach of the officer's duty *to his corporation* to impose personal liability *to a third person* upon him. Neither the evidence nor the finding support the conclusion that defendant V.M. Haidinger was personally liable to plaintiff by reason of his negligent performance of his corporate duties. . . .

Judgment against defendant Haidinger-Hayes, Inc. is affirmed . . . Judgment against defendant V.M. Haidinger is reversed.

◆◆◆

Case Question

1. What factors, if any, support a policy of exempting officers from personal liability for their corporate torts unless a physical injury resulted?

Officers can also commit crimes for which the corporation will share criminal liability. Of course, a corporation can only be fined; incarceration is impossible. The *U.S.* v. *Park* case that follows is a 1975 Supreme Court decision treating the issue of an officer's criminal liability. The criminal statute imposes liability regardless of knowledge, intent, or the consciousness of wrongdoing. The statute closely approaches the imposition of absolute liability. In that sense it differs from most criminal statutes. Nonetheless the case is important because many such statutes can apply to corporations within certain industries.

U.S. v. PARK
421 U.S. 658 (1975)

♦♦♦

MR. CHIEF JUSTICE BURGER delivered the opinion of the Court.

We granted certiorari to consider whether jury instructions in the prosecution of a corporate officer under § 301 (k) of the Federal Food, Drug, and Cosmetic Act, 21 U.S.C. § 331 (k), were appropriate under *United States* v. *Dotterweich,* 320 U.S. 277 (1943).

Acme Markets, Inc., is a national retail food chain with approximately 36,000 employees, 874 retail outlets, 12 general warehouses, and four special warehouses. Its headquarters, including the office of the president, respondent Park, who is chief executive officer of the corporation, are located in Philadelphia, Pennsylvania. In a five-count information filed in the United States District Court for the District of Maryland, the Government charged Acme and respondent with violations of the Federal Food, Drug, and Cosmetic Act. Each count of the information alleged that the defendants had received food that had been shipped in interstate commerce and that, while the food was being held for sale in Acme's Baltimore warehouse following shipment in interstate commerce, they caused it to be held in a building accessible to rodents and to be exposed to contamination by rodents. These acts were alleged to have resulted in the food being adulterated. . . .

Acme pleaded guilty to each count of the information. Respondent pleaded not guilty. The evidence at trial demonstrated that in April 1970 the Food and Drug Administration (FDA) advised respondent by letter of unsanitary conditions in Acme's Philadelphia warehouse. In 1971 FDA found that similar conditions existed in the firm's Baltimore warehouse. An FDA consumer safety officer testified concerning evidence of rodent infestation and other unsanitary conditions discovered during a 12-day inspection of the Baltimore warehouse in November and December 1971. He also related that a second inspection of the warehouse had been conducted in March 1972. On that occasion the inspectors found that there had been improvement in the sanitary conditions, but that, "there was still evidence of rodent activity in the building and in the warehouse and we found some rodent-contaminated lots of food items."

The Government also presented testimony by the Chief of Compliance of FDA's Baltimore office, who informed respondent by letter of the conditions at the Baltimore warehouse after the first inspection. There was testimony by Acme's Baltimore division vice president, who had responded to the letter on behalf of Acme and respondent and who described the steps taken to remedy the insanitary conditions discovered by both inspections. The Government's final witness, Acme's vice president for legal affairs and assistant secretary, identified respondent as the president and chief executive officer of the company and read a bylaw prescribing the duties of the chief executive officer. He testified that respondent functioned by delegating "normal operating duties," including sanitation, but that he retained "certain things, which are the big, broad, principles of the operation of the company," and had "the resonsibility of seeing that they all work together."

At the close of the Government's case-in-chief, respondent moved for a judgment of acquittal on the ground that "the evidence in chief has shown that Mr. Park is not personally concerned in this Food and Drug violation." The trial judge denied the motion, stating that *United States* v. *Dotterweich*, 320 U.S. 277 was controlling.

Respondent was the only defense witness. He testified that, although all of Acme's employees were in a sense under his general direction, the company had an "organizational structure for resonsibilities for certain functions" according to which different phases of its operation were "assigned to individuals who, in turn, have staff and departments under them." He identified those individuals responsible for sanitation and related that upon receipt of the January 1972 FDA letter, he had conferred with the vice president for legal affairs, who informed him that the Baltimore division vice president "was investigating the situation immediately and would be taking corrective action and would be preparing a summary of the corrective action to reply to the letter." Respondent stated that he did not "believe there was anything (he) could have done more constructively than what (he) found was being done."

On cross-examination, respondent conceded that providing sanitary conditions for food offered for sale to the public was something that he was "responsible for in the entire operation of the company," and he stated that it was one of many phases of the company that he assigned to "dependable subordinates." Respondent was asked about and, over the objections of his counsel, admitted receiving, the April 1970 letter addressed to him from FDA regarding insanitary conditions at Acme's Philadelphia warehouse. He acknowledged that, with the exception of the divison vice president, the same individuals had responsibility for sanitation in both Baltimore and Philadelphia. Finally, in response to questions concerning the Philadelphia and Baltimore incidents, respondent admitted that the Baltimore problem indicated the system for handling sanitation "wasn't working perfectly" and that as Acme's chief executive officer he was responsible for "any result which occurs in our company."

At the close of the evidence, respondent's renewed motion for judgment of acquittal was denied. . . . Respondent's counsel objected to the (jury) instructions on the ground that they failed to reflect our decision in *United States* v. *Dotterweich*, 320 U.S. 277, and to define ' "responsible relationship." ' The trial judge overruled the objection. The jury found respondent guilty on all counts of the information, and he was subsequently sentenced to pay a fine of $50 on each count.

The Court of Appeals reversed the conviction and remanded for a new trial. . . .

We granted certiorari because of an apparent conflict among the courts of appeals with respect to the standard of liability of corporate officers under the Federal Food, Drug, and Cosmetic Act as construed in *United States* v. *Dotterweich,* supra, and because of the importance of the question to the Government's enforcement program. We reverse.

I.

The question presented by the Government's petition for certiorari in *United States* v. *Dotterweich*, supra, and the focus of this Court's opinion, was whether "the manager of a corporation, as well as the corporation itself, may be prosecuted under the Federal Food, Drug, and Cosmetic Act of 1938 for the introduction of misbranded and adulterated articles into interstate commerce." In Dotterweich, a jury had disagreed as to the corporation, a jobber purchasing drugs from manufacturers and shipping them in interstate commerce under its own label, but had convicted Dotterweich, the corporation's president and general manager. The Court of Appeals reversed the conviction on the ground that only the drug dealer, whether corporation or individual, was subject to the criminal provision of the Act, and that where the dealer was a corporation, an individual connected therewith might be held personally only if he was operating the corporation "as his 'alter ego.' "

In reversing the judgment of the Court of Appeals and reinstating Dotterweich's conviction, this Court looked to the purposes of the Act and noted that they "touch phases of the lives and health of people which, in the circumstances of modern industrialism, are largely beyond self-protection." It observed that the Act is of "a now familiar type" which "dispenses with the conventional requirement for criminal conduct — awareness of some wrongdoing. In the interest of the larger good it puts the burden of acting at hazard upon a person otherwise innocent but standing in responsible relation to a public danger."

Central to the Court's conclusion that individuals other than proprietors are subject to the criminal provisions of the act was the reality that "the only way in which a corporation can act is through the individuals who act on its behalf." . . .

At the same time, however, the Court was aware of the concern which was the motivating factor in the Court of Appeals' decision, that literal enforcement "might operate too harshly by sweeping within its condemnation any person however remotely entangled in the prescribed shipment." A limiting principle, in the form of "settled doctrines of criminal law" defining those who "are responsible for the commission of a misdeameanor", was available. In this context, the Court concluded, those doctrines dictated that the offense was committed "by all who have . . . a responsible share in the furtherance of the transaction which the statute outlaws."

The Court recognized that, because the Act dispenses with the need to prove "consciousness of wrongdoing," it may result in hardship even as applied to those who share "a responsibility in the business process resulting in" a violation. It regarded as "too treacherous" an attempt "to define or even to indicate by way of illustration the class of employees which stands in such a responsible relation." The question of responsibility, the Court said, depends "on the evidence produced at the trial and its submission — assuming the evidence warrants it — to the jury under appropriate guidance." The Court added: "In such matters the good sense of prosecutors, the wise guidance of trial judges, and the ultimate judgment of juries must be trusted." . . .

II.

The rule that corporate employees who have "a responsible share in the furtherance of the transaction which the statute outlaws" are subject to the criminal provision of the Act was not formulated in a vacuum. Cases under the Federal Food and Drugs Act of 1906 reflected the view both that knowledge or intent were not required to be proved in prosecutions under its criminal provision, and that responsible corporate agents could be subjected to the liability thereby imposed. Moreover, the principle had been recognized that a corporate agent, through whose act, default, or omission the corporation committeed a crime, was himself guilty individually of that crime. The principle had been applied whether or not the crime required "consciousness of wrongdoing", and it has been applied not only to those corporate agents who themselves committed the criminal act, but also to those who by virtue of their managerial positions or other similar relations to the act could be deemed responsible for its commission.

In the latter class of cases, the liability of managerial officers did not depend on their knowledge of, or personal participation in, the act made criminal by the statute. Rather, where the statute under which they were prosecuted dispensed with "consciousness of wrongdoing", an omission or failure to act was deemed a sufficient basis for a responsible corporate agent's liability. It was enough in such cases that, by virtue of the relationship he bore to the corporation, the agent had the power to have prevented the act complained of. . . .

The rationale of the interpretation given the Act in Dotterweich, as holding criminally accountable the persons whose failure to exercise the authority and supervisory responsiblity reposed in them by the business organization resulted in the violation complained of, has been confirmed in our subsequent cases. Thus, the Court has reaffirmed the proposition that "the public interest in the purity of its food is so great as to warrant the imposition of the highest standard of care on distributors." In order to make "distributors of food the strictest censors of their merchandise," the Act punishes "neglect where the law requires care, or inaction where it imposes a duty." "The accused, if he does not will the violation, usually is in a position to prevent it with no more care than society might reasonably expect and no more exertion than it might reasonably exact from one who assumed his responsibilities." Similarly, in cases decided after Dotterweich, the court of appeals have recognized that those corporate agents vested with the responsibility, and power commensurate with that responsibility, to devise whatever measures are necessary to ensure compliance with the Act bear a "responsible relationship" to, or have a "responsible share" in, violations.

Thus, Dotterweich and the cases which have followed reveal that in providing sanctions which reach and touch the individuals who execute the corporate mission — and this is by no means necessarily confined to a single corporate agent or employee — the Act imposes not only a positive duty to seek out and remedy violations when they occur but also, and primarily, a duty to implement measures that will insure that violations will not occur. The requirements of foresight and vigilance imposed on responsible corporate agents are beyond question demanding, and perhaps onerous, but they are no more stringent than the public has a right to expect of those who voluntarily assume positions of authority in business enterprises whose services and products affect the health and well-being of the public that supports them. . . .

The Act does not, as we observed in Dotterweich, make criminal liability turn on "awareness of some wrongdoing" or "conscious fraud." The duty imposed by Congress on responsible corporate agents is, we emphasize, one that requires the highest standard of foresight and vigilance, but the Act, in its criminal aspect, does not require that which is objectively impossible. The theory upon which responsible corporate agents are held criminally accountable for "causing" violations of the Act permits a claim that a defendant was "powerless" to prevent or correct the violation to "be raised defensively at a trial on the merits." If such a claim is made, the defendant has the burden of coming forward with evidence, but this does not alter the Government's ultimate burden of proving beyond a reasonable doubt the defendant's guilt, including his power, in light of the duty imposed by the Act, to prevent or correct the prohibited condition. Congress has seen fit to enforce the accountability of responsible corporate agents dealing with products which may affect the health of consumers by penal sanctions cast in rigorous terms, and the obligation of the courts is to give them effect so long as they do not violate the Constitution. . . .

III.

Turning to the jury charge in this case, it is of course arguable that isolated parts can be read as intimating that a finding of guilt could be predicated solely on respondent's corporate position. But this is not the way we review jury instructions, because "a single instruction to a jury may not be judged in artificial isolation, but must be viewed in the context of the overall charge." . . .

Reading the entire charge satisfied us that the jury's attention was adequately focused on the issue of respondent's authority with respect to the conditions that formed the basis of the alleged violations. Viewed as a whole, the charge did not permit the jury to find guilt solely on the basis of respondent's position in the corporation; rather, it fairly advised the jury that to find guilt it must find respondent "had a responsible relation to the situation" and "by virtue of his position . . . had authority and responsiblity" to deal with the situation. The situation referred to could only be "food . . . held in unsanitary conditions in a warehouse with the result that it consisted, in part, of filth or . . . may have been contaminated with filth."

Moreover, in reviewing jury instructions, our task is also to view the charge itself as part of the whole trial. . . . The record in this case reveals that the jury could not have failed to be aware that the main issue for determination was not respondent's position in the corporate hierachy, but rather his accountability, because of the responsibility and authority of his position, for the conditions which gave rise to the charges against him.

We conclude that, viewed as a whole and in the context of the trial, the charge was not misleading and contained an adequate statement of the law to guide the jury's determination. . . .

◆◆◆

Case Questions

1. What conceivable reason could Park have for appealing a case all the way to the Supreme Court when his fine only totaled $250.00?
2. Do you think that Park or the corporation paid for his legal expenses? If the corporation financed Park's litigation, do you believe it was a wise decision when one compares a $250.00 fine to the tremendous cost of an appeal?
3. Why would the corporation plead guilty while the chief executive officer pleads innocent?

4. Since the board of directors has the legal authority to manage the corporation, would it not be more appropriate to prosecute the board instead of a corporate officer?
5. Is this an instance where the buck stops at the corporate president's desk?

INDEMNIFICATION OF DIRECTORS AND OFFICERS

Who bears a director's or officer's expenses incurred in defending his actions in a lawsuit? Are such expenses a personal risk that accompany the position? Should they be reimbursed if their defense is successful? What is to be done if an out-of-court settlement is reached, which is a common occurrence? The problem is to balance the interests of the corporation vis-a-vis its directors and officers. It seems only fair that the directors and officers should be reimbursed for their reasonable expenses if they acted in good faith and did not breach any duties owed the corporation. It would be unfair to allow them to violate their obligations with impunity and, when called to account in court, have the wronged shareholders bear the expenses.

Many business corporation statutes are silent on the matter of indemnification. To fill this gap many corporations have adopted a by-law to cover the situation. In 1975 section 15 of by-laws of Pan Am read as follows:

> To the full extent permitted by law, the Corporation shall indemnify each person made or threatened to be made a party to any civil or criminal action or proceeding by reason of the fact he, or his testator or intestate, is or was a director or officer of the Corporation or served any other corporation of any type or kind, domestic or foreign, in any capacity at the request of the Corporation.

Pam Am is a New York corporation. The New York Business Corporation Law, sections 721-726 permit indemnification for, among other things, 1) reasonable expenses incurred in the defense of an action by or in the right of the corporation, except in relation to matters as to which he is adjudged to have breached his duty; 2) judgments, fines, or monetary settlements and the reasonable expenses incurred as a result of the action (other than by or in the right of the corporation) if the individual acted in good faith and in what he reasonably believed to be in the best interests of the corporation; 3) fines and expenses of a criminal proceeding if the criteria of number 2 are met in addition to a showing that he had no reasonable cause to believe that his conduct was illegal; and 4) indemnification ordered by a court.

Because the exposure to indemnification could place a severe strain upon a company's assets, a protective device is to acquire insurance coverage. Section 727 of the New York statute explicitly permits the purchase of such a liability policy. Purchase of such an insurance policy covering the indemnification of directors and officers, called D & O insurance, contains other advantages. Some states prohibit indemnification where an out of court settlement was reached. D & O insurance can supply the necessary reimbursement. Or, suppose bankruptcy intervenes prior to the termination of litigation. A by-law may give the director or officer the legal right to reimbursement but, that is of little solace when the corporate treasury is empty. Again, insurance can fill such a gap.

What is contained in a typical D & O policy? The policy will be written to cover the wrongful or negligent acts of the corporate directors and named officers (of both the parent and subsidiaries). If the corporate by-law is written in broad language reimbursing individuals outside the above category, added insurance, with its extra premium, need be purchased. The policy will contain exclusions for such matters as: 1) any fine or penalty imposed by law; 2) antitrust violations; 3) profits derived from violations of § 16 (b) of the securities laws; and 4) defamation.[1] Of course, the policy will contain a dollar limitation. It is important to ascertain whether the costs and expenses incurred in defending a suit are included in the policy limits. Typically there is a deductible and, other insurance will be deemed to provide primary coverage. The latter prevents the corporation from receiving multiple recoveries on a single claim. The policy will cover claims filed during the policy life even though the wrongful act occurred prior to the commencement of the policy.

Since a D & O policy will cover claims for incidents occurring prior to the policy's starting date, what if the corporation concealed facts about a prior incident on its insurance application? Can the insurer raise this as a defense to avoid paying the claim? At this time, the answers to these questions are uncertain. These issues are currently being litigated. The D & O insurance carriers for Penn Central are attempting to rescind their policy and return the premiums. The insurers assert that the policy is null and void because of alleged fraudulent concealment of certain facts by Penn Central in procurement of the policy.

For practical reasons, D & O insurance may not be available at a reasonable cost to all corporations. The insurer obviously attempts to measure the risk involved in insuring a particular company. An established corporation with substantial assets and a good history of earnings should experience little trouble in acquiring a policy. A newly formed corporation, a closely held corporation, a corporation dominated by a small group of shareholders or, a conglomerate may face substantial difficulty. Each one presents risks that are hard to measure and/or risks that an insurer may not be willing to bear.

EXECUTIVE COMPENSATION

Compensation is the carrot that stimulates corporate officers to a high level of performance. Compensation is not synonymous with cash; although salary is the primary form of corporate remuneration. Compensation can also take the form of: 1) cash bonuses based upon the corporation's performance; 2) stock options granting the executive the right to purchase a given number of corporate shares within a specified future period at a specified price (frequently the market price as of the date the option is granted); 3) phantom stock when he need not buy the stock but is paid cash equal to the dividends that he would receive if he did own the stock; 4) pension benefits, life insurance, health insurance, etc., and 5) deferred compensation where the executive will be paid as a consultant after his retirement when he is in a lower tax bracket.

Different compensation forms enjoy varying degrees of popularity depending upon the current tax law provisions, the health of the stock market and general economic conditions. When a lawyer is putting together a compensation package he must balance many interests, even conflicting ones! The plan should be as inexpensive to the company as possible yet, sufficiently generous to attract and retain high quality individuals. It must recognize and reward achievement. Tax liability for both the corporation and any recipient should be the absolute minimum. It cannot be so high as to attract and unduly upset the shareholders.

When shareholders do object so vehemently to the level of executive compensation as to bring a lawsuit, they usually allege the gift or waste of corporate assets. The *Rogers* v. *Hill* case is the most famous case on executive compensation. The *Winkleman* v. *General Motors* case shows the typical outcome of such a challenge—the shareholders lose. The courts have been extremely reluctant to strike down executive compensation as constituting waste. Under the Internal Revenue Code of 1954, if salary is to be deductible as an expense from corporate revenues, it must be reasonable. In the tax realm the courts have not been hobbled by any reluctance to declare salaries so high as to be unreasonable. Are the courts applying a different standard of reasonableness in measuring executive compensation for corporation law purposes vis-a-vis tax law? If so, why?

ROGERS v. HILL
289 U.S. 582 (1933)

◆◆◆

Mr. Justice Butler

The American Tobacco Company is a corporation organized under the laws of New Jersey. The petitioner, plaintiff below, acquired in 1916 and has since been the owner of 200 shares of its common stock. He also has 400 shares of common stock B. In accordance with by-law XII, adopted by the stockholders at their annual meeting, March 13, 1912, the company for many years has annually paid its president and vice-president large amounts in addition to their fixed salaries and other sums allowed them as compensation for services.

Plaintiff maintains that the by-law is invalid and that, even if valid, the amounts paid under it are unreasonably large and therefore subject to revision by the courts. In March, 1931, he demanded that the company bring suit against the officers who have received such payments to compel them to account to the company for all or such part thereof as the court may hold illegal. The company, insisting that such a suit would be without basis in law or fact, refused to comply with his demand. . . .

It follows from what has been shown that when adopted the by-law was valid. But plaintiff alleges that the measure of compensation fixed by it is not now equitable or fair. And he prays that the court fix and determine the fair and reasonable compensation of the individual defendants, respectively, for each of the years in question. . . . The only payments that plaintiff by this suit seeks to have restored to the company are the payments made to the individual defendants under the by-law.

We come to consider whether these amounts are subject to examination and revision in the district court. As the amounts payable depend upon the gains of the business, the specified percentages are not per se unreasonable. The by-law was adopted in 1912 by an almost unanimous vote of the shares represented at the annual meeting and presumably the stockholders supporting the measure acted in good faith and according to their best judgment. ... Regard is to be had to the enormous increase of the company's profits in recent years. The 2½ percent yielded President Hill $447,870.30 in 1929 and $842,507.72 in 1930. The 1½ percent yielded to each of the vice-presidents, Neily and Riggio, $115,141.86 in 1929 and $409,495.25 in 1930 and for these years payments under the by-law were in addition to the cash credits and fixed salaries shown in the statement.

While the amounts produced by the application of the prescribed percentages give rise to no inference of actual or constructive fraud, the payments under the by-law have by reason of increase of profits become so large as to warrant investigation in equity in the interest of the company. Much weight is to be given to the action of the stockholders, and the by-law is supported by the presumption of regularity and continuity. But the rule prescribed by it cannot, against the protest of a shareholder, be used to justify payments of sums as salaries so large as in substance and effect to amount to spoliation or waste of corporate property. The dissenting opinion of Judge Swan indicates the applicable rule: "If a bonus payment has no relation to the value of services for which it is given, it is in reality a gift in part and the majority stockholders have no power to give away corporate property against the protest of the minority." 60 F. (2d) 109, 113. The facts alleged by plaintiff are sufficient to require that the district court, upon a consideration of all the relevant facts brought forward by the parties, determine whether and to what extent payments to the individual defendants under the by-law constitute misuse and waste of the money of the corporation. ...

The statement below shows for the years specified the amounts alleged to have been paid by the company to the named defendants as salary, credits, and under by-law XII.

	Salary	Cash Credits	By-Law
Hill			
1921...			$ 89,833.94
1922...			82,902.61
1923...			77,336.54 Vice President
1924...			88,894.26
1925...			97,059.38
1926...	$ 75,000		188,643.45
1927...	75,000		268,761.45
1928...	75,000		280,203.68 President
1929...	144,500	$136,507.71	447,870.30
1930...	168,000	273,470.76	842,507.72
Neiley			
1929...	$ 33,333.32	$ 44,897.89	$115,141.87
1930...	50,000.00	89,945.52	409,495.25
Riggio			
1929...	$ 33,333.30	$ 45,351.40	$115,141.86
1930...	50,000.00	90,854.06	409,495.25

◆◆◆

Note

Notice the years of the payments in dispute — the start of the depression. Speaking of these same sums in later litigation a judge, who did not reduce them, characterized them as follows:

> Now, even a high-bracketer would deem these stipends munificent. To the person of moderate income they would be princely — perhaps something unattainable; to the wage-earner ekeing out an existence, they would be fabulous, and the unemployed might regard them as fantastic, if not criminal. To others they would seem immoral, inexcusably unequal, and an indictment of our economic system. *Heller* v. *Boylan,* 29 N.Y.S. 2d 653 (1941).

To add some perspective to the disputed amount of compensation, it might be of value to examine more recent corporate compensation figures. The following figures are taken from the respective company's 1975 proxy statement. They reflect the aggregate remuneration for the highest paid individual within that company.

Sears, Roebuck & Company	$240,000
Polaroid Corporation	212,278
Pan American World Airways	184,319

After the Supreme Court's ruling in *Rogers* v. *Hill,* the parties negotiated a settlement. Under the terms of the settlement the bonus base was reduced and the employee's stock subscription plan was revised. By March of 1940 these adjustments saved the corporation $8,450,000. Rogers, the plaintiff shareholder, who was an attorney and represented himself, was paid legal fees of $525,000 (after taxes he received $263,000) or less than the 8½ percent of the savings enjoyed by the corporation. Other shareholders then attacked Roger's fee alledging that he sold out the real interests of the shareholders for the payment from American Tobacco. His fee was upheld as reasonable and the judge cleared him of any wrongdoing. *Rogers* v. *Hill,* 34 F. Supp 358 (1940).

Subsequently other shareholders challenged the amount of the officers' compensation. Their suit was unsuccessful. *Heller* v. *Boylan,* 29 N.Y.S. 2d 653 (1941). The judge said that he lacked a reliable standard to measure them against and since the great majority of storkholders had approved them, he would permit them to stand.

What factors does a court examine in determining whether an executive's compensation is matched by his value to the corporation or is so excessive as to constitute an impermissable gift and waste of corporate assets? The case that follows provides some indication.

WINKELMAN v. GENERAL MOTORS CORPORATION
44 F. Supp. 960 (1942)

◆◆◆

Among the issues presented by this litigation is the propriety of the total compensation, salary plus bonus, paid to certain executives and managers of

General Motors Corporation, many of whom were directors. (Ex 31-1 to 42.) I am of the opinion that for the years 1930 to 1940 inclusive, these amounts were not in excess of the value of the services rendered by those individuals, excepting from said amounts the alleged equalization payment of February 11, 1931. A large part of the record in this case consists of testimony concerning the nature, extent and importance of the services of the recipients in the various corporate postions they held. The responsibilities they assumed and the broad scope of their duties as active and efficient members of the staff of General Motors Corporation are all in the record.

I stated in an opinion, filed in August 1940 on the motion of the three of the defendants, Whitney, Morgan, and Prosser, for summary judgment, that there were several of the years, to wit, 1930, 1935, 1936, and 1937, where the amounts awarded were so large that they required an investigation by a court of equity in the suit brought by plaintiff stockholders. *Rogers* v. *Hill*, 289 U.S. 582, 591, 53 S. Ct. 731, 77 L. Ed. 1385, 88 A.L.R. 744. This investigation has been had during the course of this trial and I am now satisfied that the compensation of these executives was not excessive as to those years also.

Concerning the compensation of executives, I have made the following findings, among others:

"There has always been keen rivalry for executives in the automobile industry. For example, General Motors lost to competitors — Charles W. Nash, who became head of the Nash Motors Company; Walter P. Chrysler, who developed the Chrysler Corporation; and K.T. Keller, who is now President of the Chrysler Corporation. Offers were made by competitors to Messrs. Knudsen and Raskob. It was necessary for the Corporation to hold out attractive financial benefits to prevent the loss of valuable executives.

"From the end of 1922 through 1929, total assets of the corporation (less depreciation) increased 140 percent. Net sales for 1929 increased nearly 225 percent over 1922 and income available for dividends increased 355 percent. Net income for the period 1923-1929 equalled $1,185,000,000, and average return on stockholder capital of 29.45 percent. After payment of 61.6 percent of such net income as cash dividends to stockholders, more than $445,000,000 was reinvested in the business during that period and constituted 40 percent of the total assets (less depreciation) owned by the Corporation at the end of 1929.

"General Motors earned more in the decade of the thirties than in that of the twenties although almost a third of the period 1930-1940 was a time of severe economic depression. In 1930-1940 inclusive, it earned $1,500,000,000 upon net sales totalling more than $12,000,000,000. Return on stockholder capital averaged 14.3 percent, a performance equalled by few companies. Over this period General Motors increased its share of the total passenger car output from approximately 34 percent in 1930 to as much as 50 percent in 1941.

"A comparison of General Motors passenger car sales with those of the Ford Motors Company, the dominant automobile manufacturer in 1923, illustrates the growth in market strength of General Motors to the present day. In 1923, Ford's sales totalled approximately 1,773,000 units; General Motors sold about 774,000 cars, only 44 percent of Ford's sales. In 1940, General Motors sales totalled approximately 1,748,000 cars; Ford sold about 717,000 cars, only 41 percent of General Motors sales."

Is a $500,000 total of salary plus bonus for the chief executive of a corporation of this magnitude, in very prosperous years, so excessive that its payment should be legally condemned as a waste of corporate assets? Having heard all the testimony and considered the exhibits I am of the opinion that the directors are not chargeable with waste for having approved these payments. These executives have built up a great industry; managed it successfully; given employment to hundreds of thousands of skilled workers; earned tremendous profits for the stockholders and contributed largely to the prosperity of the nation. Although in certain instances, hereinafter discussed, some of them have taken advantage of their position of influence to the detriment of the corporation, there is no denying the compentence of their business management of its value to the Corporation.

The plaintiffs offered nothing as a yardstick or comparison for determining the reasonableness of the salaries and bonuses. On the other hand the defendants have referred the Court to several reported stockholders' suits . . . in which it was held that compensation which was about twice the amount of the highest total compensation paid to any of these executives, was not excessive. In determining that the salaries and bonus allotments in the present case were not excessive, that they were earned by the recipients. . . .

◆◆◆

Case Questions

1. Should a court more closely scrutinize a compensation plan established by the directors, as opposed to a plan approved by the shareholders?
2. Can any man or woman be worth $1,000,000 a year?
3. If bonus compensation is to be based upon the performance of the corporation, what is to be done when factors, over which officers have no control, dramatically increase or decrease corporation performance? What if car sales slump because of an oil embargo imposed by foreign producing nations? What if a favorable tax revision, coupled with a change in accounting methods, cause a non-recurring jump in profits?
4. If the courts are unable to devise a standard against which to measure the reasonableness of executive compensation, does that mean that there will exist no limitation upon such compensation?
5. The 1954 Internal Revenue Code only permits a corporation to deduct reasonable compensation as a business expense. Should the IRS challenge the deductability of some of today's corporate salaries?

REVIEW PROBLEMS

1. A stockholder brings a suit in equity seeking the appointment of a receiver for the defendant corporation and the dissolution of the corporation. The president and treasurer of the corporation, who was also a director, orally employed an attorney to defend the suit for $2,000. The board of directors had no knowledge of the contract. When the attorney was not paid for his services, he brought suit for his fee. Will the attorney prevail? [*Kelley* v. *Citizens Finance Co.*, 28 N.E. 2d 1005 (1940)]
2. The board of directors of American Airlines, a majority of which is disinterested, approve a restricted stock option plan. The shareholders approve the plan at the annual meeting. A committee of disinterested directors issue the options to 289 employees over a two year time span. Several shareholders bring suit seeking to cancel the options as waste and as

impermissable gifts of corporate assets. The directors contend that they have determined, in the exercise of their business judgment, that the corporation will receive benefits from the grant of this type of executive compensation. What decision? [*Beard* v. *Elster,* 160 A. 2d 731 (1960)]

3. Would your opinion differ if the stock option plan in the problem above had been approved by an interested board? [*Gottleib* v. *Heyden Chemical* 90 A. 2d 660, on limited reargument, 91 A. 2d 57]

4. Allis-Chalmers and four non-director employees entered guilty pleas in the famous 1960 electrical equipment price fixing conspiracy. Thereafter a stockholder's derivative action was brought against the directors to recover damages which Allis-Chalmers was claimed to have suffered by reason of these violations. The corporation employed in excess of 31,000 people, had 24 plants, 145 sales officers, 5,000 dealers and distributors, and a sales volume in excess of $500,000,000 annually. Its operating policy was to decentralize by delegating authority to the lowest possible management level. The evidence showed that no director had actual knowledge of the antitrust violations, nor did they have actual knowledge of any facts that should have put them on notice that illegal antitrust activities were being carried out. Nonetheless, the plaintiffs contend that the directors are liable as a matter of law by reason of their failure to take action designed to learn of and prevent antitrust activity on the part of any Allis-Chalmers employees. Is liability to be fixed upon the directors? [*Graham* v. *Allis Chalmers,* 188 A.2d 125 (1963)]

5. Is it realistic to believe that directors could be completely ignorant of massive antitrust violations occuring within a large industry over a several year period?

6. Should the labor unions that represent the corporation's employees have representatives on the board of directors, as they do in West Germany?

ENDNOTE

1. Hinsey, Delancey, Stahl & Kramer, "What Existing D & O Policies Cover," *27 Bus. Lawyer 153* (1972). The entire issue of this journal is devoted to an excellent presentation on officers' and directors' legal responsibilities and liabilities.

A corporation pays dividends when it distributes its assets to the shareholders in respect to their stock holdings. Dividends can take the form of cash, property (including stock of another corporation), or the corporation's own shares. Typically, dividends are paid from the corporation's "profits" or "surplus." However, it is possible to pay a liquidating dividend thereby invading the corporation's "capital."

There are three potentially conflicting interests that must be reconciled in matters of dividend distribution: shareholders, directors and creditors. The shareholders want income. In a close corporation dividends will frequently be significant, or even primary, source of income to the shareholders. The average shareholder in the publicly traded corporation also desires income. His investment is based on the expectation of income, not upon any desire for corporate control. Of course the shareholders can disagree among themselves as to what form this income should assume. Depending upon their tax bracket, etc. they may desire their income in the form of current dividends or prefer that it take the form of capital gains. The directors have a different perspective. The law has given them the responsibility of managing the corporation. The best interest of the corporation can differ from the stockholders desire for high dividends. The directors may wish to finance plant expansion from earnings rather than borrowing funds in the money markets. Or, there may be some other sound basis for retaining a large amount of the earnings. The corporate creditors are governed by their own economic self interest. They do not want to see the corporate assets depleted before they are paid. Since the shareholders have no personal liability for the debts of the corporation, the corporate assets are the creditors' only recourse if they are not paid.

SOURCES FOR DIVIDENDS

The dividends provisions of the various business corporation statutes are designed to protect the corporate creditors. These statutory provisions vary among jurisdictions but they all have the aim of preseving the corporation's capital for the benefit of creditors. Section 41(a) of the Illinois Business Corporation Act provides that "no dividend shall be declared or paid at a time when the corporation is insolvent or its net assets are less than its stated capital, or when the payment thereof would render the corporation insolvent or reduce its net assets below its stated capital." "Insolvency" is defined in Illinois as the inability to pay debts as they become due in the usual course of business (Some statutes use the bankruptcy definition of insolvency — when liabilities exceed assets). "Net assets" means what remains after liabilties and capital are subtracted from assets. Frequently net assets are called "earned surplus," or what the accountants refer to as "retained earnings." "Stated capital" means at any particular time, the sum of (a) the par value of all shares then issued having a par value and (b) the consideration received by the corporation for all shares then issued without par value, except such part thereof as may have been allocated otherwise than to stated capital in a manner permitted by law, and (c) such amounts not included in clauses (a) or (b) of this Section as may have been transferred to the stated capital account of the corporation, whether upon the issue of shares as a share dividend or otherwise, minus such formal reductions from said sum as may have been effected in manner permitted by law.

The complexity of questions involved in dividend distributions cannot be over stressed. As previously mentioned, the statutes vary among jurisdictions. Not only do the statutory provisions vary, but also the definition of basic terms. The form that the dividend distribution is to take can also vary widely. While most dividends are distributed as cash, other methods of payment are possible. The rights of the stockholders of different classes must be recognized. The accountants and the SEC must be satisfied that the nature and result of the distribution be accurately reported. The provisions of the internal revenue code must be met. The IRS will be concerned both that excessive earnings not be retained and that dividends (non-deductible by the corporation and taxable income to the shareholder) be properly reported as such. Sometimes the IRS will challenge the validity of interest payments or the amount of corporate salaries as being a mere disguise for a dividend distribution.

In addition to the determination of when a "surplus" is available to pay a dividend, questions can arise as to which items are properly taken into account in the computation of a surplus. Corporate goodwill is not normally included as an asset. Arriving at a reasonable valuation for goodwill is usually impossible, except where something like a trademark is purchased in an arms length transaction. What of appreciating and depreciating assets? These also present questions of valuation. How does one know that "true" amount of unrealized appreciation when that asset has not been sold or lacks an established market value? The availability of accepted depreciation methods and schedules for tax purposes can lessen, but not completely eliminate, the asset valuation questions involved in depreciation. It is impossible to generalize whether appreciation and depreciation of assets may or must be taken into account in surplus determination. The given state's statute or court opinions must be examined. Illinois, section 41 (c) provides that "no dividend except a dividend payable in its own shares, shall be declared or paid out of surplus arising from unrealized appreciation in value, or revaluation, of assets."

Then there is the "nimble dividend" situation. Suppose a corporation has suffered through several years of losses and now has a deficit of $100,000.00. The corporation then enjoys a return to prosperity and for the current year shows a profit of $20,000.00. A surplus remains absent, but is that $20,000.00 nonetheless available for dividends? The majority of states do not permit "nimble dividend" distributions. The concept is that only the corporation's net profits from its entire existence should be available for dividends. The Model Business Corporation Act and a handful of states permit nimble dividends. Section 45 Model Act provides:

> [Alternative] (a) Dividends may be declared and paid in cash or property only out of the unreserved and unrestricted earned surplus of the corporation, or out of the unreserved and unrestricted net earnings of the current fiscal year and the next preceding fiscal year taken as a single period, except as otherwise provided in this section.[1]

Is "capital surplus" or "paid-in surplus" available as a dividend source? Earned surplus is the profit derived from the operation of the corporation. Capital surplus or paid-in surplus is derived from the sale of stock at a price in excess of its par or stated value, from a reduction in the par or stated value after issuance, or the profits received by the corporation from the purchase and sale of its own stock. Section 2.12 of the Illinois statute defines it thus:

> Paid-in surplus means all that part of the consideration received by the corporation for, or on account of, all shares issued which does not constitute stated capital, less expenses, including commissions, paid or incurred by the corporation on account of the issuance of such shares whether such paid-in surplus has been heretofore or is hereafter created by (a) the receipt by the corporation for, or on account of, the issuance of shares having a par value of consideration in excess of the par value of such shares or (b) the allocation of any part of the consideration received by the corporation for, or on account of, the issuance of shares in a manner permitted by law or (c) a reduction of stated capital under this Act or of capital stock under any prior Act of this State, minus such formal reductions of paid-in surplus as may have been effected in a manner permitted by law.

Most states place some form of restriction upon the use of paid-in surplus for dividend distributions. Frequently it can only be used to pay dividends upon preferred stock and then the stockholder must be told the source of dividends. This notice requirement should alert the shareholder that the corporation is not paying the dividends from ordinary corporate profits. Continuing with our Illinois example, section 41 (b) provides:

> Dividends may be paid out of paid-in surplus or surplus arising from the surrender to the corporation of any of its shares only upon shares having a preferential right to receive dividends, provided that the source of such dividends is disclosed to the shareholders receiving such dividends, concurrently with payment thereof.

Finally, let us examine the matter of dividends in partial liquidation of the corporation. The declaration of a liquidating dividend is an extraordinary matter that usually requires specific stockholder approval by a two-thirds majority vote of the outstanding shares of each class. Illinois protects the corporate creditors by limiting liquidating dividends in section 41 a (d) as follows:

> No such distribution shall be made at a time when the corporation is insolvent or its net assets are less than its stated capital, or when such distribution would render the corporation insolvent or reduce its net assets below its stated capital.

DECLARATION OF DIVIDENDS

Dividends are declared by a resolution of the board of directors. Shareholders cannot declare dividends, even by a unanimous vote. The board resolution will specify the amount of dividend per share declared to shareholders of record on a given future date. The dividends will then be payable on a specified date subsequent to the record date.

It is possible that a shareholder may sell his shares after the record date but prior to the date of payment. Is the buyer or seller entitled to the dividends?

The seller. This problem is easily handled on the national securities exchanges. The shares are traded "ex dividend" or without the dividend. The price of ex dividend stock will be reduced to reflect the absence of the dividend.

DIRECTORS' LIABILITY
FOR IMPERMISSIBLE DIVIDENDS

Most statutes impose civil liability upon directors that vote for or assent to the declaration and distribution of a dividend from an unallowable source. The directors will have joint and several liability and be entitled to contribution from the other assenting directors. Illinois' section 42.8 imposes criminal liability on directors who vote for or assent to payment of an illegal dividend. Several other states also impose criminal sanctions in this situation.

Oftentimes a state will exempt from liability a director who acted in good faith in declaring the illegal dividend. Section 42.10 of the Illinois Business Corporation Act is typical:

A director shall not be liable under . . . this section relating to the declaration of dividends and distribution of assets if he relied and acted in good faith upon a balance sheet and profit and loss statement of the corporation represented to him to be correct by the president or the officer of such corporation having charge of its books of account, or certified by an independent public or certified public accountant or firm of such accountants to fairly reflect the financial condition of such corporation, nor shall he be so liable if in good faith in determining the amount available for any such dividend or distribution he considered the assets to be of their book value.

What of the shareholders that received the illegal dividends; are they permitted to retain them? Some statutes are silent on the matter. In such cases it would appear that if the shareholders innocently received the dividends, and if the corporation is solvent, the dividends may be retained. If the corporation was insolvent the dividends would constitute a fraudulent conveyance and could be recovered. Section 48 of the Model Act and § 42.11 of the Illinois statute make the recipient shareholders liable through contribution to the liable directors if the shareholders knowingly accepted or received an illegal dividend.

TYPES OF DIVIDENDS

The most common form for dividends is a cash distribution. Another popular type is a stock dividend, paying the shareholders a dividend with stock of the distributing corporation. In one sense, it is no dividend at all. Consider the following:

Shareholder A owns ten shares of Corporation X's common stock. X has only 100 issued and outstanding shares. Thus A is a 10 percent shareholder and his shares represent one tenth of the value of the corporation. The directors then declare and pay a 20 percent stock dividend. A now owns twelve shares out of X's 120 shares. A now owns more shares but their value and percentage ownership remain static.

Despite these facts, stock dividends are of value to the shareholder. In a publicly traded corporation the per share price frequently will not drop far enough to accurately reflect each share's reduced ownership ratio. If the corporation continues to be a financial success it will not take long for the per share price to climb back up to or exceed the quoted predividend market price. The corporation need not part with any cash when it distributes a stock dividend. The corporation will be required to make a transfer from earned surplus to the capital account. What amount is to be transferred is open to some debate. Legally all that is required to be transferred is the par or stated value multiplied by the number of distributed shares. However, from an accounting standpoint, a good argument can be made that the transfer should reflect the fair market value of the distributed shares.

Do not confuse a stock dividend with a stock split; legally they are two entirely different actions. A stock split is designed to reduce the per share market price of a stock thereby both increasing demand and further broadening the number of shareholders. Suppose stock is selling at 400 dollars per share. For most individuals that is a prohibitive price. If a 4 for 1 stock split occurs the price will drop to 100 dollars per share and four shares of stock will be distributed for each one share of the previous stock. The articles will require amending, either by the board or the shareholders as the case may be, to approve a commensurate reduction in the par or stated value of each share. This is not necessary for a stock dividend. However, with both stock dividends and stock splits, it will be necessary to amend the articles if there are an insufficient number of authorized shares to effectuate the dividend or split.

It is possible to have a reverse stock split. Suppose the per share price is only 2 dollars. Under the current margin requirements an investor cannot borrow funds to purchase stock priced below 5 dollars per share. Thus, the 2 dollar price can harm the attractiveness of the stock. So, the directors declare a 1 for 4 reverse stock split. For each four 2 dollar shares they issue one 8 dollar share (also multiplying the par or stated value by four).

Property dividends are a rarity. They can fulfill a useful purpose. E.I. du Pont de Nemours & Company once held a 23 percent stock interest in General Motors. In 1957 the Supreme Court held this ownership constituted a violation of the antitrust laws. It was ordered to divest itself of the GM stock within ten years. The stock had a 3.4 billion dollar value and represented about 63 million shares of approximately 281 million GM shares then outstanding. Du Pont faced a myriad of problems. It couldn't just sell in one lump sum. Dumping six million shares annually for the next decade would severely depress the value of the stock. At that time the typical yearly GM trading volume did not approach six million shares. Du Pont solved its problem by distributing the GM shares as dividends to its own shareholders. Standard Oil of Indiana distributed its shares in Standard Oil of New Jersey in a similar antitrust divestiture.

DIRECTORS' DISCRETION IN DIVIDEND MATTERS

The directors decide whether a dividend is to be paid and, if so, in what amount and in what form. The courts will not interfere with the directors' discretion in these matters unless there is a showing of bad faith, abuse of discretion, unreasonableness or, willful neglect on the part of the directors. The declaration of dividends is a classic example of the application of the business judgment rule.

Because of the deference afforded the directors' business judgment successful shareholder suits to compel dividends are sparse. Following we list a few of the successful cases. In *Patton* v. *Nicholas,* 302 S.W. 2d 441 (1957), a 61 percent stockholder maliciously suppressed the payment of any dividends for a ten year period. The court ordered $112,000 in dividends to be paid. In *Channon* v. *Channon Co.,* 218 Ill. App. 397 (1920), an Illinois court held it to be an abuse of discretion where the dominant shareholder-director who was the father of the plaintiff, stated that no further dividends would be declared for as long as he lived. In *Von Au* v. *Magenheimer,* 89, N.E. 1114, dividends were ordered because they had been withheld in an effort to freeze out the minority shareholders. The directors, in an effort to depress the value of the stock and then buy it for less than its true value, declared low dividends, inflated salaries and represented to the minority shareholders that the company had suffered financial reverses. Dividends have also been ordered where the directors, acting in collusion with a bankrupt shareholder, fraudulently withheld dividends to prevent the shareholder's creditors from obtaining them, *In re Brantman,* 244 F. 101 (1917).

Strange as it may seem, shareholders have complained to the courts of excessive dividends. The shareholder was unsuccessful in the following two instances. In *Sinclair Oil Co.* v. *Levien,* 280 A. 2d 717 (Del. S. Ct. 1971) the shareholder alleged that the subsidiary was paying out excessive dividends to the parent to finance the parent's expansion. In *ADT* v. *Grinnell,* 306 N.Y.S. 2d 209 (1969) a shareholder complained that a subsidiary was paying unreasonable and excessive dividends. It was argued that the parent, who owned 80 percent of the stock, was attempting to milk the corporation prior to being forced to divest the subsidiary for antitrust violations.

Lawsuits in equity to compel the declaration of dividends usually arise within the context of a close corporation. The Ford Motor and Gottfried cases that follow are two examples. The Ford case illustrates director abuse while in Gottfried the directors' actions were proper. Ford Motor also presents interesting social and economic issues. The almost five decades that have ensued since the decision have observed significant social, economic, political, and legal changes. One can speculate whether these shifts in attitude would alter the result if the case were to be decided today.

DODGE v. FORD MOTOR CO.
204 Mich. 459; 170 N.W. 668 (1919)

◆◆◆

Action by John F. Dodge and Horace E. Dodge against the Ford Motor Company and others. Decree for plaintiffs, and defendants appeal. Affirmed in part and reversed in part. . . .

The parties in the first instance associating, who signed the articles, included Henry Ford, whose subscription was for 255 shares, John F. Dodge, Horace E. Dodge, the plaintiffs, Horace H. Rackham and James Couzens, who each subscribed for 50 shares, and several other persons. The company began business in the month of June, 1903. In the year 1908, its articles were amended and the capital stock increased from $150,000 to $2,000,000, the number of shares being increased to 20,000; . . .

The business of the company continued to expand. The cars it manufactured met a public demand, and were profitably marketed, so that, in addition to regular quarterly dividends equal to 5 percent monthly on the capital stock of $2,000,000, its board of directors declared and the company paid . . . a total of $41,000,000 in special dividends. . . .

The surplus above capital stock was September 30, 1912, $14,745,095.67, . . . July 31, 1916, it was $111,960,907.53. Originally, the car made by the Ford Motor Company sold for more than $900. From time to time, the selling price was lowered and the car itself improved until in the year ending July 31, 1916, it sold for $440. Up to July 31, 1916, it had sold 1,272,986 cars at a profit of $173,895,416.06. . . . For the year beginning August 1, 1916, the price of the car was reduced $80 to $360.

From a mere assembling plant, the plant of the Ford Motor Company came to be a manufacturing plant, in which it made many of the parts of the car which in the beginning it had purchased from others. At no time has it been able to meet the demand for its cars or in a large way to enter upon the manufacture of motor trucks.

No special dividend having been paid after October, 1915 . . . the plaintiffs, who together own 2,000 shares, or one-tenth of the entire capital stock of the Ford Motor Company, on the 2nd of November, 1916, filed in the circuit court for the county of Wayne, . . . their bill of complaint, . . . in which bill they charge that since 1914 they have not been represented on the board of directors of the Ford Motor Company, and that since that time the policy of the board of directors has been dominated and controlled absolutely by Henry Ford, the president of the company, who owns and for several years has owned 58 percent of the entire capital stock of the company; . . . Setting up that on the 31st of July, 1916, the end of its last fiscal year, the said Henry Ford gave out for publication a statement of the financial condition of the company (the same as hereinabove set out), that for a number of years a regular dividend, payable quarterly, equal to 5 percent monthly upon the authorized capital stock, and the special dividends hereinbefore referred to, had been paid, it is charged that notwithstanding the earnings for the fiscal year ending July 31, 1916, the Ford Motor Company has not since that date declared any special dividends:

"And the said Henry Ford, president of the company, has declared it to be the settled policy of the company not to pay in the future any special dividends, but to put back into the business for the future all of the earnings of the company, other than the regular dividend of five percent (5%) monthly upon the authorized capital stock of the company — two million dollars ($2,000,000)."

This declaration of the future policy, it is charged in the bill, was published in the public press in the city of Detroit and throughout the United States in substantially the following language:

'My ambition,' declared Mr. Ford, 'is to employ still more men; to spread the benefits of this industrial system to the greatest possible number, to help them build up their lives and their homes. To do this, we are putting the greatest share of our profits back into the business.' "

It is charged further that the said Henry Ford stated to plaintiffs personally, in substance, that as all the stockholders had received back in dividends more than they had invested they were not entitled to receive anything additional to the regular dividend of 5 percent a month, and that it was not his policy to have larger dividends declared in the future, and that the profits and earnings of the company would be put back into the business for the purpose of extending its operations and increasing the number of its employees, and that, inasmuch as the profits were to be represented by investment in plants and capital investment, the stockholders would have no right to complain. ...

The said Henry Ford, "dominating and controlling the policy of said company, has declared it to be his purpose — and he has actually engaged in negotiations looking to carrying such purposes into effect — to invest millions of dollars of the company's money in the purchase of iron ore mines in the Northern Peninsula of Michigan or state of Minnesota; to acquire by purchase or have built ships for the purpose of transporting such ore to smelters to be erected on the River Rouge adjacent to Detroit in the county of Wayne and state of Michigan; and to construct and install steel manufacturing plants to produce steel products to be used in the manufacture of cars at the factory of said company; and by this means to deprive the stockholders of the company of the fair and reasonable returns upon their investment by way of dividends to be declared upon their stockholding interest in said company."

Setting up that the present invested assets of the company, exclusive of cash on hand, as of July 31, 1916, represented more than 30 times the present authorized capital of the company, and 2½ times the maximum limit ($25,000,000) fixed by the laws of the state of Michigan for capitalization of such companies (now $50,000,000), it is charged that the present investment in capital and assets constitutes an unlawful investment of the earnings, and that the continued investment of earnings would be a continuation of such unlawful policy. ...

Plaintiffs ask for an injunction to restrain the carrying out of the alleged declared policy of Mr. Ford and the company, for a decree requiring the distribution to stockholders of at least 75 percent of the accumulated cash surplus, and for the future that they be required to distribute all of the earnings of the company except such as may be reasonably required for emergency purposes in the conduct of the business.

The answer of the Ford Motor Company, which was filed November 28, 1916, admits most of the allegations in the plaintiffs' bill of complaint, ... and declining to answer those charges personal to Mr. Henry Ford. ... It denies that Henry Ford forced upon the board of directors his policy of reducing the price of cars by $80, and says that the action of the board in that behalf was unanimous and made after careful consideration. ...

The cause came on for hearing in open court on the 21st of May, 1917. A large volume of testimony was taken, with the result that a decree was entered December 5, 1917, in and by which it is decreed that within 30 days from the entry thereof the directors of the Ford Motor Company declare a dividend upon all of the shares of stock in an amount equivalent to one-half of, and payable out of, the accumulated cash surplus of said Ford Motor Company, on hand at the close of the fiscal year ending July 31, 1916. ...

Defendants have appealed, plaintiffs have not appealed, from the decree. In the briefs, appellants state and discuss the following propositions: ...

"(4) The management of the corporation and its affairs rests in the board of directors, and no court will interfere or substitute its judgment so long as the proposed actions are not ultra vires or fraudulent. They may be ill advised, in the opinion of the court, but this is no ground for exercise of jurisdiction.

"(5) The board has full power over the matter of investing the surplus and as to dividends so long as they act in good faith.

"(6) Such rights of management and control over investments and dividends are not only rules of law, they are rights fixed by the contract between the parties in the formation of the corporation.

"(7) These things are so although the majority of the stock is held by one man.

"It is the right and the duty of the majority to control. This duty must be exercised, and the responsibility cannot be shifted or evaded.

"(8) Motives of the board members are not material and will not be inquired into by the court so long as the acts are within their lawful powers.

"(9) Motives of a humanitarian character will not invalidate or form the basis of any relief so long as the acts are within the lawful powers of the board, if believed to be for the permanent welfare of the community. . . .

The rule which will govern courts in deciding these questions is not in dispute. It is, of course, differently phrased by judges and by authors, and, as the phrasing in a particular instance may seem to lean for or against the exercise of the right of judicial interference with the actions of corporate directors, the context, or the facts before the court, must be considered. . . ."

In Cook on Corporations (7th Ed.) § 545, it is expressed as follows:

"The board of directors declare the dividends, and it is for the directors, and not the stockholders, to determine whether or not a dividend shall be declared.

"When, therefore, the directors have exercised this discretion and refused to declare a dividend, there will be no interference by the courts with their decision, unless they are guilty of a willful abuse of their discretionary powers, or of bad faith or of a neglect of duty. It requires a very strong case to induce a court of equity to order the directors to declare a dividend, inasmuch as equity has no jurisdiction, unless fraud or a breach of trust is involved. There have been many attempts to sustain such a suit, yet, although the courts do not disclaim jurisdiction, they have quite uniformly refused to interfere. The discretion of the directors will not be interfered with by the courts, unless there has been bad faith, willful neglect, or abuse of discretion. . . ."

It is not necessary to multiply statements of the rule.

To develop the points now discussed, and to considerable extent they may be developed together as a single point, it is necessary to refer with some particularity to the facts. . . .

The record, and especially the testimony of Mr. Ford, convinces that he has to some extent the attitude towards shareholders of one who has dispensed and distributed to them large gains and that they should be content to take what he chooses to give. His testimony creates the impression, also, that he thinks the Ford Motor Company has made too much money, has had too large profits, and that, although large profits might be still earned, a sharing of them with the public, by reducing the price of the output of the company, ought to be undertaken. We have no doubt that certain sentiments, philanthropic and altruistic, creditable to Mr. Ford, had large influence in determining the policy to be pursued by the Ford Motor Company — the policy which has been herein referred to. . . .

There should be no confusion (of which there is evidence) of the duties which Mr. Ford conceives that he and the stockholders owe to the general public and the duties which in law he and his codirectors owe to protesting, minority stockholders. A business corporation is organized and carried on primarily for the profit of the stockholders. The powers of the directors are to be employed for that end. The discretion of directors is to be exercised in the choice of means to attain that end, and does not extend to a change in the end itself, to the reduction of profits, or to the non-distribution of profits among stockholders in order to devote them to other purposes.

There is committed to the discretion of directors, a discretion to be exercised in good faith, the infinite details of business, including the wages which shall be paid to employees, the number of hours they shall work, the conditions under which labor shall be carried on, and the price for which products shall be offered to the public.

It is said by appellants that the motives of the board members are not material and will not be inquired into by the court so long as their acts are within their lawful powers. As we have pointed out, and the proposition does not require argument to sustain it, it is not within the lawful powers of a board of directors to shape and conduct the affairs of a corporation for the merely incidental benefit of shareholders and for the primary purpose of benefiting others, and no one will contend that, if the avowed purpose of the defendant directors was to sacrifice the interests of shareholders, it would not be the duty of the courts to interfere. ...

The decree of the court below fixing and determining the specific amount to be distributed to stockholders is affirmed. In other respects, except as to the allowance of costs, the said decree is reversed. Plaintiffs will recover interest at 5 percent per annum upon their proportional share of said dividend from the date of the decree of the lower court.

◆◆◆

Case Questions

1. Does the fact that a corporation is organized and carried on primarily for the profit of its stockholders justify profits of any magnitude? During the 1973-74 Arab oil embargo, the major U.S. oil companies dramatically increased their profits over the previous year. In some instances the profit increases reached 400 percent. Some individuals labeled these profits "obscene." What are obscene profits?
2. Would the decision differ if Ford justified his price reduction policy on stimulating demand to such a degree that even greater profits would be generated despite the lower per unit profit margin?
3. Are not plant expansion, diversification into iron ore mining, shipping and steel manufacturing allowable corporate purposes, so long as they are not ultra-vires? Why then should a court inquire as to the motive of the directors in undertaking such activities?
4. Do you believe the Dodge shareholders had a valid complaint in view of the fact that regular dividends were being paid in the amount of 5 percent monthly upon the authorized capital stock (two million dollars)?

Subsequent to this litigation Henry Ford bought out the minority interests of the two Dodge brothers. The Dodges then used this money to develop what became the rival Chrysler Corporation.

GOTTFRIED v. GOTTFRIED
73 N.Y.S.2d 692 (1947)

◆◆◆

CORCORAN, Justice

This action was brought in the early part of 1945 by minority stockholders of Gottfried Baking Corporation (hereinafter called "Gottfried"), to compel the Board of Directors of that corporation to declare dividends on its common stock. The defendants are Gottfried itself, its directors, and Hanscom Baking Corporation (hereinafter called "Hanscom"), a wholly owned subsidiary of Gottfried. Gottfried is a closely held family corporation. All of its stockholders, with minor exceptions, are children of the founder of the business, Elias Gottfried, and their respective spouses.

Both corporations are engaged in the manufacture and sale of bakery products; Gottfried for distribution at wholesale, and Hanscom for distribution at retail in its own stores. Each corporation functions separately, in the manufacture and sale of its respective products.

At the end of 1946 the outstanding capitalization of Gottfried consisted of 4500 shares of "A" stock, without nominal or par value, and 20,862 shares of common stock without par value. The "A" stock is entitled to dividends of $8 per share before any dividends may be paid upon the common stock, as well as a further participation in earnings. At the end of 1944, immediately before this action was commenced, Gottfried also had outstanding preferred stock in the face amount of $79,000, and Hanscom had outstanding $86,000 face amount of preferred stock. The plaintiffs in the aggregate owned approximately 38 percent of each of these classes of securities. The individual defendants owned approximately 62 percent.

From 1931 until 1945 no dividends had been paid upon the common stock, although dividends had been paid regularly upon the outstanding preferred stock and intermittently upon the "A" stock. There seems to be no question with respect to the policy of the Board of Directors in not declaring dividends prior to 1944. An analysis of the financial statements of the corporation shows a new working capital deficit at the end of 1941, in which year a consolidated loss of $109,816 had been incurred. Moreover, until the end of 1943 the earned surplus was relatively small in relation to the volume of business done and the growing requirements of the business.

Although the action was brought in the early part of 1945 to compel the declaration of dividends upon the common stock, dividends actually were declared and paid upon said stock in 1945, and subsequently. The purpose of the action now, therefore, is to compel the payment of dividends upon the common stock in such amount as under all the circumstances is fair and adequate.

The action is predicated upon the claim that the policy of the Board of Directors with respect to the declaration of dividends is animated by considerations other than the best welfare of the corporations or their stockholders. The plaintiffs claim that bitter animosity on the part of the directors, who own the controlling stock, against the plaintiff minority stockholders, as well as a desire to coerce the latter into selling their stock to the majority interests at a grossly inadequate price, and the avoidance of heavy personal income taxes upon any dividends that might be declared, have been the motivating factors that have dominated the defendants. Plaintiffs contend, moreover, that the defendants by excessive salaries, bonuses and corporate loans to themselves or some of them, have eliminated the immediate need of dividends insofar as they were concerned, while at the same time a starvation dividend policy with respect to the minority stockholders — not on the payroll — operates designedly to compel the plaintiffs to sacrifice their stock by sale to the defendants.

There is no essential dispute as to the principles of law involved. If an adequate corporate surplus is available for the purpose, directors may not withhold the declaration of dividends in bad faith. But the mere existence of an adequate corporate surplus is not sufficient to invoke court action to compel such a dividend. There must also be bad faith on the part of the directors. ...

There are no infallible distinguishing ear-marks of bad faith. The following facts are relevant to the issue of bad faith and are admissible in evidence: Intense hostility of the controlling faction against the minority; exclusion of the minority from employment by the corporation; high salaries, or bonuses or corporate loans made to the officers in control; the fact that the majority group may be subject to high personal income taxes if substantial dividends are paid; the existence of a desire by the controlling directors to acquire the minority stock interests as cheaply as possible. But if they are not motivating causes they do not constitute "bad faith" as a matter of law.

The essential test of bad faith is to determine whether the policy of the directors is dictated by their personal interests rather than the corporate welfare. Directors are fiduciaries. Their cestui que trust are the corporation and the stockholders as a body. Circumstances such as those above mentioned and any other significant factors, appraised in the light of the financial condition and requirements of the corporation, will determine the conclusion as to whether the directors have or have not been animated by personal, as distinct from corporate, considerations.

The court is not concerned with the direction which the exercise of the judgment of the Board of Directors may take, provided only that such exercise of judgment be made in good faith. It is axiomatic that the court will not substitute its judgment for that of the Board of Directors.

It must be conceded that closely held corporations are easily subject to abuse on the part of dominant stockholders, particularly in the direction of action designed to compel minority stockholders to sell their stock at a sacrifice. But close corporation or not, the court will not tolerate directorate action designed to achieve that or any other wrongful purpose. Even in the absence of bad faith, however, the impact of dissension and hostility among stockholders falls usually with heavier force in a closely held corporation. In many such cases, a large part of a stockholder's assets may be tied up in the corporation. It is frequently contemplated by the parties, moreover, that the respective stockholders receive their major livelihood in the form of salaries resulting from employment by the corporation. If such employment be terminated, the hardship suffered by the minority stockholder or stockholders may be very heavy. Nevertheless, such situations do not in themselves form a ground for the interposition of a court of equity.

There is no doubt that in the present case bitter dissension and personal hostility have existed for a long time between the individual plaintiffs and defendants. The plaintiffs Charles Gottfried and Harold Gottfried have both been discontinued from the corporate payrolls.

It is true too that several of the defendants have in recent years received as compensation substantial sums. In the case of Maurice K. Gottfried this has taken the form of ten percent of the gross annual profits of Hanscom before corporate income taxes. During the period from January 1, 1943 to December 21, 1946, he received, in addition to a fixed salary of $15,600, an aggregate sum of $220,528.91, or an average of $45,105.78 per annum. The evidence in this connection discloses, however, that he has been the chief executive officer of Hanscom since its acquisition by Gottfried in 1933. The stock of Hanscom had been purchased in 1933 at a cost of $10,000 plus the assumption of liabilities amounting to $18,000. At that time Hanscom had 12 retail stores, a basement bakery, and volume of sales around $300,000. By way of contrast, for the year 1945 its net sales aggregated $4,614,000. For the year 1946, they had increased to $5,907,500. The number of stores had grown to 63, and operations had been expanded from the Washington Heights district of Manhattan to all the boroughs of the City of New York except Richmond. The profits before taxes and participation by Maurice Gottfried therein had increased to the large sum of $932,168.

There seems little doubt that in this tremendous expansion Maurice Gottfried played an important part. There is some dispute as to whether his profit participation was voted by the Board of Directors of Hanscom on February 16, 1942, or in the early part of 1943, shortly after the employment by the corporation of plaintiff Charles Gottfried had been terminated. There is testimony to the effect that from 1935 on Maurice was constantly requesting some such arrangement. The minutes of the Board of Directors of Hanscom, held on July 1, 1941, disclose that at that time Maurice presented a draft of a proposed contract between himself and Hanscom providing for a participation in profits on his part. The minutes state that the contract was approved generally but was left open for consideration of certain of the provisions thereof. This was long before any question of dividend policy had arisen between the parties.

The propriety and legality of Maurice's agreement for participation in the profits of Hanscom is the subject of other litigation between the parties. There is no determination in this proceeding as to such propriety or legality. The above evidence is discussed merely because it tends to show that the policy of Maurice and other directors in connection with his profit participation arrangement bore no relationship to the question of whether dividends should be declared or paid, which is the only subject of the present action. Even if it had been established that such arrangement was excessive or invalid in part or in whole that question is divorced from the present issues. It should be noted in this connection that the burden of this arrangement fell equally upon the other defendant directors and not merely upon the plaintiffs.

The only other significant extra compensation to directors relates to bonuses paid to the defendant Benjamin Gottfried of $5,000 in 1945 and $25,000 in 1946, and to the payment to defendant William Prince of $10,000 in 1946. These bonuses were all paid apparently after the commencement of the action. There is evidence that they were paid for special services rendered. It is significant that in many instances in the past, long before the dividend dispute arose, and as a matter of settled policy, bonuses had been paid to various officers and directors in recognition of outstanding services, and without objection by any party. The bonuses in question were not disproportionate to those paid in many instances in prior years. There is evidence of a long-standing bonus policy in the company which negatives any conclusion that these payments were conceived or made in lieu of dividends or in furtherance of a scheme not to pay dividends.

The evidence also discloses that substantial advances or loans have been made from time to time to several of the defendants, part of which still remain outstanding. Advances and loans of this character in varying amounts likewise had been made for many years to stockholders and directors. Without passing upon the propriety or legality of these transactions, the evidence does not sustain an inference that they were made with a view to the dividend policy of the corporation. They were incurred, in large part, long before any controversy arose with respect to dividends, nor is the aggregate amount thereof of sufficient magnitude to affect in a material way the capacity of Gottfried to pay dividends.

Plaintiff Charles Gottfried testified that Benjamin Gottfried, one of the defendants, told him that he and the other minority stockholders would never get any dividends because the majority could freeze them out and that the majority had other ways than declaring dividends of getting money out of the companies. Benjamin Gottfried denied that he had ever made such statements. There is no evidence, moreover, that such statements were made by any of the other defendants. The court does not believe that this disputed testimony carries much weight upon the question of a concerted policy on the part of the directors to refrain from declaring dividends for the purpose of "freezing out" the plaintiffs.

Nor does the evidence with respect to the financial condition of the corporation and its business requirements sustain the plaintiffs' claims. The action was started in the early part of 1945. The financial condition of Gottfried at the end of the immediately preceding year is of fundamental importance in determining the validity of plaintiffs' claim at the time that suit was brought. The consolidated balance sheet for the year ended December 30, 1944 discloses current assets of $1,055,844 against current liabilities of $468,438, or a working capital of $587,407. Of the current assets, cash represented $523,691 and inventory $357,347. The ratio of current assets to current liabilities at that time was, therefore, slightly above 2 to 1. The gross volume of business done in 1944 was $8,737,475. The net working capital, therefore, was less than 7 percent of the volume of business transacted. The net earnings for this year were $174,415.28, somewhat less than those for the two preceding war years. The earned surplus was $867,141.

The evidence discloses that at the end of 1944 expenditures in the amount of approximately $564,220 were contemplated to be made, and actually were made in 1945 in addition to ordinary operating expenses and in addition to other normal use of working capital. This sum included the retirement of the then outstanding preferred stocks of Gottfried and Hanscom in the sum of $165,000. Since all the parties held these preferred stocks in the same ratio as they held Gottfried "A" stock and common stock, each of the stockholders, including the plaintiffs, participated proportionately in the benefits of such retirement. After said retirement their respective pro rata interests in Gottfried were precisely the same as before these distributions were made. From this point of view the plaintiffs were in at least as good a position as a result of this preferred stock retirement as though dividends had been paid upon the common stock in the sum of $165,000, which is almost equivalent to the entire net earnings for the year 1944. It is noteworthy in this connection, moreover, that the retirement of the preferred stock was urged by both Charles and Harold Gottfried, two of the plaintiffs, at the annual meeting of the stockholders of Gottfried held on December 5, 1944. Harold went so far as to request that funds be borrowed from a bank in order to effect such retirement. These stockholders certainly cannot complain because a sum almost equivalent to the prior year's entire net income was defrayed, in accordance with their own request, in the form of retirement of preferred stock rather than by payment of dividends on the common stock.

Other major items of expenditure in 1945, which appear to have been contemplated at the end of 1944, were payments of dividends on Gottfried preferred stock in the sum of $5,031, dividends on Hanscom preferred stock in the sum of $5,597, and dividends on the "A" stock of $36,000. In all of these payments of dividends on stock prior to the common stock the plaintiffs were pro rata beneficiaries. In 1945 there were also payments upon outstanding mortgages in the sum of $133,626. Reduction of mortgage indebtedness seems to have been a standard policy of Gottfried when its financial condition permitted it. Payments for sites for new plants and properties deemed necessary for the corporations' operations aggregated more than $214,000.

In addition to the above-mentioned expenditures of $560,220 contemplated in 1944 and made in 1945, Gottfried in 1945 paid $31,532 in dividends on the common stock. It may be, of course, that the payment of these dividends was stimulated by the commencement of this suit. The fact remains that they were paid. Other abnormal expenditures which seem to have been contemplated at the end of 1944 were a substantial increase in inventories owing to unusual conditions in the market at the time and various post-war projects involving large sums of money which could not be effectuated during the war period.

The ratio of dividends paid in 1945 to the earnings of the immediately preceding year was 44.87 percent.

Under these circumstances, it may not be said that the directorate policy regarding common stock dividends at the time the suit was brought was unduly conservative. It certainly does not appear to have been inspired by bad faith.

Although the right (but not the measure) of recovery, even in equity, is usually determined as of the date that suit is brought . . . we shall consider the situation as of the date of the trial.

In 1945 the net earnings were $318,222.72. The current assets amounted to $1,441,408, and the current liabilities to $1,042,967, leaving a working capital of $398,441. This is less than the working capital at the end of 1944 by approximately $188,966, despite the fact that the volume of business for 1945 had increased to $9,405,726. The ratio of working capital to volume of business done was, therefore, approximately 4½ percent. This decrease in working capital at the end of 1945, as compared with the end of 1944, demonstrates fairly conclusively that maximum dividends were paid during 1945. At the end of 1945 the ratio of current assets to current liabilities was 1.38.

At the end of 1945 it was contemplated that dividends would be paid in 1946 on the common stock in the sum of $42,176 and dividends on the "A" stock (in which, as above stated, the plaintiffs held a proportionate interest), of $45,000, or a total of $87,176. The actual dividends paid upon the Class "A" and common stock in 1946 was in excess of this sum and amounted to $153,926. These dividends represented 48.37 percent of the net profit for the previous year. This constituted the highest proportion since 1932 of dividends paid in any year with relation to the earnings of the preceding year.

It appears, moreover, that at the end of 1945, there were actually contemplated various expenditures amounting to $142,000 to be made in 1946 for new sites and the acquisition of other property considered necessary. The actual dividends paid in 1946 plus these further proposed expenditures aggregated $396,239, which is considerably in excess of the entire net earnings for the preceding year. . . .

The testimony discloses that many general considerations affected the policy of the Board of Directors in connection with dividend payments. Some of the major factors were as follows: The recognition that earnings during the war years might be abnormal and not representative of normal earning capacity; the pressing need for heavy expenditures for new equipment and machinery, replacement of which had been impossible during the war years; heavy expenditures required to finance the acquisition and equipment of new Hanscom stores in harmony with the steady growth of the business; the increased initial cost of opening new stores because, under present conditions, it has been difficult to lease appropriate sites necessitating actual acquisition by ownership of locations; the erection of a new bakery for Hanscom at a cost of approximately $1,000,000 inasmuch as the existing plant is incapable of producing the requirements of Hanscom sales which are running at the rate of approximately $6,000,000 per annum; unstable labor conditions with actual and threatened strikes; several pending actions involving large sums of money under the Federal Fair Labor Standards Act; a general policy of financing expansion through earnings requiring long-term debt.

The plaintiffs oppose many of these policies of expansion. There is no evidence of any weight to the effect that these policies of the Board of Directors are actuated by any motives other than their best business judgment. If they are mistaken, their own stockholdings will suffer proportionately to those of the plaintiffs. With the wisdom of that policy the court has no concern. It is this court's conclusion that these policies and the expenditures which they entail are undertaken in good faith and without relation to any conspiracy, scheme or plan to withhold dividends for the purpose of compelling the plaintiffs to sell their stock or pursuant to any other sinister design.

The plaintiffs have failed to prove that the surplus is unnecessarily large. They have also failed to prove that the defendants recognized the propriety of paying dividends but refused to do so for personal reasons.

The complaint is dismissed and judgment directed for the defendants.

◆◆◆

Case Questions

1. What courses of action are available to a minority shareholder in a close corporation who disagrees with the dividend policy of the controlling faction? Litigation is expensive. Not only did the dissidents in the instant case bear their own legal expenses but, as 38 percent shareholders, also indirectly bore 38 percent of the cost of defending the board against their suit.

2. How does one distinguish between the directors' personal interests and the corporate welfare when the directors hold such a dominant ownership position so as to almost constitute a corporate alter ego?

3. Upon reading the court's opinion in this case it seems clear that the board had legitimate reasons to support its dividend policy. If the facts were so clear, why did the minority shareholders fail to recognize them and instead institute an unsuccessful lawsuit? Did their personal feelings obscure the facts? Was their lawyer stupid? Was the action motivated by vindictiveness and merely designed to harass the controlling majority? Was it a gamble, or may the facts only appear clear in retrospect?

REVIEW PROBLEMS

1. A bankruptcy trustee sues the former directors of a company to recover dividends aggregating $3,639,058. The plaintiff claims that, despite the figures shown on the corporate books, there was no surplus and that the capital was impaired by the dividend payments. The directors claim that a proper surplus did exist. The plaintiff claims that: 1) the directors improperly "wrote-up" land that cost $1,526,157.30 to a value of $8,737,949.02. The difference represents unrealized appreciation; 2) the directors improperly declined to "write-down" to actual value the costs of investments in and advances to subsidiaries, thereby failing to take into account unrealized depreciation. What do you think of the directors' decisions? [*Randall* v. *Bailey*, 23 N.Y.S. 2d 179 (1940)] *must appro[v]e and dep[r]*

2. The state business corporation statute vests discretion in the directors as to dividend declarations. The corporate articles contain the following clause: "The holders of preferred stock shall be entitled to receive, and the Company shall be bound to pay thereon, but only out of net profits of the company, a fixed yearly dividend of fifty cents per share, payable semiannually." Are the directors obligated to declare dividends upon the preferred stock whenever the corporation enjoys net profits? [*Constantin* v. *Holding Corp.*, 153 A. 2d 378 (1959)] *st law applies*

3. The receiver of a shipbuilding company sues the five directors to compel the repayment of dividends. The corporation's original capital of $800,000 was largely impaired by a sum in excess of $760,000. Dividends of $28,000 were declared and paid in 1901; $48,000 in 1902; and $48,000 in 1903. These dividends were paid not out of profits, for there were none to divide, but out of capital. Two of the directors were also officers and had personal knowledge of the company's financial condition. The remaining three directors relied upon the reports of the treasurer as showing profits. The accounting methods used in these reports were erroneous. Items were inflated in glaring amounts. Any inquiry as to the make up of the items would have disclosed their hollow nature. Carried as an asset was "work in progress." It lists the sums spent on building three ships. Yet the sums totaled more than the contract price to be received for the boats. The company would receive

$180,000 less than the cost of the boats. Which directors should be liable?
[*Cornell* v. *Seddinger*, 85 A 446 (1912)] *YES The others 3 should have known*

ENDNOTE

1. Copyright 1969. Reprinted from § 45 (Alternative) (a), Model Business Corporation Act, with permission of the American Bar Association and its section of Corporation, Banking and Business Law.

Directors, officers, employees and, in some instances, shareholders have fiduciary obligations to their corporation. They are agents of the corporation and owe it the fiduciary duties that are owed to any other principal. They bear the duties of loyalty and good faith and many not make secret profits at the expense of the corporation, divert corporate information to their own use, place themselves in conflict of interest situations, etc. The usual principal-agent rules apply to them and they are liable to the corporation for any fiduciary violations and must disgorge any profits. However, directors and others are not automatically barred from competing with their corporation. If they act fairly and in complete good faith, no liability to the corporation will be incurred. Let us turn from general platitudes to an examination of how the rules apply in concrete situations. The law in this area is found in court decisions; the business corporation statutes are generally silent on this topic.

CORPORATE OPPORTUNITIES

Corporate employees may not divert a corporate opportunity to their own benefit. Typically it is high level management personnel who occupy positions permitting them to learn of such opportunities and then appropriate them for their own use. If the opportunity is offered to the corporation and a disinterested board rejects it, the corporate employee is then free to personally seize the opportunity. The next case is a straightforward blatant example of the wrongful diversion of a corporate opportunity. The *Guth* v. *Loft* case that immediately follows it is probably the classic case in the field.

CHICAGO FLEXOTILE FLOOR COMPANY v. CHARLES R. LANE
188 Minn. 422, 247 N.W. 517 (1933)

◆◆◆

OLSEN, Justice

Defendant appeals from an order denying his motion for a new trial and also from the judgment entered in plaintiff's favor.

The case was tried to the court, and findings of fact and conclusions of law were duly made, upon which judgment was entered. The plaintiff was and is engaged in the business of furnishing the material for and laying what is known as "Flexotile Floors" or floor coverings in buildings. It enters into contracts with owners or occupants of buildings to install such floors at a fixed price per square foot. This floor material was manufactured, or at least its sale and distribution controlled, by the Flexotile Floor Company, a corporation located at Rockford,

Illinois, which may be referred to as the Rockford company. This company did not generally engage in installing these floors or taking contracts therefor. It made what is referred to as licenses to other companies to contract for and install these floors in specified territories, including agreement by the licensees to purchase the material from and pay for same to the Rockford company at fixed prices. The Rockford company conducted a nation-wide advertising campaign and in that way got in touch with prospective customers for its product. It then referred such customers to one of its licensed installing companies and turned the correspondence and matter of contracting for and installing the floors over to such licensee. The plaintiff was organized and incorporated in January, 1927, and was licensed by the Rockford company to contract for and install flexotile floors in Cook county, Illinois and elsewhere, as might be mutually agreed upon from time to time. . . . It opened an office in Chicago for carrying on the work of obtaining contracts and installing floors in Cook county and elsewhere. Defendant was one of its incorporators and stockholders and a vice president and director of the corporation. He was employed as the manager of its Chicago office and business from the time of its organization until his resignation December 31, 1929.

The court made very complete and clear findings of fact. Three causes of action are involved. First, the court found in substance that shortly before he resigned and while acting as manager of plaintiff's Chicago office and business defendant obtained for plaintiff a contract to install flexotile floors for Carroll & Klug, at Portage, Wisconsin; that defendant fraudulently failed to report the making of this contract to plaintiff at Minneapolis, and a few days after his resignation fraudulently caused to be represented to Carroll & Klug that plaintiff was unable to perform the contract and induced them to change the contract so as to be in the name of the Rockford company, which was in fact the name under which defendant was then doing business for himself; that when he resigned defendant removed and took with him from the office and files of plaintiff the contract and all correspondence related to the Carroll & Klug job; that he thereafter did perform the contract with Carroll & Klug and received a profit therefrom amounting to $1,298.66. The plaintiff was at all times in a position to carry out the contract and would have done so if defendant had not concealed the contract and diverted it from plaintiff.

The second cause of action is as to a contract with Stone & Thomas at Wheeling, West Virginia, which the court found was obtained for plaintiff, concealed, and fraudulently diverted by defendant in substantially the same way. . . . On this contract defendant received a profit of $5,612.62.

The third cause of action on which recovery was allowed was for commissions received by defendant from the Rockford company on the price of material purchased by plaintiff from that company, which the court found were secret profits obtained by defendant from the plaintiff's business. The amount as allowed by the amended findings was $7,102.97, from which a deduction of $2,500 was allowed for money advanced by defendant to plaintiff, leaving a balance of $4,602.97.

The court in its memorandum, made a part of its findings and decision, states in reference to the Carroll & Klug contract:

> In failing to approve and turn this contract over to the plaintiff Lane violated his duty and fraudulently and dishonestly obtained the fruits of the contract for himself.

In reference to the Stone & Thomas contract the court says:

> The whole transaction constituted a fraudulent diversion of the business of the plaintiff to the defendant personally, which was an abuse of his duties as agent of the plaintiff.

If the facts as found by the court are sustained by the evidence there is not much room for discussion of the law. An officer and agent of a corporation, in charge of business for it, who secretly and fraudulently diverts corporate business within his charge to himself and receives and appropriates the profits thereof, is accountable to the corporation for such profits. He is likewise accountable to the corporation for secret commissions received by him upon goods purchased for the corporation. . . .

Under the circumstances shown, defendant is in no position to urge that no . . . contract was entered into before he resigned. Even if there had been no enforceable contract in either of these matters, after the jobs had been referred to and placed in plaintiff's hands by the Rockford company and negotiations had and (*sic*) practically completed with the parties by plaintiff, defendant could not secretly and fraudulently divert further negotiations and himself become interested and take over the jobs without becoming liable to plaintiff. . . .

As to the alleged secret commissions received by defendant from the Rockford company on sales of materials by that company to plaintiff, defendant contends that such commissions were received by him with the knowledge and consent of the plaintiff. The trial court in its memorandum has carefully analyzed the evidence on that issue. Whether defendant received such commissions secretly, without fairly disclosing the same to plaintiff, in other words without plaintiff's knowledge, and was under the evidence, a question of fact for the trial court, and its findings thereon are sustained by the evidence. . . .

◆◆◆

Case Questions

1. How could Lane's diversion of this corporate business have come to the attention of the corporation?
2. Does a company institute a lawsuit, such as in the instant case, just to recover its profits or, also to serve as a deterrent against wrongful acts by other employees?

GUTH, et al. v. LOFT, INC. and PEPSI-COLA COMPANY
23 Del Ch. 255, 5A 2d 503 (1939)

◆◆◆

Loft filed a bill in the Court of Chancery against Charles G. Guth, Grace and Pepsi seeking to impress a trust in favor of the complainant upon all shares of the capital stock of Pepsi registered in the name of Guth and in the name of Grace (approximately ninety-one percent of the capital stock), to secure a transfer of those shares to the complainant, and for an accounting.

The cause was heard at great length by the Chancellor who, on September 17, 1938, rendered a decision in favor of the complainant in accordance with the prayers of the bill. . . .

The essential facts, admitted or found by the Chancellor, briefly stated, are these: Loft was, and is, a corporation engaged in the manufacturing and selling of candies, syrups, beverages and foodstuffs, having its executive offices and main plant at Long Island City, New York. In 1931, Loft operated one hundred and fifteen stores largely located in the congested centers of population along the Middle Atlantic seaboard. While its operations chiefly were of a retail nature, its wholesale activities were not unimportant, amounting in 1931 to over $800,000. It had the equipment and the personnel to carry on syrup making operations, and was engaged in manufacturing fountain syrups to supply its own extensive needs. It had assets exceeding $9,000,000 in value, excluding goodwill; . . .

Guth a man of long experience in the candy, chocolate and soft drink business, became vice-president of Loft in August, 1929, and its president in March, 1930.

Grace was owned by Guth and his family. It owned a plant in Baltimore, Maryland, where it was engaged in the manufacture of syrups for soft drinks, and it had been supplying Loft with "Lady Grace Chocolate Syrup."

In 1931, Coca-Cola was dispensed at all of the Loft stores, and of the Coca-Cola syrup Loft made large purchases, averaging over 30,000 gallons annually. The cost of the syrup was $1.48 per gallon. Guth requested the Coca-Cola Company to give Loft a jobber's discount in view of its large requirements of syrups which exceeded greatly the purchases of some other users of the syrup to whom such discount had been granted. After many conferences, the Coca-Cola Company refused to give the discount. Guth became incensed, and contemplated the replacement of the Coca-Cola beverage with some other cola drink. On May 19, 1931, he addressed a memorandum to V.O. Robertson, Loft's vice-president asking "Why are we paying a full price for Coca-Cola? Can you handle this, or would you suggest our buying Pebsaco (Pepsi-Cola) at about $1.00 per gallon?" To this Robertson replied that Loft was not paying quite full price for Coca-Cola, it paying $1.48 per gallon instead of $1.60 but that it was too much, and that he was investigating as to Pepsi-Cola.

Pepsi-Cola was a syrup compounded and marketed by National Pepsi-Cola Company, controlled by one Megargel. The Pepsi-Cola beverage had been on the market for upwards of twenty-five years, but chiefly in southern territory. It was possessed of a secret formula and trademark. This company, as it happened, was adjudicated a bankrupt on May 26, 1931. . . .

Megargel was not unknown to Guth. In 1928, when Guth had no connection with Loft, Megargel had tried unsuccessfully to interest Guth and one Hoodless, vice-president and general manager of a sugar company, in National Pepsi-Cola Company. Upon the bankruptcy of this company Hoodless, who apparently had had some communication with Megargel, informed Guth that Megargel would communicate with him, and Megargel did inform Guth of his company's bankruptcy and that he was in a position to acquire from the trustee in bankruptcy, the secret formula and trademark for the manufacture and sale of Pepsi-Cola.

In July, 1931, Megargel and Guth entered into an agreement whereby Megargel would acquire the Pepsi-Cola formula and trademark; would form a new corporation with an authorized capital of 300,000 shares of the par value of five dollars to which corporation Megargel would transfer the formula and trademark; would keep 100,000 shares for himself, transfer a like number to Guth, and turn back 100,000 shares to the company as treasury stock, all or a part thereof to be sold to provide working capital. By the agreement between the two, Megargel was to receive $25,000 annually for the first six years, and, thereafter a royalty of two and one-half cents on each gallon of syrup.

Megargel had no money. The price of the formula and trademark was $10,000. Guth loaned Megargel $12,000 upon his agreement to repay him out of the first $25,000 coming to him under the agreement between the two, and Megargel made a formal assignment to Guth to that effect. The $12,000 was paid to Megargel in this way: $5,000 directly to Megargel by Guth, and $7,000 by Loft's certified check, Guth delivering to Loft simultaneously his two checks aggregating $7,000. Guth also advanced $426.40 to defray the cost of incorporating the company. This amount and the sum of $12,000 were afterwards repaid to Guth.

Pepsi-Cola Company was organized under the laws of Delaware in August, 1931. The formula and trademark were acquired from the trustee in bankruptcy of National Pepsi-Cola Company, and its capital stock was distributed as agreed, except that 100,000 shares were placed in the name of Grace.

At this time Megargel could give no financial assistance to the venture directly or indirectly. . . . Guth was heavily indebted to Loft, and, generally, he was in most serious financial straits, and was entirely unable to finance the enterprise. On the other hand, Loft was well able to finance it.

Guth, during the years 1931 to 1935 dominated Loft and through his control of the board of directors he drew upon Loft without limit to further the Pepsi enterprise having at one time almost the entire working capital of Loft engaged therein. He used Loft's plant facilities, materials, credit, executives and employees as he willed. Pepsi's payroll sheets were a part of Loft's and a single Loft check was drawn for both.

All the while Guth was carrying forward his play to replace Coca-Cola with Pepsi-Cola at all of the Loft stores. Loft spent at least $20,000 in advertising the beverage, whereas it never had to advertise Coca-Cola. Loft, also, suffered large losses of profits as its stores resulting from the discarding of Coca-Cola. These losses were estimated at $300,000. They undoubtedly were large.

Guth claimed that he offered Loft the opportunity to take over the Pepsi-Cola enterprise, frankly stating to the directors that if Loft did not, he would; but that the board declined because Pepsi-Cola had proved a failure, and that for Loft to sponsor a company to compete with Coca-Cola would cause trouble; that the proposition was not in line with Loft's business; that it was not equipped to carry on such business on an extensive scale; and that it would involve too great a financial risk. Yet, he claimed that, in August, 1933, the Loft directors consented, without a vote, that Loft should extend to Guth its facilities and resources without limit upon Guth's guarantee of all advances, and upon Guth's contract to furnish Loft a continuous supply of syrup at a favorable price. The guaranty was not in writing if one was made, and the contract was not produced.

The Chancellor found that Guth had never offered the Pepsi opportunity to Loft; . . . Guth's use of Loft's money, credit, facilities and personnel in the furtherance of the Pepsi venture was without the knowledge or authorization of Loft's directors; . . . *among other things*

By the decree entered the Chancellor found, inter alia, that Guth was estopped to deny that opportunity of acquiring the Pepsi-Cola trademark and formula was received by him on behalf of Loft, and that the opportunity was wrongfully appropriated by Guth to himself; that the value inhering in and represented by the 97,500 shares of Pepsi stock standing in the name of Guth and the 140,000 shares standing in the name of Grace, were, in equity, the property of Loft; that the dividends declared and paid on the shares of stock were, and had been, the property of Loft; and that for all practical purposes Guth and Grace were one.

The Chancellor ordered Guth and Grace to transfer the shares of stock to Loft; . . . Guth to account for and pay over to Loft any other dividends, profits, gains, etc., attributable or allocable to the 97,500 shares of Pepsi stock standing in his name; Grace to do likewise with respect to the 140,000 shares standing in its name; Guth to pay to Loft all salary or compensation paid him by Pepsi prior to October 21, 1935; . . . Guth and Grace to be credited with such sums of money as may be found due them from Loft or from Pepsi in respect of matters set forth in the bill of complaint; and a master to be appointed to take and state the accounts.

LAYTON, Chief Justice, delivered the opinion of the Court:

In the court below the appellants took the position that, on the facts, the complainant was entitled to no equitable relief whatever. In this court, they seek only a modification of the Chancellor's decree, not a reversal of it. . . .

Manifestly, the Chancellor found to exist facts and circumstances from which the conclusion could be reached that the Pepsi-Cola opportunity belonged in equity to Loft.

Corporate officers and directors are not permitted to use their position of trust and confidence to further their private interests. While technically not trustees, they stand in a fiduciary relation to the corporate and its stockholders. A public policy, existing through the years, and derived from a profound knowledge of human characteristics and motives, has established a rule that demands of a corporate officer or director, peremptorily and inexorably, the most scrupulous observance of his duty, not only affirmatively to protect the interests of the corporation committed to his charge, but also to refrain from doing anything that would work injury to the corporation, or to deprive it or profit or advantage which his skill and ability might properly bring to it, or to enable it to make in the reasonable and lawful exercise of its powers. The rule that requires an undivided and unselfish loyalty to the corporation demands that there shall be no conflict between duty and self-interest. The occasions for the determination of honesty, good faith, and loyal conduct are many and varied, and no hard and fast rule can be formulated. The standard of loyalty is measured by no fixed scale.

If an officer or director of a corporation, in violation of his duty as such, acquires gain or advantage for himself; the law charges the interest so acquired with a trust for the benefit of the corporation, at its election, while it denies to the betrayer all benefit and profit. The rule, inveterate and uncompromising in its rigidity, does not rest upon the narrow ground of injury or damage to the corporation resulting from the betrayal of confidence, but upon a broader foundation of a wise public policy that, for the purpose of removing all temptation, extinguishes all possibility of profit flowing from a breach of the confidence imposed by the fiduciary relation. Given the relation between the parties, a certain result follows; and a constructive trust is the remedial device through which precedence of self is compelled to give way to the stern demands of loyalty. . . .

It is true that when a business opportunity comes to a corporate officer or director in his individual capacity rather than in his official capacity, and the opportunity is one which, because of the nature of the enterprise, is not essential to his corporation, and is one in which it has no interest or expectancy, the officer or director is entitled to treat the opportunity as his own, and the corporate has no interest in it, if, of course the officer or director has not wrongfully embarked the corporation's resources therein. . . .

On the other hand, it is equally true that, if there is presented to a corporate officer or director a business opportunity which the corporation is financially able to undertake, is, from its nature, in the line of the corporation's business and is of practical advantage to it, is one in which the corporation has an interest or a reasonable expectancy, and, by embracing the opportunity the self-interest of the officer or director will be brought into conflict with that of his corporation, the law will not permit him to seize the opportunity for himself. And, if, in such circumstances, the interests of the corporation are betrayed, the corporation may elect to claim all of the benefits of the transaction for itself, and the law will impress a trust in favor of the corporation under the property interests and profits so acquired.

Duty and loyalty are inseparably connected. Duty is that which is required by one's station or occupation; is that which one is bound by legal or moral obligation to do or refrain from doing; and it is with this conception of duty as the underlying basis of the principle applicable to the situation disclosed, that the conduct and acts of Guth with respect to his acquisition of the Pepsi-Cola enterprise will be scrutinized. Guth was not merely a director and the president of Loft. He was its master. It is admitted that Guth manifested some of the qualities of a dictator. The directors were selected by him. Some of them held salaried positions in the company. All of them held their positions at his favor. Whether they were supine merely, or for sufficient reasons entirely subservient to Guth, it is not profitable to inquiry. It is sufficient to say that they either willfully or negligently allowed Guth absolute freedom of action in the management of Loft's activities, and theirs is an unenviable position whether testifying for or against the appellants.

The real issue is whether the opportunity to secure a very substantial stock interest in a corporation to be formed for the purpose of exploiting a cola beverage on a wholesale scale was so closely associated with the existing business activities of Loft, and so essential thereto, as to bring the transaction within that class of cases where the acquisition of the property would throw the corporate officer purchasing it into competition with his company. This is a factual question to be decided by reasonable inferences from objective facts. . . .

(I)t is contended that the Pepsi-Cola opportunity was not in the line of Loft's activities which essentially were of a retail nature. It is pointed out that, in 1931, the retail stores operated by Loft were largely located in the congested areas along the Middle Atlantic Seaboard, that its manufacturing operations were centered in its New York factory, and that it was a definitely localized business, and not operated on a national scale; whereas, the Megargel proposition envisaged annual sales of syrup at least a million gallons, which could be accomplished only by a wholesale distribution. Loft, however, had many wholesale activities. Its wholesale business in 1931 amounted to over $800,000. It was a large company be any standard. It had an enormous plant. It paid enormous rentals. Guth, himself, said that Loft's success depended upon the fullest utilization of its large plant facilities. Moreover, it was a manufacturer of syrups and, with the exception of cola syrup, it supplied its own extensive needs. The appellants admit that wholesale distribution of bottled beverages can best be accomplished by license agreements with bottlers. Guth, president of Loft, was an able and experienced man in that field. Loft, then, through its own personnel, possessed the technical knowledge, the practical business experience, and the resources necessary for the development of the Pepsi-Cola enterprise.

But, the appellants say that the expression, "in the line" of a business, is a phrase so elastic as to furnish no basis for a useful inference. The phrase is not within the field of precise definition, nor is it one that can be bounded by a set formula. It has a flexible meaning, which is to be applied reasonably and sensibly to the facts and circumstances of the particular case. Where a corporation is engaged in a certain business, and an opportunity is presented to its embracing an activity as to which it has fundamental knowledge, practical experience and ability to pursue, which, logically and naturally, is adaptable to its business having regard for its financial position, and is one that is consonant with its reasonable needs and aspirations for expansion, it may be properly said that the opportunity is in the line of the corporation's business.

The manufacture of syrup was the core of the Pepsi-Cola opportunity. The manufacture of syrups was one of Loft's not unimportant activities. It had the necessary resources, facilities, equipment, technical and practical knowledge and experience. The tie was close between the business of Loft and the Pepsi-Cola enterprise. . . .

Upon a consideration of all the facts and circumstances as disclosed we are convinced that the opportunity to acquire the Pepsi-Cola trademark and formula, goodwill and business belonged to the complainant, and that Guth, as its president, had no right to appropriate the opportunity to himself.

The Chancellor's opinion may be said to leave in some doubt whether he found as a fact that the Pepsi-Cola opportunity belonged to Loft. Certain it is that he found all of the elements of a business opportunity to exist. Whether he made use of the word "estopped" as meaning that he found in the facts and circumstances all of the elements of an equitable estoppel, or whether the word was used loosely in the sense that the facts and circumstances were so overwhelming as to render it impossible for Guth to rebut the conclusion that the opportunity belonged to Loft, it is needless to argue. It may be said, however, that we are not at all convinced that the elements of an equitable estoppel may not be found having regard for the dual personalty which Guth assumed.

The decree of the Chancellor is sustained.

◆◆◆

Case Questions

1. Is it possible for a dominated board of directors to reject a corporate opportunity?
2. Should the directors bear some liability for their acts of omission in not knowing that Loft's money, credit, facilities and personnel were being used in furtherance of the Pepsi venture?
3. Suppose the Pepsi venture was a financial failure. Would Loft be responsible for the Pepsi debts or for Guth's personal losses?

TO WHOM IS THE OPPORTUNITY MADE AVAILABLE?

The issue of what exactly constitutes a corporate opportunity can test one's legal prowess. Interwined with the question is the sub-issue of to whom the opportunity was presented. Was the offer in fact made to the corporation? The following case examines these matters.

JOHNSTON v. GREENE
121 A. 2d 919 (S. Ct., Del., 1956)

◆◆◆

SOUTHERLAND, Chief Justice

The ultimate question in this case is the fairness of a transaction between a corporation and its president and dominating director. The court below held that he had appropriated for himself a corporate opportunity belonging to his corporation.

The pertinent facts, either uncontroverted or found by the Chancellor, are as follows:

Airfleets, Inc., is a Delaware corporation, organized in 1948 as a wholly owned subsidiary of Consolidated Vultee Aircraft Corporation (called "Convair"). Convair sometime thereafter distributed all of the Airfleets stock to its own stockholders. Atlas Corporation, an investment company, became Airfleets' largest single stockholder, owning about 18 percent of its stock. Upon the organization of Airfleets the defendant Odlum became and has since been its president, without compensation. Odlum is also the president of Atlas, owning or controlling about 11 percent of its stock. He is a man of varied business interests. At the time here material he also was chairman of the Board of Directors of Convair, a director of United Fruit Company, a director of Wasatch Corporation, and a trustee of several foundations.

Airfleets was organized to finance aircraft that might be sold or leased to the air lines. This purpose was never carried out. Airfleets' first business venture was the sale of certain aircraft manufacturing plants, aircraft, and related assets that it had acquired from Convair. By the fall of 1951 it had nearly completed the sale of these assets, and was in a liquid position, with about $2,000,000 in cash. It also held marketable securities worth about $1,500,000. It was looking for investment "without any predisposition as to the type." ... At this time, therefore, it was not a corporation with any well-defined object or purpose, other than that of employing its liquid assets for the profit of its stockholders.

Certainly it was not then engaged in the business of manufacturing aircraft or aircraft accessories.

In late December of 1951 a business opportunity was brought to the attention of Mr. Odlum in the following circumstances:

Mr. Lester E. Hutson was the owner of all the stock of Nutt-Shel Company, a California corporation operating a plant in or near Los Angeles for the manufacture of self-locking nuts used in aircraft. Hutson also owned certain patents and patent applications covering the device. A license agreement was in effect, granting to Nutt-Shel exclusive rights in respect of the patents.

Hutson knew of Odlum by reputation as a well-known financier and president of Atlas Corporation, and as a man engaged in various enterprises. Hutson had never heard of Airfleets. Cousins was a friend of Odlum's, having known Odlum since 1942, and was to spend New Year's weekend with Odlum at the latter's ranch in California. He also knew of Odlum's association with Convair and Atlas, but had never head of Airfleets. . . .

On the Friday before New Year's Cousins broached the subject and outlined to Odlum the history and nature of the Nutt-Shel business. Odlum was interested, and a few days later Hutson came to the ranch to discuss the matter and furnish Odlum with financial data. . . .

Hutson was willing to sell the patents separately but would not sell the stock separately. He would have preferred to retain a controlling interest in the stock but Odlum said he would have to have the controlling interest. Hutson told Odlum that he had been advised by his attorney and that . . . it would be advisable to have the patents under separate ownership. The reason for this was the possibility of the disallowance of the royalty expense on renegotiation of government contracts, as payments from a wholly-owned corporation to its sole stockholder. . . .

Hutson returned a few days later with additional data. Mr. Rockefeller, Odlum's executive assistant at Convair and a director of Airfleets, was present. He sat in on the discussions and took the papers home with him. Odlum had the Nutt-Shel plant inspected by Mr. Ryan, of the Convair organization. Ryan's report was very favorable. Odlum also received a telephone call from Rockefeller, advising him of the result of Rockefeller's study of the papers. Odlum decided to make the purchase. On February 10 he talked to Hutson by telephone and confirmed the price — $350,000 dollars for the patents, $1,000,000 for the stock" — and told Hutson that he had decided to buy the entire deal. He then arranged, through his New York counsel, for the employment of attorneys in California to handle the closing of the transaction. . . .

At about this time Odlum was advised by his tax consultant that the acquisition of Nutt-Shel might fit very well into the tax problems of Airfleets. Odlum requested further study of the matter, as a result of which he concluded to submit the proposition to Airfleets' Board of Directors.

The . . . directors reached the conclusion that the stock would be a desirable investment for Airfleets, but that it would be undesirable to acquire the patents. The reasons were two: first, the undesirability of investing the additional $350,000, or a total investment of about two-thirds of Airfleets' net assets, in one enterprise; and second, the possibility of the disallowance of royalty payments. Odlum told them that in those circumstances, in order to make it possible for the company to buy the stock, he would undertake to find buyers for the patents, and if necessary would take himself whatever interest was not so disposed of.

A formal meeting of the Board was held on January 28th. . . . The board (Odlum not voting) voted to acquire the stock but not the patents. The Chancellor found that Odlum dominated the other directors and that the decision not to acquire the patents was his. This finding we accept.

On February 8th formal contracts of sale between Hutson and Airfleets, covering the stock, and between Hutson and Odlum, covering the patents, were signed. The transaction was closed in the latter part of the month.

In the meantime Odlum had arranged for the purchase of the patents for $350,000 . . . by 37 different persons and corporations, including himself. His own retained interest is about 7½ percent. Odlum testified that he had expected to sell this interest, but after the propriety of the transaction had been questioned by an Airfleets stockholder, his position became "frozen."

The rejection of the opportunity to buy the patents is attacked as a breach of Odlum's fiduciary duty to Airfleets. The complaint charges (1) that Hutson offered to sell the patents to Airfleets for $350,000; (2) that the patents were useful and necessary to Airfleets in the conduct of the Nutt-Shel business, and the opportunity to purchase them was a valuable asset of Airfleets; (3) that the directors, under the domination of Odlum, who controlled the management of Airfleets, caused Airfleets to reject the offer, in violation of their fiduciary duty; and (4) that Odlum caused the patents to be purchased for himself and certain of his associates subject to his control.

The case made by the complaint is thus one of the unlawful diversion of a corporate opportunity for the benefit of the president and dominating director of a corporation

The general principles of the law pertaining to corporate opportunity are settled in this state. *Guth* v. *Loft*, 23 Del. Ch. 255, 5 A.2d 503, 510. Speaking for the Supreme Court, Chief Justice Layton said:

> It is true that when a business opportunity comes to a corporate officer or director in his individual capacity rather than in his official capacity, and the opportunity is one which, because of the nature of the enterprise, is not essential to his corporation, and is one in which it has no interest or expectancy, the officer or director is entitled to treat the opportunity as his own, and the corporation has no interest in it, if, of course, the officer or director has not wrongfully embarked the corporation's resources therein.

*   *   *

> On the other hand, it is equally true that, if there is presented to a corporate office or director a business opportunity which the corporation is financially able to undertake, is, from its nature, in the line of the corporation's business and is of practical advantage to it, is one in which the corporation has an interest or a reasonable expectancy, and, by embracing the opportunity, the self-interest of the officer or director will be brought into conflict with that of his corporation, the law will not permit him to seize the opportunity for himself.

The Chancellor found that the purchase of the patents was not essential to Airfleets' business, and assumed that it was not one in which the corporation had an expectancy. But he held that it was one in which Airfleets had an interest in the sense that through Odlum it was actively seeking valuable investments, for which it had available funds, and that it was Odlum's duty to find such opportunities.

He also found that Odlum's decision to reject the opportunity to buy the patents was taken in his own interest because by affording friends, associates, and others the opportunity to buy the patents Odlum was satisfying obligations of his own. . . .

The first important fact that appears in that Hutson's offer, which was to sell the patents and at least part of the stock, came to Odlum, not as a director of Airfleets, but in his individual capacity. The Chancellor so found. The second important fact is that the business of Nutt-Shel — the manufacture of self-locking nuts — had no direct or close relation to any business that Airfleets was engaged in or had ever been engaged in, and hence its acquisition was not essential to the conduct of Airfleets' business. Again, the Chancellor so found. The third fact is that Airfleets had no interest or expectancy in the Nutt-Shel business, in the sense that those words are used in the decisions dealing with the law of corporate opportunity.

> Whether in any case an officer of a corporation is in duty bound to purchase property for the corporation, or to refrain from purchasing property for himself, depends upon whether the corporation has an interest, actual or in expectancy, in the property, or whether the purchase of the property by the officer or director may hinder or defeat the plans and purposes of the corporation in the carrying on or development of the legitimate business for which it was created. . . . For the corporation to have an actual or expectant interest in any specific property, there must be some tie between that property and the nature of the corporate business. . . .

We accordingly find ourselves compelled to disagree with the Chancellor's decision. Recognizing that Airfleets had no expectancy in the Nutt-Shel business and that its acquisition was not essential to Airfleets, he nevertheless held that Airfleets' need for investments constituted an "interest" in the opportunity to acquire that business. Now, this is an application of the rule of corporate opportunity that requires careful examination. It is one thing to say that a corporation with funds to invest has a general interest in investing those funds; it is quite another to say that such a corporation has a specific interest attaching in equity to any and every business opportunity that may come to any of its directors in his individual capacity. This is what the Chancellor appears to have held. Such a sweeping extension of the rule of corporate opportunity finds no support in the decisions and is, we think, unsound.

We cannot find any such circumstances in this case. At the time when the Nutt-Shel business was offered to Odlum, his position was this: He was the part-time president of Airfleets. He was also president of Atlas — an investment company. He was a director of other corporations and a trustee of foundations interested in making investments. If it was his fiduciary duty, upon being offered any investment opportunity, to submit it to a corporation of which he was a director, the question arises, which corporation? Why Airfleets instead of Atlas?

Why Airfleets instead of one of the foundations? So far as appears, there was no specific tie between the Nutt-Shel business and any of these corporations or foundations. Odlum testified that many of his companies had money to invest, and this appears entirely reasonable. How, then, can it be said that Odlum was under any obligation to offer the opportunity to one particular corporation? And if he was not under such an obligation, why could he not keep it for himself? . . .

It was unnecessary to labor the point further. We are of opinion that the opportunity to purchase the Nutt-Shel business belonged to Odlum and not to any of his companies.

This conclusion requires the rejection of the plaintiffs' contention, and of the Chancellor's holding, that the opportunity to buy the Nutt-Shel business belonged to Airfleets. But it does not in itself dispose of the case.

The refusal of the directors of Airfleets to buy the patents was, under the Chancellor's finding, a transaction between the dominating director and his corporation. It is therefore subject to strict scrutiny, and the defendants have the burden of showing that it was fair. . . .

Now a fair way to determine the propriety of Odlum's action "is to consider whether the proposition submitted would have commended itself to an independent corporation." . . . It is clear to us that if a wholly independent board of directors had determined, upon the information received by Odlum, that it was undesirable for Airfleets to buy the patents and that they should be transferred to third persons, a reviewing court would not think of disturbing its judgment upon the matter. Moreover, it is a fair conclusion that in the light of this information received from four separate sources the separation of the ownership of the patents would have commended itself to an independent board of directors.

We cannot say, of course, that on this matter an independent board would have in all likelihood agreed with Odlum; they might, or they might not. But certainly such a consideration is more than a mere pretext or excuse for rejecting the purchase of the patents. The Chancellor thought it not persuasive because Airfleets' existing investments were of a temporary nature, and could readily have been sold to provide more cash. This hardly seems to touch the point of the proportion of the required investment — $1,350,000 — to total net assets; moreover, whether and at what time any investment should be sold is peculiarly a matter of business judgment.

Now, as the Chancellor found, Odlum made these decisions on behalf of Airfleets. If, after making them, he had elected to keep the patents for himself, a serious question would be presented whether he had sustained the burden of establishing fairness. . . .

But Odlum did not seek to profit personally by what he had done. He promptly divested himself, prior to the closing of the transaction, of almost the entire interest in the patents. . . .

We do not think that it can be fairly said that Odlum profited personally from the sale. The Chancellor's finding that the sale of the patents was improper was, we think, based on his holding that the Nutt-Shel business, including the patents, was a corporate opportunity belonging to Airfleets. If that were so, then his conclusion would be sound, since, as he said Odlum's motive in allowing friends, associates and others by buying the patents could not justify the diversion from

Airfleets of an asset belonging to it. But we are of opinion, as above stated, that this is not a case of corporate opportunity, and is to be judged by the test applicable to a transaction between the dominating director and his corporation — the test of fairness.

Our conclusions upon a careful review of this record are: first, that the opportunity to acquire the Nutt-Shel business did not belong to Airfleets second, that the transaction between Odlum and Airfleets involving the patents was fair and free of any overreaching or inequitable conduct.

It follows that the judgment of the Court of Chancery must be reversed. This cause is remanded to that court, with directions to vacate the judgment and dismiss the complaint.

◆◆◆

Case Questions

1. Suppose Odlum sat on the board of both an aircraft manufacturer and a manufacturer of metal fasteners, including nuts and bolts. Both businesses would have a close relationship and an interest in the Nutt-Shel business. What would Odlum's obligations be in such a situation? Should he make the opportunity known to both companies and let them bid for it? If he reveals the opportunity to just one, would the other have a valid complaint? Suppose he neither seizes the opportunity for himself, nor reveals it to either company. Could both corporations successfully assert a violation of Odlum's fiduciary duties to them?

2. What difficulties does a court face in deciding whether an opportunity came to a person in his capacity as a director or as an individual? If the evidence is evenly balanced, will a court decide in favor of the corporation? Court will vote against the agent - conservative approach

3. Do you agree that the Chancellor gave too broad a meaning to the phrase "corporate opportunity" when he held that Airfleet had an interest in Nutt-Shel because it had a need for valuable investments?

CORPORATE OPPORTUNITIES IN TIMES OF FINANCIAL STRESS

May corporate fiduciaries avail themselves of an opportunity if the corporation lacks the necessary financial resources? The *Irving Trust* v. *Deutsch* case answers the question in the negative and explains the reasons behind that answer. While not a true corporate opportunity case, the circumstances in *Manufacturers Trust* v. *Becker* also examine a fiduciary's dealings with a corporation experiencing financial problems, in this instance an insolvent corporation.

IRVING TRUST CO. v. DEUTSCH
73 F 2d. 121 (1934)

◆◆◆

SWAN, Circuit Judge.

A very complete statement of the facts may be found in the opinion of the District Court which by the terms of the decree appealed from stands as the findings of facts and the conclusions of law. For an understanding of the main issues raised by the appeal, the following summary will serve as an adequate introduction:

The plaintiff is the trustee in the bankruptcy of a Delaware corporation, Sonora Products Corporation of America, whose corporate name was formerly Acoustic Products Company. For convenience the bankrupt will be referred to as Acoustic. It was chartered in 1927 to deal in phonographs, radios, and similar apparatus. In March, 1928, it was essential for Acoustic to acquire rights to manufacture under basic patents in the radio art, and it was believed that such rights might be acquired through the De Forest Radio Company, which was then in receivership in the Chancery Court of New Jersey. The defendant Bell was employed by Acoustic to negotiate with the defendants Reynolds and W. R. Reynolds and Co., who were in control of the De Forest situation by reason of a contract under which they expected to purchase 600,000 shares of stock at 50 cents per share, lift the receivership, and reorganize the De Forest Company. Although Bell's negotiations did not produce an arrangement of the sort originally contemplated by Acoustic, he did succeed, with the assistance of the defendant Biddle, in obtaining from Reynolds & Co. an offer of a one-third participation in the purchase of the 600,000 shares of De Forest stock; that is 200,000 shares for $100,000 cash. The offer was directed to Messrs. Biddle and Bell and provided:

> Your signatures on a signed copy hereof will constitute an agreement between us which will be subject to the approval of your board of directors not later than April 9th 1928.

It also provided that, if the stock was taken, Acoustic's nominees should hold four of the nine places on the De Forest Company's directorate and that Acoustic should have the right to enter into a contract, subject to the approval of the De Forest board of directors, "to handle the managing, operating and selling of the De Forest products." This offer was presented to a meeting of the board of directors of Acoustic on April 3, 1928, and a resolution was passed instructing its president, the defendant Deutsch, to endeavor to obtain sufficient funds to enable Acoustic to carry out its obligations in the event of its final acceptance of the offer. On April 9th, at an adjourned meeting of the board, Mr. Deutsch reported his inability to procure the necessary funds for Acoustic, and announced that "several individuals were desirous of accepting said proposition on their own behalf" and were willing to make arrangements so as to extend to Acoustic the benefits contemplated by the acquisition of the stock. Thereupon a resolution was adopted approving Mr. Biddle's acceptance on behalf of Acoustic and directing the proper officers to notify its acceptance to Reynolds & Co. On April 10th, Mr. Deutsch telegraphed Mr. Biddle of this action, with the explanation that it was understood by the directors that, if Acoustic could not finance the purchase when time for payment came, the directors would individually acquire the stock. Partial payment for the 200,000 shares was made on April 24th by the personal checks of Biddle, Deutsch, and Hammond, for which Reynolds & Co. gave a receipt to Acoustic. The balance was paid on May 25, 1928, at which time it was explained to Reynolds that the stock was being purchased by individuals since Acoustic was without available funds. He acquiesced and caused the stock certificates to be issued to Messrs. Bell, Biddle, Deutsch, Hammond, Stein, and White. For convenience these gentlemen are referred to as the Biddle syndicate. . . . An active market for De Forest shares was created on the Curb Exchange, and defendants made large profits in selling their shares. The bill of complaint seeks to hold the defendants jointly and severally to account for such profits. . . .

Concretely, the argument is that members of the Biddle syndicate, three of whom, Messrs. Biddle, Deutsch, and Hammond, were directors and one, Mr. Bell, its agent in procuring the contract, appropriated to themselves Acoustic's rights under its contract with Reynolds & Co. for 200,000 shares of De Forest stock, when as fiduciaries they were obligated to preserve those rights for Acoustic and were forbidden to take a position where personal interest would conflict with the interest of their principal. . . . In answer to this argument, the defendants do not deny the principle, but dispute its applicability to the facts. . . .

It is next contended that the contract was ultra vires Acoustic, and hence its directors and officers violated no fiduciary duty in taking stock which the corporation could not legally acquire. . . . Without pausing to determine the soundness of the asserted conclusion, we pass to a consideration of the premise. Access to the De Forest patents was concededly essential to Acoustic. It was thought that access to them could be obtained by buying a minority stock interest because four of the De Forest Company's nine directors were to be named by Acoustic and it was to have the opportunity to make a contract to manage the De Forest Company. It is true that the terms of such contract were yet to be drafted and submitted to the De Forest board of directors, but, with four directors committed to it, the prospect of getting the contract seemed bright. The management contract, carrying access to the patents, was a legitimate corporate purpose. So was stock ownership in the De Forest Company as a going concern. By Acoustic's investment, together with that of Reynolds & Co., the receivership was to be lifted and the De Forest restored to the position of a going concern. No stock market operation was contemplated by Acoustic when it accepted the offer; that was a later development arranged between Reynolds and the Biddle syndicate on May 25th. In the light of these facts, we think the purchase was within the corporation's charter powers. . . .

The main defense asserted is that Acoustic by reason of its financial straits had neither the funds nor the credit to make the purchase and that the directors honestly believed that by buying the stock for themselves they could give Acoustic the advantage of access to the De Forest patents, while at the same time taking a stock speculation for their own benefit. . . . That the prohibition against corporate officers acting on their own behalf is removed if the corporation is itself financially unable to enter into the transaction, . . .

The facts in the case at bar are . . . strong against the defendant directors since . . . the directors absolutely bound Acoustic by contract to make the payments to Reynolds & Co., and thus subjected it to the risk of an action for damages for nonperformance, without committing themselves to it to relieve it of this obligation if necessary when time for payment should arrive. The defendants' argument, . . . that the equitable rule that fiduciaries should not be permitted to assume a position in which their individual interests might be in conflict with those of the corporation can have no application where the corporation is unable to undertake the venture, is not convincing. If directors are permitted to justify their conduct on such a theory, there will be a temptation to refrain from exerting their strongest efforts on behalf of the corporation since, if it does not meet the obligations, an opportunity of profit will be open to them personally. Indeed, in the present suit it is at least open to question whether a stronger effort might not have been made on the part of the management to procure for Acoustic the necessary funds or credit. Thus it appears that Deutsch owed Acoustic $125,000 on his note due February 2, 1928, and secured by collateral. No effort was made to collect it or to realize on the collateral. The directors contend that they took no action because Deutsch thought that he had a defense to his note; but the validity of such defense, as well as whether the possibility of resorting to this asset was fully considered, is very doubtful. After April 9th no efforts appear to have been made to raise for Acoustic the $100,000 required for the De Forest stock. Moreover, Acoustic did have substantial banking accommodations on June 6th, and, if these had been made available a few weeks earlier, it would have been able to perform its contract with Reynolds & Co. While these facts raise some question whether Acoustic actually lacked the funds or credit necessary for carrying out its contract, we do not feel justified in reversing the District Court's finding that it did. Nevertheless, they tend to show the wisdom of a rigid rule forbidding directors of a solvent corporation to take over for their own profit a corporate contract on the plea of the corporation's financial inability to perform. If the directors are uncertain whether the corporation can make the necessary outlays, they need not embark it upon the venture; if they do, they may not substitute themselves for the corporation any place along the line and divert possible benefits into their own pockets. . . .

For the foregoing reasons, the decree of dismissal is reversed as against Bell, Biddle, Deutsch, and Hammond; . . .

◆◆◆

Case Questions

1. Since certain of the directors had sufficient funds to purchase the stock for themselves, why didn't they lend the necessary funds to Acoustic with the De Forest stock as collateral?
2. Why didn't the directors purchase the stock and simultaneously grant Acoustic a purchase option to cover those shares?
3. Once an active market in the De Forest shares had been established on the Curb Exchange, would the directors have been free to purchase the stock as a personal investment? YES

MANUFACTURERS TRUST CO., TRUSTEE v. BECKER ET AL.
338 U.S. 304 (1949)

◆◆◆

MR. JUSTICE CLARK delivered the opinion of the Court.

This proceeding in bankruptcy is on objections to the allowance of claims equal to the principal amount of bonds of the debtor acquired at a discount during its insolvency by close relatives and an office associate of directors of debtor. Petitioner's objection that equitable considerations require limitation of the claims was dismissed by the referee, and the District Court affirmed. ... Following affirmance by a divided Court of Appeals for the Second Circuit ... we granted certiorari because the issue presented has importance in the administration of the arrangement and corporate reorganization provisions of the Bankruptcy Act.

On January 8, 1946, Calton Crescent, Inc., sold its only property, an apartment house located in New Rochelle, New York, for $300,000 pursuant to a contract entered into in October, 1945. Being unable to discharge in full its obligations under debenture bonds maturing in 1953, outstanding in principal amount of $254,450, debtor filed in May, 1946, a petition under CH. XI of the Bankruptcy Act. ... Under the plan of arrangement, authorizing a dividend of 43.61 percent of the principal amount of the bonds, respondents Regine Becker, Emily K. Becker, and Walter A. Fribourg were to receive an aggregate dividend of $64,237.53 on allowance of claims based on respective individual holdings of debentures which total $147,300 in principal sum but were acquired at a total cost of $10,195.43.[1] Petitioner, Manufacturers Trust Company, appearing individually as creditor for fees and disbursements due it as indenture trustee and also as original trustee under said indenture, objected to allowance of respondents' claims as filed, on the ground that the circumstances of respondents' acquisitions require limitation of their claims to the cost of the debenture plus interest.

The circumstances pertinent to our consideration of petitioner's objections are as follows: The debtor was organized in 1933 to take title to the apartment property. ... By January 1942 debtor had defaulted under the terms of the first mortgage and was operating with a deficit; at no time in the previous several years had its debentures been selling on the market at more than 8 percent of face value.

While debtor was then considering a sale of the property for $220,000, a suit to enjoin the sale was brought by Sanford Becker, son of respondent Regine Becker and husband of respondent Emily Becker. Thereafter he proposed to arrange a loan on second mortgage to debtor of $15,000 to pay off the arrearages on the first mortgage, all share and debenture holders being invited to participate. In April, 1942, debtor accepted the offer, but none of its share or debenture holders elected to participate other than respondent Fribourg, who had desk room in the offices of Sanford Becker and his brother Norman Becker and was a long-time friend of the former. The loan was made by respondents Regine Becker, Emily Becker, and Fribourg. The second mortgage thus created was in default by the end of 1942, and in 1943 respondents took an assignment of rents but did not foreclose; nor was there change in management of the property. The second mortgage and interest were paid upon sale of the property in 1946. In addition to the second mortgage, sums aggregating $7,921.63 were advanced by respondents to pay taxes; this amount was repaid without interest

---

[1] The amount and cost of the respective holdings of the respondents, insofar as objected to, are as follows:

	Principal Amount	Cost
Regine Becker	$44,500	$3,060.63
Emily K. Becker	52,800	5,010.00
Walter A. Fribourg	50,000	2,124.80

in 1944 and 1945. Pursuant to provisions of the loan agreement in 1942, Sanford and Norman Becker were made directors of debtor, and when the remaining three directors resigned in 1944, the vacancies were filled by nominees of the Becker brothers.

The referee found that from early 1942 the market value of the property of debtor was insufficient to pay its debts. However, the record shows a tax valuation during the period of only slightly less than the outstanding indebtedness. And although the debtor's operating account frequently ran in arrears, it revealed a surplus in 1945. Prior to disposing of its property debtor was at all times a going concern.

It was the referee's finding, left undisturbed by both courts below, that respondents' purchases were without overreaching or failure to disclose any material fact to the selling bondholders. Petitioner does not here contend that respondents' claims should be limited because of conduct by the Becker directors or by respondents amounting to bad faith or abuse of fiduciary advantage. Nor does petitioner contend that respondents' bondholdings influenced the conduct of corporate affairs to the injury of the corporation or other creditors. Indeed, the referee found that the purchases were not unfair to debtor, that at the time of respondents' purchases debtor was not in the field to settle its indebtedness on the debentures, and that the assistance rendered to debtor by respondents materially aided in its grave financial situation. Moreover, the findings indicate that the most generous suggestion of an offer for the apartment building after the Beckers became directors and prior to the sale was at a figure substantially less than the sale price.

Petitioner urges broadly that directors are precluded from profiting by the purchase of claims against an insolvent corporation. And, it contends, if directors may claim only the cost of debt securities acquired at a discount during a debtor's insolvency, those related as respondents are to the Becker directors and should not be permitted to do more. Thus we view respondents' claims initially as if they were claims of directors.

This Court has repeatedly insisted on good faith and fair dealing on the part of corporate fiduciaries. It is especially clear, when claims in bankruptcy accrue to the benefit of a corporate officer or director, that the court must refuse any claim that would not be fair and equitable to other creditors. . . .

Claims of a corporate officer or director arising out of transactions with the corporation have been enforced when good faith and fairness were found. . . .

When the transactions underlying respondents' claims here are drawn alongside a good faith standard of fiduciary obligation, they appear unobjectionable. There is no component of unfair dealings or bad faith. The findings negative any misrepresentation or deception, any utilization of inside knowledge or strategic position, or any rivalry with the corporation. During the period of the purchases the conduct of the Becker directors and of respondents with reference to the affairs of the debtor was to its substantial benefit and to the advantage of the other debenture holders. And there is nothing to suggest that had the debentures been acquired by the Becker directors they would have been unjustly enriched.

However, it is the contention of petitioner, and of the Securities and Exchange Commission as amicus curiae, that a standard of good faith and fair dealings is inadequate here. . . . (T)hey invoke the principle that a trustee can make no profit from his trust. But . . . even during insolvency corporate assets "are not in any true and complete sense trusts." . . .

The Commission asserts, also, that if a director is free to acquire corporate obligations at a discount during insolvency and later enforce them in full, he will be subject to a possible conflict of interests inconsistent with his role as fiduciary to creditors of the corporation. Specifically it is argued that he may seek to postpone adjustment of claims or the institution of proceedings for relief, when such action would serve the interests of the corporation and its creditors, in order to continue his own purchase of corporate obligations at a market price lower than the valuation which he has made with the benefit of inside information.

This court has recognized that equity must apply not only the doctrines of unjust enrichment when fiduciaries have yielded to the temptation of self-interest but also a standard of loyalty which will prevent a conflict of interests from arising. . . . In this case the consideration is whether or to what extent a conflict of interests would arise from a director's opportunity to purchase unmatured obligations of a corporation which, though technically insolvent, remains nevertheless a going concern. That "there is no such conflict in the ordinary case of the purchase by a director in a going corporation of its outstanding obligations," *Seymour* v. *Spring Forest Cemetery Assn.,* 144 N.Y. 333, 344 . . . (1895), would seem true not only of solvent corporations. Certainly the present record does not tend to establish that the opportunity for such purchases during insolvency would deprive a going corporation of the sound judgment of its officer. And in any event the potentiality of conflict must be weighed against the desirability of permitting reinforcement of the insolvent's position insofar as a director's acquisition of claims may help. On this record the probability that an actual conflict of loyalties arose from the opportunity to purchase respondents' claims, while the debtor was a going concern, is not great enough to justify the exercise of equity jurisdiction which petitioner urges.

Undoubtedly the possibilities of a conflict of interests for the purchasing director are intensified as the corporation becomes less a going concern and more a prospective subject of judicial relief. And if it is clear that a fiduciary may ordinarily purchase debt claims in fair transactions during solvency of the corporation, the lower federal courts seem equally agreed that he cannot purchase after judicial proceedings for the relief of a debtor are expected or have begun. In this case, which lies between, it is unnecessary to determine precisely at what point the probability of conflict requires that equity declare ended the opportunity for profitable trading. It could hardly have been prior to the latest purchases of Regine and Emily Becker.

The decision of the Court of Appeals is Affirmed.

MR. JUSTICE BURTON, with whom MR. JUSTICE BLACK joins, dissenting.

While corporate directors are not classed as express trustees, their obligations to their respective corporations are fiduciary in character. The more precarious the condition of the corporation, the more it needs the undivided loyalty of its directors. Conflicts of interest must be resolved in its favor. An example of the need for doing so arises whenever, in the face of a prospect of the corporation's liquidation, some of its directors invest in its notes at a substantial discount. An inherent conflict of interests is thereby created. It may be necessary for them to choose between a corporate policy of reorganization which might be best for the corporation and one of liquidation which might yield more certain profits to them as noteholding directors. The fiduciary obligation of such directors to their corporation might thus conflict with their personal interest as noteholders. Their access to confidential corporate information emphasizes the good faith expected of them. The solution lies in making them accountable to their corporation for their profits from such an investment, much as a trustee must account to his beneficiaries for his profits from dealings in the subject matter of his trust. This result would spring wholly from the fiduciary nature of the obligations of directors to their corporation. It would need no proof of a breach of trust or of the actual overreaching of anyone. . . .

A mere excess of a corporation's liabilities over its assets may not subject its directors to . . . accountability. Nevertheless, any evidence of the financial instability of their corporation obligates the directors to overcome whatever presumption of conflict of interests between their own and those of the corporation or of its creditors that such evidence presents.

In the instant case there should be a finding whether or not, at the time of the purchases of the debentures in question, there was a sufficient prospect of liquidation to bring the interests of directors as debenture purchasers into conflict with the interests of their corporation. If such a conflict is established, it then will be necessary to determine the extent, if any, to which the relatives and associates of such directors are to be identified with them.

I agree with the reasoning of the dissent below. . . . Accordingly, I would reverse the judgment and remand the cause for further findings in accordance with this opinion.

◆◆◆

Case Questions

1. Would the dissenting justices annunciate a rule absolutely prohibiting directors from profiting in their corporation's debt securities purchased at a discount during insolvency?
2. Could the petitioner have seriously thought that he would be victorious when he concedes that the respondents had not acted in bad faith, had not abused any fiduciary advantage, and had not adversely influenced corporate affairs vis-a-vis the corporate creditors?
3. It is unconscionable that relatives of directors of an insolvent corporation expend only $10,195 to purchase bonds at discount and then recover $64,237 for those same bonds in a bankruptcy proceeding? Was there anything that would have prevented the petitioner from purchasing these same bonds on the market at a substantial discount and then enjoying a windfall profit in the bankruptcy action?

SALE OF CONTROL

A shareholder need not own an absolute majority of a corporation's voting stock to control that corporation. If the shares are sufficiently widely scattered, an individual with as little as 10 to 15 percent of the shares can elect a majority of the board of directors; such a shareholder is said to have "working control." When a controlling stockholder sells his shares he can expect to receive more money per share than can the ordinary shareholder. Why is he receiving a premium for his shares? Because the purchaser is not just acquiring the shares; he is also gaining control of the corporation. That element of control has an inherent economic value.

The question that should immediately come to mind is whether control constitutes an asset of the corporation. Normally, the seller of a controlling bloc of stock is permitted to retain the premium. The idea is that the voting power is inherent in the stock and transfer of the stock transfers the voting rights. However, a controlling shareholder may not sell his stock with impunity. Sale of control is allowable in some instances and impermissable in others. The controlling shareholder does owe certain fiduciary duties to the corporation and the other shareholders. Just as the purchase of votes is illegal in the political sphere, so too is it in the corporate sphere. One cannot retain his shares but sell his votes. (Don't confuse this with proxies, where one can give one's voting rights to another.) When the sale of control is challenged, the court will focus on the legitimacy of the buyer's purpose. If the new regime intends some illegal or fraudulent activities or, will cause injury to the corporation, the seller will be liable to the corporation. If a corporation enjoys a large amount of liquid assets the purchaser may intend to come in and loot the corporation of those assets. Possibly the new directors have no intention of responsibly exercising their management responsibilities. In either of these situations the seller will have breached his fiduciary obligations, if he knew, or should have known, of these plans.

The *Perlman* v. *Feldmann* case that follows is a famous example of the improper sale of control. It contains two somewhat unique elements. First, the sale of control is declared unallowable even though the purchasers did not engage in any illegitimate activity. Secondly, the selling shareholder must disgorge a pro rata share of the premium directly to the other shareholders and not to the corporation, as is the rule in the typical derivative suit. However, it is important to remember that one may generally sell control without liability. The Perlman case represents an exception to the general rule.

The *Essex* v. *Yates* case examines the legality of the sale of a controlling block of stock coupled with the seriatim resignation of a majority of the board. When a corporation has directors serving staggered terms of office the purchaser cannot gain immediate control. Therefore, the seller will agree to use his influence to have the directors resign, in turn to be replaced by the purchaser's slate. Such an agreement is allowable if the corporation does not thereby suffer any injury.

PERLMAN v. FELDMANN
219 F.2d 173 (1955)

◆◆◆

CLARK, Chief Judge.

This is a derivative action brought by minority stockholders of Newport Steel Corporation to compel accounting for, and restitution of, allegedly illegal gains which accrued to defendants as a result of the sale in August, 1950, of their controlling interest in the corporation. The principal defendant, C. Russell Feldmann, who represented and acted for the others, members of his family, was at that time not only the dominant stockholder, but also the chairman of the board of directors and the president of the corporation. Newport, an Indiana corporation, operated mills for the production of steel sheets for sale to manufacturers of steel products, first at Newport, Kentucky, and later also at other places in Kentucky and Ohio. The buyers, a syndicate organized as Wilport Company, a Delaware corporation, consisted of end-users of steel who were interested in securing a source of supply in a market becoming ever tighter in the Korean War. Plaintiffs contend that the consideration paid for the stock included compensation for the sale of a corporate asset, a power held in trust for the corporation by Feldmann as its fiduciary. This power was the ability to control the allocation of the corporate product in a time of short supply, through control of the board of directors; and it was effectively transferred in this sale by having Feldmann procure the resignation of his own board and the election of Wilport's nominees immediately upon consummation of the sale. . . . Plaintiffs argue here, as they did in the court below, that in the situation here disclosed the vendors must account to the nonparticipating minority stockholders for that share of their profit which is attributable to the sale of the corporate power. Judge Hincks denied the validity of the premise, holding that the rights involved in the sale were only those normally incident to the possession of a controlling block of shares, with which a dominant stockholder, in the absence of fraud or foreseeable looting, was entitled to deal according to his own best interests. Furthermore, he held that plaintiffs had failed to satisfy their burden of proving that the sales price was not a fair price for the stock *per se.* Plaintiffs appeal from these rulings of law which resulted in the dismissal of their complaint.

The essential facts found by the trial judge are not in dispute. Newport was a relative newcomer in the steel industry with predominantly old installations which were in the process of being supplemented by more modern facilities. Except in times of extreme shortage Newport was not in a position to compete profitably with other steel mills for customers not in its immediate geographical area. Wilport, the purchasing syndicate, consisted of geographically remote end-users of steel who were interested in buying more steel from Newport than they had been able to obtain during recent periods of tight supply. The price of $20 per share was found by Judge Hincks to be a fair one for a control block of stock, although the over-the-counter market price had not exceeded $12 and the book value per share was $17.03. But this finding was limited by Judge Hincks' statement that "(w)hat value the block would have had if shorn of its appurtenant power to control distribution of the corporate product, the evidence does not show." It was also conditioned by his earlier ruling that the burden was on plaintiffs to prove a lesser value for the stock.

Both as director and as dominate storkholder, Feldmann stood in a fiduciary relationship to the corporation and to the minority storkholders as beneficiaries thereof. . . . His fiduciary obligation must in the first instance be measured by the law of Indiana, the state of incorporation of Newport. . . . Although there is no Indiana case directly in point, the most closely analogous one emphasizes the close scrutiny to which Indiana subjects the conduct of fiduciaries when personal benefit may stand in the way of fulfillment of trust obligations. In *Schemmel* v. *Hill*, 91 Ind.App. 373, 169 N.E. 678,682,683, McMahan, J., said: "Directors of a business corporation act in a strictly fiduciary capacity. Their office is a trust. ... When a director deals with his corporation, his acts will be closely scrutinized. ... Directors of a corporation are its agents, and they are governed by the rules of law applicable to other agents, and, as between themselves and their principal, the rules relating to honesty and fair dealing in the management of the affairs of their principal are applicable. They must not, in any degree, allow their official conduct to be swayed by their private interest, which must yield to official duty. ... In a transaction between a director and his corporation, where he acts for himself and his principal at the same time in a matter connected with the relation between them, it is presumed, where he is thus potential on both sides of the contract, that self-interest will overcome his fidelity to his principal, to his own benefit and to his principal's hurt." And the judge added: "Absolute and most scrupulous good faith is the very essence of a director's obligation to his corporation. The first principal duty arising from his official relation is to act in all things of trust wholly for the benefit of his corporation."

In Indiana, then, as elsewhere, the responsibility of the fiduciary is not limited to a proper regard for the tangible balance sheet assets of the corporation, but includes the dedication of his uncorrupted business judgment for the sole benefit of the corporation, in any dealings which may adversely affect it. ... Although the Indiana case is particularly relevant to Feldmann as a director, the same rule should apply to his fiduciary duties as majority stockholder, for in that capacity he chooses and controls the directors, and thus is held to have assumed their liability. ... This, therefore, is the standard to which Feldmann was by law required to conform in his activities here under scrutiny.

It is true, as defendants have been at pains to point out, that this is not the ordinary case of breach of fiduciary duty. We have here no fraud, no misuse of confidential information, no outright looting of a helpless corporation. But on the other hand, we do not find compliance with that high standard which we have just stated and which we and other courts have come to expect and demand of corporate fiduciaries. In the often-quoted words of Judge Cardozo: "Many forms of conduct permissible in a workaday world for those acting at arm's length, are forbidden to those bound by fiduciary ties. A trustee is held to something stricter than the morals of the market place. Not honesty alone, but the punctilio of an honor the most sensitive, is then the standard of behavior. As to this there has developed a tradition that is unbending and inveterate. Uncompromising rigidity has been the attitude of courts of equity when petitioned to undermine the rule of undivided loyalty by the 'disintegrating erosion' of particular exceptions." *Meinhard* v. *Salmon,* supra, 249 N.Y. 458, 464, 164 N.E. 545, 546, 62 A.L.R. 1. The actions of defendants in siphoning off for personal gain corporate advantages to be derived from a favorable market situation do not betoken the necessary undivided loyalty owed by the fiduciary to his principal.

The corporate opportunities of whose misappropriation the minority stockholders complain need not have been an absolute certainty in order to support this action against Feldmann. If there was possibility of corporate gain, they are entitled to recover. In *Young* v. *Higbee Co.*, supra, 324 U.S. 204, 65

S.Ct. 594, two stockholders appealing the confirmation of a plan of bankruptcy reorganization were held liable for profits received for the sale of their stock pending determination of the validity of the appeal. They were held accountable for the excess of the price of their stock over its normal price, even though there was no indication that the appeal could have succeeded on substantive grounds. And in *Irving Trust Co.* v. *Deutsch,* supra, 2 Cir., 73 F.2d 121, 124, an accounting was required of corporate directors who bought stock for themselves for corporate use, even though there was an affirmative showing that the corporation did not have the finances itself to acquire the stock. Judge Swan speaking for the court pointed out that "The defendants' argument . . . that the equitable rule that fiduciaries should not be permitted to assume a position in which their individual interests might be in conflict with those of the corporation can have no application where the corporation is unable to undertake the venture, is not convincing. If directors are permitted to justify their conduct on such a theory, there will be a temptation to refrain from exerting their strongest efforts on behalf of the corporation since, if it does not meet the obligations, an opportunity of profit will be open to them personally."

This rationale is equally appropriate to a consideration of the benefits which Newport might have derived from the steel shortage. In the past Newport had used and profited by its market leverage by operation of what the industry had come to call the "Feldmann Plan." This consisted of securing interest-free advances from prospective purchasers of steel in return for firm commitments to them from future production. The funds thus acquired were used to finance improvements in existing plants and to acquire new installations. In the summer of 1950 Newport had been negotiating for cold-rolling facilities which it needed for a more fully integrated operation and a more marketable product, and Feldmann plan funds might well have been used toward this end.

Further, as plaintiffs alternatively suggest, Newport might have used the period of short supply to build up patronage in the geographical area in which it could compete profitably even when steel was more abundant. Either of these opportunities was Newport's, to be used to its advantage only. Only if defendants had been able to negate completely any possibility of gain by Newport could they have prevailed. It is true that a trial court finding states: "Whether or not, in August, 1950, Newport's position was such that it could have entered into 'Feldmann Plan' type transactions to procure funds and financing for the further expansion and integration of its steel facilities and whether such expansion would have been desirable for Newport, the evidence does not show." This, however, cannot avail the defendants, who — contrary to the ruling below — had the burden of proof on this issue, since fiduciaries always have the burden of proof in establishing the fairness of their dealings with trust property. . . .

Defendants seek to categorize the corporate opportunities which might have accrued to Newport as too unethical to warrant further consideration. It is true that reputable steel producers were not participating in the gray market brought about by the Korean War and were refraining from advancing their prices, although to do so would not have been illegal. But Feldmann plan transactions were not considered within this self-imposed interdiction; the trial court found that around the time of the Feldmann sale Jones & Laughlin Steel Corporation, Republic Steel Company, and Pittsburgh Steel Corporation were all participating in such arrangements. In any event, it ill becomes the defendants to disparage as unethical the market advantages from which they themselves reaped rich benefits.

We do not mean to suggest that a majority stockholder cannot dispose of his controlling block of stock to outsiders without having to account to his corporation for profits or even never do this with impunity when the buyer is an interested customer, actual or potential, for the corporation's product. But when the sale necessarily results in a sacrifice of this element of corporate good will and consequent unusual profit to the fiduciary who has caused the sacrifice, he should account for his gains. So in a time of market shortage, where a call on a corporation's product commands an unusually large premium, in one form or another, we think it sound law that a fiduciary may not appropriate to himself the value of this premium. Such personal gain at the expense of his coventurers seems particularly reprehensible when made by the trusted president and director of his company. In this case the violation of duty seems to be all the clearer because of this triple role in which Feldmann appears, though we are unwilling to say, and are not to be understood as saying, that we should accept a lesser obligation for any one of his roles alone.

Hence to the extent that the price received by Feldmann and his codefendants included such a bonus, he is accountable to the minority stockholders who sue here. *Restatement,* Restitution §§ 190, 197 (1937); ... And plaintiffs, as they contend, are entitled to a recovery in their own right, instead of in right of the corporation (as in the usual derivative actions), since neither Wilport nor their successors in interest should share in any judgment which may be rendered. ... Defendants cannot well object to this form of recovery, since the only alternative, recovery for the corporation as a whole, would subject them to a greater total liability.

The case will therefore be remanded to the district court for a determination of the question expressly left open below, namely, the value of defendants' stock without the appurtenant control over the corporation's output of steel. We reiterate that on this issue, as on all others relating to a breach of fiduciary duty, the burden of proof must rest on the defendants. ... Judgment should go to these plaintiffs and those whom they represent for any premium value so shown to the extent of their respective stock interests. ...

SWAN, Circuit Judge (dissenting).

With the general principles enunciated in the majority opinion as to the duties of fiduciaries I am, of course, in thorough accord. But, as Mr. Justice Frankfurter stated in *Securities and Exchange Commission* v. *Chenery Corp.,* 318 U.S. 80, 85 ... "to say that a man is a fiduciary only begins analysis; it gives direction to further inquiry. To whom is he a fiduciary? What obligations does he owe as a fiduciary? In what respect has he failed to discharge these obligations?" My brothers' opinion does not specify precisely what fiduciary duty Feldmann is held to have violated or whether it is a duty imposed upon him as the dominant stockholder or as a director of Newport. Without such specification I think that both the legal profession and the business world will find the decision confusing and will be unable to foretell the extent of its impact upon customary practices in the sale of stock.

The power to control the management of a corporation, that is, to elect directors to manage its affairs, is an inseparable incident to the ownership of a majority of its stock, or sometimes, as in the present instance, to the ownership of enough shares, less than a majority, to control an election. Concededly a majority or dominant shareholder is ordinarily privileged to sell his stock at the best price obtainable from the purchaser. In so doing he acts on his own behalf, not as an agent of the corporation. If he knows or has reason to believe that the purchaser intends to exercise to the detriment of the corporation the power of management acquired by the purchase, such knowledge or reasonable suspicion will terminate the dominant shareholder's privilege to sell and will create a duty not to transfer the power of management to such purchaser. The duty seems to me to resemble the obligation which everyone is under not to assist another to commit a tort rather than the obligation of a fiduciary. But whatever the nature of the duty, a violation of it will subject the violator to liability for damages sustained by the corporation. Judge Hincks found that Feldmann had no reason to think that Wilport would use the power of management it would acquire by the purchase to injure Newport, and that there was no proof that it ever was so used. Feldmann did know, it is true, that the reason Wilport wanted the stock was to put in a board of directors who would be likely to permit Wilport's members to purchase more of Newport's steel than they might otherwise be able to get. But there is nothing illegal in a dominant shareholder purchasing from his own corporation at the same prices it offers to other customers. That is what the members of Wilport did, and there is no proof that Newport suffered any detriment therefrom.

My brothers say that "the consideration paid for the stock included compensation for the sale of a corporate asset," which they describe as "the ability to control the allocation of the corporate product in a time of short supply, through control of the board of directors; and it was effectively transferred in this sale by having Feldmann procure the resignation of his own board and the election of Wilport's nominees immediately upon consummation of the sale." The implications of this are not clear to me. If it means that when market conditions are such as to induce users of a corporation's product to wish to buy a controlling block of stock in order to be able to purchase part of the corporation's output at the same mill list prices as are offered to other customers, the dominant stockholder is under a fiduciary duty not to sell his stock, I cannot agree. For reasons already stated, in my opinion Feldmann was not proved to be under any fiduciary duty as a stockholder not to sell the stock he controlled.

Feldmann was also a director of Newport. Perhaps the quoted statement means that as a director he violated his fiduciary duty in voting to elect Wilport's nominees to fill the vacancies created by the resignations of the former directors of Newport. As a director Feldmann was under a fiduciary duty to use an honest judgment in acting on the corporation's behalf. A director is privileged to resign, but so long as he remains a director he must be faithful to his fiduciary duties and must not make a personal gain from performing them. Consequently, if the price paid for Feldmann's stock included a payment for voting to elect the new directors, he must account to the corporation for such payment, even though he honestly believed that the men he voted to elect were well qualified to serve as directors. He cannot take pay for performing his fiduciary duty. There is no

418

suggestion that he did do so, unless the price paid for his stock was more than its value. . . .

Judge Hincks went into the matter of valuation of the stock with his customary care and thoroughness. He made no error of law in applying the principles relating to valuation of stock. Concededly a controlling block of stock has greater sale value than a small lot. While the spread between $10 per share for small lots and $20 per share for the controlling block seems rather extraordinarily wide, the $20 valuation was supported by the expert testimony of Dr. Badger, whom the district judge said he could not find to be wrong. I see no justification for upsetting the valuation as clearly erroneous. Nor can I agree with my brothers that the $20 valuation "was limited" by the last sentence in finding 120. The controlling block could not by any possibility be shorn of its appurtenant power to elect directors and through them to control distribution of the corporate product. It is this "appurtenant power" which gives a controlling block its value as such block. What evidence could be adduced to show the value of the block "if shorn" of such appurtenant power, I cannot conceive, for it cannot be shorn of it.

The opinion also asserts that the burden of proving a lesser value than $20 per share was not upon the plaintiffs but the burden was upon the defendants to prove that the stock was worth that value. Assuming that this might be true as to the defendants who were directors of Newport, they did show it, unless finding 120 be set aside. Furthermore, not all the defendants were directors; upon what theory the plaintiffs should be relieved from the burden of proof as to defendants who were not directors, the opinion does not explain.

The final conclusion of my brothers is that the plaintiffs are entitled to recover in their own right instead of in the right of the corporation. This appears to be completely inconsistent with the theory advanced at the outset of the opinion, namely, that the price of the stock "included compensation for the sale of a corporate asset." If a corporate asset was sold, surely the corporation should recover the compensation received for it by the defendants. Moreover, if the plaintiffs were suing in their own right, Newport was not a proper party. The case of *Southern Pacific Co.* v. *Bogert,* 250 U.S. 483, 39 S.Ct. 533, 63 LEd. 1099, relied upon as authority for the conclusion that the plaintiffs are entitled to recover in their own right, relates to a situation so different that the decision appears to me to be inapposite.

I would affirm the judgment on appeal.

◆◆◆

Case Questions

1. Does this decision declare it to be illegal *per se* for a controlling shareholder to derive a premium from the sale of a controlling block of stock?
2. Is this decision relatively unimportant in that the circumstances are so unique that it is unlikely for a similar situation to arise again?
3. In measuring a fiduciary's activities against his legally imposed duties does a court focus upon the degree of harm caused his corporation or the amount of advantages it was unable to secure?

4. Could a fiduciary fulfill his obligations by offering the minority shareholders the opportunity of selling a pro rata share of their holdings to the new controlling shareholder, i.e., if the new shareholder desires to purchase 40 percent ownership and the fiduciary owns 45 percent, then the fiduciary would sell 45 percent of the total number of shares necessary to constitute 40 percent ownership with the minority having the chance to sell the remaining number of shares according to their proportionate ownership?

5. Did Wilport pay a premium for control of Newport or was it actually paying a premium for Newport's steel products? Is it legally significant to know which item Wilport was purchasing at a premium?

Case Comment

The defendants sold their stock for 20 dollars per share although the over-the-counter price had not exceeded 12 dollars. On remand the district court had the task of determining what portion of the 20 dollars per share was attributable to its control aspects. It valued this control at $5.33 per share. The Feldmann group sold 398,927 shares to Wilport. Multiplying this times $5.33 yields a total premium of $2,126,280.91. The court, as you remember, in a somewhat unique ruling for a derivative suit, held that the recovery should not go to the corporation but to the individual minority shareholders. The Wilport shares constituted 36.99 percent of the outstanding shares of Newport. Under the ruling Wilport was barred from recovering any of the premium. Its percentage share of the premium would have been $786,511.29. After this amount was subtracted from the total premium it left $1,339,769.62 due the minority shareholders [154 F. Supp. 436 (1957)].

The *Blue Chip Stamps* v. *Manor Drug* case, *supra* chapter 16 discusses Rule 10b-5 in connection with the "Birnbaum rule." That litigation, 193 F. 2d 461 (1952), arose when some minority shareholders of Newport unsuccessfully sued Feldmann over the alleged rejection of a favorable merger prior to the Wilport transaction.

ESSEX UNIVERSAL CORPORATION v. YATES
305 F.2d 572 (2nd Cir., 1962)

◆◆◆

LUMBARD, Chief Judge.

This appeal from the district court's summary judgment in favor of the defendant raises the question whether a contract for the sale of 28.3 percent of the stock of a corporation is, under New York law, invalid as against public policy solely because it includes a clause giving the purchaser an option to require a majority of the existing directors to replace themselves, by a process of seriatim resignation, with a majority designated by the purchaser. . . .

Since we are in agreement on certain preliminary questions, this opinion constitutes the opinion of the court up to the point where it is indicated that it thenceforth states only my individual views.

The defendant Herbert J. Yates, a resident of California, was president and chairman of the board of directors of Republic Pictures Corporation, a New

York corporation which at the time relevant to this suit had 2,004,190 shares of common stock outstanding. Republic's stock was listed and traded on the New York Stock Exchange. In August 1957, Essex Universal Corporation, a Delaware corporation owning stock in various diversified businesses, learned of the possibility of purchasing from Yates an interest in Republic. Negotiations proceeded rapidly, and on August 28 Yates and Joseph Harris, the president of Essex, signed a contract in which Essex agreed to buy, and Yates agreed "to sell or cause to be sold" at least 500,000 and not more than 600,000 shares of Republic stock. The price was set at eight dollars a share, roughly two dollars above the then market price on the Exchange. Three dollars per share was to be paid at the closing on September 18, 1957 and the remainder in twenty-four equal monthly payments beginning January 31, 1958. The shares were to be transferred on the closing date, but Yates was to retain the certificates, endorsed in blank by Essex, as security for full payment. In addition to other provisions not relevant to the present motion, the contract contained the following paragraph:

6. Resignations.

Upon and as a condition to the closing of this transaction if requested by Buyer at least ten (10) days prior to the date of the closing:

(a) Seller will deliver to Buyer the resignations of the majority of the directors of Republic.

(b) Seller will cause a special meeting of the board of directors of Republic to be held, legally convened pursuant to law and the by-laws of Republic, and simultaneously with the acceptance of the directors' resignations set forth in paragraph 6(a) immediately preceding will cause nominees of Buyer to be elected directors of Republic in place of the resigned directors.

Before the date of the closing, as provided in the contract, Yates notified Essex that he would deliver 566,223 shares, or 28.3 percent of the Republic stock then outstanding, and Essex formally requested Yates to arrange for the replacement of a majority of Republic's directors with Essex nominees pursuant to paragraph 6 of the contract. This was to be accomplished by having eight of the fourteen directors resign seriatim, each in turn being replaced by an Essex nominee elected by the others; such a procedure was in form permissible under the charter and by-laws of Republic, which empowered the board to choose the successor of any of its members who might resign.

On September 18, the parties met as arranged for the closing at Republic's office in New York City. Essex tendered bank drafts and cashier's checks totalling $1,698,690, which was the 37½ percent of the total price of $4,529,784 due at this time. The drafts and checks were payable to one Benjamin C. Cohen, who was Essex' banker and had arranged for borrowing of the necessary funds. Although Cohen was prepared to endorse these to Yates, Yates upon advice of his lawyer rejected the tender as "unsatisfactory" and said, according to his deposition testimony, "Well, there can be no deal. We can't close it."

Essex began this action in the New York Supreme Court, and it was removed to the district court on account of diversity of citizenship. Essex seeks damages of $2,700,000, claiming that at the time of the aborted closing the stock was in actuality worth more than $12.75 a share. Yates' answer raised a number of defenses, but the motion for summary judgment now before us was made and decided only on the theory that the provision in the contract for immediate transfer of control of the board of directors was illegal *per se* and tainted the entire contract. We have no doubt, and the parties agree, that New York law governs. . . .

The terms of the contract . . . express the unwillingness of Essex to pay the agreed price if Yates did not bring about the transfer of directorships, and surely no court would have forced it to make payment in that event. Since Yates could thus not have chosen to excise the hypothetically illegal term of the contract to make the provision for the sale of stock enforceable, it would be unjust to allow Essex the option of waiving it to make the sale enforceable should it suit its purposes to do so. . . .

We are strongly influenced by those New York cases holding invalid agreements to sell stock because accompanied by illegal agreements for the transfer of management control, even though they contain no indication that the issue of separability was explicitly raised. . . . Accordingly, we hold the provision regarding directors inseparable from the sale of shares, and proceed to a consideration of its legality.

Up to this point my brethren and I are in agreement. The following analysis is my own, except insofar as the separate opinions of Judges Clark and Friendly may indicate agreement.

It is established beyond question under New York law that it is illegal to sell corporate office or management control by itself (that is, accompanied by no stock or insufficient stock to carry voting control). . . . The same rule apparently applies in all jurisdictions where the question has arisen. . . . The rationale of the rule is undisputable: persons enjoying management control hold it on behalf of the corporation's stockholders, and therefore may not regard it as their own personal property to dispose of as they wish. Any other rule would violate the most fundamental principle of corporate democracy, that management must represent and be chosen by, or at least with the consent of, those who own the corporation.

Essex was, however, contracting with Yates for the purchase of a very substantial percentage of Republic stock. If, by virtue of the voting power carried by this stock, it could have elected a majority of the board of directors, then the contract was not a simple agreement for the sale of office to one having no ownership interest in the corporation, and the question of its legality would require further analysis. Such stock voting control would incontestably belong to the owner of a majority of the voting stock, and it is commonly known that equivalent power usually accrues to the owner of 28.3 percent of the stock. For the purpose of this analysis, I shall assume that Essex was contracting to acquire a majority of the Republic stock, deferring consideration of the situation where, as here, only 28.3 percent is to be acquired.

Republic's board of directors at the time of the aborted closing had fourteen members divided into three classes, each class being "as nearly as may be" of the same size. Directors were elected for terms of three years, one class being elected at each annual shareholder meeting on the first Tuesday in April. Thus, absent the immediate replacement of directors provided for in this contract, Essex as the hypothetical new majority shareholder of the corporation could not have obtained managing control in the form of a majority of the board in the normal course of events until April 1959, some eighteen months after the sale of the stock. The first question before us then is whether an agreement to accelerate the transfer of management control, in a manner legal in form under the corporation's charter and by-laws, violates the public policy of New York.

There is no question of the right of a controlling shareholder under New York law normally to derive a premium from the sale of a controlling block of stock. In other words, there was no impropriety *per se* in the fact that Yates was to receive more per share than the generally prevailing market price for Republic stock. . . .

The next question is whether it is legal to give and receive payment for the immediate transfer of management control to one who has achieved majority share control but would not otherwise be able to convert that share control into operating control for some time. I think that it is.

Of course under some circumstances controlling shareholders transferring immediate control may be compelled to account to the corporation for that part of the consideration received by them which exceeds the fair value of the block of stock sold, as well as for the injury which they may cause to the corporation. . . .

In *Perlman* v. *Feldmann*, 219 F.2d 173, . . . (2 Cir.), cert. denied, 349 U.S. 952 (1955), this court, in a decision based only nominally on Indiana law, went beyond this rule to hold liable controlling shareholders who similarly sold immediate control even in the absence of illegitimate activity on the part of the purchasers. Our theory was basically that the controlling shareholders in selling control to a potential customer had appropriated to their personal benefit a corporate asset: the premium which the company's product could command in a time of market shortage. . . .

A fair generalization . . . may be that a holder of corporate control will not, as a fiduciary, be permitted to profit from facilitating actions on the part of the purchasers of control which are detrimental to the interests of the corporation or the remaining shareholders. There is, however, no suggestion that the transfer of control over Republic to Essex carried any such threat to the interests of the corporation or its other shareholders.

Our examination of the New York cases discussed thus far gives us no reason to regard as impaired the holding of the early case of *Barnes* v. *Brown,* 80 N.Y. 527 (1880), that a bargain for the sale of a majority stock interest is not made illegal by a plan for immediate transfer of management control by a program like that provided for in the Essex-Yates contract. . . .

Given this principle that it is permissible for a seller thus to choose to facilitate immediate transfer of management control, I can see no objection to a contractual provision requiring him to do so as a condition of the sale. Indeed, a New York court has upheld an analogous contractual term requiring the board of directors to elect the nominees of the purchasers of a majority stock interest to officerships. *San Remo Copper Mining Co.* v. *Moneuse,* 149 App.Div. 26, 133 N.Y.S. 509 (1st Dept. 1912). . . .

The most troublesome, and most recent, of the relevant New York decisions, . . . is *Benson* v. *Braun,* 8 Misc.2d 67, 155 N.Y.S.2d 622 (Nassau County Sup.Ct.1956). That case was a derivative action by minority shareholders seeking to recover an alleged premium received by the sellers of a majority share interest for transferring control over the board of directors in the manner provided for in the Essex-Yates contract; there was, however, no such explicit contractual provision. The complaint . . . alleged that this premium had been for the immediate transfer of control under circumstances raising a reasonable suspicion that the purchasers intended to loot the corporation. At the trial, the court found no reason for the sellers to have suspected looting, but went on to say that it was necessary to determine "whether the price paid for the stock is so great that it can be explained in no other way than as a payment for resigning from office." . . .

The payment of a large premium for resigning (alleged to be $800,000 in *Benson* v. *Braun*) is, of course, relevant to the question whether the sellers had any reason for suspecting that the purchasers had improper intentions in acquiring control. . . .

The easy and immediate transfer of corporate control to new interests is ordinarily beneficial to the economy and it seems inevitable that such transactions would be discouraged if the purchaser of a majority stock interest were required to wait some period before his purchase of control could become effective. Conversely it would greatly hamper the efforts of any existing majority group to dispose of its interest if it could not assure the purchaser of immediate control over corporation operations. I can see no reason why a purchaser of majority control should not ordinarily be permitted to make his control effective from the moment of the transfer of stock. . . .

Because 28.3 percent of the voting stock of a publicly owned corporation is usually tantamount to majority control, I would place the burden of proof on this issue on Yates as the party attacking the legality of the transaction. Thus, unless on remand Yates chooses to raise the question whether the block of stock in question carried the equivalent of majority control, it is my view that the trial court should regard the contract as legal and proceed to consider the other issues raised by the pleadings. If Yates chooses to raise the issue, it will, on my view, be necessary for him to prove the existence of circumstances which would have prevented Essex from electing a majority of the Republic board of directors in due course. It will not be enough for Yates to raise merely hypothetical possibilities of opposition by the other Republic shareholders to Essex' assumption of management control. Rather, it will be necessary for him to show that, assuming neutrality on the part of the retiring management, there was at the time some concretely foreseeable reason why Essex' wishes would not have prevailed in shareholder voting held in due course. In other words, I would require him to show that there was at the time of the contract some other organized block of stock of sufficient size to outvote the block Essex was buying, or else some circumstance making it likely that enough of the holders of the remaining Republic stock would band together to keep Essex from control.

Reversed and remanded for further proceedings not inconsistent with the judgment of this court.

CLARK, Circuit Judge (concurring in the result). * * *

My concern is lest we may be announcing abstract moral principles which have little validity in daily business practice other than to excuse a defaulting vendor from performance of his contract of sale. Thus for fear of a possible occasional contract inimical to general stockholder interest we may be condemning out of hand what are more often normal and even desirable business relationships. As at present advised I would think that the best we can do is to consider each case on its own facts and with the normal presumption that he who asserts illegality must prove it.

. . . I am constrained to point out that I do not believe a district court determination as to whether or not "working control" was transferred to the vendee can or should affect the outcome of this case. The contract provides for transfer of 28.3 percent of the outstanding stock and effective control of the board of directors, and there is no evidence at this stage that the vendor's power to transfer control of the board was to be secured unlawfully, as, for example, by bribe or duress. Surely in the normal course of events a management which was behind it 28.3 percent of the stock has working control, absent perhaps a pitched proxy battle which might unseat it. But the court cannot foresee such an unlikely event or predict its outcome; thus it is difficult to see what further evidence on the question of control could be adduced. My conclusion that there is no reason to declare this contract illegal on its face would remain unaffected by any hypothetical findings on "control." . . .

FRIENDLY, Circuit Judge (concurring).

Chief Judge Lumbard's thoughtful opinion illustrates a difficulty, inherent in our dual judicial system, which has let at least one state to authorize its courts to answer questions about its law that a Federal court may ask. Here we are forced to decide a question of New York law, of enormous importance to all New York corporations and their stockholders, on which there is hardly enough New York authority for a really informed prediction what the New York Court of Appeals would decide on the facts here presented, . . .

I have no doubt that many contracts, drawn by competent and responsible counsel, for the purchase of blocks of stock from interests thought to "control" a corporation although owning less than a majority, have contained provisions like paragraph 6 of the contract *sub judice*. However, developments over the past decades seem to me to show that such a clause violates basic principles of corporate democracy. To be sure, stockholders who have allowed a set of directors to be placed in office, whether by their vote or their failure to vote, must recognize that death, incapacity or other hazard may prevent a director from serving a full term, and that they will have no voice as to his immediate successor. But the stockholders are entitled to expect that, in that event, the remaining directors will fill the vacancy in the exercise of their fiduciary responsibility. A mass seriatim resignation directed by a selling stockholder, and the filling of vacancies by his henchmen at the dictation of a purchaser and without any consideration of the character of the latter's nominees, are beyond what the stockholders contemplated or should have been expected to contemplate. This seems to me a wrong to the corporation and the other stockholders which the law ought not countenance, whether the selling stockholder has received a premium or not. Right in this Court we have seen many cases where sudden shifts of corporate control have caused serious injury; . . . A special meeting of stockholders to replace a board may always be called, and there could be no objection to making the closing of a purchase contingent on the results of such an election. I perceive some of the difficulties of mechanics such a procedure presents, but I have enough confidence in the ingenuity of the corporate bar to believe these would be surmounted.

Hence I am inclined to think that if I were sitting on the New York Court of Appeals, I would hold a provision like Paragraph 6 violative of public policy save when it was entirely plain that a new election would be a mere formality — i.e., when the seller owned more than 50 percent of the stock. . . .

◆◆◆

Case Questions

1. Why would Yates attempt to back out of the deal with Essex, after so eagerly having made the agreement?
2. Is it valid to criticize the concept that the new owner of a controlling block of stock should immediately enjoy majority status on the board of directors?

INTERESTED DIRECTORS AND INTERLOCKING DIRECTORATES

The conflict of interest that exists when a director engages in transactions with his corporation should be crystal clear. On the one hand are his fiduciary duties, on the other, his individual self-interest. Nevertheless such transactions are common and can be of benefit to the corporation. The general rules governing such circumstances are: 1) If the director's presence is necessary for purposes of a quorum or his vote is necessary to pass the resolution the contract will be voidable at the option of the corporation. 2) If the director's presence is neither necessary for a quorum nor for passage of the resolution the contract will be valid if it is a fair one. If challenged, the interested director bears the burden of proving its fairness.

Some jurisdictions handle the matter by statute. Illinois absolutely prohibits certain transactions. Section 41b of its corporation act provides that "No loans shall be made by a corporation to its officers or directors, and no loans shall be made by a corporation secured by its shares." Section 42.8 declares any violation to be a criminal offense. Section 144 of the Delaware statute reads:

> (a) No contract or transaction between a corporation and one or more of its directors or officers, or between a corporation and any other corporation, partnership, association, or other organization in which one or more of its directors or officers, are directors or officers, or have a financial interest, shall be void or voidable solely for this reason, or solely because the director or officer is present at or participates in the meeting of the board or committee which authorizes the contract or transaction, or solely because his or their votes are counted for such purpose, if:
>> (1) The material facts as to his relationship or interest and as to the contract or transaction are disclosed or are known to the board of directors or the committee, and the board or committee in good faith authorizes the contract or transaction by the affirmative votes of a majority of the disinterested directors, even though the disinterested directors be less than a quorum; or
>> (2) The material facts as to his relationship or interest and as to the contract or transaction are disclosed or are known to the shareholders

entitled to vote thereon, and the contract or transaction is specifically approved in good faith by vote of the shareholders; or

(3) The contract or transaction is fair as to the corporation as of the time it is authorized, approved or ratified, by the board of directors, a committee, or the shareholders.

(b) Common or interested directors may be counted in determining the presence of a quorum at a meeting of the board of directors or of a committee which authorizes the contract or transaction.

The presence of an interlocking directorate compounds the problem. Suppose director X sits on the board of both company A and company B. Companies A and B now wish to do business with each other. Not only may X have his own self-interest, he now owes fiduciary duties to two corporations that have potentially conflicting interests.

Although it is a 1918 case, *Globe Woolen Co.* v. *Utica Gas & Elec. Co.,* 121 N.E. 378, remains the leading case on interlocking directorates. An individual by the name of Maynard was a director, officer and large shareholder of Globe. He was also a director, but not a shareholder, of Utica. Globe operated a woolen mill in Utica whereas the defendant generated and sold electricity. For several years the defendant had studied the possibility of supplying electricity for the operation of the plaintiff's plants in place of steam. An agreement was reached establishing a certain per kilowatt hour price. The contracts also guaranteed the plaintiff a $300 per month saving on its heat, light and power as compared to the corresponding month in the year previous to the switch to electricity. The contracts had a duration of five years with a renewal option of another five years. The required plant installations cost Globe $21,000. The defendant had miscalculated Globe's power requirements; compounding the problem were changes in Globe's production methods that increased electrical consumption. As a result, by February 1911 the defendant had supplied Globe with approximately $60,000 of electricity, had received no money, and owed Globe $11,000 under its guarantee. When the defendant attempted to avoid the contract Globe sued for specific performance. The court refused to enforce the contract but did require that Utica reimbuse Globe for its installation expenses.

When the contracts came up for approval by the respective boards, Maynard introduced the resolution but neither spoke on the matter nor voted. Globe sought to uphold the validity of the contracts on this ground. The court pointed out that the absence of his vote gave the transaction the presumption of propriety but that a challenge to it would lead to a probe beneath its surface. The court remarked that a "dominating influence may be exerted in other ways than by a vote. ... A beneficiary, about to plunge into a ruinous course of dealing, may be betrayed by silence as well as by the spoken word." Maynard had negotiated the contract and had dealt with his subordinates in both companies. The board members knew that he had framed the transaction and, in his presence, they were assured of its justice and equitability. The court characterized the unfairness of the contracts as "startling" and their consequences as "disastrous." In the words of the court:

The mischief consists in this: That the guaranty has not been limited by a statement of the conditions under which the mills are to be run. No matter how large the business, no matter how great the increase in the price of labor or of fuel, no matter what the changes in the nature or the proportion of the products, no matter even though there be extensions of the plant, the defendant has pledged its word that for ten years there will be a saving of $600 a month, $300 for each mill, $7,200 a year. As a result of that pledge it has supplied the plaintiff with electric current for nothing, and owes, if the contract stands, about $11,000 for the privilege. These elements of unfairness Mr. Maynard must have known, if indeed his knowledge be material. He may not have known how great the loss would be. He may have trusted to the superior technical skill of Mr. Greenidge to compute with approximate accuracy the comparative cost of steam and electricity. But he cannot have failed to know that he held a one-sided contract which left the defendant at his mercy. He was not blind to the likelihood that in a term of ten years there would be changes in the business. The swiftness with which some of the changes followed permits the inference that they were premeditated.

In holding the contracts voidable at the election of the defendant, the opinion ended upon the following note:

We hold, therefore, that the refusal to vote does not nullify as of course an influence and predominance exerted without a vote. We hold that the constant duty rests on a trustee to seek no harsh advantage to the detriment of his trust, but rather to protest and renounce if through the blindness of those who treat with him he gains what is unfair. And, because there is evidence that in the making of these contracts that duty was ignored, the power of equity was fittingly exercised to bring them to an end.

While direct regulation of corporations is within the states' domain, a substantial amount of federal legislation interlaces with it. The antitrust, securities, labor and tax laws all bear a significant impact on corporations. Section 8 of the Clayton Act, 15 U.S.C.A. § 19, provides:

No person at the same time shall be a director in any two or more corporations, any one of which has capital, surplus, and undivided profits aggregating more than $1,000,000, engaged in whole or in part in commerce ... if such corporations are or shall have been theretofore, by virtue of their business and location of operations, competitors, so that the elimination of competition by agreement between them would constitute a violation of any of the provisions of any of the antitrust laws.

Notice that the statute does not prohibit: 1) vertical interlocks between a parent and subsidiary or a supplier and a manufacturer; or 2) a circuitous interlock such as: a) Corporation A, a non-competitor, has one of its directors on the board of Corporation B and another on Corporation C, with both B and C being competitors or, b) B and C are competitors and each has one of its directors on the board of A, a non-competitor.

EMPLOYEE-COMPETITOR

The law proscribes an employee from using confidential information for his own benefit. The federal securities laws, § 16(b) and Rule 10-b-5, explicitly forbid the use of such information in certain transactions involving the company's securities. The employee is also barred from passing confidential information to a competitor of the employer. If it is transferred, the employee must pay back any profit he derived and the competitor will be enjoined from further use of the information, in addition to compensating the former employer for damages suffered thereby. The wrong is using the confidential information; it is irrelevant whether or not the corporation sustained damage. Confidential information is just that, *confidential*. It is information that is not readily available to the public. It can take numerous forms including: customer lists, salary information, trade secrets, the marketing strategy for a new product, schematic drawings for new production machinery, etc.

The *Bancroft-Whitney Co.* v. *Glen* case illustrates the wrongful appropriation of confidential corporate information. In the last two cases we shift gears. *Hobbs* v. *United States* defines the shop rights doctrine. *Wellington Print Works Inc.* v. *Magid* illustrates the application of the doctrine. One cannot properly characterize the shop rights doctrine as involving confidential information or fiduciary obligations. It is the employee that has the idea and the skill, but he utilizes the company's time, material, or equipment to bring his idea to fruition. The issue is how to achieve a proper balance between their respective interests in the finished product.

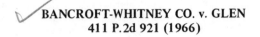

BANCROFT-WHITNEY CO. v. GLEN
411 P.2d 921 (1966)

◆◆◆

MOSK, Justice.

This is an action for breach of fiduciary duty by a corporate officer and for unfair competition.

In July 1961 Glen, while ostensibly serving as president of plaintiff, and defendants Bender and Bender Co. commenced negotiations for the purpose of establishing a western division of Bender Co.

During November 1961, Glen, without resigning or giving notice to plaintiff or its officers, directors, or shareholders, signed a contract with Bender Co. to become president of the contemplated western division, commencing on or about January 1, 1962.

In analyzing the legal principles applicable in this case, it should be repeated that we are not concerned with the simple right of one competitor to offer the employees of another a job at more favorable terms than they presently enjoy or the right of an employee (or an officer of a corporation) to seek a better job. The question here is whether the president of a corporation is liable for the breach of his fiduciary duty because of the conduct described above relating to other employees of the corporation and whether, under these facts, those who hire the employees are guilty of unfair competition for acting in concert with the president.

Corporate officers and directors are not permitted to use their position of trust and confidence to further their private interests.

The mere fact that the officer makes preparations to compete before he resigns his office is not sufficient to constitute a breach of duty. It is the nature of his preparations which is significant.

It is beyond question that a corporate officer breaches his fiduciary duties when, with the purpose of facilitating the recruiting of the corporation's employees by a competitor, he supplies the competitor with a selective list of the corporation's employees who are, in his judgment, possessed of both ability and the personal characteristics desirable in an employee, together with the salary the corporation is paying the employee and a suggestion as to the salary the competitor should offer in order to be successful in recruitment. This conclusion is inescapable even if the information regarding salaries is not deemed to be confidential.

The *Restatement of Agency* provides that the rule prohibiting the disclosure of confidential information by an agent applies "not only to those communications which are stated to be confidential, but also to information which the agent should know his principal would not care to have revealed to others or used in competition with him. It applies to unique business methods of the employer, trade secrets, *lists of names,* and all other matters which are peculiarly known in the employer's business. It does not apply to matters of common knowledge in the community nor to special skill which the employee has acquired because of his employment." (Rest. 2d Agency, § 395, com. b.) The salaries paid by a corporation to its employees are not matters of common knowledge and, even among corporation employees, they are divulged only to those persons or organizations directly concerned with personnel matters or to responsible fiduciaries.

Defendants argue that the salary information is not confidential because the employees could have revealed their own salaries to Bender Co. or anyone else. It requires little talent to distinguish between a situation in which an individual voluntarily discloses his own salary to another and one in which the unpublished salary list of a group of prospective employees is revealed to a competitor for the purpose of facilitating the recruitment of the corporations personnel.

It is clear from the evidence set forth above that Bender was aware of or ratified Glen's breach of his fiduciary duties in all but a few respects, that he cooperated with Glen in the breach, and that he received the benefits of Glen's infidelity. It cannot be said here, as was stated in another context . . . that Bender Co. did not "reap where it has not sown." Under all the circumstances, Bender and Bender Co. must be held liable for their part in Glen's breach of his fiduciary duties. They encouraged the sowing and reaped the benefit. They cannot now disclaim the burden.

◆◆◆

Case Questions

1. Suppose an individual is employed in the tax department of an accounting firm. Over a period of years, because of his exposure to the tax problems of the firm's clients, he becomes an expert in the tax aspects of mergers. May he join a competing firm and put his tax expertise to work for their clients?
2. May an employee, in anticipation of taking a position with another company, solicit the business of his current employer's clients? Upon leaving his old employer, may he accept work from his old clients?
3. If a corporation is contemplating entering a new field or expanding its current geographic territory, is it wiser to build a staff from scratch or raid the personnel of a competitor?

HOBBS v. UNITED STATES
376 F. 2d 488 (1967)

◆◆◆

The classic shop rights doctrine ordains that when an employee makes and reduces to practice an invention on his employer's time, using his employer's tools and services of other employees, the employer is the recipient of an implied, nonexclusive, royalty-free license.

Shop rights generally arise only when there is a direct employer-employee relationship.

At least two considerations underlie the shop rights doctrine. First, it seems only fair that when an employee has used his employer's time and equipment to make an invention, the employer should be able to use the device without paying a royalty. Second, under the doctrine of estoppel if an employee encourages his employer to use an invention, and then stands by and allows him to construct and operate the new device without making any claim for compensation or royalties, it would not be equitable to allow the employee later to assert a claim for royalties or other compensation.

Part of the reasoning behind the first consideration is that the employer is in a position to reward the inventive employee through salary increases, promotions, bonuses and the like.

◆◆◆

WELLINGTON PRINT WORKS, INC. v. MAGID
242 F. Supp. 614 (1965)

◆◆◆

This is an action for a permanent injunction to determine whether the plaintiff, a family-owned corporation, has an ownership interest in inventions or discoveries of the defendant, a member of the family, and a former employee of the plaintiff corporation.

David B. Magid (D. B. Magid) is the father of the defendant, Eugene A. Magid. From 1955 to March 15, 1961, D. B. Magid was the principal and only shareholder of the plaintiff corporation. Eugene A. Magid was President of Wellington Print Works, Inc., (Wellington) from 1955 until March 15, 1961, and D. B. Magid was Secretary-Treasurer during this period.

On March 15, 1961, D. B. Magid became President of Wellington; Eugene was appointed Treasurer, and a younger brother, Robert P. Magid, became Secretary. This arrangement continued until March 21, 1962.

Wellington had been acquired by D. B. Magid in 1949, and he sent the defendant, Eugene A. Magid, to Wellington to be his "eyes" to protect the family's interests. As previously stated, Eugene was President until 1961 with no definitely defined duties except to sign checks, audit purchase orders and settle labor disputes.

While employed at Wellington Eugene A. Magid apparently accounted to no one except his father. He set his own hours, and no one restricted his activities in the plant. Although Eugene was not a technically trained person he began to experiment with techniques for superimposing patterns on particular materials, and also, the laminating of the materials themselves.

During the year 1962, he began to devote considerable time to these experiments. Eugene submitted samples or "patches" of his work to his brother Robert and M. Danson, sales manager of Hartford. He also prepared diagrams of his inventions which reflected Wellington's machines. He also used Wellington's equipment and personnel to conduct his experiments which interrupted the normal assembly line production of the company. The time that he spent in these endeavors was not confined to the daylight hours alone, and he frequently ran samples of the machines during the two later shifts at the Wellington plant.

Initially, no one showed much interest in his samples until it became apparent that Eugene exhibited a natural talent in his inventive work. In fact, D. B. Magid expressed irritation when he was questioned by a son-in-law as to why Eugene was working such long hours. He said that if Eugene would stop playing around with the machines and do the work that he was supposed to perform, he could go home at a decent hour.

Hundreds of samples produced by Eugene were sent to the sales manager of Hartford and many of the new patterns produced by Eugene were sold. Of these numerous samples five particular discoveries which are the subject matter of this suit created great interest in Robert P. Magid. These five inventions had been submitted to Wellington's patent attorney for an opinion as to their patentability. He determined that three of the developments were patentable, and Eugene applied for patents on these discoveries.

In March of 1964, Eugene asked for commissions for the products which he had invented. Prior to this time he had not asked for any additional compensation for his inventive efforts. Robert declined to authorize these commissions and directed Eugene to assign the patent applications on the inventions to Wellington. Eugene refused and on June 23, 1964, Robert P. Magid proffered a contract of employment to Eugene which required him to assign any patent applications to Wellington and that any future inventions would be the property of Wellington.

Eugene then met with D. B. Magid who told him to sign the contract or be fired, and also, that he must assign his patent applications to the plaintiff. Eugene refused to meet these terms, and on July 31, 1964, he was discharged.

The law is clear that absent a contrary understanding the mere existence of an employer-employee relationship does not entitle the employer to ownership of invention of the employee even though the employee uses the time and facilities of the employer. However, if the employee does use his employer's time and facilities, the employer is entitled to a shop right in the invention. Such a shop right passes from the employee to his employer immediately upon the making of the invention by the employee. A shop right is limited to a non-exclusive right in the employer to practice the employee's invention.

The record in this case compels the conclusion that no agreement either express or implied existed between the plaintiff and the defendant, whereby the defendant was obligated to assign his inventions to the plaintiff.

However, we do conclude that because the defendant used his employer's time and facilities in developing these inventions that the plaintiff does have a non-exclusive license to practice them.

432

We reject the defendant's contention that because he experimented primarily on the late shifts that he was working on his own time and not Wellington's. When an employee receives a large salary of $25,000.00 a year and is an officer of a corporation his obligations do not cease at the close of normal business hours. Particularly is this true in a situation where the employer functions 24 hours a day. The method of production employed by Wellington in operating around the clock made the defendant's inventions possible.

◆◆◆

Case Questions

1. Does the shop rights doctrine strike a fair balance between the employee-inventor and the employer?
2. Does the employer's shop right prevent the employee-inventor from granting a license to a competitor of the employer?
3. Would it be wise for a company to offer employment contracts, with a clause assigning all patent rights to the employer, to each of its employees?
4. Would the shop rights doctrine have an application to a university student who makes an important discovery during a chemistry lab experiment? Would it apply to a professor that was using the university laboratory?

REVIEW PROBLEMS

1. Keebler acquires full stock ownership of Meadors. It subsequently sells all its Meadors stock to Atlantic Services, who in turn sells the stock to Flora Mir Distributing Company. The purchase by Atlantic and Flora were financed by Meador's own liquid assets. Certain Meadors' debenture holders now sue Keebler alleging that Keebler owed a fiduciary duty to Meadors' creditors as well as its stockholders when it sold its controlling interests. The holders allege that Keebler violated this duty by not inquiring into Atlantic's purposes behind the purchase. At the time of the sale Keebler knew: 1) No one from Atlantic had experience in the candy business; 2) Atlantic did not inspect the Meadors operation prior to executing the purchase agreement; 3) At the time of the closing only Atlantic's accountant had examined Meadors to any extent and his primary interest was in the books and inventory; 4) An outsider could not accept Meadors' profit at face value because it had no market of its own; 5) Prior to the closing, Atlantic failed to negotiate with Meadors' key employees about continuing the business. Keebler acknowledges that Atlantic looted Meadors with dispatch but argues that it must have had knowledge of the intended looting to be held liable therefor. The debenture holders argue that Keebler knew sufficient suspicious circumstances that it had the duty to investigate the prospective purchaser. What decision? [*Swinney* v. *Keebler Co.*, 329 F. Supp. 216 (1971)].

2. Lincoln Stores operated retail department stores in fourteen cities scattered throughout several states. One store was located in Norwich, Conn. The store was successful although it lacked sufficient space. Acquisition of additional space was frequently discussed although in 1932 the corporation declined to exercise an option for leasing added space in the same building. It was decided that the extra sales would be outweighed by the lease expenses. Expansion was not thereafter considered until 1938. In April 1937 the Reid

& Hughes department store in Norwich was put up for sale. It was on the same side of the street as the Lincoln Store and ninety feet distant but afforded it slight competition. Grant, Martin and Haley secretly purchase it; all three were employed by Lincoln Stores. Grant and Martin were directors. Martin was the general manager of all the stores. Grant managed one store and supervised two others. Haley was a buyer. Shortly after the purchase Haley resigned to take over the Reid & Hughes store. Grant and Martin concealed their ownership interests while continuing in the employ of Lincoln Stores. The three had various meetings in several states concerning the purchase and billed their travelling expenses to the corporation. To ascertain the inventory and capital requirements of their new store, Grant used certain of the company's confidential information. The knowledge and experience they acquired in working for Lincoln Stores would be directly used in the operation of Reid & Hughes. In June 1937 Grant and Martin were discharged as employees and directors. Lincoln Stores seeks an injunction to enjoin Grant, Martin and Haley from operating the competing store and from using information they acquired as employees. It also seeks an accounting to determine the amount of the damages it sustained through their alleged illegal activities. Later they added a petition to have a constructive trust declared upon the shares owned by Grant, Martin and Haley. What, if any, relief should be granted Lincoln Stores? [*Lincoln Stores* v. *Grant*, 34 N.E. 2d 704 (1941)]. *Lincoln can collect wages & TE paid for*

3. Seagrave Corp. proposes to merge with Fyr-Fyter Co. by purchasing all of its common stock. As part of the overall plan Wetzel, who owns Post, Inc., that in turn owns Fyr-Fyter, contracts with about thirty Seagrave shareholders to purchase 35,000 shares at 20 dollars per share. This price is 5 dollars or more per share than is available on the open market. This stock purchase is conditioned upon the consummation of the merger and the delivery by the seller-stockholders of the written resignations of four Seagrave directors to Wetzel on the closing date. Seagrave had a seven person board of directors. The selling shareholders had working control of Seagrave and elected four members of the board. Two of the selling shareholders were themselves directors. This seller stockholder group is called the Wilkes group. The remaining three directors, called the Spain group, were also officers of Seagrave and constituted its active management. The two directors groups strongly oppose each other and the resignations of the Spain group are probable if the Wilkes group continues to dominate the board. The Spain group desires to get rid of the Wilkes group. It was Wetzel's stated intention to make no substantial changes in the operating management of Seagrave. Actually, Wetzel did not need to purchase any stock from the selling stockholders to gain a majority of Seagrave's voting stock. Minority shareholders bring a derivative suit to halt the proposed merger. They contend that the directors have placed themselves in a position of conflict of interest between their fiduciary obligation and their own private interests. Should the merger be enjoined? [*Seagrave Corp.* v *Mount*, 212 F.2d 389 (1954)]. *yes*

4. Duane Jones Co. is an advertising company. The founder, Duane Jones, was the majority stockholder. In 1951 trouble arose within the company resulting in several resignations and the loss of several large advertising accounts. The company did not have employment contracts with its employees nor was it under contract to its advertising clients. A group of directors, officers and employees decided to make an attempt to buy out Duane Jones. During June 1951 they told Jones that if he would not sell, they would leave en masse and some of the accounts had already agreed to shift their work. Under this pressure Jones agreed but he never completed the transaction. In August

1951 the board discharged most of this employee group. They then formed their own advertising agency, Scheideler, Beck and Werner, Inc., which began business during September. In less than two months in excess of 50 percent of the Duane Jones Co. employees joined the new firm. A number of important advertising accounts also shifted. The new agency invited some former Duane Jones Co. accounts to make the shift. Duane Jones Co. brings suit seeking monetary damages. It alleges that the former employees breached their fiduciary duties of utmost good faith and loyalty. It argues that the defendants, while employees, determined upon a course of conduct which, when carried out, resulted in benefit to themselves through destruction of the Duane Jones Co. business. Defendants contend that they were fired and did not complete until after their discharge. They also argue that the advertising accounts had no contractual obligation to remain with Duane Jones Co. and were free to shift. How should this case be decided? [*Duane Jones Co.* v *Burke,* 117 N.E. 2d 237 (1954)].

Duane Jones wins

The way an employee goes & what he takes with him of a confidential nature

ALTERING THE CORPORATE STRUCTURE AND DISSOLUTION

We have observed that the directors have the exclusive authority to manage the business and affairs of a corporation. However, certain fundamental changes in the corporate structure, i.e., mergers, consolidations, the sale or lease of virtually all the corporate assets, amendments to the articles, and dissolution require shareholder approval. Depending upon the jurisdiction involved, such action usually will require either a simple majority or a two-thirds vote of the voting shares outstanding. Thus, the shareholders have veto power over any proposed plan that would alter the basic nature of the present corporation.

Actions affecting the fundamental nature of the corporation may be subject to a complex variety of rules of law. If shareholder approval is required, then one must conform, not only to the state's business corporation act, but also to the federal rules on proxy solicitation. If the transaction is to be consummated through the purchase of securities, it may be necessary to comply with the '34 Act's tender offer provisions. Insiders must be careful that their activities do not violate Section 16(b) or Rule 10b-5. One must be aware of the potential antitrust repercussions inherent in a corporate acquisition. There are the technical accounting aspects that must be surmounted. Finally, there are those inevitable tax consequences to be faced. The corporations and their respective shareholders may well desire that reorganization qualify as "tax free" under the Internal Revenue Code of 1954. The parties involved can avoid federal tax liability if the reorganization is: 1) a statutory merger; 2) a statutory consolidation; 3) achieved by an exchange of stock and a minimum of 80% of the stock of each class of the one corporation is acquired by the other; 4) a sale of assets for the shares of the corporation that is to survive. Occasionally the parties may desire, or be unable to avoid, a taxable reorganization with its resulting gains or losses. The typical cash tender offer is a common example. Also, one who ignores the state tax consequences of a reorganization does so at his own peril.

AMENDING THE ARTICLES

From time to time a corporation may wish to amend its articles of incorporation. It may do so in any and as many respects as may be desired. However, the amendments can contain only such provisions as might be lawfully contained in original articles of incorporation made at the time of making such amendments. Section 53 of the Illinois business corporation act sets forth the typical amendment procedure. It requires that the board of directors adopt a resolution setting forth the proposed amendment and directing that it be submitted to a vote of the shareholders at either an annual or special meeting. Written or printed notice setting forth the proposed amendment or a summary of the changes to be effected thereby must be given to each shareholder of record entitled to vote at the meeting. To be adopted the proposed amendment must receive the affirmative vote of the holders of at least two-thirds of the outstanding shares entitled to vote at such meeting. If any class of shares is entitled to vote as a class, the proposed amendment must receive the affirmative vote of the holders of at least two-thirds of the outstanding shares of each class of shares entitled to vote as a class and two-thirds of the total outstanding shares entitled to vote at the meeting.

Section 54 of the Illinois statute provides that holders of outstanding shares of a class shall be entitled to vote as a class if the proposed amendment would:

(a) Increase or decrease the aggregate number of authorized shares of such class.

(b) Increase or decrease the par value of the shares of such class.

(c) Effect an exchange, reclassification, or cancellation of all or part of the shares of such class.

(d) Change the designations, preferences, qualifications, limitations, restrictions, or special or relative rights of the shares of such class.

(e) In the case of a preferred or special class of shares, divide the shares of such class into series and fix and determine the designation of such series and the variations in the relative rights and preferences between the shares of such series.

(f) Change the shares of such class, whether with or without par value, into the same or a different number of shares, either with or without par value, of the same class or another class or classes.

(g) Create a right of exchange, of all or any part of the shares of another class into the shares of such class.

(h) Create a new class of shares having rights and preferences prior and superior to the shares of such class, or increase the rights and preferences of any class having rights and preferences prior or superior to the shares of such class.

(i) Limit or deny the existing preemptive rights of the shares of such class.

(j) Cancel or otherwise affect dividends on the shares of such class which had accrued but had not been declared.

The holders of the outstanding shares of a class shall not be entitled to vote as a class upon a proposed amendment if such class is divided into series, and the proposed amendment would change the designations, preferences, qualifications, restrictions or special or relative rights of one or more but not all of such series. In such event, the holders of the outstanding shares of any series to be changed by the proposed amendment shall be entitled to vote as a class thereon.

After the amendments have received shareholder approval, they are to be executed in duplicate and vertified by the president or a vice-president, and the secretary is to affix the corporate seal. Both copies are to be delivered to the Secretary of State. If he finds that they conform to the law, and if all franchise taxes, fees and charges have been paid, the Secretary will file them and affix a certificate of amendment. The original will be retained in his office and the duplicate returned to the corporation.

MERGER, CONSOLIDATION AND SALE OF ASSETS

The mechanical process involved in a merger, consolidation, sale, lease, exchange, mortgage, or other disposition of all, or substantially all, the corporate assets, other than in the regular course of business, is for the board of directors to adopt a resolution approving the transaction followed by a vote of the shareholders. In Illinois §§ 64, 72 require the approval of at least two-thirds of the outstanding shares while Delaware, § 271, requires only the approval by a majority of the outstanding stock.

A merger differs from a consolidation. In a statutory merger, corporation A and corporation B are combined. Corporation A will cease to exist while corporation B, the surviving corporation, will continue in operation. In a statutory consolidation both A and B will cease to exist and will be replaced by a new corporation C. In either a merger or consolidation, the surviving, or new corporation, will take title to all the assets and be responsible for all the liabilities of the constituent corporations. (See § 69 of the Illinois statute.) When a corporation sells all of its assets in a bona fide transaction, the purchaser is not liable for the debts of the corporate seller. However, there are four exceptions to this general rule: 1) where the purchaser expressly or impliedly agrees to assume such debts; 2) where the transaction is really a consolidation or a merger; 3) when the purchasing corporation is merely a continuation of the selling corporation; and 4) where the transaction was fraudulently made in order to escape liability for such debts. [*Lamb v. Leroy Corp.*, 454 P. 2d 24 (1969)]. Caveat: a sale of assets may require compliance with the Uniform Commercial Code's Article 6 Bulk Transfer provisions.

Naturally, mergers, consolidations, or sale of assets do not exhaust the list of possible forms of corporate structural changes. The methods available to combine, expand or contract the corporate structure are only limited by man's imagination and ingenuity.

It is not unexpected that a shareholder may oppose the merger or consolidation. Despite his opposition, the corporate reorganization may be approved. Is his position now untenable; will he be forced to remain an owner of a corporation that he opposes? What is he to do if he is in a close corporation that has no market for its shares? In order to protect the interests of such a shareholder the business corporation statutes contain a *dissent and appriasal remedy*. If the shareholder complies with the statutory requirements the surviving corporation must purchase his shares.

The New York Business Corporation Law, § 806 provides:

(b)The following provisions shall apply to amendments and changes . . .

(6)A holder of any adversely affected shares who does not vote for or consent in writing to the taking of such action shall, subject to and by complying with the provisions of section 623 (Procedure to enforce shareholder's right to receive payment for shares), have the right to dissent and to receive payment for such shares, if the certificate of amendment (A) alters or abolishes any preferential right of such shares having preferences; or (B) creates, alters or abolishes any provision or right in respect of the redemption of such shares or any sinking fund for the redemption or purchase of such shares; or (C) alters or abolishes any preemptive right of such holder to acquire shares or other securities; or (D) excludes or limits the right of such holder to vote on any matter, except as such right may be limited by the voting rights given to new shares then being authorized of any existing or new class.

The Delaware General Corporation Law, § 262 provides:

(b)The corporation surviving or resulting from any merger or consolidation shall within 10 days after the effective date of the merger or consolidation, notify each stockholder of any corporation of this State so merging or consolidating who objected in writing and whose shares either were not entitled to vote or were not voted in favor of the merger or consolidation, and who filed such written objection with the corporation before the taking of the vote on the merger or consolidation, that the merger or consolidation has become effective. ... If any such stockholder shall within 20 days after the date of mailing of the notice demand in writing, from the corporation surviving or resulting from the merger or consolidation, payment of the value of his stock, the surviving or resulting corporation shall, within 30 days after the expiration of the period of 20 days, pay to him the value of his stock on the effective date of the merger or consolidation, exclusive of any element of value arising from the expectation or accomplishment of the merger or consolidation.

(k)This section shall not apply to the shares of any class or series of a class of stock, which, ... were either listed on a national securities exchange, or held of record by more than 2,000 stockholders, unless the certificate of incorporation of the corporation issuing such stock shall otherwise provide; nor shall this section apply to any of the shares of stock of the constituent corporation surviving a merger if the merger did not require for its approval the vote of the stockholders of the surviving corporation, as provided in subsection (f) of § 251 of this title. This subsection shall not be applicable to shares of any class or series of a class of stock of a constituent corporation if under the terms of a merger or consolidation ... the holders thereof are required to accept for such stock anything except (1) shares of stock or shares of stock and cash in lieu of fractional shares of the corporation surviving or resulting from such merger or consolidation; or (2) shares of stock or shares of stock and cash in lieu of fractional shares of any other corporation, which ... will be either listed on a national securities exchange or held of record by more than 2,000 stockholders; or a combination of shares of stock or shares of stock and cash in lieu of fractional shares as set forth in (1) and (2) of this subsection.

Delineating a merger or consolidation from a sale of assets is not necessarily an easy matter. Lawyers and accountants have used their ingenuity to develop hybrid forms that are advantageous under a given set of circumstances. The *Farris* v. *Glen Alden* case that follows illustrates the legal complexities inherent in such situations.

FARRIS v. GLEN ALDEN CORPORATION
393 Pa. 427; 143 A. 2d 25 (1958)

◆ ◆ ◆

COHEN, Justice.

We are required to determine on this appeal whether, as a result of a "Reorganization Agreement" executed by the officers of Glen Alden Corporation and List Industries Corporation, and approved by the shareholders of the former company, the rights and remedies of a dissenting shareholder accrue to the plaintiff.

Glen Alden is a Pennsylvania corporation engaged principally in the mining of anthracite coal and lately in the manufacture of air conditioning units and fire-fighting equipment. In recent years the company's operating revenue has declined substantially, and in fact, its coal operations have resulted in tax loss carryovers of approximately $14,000,000. In October 1957, List, a Delaware holding company owning interests in motion picture theaters, textile companies and real estate, and to a lesser extent, in oil and gas operations, warehouses and aluminum piston manufacturing, purchased through a wholly owned subsidiary 38.5 percent of Glen Alden's stock. This acquisition enabled List to place three of its directors on the Glen Alden board.

On March 20, 1958, the two corporations entered into a "reorganization agreement," subject to stockholder approval, which contemplated the following actions:

1. Glen Alden is to acquire all of the assets of List, excepting a small amount of cash reserved for the payment of List's expenses in connection with the transaction. These assets include over $8,000,000 in cash held chiefly in the treasuries of List's wholly owned subsidieries.

2. In consideration of the transfer, Glen Alden is to issue 3,621,703 shares of stock to List. List in turn is to distribute the stock to its shareholders at a ratio of five shares of Glen Alden stock for each six shares of List stock. In order to accomplish the necessary distribution, Glen Alden is to increase the authorized number of its shares of capital stock from 2,500,000 shares to 7,500,000 shares without according pre-emptive rights to the present shareholders upon the issuance of any such shares.

3. Further, Glen Alden is to assume all of List's liabilities including a $5,000,000 note incurred by List in order to purchase Glen Alden stock in 1957, outstanding stock options, incentive stock options plans, and pension obligations.

4. Glen Alden is to change its corporate name from Glen Alden Corporation to List Alden Corporation.

5. The present directors of both corporations are to become directors of List Alden.

6. List is to be dissolved and List Alden is to then carry on the operations of both former corporations.

Two days after the agreement was executed notice of the annual meeting of Glen Alden to be held on April 11, 1958, was mailed to the shareholders together with a proxy statement analyzing the reorganization agreement and recommending its approval as well as approval of certain amendments to Glen Alden's articles of incorporation and bylaws necessary to implement the agreement. At this meeting the holders of a majority of the outstanding shares, (not including those owned by List), voted in favor of a resolution approving the reorganization agreement.

On the day of the shareholders' meeting, plaintiff, a shareholder of Glen Alden, filed a complaint in equity against the corporation and its officers seeking to enjoin them temporarily until final hearing, and perpetually thereafter, from executing and carrying out the agreement.

The gravamen of the complaint was that the notice of the annual shareholders' meeting did not conform to the requirements of the Business Corporation Law, 15 P.S. § 2852-1 et seq., in three respects: 1) It did not give notice to the shareholders that the true intent and purpose of the meeting was to effect a merger or consolidation of Glen Alden and List; 2) It failed to give notice to the shareholders of their right to dissent to the plan of merger or consolidation and claim fair value for their shares, and 3) It did not contain copies of the text of certain sections of the Business Corporation Law as required.[1]

By reason of these omissions, plaintiff contended that the approval of the reorganization agreement by the shareholders at the annual meeting was invalid and unless the carrying out of the plan were enjoined, he would suffer irreparable loss by being deprived of substantial property rights.

The defendants answered admitting the material allegations of fact in the complaint but denying that they gave rise to a cause of action because the transaction complained of was a purchase of corporate assets as to which shareholders had no rights of dissent or appraisal. For these reasons the defendants then moved for judgment of the pleadings.[2]

The court below concluded that the reorganization agreement entered into between the two corporations was a plan for a *de facto* merger and that therefore the failure of the notice of the annual meeting to conform to the pertinent requirements of the merger provisions of the Business Corporation Law rendered the notice defective and all proceedings in furtherance of the agreement void. Wherefore, the court entered a final decree denying defendant's motion for judgment on the pleadings, entering judgment upon plaintiff's complaint and granting the injunctive relief therein sought. This appeal followed.

When use of the corporate form of business organization first became widespread, it was relatively easy for courts to define a "merger" or a "sale of assets" and to label a particular transaction as one or the other. ... But prompted by the desire to avoid the impact of adverse, and to obtain the benefits of favorable, government regulations, particularly federal tax laws, new accounting and legal techniques were developed by lawyers and accountants which interwove the elements characteristic of each, thereby creating hybrid forms of corporate amalgamation. Thus, it is no longer helpful to consider an individual transaction in the abstract and solely by reference to the various elements therein determine whether it is a "merger" or a "sale." Instead, to determine properly the nature of a corporate transaction, we must refer not only to all the provisions of the agreement, but also to the consequences of the transaction and to the purposes of the provisions of the corporation law said to be applicable. We shall apply this principle to the instant case.

Section 908, subd. A of the Pennsylvania Business Corporation Law provides: "If any shareholder of a domestic corporation which becomes a party to a plan of merger or consolidation shall object to such plan of merger or consolidation * * * such shareholder shall be entitled to * * * (the fair value of his shares upon surrender of the share certificate or certificates representing his shares)." ...

---

[1] The proxy statement included the following declaration: "Appraisal Rights. In the opinion of counsel, the shareholders of neither Glen Alden nor List Industries will have any rights of appraisal or similar rights of dissenters with respect to any matter to be acted upon at their respective meetings."

[2] Counsel for the defendants concedes that if the corporation is required to pay the dissenting shareholders the appraised fair value of their shares, the resultant drain of cash would prevent Glen Alden from carrying out the agreement. On the other hand, plaintiff contends that if the shareholders had been told of their rights as dissenters, rather than specifically advised that they had no such rights, the resolution approving the reorganization agreement would have been defeated.

The rationale . . . of the present section of the Business Corporation Law . . . is that when a corporation combines with another so as to lose its essential nature and alter the original fundamental relationships of the shareholders among themselves and to the corporation, a shareholder who does not wish to continue his membership therein may treat his membership in the original corporation as terminated and have the value of his shares paid to him. . . .

Does the combination outlined in the present "reorganization" agreement so fundamentally change the corporate character of Glen Alden and the interest of the plaintiff as a shareholder therein, that to refuse him the rights and remedies of a dissenting shareholder would in reality force him to give up his stock in one corporation and against his will accept shares in another? If so, the combination is a merger within the meaning of section 908, subd. A of the corporation law. . . .

If the reorganization agreement were consummated plaintiff would find that the "List Alden" resulting from the amalgamation would be quite a different corporation than the "Glen Alden" in which he is now a shareholder. Instead of continuing primarily as a coal mining company, Glen Alden would be transformed, after amendment of its articles of incorporation, into a diversified holding company whose interests would range from motion picture theaters to textile companies, Plaintiff would find himself a member of a company with assets of $169,000,000 and a long-term debt of $38,000,000 in lieu of a company one-half that size and with but one-seventh the long-term debt.

As an aftermath of the transaction plaintiff's porportionate interest in Glen Alden would have been reduced to only two-fifths of what it presently is because of the issuance of an additional 3,621,703 shares to List which would not be subject to pre-emptive rights. In fact, ownership of Glen Alden would pass to the stockholders of List who would hold 76.5 percent of the outstanding shares as compared with but 23.5 percent retained by the present Glen Alden shareholders.

Perhaps the most important consequence to the plaintiff, if he were denied the right to have his shares redeemed at their fair value, would be the serious financial loss suffered upon consummation of the agreement. While the present book value of his stock is $38 a share after combination it would be worth only $21 a share. In contrast, the shareholders of List who presently hold stock with a total book value of $33,000,000 or $7.50 a share, would receive stock with a book value of $76,000,000 or $21 a share.

Under these circumstances it may well be said that if the proposed combination is allowed to take place with right of dissent, plaintiff would have his stock in Glen Alden taken away from him and the stock of a new company thrust upon him in its place. He would be projected against his will into a new enterprise under terms not of his own choosing. It was to protect dissident shareholders against just such a result that . . . the legislature . . . in section 908, subd. A, granted the right of dissent. And it is to accord that protection to the plaintiff that we conclude that the combination proposed in the case at hand is a merger within the intendment of section 908, subd. A.

We hold that the combination contemplated by the reorganization agreement, although consummated by contract rather than in accordance with the statutory procedure, is a merger within the protective purview of sections 908, subd. A and 515 of the corporation law. The shareholders of Glen Alden should have been notified accordingly and advised of their statutory rights of dissent and appraisal. The failure of the corporate officers to take these steps renders the stockholder approval of the agreement at the 1958 shareholders' meeting invalid. The lower court did not err in enjoining the officers and directors of Glen Alden from carrying out this agreement.

Decree affirmed at appellants' cost.

◆◆◆

Case Questions

1. How can fair value be ascertained when the shares involved are in a close corporation and are not publicly traded on an exchange? What if the shares in a publicly traded corporation are selling below book value because of a severely depressed stock market?
2. Would the rationale underlying a stockholder's right of dissent or appraisal in a merger or consolidation be equally applicable in a purchase of corporate assets?
3. Could the directors of Glen Alden and List have purposely characterized the arrangement as a purchase of assets in an effort to avoid the dissent and appraisal right?
4. Was this a "de facto" merger?
5. It is possible for a minority shareholder, through the successful assertion of his right of dissent, to frustrate a corporate merger when he would be unable to do so in a stockholder's vote. Does this fact open the dissent and appraisal remedy to valid criticism?

Case Comments

The Pennsylvania legislature indicated their agreement with the court ruling in *Farris* v. *Glen Alden* by codifying its result. Pa. Stat. Ann Title 15 section 1311 (F) (1968) provides as follows:

> The shareholders of a business corporation which acquires by purchase, lease or exchange all or substantially all of the property of another corporation by the issuance of shares . . . shall be entitled to the rights and remedies of dissenting shareholders . . . if, but only if, such acquisition shall have been accomplished by the issuance of voting shares of such corporation to be outstanding immediately after the acquisition sufficient to elect a majority of the directors of the corporation.

SHORT FORM MERGERS

Some jurisdictions provide a shortcut method of merging when the merger involves a parent and subsidiary corporations. Section 253 of the Delaware General Corporation Law is a good illustration. Under its provisions, if at least 90 percent of the outstanding shares of each class of the stock of a corporation is owned by another corporation, all that is required for a merger is approval by the boards of directors. No vote by the shareholders is necessary; although they do retain their right of dissent and appraisal. These short form merger statutes are designed to give the parent corporation a means of eliminating the minority stockholders' interest in the enterprise. [See *Stauffer* v. *Standard Brands,* 187 A.2d 78 (Del.)]. If the parent so desires, it may permit the minority to remain in the resultant going enterprise; or it may elect to force them out by paying them the value of their shareholdings.

THE APPRAISAL PROCESS

If the objecting shareholder and the corporation are unable to agree upon the value of the stock, either may petition the court for the appointment of an appraiser to determine its value. Notice that Delaware has adopted an unusual position in § 262(k) by declaring the appraisal remedy inapplicable to shares in certain publicly held corporations. Under § 262(h) the Delaware courts have discretion to tax the appraisal costs, exclusive of attorneys' fees, upon one or both of the parties. Such power exerts pressure on the parties to make, and alternatively to accept, a reasonable offer for the shares.

The next case illustrates the difficult process of arriving at a valuation for the stock.

APPLICATION OF DELAWARE RACING ASSOCIATION
213 A.2d 203 (S. Ct. Del. 1965)

♦♦♦

WOLCOTT, Chief Justice.

This is an appeal by stockholders of Delaware Steeplechase and Race Association (Steeplechase) from a judgment of the Vice Chancellor in an appraisal proceeding fixing the value of the Steeplechase stock.

Delaware Racing Association (Racing) filed a petition for an appraisal of the value of Steeplechase shares. Steeplechase, on July 31, 1963, under the provisions of 8 Del.C., § 253, had been merged into Racing. Stockholders of Steeplechase owning 77 common shares of the 1519 outstanding were determined to be entitled to an appraisal. The Vice Chancellor appointed an Appraiser who submitted a final report fixing the per share value of Steeplechase stock at $3,472.90. To this report both Racing and the stockholders filed exceptions. The Vice Chancellor fixed the per share value of Steeplechase at $2,321.30. This appeal followed.

A brief summary of the factual background is required. Steeplechase, between 1937 and July 31, 1963, owned and operated, with the exception of 1943, Delaware Park near Stanton, Delaware, a track for thoroughbred horse racing. On-track parimutuel betting was carried on with a percentage of the pool going to the State in the form of a tax, and a percentage of the pool going to Steeplechase in the form of earnings. ... Authority to control the carrying on of horse racing for stakes or purses was granted to the Delaware Racing Commission. ...

The Commission, by statute, is further authorized to allow a licensee out of net revenue a sum not in excess of 4 percent of its "capital investment" as return on such investment. It is further required that all of the net revenue in excess of the 4 percent return on investment be set aside by the licensee for the retirement of debt and preferred stock, and for the maintenance of plant and purses, stakes and awards. . . .

Steeplechase was organized and licensed and by 1938 had invested approximately $1,170.000 in fixed assets, of which only $15,190.000 was supplied by the paid-in value of 1519 issued shares of $10 par common stock. The balance of the money invested by Steeplechase came from an issue of debentures and an issue of preferred stock. By 1945 the entire debenture issue had been redeemed, and by 1953 all of the preferred stock had been retired out of earnings, leaving as the sole corporate security outstanding 1519 shares of common stock. Meanwhile, from 1938 to July 31, 1963, the original investment of $1,170,000 in fixed assets had increased to $8,741,000.00. This increase had been financed out of earnings.

Since the inception of the racing enterprise, Steeplechase has paid no dividends on its common stock. It paid stated dividends on its preferred stock, retired since 1953. No dividends have been paid on the common stock by reason of the described statutory restrictions, restrictions imposed by the Racing Commission, limitations prescribed in loan agreements for the expansion of Steeplechase's facilities, and, finally, by reason of the policy of the promoters and managers to plow back all earnings for the constant betterment of racing facilities and the improvement of thoroughbred racing. This management policy has long been known to the public.

In April, 1962, William duPont, a director and large stockholder of Steeplechase, made an offer to all of Steeplechase's common stockholders to join with him in giving their shares to Delaware Park, Inc., a charitable corporation and sole owner of Racing, or, in the alternative, to sell their shares to him at a price of $1,530 per share, in which event he undertook to give such shares to Delaware Park, Inc. His offer was based upon an appraisal of Steeplechase stock made by Standard Research Consultants which fixed the fair market value of Steeplechase common stock as of December 31, 1962 at $1,530 per share. A summary of the appraisal report accompanied Mr. duPont's offer.

As a result of this offer a total of 1390 shares of Steeplechase was acquired by Delaware Park, Inc., either as a gift from Mr. duPont or as gifts from other registered shareholders of Steeplechase.

Delaware Park, Inc., thereupon, as the owner in excess of 90 percent of the shares of Steeplechase, caused Steeplechase to be merged into Racing pursuant to 8 Del.C., § 253, the short-form merger statute. . . .

[Omitted is the court's discussion of its scope of review and how value is to be measured. It held that the measurement of value is the same in both a short form and a long form merger. It said the shareholders are entitled to be paid the intrinsic value of their shares determined on a going concern basis, which excludes a valuation based solely upon the liquidating value, or an aliquot share in the value of the merged corporation.]

Asset Value

Both the Appraiser and the Vice Chancellor made findings as to the value of the assets of Steeplechase. The stockholders accept these findings as to the value of the assets of Steeplechase. The stockholders accept these findings but object to the deduction from the total asset value of 27 percent for obsolescence, to the refusal to include in the asset valuation a figure representing construction in progress and leasehold improvements, and to the deduction of a figure representing demolition costs from the value of the land.

Obsolescence

Delaware Park, the racing plant of Steeplechase, was built in 1937 when most of the patrons of the track arrived by railroad. At this time Delaware Park was favorably situated in close proximity to the tracks of the Pennsylvania and B. & O. Railroads. The establishment was laid out to take advantage of this then fortunate situation.

However, following the War, the pattern of transportation changed. Most, if not the greatly larger number of patrons now come to the track by automobile. The change in patron transportation habits was unfortunate from the point of view of Delaware Park. It now finds itself hemmed in by the railroad tracks which formerly served it so well.

Of primary concern are traffic and parking problems occasioned by the fact that the main entrance to the track for vehicular traffic is now an entrance across the racing oval from the grandstand and clubhouse. This causes traffic flow inside the park where none or little had been encountered before. In addition, the close proximity of the tracks to the rear of the grandstand has prevented the expansion of it to give more required space to accommodate the wagering public and for pari-mutuel ticket and money-handling problems. In addition, the change in traffic patterns has created problems in the supplying of facilities for animals and employees at the track.

The Appraiser found these items to be incurable functional and economic obsolescence, and concluded that a deduction for such obsolescence should be made. He concluded to apply the "age-life" method in order to determine what this deduction should be. This is one of the methods generally accepted for such purpose. The Appriasal of Real Estate, 212-213, 217-219.

The Appraiser's rationale in determining the percentage factor to be applied to determine obsolescence was that the racing facility had a life expectancy of 33 1/3 years which meant an age-life rate of 3 percent per year. He concluded that 1 percent of this was attributable to combined functional and economic obsolescence. Since the plant had been in existence for 27 years, he applied a 27 percent rate to the entire installation as an operational whole. This finding was approved by the Vice Chancellor.

The stockholders do not argue that no deduction should be made for obsolescence. They say, however, that the rate applied was far too high; that the rate should have been perhaps not more than 2 percent, and that in any event it should not have been applied in addition to depreciation to "equipment and personal property" and to the "newly refurbished clubhouse." They say that obsolescence is applicable only to the clubhouse and grandstand, and perhaps to the former main parking lot on Kirkwood Highway, not used at present to its former extent by reason of the change in transportation patterns.

We think, however, the stockholders misconceive what it was the Appraiser and the Vice Chancellor did. They concluded, and properly so we think upon this record, that the functional layout of Delaware Park was obsolete to a substantial degree because of the changes in the habits of the betting public, and because of the physical inability to adapt existing facilities to serve the public more efficiently.

This being so, they applied the obsolescence rate to the value of the plant as a whole, not to individual items as the stockholders would have them do. In so doing, we think they were correct for the test of the modernity of any facility to serve the public is its ability to do the job. If, by reason of the passage of time and the change of public habits, a racing plant, originally well designed for the purpose, has become less efficient to serve the purpose for which it is used, it has to some extent at least become obsolete as a whole — not merely the separate installations which together go to make up the whole plant.

We therefore affirm the ruling of the Appraiser and the Vice Chancellor that an obsolescence rate must be applied to the depreciated value of Steeplechase's racing plant as a whole. What that rate should be is a matter of judgment. The rate of 27 percent was determined in accordance with accepted theories and, in the judgment of both the Appraiser and Vice Chancellor, was proper. Since it is apparent that it was not arbitrarily determined, we will not disturb it.

We affirm the application of an obsolescence rate of 27 percent to the asset value of Steeplechase.

Construction in Progress and Leasehold Improvements

The stockholders object to the refusal of the Appraiser and the Vice Chancellor to include specifically in the assets of Steeplechase the sum of $192,607.00 which, apparently, was money paid for steel for future construction and for architects' fees. The difficulty with the argument made with respect to this is that at the hearing before him the Appraiser invited the stockholders to produce proof that the items in question were not included by the Appraiser in Current Assets as Deferred Charges. No such proof was offered and we think, therefore, the argument falls.

Deduction of Demolition Cost

The real estate appraiser for Steeplechase testified that the best possible use for its land was for residential purposes. The stockholders on the other hand produced witnesses who testified that probably the land would be used for industrial purposes and put a much higher value upon it. However, the Appraiser and the Vice Chancellor accepted the valuation of $2,754,000.00 based upon residential use as the more justified. The stockholders in this appeal do not take exception to this valuation.

They do, however, argue that it was improper to deduct from that valuation the sum of $457,000.00 representing the cost of demolition of existing structures in order to make the land available for residential use. They do not object to the amount estimated for demolition cost, but do object to any deduction at all for that purpose.

We think the stockholders are wrong. The land in question is being used, not for residential purposes, but for a racing plant. Since residential use is conceded to be the best possible use, presumably the land would be more valuable for that purpose than for any other. Accordingly, a different use would necessarily discount the value of the land. Furthermore, it seems quite obvious to us that if the land were to be sold for residential use the purchaser in fixing the amount he was willing to pay would take into consideration the cost of demolishing existing structures in order to devote the land to the use intended.

It should be remembered, furthermore, that the value of the land to Steeplechase is its value as the location of a racing plant. Since we are concerned with a going concern value, we think the land value should reflect its value with respect to that going concern, and not with respect to a theoretical use. We accordingly affirm the deduction from land value of the cost of demolition of existing structures.

Market Value

The stockholders object to the Appraiser's finding, based upon the duPont offer to Steeplechase stockholders, of a market value of $1,530.00. They also object to the Vice Chancellor's use of the figure of $1,305.00 on the basis of a subsequent appraisal some year and a half after the fixing of the higher figure but reflecting the 1962 and 1963 earnings of Steeplechase. The stockholders take the position that there was no established market for Steeplechase shares and that the trading in the stock was so thin that none could be constructed.

It is, of course, axiomatic that if there is an established market for shares of a corporation the market value of such shares must be taken into consideration in an appraisal of their intrinsic value. *Chicago Corporation* v. *Munds,* 20 Del.Ch. 142, 172A. 452. And if there is no reliable established market value for the shares a reconstructed market value, if one can be made, must be given consideration. *Tri-Continental Corp.* v. *Battye, supra.* It is, of course, equally axiomatic that market value, either actual or constructed, is not the sole element to be taken into consideration in the appraisal of stock.

The argument of the stockholders, we think, does not dispute this. They argue that market value is not an element to be considered in this appraisal because no reliable market existed, and none could be constructed.

The Appraiser found a market in the duPont offer to purchase Steeplechase shares at $1,530 and gave effect to this value in his ultimate appraisal. The stockholders attack this finding, citing in support *Sporborg* v. *City Specialty Stores,* 35 Del.Ch. 560, 123 A.2d 121. That case, however, is not apposite. It dealt with a situation in which a controlling stockholder for a period of almost two years prior to the merger had maintained a market in the stock. The use of a value based upon such an artificially maintained market was rejected because it was a market made only by one party in interest and which, consequently, was maintained at an artificially high level.

This is not the fact with respect to the duPont offer. He was not the controlling stockholder of Steeplechase. His offer was made, not on the basis of a socalled market figure, but was based on the true value of the stock as determined by a very exhaustive appraisal made by an independent appraiser. Under the circumstances, we think, a market value was established by the sale or gift of over 93 percent of Steeplechase stock over less than two years at a value of $1,530. Consequently, it was not error for the Appraiser to conclude that there was a market value at this amount.

The Vice Chancellor, however, did not accept this finding of the Appraiser. He preferred to adopt a "reconstructed market value" of $1,305 per share as of the date of the merger. The reconstructed market value as of the date of merger was made by the same appraisers who had, in February, 1962, fixed the market value of Steeplechase stock at $1,530 per share. The reason for the reduction in amount is that by the date of the merger the 1962 and 1963 earnings of Steeplechase were known. These earnings had declined and this fact led to a reduction in the figure representing market value.

We think it was proper for the Vice Chancellor to accept this reconstructed market value related precisely to the date of merger. Since value, particularly market value, is dependent to a large extent on earnings, it is proper to take into consideration a reduction in those earnings in constructing a market value. If this is a matter entering into the realm of judgment, as we think it probably is, we can find nothing in this record to indicate an erroneous exercise of judgment by the Vice Chancellor. We therefore affirm his finding as to market value.

Earnings Value

Using an average of the five-year period 1958-1962, the Appraiser fixed the earnings per share of Steeplechase stock at $182.13. The Vice Chancellor rejected this finding and using the five-year period 1959-1963 fixed the earnings per share of Steeplechase stock at $120.19. The Appraiser in order to capitalize these earnings used a multiplier of 15.2, while the Vice Chancellor used a multiplier of 10. The stockholders except to the findings with respect to earnings value of both the Appriaser and the Vice Chancellor.

The main contention of the stockholders in this respect is a complaint against the use by Steeplechase of the sum-of-the-years digit method of depreciation which permitted Steeplechase to depreciate the major part of the cost of assets over the early years of their existence, thus reducing annual net income by a substantial amount. Accordingly, the stockholders' accountant divided Steeplechase's assets into those acquired prior to January 1, 1959 and those acquired or improved subsequent to that date. Depreciation on each of these assets was then recomputed on a basis which the accountant felt to be more proper. In so doing, the accountant materially increased the annual net earnings of Steeplechase.

Delaware law requires that earnings value be determined on the basis of historical earnings rather than on the basis of prospective earnings. *Cottrell* v. *Pawcatuck Company*, 36 Del.Ch. 169, 128 A.2d 225. Average earnings over the five-year period immediately preceding the merger have ordinarily been used as the basis for determining earnings value.

We therefore are of the opinion that the Vice Chancellor was correct in averaging earnings over the five years 1959-1963, since that was the period immediately preceding the merger. Even though the merger took place on July 31, 1963, the annual race meeting of that year had terminated by that time and all of Steeplechase's 1963 earnings had been made.

Furthermore, to start the period to be averaged with the year 1958 was to give a distorted effect to Steeplechase's earnings for the reason that 1958 was the first year of the so-called "long meeting," about 50 days, whereas theretofore meetings had been limited to 30 days. By reason of this, the earnings for 1958 were greatly increased. Furthermore, the new clubhouse had not been completed in 1958, although it was in progress, and there was no charge against 1958 earnings for this expense. All in all, we think it was more proper to take the five years 1959-1963 as the period to determine average earnings.

The argument of the stockholders based on the recalculation of depreciation by their accountant in reality comes down to nothing more than a disagreement among accountants as to what method should be followed in the depreciation of assets. The method of depreciation followed by Steeplechase was admittedly an acceptable accounting method and was accepted and approved by the Racing Commission and the Internal Revenue Service. This being so, we think the Appraiser and the Vice Chancellor did not err in accepting the method also.

Finally, the stockholders object to the use by the Vice Chancellor of a multiplier of 10 to fix the capitalized value of earnings. They argue that the multiplier of 15.2, that used by the Appraiser, should be applied. They point to the fact that Steeplechase is not an industrial-type business, not a retail store, nor a closed-end investment company. They liken it to a public utility as to which a proper multiplier is 15.2.

We think, however, that there are strong reasons why Steeplechase is not comparable to a public utility. In the first place, it is not a monopoly. It, in fact, operates in a field in which there is strong competition from other nearby tracks in neighboring states. In the second place, the State does not guarantee Steeplechase a fair return on its investment as it does with respect to public utilities. We think the two are not comparable. In fact, we believe Steeplechase to be unique.

In any event, the application of a multiplier to average earnings in order to capitalize them lies within the realm of judgment. There is no hard and fast rule to govern the selection. The multiplier of 10 used by the Vice Chancellor finds support in Dewing, *The Financial Policies of Corporations* (5th Ed.) 338-40, a book relied on in the past by the courts of this State. We cannot say, therefore, that reliance on this authority by the Vice Chancellor was improper. We affirm his use of a multiplier of 10.

Dividend Value

Both the Appraiser and the Vice Chancellor found that the dividend value of Steeplechase was zero and gave it 10 percent weight. The stockholders object to this and argue that dividend value should be given no independent weight whatsoever independent of earnings. Their reason for this is that earnings and dividends are so clearly related that they largely reflect the same value factor.

In *Tri-Continental Corp.* v. *Battye, supra,* we pointed out that the object of an appraisal was to give the dissenting stockholder the equivalent of that which he could expect to receive in one way or another if he had remained as a stockholder in the going concern. This means, of course, that dividends paid, or the possibility of them being paid in the future, is of special significance in questions of valuation since receipt of dividends is ordinarily the most usual way for the stockholder to realize upon the value of his stock.

In the case of Steeplechase, no dividends have ever been paid on the common stock, and at the time of the merger it did not appear that the prospect of payment in the future was any brighter. This stemmed from the admittedly no-profit policy of the management, the restrictions imposed by the Racing Commission upon the payment of dividends on the common stock, and the plain fact that earnings in any substantial amount would not be available for the payment of dividends in the foreseeable future.

450

By reason of these facts, both the Appraiser and the Vice Chancellor gave the non-payment of dividends "substantial negative recognition." This conclusion is in accord with *Adams* v. *R.C. Williams & Co.,* Del.Ch., 158 A.2d 797, in which the Chancellor referred back an appraisal proceeding to the Appraiser with instructions to give some weight to a negative dividend factor. On further hearing the Appraiser gave 40 percent weight to the zero earnings value, which was later affirmed by the Chancellor in an unreported opinion.

Since a negative dividend value clearly is pertinent in fixing the value of stock, we cannot say that the judgment of the Appraiser and the Vice Chancellor was in error in giving it a negative weighting. We affirm that decision.

Weighting

The Vice Chancellor reversed the weighting given by the Appraiser to the various elements of value and weighted those elements of value and weighted those elements according to his own judgment. His weighting was as follows:

Asset Value	25 percent
Market Value	40 percent
Earnings Value	25 percent
Dividend Value	10 percent

In so doing the Vice Chancellor disagreed with the Appraiser who had weighted asset value at 40 percent and market value at 25 percent. The Vice Chancellor reduced the weight to be given asset value for the reason that there were no plans to liquidate the Steeplechase assets and, therefore, the assets would continue to be held for the purpose of future earnings.

Since the value of Steeplechase shares is not to be determined on the basis of a liquidation, we cannot say as a matter of law that the Vice Chancellor's judgment on this was clearly wrong.

The Vice Chancellor weighted market value at 40 percent because of his judgment that in the long run the most likely way in which an investor in Steeplechase stock, if permitted to continue in the resulting enterprise, could have realized on his investment was by way of a sale of his shares. This conclusion accords with the Tri-Continental case and, we think, is a proper reason for changing the weighting given this element by the Appraiser.

The question of what weight to give the various elements of value lies always within the realm of judgment. There is no precise criterion to apply to determine the question. It is a matter of discretion with the valuator. In the absence of a clear indication of a mistake of judgment or a mistake of law, we think this Court should accept the reasoned exercise of judgment of the Vice Chancellor and not substitute its own guess as to what the proper weightings should be. Since there has been no showing of an improper or arbitrary exercise of judgment by the Vice Chancellor, we accept his findings in this respect.

By reason of the foregoing, the judgment of the Vice Chancellor fixing the value of the stockholders' stock in Steeplechase at $2,321.30 per share is *affirmed.*

Case Questions

1. The court states that Delaware law requires that earnings value be determined on the basis of historical earnings rather than on prospective earnings. Future earnings are speculative but should they be disregarded entirely? Undoubtedly future earnings, whether the forecast was bright or dim, played some part in the directors' merger decision. Shouldn't the appraiser likewise consider them?

2. In the discussion of market value the court remarks that it is largely dependent on earnings. Therefore, a reduction in earnings is properly taken into consideration in constructing market value. Suppose the Racing Commission adopts regulations that will reduce earnings in future years. Under such circumstances do you think the court would ignore future earnings in its calculations?

3. Is it logical to ignore future earnings when determining earnings value yet, possibly consider it when ascertaining market value?

4. Does one transaction, which occurred two years previous, establish market value, even though 93 percent of the outstanding stock was involved?

5. At many points in the opinion the court, in affirming the Vice Chancellor's decision, remarks that the determination was not arrived at arbitrarily or was properly within the realm of discretion. Does this reflect excessive deference to the judgment of the Vice Chancellor?

DISSOLUTION

Thus far we have considered the ways in which the corporate structure may be altered. In each, the business enterprise continues, although it may assume a revised corporate structure. Circumstances may exist where the cessation of the corporate enterprise is desired. The termination of corporate existence is called dissolution. Let us now focus our attention upon the techniques and rationale of dissolution.

VOLUNTARY DISSOLUTION

A corporation may elect to dissolve voluntarily by the board adopting a resolution recommending dissolution and the affirmative vote of the shareholders at either an annual or special meeting. Again, many jurisdictions require a majority vote of the outstanding stock, i.e., Del. § 275, whereas others, i.e., Ill. § 76, require a two-thirds affirmative vote. The necessity of board action and a vote of the shareholders can be dispensed with if the holders of record of all its outstanding shares consent in writing to the dissolution, Del. § 275(c); Ill. § 75.

A corporation may also dissolve voluntarily through the expiration of its charter. While standard incorporating practice is to grant a corporation perpetual life, occasionally the incorporators will specify existence for a definite period of time. When that period of time expires, so does the corporation.

INVOLUNTARY DISSOLUTION

The Attorney General of the state of incorporation can petition the court for the revocation or forfeiture of a corporation's charter. Grounds for revocation in Delaware listed in § 283 are abuse, misuse or nonuse of its corporate powers, privileges or franchises. However, nonuse of corporate powers during the first two years after its incorporation cannot lead to dissolution. Illinois has a different approach in § 82 of its Business Corporation Act by listing a series of specific grounds for forfeiture including: failure to file an annual report; failure to pay its franchise tax; fraudulent procurement of the charter; substantial and willful violation of the state's consumer fraud act; etc.

The shareholders may petition a court of equity seeking the involuntary dissolution of their corporation. The power of the courts' in this regard is discretionary and, as a general rule, they are extremely reluctant to use it. Such a suit will be successful only if the court is convinced that dissolution is necessary to protect the creditors' or shareholders' interests. Circumstances justifying dissolution include: the misapplication or waste of corporate assets; oppressive, illegal or fraudulent acts on the part of the directors or those in control of the corporation; and deadlock in the management of the corporate affairs resulting in, or threatening, irreparable injury to the corporation. The *In re Radom & Neidorff, Inc.* case that follows is a fine illustration of a court's reluctance to order dissolution.

In re RADOM & NEIDORFF, INC.
307 N.Y. 1, 119 N.E.2d 563, (Ct. of App., N.Y., 1954)

◆◆◆

DESMOND, Judge.

Radom & Neidorff, Inc., the proposed dissolution of which is before us here, is a domestic corporation which has for many years, conducted, with great success, the business of lithographing or printing musical compositions. For some thirty years prior to February 18, 1950, Henry Neidorff, now deceased, husband of respondent Anna Neidorff, and David Radom, brother-in-law of Neidorff and brother of Mrs. Neidorff, were the sole stockholders, each holding eighty shares. Henry Neidorff's will made his wife his executrix and bequeathed her the stock, so that, ever since his death, petitioner-appellant David Radom and Anna Neidorff, brother and sister, have been the sole and equal stockholders. Although brother and sister, they were unfriendly before Neidorff's death and their estrangement continues. On July 17, 1950, five months after Neidorff's death, Radom brought this proceeding, praying that the corporation be dissolved under section 103 of the General Corporation Law, Consol.Laws, c.23, the applicable part of which is as follows:

> "§ 103. Petition in case of deadlock
> Unless otherwise provided in the certificate of incorporation, if a corporation has an even number of directors who are equally divided respecting the management of its affairs, or if the votes of its stockholders are so divided that they cannot elect a board of directors, the holders of one-half of the stock entitled to vote at an election of directors may present a verified petition for dissolution of the corporation as prescribed in this article. . . .

The petition here stated to the court that the corporation is solvent and its operations successful, but that, since Henry Neidorff's death, his widow (respondent here) has refused to co-operate with petitioner as president, and that she refuses to sign his salary checks, leaving him without salary, although he has the sole burden of running the business. It was alleged, too, that, because of "unresolved disagreements" between petitioner and respondent, election of any directors, at a stockholders' meeting held for that purpose in June, 1950, had proved impossible. A schedule attached to the petition showed corporate assets consisting of machinery and supplies worth about $9,500, cash about $82,000, and no indebtedness except about $17,000 owed to petitioner (plus his salary claim). Mrs. Neidorff's answering papers alleged that, while her husband was alive, the two owners had each drawn about $25,000 per year from the corporation, that, shortly after her husband's death, petitioner had asked her to allow him alone to sign all checks, which request she refused, that he had then offered her $75,000 for her stock, and, on her rejection thereof, had threatened to have the corporation dissolved and to buy it in at a low price or, if she should be the purchaser, that he would start a competing business. She further alleged that she has not, since her husband's death, interfered with Radom's conduct of the business and has signed all corporate checks sent her by him except checks for his own salary which, she says, she declined to sign because of a stockholder's derivative suit brought by her against Radom, and still pending, charging him with enriching himself at this corporation's expense. . . .

From the answering papers it appears, without dispute, that for . . . three years, the corporation's profits before taxes had totaled about $242,000, or an annual average of about $71,000, on a gross annual business of about $250,000, and that the corporation had, in 1953, about $300,000 on deposit in banks. There are many other accusations and counteraccusations in these wordy papers, but the only material facts are undisputed: first, that these two equal stockholders dislike and distrust each other; second, that, despite the feuding and backbiting, there is no stalemate or impasse as to corporate policies; third, that the corporation is not sick but flourishing; fourth, that dissolution is not necessary for the corporation or for either stockholders; and, fifth, that petitioner, though he is in an uncomfortable and disagreeable situation for which he may or may not be at fault, has no grievance cognizable by a court except as to the nonpayment of his salary, hardly a ground for dissolving the corporation. . . .

The Appellate Division reversed the order (of the trial court) and dismissed the petition, pointing out, among other things, that not only have the corporation's activities not been paralyzed but that its profits have increased and its assets trebled during the pendency of this proceeding, that the failure of petitioner to receive his salary did not frustrate the corporate business and was remediable by means other than dissolution. The dismissal of the proceeding was "without prejudice, however, to the bringing of another proceeding should a deadlock in fact arise in the selection of a board of directors, at a meeting of stockholders to be duly called, or if other deadlock should occur threatening impairment or in fact impairing the economic operations of the corporation." . . .

It is worthy of passing mention, at least, that respondent has, in her papers, formally offered, and repeated the offer on the argument of the appeal before us, "to have the third director named by the American Arbitration Association, any Bar Association or any recognized and respected public body."

Clearly, the dismissal of this petition was within the discretion of the Appellate Division. ... There is no Absolute right to dissolution under such circumstances. Even when majority stockholders file a petition because of internal corporate conflicts, the order is granted only when the competing interests "are so discordant as to prevent efficient management" and the "object of its corporate existence cannot be attained." *Hitch* v. *Hawley,* 132 N.Y. 212, 221, 30 N.E. 401, 404, see Matter of Niagara Ins. Co., 1 Paige Ch. 258. The prime inquiry is, always, as to necessity for dissolution, that is, whether judicially-imposed death "will be beneficial to the stockholders or members and not injurious to the public". ... Taking everything in the petition as true, this was not such a case, and so there was no need for a reference, or for the taking of proof, under sections 106 and 113 of the General Corporation Law.

The order should be affirmed, with costs.

FULD, Judge (dissenting).

Section 103 of the General Corporation Law, insofar as here relevant, permits a petition for dissolution of a corporation by the holders of one half of the shares of stock entitled to vote for directors "if the votes of its stockholders are so divided that they cannot elect a board of directors". That is the precise situation in the case before us, for the petition explicitly recites that petitioner Radom and respondent Neidorff "are hopelessly deadlocked with respect to the management and operation of the corporation" and that serious disputes have developed between them with the result that "the votes of the two stockholders are so divided that they cannot elect a Board of Directors." ...

For upwards of thirty years, petitioner Radom and Henry Neidorff, respondent's husband, shared equally in the ownership and management of Radom & Neidorff, Inc. Through all that time, their relationship was harmonious as well as profitable. Neidorff died in 1950, at which time respondent, through inheritance, acquired her present 50 percent stock interest in the business. Since then, all has been discord and conflict. The parties, brother and sister, are at complete loggerheads; they have been unable to elect a board of directors; dividends have neither been declared nor distributed, although the corporation has earned profits; debts of the corporation have gone unpaid, although the corporation is solvent; petitioner, who since Neidorff's death has been the sole manager of the business, has not received a penny of his salary — amounting to $25,000 a year — because respondent has refused to sign any corporate check to his order. More, petitioner's business judgment and integrity, never before questioned, have been directly attacked in the stockholder's derivative suit, instituted by respondent, charging that he has falsified the corporation's records, converted its assets and otherwise enriched himself at its expense. Negotiations looking to the purchase by one stockholder of the other's interest were begun — in an effort to end the impasse — but they, too, have failed.

In very truth, as petitioner states in his papers, "a corporation of this type, with only two stockholders in it cannot continue to operate with incessant litigation and feuding between the two stockholders, and with differences as fundamental and wholly irreconcilable as are those of Mrs. Neidorff and myself. * * * settlement of these differences cannot be effected, while continuance on the present basis is impossible, so that there is no alternative to judicial dissolution." Indeed, petitioner avers, in view of the unceasing discord and the fact that he has had to work without salary and advance his own money to the corporation, he does not, whether or no dissolution be granted, "propose to continue to labor in and operate this business". . . .

"Dissolution will serve the interests of the shareholders as well as public policy. * * * And, if the statutory authority be deemed discretionary in essence, there is no ground for withholding its affirmative exercise here, for there is no alternative corrective remedy. * * * The dissension is such as to defeat the end for which the corporation was organized."

Here, too, the asserted dissension, the court could find, permits of no real or effective remedy but a section 103 dissolution. And that is confirmed by a consideration of the alternatives seemingly open to petitioner. He could remain as president and manager of the corporation, without compensation, completely at odds with his embittered sister — certainly neither a natural nor a satisfying way in which to conduct a business. Or he could carry out his present plan to quit the enterprise — and thereby risk a loss, to corporation and stockholders, far greater than that involved in terminating the business. Or he could, without quitting, set up a competing enterprise — and thereby expose himself to suit for breach of fiduciary duty to the corporation. . . . It is difficult to believe that the legislature could have intended to put one in petitioner's position to such a choice. Reason plainly indicates, and the law allows, the reasonable course of orderly dissolution pursuant to section 103. . . .

The order of the Appellate Division should be reversed. . . .

CONWAY, DYE and VAN VOORHIS, JJ., concur with DESMOND, J.
FULD, J., dissents in opinion in which LEWIS, C. J., and FROESSEL, J. concur.

Order affirmed.

◆◆◆

Case Questions

1. Why didn't the corporate articles or by-laws contain a provision as to a method of settling deadlocks over the selection of directors?
2. Is it conceivable that an acute situation like this could arise in a publicly traded corporation?
3. What do you think the decision would be if, instead of increasing profits and the trebling of assets, the corporation, although profitable, was experiencing steadily declining earnings?
4. Is the court stating, in effect, that before it will exercise its discretion and order involuntary dissolution a corporation must experience red ink?

CORPORATE EXISTENCE AFTER DISSOLUTION

Once a corporation is dissolved it does not instantly disappear, as if by magic. There are corporate assets to collect, creditors to be paid and distributions to be made to shareholders. The corporation is in a state of limbo, able to wind up its affairs but incapable of undertaking new business. Once the winding up process is complete the corporate existence will terminate.

Delaware Corporation Law § 278 states:

> All corporations, whether they expire by their own limitation or are otherwise dissolved, shall nevertheless be continued, for the term of three years from such expiration or dissolution or for such longer period as the Court of Chancery shall in its discretion direct, bodies corporate for the purpose of prosecuting and defending suits, whether civil, criminal or administrative, by or against them, and of enabling them gradually to settle and close their business, to dispose of and convey their property, to discharge their liabilities, and to distribute to their stockholders any remaining assets, but not for the purpose of continuing the business for which the corporation was organized. . . .

REVIEW PROBLEMS

1. Bellanca Corp. is an empty shell. For many years it manufactured airplanes, but then it ceased business operations and was delisted by the American Stock Exchange. It had accumulated large losses that were available for Federal tax loss carry-over purposes. In 1961 it purchased all the capital stock of seven California corporations engaged in the egg business. The result, under the terms of the purchase agreement, was to leave the former owners of the California corporations in control of Bellanca. A Bellanca stockholder challenges the transaction. She alleges that a merger has in fact taken place without compliance with the merger provisions of the Delaware law, including the right of the dissenting shareholder to withdraw and be paid the value of his stock. The corporation argues that the state statute specifically allows one corporation to purchase all the stock of another corporation, thereby becoming a stockholder and not the owner of the assets of the other corporation. The corporation argues further that action taken in accordance with different sections of the law are acts of independent legal significance even though the end result may be the same under different sections. What decision? [*Orzeck* v. *Englehart*, 195 A.2d 375 (S. Ct. Del. 1963)].

2. Community Hotel Corp. has 2,106 issued and outstanding shares of no par common stock. It also has 4,335 outstanding $100 par value 6 percent cumulative preferred shares. There are 24 years of accrued but undeclared dividends on the preferred stock. This totals $645,000. Newport Hotel Corp. is incorporated with one purpose — to merge with Community. Newport would completely own the assets of Community. Each share of Community preferred would be converted into five shares of $1 par common stock, while each share of no par common stock would be converted into one share of $1 par common stock of the surviving corporation. If this recapitalization were to be accomplished by amending Community's articles, Rhode Island law would require the unanimous vote of the preferred shareholders. Under the merger statute, only a two-thirds vote is necessary. Some of the preferred shareholders object upon the following grounds, inter alia: 1) the merger device has been resorted to solely to obviate the necessity of a unanimous vote, and 2) it is unfair and inequitable because, if they dissent, their dividend accruals will not be given due consideration in the appraisal. What result? [*Bove* v. *Community Hotel Corp.*, 249 A.2d 89 (S. Ct. R.I. 1969)].

3. The usual statutory remedy for the shareholder that unsuccessfully opposes a merger is one of dissent and appraisal. Is it the exclusive remedy or may a

shareholder resort to equitable relief? Should equity set a merger aside on grounds of unfairness or only upon the showing of actual fraud? [*Matteson* v. *Ziebarth*, 242 P.2d 1025 (1952)].

4. Corporation X and Corporation Y are properly consolidated into a new corporation CC. The holders of some of X's cumulative preferred shares, whose dividends are in arrears, sue CC. These shareholders seek the liquidation value of their shares plus the dividend arrearages. A clause in the preferred share contract states that upon the voluntary dissolution of the corporation the preferred shareholders are entitled to $102.50 per share plus dividend arrearages, before any distribution of assets is made to the common shareholders. The shareholders claim that the consolidation worked a voluntary dissolution of corporation X. CC contends that the preferred share contract's use of the term "dissolution" means a statutory dissolution. It points out that the consolidated company assumes the debts and liabilities of the constituent companies including existing dividend arrearages. CC further argues that the preferred shareholders will be fairly treated because the consolidation agreement must recognize the dividend arrearages in determining a fair basis of conversion of shares or distribution of property in lieu of shares in the consolidated corporation. Do the preferred shareholders receive the cash that they desire? [*Anderson* v. *Cleveland-Cliffs Iron Co.*, 87 N.E. 2d 384 (1948)].

5. Minority shareholders petition the court for the involuntary dissolution of their corporation. They prove that prior to 1913 the company was a thriving enterprise. Its profits in 1912 were $45,465.50 and sales amounted to $310,697.23. A new president and general manager took office in 1913. Profits for 1913 amounted to only $11,617.64. In 1914 it suffered a $21,260.85 loss. The period from January 1, 1915, to March, 1916, observed a loss of $52,365.00. The 1914 sales were only $164,508.45. Sales for 1915 were approximately $41,000. The four primary sales agents quit the company as a result of disagreements with the company's president. Does this situation merit the granting of a decree of involuntary dissolution? [*Goodwin* v. *Milwaukee Lithographing Co.*, 177 N.W. 618 (1920)]. *YES*

6. The NLM Corporation owes a creditor $15,000. Subsequently, NLM sells its assets to Leroy Corporation in exchange for stock. The transaction was a bona fide sale. When approached earlier by NLM with a proposed merger, Leroy rejected it and countered with a purchase of assets proposal. While the assets did not exceed $165,000, NLM received Leroy stock valued at approximately $700,000. Later NLM had Leroy transfer the stock from its ownership to the NLM shareholders. The shareholders then proceeded to dissolve NLM without satisfying the $15,000 debt. The creditor now brings suit against Leroy alleging that the transaction was a de facto merger and, therefore, Leroy is responsible for NLM's liabilities. Leroy contends that the transaction was a legitimate sale of assets and fair consideration was paid. In such circumstances, the purchaser is not liable for the debts of the seller. Who will be victorious, the creditor or Leroy? [*Lamb* v. *Leroy Corporation*, 454 P.2d 24 (Nev. 1969)]. *creditor lost*

PART V
SECURITIES REGULATION

The most dynamic and significant area of corporation law today is that of securities regulation. The past several years have observed court decisions whose effects have reverberated throughout the corporate, financial, accounting and legal field. Reactions to these controversial decisions have been strong and varied. At one end of the spectrum are those applauding the recent developments as the beginning of effective regulation over heretofore ignored financial shenanigans. Others perceive it as a meddling judiciary, lacking the necessary expertise, second guessing good faith business or professional judgment. The controversy is of such intensity that the popular press occassionally gives it coverage. It is quite a change from the pre 1968 days when securities law was regarded merely as just another quiet esoteric subject.

BLUE SKY LAWS

Regulation over securities transactions can come from two sources: the federal government and/or the states. State regulation is by statutes called "blue sky laws". The phrase received common acceptance after a judge's decision referred to "speculative schemes which have no more basis than so many feet of blue sky".[1] Prior to 1933 state statutes provided the sole regulation of securities in the United States. While these statutes vary from state to state, there are three general types.

The Fraud Type.

They usually proscribe as illegal the use of "fraud" in the issuance, promotion, distribution, sale or purchase of securities. The term fraud is broadly defined but typically involves some form of deception or misrepresentation. Violations can lead to criminal prosecution for past activities and injunctions barring the future utilization of such practices.

The Dealer Type.

These mandate the registration of brokers, dealers and salesman with the state. Requirements necessary to fulfill this obligation differ in the various jurisdictions.

The Registration Type.

This type of statute requires that before securities can be traded in the state, they must be first registered or "qualified." Again the specifics vary. They range from requiring the filing of only minimal information to disclosing such data as the state official deems appropriate. Finally, some states have hybrid statues that blend together elements of the three basic types.

How important, effective or significant are the blue sky laws within the regulatory scheme? Opinion varies. Generally, state supervision of securities transactions is regarded as less effective than the federal. Federal law has the advantage of being uniform and enforceable throughout the United States. The state has only abbreviated power since it terminates at its geographical boundaries. Typically the state law will receive only perfunctory execution. Securities legislation is often not a topic of great import in a state legislature and, consequently, appropriations to the agency enforcing the law may be small. There is the attitude of "let's leave it to Uncle Sam." The minority view is that one is incorrect in downplaying the significance of such laws. Some securities are exempted from federal legislation and therefore blue sky laws are the only control. And, a few state blue sky statutes contain requirements extending beyond the federal and thus yield greater protection to the investor.

FEDERAL SECURITIES REGULATION

The federal government did not enter the securities regulation arena until the early 1930s. Remember this was the time of the Great Depression. The 1920s had seen great prosperity. The business of America was business and there were no dark clouds on the horizon. Prices on the stock market reached dizzying heights as more and more people engaged in an almost euphoric speculation. Many investors lacked the requisite knowledge to prudently invest in stocks. Even worse, some went beyond investing only their own savings — they borrowed money with which to purchase stock on margin. Then in 1929 came the great stock market crash. Stock prices plummeted and citizens watched their life savings disappear. The personal despair was so great for some that they committed suicide. Men tramped the streets in search of work, farms were foreclosed with the fall of the auctioneer's hammer, banks failed and all efforts by business to halt the economic decline proved fruitless. It was in this social, economic and political milieu that Franklin D. Roosevelt was swept into the White House on the electoral tide of 1932. Governmental efforts to aid the economy came so swiftly that the legislative branch was dubbed the "Hundred Day" Congress. The alphabet agencies were spewed forth by Congress in a torrent. Areas traditionally regarded as being within the exclusive jurisdiction of the states were subjected to federal control. While some vehemently objected to this as a distortion of our basic governmental system, most accepted it as being necessary and proper. It was against this background that the Securities Act of 1933 (also called the '33 Act) and the Securities Exchange Act of 1934 (referred to as the '34 Act) were enacted.

The two-fold objectives of the federal securities laws are disclosure and prevention of fraud. They mandate full and fair disclosure to investors of all material information, be it financial or otherwise. They also prohibit deceitful and fraudulent practices, or other acts of misrepresentation, in the sale of securities. It is important to recognize that the Securities Exchange Commission does not make a judgment as to the merits of a securities issue when it allows their sale. If one complies with the law, one can sell the securities. If the venture is highly speculative and the enterprise's success appears dubious the individual investor must be told. Once this is done, it is the individual's decision whether he desires to assume the risk and make a purchase. The Securities Exchange Commission's approval of an issue is no guarantee that the investor will make a profit. Nor is it a warranty as to the accuracy of the information contained in the registration statement and prospectus. However, the inclusion of incomplete, deceptive or false data can lead to civil and/or criminal penalties and the law does provide a mechanism for the investor to recover any loss suffered thereby.

Although our primary concern will be with the '33 and '34 Acts, other federal statutes have an important impact on certain aspects of the securities field and deserve mention. They are: the Public Utility Holding Company Act of 1935, the Trust Indenture Act of 1939, the Investment Company Act of 1940, the Investment Advisors Act of 1940, and Chapter X of the Bankruptcy Act as it applies to corporate reorganizations. The Securities Exchange Commission (S.E.C.) oversees the operations of these statutes, except the latter where it serves in an advisory capacity to the federal court.

THE SECURITIES ACT OF 1933

The '33 Act mandates that any corporation issuing securities for sale to the public make available all material information concerning those securities. The information, which is not limited to only financial data, is supplied to the S.E.C. in the form of a registration statement. A prospectus must be made available to the investor. A prospectus is like a coin, it has two sides. On the one side it provides information, much of which is duplicative of the registration statement, to the investor so he may judge the merits of the securities. On the reverse side, a prospectus is a sales device. It makes the potential investor aware of the corporation and of the financial product that it is selling — its corporate securities. It aims to convince the investor of the wisdom of making a purchase by holding out the hope of future financial gain. The second basic element of the '33 Act is its prohibition of fraudulent, deceptive or misleading activities in the sale of securities. Its fraud provisions apply only to sellers; the fraud provisions of the '34 Act apply to both sellers and buyers. These anti-fraud provisions are applicable regardless of whether registration of the securities is required.

THE SECURITIES EXCHANGE ACT OF 1934

This law created the Securities and Exchange Commission. The statute requires the disclosure of specified information by companies whose securities are listed and traded on the national stock exchanges. A 1964 amendment placed these requirements on companies whose equity securities are traded over-the-counter. The disclosures resemble those of the '33 Act. It requires the registration with the SEC of national stock exchanges and broker-dealers conducting over-the-counter activities of an interstate nature. It contains prohibitions on the use of inside information in securities transactions. It regulates the process of proxy (a shareholder's vote) solicitations and governs tender offer solicitations (corporate take-over attempts through a stock acquisition). It grants the Federal Reserve System's Board of Governors the power to establish margin requirements-the amount of credit that can be extended to purchase or carry securities. The objective is to prevent the excessive use of credit in the securities market.

THE SECURITIES AND EXCHANGE COMMISSION

The Securities and Exchange Commission (SEC) was created by Congress in 1934 to administer the various federal securities laws. It is an independent quasi-judicial agency of the federal government.

The Commission consists of five persons appointed by the President with the advice and consent of the Senate. The President designates which person shall serve as Chairman. They serve staggered five year terms with a vacancy being created in June of each year. A commission member is eligible for reappointment. Not more than three commissioners can be members of the same political party. However, it should be clear that a President can appoint a majority of the Commission before the expiration of his first term of office, or even sooner, if vacancies are created by death or resignation.

The SEC has enjoyed a sterling reputation for expertise, integrity and political independence. This reputation was tarnished somewhat during 1972, and 1973. In 1973, G. Bradford Cook resigned as Chairman of the SEC. His resignation followed charges that he had deleted from a SEC lawsuit, all reference to a secret $200,000 cash contribution by Robert Vesco to the Nixon campaign fund. It was alleged that the deletion was a political favor to fund raiser Maurice Stans. Several months after the deletion, Nixon had promoted Cook from General Counsel to Chairman of the Commission.

The Commission directs a staff that is organized along functional lines. The staff is separated into five divisions: corporation finance; market regulation; corporate regulation; investment management regulation; and enforcement. There is also an office of the general counsel and chief accountant to provide technical advice to the Commission and staff. Regional offices are maintained around the country to conduct investigations and otherwise carry out the duties of the Commission.

The Commission investigates complaints of possible violations in securities transactions. These investigations are essentially fact finding inquiries. If there is a prima facie indication of a violation, the Commission can select from several courses of action. It may seek a civil injunction. The case can be referred to the Justice Department for criminal prosecution if fraud or other willful law violation is indicated. The Commission can impose an administrative remedy after holding an administrative hearing. Such a remedy could take the form of censuring an individual or barring him from employment with a registered firm; suspending or expelling members from the exchange; or denying, suspending or revoking the registration of broker-dealers.

It is important to remember that private individuals can bring damage actions to collect the damages they incurred because of the violations.

The Commission also promulgates rules that have the force of law. It gives public notice of suggested rules and invites comments and criticisms which are considered in determining the nature and scope of the rules to be adopted. The operation of these rules receive regular review so as to provide pragmatic up-to-date protection for investors.

GOING PUBLIC

Once an entrepreneur has successfully developed his corporation, he may consider taking it public. Just as the original selection of the form of business association to be adopted involved advantages and disadvantages, so too, does the decision on going public.

The advantages inherent in going public are:
1. Develops a new source of funds. The proceeds from the sale of the securities to the public are available to the corporation for expansion,

retirement of existing debt, etc. If the corporation is successful, the public can furnish a recurring source of new funds.

2. Prestige. There is a certain degree of prestige attached to an association with a publicly owned corporation. The founders can derive a tremendous psychological feeling of achievement in the development of the corporation. The company and its products will enjoy greater visibility.

3. Enhances the capability to attract and retain high quality personnel. The availability of publicly traded stock, with its potential for capital gains treatment, can be an important incentive to some prospective managers.

4. Establishes a ready market for the company's securities. As a private concern, there is no ready market available for trading the securities and difficulties are encountered in valuation of those securities.

5. An alternate method of financing acquisitions is created. Instead of using cash, the corporation can use its securities to purchase a desired business. In the late 1960s many of the conglomerates were built through such stock acquisitions.

6. Going public can make the founders wealthy. They can sell off a portion of their stock, yielding a large amount of cash, while retaining a sufficiently large interest to retain corporate control.

7. It can provide the cash to pay estate taxes. Occasionally a large family concern will go public in order to raise the large amount of money necessary to pay federal estate taxes.

The disadvantages usually cited in going public are:

1. It is very expensive. The legal fees and auditors' fees can be quite large. Printing the necessary documents, such as the prospectus, can be costly. It is not uncommon for these three items to total in excess of $100,000. Added to this is the largest expense — the fee of the underwriter that is handling the issue. The underwriter typically charges a percentage commission (7 to 10%) based upon the public offering price.[2]

2. New expenses of an ongoing nature are created. While the underwriter's commission and certain other expenses only accompany the actual issuance and distribution of securities, other expenses constantly recur. Extra legal and accounting expenses are entailed in filing required reports with the SEC. Annual shareholder reports and proxy materials involve administrative costs of preparation plus printing and mailing expenses.

3. Privacy is lost. The shareholders have access to a great deal of information on corporate activities that a private corporation would not publicly reveal.

4. Loss of independence. Managing a privately held corporation involves important differences from running a publicly held corporation. Certain actions can require approval by the shareholders or an independent board of directors. In addition to such legal requirements, there can be practical obstacles in regard to certain matters. Purchase of a corporate jet or a nepotistic hiring policy is one thing in a private corporation and quite a different matter in a public concern.

5. Accountability to the public. Required disclosure of information can involve justification for particular corporate policies. Both the shareholders and public at large may demand an explanation of a certain

matter. This can demand the attention of high level executives. If satisfactory answers are not forthcoming, the corporation may face a stockholders' derivative suit.

6. The creation of conflicting interests may be inevitable. The company founders may be in a tax bracket where they do not want dividends to be paid. Other shareholders may well desire dividend income. A particular course of action may appear highly attractive over the long run, yet would cause a plunge in the current market price of the stock. Reconciliation of such issues can prove troublesome.

7. Loss of control. In the long run, the founders may face loss of control or a severe diminution of power. Outsiders can gain progressively larger holdings if subsequent stock offerings are necessary or if a series of acquisitions occur by means of stock swaps.

WHAT IS A SECURITY?

Although we have been frequently using the word, we have not as yet defined "security." It has an extremely broad meaning! Section 2(1) of the '33 Act defines it thus:

> The term "security" means any note, stock, treasury stock, bond, debenture, evidence of indebtedness, certificate of interest or participation in any profit-sharing agreement, collateral-trust certificate or subscription, transferable share, investment contract, voting-trust certificate, certificate of deposit for a security, fractional undivided interest in oil, gas, or other mineral rights, or, in general, any interest or instrument commonly known as a "security," or any certificate of interest or participation in, temporary or interim certificate for, receipt for, guarantee of, or warrant or right to subscribe to or purchase, any of the foregoing.

Despite this lengthy recitation, it is neither exhaustive nor all-inclusive. The definition expands to meet the ever expanding ingenuity of promoters. As the Supreme Court has stated it will examine the substance of the transaction and not be guided merely by the form it takes. The sale of silver foxes for breeding purposes, where the seller retained possession and provided the necessary management, has been held to constitute the sale of a security.[3] So has the sale of withdrawable capital shares in a savings and loan association[4] and the sale of memberships in a country club.[5]

The case that follows demonstrates the breadth given to the term "security." It should alert one to the fact that the securities laws apply not only to the fraudulent schemes of fly-by-night promoters, but also to some commercial transactions of the legitimate businessman. He may never conceive that the transaction has securities consequences. One must guard against the naive concept that "security" equates only to stocks and bonds. As the court points out, the law does not excuse one who fails to abide by it, even though he does so because of a bona fide mistake.

SEC v. HOWEY
328 U.S. 293 (1946)

◆◆◆

Mr. Justice Murphy

The Securities and Exchange Commission instituted this action to restrain the respondents from using the mails and instrumentalities of interstate commerce in the offer and sale of unregistered and non-exempt securities in violation of § 5 (a) of the Act. The District Court denied the injunction, . . . and the Fifth Circuit Court of Appeals affirmed the judgment. . . .

Most of the facts are stipulated. The respondents, W.J. Howey Company and Howey-in-the-Hills Service, Inc., are Florida corporations under direct common control and management. The Howey Company owns large tracts of citrus acreage in Lake County, Florida. During the past several years it has planted about 500 acres annually, keeping half of the groves itself and offering the other half to the public "to help us finance additional development." Howey-in-the-Hills Service, Inc., is a service company engaged in cultivating and developing many of these groves, including the harvesting and marketing of the crops.

Each prospective customer is offered both a land sales contract and a service contract, after having been told that it is not feasible to invest in a grove unless service arrangements are made. While the purchaser is free to make arrangements with other service companies, the superiority of Howey-in-the-Hills Service, Inc., is stressed. Indeed, 85 percent of the acreage sold during the 3-year period ending May 31, 1943 was covered by service contracts with Howey-in-the-Hills Service, Inc.

The land sales contract with the Howey Company provides for a uniform purchase price per acre or fraction thereof, varying in amount only in accordance with the number of years the particular plot has been planted with citrus trees. Upon full payment of the purchase price the land is conveyed to the purchaser by warranty deed. Purchases are usually made in narrow strips of land arranged so that an acre consists of a row of 48 trees. During the period between February 1, 1941, and May 31, 1943, 31 of the 42 persons making purchases bought less than 5 acres each. These tracts are not separately fenced and the sole indication of several ownership is found in small land marks intelligible only through a plat book record.

The service contract, generally of a ten year duration without option of cancellation, gives Howey-in-the-Hills Service, Inc., a leashold interest and "full and complete" possession of the acreage. For a specified fee plus the cost of labor and materials, the company is given full discretion and authority over the cultivation of the groves and the harvest and marketing of the crops. Without the consent of the company, the land owner or purchaser has no right of entry to market the crop; thus there is ordinarily no right to specific fruit. The company is accountable only for an allocation of the net profits based upon a check made at the time of picking. All the produce is pooled by the respondent companies, which do business under their own names.

The purchasers for the most part are non-residents of Florida. They are predominantly business and professional people who lack the knowledge, skill and equipment necessary for the care and cultivation of citrus trees. They are attracted by the expectation of substantial profits. It was represented, for example, that profits during the 1943-1944 season amounted to 20 percent and that even greater profits might be expected during the 1944-1945 season, although only a 10 percent annual return was to be expected over a ten year period. . . .

Section 2 (1) of the Act defines the term "security" to include the commonly known documents traded for speculation or investment. This definition also includes . . . "investment contract". . . . The legal issue in this case turns upon a determination of whether, under the circumstances, the land sales contract, the warranty deed and the service contract together constitute an "investment contract" within the meaning of § 2 (1). The lower courts, in reaching a negative answer to this problem, treated the contracts and deeds as separate transactions involving no more than an ordinary real estate sale and an agreement by the seller to manage the property for the buyer.

The term "investment contract" is undefined by the Securities Act or by relevant legislative reports. But the term was common in many state "blue sky" laws in existence prior to the adoption of the federal statute and, although the term was also undefined by the state law, it had been broadly construed by state courts so as to afford the investing public a full measure of protection. Form was disregarded for substance and emphasis was placed upon economic reality. An investment contract thus came to mean a contract or scheme for "the placing of capital or laying out of money in a way intended to secure income or profit from its employment." . . . This definition was uniformly applied by state courts to a variety of situations where individuals were led to invest money in a common enterprise with the expectation that they would earn a profit solely through the efforts of the promoter or of some one other than themselves.

By including an investment contract within the scope of §2 (1) of the Securities Act, Congress was using the term the meaning of which had been crystallized by this prior judicial interpretation. In other words, an investment contract for purposes of the Securities Act means a contract, transaction or scheme whereby a person invests his money in a common enterprise and is led to expect profits solely from the efforts of the promoter or a third party, it being immaterial whether the shares in the enterprise are evidenced by formal certificates or by nominal interests in the physical assets employed in the enterprise. It permits the fulfillment of the statutory purpose of compelling full and fair disclosure relative to the issuance of "the many types of instruments that in our commercial world fall within the ordinary concept of a security." It embodies a flexible rather than a static principle, one that is capable of adaptation to meet the countless and variable schemes devised by those who seek the use of the money of others on the promise of profits.

The transactions in this case clearly involve investment contracts as so defined. The respondent companies are offering something more than fee simple interests in land, something different from a farm or orchard coupled with management services. They are offering an opportunity to contribute money and to share in the profits of a large citrus fruit enterprise managed and partly owned by respondents. They are offering this opportunity to persons who reside in distant localities and who lack the equipment and experience requisite to the cultivation, harvesting and marketing of the citrus products. Such persons have no desire to occupy the land or to develop it themselves; they are attracted solely by the prospects of a return on their investment. Indeed, individual development of the plots of land that are offered and sold would seldom be economically feasible due to their small size. Such tracts gain utility as citrus groves only when cultivated and developed as component parts of a larger area. A common enterprise managed by respondents or third parties with adequate personnel and equipment is therefore essential if the investors are to achieve their paramount aim of a return on their investments. Their respective shares in this enterprise are evidenced by land sales contracts and warranty deeds, which serve as a convenient method of determining the investors' allocable shares of the profits. The resulting transfer of rights in land is purely incidental.

Thus all the elements of a profit-seeking business venture are present here. The investors provide the capital and share in the earnings and profits; the promoters manage, control and operate the enterprise. It follows that the arrangements whereby the investors' interests are made manifest involve investment contracts, regardless of the legal terminology in which such contracts are clothed. The investment contracts in this instance take the form of land sales contracts, warranty deeds and service contracts which respondents offer to prospective investors. And respondents' failure to abide by the statutory and administrative rules in making such offerings, even though the failure result from a bona fide mistake as to the law, cannot be sanctioned under the Act.

This conclusion is unaffected by the fact that some purchasers choose not to accept the full offer of an investment contract by declining to enter into a service contract with the respondents. The Securities Act prohibits the offer as well as the sale of unregistered, non-exempt securities. Hence it is enough that the respondents merely offer the essential ingredients of an investment contract. . . .

The test is whether the scheme involves an investment of money in a common enterprise with profits to come solely from the efforts of others. If that test be satisfied, it is immaterial whether the enterprise is speculative or non-speculative or whether there is a sale of property with or without intrinsic value. The statutory policy of affording broad protection to investors is not to be thwarted by unrealistic and irrelevant formulae.

Reversed.

◆◆◆

Case Questions

1. Does this decision reflect pragmastism on the part of the court when examining a legal issue within the context of a commercial venture?
2. Is it possible to design the sale of an orchard coupled with management services without the securities law applying to the transaction? How?
3. Is it realistic to attribute to Congress, when it enacts legislation, knowledge of various state court decisions interpreting the term "investment contract"?

The next case is the most recent Supreme Court decision on the issue of what constitutes a security. The court rejects a literal application of the statute and holds that the instruments in dispute are not securities. It emphasizes the substance of the transaction and disregards mere form.

UNITED HOUSING FOUNDATION v. FORMAN
421 U.S. 837 (1975)

◆◆◆

Mr. Justice Powell delivered the opinion of the Court.

The issue in this case is whether shares of stock entitling a purchaser to lease an apartment in Co-Op City, a state subsidized and supervised non-profit housing cooperative, are "securities" within the purview of the Securities Exchange Act of 1934.

Co-Op City is a massive housing cooperative in New York City. Built between 1965 and 1971, it presently houses approximately 50,000 people on a 200-acre site containing 35 high rise buildings and 236 town houses. The project was organized, financed, and constructed under the New York State Private Housing Finance Law, commonly known as the Mitchell-Lama Act, enacted to ameliorate a perceived crisis in the availability of decent low-income urban housing. . . .

The United Housing Fundation (UHF), a nonprofit membership corporation established for the purpose of "aiding and encouraging" the creation of "adequate, safe and sanitary housing accommodations for wage earners and other persons of low and moderate income," . . . was responsible for initiating and sponsoring the development of Co-Op City. Acting under the Mitchell-Lama Act, UHF organized the Riverbay Corporation (Riverbay) to own and operate the land and buildings constituting Co-Op City. Riverbay, a nonprofit cooperative housing corporation, issued the stock that is the subject of this litigation. . . .

To acquire an apartment in Co-Op City an eligible prospective purchaser must buy 18 shares of stock in Riverbay for each room desired. The cost per share is $25, making the total cost $450 per room, or $1,800 for a four-room apartment. The sole purpose of acquiring these shares is to enable the purchaser to occupy an apartment in Co-Op City; in effect, their purchase is a recoverable deposit on an apartment. The shares are explicitly tied to the apartment; they cannot be transferred to a nontenant, nor can they be pledged or encumbered; and they descend, along with the apartment, only to a surviving spouse. No voting rights attach to the shares as such: participation in the affairs of the cooperative appertains to the apartment, with the residents of each apartment being entitled to one vote irrespective of the number of shares owned.

Any tenant who wants to terminate his occupancy, or who is forced to move out, must offer his stock to Riverbay at its initial selling price of $25 per share. In the extremely unlikely event that Riverbay declines to repurchase the stock, the tenant cannot sell it for more than the initial purchase price plus a fraction of the portion of the mortgage that he has paid off, and then only to a prospective tenant satisfying the statutory income eligibility requirements. . . .

In May 1965, subsequent to the completion of the initial planning, Riverbay circulated an Information Bulletin seeking to attract tenants for what would someday be apartments in Co-Op City. After describing the nature and advantages of cooperative housing generally and of Co-Op City in particular, the Bulletin informed prospective tenants that the total estimated cost of the project, based largely on an anticipated construction contract with CSI, was $283,695,550. Only a fraction of this sum, $32,795,550, was to be raised by the sale of shares to tenants. The remaining $250,900,000 was to be financed by a 40-year low-interest mortgage loan from the New York Private Housing Finance Agency. After construction of the project the mortgage payments and current operating expenses would be met by monthly rental charges paid by the tenants. While these rental charges were to vary, depending on the size, nature, and location of an apartment, the 1965 Bulletin estimated that the "average" monthly cost would be $23.02 per room, or $92.08 for a four-room apartment.

Several times during the construction of Co-Op City, Riverbay, with the approval of the State Housing Commissioner, revised its contract with CSI to allow for increased construction costs. In addition, Riverbay incurred other expenses that had not been reflected in the 1965 Bulletin. To meet these increased expenditures, Riverbay, with the Commissioner's approval, repeatedly secured increased mortgage loans from the State Housing Agency. Ultimately the construction loan was $125 million more than the figure estimated in the 1965 Bulletin. As a result, while the initial purchasing price remained at $450 per room, the average monthly rental charges increased periodically, reaching a figure of $39.68 per room as of July 1974.

These increases in the rental charges precipitated the present lawsuit. Respondents, 57 residents of Co-Op City, sued in federal court on behalf of all 15,372 apartment owners, and derivatively on behalf of Riverbay, seeking upwards of $30 million in damages, forced rental reductions, and other "appropriate" relief. . . .

The heart of respondents' claim was that the 1965 Co-Op City Information Bulletin falsely represented that CSI would bear all subsequent cost increases due to factors such as inflation. Respondents further alleged that they were misled in their purchases of shares since the Information Bulletin failed to disclose several critical facts. On these bases, respondents asserted two claims under the fraud provisions of the federal Securities Acts of 1933 and 1934, . . .

Petitioners, while denying the substance of these allegations, moved to dismiss the complaint on the ground that federal jurisdiction was lacking. They maintained that shares of stock in Riverbay were not "securities" within the definitional sections of the federal Securities Acts. . . .

The District Court granted the motion to dismiss. 366 F. Supp. 1117 (1973). It held that the denomination of the shares in Riverbay as "stock" did not, by itself, make them securities under the federal Acts. The court further ruled, relying primarily on this Court's decisions in *SEC* v. *C. M. Joiner Leasing Corp.,* 320 U.S. 344 (1943), and *SEC* v. *W. J. Howey Co.,* 328 U.S. 293 (1946), that the purchase in issue was not a security transaction since it was neither induced by an offer of tangible material profits, nor could such profits realistically be expected. In the District Court's words, it was "the fundamental nonprofit nature of this transaction" which presented "the insurmountable barrier to [respondents'] claims in th[e] federal court." . . .

The Court of Appeals for the Second Circuit reversed. 500 F. 2d 1246 (1974). It rested its decision on two alternative grounds. First, the court held that since the shares purchased were called "stock" the Securities Acts, which explicitly include "stock" in their definitional sections, were literally applicable. Second, the Court of Appeals concluded that the transaction was an investment contract within the meaning of the Acts and as defined by *Howey,* since there was an expectation of profits. . . .

In making this determination in the present case we do not write on a clean slate. Well-settled principles enunciated by this Court establish that the shares purchased by respondents do not represent any of the "countless and variable schemes devised by those who seek the use of the money of others on the promise of profits," *Howey, supra,* 328 U.S., at 299, and therefore do not fall within "the ordinary concept of a security."

We reject at the outset any suggestion that the present transaction, evidenced by the sale of shares called "stock," must be considered a security transaction simply because the statutory definition of a security includes the words "any . . . stock." Rather we adhere to the basic principle that has guided all of the Court's decisions in this area:

> "[I]n searching for the meaning and scope of the word 'security' in the Act[s], form should be disregarded for substance and the emphasis should be on economic reality. . . .

The primary purpose of the Securities Acts of 1933 and 1934 was to eliminate serious abuses in a largely unregulated securities market. The focus of the Acts is on the capital market of the enterprise system: the sale of securities to raise capital for profit-making purposes, the exchanges on which securities are traded, and the need for regulation to prevent fraud and to protect the interest of investors. Because securities transactions are economic in character Congress intended the application of these statutes to turn on the economic realities underlying a transaction, and not on the name appended thereto. Thus, in construing these Acts against the background of their purpose, we are guided by a traditional canon of statutory construction:

> that a thing may be within the letter of the statute and yet not within the statute, because not within its spirit, nor within the intention of its makers. . . .

Respondents' reliance on *Joiner* as support for a "literal approach" to defining a security is misplaced. The issue in *Joiner* was whether assignments of interests in oil leases, coupled with the promoters' offer to drill an exploratory well, were securities. Looking to the economic inducement provided by the proposed exploratory well, the Court concluded that these leases were securities even though "leases" as such were not included in the list of instruments mentioned in the statutory definition. In dictum the Court noted that "[i]nstruments *may* be included within [the definition of a security], as [a] matter of law, if on their face they answer to the name or description." . . . And later, again in dictum, the Court stated that a security *"might"* be shown "by proving the document itself, which on its face would be a note, a bond or a share of stock." . . . By using the conditional words "may" and "might" in these dicta the Court made clear that it was not establishing an inflexible rule barring inquiry into the economic realities underlying a transaction. On the contrary, the Court intended only to make the rather obvious point that, in contrast to the instrument before it which was not included within the explicit statutory terms, most instruments bearing these traditional titles are likely to be covered by the statutes.

In holding that the name given to an instrument is not dispositive, we do not suggest that the name is wholly irrelevant to the decision whether it is a security. There may be occasions when the use of a traditional name such as "stocks" or "bonds" will lead a purchaser justifiably to assume that the federal securities laws apply. This would clearly be the case when the underlying transaction embodies some of the significant characteristics typically associated with the named instrument.

In the present case respondents do not contend, nor could they, that they were misled by use of the word "stock" into believing that the federal securities laws governed their purchase. Common sense suggests that people who intend to acquire only a residential apartment in a state-subsidized cooperative, for their personal use, are not likely to believe that in reality they are purchasing investment securities simply because the transaction is evidenced by something called a share of stock. These shares have none of the characteristics "that in our commercial world fall within the ordinary concept of a security." . . . Despite their name, they lack what the Court in *Tcherepnin* deemed the most common feature of stock: the right to receive "dividends contingent upon an apportionment of profits." . . . Nor do they possess the other characteristics traditionally associated with stock: they are not negotiable; they cannot be pledged or hypothecated; they confer no voting rights in proportion to the number of shares owned; and they cannot appreciate in value. In short, the inducement to purchase was solely to acquire subsidized low-cost living space; it was not to invest for profit.

The court of Appeals, as an alternative ground for its decision, concluded that a share in Riverbay was also an "investment contract" as defined by the Securities Acts. Respondents further argue that in any event what they agreed to purchase is "commonly known as a 'security' " within the meaning of these laws. In considering these claims we again must examine the substance — the economic realities of the transaction — rather than the names that may have been employed by the parties. We perceive no distinction, for present purposes, between an "investment contract" and an "instrument commonly known as a security." In either case, the basic test for distinguishing the transaction from other commercial dealings is

> whether the scheme involves an investment of money in a common enterprise with profits to come solely from the efforts of others. (*Howey, supra,* 328 U.S., at 301.)

This test, in shorthand form, embodies the essential attributes that run through all of the Court's decisions defining a security. The touchstone is the presence of an investment in a common venture premised on a reasonable expectation of profits to be derived from the entreprenurial or managerial efforts of others. By profits, the Court has meant either capital appreciation resulting from the development of the initial investment, as in *Joiner, supra* (sale of oil leases conditioned on promoters' agreement to drill exploratory well), or a participation in earnings resulting from the use of investors' funds, as in

Tcherepnin v. *Knight, supra* (dividends on the investment based on savings and loan association's profits). In such cases the investor is "attracted solely by the prospects of a return" on his investment. *Howey, supra,* 328 U.S., at 300. By contrast, when a purchaser is motivated by a desire to use or consume the item purchased — "to occupy the land or to develop it themselves," as the *Howey* Court put it, 328 U.S., at 300 — the securities laws do not apply. See also *Joiner, supra.*

In the present case there can be no doubt that investors were attracted solely by the prospect of acquiring a place to live, and not by financial returns on their investments. . . .

Nowhere does the Bulletin seek to attract investors by the prospect of profits resulting from the efforts of the promoters or third parties. On the contrary, the Bulletin repeatedly emphasizes the "nonprofit" nature of the endeavor. It explains that if rental charges exceed expenses the difference will be returned as a rebate, not invested for profit. It also informs purchasers that they will be unable to resell their apartments at a profit since the apartment must first be offered back to Riverbay "at the price . . . paid for it." . . . In short, neither of the kinds of profits traditionally associated with securities were offered to respondents.

The Court of Appeals recognized that there must be an expectation of profits for these shares to be securities, and conceded that there is "no possible profit on a resale of [this] stock." 500 F. 2d, at 1254. The court correctly noted, however, that profit may be derived from the income yielded by an investment as well as from capital appreciation, and then proceeded to find "an expectation of 'income' in at least three ways." *Ibid.* Two of these supposed sources of income or profits may be disposed of summarily. We turn first to the Court of Appeals' reliance on the deductibility for tax purposes of the portion of the monthly rental charge applied to interest on the mortgage. We know of no basis in law for the view that the payment of interest, with its consequent deductibility for tax purposes, constitutes income or profits. These tax benefits are nothing more than that which is available to any homeowner who pays interest on his mortgage. . . .

The Court of Appeals also found support for its concept of profits in the fact that Co-Op City offered space at a cost substantially below the going rental charges for comparable housing. Again, this is an inappropriate theory of "profits" that we cannot accept. The low rent derives from the substantial financial subsidies provided by the State of New York. This benefit cannot be liquidated into cash; nor does it result from the managerial efforts of others. In a real sense, it no more embodies the attributes of income or profits than do welfare benefits, food stamps or other government subsidies.

The final source of profit relied on by the Court of Appeals was the possibility of net income derived from the leasing by Co-Op City of commercial facilities, professional offices and parking spaces, and its operation of community washing machines. The income, if any, from these conveniences, all located within the common areas of the housing project, is to be used to reduce tenant rental costs. Conceptually, one might readily agree that net income from the leasing of commercial and professional facilities is the kind of profit traditionally associated with a security investment. . . . But in the present case this income — if indeed there is any — is far too speculative and insubstantial to bring the entire transaction within the Securities Acts. . . .

There is no doubt that purchasers in this housing cooperative sought to obtain a decent home at an attractive price. But that type of economic interest characterizes every form of commercial dealing. What distinguishes a security transaction — and what is absent here — is an investment where one parts with his money in the hope of receiving profits from the efforts of others, and not where he purchases a commodity for personal consumption or living quarters for personal use. . . .

We decide only that the type of transaction before us, in which the purchasers were interested in acquiring housing rather than making an investment for profit, is not within the scope of the federal securities laws.

Reversed.

◆◆◆

Case Questions

1. Is this decision indicative that the Supreme Court is drifting away from a liberal interpretation of the term "security"?
2. Since the issuer labeled his instrument "stock" and since the definition of security includes the term "stock", how can the court say that the name given to an instrument is not dispositive of the issue? Is that not a blatant disregard of the literal mandate of Congressional legislation?

REGISTRATION REQUIREMENTS

Not every security is required to be registered under the '33 Act. There are several exemptions from the registration requirement. Some of the more important exemptions listed in Section 3 of the Act are:

1. securities of the states on Federal government or their political subdivisions;
2. securities of banks, charitable organizations, common carriers subject to the Interstate Commerce Act and savings and loan associations;
3. insurance policies, commercial paper with a maturity not exceeding nine months, and securities issued by small business investment companies;
4. intrastate issues offered and sold only to residents within the state where the corporation is incorporated and doing business;
5. the small issue exemption of securities not exceeding $500,000 offered during one year. The S.E.C. has promulgated "Regulation A" setting forth the terms and conditions that must be met to qualify for this exemption;
6. Section 4(2) exempts transactions by an issurer not involving any public offering, i.e. private offerings.

It is worthwhile to again repeat the fact that the law's anti-fraud provisions can apply to securities offerings even though they are exempt from registration. Section 17 of the '33 Act makes it unlawful to utilize any instrumentality of interstate commerce or the mails in the fraudulent sale of securities. Section 10 of the '34 Act declares it to be a violation in the case of both a purchase and the sale of a security.

Oftentimes a concept can be illuminated by showing how it does not apply to a specific situation. This is what is done in the Ralston Purina case. The court provides some perspective on what constitutes an exempted private offering by holding that the plan in question constitutes a public offering.

SEC v. RALSTON PURINA COMPANY
346 U.S. 119 (1953)

◆◆◆

Mr. Justice Clark delivered the opinion of the Court.

Section 4 (1) of the Securities Act of 1933 exempts "transactions by an issuer not involving any public offering" from the registration requirements of § 5. We must decide whether Ralston Purina's offerings of treasury stock to its "key employees" are within this exemption. . . .

Ralston Purina manufactures and distributes various feed and cereal products. Its processing and distribution facilities are scattered throughout the United States and Canada, staffed by some 7,000 employees. At least since 1911 the company has had a policy of encouraging stock ownership among its employees; more particularly, since 1942 it has made authorized but unissued common shares available to some of them. Between 1947 and 1951, the period covered by the record in this case, Ralston Purina sold nearly $2,000,000 of stock to employees without registration and in so doing made use of the mails.

In each of these years, a corporate resolution authorized the sale of common stock "to employees . . . who shall, without any solicitation by the Company or its officers or employees, inquire of any of them as to how to purchase common stock of Ralston Purina Company." A memorandum sent to branch and store managers after the resolution was adopted advised that "The only employees to whom this stock will be available will be those who take the initiative and are interested in buying stock at present market prices." Among those responding to these offers were employees with the duties of artist, bakeshop foreman, chow loading foreman, clerical assistant, copywriter, electrician, stock clerk, mill office clerk, order credit trainee, production trainee, stenographer, and veterinarian. . . .

The company bottoms its exemption claim on the classification of all offerees as "key employees" in its organization. Its position on trial was that "A key employee . . . is not confined to an organizational chart. It would include an individual who is eleigible for promotion, an individual who especially influences others or who advises others, a person whom the employees look to in some special way, an individual, of course, who carries some special responsibility, who is sympathetic to management and who is ambitious and who the management feels is likely to be promoted to a greater responsibility." That an offering to all of its employees would be public is conceded.

The Securities Act nowhere defines the scope of § 4 (1)'s private offering exemption. Nor is the legislative history of much help in staking out its boundaries. . . .

Decisions under comparable exemptions in the English Companies Acts and state "blue sky" laws, the statutory antecedents of federal securities legislation, have made one thing clear — to be public and offer need not be open to the whole world. In *Securities and Exchange Comm'n* v. *Sunbeam Gold Mines Co.*, 95 F 2d 699 (C.A. 9th Cir. 1938), this point was made in dealing with an offering to the stockholders of two corporations about to be merged. Judge Denman observed that:

> In its broadest meaning the term "public" distinguishes the populace at large from groups of individual members of the public segregated because of some common interest or characteristic. Yet such a distinction is inadequate for practical purposes; manifestly, an offering of securities to all red-headed men, to all residents of Chicago or San Francisco, to all existing stockholders of the General Motors Corporation or the American Telephone & Telegraph Company, is no less "public", in every realistic sense of the word, than an unrestricted offering to the world at large. Such an offering, though not open to everyone who may choose to apply, is none the less "public" in character for the means used to select the particular individuals to whom the offering is to be made bear no sensible relation to the purposes for which the selection is made. . . .

The courts below purported to apply this test. The District Court held, in the language of the Sunbeam decision, that "The purpose of the selection bears a 'sensible relation' to the class chosen," finding that "the sole purpose of the 'selection' is to keep part stock ownership of the business within the operating personnel of the business and to spread ownership throughout all departments and activities of the business." The Court of Appeals treated the case as involving "an offering, without solicitation, of common stock to a selected group of key employees of the issuer, most of whom are already stockholders when the offering is made, with the sole purpose of enabling them to secure a proprietary interest in the company or to increase the interest already held by them."

Exemption from the registration requirements of the Security Act is the question. The design of the statute is to protect investors by promoting full disclosure of information thought necessary to informed investment decisions. The natural way to interpret the private offering exemption is in light of the statutory purpose. Since exempt transactions are those as to which "there is no practical need for (the bill's) application," the applicability of § 4 (1) should turn on whether the particular class of persons affected needs the protection of the Act. An offering to those who are shown to be able to fend for themselves is a transaction "not involving any public offering."

The Commission would have us go one step futher and hold that "an offering to a substantial number of the public" is not exempt under § 4 (1). We are advised that "whatever the special circumstances, the Commission has consistently interpreted the exemption as being inapplicable when a large number of offerees is involved." But the statute would seem to apply to a "public offering" whether to few or many. It may well be that offerings to a substantial number of persons would rarely be exempt. Indeed nothing prevents the commission, in enforcing the statute, from using some kind of numerical test in deciding when to investigate particuular exemption claims. But there is no warrant for superimposing a quantity limit on private offerings as a matter of statutory interpretation.

The exemption, as we construe it, does not deprive corporate employees, as a class, of the safeguards of the Act. We agree that some employee offerings may come within § 4 (1) e.g., one made to executive personnel who because of their position have access to the same kind of information that the Act would make available in the form of a registration statement. Absent such a showing of special circumstances, employees are just as much members of the investing "public" as any of their neighbors in the community. . . .

Keeping in mind the broadly remedial purposes of federal securities legislation, imposition of the burden of proof on an issuer who would plead the exemption seems to us fair and reasonable. *Schlemmer* v. *Buffalo, R & P.R. Company* 205 U.S. 1, 10 (1907). Agreeing, the court below thought the burden met primarily because of the respondent's purpose in singling out its key employees for stock offerings. But once it is seen that the exemption question turns on the knowledge of the offerees, the issuer's motives, laudable though they may be, fade into irrelevance. The focus of inquiry should be on the need of the offerees for the protections afforded by registration. The employees here were not shown to have access to the kind of information which registration would disclose. The obvious opportunities for pressure and imposition make it advisable that they be entitled to compliance with § 5.

Reversed

♦♦♦

Case Questions:

1. Is it a valid argument to contend that "key employees" can include such personnel as a stock clerk, production trainee and bakeshop foreman?
2. Did the court err in not giving more weight to the fact that these employees solicited the stock on their own initiative?
3. Why did the court not hold that an offering to a substantial number of the public is not exempt?
4. Is is correct to delineate private versus public offerings on the basis of the financial sophistication of the purchaser?

RULE 146: TRANSACTIONS BY AN ISSUER DEEMED NOT TO INVOLVE ANY PUBLIC OFFERING

In an effort to deal with the uncertainties over what constitutes a private or non-public offering, the SEC adopted Rule 146 in April of 1974. The rule operates prospectively from June 10, 1974 and any issuer meeting its conditions will be regarded by the SEC as having made an exempt nonpublic offering. However, failure to comply will probably yield a challenge by the SEC and the expense and burden of convincing a federal court that the offering is in fact exempt under the statute. The criteria established by the rule provide generally that to constitute a non public offering: the number of purchasers cannot exceed 35 (exclusive of institutional investors); promotional advertisements and solicitations by means of investment seminars should be shunned; the prospective purchaser must have access to the type of information contained in a registration statement; precautions must be established to prevent the purchaser from reselling the unregistered securities and; the prospective purchaser must be a sophisticated investor with the ability to evaluate the quality of the securities being offered. The last requirement can be met by an individual of sufficient financial means to risk the investment who, lacking the requisite sophistication, utilizes the advice of one with the necessary knowledge and experience.

It is important to keep in mind that the antifraud provisions of the law apply to both registered and exempt unregistered securities. Why does an issuer risk running afoul of the SEC by making a private offering, would it not prove easier to register the securities? Typically, the answer is financial. The legal, accounting, administrative and underwriting expenses that accompany a securities registration can assume substantial proportions.

RULE 144: PERSONS DEEMED NOT TO BE ENGAGED IN A DISTRIBUTION AND THEREFORE NOT UNDERWRITERS

Mention should be made of an additional point of confusion involving exempt non-public offerings and exempt transactions by any person other than an issuer, underwriter, or dealer. The problem arises thus: An issuer sells exempt non-registered stock to A, who purchases the stock for investment purposes. A now desires to resell the stock. Is resale permissable, absent registration of the stock? An underwriter is defined by the 33 Act as, among other things, one who purchased from an issuer with a view to distribution. Securities transactions by underwriters are not exempt from registration. So, may A legally sell? If A does sell, has the issuer also violated the Act by virtue of A serving as a mere conduit in the transfer of those securities to the public? Lacking concrete answers to such questions the securities industry developed the concept of "letter stock." The purchaser would sign an "investment letter" acknowledging receipt of information concerning the issuing company and attesting to the availability of any further data, their personal contact with corporate officials, their knowledge of the investment risks and the fact that the stock was unregistered and, that they were purchasing the stock with the intention of holding it for investment and not for resale. Another device designed to provide some guidance was the "change of circumstances" doctrine. If the investor purchased the non-registered securities under one set of conditions, but then experienced a "change of circumstances" this change might permit their resale. These subsequently experienced circumstances would be studied in an attempt to ascertain whether the original purchase was strictly for investment purposes. Coupled with this doctrine was the element of a time requirement. If the investor held the securities for a lengthy period of time, this could serve as an indication of his investment intentions at the time of the original purchase. No holding period was ever officially established but a rough rule of thumb developed specifying a minimum two year holding period. However, both the investment letter concept and the change in circumstances doctrine lacked official legal sanction. Thus, an important area of securities law was uncharted and dangerous. In 1972 the SEC ended much of the uncertainty by adopting Rule 144.

Just as with Rule 146, Rule 144 is not the exclusive method of meeting the statutory requirements. However, those not complying with the rule again do so at their own risk and face a substantial burden in establishing that the offers and resale are exempt from registration. The rule provides that a person who sells restricted securities is not deemed to be engaged in a distribution of the securities, and therefore is not an underwriter, if the securities are sold in accordance with the terms of the rule. The rule contains basically the following provisions: the restricted securities must have been beneficially owned for a period of at least two years; the amount sold cannot exceed one percent of the class outstanding, or if traded on an exchange, the lesser of that amount or the average weekly volume on all such exchanges during the four weeks preceding the sale; the securities must be sold in brokers' transactions (the broker is restricted to only executing the order, he cannot solicit buy orders and he may be paid only the customary commission); adequate information in regard to the issuer must be available to the public and; the person desiring to sell the securities must file with the SEC a notice to that effect.

In conjunction with the adoption of Rule 144, the SEC made several important observations. They put all persons on notice that the "change in circumstances" concept would no longer be considered as one of the factors in determining whether a person is an underwriter. The Commission now regards that concept as failing to meet the objective of the '33 Act since the circumstances of the seller are unrelated to the need of investors for the protections afforded by registration. For restrictive securities not sold pursuant to the rule, the SEC will consider the length of time the securities have been held in deciding whether the seller is an underwriter. However, the fact that securities have been held for a particular period of time does not establish per se the availability of an exemption from registration. Finally, the Commission strongly suggests that the issuer use an appropriate legend on the stock certificates, noting the fact that they are unregistered, and provide stop-transfer instructions to stock transfer agents. It will consider these as a factor in determining whether the issuer had in fact made an initial private placement.

The following case presents an excellent illustration of what constitutes the use of an instrumentality of interstate commerce, thereby subjecting the transaction to the federal securities' laws anti-fraud provisions. Note two things: 1) the stock is of a closed corporation and, 2) the telephone was used only on an instrastate basis.

MYZEL v. FIELDS
386 F. 2d 718 (1967)

LAY, Circuit Judge

The four cases here considered are actions brought under Securities and Exchange Commission Rule 10b-5, 17 C.F.R. § 240.10b-5 (hereinafter Rule 10b-5), which implements Section 10(b) of the Securities Exchange Act of 1934, 15 U.S.C. § 78a et seq., arising out of the sale of stock of a closed corporation. Trial was held before a jury and jury verdicts totaling $441,000 were returned in favor of the plaintiff. . . . We affirm the verdicts and judgments below.

The basic issues are: (1) juridiction over intrastate sales. . . .

I. JURISDICTION. Both Section 10 of the Act [15 U.S.C. § 78j (b)] and Rule 10b-5 require as a jurisdictional basis "the use of any means or instrumentality of interstate commerce or of the mails, or of any facility of any national securities exchange."

The evidence is undisputed that the telephone was used only on an intrastate basis in the solicitation or purchase of each of the appellees' stock. Appellees claim that federal jurisdiction exists because the telephone is an "instrumentality of interstate commerce" and, therefore, the cases fall within the prohibition of the statute. Despite reasoning to the contrary,[1] we are convinced that Congress, in the interest of fairly regulating interstate commerce, intended to supervise those intrastate activities in violation of Rule 10b-5 which are "inimical to the welfare and public policy of the country as a whole". . . . We hold, consequently, that intrastate use of the telephone comes within prohibition of the Act. . . . In interpreting other grants of federal power, it has long been acknowledged that Congress may regulate intrastate activity if simultaneously it is an integral part of or constitutes an instrumentality of interstate commerce. . . .

Thus, in order to protect interstate commerce, intrastate telephonic messages have been placed under the statutory prohibition pertaining to unauthorized publication or use of communications under 47 U.S.C. §605. *Weiss* v. *United States,* 308 U.S. 321, 60 S Ct. 269, 84 L.Ed. 298 (1939). We recognize that the telephone system and its voice transmission by wire is an integrated system of both intrastate and interstate commerce. . . . As such, proof of the interstate telephone message is not a prerequisite to jurisdiction over a Section 10(b) action. As long as the instrumentality itself is an integral part of an interstate

---

[1] See *Rosen* v. *Albern Color Research, Inc.,* 218 F. Supp, 473 (E.D. Pa. 1963). The Rosen case relies upon *Northern Trust Co.* v. *Essaness Theatres Corp.,* 103 F. Supp. 954 at 964 (N.D. Ill. 1952), wherein the district court states:
"The purpose of Section 17 (a) of the 1933 Act and Section 10(b) of the 1934 Act are similar and the phraseology employed is substantially similar."
Section 17(a) of the Securities Act of 1933, 15 U.S.C. § 77q(a), provides in part:

"It shall be unlawful for any person in the offer or sale of any securities by the use of any means or instruments of transportation or communication in interstate commerce or by the use of the mails, directly or indirectly * * *."

Judge Kraft in the Rosen opinion reasons that it is the interstate communication which is the essence of the offense. Despite the similarity there is a crucial omission from § 10(b) of the § 17(a) requirement that there be a communication in interstate commerce; the requirement of § 10(b) is "By the use of any means or instrumentality of interstate commerce." The legislative history does not serve to explain the difference in the wording of the two statutes. As we indicated in *Little* v. *United States,* 331 F. 2d 287, 292-293 (8 Cir. 1964), the use of the mails is not the gist of the offense:

"That the scheme to defraud is the evil intended to be controlled and remedied by passage of the Securities Act, supra cannot be in doubt * * *"

See also *Creswell-Keith, Inc.* v. *Willingham,* 264 F. 2d. 76, 80, 82 (9 Cir. 1959). All the other sections of the Securities Exchange Act of 1934 incorporate similar language, as does the Act controlling investment companies, 15 U.S.C. §80a-1 et seq. In each case the language reads "use of the mails and means and instrumentalities of interstate commerce." The Supreme Court when faced with an analogous argument under Section 605 of the Communications Act of 1934, 47 U.S.C. §605, stated:

"In making the alterations in the phraseology of the similar section of the earlier act of Congress must have had some purpose." *Weiss* v. *United States,* 308 U.S. 321, 329, 60 S. Ct. 269, 272 84 L.Ed. 298 (1939).

system, nothing in the Constitution requires Congress to exclude intrastate activities from the regulatory control. ...

But there exists additional grounds to sustain jurisdiction. It is the rule that where any interstate use is made to perpetuate the original fraudulent concealment or transaction, even though not part of the original solicitation or inducement of sales involved, that nevertheless the subsequent use of interstate facilities in furthering the scheme is sufficient to establish federal jurisdiction. ...

Appellees contended that they were fraudulently induced to sell their stock to the appellants, that the purchases were made by parties (the Myzels) other than the true buyers (the Levines) and that an Illinois corporation owned by some of the appellants was used as a conduit of concealment. The transfers of the stock to the Illinois corporation, although occurring several months and even years later, involved the delivery of checks written by the Illinois corporation on Chicago, Illinois banks to a Minnesota citizen. ... Thus, under appellees' theory, there was also sufficient evidence of interstate transactions to sustain jurisdiction.

◆◆◆

REVIEW PROBLEMS

1. Section 5(c) of the '33 Act declares it unlawful for any person to make use of any means of communication in interstate commerce or of the mails to offer to sell or buy through the use of any prospectus or otherwise any security, unless a registration statement has been filed as to such security. SEC Rule 135 (a) (2) provides that it is not an offer to sell where a notice is communicated to any class of security holders of such issuer or of another issuer advising them that it proposes to offer its securities to them in exchange for other securities presently held by such security holders. Chris-Craft is battling Bangor Punta for Control of Piper Aircraft. The Piper family agrees to exchange their stock for Bangor Punta securities. Bangor Punta in turn will attempt to gain control of Piper by acquiring in excess of 50 percent of Piper's outstanding stock. The management of both companies make this announcement through the issuance of a press release. The release mentions that Bangor Punta will make an exchange offer to all Piper shareholders for a package of Bangor Punta securities to be valued at not less than $80 per Piper share. The release mentions that a registration statement will be filed. Chris-Craft sues alleging, inter alia, that the press release is an unlawful offer to sell. Is it? [*Chris-Craft* v. *Bangor Punta*, 426 F. 2d 569, (1970)].

2. A mutual fund purchases Letter stock for $2 per share. That price is below the current market value. The issuer was willing to make such a private placement at less than market value in view of its need to quickly raise a large sum of money and by virtue of the savings realized by foregoing the expenses of SEC registration. Six months later the market price is $10 per share. In calculating the value of the shares of the mutual fund itself, what price should the mutual fund place on its Letter stock? What happens if the business fortunes of the company decline so greatly that it files bankruptcy while the mutual fund is legally prevented from unloading its Letter stock?

3. Continental Tobacco is a South Carolina corporation organized for the purpose of manufacturing cigarettes. It held a series of sales presentations for prospective purchasers of its unregistered debentures at a Florida hotel. The SEC obtained preliminary injunctions halting these promotions, which the court concluded were unlawful public offerings. Shortly thereafter the company underwent a Chapter XI Bankruptcy reorganization. Following its discharge from these proceedings, it sought to raise funds through the sale of unregistered common stock. Promotional meetings were held at private homes and hotels. The father and son operating Continental enlisted the aid of acquaintances in promoting the stock. A dentist, who was himself a purchaser, had his dental assistant display a brochure on the company to his patients. The stock was offered to 38 individuals, 35 of whom made purchases. The purchasers were dentists, physicians, businessmen and housewives. They signed "investment letters" acknowledging that they knew the stock was unregistered and were purchasing it for investment purposes. The stock certificates carried a legend noting that the stock was unregistered and that a legal opinion would be required before the stock could be resold. Do the activities, subsequent to the bankruptcy proceedings, constitute a public offering? [*SEC* v. *Continental Tobacco*, 463 F. 2d 137 (1972)].

4. Scotch whiskey warehouse receipts are being promoted for sale through direct mail and newspaper advertisements. A typical statement contained in such ads reads as follows: "Invest in Scotch Whiskey for Profit. Exceptional Capital Growth is Possible When You Buy Scotch Whiskey Reserves by the Barrel. Insured Investment for Profit and Growth in Scotch Whiskey." In addition to the phrase "Insured Investment" some ads carried the phrase "insured no loss policy." If a potential investor read a brochure prepared by the promoters he could learn that his investment was not being insured. Instead the whiskey was insured against loss from fire and cask leakage. The SEC contends that the defendants are violating the '33 Act by selling unregistered securities and the '34 Act by utilizing deceptive and fraudulent promotional advertisements. What do you think? [*SEC* v. *Lundy Associates*, 362 F. Supp 226 (1973)].

ENDNOTES

1. *Hall* v. *Geiger Jones & Co.*, 242 U.S. 539, 550 (1917).
2. Schneider & Manko, "Going Public: Practice, Procedure and Consequences," *Villanova Law Review*, Vol. 15, No. 2, PP. 283-313.
3. *SEC* v. *Payne*, 35 F. Supp. 873 (1940).
4. *Tcherepnin* v. *Knight*, 389 U.S. 332 (1967).
5. *Silver Hills Country Club* v. *Sobieski*, (Cal. S.Ct.) (1961).

When Congress held hearings on the '33 and '34 Acts it heard a great deal about gross unfairness and abuses in the securities markets resulting from persons trading upon facts not available to the general investing public. Two sections of the '34 Act are designed to outlaw such activities. One section prohibits certain individuals from making a profit in stock transactions during a certain time period. The other section outlaws all transactions based upon material inside information.

SHORT-SWING PROFITS (SECTION 16(b) OF THE '34 ACT)

Section 16 applies to every person who is directly or indirectly the beneficial owner of more than 10 percent of any class of any registered equity security, or who is a director or an officer of the issuer of such security. The word "beneficial" is extremely important. One can beneficially own securities without being the legal owner. For example, one usually will be the beneficial owner of securities legally owned by a spouse or minor children.

Section 16(b) provides:

> For the purpose of preventing the unfair use of information which may have been obtained by such beneficial owner, director, or officer by reason of his relationship to the issuer, any profit realized by him from any purchase and sale, or any sale and purchase, of any equity security of such issuer . . . within any period of less than six months, unless such security was acquired in good faith in connection with a debt previously contracted, shall inure to and be recoverable by the issuer, irrespective of any intention on the part of such beneficial owner, director, or officer in entering into such transaction of holding the security purchased or of not repurchasing the security sold for a period exceeding six months. . . . This subsection shall not be construed to cover any transaction where such beneficial owner was not such both at the time of the purchase and sale, or the sale and purchase, of the security involved, or any transaction or transactions which the Commission by rules and regulations may exempt as not comprehended within the purpose of this subsection.

The courts mechanically, yet rigorously, apply this section. It is immaterial whether one actually used inside information. The specified transactions are absolutely prohibited. If they do occur, the short-swing profits belong to the corporation. The concept is that individuals in these categories, by virtue of the positions they hold, may have access to inside information. However, if they are barred from trading at a profit in their stock, the inside information will likely become available to the investing public in the intervening six month period. The statute has a self-enforcing mechanism. If there is a change in the stock ownership of the respective director, officer or principal stockholder, during any month he must report this change to the SEC and the national securities exchange. This information is public and oftentimes is printed in financial papers such as *The Wall Street Journal.* Either the issuer of the security or a stockholder (it is not necessary that he owned stock at the time of the transaction in dispute) can sue to recover the profits for the corporation. The shareholder may bring the suit only if the issuer has failed to bring the suit within sixty days after request or has failed to diligently prosecute the suit. The shareholder does not benefit directly from any recovery. The profits go to the corporate treasury. However, the shareholder's attorney is paid a percentage of the recovered profits. The amount usually varies between 10 and 33 percent; the larger the recovery the smaller the percentage. Generally the courts are not niggardly in their allowance of attorney's fees because it serves as an important stimulus for enforcement of the law.

The statute does not give any guidance as to how a "profit" is to be calculated. In their interpretation the courts arbitrarily match purchases and sales so as to achieve the maximum profit. One cannot escape liability by showing that the specific share certificates sold (or purchased) are not the same ones purchased (or sold) during the specific six month period. In *Smolowe* v. *Delendo Corp.,* 136 F. 2d 231 (1943), the court rejected such formulas as first in first out and average purchase price average sales price. The court also held that any losses incurred during the six month period cannot be set off against the profits to reduce them. If this seems harsh consider the words of the court in *Gratz* v. *Claughton,* 187 F.2d 46 (1951), ". . . (the) crushing liability of 16(b) should serve as a warning and may prove a deterrent." The application of these rules is illustrated in the following example.

Determination of what constitutes a profit under Section 16(b) is not as easy as it may appear to be at first blush. Consider the following situation:

Day 1 An insider owns 100 shares of stock.

Day 2 He purchases 10 shares at $7 per share.

Day 3 He sells 10 shares at $5 per share.

Day 4 He purchases 10 shares at $3 per share.

Day 5 He sells 10 shares at $1 per share.

The result of these transactions is to leave him still owning 100 shares of stock. However, since he paid $100 for his additional purchases and only received $60 from his sales, it would appear that he has suffered a net loss of $40, plus commissions. Yet, amazing as it may seem, he has made a short swing profit in the amount of $20. This profit is arrived at by matching the purchase at $3 and the sale at $5 (keeping in mind that one cannot deduct the loss of $60 by matching the purchase at $7 and the sale at $1). Using this formula in an actual case a court concluded that the individual had made a profit in excess of $300,000 while in reality he had suffered a loss of several hundred thousand dollars.

There had been a long standing controversy over the interpretation of the last sentence of 16(b). The sentence provides that the section does not cover a transaction where the "beneficial owner was not such both at the time of the purchase and sale" and vice versa. The argument was over whether "at the time of purchase" means before the purchase or immediately after the purchase. In January 1976 the Supreme Court adopted the former interpretation in *Foremost-McKesson . v. Provident Securities,* 423 U.S. (1976). Foremost purchased two-thirds of Provident's assets for cash and convertible debentures. When Provident received the debentures they were immediately convertible into more than 10 percent of Foremost's outstanding common stock. Provident disposed of these securities within six months. It sought a court declaration that it was not liable to Foremost for any profits under § 16(b). The Supreme Court affirmed the grant of a declatory judgment in Provident's favor in an opinion heavily based upon legislative history. The Court acknowledged that it was creating a loophole but said that other statutory provisions against insider trading protect the investing public. Previously the Court had affirmed a ruling that a 13.2 percent shareholder, who sold 3.24 percent within six months, was liable for any profits on that sale but, was now free to sell the remaining 9.96 percent within the same six month period and retain any profits. *Reliance Elec. Co.* v. *Emerson Elec. Co.,* 404 U.S. 418 (1972).

What time period constitutes less than six months? December 1 to the following May 30, rather than June 1, does for example.

The following case provides a U.S. Supreme Court interpretation of § 16(b) within an interesting context.

BLAU v. LEHMAN
368 U.S. 403 (1962)

◆◆◆

Mr. Justice Black delivered the opinion of the Court.

The petitioner Blau, a stockholder in Tide Water Associated Oil Company, brought this action in a United States District Court on behalf of the company under § 16 (b) of the Securities Exchange Act of 1934 to recover with interest "short swing" profits, that is, profits earned within a six months' period by the purchase and sale of securities, alleged to have been "realized" by respondents in Tide Water securities dealings. Respondents are Lehman Brothers, a partnership engaged in investment banking, securities brokerage and in securities trading for its own account, and Joseph A. Thomas, a member of Lehman Brothers and a director of Tide Water. The complaint alleged that Lehman Brothers "deputed . . . Thomas, to represent its interests as a director on the Tide Water Board of Directors," and that within a period of six months in 1954 and 1955 Thomas, while representing the interests of Lehman Brothers as a director of Tide Water and "by reason of his special and inside knowledge of the affairs of Tide Water, advised and caused the defendants, Lehman Brothers, to purchase and sell 50,000 shares of . . . stock of Tide Water, realizing profits thereon which did not inure to and [were] not recovered by Tide Water."

The case was tried before a district judge without a jury. The evidence showed that Lehman Brothers had in fact earned profits out of short-swing transactions in Tide Water securities while Thomas was a director of that company. But as to the charges of deputization and wrongful use of "inside" information by Lehman Brothers, the evidence was in conflict.

First, there was testimony that respondent Thomas had succeeded Hertz, another Lehman partner, on the board of Tide Water; that Hertz had "joined Tidewater Company thinking it was going to be in the interests of Lehman Brothers;" and that he had suggested Thomas as his successor partly because it was in the interest of Lehman. There was also testimony, however, that Thomas, aside from having mentioned from time to time to some of his partners and other people that he thought Tide Water was "an attractive investment" and under "good" management, had never discussed the operating details of Tide Water affairs with any member of Lehman Brothers; that Lehman had bought the Tide Water securities without consulting Thomas and wholly on the basis of public announcements by Tide Water that common shareholders could thereafter convert their shares to a new cumulative preferred issue; that Thomas did not know of Lehman's intent to buy Tide Water stock until after the initial purchases had been made; that upon learning about the purchases he immediately notified Lehman that he must be excluded from "any risk of the purchase or any profit or loss from the subsequent sale;" and that this disclaimer was accepted by the firm.

From the foregoing and other testimony the District Court found that "there was no evidence that the firm of Lehman Brothers deputed Thomas to represent its interests as director on the board of Tide Water" and that there had been no actual use of inside information, Lehman Brothers having bought its Tide Water stock "solely on the basis of Tide Water's public announcements and without consulting Thomas."

On the basis of these findings the District Court refused to render a judgment, either against the partnership or against Thomas individually, for the $98,686.77 profits which it determined that Lehman Brothers had realized, holding:

> The law is now well settled that the mere fact that a partner in Lehman Brothers was a director of Tide Water, at the time that Lehman Brothers had this short swing transaction in the stock of Tide Water, is not sufficient to make the partnership liable for the profits thereon, and that Thomas could nót be held liable for the profits realized by the other partners from the firm's short swing transactions. *Rattner* v. *Lehman,* 2 Cir., 1952, 193 F. 2d 564, 565, 567. This precise question was passed upon in the Rattner decision. (173 F. Supp. 590, 593).

Despite its recognition that Thomas had specifically waived his share of the Tide Water transaction profits, the trial court nevertheless held that within the meaning of § 16 (b) Thomas had "realized" $3,893.41, his proportionate share of the profits of Lehman Brothers. The court consequently entered judgment against Thomas for that amount but refused to allow interest against him. On appeal, taken by both sides, the Court of Appeals for the Second Circuit adhered to the view it had taken in *Rattner* v. *Lehman,* and affirmed the District Court's judgment in all respects, Judge Clark dissenting. 286 F. 2d 786. ... We granted certiorari on the petition of Blau, filed on behalf of himself, other stockholders and Tide Water, and supported by the Commission. 366 U.S. 902. The questions presented by the petition are whether the courts below erred: (1) in refusing to render a judgment against the Lehman partnership for the $98,686.77 profits they were found to have "realized" from their "short-swing" transactions in Tide Water stock, (2) in refusing to render judgment against Thomas for the full $98,686.77 profits, and (3) in refusing to allow interest on the $3,893.41 recovery allowed against Thomas.[1]

Petitioner apparently seeks to have us decide the questions presented as though he had proven the allegations of his complaint that Lehman Brothers actually deputized Thomas to represent its interests as a director of Tide Water, and that it was his advice and counsel based on his special and inside knowledge of Tide Water's affairs that caused Lehman Brothers to buy and sell Tide Water's stock. But the trial court found otherwise and the Court of Appeals affirmed these findings. Inferences could perhaps have been drawn from the evidence to support petitioner's charges, but examination of the record makes it clear to us that the findings of the two courts below were not clearly erroneous. ... We must therefore decide whether Lehman Brothers, Thomas or both have an absolute liability under § 16(b) to pay over all profits made on Lehman's Tide Water stock dealings even though Thomas was not sitting on Tide Water's board to represent Lehman and even though the profits made by the partnership were on its own initiative, independently of any advice or "inside" knowledge given it by director Thomas.

First. The language of § 16 does not purport to impose its extraordinary liability on any "person," "fiduciary" or not, unless he or it is a "director", "officer" or "beneficial owner of more than 10 percentum of any class of any equity security . . . which is registered on a national securities exchange." Lehman Brothers was neither an officer nor a 10 percent stockholder of Tide Water, but petitioner and the Commission contend that the Lehman partnership is or should be treated as a director under § 16 (b).

(a) Although admittedly not "literally designated" as one, it is contended that Lehman is a director. No doubt Lehman Brothers, though a partnership, could for purposes of § 16 be a "director" of Tide Water and function through a deputy, since § 3 (a) (9) of the Act provides that " 'person' means . . . partnership" and § 3 (a) (7) that "director" means any director of a corporation or any person performing similar functions with respect to any organization, whether incorporated or unincorporated." Consequently, Lehman Brothers would be a "director" of Tide Water, if as petitioner's complaint charged Lehman actually functioned as a director through Thomas, who had been deputized by Lehman to perform a director's duties not for himself but for Lehman. But the findings of the two courts below, which we have accepted, preclude such a holding. It was Thomas, not Lehman Brothers as an entity, that was the director of Tide Water.

(b) It is next argued that the intent of § 3 (a) (9) in defining "person" as including a partnership is to treat a partnership as an inseparable entity. Because Thomas, one member of this inseparable entity, is an "insider," it is contended that the whole partnership should be considered the "insider." But the obvious intent of § 3 (a) (9), as the Commission apparently realizes, is merely to make it clear that a partnership can be treated as an entity under the statute, not that it

---

[1] In the two courts below it was contended both that Thomas, because of his disclaimer of all participation in these partnership transactions, had realized no profits at all, and also that, even if he did realize some profits the amount was less than that found. See the opinion of Judge Swan dissenting in part below. 286 F. 2d, at 793. We express no view on these questions since the Thomas judgment is not challenged here.

must be. This affords no reason at all for construing the word "director" in § 16 (b) as though it read "partnership of which the director is a member." And the fact that Congress provided in § 3 (a) (9) for a partnership to be treated as an entity in its own right likewise offers no support for the argument that Congress wanted a partnership to be subject to all the responsibilities and financial burdens of its members in carrying on their other individual business activities.

(c) Both the petitioner and the Commission contend on policy grounds that the Lehman partnership should be held liable even though it is neither a director, officer, nor a 10 percent stockholder. Conceding that such an interpretation is not justified by the literal language of § 16 (b) which plainly limits liability to directors, officers, and 10 percent stockholders, it is argued that we should expand § 16 (b) to cover partnerships of which a director is a member in order to carry out the congressionally declared purpose "of preventing the unfair use of information which may have been obtained by such beneficial owner, director, or officer by reason of his relationship to the issuer . . ." Failure to do so, it is argued, will leave a large and unintended loophole in the statute — one "substantially eliminating the great Wall Street trading firms from the statue's operation." 286 F. 2d, at 799. These firms it is claimed will be able to evade the Act and take advantage of the "inside" information available to their members as insiders of countless corporations merely by trading "inside" information among the various partners.

The argument of petitioner and the Commission seems to go so far as to suggest that § 16 (b)'s forfeiture of profits should be extended to include all persons realizing "short swing" profits who either act on the basis of "inside" information or have the possibility of "inside" information. One may agree that petitioner and the Commission present persuasive policy arguments that the Act should be broadened in this way to prevent "the unfair use of information" more effectively than can be accomplished by leaving the Act so as to require forfeiture of profits only by those specifically designated by Congress to suffer those losses. But this very broadening of the categories of persons on whom these liabilities are imposed by the language of § 16 (b) was considered and rejected by Congress when it passed the Act. Drafts of provisions that eventually became § 16 (b) not only would have made it unlawful for any director, officer or 10 percent stockholder to disclose any confidential information regarding registered securities, but also would have made all profits received by anyone, "insider" or not, "to whom such unlawful disclosure" had been made recoverable by the company.

Not only did Congress refuse to give § 16 (b) the content we are now urged to put into it by interpretation, but with knowledge that in 1952 the Second Circuit Court of Appeals refused, in the Rattner case, to apply § 16 (b) to Lehman Brothers in circumstances substantially like those here, Congress has left the Act as it was. And so far as the record shows this interpretation of § 16 (b) was the view of the Commission until it intervened last year in this case. Indeed in· the Rattner case the Court of Appeals relied in part on Commission Rule X-16A-3 (b) which required insider-partners to report only the amount of their own holdings and not the amount of holdings by the partnership. While the Commission has since changed this rule to require disclosure of partnership holdings too, its official release explaining the change stated that the new rule was "not intended as a modification of the principles governing liability for short-swing transactions under Section 16 (b) as set forth in the case of *Rattner* v. *Lehman*. ...." Congress can and might amend § 16 (b) if the Commission would present to it the policy arguments it has presented to us, but we think that Congress is the proper agency to change an interpretation of the Act unbroken since its passage, if the change is to be made.

Second. The petitioner and the Commission contend that Thomas should be required individually to pay to Tide Water the entire $98,686.77 profit Lehman Brothers realized on the ground that under partnership law he is co-owner of the entire undivided amount and has therefore "realized" it all. "[O]nly by holding the partner-director liable for the entire short-swing profits realized by his firm," it is urged, can "an effective prophylactic to the stated statutory policy . . . be fully enforced." But liability under § 16 (b) is to be determined neither by general partnership law nor by adding to the "prophylactic" effect Congress itself clearly prescribed in § 16 (b). That section leaves no room for judicial doubt that a director is to pay to his company only "any profit realized by him" from short-swing transactions. (Emphasis added.) It would be nothing but a fiction to say that Thomas "realized" all the profits earned by the partnership of which he was a member. It was not error to refuse to hold Thomas liable for profits he did not make.

Third. It is contended that both courts below erred in failing to allow interest on the recovery of Thomas' share of the partnership profits. Section 16 (b) says nothing about interest one way or the other. This Court has said in a kindred situation that "interest is not recovered according to a rigid theory of compensation for money withheld, but is given in response to considerations of fairness. It is denied when its exaction would be inequitable." *Board of Commissioners* v. *United States,* 308 U.S. 343, 352. Both courts below denied interest here and we cannot say that the denial was either so unfair or so inequitable as to require us to upset it.

Affirmed.

Mr. Justice Douglas, with whom The Chief Justice concurs, dissenting.

What the Court does today is substantially to eliminate "the great Wall Street trading firms" from the operation of § 16(b), as Judge Clark stated in his dissent in the Court of Appeals. 286 F. 2d 786, 799. This result follows because of the wide dispersion of partners of investment banking firms among our major corporations. Lehman Brothers has partners on 100 boards. Under today's ruling that firm can make a rich harvest on the "inside information" which §16 of the Act covers because each partner need account only for his distributive share of the firm's profits on "inside information," the other partners keeping the balance. This is a mutilation of the Act.

If a partnership can be a "director" within the meaning of § 16 (a), then "any profit realized by him," as those words are used in § 16 (b), includes all the profits, not merely a portion of them, which the partnership realized on the "inside information." There is no basis in reason for saying a partnership cannot be a "director" for the purposes of the Act. ... Everyone knows that the investment banking-corporation alliances are consciously constructed so as to increase the profits of the bankers. In partnership law a debate has long raged over whether a partnership is an entity or an aggregate. Pursuit of that will-o'-the-wisp is not profitable. For even New York with its aggregate theory recognizes that a partnership is or may be considered a entity for some purposes. It is easier to make this partnership a "director" for purposes of § 16 than to hold the opposite. . . .

At the root of the present problem are the scope and degree of liability arising out of fiduciary relations. In modern times that liability has been strictly construed. The New York Court of Appeals, speaking through Chief Judge Cardozo in *Meinhard* v. *Salmon,* 249 N.Y. 458, 164 N.E. 545, held a joint adventurer to a higher standard than we insist upon today:

> Many forms of conduct permissable in workaday world for those acting at arm's length, are forbidden to those bound by fiduciary ties. A trustee is held to something stricter than the morals of the market place. Not honesty alone, but the punctilio of an honor the most sensitive, is then the standard of behavior. As to this there has developed a tradition that is unbending and inveterate. Uncompromising rigidity has been the attitude of courts of equity when petitioned to undermine the rule of undivided loyalty by the 'disintegrating erosion' of particular exceptions (*Wendt* v. *Fischerm* 243 N.Y. 439, 444). Only thus has the level of conduct for fiduciaries been kept at a level higher than that trodden by the crowd. It will not consciously be lowered by any judgment of this court. (249 N.Y., at 464, 164 N.E., at 546. . . .)

We forget much history when we give § 16 a strict and narrow construction. Brandeis in *Other People's Money* spoke of the office of "director" as "a happy hunting ground" for investment bankers. He said that "The goose that lays golden eggs has been considered a most valuable possession. But even more profitable is the privilege of taking the golden eggs laid by somebody else's goose. The investment bankers and their associates now enjoy that privilege." Id., at 12. . . .

What we do today allows all but one partner to share in the feast which the one places on the partnership table. They in turn can offer feasts to him in the 99 other companies of which they are directors. . . . This result is a dilution of the fiduciary principle that Congress wrote into § 16 of the Act. It is, with all respect, a dilution that is possible only by a strained reading of the law. Until now, the courts have given this fiduciary principle a cordial reception. We should not leave to Congress the task of restoring the edifice that it erected and that we tear down.

◆◆◆

Case Question

1. Does this decision mean that a partnership, one member of which sits on the board of a corporation, can never be held liable for short swing profits?

SECTION 10(b) OF THE '34 ACT AND RULE 10B-5

Section 10(b) and its accompanying Rule 10b-5 prohibit persons from trading on the basis of material inside information. The focus is not upon the individual's position in the corporate hierarchy, but, whether he possesses material inside information. If so, he is prohibited from trading in that corporation's securities until that information has been made available to the general investing public. Material inside information is any fact that might reasonably affect the value of a corporation's securities. One is not prohibited from studying available public annual reports, quarterly reports, economic trends, etc. and on the basis of that analysis and one's own expertise making successful investment decisions. Such data is available to whoever wishes to study it. The concept behind the prohibition against trading on the basis of material inside information is to permit all investors to stand on an equal basis when it comes to access to information affecting the value of a corporate security.

Individuals are often amazed to learn that it is illegal to trade on the basis of inside information. They incorrectly regard it as being within the "rights" of a corporate executive, as simply another permissable form of executive compensation. It is not! Such trading violates both the securities laws and their fiduciary duties. This information belongs to their corporation and they may not convert it to their own personal use. The law regards the corporate employee as receiving adequate official compensation and demands in return that he devote his full efforts to the corporate welfare. The search for personal enrichment through inside trading is an unallowable distraction.

Mention should also be made of the "special circumstances" doctrine. Under this rule created by the Supreme Court, a director before purchasing the stock of other shareholders must inform them of any special circumstances that may affect the value of their stock. In one well known case a 75 percent shareholder-director purchased the interest of another shareholder without revealing that the U.S. would probably purchase certain corporate property, thereby enhancing the stocks value [*Strong* v. *Repide,* 213 U.S. 419 (1909)]. The failure to reveal these special circumstances to the seller was impermissable. Today, such legal actions would usually be brought under the federal securities laws.

Let us actually look at the provisions of Section 10(b) and Rule 10b-5, then examine two cases. *Cady Roberts* is a classic straightforward example of impermissably trading on the basis of inside information. *Texas Gulf Sulphur* is "the" famous inside trading case. It is lengthy, complex and highly controversial.

Regulation of the Use of Manipulative and Deceptive Devices

Sec. 10. It shall be unlawful for any person, directly or indirectly, by the use of any means or instrumentality of interstate commerce or of the mails, or of any facility of any national securities exchange –

(b) To use or employ, in connection with the purchase or sale of any security registered on a national securities exchange or any security not so registered, any manipulative or deceptive device or contrivance in contravention of such rules and regulations as the Commission may prescribe as necessary or appropriate in the public interest or for the protection of investors.

Employment of Manipulative and Deceptive Devices

Rule 10b-5. It shall be unlawful for any person, directly or indirectly, by the use of any means or instrumentality of interstate commerce, or of the mails, or of any facility of any national securities exchange,

(1) to employ any device, scheme, or artifice to defraud,

(2) to make any untrue statement of a material fact or to omit to state a material fact necessary in order to make the statements made, in the light of the circumstances under which they were made, not misleading, or

(3) to engage in any act, practice or course of business which operates or would operate as a fraud or deceit upon any person, in connection with the purchase or sale of any security.

IN THE MATTER OF CADY, ROBERTS & CO.
40 S.E.C. 907 (1961)

◆◆◆

These proceedings were instituted to determine whether Cady, Roberts & Co. ("registrant") and Robert M. Gintel ("Gintel"), the selling broker and a partner of the registrant, willfully violated the "anti-fraud" provisions of Section 10(b) of the Securities Exchange Act of 1934 ("Exchange Act"), Rule 10b-5 issued under that Act, and Section 17 (a) of the Securities Act of 1933 ("Securities Act"). . . .

From November 6, through November 23, Gintel had purchased approximately 11,000 shares of Curtiss-Wright stock for about 30 discretionary accounts of customers of registrant. With the rise in the price on November 24, he began selling Curtiss-Wright shares for these accounts and sold on that day a total of 2,200 shares on the Exchange.

On the morning of November 25, the Curtiss-Wright directors, including J. Cheever Cowdin ("Cowdin")[1], then a registered representative of registrant, met to consider, among other things the declaration of a quarterly dividend. The company had paid a dividend, although not earned, of $.625 per share for each of the first three quarters of 1959. The Curtiss-Wright board, . . . approved a dividend for the fourth quarter at the reduced rate of $.375 per share. At approximately 11:00 a.m., the board authorized transmission of information of this action by telegram to the New York Stock Exchange. The Secretary of Curtiss-Wright immediately left the meeting room to arrange for this communication. There was a short delay in the transmission of the telegram because of a typing problem and the telegram, although transmitted to Western Union at 11:12 a.m., was not delivered to the Exchange until 12:29 p.m. It had been customary for the company also to advise the Dow Jones News Ticker Service of any dividend action. However, apparently through some mistake or inadvertence, the Wall Street Journal was not given the news until approximately 11:45 a.m. and the announcement did not appear on the Dow Jones ticker tape until 11:48 a.m.

Sometime after the dividend decision, there was a recess of the Curtiss-Wright directors' meeting, during which Cowdin telephoned registrant's office and left a message for Gintel that the dividend had been cut. Upon receiving this

---

[1] Mr. Cowdin died in September 1960.

information, Gintel entered two sell orders for execution on the Exchange, one to sell 2,000 shares of Curtiss-Wright stock for 10 accounts, and the other to sell short 5,000 shares for 11 accounts. Four hundred of the 5,000 shares were sold for three of Cowdin's customers. According to Cowdin, pursuant to directions from his clients, he had given instructions to Gintel to take profits on these 400 shares if the stock took a "run-up." These orders were executed at 11:15 and 11:18 a.m. at 40 1/4 and 40 3/8, respectively.

When the dividend announcement appeared on the Dow Jones tape at 11:48 a.m., the Exchange was compelled to suspend trading in Curtiss-Wright because of the large number of sell orders. Trading in Curtiss-Wright stock was resumed at 1:59 p.m. at 36 1/2 ranged during the balance of the day between 34 1/8 and 37, and closed at 34 7/8.

Violation of Anti-Fraud Provisions

These anti-fraud provisions are not intended as a specification of particular acts or practices which constitute fraud, but rather are designed to encompass the infinite variety of devices by which undue advantage may be taken of investors and others.

An affirmative duty to disclose material information has been traditionally imposed on corporate "insiders," particularly officers, directors, or controlling stockholders. We, and the courts have consistently held that insiders must disclose material facts which are known to them by virtue of their position but which are not known to persons with whom they deal and which, if known, would affect their investment judgment. Failure to make disclosure in these circumstances constitutes a violation of the anti-fraud provisions. If, on the other hand, disclosure prior to effecting a purchase or sale would be improper or unrealistic under the circumstances, we believe the alternative is to forego the transaction.

... we accordingly find that Gintel willfully violated Sections 17(a) and 10(b) and Rule 10b-5. We also find a similar violation by the registrant, since the actions of Gintel, a member of registrant, in the course of his employment are to be regarded as actions of registrant itself. It was obvious that a reduction in the quarterly dividend by the Board of Directors was a material fact which could be expected to have an adverse impact on the market price of the company's stock. The rapidity with which Gintel acted upon receipt of the information confirms his own recognition of that conclusion.

The facts here impose on Gintel the responsibilities of those commonly referred to as "insiders." He received the information prior to its public release from a director of Curtiss-Wright, Cowdin, who was associated with the registrant. Cowdin's relationship to the company clearly prohibited him from selling the securities affected by the information without disclosure. By logical sequence, it should prohibit Gintel, a partner of registrant. This prohibition extends not only over his own account, but to selling for discretionary accounts and soliciting and executing other orders. In somewhat analogous circumstances, we have charged a broker-dealer who effects securities transactions for an insider and who knows that the insider possesses non-public material information with the affirmative duty to make appropriate disclosures or dissociate himself from the transaction.

... knowledge of this action was not arrived at as a result of perceptive analysis of generally known facts, but was obtained from a director (and associate). ...

... all the registered broker-dealer need do is to keep out of the market until the established procedures for public release of the information are carried out instead of hastening to execute transactions in advance of, and in frustration of, the objectives of the release.

Finally, we do not accept respondents' contention that Gintel was merely carrying out a program of liquidating the holdings in his discretionary accounts — determined and embarked upon prior to his receipt of the dividend information. In this connection, it is further alleged that he had a fiduciary duty to these accounts to continue the sales, which overrode any obligations to unsolicited purchasers on the Exchange.

The record does not support the contention that Gintel's sales were merely a continuance of his prior schedule of liquidation. Upon receipt of the news of the dividend reduction, which Gintel knew was not public, he hastened to sell before the expected public announcement all of the Curtiss-Wright shares remaining in his discretionary accounts, contrary to his previous moderate rate of sales. In so doing, he also made short sales of securities which he then allocated to his wife's account and to the account of a customer whom he had never seen and with whom he had had no prior dealings. Moreover, while Gintel undoubtedly occupied a fiduciary relationship to his customers, this relationship could not justify any actions by him contrary to law.

◆◆◆

Case Questions

1. If Gintel, the "tippee", had not been a partner of the same firm as Cowdin, the "tipper", would he have violated the securities law?
2. What arguments support a brokerage firm policy prohibiting members of the firm from sitting on corporate boards? What reasons support allowing a member of the firm to occupy a board seat?

SECURITIES AND EXCHANGE COMMISSION
v.
TEXAS GULF SULPHUR CO., et. al.
401 F.2d 833 (1968)

◆◆◆

WATERMAN, Circuit Judge

This action was commenced in the United States District Court for the Southern District of New York by the Securities and Exchange Commission (the SEC) pursuant to Sec. 21(e) of the Securities Exchange Act of 1934 (the Act), 15 U.S.C. § 78u(e), against Texas Gulf Sulphur Company (TGS) and several of its officers, directors and employees, to enjoin certain conduct by TGS and the individual defendants said to violate Section 10(b) of the Act, 15 U.S.C. Section

78j(b), and Rule 10b-5 (17 CFR 240.10b-5) (the Rule), promulgated thereunder, and to compel the rescission by the individual defendants of securities transaction assertedly conducted contrary to law. The complaint alleged (1) that defendants Fogarty, Mollison, Darke, Murrary, Huntington, O'Neill, Clayton, Crawford, and Coates had either personally or through agents purchased TGS stock or calls thereon from November 12, 1963 through April 16, 1964 on the basis of material inside information concerning the results of TGS drilling in Timmins, Ontario, while such information remained undisclosed to the investing public generally or to the particular sellers; (2) that defendants Darke and Coates had divulged such information to others for use in purchasing TGS stock or calls[2] or recommended its purchase while the information was undisclosed to the public or to the sellers: that defendants Stephens, Fogarty, Mollison, Holyk, and Kline had accepted options to purchase TGS stock on Feb. 20, 1964 without disclosing the material information as to the drilling progress to either the Stock Option Committee or the TGS Board of Directors; and (4) that TGS issued a deceptive press release on April 12, 1964. The case was tried at length before Judge Bonsal of the Southern District of New York, sitting without a jury. Judge Bonsal in a detailed opinion decided, *inter alia,* that the insider activity prior to April 9, 1964 was not illegal because the drilling results were not "material" until then; that Clayton and Crawford had traded in violation of law because they traded after that date; that Coates had committed no violation as he did not trade before disclosure was made; and that the issuance of the press release was not unlawful because it was not issued for the purpose of benefiting the corporation, there was no evidence that any insider used the release to his personal advantage and it was not "misleading, or deceptive on the basis of the facts then known," 258 F. Supp. 262, at 292-296 (SDNY 1966). Defendants Clayton and Crawford appeal from that part of the decision below which held that they had violated Sec. 10(b) and Rule 10b-5 and the SEC appeals from the remainder of the decision which dismissed the complaint against defendants TGS, Fogarty, Mollison, Holyk, Darke, Stephens, Kline, Murray, and Coates.

For reasons which appear below, we decide the various issues presented as follows:

(1) As to Clayton and Crawford, as purchasers of stock on April 15 and 16, 1964, we affirm the finding that they violated 15 U.S.C. § 78j(b) and Rule 10b-5 and remand, pursuant to the agreement by all the parties, for a determination of the appropriate remedy.

(2) As to Murray, we affirm the dismissal of the complaint.

(3) As to Mollison and Holyk, as recipients of certain stock options, we affirm the dismissal of the complaint.

(4) As to Stephens and Fogarty, as recipients of stock options, we reverse the dismissal of the complaint and remand for a further determination as to whether an injunction, in the exercise of the trial court's discretion, should issue.

(5) As to Kline, as a recipient of a stock option, we reverse the dismissal of the complaint and remand with directions to issue an order rescinding the

[2]A "call" is a negotiable option contract by which the bearer has the right to buy from the writer of the contract a certain number of shares of a particular stock at a fixed price on or before a certain agreed-upon date.

option and for a determination of any other appropriate remedy in connection therewith.

(6) As to Fogarty, Mollison, Holyk, Darke, and Huntington, as purchasers of stock or calls thereon between November 12, 1963, and April 9, 1964, we reverse the dismissal of the complaint and find that they violated 15 U.S.C. § 78j(b) and Rule 10b-5, and remand, pursuant to the agreement of all the parties, for a determination of the appropriate remedy.

(7) As to Clayton, although the district judge did not specify that the complaint be dismissed with respect to his purchases of TGS stock before April 9, 1964, such a dismissal is implicit in his treatment of the individual appellees who acted similarly. Consequently, although Clayton is named only as an appellant our decision with respect to the materiality of K-55-1 renders it necessary to treat him also as an appellee. Thus, as to him, as one who purchased stock between November 12, 1963 and April 9, 1964, we reverse the implicit dismissal of the complaint, find that he violated § 78j(b) and Rule 10b-5, and remand, pursuant to the agreement by all the parties, for a determination of the appropriate remedy.

(8) As to Darke, as one who passed on information to tippees, we reverse the dismissal of the complaint and remand, pursuant to the agreement by all the parties, for a determination of the appropriate remedy.

(9) As to Coates, as one who on April 16th purchased stock and gave information on which his son-in-law broker and the broker's customers purchased shares, we reverse the dismissal of the complaint, find that he violated 15 U.S.C. § 78j(b) and Rule 10b-5, and remand, pursuant to the agreement by all the parties, for a determination of the appropriate remedy.

(10) As to Texas Gulf Sulphur, we reverse the dismissal of the complaint and remand for a further determination by the district judge in the light of the approach taken in this opinion.

THE FACTUAL SETTING

This action derives from the exploratory activities of TGS begun in 1957 on the Canadian Shield in eastern Canada. In March of 1959, aerial geophysical surveys were conducted over more than 15,000 square miles of this area by a group led by defendant Mollison, a mining engineer and a Vice President of TGS. The group included defendant Holyk, TGS's chief geologist, defendant Clayton, an electrical engineer and geophysicist, and defendant Darke, a geologist. These operations resulted in the detection of numerous anomalies, i.e., extraordinary variations in the conductivity of rocks, one of which was on the Kidd 55 segment of land located near Timmins, Ontario.

On October 29 and 30, 1963, Clayton conducted a ground geophysical survey on the northeast portion of the Kidd 55 segment which confirmed the presence of an anomaly and indicated the necessity of diamond core drilling for further evaluation. Drilling of the initial hole, K-55-1, at the strongest part of the anomaly was commenced on November 8 and terminated on November 12 at a depth of 655 feet. Visual estimates by Holyk of the core of K-55-1 indicated an average copper content of 1.15 percent and an average zinc content of 8.64 percent over a length of 599 feet. This visual estimate convinced TGS that it was desirable to acquire the remainder of the Kidd 55 segment, and in order to facilitate this acquisition TGS President Stephens instructed the exploration group to keep the results of K-55-1 confidential and undisclosed even as to other officers, directors, and employees of TGS. The hole was concealed and a barren core was intentionally drilled off the anomaly. Meanwhile, the core of K-55-1 had been shipped to Utah for chemical assay which, when received in early December, revealed an average mineral content of 1.18 percent copper, 8.26 percent zinc, and 3.94 percent ounces of silver per ton over a length of 602 feet. These results were so remarkable that neither Clayton, an experienced geophysicist, nor four other TGS expert witnesses, had ever seen or heard of a comparable initial exploratory drill hole in a base metal deposit. So, the trial court concluded, "There is no doubt that the drill core of K-55-1 was unusually good and that it excited the interest and speculation of those who knew about it." By March 27, 1964, TGS decided that the land acquisition program had advanced to such a point that the company might well resume drilling, and drilling was resumed on March 31.

During this period, from November 12, 1963 when K-55-1 was completed to March 31, 1964 when drilling was resumed, certain of the individual defendants and persons said to have received "tips" from them, purchased TGS stock or calls thereon. Prior to these transactions these persons had owned 1135 shares of TGS stock and possessed no calls; thereafter they owned a total of 8,235 shares and possessed 12,300 calls.

On February 20, 1964, also during this period, TGS issued stock options to 26 of its officers and employees whose salaries exceeded a specified amount, five of whom were the individual defendants Stephens, Fogarty, Mollison, Holyk and Kline. Of these, only Kline was unaware of the detailed results of K-55-1, but he, too, knew that a hole containing favorable bodies of copper and zinc ore had been drilled in Timmins. At this time, neither the TGS Stock Option Committee nor its Board of Directors had been informed of the results of K-55-1, presumably because of the pending land acquisition program which required confidentiality. All of the foregoing defendants accepted the options granted them.

When drilling was resumed on March 31, hole K-55-3 was commenced 510 feet west of K-55-1 and was drilled easterly at a 45° angle so as to cross K-55-1 in a vertical plane. Daily progress reports of the drilling of this hole K-55-3 and of all subsequently drilled holes were sent to defendants Stephens and Fogarty (President and Executive Vice President of TGS) by Holyk and Mollison. Visual estimates of K-55-3 revealed an average mineral content of 1.12 percent copper and 7.93 percent zinc over 641 of the hole's 876 foot length. On April 7, drilling of a third hole, K-55-4, 200 feet south of and parallel to K-55-1 and westerly at a 45° angle, was commenced and mineralization was encountered over 366 of its 579 foot length. Visual estimates indicated an average content of 1.44 percent copper and 8.24 percent zinc. Like K-55-1, both K-55-3 and K-55-4 established substantial copper mineralization on the eastern edge of the anomaly. On the basis of these findings relative to the foregoing drilling results, the trial court concluded that the vertical plane created by the intersection of K-55-1 and K-55-3, which measured at least 350 feet wide by 500 feet deep extended southward 200 feet to its intersection with K-55-4, and that "There was real evidence that a body of commercially mineable ore might exist."

On April 8 TGS began with a second drill rig to drill another hole, K-55-6, 300 feet easterly of K-55-1. This hole was drilled westerly at an angle of 60° and was intended to explore mineralization beneath K-55-1. While no visual estimates of its core were immediately available, it was readily apparent by the evening of April 10 that substantial copper mineralization had been encountered over the last 127 feet of the hole's 569 foot length. On April 10, a third drill rig commenced drilling yet another hole, K-55-5, 200 feet north of K-55-1, parallel to the prior holes, and slanted westerly at a 45° angle. By the evening of April 10 in this hole, too, substantial copper mineralization had been encountered over the last 42 feet of its 97 foot length.

Meanwhile rumors that a major ore strike was in the making had been circulating throughout Canada. On the morning of Saturday, April 11, Stephens at his home in Greenwich, Conn. read in the New York Herald Tribune and in the New York Times unauthorized reports of the TGS drilling which seemed to infer a rich strike from the fact that the drill cores had been flown to the United States for chemical assay. Stephens immediately contacted Fogarty at his home in Rye, NY., who in turn telephoned and later that day visited Mollison at Mollison's home in Greenwich to obtain a current report and evaluation of the drilling progress. The following morning, Sunday, Fogarty again telephoned Mollison, inquiring whether Mollison had any further information and told him to return to Timmins with Holyk, the TGS Chief Geologist, as soon as possible "to move things along." With the aid of one Carroll, a public relations consultant, Fogarty drafted a press release designed to quell the rumors, which release after having been channeled through Stephens and Huntington, a TGS attorney, was issued at 3:00 P.M. on Sunday, April 12, and which appeared in the morning newspapers of general circulation on Monday, April 13. It read in pertinent part as follows:

NEW YORK, April 12-The following statement was made today by Dr. Charles F. Fogarty, executive vice president of Texas Gulf Sulphur Company, in regard to the company's drilling operations near Timmins, Ontario, Canada. Dr. Fogarty said:

"During the past few days, the exploration activities of Texas Gulf Sulphur in the area of Timmins, Ontario, have been widely reported in the press, coupled with rumors of a substantial copper discovery there. These reports exaggerate the scale of operations, and mention plans and statistics of size and grade of ore that are without factual basis and have evidently originated by speculation of people not connected with TGS.

"The facts are as follows. TGS has been exploring in the Timmins area for six years as part of its overall search in Canada and elsewhere for various minerals-lead, copper, zinc, etc. During the course of this work, in Timmins as well as in Eastern Canada, TGS has conducted exploration entirely on its own, without the participations by others. Numerous prospects have been investigated by geophysical means and a large number of selected ones have been core-drilled. These cores are sent to the United States for assay and detailed examinations as a matter of routine and on advice of expert Canadian legal counsel. No inferences as to grade can be drawn from this procedure.

"Most of the areas drilled in Eastern Canada have revealed either barren pyrite or graphite without value; a few have resulted in discoveries of small or marginal sulphide ore bodies.

"Recent drilling on one property near Timmins has led to preliminary indications that more drilling would be required for proper evaluation of this prospect. The drilling done to date has not been conclusive, but the statements made by many outside quarters are unreliable and include information and figures that are not available to TGS.

"The work done to date has not been sufficient to reach definite conclusions and any statement as to size and grade of ore would be premature and possibly misleading. When we have progressed to the point where reasonable and logical conclusions can be made, TGS will issue a definite statement to its stockholders and to the public in order to clarify the Timmins project."

The release purported to give the Timmins drilling results as of the release date, April 12. From Mollison Forgarty had been told of the developments through 7:00 P.M. on April 10, and of the remarkable discoveries made up to that time, detailed supra, which discoveries, according to the calculations of the experts who testified for the SEC at the hearing, demonstrated that TGS had already discovered 6.2 to 8.3 million tons of proven ore having gross assay values from $26 to $29 per ton. TGS experts, on the other hand, denied at the hearing that proven or probable ore could have been calculated on April 11 or 12 because there was then no assurance of continuity in the mineralized zone.

The evidence as to the effect of this release on the investing public was equivocal and less than abundant. On April 13 the New York Herald Tribune in an article head-noted "Copper Rumor Deflated" quoted from the TGS release of April 12 and backtracked from its original April 11 report of a major strike but nevertheless inferred from the TGS release that "recent mineral exploratory activity near Timmins, Ontario, has provided preliminary favorable results, sufficient at least to require a step-up in drilling operations." Some witnesses who testified at the hearing stated that they found the release encouraging. On the other hand, a Canadian mining security specialist, Roche, stated that "earlier in the week [before April 16] we had a Dow Jones saying that they [TGS] didn't have anything basically" and a TGS stock specialist for the Midwest Stock Exchange became concerned about his long position in the stock after reading the release. The trial court stated only that "While, in retrospect the press release may appear gloomy or incomplete, this does not make it misleading or deceptive on the basis of the facts then known."

Meanwhile, drilling operations continued. By morning of April 13, in K-55-5, the fifth drill hole, substantial copper mineralization had been encountered to the 580 foot mark, and the hole was subsequently drilled to a length of 757 feet without further results. Visual estimates revealed an average content of 0.82 percent copper and 4.2 percent zinc over a 525 foot section. Also by 7:00 A.M. on April 13, K-55-6 had found mineralization to the 946 foot mark. On April 12 a fourth drill rig began to drill K-55-7, which was drilled westerly at a 45° angle, at the eastern edge of anomaly. The next morning the 137 foot mark had been reached, fifty feet of which showed mineralization. By 7:00 P.M. on April 15, the hole had been completed to a length of 707 feet but had only encountered additional mineralization during a 26 foot length between the 425 and 451 foot marks. A mill test hole, K-55-8, had been drilled and was complete by the evening of April 13 but its mineralization had not been reported upon prior to April 16. K-55-10 was drilled westerly at a 45° angle commencing April 14 and had encountered mineralization over 231 of its 249 foot length by the evening of April 15. It, too, was drilled at the anomaly's eastern edge.

While drilling activity ensued to completion, TGS officials were taking steps toward ultimate disclosure of the discovery. On April 13, a previously-invited reporter for The Northern Miner, a Canadian mining industry journal, visited the drillsite, interviewed Mollison, Holyk and Darke, and prepared an article which confirmed a 10 million ton ore strike. This report, after having been submitted to Mollison and returned to the reporter unamended on April 15, was published in the April 16 issue. A statement relative to the extent of the discovery, in substantial part drafted by Mollison, was given to the Ontario Minister of Mines for release to the Canadian media. Mollison and Holyk expected it to be released over the airways at 11 P.M. on April 15th but for undisclosed reasons, it was not released until 9:40 A.M. on the 16th. An official detailed statement, announcing a strike of at least 25 million tons of ore, based on the drilling data set forth above, was read to representatives of American financial media from 10:00 A.M. to 10:10 or 10:15 A.M. on April 16, and appeared over Merill Lynch's private wire at 10:29 A.M. and somewhat later than expected, over the Dow Jones ticker tape at 10:54 A.M.

Between the time the first press release was issued on April 12 and the dissemination of the TGS official announcement on the morning of April 16, the only defendants before us on appeal who engaged in market activity were Clayton and Crawford and TGS director Coates. Clayton ordered 200 shares of TGS stock through his Canadian broker on April 15, and the order was executed that day over the Midwest Stock Exchange. Crawford ordered 300 shares at midnight on 15th and another 300 shares at 8:30 A.M. the next day, and these orders were executed over the Midwest Exchange in Chicago at its opening on April 16. Coates left the TGS press conference and called his broker son-in-law Haemisegger shortly before 10:20 A.M. on the 16th and ordered 2,000 shares of TGS for family trust accounts which Coates was a trustee but not a beneficiary; Haemisegger executed this order over the New York and Midwest Exchanges, and he and his customers purchased 1500 additional shares.

During the period of drilling Timmins the market price of TGS stock fluctuated but steadily gained overall. On Friday, November 8, when the drilling began, the stock closed at 17 3/8; on Friday, November 15, after K-55-1 had been completed, it closed at 18. After a slight decline to 16 3/8 by Friday, November 22, the price rose to 20 7/8 by December 13, when the chemical assay results of K-55-1 were recieved, and closed at a high of 24 1/8 on February 21, the day after the stock options had been issued. It had reached a price of 26 by March 31, after the land acquisition program had been completed and drilling had been resumed, and continued to ascend to 30 1/8 by the close of trading on April 10, at which time the drilling progress up to then was evaluated for the April 12th press release. On April 13, the day on which the April 12 release was disseminated, TGS opened at 30 1/8, rose immediately to a high of 32 and gradually tapered off to close at 30 7/8. It closed at 30 1/4 the next day, and at 29 3/8 on April 15. On April 16, the day of the official announcement of the Timmins discovery, the price climbed to a high of 37 and closed at 36 3/8. By May 15, TGS stock was selling at 58 1/4.

An insider is not, of course, always foreclosed from investing in his own company merely because he may be more familiar with company operations than are outside investors. An insider's duty to disclose information or his duty to abstain from dealing in his company's securities arises only in "those situations which are essentially extraordinary in nature and which are reasonably certain to have a substantial effect on the market price of the security if [the extraordinary situation is] disclosed."

Nor is an insider obligated to confer upon outside investors the benefit of his superior financial or other expert analysis by disclosing his educated guesses or predictions.

The only regulatory objective is that access to material information be enjoyed equally, but this objective requires nothing more than the disclosure of basic facts so that outsiders may draw upon their own investment decisions with knowledge equal to that of the insiders.

This is not to suggest, however, as did trial court, that "the test of materiality must necessarily be a conservative one, particularly since many actions under Section 10(b) are brought on the basis of hindsight," . . . in the sense that the materiality of facts is to be assessed solely by measuring the effect the knowledge of the facts would have upon prudent or conservative investors. As we stated in *List* v. *Fashion Park, Inc.*, 340 F.2d 457, 462. "The basic test of materiality * * * is whether a reasonable man would attach importance * * * in determining his choice of action in the transaction in question. This, of course, encompasses any fact" * * * which in reasonable and objective contemplation might affect the value of the corporation's stock of securities * * *." Thus, material facts include not only information of a company but also those facts which affect the probable future of the company and those which may affect the desire of investors to buy, sell, or hold the company's securities.

In each case, then, whether facts are material within Rule 10b-5 when the facts relate to a particular event and are undisclosed by those persons who are knowledgeable thereof will depend at any given time upon a balancing of both the indicated probability that the event will occur and the anticipated magnitude of the event in light of the totality of the company activity.

Our survey of the facts found below conclusively establishes that knowledge of the results of the discovery hole, K-55-1, would have been important to a reasonable investor and might have affected the price of stock. On April 16, The Northern Miner, a trade publication in wide circulation among mining stock specialists, called K-55-1, the discovery hole, "one of the most impressive drill holes completed in modern times." Roche, a Canadian broker whose firm specialized in mining securities, characterized the importance to investors of the results of K-55-1. He stated that the completion of "first drill hole" with "a 600 foot drill core is very very significant * * * anything over 200 feet is considered very significant and 600 feet is just beyond your wildest imagination."

Finally, a major factor in determining whether the K-55-1 discovery was a material fact is the importance attached to the drilling results by those who knew about it. In view of other unrelated recent developments favorably affecting TGS, participation by an informed person in a regular stock-purchase program, or even sporadic trading by an informed person, might lend only nominal support to the inference of the materiality of the K-55-1 discovery; nevertheless, the timing by those who knew of it of their stock purchases and their purchases of short-term calls-purchases in some cases by individuals who had never before purchased calls or even TGS stock-virtually compels the inference that the insiders were influenced by the drilling results. This insider trading activity, which surely constitutes highly pertinent evidence and the only truly objective evidence of the materiality of the K-55-1 discovery, was apparently disregarded by the court below in favor of the testimony of defendants, expert witnesses, all of whom "agreed that one drill core does not establish an ore body, much less a mine."

Our decision to expand the limited protection afforded outside investors by the trial court's narrow definition of materiality is not all shaken by fears that the elimination of insider trading benefits will deplete the ranks of capable corporate managers by taking away an incentive to accept such employment. Such benefits, in essence, are forms of secret corporate compensation ... derived at the expense of the uninformed investing public and not at the expense of corporation which receives the sole benefit from insider incentives. Moreover, adequate incentives for corporate officers may be provided by properly administered stock options and employee purchase plans of which there are many in existence. In any event, the normal motivation induced by stock ownership., i.e., the identification of an individual with corporate progress, is ill-promoted by condoning the sort of speculative insider activity which occurred here; for example, some of the corporation's stock was sold at market in order to purchase short-term calls upon that stock calls which would never be exercised to increase a stockholder equity in TGS unless the market price of that stock rose sharply.

It was the intent on Congress that all members of the investing public should be subject to identical market risks, which market risks include, of course the risk that one's evaluative capacity or one's capital available to put at risk may exceed another's capacity or capital. The insiders here were not trading on an equal footing with the outside investors. They alone were in a position to evaluate the probability and magnitude of what seemed from the outset to be a major ore strike; they alone could invest safely, secure in the expectation that the price of TGS stock would rise substantially in the event such a major strike should materialize, but would decline little, if at all, in the event of failure, for the public ignorant at the outset of the favorable probabilities would likewise be unaware of the unproductive exploration, and the additional exploration cost would not significantly affect TGS market prices. Such inequities based upon unequal access to knowledge should not be shrugged off as in inevitable in our way of life, or, in view of the congressional concern in the area, remain uncorrected.

We hold, therefore, that all transactions in TGS stock or calls by individuals apprised of the drilling results of K-55-1 were made in violation of Rule 10b-5. Inasmuch as the visual evaluation of that drill core (generally reliable estimate though less accurate than a chemical assay) constituted material information, those advised of the results of the visual evaluation as well as those informed of the chemical assay traded in violation of law. The geologist Darke possessed undisclosed material information and traded in TGS securities. Therefore we reverse the dismissal of the action as to him and his personal transactions. The trial court also found, 258 F. Supp. at 284, that Darke, after the drilling of K-55-1 had been completed and with detailed knowledge of the results thereof, told certain outside individuals that TGS "was a good buy." These individuals thereafter acquired TGS stock and calls. The trial court also found that later, as of March 30, 1964, Darke not only used his material knowledge for his own purchases but that the substantial amounts of TGS stock and calls purchases by these outside individuals on that day was "strong circumstantial evidence that Darke must have passed the word to one or more of his "tippees" that drilling on the Kidd 55 segment was about to be resumed." Obviously if such a resumption were to have any meaning to such "tippees," they must have previously been told of K-55-1.

Unfortunately, however, there was no definitive resolution below of Darke's liability in these premises for the trial court held as to him, as it held as to all the other individual defendants, that this "undisclosed information" never became material until April 9. As it is our holding that the information acquired after the drilling of K-55-1 was material, we on the basis of the findings of direct and circumstantial evidence on the issue that the trial court had already expressed, hold that Darke violated Rule 10b-5 (3) and Section 10 (b) by "tipping" and we demand, pursuant to the agreement of the parties, for a determination of the appropriate remedy. As Darke's "tippees" are not defendants in this action, we need not decide whether, if they acted with actual or constructive knowledge that the material information was undisclosed, their conduct is as equally violative of the Rule as the conduct of their insider source, though we note that it certainly could be equally reprehensible.

With reference to Huntington, the trial court found that he "had no detailed knowledge as to the work" on the Kidd-55 segment, 258 F. Supp. 281. Nevertheless, the evidence shows that he knew about and participated in TGS's land acquisition program which followed the receipt of the K-55-1 drilling results, and that on February 26, 1964 he purchased 50 shares of TGS stock. Later, on March 16, he helped prepare a letter for Dr. Holyk's signature in which TGS made a substantial offer for lands near K-55-1 and on the same day he, who had never before purchased calls on any stock, purchased a call on 100 shares of TGS stock. We satisfied that these purchases in February and March coupled with his readily inferable and probably reliable, understanding of the highly favorable nature of preliminary operations on the Kidd segment, demonstrate that Huntington possessed material inside information such as to make his purchase violative of the Rule and the Act.

Appellant Crawford, who ordered the purchase of TGS stock shortly before the TGS April 16 official announcement, and defendant Coates, who placed orders with and communicated the news to his broker immediately after the official announcement was read at the TGS-called press conference, concede that they were in possession of material information. They contend, however, that their purchases are not proscribed purchases for the news had already been effectively disclosed. We disagree.

Crawford telephoned his orders to his Chicago broker about midnight on April 15 and again at 8:30 in the morning of the 16th, with instructions to buy at the opening of the Midwest Stock Exchange that morning. The trial court's finding that "he sought to, and did, 'beat the news' " 258 F. Supp. at 287, is well documented by the record. The rumors of a major ore strike which had been circulated in Canada and, to a lesser extent, in New York, had been disclaimed by the TGS press release of April 12, which significantly promised the public an official detailed announcement when possibilities had ripened into actualities. The abbreviated announcement to the Canadian press at 9:40 A.M. on the 16th by the Ontario Minister of Mines and the report carried by The Northern Miner, parts of which had sporadically reached New York on the morning of the 16th through reports from Canadian affiliates a few New York investment firms, are assuredly not the equivalent of the official 10-15 minute announcement which was not released to the American financial press until after 10:00 A.M. Crawford's orders had been placed before that. Before insiders may act upon material information, such information must have been effectively disclosed in a manner sufficient to insure its availability to the investing public. Particularly here, where a formal announcement to the entire financial news media had been promised in a prior official release known to the media, all insider activity must await dissemination of the promised official announcement.

Coates was absolved by the court below because his telephone order was placed shortly before 10:20 A.M. on April 16 which was after the announcement had been made even though the news could not be considered already a matter of public information. This result seems to have been predicated upon a misinterpretation of dicta in Cady, Roberts, where the SEC instructed insiders to "keep out of the market until the established procedures for public release of the information are carried out instead of hastening to execute transactions in advance of, and in frustration of, the objectives of the release." The reading of a news release, which prompted Coates into action, is merely the first step in the process of dissemination required for compliance with the regulatory objective of providing all investors with an equal opportunity to make informed investment judgments. Assuming that the contents of the official release could instantaneously be acted upon, at the minimum Coates should have waited until the news could reasonably have been expected to appear over the media of widest circulation, the Dow Jones broad tape, rather than hastening to insure an advantage to himself and his broker son-in-law.

IS AN INSIDER'S GOOD FAITH A DEFENSE UNDER 10b-5?

Coates, Crawford and Clayton, who ordered purchases before the news could be deemed disclosed, claim, nevertheless, that they were justified on doing so because they honestly believed that the news of the strike had become public at the time they placed their orders. However, whether the case before us is treated solely as an SEC enforcement proceeding or as a private action, proof of a specific intent to defraud is unnecessary. Thus, the beliefs of Coates, Crawford and Clayton that the news of the ore strike was sufficiently public at the time of their purchase orders are to no avail if those beliefs were not reasonable under the circumstances. Crawford points to the scattered rumors of the discovery which had been circulating for some time before April 15, to the release of the information to The Northern Miner on April 15 to be published by it on the 16th, to the arrangement made by TGS with the Ontario Minister of Mines for the release of an abbreviated report on the evening of the 15th (which did not eventuate until 9:40 A.M., April 16), and to the corporation's official announcement at 10:00 A.M. on the 16th, all of which transpired prior to anticipated execution of his purchase orders that had been placed by him after trading had closed on the Midwest Exchange on April 15. However, the rumors and casual disclosure through Canadian media, especially in view of the April 12 "gloomy" or incomplete release denying the rumors and promising official confirmation, hardly sufficed to inform traders on American Exchanges affected by Crawford's purchases. Moreover, the formal announcement could not reasonably have been expected to be disseminated by the time of the opening of the exchanges on the morning of April 16, when Crawford must have expected his orders would be executed.

Clayton, who was unaware of the April 16 disclosure announcement TGS was to make can, in support of his claim that the favorable news was public, rely only on the rumors and on the phone calls received by TGS prior to the placing of his order from those who seemed to have heard some version or rumors of the news. His awareness of the contents of the April 12 release renders unreasonable any claim that he believed the news was truly public.

Finally, Coates, as we have already indicated, supra, could not reasonably have expected the official release to have been disseminated when he placed his order before 10:20 for immediate execution nor were the Canadian disclosures relied on by Crawford sufficient to render the conduct of Coates permissable under the circumstances.

MAY INSIDERS ACCEPT STOCK OPTIONS WITHOUT DISCLOSING MATERIAL INFORMATION TO THE ISSUER?

On February 20, 1964, defendants Stephens, Fogarty, Mollison, Holyk and Kline accepted stock options issued to them and a number of other top officers of TGS, although not one of them had informed the Stock Option Committee of the Board of Directors of the Board of the results of K-55-1, which information we have held was then material. The SEC sought rescission of these options. In view of our conclusion as to materiality we hold that Stephens and Fogarty violated the Rule by accepting them.

Contrary to the belief of the trial court that Kline had no duty to disclose his knowledge of the Kidd project before accepting the stock option offered him we believe that he, a vice president, who had become the general counsel of TGS in January 1964, but who had been secretary of the corporation since January 1961, and was present in that capacity when the options were granted, and who was in charge of the mechanics of issuance and acceptance of the options, was a member of top management and under a duty before accepting his option to disclose any material information he may have possessed, and, as he did not disclose such information to the Option Committee we direct rescission of the option he received. As to Holyk and Mollison, the SEC has not appealed the holding below that they, not being then members of top management (although Mollison was a vice president) had no duty to disclose their knowledge of the drilling before accepting their options. Therefore, the issue of whether, by accepting, they violated the Act, is not before us, and the holding below is undisturbed.

THE CORPORATE DEFENDANT

At 3:00 P.M. on April 12, 1964, evidently believing it desirable to comment upon the rumors concerning the Timmins project, TGS issued the press release quoted in pertinent part in the text. The SEC argued below and maintains on this appeal that this release painted a misleading and deceptive picture of the drilling progress at the time of its issuance, and hence violated Rule 10b-5(2). TGS relies on the holding of the court below that "The issuance of the release produced no unusual market action" and "In the absence of a showing that the purpose of the April 12 press release was to affect the market price of TGS stock to the advantage of TGS or its insiders, the issuance of the press release did not constitute a violation of Section 10(b) or Rule 10b-5 since it was not issued "in connection with the purchase or sale of any security' " and, alternatively, "even if it had been established that the April 12 release was issued in connection with the purchase or sale of any security, the Commission has failed to demonstrate that it was false, misleading or deceptive."

Therefore it seems clear from the legislative purpose Congress expressed in the Act, and the legislative history of Section 10(b) that Congress when it used the phrase "in connection with the purchase or sale of any security" intended only that the device employed, whatever it might be, be of a sort that would cause reasonable investors to rely thereon, and, in connection therewith, so relying, cause them to purchase or sell a corporation's securities. There is no indication that Congress intended that the corporations or persons responsible for the issuance of a misleading statement would not violate the section unless they engaged in related securities transactions or otherwise acted with wrongful motives; . . .

And, of course, as we have already emphasized, a corporation's misleading material statement may injure an investor irrespective of whether the corporation itself, or those individuals managing it, are contemporaneously buying or selling the stock of the corporation.

Accordingly, we hold that Rule 10b-5 is violated whenever assertions are made as here, in a manner reasonably calculated to influence the investing public, e.g., by means of the financial media, if such assertions are false or misleading or are so incomplete as to mislead irrespective of whether the issuance of the release was motivated by corporate officials for ulterior purposes. It seems clear, however, that if corporate management demonstrates that it was diligent in ascertaining that the information it published was the whole truth and that such diligently obtained information was disseminated in good faith, Rule 10b-5 would not have been violated.

DID THE ISSUANCE OF THE APRIL 12 RELEASE VIOLATE RULE 10b-5?

Turning first to the question of whether the release was misleading, i.e., whether it conveyed to the public a false impression of the drilling situation at the time of its issuance, we note initially that the trial court did not actually decide this question. . . . we cannot, from the present record, by applying the standard Congress intended, definitively conclude that it was deceptive or misleading to the reasonable investor, or that he would have been misled by it. Accordingly, we remand that issue to the district court that took testimony and heard and saw the witnesses for a determination of the character of the release in the light of the facts existing at the time of the release, by applying the standard of whether the reasonable investor, in the exercise of due care, would have been misled by it.

In the event that it is found that the statement was misleading to the reasonable investor it will then become necessary to determine whether its issuance resulted from a lack of due diligence. The only remedy the Commission seeks against the corporation is an injunction, and therefore we do not find it necessary to decide whether just a lack of due diligence on the part of TGS, absent a showing of bad faith, would subject the corporation to any liability for damages.

MOORE, Circuit Judge (dissenting) (with whom Chief Judge LUMBARD concurs):

In their opinion, the majority have become so involved in usurping the function of the trial court, in selecting the witnesses they (at variance with the trial court) choose to believe, in forming their own factual conclusions from the evidence, in deciding with, of course, the benefit of the wisdom of hindsight, how they, had they been executives of Texas Gulf Sulphur Company (TGS), would have handled the publicity attendant to the exploration of the Timmins property, in determining (to their own satisfaction) the motives which prompted each of the individual defendants buy TGS stock and in becoming mining engineering experts in their own right, that I find it desirable — in fact, essential — to state my opinion as to the fundamental jurisdiction of the Court of Appeals and the issues properly before us. Primarily, our task should be to review errors of law. Conversely, we are not a jury of nine with no requirement of a unanimous verdict.

Assuming the majority's and the Commission's full disclosure theory, would the facts as then developed have given the buying or selling public the so-called advantages possessed by the insiders? TGS could have announced by November 15, 1963 that it had completed a first exploratory hole, the core of which by visual examination revealed over a length of 599 of 655 feet drilled, an average copper content of 1.15 percent, zinc 8.64 percent or, had TGS waited until mid-December, by chemical analysis 1.18 percent copper, 8.26 percent zinc and 2.94 percent ounces of silver per ton; that TGS would try to acquire the other three-quarters of the segment unless the announcement boosted prices to unwarranted heights; that if the property could be acquired further exploratory holes would be drilled to ascertain the nature and extent, if any, of the ore body; that reports of developments would be made from time to time but that the SEC had indicated that TGS should advise its stockholders and the public that there was no proof as yet that a body of commercial ore exists on the property. Such an announcement would, of course, have been of no value to anyone except possibly a few graduates of Institutes of Technology and they, as the expert witnesses here, would have recognized that one drill hole does not reveal a commercially profitable mine.

The final question to be answered is: were these officers and employees disqualified as the result of possessing information gleaned by the first drill core from purchasing TGS stock? The number of possibilities for Congressional legislation and Commission rulings are legion. They extend over a gamut between definite extremes. At one extreme is a rule that no officer or employee or any member of their families shall own stock of the company for which they work or purchase stock if he possesses "material" inside information. This assumption raises the question of what is material and who is to make such a determination. Materiality must depend upon the facts and their resolution is for the fact-finder, court or jury. The majority state that the K-55-1 drilling results were material because they "might well have affected the price of TGS stock." But such a statement could be made of almost any fact related to TGS. If a labor strike had kept its plants idle for months, encouraging news of a possible settlement hoped for by the TGS labor negotiators might cause the negotiators to buy. Their belief that the strike would be protracted might cause them to sell.

Either announcement might well have affected the market and would to those who bought or sold have seemed misleading and deceptive if the anticipated event did not come to pass. Yet the requirement of hourly bulletins to the press from the conference room would not be compatible with common sense. Scores of day by day intra-company situations come to mind which in the individual opinions of company officers or employees might well affect the price of TGS stock, each individual reacting according to his own judgment. However, companies listed on a national exchange can scarcely broadcast to the nation on a daily basis their hopes and/or expectations from the developments in, for example, their research departments. An even more striking illustration would be found within the structure of a large pharmaceutical company where discoveries of panaceas to cure human disease occupies the workdays of thousands of scientists. Premature announcements of import discoveries would be branded as false and misleading if unfulfilled and all stock purchases made during the course of the research, if ultimately successful would be said to have been made with the advantage of inside information. At the other extreme is an equally easy-to-resolve *Cady, Roberts* situation where a definite fact (the reduction of the dividend) was known by an insider, who participated in the meeting where the decision had already been made, whose knowledge of the probable reaction of the market to such an announcement, namely, a substantial sell-off, caused him to leave the meeting ahead of everyone else and before the potential buyers learned of the bad news to foist his selling orders on the market and his stock on uninformed purchasers. Between these extremes there should be a rule of reason.

There can be little doubt but that those familiar with the results of K-55-1 were influenced thereby in making their purchases. The conclusion of the majority is based primarily on this assumption. They call it "a major factor in determining whether the K-55-1 discovery was a material fact" and say that this "virtually compels the inference that the insiders were influenced by the drilling results." To them, completely disregarding the trial court's findings and substituting themselves as a jury, these purchases are "the only truly objective evidence of the materiality of the K-55-1 discovery." In so holding, they confuse the inducing motive of the individual purchaser with knowledge of material facts which ought to be revealed to the public at large. The inconsistency of the majority's position is immediately apparent. Those who purchased were apparently willing on the basis of the inconclusive first hole and other information to risk a certain amount of their funds in TGS stock, hopeful that future developments would be favorable. Their motive for purchase does not establish the materiality of the facts which influenced them.

STOCK OPTIONS

As to Stephens and Fogarty, the majority decision places insider recipients of stock options in a difficult dilemma. Under the majority's decision, an insider must perform the uncommon act of refusing such an option, promoting speculation as to the reasons therefor, or accept the option and face possible ·10b-5 liability. The objective of protecting a corporation from selling securities to insiders at a price below their true worth is fully served by requiring nondisclosing insiders to abstain, not from accepting the stock options, but merely from exercising them — an event likely to occur after the inside information has become public. In any case, the failure to exercise an option is less likely to suggest that the insider possessed material information than the failure to accept such an option.

THE APRIL 12, 1964 PRESS RELEASE

With the aid of hindsight the release may indeed seem gloomy, but that is because it is now known that a very substantial tonnage of ore exists. Hindsight, however, is not the test. Furthermore, even if some investors considered the release to be discouraging compared to the rumors afloat, if the facts and conclusions presented were accurate (as they were) and if they were not presented in a manner that would mislead a reasonable investor (which they were not) then there can be no violation of 10b-5.

CONCLUSION

In summary, the most disturbing aspect of the majority opinion is its utterly unrealistic approach to the problem of the corporate press release. If corporations were literally to follow its implications, every press release would have to have the same SEC clearance as a prospectus. Even this procedure would not suffice if future events should prove the facts to have been over or understated — or too gloomy or optimistic — because the courts will always be ready and available to substitute their judgment for that of the business executives responsible therefor. But vulnerable as the news release may be, what of the many daily developments in the Research and Development departments of giant corporations. When and how are promising results to be disclosed. If they are not disclosed, the corporation is concealing information; if disclosed and hoped-for results do not materialize, there will always be those with the advantage of hindsight to brand them as false or misleading. Nor is it consonant with reality to suggest, as does the majority, that corporate executives may be motivated in accepting employment by the opportunity to make "secret corporate compensation * * * derived at the expense of the uninformed public." Such thoughts can only arise from unfounded speculative imagination. And finally there is the sardonic anomaly that the very members of society which Congress has charged the SEC with protecting, i.e., the stockholders, will be the real victims of its misdirected zeal. May the Future, the Congress or possibly the SEC itself be able to bring some semblance of order by means of workable rules and regulations in this field so that the corporations and their stockholders may not be subjected to countless lawsuits at the whim of every purchaser, seller or potential purchaser who may claim he would have acted or refrained from acting had a news release been more comprehensive, less comprehensive or had it been adequately published in the news media of the 50 States.

◆◆◆

Case Questions

1. Was it not hard for the defendants to argue the unimportance of the drilling results in light of their stock buying activities? If you sat as a juror in this case, would their stock purchases have been decisive in reaching a decision.
2. In deciding cases after-the-fact, how can one avoid having his judgement clouded by the wisdom of hindsight?
3. This decision was bitterly criticized by some when it was handed down. Does it appear to be an unreasonable decision?

Case Comment

NOTE:

Texas Gulf Sulphur Co. is now known as Texasgulf Inc.

While it may be true that one drill core does not establish an ore body, much less a mine, this discovery turned into a lucrative one. The Kidd Creek mine in Timmons, Ontario is among the richest base metal mines in the world.

TIPPER AND TIPPEE LIABILITY

What is the liability of non-trading "tippers" and trading "tippees?" In Texas Gulf Sulphur a trading tipper, Drake, was held to have violated the law. The culpability of tippees was not determined although the court remarked that their conduct "could be equally reprehensible." The same court that decided *Texas Gulf Sulphur* provided answers in *Shapiro* v. *Merrill Lynch, Pierce, Fenner & Smith, Inc.*, 495 F 2d 228 (1974). Merrill Lynch, a prospective managing underwriter of a Douglas Aircraft debenture issue, divulged to some of its customers material adverse inside information regarding Douglas' earnings. Without disclosing this information these customers sold Douglas' common stock on a national securities exchange. As a result, Merrill Lynch received commissions, the customers minimized their losses, but the investing public who purchased Douglas stock during this same period sustained substantial losses.

The plaintiffs, although they purchased Douglas stock during this time period, did not purchase the actual stock sold by the Merrill Lynch customers. The plaintiffs sued both Merrill Lynch and its customers in a private damage action. The court held that the defendants violated Section 10(b) and Rule 10 b-5. The court held them liable for damages not only to the purchasers of the actual shares sold by the defendants, but to all persons who purchased stock in the open market without knowledge of the inside information. Merrill Lynch, the non-trading "tipper" was under a duty to the investing public not to recommend trading in Douglas stock without publicly disclosing the revised earnings figures in its possession. The trading "tippees" argued that they were unable to make effective public disclosure of information about a company with which they were not associated. The court rejected this argument and pointed out that the duty is not a naked one to disclose, but a duty to refrain from trading unless they do disclose.

In breaching their duty, the "tippers" and "tippees" incurred massive potential liability. Douglas common suffered a severe drop in its market price during June, 1970 (the time at issue in the case). The number of persons who purchased in the open market during the requisite time period is probably substantial. The amount of a resulting judgment for damages does not change the application of the law. The court mentioned that, in deciding the case, it was not unmindful of the defendants' possible "Draconian liability."

The Merrill Lynch case should alert one to the potential application of the insider rules to more than just corporate employees. In addition to underwriters, banks, law firms and accounting firms oftentimes have access to inside information by virtue of their work. In an effort to avoid becoming unnecessarily embroiled in litigation, one major accounting firm has imposed the following rules upon all its employees.

1. Investments in companies that are clients of the firm are prohibited.
2. Investments in companies where an employee of the firm sits on the board of directors are prohibited.
3. All securities transactions by an employee, the employee's spouse, or the employee's dependants are to be reported to the firm.

Who is an insider? Consider the Equity Funding case. Equity Funding wrote tens of thousands of phony insurance policies which it then sold to reinsurers for cash. Its books reflected millions of dollars of non-existent assets. It may be the biggest fraud scheme in U.S. history, and has dramatized the problem of computer fraud. A number of corporate officials now stand convicted of various criminal offenses.

The fraud was exposed in 1973 by an insurance securities analyst, Raymond Dirks. He had been told of the fraud by a former Equity Funding employee, Ronald Secrist. Dirks revealed this information to some of his clients who sold Equity Funding stocks before trading in the stock was halted.

Are former employees, such as Secrist, insiders? Is Dirks an insider or is he a "tippee?" Was the information material? Confusing the problem further is the fact that Dirks received contradictory information. High corporate officials categorically denied the allegations of fraud. Low level employees and former employees confirmed Secrist's version.

WHO MAY RECOVER FOR SECTION 10(b) AND RULE 10b-5 VIOLATIONS?

Both Section 10(b) and Rule 10b-5 leave a good deal unsaid and therefore the courts must provide answers. The statute and rule are both silent on the method of computing damages when violations occur. They are also silent as to what classes of individuals are entitled to recover for violations. The next two cases explore the latter area.

SCHEIN v. CHASEN
313 So. 2d 739 (1975) (Fla. S. Ct.)

◆◆◆

ROBERTS, J.

This cause is before us for consideration of questions certified to us by the United States Court of Appeals for the Second Circuit pursuant to Rule 4.61, Florida Appellate Rules. The following questions have been certified:

Are investors, who sell stock on the basis of inside information about the issuer corporation which they received from a stockbroker who in turn received the information from the president of the issuer corporation, liable to the corporation in a shareholder derivation suit under Florida law for the profits realized by the investors on the sale of that stock? Is the stockbroker, who relayed the material information from the president of the issuing corporation to the investors, jointly and severally liable with them for the profits they realized on the sale in a shareholder's derivative suit under Florida law?

The plaintiffs, appellants, Schein, Schein and Gregorio, are shareholders of Lum's, Inc., a Florida corporation (which has subsequent to the filing of their complaints been renamed Ceasar's World, Inc.) and sue derivatively on behalf of Lum's, Inc. Invoking the diversity jurisdiction of the court, they sued derivatively in the Southern District of New York alleging that defendants were jointly and severally liable to Lum's for actionable wrongs committed against Lum's. Lum's, Inc. is a nominal defendant in each of the cases. Chasen was, at the time of the events in issue, the chief operating officer of Lum's, Inc. Lehman Brothers (defendant-appellee) was a stock brokerage firm, and Benjamin Simon (defendant-appellee) was a registered representative employed by it in its Chicago office. Investors Diversified Services, Inc. (defendant-appellee) was the investment advisor for Investors Variable Payment Fund, Inc., and IDS New Dimensions Fund, Inc., two mutual funds based in Minneapolis. Eugene Sit was portfolio manager for IDS New Dimensions Fund, Inc., and James Jundt was portfolio manager for Investors Variable Payment Fund, Inc. – both were employees of Investors Diversified Services, Inc. The defendants Chasen, Sit and Jundt were dismissed by the Federal District Court, Southern District of New York, for lack of personal jurisdiction. These dismissals were not appealed and these defendants are no longer involved in the suit. . . .

The only question before the United States Court of Appeals is the sufficiency of the complaints to state a cause of action under Florida law.

The following explication of the factual situation alleged in the pleadings as the basis for the controversy sub judice is found in the decision of the Circuit Court of Appeals, 478 F.2d 817:

"In November of 1969 Chasen, who was president and chief operating officer of Lum's, addressed a seminar of about sixty members of the securities industry with reference to Lum's earning prospects for its fiscal year ending July 31, 1970. He informed them that Lum's earnings would be approximately $1.00 to $1.10 per share. On January 5, 1970, he learned that his estimate was too optimistic and that, in fact, Lum's earnings would be only approximately $.76 per share. Three days later, prior to announcing the information to the public, Chasen telephoned Simon in Chicago and told Simon that Lum's would not have as profitable a year as had been expected. He specified to Simon that earnings would be approximately $.76 per share rather than the $1.00 per share which he had earlier announced. Simon knew the information was confidential corporate property which Chasen had not given out publicly. Simon immediately telephoned this information to Sit, and employee of defendant Investors Diversified Services, Inc. (IDS), and Sit immediately telephoned it to Jundt, ·another employee of IDS. Sit and Jundt managed the stock portfolios of defendant mutual funds Investors Variable Payment Fund, Inc. (Investors) and IDS New Dimensions Fund, Inc. (Dimensions). Upon receiving the information Sit and Jundt directed the Funds to sell their entire stock holdings in Lum's and, on the morning of January 9, 1970, prior to any public announcement, Investors sold 43,000 shares of Lum's and Dimensions sold 40,000 shares. The sales were executed on the New York Stock Exchange at about 10:30 A.M. at a price of approximately $17.50 per share. At 1:30 P.M. on the same day, the New York Stock Exchange halted further trading in Lum's stock pending a company announcement. At 2:45 P.M., Lum's issued a release which appeared on the Dow Jones News Wire Service and announced that the corporation's projected earnings would be lower than had been anticipated. When trading in Lum's was resumed on Monday, January 12, 1970, volume was heavy and the stock closed at a price of $14.00 per share − $3.50 per share lower than the Funds had realized from the sale of their shares on the previous Friday.

"The present defendants in this case are Lehman Brothers, Simon and the two Mutual Funds. Chasen, Sit and Jundt have been dismissed as defendants in that they have not been validly served under the New York State Long Arm Statute. Plaintiffs-appellants' theory of recovery is that the participants in this chain of wrongdoing are jointly and severally liable to the corporation under Florida law for misusing corporate information to thier own advantage in violation of the duty they owed to Lum's, and that they must account to Lum's for the profits realized by the Mutual Funds. They do not allege in these complaints that defendants have violated any of the federal securities laws, and they concede that the substantive law of Florida governs the rights and liabilities of the parties. They urge, however, that inasmuch as there are no Florida cases directly in point, the Florida court, if it were deciding the case, would look to other jurisdictions and would take a particular and special interest in the decision of *Diamond* v. *Oreamuno*, 29 A.D. 2d 285, 287 N.Y.S. 2d 300 (1st Dep't. 1968), aff'd. 24 N.Y. 2d 494, 301 N.Y.S. 2d 78, N.E. 2d 910 (1969), a case which plaintiffs contend supports the position they urge on this appeal."

Defendants moved to dismiss the consolidated actions upon the ground that the complaints failed to state a claim upon which relief could be granted. ... The United States District Court proceeded to examine Florida law and concluded that although the Florida Supreme Court has not considered the question presented in the instant cause, several Florida District Courts of Appeal have indicated that a complaint in a stockholders' derivative action which fails to allege both wrongful acts and damage to the corporation must be dismissed. ... Specifically, the United States District Court asserted:

> Under present Florida case law, a plaintiff in a derivative action must prove that the corporation has been damaged by the alleged breach of fiduciary trust.

The United States District Court considered the possibility that Florida courts might follow the rationale of the New York decision in *Diamond* v. *Oreamuno*, supra, and therefore considered whether defendants would be liable under the rationale of *Diamond* and concluded, as follows:

"It is clear that the complaints in these actions go far beyond the narrow holding of *Diamond*. In that case, the New York Court of Appeals held that a corporate fiduciary is liable for profits which he realizes from a sale of stock motivated by inside information received by him in his corporate position. None of the defendants in these actions fit into this mold. Chasen, as president and chief operating officer of Lum's was certainly a fiduciary of that corporation. None of the complaints, however, allege that he did anything more than pass the inside information to defendant Simon, and there are no allegations that Chasen sold any of his Lum's stock or derived any gain, monetary or otherwise, from the sales that ultimately occurred. On the other hand, the mutual fund defendants would have profited if, as alleged, they sold their 83,000 shares of Lum's stock on the basis of Chasen's inside information. It can scarcely be maintained, however, that the mutual fund defendants were officers or directors of Lum's or owed any fiduciary duties whatsoever to that corporation. The broker-dealer defendants fail to come within either of the *Diamond* perimeters as they were not fiduciaries of the corporation and, did not profit by virtue of the sales."

With regard to Chasen, the District Court opined that as a corporate officer, he may come within the holding of Diamond, but that this question need not be reached because service of process on him was improper. The Circuit Court of Appeals by divided vote reversed the District Court and found that although Florida law was controlling, it could find none that was decisive, and, therefore, it turned to the law of New York, in particular *Diamond,* supra. The Circuit Court of Appeal stated its objective to be to interpret *Diamond* as the Florida Court would probably interpret it and apply it to the facts sub judice. The Court of Appeals concluded that defendants had engaged with Chasen to misuse corporate property although the Circuit Court recognized that there was no allegation in the complaints that a prior agreement existed between Chasen and the defendants, and that *Diamond,* supra, encompassed such a situation, and determined that such a construction of *Diamond* would have the "prophylactic effect of providing a disincentive to insider trading." The Circuit Court opined that the cleansing effect of the *Diamond* rationale ought to reach third parties who, through breach of fiduciary relationship, become traders advantageously possessed of confidential insider knowledge. . . .

Judge Kaufman, dissented to this decision and explained: . . .

"The court holds today that a person with no relationship whatsoever — fiduciary or otherwise — to a corporation, who trades its shares on the basis of material inside information becomes, *ipso facto,* a fiduciary of the corporation whose shares he traded and, accordingly, may be required in a *shareholders' derivative action* — not a Section 10(b) or 16(b) action — to pay his profits to the corporation. With all due respect to my brothers, the tortured reasoning to which they are compelled to resort in reaching this conclusion represents a distortion of the law of agency and the law of fiduciary responsibility in which I am unable to join. . . .

"It is important to note at the outset that the plaintiffs in these actions, shareholders of Lum's, do not claim to have suffered any damages themselves. Rather, these derivative suits are brought 'on behalf of and for the benefit of Lum's.' They seek to recover for Lum's treasury the windfall profit garnered by the IDS mutual funds, and assert that all defendants are jointly and severally liable for this amount. Thus, the proper method of analysis is not to focus on the unfairness of the mutual funds' profit at the expense of their purchasers — who have their own recourse for any wrongdoing — but on the strands of duty running to the corporation from the various individuals involved. . . .

Despite the manner in which the majority opinion convolutes the law and the facts in this case, a view that a tippee is cloaked with state law fiduciary obligations to the corporation whose shares he trades is an unknown and untenable legal concept. *Neither Diamond — itself a significant alteration of the common law principles applicable to an officer's or director's trading in his corporation's shares — nor the law of agency support such a holding."* (e.s.)

We quote with approval the dissent of Judge Kaufman and we hold it to be responsive and to be dispositive of the controlling questions posited by the United States Circuit Court of Appeals, which we answer in the negative. Not only will we not give the unprecedented expansive reading to *Diamond* sought by appellants but furthermore, we do not choose to adopt the innovative ruling of the New York Court of Appeals in *Diamond*, supra. We adhere to previous precedent established by the courts in this state that actual damage to the corporation must be alleged in the complaint to substantiate a stockholders' derivative action. . . . In *Talcott* v. *McDowell,* supra, the court opined:

Thus, in order for a complaint to state a cause of action entitling the stockholder to relief, it must allege two distinct wrongs: the act whereby the corporation was caused to suffer damage, and a wrongful refusal by the corporation to seek redress for such act. . . .

Accordingly, we find that the rationale of Judge Kaufman in his dissent and the opinion of the United States District Court comport with Florida law and we would approve Judge Kaufman's reasoning as dispositive of the issues presented sub judice which we answer in the negative. . . .

We conclude that under the facts alleged in the complaint, Florida law does not permit the maintenance of shareholders' derivative suit on behalf of Lum's.

◆◆◆

Case Questions

1. Can a corporation suffer damage in a form other than financial? Was there an injury to Lum's when Chasen passed confidential corporate property to an outsider, thereby violating his fiduciary duties?
2. Which decision is most appealing: a) the innovative Court of Appeals decision with its resulting cleansing effect or; b) the traditional legalistic approach of Florida's highest court?
3. Since Section 10 (b) and 16 (b) do exist, does this decision weaken the drive against fraudulent stock activities?

BLUE CHIP STAMPS v. MANOR DRUG STORES
421 U.S. 723 (1975)

◆◆◆

Mr. Justice Rehnquist, delivered the opinion of the Court.

This case requires us to consider whether the offerees of a stock offering . . . may maintain a private cause of action for money damages where they allege that the offeror has violated the provisions of Rule 10b-5 of the Securities and Exchange Commission, but where they have neither purchased nor sold any of the offered shares. . . .

I

In 1963 the United States filed a civil antitrust action against Blue Chip Stamp Company ("Old Blue Chip"), a company in the business of providing trading stamps to retailers, and nine retailers who owned 90 percent of its shares. In 1967 the action was terminated by the entry of a consent decree. . . . The decree contemplated a plan of reorganization whereby Old Blue Chip was to be merged into a newly formed corporation "New Blue Chip." The holdings of the majority shareholders of Old Blue Chip were to be reduced, and New Blue Chip, one of the petitioners here, was required under the plan to offer a substantial number of its shares of common stock to retailers who had used the stamp service in the past but who were not shareholders in the old company. . . .

The reorganization plan was carried out, the offering was registered with the SEC as required by the 1933 Act, and a prospectus was distributed to all offerees as required by § 5 of that Act, 15 U.S.C. § 77e. Somewhat more than 50 percent of the offered units were actually purchased. In 1970, two years after the offering, respondent, a former user of the stamp service and therefore an offeree of the 1968 offering, filed this suit. . . . Defendants below and petitioners here are Old and New Blue Chip, eight of the nine majority shareholders of Old Blue Chip, and the directors of New Blue Chip (collectively called "Blue Chip").

Respondent's complaint alleged, *inter alia,* that the prospectus prepared and distributed by Blue Chip in connection with the offering was materially misleading in its overly pessimistic appraisal of Blue Chip's status and future prospects. It alleged that Blue Chip intentionally made the prospectus overly pessimistic in order to discourage respondent and other members of the allegedly large class whom it represents from accepting what was intended to be a bargain offer, so that the rejected shares might later be offered to the public at a higher price. The complaint alleged that class members because of and in reliance on the false and misleading prospectus failed to purchase the offered units. Respondent therefore sought on behalf of the alleged class some $21,400,000 in damages representing the lost opportunity to purchase the units; the right to purchase the previously rejected units at the 1968 price, and in addition, it sought some $25,000,000 in exemplary damages. . . .

Section 10 of the Act of 1934 made it "unlawful for any person . . . (b) to use or employ, in connection with the purchase or sale of any security registered on a national securities exchange or any security not so registered, any manipulative or deceptive device or contrivance in contravention of such rules and regulations as the Commission may prescribe as necessary or appropriate in the public interest or for the protection of investors." . . .

In 1942, acting under the authority granted to it by § 10(b) of the Act of 1934, the Commission promulgated Rule 10b-5, providing as follows:

§ 240.10b-5 Employment of manipulative and deceptive devices.

It shall be unlawful for any person, directly or indirectly, by the use of any means or instrumentality of interstate commerce, or of the mails or of any facility of any national securities exchange,

(a) To employ any device, scheme, or artifice to defraud,

(b) To make any untrue statement of a material fact or to omit to state a material fact necessary in order to make the statements made, in the light of the circumstances under which they were made, not misleading, or

(c) To engage in any act, practice, or course of business which operates or would operate as a fraud or deceit upon any person, "in connection with the purchase or sale of any security."

Section 10(b) of the 1934 Act does not by its terms provide an express civil remedy for its violation. Nor does the history of this provision provide any indication that Congress considered the problem of private suits under it at the time of its passage. . . . Similarly there is no indication that the Commission in adopting Rule 10b-5 considred the question of private civil remedies under this provision. . . .

Despite the contrast between the provisions of Rule 10b-5 and the numerous carefully drawn express civil remedies provided in both the Acts of 1933 and 1934, it was held in 1946 by the United States District Court for the Eastern District of Pennsylvania that there was an implied private right of action under the Rule. *Kardon* v. *National Gypsum Co.*, 69 F. Supp. 512 (1946). This Court had no occasion to deal with the subject until 20-odd years later, and at that time we confirmed with virtually no discussion the overwhelming consensus of the district courts and courts of appeals that such a cause of action did exist. *Superintendent of Insurance* v. *Bankers Life and Casualty Co.*, 404 U.S. 6, 13 n. 9 (1971); *Affiliated Ute Citizens* v. *United States,* 406 U.S. 128, 150-154 (1972). Such a conclusion was, of course, entirely consistent with the Court's recognition in *J. I. Case Corp.* v. *Borak,* 377 U.S. 426, 432 (1964), that private enforcement of Commission rules may "[provide] a necessary supplement to Commission action."

Within a few years after the seminal *Kardon* decision, the Court of Appeals for the Second Circuit concluded that the plaintiff class for purposes of a private damage action under § 10(b) and Rule 10B-5 was limited to actual purchasers and sellers of securities. *Birnbaum* v. *Newport Steel Corp., supra.* . . .

Just as this Court had no occasion to consider the validity of the *Kardon* holding that there was a private cause of action under Rule 10b-5 until 20-odd years later, nearly the same period of time has gone by between the *Birnbaum* decision and our consideration of the case now before us. As with *Kardon,* virtually all lower federal courts facing the issue in the hundreds of reported cases presenting this question over the past quarter century have reaffirmed *Birnbaum's* conclusion that the plaintiff class for purposes of § 10(b) and Rule 10b-5 private damage action is limited to purchasers and sellers of securities. . . .

In 1957 and again in 1959, the Securities and Exchange Commission sought from Congress amendment of § 10(b) to change its wording from "in connection with the purchase or sale of any security" to "in connection with the purchase or sale of, *or any attempt to purchase or sell,* any security." (Emphasis added.) . . . In the words of a memorandum submitted by the Commission to a congressional committee, the purpose of the proposed change was "to make section 10(b) also applicable to manipulative activities in connection with any attempt to purchase or sell any security." . . . Opposition to the amendment was based on fears of the extension of civil liability under § 10(b) that it would cause. . . . Neither change was adopted by Congress.

The longstanding acceptance by the courts, coupled with Congress' failure to reject *Birnbaum's* reasonable interpretation of the wording of § 10(b), wording which is directed towards injury suffered "in connection with the purchase or sale" of securities, argues significantly in favor of acceptance of the *Birnbaum* rule by this Court. . . .

Available extrinsic evidence from the texts of the 1933 and 1934 Acts as to the congressional scheme in this regard, though not conclusive, supports the result reached by the *Birnbaum* court. The wording of § 10(b) directed at fraud "in connection with the purchase or sale" of securities stands in contrast with the parallel antifraud provision of the 1933 Act, § 17(a), 15 U.S.C. § 77q, reaching fraud "in the offer or sale" of securities. Cf. § 5 of the 1933 Act, 15 U.S.C. 77e. When Congress wished to provide a remedy to those who neither purchase nor sell securities, it had little trouble in doing so expressly. Cf. § 16(b) of the 1934 Act, 15 U.S.C. § 78p.

Section 28(a) of the 1934 Act, 15 U.S.C. § 78bb, which limits recovery in any private damage action brought under the 1934 Act to "actual damages," likewise provides some support for the purchaser-seller rule. . . . While the damages suffered by purchasers and sellers pursuing a § 10(b) cause of action may on occasion be difficult to ascertain, . . . in the main such purchasers and sellers at least seek to base recovery on a demonstrable number of shares traded. In contrast, a putative plaintiff, who neither purchases nor sells securities but sues instead for intangible economic injury such as loss of a noncontractual opportunity to buy or sell, is more likely to be seeking a largely conjectural and speculative recovery in which the number of shares involved will depend on the plaintiff's subjective hypothesis. . . .

Having said all this, we would by no means be understood as suggesting that we are able to divine from the language of § 10(b) the express "intent of Congress" as to the contours of a private cause of action under Rule 10b-5. When we deal with private actions under Rule 10b-5, we deal with a judicial oak which has grown from little more than a legislative acorn. Such growth may be quite consistent with the congressional enactment and with the role of the federal judiciary in interpreting it, . . . but it would by disingenuous to suggest that either Congress in 1934 or the Securities and Exchange Commission in 1942 foreordained the present state of the law with respect to Rule 10b-5. It is therefore proper that we consider, in addition to the factors already discussed, what may be described as policy considerations when we come to flesh out the portions of the law with respect to which neither the congressional enactment nor the administrative regulations offer conclusive guidance.

Three principal classes of potential plaintiffs are presently barred by the *Birnbaum* rule. First are potential purchasers of shares, either in a new offering or on the Nation's post-distribution trading markets, who allege that they decided not to purchase because of an unduly gloomy representation or the omission of favorable material which made the issue appear to be a less favorable investment vehicle than it actually was. Second are actual shareholders in the issuer who allege that they decided not to sell their shares because of an unduly rosy representation or a failure to disclose unfavorable material. Third are shareholders, creditors, and perhaps others related to an issuer who suffered loss in the value of their investment due to corporate or insider activities in connection with the purchase or sale of securities which violate Rule 10b-5. It has been held that shareholder members of the second and third of these classes may frequently be able to circumvent the *Birnbaum* limitation through bringing a derivative action on behalf of the corporate issuer if the latter is itself a purchaser or seller of securities. . . . But the first of these classes, of which respondent is a member, can not claim the benefit of such a rule.

A great majority of the many commentators on the issue before us have taken the view that the *Birnbaum* limitation on the plaintiff class in Rule 10b-5 action for damages is an arbitrary restriction which unreasonably prevents some deserving plaintiffs from receiving damages which have in fact been caused by violations of Rule 10b-5. . . . The Securities and Exchange Commission has filed an *amicus* brief in this case espousing that same view. We have no doubt that this is indeed a disadvantage of the *Birnbaum* rule, and if it had no countervailing advantages it would be undesirable as a matter of policy, however much it might be supported by precedent and legislative history. But we are of the opinion that there are countervailing advantages of the *Birnbaum* rule, purely as a matter of policy, although those advantages are more difficult to articulate than is the disadvantage.

There has been widespread recognition that litigation under Rule 10b-5 presents a danger of vexatiousness different in degree and in kind from that which accompanies litigation in general. . . .

We believe that the concern expressed for the danger of vexatious litigation which could result from a widely expanded class of plaintiffs under Rule 10b-5 is founded in something more substantial than the common complaint of the many defendants who would prefer avoiding lawsuits entirely to either settling them or trying them. These concerns have two largely separate grounds.

The first of these concerns is that in the field of federal securities laws governing disclosure of information even a complaint which by objective standards may have very little chance of success at trial has a settlement value to the plaintiff out of any proportion to its prospect of success at trial so long as he may prevent the suit from being resolved against him by dismissal or summary judgment. The very pendency of the lawsuit may frustrate or delay normal business activity of the defendant which is totally unrelated to the lawsuit. . . .

Congress itself recognized the potential for nuisance or "strike" suits in this type of litigation, and in the 1934 Act amended § 11 of the 1933 Act to provide that:

> In any suit under this or any other section of this Title the Court may, in its discretion, require an undertaking for the payment of the costs of such suit, including reasonable attorney's fees. . . . (48 Stat. 881, 908.). . . .

Where Congress in those sections of the 1933 Act which expressly conferred a private cause of action for damages, adopted a provision uniformly regarded as designed to deter "strike" or nuisance actions, . . . that fact alone justifies our consideration of such potential in determining the limits of the class of plaintiffs who may sue in an action wholly implied from the language of the 1934 Act.

The potential for possible abuse of the liberal discovery provisions of the federal rules may likewise exist in this type of case to a greater extent than they do in other litigation. The prospect of extensive depositon of the defendant's officers and associates and the concomitant opportunity for extensive discovery of business documents, is a common occurrence in this and similar types of litigation. To the extent that this process eventually produces relevant evidence which is useful in determining the merits of the claims asserted by the parties, it bears the imprimatur of the Federal Rules of Civil Procedure and of the many cases liberally interpreting them. But to the extent that it permits a plaintiff with a largely groundless claim to simply take up the time of a number of other people, with the right to do so representing an *in terrorem* increment of the settlement value, rather than a reasonably founded hope that the process will reveal relevant evidence, it is a social cost rather than a benefit. Yet to broadly expand the class of plaintiffs who may sue under Rule 10b-5 would appear to encourage the least appealing aspect of the use of the discovery rules.

Without the *Birnbaum* rule, an action under § 10b-5 will turn largely on which oral version of a series of occurrences the jury may decide to credit, and therefore no matter how improbable the allegations of the plaintiff, the case will be virtually impossible to dispose of prior to trial other than by settlement. . .

The *Birnbaum* rule, on the other hand, permits exclusion prior to trial of those plaintiffs who were not themselves purchasers or sellers of the stock in question. The fact of purchase of stock and the fact of sale of stock are generally matters which are verifiable by documentation, and do not depend upon oral recollection, so that failure to qualify under the *Birnbaum* rule is a matter that can normally be established by the defendant either on a motion to dismiss or on a motion for summary judgment. . . .

The *Birnbaum* rule undoubtedly excludes plaintiffs who have in fact been damaged by violations of Rule 10b-5, and to that extent it is undesirable. But it also separates in a readily demonstrable manner the group of plaintiffs who actually purchased or actually sold, and whose version of the facts is therefore more likely to be believed by the trier of fact, from the vastly larger world of potential plaintiffs who might successfully allege a claim but could seldom succeed in proving it. And this fact is one of its advantages.

The second ground for fear of vexatious litigation is based on the concern that, given the generalized contours of liability, the abolition of the *Birnbaum* rule would throw open to the trier of fact many rather hazy issues of historical fact the proof of which depended almost entirely on oral testimony. We in no way disparage the worth and frequent high value of oral testimony when we say that dangers of its abuse appear to exist in this type of action to a peculiarly high degree. . . .

In the absence of the *Birnbaum* doctrine, bystanders to the securities marketing process could await developments on the sidelines without risk, claiming that inaccuracies in disclosure caused nonselling in a falling market and that unduly pessimistic predictions by the issuer followed by a rising market caused them to allow retrospectively golden opportunities to pass. . . .

Thus we conclude that what may be called considerations of policy, which we are free to weigh in deciding this case, are by no means entirely on one side of the scale. Taken together with the precedental support for the *Birnbaum* rule over a period of more than 20 years, and the consistency of that rule with what we can glean from the intent of Congress, they lead us to conclude that it is a sound rule and should be followed. . . .

We therefore hold that respondent was not entitled to sue for violation of Rule 10b-5, and the judgment of the Court of Appeals is

Reversed.

Mr. Justice Blackmun, with whom Mr. Justice Douglas and Mr. Justice Brennan join, dissenting.

Today the Court graves into stone *Birnbaum's* arbitrary principle of standing. For this task the Court, unfortunately, chooses to utilize three blunt chisels: (1) reliance on the legislative history of the 1933 and 1934 Securities Acts, conceded as inconclusive in this particular context; (2) acceptance as precedent of two decades of lower court decisions following a doctrine, never before examined here, that was pronounced by a justifiably esteemed panel of that Court of Appeals regarded as the "Mother Court" in this area of the law, but under entirely different circumstances; and (3) resort to utter pragmaticality and a conjectural assertion of "policy considerations" deemed to arise in distinguishing the meritorious Rule 10b-5 suit from the meretricious one. In so doing, the Court exhibits a preternatural solicitousness for corporate well-being and a seeming callousness toward the investing public quite out of keeping, it seems to me, with our own traditions and the intent of the securities laws. ...

From a reading of the complaint in relation to the language of § 10(b) of the 1934 Act and of Rule 10b-5, it is manifest that plaintiffs have alleged the use of a deceptive scheme "in connection with the purchase or sale of any security." To my mind, the word "sale" ordinarily and naturally may be understood to mean not only a single, individualized act transferring property from one party to another, but also the generalized event of public disposal of property through advertisement, auction, or some other market mechanism. Here there is an obvious, indeed a court-ordered, "sale" of securities in the special offering of New Blue Chip shares and debentures to former users. Yet the Court denies these plaintiffs the right to maintain a suit under Rule 10b-5 because they do not fit into the mechanistic categories of either "purchaser" or "seller." This, surely, is anomaly, for the very purpose of the alleged scheme was to inhibit these plaintiffs from ever acquiring the status of "purchaser." Faced with this abnormal divergence from the usual pattern of securities frauds, the Court pays no heed to the unremedied wrong or to the portmanteau nature of § 10(b). ...

The question under both Rule 10b-5 and its parent statute, § 10(b), is whether fraud was employed — and the language is critical — by "any person ... in connection with the purchase or sale of any security." On the allegations here, the nexus between the asserted fraud and the conducting of a "sale" is obvious and inescapable, and no more should be required to sustain the plaintiff's complaint against a motion to dismiss. ...

Perhaps it is true that more cases that come within the *Birnbaum* doctrine can be properly proved than those that fall outside it. But this is no reason for denying standing to sue to plaintiffs, such as those in this case, who allegedly are injured by novel forms of manipulation. We should be wary about heeding the seductive call of expediency and about substituting convenience and ease of processing for the more difficult task of separating the genuine claim from the unfounded one.

Instead of the artificiality of *Birnbaum,* the essential test of a valid Rule 10b-5 claim, it seems to me, must be the showing of a logical nexus between the alleged fraud and the sale or purchase of a security. It is inconceivable that Congress could have intended a broad-ranging antifraud provision, such as § 10(b), and, at the same time, have intended to impose, or be deemed to welcome, a mechanical overtone and requirement such as the *Birnbaum* doctrine. The facts of this case, if proved and accepted by the factfinder, surely are within the conduct that Congress intended to ban. Whether these particular

524

plaintiffs, or any plaintiff, will be able eventually to carry the burdens of proving fraud and of proving reliance and damage — that is, causality and injury — is a matter that should not be left to speculations of "policy" of the kind now advanced in this forum so far removed from witnesses and evidence.

Finally, I am uneasy about the type of precedent the present decision establishes. Policy considerations can be applied and utilized in like fashion in other situations. The acceptance of this decisional route in this case may well come back to haunt us elsewhere before long. I would decide the case to fulfill the broad purpose that the language of the statutes and the legislative history dictate, and I would avoid the Court's pragmatic solution resting upon a 20-year-old, severely criticized doctrine enunciated for a factually distinct situation.

In short, I would abandon the *Birnbaum* doctrine as a rule of decision in favor of a more general test of nexus, just as the Seventh Circuit did in *Eason* v. *General Motors Acceptance Corp.,* 490 F. 2d 654, 661 (1973), cert. denied, 416 U.S. 960 (1974). I would not worry about any imagined inability of our federal trial and appellate courts to control the flowering of the types of cases that the Court fears might result. Nor would I yet be disturbed about dire consequences that a basically pessimistic attitude foresees if the *Birnbaum* doctrine were allowed quietly to expire. Sensible standards of proof and of demonstrable damages would evolve and serve to protect the worthy and shut out the frivolous.

◆◆◆

Case Questions

1. Does this decision indicate that the Supreme Court has a pro-business tilt?
2. Is it proper to have policy considerations as the determining factor in a case of this importance? Are policy considerations just another name for a judge's personal, political, social and economic opinions?
3. When the Supreme Court is considering a case, what role should a concern over the judiciary's case-load (vexatious litigation) occupy?

OTHER FRAUDULENT ACTIVITIES

Rule 10b-5(3) outlaws practices that operate as a fraud or deceit in the purchase or sale of any security. The Investment Advisors Act of 1940 prohibits practices that operate as a fraud or deceit upon clients. Fraud can assume many forms. The Capital Gains case that follows illustrates a unique form of fraud under the latter statute.

S.E.C. v. CAPITAL GAINS RESEARCH BUREAU
375 U.S. 180 (1963)

◆◆◆

Mr. Justice Goldberg delivered the opinion of the Court.

We are called upon in this case to decide whether under the Investment Advisers Act of 1940 the Securities and Exchange Commission may obtain an injunction compelling a registered investment adviser to disclose to his clients a practice of purchasing shares of a security for his own account shortly before recommending that security for long-term investment and then immediately selling the shares at a profit upon the rise in the market price following the recommendation. The answer to this question turns on whether the practice — known in the trade as "scalping" — "operates as a fraud or deceit upon any client or prospective client" within the meaning of the Act. We hold that it does and that the Commission may "enforce compliance" with the Act by obtaining an injunction requiring the adviser to make full disclosure of the practice to his clients. . . .

Respondents publish two investment advisory services, one of which — "A Capital Gains Report" — is the subject of this proceeding. The Report is mailed monthly to approximately 5,000 subscribers who each pay an annual subscription price of $18. It carries the following description.

> An Investment Service devoted exclusively to (1) The protection of investment capital. (2) The realization of a steady and attractive income therefrom. (3) The accumulation of CAPITAL GAINS thru the timely purchase of corporate equities that are proved to be undervalued.

Between March 15, 1960, and November 7, 1960, respondents, on six different occasions, purchased shares of a particular security shortly before recommending it in the Report for long-term investment. On each occasion, there was an increase in the market price and the volume of trading of the recommended security within a few days after the distribution of the Report. Immediately thereafter, respondents sold their shares of these securities at a profit. They did not disclose any aspect of these transactions to their clients or prospective clients. . . .

The decision in this case turns on whether Congress, in empowering the courts to enjoin any practice which operates "as a fraud or deceit upon any client or prospective client," intended to require the Commission to establish fraud and deceit "in their technical sense," including intent to injure and actual injury to clients, or whether Congress intended a broad remedial construction of the Act which would encompass nondisclosure of material facts. . . .

The Investment Advisers Act of 1940 was the last in a series of Acts designed to eliminate certain abuses in the securities industry, abuses which were found to have contributed to the stock market crash of 1929 and the depression of the 1930's. . . . A fundamental purpose, common to these statutes, was to substitute a philosophy of full disclosure for the philosophy of caveat emptor and thus to achieve a high standard of business ethics in the securities industry. As we recently said in a related context, "It requires but little appreciation . . . of what happened in this country during the 1920's and 1930's to realize how essential it is that the highest ethical standards prevail" in every facet of the securities industry. *Silver* v. *New York Stock Exchange,* 373 U.S. 341, 366. . . .

(The Court then discussed the legislative history of the bill, omitted here.)

The Investment Advisers Act of 1940 thus reflects a congressional recognition "of the delicate fiduciary nature of an investment advisory relationship," as well as a congressional intent to eliminate, or at least to expose, all conflicts of interest which might include an investment adviser consciously or unconsciously — to render advice which was not disinterested. . . .

Courts have imposed on a fiduciary an affirmative duty of "utmost good faith, and full and fair disclosure of all material facts," as well as an affirmative obligation "to employ reasonable care to avoid misleading" his clients. There has also been a growing recognition by common-law courts that the doctrines of fraud and deceit which developed around transactions involving land and other tangible items of wealth are ill-suited to the sale of such intangibles as advice and securities, and that, accordingly, the doctrines must be adapted to the merchandise in issue. . . .

An adviser who, like respondents, secretly trades on the market effect of his own recommendation may be motivated − consciously or unconsciously − to recommend a given security not because of its potential for long-run price increase (which would profit the client), but because of its potential for short-run price increase in response to anticipated activity from the recommendation (which would profit the adviser). An investor seeking the advice of a registered investment adviser must, if the legislative purpose is to be served, be permitted to evaluate such overlapping motivations, through appropriate disclosure, in deciding whether an adviser is serving "two masters" or only one, "especially . . . if one of the masters happens to be economic self-interest." *United States* v. *Mississippi Valley Co.*, 364 U.S. 520, 549. Accordingly, we hold that the Investment Advisers Act of 1940 empowers the courts, upon a showing such as that made here, to require an adviser to make full and frank disclosure of his practice of trading on the effect of his recommendations. . . .

Respondents argue, finally, that their advice was "honest" in the sense that they believed it was sound and did not offer it for the purpose of furthering personal pecuniary objectives. This, of course, is but another way of putting the rejected argument that the elements of technical common-law-fraud − particularly intent − must be established before an injunction requiring disclosure may be ordered. It is the practice itself, however, with its potential for abuse, which "operates as a fraud or deceit" within the meaning of the Act when relevant information is suppressed. . . . Failure to disclose material facts must be deemed fraud or deceit within its intended meaning, for as the experience of the 1920's and 1930's amply reveals, the darkness and ignorance of commercial secrecy are the conditions upon which predatory practices best thrive. . . . The statute, in recognition of the adviser's fiduciary relationship to his clients, requires that the advice be disinterested. To insure this it empowers the courts to require disclosure of material facts. . . . The high standards of business morality exacted by our laws regulating the securities industry do not permit an investment adviser to trade on the market effect of his own recommendations without fully and fairly revealing his personal interests in these recommendations to his clients.

Experience has shown that disclosure in such situations, while not onerous to the adviser, is needed to preserve the climate of fair dealing which is so essential to maintain public confidence in the securities industry and to preserve the economic health of the country. . . .

◆◆◆

Case Question

1. What arguments, both pro and con, can you list for purchasing stock recommended by an investment adviser, who has himself purchased that particular stock?

REVIEW PROBLEMS

1. G-P owns 6¼% of the outstanding stock of Kaiser-Frazer. G-P then transfers its assets to Kaiser-Frazer and receives in return a large block of stock, swelling its holdings to 21 percent. Within six months G-P sells some of its stock at a profit. Does receipt of the stock, in return for the transfer of assets, constitute a "purchase"? If so, did G-P become the beneficial owner of 10 percent of Kaiser-Frazer stock at the very moment it purchased the stock, thereby making the short swing profits provision applicable? [*Stella* v. *Graham-Paige Motors Corporation*, 232 F2d 299 (1956)].

2. Klawans purchased 9,900 shares of stock of Williams-McWilliams Industries at various times between October 1, 1956 and January 17, 1957. These holdings amount to less than 10 percent of the corporation's stock and Klawans was neither a director nor officer during this time period. He became a director on March 18, 1957 about sixty days after the last purchase of stock. He made no further purchases but within ten days of his election as director he sold 7,900 shares at a profit. Thereafter, he sold the remaining shares at a loss. Under 16(b), do his profits belong to the corporation? If he is accountable for the profits, may he offset losses in transactions in the same stock within the six month period covered by the statute? [*Adler* v. *Klawans*, 267 F2d 840 (1959)].

3. Oreamuno and Gonzalez are directors of Management Assistants, Inc. With their wives they own approximately 14 percent of the company's common stock. In August, 1966 they learned that corporate earnings will be sharply reduced from earlier figures. This information did not become available to the other shareholders and investing public until October 18, 1966. In September, 1966 Oreamuno sold 28,500 shares of common stock and Gonzalez sold 28,000 shares. The selling price was $23.75 a share; after release of the earnings report the stock fell to $11 per share. Diamond, another shareholder, now brings a stockholders derivative suit to recover the difference between the two prices. Neither Diamond nor the corporation purchased any of the shares that were sold. The corporation sustained no loss. Should Diamond's lawsuit be dismissed? Can the purchasers of the stock also bring suit? If the answer to both questions is "yes," do you think potential double liability is a wise policy? [*Diamond* v. *Oreamuno*, 287 N.Y.S. 2d 300 (1968); 248 N.E. 2d 910 (1969)].

4. Crane Co. makes a tender offer to the shareholders of Westinghouse Air Brake Co. on April 6, 1968. Under the tender offer Crane acquired 32 percent of Air Brake's stock. However, prior to the offer, Air Brake's directors approved a merger with American Standard. After the tender offer expires, the Air Brake stockholders approve the merger. The merger is then consummated. Crane is a competitor of Standard. To avoid the antitrust problems inherent in having significant stock ownership in a competitor, Crane sells its stock during June 1968 at a profit. Standard now brings suit to recover these short swing profits. Crane argues that the antitrust laws forced the sale and 16(b) does not govern such "forced" sales. It points out that 16(b) is aimed at trading abuses arising out of access to inside information. Although by statutory definition it is an insider, it is an outsider who failed in its takeover bid. Should Crane disgorge its short swing profits? [*American Standard* v. *Crane* — F2d — (CA-2, 1974)].

LIABILITY OF DIRECTORS, ACCOUNTANTS, AND ATTORNEYS UNDER THE SECURITIES LAW

17

Currently in the mid-1970s there is extensive discussion and disagreement over what constitutes the proper role of directors, accountants and attorneys under the securities laws. Are their duties restricted to serving their client corporation or do they also encompass a duty to the public and the S.E.C.? The collapse of the Penn Central, the Home-Stake Oil Affair, the Stirling Homex scandal, the Equity Funding debacle, the National Student Marketing fraud, illegal political contributions by such corporations as American Airlines, and, finally, bribery of foreign officials by United Brands and Gulf Oil raise questions as to what the directors, accountants and attorneys were doing when certain activities occurred. Did they have knowledge of what was taking place? If not, why not? Would a reasonable director, accountant or attorney have uncovered the shenanigans? Do they have a duty of disclosure? If so, to whom does this duty run? The final answers to some of these queries remain unsettled. Yet, in other areas the securities laws are specific as to the legal responsibility of various individuals. Let us now examine various aspects of these responsibilities.

DIRECTOR'S LIABILITY

A director's liability under the securities law does not vary according to his status as an inside or outside director. The securities laws do not distinguish between the two. They impose a more rigorous responsibility than does general corporate and common law. Yet, a director does not bear absolute liability. The BarChris case that follows examines the liability of those that sign a materially false registration statement, including directors. Notice that a director incurs civil liability unless he can prove, 1) he relied upon the authority of an expert and had no reasonable grounds to believe that the expert's statements were untrue or, 2) that he made a reasonable investigation and had reasonable grounds to believe that the statements were true.

BarChris is a very significant and noteworthy case. In its own way, it is as important as the Texas Gulf Sulphur case. As you read it, you will note that it deals with accountants' and underwriters' liability in addition to that of directors.

ESCOTT v. BARCHRIS CONSTRUCTION CORP.
283 F. Supp. 643 (1968)

McLean, District Judge.

This is an action by purchasers of 5½ percent convertible subordinated fifteen year debentures of BarChris Construction Corporation (BarChris). Plaintiffs purport to sue on their own behalf and "on behalf of all other and present and former holders" of the debentures. . . .

The action is brought under Section 11 of the Securities Act of 1933 (15 U.S.C. § 77k). Plaintiffs allege that the registration statement with respect to these debentures filed with the Securities and Exchange Commission, which became effective on May 16, 1961, contained false statements and material omissions.

Defendants fall into three categories: (1) the persons who signed the registration statement; (2) the underwriters, consisting of eight investment banking firms, led by Drexel & Co. (Drexel); and (3) BarChris's auditors, Peat, Marwick, Mitchell & Co. (Peat, Marwick).

The signers, in addition to BarChris itself, were the nine directors of BarChris, plus its controller, who was not a director. . . .

On the main issue of liability, the questions to be decided are (1) did the registration statement contain false statements of fact, or did it omit to state facts which should have been stated in order to prevent it from being misleading; (2) if so, were the facts which were falsely stated or omitted "material" within the meaning of the Act; (3) if so, have defendants established their affirmative defense? . . .

At the time relevant here, BarChris was engaged primarily in the construction of bowling alleys. . . .

It is estimated that in 1960 BarChris installed approximately three percent of all lanes built in the United States. . . .

In general, BarChris's method of operation was enter into a contract with a customer, receive from him at that time a comparatively small down payment on the purchase price, and proceed to construct and equip the bowling alley. When the work was finished and the building delivered, the customer paid the balance of the contract price in notes, payable in installments over a period of years. BarChris discounted these notes with a factor and received part of their face amount in cash. The factor held back part as a reserve.

In 1960 BarChris began a practice which has been referred to throughout this case as the "alternative method of financing." In substance this was a sale and leaseback arrangement. It involved a distinction between the "interior" of a building and the building itself, i.e., the outer shell. In instances in which this method applied, BarChris would build and install what it referred to as the "interior package." Actually this amounted to constructing and installing the equipment in a building. When it was completed, it would sell the interior to a factor, James Talcott Inc. (Talcott), who would pay BarChris the full contract price therefor. The factor then proceeded to lease the interior either directly to BarChris's customer or back to a subsidiary of BarChris. In the latter case, the subsidiary in turn would lease it to the customer.

Under either financing method, BarChris was compelled to expend considerable sums in defraying the cost of construction before it received reimbursement. As a consequence, BarChris was in constant need of cash to finance its operations, a need which grew more pressing as operations expanded. . . .

By early 1961, BarChris needed additional working capital. The proceeds of the sale of the debentures involved in this action were to be devoted, in part at least, to fill that need.

Although BarChris continued to build alleys in 1961 and 1962, it became increasingly apparent that the industry was overbuilt. . . .

On October 29, 1962, it filed in this court a petition for an arrangement under Chapter XI of the Bankruptcy Act. . . .

The registration statement in its final form contained a prospectus as well as other information.

The prospectus contained, among other things, a description of BarChris's business, a description of its real property, some material pertaining to certain of its subsidiaries, and remarks about various other aspects of its affairs. It also contained financial information. It included a consolidated balance sheet as of December 31, 1960, with elaborate explanatory notes. These figures had been audited by Peat, Marwick. It also contained unaudited figures as to net sales, gross profit and net earnings for the first quarter ended March 31, 1961, as compared with the similar quarter for 1960. In addition, it set forth figures as to the company's backlog of unfilled orders as of March 31, 1961, as compared with March 31, 1960, and figures as to BarChris's contingent liability, as of April 30, 1961, on customers' notes discounted and its contingent liability under the so-called alternative method of financing.

Plaintiffs challenge the accuracy of a number of these figures. They also charge that the text of the prospectus, apart from the figures, was false in number of respects, and that material information was omitted. . . .

For convenience, the various falsities and omissions . . . are recapitulated here. They were as follows:

1. **1960 Earnings**

    (a) **Sales**

As per prospectus	$9,165,320
Correct figure	8,511,420
Overstatement	$ 653,900

    (b) **Net Operating Income**

As per prospectus	$1,742,801
Correct figure	1,496,196
Overstatement	$ 246,605

    (c) **Earnings per Share**

As per prospectus	$ .75
Correct figure	.65
Overstatement	$ .10

2. **1960 Balance Sheet**

    Current Assets

As per prospectus	$4,524,021
Correct figure	3,914,332
Overstatement	609,689

3. **Contingent Liabilities as of December 31, 1960 on Alternative Method of Financing**

As per prospectus	$ 750,000
Correct figure	1,125,795
Understatement	$ 375,795
Capitol Lanes should have been shown as a direct liability	$ 325,000

4. **Contingent Liabilities as of April 30, 1961**

As per prospectus	$ 825,000
Correct figure	1,443,853
Understatement	$ 618,853
Capitol Lanes should have been shown as direct liability	$ 314,166

5. **Earnings Figures for Quarter ending March 31, 1961**

(a) Sales

As per prospectus	$2,138,455
Correct figure	1,618,645
Overstatement	$ 519,810

(b) Gross Profit

As per prospectus	$ 483,121
Correct figure	252,366
Overstatement	$ 230,755

6. **Backlog as of March 31, 1961**

As per prospectus	$6,905,000
Correct figure	2,415,000
Overstatement	$4,490,000

7. **Failure to Disclose Officers' Loans Outstanding and Unpaid on May 16, 1961** $ 386,615

8. **Failure to Disclose Use of Proceeds in Manner not Revealed in Prospectus**

Approximately	$1,160,000

9. **Failure to Disclose Customers' Delinquencies in May 1961 and BarChris's Potential Liability with Respect Thereto**   Over $1,350,000

10. **Failure to Disclose the Fact that BarChris was Already Engaged, and was about to be More Heavily Engaged, in the Operation of Bowling Alleys**

It is a prerequisite to liability under Section 11 of the Act that the fact which is falsely stated in a registration statement, or the fact that is omitted when it should have been stated to avoid misleading, be "material." . . .

Early in the history of the Act, a definition of materiality was given in Matter of Charles A. Howard, 1 S.E.C. 6.8 (1934), which is still valid today. A material fact was there defined as:

"* * * a fact which if it had been correctly stated or disclosed would have deterred or tended to deter the average prudent investor from purchasing the securities in question." . . .

Judged by this test, there is no doubt that many of the misstatements and omissions in this prospectus were material. This is true of all of them which relate to the state of affairs in 1961, i.e., the overstatement of sales and gross profit for the first quarter, the understatement of contingent liabilities as of April 30, the overstatement of orders on hand and the failure to disclose the true facts with respect to officers' loans, customers' delinquencies, application of proceeds and the prospective operation of several alleys.

The misstatements and omissions pertaining to BarChris's status as of December 31, 1960, however, present a much closer question. The 1960 earnings figures, the 1960 balance sheet and the contingent liabilities as of December 31, 1960 were not nearly as erroneous as plaintiff's have claimed. But they were wrong to some extent, as we have seen. Would it have deterred the average prudent investor from purchasing these debentures if he had been informed that the 1960 sales were $8,511,420 rather than $9,165,320, that the net operating income was $1,496,196 rather than $1,742,801 and that the earnings per share in 1960 were approximately 65 cents rather than 75 cents? According to the unchallenged figures, sales in 1959 were $3,320,121, net operating income was $441,103, and earnings per share were 33 cents. Would it have made a difference to an average prudent investor if he had known that in 1960 sales only 256 percent of 1959 sales, not 276 percent; that net operating income was up by only $1,055,093, not by $1,301,698, and that earnings per share, while still approximately twice those of 1959, were not something more than twice? These debentures were rated "B" by the investment rating services. They were thus characterized as speculative, as any prudent investor must have realized. It would seem that anyone interested in buying these convertible debentures would have been attracted primarily by the conversion feature, by the growth potential of the stock. The growth which the company enjoyed in 1960 over prior years was striking, even on the correct figures. It is hard to see how a prospective purchaser of this type of investment would have been deterred from buying if he had been advised of these comparatively minor errors in reporting 1960 sales and earnings.

Since no one knows what moves or does not move the mythical "average prudent investor," it comes down to a question of judgment, to be exercised by the trier of the fact as best he can in the light of all the circumstances. It is my best judgment that the average prudent investor would not have cared about there errors in the 1960 sales and earnings figures, regrettable though they may be. I therefore find that they were not material within the meaning of Section 11.

The same is true of the understatement of contingent liabilities in footnote 9 by approximately $375,000. . . .

This leaves for consideration the errors in the 1960 balance sheet figures which have previously been discussed in detail. . . .

There must be some point at which errors in disclosing a company's balance sheet position become material, even to a growth-oriented investor. On all the evidence I find that these balance sheet errors were material within the meaning of Section 11. . . .

The "Due Diligence" Defenses

Section 11(b) of the Act provides that:

"* * * no person, other than the issuer, shall be liable * * * who shall sustain the burden of proof —

* * *

(3) that (A) as regards any part of the registration statement not purporting to be made on the authority of an expert * * * he had, after reasonable investigation, reasonable ground to believe and did believe, at the time such part of the registration statement became effective, that the statements therein were true and that there was no omission to state a material fact required to be stated therein or necessary to make the statements therein not misleading; * * * and (C) as regards any part of the registration statement purporting to be made on the authority of an expert (other than himself) * * * he had no reasonable ground to believe and did not believe, at the time such part of the registration statement became effective that the statements therein were untrue or that there was an omission to state a material fact required to be stated therein or necessary to make the statements therein not misleading * * *".

Section 11(c) defines "reasonable investigation" as follows:

"In determining, for the purpose of paragraph (3) of subsection (b) of this section, what constitutes reasonable investigation and reasonable ground for belief, the standard of reasonableness shall be that required of a prudent man in the management of his own property."

Every defendant, except BarChris itself, to whom as the issuer, these defenses are not available, and except Peat, Marwick, whose position rests on a different statutory provision, has pleaded these affirmative defenses. Each claims that (1) as to the part of the registration statement purporting to be made on the authority of an expert (which for convenience, I shall refer to as the "expertised portion"), he had no reasonable ground to believe and did not believe that there were any untrue statements or material omissions, and (2) as to the other parts of the registration statement, he made a reasonable investigation, as a result of which he had reasonable ground to believe and did believe that the registration statement was true and that no material fact was omitted. . . .

The only expert, in the statutory sense, was Peat, Marwick, and the only parts of the registration statement which purported to be made upon the authority of an expert were the portions which purported to be made on Peat, Marwicks's authority. . . .

The registration statement contains a report of Peat, Marwick as independent public accountants dated February 23, 1961. This relates only to the consolidated balance sheet of BarChris and consolidated subsidiaries as of December 31, 1960, and the related statement of earnings and retained earnings for the five years then ended. This is all that Peat, Marwick purported to certify. It is perfectly clear that it did not purport to certify the 1961 figures, some of which are expressly stated in the prospectus to have been unaudited. . . .

I turn now to the question of whether defendants have proved their due diligence defenses.

Russo   *Liable*

Russo was, to all intents and purposes, the chief executive officer of BarChris. He was a member of the executive committee. He was familiar with all aspects of the business. He was personally in charge of dealings with the factors. He talked with customers about their delinquencies.

Russo prepared the list of jobs which went into the backlog figure. He knew the status of those jobs. . . .

It was Russo who arranged for the temporary increase in BarChris's cash in banks on December 31, 1960, a transaction which borders on the fraudulent. . . .

In short, Russo knew all the relevant facts. He could not have believed that there were no untrue statements or material omissions in the prospectus. Russo has no due diligence defenses.

Vitolo and Pugliese

They were the founders of the business who stuck with it to the end. Vitolo was president and Pugliese was vice president. Despite their titles, their field of responsibility in the administration of BarChris's affairs during the period in question seems to have been less all-embracing than Russo's. . . .

Vitolo and Pugliese are each men of limited education. It is not hard to believe that for them the prospectus was difficult reading, if indeed they read it at all. . . .

The liability of a director who signs a registration statement does not depend upon whether or not he read it or, if he did, whether or not he understood what he was reading.

And in any case, Vitolo and Pugliese were not as naive as they claim to be. They were members of BarChris's executive committee. At meetings of that committee BarChris's affairs were discussed at length. They must have known what was going on. Certainly they knew of the inadequacy of cash in 1961. They knew of their own large advances to the company which remained unpaid. They knew that they had agreed not to deposit their checks until the financing proceeds were received. They knew and intended that part of the proceeds were to be used to pay their own loans.

All in all, the position of Vitolo and Pugliese is not significantly different, for present purposes, from Russo's. They could not have believed that the registration statement was wholly true and that no material facts had been omitted. And in any case, there is nothing to show that they made any investigation of anything which they may not have known about or understood. They have not proved their due diligence defenses.

Kircher

Kircher was treasurer of BarChris and its chief financial officer. He is a certified public accountant and an intelligent man. He was thoroughly familiar with BarChris's financial affairs. He knew the terms of BarChris's agreements with Talcott. He knew of the customers' deliquency problem. . . .

Moreover, as a member of the executive committee, Kircher was kept informed as to those branches of the business of which he did not have direct charge. . . .

Kircher worked on the preparation of the registration statement. He conferred with Grant and on occasion with Ballard. He supplied information to them about the company's business. He read the prospectus and understood it. He knew what it said and what it did not say.

Kircher's contention is that he had never before dealt with a registration statement, that he did not know what it should contain, and that he relied wholly on Grant, Ballard and Peat, Marwick to guide him. He claims that it was their fault, not his, if there was anything wrong with it. He says that all the facts were recorded in BarChris's books where these "experts" could have seen them if they had looked. He says that he truthfully answered all their questions. In effect, he says that if they did not know enough to ask the right questions and to give him the proper instructions, that is not his responsibility.

There is an issue of credibility here. In fact, Kircher was not frank in dealing with Grant and Ballard. He withheld information from them. But even if he had told them all the facts, this would not have constituted the due diligence contemplated by the statute. Knowing the facts, Kircher had reason to believe that the expertised portion of the prospectus, i.e., the 1960 figures, was in part incorrect. He could not shut his eyes to the facts and rely on Peat, Marwick for that portion.

As to the rest of the prospectus, knowing the facts, he did not have a reasonable ground to believe it to be true. On the contrary, he must have known that in part it was untrue. Under these circumstances, he was not entitled to sit back and place the blame on the lawyers for not advising him about it.

Kircher has not proved his due diligence defenses.

Trilling

Trilling's position is somewhat different from Kircher's. He was BarChris's controller. He signed the registration statement in that capacity, although he was not a director.

Trilling entered BarChris's employ in October 1960. He was Kircher's subordinate. When Kircher asked him for information, he furnished it. On at least one occasion he got it wrong.

Trilling was not a member of the executive committee. He was a comparatively minor figure in BarChris. The description of BarChris's "management" on page 9 of the prospectus does not mention him. He was not considered to be an executive officer.

Trilling may well have been unaware of several of the inaccuracies in the prospectus. But he must have known of some of them. As a financial officer, he was familiar with BarChris's finances and with its books of account. He knew that part of the cash on deposit on December 31, 1960 had been procured temporarily by Russo for window dressing purposes. He knew that BarChris was operating Capitol Lanes in 1960. He should have known, although perhaps through carelessness he did not know at the time, that BarChris's contingent liability on Type B lease transactions was greater than the prospectus stated. In the light of these facts, I cannot find that Trilling believed the entire prospectus to be true.

But even if he did, he still did not establish his due diligence defenses. He did not prove that as to the parts of the prospectus expertised by Peat, Marwick he had no reasonable ground to believe that it was untrue. He also failed to prove, as to the parts of the prospectus not expertised by Peat, Marwick, that he made a reasonable investigation which afforded him a reasonable ground to believe that it was true. As far as appears, he made no investigation. He did what was asked of him and assumed that others would properly take care of supplying accurate data as to the other aspects of the company's business. This would have been well enough but for the fact that he signed the registration statement. As a signer, he could not avoid responsibility by leaving it up to others to make it accurate. Trilling did not sustain the burden of proving his due diligence defenses.

Birnbaum

Birnbaum was a young lawyer, admitted to the bar in 1957, who, after brief periods of employment by two different law firms and an equally brief period of practicing in his own firm, was employed by BarChris as house counsel and assistant secretary in October 1960. Unfortunately for him, he became secretary and a director of BarChris on April 17, 1961, after the first version of the registration statement had been filed with the Securities and Exchange Commission. He signed the later amendments, thereby becoming responsible for the accuracy of the prospectus in its final form.

Although the prospectus, in its description of "management," lists Birnbaum among the "executive officers" and devotes several sentences to a recital of his career, the fact seems to be that he was not an executive officer in any real sense. He did not participate in the management of the company. As house counsel, he attended to legal matters of a routine nature. Among other things, he incorporated subsidiaries, with which BarChris was plentifully supplied. He was thus aware of that aspect of the business.

Birnbaum examined contracts. In that connection he advised BarChris that the T-Bowl contracts were not legally enforceable. He was thus aware of that fact.

One of Birnbaum's more important duties, first as assistant secretary and later as full-fledged secretary, was to keep the corporate minutes of BarChris and its subsidiaries. This necessarily informed him to a considerable extent about the company's affairs. Birnbaum was not initially a member of the executive committee, however, and did not keep its minutes at the outset. According to the minutes, the first meeting which he attended, "upon invitation of the Committee," was on March 22, 1961. He became a member shortly thereafter and kept the minutes beginning with the meeting of April 24, 1961.

It seems probable that Birnbaum did not know of many of the inaccuracies in the prospectus. He must, however, have appreciated some of them. In any case, he made no investigation and relied on the others to get it right. Unlike Trilling, he was entitled to rely upon Peat, Marwick for the 1960 figures, for as far as appears, he had no personal knowledge of the company's books of account or financial transactions. But he was not entitled to rely upon Kircher, Grant and Ballard for the other portions of the prospectus. As a lawyer, he should have known his obligations under the statute. He should have known that he was required to make a reasonable investigation of the truth of all the statements in the unexpertised portion of the document which he signed. Having failed to make such an investigation, he did not have reasonable ground to believe that all these statements were true. Birnbaum has not established his due diligence defenses except as to the audited 1960 figures.

Auslander

Auslander was an "outside" director, i.e., one who was not an officer of BarChris. He was chairman of the board of Valley Stream National Bank in Valley Stream, Long Island. In February 1961 Vitolo asked him to become a director of BarChris. Vitolo gave him an enthusiastic account of BarChris's progress and prospects. As an inducement, Vitolo said that when BarChris received the proceeds of a forthcoming issue of securities, it would deposit $1,000,000 in Auslander's bank.

In February and early March 1961, before accepting Vitolo's invitation, Auslander made some investigation of BarChris. He obtained Dun & Bradstreet reports which contained sales and earnings figures for periods earlier than December 31, 1960. He caused inquiry to be made of certain of BarChris's banks and was advised that they regarded BarChris favorably. . . .

On March 3, 1961, Auslander indicated his willingness to accept a place on the board. Shortly thereafter, on March 14, Kircher sent him a copy of BarChris's annual report for 1960. Auslander observed that BarChrist's auditors were Peat Marwick. They were also the auditors for the Valley Stream National Bank. He thought well of them.

Auslander was elected a director on April 17, 1961. The registration statement in its original form had already been filed, of course without his signature. On May 10, 1961, he signed a signature page for the first amendment to the registration statement which was filed on May 11, 1961. This was a separate sheet without any document attached. Auslander did not know that it was a signature page for a registration statement. He vaguely understood that it was something "for the SEC."

Auslander attended a meeting of BarChris's directors on May 15, 1961. At that meeting he, along with the other directors, signed the signature sheet for the second amendment which constituted the registration statement in its final form. Again, this was only a separate sheet without any document attached. Auslander never saw a copy of the registration statement in its final form.

At the May 15 directors' meeting, however, Auslander did realize that what he was signing was a signature sheet to a registration statement. This was the first time that he had appreciated that fact. A copy of the registration statement in its earlier form as amended on May 11, 1961 was passed around at the meeting. Auslander glanced at it briefly. He did not read it thoroughly.

At the May 15 meeting, Russo and Vitolo stated that everything was in order and that the prospectus was correct. Auslander believed this statement.

In considering Auslander's due diligence defenses, a distinction is to be drawn between the expertised and nonexpertised portions of the prospectus. As to the former, Auslander knew that Peat, Marwick had audited the 1960 figures. He believed them to be correct because he had confidence in Peat, Marwick. He had no reasonable ground to believe otherwise.

As to the non-expertised portions, however, Auslander is in a different position. He seems to have been under the impression that Peat, Marwick was responsible for all the figures. This impression was not correct, as he would have realized if he had read the prospectus carefully. Auslander made no investigation of the accuracy of the prospectus. He relied on the assurance of Vitolo and Russo, and upon the information he had received in answer to his inquiries back in February and early March. These inquiries were general ones, in the nature of a credit check. The information which he received in answer to them was also general, without specific reference to the statements in the prospectus, which was not prepared until some time thereafter.

It is true that Auslander became a director on the eve of the financing. He had little opportunity to familiarize himself with the company's affairs. The question is whether, under such circumstances, Auslander did enough to establish his due diligence defense with respect to the non-expertised portions of the prospectus.

Although there is a dearth of authority under Section 11 on this point, an English case under the analogous Companies Act is of some value. In *Adams* v. *Thrigt*, (1915) 1 Ch. 557, aff'd. (1915) 2 Ch. 21, it was held that a director who knew nothing about the prospectus and did not even read it, but who relied on the statement of the company's managing director that it was "all right," was liable for its untrue statements. . . .

Section II imposes liability in the first instance upon a director, no matter how new he is. He is presumed to know his responsibility when he becomes a director. He can escape liability only by using that reasonable care to investigate the facts which a prudent man would employ in the management of his own property. In my opinion, a prudent man would not act in an important matter without any knowledge of the relevant facts, in sole reliance upon respresentations of persons who are comparative strangers and upon general information which does not purport to cover the particular case.

To say that such minimal conduct measures up to the statutory standard would, to all intents and purposes absolve new directors from responsibility merely because they are new. This is not a sensible construction of Section 11, when one bears in mind its funcamental purpose of requiring full and truthful disclosure for the protection of investors.

I find and conclude that Auslander has not established his due diligence defense with respect to the misstatements and omissions in those portions of the prospectus other than the audited 1960 figures.

Rose

Rose, another "outside" director, is in a position comparable to Auslander's. He is a civil engineer. Peat, Marwick were the auditors for his firm and Kircher, when he was employed by Peat, Marwick, had worked on his firm's books in 1957 and 1958. Rose was favorably impressed by Kircher at that time.

Rose had not seen Kircher after the spring of 1959 until March 1961 when Kircher met with him, at Kircher's request, and invited him to become a director of BarChris. Kircher explained that BarChris did a good deal of construction work. He hinted that there might be a need for Rose's services as an engineer.

Shortly after this meeting, Kircher sent Rose a copy of BarChris's annual report for 1960. Rose observed that Peat, Marwick were BarChris's auditors. Subsequently, in March, he inquired about BarChris of three different brokers. They informed him that BarChris was apparently well managed, that it had enjoyed a steady growth, and that its stock had gone up considerably, although it paid no dividends.

Rose visited BarChris's office in mid-March and was interested in the bowling exhibit on display there. He had dinner with Vitolo who explained BarChris's plans for expansion. The other officers talked to him in a similar vein.

Rose agreed to become a director and was elected on April 17, 1961, along with Auslander and the others. Rose was present at that meeting and there learned of the proposed financing for the first time. He read the first (March 30) version of the registration statement for "about ten minutes."

On May 10, Rose signed a separate signature sheet for the first amendment. Unlike Auslander, Rose did know that the signature sheet pertained to a registration statement.

Rose attended the directors' meeting on May 15. He signed the signature sheet for the registration statement in its final form. The entire document was not submitted to the meeting.

Immediately prior to the May 15 meeting, Kircher told Rose that the progress of the company for the first quarter "was very much in line with the preceding year," but that BarChris expected to have a better year in 1961 than in 1960. At the meeting Rose inquired if the information in the registration statement was correct. Vitolo and Russo said it was.

Up to May 16, Rose had not participated in BarChris's affairs. He made no investigation. He believed that the registration statement was true. The only basis for his belief was his reliance upon Peat, Marwick and upon the BarChris officers.

What has been said with respect to Auslander applies equally to Rose. He has not sustained the burden of proving his due diligence defense as to the portions of the registration statement other than the audited 1960 figures.

Grant

Grant became a director of BarChris in October 1960. His law firm was counsel to BarChris in matters pertaining to the registration of securities. Grant drafted the registration statement for the stock issue in 1959 and for the warrants in January 1961. He also drafted the registration statement for the debentures. In the preliminary division of work between him and Ballard, the underwriters' counsel, Grant took initial responsibility for preparing the registration statement, while Ballard devoted his efforts in the first instance to preparing the indenture.

Grant is sued as a director and as a signer of the registration statement. This is not an action against him for malpractice in his capacity as a lawyer. Nevertheless, in considering Grant's due diligence defenses, the unique position which he occupied cannot be disregarded. As the director most directly concerned with writing the registration statement and assuring its accuracy, more was required of him in the way of reasonable investigation than could fairly be expected of a director who had no connection with this work. . . .

I find that Grant honestly believed that the registration statement was true and that no material facts had been omitted from it.

In this belief he was mistaken, and the fact is that for all his work, he never discovered any of the errors or omissions which have been recounted at length in this opinion, with the single exception of Capitol Lanes. He knew that BarChris had not sold this alley and intended to operate it, but he appears to have been under the erroneous impression that Peat, Marwick had knowingly sanctioned its inclusion in sales because of the allegedly temporary nature of the operation.

Grant contends that a finding that he did not make a reasonable investigation would be equivalent to a holding that a lawyer for an issuing company, in order to show due diligence, must make an independent audit of the figures supplied to him by his client. I do not consider this to be a realistic statement of the issue. There were errors and omissions here which could have been detected without an audit. The question is whether, despite his failure to detect them, Grant made a reasonable effort to that end.

Much of this registration statement is a scissors and paste-pot job. Grant lifted large portions from the earlier prospectuses, modifying them in some instances to the extent that he considered necessary. But BarChris's affairs had changed for the worse by May 1961. Statements that were accurate in January were no longer accurate in May. Grant never discovered this. He accepted the assurances of Kircher and Russo that any change which might have occurred had been for the better, rather than the contrary.

It is claimed that a lawyer is entitled to rely on the statements of his client and that to require him to verify their accuracy would set an unreasonably high standard. This is too broad a generalization. It is all a matter of degree. To require an audit would obviously be unreasonable. On the other hand, to require a check of matters easily verifiable is not unreasonable. Even honest clients can make mistakes. The statute imposes liability for untrue statements regardless of whether they are intentionally untrue. The way to prevent mistakes is to test oral information by examining the original written record.

There were things which Grant could readily have checked which he did not check. For example, he was unaware of the provisions of the agreements between BarChris and Talcott. He never read them. Thus, he did not know, although he readily could have ascertained, that BarChris's contingent liability on Type B leaseback arrangements was 100 percent, not 25 percent. . . .

As to the backlog figure, Grant appreciated that scheduled unfilled orders on the company's books meant firm commitments, but he never asked to see the contracts which, according to the prospectus, added up to $6,905,000. Thus, he did not know that this figure was overstated by some $4,490,000.

Grant was unaware of the fact that BarChris was about to operate Bridge and Yonkers. He did not read the minutes of those subsidiaries which would have revealed that fact to him. On the subject of minutes, Grant knew that minutes of certain meetings of the BarChris executive committee held in 1961 had not been written up. Kircher, who had acted as secretary at those meetings, had complete notes of them. Kircher told Grant that there was no point in writing up the minutes because the matters discussed at those meetings were purely routine. Grant did not insist that the minutes be written up, nor did he look at Kircher's notes. If he had, he would have learned that on February 27, 1961 there was an extended discussion in the executive committee meeting about customers' delinquencies, that on March 8, 1961 the committee had discussed the pros and cons of alley operation by Bar Chris, that on March 18, 1961 the committee was informed that BarChris was constructing or about to begin constructing twelve alleys for which it had no contracts, and that on May 13, 1961 Dreyfuss, one of the worst delinquents, had filed a petition in Chapter X.

Grant knew that there had been loans from officers to BarChris in the past because that subject had been mentioned in the 1959 and January 1961 prospectuses. In March Grant prepared a questionnaire to be answered by officers and directors for the purpose of obtaining information to be used in the prospectus. The questionnaire did not inquire expressly about the existence of officers' loans. At approximately the same time, Grant prepared another questionnaire in order to obtain information on proxy statements for the annual stockholders' meeting. This questionnaire asked each officer to state whether he was indebted to BarChris, but it did not ask whether BarChris was indebted to him.

Despite the inadequacy of these written questionnaires, Grant did, on March 16, 1961, orally inquire as to whether any officers' loans were outstanding. He was assured by Russo, Vitolo and Pugliese that all such loans had been repaid. Grant did not ask again. He was unaware of the new loans in April. He did know, however, that, at Kircher's request, a provision was inserted in the indenture which gave loans from individuals priority over the debentures. Kircher's insistence on this clause did not arouse his suspicions. . . .

Grant was entitled to rely on Peat, Marwick for the 1960 figures. He had no reasonable ground to believe them to be inaccurate. But the matters which I have mentioned were not within the expertised portion of the prospectus. As to this, Grant was obliged to make a reasonable investigation. I am forced to find that he did not make one. After making all due allowances for the fact that BarChris's officers misled him, there are too many instances in which Grant failed to make an inquiry which he could easily have made which, if pursued, would have put him on his guard. In my opinion, this finding on the evidence in this case does not establish an unreasonably high standard in other cases for company counsel who are also directors. Each case must rest on its own facts. I conclude that Grant has not established his due diligence defenses except as to the audited 1960 figures.

The Underwriters and Coleman

The underwriters other than Drexel made no investigation of the accuracy of the prospectus. They all relied upon Drexel as the "lead" underwriter.

Drexel did make an investigation. The work was in charge of Coleman, a partner of the firm, assisted by Casperson, as associate. Drexel's attorneys acted as attorneys for the entire group of underwriters. Ballard did the work, assisted by Stanton.

On April 17, 1961 Coleman became a director of BarChris. He signed the first amendment to the registration statement filed on May 11 and the second amendment, constituting the registration statement in its final form, filed on May 16. He thereby assumed a responsibility as an underwriter.

The facts as to the extent of the investigation that Coleman made may be briefly summarized. He was first introduced to BarChris on September 15, 1960. Thereafter he familiarized himself with general conditions in the industry, primarily by reading reports and prospectuses of the two leading bowling alley builders, American Machine & Foundry Company and Brunswick. These indicated that the industry was still growing. He also acquired general information on BarChris by reading the 1959 stock prospectus, annual reports for prior years, and an unaudited statement for the first half of 1960. He inquired about BarChris of certain of its banks and of Talcott and received favorable replies.

The purpose of this preliminary investigation was to enable Coleman to decide whether Drexel would undertake the financing. Coleman was sufficiently optimistic about BarChris's prospects to buy 1,000 shares of its stock, which he did in December 1960.

On January 24, 1961, Coleman held a meeting with Ballard, Grant and Kircher, among others. By that time Coleman had about decided to go ahead with the financing, although Drexel's formal letter of intent was not delivered until February 9, 1961 (subsequently revised on March 7, 1961). . . .

Coleman continued his general investigation. He obtained a Dun & Bradstreet report on BarChris on March 16, 1961. He read BarChris's annual report for 1960 which was available in March.

By mid-March, Coleman was in a position to make more specific inquiries. Coleman attended three meetings to discuss the prospectus with BarChris's representatives. . . .

At these discussions, which were extensive, successive proofs of the prospectus were considered and revised. At this point the 1961 figures were not available. They were put in the prospectus in May.

Coleman and Ballard asked pertinent questions and received answers which satisfied them. Among other things, the following transpired.

Logan explained some of the 1960 figures, including the reserve for bad debts, which he considered adequate.

There was a discussion of the application of proceeds section. . . .

As to the backlog of orders on hand, Ballard said that the figure, not then available, must be "hard and fast," not "puffy." Grant and Kircher "concurred." . . .

Most important for our purposes, there was a discussion of the one-half of one percent figure with respect to BarChris's past experience in repurchasing discounted customers' notes. . . .

The alternative method of financing was explained. . . .

There was talk about operating alleys. . . .

There was discussion of officers' loans. . . .

Coleman did not participate personally in any further meetings of this sort. Casperson attended some and reported to Coleman. Ballard advised Coleman as to what he was doing.

After Coleman was elected a director on April 17, 1961, he made no further independent investigation of the accuracy of the prospectus. He assumed that Ballard was taking care of this on his behalf as well as on behalf of the underwriters.

In April 1961 Ballard instructed Stanton to examine BarChris's minutes for the past five years and also to look at "the major contracts of the company." Stanton went to BarChris's office for that purpose on April 24. He asked Birnbaum for the minute books. He read the minutes of the board of directors and discovered interleaved in them a few minutes of executive committee meetings in 1960. He asked Kircher if there were any others. Kircher said that there had been other executive committee meetings but that the minutes had not been written up.

Stanton read the minutes of a few BarChris subsidiaries. His testimony was vague as to which ones. . . .

As to the "major contracts," all that Stanton could remember seeing was an insurance policy. Birnbaum told him that there was no file of major contracts. Stanton did not examine the agreements with Talcott. He did not examine the contracts with customers. He did not look to see what contracts comprised the backlog figure. Stanton examined no accounting records of BarChris. His visit, which lasted one day, was devoted primarily to reading the directors' minutes. . . .

Ballard did not insist that the executive committee minutes be written up so that he could inspect them, although he testified that he knew from experience that executive committee minutes may be extremely important. If he had insisted, he would have found the minutes highly informative, as has previously been pointed out (supre at p. 691). Ballard did not ask to see BarChris's schedule of delinquencies or Talcott's notices of delinquencies, or BarChris's correspendence with Talcott.

Ballard did not examine BarChris's contracts with Talcott. He did not appreciate what Talcott's rights were under those financing agreements or how serious the effect would be upon BarChris of any exercise of those rights.

Ballard did not investigate the composition of the backlog figure to be sure that it was not "puffy." He made no inquiry after March about any new officers' loans, although he knew that Kircher had insisted on a provision in the indenture which gave loans from individuals priority over the debentures. He was unaware of the seriousness of BarChris's cash position and of how BarChris's officers intended to use a large part of the proceeds. He did not know that BarChris was operating Capitol Lanes.

Like Grant, Ballard, without checking, relied on the information which he got from Kircher. He also relied on Grant who, as company counsel, presumably was familiar with its affairs. . . .

Coleman testified that Drexel had an understanding with its attorneys that "we expect them to inspect on our behalf the corporate records of the company including, but not limited to, the minutes of the corporation, the stockholders and the committees of the board authorized to act for the board." Ballard manifested his awareness of this understanding by sending Stanton to read the minutes and the major contracts. It is difficult to square this understanding with the formal opinion of Ballard's firm which expressly disclaimed any attempt to verify information supplied by the company and its counsel. In any event, it is clear that no effectual attempt at verification was made. The question is whether due diligence required that it be made. Stated another way, is it sufficient to ask questions, to obtain answers which, if true, would be thought satisfactory, and to let it go at that, without seeking to ascertain from the records whether the answers in fact are true and complete?

I have already held that this procedure is not sufficient in Grant's case. Are underwriters in a different position, as far as due diligence is concerned?

The underwriters say that the prospectus is the company's prospectus, not theirs. Doubtless this is the way they customarily regard it. But the Securities Act makes no such distinction. The underwriters are just as responsible as the company if the prospectus is false. And prospective investors rely upon the reputation of the underwriters in deciding whether to purchase the securities.

There is no direct authority on this question, no judicial decision defining the degree of diligence which underwriters must exercise to establish their defense under Section 11.

There is some authority in New York for the proposition that a director of a corporation may rely upon information furnished him by the officers without independently verifying it. See *Litwin* v. *Allen*, 25 N.Y.S.2d 667 (Sup. Ct.1940).

In support of that principle, the court in Litwin (25 N.Y.S.2d at 719) quoted from the opinion of the Lord Halsbury in *Dovey* v. *Cory*, (1901) App.Cas.447,486, in which he said:

> The business of life could not go on if people could not trust those who are put into a position of trust for the express purpose of attending to details of management.

Of course, New York law does not govern this case. The construction of the Securities Act is a matter of federal law. But the underwriters argue that Litwin is still in point, for they say that it establishes a standard of reasonableness for the reasonably prudent director which should be the same as the standard for the reasonably prudent underwriter under the Securities Act.

In my opinion the two situations are not analogous. An underwriter has not put the company's officers "into a position of trust for the express purpose of attending to details of management." The underwriters did not select them. In a sense, the positions of the underwriter and the company's officers are adverse. It is not unlikely that statements made by company officers to an underwriter to induce him to underwrite may be self-serving. They may be unduly enthusiastic. As in this case, they may, on occasion, be deliberately false.

The purpose of Section 11 is to protect investors. To that end the underwriters are made responsible for the truth of the prospectus. In order to make the underwriters' participation in this enterprise of any value to the investors, the underwriters must make some reasonable attempt to verify the data submitted to them. They may not rely solely on the company's officers or on the company's counsel. A prudent man in the management of his own property would not rely on them.

It is impossible to lay down a rigid rule suitable for every case defining the extent to which such verification must go. It is a question of degree, a matter of judgment in each case. In the present case, the underwriters' counsel made almost no attempt to verify management's representations. I hold that that was insufficient.

On the evidence in this case, I find that the underwriters' counsel did not make a reasonable investigation of the truth of those portions of the prospectus which were not made on the authority of Peat, Marwick as an expert. Drexel is bound by their failure. It is not a matter of relying upon counsel for legal advice. Here the attorneys were dealing with matters of fact. Drexel delegated to them, as its agent, the business of examining the corporate minutes and contracts. It must bear the consequences of their failure to make an adequate examination.

The other underwriters, who did nothing and relied solely on Drexel and the lawyers, are also bound by it. It follows that although Drexel and the other underwriters believed that those portions of the prospectus were true, they had no reasonable ground for that belief, within the meaning of the statute. Hence, they have not established their due diligence defense, except as to the 1960 audited figures.

The same conclusions must apply to Coleman. He made no investigation after he became a director. When it came to verification, he relied upon his counsel to do it for him. Since counsel failed to do it, Coleman is bound by that failure. Consequently, in his case also, he has not established his due diligence defense except as to the audited 1960 figures.

Peat, Marwick

Section 11(b) provides:

> Notwithstanding the provisions of subsection (a) no person * * * shall be liable as provided therein who shall sustain the burden of proof —
>
> * * *
>
> (3) that * * * (B) as regards any part of the registration statement purporting to be made upon his authority as an expert * * * (i) he had, after reasonable investigation, reasonable ground to believe and did believe, at the time such part of the registration statement became effective, that the statements therein were true and that there was no omission to state a material fact required to be stated therein or necessary to make the statements therein not misleading * * *.

This defines the due diligence defense for an expert. Peat, Marwick has pleaded it.

The part of the registration statement purporting to be made upon the authority of Peat, Marwick as an expert was, as we have seen, the 1960 figures. But because the statute requires the court to determine Peat, Marwick's belief, and the grounds thereof, "at the time such part of the registration statement became effective," for the purposes of this affirmative defense, the matter must be viewed as of May 16, 1961, and the question is whether at that time Peat, Marwick, after reasonable investigation, had reasonable ground to believe and did believe that the 1960 figures were true and that no material fact had been omitted from the registration statement which should have been included in order to make the 1960 figures not misleading. In deciding this issue, the court must consider not only what Peat, Marwick did in its 1960 audit, but also what it did in its subsequent "S-1 review." The proper scope of that review must also be determined.

It may be noted that we are concerned at this point only with the question of Peat, Marwick's liability to plaintiffs.

Most of the actual work was performed by a senior accountant, Berardi, who had junior assistants, one of whom was Kennedy.

Berardi was then about thirty years old. He was not yet a C.P.A. He had had no previous experience with the bowling industry. This was his first job as a senior accountant. He could hardly have been given a more difficult assignment.

After obtaining a little background information on BarChris by talking to Logan and reviewing Peat, Marwick's work papers on its 1959 audit, Berardi examined the results of test checks of BarChris's accounting procedures which one of the junior accountants had made, and he prepared an "internal control questionnaire" and an "audit program." Thereafter, for a few days subsequent to December 30, 1960, he inspected BarChris's inventories and examined certain alley construction. Finally, on January 13, 1961, he began his auditing work which he carried on substantially continuously until it was completed on February 24, 1961. Toward the close of the work, Logan reviewed it and made various comments and suggestions to Berardi.

It is unnecessary to recount everything that Berardi did in the course of the audit. We are concerned only with the evidence relating to what Berardi did or did not do with respect to those items which I have found to have been incorrectly reported in the 1960 figures in the prospectus. More narrowly, we are directly concerned only with such of those items as I have found to be material.

First and foremost is Berardi's failure to discover that Capitol Lanes had not been sold. This error affected both the sales figure and the liability side of the balance sheet.

As to factors' reserves, it is hard to understand how Berardi could have treated this item as entirely a current asset when it was obvious that most of the reserves would not be released within one year. If Berardi was unaware of that fact, he should have been aware of it.

Berardi erred in computing the contingent liability on Type B leaseback transactions at 25 percent. Berardi did not examine the documents which are in evidence which establish that BarChris's contingent liability on this type of transaction was in fact 100 percent. Berardi did not make a reasonable investigation in this instance.

The S-1 Review

The purpose of reviewing events subsequent to the date of a certified balance sheet (referred to as an S-1 reivew when made with reference to a registration statement) is to ascertain whether any material change has occured in the company's financial position which should be disclosed in order to prevent the balance sheet figures from being misleading. The scope of such a review, under generally accepted auditing standards, is limited. It does not amount to a complete audit.

Peat, Marwick prepared a written program for such a review. I find that this program conformed to generally accepted auditing standards. Among other things, it required the following:

1. Review minutes of stockholders, directors and committees. * * *
2. Review latest interim financial statements and compare with corresponding statements of preceding year. Inquire regarding significant variations and changes.
   * * *
4. Review the more important financial records and inquire regarding material transactions not in the ordinary course of business and any other significant items.
   * * *

6. Inquire as to changes in material contracts * * *

* * *

10. Inquire as to any significant bad debts or accounts in dispute for which provision has not been made.

* * *

14. Inquire as to * * * newly discovered liabilities, direct or contingent * * *.

Berardi made the S-1 review in May 1961. He devoted a little over two days to it, a total of 20½ hours. He did not discover any of the errors or omissions pertaining to the state of affairs in 1961 which I have previously discussed at length, all of which were material. The question is whether, despite his failure to find out anything, his investigation was reasonable within the meaning of the stature.

What Berardi did was to look at a consolidating trial balance as of March 31, 1961 which had been prepared by BarChris, compare it with the audited December 31, 1960 figures, discuss with Trilling certain unfavorable developments which the comparison disclosed, and read certain minutes. He did not examine any "important financial records" other than the trial balance. As to minutes, he read only what minutes Birnbaum gave him, which consisted only of the board of directors' minutes of BarChris. He did not read such minutes as there were of the executive committee. He did not know that there was an executive committee hence he did not discover that Kircher had notes of executive committee minutes which had not been written up. He did not read the minutes of any subsidiary.

In substance, what Berardi did is similar to what Grant and Ballard did. He asked questions, he got answers which he considered satisfactory, and he did nothing to verify them. For example, he obtained from Trilling a list of contracts. The list included Yonkers and Bridge. Since Berardi did not read the minutes of subsidiaries he did not learn that Yonkers' and Bridge were intercompany sales.

Since he never read the prospectus, he was not even aware that there had ever been any problem about loans from officers.

There had been a material change for the worse in BarChris's financial position. That change was sufficiently serious so that the failure to disclose it made the 1960 figures misleading. Berardi did not discover it. As far as results were concerned, his S-1 review was useless.

Accountants should not be held to a standard higher than that recognized in their profession. I do not do so here. Berardi's review did not come up to that standard. He did not take some of the steps which Peat, Marwick's written program prescribed. He did not spend an adequate amount of time on a task of this magnitude. Most important of all, he was too easily satisfied with glib answers to his inquiries.

This is not to say that he should have made a complete audit. But there were enough danger signals in the materials which he did examine to require some further investigation on his part. Generally accepted accounting standards required such further investigation under these circumstances. It is not always sufficient merely to ask questions.

Here again, the burden of proof is on Peat, Marwick. I find that that burden has not been satisfied, I conclude that Peat, Marwick has not established its due diligence defense.

◆◆◆

Case Questions

1. How does one explain the significant accounting errors in this case — incompetence? negligence? inexperience? or one of those things that inexplicably occur?
2. What lesson does this case hold for the individual that occupies a position on the board of numerous corporations?
3. How do sophisticated businessmen, underwriters and lawyers get in the position of relying upon another individual, with little or no personal verification, on matters as important as these? Is it practical to demand personal verification as an alternative to liability? Are there policy considerations supporting a strict standard of personal verification?

ACCOUNTANT'S LIABILITY

The past decade has observed increased shareholder lawsuits filed against a corporation's auditor. Naturally, the accounting profession deplores such developments. In some instances the profession believes it is being unfairly accused; that the SEC and investing public misunderstand its role. The annual audit of a publicly owned corporation plays a central role in the SEC regulatory scheme. CPA's regard such an audit as merely an affirmation that a company's transactions reflect generally accepted accounting standards. It does not mean that no fraud has occurred, since such a routine audit is not designed to ferret out fraud, particularly if management is intentionally lying to the auditors. Checking every transaction is a practical and financial impossibility. The SEC and stockholders view the accountant's role as encompassing more. The Commission is asserting that both the accounting and legal professions owe a duty beyond the one to their corporate client. The Commission has been pressuring the two professions to be more vigorous in their activities, to ask more searching questions and not to be satisfied by only verbal reassurances from top management. Thus, the evolving standard of professional liability is that when something fraudulent is discovered, report it to the SEC if the company refuses disclosure.

Liability of Peat, Marwick in the BarChris case should be easily understood. Their written program for conducting the S-1 review conformed to generally accepted auditing standards. However, their accountant failed to carry out all the steps outlined in that program. What happens if the accountants do conduct the audit in conformance with generally accepted auditing standards but the resulting financial statement is still materially false? The Simon case that follows provides the answer. Note that Simon is a criminal case, carrying with it the possibility of jail and/or a fine upon conviction. Conviction may also cost an accountant his C.P.A. certificate.

UNITED STATES v. SIMON
425 F.2d 796 (1969)

◆◆◆

Defendant Carl Simon was a senior partner, Robert Kaiser a junior partner, and Melvin Fishman a senior associate in the internationally known accounting firm of Lybrand, Ross Bros. & Montgomery. They stand convicted after trial . . . under three counts of an indictment charging them with drawing up and certifying a false or misleading financial statement of Continental Vending Machine Corporation (hereafter Continental) for the year ending September 30, 1962.

While every criminal conviction is important to the defendant, there is a special poignancy and a corresponding responsibility on reviewing judges when, as here, the defendants have been men of blameless lives and respected members of a learned profession. This is no less true because the trial judge, wisely in our view, imposed no prison sentences.

The trial hinged on transactions between Continental and an affiliate, Valley Commercial Corporation (hereafter Valley). The dominant figure in both was Harold Roth, who was president of Continental, supervised the day-to-day operations of Valley, and owned about 25 percent of the stock of each company.

Valley, which was run by Roth out of a single office on Continental's premises, was engaged in lending money at interest to Continental and others in the vending machine business. Continental would issue negotiable notes to Valley, which would endorse these in blank and use them as collateral for drawing on two lines of credit, of $1 million each, at Franklin National Bank (Franklin) and Meadowbrook National Bank (Meadowbrook), and would then transfer to Continental the discounted amount of the notes. These transactions, beginning as early as 1956, gave rise to what is called "the Valley payable." By the end of fiscal 1962, the amount of this was $1,029,475, of which $543,345 was due within the year.

In addition to the Valley payable, there was what is known as the "Valley receivable," which resulted from Continental loans to Valley. Most of these stemmed from Roth's custom, dating from mid-1957, of using Continental and Valley as sources of cash to finance his transactions in the stock market. At the end of fiscal 1962, the amount of the Valley receivable was $3.5 million, and by February 15, 1963, the date of certification, it had risen to $3.9 million. The Valley payable could not be offset, or "netted," against the Valley receivable since, as stated, Continental's obligations to Valley were in the form of negotiable notes which Valley had endorsed in blank to the two banks and used as collateral to obtain the cash which it then lent to Continental.

By the certification date, the auditors had learned that Valley was not in a position to repay its debt, and it was accordingly arranged that collateral would be posted. Roth and members of his family transferred their equity in certain securities to Arthur Field, Continental's counsel, as trustee to secure Roth's debt to Valley and Valley's debt to Continental. Some 80 percent of these securities consisted of Continental stock and convertible debentures.

The 1962 financial statements of Continental, which were dismal by any standard, reported the status of the Valley transactions as follows:

ASSETS

Current Assets:

Accounts and notes receivable:

Valley Commercial Corp., affiliate
(Note 2) $2,143,335

Valley Commercial Corp., affiliate
(Note 2) $1,400,000

LIABILITIES

Current Liabilities:

Long-term debt,
portion due within one year $8,203,788

Long-term debt (Note 7)

Valley Commercial Corp., affiliate
(Note 2)   486,130

NOTES TO CONSOLIDATED FINANCIAL STATEMENTS

2. The amount receivable from Valley Commercial Corp. (an affiliated company of which Mr. Harold Roth is an officer, director and stockholder) bears interest at 12 percent a year. Such amount, less the balance of the notes payable to that company, is secured by the assignment to the Company of Valley's equity in certain marketable securities. As of February 15, 1963, the amount of such equity at current market quotations exceeded the net amount receivable.

7. * * * The amounts of long-term debt, including the portion due within one year, on which interest is payable currently or has been discounted in advance, are as follows:

Valley Commerical Corp., affiliate $1,029,475

* * * * *

The case against the defendants can be best encapsulated by comparing what Note 2 stated and what the Government claims it would have stated if defendants had included what they knew:

The amount receivable from Valley Commercial Corp. (an affiliated company of which Mr. Harold Roth is an officer, director and stockholder), which bears interest at 12 percent a year, was uncollectible at September 30, 1962, since Valley had loaned approximately the same amount to Mr. Roth who was unable to pay. Since that date Mr. Roth and others have pledged as security for the repayment of his obligation to Valley and its obligation to Continental (now $3,900,000, against which Continental's liability to Valley cannot be offset) securities which, as of February 15, 1963, had a market value of $2,978,000. Approximately 80 percent of such securities are stock and convertible debentures of the Company.

Striking as the difference is, the latter version does not reflect the Government's further contention that in fact the market value of the pledged securities on February 15, 1963, was $1,978,000 rather than $2,978,000 due to liens of

James Talcott, Inc. and Franklin for indebtedness other than Roth's of which defendants knew or should have known.

Roth engaged the Lybrand firm as Continental's auditors in 1956.

The Valley receivable had attracted attention early in Lybrand's engagement. In the late fall of 1958, Yoder, who was then manager of the Continental audit, discussed it with Roth. In a memorandum to Simon in November 1960, Yoder again discussed the Valley receivable, noting that the payments were frequent, in round amounts, and unaccompanied by written explanations.

In 1961 and 1962, the cash payments giving rise to the Valley receivable continued to be frequent, in round amounts, and without written explanation.

Although the figure for the end of 1961 was more than double that at the end of the two preceding years, and had increased to about $2 million by December 31, 1961, prior to the certification date, the 1961 financial statement made no comment on the receivable, and none of the defendants asked whether Continental's directors had been informed of the transactions. Simon merely warned Roth that an examination of Valley's books would be required if the receivable at the end of fiscal 1962 was as large as at the end of 1961.

In December [1962] Fishman phoned Simon that the Valley receivable as of September 30 was about $3.5 million.

Meanwhile, according to Roth, he had contacted Simon in December and said that although Valley had a net worth of $2 million, it was not in a position to repay its $3.5 million debt to Continental as it had lent him approximately the same amount which he was unable to repay. He suggested that he secure the indebtedness with his equity in stocks, bonds and other securities of Continental and Hoffman International if this would be acceptable.

Late in January 1963 Fishman visited Roth and showed him a draft of Note 2 substantially identical with the final form; he told Roth that Simon wanted to see him. They met in the Lybrand office on February 6. Defendants concede that at this meeting Roth informed Simon that Valley could not repay Continental and offered to post securities for the Valley receivable, and also to post as collateral a mortgage on his house and furnishings. Simon agreed that if adequate collateral were posted, a satisfactory legal opinion were obtained, and Continental's board approved the transactions, Lybrand could certify Continental's statements without reviewing Valley's, which still were not available.

The financial statements were mailed as part of Continental's annual report on February 20. By that time the market value of the collateral had declined some $270,000 from its February 15 value. The value of the collateral fell an additional $640,000 on February 21. When the market reopened on February 25 after the long Washington's birthday recess, it fell another $2 million and was worth only $395,000. The same day a Continental check to the Internal Revenue Service bounced. Two days later the Government padlocked the plant and the American Stock Exchange suspended trading in Continental stock. Investigations by the SEC and bankruptcy rapidly ensued.

The defendants called eight expert independent accountants, an impressive array of leaders of the profession. They testified generally that, except for the error with respect to netting, the treatment of the Valley receivable in Note 2 was in no way inconsistent with generally accepted accounting principles or generally accepted auditing standards, since it made all the informative disclosures reasonably necessary for fair presentation of the financial position of Continental as of the close of the 1962 fiscal year. Specifically, they testified that neither generally accepted accounting principles nor generally accepted auditing standards required disclosure of the make-up of the collateral or of the increase of the receivable after the closing date of the balance sheet, although three of the eight stated that in light of hindsight they would have preferred that the make-up of the collateral be disclosed. The witnesses likewise testified that disclosure of the Roth borrowings from Valley was not required, and seven of the eight were of the opinion that such disclosure would be inappropriate.

Defendants asked for two instructions which, in substance, would have told the jury that a defendant could be found guilty only if, according to generally accepted accounting principles, the financial statements as a whole did not fairly present the financial condition of Continental at September 30, 1962, and then only if his departure from accepted standards was due to willful disregard of those standards with knowledge of the falsity of the statements and an intent to deceive. The judge declined to give these instructions. Dealing with the subject in the course of his charge, he said that the "critical test" was whether the financial statement as a whole "fairly presented the financial position of Continental as of September 30, 1962, and whether it accurately reported the operations for fiscal 1962." If they did not, the basic issue became whether defendants acted in good faith. Proof of compliance with generally accepted standards was "evidence which may be very persuasive but not necessarily conclusive that he acted in good faith, and that the facts as certified were not materially false or misleading."

"The weight and credibility to be extended by you to such proof, and its persuasiveness, must depend, among other things, on how authoritative you find the precedents and the teachings relied upon by the parties to be, the extent to which they contemplate, deal with, and apply to the type of circumstances found by you to have existed here, and the weight you give to expert opinion evidence offered by the parties. Those may depend on the credibility extended by you to expert witnesses, the definiteness with which they testified, the reasons given for their opinions, and all the other facts affecting credibility, * * *"

We think the judge was right in refusing to make the accountants' testimony so nearly a complete defense. The critical test according to the charge was the same as that which the accountants testified was critical. We do not think the jury was also required to accept the accountants' evaluation whether a given fact was material to overall fair presentation, at least not when the accountants' testimony was not based on specific rules or prohibitions to which they could point, but only on the need for the auditor to make an honest judgment and their conclusion that nothing in the financial statements themselves negated the conclusion that an honest judgment had been made. Such evidence may be highly persuasive, but it is not conclusive, and so the trial judge correctly charged.

Defendants next contend that, particularly in light of the expert testimony, the evidence was insufficient to allow the jury to consider the failure to disclose Roth's borrowings from Valley, the make-up of the collateral, or the post-balance sheet increase in the Valley receivable. They concentrate their fire on what they characterize as the "primary, predominant and pervasive" issue, namely the failure to disclose that Continental's loans to Valley were not for a proper business purpose but to assist Roth in his personal financial problems. It was "primary, predominant and pervasive" not only because it was most featured by the prosecution but because defendants' knowledge of Roth's diversion of corporate funds colored everything else. We join defendants' counsel in assuming that the mere fact that a company has made advances to an affiliate does not ordinarily impose a duty on an accountant to investigage what the affiliate has done with them or even to disclose that the affiliate has made a loan to a common officer if this has come to his attention. But it simply cannot be true that an accountant is under no duty to disclose what he knows when he has reason to believe that, to a material extent, a corporation is being operated not to carry out its business in the interest of all the stockholders but for the private benefit of its president. Generally accepted accounting principles instruct an accountant what to do in the usual case where he has no reason to doubt that the affairs of the corporation are being honestly conducted. Once he has reason to believe that this basic assumption is false, an entirely different situation confronts him. Then, as the Lybrand firm stated in its letter accepting the Continental engagement, he must "extend his procedures to determine whether or not such suspicions are justified." If as a result of such an extension or, as here, without it, he finds his suspicions to be confirmed, full disclosure must be the rule, unless he has made sure the wrong has been righted and procedures to avoid a repetition have been established. At least this must be true when the dishonesty he has discovered is not some minor peccadillo but a diversion so large as to imperil if not destroy the very solvency of the enterprise.

Fishman was proved to have known what was going on since 1958, Simon must have had a good idea about it from the spring of 1960 . . . and the jury could infer that Kaiser also was not unaware. In any event they concede knowledge prior to the certification.

Defendants properly make much of the alleged absence of proof of motivation.

It is quite true that there was no proof of motive in the form usual in fraud cases. None of the defendants made or could make a penny from Continental's putting out false financial statements. Neither was there evidence of motive in the sense of fear that telling the truth would lose a valuable account.

The Government finds motive in defendants' desire to preserve Lybrand's reputation and conceal the alleged dereliction of their predecessors and themselves in former years.

Even if there were no satisfactory showing of motive, we think the Government produced sufficient evidence of criminal intent. Its burden was not to show that defendants were wicked men with designs on anyone's purse, which they obviously were not, but rather that they had certified a statement knowing it to be false.

[W]e find it impossible to say that a reasonable jury could not be convinced beyond a reasonable doubt that the striking difference between what Note 2 said and what it needed to say in order to reveal the truth resulted not from mere carelessness but from design. That some other jury might have taken a more lenient view, as the trial judge said he would have done, is a misfortune for the defendants but not one within our power to remedy.

◆◆◆

Case Questions

1. Was it, in your opinion, a wise decision not to impose prison sentences on the defendants?
2. White collar criminals receive more lenient treatment at the hands of judges than do other types of criminals. Rarely is a jail sentence imposed. What does this fact do to the concept of equal justice under law?
3. Congress passed the securities laws which theoretically reflect the viewpoint and interests of all citizens. The accounting profession establishes the standard of generally accepted accounting principles. If compliance with these accounting principles constituted a complete defense in a case such as this, would not one small segment of society be determining the interpretation and applicability of national legislation?

Case Comment

President Richard Nixon granted a pardon to the defendants in the Simon litigation.

An individual can have both civil and criminal liability under the securities laws. The SEC is beginning to press criminal charges when it believes that more than a simple audit oversight is involved. In July 1975 three outside auditors of Equity Funding were sentenced to short jail terms for their conviction on numerous counts of securities fraud and filing false financial statements with the SEC. Two Peat, Marwick, Mitchell & Co. accountants have been tried for their actions in the 1968 audit of National Student Marketing and the resulting figures contained in a 1969 proxy statement. It was alleged that they improperly permitted National Student Marketing to report about $1 million in sales in 1968, then wrote the sales off as being nonexistent but, failed to disclose the write off in the 1969 proxy statement. Both men were convicted in a jury trial, fined and given short jail terms. In July 1975 the U.S. Court of Appeals for the Second Circuit upheld the conviction of the audit partner but granted a new trial to the audit supervisor.

Also in July 1975, the SEC settled administrative proceedings with the Peat, Marwick firm. The proceedings grew out of Peat, Marwick's role in auditing several clients, including National Student Marketing. As part of the settlement, Peat, Marwick was prohibited from accepting certain new clients for a six month period.

ACCOUNTANTS AND SECTION 10(b) OF THE '34 ACT

The treatment of Section 10(b) and Rule 10b-5 in Chapter 16 did not discuss the legal liability of accountants, attorneys and underwriters when their clients violate securities laws. If they intentionally participate in the fraudulent or misleading scheme of their client, it should be clear that they have violated the law. However, what if the accountant failed to expose the client's fraud merely because he conducted the audit negligently? The Ernst & Ernst case examines this specific question.

ERNST & ERNST v. HOCHFELDER
425 U.S. – (1976)

♦♦♦

Mr. Justice Powell delivered the opinion of the Court.

Petitioner, Ernst & Ernst, is an accounting firm. From 1946 through 1967 it was retained by First Securities Company of Chicago (First Securities), a small brokerage firm and member of the Midwest Stock Exchange and of the National Association of Securities Dealers, to perform periodic audits of the firm's books and records. In connection with these audits Ernst & Ernst prepared for filing with the Securities and Exchange Commission (the Commission) the annual reports required of First Securities under § 17(a) of the 1934 Act, 15 U.S.C., § 78q (a). It also prepared for First Securities responses to the financial questionnaires of the Midwest Stock Exchange (the Exchange).

Respondents were customers of First Securities who invested in a fraudulent securities scheme perpetrated by Leston B. Nay, president of the firm and owner of 92 percent of its stock. Nay induced the respondents to invest funds in "escrow" accounts that he represented would yield a high rate of return. Respondents did so from 1942 through 1966, with the majority of the transactions occurring in the 1950's. In fact, there were no escrow accounts as Nay converted respondents' funds to his own use immediately upon receipt. These transactions were not in the customary form of dealings between First Securities and its customers. The respondents drew their personal checks payable to Nay or a designated bank for his account. No such escrow accounts were reflected on the books and records of First Securities, and none was shown on its periodic accounting to respondents in connection with their own investments. Nor were they included in First Securities' filings with the Commission or the Exchange.

This fraud came to light in 1968 when Nay committed suicide, leaving a note that described First Securities as bankrupt and the escrow accounts as "spurious." Respondents subsequently filed this action for damages against Ernst & Ernst. ... The complaint charged that Nay's escrow scheme violated § 10(b) and Commission Rule 10b-5, and that Ernst & Ernst had "aided and abetted" Nay's violations by its "failure" to conduct proper audits of First Securities. As revealed through discovery, respondents' cause of action rested on a theory of negligent nonfeasance. The premise was that Ernst & Ernst had failed to utilize "appropriate auditing procedures" in its audits of First Securities, thereby failing to discover internal practices of the firm said to prevent an effective audit. The practice principally relied on was Nay's rule that only he could open mail addressed to him at First Securities or addressed to First Securities to his attention, even if it arrived in his absence. Respondents contended that if Ernst & Ernst had conducted a proper audit, it would have discovered this "mail rule." The existence of the rule then would have been disclosed in reports to the Exchange and to the Commission by Ernst & Ernst as an irregular procedure that prevented an effective audit. This would have revealed the fraudulent scheme. Respondents specifically disclaimed the existence of fraud or intentional misconduct on the part of Ernst & Ernst.

After extensive discovery the District Court granted Ernst & Ernst's motion for summary judgment and dismissed the action. The court rejected Ernst & Ernst's contention that a cause of action for aiding and abetting a securities fraud could not be maintained under § 10(b) and Rule 10b-5 merely on allegations of negligence. It concluded, however, that there was no genuine issue of material fact with respect to whether Ernst & Ernst had conducted its audits in accordance with generally accepted auditing standards.

The Court of Appeals for the Seventh Circuit reversed and remanded, holding that one who breaches a duty of inquiry and disclosure owed another is liable in damages for aiding and abetting a third party's violation of Rule 10b-5 if the fraud would have been discovered or prevented but for the breach. 503 F.2d 1100 (1974). The court reasoned that Ernst & Ernst had a common-law and statutory duty of inquiry into the adequacy of First Securities' internal control system because it had contracted to audit First Securities and to prepare for filing with the Commission the annual report of its financial condition. . .. The Court further reasoned that respondents were beneficiaries of the statutory duty to inquire and the related duty to disclose any material irregularities that were discovered. The court concluded that there were genuine issues of fact as to whether Ernst & Ernst's failure to discover and comment upon Nay's mail rule constituted a breach of its duties of inquiry and disclosure, and whether inquiry and disclosure would have led to the discovery or prevention of Nay's fraud.

We granted certiorari to resolve the question whether a private cause of action for damages will lie under § 10(b) and Rule 10b-5 in the absence of any allegation of "scienter" − intent to deceive, manipulate, or defraud.[1] We conclude that it will not and therefore we reverse. . . .

Although § 10(b) does not by its terms create an express civil remedy for its violation, and there is no indication that Congress, or the Commission when adopting Rule 10b-5, contemplated such a remedy, the existence of a private cause of action for violations of the statute and the rule is now well established. . . . During the 30-year period since a private cause of action was first implied under § 10(b) and Rule 10b-5, a substantial body of case law and commentary has developed as to its elements. Courts and commentators long have differed with regard to whether scienter is a necessary element of such a cause of action, or whether negligent conduct alone is sufficient. . . .

A

Section 10(b) makes unlawful the use or employment of "any manipulative or deceptive device or contrivance" in contravention of Commission rules. The words "manipulative or deceptive" used in conjunction with "device or contrivance" strongly suggest that § 10(b) was intended to proscribe knowing or intentional misconduct. . . .

---

[1] In this opinion the term "scienter" refers to a mental state embracing intent to deceive, manipulate, or defraud. In certain areas of the law recklessness is considered to be a form of intentional conduct for purposes of imposing liability for some act. We need not address here the question whether, in some circumstances, reckless behavior is sufficient for civil liability under § 10(b) and Rule 10b-5.

Since this case concerns an action for damages we also need not consider the question whether scienter is a necessary element in an action for injunctive relief under § 10(b) and Rule 10b-5. Cf. *SEC* v. *Capital Gains Research Bureau, Inc.*, 375 U.S. 180 (1963).

In its *amicus curiae* brief, however, the Commission contends that nothing in the language "manipulative or deceptive device or contrivance" limits its operation to knowing or intentional practices. In support of its view, the Commission cites the overall congressional purpose in the 1933 and 1934 Acts to protect investors against false and deceptive practices that might injure them. . . . The Commission then reasons that since the "effect" upon investors of given conduct is the same regardless of whether the conduct is negligent or intentional, Congress must have intended to bar all such practices and not just those done knowingly or intentionally. The logic of this effect-oriented approach would impose liability for wholly faultless conduct where such conduct results in harm to investors, a result the Commission would be unlikely to support. But apart from where its logic might lead, the Commission would add a gloss to the operative language of the statute quite different from its commonly accepted meaning. . . . The argument simply ignores the use of the words "manipulative," "device," and "contrivance," terms that make unmistakable a congressional intent to proscribe a type of conduct quite different from negligence. Use of the word "manipulative" is especially significant. It is and was virtually a term of art when used in connection with securities markets. It connotes intentional or willful conduct designed to deceive or defraud investors by controlling or artifically affecting the price of securities.

In addition to relying upon the Commission's argument with respect to the operative language of the statute, respondents contend that since we are dealing with "remedial legislation," . . . it must be construed " 'not technically and restrictively, but flexibly to effectuate its remedial purposes.' " . . . They argue that the "remedial purposes" of the Acts demand a construction of § 10(b) that embraces negligence as a standard of liability. But in seeking to accomplish its broad remedial goals, Congress did not adopt uniformly a negligence standard even as to express civil remedies. In some circumstances and with respect to certain classes of defendants, Congress did create express liability predicated upon a failure to exercise reasonable care. E.g., 1933 Act § 11(b)(3)(B), 48 Stat. 82 as amended 15 U.S.C. § 77k(b)(3)(B) (liability of "experts," such as accountants, for misleading statements in portions of registration statements for which they are responsible). But in other situations good faith is an absolute defense. 1934 Act § 18, 48 Stat. 897, as amended 15 U.S.C. § 78r (misleading statements in any document filed pursuant to the 1934 Act). And in still other circumstances Congress created express liability regardless of the defendant's fault, 1933 Act § 11(a) (issuer liability for misleading statements in the registration statement).

It is thus evident that Congress fashioned standards of fault in the express civil remedies in the 1933 and 1934 Acts on a particularized basis. Ascertainment of congressional intent with respect to the standard of liability created by a particular section of the Acts must therefore rest primarily on the language of that section. Where, as here, we deal with a judicially implied liability, the statutory language certainly is no less important. In view of the language of § 10(b) which so clearly connotes intentional misconduct, and mindful that the language of a statute controls when sufficiently clear in its context, . . . further inquiry may be unnecessary. We turn now, nevertheless, to the legislative history of the 1934 Act to ascertain whether there is support for the meaning attributed to § 10(b) by the Commission and respondents.

B

Although the extensive legislative history of the 1934 Act is bereft of any explicit explanation of Congress' intent, we think the relevant portions of that history support our conclusion that § 10(b) was addressed to practices that involve some element of scienter and cannot be read to impose liability for negligent conduct alone. ...

C

The 1933 and 1934 Acts constitute interrelated components of the federal regulatory scheme governing transactions in securities. ... As the court indicated ..., "the interdependence of the various sections of the securities laws is certainly a relevant factor in any interpretation of the language Congress has chosen. ...." Recognizing this, respondents and the Commission contrast § 10(b) to other sections of the Acts to support their contention that civil liability may be imposed upon proof of negligent conduct. We think they misconceive the significance of the other provisions of the Acts.

The Commission argues that Congress has been explicit in requiring willful conduct when that was the standard of fault intended, Citing § 9 of the 1934 Act, 48 Stat. 889, 15 U.S.C. § 78i, which generally proscribes manipulation of securities prices. Sections 9 (a)(1) and (a)(2), for example, respectively prohibit manipulation of security prices "[f]or the purpose of creating a false or misleading appearance of actual trading in any security ... or ... with respect to the market for any such security," and "for the purpose of including the purchase or sale of such security by others." See also § 9(a)(4). Section 9(e) then imposes upon "[a]ny person who willfully participates in any act or transaction in violation of" other provisions of § 9 civil liability to anyone who purchased or sold a security at a price affected by the manipulative activities. From this the Commission concludes that since § 10(b) is not by its terms explicitly restricted to willful, knowing, or purposeful conduct, it should not be construed in all cases to require more than negligent action or inaction as a precondition for civil liability.

The structure of the Acts does not support the Commission's argument. In each instance that Congress created express civil liability in favor of purchasers or sellers of securities it clearly specified whether recovery was to be premised on knowing or intentional conduct, negligence, or entirely innocent mistake. See 1933 Act, §§ 11, 12, 15, 48 Stat. 82, 84, as amended 15 U.S.C. §§ 77k, 77l, 77o; 1934 Act §§ 9, 18, 20, 48 Stat. 889, 897, 899, as amended 15 U.S.C. §§ 78i, 78r, 78t. For example, § 11 of the 1933 Act unambiguously creates a private action for damages when a registration statement includes untrue statements of material facts or fails to state material facts necessary to make the statements therein not misleading. Within the limits specified by § 11(e), the issuer of the securities is held absolutely liable for any damages resulting from such misstatement or omission. But experts such as accountants who have prepared portions of the registration statement are accorded a "due diligence" defense. In effect, this is a negligence standard. An expert may avoid civil liability with respect to the portions of the registration statement for which he was responsible by showing that "after reasonable investigation" he had "reasonable ground[s] to believe" that the statements for which he was responsible were true and there was no omission of a material fact. § 11(b)(3)(B)(i). ... The express recognition of a case of action premised on negligent behavior in § 11 stands in sharp contrast to the language of § 10(b), and significantly undercuts the Commission's argument.

We also consider it significant that each of the express civil remedies in the 1933 Act allowing recovery for negligent conduct, see §§ 11, 12(2), 15 15 U.S.C. §§ 77k, 77l, 77o, is subject to significant procedural restrictions not applicable under § 10(b). Section 11(e) of the 1933 Act, for example, authorizes the court to require a plaintiff bringing a suit under § 11, § 12(2), or § 15 thereof to post a bond for costs, including attorneys' fees and in specified circumstances to assess costs at the conclusion of the litigation. Section 13 specifies a statute of limitations of one year from the time the violation was or should have been discovered, in no event to exceed three years from the time of offer or sale, applicable to actions brought under § 11, § 12(2), of § 15. These restrictions, significantly, were imposed by amendments to the 1933 Act adopted as part of the 1934 Act. ... We think these procedural limitations indicate that the judicially created private damage remedy under § 10(b) — which has no comparable restrictions — cannot be extended, consistently with the intent of Congress, to actions premised on negligent wrongdoing. Such extension would allow causes of action covered by § 11, § 12(2), and § 15 to be brought instead under § 10(b) and thereby nullify the effectiveness of the carefully drawn procedural restrictions on these express actions. ... We would be unwilling to bring about this result absent substantial support in the legislative history, and there is none.

D

We have addressed, to this point, primarily the language and history of § 10(b). The Commission contends, however, that subsections (2) and (3) of Rule 10b-5 are cast in language which — if standing alone — could encompass both intentional and negligent behavior. These subsections respectively provide that it is unlawful "[t]o make any untrue statement of a material fact or to omit to state a material fact necessary in order to make the statements made, in light of the circumstances under which they were made, not misleading ..." and "to engage in any act, practice, or course of business which operates or would operate as a fraud or deceit upon any person. ...." Viewed in isolation the language of subsection (2), and arguably that of subsection (3), could be read as proscribing, respectively, any type of material misstatement or omission, and any course of conduct, that has the effect of defrauding investors, whether the wrongdoing was intentional or not.

We note first that such a reading cannot be harmonized with the administrative history of the rule, a history making clear that when the Commission adopted the rule it was intended to apply only to activities that involved scienter. More importantly, Rule 10b-5 was adopted pursuant to authority granted the Commission under § 10(b). The rulemaking power granted to an administrative agency charged with the administration of a federal statute is not the power to make law. Rather, it is " 'the power to adopt regulations to carry into effect the will of Congress as expressed by the statute.' " ... Thus, despite the broad view of the Rule advanced by the Commission in this case, its scope cannot exceed the power granted the Commission by Congress under § 10(b). For the reasons stated above, we think the Commission's original

interpretation of Rule 10b-5 was compelled by the language and history of §
10(b) and related sections of the Acts. . . . When a statute speaks so specifically
in terms of manipulation and deception, and of implementing devices and
contrivances — the commonly understood terminology of international
wrongdoing — and when its history reflects no more expansive intent, we are
quite unwilling to extend the scope of the statute to negligent conduct. . . .

The judgment of the Court of Appeals is *Reversed.*

MR. JUSTICE STEVENS took no part in the consideration or decision of this
case.

MR. JUSTICE BLACKMUN, with whom MR. JUSTICE BRENNAN joins,
dissenting.

Once again — see *Blue Chip Stamps* v. *Manor Drug Stores,* 421 U.S. 723, 730
(1975) — the Court interprets § 10(b) of the Securities Exchange Act of
1934 . . . and . . . Rule 10b-5, . . . restrictively and narrowly and thereby
stultifies recovery for the victim. This time the Court does so by confining the
statute and the Rule to situations where the defendant has "scienter," that is,
the "intent to deceive, manipulate, or defraud." Sheer negligence, the Court
says, is not within the reach of the statute and the Rule, and was not
contemplated when the great reforms of 1933, 1934, and 1942 were effectuated
by Congress and the Commission.

Perhaps the Court is right, but I doubt it. The Government and the
Commission doubt it too, as is evidenced by the thrust of the brief filed by the
Solicitor General on behalf of the Commission, as *amicus curiae.* The Court's
opinion, ante, to be sure, has a certain technical consistency about it. It seems to
me, however, that an investor can be victimized just as much by negligent
conduct as by positive deception, and that it is not logical to drive a wedge
between the two, saying that Congress clearly intended the one but certainly not
the other.

No one questions the fact that the respondents here were the victims of an
intentional securities fraud practiced by Leston B. Nay. What is at issue, of
course, is the petitioner-accountant firm's involvement and that firm's
responsibility under Rule 10b-5. The language of the Rule, making it unlawful
for any person "in connection with the purchase or sale of any security"

(b) To make any untrue statement of a material fact or to omit to state a
material fact necessary in order to make the statements made, in the
light of the circumstances under which they were made, not misleading,
or

(c) To engage in any act, practice, or course of business which operates or
would operate as a fraud or deceit upon any person, seems to me,
clearly and succinctly, to prohibit negligent as well as intentional
conduct of the kind proscribed, to extend beyond common law fraud,
and to apply to negligent omission and commission. This is consistent
with Congress' intent, repeatedly recognized by the Court, that
securities legislation enacted for the purpose of avoiding frauds be
construed "not technically and restrictively, but flexibly to effectuate
its remedial purposes."

On motion for summary judgment, therefore, the respondents' allegations, in my view, were sufficient, and the District Court's dismissal of the action was improper to the extent that the dismissal rested on the proposition that suit could not be maintained under § 10(b) and Rule 10b-5 for mere negligence. The opposite appears to be true, at least in the Second Circuit, with respect to suits by the SEC to enjoin a violation of the Rule. *SEC* v. *Management Dynamics, Inc.,* 515 F.2d 881 (1975); *SEC* v. *Spectrum, Ltd.,* 489 F.2d 535, 541 (1973); *SEC* v. *Texas Gulf Sulphur Co.,* 401 F.2d 833, 854-855 (1968), cert. denied *sub nom. Kline* v. *SEC,* 394 U.S. 976 (1969). I see no real distinction between that situation and this one, for surely the question whether negligent conduct violates the Rule should not depend upon the plaintiff's identity. If negligence is a violation factor when the SEC sues, it must be a violation factor when a private party sues. And, in its present posture, this case is concerned with the issue of violation, not with the secondary issue of a private party's judicially created entitlement to damages or other specific relief. . . .

The critical importance of the auditing accountant's role in insuring full disclosure cannot be overestimated. The SEC has emphasized that in certifying statements the accountant's duty "is to safeguard the public interest, not that of his client." . . . "In our complex society the accountant's certificate and the lawyer's opinion can be instruments for inflicting pecuniary loss more potent than the chisel or the crowbar." . . . In this light, the initial inquiry into whether Ernst & Ernst's preparation and certification of the financial statements of First Securities Company of Chicago were negligent, because of the failure to perceive Nay's extraordinary mail rule, and in other alleged respects, and thus whether Rule 10b-5 was violated, should not be thwarted.

But the Court today decides that it is to be thwarted; and so once again it rests with Congress to rephrase and to re-enact, if investor victims, such as these, are ever to have relief under the federal securities laws that I thought had been enacted for their broad, needed, and deserving benefit.

◆◆◆

Case Questions

1. Is the dissent correct in its claim that the decision establishes a double standard — one requiring private individuals to show fraud or intentional misconduct in order to maintain a 10b action whereas, the government (SEC) need only show mere negligence?
2. Is this decision technically correct yet, violative of the law's spirit?
3. Was the plaintiffs' decision to sue Ernst & Ernst influenced by the fact that Nay was deceased and First Securities bankrupt?
4. Can the legal rationale of this decision also be applied to situations , where attorneys or underwriters were negligent in the performance of their duties?

ATTORNEY'S LIABILITY

Recently questions have arisen over what responsibility attorneys bear in cases of securities law violations. What makes the questions in this area unusually sticky is the presence of the attorney-client privilege, under which the attorney has the legal duty not to divulge any of his client's secrets (including past criminal activity) without the client's permission. The National Student Marketing case that follows provides a preliminary exploration of some issues. The SEC position in the case is that the attorneys should have ceased representing their clients and notified the Commission of the violations.

Other issues can also arise. What is a law firm to do when an accounting firm approaches it and demands information on a mutual client, information the client refuses to supply? The accountants may claim that the information is necessary to ascertain the client's contingent liabilities. Without such data they cannot render a "clean opinion letter" or will become a likely candidate as a defendant in a subsequent shareholders' suit. The law firm, beyond citing attorney client privilege, may claim that such information would be a practical invitation to a lawsuit or might aid an opponent in current litigation.

Whatever the answers are to these varied and perplexing questions, the fact remains that accountants and attorneys occupy a unique position as licensed professionals. They bear a twofold responsibility to their clients and the public. The parameters of latter duty remain in flux.

SEC v. NATIONAL STUDENT MARKETING
360 F. SUPP. 284 (1973)

◆◆◆

PARKER, District Judge

Alleging violations and aiding and abetting in violations of the anti-fraud, proxy and reporting sections of the securities laws, the Securities and Exchange Commission ("SEC" or "Commission") has brought suit for injunctive relief against National Student Marketing Corporation ("NSMC"), its officers, directors, outside legal counsel and independent auditors and the officers, directors, and legal advisors of Interstate National Corporation ("Interstate"), a company which was merged into NSMC, seeking to prevent future violations of those laws.

Defendants White & Case, a New York City law firm which at all relevant times was NSMC's outside legal adviser, and Marion Jay Epley, III ("Epley"), a partner in that firm, have requested this Court . . . to enter an order dismissing the proceedings on the grounds that venue is improper as to them in the District of Columbia and that in personam jurisdiction is lacking. Alternatively, these defendants . . . have moved to sever and transfer the claims against them to the United States District Court for the Southern District of New York.

Defendants Cameron and Brown ("Brown"), at all relevant times the president and a director of Interstate, Lord, Bissell & Brook, a Chicago Law firm which represented Interstate, Max E. Meyer ("Meyer"), a partner in that firm and a director of Interstate, and Louis F. Schauer ("Schauer"), also a member of Lord, Bissell & Brook, have moved pursuant to Rule 12(b) (6) of the Federal Rules of Civil Procedure to dismiss the proceedings for failure to state a claim upon which relief can be granted. Alternatively these defendants move for summary judgment in their favor pursuant to Rules 12(b) and 56 of the Federal Rules. Defendants Paul E. Allison ("Allison"), Robert P. Tate ("Tate"), and

William J. Bach ("Bach"), all of whom were directors of Interstate, have likewise requested this Court to grant summary judgment in their behalf pursuant to Rules 12(b) and 56.

The Court, after careful consideration of the memoranda of points and authorities, affidavits, exhibits and the representations of counsel during oral argument and for the reasons set forth below, denies the motions of White & Case, Epley, Brown, Lord, Bissell & Brook, Meyer and Schauer. The motions of Allison, Bach and Tate are granted and summary judgment is entered in their favor.

Background

In this proceeding the Commission has set forth a pleading, the First Amended Complaint For Injunctive and Other Relief, which contains four claims. The First Claim of the Amended Complaint, which does not involve any of the movants, recounts an alleged mammoth securities fraud scheme perpetrated by the principal officers, directors and accountants of NSMC and details the purchase and sale of over eleven million shares of NSMC stock between 1968 and 1970. Lying at the heart of this alleged scheme is the preparation, issuance, dissemination and promotion of false and misleading financial statements which artificially inflated the price of NSMC stock and enabled NSMC to fruadulently acquire approximately twenty-five companies in exchange for its own stock.

A significant portion of the remainder of the Amended Complaint concerns the October, 1969 acquisition of Interstate by NSMC. During the spring and summer of 1969 Interstate, an Illinois corporation, explored the possibility of merging with NSMC, which at the time was a District of Columbia corporation. Interstate engaged the investment banking firm of White, Weld & Company ("White, Weld") to make an investigation into the background, history and finances of NSMC, and to make recommendations as to the advisability of the merger. A preliminary report on NSMC, presented to the Interstate Board of Directors on August 12, 1969, and a final draft, dated September 22, 1969, were generally favorable to the merger. An Agreement and Plan of Merger ("Merger Agreement") was executed by the Interstate Board of Directors on August 15, 1969. The Merger Agreement, which was subject to Interstate and NSMC shareholder approval, contained, inter alia, the following significant provisions: Interstate was to receive from NSMC's counsel, White & Case, an opinion letter satisfactory to Lord, Bissell & Brook, that NSMC had taken all actions required of it by law and that all transactions in connection with the merger had been duly and validly taken; NSMC would receive from Lord, Bissell & Brook, a similar letter satisfactory to White & Case, that Interstate had taken all necessary steps to effectuate the transaction and that the merger was reached in accordance with law; and Peat, Marwick, Mitchell & Co. ("PMM") as NSMC's independent accountants would issue to Interstate a "comfort letter" stating that there was no reason to believe that NSMC's unaudited nine month financial statements for the period ending May 31, 1969 were not prepared in accordance with standard and accepted accounting procedures or that any material in those financials were required. It was further understood that the letter would indicate that NSMC had experienced no material adverse change in its financial posture from May 31, 1969, until five days prior to the effective date of the merger.

After receiving and having the opportunity to review the proxy material mailed to them, which included copies of the proposed agreement, shareholders of each corporation approved the merger at specially held meetings in early October, 1969. The material mailed to Interstate stockholders included the required nine month financial statements of NSMC which reflected a profit of approximately $700,000.00

The closing meeting took place at the office of White & Case in New York on Friday afternoon, October 31, 1969. In attendance were representatives of NSMC; officers and directors of Interstate, including Brown, Allison, Bach and Tate; Meyer, Schauer representing Lord, Bissell & Brook; and Epley on behalf of White & Case. During the progress of the meeting PMM telephonically transmitted from its Washington, D.C. office to White & Case an unsigned draft of the comfort letter which was to be prepared in accordance with the Merger Agreement. Providing less than the anticipated degree of comfort, the letter, which had been typewritten and distributed to those present at the closing, noted in pertinent part that:

> our examination in connection with the year ended August 31, 1969 which is still in process, disclosed the following significant adjustments which in our opinion should be reflected retroactive to May 31, 1969:
> 1. In adjusting the amortization of deferred costs at May 31, 1969, to eliminate therefrom all costs for programs substantially completed or which commenced 12 months or more or prior, an adjustment of $500,000 was required. Upon analysis of the retroactive effect of this adjustment, it appears that the entire amount could be determined applicable to the period prior to May 31, 1969.
> 2. In August 1969 management wrote off receivables in amounts of $300,000. It appears that the uncollectibility of these receivables could have been determined at May 31, 1969 and such charge off should have been reflected as of that date.
> 3. Acquisition costs in the amount of $84,000 for proposed acquisitions which the Company decided not to pursue were transferred from additional paid-in capital to general and administrative expenses. In our opinion, these should have been so transferred as of May 31, 1969.

On the date of closing but prior to consummation of the merger PMM allegedly informed White & Case and Epley of its desire to add to the draft letter an additional paragraph to the effect that with the noted adjustments properly made, NSMC's unaudited consolidated statement for the nine month period would not reflect a profit as had been indicated but rather a net loss and the consolidated operations of NSMC as it existed at May 31, 1969, would show a break-even as to net earnings for the year ended August 31, 1969. It is averred that White & Case and Epley did not inform the others of this information. Despite the unexpected revelations of the comfort letter, and without its contents being disclosed by any of the defendants who had knowledge of such, the merger was completed on schedule and the Articles of Merger were filed and recorded in the Corporation Division of the Office of the Recorder of Deeds of the District of Columbia. The final copy of the comfort letter which was received by White & Case approximately one hour after the closing was consummated and by the Interstate representatives several days after closing did in fact contain two supplemental paragraphs:

Your attention is called, however, to the fact that if the aforementioned adjustments had been made at May 31, 1969, the unaudited consolidated statement of earnings of National Student Marketing Corporation would have shown a net loss of approximately $80,000. It is presently estimated that the consolidated operations of the company as it existed at May 31, 1969, will be approximately a breakeven as to net earnings for the year ended August 31, 1969.

In view of the above mentioned facts, we believe the companies should consider submitting corrected interim unaudited financial information to the shareholders prior to proceeding with the closing.[2]

After receiving the contents of the comfort letter counsel for both companies rendered legal opinions, as required of them by the Merger Agreement, that all transactions in connection with the merger had been duly and validly taken.

The gravemen of the SEC's charges against the attorney defendants, as they relate to the events of October 31, is found in paragraph 48 (i) of the Second Claim:

As part of the fraudulent scheme White & Case, Epley, Lord, Bissell & Brook, Meyer and Schauer failed to refuse to issue their opinions . . . and failed to insist that the financial statements be revised and shareholders be resolicited, and failing that, to cease representing their respective clients and, under the circumstances, notify the plaintiff Commission concerning the misleading nature of the nine month financial statements.

The Interstate shareholders were not apprised of PMM's suggested adjustments to NCMC's financials. The SEC maintains that such concealment by Brown, Meyer, Allison, Bach and Tate constituted conduct proscribed by the securities laws and so charges in paragraph 48 (f) of the Amended Complaint.

Defendants White & Case and Epley are further charged in the Second Claim with continuing in their attempts to conceal the nature of the comfort letters by transmitting to the Commission a Form 8-K report for the month of October 1969 which, by reason of its omission of any reference to the letters' contents, was materially false and misleading.

The Third Claim alleges that on the day of closing Brown, Meyer, Allison, Bach and Tate furthered their participation in the fraudulent scheme by selling a portion of NSMC stock they had acquired as a result of the merger without publicly disclosing the new information they had received earlier that day concerning NSMC's financials. Lord, Bissell & Brook, through Meyer and/or Schauer, and at the request of White & Case, rendered an opinion as to the legality of these sales. The failure of the opinion to make mention of the comfort letter and the possible necessity of its disclosure before the stocks would be sold, serves as the basis for the charges brought against both groups of attorneys in this Claim.

The Fourth Claim, which does not relate to the Interstate NSMC merger, charges White & Case with issuing to their client a materially false and misleading opinion concerning the sale of two NSMC subsidiaries. Finally, White & Case and Epley are alleged to have participated in the preparation of a false and

---

[2] The contents of the second paragraph were allegedly related by PMM to White & Case and Epley one hour after the closing had been completed.

misleading annual report which was filed with the Commission in the District of Columbia.

MOTION OF WHITE & CASE AND EPLEY TO DISMISS BECAUSE OF IMPROPER VENUE AND LACK OF IN PERSONAM JURISDICTION

White & Case and Epley claim that the wrongdoing, if any, of which they are accused was pursued in their representative capacity as attorneys and that they are not and were never principals in nor beneficiaries of any alleged fraudulent scheme. They contend that there is no authority to support the Commission's theory that attorneys serving in representative capacities can be held accountable under the co-conspirator theory. Accordingly, they have urged the Court to distinguish the facts as related to them from those in which the co-conspirator doctrine has been accepted and applied. Further, they assail the use of the doctrine in this instance as being dangerously expansive because of its possible serious implications for members of securities law bar and for attorneys who appear before other administrative agencies in the District of Columbia. . . .

The Court is fully aware of the importance and possible precedent setting nature of the issues raised in this entire litigation as related to an attorney's responsbility under the securities laws. However, a ruling on the instant motion based upon those considerations as urged by the defendants would in effect constitute a premature determination of matters yet to be fully ventilated and tried on the merits. . . .

ALTERNATIVE MOTION OF WHITE & CASE AND EPLEY TO SEVER AND TRANSFER CLAIMS (omitted)

MOTIONS OF LORD, BISSELL & BROOK, MEYER, SCHAUER, BROWN, ALLISON, BACH AND TATE TO DISMISS AND FOR SUMMARY JUDGMENT

Defendants Lord, Bissell & Brook, Meyer, Schauer, Brown, Allison, Bach and Tate, have moved to dismiss and for summary judgment alleging that neither the Amended Complaint nor the undisputed facts provide a basis for the issuance of a permanent injunction against them under the Securities Act or the Exchange Act. These seven defendants are charged with violations of the securities laws only in the Second and Third Claims.

Section 21(e) of the Exchange Act provides in pertinent part with respect to the issuance of a permanent injunction:

> Whenever it shall appear to the Commission that any person is engaged or about to engage in any acts or practices which constitute or will constitute a violation of the provisions of this [title], or any rule or regulation thereunder, it may in its discretion bring an action in . . . [the United States District Court for the District of Columbia] . . . to enjoin such acts or practices, and upon a proper showing a permanent . . . injunction . . . shall be granted.

Section 20(b) of the Securities Act is to the same effect.

The standard to be applied in determining whether to issue a permanent injunction is whether there is a reasonable likelihood, in view of a defendant's past conduct, that there will be future illegal acticity. . . . "The necessary determination is that there exists some cognizable danger of recurrent violation, something more than the mere possibility which serves to keep the case alive." At this posture of the proceedings the Court is not called upon to issue an injunction. Before the Court are defendants' motions to dismiss which assert that the conclusory allegations of the Commission's complaint do not admit of facts sufficient to support the issuance of an injunction, and defendants' motions for summary judgment which claim that there is no genuine factual issue to be tried and that the uncontested facts show that the Commission is not entitled to an injunction. For the purposes of a motion to dismiss, a complaint should not be dismissed for insufficiency unless it appears to a certainty that plaintiff is entitled to no relief under any state of facts which could be proved in support of the claim. The pleadings are to be liberally construed. In ruling on a motion for summary judgment a court's function is to determine whether a genuine issue exists, not to resolve any existing factual issues. The movants have the burden of showing the absence of any genuine issue as to all material facts.

The purpose of injunctive relief is to protect the public from future violations and the Court retains broad discretion in determining whether the likelihood of future violations is such that an injunction should issue for this purpose. The case law identifies several factors which are deemed relevant to the probability of recurrent violàtions. The character of the past violations, the effectiveness of the discontinuance and the bona fides of the expressed intent to comply are considered. The number and duration of past wrongs, the time which has elapsed since the last violation, the opportunity to commit further illegal acts, the novelty of the violation, and the harmful impact of the injunction on the defendant are objective factors which the courts have examined. Subjective inquiries into the wilfulness or bad faith in a defendants's prior conduct and the sincerity of his representations not to violate the law are also pertinent.

The Amended Complaint alleges that a draft comfort letter was received by the movants during the closing of the NSMC-Interstate merger on October 31, 1969, and that a final comfort letter was received the following week. In the Second Claim the Interstate officers and directors are accused of consummating the merger without disclosing the contents of the draft comfort letter and of failing to disclose the final comfort letter. The law firm of Lord, Bissell & Brook and Meyer and Schauer are charged with issuing an opinion upholding the validity of the merger, failing to insist that the NSMC financial statements be revised and the shareholders resolicited, continuing to represent their clients, and failing to notify the Commission of the misleading nature of the nine month financial statement. In the Third Claim, the Interstate officers and directors are accused of having sold NSMC common stock on or about October 31, 1969, after receiving and reading, and without disclosing, the contents of the draft comfort letter, and Lord, Bissell & Brook, Meyer and Schauer are charged with issuing an opinion that this NSMC stock could lawfully be sold.

The acts with which the movants are charged, if performed with an awareness that previously received information concerning NSMC's earnings was false and misleading, could reasonably have been knowing and willful violations of the securities laws. The motive, intent and state of mind of the movants are highly relevant to the Court's determination of the appropriateness of injunctive relief. Well pleaded allegations which support a showing of knowledge and willfulness could provide a basis for the issuance of an injunction and would necessitate denial of a motion to dismiss. The existence of knowing and willful violations is sufficiently supported by the complaint's allegations concerning the receipt of the comfort letters, because knowledge of the false and misleading nature of prior information about NSMC's earnings could reasonably be inferred from the fact of the receipt by the movants of the draft and final comfort letters.

NSMC's May 31, 1969 financial statement, with which shareholder approval for the Interstate merger was solicited, stated NSMC's nine month earnings to be $700,000. White, Weld, Interstate's financial advisor, issued reports in August and September of 1969 which indicated that NSMC's consolidated net earnings for the year ended August 31, 1969 were projected to be $3.5 million. Acquisitions were to provide 84 percent of NSMC's consolidated net earnings, with Interstate itself providing 44 percent. Although the September report was generally favorable to the merger, it did, however, point out that part of the reason for its favorable impression of NSMC and for its belief that the Interstate shareholders would be reasonably well insulated from a major price decline in their NSMC holdings was the ability of NSMC to accomplish substantial internal earnings growth.

The draft comfort letter received at the closing pronounced that in connection with the PMM examination of NSMC's financial statements for the year ended August 31, 1969, significant adjustments of $884,000 should be reflected retroactive to May 31, 1969.

From this letter, the movants reasonably could have ascertained that previous communications concerning NSMC's earnings, including the figures upon which the Interstate shareholders had been solicited, were incorrect, and that NSMC's earnings could be substantially reduced. The final comfort letter, received by the movants several days later, actually stated that NSMC would earn no profit for the year ended August 31, 1969, and suggested resolicitation of the shareholders. The receipt of either of these letters would provide the basis for an inference of an awareness that previously received financial information was false and misleading, and consequently, that the acts performed by the movants were done knowingly and willfully.

In support of their motions movants aver that there is nothing to establish that they did not act reasonably and in good faith. It is claimed, among other things, that the draft comfort letter merely reflected a change in the time when the $884,000 adjustment should be made, that the draft letter was ambiguous and its impact uncertain, that inquiry was made of the effect of the draft letter and movants were told in response that the predicted August 31, 1969 earnings would remain substantially unchanged, and that the movants exercised reasonable business and legal judgment under the circumstances following the receipt of the draft and final letters. The stock sales by the movants were said to have been prearranged and transacted without any intent to defraud.

Because the circumstances surrounding the receipt of the draft comfort letter have not been fully developed, its probable financial impact can not be authoritatively judged. It is nevertheless clear that the draft letter can not be dismissed as merely an indication of a dispute as to the proper quarter in which to make the $884,000 adjustment, devoid of any effect on NSMC's earnings; the draft letter revealed that NSMC's May 31, 1969 earnings could be $884,000 less than the movants and the Interstate shareholders had anticipated, actually reflecting a loss for the nine month period, and that the August 31, 1969 figures, of which neither the movants nor the Interstate shareholders were aware, could be correspondingly reduced.

Movant's contentions do not resolve the matter of the good faith and the reasonableness of their actions but emphasize the need for further proceedings in which their motive, intent and state of mind may be examined. In view of the receipt by the movants of the draft and final comfort letters, whether their actions were done knowingly and willfully is a question of fact which can not and should not be resolved simply on the basis of the pleadings and affidavits. Evaluation of the character of the movants' past conduct and the sincerity of their representations not to engage in future unlawful activity would involve the resolution of factual issues and is not appropriate on a motion for summary judgment.

Other arguments have been urged upon the Court which pertain to matters of a more objective nature than willfullness and state of mind. It has been claimed that the alleged violations constituted a single isolated event which took place more than three years ago, that the acts of alleged wrongdoing are of a novel quality, and that the issuance of an injunction would severely harm the movants. These points are undoubtedly relevant to the ultimate question of whether an injunction would be proper. However, the singleness of the violations and the time elapsed since their performance would not by themselves preclude such relief if the violations were found to have been performed knowingly and willfully. The issue of the novelty of the theories of liability as to the movants, although it may later become material, is not before the Court since movants have conceded violations of the securities laws for the purposes of their motions. Until the matter of scienter is resolved, the Court can not accurately determine the likelihood of future violations, or thoroughly weigh the need for an injunction against the harm it would cause.

The question of the opportunity of the defendants to engage in future violations of the securities laws, however, is largely independent of past conduct, and can be dispositive of the need for injunctive relief, even if a knowing and willful past violation is presumed.

Brown, president and a director of Interstate at the time of the alleged violations, is currently chairman of the board of directors of NSMC and president of Interstate. Lord, Bissell & Brook and its partners and associates are presently involved in securities law practice. Meyer and Schauer are active partners in the firm, and Schauer devotes a substantial portion of his practice to corporate and securities law. It can not be concluded that Lord, Bissell & Brook, Meyer, Schauer and Brown have an insignificant opportunity to participate in future securities laws violations.

On the other hand, the undisputed facts place Allison, Bach and Tate in a different situation. Allison and Tate have both retired and, with certain minor exceptions, are not connected with the securities field or with the management of any public corporation. Bach, although he now practices law in Bloomington, Illinois, maintains no involvement in any corporate or securities-related activity and is approaching retirement. All three have claimed, and the Commission has admitted, that they are not and do not expect to be directors or insiders of any public company. In view of the apparent lack of opportunity for Allison, Bach and Tate to engage in future violations of the securities laws, the Court, in its discretion, finds that the purpose of protecting the public by means of a permanent injunction would not be furthered significantly by maintaining these three defendants in this action. Assuming that Allison, Bach and Tate knowingly and willfully violated the securities laws, there is no reasonable likelihood of a similar violation since these defendants are not, and are not expected to be directors or insiders of any public company. Accordingly, summary judgment will be entered in their favor. However, the entry of judgment against the Commission will not bar it from seeking appropriate relief in the event of possible future violations.

◆◆◆

Case Questions

1. How much trust would a client place in an attorney knowing that the attorney would reveal any securities law violations to the S.E.C.?
2. What considerations could have led the lawyers in this instance to have remained silent about the comfort letter permitting the closing to proceed?
3. Did the accountants discharge their duty by communicating the comfort letter to the lawyers? Since their client was the corporation, should they have not also sent a copy of the comfort letter to the respective corporate boards?

The legal fallout from the National Student Marketing case is continuing. Cortes W. Randell, the president and founder of the company plead guilty to several stock fraud charges. Liability of the law firms involved remains to be decided.

STATUTORY LIABILITY FOR SECURITIES LAW VIOLATIONS   *SKIM*

Section 17 of the '33 Act contains a general fraud prohibition applicable to the sellers of securities. Section 10 and Rule 10 b-5 of the '34 Act prohibit the use of deceptive practices in the purchase and sale of securities. Section 16 (b) outlaws short swing profits. We have already examined these provisions in some depth. Several other possible sources of liability should be mentioned.

Under the '33 Act: Section 11 imposes civil liability on those participating in the preparation of a false registration statement. A purchaser who sustained a loss by reason of such mis-statements or omissions can recover such losses plus attorneys fees. The defendants are jointly and severally liable. Section 12 (1) imposes liability upon persons who offer or sell a security in violation of the registration and prospectus provisions of the statute. Section 12 (2) imposes liability for the sale of a security, whether registered or exempt from registration, by means of a material mis-statement or omission of a material fact. If the purchaser suffered any loss he may bring a private damage action to recover that loss.

Under the '34 Act: Section 9(e) imposes civil liability for manipulating the prices of securities. An individual that has been injured by such activities may recover his losses plus attorneys fees. Section 18 creates liability for any person that files any false document that is required to be filed by law. Any person who relied upon that document, thereby suffering a loss, can recover that loss plus attorneys fees.

SEC must get justice dept to initiate criminal liabilities

Whenever the Commission believes that any provision has been, or is about to be violated, it may seek injunctive relief (Section 20(b) of '33 Act and Section 21 (e) of the '34 act). A willful violation of the '33 Act is a crime punishable by a fine not to exceed $5,000 and/or a prison term not to exceed five years (Section 24). A willful violation of the '34 Act is also punishable by a fine and/or jail term. The maximum penalty varies according to the type of violation. (Section 32).

REVIEW PROBLEMS

Penn Central

1. High Baller is the largest trucking firm in the U.S. On February 1, 1968, Overdrive Express had merged with it. However, poor planning, lack of capital, poor service and executive in-fighting doomed the venture from the start. During 1970 it fell over the brink into bankruptcy. Several months after the merger, High Baller stock reached a high of $88.50; it dropped to a low of $10 a share in June, 1970, just prior to the filing of the bankruptch petition. Good-as-Gold, a prestigious investment banking and securities firm handled the bulk of High Baller's securities offerings. A member of the firm sat on High Baller's board of directors. He was aware of High Baller's financial problems but his investment banking firm had a buy recommendation on its stock. However, his firm quietly informed several favored clients to sell. The client's did`so before the real bottom dropped out of the stock and prior to the filing of the bankruptcy petition.

As the company was financially declining, various officers and directors contrived various transactions with subsidiaries and improperly recorded revenue to give the impression that the company was financially sound. This fraudulent activity assumed massive proportions. The national accounting firm that handled High Baller's accounting work failed to ferret out the fraud. It conducted no search for fraud nor did it review the entire financial condition of the company. It confined its review to the legitimacy of certain transactions and accounts.

As the deepending financial plight of High Baller gradually came to the notice of the public, the stock began a sustained price decline. Some officers and directors sold their stock prior to and during this decline. Included in this group were the top officials of the finance department that dealt on a daily basis with the company's cash problems. Stock sales ranged from isolated, sporadic and small to stunning examples of bailouts.

Not all the directors actively participated in the massive fraud scheme that preceded the company's financial collapse. The directors ranged in quality from the most sophisticated businessmen to individuals that obtained the position merely on the basis of their wealth and social status. The board consisted of both inside and outside directors. Some directors did not attend all board meetings, however, they were given the required legal notice. Some board members took an active part in the meetings, making numerous inquiries and requesting documentation from management. Others merely served as rubber stamps for the high company officers. A third small category often times sat mute and would typically vote "present" on board resolutions.

What legal and ethical issues can one perceive in a situation such as this?

2. Would the investing public be afforded an increased degree of protection if the SEC licensed the attorneys and accountants that practice before it?

REGULATION OF THE PROXY PROCESS AND TENDER OFFERS

18

A proxy is the device whereby a shareholder gives to another the right to vote his shares of stock. It is an agency relationship and, as such, it is revocable.

PROXY REGULATION ✓ *Federal law important*

The proxy process is governed by the law of agency, the state's corporation statute and the '34 Act. Our focus here will be upon the regulatory process under section 14(a) of the '34 Act. That section provides that it is unlawful for any person, by the use of the mails or by any means or instrumentality of interstate commerce or of any facility of a national securities exchange or otherwise, in contravention of such rules and regulations as the Commission may prescribe as necessary or appropriate in the public interest or for the protection of investors, to solicit or to permit the use of his name to solicit any proxy or consent or authorization in respect of any security (other than an exempted security) registered pursuant to section 12 of this title. These regulations apply whether the proxy solicitation is for the election of directors or for approval of other corporate action.

At one time the proxy process was rather staid. Occasionally, a bitter proxy battle occurred, when two or more groups struggled for control of a corporation, but these tended to be few in number. The late 1960s saw a dramatic change as social activist groups seized upon the proxy process as a method of dramatizing their positions. A group called the Medical Committee for Human Rights sought to present a proposal to Dow Chemical shareholders to restrict the sale of napalm. The Project on Corporate Responsibility began its Campaign GM to include various proposals in the General Motors proxy statement. These and other such efforts led to extensive litigation over what is a proper subject for action by security holders. The result was the adoption of important amendments, which took effect January 1, 1973, to the proxy rules.

The proxy is accompanied by a proxy statement. Its contents are also highly regulated by section 14. The shareholder votes by proxy and must be given the opportunity to vote "yes" or "no" on each item. The proxy statement is designed to provide him with sufficient information to cast an intelligent ballot. Even when management does not solicit proxies, it is still required by section 14(c) to supply annually to the security holders information substantially equivalent to that which would be required in a proxy statement. The detailed regulation of the proxy process is set forth in Rule 14.

SHAREHOLDER PROPOSALS [1]

Any security holder entitled to vote at a shareholders' meeting is entitled to submit a proposal to be voted upon by the shareholders. He must submit his proposal accompanied by notice of his intention to present the proposal for

[1] In November 1976, the SEC adopted some changes to its rules on shareholder proposals.

574

action at the meeting. The management of the issuer shall set forth the proposal in its proxy statement and identify it in its proxy form so that the shareholders may vote on it. Management need not include the proposal unless it is received at the issuer's principal executive offices not less than seventy days in advance of the annual meeting date listed in the proxy statement for the last annual meeting. If that date is changed, the proposal must be received within a reasonable time. Excluded from these provisions are elections to office and counter proposals to matters to be submitted by management. [Rule 14a-8(a)]

The proxy statement shall contain the name and address of the security holder making the proposal, or state that the issuer or Commission will furnish the information upon request. If management opposes the proposal, it shall, at the request of the security holder, include in the proxy statement a statement of the security holder, in not more than 200 words, in support of the proposal. [Rule 14a-8(b)]

IMPROPER SHAREHOLDER PROPOSALS

Management may exclude a proposal:

1. If the proposal as submitted is, under the laws of the issuer's domicile, not a proper subject for action by security holders; or
2. If the proposal:
   a. relates to the enforcement of a personal claim or the redress of a personal grievance against the issuer, its management, or any other person; or
   b. consists of a recommendation, request or mandate that action be taken with respect to any matter, including a general economic, political, racial, religious, social or similar cause, that is not significantly related to the business of the issuer or is not within the control of the issuer;
   NOTE. Proposals not within an issuer's control are those which are beyond its power to effectuate.
3. If the proposal consists of a recommendation or request that the management take action with respect to a matter relating to the conduct of the ordinary business operations of the issuer.

Management may also omit the proposal if it was included at either of the last two annual meetings and the security holder failed without good cause to present the proposal for action. If substantially the same proprosal has been previously presented in management's proxy statement within the preceding five calendar years, it may be omitted from any meeting held within the next three calendar years, provided that: 1) if submitted at only one meeting during the preceding period it received less than 3 percent of the total votes cast on the proposal; or 2) if submitted at two meetings, it received less than 6 percent of the votes at the time of its second submission; or 3) if submitted at three or more meetings, it received less than 10 percent of the vote at the time of its latest submission. [Rule 14a-8(c)]

If management asserts that a proposal may properly be omitted, it must notify the Commission not later than thirty days prior to the date that the preliminary copies of the proxy materials are filed. The SEC requires advance filing of proxy material so that it may examine it for compliance with the applicable disclosure requirements. A copy of the proposal, with its supporting statement, is to be included accompanied by a statement of reasons why management deems omission to be proper in the particular case. At the same time, management must notify the security holder and supply him with a copy of the reasons for omission. [Rule 14a-8(d)] If the secuirty holder wishes to dispute the omission, the SEC will determine the issue, with appeal to the courts being available.

PROXY EXPENSES

Who pays for the expense of a proxy fight and whose expenses are to be paid? Expenses incurred in a proxy fight can reach large sums. There is the expense of printing and mailing the items required under the proxy rules. There are newspaper ads, counter-mailings to reply to the oppositions, and even attorneys' fees. Often a professional proxy soliciting firm is hired to handle and manage the campaign and, of course, it must be paid. In one case, the following fees were incurred:

1. $106,000 incurred by the old board to defend its position
2. $28,000 allowed by the new board to pay unreimbursed expenses of the old board
3. $127,000 expenses incurred by the new board in waging their successful contest.

The shareholders ratified this action. These expenses were incurred at 1950s prices. The expenses today would be much greater. In upholding the payment of these expenses the court stated:

> The rule then which we adopt is simply this: In a contest over policy, as compared to a purely personal power contest, corporate directors have the right to make reasonable and proper expenditures, subject to the scrutiny of the courts when duly challenged, from the corporate treasury for the purpose of persuading the stockholders of the correctness of their position and soliciting their support for policies which the directors believe, in all good faith, are in the best interests of the corporation. The stockholders, moreover, have the right to reimburse successful contestants for the reasonable and bona fide expenses incurred by them in any such policy contest, subject to like court scrutiny. That is not to say, however, that corporate directors can, under any circumstances, disport themselves in a proxy contest with the corporation's moneys to an unlimited extent. Where it is established that such moneys have been spent for personal power, individual gain or private advantage, and not in the belief that such expenditures are in the best interests of the stockholders and the corporation, or where the fairness and reasonableness of the amounts allegedly expended are duly and successfully challenged, the courts will not hesitate to disallow them. . . . [*Rosenfeld* v. *Fairchild Engine & Airplaine Corp.*, 128 N.E. 2d 291 (1955) (N.Y. Ct. of App.).]

Case Questions

1. Does it appear odd that when the shareholders throw out the old board, thereby determining that its policies were not in the best interests of the corporation, they must pay the expenses of the discredited board?
2. Realistically, how can a court distinguish between instances where the directors are seeking personal power, as opposed to the corporation's best interests? In most situations will not the two elements be interwined?

The Transamerica case that follows illustrates the mechanism for enforcement of the proxy rules. It also provides one perspective on what constitutes proper matters for stockholder action.

SECURITIES AND EXCHANGE COMMISSION v. TRANSAMERICAN CORPORATION
67 F. Supp. 326 (1946)

◆◆◆

Action by the Securities and Exchange Commission against the Transamerica Corporation and its officers and directors to enforce compliance with the proxy rules of the commission under the Securities Exchange Act. On motion by plaintiff for summary judgment.

Relief granted only in part. . . .

No facts are disputed. Defendant Transamerica Corporation is a Delaware corporation. It has 9,935,000 voting shares outstanding, held by approximately 150,000 shareholders. In January 1946, John J. Gilbert, a stockholder, submitted by letter four proposals which he wished presented for action at the annual stockholders' meeting to be held April 25, 1946. Three of the proposals were: (1) To have indenpendent public auditors of the books of the corporation elected by the stockholders, beginning with the annual meeting of 1947, and a representative of the auditing firm last chosen attend the annual meeting each year; (2) to repeal By-Law 47 and enact a new one which would eliminate requirement that notice of any proposed alteration or amendment of the By-Laws be contained in the notice of meeting; and (3) to change the place of annual meeting of the corporation from Wilmington, Delaware, to San Francisco, California. As the directors amended the by-laws on March 26, 1946, changing the place of the annual meeting to San Francisco instead of Wilmington, the third proposal drops from the case.

The other proposal which Gilbert intended to present for action by shareholders at the annual meeting was a "resolution," which provided a report of the proceedings at annual meetings should be sent to all stockholders after the meeting.

Under Proxy Rule X-14A-7, Gilbert requested the proposals be set forth in the management's proxy material; if the management intended to oppose the proposals, then he desired his name and address and his supporting statements of less than one hundered words each to be included in such proxy material. On February 1, 1946, defendant, acknowledging receipt of the proposals and requests, indicated if the resolutions were introduced, the presiding officer at the meeting would rule them out of order. On February 12, 1946, SEC suggested defendant's compliance with the proxy rules, i.e., to include the Gilbert proposals in the proxy material and to provide a proxy form whereby solicited security holders could ballot for or against such proposals. SEC's position was reiterated by telegrams dated February 15 and 20, 1946, and letter of March 29, 1946. The notice of the meeting, proxy statement and proxy — making no mention of Gilbert's name, address, his proposals or statements in support thereof, and not containing provision for ballot so that stockholders could specify their approval or disapproval — were mailed to stockholders beginning March 18, 1946. . . .

Defendant, its officers and directors, have used the mails, instrumentalities of interstate commerce, and facilities of three national securities exchanges to transmit management's proxy material. On March 29, 1946, SEC notified management that its failure to comply with Gilbert's requests was a violation of proxy rules and enforcement would be sought by court action should management proceed in its refusal to comply. On April 5, 1946, defendant's counsel indicated it would not deviate from its previous course of conduct. SEC then filed the instant action to enjoin defendant from exercising any power conferred by any of the proxies solicited or from any further proxy solicitation in violation of the proxy rules.

The matter came on for hearing on April 24, 1946, the day before the scheduled annual meeting, on plaintiff's motion for a preliminary injunction. The court then decided if defendant had solicited the proxies in violation of the proxy rules in failing to include the Gilbert proposals, such failure did not invalidate the proxies from use for the election of directors. The court directed that the meeting be held the next day, on April 25, 1946, for the sole purpose of an election of directors. It then was ordered that the meeting would be . . . required to adjourn to a date before which defendant must give a new notice of the meeting, specifying the Gilbert proposals as suggestions for action and solicit new proxies with authority to vote them on these proposals. As no facts were in dispute, after argument on the motion for injunction, plaintiff asked for summary judgment. . . .

1. The inquiry applicable to the Gilbert proposals is whether they are a "proper subject for action by security holders" at an annual meeting. This inquiry must be answered not by federal but by Delaware law.[2]

I shall first consider the proposal that defendant send a report as to what occurred at all annual meetings to its stockholders. This resolution was not intended by Gilbert to be offered as a by-law amendment but as a straight resolution. Under Delaware law this resolution is not "a proper subject for action" by stockholders. Sec. 9 of the Delaware Corporation Law provides: "The business of every corporation organized under the provisions of this Chapter shall be managed by a Board of Directors, except as hereinafter or in its Certificate of Incorporation otherwise provided * * *." Sec. 5(8) of the Delaware Corporation Law provides that a certificate of incorporation may set forth "* * * any provision which the incorporators may choose to insert for the management of the business and for the conduct of the affairs of the corporation, and any provisions creating, defining, limiting and regulating the powers of the corporation, the directors and the stockholders, or any class of stockholders * * * provided, such provisions are not contrary to the laws of this State." In accordance with the statutory power conferred by Sec. 5(8), Article

─────────────────────────
[2]Release of January 3, 1945, Securities Exchange Act of 1934, Release No. 3638; Holding Company Act of 1935, Release No. 5536; Investment Company Act of 1940, Release No. 735:

"Speaking generally, it is the purpose of Rule X-14 A-7 to place stockholders in a position to bring before their fellow stockholders matters of concern to them as stockholders in such corporation; that is, such matters relating to the affairs of the company concerned *as are proper subjects for stockholders' action under the laws of the State under which it is organized*. It is not the intent of Rule X-14 A-7 to permit stockholders to obtain the consensus or other stockholders with respect to matters which are of a general political, social or economic nature. Other forums exist for the presentation of such views." (Emphasis added.)

XIII of the Certificate of Incorporation of Transamerica was adopted by the incorporators. This article reads: "All of the powers of this corporation in so far as the same may be lawfully vested by this Certificate of Incorporation in the Board of Directors, are hereby conferred upon the board of directors of this corporation." Article XIII is a comprehensive grant of powers to the Board of Directors and, read in connection with Sec. 5(8) of the Delaware Corporation Law, makes clear that the directors are vested not only with the management of the business, but also with "the conduct of the affairs of the corporation."

Article XIII gives directors and not stockholders the right to determine whether a report of the annual meeting must be sent to stockholders, for the propriety of the expense and the issuance of such a report is clearly related to the conduct of the affairs of the corporation. It is both good law and good sense, based on business expediency, that such matters must be determined by the Board of Directors. . . . In one of the leading cases, Judge Lehman said: "* * * The directors are constituted managers of the corporate affairs. They determine the corporate policies, they elect the corporate officers. In the functioning of the corporate machinery the power of control of the holders of the majority stock is, as in such matters, exhausted with the election of the directors." The only power which stockholders normally have to control the corporate machinery is exhausted when they elect corporate directors. The rule is not a harsh one because, if a sufficient number of stockholders are interested in a particular matter or policy which is opposed to that followed by management, they are at liberty to band together and elect a Board of Directors who will be sympathetic toward the particular policies which the stockholders espouse.

The particular resolution which Gilbert proposes, even if carried by a majority vote of the stockholders, would not be binding upon the officers and directors. In short, the resolution is not "a proper subject for action by the security holders" within the meaning of Rule X-14A-7; . . .

2. Gilbert's letter of January 2, 1946, shows he intended to propose a resolution to amend Sec. 47 of the by-laws so as to eliminate the giving of notice when stockholders desired to amend the by-laws. Sec. 47 provides by-laws may be amended either by directors or stockholders but to adopt a valid amendment the proposed amendment must be set forth in the notice of meeting. Such a by-law is valid. . . .

There is nothing in the General Corporation Law of Delaware or in the charter or by-laws of Transamerica Corporation which requires it to give stockholders notice of any by-law amendment which a shareholder desires to submit at an annual meeting. If the Board of Directors refuses to notice an amendment which a shareholder deems desirable, he must seek his remedy in other channels. . . .

The stockholders, then, are authorized to amend the by-laws of a corporation at any annual meeting if the directors, in the exercise of their discretion, determine to give notice that the question of amending the by-laws is one of the matters to come before the meeting. If the directors are recalcitrant, any stockholder who desires action may, by banding together with the majority of the stockholders, require the calling of a special meeting for the purpose of amending the by-laws. . . .

This seems to me a very reasonable way to conduct the internal affairs of a modern corporation. If the rule were otherwise, any of the several hundred thousand stockholders, or all of them, might have suggestions as to by-law changes and the directors who, of necessity, are charged with the general management of the corporation would have to involve the corporation in great expense to print the great number of suggested by-law changes, with no defense against the requests of cranks. Moreover, it is doubtful whether such meetings could be concluded before the time for the succeeding annual meeting. However, if the majority of the stockholders in accordance with the usual democratic principle, desire to have their corporation managed in such a Pickwickian fashion they may, of course, do so under their power to amend the by-laws at a special meeting. ... I accordingly conclude that the Gilbert proposal to amend the by-law, as discussed, is not a proper suggestion for stockholders' action.

3. ... No cogent reason has been advanced why the proposal to have independent public auditors of the books of the corporation elected by stockholders (beginning with the annual meeting of 1947, and a representative of the auditing firm so chosen attend the annual meeting each year) is not a proper subject matter to come before the annual meeting, ... With respect to the annual meeting of defendant Transamerica, management by the exercise of procedural limitations had no right to omit this particular Gilbert proposal from the notice of the annual meeting to be sent to all stockholders. The selection of independent auditors is such a proper and common subject for action by stockholders that the mechanics of treatment of this type of proposal has been set forth in items 8 and 10 of schedule 14(a) of the Commission's proxy rules. ...

The SEC concluded that management's failure to notice and present to the stockholders the Gilbert proposal with respect to the selection of independent auditors was in violation of the proxy rules. That conclusion is adopted here.

The Delaware Corporation Law, which admittedly controls, contains no specific statutory provision expressly denying to stockholders the right to vote or select independent auditors. And in this case, there is no limitation in the charter or by-laws restricting that right to directors rather than to stockholders. Furthermore, there is no provision in the Delaware Corporation Law from which the conclusion is inescapable that such a right must be exclusively exercised by the directors on the theory that the stockholders have delegated every conceivable piece of business, with respect to the affairs of the corporation, to the directors. Here, the stockholders, as beneficial owners of the enterprise, may prefer to consider the selection of independent auditors to review what is no more than the trust relationship which exists between the directors and stockholders. Truly it would be an odd legal relationship whereby trustee has conclusive discretion over the method and person who shall review the trustee's accounts. The matter of independent auditors is obviously a proper subject matter to come before a stockholders' annual meeting or any special meeting. ...

In order to protect the stockholders, defendant should be required to comply with the Securities Exchange Act of 1934 and all apposite rules and regulations of the SEC promulgated thereunder; and in this instance, an order should be prepared directing defendant to notice and set forth the Gilbert proposal as to independent auditors for a vote of stockholders at the adjourned meeting of the company. ...

◆◆◆

Note: On appeal the court also compelled the resolicitation of Gilbert's proposals (2) and (4). 163 F.2d 511(1947).

FALSE OR MISLEADING PROXY STATEMENTS

When one alleges that a proxy statement is materially false or misleading, what is the requisite burden of proof? Is it sufficient to merely prove that a reasonable shareholder "might" have considered the statement important? Or does one bear the heavier burden of showing that the statement had a "significant propensity" to affect the shareholder's decision? The Northway case that follows examines the question in the context of proxy solicitation. Caveat: This Seventh Circuit decision breaks new ground and there is no assurance that the Supreme Court holds a similar view of the question.

NORTHWAY, INC. v. TSC INDUSTRIES, INC.
512 F. 2d 324 (1975)

♦♦♦   *Disclosure not accurate*

This appeal concerns violations of Rules 14a-3 and 14a-9 issued by the Securities Exchange Commission pursuant to section 14(a) of the Securities Exchange Act of 1934, 15 U.S.C. § 78n(a). This section makes it unlawful for any person to solicit by mail or other means of interstate commerce proxies of a registered security in violation of rules promulgated by the Commission pursuant to the statute. The appeal also concerns alleged violations of section 78j(b) of the Securities Exchange Act of 1934 and Rule 10b-5 thereunder.

Plaintiff Northway, Inc. brought this action against defendants National Industries, Inc. and TSC Industries, Inc. for alleged violations of section 14(a) in connection with the acquisition of TSC by National in a stock-for-stock purchase. Northway alleges that these corporate defendants issued a joint proxy statement in connection with a takeover, which statement was incomplete and materially misleading. In addition, Northway brought suit against Charles E. Schmidt and various members of his family alleging that these defendants also violated the Securities and Exchange Act by selling their controlling interest in TSC without adequately protecting the interests of its other shareholders. The Schmidt defendants were also charged with aiding and abetting the corporate defendants. . . .

We affirm the granting of summary judgment for the Schmidt defendants, but reverse the denial of summary judgment as to the liability of the corporate defendants.

I

Plaintiff Northway is a Delaware corporation doing business in Illinois, where it maintains its principal place of business. In January and February of 1969 Northway owned 200 shares of Common Stock in TSC Industries, also a Delaware corporation. Northway continued to own the TSC stock throughout the period of the transactions challenged in this lawsuit.

As of January 16, 1969 Charles E. Schmidt, Sr. and various members of his family owned approximately one third of the outstanding voting shares in TSC. In addition, Mr. Schmidt and his son, Charles E. Schmidt, Jr., were members of the TSC board of directors. On that day, Mr. Schmidt was approached by representatives of National Industries, Inc., a Kentucky corporation, who inquired into the possibility of acquiring all of the Schmidt family interest in TSC. After reviewing his own financial position and after an evaluation of National Industries and its key personnel, Mr. Schmidt determined that he would move ahead with the sale. On January 30, 1969 a stock purchase agreement was signed. Under the agreement, the Schmidt defendants were to receive substantially the then market value for their TSC securities. Payment was to be in cash and National's 5 percent notes payable in six annual installments. Immediately after signing the agreement Mr. Schmidt tendered his resignation from the board of directors of TSC. Mr. Schmidt's son, Charles E. Schmidt, Jr., tendered his resignation from the TSC board of directors on February 7, 1969, the date of closing of the stock transfer. The Schmidt defendants had no further contact with TSC or National after February 7, 1969.

Shortly after the acquisition of the Schmidt interests, on March 31, 1969, four National nominees were elected to the ten-man board of directors of TSC. On that same day, Stanley R. Yarmuth, president and chief executive officer of National, became the chairman of the TSC board of directors and Charles F. Simonelli, executive vice president of National became chairman of the TSC executive committee.

On October 16, 1969, a proposal to liquidate and dissolve TSC and to sell all its assets to National was considered at a meeting of the TSC board of directors. Under the proposal National was to acquire all TSC assets in return for National securities. Eight members of the TSC board of directors attended this meeting. The proposition received the affirmative votes of four non-National directors. The three National nominees on the TSC board attending the meeting abstained from voting on the advice of their attorneys. One non-National director also abstained.

On November 12, 1969, TSC and National issued a joint proxy statement to the shareholders of TSC concerning the proposed liquidation and sale. The statement urged TSC shareholders to approve the transaction. Sufficient proxies were received and voted in favor of the proposal to cause it to be approved. TSC was placed in liquidation and dissolution and notices were sent to all TSC stockholders advising them that they were required to exchange their TSC shares for National securities. Shares were exchanged and the transaction completed.

II

Corporate defendants National Industries, Inc., and TSC, Inc. are charged with violations of § 14(a) of the Securities Exchange Act of 1934, 15 U.S.C. § 78n(a), and Rules 14a-3 and 14a-9 thereunder. The 14a-3 claim is based on the failure of the corporate defendants to include in the joint proxy statement the conclusion that a change in control of TSC had taken place as a result of the transfer of the Schmidt interests in TSC to National. . . .

We agree with the district court that the issue of control is a factual issue presently in dispute and that summary judgment as to the Rule 14a-3 claim would have been inappropriate. . . . The trial court properly denied Northway's motion in the face of this bona fide dispute.

Plaintiff's Rule 14a-9 motion for summary judgment is quite different from the 14a-3 motion. The central question under Rule 14a-9 is whether, considering all of the circumstances which existed at the time the joint proxy statement was issued, the proxy statement was false or misleading in its presentation of a material fact or in its failure to include such a fact. Northway contends that the statement was misleading because of five omissions of fact, all of which it says were material. To prevail on the 14a-9 issue Northway must establish undisputed facts sufficient to show that one or more of the omitted items is material as a matter of law. To do this, it must demonstrate that reasonable minds could not differ on the question of materiality. . . .

In *Mills* v. *Electric Autolite Co.,* 396 U.S. 375, (1970), . . . the Supreme Court addressed itself to the elements of a cause of action brought under Rule 14a-9. The Court held that once materiality is established, specific proof of a causation is unnecessary providing it is shown that the proxy statement itself was an essential link in the transaction. The Court thus recognized that the concept of materiality is itself defined in terms of potential causative effects.

Since *Mills,* some uncertainty has developed as to which language in that opinion represents the proper test to apply in determining the materiality of an omitted fact. Different results could flow from a test requiring only that the omitted fact "might have been considered important by a reasonable shareholder who was in the process of deciding how to vote" than would flow from a test requiring that the fact have "a significant *propensity* to affect the voting process." On a motion for summary judgment, the "might have" test would ask whether a reasonable mind could conclude that the omitted fact is so irrelevant that it would never reasonably be considered important. The "significant propensity" test would ask whether a reasonable mind could conclude that the fact is less than significant in its potential to affect the voting process. Many facts which are relevant within the first test could reasonably be said to have less than a significant propensity to affect the voting process taken as a whole, even though for some few stockholders these same facts could be determinative.

We believe the policies which underlie § 14(a) and Rule 14a-9 are best served by a test that includes all facts which a reasonable stockholder might consider important. We are mindful of Judge Friendly's thorough consideration of this question and of the criticism that such a test is "too suggestive of a mere possibility, however unlikely." *Gerstle* v. *Gamble-Skogmo, Inc.,* 478 F.2d 1281, 1302 (2d Cir. 1973). Yet we think any test which does not require the inclusion of facts which *could* influence a reasonable stockholder would seriously undercut the intended prophylactic effect of these disclosure provisions. Any speculation under such a test is limited by the "reasonable stockholder" language therein and by the overriding purposes of § 14(a), from which any test must take its meaning and to which Justice Harlan specifically referred in *Mills.* This test will not reach "trivial" and "unrelated" facts; neither will it fail to reach facts which may be relevant for some, but not for others.

We are convinced that the test we adopt is supported by the reasoning of the Supreme Court in *Mills* and in *Affiliated Ute Citizens* v. *United States,* 406 U.S. 128, (1972). . . . These cases held that proof of causation or actual reliance is unnecessary to establish liability under Rules 14a-9 and 10b-5 in connection with a failure to disclose, and that causation is established once it is shown that the facts in question might have been considered important by a reasonable stockholder. It would make little sense to hold that causation is established by a more lenient standard than materiality. In fact any test of materiality which requires a finding of some probability that the omitted fact would affect the voting process necessitates the same difficult proofs the Supreme Court sought to avoid by eliminating the need for independent proof of causation or reliance. ...

Having concluded that the proper test of materiality is whether the omitted fact is "of such a character that it might have been considered important by a reasonable shareholder who was in the process of determining how to vote," ... we consider the five separate facts omitted from the joint proxy statement in this case.

A

Northway's initial charge is that the joint proxy statement failed to disclose two material facts related to the question of National's potential influence over the management of TSC. Specifically, the proxy failed to show that both TSC and National had filed special reports with the Securities Exchange Commission indicating that the transfer of the Schmidt interests had resulted in a change in control of TSC and that National could be deemed the "parent" of TSC as a result of that transfer. The statement also failed to show that at the time the TSC board of directors considered the proposed merger transaction and at the time the joint statement was issued, the chairman of the TSC board of directors was Stanley Yarmuth, National's president and chief executive officer, and the chairman of the TSC executive committee was Charles Simonelli, National's executive vice president.

Northway contends that failure to include these facts was misleading since TSC stockholders were relying on the TSC board of directors to negotiate on their behalf for the best possible rate of exchange with National. Because these facts were persuasive indicators that the TSC board was in fact under the control of National, and that National thus "sat on both sides of the table" in setting the terms of the exchange, Northway says these facts were material to a decision whether or not to approve the terms of the transaction as a matter of law. We agree.

While the proxy statement did indicate that five of the ten positions on the TSC board of directors were held by nominees of National and that National held a substantial equity position in TSC amounting to thirty-four percent of outstanding voting securities, this did not render the additional information bearing on National's influence over TSC merely cumulative or trivial. Indeed, there is a vast difference between the picture presented by these facts alone and the picture which would have resulted from the addition of the facts that National nominees occupied the chairmanships of both the board of directors and the executive committee of TSC and that even before the National nominees became TSC board members, both National and TSC thought it necessary to inform the Securities Exchange Commission that National could be deemed to be in control of TSC. The picture presented in the joint proxy statement may well have indicated to "those aware of [the] corporate mechanism," ... that National was in a position to exert considerable influence over TSC, but all stockholders, unsophisticated and sophisticated alike, were entitled to the full picture: that a substantial likelihood existed that National's influence in fact amounted to control.

We hold that failure to disclose the prior filings with the Securities Exchange Commission and the failure to disclose the crucial positions held by National nominees Yarmuth and Simonelli on the TSC board of directors were materially misleading within the meaning of § 14(a) of the Securities Exchange Act of 1934 and Rule 14a-9 thereunder as a matter law. The order of the district court denying summary judgment against the corporate defendants on the issue of liability must therefore be reversed on this ground alone.

B

Northway further contends that the proxy statement was materially misleading in its failure to disclose two sets of facts relating to the favorability of the terms of the proposed merger transaction to TSC shareholders. The first omission involves a series of acquisitions of National Industries Common Stock by National and by Madison Fund, Inc., a large mutual fund, during the two years immediately preceding the issuance of the proxy statement. The second omission involves a reference in the statement to an opinion letter from Hornblower & Weeks-Hemphill, Noyes indicating their favorable evaluation of the proposed transaction, when no similar reference was made to a subsequent letter from that firm which more particularly described the basis for the original opinion and indicated that Hornblower expected the market value of the National Warrants being offered to decline substantially prior to the proposed exchange. We hold that these omissions were also material and in violation of Rule 14a-9.

The joint proxy statement contained a major section entitled "Proposed Agreement to Sell TSC's Assets to National and Liquidation and Dissolution of TSC." The first information which appeared in this section concerned the approval of the proposed agreement by the boards of directors of National and TSC. The shareholders were told that the boards of directors of both corporations believed the proposal to be in the best interests of their shareholders, based in part on "recent market prices of the securities of the two corporations." The shareholders were also informed of the favorable opinion of the Hornblower firm regarding the fairness of the transaction to the stockholders of TSC. Current market values of the securities involved were listed as one of the bases for the Hornblower opinion, with specific reference to a "substantial premium over current market values represented by the securities being offered to TSC stockholders."

Following this information the terms of the proposed exchange were set out. According to those terms holders of TSC Series 1 Preferred Stock were to receive .6 share of National Series B Preferred Stock and one National Warrant for each of their shares. Each holder of TSC Common Stock was to receive .5 share of National Series B Preferred Stock and 1.5 National Warrants for each of his shares. One of the characteristics of National Series B Preferred was that each such share would be convertible into National Common Stock. Each National Warrant entitled its holder to purchase one share of National Common at $21.40 per share until October 31, 1978.

By linking the evaluation of the proposed exchange to current market values, the proxy statement invited shareholders to rely on a table of market values which appeared three pages later in that statement. The table included market prices of all of the securities involved in the proposed exchange for 1967, 1968 and 1969 up to November 7, 1969; the closing prices on November 7 were set out separately at the bottom of the same page. By using simple arithmetic, any TSC shareholder could thus determine the apparent premium which would result from the proposed rates of exchange based on the latest market figures. Based on these simple calculations, the premiums disclosed were indeed "substantial" as had been indicated earlier in the proxy statement. Each holder of TSC Series 1 Preferred, which closed on November 7 at $12.00, would be receiving National securities worth $15.23 at that closing, while each holder of TSC Common, which closed at $13.25 on that day, would be receiving National securities worth $16.19.

The shareholders were not told that in a subsequent communication the Hornblower firm had predicted that when issued, the National Warrants involved in the exchange would have declined from the November 7 closing price of $5.25 to a market value of $3.50. Such a disclosure would have reduced the apparent premium being offered TSC shareholders by fifty-four percent for holders of Series 1 Preferred and eighty-nine percent for holders of TSC Common. Both corporations were aware of the likelihood of such a decline. The topic was discussed at the TSC board meeting which considered the proposed liquidation and sale, and the subsequent Hornblower opinion letter was specifically requested by National.

In simple terms, TSC and National had received some good news and some bad news from the Hornblower firm. They chose to publish the good news and omit the bad news. Thus, TSC shareholders who relied on the joint proxy statement were led to believe that Hornblower considered the current market values disclosed in the proxy to be accurate indicators of the "profit" to be generated by the exchange being proposed. This wasn't true. The materiality of the omission is obvious.

Additionally, stockholders of TSC should have been informed of substantial purchases of National Common Stock by National and by Madison Fund, Inc. during 1968-69, and that between the Schmidt acquisition by National on January 31, 1969 and the proxy solicitation on November 12, 1969 these two corporations accounted for 8.5 percent of all reported transactions in National Common Stock. It is not disputed that Mr. Edward Merkel, president of Madison Fund, was a paid consultant of National receiving $12,000 per year for "being available" to National for at least one day per month, nor is it disputed that the chairman of National's board of directors, Bernard Barnett, was a director of Madison.

The trial judge found that these facts, coupled with the peculiar timing of the National and Madison acquisitions, showed "the opportunity for coordination." 361 F.Supp. at 116. The judge held, however, that while "the inference that might be drawn from [this] evidence might support a finding of coordination, the Court is not free to draw such inferences." But the purpose of 14a-9 is to allow the stockholders to draw such inferences as they see fit before their final decision on proxy questions. While we agree that collusion is not conclusively established by the omitted facts, it is certainly suggested. Stockholders contemplating an offer involving preferred shares convertible to common stock and warrants for the purchase of common stock must be informed of circumstances which tend to indicate that the current selling price of the common stock involved may be affected by apparent market manipulations. It was for the shareholders to determine whether the market price of the common shares was relevant to their evaluation of the convertible preferred shares and warrants, or whether the activities of Madison and National actually amounted to manipulation at all. This is the very purpose of disclosure.

We therefore hold that failure to disclose the unfavorable opinion letter from Hornblower and the facts surrounding the National-Madison acquisitions also violated Rule 14a-9 as a matter of law.

C

Northway's final claim under 14a-9 is that the proxy statement was materially misleading in its unqualified assertion that the TSC board of directors had approved the proposed liquidation and sale. First, Northway asserts that the proposal was never legally approved under the applicable Delaware law. The district judge found that § 144 of the Delaware Corporation Law covered the approval procedure in this case and that under that section, the approval vote was legally sufficient. In view of our disposition of Northway's other claims, and in view of the fact that this issue has not been resolved by the courts of Delaware, we decline to reach the question. ...

A second facet of Northway's final claim remains. The resolution of dissolution and liquidation was presented to a meeting of the TSC board on October 16, 1969. Attending that meeting were eight of the ten directors who comprised the board at that time. Charles F. Simonelli and Hyman Ullner, both National nominees, were absent from the meeting. The proposal was summarized for the board by Mr. Allan Solomon, another National nominee. A period of discussion ensued and a vote was called. The three National nominees attending the meeting announced that though they felt this was a good proposal, they had been advised by their attorneys not to vote on the matter. Orville E. Peterson, who had just negotiated the sale of his TSC stock to National for cash and notes payable over five years, also abstained in view of this recent sale. The four remaining directors voted in favor of the proposal to liquidate and to sell to National.

Northway points out that the resolution of dissolution and liquidation was thus passed upon by a minority of the entire board and that the resolution never received a simple majority of those present and eligible to vote at the October 16th meeting. They contend that these facts are so unusual that even if Delaware law allows such a procedure, the stockholders would want to know that the proposal received only four affirmative votes and that those interested directors who could have voted were cautioned against doing so by their legal advisors.

While we agree that the passage of an extraordinary resolution by four affirmative votes out of a total of ten board members is highly unusual, we do not think that this, standing alone, is the type of information which is clearly relevant to a shareholder's decision to approve the underlying proposal. We further believe that reasonable minds could differ on the question of whether or not a reasonable shareholder might consider this information important to his decision. Such information is not related to the substance of the liquidation and sale proposal as is information which reflects on the market value of securities involved, nor is it as suggestive of self-dealing as is information related to possible control relationships between the participating corporations. Without other facts, this information may only indicate that those who favored the transaction but felt a possible conflict did not wish to taint the vote of the disinterested board members who also approved of the proposal. The materiality of this omission is not properly determined on motion for summary judgment.

[The Court then discussed why Charles E. Schmidt and members of his family had not violated the securities laws and had not aided and abetted the corporate defendants.]

♦♦♦

Case Questions

1. Why did TSC and National fail to mention in the proxy statement that National nominees occupied the chairmanships of the TSC board and executive committee and the unfavorable opinion letter from Hornblower?
2. Is the court correct in saying that the circumstances surrounding the board's vote on the resolution is not relevant to the shareholders?

Note: The Supreme Court subsequently held that the court had applied the wrong legal test and remanded the case for further proceedings, 96 S. Ct. 2126 (1976).

TENDER OFFERS

Although neither defined by statute nor Commission rule, the term "tender offer" is generally understood to mean a public offer or solicitation to purchase securities during a given time at a given price. The tender offer can take three forms: 1) an offer for cash; 2) an offer to exchange for securities of another corporation or; 3) a combination of cash and securities.

ACQUISITION OF 5 PERCENT OR MORE OF A COMPANY'S SECURITIES

Section 13(d) of the '34 Act requires that any person acquiring directly or indirectly beneficial ownership of more than 5 percent of any registered equity security of a class file a report disclosing his acquisition. He must file a Schedule 13D with the SEC, the issuer of the security and each exchange where the security is traded within ten days of such acquisition. Schedule 13D requires such information as the identity of all persons on whose behalf the purchases have been made, the number of shares owned, the source and amount of the funds used in making the purchases, and the purpose in making the purchases. If the purpose is to acquire control of the issuer of the securities then any plans to liquidate the issuer, sell its assets, merge it, or make any major change in its business or corporate structure must be disclosed. The purpose of this disclosure requirement is to supply public shareholders, facing a cash tender offer for their shares, with information regarding the qualifications and intentions of the offeror. This enables the incumbent management the opportunity to present its position to the shareholders. The legislation was drafted for the benefit of shareholders and to neither aid nor hamper either managment or the corporate raider. Lacking such data a shareholder confronts several unknowns. He could simply sell his shares in the market. Or, he might await a more favorable tender offer. If one never appears, it may be too late to tender his shares. He might tender all of his shares in the hope that they will all be taken. Lastly, he might simply refuse the offer and continue to hold the stock. The decision is a hard one but the risks should be reduced if he has the Schedule 13D information to give some guidance.

REGULATION OF TENDER OFFERS

It is unlawful for any person, directly or indirectly, to make a tender offer for any registered security if, after consummation he would be the beneficial owner of more than 5 percent of that security, unless at the time the offer is first made such person has filed the requisite documents with the SEC. Section 14(d)(1) of the '34 Act requires the filing of the information specified in section 13(d) and such other information as the Commission may prescribe by rule as in the public interest or for the protection of investors. Copies of all requests or invitations for tenders and advertisements making such a tender offer must also be filed with the Commission. Any additional material subsequent to the initial solicitation shall be filed not later than the time such material is first published or sent or given to security holders. Copies of all statements furnished to security holders and the Commission shall be sent to the issuer not later than the date such material is first published or sent or given to any security holder.

Tender offers that involve the offer of securities in exchange for the target company's securities must be registered under the terms of the '33 Act. Otherwise, the information that must be furnished the security holders, issuer and Commission is similar to that of a cash tender offer.

COMMUNICATIONS BY MANAGEMENT DURING THE TENDER OFFER

The management of the company subject to the tender offer may support it, oppose it, or remain neutral. Management has no legal duty to comment on the offer. However, if management or any other person (such as a competing tender offeror) wishes to recommend acceptance or rejection of the offer, he must file a Schedule 14D with the Commission. Schedule 14D includes copies of all solicitations or recommendations to accept or reject the offer; the identity of the security involved and the name and address of the issuer; the reasons for recommending acceptance or rejection; the name, address and relationship to the issuer or maker of the tender offer of the persons filing the schedule; the identity of anyone retained by the person filing the schedule to engage in solicitation or make recommendations regarding the offer, accompanied by the terms of such employment [§ 14(d)(4)(a)]. This schedule must be filed at the time that copies are first published, sent or given to the security holders.

Management need not file this schedule if it is merely sending a "wait and see" communication. Such a communication is exempt under Rule 14(d)-2 if it only requests that the security holders defer making a decision while management studies the offer. To avoid undue stalling, management must communicate their recommendation at least ten days prior to the expiration of the tender offer.

WITHDRAWAL AND PRORATION

Under section 14(d)(5) the depositor of securities may withdraw them at any time until the expiration of seven days after the time definitive copies of the offer are first published or sent or given to security holders, and at any time after sixty days from the date of the original tender offer. The effect of this provision is to create a minimum tender offer duration of seven days.

Where the tender offer is for less than all the outstanding equity securities of a class, and where a greater number of securities is deposited within the first ten days than the person is bound or willing to take up, the securities shall be taken up on a pro rata basis [14(d)(6)]

FRAUDULENT, DECEPTIVE OR MANIPULATIVE PRACTICES

Under section 14(e) it is unlawful for any person to make any untrue statement of a material fact or omit to state any material fact necessary in order to make the statements made, in the light of the circumstances under which they are made, not misleading, or engage in any fraudulent, deceptive, or manipulative acts or practices, in connection with any tender offer or request or invitation for tenders, or any solicitation of security holders in opposition to or in favor of any such offer, request, or invitation.

ISSUER'S TENDER OFFER FOR ITS OWN SECURITIES

If the issuer is making a cash tender offer for its own securities it is exempt from the foregoing rules [§14(d)(8)]. However, the issuer must be cognizant of both section 10(b) and Rule 10b-5. If all material information was not disclosed and the market price rises, individuals that tendered shares may sue. If the market price drops, individuals who declined the tender offer may sue.

CORPORATE REPORTING

Since one purpose of the securities laws is disclosure, it should not be surprising that corporations must file a significant number of reports with the S.E.C. Under the '33 Act, an issuing company must file a registration statement prior to the public offering of its securities. The purpose is to provide disclosure of financial and other data upon which investors can judge the security's merits. The investor must be supplied with a prospectus (selling circular) containing the salient data from the registration statement. (A copy of the prospectus is made a part of the registration statement). The '34 Act requires corporations having their shares publicly traded on an exchange or having one million dollars in assets and 500 or more shareholders to file a registration form with the Commission. This data is less extensive than that filed under the '33 Act. To keep this information current such companies must file periodic reports with the Commission.

A company's annual report is neither mandated by law, nor cleared in advance by the S.E.C. The S.E.C. has a certain degree of indirect control over it however, because of its control over the proxy solicitation process. Companies are required to file an annual report with the Commission called the 10-K report. It contains a great deal of technical information and includes a certified financial statement. It also contains such data as a five year summary of earnings plus information relating to the company's liquidity. However, its most controversial aspect is the line of business reporting. A company with more than one line of business, and sales exceeding $50 million, is required to break down sales and pre-tax earnings of each product line that contributed in excess of ten percent of sales and pre-tax earnings. Some companies do not like the idea of publicly disclosing the company's operating results according to lines of business. The 10-K report is a public document available from the S.E.C. The Commission is using some public jaw boning to get companies to include such 10-K information in the shareholder's annual report. The results thus far are mixed.

Other reports are required, only two which we will mention. The first is the 10-Q report. It is a quarterly report filed with the Commission. By nature it is more of an interim or summary report. Its financial statements are unaudited. The second report is the 8-K. It must be filed for any month that observed the occurrence of significant events. For example, if a corporation had any unusual charges and credits to income they must be reported in an 8-K.

A corporation's duties under the securities laws do not cease with the filing of the required periodic reports. To avoid problems under Rule 10 b-5, it should publicly announce material information. The discussion of the press release in the *Texas Gulf Sulphur* case makes clear that such an announcement must be accurate.

SECURITIES AND THE UNIFORM COMMERCIAL CODE

Article 8, "Investment Securities" of the Uniform Commercial Code governs securities. It does not regulate securities in the same manner as do the blue sky or federal securities laws. Rather it regulates the mechanical process of negotiating and transferring securities. While securities are negotiable instruments they do not operate under Article 3's rules on commercial paper.

TRANSFER

A security that is delivered without an indorsement gives the purchaser the right to have the necessary indorsement supplied (8-307). The purchaser will not become a bona fide purchaser until the indorsement is supplied. A security can be indorsed in blank (including bearer) or with a special indorsement. Unless otherwise agreed the indorser assumes no obligation that the security will be honored by the issuer. An indorsement purporting to be only part of a security representing units intended by the issuer to be separately transferable is effective to the extent of the indorsement (8-308). Both physical delivery and indorsement are necessary to transfer (negotiate) a security (8-309). A purchaser who purchases for value in good faith and without notice of any adverse claim and who takes delivery of a security in bearer form or with an indorsement is a bona fide purchaser (8-302). A bona fide purchaser acquires the rights in the security which his transferor had or had actual authority to convey, plus he takes the security free of any adverse claim (8-301).

RESTRICTIONS ON TRANSFER

A corporation may place restrictions upon the transfer of its stock if the state statute, corporate charter or bylaws so provide. The courts will enforce such restrictions if they are reasonable. Typically such transfer restrictions only appear in close corporations. Oftentimes the restrictions will require that the corporation or other shareholders be given the first option to purchase such shares. Under the UCC, such restrictions, unless noted conspicuously on the security, will be ineffective except against a person with actual knowledge of it (8-204).

WARRANTIES

A person that transfers a security to a purchaser for value warrants that the transfer is effective and rightful, the security is genuine and has not been materially altered, and that he knows no fact which might impair the validity of the security. A person presenting a security for registration of transfer or for payment or exchange warrants to the issuer that he is entitled to the registration, payment or exchange. A purchaser for value without notice who receives a new, reissued or re-registered security on registration of transfer warrants only that he has no knowledge of any unauthorized signature in a necessary indorsement (8-306).

WRONGFUL TRANSFERS

Any person against whom the transfer of a security is wrongful (for any reason) may reclaim possession of the security or obtain possession of a new security evidencing the same rights or have damages except against a bona fide purchaser (8-315). If the transfer is based upon a forged indorsement, the owner may reclaim the security even from a bona fide purchaser, unless the bona fide purchaser has received a new, reissued or re-registered security upon registration of transfer (8-315, 8-311). Even in the latter case, the original owner of the security transferred by a forged indorsement is protected. On demand the issuer must issue a like security to the true owner unless such delivery would result in an overissue (8-404). Overissue means the issue of securities in excess of the amount which the issuer has corporate power to issue. If delivery would result in an overissue, then the owner can force the issuer to either purchase an identical security that is reasonably available for purchase; or if unavailable, the issuer must pay the owner the last price that the owner or last purchaser for value paid for it with interest from date of demand (8-104). The issuer's recourse is against the forger or the guarantor of the forger's signature.

There is a statute of frauds section applicable to investment securities (8-319). The provisions are similar to those applicable to the sale of goods, except that it is applicable regardless of the securities' value.

REGISTRATION

Whenever a security is presented to the issuer with a request to register transfer, the issuer must honor the request if the security is properly indorsed; reasonable assurance is given that the indorsements are genuine; the issuer has no duty to inquire into adverse claims or has discharged such duty; the applicable law relating to the collection of taxes has been complied with; and it is a rightful transfer or is to a bona fide purchaser (8-401). The issuer may require a guarantee of the indorsement signature (8-402). The issuer has the duty to inquire into an adverse claim if he receives a written notification of an adverse claim at a time and in a manner that affords a reasonable opportunity to act prior to issuing the new security. The issuer can discharge this duty by any reasonable means, including notifying the adverse claimant that the transfer will be registered unless, within thirty days from date of mailing the notification, either an appropriate restraining order is issued; or a sufficient indemnity bond is filed with the issuer to protect against any loss suffered by complying with the adverse claim (8-403).

If a security is lost, destroyed or stolen, the issuer must issue a new security if the owner so requests before the issuer has notice that a bona fide purchaser has acquired the security, files a sufficient indemnity bond with the issuer; and satisfies any other reasonable requirement of the issuer (8-405).

REVIEW PROBLEMS

1. Company X has steadily been losing ground in a competitive industry. This loss is reflected in a downward slide of the market price of its stock. One shareholder attributes the problems of the company to an entrenched inefficient management. Management learns that this shareholder-critic has recently begun purchasing additional stock. Her ownership now approaches 4 percent of the outstanding shares. With her wealth and the depressed price of the stock she can probably acquire in excess of 15 percent of the stock. This will probably give her control because the stock is so widely held. Management, in total, owns less than 1 percent. To stave her off, management is considering two courses of action. 1) Redemption of a large number of shares, thereby inflating her percentage ownership above 5 percent. This would necessitate her divulging her intentions in a Schedule 13D report. 2) Issuance of convertible debentures, to friends of management, in such an amount that if immediately converted the outstanding stock would double thereby halving her percentage ownership. What do you think of such tactics? Would your views differ if a) the redemption had been previously approved to obtain treasury stock for executive stock option plans, or b) additional financing was required for plant expansion and convertible debentures offered the most attractive feature?

2. Mosinee Paper Corporation has slightly more than 800,000 shares of common stock outstanding. It has only this one class of equity security and it is registered under terms of the '34 Act. Rondeau begins making large purchases of Mosinee stock in the over-the-counter market. By May 17, 1971 he acquired 40,413 shares which is in excess of 5 percent. He did not file a Schedule 13D but continued to purchase substantial blocks of stock. By July 30, 1971 he had acquired over 60,000 shares. On that date he received a letter from the chairman of the board stating that his activity had given rise to numerous rumors and was creating problems under the securities laws. Rondeau immediately stopped his purchase and consulted his attorney. On August 25, 1971 he filed a Schedule 13D. Mosinee seeks an injunction to prohibit him from voting or pledging his stock and from acquiring additional shares, requiring divesture of the stock already owned, and for damages. Rondeau readily concedes his violation. He claims that it is merely a technical violation and proves that it was due to a lack of familiarity with the securities laws. He further claims that neither Mosinee nor its shareholders have been harmed. Would denial of the injunction be justified? [*Rondeau* v. *Mosinee Paper Corporation,* 422 U.S. 49 (1975)].

3. Is it appropriate that shareholders lack the absolute right to have their corporation adopt a stance on a political, racial, social or religious cause?

4. Should a court enforce a restriction on the transfer of stock that requires a subsequent purchaser be approved by the remaining shareholders?

5. Why would a corporation desire to restrict the free transfer of its stock? What disadvantages do stock transfer restrictions place upon a corporation?

6. If a shareholder's proposal is one that management can properly exclude from the proxy form, yet is of a harmless nature, should management permit the matter to go before the shareholders?

PART VI

RECENT FEDERAL LEGISLATION AND THE AMERICAN BUSINESS ASSOCIATION

CORPORATE DUTIES TO EMPLOYEES AND THE PUBLIC

19

The corporation in America today is by far the dominant form of business association in terms of the value of productive assets owned. Its ascendancy has been followed by increasing governmental attempts, primarily at the federal level, to impose upon it and other forms of association new legal duties intended to serve two primary objectives. The first objective has been to create new duties running from employers to employees. The traditional forces at work in the unregulated atmosphere of the marketplace-competition, the profit motive, and recently even the increasing power of labor unions-have failed to develop enforceable duties against the employer in several key circumstances. These circumstances include: employment discrimination based upon race, age, sex or national origin; employee work-place safety; and employee retirement security. Recent federal legislation in these three areas and appellate case interpretation of the legislation are the subject of the first portion of this chapter.

The second portion of this chapter presents material illustrating the federal government's attempt to fill a second perceived need, again resulting from the marketplace's failure to develop adequate measures for protection. This perceived need is in the areas of the liabilities for producing a faulty product and for environmental pollution. In both areas, the new federal duties run from the business association to the public.

It must be emphasized at this point that the federal legislation presented in the first two sections of the chapter is very new. Its application in many areas has not been attempted before. Therefore, until a body of case law develops adding stability and clarity to the application of the legislation, the legislation will be subject to varying interpretation, even, perhaps, substantial alteration by Congress or administrative agencies. Although substantial change in the legislation might diminish the value of the material here, it is still of great current significance. Like it or not "federal regulation" is here to stay. Business associations are spending millions of dollars to alter their management structures and productive processes in order to achieve compliance with this federal legislation. For example, on December 15, 1975, *Newsweek Magazine* (p. 45) reported that in 1975, Goodyear Tire and Rubber Company spent the following amounts to achieve compliance with federal regulations:

Environmental Costs (capital, equipment, manpower, etc.)	$ 17.2 Million
Occupational Safety and Health	6.9 Million
Motor Vehicle Safety Standards (equipment and testing of tires)	3.4 Million
Personnel and Administration	2.5 Million
TOTAL	$ 30.0 Million

While the impact of recent federal legislation upon business associations is weighed by social and economic commentators and scholars, it remains obvious that not all the activity, products or services generated by these associations can be subject to legislation. There remain significant issues about the conduct of business associations, especially the larger corporations, which are unresolved by legislative act. These issues are often lumped into one vaguely defined area called "social responsibility." This area of responsibility, defined by dimly perceived unenforceable duties, is the subject of the final portion of this chapter.

RECENT FEDERAL LEGISLATION
ON EMPLOYERS' DUTIES TO EMPLOYEES

In this portion of the chapter we will examine the 1964 Civil Rights Act and its amendment by the 1972 Equal Employment Opportunity Act; the 1963 Equal Pay Act; the 1967 Age Discrimination in Employment Act; the 1970 Occupational Safety and Health Act; and the Employee Retirement Security Act of 1974.

CIVIL RIGHTS LAWS

The major civil rights legislation affecting employees is contained in Title VII of the 1964 Civil Rights Act[1] and its amendment by the 1972 Equal Employment Opportunity Act.[2] Together they make it unlawful to discriminate in employment based upon race, color, religion, sex or national origin. The law as amended applies to an employer in any industry affecting commerce who has fifteen or more employees. State and local governments and their political subdivisions are now covered by the law, but employees of the federal government are not. Also, the law applies to any labor organization that operates a hiring hall or has fifteen or more members.

Under the law it is illegal for an employer to refuse to hire or to discharge any individual or otherwise to discriminate against any individual with respect to his compensation, terms, conditions, or privileges of employment, because of such individual's race, color, religion, sex, or national origin. Also, it is unlawful for a labor organization to exclude or to expel from its membership, or otherwise to discriminate against, any individual because of his or her race, color, religion, sex, or national origin.

These broad statements outlawing discrimination in employment are subject to several exceptions. It is not unlawful for a religious organization to hire employees of a particular religion to perform work connected with carrying out the activities of that organization. More importantly, it is not an unlawful employment practice for an employer to judge an individual upon his religion, sex, or national origin in those certain instances where religion, sex, or national origin is a bona fide occupational qualification (BFOQ). Note that the BFOQ provision of the 1964 Act[3] allows discrimination based only upon religion, sex or national origin. Race can never be the basis for a BFOQ.

The bona fide occupational qualification just referred to is defined as legally permissible discrimination based upon the fact that the discrimination is reasonably necessary in the normal operation of the particular enterprise. In one of the leading cases in this area Pan Am refused to hire a male applicant for the position of Cabin Attendant asserting the claim of the passengers that they preferred females. The court held that sex bore no reasonable relation to the performance of the job. (*Diaz* v. *Pan Am.,* 442 F2d 385, 1971.)

Can the physical demands of a job be a BFOQ? Suppose a company has sexually segregated employees by adopting a policy that provides women are only eligible for jobs that require lifting thrity-five pounds or less. This is unlawful. All workers, regardless of their sex, must be afforded the opportunity to demonstrate their ability to perform more strenuous jobs on a regular basis. If a woman demonstrates the capability to perform a job requiring lifting items in excess of thirty-five pounds and desires that job, it cannot be denied her because she is a woman. [*Bowe* v. *Colgate Palmolive,* 416 F2d 711 (1970)].

Under guidelines on sex discrimination issued by the federal agency charged with the enforcement of Title VII, the Equal Employment Opportunity Commission (EEOC), the BFOQ exceptions are interpreted narrowly. For example, it gives the occupation of actor or actress as a legitimate BFOQ. Also, it may be legal to discriminate against males when hiring persons to sell female cosmetics. However, these guidelines say that it is unlawful to refuse to hire a woman on the assumption that the turnover' rate for women is higher than among men. It would also be unlawful to refuse to hire an individual on stereotyped sexual characterizations — that women are less capable of aggressive salesmanship or that men are less capable of assembling intricate equipment.

It is not unlawful for an employer to apply different standards of compensation, or different terms, conditions, or privileges of employment pursuant to a bona fide seniority or merit system, or a system which measures earnings by quantity or quality of production, provided that such differences are not the result of an intention to unlawfully discriminate. Nor is it unlawful for an employer to give and to act upon the results of any professionally developed ability test provided that the test is not designed or used to discriminate because of race, color, religion, sex, or national origin. However, the Supreme Court has ruled that for such tests to be allowable, they must be "job related." Suppose a company requires that an individual pass an aptitude test to be hired or to gain a job transfer. Also suppose that the tests:

1. do not measure the ability to perform a particular job and
2. render ineligible a markedly disproportionate number of Blacks.

Such tests, even though they are neutral on their face, do discriminate and do violate the 1964 Civil Rights Law. The tests are not job related for they do not bear a demonstrable relationship to successful performance of the job. [*Griggs* v. *Duke Power Co.,* 401 U.S. 424 (1971)]. A person is not guaranteed a job regardless of qualification. However, he cannot be denied a job by an artificial, unnecessary or discriminatory barrier.

It is not sufficient for an employer to stop discriminatory practices. It must take affirmative action to remedy the effects of past illegal practices. Does this mean employers must adopt a quota system? Some individuals claim that affirmative action programs under the Civil Rights Law constitute the imposition of a quota system when the law itself does not mandate a quota system. Others argue that a remedial quota program is necessary to offset the effects of past discriminatory practices. The Act states that an employer or union is not required to grant preferential treatment to any individual or to any group because of the race, color, religion, sex or national origin of such individual or group on account of an existing imbalance in the percentage of persons in the employed.

It is generally recognized that reverse discrimination is also illegal. However, the federal courts have upheld the "Philadelphia Plan." The Philadelphia Plan was promulgated under Executive Order 11246. This Order forbids discrimination by contractors and subcontractors that do business with the federal government. In some instances the Order requires that affirmative action be taken to improve the employment opportunities of minorities. For example, if a contractor wished to be eligible for government contracts, he was required to establish specific goals for the hiring of minority workers. These goals would be based upon the minority groups' percentage representation in the construction industry in a given geographical area. The court held that such an affirmative action program did not violate the Civil Rights Act, the National Labor Relations Act or the U.S. Constitution. It said that while the plan was "color-conscious," the Civil Rights Law was not passed to freeze the status quo and does not foreclose remedial action to overcome existing evils [*Contractors Ass'n of Eastern Penn.* v. *Sec. of Labor,* 442 F2d 159 (1971)].

It is also an unlawful employment practice for an employer, union or employment agency to discriminate against any person because that person has opposed any practice made unlawful by the Civil Rights Law, or because he has made a charge, testified, assisted, or participated in any manner in an investigation, proceeding, or hearing under the law. In *McDonnell Douglas* v. *Green,* 411 U.S. 792 (1973), the Supreme Court ordered a lower court to determine a company's motivation in refusing to rehire a properly discharged employee. If the refusal was based upon the former employee's impermissable activity, it would be legal; if based upon the discharged employee's civil rights activities against the company, the refusal to rehire would be unlawful.

Finally, it is an unlawful employment practice for an employer, union or employment agency to print or publish or cause to be printed or published any advertisement relating to employment indicating any discrimination, based on race, color, religion, sex or national origin, except when each is a bona fide occupational qualification for employment.

The major issue to be faced by the courts in the latter half of the 1970s in the area of employment discrimination is how the Civil Rights Laws and the seniority system work together when layoffs become necessary. Traditionally, job seniority decides who is to be laid off — the last hired, first fired formula. The recent strong economic downturn has raised a controversial and troublesome issue. Suppose a company had, until recently, illegally discriminated against women and minorities? Then, when layoffs become necessary, the sole criterion used for laying off workers under the contract was seniority. Is it legal and fair to lay off the women and minorities when their low seniority was a result of attempts to remedy previous illegal discrimination? Is it legal and fair to lay off white males who have greater seniority and, under the terms of the contract, have job priority? As yet, we lack answers to these questions. However, some federal trial courts have recently indicated that the Civil Rights Laws supersede the seniority system. If this is so, are minorities and women to be laid off in the same proportion as the layoff in the plant's total layoff — a 5 percent layoff means 5 percent of minorities are to be laid off? Could the layoffs occur according to seniority if those laid off receive cash payments until normal attrition or new business opens up new positions? Again there are no answers.

Compliance with the 1964 and 1972 laws is achieved through the Equal Employment Opportunity Commission (EEOC). It consists of five members appointed by the President with the consent of the Senate. No more than three members can be of the same political party and they serve five-year terms. There is a General Counsel who conducts any necessary litigation under the law. This position is also filled by a presidential appointment, with the Senate's consent, and the term of office is four years.

Charges of discrimination can be brought to the EEOC by the aggrieved individual, a person acting *on behalf* of the aggrieved individual, or a Commission member. A charge must be filed within 180 days after the alleged discrimination unless the charge was initially filed with a state or local agency. If originally processed by a local or state agency, the charge must be filed with the EEOC within 300 days or 30 days after the state or local agency has terminated proceedings, whichever is earlier.

The organization charged with discrimination is then notified of the charge. The EEOC conducts an investigation and, if it believes a violation has occurred, it attempts to achieve an informal settlement by conciliation. This is a process whereby the parties meet informally and try to reach a satisfactory resolution of the allegations. All of these conciliation activities are conducted in private. If voluntary conciliation proves impossible, the General Counsel files suit on behalf of one individual or a class of individuals in an effort to eliminate the alleged unlawful practice. However, no individually initiated EEOC lawsuit can be brought against a *government* or any of its political subdivisions. Only if the EEOC can convince the Justice Department to *sue* government units will the issue reach court.

If a *state* has a fair employment practice law, as most do, the individual should first file the charge with the state agency (the EEOC must defer to the state for 60 days). After the charge has been on file with the state at least 60 days, the individual is free to file a charge with the EEOC. If the EEOC dismisses the charge, or if 180 days have passed without the EEOC achieving a conciliation agreement or filing suit, the individual may file a private lawsuit. The individual is free to sue both private parties and governments or their political subdivisions.

Recently there has been growing criticism of EEOC operation. Much of the criticism has been based on its huge backlog of cases. At the end of 1974, it had a backlog of approximately 100,000 unresolved charges. As of May, 1974, over 20,000 of those charges were at least two years old. In the fiscal year that ended June 30, 1974, the EEOC had only resolved about half of the cases that it took to conciliation.[4] During that period only about 8,600 cases reached the conciliation stage of the process. Recently there have been some changes in the EEOC membership and in the General Counsel's office in an effort to resolve some of these difficulties. It is still too early to tell whether these efforts will be successful.

EQUAL PAY ACT OF 1963

The year 1963 saw the enactment of the Equal Pay Act.[5] It amended Section 6 of the Fair Labor Standards Act and outlaws wage discrimination based upon the employee's sex. The concept that a man, because of his role in society, should be paid more than a woman for doing the same job is declared unlawful. Every employee covered by the federal minimum wage law is protected by the Equal Pay Act. On July 1, 1972, the Act's protection was extended to executive, administrative, and professional employees and to outside sales personnel who previously had been exempt from coverage.

The Act prohibits an employer from discriminating between employees on the basis of sex by paying wages to employees at a rate less than the rate at which he pays wages to employees of the opposite sex for equal work on jobs, the performance of which requires equal skill, effort, and responsibility, and which are performed under similar working conditions. Equal work does not mean that the jobs be identical, only that they be substantially equal. Artificial job classifications that do not substantially differ from genuine ones cannot be created to avoid the operation of the law. If unlawful wage differentials do exist, the employer cannot eliminate them by reducing wage rates. The employer must raise the pay rate of those being discriminated against to the higher wage level of those performing equal work. The law prohibits a union from causing or attempting to cause an employer to discriminate as to wage rates.

There are four exceptions to the equal pay for equal work mandate: differing pay to opposite sexes is permissable where it,[6] " . . . is made pursuant to 1) a seniority system; 2) a merit system; 3) a system which measures earnings by quantity or quality or production; or 4) a differential based on any other factor other than sex." Once it is shown that an employer pays workers of one sex more than workers of the opposite sex for equal work, the burden shifts to the employer to show that the differential is justified under one of these exceptions.

Litigation under the Act has begun to significantly increase since 1972. The amount of money involved can be large. In the Wheaton Glass case discussed below, the court ordered the employer to pay $901,062.00 in back pay to women inspector-packers. It is also noteworthy that in cases under the Equal Pay Act and the Age Discrimination Act the court can order the company to pay the reasonable attorneys' fees of the employees.

Let us take a brief look at three important cases to see how the courts are applying the law. In *Shultz* v. *Wheaton Glass Co.,* 421 F.2d 259 (1970), the employer paid its female selector-packers $2.14 per hour while paying its male selector-packers $2.35 per hour, 21 cents per hour more than the females received. The company denied that the females performed equal work and, in any event argued that the pay differential was based on a factor other than sex. During periodic oven shutdowns, the male workers could be assigned to perform duties of snap-up boys who were paid $2.16 per hour. The court said that the company failed to explain why the availability of men to perform work which pays two cents per hour more than women receive should result in overall payment to men of 21 cents more than women for their common work. The court said the jobs of male and female selector-packers are substantially equal and therefore the employer violated the Act.

What is a factor other than sex that can justify a wage differential? We receive a good answer in *Hodgson* v. *Robert Hall Clothes,* 473 F.2d 589 (1973). Robert Hall had men staff the men's department while all the sales personnel in the women's department were women. These sales personnel performed equal work, yet the salesmen received higher salaries than the saleswomen. Each received a base salary plus incentive payments based upon the garment sold. Robert Hall said this wage differential was based not upon sex, but on economic factors, i.e., the higher profitability of the men's department. The court held that this economic benefit to Robert Hall can be used to justify a wage differential. It also said that Robert Hall proved that it received the economic benefits upon which it based its salary differentials. Robert Hall showed that for every year of the store's operation, the men's department was substantially more profitable than the women's department. The court pointed out that while it may require equal effort to sell two different shoes for $10, if the employer receives a four dollar profit on one pair as opposed to a two dollar profit on the other, the employer can pay a higher wage to the person selling the pair yielding the higher profit.

In our last case, *Corning Glass Works* v. *Brennan*, 417 U.S. 188 (1974), the Supreme Court held an employer in violation of the Act for paying a higher base wage to male night shift inspectors than it paid to female inspectors performing the same tasks on the day shift. In this case, the higher wage was paid in addition to an added night shift differential paid to all employees for night work.

AGE DISCRIMINATION LEGISLATION

In 1967, Congress passed the Age Discrimination in Employment Act.[7] It prohibits discrimination against individuals between the ages of 40 and 65 in hiring, compensation or terms of employment. The Act applies to employers, labor organizations, and employment agencies. This Act does not require that persons between the ages of 40 and 65 must be hired. Instead, it says that a refusal to hire them cannot be based upon their age.

The law governs employers engaged in an industry affecting commerce who have 20 or more employees. It governs unions that either operate a hiring hall or have 25 or more members. The law applies to employment agencies regardless of their size or the number of persons placed. Even if the employment agency is not paid for its services, it is covered by the law if it regularly procures employees. The law applies to the states and their political subdivisions and also covers many federal governmental agencies.

Like Title VII of the Civil Rights Act, it is permissible to discriminate based upon a person's age where age is a bona fide occupational qualification (BFOQ) *reasonably necessary* to the normal operation of the particular business, or where the differentiation is based on reasonable factors other than age. In this case, the BFOQ also means discrimination is permissible to observe the terms of a bona fide seniority system or any bona fide employee benefit plan such as a retirement, pension, or insurance plan, which is not a subterfuge to evade the purposes of this Act.

Only recently have significant issues been litigated under this law. In mid 1974, for example, Standard Oil of California reached an out-of-court settlement that provided that it pay 2 million dollars to 160 "older" persons that it had discharged. Standard Oil also agreed to offer to rehire 120 of these individuals.

Thus far, there have been very few court cases completely litigated. Probably the most important one involved Greyhound Lines. Greyhound declined to consider applications for intercity bus drivers from individuals 35 years of age or older. The Secretary of Labor alleged that this violated the Act. Greyhound argued that age was a BFOQ for such drivers. Greyhound won the case. The court showed great concern for the passenger safety issue. It said that

Greyhound need only show a minimal increase of risk of harm that one or more person's safety would be jeopardized. The court ruled that Greyhound had proved its case by proving three things: 1) rigors of extra board assignments [the type of driving required of new employees]; 2) degenerative physical and changes brought on by the aging process beginning in the late thirties; and 3) statistical evidence showing its safest drivers had 16 to 20 years of experience and were between 50-55 years of age. This could not usually be attained by hiring applicants 40 years of age or over [*Hodgson* v. *Greyhound Lines,* 499 F.2d 859 (1974)]. On January 20, 1975, the Supreme Court refused to hear an appeal of the case.

The Secretary of Labor is empowered under the law to make investigations and require the keeping of records necessary for administering the Act. Voluntary settlement of disputes is encouraged. Before an individual can sue, he must give the Secretary at least 60 days notice of his intention to sue. The individual must file this notice within 180 days of the alleged unlawful discrimination. If voluntary settlement proves impossible, then the individual or the Secretary can sue. The lawsuit must be filed within two years of the violation or three years for a willful violation.

This concludes the material on employment discrimination. Obviously it is not the final word since the case law in this area is relatively new. To end this first portion of the chapter we present a recent Supreme Court decision discussing two very important issues on the duties of employers to employees. The issues concern, first, the need for and the circumstances in which the remedy of back pay will be awarded for discriminatory job practices and second, the circumstances in which employment tests may be used in hiring and promotion.

ALBEMARLE PAPER COMPANY v. JOSEPH P. MOODY, ET AL
422 U.S. 405 (U.S. SUP. CT., 1975)

◆◆◆

Mr. Justice Stewart delivered the opinion of the Court.

These consolidated cases raise two important questions under Title VII of the Civil Rights Act of 1964, 78 Stat. 253, as amended by the Equal Employment Opportunity Act of 1972, 86 Stat. 103, 42 U. S. C. § 2000 (e): First: When employees or applicants for employment have lost the opportunity to earn wages because an employer has engaged in an unlawful discriminatory employment practice, what standards should a federal district court follow in deciding whether to award or deny backpay? Second: What must an employer show to establish that pre-employment tests racially discriminatory in effect, though not in intent, are sufficiently "job related" to survive challenge under Title VII?

I

The respondents — plaintiffs in the District Court — are a certified class of present and former Negro employees at a paper mill in Roanoke Rapids, North Carolina; the petitioners — defendants in the District Court — are the plant's owner, the Albemarle Paper Company, and the plant employees' labor union, Halifax Local No. 425. In August of 1966, after filing a complaint with the Equal Employment Opportunity Commission (EEOC), and receiving notice of their right to sue, the respondents brought a class action in the United States District Court for the Eastern District of North Carolina, asking permanent injunctive relief against "any policy, practice, custom, or usage" at the plant that violated Title VII. The respondents assured the court that the suit involved no claim for any monetary awards on a class basis, but in June of 1970, after several years of discovery, the respondents moved to add a class demand for backpay. The court ruled that this issue would be considered at trial.

At the trial, in July and August of 1971, the major issues were the plant's seniority system, its program of employment testing, and the question of backpay. In its opinion of November 9, 1971, the court found that the petitioners had "strictly segregated" the plant's departmental "lines of progression" prior to January 1, 1964, reserving the higher paying and more skilled lines for whites, ... The "racial identifiability" of whole lines of progression persisted until 1968, when the lines were reorganized under a new collective-bargaining agreement. The court found, however, that this reorganization left Negro employees "locked in the lower paying job classifications," ... The formerly "Negro" lines of progression had been merely tacked on to the bottom of the formerly "white" lines, and promotions, demotions, and layoffs continued to be governed — where skills were "relatively equal" — by a system of "job seniority." Because of the plant's previous history of overt segregation, only whites had seniority in the higher job categories. Accordingly, the court ordered the petitioners to implement a system of "plantwide" seniority.

The court refused, however, to award backpay to the plaintiff class for losses suffered under the "job seniority" program. The court explained:

> In the instant case there was no evidence of bad faith non-compliance with the Act. It appears that the company as early as 1964 began active recruitment of blacks for its Maintenance Apprenticeship Program. Certain lines of progression were merged on its own initiative, and as judicial decisions expanded the then existing interpretations of the Act, the defendants took steps to correct the abuses without delay. ...

The court also refused to enjoin or limit Albermarle's testing program. Albemarle had required applicants for employment in the skilled lines of progression to have a high school diploma and to pass two tests, the Revised Beta Examination, allegedly a measure of nonverbal intelligence, and the Wonderlic Test (available in alternate Forms A and B), allegedly a measure of verbal facility.

The petitioners did not seek review of the court's judgment, but the respondents appealed the denial of a backpay award and the refusal to enjoin or limit Albemarle's use of pre-employment tests. A divided Court of Appeals for the Fourth Circuit reversed the judgment of the District Court, ruling that backpay should have been awarded and that use of the tests should have been enjoined, 474 F.2d 134. As for backpay, the Court of Appeals held that an award could properly be requested after the complaint was filed and that an award could not be denied merely because the employer had not acted in "bad faith," ...

II

Whether a particular member of the plaintiff class should have been awarded any backpay and, if so, how much, are questions not involved in this review. The equities of individual cases were never reached. Though at least some of the members of the plaintiff class obviously suffered a loss of wage opportunities on account of Albermarle's unlawfully discriminatory system of job seniority, the District Court decided that no backpay should be awarded to anyone in the class. The court declined to make such an award on two stated grounds: the lack of "evidence of bad faith noncompliance with the Act," and the fact that "the defendants would be substantially prejudiced" by an award of backpay that was demanded contrary to an earlier representation and late in the progress of the litigation. . . .

The petitioners contend that the statutory scheme provides no guidance, beyond indicating that backpay awards are within the District Court's discretion. We disagree. It is true that backpay is not an automatic or mandatory remedy; like all other remedies under the Act, it is one which the courts "may" invoke. The scheme implicitly recognizes that there may be cases calling for one remedy but not another, and — owing to the structure of the federal judiciary — these choices are of course left in the first instance to the district courts. But such discretionary choices are not left to a court's "inclination, but to its judgment; and its judgment is to be guided by sound legal principles." The power to award backpay was bestowed by Congress, as part of a complex legislative design directed at an historic evil of national proportions. A court must exercise this power "in light of the large objectives of the Act," *Hecht Co.* v. *Bowles,* 321 U.S. 321, 331.

The District Court's decision must therefore be measured against the purposes which inform Title VII. As the court observed in *Griggs* v. *Duke Power Co.,* . . . 401 U.S., at 429-430, the primary objective was a prophylactic one:

It was to achieve equality of employment opportunities and remove barriers that have operated in the past to favor an identifiable group of white employees over other employees.

Backpay has an obvious connection with this purpose. If employers faced only the prospect of an injunctive order, they would have little incentive to shun practices of dubious legality. It is the reasonably certain prospect of a backpay award that "provide[s] the spur or catalyst which causes employers and unions to self-examine and to self-evaluate their employment practices and to endeavor to eliminate, so far as possible, the last vestiges of an unfortunate and ignominious page in this country's history." *United States* v. *N. L. Industries,* 79 F.2d 354, 379.

It is also the purpose of Title VII to make persons whole for injuries suffered on account of unlawful employment discrimination. This is shown by the very fact that Congress took care to arm the courts with full equitable powers. . . . Title VII deals with legal injuries of an economic character occasioned by racial or other antiminority discrimination. The terms "complete justice" and "necessary relief" have acquired a clear meaning in such circumstances. Where racial discrimination is concerned, "the [district] court has not merely the power but the duty to render a decree which will so far as possible eliminate the discriminatory effects of the past as well as bar like discrimination in the future." *Louisiana* v. *United States,* 380 U.S. 145, 154. And where a legal injury is of an economic character,

> [t]he general rule is, that when a wrong has been done, and the law gives a remedy, the compensation shall be equal to the injury. The latter is the standard by which the former is to be measured. The injured party is to be placed as near as may be, in the situation he would have occupied if the wrong had not been committed. *Wicker* v. *Hoppock,* 6 Wall, 94, at 99.

The "make whole" purpose of Title VII is made evident by the legislative history. The backpay provision was expressly modeled on the backpay provision of the National Labor Relations Act. Under that Act, "[m]aking the workers whole for losses suffered on account of an unfair labor practice is part of the vindication of the public policy which the Board enforces." . . . We may assume that Congress was aware that the Board, since its inception, has awarded backpay as a matter of course — not randomly or in the exercise of a standardless discretion, and not merely where employer violations are peculiarly deliberate, egregious or inexcusable. Furthermore, in passing the Equal Employment Opportunity Act of 1972, Congress considered several bills to limit the judicial power to award backpay. These limiting efforts were rejected, and the backpay provision was re-enacted substantially in its original form. . . .

It follows that, given a finding of unlawful discrimination, backpay should be denied only for reasons which, if applied generally, would not frustrate the central statutory purposes of eradicating discrimination throughout the economy and making persons whole for injuries suffered through past discrimination. The courts of appeals must maintain a consistent and principled application of the backpay provision, consonant with the twin statutory objectives, while at the same time recognizing that the trial court will often have the keener appreciation of those facts and circumstances peculiar to particular cases.

The District Court's stated grounds for denying backpay in this case must be tested against these standards. The first ground was that Albemarle's breach of Title VII had not been in "bad faith." This is not a sufficient reason for denying backpay. Where an employer has shown bad faith — by maintaining a practice which he knew to be illegal or of highly questionable legality — he can make no claims whatsoever on the Chancellor's conscience. But, under Title VII, the mere absence of bad faith simply opens the door to equity; it does not depress the scales in the employer's favor. If backpay were awardable only upon a showing of bad faith, the remedy would become a punishment for moral turpitude, rather than a compensation for workers' injuries. This would read the "make whole" purpose right out of Title VII, for a worker's injury is no less real simply because his employer did not inflict it in "bad faith." Title VII is not concerned with the employer's "good intent or absence of discriminatory intent" for "Congress directed the thrust of the Act to the consequences of employment practices, not simply the motivation."

III

In *Griggs* v. *Duke Power Co.,* 401 U.S. 424, this Court unanimously held that Title VII forbids the use of employment tests that are discriminatory in effect unless the employer meets "the burden of showing that any given requirement [has] . . . a manifest relation to the employment in question." *Id.*, at 432.[1] This burden arises, of course, only after the complaining party or class has made out a prima facie case of discrimination — has shown that the tests in question select applicants for hire or promotion in a racial pattern significantly different from that of the pool of applicants. . . . If an employer does then meet the burden of proving that its tests are "job related," it remains open to the complaining party to show that other tests or selection devices, without a similarly undesirable racial effect, would also serve the employer's legitimate interest in "efficient and trustworthy workmanship." Such a showing would be evidence that the employer was using its tests merely as a "pretext" for discrimination. . . . In the present case, however, we are concerned only with the question whether Albemarle has shown its tests to be job related.

The concept of job relatedness takes on meaning from the facts of the *Griggs* case. A power company in North Carolina had reserved its skilled jobs for whites prior to 1965. Thereafter, the company allowed Negro workers to transfer to skilled jobs, but all transferees — white and Negro — were required to attain national median scores on two tests,

> the Wonderlic Personnel Test, which purports to measure general intelligence, and the Bennett Mechanical Comprehension Test. Neither was directed or intended to measure the ability to learn to perform a particular job or category of jobs. . . . Both were adopted, as the Court of Appeals noted, without meaningful study of their relationship to job-performance ability. Rather, a vice president of the Company testified, the requirements were instituted on the Company's judgment that they generally would improve the overall quality of the workforce. (*Griggs* v. *Duke Power Co., supra,* at 428 and 431.)

The Court took note of "the inadequacy of broad and general testing devices as well as the infirmity of using diplomas or degrees as fixed measures of capability," and concluded:

> Nothing in the Act precludes the use of testing or measuring procedures; obviously they are useful. What Congress has forbidden is giving these devices and mechanisms controlling force unless they are demonstrably a reasonable measure of job performance. . . . What Congress has commanded is that any tests used must measure the person for the job and not the person in the abstract. (*Id.*, at 433 and 436).

Like the employer in *Griggs*, Albemarle uses two general ability tests, the Beta Examination, to test nonverbal intelligence, and the Wonderlic Test (Forms A and B), the purported measure of general verbal facility which was also involved in the *Griggs* case. Applicants for hire into various skilled lines of progression at the plant are required to score 100 on the Beta Exam and 18 on one of the Wonderlic Test's two alternate forms.

---

[1]In *Griggs* the Court was construing 42 U.S.C. §2000e-2 (h), which provides in pertinent part that it shall not "be an unlawful employment practice for an employer to give and to act upon the results of any professionally developed ability test provided that such test, its administration or action upon the results is not designed, intended, or used to discriminate because of race, color, religion, sex, or national origin."

The question of job relatedness must be viewed in the context of the plant's operation and the history of the testing program. The plant, which now employs about 650 persons, converts raw wood into paper products. It is organized into a number of functional departments, each with one or more distinct lines of progression, the theory being that workers can move up the line as they acquire the necessary skills. The number and structure of the lines has varied greatly over time. For many years, certain lines were themselves more skilled and paid higher wages than others, and until 1964 these skilled lines were expressly reserved for white workers. In 1968, many of the unskilled "Negro" lines were "end-tailed" on to skilled "white" lines, but it apparently remains true that at least the top jobs in certain lines require greater skills than the top jobs in other lines. In this sense, at least, it is still possible to speak of relatively skilled and relatively unskilled lines.

In the 1950s while the plant was being modernized with new and more sophisticated equipment, the company introduced a high school diploma requirement for entry into the skilled lines. Though the company soon concluded that this requirement did not improve the quality of the labor force, the requirement was continued until the District Court enjoined its use. In the late 1950s, the company began using the Beta Examination and the Bennett Mechanical Comprehension Test (also involved in the *Griggs* case) to screen applicants for entry into the skilled lines. The Bennett test was dropped several years later, but use of the Beta test continued.

The company added the Wonderlic Tests in 1963, for the skilled lines, on the theory that a certain verbal intelligence was called for by the increasing sophistication of the plant's operations. The company made no attempt to validate the test for job relatedness, and simply adopted the national "norm" score of 18 as a cut-off point for new job applicants. After 1964, when it discontinued overt segregation of the lines of progression, the company allowed Negro workers to transfer to the skilled lines if they could pass the Beta and Wonderlic Tests, but few succeeded in doing so. Incumbents in the skilled lines, some of whom had been hired before adoption of the tests, were not required to pass them to retain their jobs or their promotion rights. The record shows that a number of white incumbents in high ranking job groups could not pass the tests.

Because departmental reorganization continued up to the point of trial, and has indeed continued since that point, the details of the testing program are less than clear from the record. The District Court found that, since 1963, the Beta and Wonderlic tests have been used in thirteen lines of progression, within eight departments. Albemarle contends that at present the tests are used in only eight lines of progression, within four departments.

Four months before this case went to trial, Albemarle engaged an expert in industrial psychology to "validate" the job relatedness of its testing program. He spent a half day at the plant and devised a "concurrent validation" study, which was conducted by plant officials, without his supervision. The expert then subjected the results to statistical analysis. The study dealt with ten job groupings, selected from near the top of nine of the lines of progression. Jobs were grouped together solely by their proximity in the line of progression; no attempt was made to analyze jobs in terms of the particular skills they might require. All, or nearly all, employees in the selected groups participated in the study — 105 employees in all, but only four Negroes. Within each job grouping, the study compared the test scores of each employee with an independent "ranking" of the employee, relative to each of his co-workers, made by two of the employee's supervisors. The supervisors, who did not know the test scores, were asked to:

> determine which ones they felt irrespective of the job that they were actually doing, but in their respective jobs, did a better job than the person they were rating against. . . .

For each job grouping, the expert computed the "Phi coefficient" of statistical correlation between the test scores and an average of the two supervisional rankings. Consonant with professional conventions, the expert regarded as "statistically significant" any correlation that could have occurred by chance only five times, or less, in 100 trials. On the basis of these results, the District Court found that "[t] he personnel tests administered at the plant have undergone validation studies and have been proven to be job related." Like the Court of Appeals, we are constrained to disagree.

. The EEOC has issued "Guidelines" for employers seeking to determine, through professional validation studies, whether their employment tests are job related. . . . These guidelines draw upon and make reference to professional standards of test validation established by the American Psychological Association. The EEOC Guidelines are not administrative "regulations" promulgated pursuant to formal procedures established by the Congress. But, as this Court has heretofore noted, they do constitute "[t] he administrative interpretation of the Act by the enforcing agency," and consequently they are "entitled to great deference". . . .

The message of these Guidelines is the same as that of the *Griggs* case — that discriminatory tests are impermissible unless shown, by professionally acceptable methods, to be "predictive of or significantly correlated with important elements of work behavior which comprise or are relevant to the job or jobs for which candidates are being evaluated."

Measured against the Guidelines, Albemarle's validation study is materially defective in several respects:

1. Even if it had been otherwise adequate, the study would not have "validated" the Beta and Wonderlic test battery for all of the skilled lines of progression for which the two tests are, apparently, now required. The study showed significant correlations for the Beta Exam in only three of the eight lines. . . . The study . . . involved no analysis of the attributes of, or the particular skills needed in, the studied job groups. There is accordingly no basis for concluding that "no significant differences" exist among the lines of progression, or among distinct job groupings within the studied lines of progression. Indeed, the study's checkered results appear to compel the opposite conclusion.

2. The study compared test scores with subjective supervisorial rankings. While they allow the use of supervisorial rankings in test validation, the Guidelines quite plainly contemplate that the rankings will be elicited with far more care than was demonstrated here. Albemarle's supervisors were asked to rank employees by a "standard" that was extremely vague and fatally open to divergent interpretations. . . .

There is no way of knowing precisely what criteria of job performance the supervisors were considering, whether each of the supervisors was considering the same criteria — or whether, indeed, any of the supervisors actually applied a focused and stable body of criteria of any kind. There is, in short, simply no way to determine whether the criteria actually considered were sufficiently related to the Company's legitimate interest in job-specific ability to justify a testing system with a racially discriminatory impact.

3. The company's study focused, in most cases, on job groups near the top of the various lines of progression. In *Griggs* v. *Duke Power Co., supra,* the Court left open "the question whether testing requirements that take into account capability for the next succeeding position or related future promotion might be utilized upon a showing that such long-range requirements fulfill a genuine business need." 401 U.S., at 432. The Guidelines take a sensible approach to this issue, and we now endorse it:

"If job progression structures and seniority provisions are so established that new employees will probably, within a reasonable period of time and in a great majority of cases, progress to a higher level, it may be considered that candidates are being evaluated for jobs at that higher level. However, where job progression is not so nearly automatic, or the time span is such that higher level jobs or employees' potential may be expected to change in significant ways, it shall be considered that candidates are being evaluated for a job at or near the entry level." . . .

The fact that the best of those employees working near the top of a line of progression score well on a test does not necessarily mean that that test, or some particular cutoff score on the test, is a permissible measure of the minimal qualifications of new workers, entering lower level jobs. In drawing any such conclusion, detailed consideration must be given to the normal speed of promotion, to the efficacy of on-the-job training in the scheme of promotion, and to the possible use of testing as a promotion device, rather than as a screen for entry into low-level jobs. The District Court made no findings on these issues. The issues take on special importance in a case, such as this one, where incumbent employees are permitted to work at even high-level jobs without passing the company's test battery.

4. Albemarle's validation study dealt only with job-experienced, white workers; but the tests themselves are given to new job applicants, who are younger, largely inexperienced, and in many instances nonwhite. The Standards of the American Psychological Association state that it is "essential" that

[t]he validity of a test should be determined on subjects who are at the age or in the same educational or vocational situation as the persons for whom the test is recommended in practice.

For all these reasons, we agree with the Court of Appeals that the District Court erred in concluding that Albemarle had proved the job relatedness of its testing program and that the respondents were consequently not entitled to equitable relief.

Accordingly, the judgment is vacated, and these cases are remanded to the District Court for proceedings consistent with this opinion.

It is so ordered.

Mr. Justice Powell did not participate in the consideration or decision of these cases.

♦♦♦

Case Questions

1. Why did the District Court refuse to award back pay to the plaintiffs?
2. Under what circumstances will a court award back pay to a class of employees who have been discriminated against?
3. If tests are used for job qualification and promotion what is the standard they must meet?

OCCUPATIONAL SAFETY

Job related injuries cost the work force and the economy staggering amounts. For example, it is estimated that 14,200 workers were killed in 1973 and 2.5 million were permanently or temporarily disabled by on-the-job accidents. Two hundred fifty million man-days annually are lost to job injuries in industries covered by new federal legislation.[8]

The legal history of worker compensation for work-related injuries and of worker protection from unsafe working conditions is a sorry one. As the industrial revolution grew in this country the law did not develop a corresponding duty for employers to furnish a safe work place. Indeed, the early common law provided the injured worker little chance for compensation. First, an injured worker put his job in jeopardy by suing or threatening to sue an employer who may have been negligent in providing faulty tools or an unsafe workplace. Similarly, witnesses, often fellow workers, were hesitant to testify against the employer.

The greatest deterrents to compensation, however, were the legal defenses available to the employer. The early common law developed and established three rules ordinarily used by an employer: 1) if an injury was caused by *another employee,* the common law held that the employer was not liable — this was called the Fellow-Servant Rule; 2) if the job was dangerous and had known risks, then the employer could defend on the basis of the employee's "assumption of the risks" when he took the job; and 3) if the *employee's* lack of care played a part in the injury, then the employer could defend on the basis of contributory negligence. These defenses have been limited substantially today.

In response to a growing public awareness of both the cost to our society of work-related injuries and the increasing evidence that places of work once thought relatively safe (working in air-polluted factories for example) do pose substantial threats to human life, Congress passed The Williams Steiger Occupational Safety and Health Act of 1970.[9] This Act became effective April 28, 1971. The Act establishes the Occupational Safety and Health Administration. The public has adopted the abbreviation of OSHA to refer to both the Act and the administrative agency.

The Act applies to all persons engaged in a business affecting commerce who have employees. It does not cover those places of work already covered by the Coal Mine Health and Safety Act or the Atomic Energy Act. Also, municipal, county, state and federal government workers are not directly covered by OSHA. Many states, however, do have occupational safety acts or plans which do include municipal, county, and state employees.

The Act places two major duties on employers. First, employers must furnish to employees a place of employment which is *free* from *recognized hazards* that are *likely* to cause *death* or *serious physical harm.*[10] This statement is referred to as the general duty clause of the act, but it applies *only* where no specific safety standard promulgated under the act is applicable. A second and related duty is for the employer to comply with all appropriate standards for safety. The Secretary of Labor and his agents have promulgated literally thousands of safety standards which apply to employers. Most of these safety standards were developed from earlier "national consensus standards" developed by nationally recognized standards producing organizations such as the American National Standards Institute and the National Fire Protection Association. These very specific safety standards cover subjects such as the proper construction and maintenance of equipment; machine guarding; and, fire and injury prevention procedures. They also specify the type of personal protective equipment worn by employees and training requirements necessary to insure safe work practices.

In addition to complying with the two major duties above, employers with more than 10 employees must also keep substantial records and make reports on all work-related injuries and deaths. It must be remembered that the Act does not provide for compensation for injuries nor affect workman's compensation. It is not compensatory in concept. It is preventative.

To insure compliance with the standards promulgated an agent of the federal government charged with enforcing OSHA may enter any place of work at any reasonable time and in a reasonable manner. This agent may question any employee or make any reasonable inspection or investigation. If upon inspection a violation is believed to exist, a citation will be issued. The employer is given a reasonable time to remedy the situation (not longer than six months); if the citation or one of the safety standards used is believed unreasonable the employer may seek to appeal the citation or standard to an administrative law judge assigned to the case by the Occupational Safety and Health Commission; this appeal is an adversary one with the appealing party being opposed by the Secretary of Labor. The decision of this judge becomes final unless a member of the Commission agrees to hear an appeal to the full Commission. If the Commission rules against the employer, or if the Commission refuses to hear an appeal, the employer may appeal the case to the U.S. Court of Appeals for the circuit in which the violation allegedly occurred or where the party has his principal place of business.

Any employer who *willfully* and *repeatedly* violates the general duty clause may be assessed a civil penalty of not more than $10,000 for each violation; the fine is $1,000 for a simple violation. However, any employer who fails to correct a violation may be assessed not over $1,000 each day such failure continues.

The Act takes cognizance of the lack of protection afforded employees at common law who wished to charge their employers with maintaining unsafe work areas. Under the Act, an employee may report a violation of a standard to an area OSHA office on a complaint form which allows the reporter to remain anonymous. If there is an imminent danger alleged or if the complaint appears valid an inspection will follow within a reasonable time. If the employee wishes to reveal his identity, he may walk with the inspector during the visit to the work site. If he believes he has been discriminated against because he reported the company, he may file a complaint with OSHA and, if the charges are proven, he may be compensated.

At this early stage it is not easy to assess the impact of the Act. Since many cases have now reached the appellate court level it can be assumed that enforcement activity is well underway. Much of the litigation to date centers on the interpretations of the general duty clause. Although detailed safety standards are available and cover most usual employment circumstances, they cannot cover every situation. The general duty clause was intended to impose safety duties where no specific expressed standards were available. It should be noted that where a general duty clause violation is alleged, the common law fellow-servant rule and the defenses of assumption of risk and contributory negligence are not available to the employer.

Because this new law will grow and, perhaps, change by means of court interpretations of the general duty clause, we present here some of the decisions construing its meaning. As stated above, the general duty clause requires each employer to furnish employees a place of employment free from recognized hazards which might cause death or serious physical harm. Much litigation has focused on the meaning of the words "recognized hazards." Is an employer liable for a violation of the act where injury was caused by an event it could not have foreseen? In one of the early cases a foreman of the employer was riding on the running board of a front-end loader as it descended a small hill at a construction site. The engine stalled causing a loss of control over the vehicle resulting in the death of the foreman. [*National Realty & Construction Co.* v. *OSAHRC*, 489 F. 2d 1257 (D.C. Cir., 1973).] The court held that the hazard of riding on heavy equipment was "recognized" and was "likely to cause death or serious physical harm" but held that there was no violation of the general duty clause because it was not shown what the employer could have done to eliminate the hazard. A violation of the clause does not exist when isolated and unpreventable accidents occur.

A similar result was reached when a new employee on the job only four days unexplainably cut a steel band around railroad ties which were being lifted into the air. He was killed when they fell on him. [*Brennan* v. *OSAHRC and Republic Creosoting Co.*, 487 F. 2d 438 (8th Cir., 1973).] In this case the result (the falling of the ties) was so obvious that no amount of training would have eliminated the hazard.

It is clear under some recent decisions that failure to properly train an employee may result in liability. In a 1974 decision a supervisor for an employer instructed employees to open elevator hoistway doors by tripping an emergency release device. This procedure led to an employee stepping into an open elevator shaft and falling to his death. The Commission held this was a violation of the general duty clause because the employer had instructed a person to open the doors without giving him proper warning or training. (*National Cleaning Contractors, Inc.*, OSAHRC docket #4740, Nov., 1974). The employer does not have to be aware of the hazard to be liable; it is sufficient if the hazard would be recognizable by a prudent person.

A second line of decisions involves the liability of employers who request employees to work at a work cite where employees of other employers are also working. It appears that liability is created even though the employer did not create the unsafe condition but required an employee to work where there was such a condition. One employer asserted in defense of an alleged violation that it was not responsible for the cleaning up of scrap lumber with protruding nails. Neither it nor its employees had any duty with regard to the lumber. The Commission found that the mere exposure of its employees to the hazard suffices regardless of who created the hazardous conditions. (*Johns Manville Sales Corp.,* OSAHRC docket #3163, Nov., 1974) This decision and related ones establish the principle that a place of employment is any place the employer requires the employee to work.

It has been held that even where a general contractor promises sub-contractors, it will be solely responsible for the safety conditions on the job site, this will not relieve sub-contractors from liability if the general duty clause is violated. [*Bayside Pipe Coats, Inc.,* OSAHRC #1953 (1974)]

In summary, the litigation prompted by OSHA has focused on the "recognized hazard" and "place of employment" phrases of the general duty clause. A recognized hazard (see the *American Smelting* decision below) is not one limited to detection by the human senses. Sensitive machines may be used. So, a violation of the general duty clause will exist if the hazard 1) is common knowlege or generally recognized in the particular industry in which it occurs, and is 2) detectable by the human senses or is of such wide general recognition as a hazard in the industry that there are generally accepted tests for its existence which should be known to the employer.[11]

We have presented two decisions on OSHA, below. The first, *American Smelting* deals with two issues. The first is the definition of a "recognized hazard" and the second (not so obvious) point is that a violation may occur without obvious permanent injury to the employee. The act requires that the hazards are causing or *are likely* to cause death or serious harm to employees.

The *Pecosteel-Arizona* decision illustrates that an employer can not evade liability by delegating the duty of providing a safe work place to an employee.

AMERICAN SMELTING AND REFINING COMPANY v. OSAHRC
501 F2d 504 (C.A., 82, 1974)

◆◆◆

GIBSON, Circuit Judge

Petitioner, American Smelting and Refining Company, upon complaint of the United Steelworkers of America (Union), was charged with a violation of the Occupational Safety and Health Act of 1970, 29 U.S.C. Sec. 651 et seq. (hereafter the Act or OSHA), in allowing the existence of a health hazard at its Omaha, Nebraska, plant. Specifically, Petitioner was charged with exposing its employees to hazardous airborne concentrations of lead. The Act's general purpose and its "general duty" clause evidence a clear Congressional purpose to provide employees a safe and nonhazardous environment in which business, including commercial and industrial corporations, is to be conducted.

The complaint of the Union about unsafe working conditions triggered an investigation of plant conditions and monitoring of the working environment present in the Petitioner's plant by personnel of the Secretary of Labor's office. The airborne lead concentrations within the plant varied depending on the type of industrial operation being performed in certain work areas, but the results obtained were adequate to indicate that long-range preventative engineering practices should be instituted within a six-month period, preceded by immediate administrative controls of approved respirators, rotation of employees, and any other appropriate measures.

The complaint and investigation, with its monitoring tests, resulted in a citation being issued. ... The citation was contested by Petitioner, causing the matter to be forwarded to the commission for hearing. After a hearing, the Administrative Law Judge on March 1, 1972, found that airborne concentrations in inorganic lead at American Smelting and Refining Company's Omaha plant presented "a recognized hazard that (was) likely to cause, if continued unabated, death or serious physical harm to employees, and as such, constituted a violation of Section 5(a)(1) (the general duty provision) of the Act." The Occupational Safety and Health Review Commission (the Commission) directed review and on August 17, 1973, upheld the Administrative Law Judge's finding of a violation. Chairman Moran vigorously dissented. The Petitioner filed this appeal for review of the Commission's order. ...

The petitioner, a New Jersey corporation, operates a lead refining plant in Omaha, Nebraska, and employs 390 to 400 workers there. Receiving lead bullion in solid blocks, the plant produces commercial grades of refined lead and lead alloys by separating impurities from the lead. Recovery of the impurities is also accomplished where possible. The Omaha plant, one of the Petitioner's lead refineries, was purchased before 1910 and has since produced refined lead and lead alloys.

Three representatives of the Secretary visited Petitioner's Omaha plant on June 30, 1971, to evaluate the presence of harmful concentrations of airborne lead.[1] The plant's personnel director and plant manager fully cooperated and conducted a tour of the plant. Of the 390 to 400 workers, approximately 95 work in areas that may be affected periodically by high levels of airborne concentrations of lead. ...

While inspecting the plant, the Secretary's representatives ... observed that all but one of the employees had their company-supplied respirators hanging around their necks, rather than properly wearing them over their noses and mouths. After the tour of the plant, the representatives decided to take air samples of the melting, cupel, retort, and crane areas. Respondent chose seven employees and placed an air sampling pump on each employee. ... The representatives activated the pumps on each of the seven workers, and the pumps were in place for approximately two hours and fifty-seven minutes. This period of time was sufficient to allow each worker to complete at least one complete cycle of his normal work throughout the plant. ...

---

[1] 29 U.S.C. Sec. 657(a) authorizes the Secretary to enter without delay, inspect, and investigate places of employment at reasonable times. Any employee or representative of employees may request an inspection by the Secretary. ...

The following results were obtained:

Employee's Name	His Working Area	Concentration of Lead[2]
Zandijas	Retort	2.70 mg/M^3
Gulizia	Retort (cupel)	0.75 mg/M^3
Rojas	Retort (cupel)	2.85 mg/M^3

The Respondents throughout these proceedings have maintained that the industry recognizes that any lead concentration above .2 mg/M^3 constitutes a hazardous condition. The Petitioner counters by claiming generally that air sampling is inferior to periodic biological testing of each employee's blood and urine and acting upon those results with medical care and transfers to work areas of lesser lead concentrations. Mainly because of its biological monitoring of each employee, the Petitioner argues that there was not a recognized hazard in the plant causing or likely to cause death or serious physical harm to the employees. ...

On March 1, 1972, Administrative Law Judge Brennan filed an extensive report of 47 pages. He found that .2 mg/M^3 of airborne lead concentration is generally recognized by the industry as the safe level, that a "recognized hazard" existed in violation of the general duty clause due to concentrations for airborne lead greater than .2 mg/M^3, and that the Petitioner's "preventive program" including biological monitoring, the required use of respirators, and transfers of employees with high levels of lead concentration in blood and urine samples did not negate a finding of a recognized hazard. Having found a violation of the general duty clause, the Administrative Law Judge required the Petitioner to complete feasible engineering controls to reduce the concentration of airborne lead contaminants to .2 mg/M^3 or below within six months from the entry of a final order. He also approved the Secretary's assessment of a $600 fine, specifically finding it was a civil penalty and constitutional. ...

Relying on limited though express legislative history, the Petitioner argues that the general duty clause was not intended to cover hazards that can be detected only by testing devices. Since the airborne concentrations of lead in excess of .2 mg/M^3 were discovered by air sampling pumps instead of the human senses, Petitioner argues that no recognized hazard existed. In short, "recognized" only means recognized directly by human senses without the assistance of any technical instruments. ...

We find Petitioner and Chairman Moran's views unpersuasive. Looking to the words of the Act itself, "recognized hazards" was enacted instead of "readily apparent hazards." From the commonly understood meanings of the terms themselves, "recognized" denotes a broader meaning than "readily apparent."

We further think that the purpose and intent of the Act is to protect the health of the workers and that a narrow construction of the general duty clause would endanger this purpose in many cases. To expose workers to health dangers that may not be emergency situations and to limit the general duty clause to dangers only detectable by the human senses seems to us to be a folly. Our technological age depends on instrumentation to monitor many conditions of industrial operations and the environment. Where hazards are recognized but not detectable by the senses, common sense and prudence demand that

---

[2] The symbol "mg/M^3" represents miligrams per cubic meter of air and is the commonly used measure.

instrumentation be utilized. Certain kinds of health hazards, such as carbon monoxide and asbestos poisoning, can only be detected by technical devices. . . . The Petitioner's contention, though advanced by arguable but loose legislative interpretation, would have us accept a result that would ignore the advances of industrial scientists, technologists, and hygienists, and also ignore the plain working, purpose, and intent of this Act. The health of workers should not be subjected to such a narrow construction. . . .

The Petitioner's . . . contention is that it has instituted many protective measures that prevent the likelihood of harm to the employees. We agree with the Administrative Law Judge that Petitioner's program has not reduced the likelihood of serious physical harm.

Petitioner does have a program to attempt to eliminate the dangers of lead poisoning. It has spent over $400,000 since 1960 on various engineering controls to reduce airborne lead contamination. Industrial hygienists and physicians are employed. Respirators are supplied, but admittedly are awkward to wear and seldom used.

Most important in the Petitioner's view is a reliance on a biological monitoring program, which involves the testing of each employee's blood and urine to determine the concentration of lead. Dr. Nelson, the Petitioner's Director of Environmental Sciences, stated that this testing is "a far more effective way of securing the safety of employees." Dr. Kehoe prefers biological monitoring, since air measurement "is not a standard which we regard as crucial in relation to the individual." For as yet unexplained reasons, differing individuals can be exposed to higher amounts of lead without becoming ill. The candid Dr. Kehoe, however, had this exchange with the Administrative Law Judge:

> (Administrative Law Judge) Which procedure, Doctor, in your opinion would most greatly detect a change in the lead environment of a workplace, biological sampling or air sampling?
> (Dr. Kehoe) Either one. I don't know that there is too much to choose from in this. But what I, as a physician, am concerned with is John Doe.

Although a carefully conducted biological monitoring system might prevent the likelihood of lead poisoning harm to employees, we think it was more than reasonable for the Secretary to rely on the effective and efficient air sampling method. In addition, the disadvantages of the biological sampling system are demonstrated in this case. About 10 percent of employees tested from 1970-71 were found to have unsafe levels of lead concentration in their blood and urine, yet generally these employees were not tested frequently enough, according to Petitioner's expert testimony, to ascertain whether they should be changed to another working area in the plant. In fact, the plant manager had no direct involvement with the monitoring plan. . . . The biological monitoring did not eliminate or even reduce the hazard; it merely disclosed it. Although testing of the blood and urine is the most important test for each individual, the use of air sampling tests is the most efficient and practical way for the Secretary to check for a hazard likely to cause death or serious physical harm to the workers as a group. We think it also the most efficient manner for the employer to check the existence of a hazard. . . . Workers should not be subjected to hazardous concentrations of airborne lead; biological monitoring should complement an industrial hygiene program for clean or at least safe air, it is not a substitute for a healthful working environment.

In addition, the Petitioner knew or should have known that the respirators would not reduce the likelihood of serious physical harm to the employees. During the unannounced tour of the plant by the Secretary's representatives, only one employee was properly wearing his respirator. The reasonable inference is that employees rarely used the awkward and uncomfortable respirators. It was reasonably foreseeable to the Petitioner that the respirators would not be properly worn. We hold that there was adequate evidence on the record considered as a whole that the biological monitoring program would not prevent a likelihood of harm to employees.

The Petitioner also argues that the $600 assessed . . . though labeled a civil penalty, is punitive in nature and an unconstitutional abridgment of Petitioner's right to criminal enforcement only through the courts. Civil penalties are not uncommon in federal law, and Congress here clearly intended to create a civil sanction. *Helvering* v. *Mitchell,* 303 U.S. 391, 399 (1938).

Affirming the decision of the Commission, we deny relief to the Petitioner.

◆◆◆

Case Questions

1. Of what value was the biological monitoring system? It did not eliminate the hazard. Apparently, it just provided a basis for a management decision to move the employees away from the hazard.
2. What are the duties of an employer when it finds almost all of its employees do not use the safety devices provided? The OSHA legislation does not put a duty on the employee to abide by the safety rules and standards promulgated by the employer. The matter of employee discipline for failing to follow instructions is left entirely to the employer.

SECRETARY OF LABOR v. STRUCTURAL STEEL ERECTORS, INC., D/B/A PECOSTEEL, ARIZONA
2 Occ. Safety & Health Cases 1507, 1975

(Author's note: This is a decision by the Occupational Safety & Health Review Commission.)

VAN NAMEE, Commissioner

This matter presents the question whether the hearing judge committed reversible error by finding that Respondent did not, and could not with the exercise of reasonable diligence, know that its managing foreman would leave a skylight opening unprotected contrary to the requirements of . . . section 5(a)(2) of the Occupational Safety and Health Act of 1970 (29 U.S.C. 651 *et seq.*). The matter arose out of the following facts.

Respondent had been engaged to install a roof on a water tank in Tombstone, Arizona. The tank measured 92½ feet across and 22½ feet deep. It was to be roofed over with corrugated metal sheets capable of supporting the weight of a 200-pound man. It was to be provided with four skylights each measuring 4 by 16 feet. The skylights were to be covered with plastic sheets, and the sheets were incapable of supporting a 200-pound man.

Respondent's vice-president and general manager met with other company personnel before commencement of construction. At the meeting it was recognized that the plastic sheets would constitute a safety hazard and various precautions were discussed. However, no decision regarding safety precautions was made.

Rather, job foreman Bill Manners was assigned to supervise the job, and he was given the authority to determine safety precautions. Manners had complete responsibility for the job, but he was not in attendance at the meeting.

Manners determined that once a plastic sheet was installed it was to be covered by metal sheeting and the metal sheets were temporarily secured by screws. This practice was followed. However, on November 15, 1972, thirteen metal sheets necessary for completion of the job were not delivered. Manners therefore decided to remove the metal sheets then covering the skylights and place them elsewhere. Manners and an employee performed the job. They returned the next morning and, as was their custom, warned each other of skylight hazard. A short while later Manners fell through a skylight and was killed.

On these facts Complainant issued a citation for an alleged serious violation of the above-noted standard. Respondent contested, and the matter went to hearing. The hearing judge determined that Manners unquestionably committed a serious violation, but he also determined to vacate because the record "does not establish that Respondent's supervisory personnel had actual knowledge of the foreman's actions."

One week later the same hearing judge, in a case having strikingly similar facts, said as follows:

"A corporate employer can only operate through its agents and therefore, its absolute and continuing duty to "comply with occupational safety and health standards, promulgated under this Act" (Section 5(a)(2) of the Act) necessarily has to be delegated to supervisory personnel. This delegation, however, cannot be permitted to relieve the corporate employer of its duty to comply with a particular standard: otherwise, the effectiveness of safety standards would be nullified and the manifest legislative intent of the Act defeated. If a corporate employer entrusts supervisory personnel with the performance of activities which involve compliance with safety and health standards, the employer continues to be responsible for the failure of its supervisors to comply with the standards. This principle is clearly consistent with the Congressional intent to impose on employers "final responsibility for compliance with the Act" (see S. Report No. 91-1282, 91st Cong. 2d Session, pp. 10-11).

The Respondent had assigned the task of setting the two heavy steel beams which required the use of a crane to its foreman. Thereafter, whatever action the foreman took in furtherance of carrying out this work assignment, even action resulting in violation of the crane standard, must be deemed to have been done within the scope of his employment and imputed to the Respondent. Also, just as the foreman's actions on October 2, 1972 must be attributed to the Respondent, so must the foreman's knowledge be imputed to the Respondent.

We think his statements are entirely appropriate for resolving this case. Manners was the supervisor in charge and had been so assigned by Respondent. Accordingly, his actions as well as his knowledge must be imputed to this Respondent. . . . We will therefore affirm the citation.

Turning now to the matter of an appropriate penalty we note that Respondent is small in size (its annual gross is $340,000); it has no prior history; and, it appears to have acted in good faith. We find the gravity of the violation to be moderate in that two employees were briefly exposed to the hazard but the consequences were severe. The proposed penalty of $550 is appropriate.

Accordingly, the citation for a serious violation of 29 C.F.R. 1926.500(b)(4) as amended is affirmed, and a penalty of $550 is assessed therefore. The hearing judge's decision to the contrary is reversed. It is so ORDERED.

◆◆◆

Case Questions

1. Describe the event or act for which the citation was issued. Whose responsibility was it to see that this safety hazard was eliminated?
2. Practically speaking, could Manners have refused to work since the metal coverings were not delivered? Probably not! Therefore, perhaps the best practical remedy for this type of situation is to reach the result achieved in this case.
3. Does not the Commission use the same approach here that the court struggles with but ultimately used in the *Humphrey* v. *Virginian Ry. Co.* case in Chapter 5? Also, do you see a similiarity between the reasoning of the Commission and the application of absolute liability in tort law?

The Employment Retirement Income Security Act of 1974

The Employment Retirement Income Security Act of 1974 became law on Labor Day, 1974.[12] It is a very complex piece of legislation and, like OSHA, is so new any statements about its value must be tenuous. We present here just a brief overview.

Many employers and most large corporations provide retirement plans of some kind for their employees. Usually the employee and employer both contribute to a fund which is administered for the benefit of the employee. Funds are invested conservatively so that slight growth in the fund can be expected. At retirement age, the employee typically could withdraw all or part of his share. However, at least three major events could disasterously alter one's hopes of a secure retirement: 1) the employee could be discharged or quit before any legal right to the retirement funds accrued; or 2) the firm could fail and the retirement fund might be paid over to creditors; or, 3) those in charge of the administration of the fund could abuse their position and either embezzle or squander the funds. This new legislation attempts to overcome these unfortunate results or at least minimize them. The act primarily assures participants in a pension fund program that they will get what they planned on when they retire or quit. To achieve this, the act emphasises: 1) the vesting of rights in the fund; 2) insurance against company collapse, and 3) strict duties for the administrators of the fund.

The law does not require that a corporation have a pension plan. For those that do, however, the following requirements apply. First, the plan must cover all employees who are at least 25 years old and have one year of service. If the employee is to have an immediate vested right in the retirement benefits upon payment to the fund, then three years of service may be required. Second, employers may choose one of three ways to let employees gain vested or guaranteed rights in the fund which become payable at the retirement age provided in the plan or at age 65. The first of these is to provide that rights in the pension plan become nonforfeitable after ten years of service, even if the employee quits. A second method of allowing a participant to gain vested or guaranteed rights in the plan is to provide that he be entitled to 25 percent of the accrued benefits after five years of service and this percentage would increase to 50 percent after 10 years and 100 percent after fifteen years. A third method of guaranteeing a worker benefits is to adopt the "rule of 45" which provides half of his benefits when the age of the worker and years of service total forty-five (but a minimum of five years of service is required.) For younger participants, the rule provides for full vesting after fifteen years of service. These three methods just discussed provide a measure of protection for the employee against discharge or circumstances compelling one to quit.

Another objective of the act is to protect employees benefits when the corporation fails. A study by the Labor and Treasury Departments reveals that 1,227 pension plans terminated in 1972 resulting in almost $50 million of lost benefits to approximately 20,000 participants.[13] The act creates a new Public Pension Benefit Guaranty Corporation which guarantees workers through a scheme of insurance that they will receive the benefits they are entitled to if the company fails. The premiums for this insurance are about one dollar per worker per year or 50 cents each for workers under more comprehensive multi-employer plans. The insurance will provide maximum benefits to the lesser of $750 per month or 100 percent of the employees average wages for his best paid five consecutive years of employment. This corporation could also seek to recover from the employer up to 30 percent of the collapsed firm's net worth if pension fund assets were insufficient to pay benefits.

Thirdly, some of the act's major provisions concern the standards to be observed by the fiduciaries administering the plan. Such fiduciaries are barred from engaging in such transactions as buying for the pension fund property they own personally. Pension funds holding stock and real property of the employer must reduce such holdings to 10 percent of the fund's total assets over the next ten years.

To insure compliance with the terms of the act, extensive reporting requirements must be met. Reports to employees, the Labor and Treasury Departments and the Pension Benefit Guaranty Corporation are necessary. This reporting is designed to provide detailed information to the government as well as to participants in the plan.

Some authorities such as New York's Senator Jacob Javits declare that this Act is the first major achievement since Social Security to provide for the security of workers in retirement years.[14] Although it is estimated that the act will affect over thirty million persons presently covered by private pension plans,[15] many view the act as just one more costly type of interference from the federal government.

RECENTLY DEVELOPED LEGAL DUTIES OF BUSINESS ASSOCIATIONS TO THE PUBLIC

This section of the chapter presents an overview of emerging legal duties which run from the business association to the public. Of course business associations are under the same duties as are all individuals with regard to the commission of torts, crimes or the breach of contracts. These topics have been discussed in the first portion of this book. However, the law places on business associations additional duties when that association sells a product to the public or poses a threat to the environment when it produces the product.

The general duties creating association liability for producing a faulty product or for polluting are the subjects of this portion of the chapter. The laws creating these duties are now an unclear mix of state and federal duties. The law of product liability has, until very recently, been created by the state legislatures and courts. However, for reasons explained later, federal legislation on the warranties made by sellers has recently passed Congress and is now in force. These federal duties are integrated with the state level duties discussed.

Environmental duties are also a mixture of state and federal enforcement. However, because the states vary so widely in their enforcement of their environmental laws we will focus only upon the federal effort.

PRODUCT LIABILITY

This material describes the circumstances in which the manufacturer or seller of products will be liable because the product failed to perform as promised (warranted) or failed to perform safely. As noted before in Chapters 4 and 8, it is sometimes useful to present the material by dividing it into contract and tort duties. This is certainly true of the law of product liability. Both the contract law and tort law have shown substantial growth and change in this area since the early 1960s. Much of this growth has been in state legislative and common law. Although this chapter emphasizes federal law we begin oru discussion of product liability with state law in order to present a full picture of the circumstances in which a manufacturer or seller of a product will be liable if the product does not perform as promised.

Contract Liability Through Warranty: State Law

The Uniform Commercial Code (U.C.C.) is a comprehensive piece of legislation which, in its Article 2, covers contracts for the sale of goods. Contracts for services are not covered. Work on this legislation began in the 1940s and by 1968, only Louisiana had not adopted most portions of the code in its state legislative scheme. This is the legislation referred to in Chapter 1 which supplanted much of the common law of contracts.

One of the firmly entrenched common law concepts was *caveat emptor* (buyer beware). This phrase stood for the legal principle that the buyer of a product had a duty to inspect and try out the product before purchase. If the buyer satisfied this duty or failed to exercise his privilege of a thorough inspection, and then purchased a product which subsequently failed, it was his loss. Although there are some vestiges of this principle in today's court opinions, generally speaking, it is in a state of sharp descent. As a result of the increasing complexity of consumer goods, the principle simply was no longer fair. It was impossible to tell before purchase, for example, if a complex piece of machinery such as an automobile could not only fulfill all of the expectations of the purchaser but would also last a reasonable length of time. More and more consumers were led to rely on the seller's assertions of performances and the seller's judgment in selecting the goods for the purchaser's needs.

The U.C.C. recognizes this shift in consumer reliance by providing that a seller of goods may be liable for breach of warranty in three circumstances.

Section 2-313 of Article 2 of the U.C.C. provides:

(1) Express warranties by the seller are created as follows:
    (a) Any affirmation of fact or promise made by the seller to the buyer which relates to the goods and becomes part of the basis of the bargain creates an express warranty that the goods shall conform to the affirmation or promise.
    (b) Any description of the goods which is made part of the basis of the bargain creates an express warranty that the goods shall conform to the description.
    (c) Any sample or model which is made part of the basis of the bargain creates an express warranty that the whole of the goods shall conform to the sample or model.

(2) It is not necessary to the creation of an express warranty that the seller use formal words such as "warranty" or "guarantee" or that he have a specific intention to make a warranty, but an affirmation merely of the value of the goods or a statement purporting to be merely the seller's opinion or commendation of the goods does not create a warranty.

If a consumer *relies* on a promise of the seller or manufacturer which is made on the packaging material or in advertising materials or made by the selling agent at the time of sale and the item fails to fulfill that promise then the seller is given a cause of action against the seller or manufacturer based upon Section 2-313 for a breach of the promise.

Section 2-314 provides:

(1) Unless excluded or modified . . . a warranty that the goods shall be merchantable is implied in a contract for their sale if the seller is a merchant with respect to goods of that kind. Under this section the serving for value of food or drink to be consumed either on the premises or elsewhere is a sale.

(2) Goods to be merchantable must be at least such as
    (a) pass without objection in the trade under the contract description; and
    (b) in the case of fungible goods, are of fair average quality within the description; and

> (c) are fit for the ordinary purposes for which such goods are used, and
>
> (d) run, within the variations permitted by the agreement, of even kind, quality and quantity within each unit and among all units involved; and
>
> (e) are adequately contained, packaged, and labeled as the agreement may require; and
>
> (f) conform to the promises or affirmations of fact made on the container or label if any.
>
> (3) Unless excluded or modified ... other implied warranties may arise from course of dealings or usage of trade.

Section 2-315 provides:

> Where the seller at the time of contracting has reason to know any particular purpose for which the goods are required and that the buyer is relying on the seller's skill or judgment to select or furnish suitable goods, there is unless excluded or modified under the next section an implied warranty that the goods shall be fit for such purpose.

Now that these three sections are before you, several differences in their terms should be noted. First observe that Sections 2-313 and 2-315 apply to *sellers* of goods and Section 2-314 applies to sellers who are merchants. The term "merchant" as it is used here is narrower than the term seller and refers to a person, a corporation or other legal entity who deals in goods of the kind sold or holds itself out as having knowledge or skill peculiar to the goods involved. [U.C.C. § 2-104(1)]. A seller is anyone who is selling. Secondly, note that in both Sections 2-314 and 2-315 the words "unless excluded or modified" appear.

Section 2-316 provides for the exclusion or modification of warranties. Somewhat simplified, this section provides that if an *express warranty* is made under Section 2-313 and then an attempt to exclude or modify the warranty is attempted by the seller, it will not be allowed because such an attempt is inconsistent with the making of the *expressed warranty*. Thus *express warranties* may not be excluded or modified once they are made. The Section further provides that to exclude or modify the *implied warranty of merchantability* (§ 2-314) the language so used must mention merchantability and must be conspicuous. To exclude or modify the implied warranty of fitness for a particular purpose (§ 2-315) there must be a writing and the language must be conspicuous. The U.C.C. further provides in Section 2-316 that the expression "as is" or "with all faults" or other language commonly used to exclude warranties does operate to exclude implied warranties. If the packaging states "there are no warranties which extend beyond the description on the face hereof" this will operate to exclude all warranties of fitness. There are also other provisions relating to the waiver of warranties, but the point to be made is that the waiver and modification provisions are present in the U.C.C. and they are often used by manufacturers and sellers so that little protection is afforded the consumer. This is especially true where all of the manufacturers in a market adopt the same waiver and modification provisions. (See the *Henningen* case.) The potential abuse of the waiver and modification section of the U.C.C. is one of the major reasons for the passage of recent federal legislation dealing with warranties. Before we proceed to a discussion of this legislation, however, a second problem area of the U.C.C. must be identified.

The warranty provisions already discussed do not differentiate between the various levels of distribution for a product. Typically an item is produced and packaged by a manufacturer, shipped to a wholesaler which distributes to a retailer, which sells to a consumer. At each level, title to the goods may change hands so that a "sale of goods" has taken place. If there is a breach of a warranty, against whom may the consumer bring suit? The code itself does not answer this question. One might argue that a consumer could sue his or her seller, that the seller could sue its seller and so on up the chain until the manufacturer or the one responsible for the breach is ultimately liable. This result would not only cause a needless multiplicity of law suits but might result in difficulties if one of the sellers is insolvent. Nevertheless, some courts have read the U.C.C. as compelling this result. However, the better view is that such a result is not required nor was it intended by the drafters of the U.C.C.[16]. Most recent cases have allowed an injured consumer to sue the manufacturer based upon warranties made by it. This result not only places liability on those who are ultimately responsible for the breach, but is fair in light of the massive advertising campaigns by many manufacturers inducing consumers to buy.

A related problem is to whom do the warranties extend? Section 2-318 of the U.C.C. provides in part that:

> A seller's warranty whether express or implied extends to any natural person who is in the family or household of his buyer or who is a guest in his home if it is reasonable to expect that such person may use, consume or be affected by the goods. . . .

Some courts have reasoned that since the U.C.C., Article 2, is concerned with contracts, recovery for a breach of warranty may only be awarded to one contracting with ("in privity with") a seller and that Section 2-318 was intended to expand this scope of liability. Thus Section 2-318 limited liability to buyers, family or household members and guests of the buyer.[17] This result has been criticized by some authorities[18] which argue that Section 2-318 was to be only a partial statement of those to whom the warranties extended. Indeed, bystanders injured by defective products have recovered in some states.[19]

In concluding this section we present one of the leading cases in the products liability field. This case not only illustrates how major manufacturers attempted to withdraw warranties once made, but also illustrates that in some cases court's will provide a measure of flexibility in the law to protect those at the mercy of massive concentrations of economic power. The case was decided under the Uniform Sale of Goods Law, the U.C.'s predecessor. This does not alter the viability of the court's reasoning. Under the U.C.C., this case would probably be decided the same way. It must also be noted here that as a result of the inadequate protection provided by the U.C.C. warranty provisions, two results have been manifest. The first, already noted, is that Congress has passed new federal laws on warranties. The second is that tort law has developed and expanded its concept of negligent design and absolute liability to provide remedies where the U.C.C. might not. Both of these subjects are discussed in greater detail following this case.

HENNINGSEN v. BLOOMFIELD MOTORS, INC.
and CHRYSLER CORPORATION
32 N.J. 358, 161 A.2d 69 (Sup. Ct. of N.J., 1960)

◆◆◆

Francis, J.

Plaintiff Clause H. Henningsen purchased a Plymouth automobile, manufactured by defendant Chrysler Corporation, from defendant Bloomfield Motors, Inc. His wife, plaintiff Helen Henningsen, was injured while driving it and instituted suit against both defendants to recover damages on account of her injuries. . . . The complaint was predicated upon breach of express and implied warranties and upon negligence. At the trial the negligence counts were dismissed by the court and the cause was submitted to the jury for determination solely on the issues of implied warranty of merchantability. Verdicts were returned against both defendants and in favor of the plaintiffs. Defendants appealed and plaintiffs cross-appealed from the dismissal of their negligence claim. . . .

The facts are not complicated, but a general outline of them is necessary to an understanding of the case.

On May 7, 1955 Mr. and Mrs. Henningsen visited the place of business of Bloomfield Motors, Inc., an authorized De Soto and Plymouth dealer, to look at a Plymouth. . . . They were shown a Plymouth which appealed to them and the purchase followed. The record indicates that Mr. Henningsen intended the car as a Mother's Day gift to his wife. He said the intention was communicated to the dealer. When the purchase order or contract was prepared and presented, the husband executed it alone. His wife did not join as a party.

The purchase order was a printed form of one page. On the front it contained blanks to be filled in with a description of the automobile to be sold, the various accessories to be included, and the details of the financing. . . .

The reverse side of the contract contains 8-½ inches of fine print. . . . The page is headed "Conditions" and contains ten separate paragraphs consisting of 65 lines in all. The paragraphs do not have headnotes or margin notes denoting their particular subject, as in the case of the "Owner Service Certificate" to be referred to later. In the seventh paragraph, about two-thirds of the way down the page, the warranty, which is the focal point of the case, is set forth. It is as follows:

7. It is expressly agreed that there are no warranties, express or implied, made by either the dealer or the manufacturer on the motor vehicle, chassis, of parts furnished hereunder except as follows.
The manufacturer warrants each new motor vehicle (including original equipment placed thereon by the manufacturer except tires), chassis or parts manufactured by it to be free from defects in material or workmanship under normal use and service. Its obligation under this warranty being limited to making good at its factory any part or parts thereof which shall, within ninety (90) days after delivery of such vehicle to the original purchaser or before such vehicle has been driven 4,000 miles, whichever event shall first occur, be returned to it with

transportation charges prepaid and which its examination shall disclose to its satisfaction to have been thus defective; *this warranty being expressly in lieu of all other warranties expressed or implied and all other obligations or liabilities on its part*, and it neither assumes or authorizes any other person to assume for it any other liability in connection with the sale of its vehicles * * *. (Emphasis ours.)

The new Plymouth was turned over to the Henningsens on May 9, 1955. . . . Mr. Henningsen drove it from the dealer's place of business in Bloomfield to their home in Keansburg. . . . Thereafter, it was used for short trips on paved streets about the town. It had no servicing and no mishaps of any kind before the event of May 19. That day, Mrs. Henningsen drove to Asbury Park. On the way down and in returning, the car performed in normal fashion until the accident occurred.

She was proceeding north on Route 36 in Highlands, New Jersey, at 20-22 miles per hour. The highway was paved and smooth, and contained two lanes for northbound travel. She was riding in the right hand lane. Suddenly she heard a loud noise "from the bottom, by the hood." It "felt as if something cracked." The steering wheel spun in her hands; the car veered sharply to the right and crashed into a highway sign and a brick wall. No other vehicle was in any way involved. A bus operator driving in the left-hand lane testified that he observed plaintiffs' car approaching in normal fashion in the opposite direction; "all of a sudden [it] veered at 90 degress * * * and right into this wall." As a result of the impact, the front of the car was so badly damaged that it was impossible to determine if any of the parts of the steering wheel mechanism or workmanship or assembly were defective or improper prior to the accident. The condition was such that the collision insurance carrier, after inspection, declared the vehicle a total loss. It had 468 miles on the speedometer at the time.

The insurance carrier's inspector and appraiser of damaged cars, with eleven years of experience, advanced the opinion, based on the history and his examination, that something definitely went "wrong from the steering wheel down to the front wheels" . . . "something down there had to drop off or break loose to cause the car" to act in the manner described.

As has been indicated, the trial court felt that the proof was not sufficient to make out a prime facie case as to the negligence of either the manufacturer or the dealer.

The case was given to the jury, therefore, solely on the warranty theory, with results favorable to the plaintiffs against both defendants.

I

The Claim of Implied Warranty Against the Manufacturer

In the ordinary case of sale of goods by description an implied warranty of merchantability is an integral part of the transaction. . . . If the buyer, expressly or by implication, makes known to the seller the particular purpose for which the article is required and it appears that he has relied on the seller's skill or judgment, an implied warranty arises of reasonable fitness for that purpose. . . . The former type of warranty simply means that the thing sold is reasonably fit for the general purpose for which it is manufactured and sold. . . .

Of course such sales, whether oral or written, may be accompanied by an express warranty. Under the broad terms of the Uniform Sale of Goods Law any affirmation of fact relating to the goods is an express warranty if the natural tendency of the statement is to induce the buyer to make the purchase. . . . And over the years since the almost universal adoption of the act, a growing awareness of the tremendous development of modern business methods has prompted the courts to administer that provision with a liberal hand. . . .

The uniform act codified, extended and liberalized the common law of sales. The motivation in part was to ameliorate the harsh doctrine of *caveat emptor*, and in some measure to impose a reciprocal obligation on the seller to beware. The transcendent value of the legislation, particularly with respect to implied warranties, rests in the fact that obligations on the part of the seller were imposed by operation of law, and did not depend on their existence upon express agreement of the parties. And of tremendous significance in a rapidly expanding commercial society was the recognition of the right to recover damages on account of personal injuries arising from breach of warranty. . . . Recovery of damages does not depend upon proof of negligence or knowledge of the defect.

As the Sales Act and its liberal interpretation by the courts threw this protective cloak about the buyer, the decisions in various jurisdictions revealed beyond doubt that many manufacturers took steps to avoid these ever increasing warranty obligations. Realizing that the act governed the relationship of buyer and seller, they undertook to withdraw from actual and direct contractual contact with the buyer. They ceased selling products to the consuming public through their own employees and making contracts of sale in their own names. Instead, a system of independent dealers was established; their products were sold to dealers who in turn dealt with the buying public, ostensibly solely in their own personal capacity as sellers. In the past in many instances, manufacturers were able to transfer to the dealers burdens imposed by the act and thus achieved a large measure of immunity for themselves. But, as will be noted in more detail hereafter, such marketing practices, coupled with the advent of large scale advertising by manufacturers to promote the purchase of these goods from dealers by members of the public, provided a basis upon which the existence of express or implied warranties were predicated, even though the manufacturer was not a party to the contract of sale.

With these considerations in mind, we come to a study of the express warranty on the reverse side of the purchase order signed by Clause Henningsen. . . .

The terms of the warranty are a sad commentary upon the automobile manufacturers' marketing practices. . . .

The manufacturer agrees to replace defective parts for 90 days after the sale or until the car has been driven 4,000 miles, whichever is first to occur, *if the part is sent to the factory, transportation charges prepaid, and if examination discloses to its satisfaction that the part is defective.* It is difficult to imagine a greater burden on the consumer, or less satisfactory remedy. Aside from imposing on the buyer the trouble of removing and shipping the part, the maker has sought to retain the uncontrolled discretion to decide the issue of defectiveness. Some courts have removed much of the force of that reservation by declaring that the purchaser is not bound by the manufacturer's decision. . . .

Also, suppose, as in this case, a defective part or parts caused an accident and that the car was so damaged as to render it impossible to discover the precise part or parts responsible, although the circumstances clearly pointed to such fact as the cause of the mishap. Can it be said that the impossibility of performance deprived the buyer of the benefit of the warranty?

Moreover, the guaranty is against defective workmanship. That condition may arise from good parts improperly assembled. There being no defective parts to return to the maker, is all remedy to be denied? . . .

The matters referred to represent only a small part of the illusory character of the security presented by the warranty. Thus far the analysis has dealt only with the remedy provided in the case of a defective part. What relief is provided when the breach of the warranty results in personal injury to the buyer? (Injury to third persons using the car in the purchaser's right will be treated hereafter). As we have said above, the law is clear that such damages are recoverable under an ordinary warranty. The right exists whether the warranty sued on is express or implied. . . . And, of course, it has long since been settled that where the buyer or a member of his family driving with his permission suffers injuries because of negligent manufacture or construction of the vehicle, the manufacturer's liability exists. . . . But in this instance, after reciting that defective parts will be replaced at the factory, the alleged agreement relied upon by Chrysler provides that the manufacturer's "obligation under this warranty" is limited to that undertaking; further, that such remedy is "in lieu of all other warranties, express or implied, and all other obligations or liabilities on its part." The contention has been raised that such language bars any claim for personal injuries which may emanate from a breach of the warranty. . . .

Putting aside for the time being the problem of the efficacy of the disclaimer provisions contained in the express warranty, a question of first importance to be decided is whether an implied warranty of merchantability by Chrysler Corporation accompanied the sale of the automobile to Clause Henningsen.

Chrysler points out that an implied warranty of merchantability is an incident of a contract of sale. It conceded, of course, the making of the original sale to Bloomfield Motors, Inc., but maintains that this transaction marked the terminal point of its contractual connection with the car. Then Chrysler urges that since it was not a party to the sale by the dealer to Henningsen, there is no privity of contract between it and the plaintiffs, and the absence of this privity eliminates any such implied warranty.

There is no doubt that under early common-law concepts of contractual liability only those persons who were parties to the bargain could sue for breach of it. In more recent times a noticeable disposition has appeared in a number of jurisdictions to break through the narrow barrier of privity when dealing with sales of goods in order to give realistic recognition to a universally accepted fact. The fact is that the dealer and the ordinary buyer do not, and are not expected to, buy goods, whether they be foodstuffs or automobiles, exclusively for their own consumption or use. Makers and manufacturers know that and advertise and market their products on that assumption; witness, the "family" car, the baby foods, etc. The limitations of privity in contracts for the sale of goods developed their place in the law when marketing conditions were simple, when maker and buyer frequently met face to face on an equal bargaining plane and when many of the products were relatively uncomplicated and conducive to inspection by a buyer competent to evaluate their quality. . . . With the advent of mass-marketing, the manufacturer became remote from the purchaser, sales were accomplished through intermediaries, and the demand for the product was created by advertising media. In such an economy it became obvious that the consumer was the person being cultivated. Manifestly, the connotation of "consumer" was broader than that of "buyer." He signified such a person who, in the reasonable contemplation of the parties to the sale, might be expected to use the product. Thus, where the commodities sold are such that if defectively manufactured they will be dangerous to life or limb, then society's interests can only be protected by eliminating the requirement of privity between the maker and his dealers and the reasonably expected ultimate consumer. In that way the burden of losses consequent upon use of defective articles is borne by those who are in a position to either control the danger or make an equitable distribution of the losses when they do occur. . . .

Accordingly, we hold that under modern marketing conditions, when a manufacturer puts a new automobile in the stream of trade and promotes its purchase by the public, an implied warranty that it is reasonably suitable for use as such accompanies it into the hands of the ultimate purchaser. Absence of agency between the manufacturer and the dealer who makes the ultimate sale is immaterial.

II

The Effect of the Disclaimer and Limitation of Liability Clauses on the Implied Warranty of Merchantability

The task of the judiciary is to administer the spirit as well as the letter of the law. On issues such as the present one, part of that burden is to protect the ordinary man against the loss of important rights through what, in effect, is the unilateral act of the manufacturer. The status of the automobile industry is unique. Manufacturers are few in number and strong in bargaining position. In the matter of warranties on the sales of their products, the Automotive Manufacturers Association has enabled them to present a united front. From the standpoint of the purchaser, there can be no arms length negotiating on the subject. Because his capacity for bargaining is so grossly unequal, the inexorable conclusion which follows is that he is not permitted to bargain at all. He must take or leave the automobile on the warranty terms dictated by the maker. He cannot turn to a competitor for better security.

Public policy is a term not easily defined. Its significance varies as the habits and needs of a people may vary. It is not static and the field of application is an ever increasing one. A contract, or a particular provision therein, valid in one era may be wholly opposed to the public policy of another. . . . Courts keep in mind the principle that the best interests of society demand that persons should not be unnecessarily restricted in their freedom to contract. But they do not hesitate to declare void as against public policy contractual provisions which clearly tend to the injury of the public in some way. . . .

Public policy at a given time finds expression in the Constitution, the statutory law and judicial decisions. In the area of sale of goods, the legislative will has imposed an implied warranty of merchantability as a general incident of sale of an automobile by description. The warranty does not depend upon the affirmative intention of the parties. It is a child of the law; it annexes itself to the contract because of the very nature of the transaction. The judicial process has recognized a right to recover damages for personal injuries arising from a breach of that warranty. The disclaimer of the implied warranty and exclusion of all obligations except those specifically assumed by the express warranty signify a studied effort to frustrate that protection. ... The lawmakers did not authorize the automobile manufacturer to use its grossly disproportionate bargaining power to relieve itself from liability and to impose on the ordinary buyer, who in effect has no real freedom of choice, the grave danger of injury to himself and others that attends the sale of such a dangerous instrumentality as a defectively made automobile. In the framework of this case, illuminated as it is by the facts and the many decisions noted, we are of the opinion that Chrysler's attempted disclaimer of an implied warranty of merchantability and of the obligations arising therefrom is so inimical to the public good as to compel an adjudication of its invalidity. ...

Under all of the circumstances outlined above, the judgment in favor of the plaintiffs and against the defendants is affirmed.

◆◆◆

Case Questions

1. Define the "implied warranty" created by the court. Under what circumstances will a court be likely to create such a warranty?
2. Under what circumstances will a court consider limiting or voiding a written waiver of warranties made by a consumer?

Federal Warranty Legislation

The average consumer does not know the meaning of the words, "express warranty" or "warranty of merchantability" or "warranty of fitness for a particular purpose." Moveover, if a consumer is educated enough to understand and be able to apply these rules, there is the chance that access to the legal system will prove too costly to redress the breach of such a warranty. Or, there is always the chance that the manufacturer has waived or modified the warranties when and if made. Consumer dissatisfaction with both their inability to understand the complex warranty provisions of the U.C.C. and their reluctance to enforce breaches are two of the major reasons for the passage of the Consumer Product Warranty and Federal Trade Commission Improvements Act (also called the Magnuson — Moss Warranty — Federal Trade Commission Improvement Act) which became law on July 4, 1975.[20]

The Act seeks to regulate written product warranties and service contracts provided by manufacturers and suppliers. Also, the Act places some of the burden of enforcement and promulgation of warranty standards on the Federal Trade Commission. The Act does not alter the warranties of merchantability or fitness for a particular purpose created by the U.C.C.; nor is it applicable when no warranties are made. It is applicable when a warranty is made and the cost of the item purchased exceeds $5.00.

At least three definitions are important under this act. This applies to written warranties and defines these as any affirmation of fact, promise or undertaking in writing which becomes part of the basis of the bargain. So, if the promise made is relied on to the extent that it forms part of the basis of the bargain, then the provisions of the act apply if the product was distributed in or affected interstate commerce. Remember this last requirement exists for all federal legislation. Secondly, the product sold must be bought by a *consumer* who is defined as any person who buys a consumer product for purposes other than resale, or any person to whom the product is transferred during the warranty period. Thirdly, the act defines a consumer product as any tangible personal property normally used for personal, family or household purposes. Contracts for the service of consumer products are also covered.

The items and persons covered by the act are extensive. Again we will not go into detail but will present here only an overview of the legislation. Fundamentally, the act attempts to compel sellers of consumer products to make clear to consumers the warranties made and the process which must be followed to claim a breach of the warranty. The act also imposes certain minimum standards in the making of warranties and, finally, as noted, requires the FTC to prosecute violators and promulgate added rules and regulations for the implementation of the Act.

The one who makes a warranty (called a warrantor) is required to fully and conspicuously disclose the terms and limitations of the warranty to the consumer *before* the sale. Some of the items which warrantors should disclose are, among others, the following: [21]

1. A clear identification of the names and addresses of warrantors,
2. The identity of the party or parties to whom the warranty is extended,
3. The products or parts covered,
4. A statement as to what the warrantor will do, at whose expense the work will be done, and the period of time the warranty will last, assuming that the product fails to conform to the written warranty,
5. A statement of what the consumer must do and the expenses he will bear,
6. A statement of the exceptions and exclusions from the terms of the warranty,
7. The step-by-step procedure consumers must take in order to obtain performance of any obligation under the warranty,
8. Information about the availability and required usage by the consumer of any informal dispute settlement procedure,
9. A brief summary of the legal remedies available to the consumer,
10. The time during which the warrantor will fulfill his obligations under the warranty.

Further, the Act stipulates that written warranties be conspicuously designated as either 1) a full " *state duration* − e.g. 2 year − warranty" or 2) a limited warranty. A full (*e.g., "2 year warranty"*) must conform to certain federal minimum content standards. These substantive standards state: [22]

1. Any defects, malfunctions or inability to conform to the terms of a written warranty must be corrected by the warrantor without charge and within a reasonable length of time.
2. The warrantor cannot limit the period of time within which implied warranties will be effective with respect to the consumer product.

3. The warrantor cannot limit or exclude consequential damages on a consumer product unless noted conspicuously on the face of the warranty.
4. The warrantor must allow the consumer to choose between a refund of the purchase price or replacement of the defective product or part whenever a reasonable number of attempts to remedy the defect or malfunction has occurred.

A "limited warranty" need not satisfy these standards but it must be conspicuously labled as such. Remember that a warranty is any statement of fact, promise or undertaking. So, a statement such as "satisfaction guaranteed" or the like is neither a full or limited warranty (it is sometimes referred to as seller's puffing). These "designation" requirements just referred to, apply to goods costing more than ten dollars. Do not confuse this with the "disclosure" requirements which are applicable to written warranties on consumer products costing more than five dollars.

Perhaps the most significant provision of the act is the one limiting the use of written warranties to disclaim the implied warranties created in law by the U.C.C. This is the practice revealed by the manufacturer of Plymouth in the *Henningsen* case. The act provides that a written warranty may not be used to impose any limitation on the duration of implied warranties.[23] If a written warranty of reasonable duration is given, however, an implied warranty may be limited to the same time period. Moreover, the act is clear in its statement that a supplier may not disclaim or modify an implied warranty when either a written warranty is given or a service contract is entered into at the time of sale or written ninety days thereafter.[24]

The remedy provisions of the act are also noteworthy. If the act applies to a warrantor and a breach of the warranty occurs, the warrantor or his designated representative must remedy the defect within a reasonable time and without charge. The term "without charge" means that the warrantor may not assess the consumer for any costs the warrantor or his representative incur in connection with the required remedy.[25]

In the provision referred to as an "anti-lemon" provision, the consumer may receive a refund or replacement if the warrantor does not remedy the defect after a reasonable number of attempts.[26] What is "reasonable" in this case awaits definition by the FTC.

Enforcement of the act's provisions are divided between the consumer and the government. If informal attempts to settle disputed claims are not sufficient the individual may seek redress in the courts. If there are at least 100 named plaintiffs and the claims of each exceeds $25 and the aggregate of all claims, exclusive of interest and costs exceeds $50,000, class actions are authorized.[27] If repeated violations are evident or if a warrantor fails to comply with a cease and desist order of the FTC, then either the FTC or the Justice Department may bring an action in the district court asking for an injunction. Persons or corporations knowingly violating a cease and desist order declaring conduct to be unfair and deceptive are subject to a civil penalty not exceeding $10,000 for each violation.[28]

Finally, considerable responsibility is placed on the FTC for developing efficient remedies (especially for the anti-lemon provisons) and in promulgating minimum requirements for informal dispute settlement and for developing other standards needed for the accomplishment of the act's objectives. Only if the consumer and the FTC accept the responsibilities placed on them by the act (no amount of legislation can make a consumer pursue remedies if he simply is not interested or does not take the time) will the act achieve its objectives of attempting to hold sellers liable for the warranties they make.

Tort Liability Through Negligent
Design and Strict Liability

In this section of the chapter we again return to a brief presentation of state law. An entirely separate set of legal principles which provide remedies to a consumer injured by a defectively produced product are provided by the application of tort law. These tort remedies may be sought in the same trial in which the breach of the contract-warranty remedies are also alleged. It is good to argue the tort duties even in those cases where the application of current warranty law would be applicable because the warranty arguments may fail because of some technicality. For example, it may be that the manufacturer had successfully modified or waived the warranty or perhaps the express warranty relied upon did not form the basis of the bargain. More importantly, tort law provides a remedy to those who would be denied a remedy by some courts because they were not in privity with — had not contracted with — the manufacturer.

Tort law has developed two lines of analysis. These lines are not clear and appear to overlap in many instances. The older of the two holds simply that a manufacturer has a duty to design a product reasonably fit for its intended use. Proving negligent design, however, was, and continues to be, a substantial problem. What if, for example, all of the manufacturers in the market producing the defective product used the same design and manufacturing methods? How is the standard of "reasonableness" to be derived? Moreover, how is a plaintiff to show the negligent design was *the cause* of the defect resulting in injury? One of the most interesting cases in this area, *Larsen* v. *General Motors* is used to illustrate that in some circumstances a manufacturer may be liable for a negligently designed part of an automobile where such design would expose a person to unreasonable risk or injury. In this case, can you discern how the court arrives at its decision that the negligently designed steering mechanism posed an unreasonable risk of injury?

Because of the problems of proof, tort law has developed a second line of analysis for defective products which is less rigorous. This developing line of analysis is based upon the "strict" liability of a manufacturer. This principle is well stated by the *Restatement of Torts, Second*, § 402A, 1965, which provides:

(1) One who sells any product in a defective condition unreasonably dangerous to the user or consumer or to his property is subject to liability for physical harm thereby caused to the ultimate user or consumer, or to his property, if
    (a) the seller is engaged in the business of selling such a product, and
    (b) it is expected to and does reach the user or consumer without substantial change in the condition in which it is sold.
(2) The rule stated in Sub-section (1) applies although
    (a) the seller has exercised all possible care in the preparation and sale of his product, and
    (b) the user or consumer has not bought the product from or entered into any contractual relation with the seller.

Note that this principle imposes liability on a seller without regard to fault or negligence. The key words in the statement are "unreasonably dangerous." The types of products which can be classified as unreasonably dangerous have been steadily expanding. In the nineteenth century courts held that weapons (guns), poisons, and scaffolding, if created with a defect, would create strict liability for the manufacturer. In the twentieth century courts have expanded the classification of unreasonably dangerous products to include automobiles and consumer items such as power tools. (See the *Greenman* case).

The definition of which products are unreasonably dangerous varies from state to state so differing results in the application of the principle of strict liability can be expected.

We have reproduced two famous products liability cases. The first, the *Larsen* case, presents the outlines of a negligent design cause of action. The second, the *Greenman* case, exemplifies the application of strict liability together with warranty arguments. Also note in the *Greenman* case those products which have been termed "unreasonably dangerous" thus allowing recovery based upon strict liability.

LARSEN v. GENERAL MOTORS
391 F 2d 495 (8 Cir 1968)

◆◆◆

The driver of a 1963 Chevrolet Corvair claims injury as a result of the alleged negligent design of the automobiles's steering assembly. The alleged design defect did not cause the accident. There was a head-on collision with the impact occurring on the left front corner of the car. This caused a severe rearward thrust of the steering mechanism into the plaintiff's head. The solid steering shaft extended without interruption from a point 2.7 inches in front of the leading surface of the front tire to a position directly in front of the driver. The District Court dismissed the complaint ruling that the manufacturer has no legal duty to make a vehicle that would protect the plaintiff from injury in the event of a head-on collision.

The plaintiff does not contend that the design caused the accident but that because of the design he received injuries he would not have otherwise received or, in the alternative, his injuries would not have been as severe.

General Motors contends that it has no duty to produce a vehicle in which it is safe to collide or which is accident proof or incapable of injurious misuse. It views its duty as extending only to producing a vehicle that is reasonably fit for its intended use or for the purpose for which it was made and that is free from hidden defects; and that the intended use of a vehicle and the purpose for which it is manufactured do not include its participation in head-on collisions or any other type of impact, regardless of the manufacturer's ability to foresee that such collisions may occur.

The plaintiff maintains that General Motors' view of its duty is too narrow and restrictive and that an automobile manufacturer is under a duty to use reasonable care in the design of the automobile to make it safe to the user for its foreseeable use and that its intended use or purpose is for travel on the streets and highways, including the possibility of impact or collision with other vehicles or stationary objects.

There is a line of cases directly supporting General Motors' contention that negligent design of an automobile is not actionable, where the alleged defective design is not a causative factor in the accident. The latest leading case on this point is *Evans* v. *General Motors Corporation,* 359 F.2d 822 (7 Cir. 1966). A divided court there held that General Motors in designing an "X" body frame without perimeter support, instead of an allegedly more safe perimeter body frame, was not liable for the death of a user allegedly caused by the designed defect because the defendant's design could not have functioned to avoid the collision. The Court reasoned. . . .

> A manufacturer is not under a duty to make his automobile accident proof or full-proof; nor must he render the vehicle 'more' safe where the danger to be avoided is obvious to all. Perhaps it would be desirable to require manufacturers to construct automobiles in which it would be safe to collide, but that would be a legislative function, not an aspect of judicial interpretation of existing law.
>
> The intended purpose of an automobile does not include its participation in collisions with other objects, despite the manufacturer's ability to foresee the possibility that such collisions may occur.

Accepting, therefore, the principle that a manufacturer's duty of design and construction extends to producing a product that is reasonably fit for its intended use and free of hidden defects that could render it unsafe for such use, the issue narrows on the proper interpretation of "intended use." Automobiles are made for use on the roads and highways in transporting persons and cargo to and from various points. This intended use cannot be carried out without encountering in varying degrees the statistically proved hazard of injury-producing impacts of various types. The manufacturer should not be heard to say that it does not intend its product to be involved in any accident when it can easily foresee and when it knows that the probability over the life of its product is high, that it will be involved in some type of injury-producing accident. O'Connell, in his article "Taming the Automobile," 58 *Nw. U.L. Rev.* 299, 348 (1963) cites that between one-fourth to two-thirds of all automobiles during their use at some time are involved in an accident producing injury or death.

We think the "intended use" construction urged by General Motors is much too narrow and unrealistic. Where the manufacturer's negligence in design causes an unreasonable risk to be imposed upon the user of its product, the manufacturer should be liable for the injury caused by its failure to exercise reasonable care in the design. These injuries are readily foreseeable as an incident to the normal and expected use of an automobile. While automobiles are not made for the purpose of colliding with each other, a frequent and inevitable contingency of normal automobile use will result in collisions and injury-producing impacts. No rational basis exists for limiting recovery to situations where the defect in design or manufacture was the causative factor of the accident, as the accident and the resulting injury, usually caused by the so-called "second collision" of the passenger with the interior part of the automobile, all are foreseeable. Where the injuries or enhanced injuries are due to the manufacturer's failure to use reasonable care to avoid subjecting the user of its products to an unreasonable risk of injury, general negligence principles should be applicable. The sole function of an automobile is not just to provide a means of transportation, it is to provide a means of safe transportation, or as safe as is reasonably possible under the present state of the art.

We do agree that under the present state of the art an automobile manufacturer is under no duty to design an accident proof or full-proof vehicle or even one that floats on water, but such manufacturer is under a duty to use reasonable care in the design of its vehicle to avoid subjecting the user to an unreasonable risk of injury in the event of a collision. Collision with or without fault of the user are clearly foreseeable by the manufacturer and are statistically inevitable.

The duty of reasonable care in design should be viewed in light of the risk. While all risks cannot be eliminated nor can a crash-proof vehicle be designed under the present state of the art, there are many common-sense factors in design, which are or should be well known to the manufacturer that will minimize or lessen the injurious effects of a collision. The standard of reasonable care is applied in many other negligence situations and should be applied here.

The courts . . . have held that a manufacturer of automobiles is under a duty to construct a vehicle that is free of latent and hidden defects. We can perceive of no significant difference in imposing a common law duty of a reasonable standard of care in design the same as in construction. A defect in either can cause severe injury or death and a negligent design defect should be actionable. Any design defect not causing the accident would not subject the manufacturer to liability for the entire damage, but the manufacturer should be liable for that portion of the damage or injury caused by the defective design over and above the damage or injury that probably would have occurred as a result of the impact or collision absent the defective design.

The manufacturer's duty to use reasonable care in the design and manufacture of a product to minimize injuries to its users and not to subject its users to an unreasonable risk of injury in the event of a collision or impact should be recognized by the courts. The normal risk of driving must be accepted by the user but there is no need to further penalize the user by subjecting him to an unreasonable risk of injury due to negligence in design.

If, because of the alleged undisclosed defect in design of the 1963 Corvair steering assembly, an extra hazard is created over and above the normal hazard, General Motors should be liable for this unreasonable hazard.

◆◆◆

Case Questions

1. Does the GM position on their legal and financial responsibility to automobile accident victims expose them to valid social criticism?
2. Is GM's defense a wise one from an economic perspective? What would be your position in light of the following statistics: new car sales in excess of 11 million per year, 1972 automobile accident deaths of 56,600 and disabling injuries of 2.1 million? Would your opinion differ upon learning that in 1970 the "big three" automakers had revenue in excess of 40.7 billion dollars and profits exceeding 1.1 billion dollars.

Does ownership of GM stock or GM automotive product color your view?

3. If the safety of the user is to be a concern of the manufacturer, where is the line to be drawn? Was the court's decision, in extending liability beyond accident causing defects, a wise one? Who is to draw the line? Is such a decision exclusively within the realm of the legislative branch?

4. Is the best legal defense to a lawsuit necessarily the preferable one from a public relations or social point of view?

GREENMAN v. YUBA POWER PRODUCTS, INC.
59 Cal. 2d 57, (S. Ct., Cal., 1963)

◆◆◆

TRAYNOR, Justice.

Plaintiff brought this action for damages against the retailer and the manufacturer of a Shopsmith, a combination power tool that could be used as a saw, drill, and wood lathe. He saw a Shopsmith demonstrated by the retailer and studied a brochure prepared by the manufacturer. He decided he wanted a Shopsmith for his home workshop, and his wife bought and gave him one for Christmas in 1955. In 1957 he bought the necessary attachments to use the Shopsmith as a lathe for turning a large piece of wood he wished to make into a chalice. After he had worked on the piece of wood several times without difficulty, it suddenly flew out of the machine and struck him on the forehead, inflicting serious injuries. About ten and a half months later, he gave the retailer and the manufacturer written notice of claimed breaches of warranties and filed a complaint against them alleging such breaches and negligence.

After a trial before a jury, the court ruled that there was no evidence that the retailer was negligent or had breached any express warranty and that the manufacturer was not liable for the breach of any implied warranty. Accordingly, it submitted to the jury only the cause of action alleging breach of implied warranties against the retailer and the causes of action alleging negligence and breach of express warranties against the manufacturer. The jury returned a verdict for the retailer against plaintiff and for plaintiff against the manufacturer in the amount of $65,000. The trial court denied the manufacturer's motion for a new trial and entered judgment on the verdict. The manufacturer and plaintiff appeal. Plaintiff seeks a reversal of the part of the judgment in favor of the retailer, however, only in the event that the part of the judgment against the manufacturer is reversed.

Plaintiff introduced substantial evidence that his injuries were caused by defective design and construction of the Shopsmith. His expert witnesses testified that inadequate set screws were used to hold parts of the machine together so that normal vibration caused the tailstock of the lathe to move away from the piece of wood being turned permitting it to fly out of the lathe. They also testified that there were other more positive ways of fastening the parts of the machine together, the use of which would have prevented the accident. The jury could therefore reasonably have concluded that the manufacturer negligently constructed the Shopsmith. The jury could also reasonably have concluded that statements in the manufacturer's brochure were untrue, that they constituted express warranties [1] and that plaintiff's injuries were caused by their breach.

The manufacturer contends, however, that plaintiff did not give it notice of breach of warranty within a reasonable time and that therefore his cause of action for breach of warranty is barred by section 1769 of the Civil Code. Since it cannot be determined whether the verdict against it was based on the negligence or warranty cause of action or both, the manufacturer concludes that the error in presenting the warranty cause of action to the jury was prejudicial.

Section 1769 of the Civil Code provides: "In the absence of express or implied agreement of the parties, acceptance of the goods by the buyer shall not discharge the seller from liability in damages or other legal remedy for breach of any promise or warranty in the contract to sell or the sale. But, if, after acceptance of the goods, the buyer fails to give notice to the seller of the breach of any promise or warranty within a reasonbale time after the buyer knows, or ought to know of such breach, the seller shall not be liable therefor."

Like other provisions of the uniform sales act (Civ. Code. §§ 1721-1800), section 1769 deals with the rights of the parties to a contract of sale or a sale. It does not provide that notice must be given of the breach of a warranty that arises independently of a contract of sale between the parties. Such warranties are not imposed by the sales act, but are the product of common-law decisions that have recognized them in a variety of situations. . . .

We conclude, therefore, that even if plaintiff did not give timely notice of breach of warranty to the manufacturer, his cause of action based on the representations contained in the brochure was not barred.

Moreover, to impose strict liability on the manufacturer under the circumstances of this case, it was not necessary for plaintiff to establish an express warranty as defined in section 1732 of the Civil Code. [2] A manufacturer is strictly liable in tort when an article he places on the market, knowing that it is to be used without inspection for defects, proves to have a defect that causes injury to a human being. Recognized first in the case of unwholesome food product, such liability has now been extended to a variety of other products that create as great or greater hazards if defective. *Peterson* v. *Lamb Rubber Co.,* 54 Cal. 2d 339, 347 [grinding wheel] ; *Vallis* v. *Canada Dry Ginger Ale, Inc.,* 190 Cal. App. 2d 35, 42-44 [bottle] ; *Jones Burgermeister Brewing Corp.,* 198 Cal. App. 2d 198, 204 [bottle] ; *Gottsdanker* v. *Cutter Laboratories,* 182 Cal. App. 2d 602, 607 [vaccine] ; *McQuaide* v. *Bridgport Brass Co.,* D.C. 190 F. Supp. 252, 254 [insect spray] ; *Bowles* v. *Zimmer Manufacturing Co.,* 7 Cir., 277 F. 2d 868, 875 [surgical pin] ; *Thompson* v. *Reedman D.C.,* 199 F. Supp. 120, 121 [automobile] ; *Chapman* v. *Brown.* D.C. 198 F. Supp. 78, 118, 119, affd. *Brown*

---

[1] In this respect the trial court limited the jury to a consideration of two statements in the manufacturer's brochure: (1) "WHEN SHOPSMITH IS IN HORIZONTAL POSITION — Rugged construction of frame provides rigid support from end to end. Heavy centerless-ground steel tubing insures perfect alignment [sic] of components." (2) "SHOPSMITH maintains its accuracy because every component has positive locks that hold adjustments through rough or precision work."

[2] Any affirmation of fact or any promise by the seller relating to the goods is an express warranty if the natural tendency of such affirmation or promise is to induce the buyer to purchase the goods, and if the buyer purchases the goods relying thereon. No affirmation of the value of the goods, nor any statement purporting to be a statement of the seller's opinion only shall be construed as a warranty.

v. *Chapman*, 9 Cir., 304 F. 2d 149 [skirt]; *B.F. Goodrich Co.* v. *Hammond*, 10 Cir., 269 F. 2d 501, 504 [automobile tire]; *Markovich* v. *McKesson and Robbins, Inc.*, 106 Ohio App. 265 [home permanent]; *Graham* v. *Bottenfield's Inc.*, 176 Kan. 68 [Hair dye]; *General Motors Corp.* v. *Dodson*, 47 Tenn. App. 438 [automobile]; *Henningsen* v. *Bloomfield Motors, Inc.*, 32 N.J. 358 [automobile]; *Hinton* v. *Republic Aviation Corporation*, D.C., 180 F. Supp. 31, 33 [airplaine].

Although in these cases strict liability has usually been based on the theory of an express or implied warranty running from the manufacturer to the plaintiff, the abandonment of the requirement of a contract between them, the recognition that the liability is not assumed by agreement but imposed by law . . . and the refusal to permit the manufacturer to define the scope of its own responsibility for defective products . . . make clear that the liability is not one governed by the law of contract warranties but by the law of strict liability in tort. Accordingly, rules defining and governing warranties that were developed to meet the needs of commercial transactions cannot properly be invoked to govern the manufacturer's liability to those injured by their defective products unless those rules also serve the purposes for which such liability is imposed.

 . . . The purpose of such [strict] liability is to insure that the costs of injuries resulting from defective products are borne by the manufacturers that put such products on the market rather than by the injured persons who are powerless to protect themselves. Sales warranties serve this purpose fitfully at best. . . . In the present case, for example, plaintiff was able to plead and prove an express warranty only because he read and relied on the representations of the Shopsmith's ruggedness contained in the manufacturer's brochure. Implicit in the machine's presence on the market, however, was a representation that it would safely do the jobs for which it was built. Under these circumstances, it should not be controlling whether plaintiff selected the machine because of the statements in the brochure, or because of the machine's own appearance of excellence that belied the defect lurking beneath the surface, or because he merely assumed that it would safely do the jobs it was built to do. It should not be controlling whether the details of the sales from manufacturer to retailer and from retailer to plaintiff's wife were such that one or more of the implied warranties of the sales act arose. . . . "The remedies of injured consumers ought not to be made to depend upon the intricacies of the law of sales." *Ketterer* v. *Armour & Co.*, D.C., 200 F. 323, 323: *Klein* v. *Duchess Sandwich Co.*, 14 Cal. 2d 272. To establish the manufacturer's liability it was sufficient that plaintiff proved that he was injured while using the Shopsmith in a way it was intended to be used as a result of a defect in design and manufacture of which plaintiff was not aware. . . .

The judgment is affirmed.

GIBSON, C.J., and SCHAUER, McCOMB, PETERS, TOBRINGER, and PEEK, J.J., concur.

◆◆◆

Case Questions

1. What are the policy reasons for the doctrine of strict liability?
2. Note that the judge writing this opinion is the same one that was in favor of an expanding definition of inherent authority in Chapter 4. Is Judge Traynor consistent in arguing for strict liability and an expanded scope of circumstances in which the principle of inherent authority will be applied?

RECENT FEDERAL ENVIRONMENTAL PROTECTION LAWS

Business associations have been subject to both federal and state laws intending to protect the environment since the late nineteenth century. However, these laws were not enforced and, until very recently, legal policy regarding the business association and the environment was, at best, fragmented. Today, some states have very active environmental protection agencies but, for the sake of simplicity and uniformity, we will focus only upon federal efforts to protect the environment.

The National Environmental Policy Act

The federal effort may be exemplified by analyzing one piece of legislation, The National Environmental Policy Act, and two administrative agencies: The Council on Environmental Quality (CEQ) and the Environmental Protection Agency (EPA). The National Environmental Policy Act (NEPA) became law January 1, 1970.[29] The purpose of the statute was to declare a national environmental policy which would encourage harmony between humans and the environment by promoting efforts to eliminate damage to the environment and biosphere. In general, the statute attempts to accomplish this rather broadly stated objective by requiring *federal agencies* to create environmental impact statements under some circumstances and by creating the Council on Environmental Quality. The primary duties under NEPA are not upon business associations directly, but are upon federal agencies which plan to disturb the environment. Since federal agencies hire private sector employers to accomplish much of their work, they and their employees are indirectly concerned, and they should have a basic understanding of NEPA requirements. In order to insure that environmental values are considered at all levels in the decision-making process of the federal bureaucracy, the statute requires the preparation of an impact statement by each federal agency which proposes legislation and/or any other major federal action having a significant effect on the quality of the environment. This detailed environmental impact statement must inlcude:[30]

1. The environmental impact of the proposed action.
2. Any adverse environmental effects which cannot be avoided should the proposal be implemented.
3. Alternatives to the proposed action.
4. The relationship between local short-term uses by man and the maintenance and enhancement of long-term productivity.
5. Any irreversible and irretrievable commitments of resources which would be involved in the proposed action should it be implemented.

The question of when these impact statements must be submitted is not defined clearly by the Act. The CEQ, however, has issued some guidelines which require an impact statement where the proposed federal action is likely to be highly controversial or the environment, even in a very limited geographic area, may be significantly affected.[31]

The litigation which has arisen under the provisions of the Act has been concerned primarily with proper procedures for filing the impact statements and the content of the statements themselves. There can be little doubt that the courts have not backed off in requiring the federal government to strictly adhere to the Congressional intent of the Act. We have reproduced excerpts from one of the early decisions (1971) under the Act emphasizing the necessity for strict compliance. The opinion also illustrates how the act was intended to protect the environment by requiring a deliberate, conscious weighing by decision makers of the adverse environmental impact of the activity against the benefits to be derived.

CALVERT CLIFFS' COORD. COM. v. UNITED STATES A. E. COMM'N
449 F 2d 1109 (D.C.C.A., 1971)

◆◆◆

WRIGHT, Circuit Judge

These cases are only the beginning of what promises to become a flood of new litigation — litigation seeking judicial assistance in protecting our natural environment. Several recently enacted statutes attest to the commitment of the Government to control, at long last, the destructive engine of material "progress." But it remains to be seen whether the promise of this legislation will become a reality. Therein lies the judicial role. In these cases, we must for the first time interpret the broadest and perhaps most important of the recent statutes: the National Environmental Policy Act of 1969 (NEPA). We must assess claims that one of the agencies charged with its administration has failed to live up to the congressional mandate. Our duty, in short, is to see that important legislative purposes, hearlded in the halls of Congress, are not lost or misdirected in the vast hallways of the federal bureaucracy.

NEPA, like so much other reform legislation of the last forty years, is cast in terms of a general mandate and broad delegation of authority to new and old administrative agencies. It takes the major step of requiring all federal agencies to consider values of environmental preservation in their spheres of activity, and it prescribes certain procedural measures to ensure that those values are in fact fully respected. Petitioners argue that rules recently adopted by the Atomic Energy Commission to govern consideration of environmental matters fail to satisfy the rigor demanded by NEPA. The Commission, on the other hand, contends that the vagueness of the NEPA mandate and delegation leaves much room for discretion and that the rules challenged by petitioners fall well within the broad scope of the Act. We find the policies embodied in NEPA to be a good deal clearer and more demanding than does the Commission. We conclude that the Commission's procedural rules do not comply with the congressional policy. Hence we remand these cases for further rule making. . . .

Perhaps the greatest importance of NEPA is to require the Atomic Energy Commission and other agencies to *consider* environmental issues just as they consider other matters within their mandates. This compulsion is most plainly stated in Section 102. There, "Congress authorizes and directs that, to the fullest extent possible: (1) the policies, regulations, and public laws of the United States shall be interpreted and administered in accordance with the policies set forth in this Act * * *," Congress also "authorizes and directs" that "(2) all agencies of the Federal Government shall" follow certain rigorous procedures in considering environmental values. . . . In general, all agencies must use a "systematic, interdisciplinary approach" to environmental planning and evaluation "in decision making which may have an impact on man's environment." In order to include all possible environmental factors in the decisional equation, agencies must "identify and develop methods and procedures * * * which will insure that presently unquantified environmental amenities and values may be given appropriate consideration in decision making along with economic and technical considerations." "Environmental amenities" will often be in conflict with "economic and technical considerations." To "consider" the former "along with" the latter must involve a balancing process. In some instances environmental costs may outweigh economic and technical benefits and in other instances they may not. But NEPA mandates a rather finely tuned and "systematic" balancing analysis in each instance.

To ensure that the balancing analysis is carried out and given full effect, Section 102 (2) (C) requires that responsible officials of all agencies prepare a "detailed statement" covering the impact of particular actions on the environment, the environmental costs which might be avoided, and alternative measures which might alter the cost-benefit equation. The apparent purpose of the "detailed statement" is to aid in the agencies' own decision making process and to advise other interested agencies and the public of the environmental consequences of planned federal action. Beyond the "detailed statement," Section 102 (2) (1) requires all agencies specifically to "study, develop, and describe appropriate alternatives to recommended courses of action in any proposal which involves unresolved conflicts concerning alternative uses of available resources." This requirement, like the "detailed statement" requirement, seeks to ensure that each agency decision maker has before him and takes into proper account all possible approaches to a particular project (including total abandonment of the project) which would alter the environmental impact and the cost-benefit balance. Only in that fashion is it likely that the most intelligent, optimally beneficial decision will ultimately be made. . . .

We conclude, then, that Section 102, of NEPA mandates a particular sort of careful and informed decision-making process and creates judicially enforceable duties. The reviewing courts probably cannot reverse a substantive decision on its merits, under Section 101, unless it be shown that the actual balance of costs and benefits that was struck was arbitrary or clearly gave insufficient weight to environmental values. But, individualized consideration and balancing of environmental factors conducted fully and in good faith — it is the responsibility of the courts to reverse. As one District Court has said of Section 102 requirements, "It is hard to imagine a clearer or stronger mandate to the Courts." . . .

In the cases before us now, we do not have to review a particular decision by the Atomic Energy Commission granting a construction permit or an operating license. Rather, we must review the Commission's recently promulgated rules which govern consideration of environmental values in all such individual decisions. The rules were devised strictly in order to comply with the NEPA procedural requirements but petitioners argue that they fall far short of the congressional mandate . . .

II

The question here is whether the Commission is correct in thinking that its NEPA responsibilities may "be carried out in toto outside the hearing process" — whether it is enough that environmental data and evaluations merely "accompany" an application through the review process, but receive no consideration whatever from the hearing board.

We believe that the Commission's crabbed interpretation of NEPA makes a mockery of the Act. What possible purpose could there be in the Section 102 (2) (C) requirement (that the "detailed statement" accompany proposals through agency review processes) if "accompany" means no more than physical proximity — mandating no more than the physical act of passing certain folders and papers, unopened, to reviewing officials along with other folders and papers? What possible purpose could there be in requiring the "detailed statement" to be before hearing boards, if the boards are free to ignore entirely the contents of the statement? NEPA was meant to do more than regulate the flow of papers in the federal bureaucracy. The word "accompany" in Section 102 (2) (C) must not be read so narrowly as to make the Act ludicrous. It must, rather, be read to indicate a congressional intent that environmental factors, as compiled in the "detailed statement," be considered through agency review processes.

Beyond Section 102 (2) (C), NEPA requires that agencies consider the environmental impact of their actions "to the fullest extent possible." The Act is addressed to agencies as a whole, not only to their professional staffs. Compliance to the "fullest" possible extent would seem to demand that environmental issues be considered at every important stage in the decision making process concerning a particular action at every stage where an overall balancing of environmental and non-environmental factors is appropriate and where alterations might be made in the proposed action to minimize environmental costs. . . .

IV

The sweep of NEPA is extraordinarily broad, compelling consideration of any and all types of environmental impact of federal action. However, the Atomic Energy Commission's rules specifically exclude from full consideration a wide variety of environmental issues. First, they provide that no party may raise and the Commission may not independently examine any problem of water quality — perhaps the most significant impact of nuclear power plants. Rather, the Commission indicates that it will defer totally to water quality standards devised and administered by state agencies and approved by the federal government under the Federal Water Pollution Control Act. Secondly, the rules provide for similar abdication of NEPA authority to the standards of other agencies. . . .

We believe the Commission's rule is in fundamental conflict with the basic purpose of the Act. NEPA mandates a case-by-case balancing judgment on the part of federal agencies. In each individual case, the particular economic and technical benefits of planned action must be assessed and then weighed against the environmental costs; alternatives must be considered which would effect the balance of values. The magnitude of possible benefits and possible costs may lie anywhere on a broad spectrum. Much will depend on the particular magnitudes involved in particular cases. In some cases, the benefits will be great enough to justify a certain quantum of environmental costs; in other cases, they will not be so great and the proposed action may have to be abandoned or significantly altered so as to bring the benefits and costs into a proper balance. The point of the individualized balancing analysis is to ensure that, with possible alterations the optimally beneficial action is finally taken. . . .

The Atomic Energy Commission, abdicating entirely to other agencies' certifications, neglects the mandated balancing analysis. Concerned members of the public are thereby precluded from raising a wide range of environmental issues in order to affect particular Commission decisions. And the special purpose of NEPA is subverted. . . .

V

Petitioners' final attack is on the Commission's rules governing a particular set of nuclear facilities: those for which construction permits were granted without consideration of environmental issues, but for which operating licenses have yet to be issued. These facilities, still in varying stages of construction, include the one of most immediate concern to one of the petitioners: the Calvert Cliffs nuclear power plant on Chesapeake Bay in Maryland.

The Commission's rules recognize that the granting of a construction permit before NEPA's effective date does not justify bland inattention to environmental consequences until the operating license proceedings, perhaps far in the future. The rules require that measures be taken *now* for environmental protection. Specifically, the Commission has provided for three such measures during the pre-operating license stage. First, it has required that a condition be added to all construction permits, "whenever issued," which would oblige the holders of the permits to observe all applicable environmental standards imposed by federal or state law. Second, it has required permit holders to submit their own environmental report on the facility under construction. And third, it has initiated procedures for the drafting of its staff's "detailed environmental statement" in advance of operating license proceedings.

The one thing the Commission has refused to do is take any independent action based upon the material in the environmental reports and "detailed statements." Whatever environmental damage the reports and statements may reveal, the Commission will allow construction to proceed on the original plans. It will not even consider requiring alterations in those plans (beyond compliance with external standards which would be binding in any event), though the "detailed statements" must contain an analysis of possible alternatives and may suggest relatively inexpensive but highly beneficial changes. . . . Once again, the Commission seems to believe that the mere drafting and filing of papers is enough to satisfy NEPA.

The Commission appears to recognize the severe limitation which its rules impose on environmental protection. Yet it argues that full NEPA consideration of alternatives and independent action would cause too much delay at the pre-operating license stage. It justifies its rules as the most that is "practicable, in the light of environmental needs and 'other essential considerations of national policy'." It cites in particular, the "national power crisis" as a consideration of national policy militating against delay in construction of nuclear power facilities. . . .

The special importance of the pre-operating license stage is not difficult to fathom. In cases where environmental costs were not considered in granting a construction permit, it is very likely that the planned facility will include some features which do significant damage to the environment and which could not have survived a rigorous balancing of costs and benefits. At the later operating license proceedings, this environmental damage will have to be fully considered. But by that time the situation will have changed radically. Once a facility has been completely constructed, the economic cost of any alteration may be very great. In the language of NEPA, there is likely to be an "irreversible and irretrievable commitment of resources," which will inevitably restrict the Commission's options. . . .

By refusing to consider requirement of alterations until construction is completed, the Commission may effectively foreclose the environmental protection desired by Congress. It may also foreclose rigorous consideration of environmental factors at the eventual operating license proceedings. If "irreversible and irretrievable commitment[s] of resources" have already been made, the license hearing (and any public intervention therein) may become a hollow exercise. This hardly amounts to consideration of environmental values "to the fullest extent possible."

A full NEPA consideration of alterations in the original plans of a facility, then, is both important and appropriate well before the operating license proceedings. It is not duplicative if environmental issues were not considered in granting the construction permit. And it need not be duplicated, absent new information or new developments, at the operating license stage. In order that the pre-operating license review be as effective as possible the Commission should consider very seriously the requirement of a temporary halt in construction pending its review and the "backfitting" of technological innovations. For no action which might minimize environmental damage may be dismissed out of hand. Of course, final operation of the facility may be delayed thereby. But some delay is inherent whenever the NEPA consideration is conducted whether before or at the license proceedings. It is far more consistent with the purposes of the Act to delay operation at a stage where real environmental protection may come about than at a stage where corrective action may be so costly as to be impossible.

Thus, we conclude that the Commission must go farther than it has in its present rules. It must consider action, as well as file reports and papers, at the pre-operating license stage. As the Commission candidly admits, such consideration does not amount to a retroactive application of NEPA. Although the projects in question may have been commenced and initially approved before January 1, 1970, the Act clearly applies to them since they must still pass muster before going into full operation. All we demand is that the environmental review be as full and fruitful as possible.

We hold that, in the . . . respects detailed above, the Commission must revise its rules governing consideration of environmental issues. We do not impose a harsh burden on the Commission. For we require only an exercise of substantive discretion which will protect the environment "to the fullest extent possible."

No less is required if the grand congressional purposes underlying NEPA are to become a reality.

Remanded for proceedings consistent with this opinion.

◆◆◆

Case Questions

1. List the duties placed by NEPA upon federal agencies.
2. What has the Atomic Energy Commission done to impose the consideration of potential adverse environmental alteration upon those who have received construction permits *before* NEPA's effective date?

Council On Environmental Quality (CEQ)

Title I of NEPA covers the declaration of a national environmental policy and the requirement of the creation of impact statements to be used in the decision-making process concerning almost all federal actions affecting the environment. Title II creates the CEQ and gives it the following functions (a partial listing only - parts quoted):[32]

1. "to assist and advise the President in the preparation of the Environmental Quality Report . . ." This report is submitted to Congress before July 1 of each year and is to include a current evaluation of the status and condition of the major environmental assets of the nation (land, water, air and depletable resources).
2. "to gather authoritative information concerning the conditions and trends in the quality of the environment . . ."
3. "to review and appraise the various programs and activities of the Federal Government in light of the policy set forth in Title I . . ."
4. "to develop and recommend to the President national policies to foster and promote the improvement of environmental quality . . ."

In summary, NEPA was established to oversee the development of a national environmental policy and to make sure that, within reason, the nation's most powerful producer and consumer, the federal government, conformed to that policy.

Environmental Protection Agency

The Environmental Protection Agency (EPA) was created by executive order and began operation on December 2, 1970.[33] The EPA cooperates closely with the CEQ but pursues different objectives. The EPA coordinates enforcement of federal laws, rules and regulations as they impact the *private sector.* More specifically, the EPA is responsible for conducting research and demonstrations, for establishing and enforcing environmental standards, for monitoring pollution and, perhaps most importantly, for working with state and local governments in their attempt to enforce state and local laws.

In fact, it is the policy of the EPA to leave pollution control enforcement to the states where the states have effective environmental laws. However, it is difficult for states to effectively attack major environmental polluters of the air and water, or users of pesticides or producers of radiation and noise because these substances seldom stay within state boundary lines.

We have outlined the chief areas of enforcement for the EPA. It must be remembered that environmental protection is a relatively new area for the legal system. Procedures and standards for judicial review, measures of damages, and effective remedies are just emerging. Generalization, therefore, is difficult, but rapid development in the substantive areas under the EPA's jurisdiction is expected.

AIR

The federal legislation on air quality is comprehensive. It began with the Air Pollution Act of 1955[34] which authorized the first federally funded air pollution research. The Motor Vehicle Pollution Control Act of 1965[35] gave the federal government the authority to set standards for emission discharges into the air by automobiles. The Air Quality Act of 1967[36] established comprehensive federal research in air pollution and the Clean Air Act of 1970[37] set up a new system of national air quality standards and provided for the establishment of new auto pollution levels. This 1970 Act was the first to provide for national, uniform air quality standards based on geographic regions.

No act has created more controversy and difficulty for the EPA than the Clean Air Act. Although the National Motor Vehicle Emissions Standards Act recognized in 1965 that pollution from motor vehicles could only be handled by federal (national) standards, it was the 1970 Act that accelerated the schedule for emission controls. It required that by 1975 new autos had to show a 90 percent reduction in hydrocarbon and carbon emissions over 1970 models. Also, the 1970 law prohibited the sale of a new car unless it was certified by the EPA as having complied with emission standards.

Congress gave the EPA special powers in the 1970 Act. It was specifically granted:

1. the power to require those firms under review to give all necessary information; and,
2. the emergency authority under which it could suspend the imposition of emission standards.

Also, the Act provided that willful violators of EPA regulations could be denied federal contract awards.

Most enforcement of the 1970 Act is not accomplished in court. The Administrator of the EPA notifies a polluter that he is in violation of the law, issues an order to stop the pollution and, if this fails, then court action for an injunction may be sought. A noteworthy provision of the 1970 Act is that when certain conditions are met, private citizens may bring legal action against polluters. A clear violation of a standard or EPA order must be alleged and notice must be given both the polluter and the EPA. Citizens may also bring an action against the Administrator of the EPA if he fails to perform an act required of him under the law.

WATER

Early attempts at controlling water pollution by legislation in 1886 and 1899 were unsuccessful because those in charge of enforcing the law did not enforce it. It was not until recently that enforcement of such legislation was forthcoming.

The Federal Water Pollution Control Act (FWPCA) was passed in 1948, amended in 1956, and again in 1972.[38] The 1972 amendments restructured the authority for water pollution control and consolidated this authority in the Administrator of the EPA.

The objective of the recent water pollution amendments to the FWPCA is to restore and then maintain the chemical, physical and biological integrity of the nation's navigable waters. A primary goal is the elimination of the discharge of all pollutants into the navigable waters of the U.S. by 1985. This is only a goal; not, at this date, a requirement.

A second goal is to achieve an interim level of water quality which would provide for the protection of fish, shellfish, wildlife and recreation areas by 1983.

The 1972 amendments changed the thrust of the EPA's efforts in water quality control from the promulgation of water quality standards to effluent limitations of pollutants being discharged from any discernible, confined and separate means of conveyance. Generally, the emphasis was off of setting standards for and measuring pollutants in a given body of water, and emphasis was placed on identifying the major polluters. Again, state enforcement techniques and efforts are respected by the EPA.

Under present legislation the Administrator of the EPA is directed to publish a list of toxic pollutants and effluent limitations for these pollutants. Such limitations may constitute an absolute prohibition against discharging.

Enforcement of the various water pollution laws is accomplished in much the same manner as air-pollution enforcement. Informal attempts to reach a resolution are stressed with the ultimate remedy of an injunction being provided by the court system. Also, private suits against water-polluters are allowed in some instances.

SOLID WASTE, PESTICIDES, RADIATION and NOISE

Since 1965, federal legislation aimed at controlling the interstate effects of solid waste disposal, the use of pesticides, radiation and noise has received increasing attention. Again, legislation places the enforcement of federal laws in these areas within the jurisdiction of the EPA. The mandate of the EPA in each case is much the same. It is to conduct research, develop standards, and enforce its rules and regulations as well as enforce the substantial provisions of other federal legislation in these areas.

In summary, it is difficult to assess the EPA's impact at this point. The history of "regulating" conduct through federal administrative agencies is one characterized by some successes but more failures. In no small sense, the success of the agency will depend upon the attitude and abilities of the administrator and those he or she hires as well as the money provided by Congress for agency operation.

In conclusion we again stress the risks of including new legislation in a textbook. The rules and regulations made by the appropriate administrative agencies and court interpretation of the legislation may substantially change some of the material. However, the broad range of circumstances in which new duties have been imposed can not be ignored in a book for the student of business associations. For the most part, these legislative duties are here to stay.

SOCIAL RESPONSIBILITIES OF AMERICAN BUSINESS ASSOCIATIONS

Thus far in the chapter we have presented material outlining the circumstances in which the enforcement machinery of federal administrative agencies and the court system may be used to impose duties on employers, producers, and polluters. However, many activities of business associations which have undesirable effects on human welfare remain beyond the reaches of the law. Recently, because of disclosures made during the Watergate proceedings about unethical corporate conduct (some of it illegal), the public consciousness about such activity has been aroused. This conduct by business associations (primarily corporations) which violates no expressed or recognized legal duty, yet appears to most persons to be beyond the rules of "fair play" has created the fundamental question of whether or not business associations should exercise a measure of "social responsibility."

Most humans recognize that they are subject to some social control which is beyond the formal enforcing structure of the legal system. They obey these codes of conduct because they perceive that it is in their best interests *as humans* to do so. Also, responsibility for such an act by a single person can be relatively easily affixed on the perpetrator of the act. Accountability is not much of a problem when focusing on the acts of an individual human. In applying the concept of "social responsibility" to a business association, however, at least two formidable obstacles are presented.

First, affixing responsibility for an act done in the name of the association is not the same as affixing it on a human. In a business association, the human responsibility for a decision is diffused. For example, Ralph Nader attempted for years to determine what person at General Motors was responsible for designing the Corvair automobile. To date, no satisfactory answer has been found.

If the human accountability for corporate decisions is obfuscated then what means of enforcement would be effective? Fines against the business associations hurt the shareholders more than those actually responsible for the decision prompting the fine -- the managers.

A second formidable obstacle is again presented by the very nature of the business association. By definition, the objective of business associations is to earn a profit, not, as is true of humans, to maximize one's total welfare. Thus when the task of making a profit conflicts with the proposed course of action which would maximize some other objective, the conventional wisdom dictates that business associations must opt for the profit maximizing opportunity. This view is most eloquently stated by Professor Milton Friedman, noted conservative economist. Recently, he argued that when a corporation spends time or effort on what is "socially" desirable and thereby sacrifices an economic opportunity to earn profit it is engaging in an undesirable enfringement on the political process and misleading the shareholders.[39] Social decisions, he asserts, should be made by either individual humans, or, where the need is greater, by the elected politicians whose expressed task is to protect the public welfare. Moreover, when business associations make social decisions what standards are to be applied? He continues, that if, at the expense of corporate profits, the managers of a corporation decide to hire "hardcore" unemployed instead of better-qualified workers, the corporation would be spending someone else's money — the shareholders, to the extent this reduced profits — for a general social interest. In summary, Friedman's doctrine is that the business association, especially large corporations, is chartered by the state to make a profit, and the general welfare is best served when each corporation acts to maximize this objective. Certainly our perceptions of this restatement of Adam Smith's invisible hand moving in the economy vary with the times. Nevertheless, Friedman's logic is in accord with our capitalistic tradition. It presents a modern-day manifestation of the reasoning found in the *Dodge* v. *Ford Motor Co.* opinion discussed in Chapter 12. In this case, you will recall, the court sided with the Dodge brothers and compelled Henry Ford to continue to pay massive dividends to the shareholders rather than spend some of the great quantities of revenues on employee and customer benefits.

On the other hand, the Friedman view appears to some to be simplistic. The question of when profits should be sacrificed to achieve a socially desirable result is, perhaps, one of the most important and complex questions facing the directors of large corporations. Certainly, there is precedent, both legal and otherwise, for corporate acts of compassion and humanity. For example, recall the logic and language of the court in the *A. P. Smith Mfg. Co.* v. *Barlow* case in Chapter 9. There, a court recognized that a corporate donation of $1,500 dollars to Princeton University was permissible and even desirable because so much of the wealth today is generated by this form of association that some commitment to its "social environment" should be allowed.

If these questions of the existence of social responsibilities and human accountability for corporate acts are still being formulated, one can hardly expect answers. We provide none here. One can recognize with some satisfaction that business association duties to end discrimination in employment, to provide adequate retirement security, to provide safe products and non-polluting manufacturing processes have recently been formally recognized by Congress. However, the struggle to develop the appropriate balance between profits and the needs of human welfare continues. This struggle is most dramatically highlighted today by the litigation involving the Reserve Mining Company. The following reproduced portions of this litigation are used to illustrate the complex nature of the balance being sought.

The Reserve Mining Litigation

The litigation involving the Reserve Mining Company at Silver Bay, Minnesota, is extremely complex and, at this writing, not complete. The plaintiffs are the cities of Duluth, Minnesota; and Superior, Wisconsin; and the states of Minnesota, Wisconsin and Michigan as well as the Federal Government and numerous environmental groups. The defendants are, among others, Reserve Mining Company, Armco Steel Corporation, and Republic Steel Corporation. At issue was Reserve Mining's pollution of Lake Superior. The case was tried in the U.S. District Court at Duluth. After 9½ months of trial, the district judge, Judge Lord, ordered Reserve Mining to cease its discharge into Lake Superior as of

12:01 a.m., April 21, 1974. The opinion accompanying this order is reproduced below. Not quite two days later the Eighth Circuit Court of Appeals stayed (suspended) the order of the District Court closing Reserve Mining pending a full hearing by the Circuit Court on a motion to suspend the stay. On May 15, 1974, the Circuit Court continued its stay until June 4, 1974. On this latter date the Circuit Court of Appeals granted a seventy-day continuation upon Reserve's taking prompt steps to abate its discharge into air and water. The Circuit Court remanded part of the case back to the District Court and set out a procedure by which Reserve was to submit plans for abating its discharges. On August 3, 1974, the District Court again found the attempts by Reserve to abate its discharge inadequate and suggested to the Circuit Court that the stay of the initial temporary injunction be lifted. Meanwhile, the first order of the Circuit Court staying the District Court injunction against continued discharge reached the U.S. Supreme Court on Appeal. The Supreme Court decision was announced October 11, 1974. The decision follows.

On March 14, 1975, the Circuit Court reached its decision on the merits of the case and held that Reserve was guilty of creating a risk to the public health of sufficient gravity to be legally cognizable and an abatement order on reasonable grounds might be issued but the evidence did not require that Reserve immediately terminate its operations. Reserve and its parent companies were to be given a reasonable opportunity to convert its taconite operations to on-land disposal and to restrict air emissions.

The record is silent as to the activities of the parties between the spring of 1975 and November of 1975. It is safe to assume that the pollution continued while the feasibility of various on-land disposal sites was explored. In November of 1975, the state of Minnesota asked the trial court to order the U.S. Corps of Engineers to supply filtered water to the city of Duluth, Minnesota which draws its drinking water from Lake Superior. The result of this proceeding was that Judge Lord ordered Reserve Mining to pay $100,000 to cover the cost of this filtration. Reserve Mining appealed this decision based upon three alleged errors: 1) the fact that it had no notice that it might be fined; 2) that Judge Lord exhibited prejudice toward it; and 3) that Judge Lord violated an earlier appellate court order which recognized state jurisdiction over the issue of the disposal cite. On January 6, 1976, the appellate court removed Judge Lord from the case based upon the arguments of Reserve.[40] The order of removal cites the following as evidence of judicial prejudice.[41]

> ... the trial judge announced on the record that witnesses called by Reserve could not be believed, that in every instance Reserve Mining Company hid the evidence, misrepresented, delayed and frustrated the ultimate conclusions, and that he did not have 'any faith' in witnesses to be called by Reserve.

Indeed, such statements are out of the ordinary for a trial judge. But, so is the nature of the threat posed to the public by Reserve. On February 21, 1976 Judge Edward Devitt, the apparent replacement for Judge Lord, heard arguments by the U.S. Government that Reserve should be required to pay $288,800 expended by the U.S. Army Corps of Engineers for filtration of water. The court agreed that Reserve should be liable for the expenses of filtration and ordered the parties to meet promptly to agree on the correctness of the amount sought.[42]

As of this date, spring, 1977, the parties continue to study the feasible cites for on-land disposal.

U.S. v. RESERVE MINING
6 ERC 1449 (D. Ct., Minn., 1974)

Action for injunctive relief to abate mining company's discharges of taconite tailings into air and into Lake Superior.

Injunctive relief granted. . . .

LORD, J.:

This action for injunctive relief is before the Court after 139 days of trial, which included testimony from well over 100 witnesses, over 1,621 exhibits, and over 18,000 pages of transcript. Of necessity, it will require several weeks before the Court will be able to set forth in writing its detailed findings of fact and conclusions of law. Inasmuch as the case deals with issues concerning public health, the ultimate resolution of the problem should not be delayed by this procedural matter. The Court has carefully considered all of the evidence and hereto sets forth its essential findings of fact and conclusions of law to be refined and supplemented at a later date.

Findings of Fact

1. Reserve Mining Company (Reserve) is set up and run for the sole benefit of its owners, Armco Steel Corporation (Armco) and Republic Steel Corporation (Republic), and acts as a mere instrumentality or agent of its parent corporations. Reserve is run in such a manner as to pass all its profits to the parents.

2. Reserve acting as an instrumentality and agent for Armco and Republic discharges large amounts of minute amphibole fibers into Lake Superior and into the air of Silver Bay daily.

3. The particles when deposited into the water are dispersed throughout Lake Superior and into Wisconsin and Michigan.

4. The currents in the lake, which are largely influenced by the discharge, carry many of the fibers in a southwesterly direction toward Duluth and are found in substantial quantities in the Duluth drinking water.

5. Many of these fibers are morphologically and chemically identical to amosite asbestos and an even larger number are similar to amosite asbestos.

6. Exposure to these fibers can produce asbestosis, mesothelioma, and cancer of the lung, gastrointestinal tract and larynx.

7. Most of the studies dealing with this problem are concerned with the inhalation of fibers; however, the available evidence indicates that the fibers pose a risk when ingested as well as when inhaled.

8.. The fibers emitted by the defendant into Lake Superior have the potential for causing great harm to the health of those exposed to them.

9. The discharge into the air substantially endangers the health of the people of Silver Bay and surrounding communities as far away as the eastern shore in Wisconsin.

10. The discharge into the water substantially endangers the health of the people who procure their drinking water from the western arm of Lake Superior including the communities of Beaver Bay, Two Harbors, Cloquet, Duluth, and Superior, Wisconsin.

11. The present and future industrial standard for a safe level of asbestos fibers in the air is based on the experience related to asbestosis and not to cancer. In addition its formulation was influenced more by technological limitations than health considerations.

12. The exposure of a non-worker populace cannot be equated with industrial exposure if for no other reason than the environmental exposure, as contrasted to a working exposure, is for every hour of every day.

13. While there is a dose-response relationship associated with the adverse effects of asbestos exposure and may be therefore a threshold exposure value below which no increase in cancer would be found, this exposure threshold is not now known. . . .

Memorandum

It has been clearly established in this case that Reserve's discharge creates a serious health hazard to the people exposed to it. The exact scope of this potential health hazard is impossible to accurately quantify at this time. Significant increase in diseases associated with asbestos exposure do not develop until fifteen to twenty years after the initial exposure to the fibers. The state of the scientific and medical knowledge available in this area is in its early stages and there is insufficient knowledge upon which to base an opinion as to the magnitude of the risks associated with this exposure. The fact that few fibers have been found in the tissue of certain deceased Duluth residents may indicate that the general contamination in the community of Duluth has not yet reached alarming proportions. Unfortunately, the real answer to the problem will not be available until some ten to twenty years from this date when the health experience of those exposed to the fibers emitted from Reserve's plant is reviewed. At present the Court is faced with a situation where a commercial industry is daily exposing thousands of people to substantial quantities of a known human carcinogen. Emphasis is placed upon the fact that the Court is not dealing with a situation in which a substance causes cancer in experimental animals where the effect on humans is largely speculative. Fibers identical and similar to those emitted from Reserve's plant have been directly associated with a marked increase in the incidence of cancer in humans.

The Court has been constantly reminded that a curtailment in the discharge may result in a severe economic blow to the people of Silver Bay, Babbit and others who depend on Reserve directly or indirectly for their livelihood. Certainly unemployment in itself can result in an unhealthy situation. At the same time, however, the Court must consider the people downstream from the discharge. Under no circumstances will the Court allow the people of Duluth to be continuously and indefinitely exposed to a known human carcinogen in order that the people in Silver Bay can continue working at their jobs.

Naturally the Court would like to find a middle ground that would satisfy both considerations. If an alternate method of disposal is available that is economically feasible, could be speedily implemented and took into consideration the health questions involved, the Court might be disposed to fashion a remedy that would permit the implementation of such a system. However, if there is no alternative method available, the Court has no other choice but to immediately curtail the discharge and stop the contamination of the water supply of those downstream from the plant.

With these considerations in mind, the Court on February 5, 1974, took the unusual step of relating to the parties the Court's view of the evidence to date concerning the public health issue. The Court had heard in one form or another from substantially all of the world's experts in the area. The Court was led to believe by Reserve that little had been done in the way of devising an alternative method of disposing of the tailings on land and, in fact, that Reserve knew of no feasible way to accomplish such a system. At that time, it was Reserve's posture in this litigation that the only feasible alternative to the present discharge was the creation of a pipe system that would carry the tailings to the bottom of the lake. If, in fact, the deep pipe system was unacceptable, the Court was led to believe that Reserve had no alternative method for disposing of the tailings. Hence the Court found it essential that Reserve's attention be focused directly on the problem and a possible on land disposal alternative be develped as quickly as possible.

The Court was at one and the same time hearing a motion for a temporary restraining order and a permanent injunction. The reluctance of the Court to make a formal ruling on the temporary restraining order at an early time was done out of caution with the anticipation of hearing from more of the world's experts. It was after hearing all of this evidence that the Court gave its tentative findings on the health issue with the caveat that further evidence would be taken. The statement was made with a view toward giving Reserve an impetus to start resolving its problem and to give Duluth and the Lake Shore communities time to seek clean water. It did not have the desired effect in either instance.

As it turned out, after days of testimony on the underwater disposal alternative proposed by Reserve, it became clear to the Court that this alternative in no way lessened the public health threat and possibly created additional problems relating to public health. The Court's findings in this regard turned out to be superfluous in that later testimony by representatives of Armco, half owner of Reserve, indicated that Armco had long since disregarded this underwater disposal system on the basis of engineering infeasibility alone, without any regard to its effect on the lake or public health. Upon further inquiry to officers of Armco and Republic, who also serve on the Board of Directors of Reserve, it appeared that several plans had been developed dealing with the possibility of on land disposal. Although these plans had been asked for by plaintiffs by way of interrogatories and by the Court by direct order, they were not produced nor mentioned until the representatives of Armco and Republic were deposed on March 1, 1974. The Court is apprised that defendants' failure to produce these plans for on land disposal will be the subject matter for motions by the plaintiffs to collect costs involved in the litigation so this matter will be dealt with at that time. The Court has stated on the record and will repeat here that Reserve's insistence on advocating the underwater disposal system which had been deemed infeasible by one of its owners and the failure to timely produce the documents dealing with possible on land disposal systems has substantially delayed the outcome of this litigation in a situation where a speedy resolution is essential.

The Court refers to this history in the case only to point out that since February 5, defendants were informed that the present method of discharge would stop and that if they chose to keep Reserve in operation they had to come up with an on land disposal alternative that would satisfy the health problems created by the present discharge in the air and water. It was the Court's fervent wish that the health hazard could be abated without the economic problems that would be imposed upon the people in the North Shore communities if Reserve in fact closed down permanently. The documents of Reserve's parent companies indicate that they have known for some time that they would have to make modifications in their discharge. . . . Even when faced with the evidence in this case that their discharge creates a substantial threat to the health of the people exposed to it, defendants are reluctant to curtail their discharge until the latest possible moment, presumably in order to prolong the profitability of the present discharge.

It was not until a few days ago that there was any indication to this Court that Reserve had a feasible plan for the disposal of taconite tailings on land. The testimony in the case by Reserve and representations by Reserve's counsel indicated that they not only had no such plan but that the engineering problems of such a system were insurmountable. The plaintiffs, on the other hand, introduced testimony indicating that on land disposal is feasible. Reserve took issue with this testimony even after the major engineering problems were solved and maintained that it would simply be too expensive to change their method of disposal to on land.

The evidence in the case indicates that the daily profit in the operation at Reserve is in the neighborhood of $60,000.00 per day. Each year that the plant remains in operation there is a 90 percent return on owner's equity. In other words, for every dollar Armco and Republic initially invested in Reserve, they get back ninety cents each year the plant remains in operation.

This is not to say that the companies could not afford to make modifications. The testimony adduced at trial was to the effect that (with product improvement) Reserve, Republic and Armco could afford at the very least a $180,000,000 to $200,000,000 capital outlay with reasonably associated operating costs without substantially changing their economic situation as to profitability, intraindustry position, interest coverage, bond rating, etc. This figure should come as no shock to the defendant. Their own documents, recently discovered, support this fact. In this area it should be noted that any reduction in the royalty rate paid by Reserve or the interest rate, by such devices as revenue bonds or industrial bonds, would make even larger capital outlays, with accompanying operating expenses, possible. . . . The evidence is clear that Republic and Armco are two of the largest corporations in this country. They are prosperous now and would remain prosperous even after the necessary alterations are made. Defendants have had the means to implement a feasible, economical alternative. It was their choice whether they would make the investment or abandon their employees and the State of Minnesota.

It should be noted in this regard that the State of Minnesota is here in the posture of asking the Court for fines and penalties as well as injunctive relief.

Reserve on the other hand still has outstanding counterclaims against the state. It would, therefore, be inappropriate and premature for this governmental unit to subsidize the company before these matters are decided by the Court.

Today, April 20, 1974, the chief executive officers of both Armco and Republic have testified that they are unwilling to abate the discharge and bring their operation into compliance with applicable Minnesota regulations in an acceptable manner. They proposed a plan for an on land disposal site in the Palisades Creek area adjacent to the Silver Bay plant. Although this particular plan was in existence for several years it was not brought forward until the latest stages of this proceeding. The plan, which has been rejected by the plaintiffs because it is not environmentally sound, is totally unacceptable to the Court because of the conditions imposed with it. . . .

Defendants have the economic and engineering capability to carry out an on land disposal system that satisfies the health and environmental considerations raised. For reasons unknown to this Court they have chosen not to implement such a plan. In essence they have decided to continue exposing thousands daily to a substantial health risk in order to maintain the current profitability of the present operation and delay the capital outlay (with its concommitant profit) needed to institute modifications. The Court has no other alternative but to order an immediate halt to the discharge which threatens the lives of thousands. In that defendants have no plan to make the necessary modifications, there is no reason to delay any further the issuance of the injunction.

Up until the time of writing this opinion the Court has sought to exhaust every possibility in an effort to find a solution that would alleviate the health threat without a disruption of operations at Silver Bay. Faced with the defendants' intransigence, even in the light of the public health problem, the Court must order an immediate curtailment of the discharge.

THEREFORE, IT IS ORDERED

1) That the discharge from the Reserve Mining Company into Lake Superior be enjoined as of 12:01 A.M., April 21, 1974.

2) That the discharge of amphibole fibers from the Reserve Mining Company into the air be enjoined as of 12:01 A.M., April 21, 1974 until such time as defendants prove to the Court that they are in compliance with all applicable Minnesota Regulations. . . .

◆◆◆

U.S. v. RESERVE MINING
7 ERC 1113 (U.S. Sup. Ct., 1974)

◆◆◆

The respective applications for an order vacating or modifying the stay order of the United States Court of Appeals for the Eighth Circuit, presented to MR. JUSTICE BLACKMUN and by him referred to the Court, are each denied. Four Justices, however, state explicitly that these denials are without prejudice to the applicants' renewal of their applications to vacate if the litigation has not been finally decided by the Court of Appeals by January 31, 1975.

Mr. Justice Douglas, dissenting.

I would vacate the stay issued by the Court of Appeals.

Judge Lord made detailed findings as to the health hazards of the respondent's discharges into the air and into the waters of Lake Superior, . . . The Court of Appeals disagreed with Judge Lord's conclusion but it stopped short of holding that his findings were "clearly erroneous" within the meaning of Rule 52 (a) of the Rules of Civil Procedure. Even in its view, the issue, however, was close or rather neatly balanced. It therefore decided that being a "court of law" it was "governed by rules of proof" and that "unknowns may not be substituted for proof of a demonstrable hazard to the public health."

That position, however, with all respect makes "maximizing profits" the measure of the public good, not health of human beings or life itself. Property is, of course, protected under the Due Process Clause of the Fifth Amendment against federal intrusion. But so is life and liberty. Where the scales are so evenly divided, we cannot say that the findings on health were "clearly erroneous" nor am I able to discover how "maximizing profits" becomes a governing principle overriding the health hazards. If equal justice is the federal standard, we should be as alert to protect people and their rights as the Court of Appeals was to protect "maximizing profits." If, as the Court of Appeals indicates, there is doubt, it should be resolved in favor of humanity, lest in the end our judicial system be part and parcel of a regime that makes people, the sovereign power in this Nation, the victims of the great God Progress which is behind the stay permitting this vast pollution of Lake Superior and its environs. I am not aware of a constitutional principle that allows either private or public enterprises to despoil any part of the domain that belongs to all of the people. Our guiding principle should be Mr. Justice Holmes' dictum that our waterways, great and small, are treasures, not garbage dumps or cesspools.

Case Questions

1. Who owns Reserve Mining? From the limited information available do you think it would be fair to impose responsibility for the acts of pollution upon any human in the form of a fine or imprisonment? If so, which person?
2. Assume an employee of Reserve who must breathe the polluted air of Silver Bay every day wishes to object to his employer's acts. What are his remedies? What are the remedies of the residents of the city of Duluth?
3. Do Reserve or the owners of Reserve make a product that can be identified as having been made by them so that concerned consumers might bring some form of pressure to bear on them in the form of a boycott?
4. Each year Reserve returns to its owners 90 percent of their initial investment. Is Reserve too profitable? How would Milton Friedman view this case? Is Reserve being socially responsible by maximizing its profit?
5. Is Reserve Mining beyond the law?

CONCLUSION

When science seems to confront the conventional wisdom or established practice, the response often takes years. In this case, some readjustment of Reserve Mining's industrial processes seems in order. However, no alternative appears easy or satisfactory. It could be that on-land disposal of the waste may pose as great a threat to the environment and human life as the current method of disposal. If so, perhaps we should focus on how the decision of waste disposal is made; who will make it? and, what standards will be applied? Is it sufficient that this decision should be made by private interests?

REVIEW PROBLEMS

1. List the acts declared unlawful by Title VII of the 1964 Civil Rights Act, the Equal Employment Opportunity Act of 1972, the Equal Pay Act of 1963 and the Age Discrimination in Employment Act of 1967.
2. Define the bona fide occupational qualification and describe the circumstances in which it might be properly applied.
3. What are the reasons for and the standards to be used in the award of back pay for employment discrimination?
4. Define the general duty clause of the Occupational Safety and Health Act. Specifically, what is a "recognized hazard" for purposes of the application of the Act?
5. Outline the duties placed upon employers by the Employment Retirement Income Security Act of 1974.
6. Distinguish between express warranties, implied warranties of merchantability and implied warranties of fitness for a particular purpose.
7. John purchased a drill from the local hardware store on the personal word of the salesman that the drill was "double insulated." The box in which it came also said it was double insulated. The double insulation feature meant the tool was so constructed that should there be a short in the tool, the user would not be harmed. John was insistent on this feature in his tools because his workshop was in the basement and the floors were often wet because the walls leaked rain water.

    The first time John used the tool he was standing on a damp floor. An electrical short developed in the tool and he was severely injured. John later found out that the drill was not double insulated; in fact, many of the wires on the inside were not covered with insulating material which was used by most other manufacturers and prescribed by industry standards. It was of a different type and inferior.

    List and define all of the legal principles which John may argue to state a good cause of action against the manufacturer and the seller.
8. Explain the reasons for the passage of the Consumer Product Warranty and Federal Trade Commission Improvement Act. Outline its provisions.
9. Write a short but concise paragraph explaining the attempts of Congress to establish and provide for enforcement of environmental policy. Have such efforts been successful?
10. Derive your own definition of "social responsibility" as applied to business associations.

ENDNOTES

1. 42 U.S.C.A. § 2000e (1964).
2. 42 U.S.C.A. § 2000e as amended (1972).
3. 42 U.S.C.A. § 2000e-2 (e) (1964).
4. *Wall St. Journal,* Oct. 22, 1974, p. 20, Col. 4.
5. 29 U.S.C.A. 206 as amended (1963).
6. 42 U.S.C.A. § 2000e-2(h).
7. 29 U.S.C.A. § 621-634 (1967).
8. Ill. Inst. for Con't. L. Ed., OSHA p. 1-5, 1974.
9. 29 U.S.C.A. § 651 et seq. (1970).
10. 29 U.S.C.A. § 654 (a) (1).
11. 2 OSHA Rptr., BNA, 77:3103.
12. 29 U.S.C.A. § 1001 et. seq. (1974).
13. *Wall St. Journal,* Aug. 28, 1974, p.1, Col. 6.
14. *Id.*
15. *Id.*
16. R. J. Nordstrom, *Law of Sales* 284 (1970).
17. *Id.,* 280.
18. *Id.*
19. *Id.*
20. Pub. L. No. 93-637; § 101 et seq. (Jan. 4, 1975).
21. *Id.,* § 102 (a).
22. *Id.,* § 104 (a) (1).
23. *Id.,* § 104 (a) (2).
24. *Id.,* § 108 (a).
25. *Id.,* § 104 (a) (1).
26. *Id.,* § 101.
27. *Id.,* § 110 (d).
28. *Id.,* § 204 (b).
29. 42 U.S.C.A. § 4321 et seq. (1970).
30. 42 U.S.C.A. § 4332 (2) (c).
31. 36 Fed. Reg. 7724 (1971).
32. 42 U.S.C.A. § 4344.
33. Much of the information in this section was taken from, *The Challenge of the Environment: A Primer on EPA's Statutory Authority,* 1972, U.S.G.P.O.
34. 42 U.S.C.A. § 1857 et seq. (1955).
35. 42 U.S.C.A. § 1857b-1 to 1857b-8 (1965).
36. 42 U.S.C.A. § 1857 2 (1967).
37. 42 U.S.C.A. § 1857 as amended. (1970).
38. 33 U.S.C.A. § 1155 et. seq. as amended. (1972).
39. *New York Times, Magazine,* pp. 32-33 (Sept. 13, 1970).
40. 44 LW 2306 (1976).
41. *Id.,* citing transcript of November 14, 1975 hearings at 2-5, 56, 109.
42. Environmental Reporter, Current Developments, 1873 (March 5, 1976).

PART VII
EPILOGUE

THE NEW FORM OF PROPERTY

20

An epilogue is a concluding section of a speech, play, novel or narrative serving to round out or complete the design of the work. In our view, no comprehensive treatment of the legal perspectives of American business associations would be complete without reference to the insights of Professor Adolph Berle, made public as long ago as 1932. Through the kind permission of the Columbia Law Journal we present, in an edited article, a synthesis of Professor Berle's views written by himself in 1965.

Our legal perspective has focused upon the circumstances in which courts will enforce duties between the individual members of a business association, or between the members and the association, or between the association and the public. Professor Berle's legal perspective is more narrow but considerably deeper and more profound. Specifically, he attempts to assess the impact of the form of corporate ownership and managerial devices upon the traditional conception of property and property rights. Hopefully, his keen observations, while answering some of your lingering questions about the corporate form of business association, will raise more questions than it answers. As you read this article we suggest you keep a list of the issues presented and questions raised. The seeking of the answers to these questions will provide the stimulus for continued inquiry and education in the legal perspectives of American business associations.

PROPERTY, PRODUCTION AND REVOLUTION **
Adolph A. Berle*
65 Col. L. Rev. 1 (1965)

(Authors' note: This article has been edited and the footnotes renumbered.)

More than thirty years ago, in the preface of *The Modern Corporation and Private Property,* I wrote:

> The translation of perhaps two-thirds of the industrial wealth of the country from individual ownership to ownership by the large, publicly financed corporations vitally changes the lives of property owners, the lives of workers, and the methods of property tenure. The divorce of ownership from control consequent on that process almost necessarily involves a new form of economic organization of society.[1]

Dr. Means and I had pointed out that the two attributes of ownership — risking collective wealth in profit-seeking enterprise and ultimate management of

---

*Professor Emeritus of Law, Columbia University; A.B., Harvard, 1913; A.M., 1914; LL.B., 1961; LL.D., Columbia, 1964.

**Reprinted with permission from 65 Columbia Law Review 1, Copyright © 1965.

[1] *Preface* to BERLE & MEANS, THE MODERN CORPORATION AND PRIVATE PROPERTY at vii-viii (1932).

responsibility for that enterprise — had become divorced. Accordingly we raised the questions:

> Must we not, therefore, recognize that we are no longer dealing with property in the old sense? Does the traditional logic of property still apply? Because an owner who also exercises control over his wealth is protected in the full receipt of the advantages derived from it, must it *necessarily* follow that an owner who has surrendered control of his wealth should likewise be protected to the full? May not this surrender have so essentially changed his relation to his wealth as to have changed the logic applicable to his interest in that wealth? An answer to this question cannot be found in the law itself. It must be sought in the economic and social background of law.*2*

We based these questions on the growing dominance of the corporate form, the increasing decision-making power of corporate management, the increasingly passive position of shareholders, and the increasing inapplicablility of the ethical and economic justifications given (rightly enough at the time) by classic economics.

The object of this essay is to review some aspects of this conception in the light of a generation of experience and consequent developments.

I. THE CONTINUING CURRENT OF CHANGE TO "COLLECTIVE CAPTIALISM"

Factually, the trend towards dominance of that collective capitalism we call the "corporate system" has continued unabated. Evolution of the corporation has made stock-and-security ownership the dominant form by which individuals own wealth representing property devoted to production (as contrasted with property devoted to consumption).*3* The last great bastion of individually-owned productive property — agriculture — has been dramatically declining in proportion to the total production of the United States,*4* and even in agriculture, corporations have been steadily making inroads. Outside of agriculture, well over ninety percent of all the production in the country is carried on by more than a million corporations. In all of them, management is theoretically distinct from ownership. The directors of the corporation are not the "owners"; they are not agents of the stockholders and are not obliged to follow their instructions.*5* This in itself is not determinative. Numerically most of the million corporations are "close" — the stockholders are also the directors or are so related to them that the decision-making power rests with the stockholders. Quantitatively, however, a thousand or so very large corporations whose stockholders' lists run from 10,000 to 2,500,000, as in the case of

---

2 BERLE & MEANS, *op. cit. supra* note 1, at 338-39.

3 See note 11 *infra* (sic) and accompanying text.

4 Agricultural employment declined dramatically from 11.4 in 1920 to 5.7 million in 1960. Value of owned farms and equipment rose — but far more slowly than the value of assets, chiefly corporate, employed in industry. See BERLE, THE AMERICAN ECONOMIC REPUBLIC 233 n. 24 (1963).

5 Manson v. *Curtis,* 223 N.Y. 313, 322, 119 N.E. 559, 562 (1918); *Peabdoy* v. *Interborough Rapid Transit Co.,* 121 Misc. 647, 651, 202 N.Y. Supp. 287, 291 (1923) (Lehman, J.) *modified on other grounds,* 212 App. Div. 502, 209 N.Y. Supp. 380 (1st Dep't 1925).

American Telephone and Telegraph, account for an overwhelmingly large percentage both of asset-holders and of operations. *Fortune* Magazine tabulated the 500 largest United States industrial corporations and found their combined sales were 245 billion dollars in 1963 or about sixty-two percent of all industrial sales.[6] The factor of concentration is, of course, higher in the public service industries: communications, transportation and public utilities. It is not unfair to suggest that if these industries were included (they are not in the *Fortune* tabulation), 600 to 700 large corporations, whose control nominally is in the hands of their "public" stockholders (actually, of their managers), account for seventy percent of commercial operation of the country — agriculture aside. There has been a slow but continuing trend toward corporate concentration reckoned by the percentage of industry thus controlled. Actually the total trend is more marked because, in contrast to total economic growth, the proportion of American economic activity represented by individually controlled agriculture has been relatively declining.[7] American economics at present is dominantly, perhaps overwhelmingly, industrial.

The effect of this change upon the property system of the United States has been dramatic. Individually-owned wealth has enormously increased. It is today reckoned at somewhat more than 1,800 billion dollars.[8] Of more importance is the distribution of that figure. Relatively little of it is "productive" property — land or things employed by its owners in production or commerce — though figures are hazy at the edges. The largest item of individually-owned wealth, exclusive of productive assets, is described as "owner-occupied homes" (approximately 520 billion dollars).[9] These, of course, are primarily for consumption though a fraction of them are probably farmsteads. The next largest item — consumer durables — accounts for 210 billion dollars more;[10] these are chiefly automobiles and home equipment, again chiefly used for personal convenience and not for capital or productive purposes.

The property system as applied to productive assets breaks down (as of the end of 1963) as follows: 525 billion dollars of shares of corporate stock; 210 billion dollars in fixed income financial assets (federal, state and local government securities, corporate and foreign bonds, life insurance values, etc.); and 360 billion dollars in liquid assets, chiefly cash in banks.[11] These figures mean that, far and away, the largest item of personally owned "property" representing productive assets and enterprise is in the form of stock of corporations. . . . "Individually-owned" enterprise is thus steadily disappearing. Increasingly, the American owns his home, his car, and his household appliances; these are for his consumption. Simultaneously, he increasingly owns stocks, life insurance, and rights in pension funds, social security funds and similar arrangements. And he has a job, paying him a wage, salary or commission. . . .

In crude summation, most "owners" own stock, insurance savings and pension cliams and the like, and do not manage; most managers (corporate administrators) do not own. The corporate collective holds legal title to the tangible productive wealth of the country — for the benefit of others.

---

[6] *The Fortune Directory,* Fortune, July 1964, p. 179.
[7] See note 4 *supra* and accompanying text.
[8] First Nat'l city Bank, Monthly Economic Letter, July 1964, p. 78.
[9] *Ibid.*
[10] *Ibid.*
[11] *Ibid.*

The word "revolutionary" has been justifiably applied to less fundamental change. The United States is no longer anticipating a development. It is digesting a fact.

II. THE EMERGING CONCEPTION OF PROPERTY

Lawyers are accustomed to conceive of property in terms of ancient classification. If tangible, it was "real" — that is, land or rights derived from land; or it was "personal" — mobile, capable of being used, taken away, moved, transferred and so forth by its owners. If intangible, it was a "chose of action" — a claim on or against other individuals or entities capable of being enforced or protected in the courts. Some of this was "negotiable," passing under the law-merchant or adaptations thereof. The *proprietas* (the relation of the individual or owner to this property — real, personal or chosen in action) was assumed to be fixed.

There is no occasion to change these classic definitions. They do quite well for the purposes of defining rights, methods of transfer, handling intervening claims, and the myriad minor problems of transmission and adjustment. What has changed is the conception of *proprietas*. I here suggest that a new classification has been superimposed on the old theory.

My thesis is that "property" is now divided into two categories: (a) consumption property on the one hand and (b) productive property on the other — property devoted to production, manufacture, service or commerce, and designed to offer, for a price, goods or services to the public from which a holder expects to derive a return.

In respect of productive property, the *proprietas* has now been made subject to an overall, political determination as to the kind of civilization the American state in its democratic processes has decided it wants. This is an on-going process, not yet complete.

As a corollary, productive property has been divided into two layers: 1) that fraction which, though not managed by active owners, is administered to yield a return by way of interest, dividends of distribution of profit, and 2) that layer dominated and controlled by the representatives or delegates of the passive owners whose decisions are now subject to the political process just noted. In this category, social development is at present intense and likely to continue.

This essay does not deal with forces present and emerging that now bear on or will later affect consumptive property. Unquestionably these exist. . . .

In general, however, the impact of modern and economic evolution seems to be an expansion of a very old common-law maxim: *Sic utere tuo ut alienum non laedas*. The essential aim is to preserve the greatest available degree of consumption and choice as empty land fills up, roads become congested, and the capacity to invade others' lives by esthetic horrors is enlarged by technique. American law and law schools have, happily, developed a growing number of scholars and experts in this field. Let us confine (the word is scarcely apt) ourselves to the impact of economic and social evolution on *productive* property in its two aspects: 1) managerial-productive (management) and 2) passive-receptive (stock and security ownership).

III. THE CHANGING CONTENT OF PROPERTY [12]

We must note an enormous expansion of the scope of the term "property" in this connection. Not only is it divorced from the decision-making power of its supposedly beneficial holders (stockholders and their various removes), but it has come to encompass a set of conceptions superimposed upon the central reality of domination over tangible things. Businessmen describe an enterprise, great or small, as "the property." They do not mean merely the physical plant. They include access to all the facilities necessary to produce, transport, distribute and sell. They mean an entire organization of personnel without which the physical plant would be junk; they mean a hierarchy of executives, technical experts, sales managers and men; as well as the dealer organization and the labor relations habits. These relationships are increasingly protected, not merely by the law of contract, but by an increasing body of law imposing upon individuals a measure of loyalty to the central enterprise. For example, they may not acquire and sell to others as part of their personal capacity or equipment, confidential technical information, data on sales, or customer goodwill. Underlying this extension of the property concept to management relationships is recognition of the fact that the "capital" has been projected far into the realm of intangibles. The central enterprise is spending good money — often in immense amounts — building this organization, this technical information, these relationships; it is entitled to be protected against their appropriation by individuals. . . .

A shift in attitute toward corporate property arises in part from the changed origin of finance-capital. The property of corporations is dedicated to production, not to personal consumption; but, even more significant, that property is no longer the result of individual effort or choice. This change has come silently. Its implications even yet are not understood.

Corporations were originally groups of investors pooling their individual contributions of risk capital to organize and carry on an enterprise. Since they had saved their earnings or gains and had risked them in the undertaking, they were assimilated to the owner of land, who cleared and cultivated it, and sold its products. As the economics of the time went, this was justifiable. They had sacrificed, risked and, to some extent, worked at the development of the product. Presumably they had done something useful for the community, since it was prepared to pay for the product.

A mature corporation typically does not call for investor-supplied capital. It charges a price for its products from which it can pay taxation, costs, depreciation allowances, and can realize a profit over and above all these expenses. Of this profit item, approximately half goes as income taxes to the federal government, and sixty percent of the remaining half is distributed to its shareholders. It accumulates for capital purposes the undistributed forty percent and its depreciation charges. This is a phenomenon not of "investment," but of market power. Since corporations legally have perpetual life, this process can

---

[12] The rapid increase in technical development necessarily downgrades the position of physical or tangible things and upgrades the factors or organization and technical knowledge. Organization is not reducible to a formula. Technical knowledge is rarely if ever assignable to any single individual, group of individuals or corporation. It is part of the heritage of the country and of the race. In neither case do the traditional formulae applicable to common-law property fit the current fact.

continue indefinitely. The result has been that more than sixty percent of capital entering a particular industry is "internally generated" or, more accurately, "price-generated" because it is collected from the customers. Another twenty percent of the capital the corporation uses is borrowed from banks chiefly in anticipation of this accumulative process. The corporations in aggregate do indeed tap individual "savings," but for only a little less than twenty percent of their capital, and mainly through the issuance of bonds to intermediate savings-collecting institutions (life insurance companies, trust funds, pension trusts and savings banks).[13]

The corporation becomes the legal "owner" of the capital thus collected and has complete decision-making power over it; the corporation runs on its own economic steam. On the other hand, its stockholders, by now grandsons or great-grandsons of the original "investors" or (far more often) transferees of their transferees at thousands of removes, have and expect to have through their stock the "beneficial ownership" of the assets and profits thus accumulated and realized, after taxes, by the corporate enterprise. Management thus becomes, in an odd sort of way, the uncontrolled administrator of a kind of trust having the privilege of perpetual accumulation. The stockholder is the passive beneficiary, not only of the original "trust," but of the compounded annual accretions to it.

Not surprisingly, therefore, we discover a body of law building up to protect and deal with this remarkable phenomenon. To that fact itself perhaps is due a continuing tendency: subjection of property devoted to *production* — that is, chiefly in managerial hands — to legal rules requiring a use of it, more or less corresponding to the evolving expectations of American civilization.

IV. DEVELOPMENT OF PROPERTY LAW

Inevitably, the common-law legal system moves to normalize the new areas thus comprehended within the general head of "productive property." Two major lines are observed. The first (primarily outside the scope of this essay) proceeds through taxation. The principle has been established that the federal government — and in lesser measure, state governments — both may and should take a protion of the profits of corporations through the device of direct corporate income tax. Under the recent tax reduction, the federal government presently taxes corporate profits above 25,000 dollars at the rate of fifty percent; that percentage will be reduced to forty-eight percent in 1965.[14] This virtually makes the state an equal partner as far as profits are concerned. Factually, though silently, the process recognizes a fundamental and entirely demonstrable economic premise. Corporations derive their profits partly indeed from their own operations, but partly also from their market position and increasingly from techniques resulting from state expenditures of taxpayers' money. In this sense, the American state is an investor in practically every substantial enterprise; without its activity, the enterprise, if it could exist at all, would be or would have been compelled to spend money and effort to create position, maintain access to market, and build technical development it currently takes for granted. Under these circumstances, there is little reason or justification for assuming that *all* profits should automatically accrue to

[13] Gorman & Shea, *Capital Formation, Savings & Credit,* Survey of Current Bus., May 1964, p. 11.

[14] *Internal Revenue Code* of 1954 §§ 11 (b), (c).

stockholders. Put differently, stockholders – not having created the entire enterprise – are no longer the sole residuary legatees (after production costs and depreciation) of all the profits of an industrial progress, much of which is derived from state outlay.

A second line of development impinges directly on management operation. It arises from an evolving social concept of what American civilization should look like. It began with the minimum wage legislation[15] and the Wagner Act, [16] later revised by the Taft-Hartley Act[17] and modified by the Landrum-Griffin Act.[18] These statutes, and the growing body of case and administrative law under them, limit the decision-making power of corporate mangements with respect to wages and labor relations. Of interest is the fact that these laws in the main (though not universally) are applied to general enterprise for profit-making operations in production or commerce. Slowly a distinction began to develop between both expenditures and activities for personal consumption, and enterprises directed towards the offer of goods or services to the public from whose purchase or payment a profit is expected.

The latter, it increasingly appears, are subject to the imposition of rules derived essentially from the Bill of Rights. These rules are designed to assure that the market power of enterprise shall not be used so as to create or perpetuate conditions which the state itself is forbidden to create or maintain. . . .

The political ideal invested in the Constitution and reflected in the Bill of Rights, and the fourteenth and fifteenth amendments, contemplated individuals whose personality was not to be invaded, save for police purposes designed to protect other personalities from invasion. In the simpler days of the eighteenth century, the state was the principal threat: the Bill of Rights restrained the federal government and by the fourteenth amendment extended the restraints to the state governments. As the twentieth century entered its later half, it was clear that personal freedom could be abridged or invaded by denial of economic facilities offered or provided by privately-owned enterprises. Such facilities indeed were chiefly in private hands – overwhelmingly, in fact, offered or conducted by corporations. Yet they were essential to life and personality. The result was gradual, judicial extension of constitutional law, complemented now by such statutes as the Civil Rights Act of 1964 which covers the fields of lodging, restaurant facilities, places of entertainment, establishments serving or offering to serve food, gasoline or other products. The Civil Rights Act does not extend, even remotely, to the whole field of commerce; it does not affect all productive property. Yet the point is clear: such property may by statute, if not by constitutional extension, be made subject to those limitations which inhibit state action to protect individual freedom. . . .

---

[15] See *e.g.,* Fair Labor Standards Act of 1938, § 6, 52 Stat. 1062, as amended, 29 U.S.C. § 206 (Supp. V, 1964;) District of Columbia Minimum-Wage Law, ch. 174, 40 Stat. 960 (1918), held unconstitutional in *Adkins* v. *Children's Hosp.,* 261 U.S. 525 (1923), in turn overruled by *West Coast Hotel Co.* v. *Parrish,* 300 U.S. 379 (1937); Mass. Acts 1912, ch. 706.

[16] National Labor Relations Act, 49 Stat. 453 (1935), as amended, 29 U.S.C.§§ 151-68 (1959), as amended, 29 U.S.C.§§ 153-64 (Supp. V, 1964).

[17] Labor Management Relations Act, 61 Stat. 136 (1947), as amended, 29 U.S.C. §§ 141-87 (1959), as amended, 29 U.S.C. §§ 153-87 (Supp. V, 1964).

[18] Labor-Management Reporting and Disclosure Act of 1959, 73 Stat. 519, 29 U.S.C. §§ 153-87 (Supp. V, (1964).

V. THE INSTITUTION OF PASSIVE PROPERTY

Increased size and domination of the American corporation has automatically split the package of rights and privileges comprising the old conception of property. Specifically, it splits the personality of the individual beneficial owner away from the enterprise manager. The "things" themselves — including the intangible elements noted earlier in this essay — "belong" to the corporation which holds legal title to them. The ultimate beneficial interest embodied in a share of stock represents an expectation that a portion of the profits remaining after taxes will be declared as dividends, and that in the relatively unlikely event of liquidation each share will get its allocable part of the assets. The former expectation is vivid; the latter so remote that it plays little part in giving market value to shares. Stockholders do have a right to vote which is of diminishing importance as the number of shareholders in each corporation increases — diminishing in fact to negligible importance as the corporations become giants. As the number of stockholders increases, the capacity of each to express opinions is extremely limited. No one is bound to take notice of them, though they may have quasi-political importance, similar to that of constituents who write letters to their congressman. Finally, they have a right, difficult to put into operation, to bring a stockholders' action against the corporation and its management, demanding that the corporation be made whole from any damage it may have suffered in case of theft, fraud, or wrongdoing by directors or administrators. Such actions are common, though few stockholders are involved in them. They are a useful deterrent to dishonesty and disloyalty on the part of management.

These shares nevertheless have become so desirable that they are now the dominant form of personal wealth-holding because, through the device of stock exchanges, they have acquired "liquidity" — that is, the capability of being sold for ready cash within days or hours. The stockholder, though no longer the sole residuary legatee of all profits, is the residuary legatee of about half of them, and that is a vast stake. (Sophisticated estimates indicate that dividends combined with increase in market value of shares have yielded better than eight percent per annum during the generation past). The package of passive property rights and expectations has proved sufficiently satisfactory to have induced an increasing number of Americans to place their savings in this form of property. In 1929 perhaps one million Americans owned common stock. At the close of 1963, a conservative estimate would place that figure at between seventeen and twenty million stockholders.[19] These holdings represent 525 billion dollars of current market value, comprising slightly less than one-third of individually-owned wealth in the United States.[20] Projecting the trend, one would expect twenty years from now to find between forty and fifty million Americans directly owning shares. The aggregate market value of personally-owned shares now approximates ten to fifteen percent more than the annual personally-received income in the United States (the latter will be nearly 500 billion dollars for the .year 1964). We can expect that the total market value of personally-owned shares twenty years hence will far surpass the trillion dollar mark.

---

[19] The 1962 Figure is 17,010,000 stockholders. U.S. DEP'T OF COMMERCE, STATISTICAL ABSTRACT OF THE UNITED STATES 474 (1964).

[20] See Note 11 *supra* (sic) and accompanying text.

Yet this is only the "top level" of passive property-holding. A very large number of shares are not held by individuals, but by intermediate fiduciary institutions which in turn distribute the benefits of shareholding to participating individuals. One of the two largest groups of such intermediary institutions is that of the pension trust funds maintained by corporations or groups of corporations for the benefit of employees; these collect savings in regular installments from employers to be held in trust for their employees and subsequently paid to them as old age or other similar benefits. The second is the relatively smaller group of institutions known as mutual funds; these buy a portfolio of assorted stocks and sell participations in the portfolio to individuals desiring to hold an interest in diversified groups of stock instead of directly holding shares in one or more companies. Through the pension trust funds not less than twenty million (probably a great many more) employees already have an indirect beneficial claim both to the dividends proceeding from shares and to the rise in market value in the pension portfolio — even though their interest is nonliquid, and is received only on retirement, death or (occasionally) other contingency. ...

In addition to these two categories there are other intermediate institutions which are also holders (though less significant) of stocks — namely, life insurance companies which invest about three percent of their assets in stocks, and fire and casualty companies which invest a considerably larger percentage. Comparatively speaking, all these institutions combined probably own a relatively small fraction of all stocks outstanding — perhaps between seven and ten percent.[21] Yet the rapidity of their growth — especially striking in the case of pension trusts — indicates that this form of stockholding is likely to become dominant in future years.

The significance of the intermediate institutions is twofold. First, they vastly increase the number of citizens who, to some degree, rely on the stockholding form of wealth. Second, they remove the individual still further from connection with or impact on the management and administration of the productive corporations themselves.

As might be expected, the law has moved to protect the holders of this form of wealth. It has not unnaturally moved along the lines of the interest that most preoccupies shareholders — that is, "liquidity" (capacity to turn the holding into cash), and market price. Since liquidity turns not on underlying property, but on resale of shares, legal protection is chiefly involved with the processes of the market place. Hence its preoccupation with information enabling buyers and sellers to determine the price at which they are willing to buy or sell. The entire battery of legislation set up by the Securities and Exchange Acts[22] has essentially little to do with the conduct of the corporation's affairs beyond requiring regular publication of information considered accurate by accounting standards, and prohibiting speculative activities by corporate administrators. Even more directly, this legislation deals with conduct of the stock exchanges

---

21 No one really knows the exact percentage of institutional holdings of stocks. Mutual investment funds are wholly invested in stock: they are reported to aggregate about $29 billion. No figures are available on pension trust holdings and insurance company holdings (such holdings are small due to statutory limitation on this kind of investment). A sophisticated guess on the generous side would be total holdings of around $50 billion or less than 10% of the value of outstanding stocks — hence the rough estimate. The percentage is probably slowly rising.

22 Securities Act of 1933, 48 Stat. 74, as amended, 15 U.S.C., §§ 77a-77aa (1959). ...

themselves and with practices of their members who buy or sell as brokers for the public.

Both in direction and effect, this preoccupation of the Securities and Exchange Acts recognizes a new economic fact: that stock markets are no longer places of "investment" as the word was used by classical economists. Save to a marginal degree, they no longer allocate capital. They are mechanisms for liquidity. The purchaser of stock, save in rare instances, does not buy a new issue. The price he pays does not add to capital or assets of the corporation whose shares he buys. Stock markets do not exist for, and in general are not used for (in fact are not allowed to be used for), distribution of newly-issued shares. Their rules commonly prevent shares from being listed and traded until *after* they have been sold by some other means. Occasionally, it is true, large new issues are distributed which shortly after make their way into markets (one thinks at once of the American Telephone and Telegraph Company issue of new stock in 1964). But such operations perform an insignificant percentage of the work of stock exchanges. The exchanges are institutions in which shares, arising from investment made long ago, are shifted from sellers who wish cash to buyers who wish stock. Purchases and sales on the New York and other stock exchanges do not seriously affect the business operations of the companies whose shares are the subject of trading.

We have yet to digest the social-economic situation resulting from this fact. Immense dollar values of stocks are bought and sold every day, month and year. These dollars — indeed hundreds of billions of dollars — do not, apparently, enter the stream of direct commercial or productive use. That is, they do not become "capital" devoted to productive use. A seller of stocks more likely desires to buy other stocks than to use the capital for a business he himself owns.[23]

Dr. Paul Harbrecht, at Columbia and now at Georgetown University, has been elaborating a theory that we have evolved a new wealth-holding and wealth-circulating system whose liquidity is maintained through the exchanges but is only psychologically connected with the capital gathering and capital application system on which productive industry and enterprise actually depend.[24] If this is the fact, one effect of the corporate system has been to set up a parallel, circulating "property-wealth" system, in which the wealth flows from passive wealth-holder to passive wealth-holder, without significantly furthering the functions of capital formation, capital application, capital use or risk bearing. Yet these functions were the heart of the nineteenth century "capitalist" system. Both the wealth and the wealth-holders are divorced from the productive — that is, the commercial — process through, at long last, the estimate of this wealth turns on an estimate of the productiveness, the character and effectiveness of the corporation whose shares are its vehicles.

---

[23] Though accurate figures are not available, it is estimated that between 20 and 25 percent of all trading on the New York Stock Exchange is for "institutional accounts." It represents investment funds or other institutions selling blocks of securities and buying others. In addition, there is a substantial volume of such trading which goes on off the exchange — the so called "third market." But this trading comprises only an insignificant amount of "new" stock issues. It is a shift in ownership — from the previous holder to a new holder — gradually indeed from individual investors to institutional investors.

[24] See HARBRECHT, PENSION FUNDS AND ECONOMIC POWER 273-89 (1959); Harbrecht, *The Modern Corporation Revisitted*, 64 COLUM. L. REV. 1410 (1964).

Now, clearly, this wealth cannot be justified by the old economic maxims, despite passionate and sentimental arguments of neoclassic economists who would have us believe the old system has not changed. The purchaser of stock does not contribute savings to an enterprise, thus enabling it to increase its plant or operations. He does not take the "risk" of a new or increased economic operation; he merely estimates the chance of the corporation's shares increasing in value. The contribution his purchase makes to anyone other than himself is the maintenance of liquidity for other shareholders who may wish to convert their holdings into cash. Clearly he can not and does not intend to contribute managerial or entrepreneurial effort or service.

This raises a problem of social ethics that is bound to push its way into the legal scene in the next generation. Why have stockholders? What contribution do they make, entitling them to heirship of half the profits of the industrial system, receivable partly in the form of dividends, and partly in the form of increased market values resulting from undistributed corporate gains? Stockholders toil not, neither do they spin, to earn that reward. They are beneficiaries by position only. Justification for their inheritance must be sought outside classic economic reasoning.

It can be founded only upon social grounds. There is — and in American social economy, there always has been — a value attached to individual life, individual development, individual solution of personal problems, individual choice of consumption and activity. Wealth unquestionably does add to an individual's capacity and range in pursuit of happiness and self-development. There is certainly advantage to the community when men take care of themselves. But that justification turns on the distribution as well as the existence of wealth. Its force exists only in direct ratio to the number of individuals who hold such wealth. Justification for the stockholder's existence thus depends on increasing distribution within the American population. Ideally, the stockholder's position will be impregnable only when every American family has its fragment of that position and of the wealth by which the opportunity to develop individuality becomes fully actualized.

Such distribution is indeed proceeding — rather dramatically in terms of statistics, all too slowly in terms of social ethics. The generation since 1932 has multiplied the number of direct stockholders tenfold. If indirect stockholdings through intermediate institutions are included, a vast indirect sector has grown up as well. Yet distribution of wealth generally is still in its infancy. One percent of the American population owns perhaps twenty-five percent of all personally-owned wealth[25] and undoubtedly more than that percentage of common stocks. Plainly we have a long way to go. The intermediate institutions, notably pension trusts, justify themselves not merely because they increase the benefits of the stockholder-position, but because they rationalize it as well. Through direct ownership, Nym who bought railroad stocks twenty years ago lost money, Bardolph who bought A.T. & T. trebled his stake, while Pistol who bought I.B.M. stock has multiplied it fiftyfold. This is an irrational result. The pension trust, possibly holding all of these stocks distributes the losses and the benefits (the latter being considerably greater) among a broad category of employees.

---

[25] LAMPMAN, THE SHARE OF TOP WEALTHHOLDERS IN NATIONAL WEALTH 1922-1926, at 208 (1962).

One would expect therefore that the law would increasingly encourage an even wider distribution of stocks — whether through tax policy or some other device. It would encourage pension trust or social security trust entry into stockholder position. The time may well come when the government social security funds are invested, not wholly in government bonds as at present but in a broadening list of American stocks. As social security and pension trusts increasingly cover the entire working population of the United States, the stockholder position, though having lost its ancient justification could become a vehicle for rationalized wealth distribution corresponding to and serving the American ideal of a just civilization. The institution of passive property has an advantage which, so far as we know, is new to history in that distribution and redistribution of wealth-holding can take place without interruption of the productive process. ... The corporate system, accompanied by reasonably enlightened tax policies and aided by continuously growing productivity, can achieve whatever redistribution the American people want.

Few observers would seriously deny that greater production is inevitable as well as needed. President Lyndon B. Johnson boldly embraced the propositon that "poverty" (referring to families with income of less than three thousand dollars a year) can and should be abolished, making a first tentative approach toward meeting the problem in 1964. It is scarcely open to question that present and potential productive capacity offers adequate tools to the American economy when and if the American public really desires to "abolish poverty." That is, the tools are at hand insofar as the problems are economic. Actually it is clear that problems deeper than economic — for example, problems of education and automation — will have to be met. What can be said is that the deeper problems cannot readily be met unless productive capacity can be maintained and increased to finance their solution, and unless the present technical organization of wealth can permit the shifting process to go on without interrupting or handicapping production. Both these conditions do exist.

VI. THE INSTITUTIONAL ECONOMIC REVOLUTION

Though its outline is still obscure, the central mass of the twentieth century American economic revolution has become discernible. Its driving forces are five: 1) immense increase in productivity; 2) massive collectivization of property devoted to production, with accompanying decline of individual decision making and control; 3) massive dissociation of wealth from active management; 4) growing pressure for greater distribution of such passive wealth; 5) assertion of the individual's right to live and consume as the individual chooses.

Of this revolution, the corporation has proved a vital (albeit neutral) instrument and vehicle. It has become, and now is, the dominant form of organization and production. It has progressively created, and continues to create, a passive form of wealth. It is, in great measure, emancipated from dependence on individual savings and "capital" markets. Nevertheless, like the slave of Aladdin's lamp, it must increasingly follow the mandate of the American state, embodied in social attitudes and in case, statute and constitutional law. This mandate changes and evolves as a consensus is developed on values and their priorities in American life. ...

A closely related trend (not here discussed) is, of course, emergence of the American state partly as an administrator of wealth distribution, partly as a direct distributor of certain products. In notable areas production for use rather than production for profit is emerging as the norm. Education, scientific research and development, the arts, and a variety of services ranging from roads and low-income housing to nonprofit recreation and television constitute a few illustrative fields. Health will probably be — in part now is — such a field. Increasingly it is clear that these noncommerical functions are, among other things, essential to the continued life, stability and growth of the non-statist corporate enterprise.

In typical American fashion, the revolution has come not through a single ideological or utopian burst, conceived and imposed by a few, but through an evolving concensus that insists equally on enjoying the results of mass production and on the primacy of individual life. It will go forward — as it inevitably must — as fast and as far as that consensus demands.

CONCLUSION

In summary, we are well underway toward recognition that property used in production will be made to conform to the conception of civilization worked out through American constitutional democratic processes. The Civil Rights Act of 1964 was a notable step in this process. ... This could, as I think it does, include recognition that collective operations — predominantly conducted by corporations — as they attain size and power, are assimilable to statist operations, and are governed by the same constitutional limitations. Having attained size and economic power surpassing individual operations, corporations are essentially political constructs, having perpetual life and a continued legitimacy that depends on their performance as a productive and distributive mechanisms. Both in intra-corporate operations (the corporation and its officers, agents, labor and employees) and in productive and distributive functions (relations with suppliers and customers), they will not be allowed to invade personality and freedom, or to discriminate for or against categories of men.

Passive property, on the other hand, loses its "capital" function and becomes increasingly an exclusive means for distributing liquid wealth, and a channel for distributing income whose accumulation for capital purposes is not required. Norms for that distribution are beginning to change. The anti-poverty campaign suggests a beginning, setting minimum standards of distributed income. Beyond that (police regulations aside) the right to choose consumption — to spend if and as you please — will be guarded as a defense of the individual's right to order his own life.

So far, so much. Yet, far beyond this summary, the real revolution of our time is yet perceived. If the current estimate that by 1980 ... our total productivity will double (approximately 1.2 trillion of 1960 dollars) and personnally received income will reach approximately one trillion dollars, proves true, the entire emphasis of American civilization will appreciably change. Philosophical preoccupation will become more important than economic. What is this personal life, this individuality, this search for personal development and fulfillment intended to achieve? Mere wallowing in consumption would leave great numbers of people unsatisfied; their demand will be for participation. This means, in substance, a growing demand that significant jobs be available for everyone, at a time when automation may diminish the number of all commercially created jobs as we presently know them. It may well mean that the state will be expected to create jobs wherever a social need is recognized, and irrespective of the classic requirement for a commercial base. Is it possible, as Walt Rostow maintains,[26] that the population will merely become bored? Perhaps; but if so, it will be because esthetics, the arts, the endeavor to understand and enjoy the thrilling prospects opened by science, and the endless reasearch for meaning, will have tragically lagged far behind economic advance. Not impossibly, the teacher, the artist, the poet and the philosopher will then set the pace.

Meantime, quite obviously — as a glace at Harlem (ten blocks from Columbia University) or the Appalachian coal field or the other spotted areas of rural and urban decay will forcefully demonstrate — there is plenty to be done.

26 ROSTOW, *The Stages Of Economic Growth* 91-92 (1960).

APPENDICES

APPENDICES

REVIEW PROBLEMS

A substantial drawback to current instructional efforts at the university level is that the information learned is too often fragmented by our desire to categorize bodies of knowledge. This makes instruction relatively easy by providing manageable units of knowledge. However, most problems in reality do not come in defined categories. For example, managers seldom are informed of a problem in a business by reference to the traditional compartments of knowledge. Problems do not come labled: this is a cost accounting problem; or, this is a marketing channels problem; or, this is an agency law problem. Only after serious analysis and consultation can a problem be so classified; and even when it is, it may often require the application of principles from all of those areas.

REVIEW PROBLEMS

The student of the law of business associations will almost never be presented with a problem clearly designated as a "corporation law" problem, for example. To acquaint the student with some of the problems he or she might face as a manager of a business association we have presented below some review problems which are not labled by the principles which must be applied. We start with relatively easy review questions and end with complex ones. In the more difficult problems the student is advised to first list the "legal" issues as you see them. Then recall and define the legal principle which you believe to be applicable. Finally, in a concisely worded paragraph or two, explain how the principle might be applied by a court. There may be no obvious or correct solution. The most important task here is to correctly recall, define and apply the legal principle.

Some of the questions are direct quotes from or adaptations of problems from the Uniform CPA Examinations copyrighted by the American Institute of Certified Public Accountants, Inc., and are reproduced here with their permission. These questions are identified by designating them, "CPA Exam Question" followed by the number of the question and the month, day and year they appeared on the exam.

The remainder of the review questions are fictional and were created only for purposes of review.

Indicate whether the answer for questions 1 to 9 is true or false. Then in a short paragraph give the reasons for your answer.

1. **Adaptation of CPA Exam Question 3, November 5, 1971.**
   Peters, Long and Tyler formed a general merchandising partnership. Cash capital contributions were $50,000 from Peters, and $25,000 each from Long and Tyler. The partnership agreement provides that the partners are to

share profits and loses in proportion to capital contribution balances and that the partnership is to have a duration of ten years. After the partnership was established, the partners decided to admit Kramer as a partner if he would make a capital contribution of $25,000 and Kramer agreed to this. At the time of Kramer's admission, the partnership agreement was amended to provide that no partner shall make any contract for the firm involving more than $50,000 without the express consent of all other partners.

    a. If the partnership makes a profit of $100,000 during its first year of operations, Peters is entitled to $50,000.

    b. If the partnership agreement were silent on the subject of the division of profits, the answer to the question above would be different.

    c. If a judgment is entered against the partnership, each of the partners would be personally liable for the full amount thereof and the judgment creditor could proceed to collect from any one of them.

    d. In the question above, the judgment creditor must first exhaust the assets of the partnership before he can proceed against the individual assets of the partners.

    e. If Tyler should die, the partnership would be dissolved as a matter of law.

    f. Any one of the partners may retire from the business at any time and dissolve the partnership without liability.

    g. Kramer's admission required the dissolution of the old partnership and the formation of a new partnership.

    h. Kramer would be liable personally for obligations of the partnership incurred prior to his admission.

    i. If Kramer is liable for partnership obligations incurred prior to his admission to the firm, such obligations could be collected out of both his partnership and personal assets.

2. Adaptation of CPA Exam Question 27, May 9, 1975.

Head is a crane operator for Magnum Construction Corporation. One day while operating the crane he negligently swung the crane into another building, which caused extensive damage to the other building and the crane. The accident also resulted in fracturing Head's elbow and dislocating his hip. In this situation,

    a. Head is liable for the damages he caused to the crane and the building.

    b. Magnum's liability is limited to the damage to the building only if Head was acting within the scope of his authority.

    c. Magnum will not be liable for damage to the building if Head's negligence was in clear violation of Magnum's safety standards and the rules regarding operation of the crane.

3. Adaptation of CPA Exam Question 30, May 9, 1975.

The ratification doctrine

    a. Is not applicable to situations where the party claiming to act as the agent for another has no express or implied authority to do so.

    b. Is designed to apply to situations where the principal was originally incompetent to have made the contract himself, but who, upon becoming competent, ratifies.

    c. Requires the principal to ratify the entire act of the agent and the ratification is retroactive.

    d. Applies only if the principal expressly ratifies in writing the contract made on his behalf within a reasonable time.

4. Adaptation of CPA Exam Question 31, May 9, 1975.

Normally a principal will not be liable to a third party

    a. On a contract signed on his behalf by an agent who was expressly forbidden by the principal to make it and where the third party was unaware of the agent's limitation.

    b. On a contract made by his agent and the principal is not disclosed, unless the principal ratifies it.

    c. For torts committed by an independent contractor if they are within the scope of the contract.

    d. On a negotiable instrument signed by the agent in his own name without revealing he signed in his agency capacity.

5. Adaptation of CPA Exam Question 23, May 9, 1975.

The partnership of Baker, Green, and Madison is insolvent. The partnership's liabilities exceed its assets by $123,000. The liabilities include a $25,000 loan from Madison. Green is personally insolvent, his personal liabilities exceed his personal assets by $13,500. Green has filed a voluntary petition in bankruptcy. Under these circumstances, partnership creditors

    a. Must proceed jointly against the partnership and all the general partners so that losses may be shared equitably among the partners.

    b. Rank first in payment and all (including Madison) will share proportionately in the partnership assets to be distributed.

    c. Will have the first claim to partnership property to the exclusion of the personal creditors of Green.

    d. Have the right to share pro rata with Green's personal creditors Green's personal assets.

6. Adaptation of CPA Exam Question 24, May 9, 1975.

Jack Gordon, a general partner of Visions Unlimited, is retiring. He sold his partnership interest to Don Morrison for $80,000. Gordon assigned to Morrison all his rights, title, and interests in the partnership and named Morrison as his successor partner in Visions. In this situation

    a. The assignment to Morrison dissolves the partnership.

    b. Absent any limitation regarding the assignment of a partner's interest, Gordon is free to assign it at his will.

    c. Morrison is entitled to an equal voice and vote in the management of the partnership, and he is entitled to exercise all the rights and privileges that Gordon had.

    d. Morrison does not have the status of a partner, but he can, upon demand, inspect the partnership accounting records.

7. Adaptation of CPA Exam Question 25, May 9, 1975.

Morton, a senior staff member of Wilcox & Southern, CPAs, has been offered the opportunity to become a junior partner of the firm. However, to be admitted to the partnership he must contribute $30,000 to the partnership's capital, and he does not have that amount of money. It is estimated that the partnership interest in question is worth at least

$100,000. The partnership agreement is silent on assignment of a partner's interest. Morton accepts the offer and becomes a junior partner.

a. Morton could assign his partnership interest to a bank or other lending institution as security for a loan to acquire his partnership interest.

b. Morton is personally liable for all debts of the partnership, past and present, unless the partnership agreement provides otherwise.

c. Since Morton is only a junior partner with very little say in the management of the firm and the selection of clients, he has the legal status of a quasi limited partner.

d. If Morton pledged his partnership interest as security for a loan to acquire his partnership interest, the transaction created a subpartnership between himself and the lending institution.

8. **Adaptation of CPA Exam Question 26, May 9, 1975.**
Menlow Corporation dismissed Gibson, its purchasing agent, for incompetence. It published a notice in the appropriate trade journals which stated: "This is to notify all parties concerned that Gibson is no longer employed by the Menlow Corporation and the corporation assumes no further responsibility for his acts." Gibson called on several of Menlow's suppliers with whom he had previously dealt, and when he found one who was unaware of his dismissal, he would place a substantial order for merchandise to be delivered to a warehouse in which he had rented space. Menlow had rented warehouse space in the past when its storage facilities were crowded. Gibson also called on several suppliers with whom Menlow had never dealt; he would present one of his old business cards to the secretary and then make purchases on open account in the name of Menlow. Gibson then sold all the merchandise delivered to the warehouse and absconded with the money. In this situation,

a. Gibson had continuing express authority to make contracts on Menlow's behalf with suppliers with whom he had previously dealt as Menlow's agent, if they were unaware of his dismissal.

b. The suppliers who previously had no dealings with Menlow cannot enforce the contracts against Menlow even if the suppliers were unaware of Gibson's lack of authority.

c. Menlow is liable on the Gibson contracts to all suppliers who had dealt with Gibson in the past as Menlow's agent.

d. Constructive notice via publication in the appropriate trade journals is an effective notice to all third parties regardless of whether they had dealt with Gibson or read the notice.

9. **Adaptation of CPA Exam Question 3, May 11, 1973.**
A. The examination of the financial statements of the Franklin Grocery Company revealed the following dispute relating to a balance due on open account. The item in dispute was a certain quantity of canned goods allegedly purchased by the Birch Steamship Company. On October 10, 1972, Arthur Snead, one of Franklin's salesmen, called upon Birch Steamship to solicit business. He had done business for several years with Ken Small, one of Birch Steamship's purchasing agents. Upon asking for Small at the receptionist's desk, he was told that Small was not there. The receptionist then called James Drew, another purchasing agent. She

informed Drew that Arthur Snead of Franklin Grocery was looking for Small. Drew told the secretary that Small was at pier 30 supervising the loading of provisions. Snead found Small at pier 30 and took the disputed order for the canned goods, which were duly shipped to Birch Steamship. Unknown to Snead, Small had been relieved of his position as purchasing agent due to incompetency. Small obtained possession of the canned goods shipped to Birch Steamship and sold them. Birch refuses to pay.

1. Small had no express authority to make the purchase on Birch Steamship's behalf.
2. Small had the apparent authority to bind Birch Steamship.
3. To defeat Franklin Grocery, Birch Steamship must show knowledge by Franklin of Small's dismissal as a purchasing agent.
4. A publication in local papers and trade publications of the removal of Small as a purchasing agent would give effective notice to new suppliers of Birch Steamship.
5. Birch Steamship is liable on the contract made by Small as its purported agent.
6. Had Birch Steamship learned of the unauthorized contract made on its behalf by Small, it could have ratified the transaction.

B. During your examination of the financial statements of Bonanza Development Corporation, you reviewed certain land transactions involving John Walters as agent for Bonanza. Bonanza feared the price of land would skyrocket if it became known that it was trying to purchase a large number of tracts of land to develop a shopping center. It, therefore, instructed Walters not to disclose to prospective sellers that he was acting as an agent on its behalf. The agreement between Walters and Bonanza was in writing and signed by both parties.

1. Bonanza is an undisclosed principal.
2. Unless Bonanza ratifies the contracts made by Walters, it has no liability thereon.
3. Walters has committed a fraud in failing to notify prospective buyers of the fact he is acting as Bonanza's agent.
4. Bonanza cannot enforce the contracts made by Walters secretly on its behalf.
5. Walters will not be entitled to the commissions agreed to by Bonanza in that he has entered into an illegal bargain.
6. If Walters gave the usual warranties in connection with the purchase of the land, Bonanza would be liable on them even though Walters was not authorized to make them.

C. Your client, Sanitary Dairies, Inc., had employed Harold Stone as a milk-truck driver. Stone negligently ran the truck into the car of Ronald Green, injuring Green, his wife, and damaging Green's car. Stone was also injured in the collision.

1. If Stone had never had a previous accident, Sanitary Dairies would not be liable.
2. Stone can avoid liability in that he was engaged in the performance of his principal's business.
3. Had Stone left his assigned route in order to pick up his wife and take her shopping, Sanitary Dairies would not be liable.

4. Stone has breached one of his duties to his principal.

D. Charles Golden, a promoter, contacted an inventor, a plant owner, and several investors to join him in creating the Meglo Corporation. Golden made several contracts on behalf of the corporation prior to its coming into existence. The principals other than Golden subsequently decided to disassociate themselves from Golden and the contracts that he made and independently created the Meglo Corporation. You have been engaged as the CPA for Meglo.

1. Meglo is liable on the contracts made by Golden on behalf of the corporation.
2. Golden was the agent for a nonexistent principal.
3. The ratification doctrine does not apply to the contracts made by Golden on Meglo's behalf.
4. Golden is a principal.

10. CPA Exam Question 6, May 11, 1973.

A. Charles Meskill has decided to invest $600,000 in a new business venture. Meskill will be joined by two, possibly three, former business associates. He has purchased the patent rights to a revolutionary adhesive substance known as "sticko." In connection with the transaction, he is considering the various forms of business organization he might use in establishing the business. You have been engaged to study the accounting and business problems he should consider in choosing to operate as a general partnership limited partnership, or corporation. Meskill requests specific advice on the following aspects as they relate to the operation of a business as one of these three forms of business organization: 1) personal liability in the event the venture proves to be a disaster; 2) the borrowing capacity of the entity; 3) requirements for doing a multi-state business; 4) the liability of the entity for the acts of its agents; and 5) the recognition of the entity for income tax purposes and major income tax considerations in selecting one of the three forms of business organization.

Required:

Discuss the various legal implications of each specific aspect for which Meskill seeks advice for operating a business in the above mentioned forms of business organization.

B. Selecting the general partnership versus the corporation as a form of business organization requires consideration of: 1) the right to compensation for services rendered; 2) the fiduciary duty; and 3) management prerogatives.

Required:

Compare and contrast the rights and responsibilities of a common stockholder with a general partner for each of the three areas stated above.

11. CPA Examination Question 4, May 11, 1973.

A. Parker Pastry, Inc., is a closely held corporation. Curtis and Smith, two of Parker's directors, together own 55 percent of the corporations's outstanding stock. Devlin, an elderly retired executive, owns 25 percent of Parker's outstanding stock. The remaining 20 percent of the outstanding stock is held by five other unrelated persons. There have been no ownership changes in recent years. Parker's stock has no-par value and a present book value of $50 per share.

Baxter Bakeries Corp. is a large, publicly held corporation whose stock is traded on a national securities exchange. The Baxter stock has a par value of $75 per share and is presently being traded at about $100 per share.

Baxter is seeking control of Parker. For tax reasons, Baxter must acquire 80 percent of Parker's stock to make the acquisition economically feasible. It is not interested at this time in acquiring more than this 80 percent. Baxter's president proposes to Curtis and Smith that Baxter exchange one share of its stock for one share of Parker stock provided that no less than 80 percent nor more than 85 percent of Parker's stock is thus acquired by Baxter.

Without revealing Baxter's offer, Curtis and Smith purchase the Parker stock owned by Devlin at book value. Thereafter, Smith and Curtis deliver their now 80 percent of Parker's outstanding stock to Baxter in exchange for Baxter stock.

Required:

What rights does Devlin have against Curtis and Smith under the federal Securities Exchange Act of 1934? Explain.

B. In order for Baxter to acquire the Parker stock, as described in part A. above, Baxter was required to deliver 30,000 of its shares in exchange for the Parker stock. Baxter had 12,000 shares in its treasury and was currently authorized by its charter to issue 100,000 additional shares. The Baxter directors formally authorized the delivery of the 12,000 treasury shares and the issuance of 18,000 additional shares to acquire the Parker stock. As the auditor of Baxter's financial statements, you are concerned about the contingency that Baxter might incur a liability from stockholders' objections to this Board action. Baxter stockholders might argue that the exchange was unfair, considering the fact that the Parker stock had a book value of $50 per share and was being exchanged for Baxter stock on a share-for-share basis.

Required:

1. Was the action of Baxter's directors proper? Explain.
2. Could any Baxter stockholder successfully assert a preemptive right to acquire any of the shares to be delivered by Baxter? Explain.

C. The 12,000 Baxter shares delivered equally to Curtis and Smith, as described in part B. above, had been issued originally in connection with a public offering registered under the federal Securities Act of 1933. The 18,000 newly issued shares had not been registered by Baxter.

Shortly after acquiring his Baxter shares, Curtis sold them to the public in a regular stock exchange transaction, a plan he had in mind at the time he acquired the shares. Smith retained his shares for several years, having viewed his acquisition as an investment. Smith then sold his stock to the public in a regular stock exchange transaction in order to meet unexpected financial reverses. At the time of their respective sales, neither Curtis nor Smith was employed by Baxter in any capacity and neither owned 10 percent of Baxter's stock. Neither Curtis nor Smith registered their sales with the Securities and Exchange Commission.

Required:

Will persons who purchased Curtis' and Smith's stock have any rights against Baxter under the federal Securities Act of 1933? Explain.

D. Several years after acquiring 80 percent of the stock of Parker, Baxter decided to merge Parker into itself. Under applicable state law, the merger required approval of only two-thirds of the Parker shares. Baxter voted its 80 percent of Parker's stock in favor of the merger which provided that each minority stockholder of Parker receive one share of Baxter stock in exchange for three shares of Parker stock. In connection with your examination of Baxter's financial statements, you have discovered that some of the minority stockholders voted against the merger. You are concerned that Baxter properly disclose in its financial statements the liability, if any, to the minority stockholders voting against the merger.

Required:

1. What are the rights of Parker stockholders who oppose the merger?
2. What steps must a stockholder ordinarily take to protect his rights in these circumstances?

12. CPA Exam Question 5, November 7, 1975.

A. Boswell Realty Corporation, whose sole business is land development, purchased a large tract of land on which it intended to construct a high-rise apartment-house complex. In order to finance the construction, Boswell offered to sell $3,000,000 worth of shares in Boswell Realty to about 1,000 prospective investors located throughout the United States.

Required:

1. Discuss the implications of the Securities Act of 1933 to Boswell's offering to sell shares in the corporation.
2. The Securities Act of 1933 is considered a disclosure statute. Briefly describe the means provided and the principal types of information required to accomplish this objective of disclosure.
3. If an investor acquires shares of stock in Boswell Realty Corporation, is his interest real or personal property? Explain.

B. Taylor Corporation, incorporated and doing business in Delaware, is a manufacturing company whose securities are registered on a national securities exchange. On February 6, 1975, one of Taylor's engineers disclosed to management that he had discovered a new product which he believed would be quite profitable to the corporation. Messrs. Jackson and Wilson, the corporation's president and treasurer and members of its board of directors, were very impressed with the prospects of the new product's profitability. Because the corporation would need additional capital to finance the development, production, and marketing of the new product, the board of directors proposed that the corporation issue an additional 100,000 shares of common stock.

Wilson was imbued with such confidence in the corporation's prospects that on February 12, 1975, he purchased on the open market 1,000 shares of the corporation's common stock at $10 per share. This was before news of the new product reached the public in late February and caused a rise in the market price to $30 per share. Jackson did not purchase any shares in February because he had already purchased 600 shares of the corporation's common stock on January 15, 1975, for $10 per share.

In late February, when the market price of the corporation's common stock was $30 per share, Wilson approached two insurance companies to discuss the proposed issuance of an additional 100,000 shares of common stock. In March, Wilson reported to the board of directors that negotiations had been successful and one of the insurance companies had agreed to purchase the entire 100,000 shares for $3,000,000. The insurance company signed an investment letter, and a legend restricting transfers was imprinted on the face of each certificate issued to it. Moreover, the appropriate stock-transfer instructions were given to the corporation's stock-transfer agent.

Due to unexpected expenses arising from a fire in his home, on April 16, 1975, Jackson sold at $35 per share on the open market the 600 shares of stock he purchased in January, Wilson continues to hold his 1,000 shares.

What questions arising out of the federal securities laws are suggested by these facts? Discuss.

13. **Adaptation of CPA Exam Question 4, May 9, 1975.**

Byron Corporation acquired more than 70 percent of the outstanding common stock of Sage, Inc., during the last twelve months; most of the shares were purchased from five of Sage's directors who owned approximately 60 percent of Sage's outstanding common stock which they sold to Byron. These five individuals were on the board of directors of both Sage and Byron for many year and still remain on both boards. Also, Byron utilized its ownership control to elect the remaining members of the board of directors and its own slate of officers of Sage.

You have just begun your first examination of the financial statements of Burke Corporation. Your examination is for the year ended December 31, 1974. Burke has never been audited before and is not subject to the Securities Act of 1933 or the Securities Exchange Act of 1934.

You have extracted the following information from Burke's general ledger and the corporation's Articles of Incorporation.

Stockholder's Equity

8%, cumulative, nonvoting preferred stock; par value, $100 per share; authorized, issued, and outstanding, 10,000 shares; liquidation preference, $115 per share aggregating $1,150,000	$1,000,000
Common stock; par value, $10 per share; authorized, 100,000 shares; issued and outstanding 10,000 shares	100,000
Additional paid-in capital	50,000
Retained earnings	110,000
Total	$1,260,000

Your preliminary inquiry has revealed the following information:
- Burke was incorporated in 1965 in a state which had adopted the Model Business Corporation Act.

- No dividends have been declared or paid on the preferred stock for 1973 and 1974. Dividends on the preferred stock had been declared and paid in all prior years. The preferred stock was issued six years ago at par to a group of local investors different from the common stockholders.
- Dividends of $20,000 were declared and paid on the common stock in both 1973 and 1974. Annual dividends have been declared and paid on the 10,000 shares of common stock outstanding since Burke's incorporation. The common stock is closely held and most of the common stockholders are members of the board of directors, officers, or employees.
- Burke's net income was $50,000 and $40,000 for 1973 and 1974, respectively. The $110,000 balance of retained earnings at December 31, 1974, was after closing the books on that date.
- Burke is and has been solvent since its incorporation.
  Required:
  Discuss the legal implications of the above facts to Burke, its directors, and its stockholders.

14. In 1971, S learned that A, B, and C were planning to form a corporation for the purpose of manufacturing and marketing a line of novelty-type items to wholesale outlets. S had patented a self-locking gas tank cap, but lacked the financial backing to market it profitably. He negotiated with A, B, and C, who agreed to purchase the patent rights for $5,000 to be paid in cash and 200 shares of $100 par value preferred stock in the corporation to be performed. The agreement was signed in December, 1971. The corporation was formed and properly registered with the Secretary of State in January, 1972 and S's stock was issued to him in the Spring of 1972 but the corporation has refused to pay the $5,000 cash and to declare dividends although the business grew very profitable due to the value of S's patent. What are S's rights?

15. C, the president of C Corp. is a good friend of yours and asked you to buy a few of the common shares of C Corp. when the initial issue came out. This you did. Shortly thereafter, he asked you if you would be willing to stand for election to the board. At first you refused, but he finally won out by convincing you that all you had to do was to sign the annual report; you did not have to attend lengthy board meetings or make any decisions or read any of the financial statements. Based upon C's assertions above you accepted the nomination and were elected to the board. You attended no meetings and did not read any of the corporate reports. You did feel some responsibility to the other shareholders and from time to time you questioned C about the company. You always relied upon C's verbal responses to your questions as the financial condition of the company.

At the end of your second year on the board you were horrified to learn that the corporation had filed for bankruptcy. It was revealed that during the last year's operation, your friend, C, received a loan of $10,000 from the company which was secured by some of the company's most valuable and liquid assets. His drinking problem, of which you were aware, had caused his competent sales force to quit and he replaced it with dishonest men interested in looting the company. In 1970 net profits of the C Corp. were $25,000, in 1971 they were $150 and in 1972 the corporation was unable to meet some of its obligations as they became due.

A minority shareholder sues you and the president, C, for the recovery of the $10,000 loan, and for $50,000 he alleges is due for mismanagement.

    a. Decide the case against the president. What are the legal cause(s) of action, the defenses and how much should be recovered?

    b. Decide the case against yourself; what are the causes of action, the defenses and will recovery be successful?

16. As president of C Corp. discussed above, C hired a supposed super salesman, S, to develop the Chicago sales region. His official title was general agent and salesman. C furnished him with a list of potential customers in the region and told him to do everything he could to increase the business of C Corp. This was in 1966. On his first visit to Chicago S discovered that Y Corp. of Indianapolis, Indiana was a close competitor of C Corp. in the region. S, therefore, adopted a strategy of relating the falsified results of a test that was conducted by one of the consumer agencies which revealed that Y Corp.'s products had been declared unsafe and had been or would soon be banned. Soon the word that S was spreading took effect. The sales of Y Corp. dropped off sharply and the sales of C Corp. zoomed upward.

Y Corp. received word that S was spreading false and malicious information about the company's product which was an obvious tort (civil wrong) called intentional disparaging another's product. As soon as C Corp.'s president found out about this he fired S. Soon thereafter Y Corp. sues C Corp. for $250,000 in lost business.

Describe the circumstances or facts that must be established in order to hold C Corp. liable for the $250,000.

17. Y Corporation, an engine manufacturer, desired to enter the boat building business. It decided upon a vote of 5 to 2 of the board to form a subsidiary corporation to engage in that business and sell its motors to the subsidiary. Thereupon it formed the Z Yacht Company for the purpose, with an initial capitalization of $250,000 and loaned the Yacht Company $750,000 secured by promissory notes.

A was the Vice President in charge of development for the Y Corporation and was appointed by the board to develop the Z Yacht Company. He moved his office from the Y Corporation headquarters into the building which Z Yacht Company rented for its operation. A hired a chief naval architect, N, to do all of the designing and A promised to pay him a salary of $20,000 per year plus 10 percent of the Z Yacht Company profits arising from the sale of the new boats, plus he was promised stock options in Y Corp. A also acted as the chief purchasing agent and ordered raw materials from creditors, C, D, and E for a total of $220,000 of which $120,000 was paid in cash and the balance was to be paid upon the sale of boats. Another supplier, F, decided not to do business with A and Z Yacht Company because he just didn't ". . . like the looks of the situation."

Y Corporation provided $250,000 worth of motors for no cash payment to Z Yacht Company. The agreement between Y and Z was that Y would be paid as soon as the boats were sold.

In order to impress the prospective purchasers of the yachts A bought a . Cadillac convertible special monarch deluxe for $20,000 on credit from Kady, the local Cadillac dealer and he signed the security agreement and purchase contract in his capacity as a representative of Z Yacht Company.

Unfortunately, A was much better at developing sales campaigns for new products than he was at developing a new manufacturing company. Most of the cash in the company *was* paid out for exorbitant salaries and huge promotional parties. Within a short time from the period that all of the above arrangements were made, the Z Yacht Company filed for bankruptcy. N had been paid only for the first two months of work, then was not paid for the next three months time he put in; C, D, E and Kady were never paid and neither was Y. What are the rights, remedies of N, C, D, E, Kady and Y? Who gets what from whom and why based upon what possible legal agreements.

Deciding whether or not a party will ultimately prevail in the courts is not as important as recognizing and discussing all legal issues. If you think a fact which is not stated is important, state what it is, and that you are assuming its existence.

18. Three engineers who lived in San Francisco designed and made, in their spare time, a People Powered Car (hereafter, "PPC") which was propelled by pumping pedals much like a bicycle. They were so impressed with the ease by which PPC's could be manufactured that they formed the PPC Company to manufacture and market the PPC's. This company sold shares to the public on the west coast. An elderly retired man, R, purchased some shares.

Having raised $500,000 by the sale of stock, PPC Company began business and the three engineers, A, B, and C, were elected directors along with D & E. D & E were very wealthy businessmen who bought large amounts of stock because the PPC looked like a sure thing. However, they never took an interest in the business and rarely came to board meetings. They left the enterprize to A, B, and C, to operate. Unfortunately, A, B, and C were much better engineers than businessmen. At their first board meeting, they hired O as president of the company. O was a hot-shot-promoter type who had just been discharged from the Detroit fraternity of top automobile manufacturing managers for questionable deals. O was given the express assignment of developing the marketing and promotion for the PPC as well as overseeing staff operations. A, B, and C were to concentrate on manufacturing, research and development.

O realized when he was hired that $500,000 in paid-in capital was not going to take the company far. He negotiated an unsecured loan from L lending institution for one million dollars. This was possible because he altered the books of the corporation to make it appear five million dollars was paid in, instead of $500,000. O reported at the next board meeting that this loan had been received. A, B, and C said nothing; D, who was present, was reading the Wall Street Journal and not paying attention. O asked for a vote of approval and it passed unanimously. (E was absent).

Surprised with the easy affirmation by the board obtained for the loan, O transferred to the PPC Company for a very small price the ownership of his home and his two family autos. He did this because he was expecting to be sued, individually, by all of his Detroit creditors for debts incurred there.

Again, the board acquiesced to this transaction upon O's pointing out that his home and cars were used sometimes to entertain business clients, and thus the PPC Company benefited.

O entered into a contract to purchase a $250,000 airplane for the corporation. O signed the name of the PPC Company on the contract. The seller of the airplane, S, asked O if he were authorized to make the purchase. O said he was authorized to enter into all contracts which concerned the marketing of the PPC. He used the plane a few times to fly from coast to coast to promote the sale of the PPC. The first time the directors learned of the airplane, they held a special board meeting and passed a resolution directing O to cancel the airplane contract because it was unauthorized. O does this, S repossesses the plane and sues PPC Company for breach of contract.

Meanwhile, A, in his capacity as Vice President for Development, hired N to test drive all of the PPC's which were manufactured. He was instructed to drive each one around town, up and down hills and to maintain a speed of 30 m.p.h. for three minutes on each car. While going down a steep hill, N lost control of the PPC and it ran over T, standing on the sidewalk. T sues N and PPC Company for $500,000 because both of his legs were broken.

Sales of the PPC never developed. GM and Ford began to manufacture much smaller autos and the consumers opted for these or motorcycles. The roof began to fall in. L demanded a $125,000 payment which was due, O had judgments of $80,000 against him in Detroit and PPC Company already faced two large law suits from S and T; and R has demanded the PPC Company sue O for fraud.

Write a well organized essay answer explaining the legal liability, if any, of PPC Company to L, Detroit creditors of O, S, and T.

Deciding whether or not a party will ultimately prevail in the courts is not as important as recognizing and discussing all legal issues. If you think a fact which is not stated is important state the fact and that you are assuming its existence.

19. X is a large shareholder in the Midwest Real Estate Development Corporation (hereafter referred to as, "The Corp."), its president and chairman of the Board of Directors. The Corp. is a publicly held corporation with its shares being traded on the American Stock Exchange. The activities of the Corp. primarily include the purchase of large tracts of real estate in the Midwest and the development of them into condominiums, large apartment complexes and shopping centers. The Corp. has been very successful. It is now the largest real estate development firm between Chicago and Cleveland and it's branching out into the manufacturing of preconstructed housing modules which will be built in a large 50,000 square foot plant and delivered to construction sites.

X's uncle, Y, is President of an Elkhart, Indiana firm which, in the past, has concentrated on constructing recreational vehicles. The name of this corporation is Mooncraft International (hereafter called "Moon"). Moon is very research oriented for a firm of its size and employs several ex-NASA metalurgical engineers to research and develop new materials for recreational vehicle construction. In January of 1973, Moon's engineers discovered a process which combines aluminum, fiberglass, soybeans and water into a building material which is as strong as steel, as workable as wood and has better insulating qualities than any commercially available insulation material. It can be made into sheets (up to 5 inches thick), beams, tubes, posts, or almost any shape. This substance can be manufactured at 1/2 the cost of an equal amount of other building material and is 2/3 the cost of wood. In February, 1973, Moon secured patents on the primary process and the related processes required to manufacture this material.

Moon was controlled by Y and other members of his family; about 20 percent of Moon was owned by persons unrelated to Y in any way. X has purchased 10 percent of Moon for his wife who sat on Moon's Board of Directors.

The discovery of this material had not been made public. In March, 1973, X and Y had preliminary discussions about the Corp's acquiring a controlling interest in Moon from Y and members of his family. On March 30, 1973, the Corp., through its president X, and Y and Y's family agreed in a lengthy contract entitled, "Memorandum of Understanding" that the Corp. would acquire about 80 percent of the stock of Moon which was held by Y, his family and X's wife for $30 per share. The book value of the stock was $10 per share and the 20 percent that was owned by the public had never traded at more than $15 per share. Of course, the Memorandum was to be voted on at ·the Corp's board meeting on April 10.

The proposal passed the April 10 board meeting. A provision in the Memorandum which was not specifically pointed out at this meeting nor was it discussed, states, "36. Until the final date of sale, Moon reserves the right to sell licenses to produce under the new patents to whomever it selects." The patent was owned by Moon and was, at this point, a major asset.

On April 10, X purchased 500 shares of the Corp. for his two sons and then did the same thing on April 12 for his two daughters.

On April 11, the Corp. issued an announcement to the public which states, "The Midwest Real Estate Development Corporation has made arrangements to purchase Mooncraft International, an Elkhart, Indiana firm which manufactures recreational vehicles."

On April 20 Moon gave a license to produce the material for the next fifteen years to a new corporation (Called "New Corp.") owned by X and Y and their families.

ASSUME: 1. You have owned shares of Moon since 1970 and you were not offered $50/share for your stock.
2. The common stock of the Corp. sold for about $8 per share from 1971 to April 27, 1973. You owned some shares of the Corp. and sold them for $8.25 on April 15, 1973. Between April 27, 1973 and August 1, 1973 the price of the Corp.'s common went from $8.25 to $48.00/share. This was due to the publicity given to the new building material and process in June and July, 1973.
3. Assume New Corp. is sold in July by X and Y for 1000 percent profit to a firm which plans to develop and expand activities in the Midwest.

Write a well organized essay about the legal problems you discern in the above problem. Specifically, what remedies do you have. What breaches of duty do you see. Where is the legal liability and to whom. If you see an issue but feel uncomfortable about reaching a definite conclusion you may argue both sides of the issue.

20. Additrol (hereafter "A") is a midwest corporation which manufactures additives for engine oil and gasoline. These additives are combined with the refined gas and oil and are intended to make the automobile engine run without knocking. A is publicly owned and its shares are traded on the American Stock Exchange. Last year, the gross sales amounted to 77 million dollars, and the company earned almost 9.5 million dollars net profit.

A was founded by the Smith family, and currently 30 percent of the outstanding shares are owned by the Smith family giving them voting control of A. They usually can elect three out of five directors. Bob Smith is Chairman of the Board and his brother, Carl, is President and Chief Executive Officer of A.

A's competitors are Standard Oil of New Jersey and Gulf Oil, each of which manufacture additives for their own refined gas and oil as well as sell these additives to other major refiners. A can maintain its competitiveness only by expending large amounts for research and development. Much of A's success has been attributed to its ability to develop patents for new additives. After a patent is received A then sells a license to produce the substance to other manufacturers.

In March of 1973, an inventor, "I" approached Carl Smith with an idea of making a chemical compound out of clay which would eliminate much of the smoke (produced by the internal combustion engine) when added to the gas supply. Carl referred the matter to his research staff and they recommended A buy the complete rights to develop the idea of I. Carl took the matter to a board meeting and suggested A buy the concept from I. Although all of the five directors were notified, only two of the Smith directors and two of the others attended. The others, named "C" and "D" were very perceptive businessmen and could see that in the near future the price of crude oil was going to double. This made them fear that the long-run outlook for the additive market which was directly linked to the automobile market was rather speculative. These directors believed that the resources of A should be directed into developing large batteries or energy storing cells which could be used in electric cars. Therefore, they voted against the proposal of Carl's that I's invention be purchased by A. Therefore, the matter failed because it did not receive a majority vote. It would be three months until the next board meeting and Bob and Carl thought they should not wait. Together, they personally purchased the rights to the development of I's idea for $500,000.

A month later, the price of oil began to climb. Since most of the additives were derivatives from petroleum, A's costs began to climb. Most oil companies had the market leverage to raise prices, and most raised their prices more than their costs were rising; therefore, they showed large profits. A, however, was a family-run corporation and they had refused to promote good managers to top positions in the corporation. Their profits did not rise and it was felt that at last Standard Oil and Gulf were going to squeeze A out of the market. At the next board meeting in June, Bob and Carl made an impassioned plea for A to buy the rights for I's invention from them. This time, all of the Smith family directors were present and the vote was 3 to 2 to buy I's invention from Bob and Carl for 1 million dollars. It was made clear that Bob and Carl were the present owners.

The 1 million dollars was paid in July, August, and September; and, by September it was realized that A was going to show a loss for the first time in 20 years due in part to the large cash payment to Bob and Carl.

On August 30, 1973, the shares of A were selling at $25 per share. By September 15, Bob and Carl had information to indicate that due to their rising costs and their inability to raise the selling price of their product and due to a severe lack of cash, A was approaching insolvency. They each sold 10,000 shares of A on September 16 at $24 per share. The third quarter earnings report was made public on September 30, indicating a severe loss. The selling price of A's shares dropped to $15 per share as soon as the market absorbed the news of the loss.

Shortly thereafter, Bob and Carl agreed to sell their remaining shares to a subsidiary of ITT for $25 per share. This sale was to take place November 3, 1973 and this sale would give ITT voting control of A. ITT was really after A's patents and, in particular, they were most interested in I's invention. A had put much money into the development of I's concept and it now appeared, at least in the short run, that I's invention was truly miraculous.

Shortly before the sale of Bob and Carl's shares to ITT was finalized, Carl Smith, as president, sold on behalf of the corporation an "irrevocable" license to use I's invention to Family Corporation owned by Bob and Carl and recently formed just to own the license. The contract price was $25,000. At this time, one of the chief assets which A owned was I's invention. Bob and Carl insist that the $25,000 was needed to keep A in operation.

Write a well organized essay about the legal issues you discern in the above fact pattern. After discussing the causes of action, if any, describe the *remedies* available. What defenses may be argued and do you anticipate that they will be successful? If you see an issue but feel uncomfortable about reaching a definite conclusion you may argue both sides of the issue. Finally, be sure to discuss the maner in which D may seek a remedy.

UNIFORM PARTNERSHIP ACT*

PART I
PRELIMINARY PROVISIONS

1. Name of Act

This act may be cited as Uniform Partnership Act.

2. Definition of Terms

In this act, "Court" includes every court and judge having jurisdiction in the case.

"Business" includes every trade, occupation, or profession.

"Person" includes individuals, partnerships, corporations, and other associations.

"Bankrupt" includes bankrupt under the Federal Bankruptcy Act or insolvent under any state insolvent act.

"Conveyance" includes every assignment, lease, mortgage, or encumbrance.

"Real Property" includes land and any interest or estate in land.

3. Interpretation of Knowledge and Notice

1. A person has "knowledge" of a fact within the meaning of this act not only when he has actual knowledge thereof, but also when he has knowledge of such other facts as in the circumstances shows bad faith.
2. A person has "notice" of a fact within the meaning of this act when the person who claims the benefit of the notice:
   a. States the fact to such person, or
   b. Delivers through the mail, or by other means of communication, a written statement of the fact to such person or to a proper person at his place of business or residence.

4. Rules of Construction

1. The rule that statutes in derogation of the common law are to be strictly construed shall have no application to this act.
2. The law of estoppel shall apply under this act.
3. The law of agency shall apply under this act.
4. This act shall be so interpreted and construed as to effect its general purpose to make uniform the law of those states which enact it.
5. This act shall not be construed so as to impair the obligations of any contract existing when the act goes into effect, nor to affect any action or proceedings begun or right accrued before this act takes effect.

5. Rules for Cases Not Provided for in This Act

In any case not provided for in this act the rules of law and equity, including the law merchant, shall govern.

---

*The Uniform Partnership Act was originally developed by the National Conference of Commissioners on Uniform State Laws.

PART II
NATURE OF PARTNERSHIP

6. Partnership Defined

1. A partnership is an association of two or more persons to carry on as co-owners a business for profit.
2. But any association formed under any other statute of this state, or any statute adopted by authority, other than the authority of this state, is not a partnership under this act, unless such association would have been a partnership in this state prior to the adoption of this act; but this act shall apply to limited partnerships except in so far as the statutes relating to such partnerships are inconsistent herewith.

7. Rules for Determining the Existence of a Partnership

In determining whether a partnership exists, these rules shall apply:

1. Except as provided by section 16 persons who are not partners as to each other are not partners as to third persons.
2. Joint tenancy, tenancy in common, tenancy by the entireties, joint property, common property, or part ownership does not of itself establish a partnership, whether such co-owners do or do not share any profits made by the use of the property.
3. The sharing of gross returns does not of itself establish a partnership, whether or not the persons sharing them have a joint or common right or interest in any property from which the returns are derived.
4. The receipt by a person of a share of the profits of a business is prima facie evidence that he is a partner in the business, but no such inference shall be drawn if such profits were received in payment:
   a. As a debt by installments or otherwise,
   b. As wages of an employee or rent to a landlord,
   c. As an annuity to a widow or representative of a deceased partner.
   d. As interest on a loan, though the amount of payment varies with the profits of the business,
   e. As the consideration for the sale of a good-will of a business or other property by installments or otherwise.

8. Partnership Property

1. All property originally brought into the partnership stock or subsequently acquired by purchase or otherwise, on account of the partnership, is partnership property.
2. Unless the contrary intention appears, property acquired with partnership funds is partnership property.
3. Any estate in real property may be acquired in the partnership name. Title so acquired can be conveyed only in the partnership name.
4. A conveyance to a partnership in the partnership name, though without words of inheritance, passes the entire estate of the grantor unless a contrary intent appears.

PART III
RELATIONS OF PARTNERS TO PERSONS DEALING
WITH THE PARTNERSHIP

9. Partner Agent of Partnership as to Partnership Business

1. Every partner is an agent of the partnership for the purpose of its business, and the act of every partner, including the execution in the partnership name of any instrument, for apparently carrying on in the usual way the business of the partnership of which he is a member binds the partnership, unless the partner so acting has in fact no authority to act for the partnership in the particular matter, and the person with whom he is dealing has knowledge of the fact that he has no such authority.

2. An act of a partner which is not apparently for the carrying on of the business of the partnership in the usual way does not bind the partnership unless authorized by the other partners.

3. Unless authorized by the other partners or unless they have abandoned the business, one or more but less than all the partners have no authority to:
   a. Assign the partnership property in trust for creditors or on the assignee's promise to pay the debts of the partnership,
   b. Dispose of the good-will of the buiness,
   c. Do any other act which would make it impossible to carry on the ordinary business of a partnership,
   d. Confess a judgement,
   e. Submit a partnership claim or liability to arbitration or reference.

4. No act of a partner in contravention of a restriction on authority shall bind the partnership to persons having knowledge of the restriction.

10. Conveyance of Real Property of the Partnership

1. Where title to real property is in the partnership name, any partner may convey title to such property by a conveyance executed in the partnership name; but the partnership may recover such property unless the partner's act binds the partnership under the provisions of paragraph (1) of section 9, or unless such property has been conveyed by the grantee or a person claiming through such grantee to a holder for value without knowledge that the partner, in making the conveyance, has exceeded his authority.

2. Where title to real property is in the name of the partnership, a conveyance executed by a partner, in his own name, passes the equitable interest of the partnership, provided the act is one within the authority of the partner under the provisions of paragraph (1) of section 9.

3. Where title to real property is in the name of one or more but not all the partners, and the record does not disclose the right of the partnership, the partners in whose name the title stands may convey title to such property, but the partnership may recover such property if the partners' act does not bind the partnership under the provisions of paragraph (1) of section 9, unless the purchaser or his assignee, is a holder for value, without knowledge.

4. Where the title to real property is in the name of one or more or all the partners or in a third person in trust for the partnership name, a conveyance executed by a partner in the partnership name, or in his own name, passes the equitable interest of the partnership, provided the act is one within the authority of the partner under the provisions of paragraph (1) of section 9.
5. Where the title to real property is in the names of all the partners a conveyance executed by all the partners passes all their rights in such property.

11. Partnership Bound by Admission of Partner

An admission or representation made by any partner concerning partnership affairs within the scope of his authority as conferred by this act is evidence against the partnership.

12. Partnership Charged with Knowledge of or Notice to Partner

Notice to any partner of any matter relating to partnership affairs, and the knowledge of the partner acting in the particular matter, acquired while a partner or then present to his mind, and the knowledge of any other partner who reasonably could and should have communicated it to the acting partner, operate as notice to or knowledge of the partnership, except in the case of a fraud on the partnership committed by or with the consent of that partner.

13. Partnership Bound by Partner's Wrongful Act

Where, by any wrongful act or omission of any partner acting in the ordinary course of the business of the partnership or with the authority of his co-partners, loss or injury is caused to any person, not being a partner in the partnership, or any penalty is incurred, the partnership is liable therefore to the same extent as the partner so acting or omitting to act.

14. Partnership Bound by Partner's Breach of Trust

The partnership is bound to make good the loss:
a. Where one partner acting within the scope of his apparent authority receives money or property of a third person and misapplied it; and
b. Where the partnership in the course of its business receives money or property of a third person and the money or property so received is misapplied by any partner while it is in the custody of the partnership.

15. Nature of Partner's Liability

All partners are liable
a. Jointly and severally for everything chargeable to the partnership under sections 13 and 14.
b. Jointly for all other debts and obligations of the partnership; but any partner may enter into a separate obligation to perform a partnership contract.

16. Partner by Estoppel

1. When a person, by words spoken or written or by conduct, represents himself, or consents to another representing him to any one, as a partner in an existing partnership or with one or more persons not actual partners, he is liable to any such person to whom such representation has been made, who has, on the faith of such representation, given credit to

the actual or apparent partnership, and if he has made such representation or consented to its being made in a public manner, he is liable to such person, whether the representation has or has not been made or communicated to such person so giving credit by or with the knowledge of the apparent partner making the representation or consenting to its being made.

    a. When a partnership liability results, he is liable as though he were an actual member of the partnership.

    b. When no partnership liability results, he is liable jointly with the other persons, if any, so consenting to the contract or representation as to incur liability, otherwise separately.

2. When a person has been thus represented to be a partner in an existing partnership, or with one or more persons not actual partners, he is an agent of the persons consenting to such representation to bind them to the same extent and in the same manner as though he were a partner in fact, with respect to persons who rely upon the representation. Where all the members of the existing partnership consent to the representation, a partnership act or obligation results; but in all other cases it is the joint act or obligation of the person acting and the persons consenting to the representation.

17. Liability of Incoming Partner

A person admitted as a partner into an existing partnership is liable for all the obligations of the partnership arising before his admission as though he had been a partner when such obligations were incurred, except that this liability shall be satisfied only out of partnership property.

PART IV
RELATIONS OF PARTNERS TO ONE ANOTHER

18. Rules Determining Rights and Duties of Partners

The rights and duties of the partners in relation to the partnership shall be determined, subject to any agreement between them, by the following rules:

    a. Each partner shall be repaid his contributions, whether by way of capital or advances to the partnership property and share equally in the profits and surplus remaining after all liabilities, including those to partners, are satisfied; and must contribute towards the losses, whether of capital or otherwise, sustained by the partnership according to his share in the profits.

    b. The partnership must indemnify every partner in respect of payments made and personal liabilities reasonably incurred by him in the ordinary and proper conduct of its business, or for the preservation of its business or property.

    c. A partner who in aid of the partnership makes any payment or advance beyond the amount of capital which he agreed to contribute, shall be paid interest from the date of the payment or advance.

    d. A partner shall receive interest on the capital contributed by him only from the date when repayment should be made.

   e. All partners have equal rights in the management and conduct of the partnership business.

   f. No partner is entitled to remuneration for acting in the partnership business, except that a surviving partner is entitled to reasonable compensation for his services in winding up the partnership affairs.

   g. No person can become a member of a partnership without the consent of all the partners.

   h. Any difference arising as to ordinary matters connected with the partnership business may be decided by a majority of the partners; but no act in contravention of any agreement between the partners may be done rightfully without the consent of all the partners.

19. Partnership Books

The partnership books shall be kept, subject to any agreement between the partners, at the principal place of business of the partnership, and every partner shall at all times have access to and may inspect and copy any of them.

20. Duty of Partners to Render Information

Partners shall render on demand true and full information of all things affecting the partnership to any partner or the legal representative of any deceased partner or partner under legal disability.

21. Partner Accountable as a Fiduciary

1. Every partner must account to the partnership for any benefit, and hold as trustee for it any profits derived by him without the consent of the other partners from any transaction connected with the formation, conduct, or liquidation of the partnership or from any use by him of its property.

2. This section applies also to the representatives of a deceased partner engaged in the liquidation of the affairs of the partnership as the personal representatives of the last surviving partner.

22. Rights to an Account

Any partner shall have the right to a formal account as to partnership affairs:

   a. If he is wrongfully excluded from the partnership business or possession of its property by his co-partners,

   b. If the right exists under the terms of any agreement,

   c. As provided by section 21,

   d. Whenever other circumstances render it just and reasonable.

23. Continuation of Partnership Beyond Fixed Term

1. When a partnership for a fixed term or particular undertaking is continued after the termination of such term or particular undertaking without any express agreement, the rights and duties of the partners remain the same as they were at such termination, so far as is consistent with a partnership at will.

2. A continuation of the business by the partners or such of them as habitually acted therein during the term, without any settlement or liquidation of the partnership affairs, is prima facie evidence of a continuation of the partnership.

PART V
PROPERTY RIGHTS OF A PARTNER

24. Extent of Property Rights of a Partner

The property rights of a partner are 1) his rights in specific partnership property, 2) his interest in the partnership, and 3) his right to participate in the management.

25. Nature of a Partner's Right in Specific Partnership Property

1. A partner is co-owner with his partners of specific partnership property holding as a tenant in partnership.
2. The incidents of this tenancy are such that:
   a. A partner, subject to the provisions of this act and to any agreement between the partners, has an equal right with his partners to possess specific partnership property for partnership purposes; but he has no right to possess such property for any other purpose without the consent of his partners.
   b. A partner's right in specific partnership property is not assignable except in connection with the assignment of rights of all the partners in the same property.
   c. A partner's right in specific partnership property is not subject to attachment or execution, except on a claim against the partnership. When partnership property is attached for a partnership debt the partners, or any of them or the representatives of a deceased partner, cannot claim any right under the homestead or exemption laws.
   d. On the death of a partner his right in specific partnership property vests in the surviving partner or partners, except where the deceased was the last surviving partner, when his right in such property vests in his legal representative. Such surviving partner or partners, or the legal representative of the last surviving partner, has no right to possess the partnership property for any but a partnership purpose.
   e. A partner's right in specific partnership property is not subject to dower, curtesy, or allowances to widows, heirs, or next of kin.

26. Nature of Partner's Interest in the Partnership

A partner's interest in the partnership is his share of the profits and surplus, and the same is personal property.

27. Assignment of Partner's Interest

1. A conveyance by a partner of his interest in the partnership does not of itself dissolve the partnership, nor, as against the other partners in the absence of agreement, entitle the assignee, during the continuance of the partnership, to interfere in the management or administration of the partnership business or affairs, or to require any information or account of partnership transactions, or to inspect the partnership books; but it merely entitles the assignee to receive in accordance with his contract the profits to which the assigning partner would otherwise be entitled.
2. In case of a dissolution of the partnership, the assignee is entitled to receive his assignor's interest and may require an account from the date only of the last account agreed to by all the partners.

28. Partner's Interest Subject to Charging Order

1. On due application to a competent court by any judgment creditor of a partner, the court which entered the judgment order, or decree or any other court, may charge the interest of the debtor partner with payment of the unsatisfied amount of such judgment debt with interest thereon; and may then or later appoint a receiver of his share of the profits, and of any other money due or to fall due to him in respect of the partnership, and make all other orders, directions, accounts and inquiries which the debtor partner might have made, or which the circumstances of the case may require.

2. The interest charged may be redeemed at any time before foreclosure, or in case of a sale being directed by the court may be purchased without thereby causing a dissolution;
   a. With separate property, by any one or more of the partners, or
   b. With partnership property, by any one or more of the partners with the consent of all the partners whose interests are not so charged or sold.

3. Nothing in this act shall be held to deprive a partner of his right, if any, under the exemption laws, as regards his interest in the partnership.

PART VI
DISSOLUTION AND WINDING UP

29. Dissolution Defined

The dissolution of a partnership is the change in the relation of the partners caused by any partner ceasing to be associated in the carrying on as distinguished from the winding up of the business.

30. Partnership not Terminated by Dissolution

On dissolution the partnership is not terminated, but continues until the winding up of partnership affairs is completed.

31. Causes of Dissolution

Dissolution is caused:

1. Without violation of the agreement between the partners,
   a. By the termination of the definite term or particular undertaking specified in the agreement,
   b. By the express will of any partner when no definite term or particular undertaking is specified,
   c. By the express will of all the partners who have not assigned their interests or suffered them to be charged for their separate debts, either before or after the termination of any specified term or particular undertaking,
   d. By the expulsion of any partner from the business bona fide in accordance with such a power conferred by the agreement between the partners;

2. In contravention of the agreement between the partners, where the circumstances do not permit a dissolution under any other provision of this section, by the express will of any partner at any time;

3. By any event which makes it unlawful for the business of the partnership to be carried on or for the members to carry it on in partnership;
4. By the death of any partner;
5. By the bankruptcy of any partner or the partnership;
6. By decree of court under section 32.

32. Dissolution by Decree of Court

1. On application by or for a partner the court shall decree a dissolution whenever:
   a. A partner has been declared a lunatic in any judicial proceeding or is shown to be of unsound mind,
   b. A partner becomes in any other way incapable of performing his part of the partnership contract,
   c. A partner has been guilty of such conduct as tends to affect prejudicially the carrying on of the business,
   d. A partner willfully or persistently commits a breach of the partnership agreement, or otherwise so conducts himself in matters relating to the partnership business that it is not reasonably practicable to carry on the business in partnership with him,
   e. The business of the partnership can only be carried on at a loss,
   f. Other circumstances render a dissolution equitable.
2. On the application of the purchaser of a partner's interest under sections 28 or 29;
   a. After the termination of the specified term or particular undertaking.
   b. At any time if the partnership was a partnership at will when the interest was assigned or when the charging order was issued.

33. General Effect of Dissolution on Authority of Partner

Except so far as may be necessary to wind up partnership affairs or to complete transactions begun but not then finished, dissolution terminates all authority of any partner to act for the partnership.

1. With respect to the partners,
   a. When the dissolution is not by the act, bankruptcy or death of a partner; or
   b. When the dissolution is by such act, bankruptcy or death of a partner, in cases where section 34 so requires.
2. With respect to persons not partners, as declared in section 35.

34. Right of Partner to Contribution from Co-Partners after Dissolution

Where the dissolution is caused by the act, death or bankruptcy of a partner, each partner is liable to his co-partners for his share of any liability created by any partner acting for the partnership as if the partnership had not been dissolved unless

a. The dissolution being by act of any partner, the partner acting for the partnership had knowledge of the dissolution, or
b. The dissolution being by the death or bankruptcy of a partner, the partner acting for the partnership had knowledge or notice of the death or bankruptcy.

35. Power of Partner to Bind Partnership to Third Persons after Dissolution

1. After dissolution a partner can bind the partnership except as provided in Paragraph (3).

   a. By any act appropriate for winding up partnership affairs or completing transactions unfinished at dissolution;

   b. By any transaction which would bind the partnership if dissolution had not taken place, provided the other party to the transaction

     I. Had extended credit to the partnership prior to dissolution and had no knowledge or notice of the dissolution; or

     II. Though he had not so extended credit, had nevertheless known of the partnership prior to dissolution, and, having no knowledge or notice of dissolution, the fact of dissolution had not been advertised in a newspaper of general circulation in the place (or in each place if more than one) at which the partnership business was regularly carried on.

2. The liability of a partner under Paragraph (1b) shall be satisfied out of partnership assets alone when such partner had been prior to dissolution

   a. Unknown as a partner to the person with whom the contract is made; and

   b. So far unknown and inactive in partnership affairs that the business reputation of the partnership could not be said to have been in any degree due to his connection with it.

3. The partnership is in no case bound by any act of a partner after dissolution

   a. Where the partnership is dissolved because it is unlawful to carry on the business, unless the act is appropriate for winding up partnership affairs; or

   b. Where the partner has become bankrupt; or

   c. Where the partner has no authority to wind up partnership affairs; except by a transaction with one who

     I. Had extended credit to the partnership prior to dissolution and had no knowledge or notice of his want of authority; or

     II. Had not extended credit to the partnership prior to dissolution, and, having no knowledge or notice of his want of authority, the fact of his want of authority has not been advertised in the manner provided for advertising the fact of dissolution in Paragraph (1bII).

4. Nothing in this section shall affect the liability under Section 16 of any person who after dissolution represents himself or consents to another representing him as a partner in a partnership engaged in carrying on business.

36. Effect of Dissolution on Partner's Existing Liability

1. The dissolution of the partnership does not of itself discharge the existing liability of any partner.

2. A partner is discharged from any existing liability upon dissolution of the partnership by an agreement to that effect between himself, the partnership creditor and the person or partnership continuing the business; and such agreement may be inferred from the course of dealing between the creditor having knowledge of the dissolution and the person or partnership continuing the business.

3. Where a person agrees to assume the existing obligations of a dissolved partnership, the partners whose obligations have been assumed shall be

discharged from any liability to any creditor of the partnership who, knowing of the agreement, consents to a material alteration in the nature of time of payment of such obligations.

4. The individual property of a deceased partner shall be liable for all obligations of the partnership incurred while he was a partner but subject to the prior payment of his separate debts.

37. Right to Wind Up

Unless otherwise agreed the partners who have not wrongfully dissolved the partnership or the legal representative of the last surviving partner, not bankrupt, has the right to wind up the partnership affairs; provided however, that any partner, his legal representative or his assignee, upon cause shown, may obtain winding up by the court.

38. Rights of Partners to Application of Partnership Property

1. When dissolution is caused in any way, except in contravention of the partnership agreement, each partner, as against his co-partners and all persons claiming through them in respect of their interests in the partnership, unless otherwise agreed, may have the partnership property applied to discharge its liabilities, and the surplus applied to pay in cash the net amount owing to the respective partners. But if dissolution is caused by expulsion of a partner, bona fide under the partnership agreement and if the expelled partner is discharged from all partnership liabilities, either by payment or agreement under section 36(2), he shall receive in cash only the net amount due him from the partnership.

2. When dissolution is caused in contravention of the partnership agreement the rights of the partners shall be as follows:

   a. Each partner who has not caused dissolution wrongfully shall have,
      I. All the rights specified in paragraph (1) of this section, and
      II. The right, as against each partner who has caused the dissolution wrongfully, to damages for breach of the agreement.

   b. The partners who have not caused the dissolution wrongfully, if they all desire to continue the business in the same name, either by themselves or jointly with others, may do so, during the agreed term for the partnership and for that purpose may possess the partnership property, provided they secure the payment by bond approved by the court, or pay to any partner who has caused the dissolution wrongfully, the value of his interest in the partnership at the dissolution, less any damages recoverable under clause (2a,II) of this section, and in like manner indemnify him against all present or future partnership liabilities.

   c. A partner who has caused the dissolution wrongfully shall have:
      I. If the business is not continued under the provisions of paragraph (2b) all the rights of a partner under paragraph (1), subject to clause (2aII), of this section,
      II. If the business is continued under paragraph (2b) of this section the right as against the co-partners and all claiming through them in respect of their interests in the partnership, to have the value of his interest in the partnership, less any damages caused to his co-partners by the dissolution, ascertained and paid to him in

cash, or the payment secured by bond approved by the court, and to be released from all existing liabilities of the partnership; but in ascertaining the value of the partner's interest the value of the business shall not be considered.

39. Rights Where Partnership is Dissolved for Fraud or Misrepresentation

Where a partnership contract is rescinded on the ground of the fraud or misrepresentation of one of the parties thereto, the party entitled to rescind is, without prejudice to any other right, entitled,

    a. To a lien on, or a right of retention of, the surplus of the partnership property after satisfying the partnership liabilities to third persons for any sum of money paid by him for the purchase of an interest in the partnership and for any capital or advances contributed by him; and

    b. To stand, after all liabilities to third persons have been satisfied, in the place of the creditors of the partnership for any payments made by him in respect of the partnership liabilities; and

    c. To be indemnified by the person guilty of the fraud or making the representation against all debts and liabilities of the partnership.

40. Rules for Distribution

In settling accounts between the partners after dissolution, the following rules shall be observed, subject to any agreement to the contrary:

    a. The assets of the partnership are:
      I. The partnership property,
      II. The contributions of the partners necessary for the payment of all the liabilities specified in clause (b) of this paragraph.

    b. The liabilities of the partnership shall rank in order of payment, as follows:
      I. Those owing to creditors other than partners,
      II. Those owing to partners other than for capital and profits.
      III. Those owing to partners in respect of capital.
      IV. Those owing to partners in respect of profits.

    c. The assets shall be applied in order of their declaration in clause (a) of this paragraph to the satisfaction of the liabilities.

    d. The partners shall contribute, as provided by section 18 (a) the amount necessary to satisfy the liabilities; but if any, but not all, of the partners are insolvent, or not being subject to process, refuse to contribute, the other partners shall contribute their share of the liabilities and, in the relative proportions in which they share the profits, the additional amount necessary to pay the liabilities.

    e. An assignee for the benefit of creditors or any person appointed by the court shall have the right to enforce the contributions specified in clause (d) of this paragraph.

    f. Any partner or his legal representative shall have the right to enforce the contributions specified in clause (d) of this paragraph, to the extent of the amount which he has paid in excess of his share of the liability.

    g. The individual property of a deceased partner shall be liable for the contributions specified in clause (d) of this paragraph.

    h. When partnership property and the individual properties of the partners are in possession of a court for distribution, partnership creditors shall have priority on partnership property and separate creditors on individual property, saving the rights of lien or secured creditors as heretofore.

    i. Where a partner has become bankrupt or his estate is insolvent the claims against his separate property shall rank in the following order:

        I. Those owing to separate creditors,

        II. Those owing to partnership creditors,

        III. Those owing to partners by way of contribution.

41. Liability of Persons Continuing the Business in Certain Cases

1. When any new partner is admitted into an existing partnership, or when any partner retires and assigns (or the representative of the deceased partner assigns) his rights in partnership property to two or more of the partners, or to one or more of the partners and one or more third persons, if the business is continued without liquidation of the partnership affairs, creditors of the first or dissolved partnership are also creditors of the partnership so continuing the business.

2. When all but one partner retire and assign (or the representative of a deceased partner assigns) their rights in partnership property to the remaining partner, who continues the business without liquidation of partnership affairs, either alone or with others, creditors of the dissolved partnership are also creditors of the person or partnership so continuing the business.

3. When any partner retires or dies and the business of the dissolved partnership is continued as set forth in paragraphs (1) and (2) of this section, with the consent of the retired partners or the representative of the deceased partner, but without any assignment of his right in partnership property, rights of creditors of the dissolved partnership and of the creditors of the person or partnership continuing the business shall be as if such assignment had been made.

4. When all the partners or their representatives assign their rights in partnership property to one or more third persons who promise to pay the debts and who continue the business of the dissolved partnership, creditors of the dissolved partnership are also creditors of the person or partnership continuing the business.

5. When any partner wrongfully causes a dissolution and the remaining partners continue the business under the provisions of section 38 (2b) either alone or with others, and without liquidation of the partnership affairs, creditors of the dissolved partnership are also creditors of the person or partnership continuing the business.

6. When a partner is expelled and the remaining partners continue the business either alone or with others, without liquidation of the partnership affairs, creditors of the dissolved partnership are also creditors of the person or partnership continuing the business.

7. The liability of a third person becoming a partner in the partnership continuing the business, under this section, to the creditors of the dissolved partnership shall be satisfied out of partnership property only.

8. When the business of a partnership after dissolution is continued under any conditions set forth in this section the creditors of the dissolved partnership, as against the separate creditors of the retiring or deceased partner or the representative of the deceased partner, have a prior right to any claim of the retired partner or the representative of the deceased partner against the person or partnership continuing the business, on account of the retired or deceased partner's interest in the dissolved partnership or on account of any consideration promised for such interest or for his right in partnership property.

9. Nothing in this section shall be held to modify any right or creditors to set aside any assignment on the ground of fraud.

10. The use by the person or partnership continuing the business of the partnership name, or the name of a deceased partner as part thereof, shall not of itself make the individual property of the deceased partner liable for any debts contracted by such person or partnership.

42. Rights of Retiring or Estate of Deceased Partner When the Business is Continued

When any partner retires or dies, and the business is continued under any of the conditions set forth in section 41 (1, 2, 3, 5, 6), or section 38 (2b) without any settlement of accounts as between him or his estate and the person or partnership continuing the business, unless otherwise agreed, he or his legal representative as against such persons or partnership may have the value of his interest at the date of dissolution ascertained, and shall receive as an ordinary creditor an amount equal to the value of his interest in the dissolved partnership with interest, or, at his option or at the option of his legal representative, in lieu of interest, the profits attributable to the use of his right in the property of the dissolved partnership; provided that the creditors of the dissolved partnership as against the separate creditors, or the representative of the retired or deceased partner, shall have priority on any claim arising under this section, as provided by section 41 (8) of this act.

43. Accrual of Actions

The right to an account of his interest shall accrue to any partner, or his legal representative, as against the winding up partners or the surviving partners or the person or partnership continuing the business, at the date of dissolution, in the absence of any agreement to the contrary.

PART VII
MISCELLANEOUS PROVISIONS

44. When Act Takes Effect

This act shall take effect on the _____ day of _____ one thousand nine hundred and _____ .

45. Legislation Repealed

All acts or parts of acts inconsistent with this act are hereby repealed.

GLOSSARY OF LEGAL TERMS

AB INITIO, Latin — From the beginning. An agreement or act may be illegal ab initio.

ABSOLUTE/STRICT LIABILITY — Tort liability imposed without regard to fault.

ACCOUNTING — As used in this text, refers to a remedy available to a partner which compels disclosure to the partner of all financial matters of the partnership. A complete statement of all accounts.

ACTUAL AUTHORITY — A classification of authority in which a principal expressly or impliedly authorizes an agent to act for the principal.

ACTUAL NOTICE — Notice or knowledge of an event actually received.

ADJUDICATION — The rendering of a judgment in a court case.

ADMINISTRATIVE AGENCY — A federal or state unit invested by the legislature or executive with rule making and enforcing authority.

ADMINISTRATOR — A person appointed by a probate court to wind up the affairs of a deceased person when the deceased left no will or, if a will existed, it did not name an executor.

AEQUITAS, Latin — A term usually denoting equity law or equitable principles.

AFFIDAVIT — A written declaration of facts made voluntarily and confirmed by an oath of the party making it.

AGENCY — A consensual, fiduciary relation between two persons, created by law by which one, the principal, has a right to control the conduct of the agent, and the agent has the power to affect the legal relations of the principal.

AGENT — The legal entity acting for another in the agency relationship.

ANSWER — A pleading document usually submitted by the defendant in which the party asserts matters of fact as a defense to facts asserted in a complaint or petition.

APPARENT AUTHORITY — An agent's power to affect the legal relations of a principal arising from the principal's manifestation of authority to the third person and the latter's reasonable reliance on the manifestation.

APPELLANT — (also sometimes called PETITIONER) — The party initiating the appeal from one court to another.

APPELLATE COURT — A court with three or more judges sitting in judgment on appeals to it from a lower appellate court or other tribunal of original jurisdiction.

APPELLEE — (sometimes also called RESPONDENT) — The party in an appellate case against whom the appeal is taken. The one responding to the appellant.

ARTICLES OF INCORPORATION — The articles of incorporation is the document filed with the secretary of state to incorporate an enterprise. It establishes the basic structure and conduct of the corporation. It is also called the charter or certificate of incorporation.

ASSAULT — An intentional, unlawful threat of injury to another by the use of force under such circumstances as create a well founded fear of injury to the one threatened.

ASSUMPSIT — An older form of a cause of action based primarily upon a promise implied in the law.

ASSUMPTION OF RISK — A defense in a tort action available to employers which permits the employer to avoid liability to an injured employee caused by the employer or one of its other agents on the basis that the injured employee knowingly undertook a dangerous task and therefore agreed that the risk of injury was his own.

ATTACHMENT — The act of a sheriff, marshall or other officer of the court in seizing a person's property by authority of a court order. The property is usually sold by the sheriff or marshall.

AUDIT – The process of investigating and reporting on an association's financial accounts.

AUTHORITY – A broad legal term denoting some of the circumstances in which courts will hold the principal liable for an agent's promises or acts made for the principal. (See specific types of authority – express, implied, apparent, estoppel, inherent, incidental).

BALANCE SHEET – A financial statement showing the assets, liabilities and owners' equity of a business association as of a certain date.

BATTERY – A forceful unlawful touching of another person without the consent of the injured person.

BLUE SKY LAWS – State securities law statutes.

BONA FIDE, Latin – In good faith.

BONA FIDE OCCUPATIONAL QUALIFICATION – (BFOQ) – An exception to Title VII of the 1964 Civil Rights Act allowing employment discrimination when it is reasonably necessary in the normal operation of the enterprize. Discrimination based upon race can never be a bona fide occupational qualification.

BOND – A corporate debt instrument which matures at a specified date in the future and usually provides for the regular payment of interest until the maturity date. A bondholder is a creditor of the corporation.

BREACH OF DUTY – See CAUSE OF ACTION.

BRIEF – Appellate – A formal legal document setting forth the detailed legal arguments made to an appellate court.
Study – an informal method of student note taking on appellate cases.

BY-LAWS – The document containing the detailed requirements that regulate the internal affairs of the corporation. They are subordinate to the articles.

CAPACITY – The legal ability to act as defined primarily by state statute.

CAPITAL SURPLUS – Capital derived from the sale of stock at a price in excess of its par or stated value. It is also called paid-in surplus.

CAUSE OF ACTION – The heart of the plaintiff's case composed of at least two elements: the assertion of the existence of a legal duty and its breach.

CAVEAT EMPTOR, Latin – Let the buyer beware.

CERTIORARI – A discretionary writ of review. Usually filed with an appellate court asking that court to review judicial actions.

CHANCERY – Equity, the system of jurisprudence administered by a court of equity.

CHATTEL – Personal property, moveables.

CHOSE IN ACTION – A cause of action for the return of personal property held by another.

CIRCUMSTANTIAL AUTHORITY – Authority of an agent to act created by circumstances. (See APPARENT, INHERENT AUTHORITY AND ESTOPPEL.)

CIVIL LAW – The system of jurisprudence indicating the private rights and remedies of citizens in contrast to those which are public, the violation of which is prosecuted under the criminal law.

CLASS ACTION – A type of civil case in which one person sues or is sued as a representative of a class of persons. It will be allowed if 1) the class is so numerous joinder of all is impracticable, 2) there are questions of fact and law common to all, 3) the claims asserted are typical of those assertable by the class, 4) the representative will fairly represent the class, and such a method of trying the case is superior to others.

CLOSE CORPORATIONS – A corporation that has a small number of shareholders.

COMMON LAW – That body of law which derives its authority from usage and customs and is expressed in judicial opinions, not legislative acts.

COMPLAINT – The formal document filed by a plaintiff to initiate the trial of a civil case.

CONDITION PRECEDENT – Describes an event which must occur before other acts or promises become legally operative.

CONSIDERATION – That exchange of promises or value which will support an enforceable contract.

CONSIGNMENT – The act or process of allowing another to hold your goods for sale, storage or shipment.

CONSOLIDATION — An alteration of corporate structure whereby corporations A and B will cease to exist and will be replaced by a new corporation C.

CONSTRUCTIVE NOTICE — A form of notice of an event or information which the law implies in circumstances in which actual notice is impracticable.

CONTRIBUTORY NEGLIGENCE — A defense to a negligence case in some jurisdictions in which recovery for injury caused by a defendant's negligence will be denied if the injured party was negligent in causing the injury.

CONVERSION — A tort in which one exercises unauthorized control over the personal property of another to the owner's damage.

COOPERATIVE ASSOCIATION — A form of business association formed primarily to provide an economic service to its members.

CORPORATION — A legal entity created, most often, by state statute which provides for the limited liability of its owners and for perpetual existence.

COUNTER CLAIM — A cause of action asserted by a defendant against another party in a law suit, usually the plaintiff.

COVENANT — An agreement or promise.

CRIMINAL LAW — That system of jurisprudence which is prosecuted by governmental personnel and is intended to punish the wrongful intent of the defendant. Imprisonment or a fine are the possible results.

CUMULATIVE PREFERRED STOCK — If dividends are not paid on the stock they are not lost but will cumulate until paid.

CUMULATIVE VOTING — Allows a shareholder to multiply the number of votes given him by his shares times the number of directors to be elected. It is designed to allow minority shareholders to gain representation on the board.

DEBENTURE — An unsecured corporate debt instrument.

DECEIT — (See MISREPRESENTATION)

DE FACTO, Latin — In fact, in actuality.

DEFAMATION — The tort of injuring a person's character, fame or reputation by publishing or speaking falsely about the person.

DEFAULT JUDGMENT — A judgment rendered when one of the parties fails to respond or appear before the court.

DEFENDANT — The party being sued in a court case.

DE JURE CORPORATION — A legally formed corporation, one formed in compliance with the state statute.

DELEGATION, of authority — A grant of authority by an agent to another agent with the permission or knowledge of the principal.

DEMURRER — An older form of pleading usually used by the defendant to challenge the legal sufficiency of the plaintiff's complaint; this pleading is construed to mean that the party using it admits the facts alleged but asserts they have no legal consequences.

DEPOSITION — The written testimony of a party or a witness taken out of court but under oath.

DERIVATIVE SUIT — A lawsuit brought by a shareholder on behalf of the corporation for damage suffered by the corporation. Also called a representative suit. The recovery goes to the corporation.

DESCENT — Hereditary succession of property.

DIRECTED VERDICT — A verdict entered by the court when one of the parties has made a motion for the directed verdict and the judge believes, after resolving all inferences against the moving party, that reasonable minds could reach but one conclusion and that is in favor of the moving party.

DIRECTORS AND OFFICERS INSURANCE — Insurance purchased by the corporation to indemnify directors and officers for the expense of defending their actions in a lawsuit against them arising because of corporate business. Also called D & O insurance.

DISCLOSED PRINCIPAL — A principal which can be identified by a third party.

DISCOVERY – Procedure – a set of procedures available for use in the trial of a case which enable all parties to obtain all relevant evidence from the other parties.
Devices – (See DEPOSITION, INTERROGATORIES)

DISMISSAL WITH PREJUDICE – Dismissal of a case under circumstances in which the issues presented may not be litigated again.

DISSENT AND APPRAISAL – A remedy available to a shareholder that objects to a merger or other special corporate transaction as defined by state statute. The corporation must purchase the dissenting shareholder's stock for its agreed upon or appraised value.

DISSOLUTION – Corporation – The termination of the corporation's legal existence.
Partnership – the change in the relation of the partners caused by any partner ceasing to be associated in the carrying on of the business. This change usually terminates the authority of the partners to act for the partnership in the usual course of business.

DIVERSITY JURISDICTION – The power of federal district courts to hear a dispute based upon a breach of state law if it is between residents of different states and the amount in controversy exceeds $10,000.

DIVIDEND – An amount of money or other property set aside out of corporate profits by the board of directors for payment to the shareholders.

DUE PROCESS – The exercise of the powers of government as the settled maxims of law permit. Basic procedural and substantive rights of individuals as expressed in the U. S. and state constitutions as interpreted by the courts.

EARNED SURPLUS – The profit derived from the operation of the corporation. Accountants sometimes call it retained earnings.

EQUITY LAW, EQUITABLE PRINCIPLES – That body of law which relies for its authority upon the conscience of the chancellor or judge.

ESTOPPEL – A bar raised by the law which stops a party from alleging or from denying facts when, if allowed, it would permit the party to work an injustice by allowing the allegation or denial.

EX PARTE, Latin – By or for one party only.

EXPRESS AUTHORITY – Authority of an agent based upon explicit instructions either oral or written.

EXPRESSED WARRANTY – Any affirmation of fact made by a seller of goods to the buyer which relates to the goods and becomes part of the basis of the bargain.

FALSE IMPRISONMENT – A tort committed when one intentionally restrains another against the latter's will.

FELLOW-SERVANT RULE – The rule relieving a master of liability for injury to a servant caused through the negligence of a fellow servant.

FELONY – A criminal offense that carries a penitentiary or a death sentence. It is a more serious crime than a misdemeanor.

FIDUCIARY – An individual who, because of the relationship of trust and confidence that he enjoys with another person, is in the position of a trustee. The law demands the utmost good faith and loyalty from the fiduciary in fulfilling his duties. The word is used as both a noun and an adjective.

GRAVAMEN – The significant portion of a legal complaint or charge.

IMPLIED AUTHORITY – That authority which the law recognizes the agent has which is reasonably necessary to carry out the expressed authority of the principal. It may also be referred to as incidental authority.

IMPLIED WARRANTY OF FITNESS FOR A PARTICULAR PURPOSE – A warranty (guarantee or promise) that is implied in a contract for the sale of goods by the U.C.C., §2-315, which provides that where the seller at the time of contracting has reason to know any particular purpose for which the goods are required and that the buyer is relying on the seller's skill or judgment to select or furnish suitable goods, then the goods sold shall be fit for such purpose.

IMPLIED WARRANTY OF MERCHANTABILITY – The warranty (guarantee) automatically created by the U.C.C., §2-314, when a merchant sells an item of personal property. Under this warranty the item is guaranteed to be of fair average quality and fit for the ordinary purposes for which such goods are used.

INCIDENTAL AUTHORITY − (See IMPLIED AUTHORITY)

INCOME STATEMENT − The accounting statement that reports the revenues and expenses of an enterprize for a period of time.

INDEMNITY − A duty requiring one person to make good any loss incurred by another while acting at the request or for the benefit of the former.

INDEPENDENT CONTRACTOR − A person who performs a task according to his own methods and judgment. His employer exercises no control over him except as to the resulting product.

INHERENT AUTHORITY − The power of an agent derived not from the principal's authority but from the position of the agent in the principal's business together with reasonable reliance by a third party upon the power which usually accompany the position.

INJUNCTION − An order issued by a court of equity that orders a person to do or cease doing a particular activity.

INSIDE DIRECTOR − A director that is also a corporate employee.

INSTRUCTION, from judge − The statement made by the trial judge to the jury informing them of the applicable law they are to use in their deliberations.

INTER ALIA, Latin − Among other things.

INTERESTED DIRECTOR − A director who has a personal interest in a matter to be considered by the board.

INTERLOCKING DIRECTORATE − A situation where one individual sits on the board of directors of two or more corporations which do business with one another or are otherwise connected.

INTERMEDIATE APPELLATE COURT − The court to which decisions of a trial court or an administrative agency are appealed. It is the court just below the highest appellate court of the jurisdiction, usually called the supreme court.

INTERROGATORIES − Written questions directed to a witness or a party to a lawsuit. The questions must be answered in writing and under oath. Interrogatories form one part of the pre-trial discovery process.

JOINT OBLIGATIONS − Obligations or liability that is incurred by two or more persons. Their liability is undivided and they must be sued jointly. They do not bear individual liability as do persons who have joint and several liability.

JOINT AND SEVERAL LIABILITY − Liability incurred by two or more persons who may then be sued individually or as a group.

JOINT VENTURE − A combination of two or more legal persons to conduct a profit making enterprise. Usually the combination involves a single business transaction. Although the parties incur joint liability, it is distinguished from a partnership by its limited nature and scope.

JUDGMENT − The official judicial determination upon the issues in a lawsuit.

JUDGMENT CREDITOR − A creditor who has established, through court action, the existence, and non-payment of a debt owed by his debtor.

JUDGMENT NOTWITHSTANDING THE VERDICT − Also called JUDGMENT N.O.V. Judgment entered by a court that overturns or reverses the verdict of the jury. Judgment N.O.V.'s are quite rare and only granted when absolutely no legal basis exists for the jury's decision.

JUDGMENT ON THE PLEADINGS − Judgment entered by the court in favor of a party based only upon the pleadings filed before a trial. It will be granted only where there is no genuine issue as to any material fact and the moving party is entitled to a judgment as a matter of law. It accomplishes the same purpose as summary judgment.

JURISDICTION − The "power" of a court to hear and decide a lawsuit. It is contrasted to venue which refers to the geographical location where the lawsuit is brought.

LACHES − An equitable doctrine that bars a person from enforcing a claim. This doctrine is utilized when the person has delayed enforcing his claim for such an unreasonable period of time that the adverse party's cause has been unfairly prejudiced.

LAW − As used in this text means a statement of the circumstances when courts or law enforcement agencies will act.

LEGAL DUTY – An obligation that is imposed by either a state or federal statute, an administrative agency or an appellate court relying upon the common law.

LEGISLATURE – The branch of government that passes the statutes.

LIABILITY – An extremely broad legal term meaning an obligation, debt, unliquidated claim, legal responsibility, or the possibility of incurring the judgment of a court.

LIBEL – Written defamation. Oral defamation is called slander.

LIMITED LIABILITY – Liability the extent of which is in some measure limited, not absolute. Oftentimes limited liability is used in a context meaning a person's financial liability has a ceiling. Most often applied to shareholders of corporations to limit their liability to corporate creditors to the amount of money promised or paid into the corporation in exchange for the shares.

LIMITED PARTNERSHIP – A partnership consisting of one or more general partners, with the normal partnership rights and liabilities, and one or more limited partners, who do not conduct the partnership business and whose liability is limited to the extent of their capital contribution.

LITIGANT – A party to a lawsuit.

LOANED/BORROWED SERVANT – A servant who is loaned by his master to another. The borrower is liable for acts of the servant performed in his employment if he has direct control over the servant.

MASTER – The principal that engages another, called a servant, to perform services on his behalf and who exercises control over the physical acts of the servant. In the area of contracts the usual terms are: principal-agent, whereas when tort law is involved the terms used respectively are: master – servant.

MATERIAL INFORMATION – A technical term used in the application of the federal securities laws to denote information about corporate activities which would cause a reasonably prudent investor in the securities market to either buy, sell or refrain from buying or selling.

MERGER – An alteration of corporate structure where corporation A and B are combined. Corporation A ceases to exist while B, the surviving corporation, will continue in operation.

MISDEMEANOR – A criminal offense that is not as serious as a felony. Typically the penalty is a fine and/or imprisonment in a facility other than a penitentiary.

MISREPRESENTATION – A misstatement, either by word or conduct, of fact. Sometimes the word "fraud" is used to indicate an intentional misstatement while misrepresentation is used to indicate non-willful misstatements.

MOTION TO DISMISS FOR FAILURE TO STATE A CLAIM – A procedural device whereby a litigant admits the facts stated in the opponent's pleading, but asserts that they are insufficient in law to support the legal action. This motion accomplishes the same purpose as the older pleading called a demurrer.

MUNICIPAL CORPORATION – A public corporation organized under congressional or legislative authority to carry out political or governmental purposes. Cities and towns are prime examples.

NEGLIGENCE – The failure to exercise the ordinary care that a reasonable person would exercise under those circumstances. An act of negligence may be one of commission or omission.

NOTICE, KNOWLEDGE – Knowledge of, or information about, the existence of facts. Notice can be either actual or constructive.

ORDINANCE – Those statutes created by the legislative arm of a municipal corporation.

OUTSIDE DIRECTOR– A director who is not an employee of the corporation.

PARTIALLY DISCLOSED PRINCIPAL – The situation where a person knows that he is dealing with an agent, thereby knowing the existence of the principal but not his identity.

PARTNERSHIP – An association of two or more persons to carry on as co-owners a business for profit.

PARTNERSHIP INTEREST – A technical term used by the U.P.A., §26 to refer to a partner's right to share in the profits of the firm.

PARTNERSHIP PROPERTY — Assets or property of any kind that belongs to the partnership. Partnership property is not the property of individual partners.

PETITIONER — The person who files a petition with a court. The person opposing the petition is called the "respondent." Sometimes used as a synonym for appellant.

PLAINTIFF — The person who initiates a lawsuit by filing a complaint.

PLEADINGS — A term designating both the complaint filed by the plaintiff and the answer filed by the defendant in a lawsuit plus supplementary documents which are the formal allegations or denials forming the basis of the suit.

POLICE POWER — The inherent power of a state to enact legislation necessary for the protection of the public's safety, health and welfare.

PRE-EMPTIVE RIGHTS — The right of a shareholder to purchase his pro rata share of any newly authorized and issued shares of the corporation.

PREFERRED STOCK — Stock that is entitled to certain preferences, usually in the payment of dividends, over that of common stock. Oftentimes, preferred stock will not have voting rights and will be preferred over common upon the liquidation of the corporation.

PRIMA FACIE, Latin — On its face. Evidence sufficient to establish one's claim unless rebutted by the opposing party.

PRINCIPAL — The person who engages another (called an agent) to act for him and upon his behalf.

PRINCIPLE — A basic truth or rule.

PRIVITY — A relationship between two or more persons that is mutual or successive, i.e., seller — buyer, heir — ancestor, etc.; historically, it denoted a relationship between contracting parties that was necessary in order to support a suit based upon a breach of contract.

PROMOTER — The individual that performs all the items necessary for incorporation.

PROPRIETORSHIP — The form of business association that is owned and operated by a single owner. The owner is called the "sole—proprietor."

PUBLIC CORPORATION — A corporation organized by Congress or a state to carry out a governmental purpose. (See MUNICIPAL CORPORATION.) A corporation serving the public interest, such as a railroad or utility, are sometimes called a public or public service corporation. A publicly held corporation is a private corporation whose shares are owned by members of the general public.

PUBLIC POLICY — A very broad term usually denoting the legal duties of persons to the community as expressed in legislative and judicial pronouncements.

RATIFICATION — A person's approval of a prior act which was done on his behalf but was not binding on him when done. One cannot ratify an act unless he has knowledge of all the material facts.

RESPONDEAT SUPERIOR, Latin — Let the master answer. This doctrine makes a master liable for the acts of his servant committed within the course and scope of the servant's employment. It includes liability for acts incidental to acts within the scope of employment.

RESPONDENT — The person who is the opposing party in a court petition or appellate proceeding.

RESTATEMENT OF THE LAW (of Agency, of Negligence, etc.) — A compilation of legal principals published by the American Law Institute which represent a desired statement of the law.

RESTRICTIVE COVENANT — Usually refers to an expressed promise made by an employee not to compete with the employer in a defined geographical area and in a defined line of work after the employment is terminated.

SECTION 1244 STOCK — Stock issued by a corporation which meets the requirements of Section 1244 of the Internal Revenue Code which allows the loss sustained upon sale of the stock to be treated as an ordinary loss of the individual up to $25,000.

SERVANT — A person acting on behalf of, and controlled by, another called a master.

SERVICE OF PROCESS — The delivery of the legal papers in a lawsuit (usually the complaint) to the correct person.

SHOP RIGHTS – The nonexclusive royalty-free license enjoyed by an employer in an employee's invention when the employer's time, tools or services were used in developing the invention.

SHORT SALE – selling short – The sale of shares of stock by a seller who does not own them. At a later date the seller replaces the shares by purchasing them on the open market, hopefully at a lower price than he sold them for, thereby making a profit.

SHORT SWING PROFITS – Profits realized by a director, officer or beneficial owner of more than 10 percent of any class of stock from transactions in his corporation's stock within any period of less than six months. Under §16(b) of the Securities Exchange Act of 1934 such profits belong to the corporation.

SLANDER – Oral defamation. Defamation that is published in written form is called libel.

SPECIFIC PERFORMANCE – Performance of a contract according to its exact liberal terms. It is an extraordinary legal remedy ordered by a court only when money damages are inadequate compensation for the breach of the contract.

STATUTE, STATUTORY LAW – A law enacted by a legislature.

STATUTE OF LIMITATIONS – Statutes or laws prescribing the time within which legal action must be instituted upon certain claims or forever be barred from bringing suit.

STOCK OPTION – A form of corporate compensation that grants an executive the right to purchase a given number of corporate shares within a specified future period at a specified price.

STOCK SPLIT – A device designed to reduce the per share market price of a stock thereby increasing demand and broadening the number of shareholders. If stock is priced at $400 per share it is relatively unattractive to small investors. If a 4 for 1 stock split occurs, four shares valued at $100 per share will be issued for each one share of the previous stock.

STRIKE SUIT – A stockholder's derivative suit wholly lacking in merit.

SUB AGENTS – An agent appointed by another agent who is empowered to do so to perform acts undertaken by the appointing agent for the principal but for whose conduct the principal remains primarily liable.

SUBCHAPTERS CORPORATIONS – A corporation with ten or fewer shareholders who are individuals or estates (not partnerships or corporations) with one class of stock and which meet the other requirements of Sections 1371-1379 of the Internal Revenue Code. These sections allow the qualifying corporation to elect to avoid paying any corporate tax on its income and instead have the shareholders taxed on the taxable income of the corporation in proportion to their shareholdings. If the corporation has a net operating loss, it can be deducted directly by the shareholders against their individual incomes.

SUBSIDIARY – A corporation substantially owned and controlled by another corporation called the parent corporation.

SUMMONS – A writ directing the sheriff to notify the defendant that a lawsuit has been filed against him and that he has a certain number of days to answer or have judgment entered against him.

SURETY – A person who serves as an insurer of the debt or obligation of his principal. The surety's liability is contingent on default by the principal.

TENDER OFFER – An offer to buy shares directed at the shareholders of a target company over which the offeror is seeking to gain control. Federal securities laws govern such offers.

THIRD PARTY – A person that is not a party to the immediate contract, relationship, matter or transaction.

TIPPEE – The recipient of material corporate information.

TIPPER – The individual who passes material information affecting the price of a corporation's securities to another, called a tippee.

TORT – A civil wrong or injury committed by one person against another. Assault, battery, slander, and negligence are just some examples of a tort.

TRADE MARK, TRADE NAME – A trade mark is a symbol, emblem, or words attached to goods to identify them as the product of a specific manufacturer. A trade name is a name used to identify a specific business.

TRADE SECRET – Any formula, pattern, device or compilation of information which is used in one's business, and which gives him an opportunity to obtain an advantage over competitors who do not know or use it.

TREASURY STOCK – Stock that has been repurchased by the issuing corporation.

TRESPASS – A non-consensual transgression against another's person or property.

UNDERWRITER – An individual or company whose business is the distribution of securities for sale. The term can have a more technical definition under the federal securities law which regulates the activities of the defined underwriters.

UNDISCLOSED PRINCIPAL – The situation where a person lacks the knowledge that the one with whom he is dealing is not acting on his own behalf but is an agent of another. The existence and the identity of the principal is unrevealed.

ULTRA VIRES, Latin – Beyond the powers. An act outside the powers granted a corporation in its articles.

VERDICT – The formal decision rendered by the jury in a lawsuit.

VICARIOUS LIABILITY – Liability which the law imposes upon one for the illegal acts of another. In agency law vicarious liability is accomplished by the application of the common law doctrine of Respondeat Superior.

VOIRE DIRE – The process of questioning prospective jurors to determine their objectivity and the presence or lack of bias or prejudice.

WAIVER – The voluntary reliquishing of one's legal rights or claims.

WARRANTY – An expressed or implied legal guarantee or promise that certain specified facts are true.

INDEX

Accoutant's Liability under Securities Laws
  generally, 529, 546-562
Agency
  creation, 60
  defined, 60
  delegation, 174
  husband and wife, 78
  operation, 165-166
  scope of employment, 127
  termination, 182-185
  type of business association, 37
Agent
  contractual liability of, 105-107
  duties of, 62
Answer
  defined, 14
Apparent authority
  generally, 90-91
Appeals
  courts of, 19
  process, 18
  study of appellate cases, 21
Appellant
  defined, 18
Appellee
  defined, 18
Articles Of Incorporation
  amendment, 435-436
  generally, 268-271
  specimen, 268-270
Assault
  defined, 113
Attorneys' liability under Securities Law
  generally, 529, 562-571
Authority
  actual, 84
  circumstantial, 90
  for other types, *see individual headings,*
    e.g., Express authority
  to commit a tort, 144

Battery
  defined, 113
Blue Sky Laws
  generally, 461-462
Board of directors, *see* Directors
Bonds
  generally, 295
Briefing
  generally, 21, 25-27
Business associations
  types, 37-45

By-laws
  generally, 271

Capacity
  of principal & agent, 77-78
  to form a partnership, 196-197
Certificate Of Incorporation, see Articles
    Of Incorporation
Charter, *see* Articles Of Incorporation
Circumstantial authority, *see* Authority
Civil law
  defined, 6-7
Civil rights
  Act of 1964, 596-598
  age discrimination, 601
  bona fide occupational
    qualifications, 596
  Equal Employment Opportunity
    Act, 596
  Equal Employment Opportunity
    Commission, 599
  Equal Pay Act, 599-601
  seniority, 598
Class actions
  defined, 14
Close corporations
  defined, 308
  generally, 308-314
  special statutory provisions, 313-314
Common law
  defined, 5
Complaint
  defined, 9
Consolidation
  generally, 436-442
Consumer Product Warranty Act
    (Magnuson-Moss Act)
  generally, 630
Cooperatives
  generally, 43-44
Corporate entity
  defective incorporation, 271-272
  disregard of, 272-281
  nature of, 260-261
  powers of, 287-291
Corporations
  advantages of corporate form, 55
  by-laws, *see* By-laws
  capital structure, 295-300
  characteristics, 40
  close, *see* Close corporations

Corporations (*continued*)
    compared with other business
      associations, 55
    consolidation, *see* Consolidation
    control, 293-295, 323, 435
    de facto, 271
    de jure, 271
    directors, *see* Directors
    dissolution, 451-456
    dividends, *see* Dividends
    foreign, 282-287
    incorporation, 268-272
    merger, *see* Merger
    municipal, 42
    officers, *see* Officers
    piercing the veil, 272-281
    powers of, 287-291
    public vs. private, 42
    restrictions on, 42-43
    sales of assets, *see* Sale of Assets
    social responsibility of, 649
    structural changes, 435-451
    Subchapter S, 41-42
    subsidiaries, *see* Subsidiaries
    tender offers, *see* Tender Offers
    varieties of, 259
Crimes
    defined, 6
    felony, 7
    misdemeanor, 7
Cumulative voting
    generally, 306

Deceit
    defined, 114
Defamation
    defined, 114
Delegation
    of agency duties, 174
Demurrer, *see* Motion to dismiss
Deposition
    defined, 15
Derivative suits
    costs, 315
    defined, 316
    demand on directors and
      shareholders, 316-320
    indemnification, 364-365
    security for expenses, 316-317
Directed verdict
    defined, 17
Directors
    authority, 323, 325
    business judgment, defense of 327-343
    compensation, 326
    election, 323-324, 326-327
    executive committees, 324, 326
    fiduciary duties, 327-328, 391-432
    informal action, 325-326
    inside, 326

Directors (*continued*)
    insurance, *see* Directors' and Officers'
      Insurance
    interested, 425
    interlocking, 426-427
    liability for impermissible dividends, 376
    liability under Securities Law, 529-549
    management by, 323, 325
    meetings, 324-325
    outside, 326
    removal, 326-327
Directors' and Officers' Insurance
    generally, 364-365
Discovery
    defined, 15-16
Discrimination, *see* Civil Rights
Dissolution of corporation
    involuntary, 451-456
    voluntary, 451
Dissolution of partnership, *see* Partnership
Diversity jurisdiction
    explained, 8
Dividends
    directors' discretion, 377-389
    forms of, 376-377
    impermissible, 376
    nimble dividends, 374
    payment of, 375
    policy considerations, 373
    shareholders right to, 375, 377-378
    statutory limitations, 373-375
    stock dividends, 376-377

Employees
    fiduciary duties of, 427-432
Employment Retirement Income
    Security Act (ERISA)
    Act of 1974, 619
Environmental protection
    Council on Environmental Quality
      (CEQ), 646
    Environmental Protection Agency
      (EPA), 646-49
    National Environmental Policy Act
      (NEPA), 640
    Reserve Mining Litigation, 650-57
Equal Pay Act
    generally, 599-601
Equity law
    defined, 5
Estoppel
    defined, 91-92
Express authority
    generally, 84-85

False imprisonment
    defined, 113
Fiduciary duties
    care, 327-328
    control, sale of, 411-425

Fiduciary duties (*continued*)
   corporate opportunities, 391-411
   defined, 62, 65-66
   generally, 391-432
   insider trading, *see* Insider trading
   interested directors, *see* Directors
   interlocking directors, *see* Directors
   partner as fiduciary, 208
Foreign corporations, *see* Corporations

Husband and wife
   as agents for one another, 78

Implied authority
   defined, 84-85
Incorporation, *see* Corporations
Independent contractor
   generally, 125-126, 129
Inherent authority
   generally, 97-98
Insider Trading
   common law rule (special circumstances
     doctrine), 493
   generally, 485-527
   materiality, 502-506
   Rule 10b-5, 492-495
   sale of control, *see* Sale of control
   Section 16(b), 485
   tippers and tippees, 512
   who can recover for violations, 513-524
Instructional objectives
   generally, 20-21
Instructions
   judicial, 17
Interrogatories
   defined, 15

Joint and Several Liability
   of partners, 234
Joint venture
   generally, 39, 214
Judgment N.O.V.
   defined, 18
Judgment on the pleadings
   defined, 16
Judicial Systems
   generally, 7
Jury trial
   generally, 16-17

Law
   defined, 3
Loaned or borrowed servant
   generally, 176
Licenses
   from state, 31
Limited partnership
   generally, 39, 214-215

Master
   defined, 125
   liability of, 125-128
Merger
   de facto, 438-442
   dissent and appraisal rights, 437-438, 443
   generally, 436-442
   shareholder vote, 437
   short form, 442-443
Motion to dismiss
   for failure to state a claim, 15

Negligence
   generally, 17
   in design of product, 633
Non-servant agent
   defined, 127, 129
Notice
   given to agent, 165-166
   of agency termination, 182, 185
   of partnership dissolution, 241-242

Occupational safety
   Occupational Safety & Health Act
     (OSHA), 610-613
Officers
   authority, 343-355
   compensation, 365-370
   fiduciary duties, 391
   insiders under § 16(b), 485
   liability for torts and crimes, 355-363
   president, 344-345
   secretary, 345
   treasurer, 345
   vice-president, 345

Partners
   incoming, 238
   interest in partnership, 206-209
   joint & several liability of, 234
   liability upon dissolution, 248-251
   property, 206-208
Partnership
   advantages, 39
   agreement, sample, 204-206
   compared with other business
     associations, 55
   contractual liability, 221-222
   creation, 196-198
   definition, 195-197
   dissolution, 241-242, 247, 251
   property, 206-208
   separate entity, 38
   tort liability, 227, 234
Payment
   to agent, 165-166
Pensions, *see* Employment Retirement
   Income Security Act

Petition, *see* Complaint
Petitioner, *see* Appellant
Preemptive rights, *see* Shareholders
Preferred stock
  generally, 299
Principal
  disclosed, 106-107
  duties, 75
  liability
    contract, 83-105
    loaned or borrowed servant, 176
    on public policy or statute, 155-156
    sub-agents, 168-169
    vicarious, 118-128
    partially disclosed, 106-107
    undisclosed, 106-107
Product liability
  federal warranty legislation, 630-632
  negligent design, 633
  strict liability, 633
  U.C.C. warranties, 622-623
Professional corporations
  generally, 261
Promoters
  contracts by, 263-268
  secret profits by, 263
Proprietorship
  compared to other business
    associations, 55
  generally, 38
Proxies
  forms of, 304
  generally, 303-304, 573
  regulation under Federal Securities
    Law, 573-587
  revocability, 304
  solicitation, 573
    costs, 575
    misleading statements, 580-587
    shareholder proposals, 573-575
  specimen, 304

Ratification
  of agent's contracts, 101-102
  of agent's torts, 144
Registration
  of securities under federal law, *see*
    Securities regulation
Remedies
  for breach of fiduciary duties, 74-75
Reorganization, Corporate, *see* Merger and
    Consolidation
Respondeat superior
  generally, 118-128
Respondent, *see* Appellee
Restatement of the law
  defined, 5, 59
Restrictions on business associations
  federal, 36-37
  state, 29-31

Restrictive covenant
  generally, 66
Rule
  individual, 4
  judicial, 5
  legislative, 3
  types, 6

Sale of assets
  generally, 436-442
Sale of control
  liability of shareholder seller, 411-418
Securities and Exchange Commission
  generally, 463-464
Securities regulation
  fraudulent activities, 524-527
  Insider Trading, *see* Insider Trading
  liability for violations, 571-572
  nonpublic (private) offerings, 475-479
  registration of securities, 462-463,
    475-476
  regulation of proxies, 573-587
  regulation of tender offers, 587-589
  Securities Act of 1933, 463
  securities defined, 466-475
  Securities Exchange Act of 1934, 463
  state regulation, *see* Blue Sky Laws
  underwriters, 479-480
Servant
  generally, 125, 129
  loaned or borrowed, 176
Shareholders
  cumulative voting, 306
  derivative suits, 315-320
  fiduciary duties, 411-425
  inspection rights, 315
  liabilities,
    debts of corporation, 295
    piercing the corporate veil, 272-281
    subscription agreements, 298
  meetings, 307
  power of, 293-295, 435
  preemptive rights, 305-306
  proxies, *see* Proxies
  right of dissent and appraisal, 437-438,
    443
  voting trusts, 304-305
Shop rights doctrine
  generally, 430-432
Social responsibilities of business
  generally, 649
Stock
  common, 299
  dividends, *see* Dividends
  nonvoting, 298-299
  no par, 298
  options, 507, 510
  par value, 298
  preemptive rights, 305-306
  preferred, 299

Stock (*continued*)
    registration, 462-463, 475-476
    restriction on transfer of, 590
    Section 1244, 41
    specimen, 296-297
    splits, 377
    subscriptions, 298
    treasury stock, 298
    voting, 298-299
    watered stock, 263
Strict liability, *see* Product liability
Sub-agents
    generally, 168-169
Subsidiaries
    generally, 272-273
    liability of parent, 273, 278-281
Summary judgment, *see* Judgment on the
    pleadings
Summons
    defined, 14

Tender offers
    regulation of, *see* Securities Regulation
Termination
    of agency, *see* Agency
    of partnership, *see* Partnership
Tort
    defined, 113
    types, 113-114
Trade mark, Trade names
    generally, 30
Trade secret
    generally 66
Trial process
    explained, 9-18

Underwriters, *see* Securities Regulation
Uniform Partnership Act, *see* Appendix

Voting trust, *see* Shareholders

Warranties, *see* Product liability